2

CampingCard ACSI 2016

This year you can take advantage of large discounts at no fewer than 3,142 campsites in 20 countries.

13	in	Norway
26	in	Sweden
56	in	Denmark
388	in	The Netherlands
57	in	Belgium
25	in	Luxembourg
323	in	Germany
47	in	Switzerland
96	in	Austria
20	in	The Czech Republic
13	in	Hungary
14	in	Slovenia
72	in	Croatia
32	in	Greece
45	in	Great Britain
15	in	Ireland
1,345	in	France
243	in	Spain
23	in	Portugal
289	in	Italy

Did you hear about...

our handy website: www.CAMPINGCARD.com. See page **26**.

the CampingCard ACSI app: all campsite information at your fingertips, even without internet. See page **30**.

the ACSI Club ID: the Camping Carnet for Europe. See page **20**.

You will find your discount card in part 2.

Check the CampingCard ACSI app or **www.CAMPINGCARD.com/modifications** before you leave for the most up to date information.

Validity of CampingCard ACSI

The CampingCard ACSI card is valid for one calendar year and is non-transferable. We ask you therefore to complete the back of the card in full and sign it. A campsite has the right to ask you for additional identification.

The information in this guide applies specifically to 2016. Each year new campsites join, other sites change the period in which the discount card is accepted or their rates. The details in this guide are therefore updated annually.
Check the CampingCard ACSI app or www.CAMPINGCARD.com/modifications for the most up to date information.

Take note! Only campsites which appear in this guide display the blue CC logo, and you will only get a discount on your overnight stay with your CampingCard ACSI discount card at these sites. See also 'Only campsites with the CC logo' on page 9.

Please also note that expired discount cards will not be accepted at campsites.

Visit: **www.CAMPINGCARD.com**

VALDERROBRES * R C7 34 N40°52.429' E000°09.364' 44580

Directions: Calle Elvira Hidalgo. From Arnes follow A231 east into Valderrobres. Turn left, sp 'Alcaniz', and cross river bridge; the Aire is visible on right. Turn 1st right into Calle Elvira Hidalgo, then 1st right again into riverside car park, signed. A231 is a pleasant drive.

20; Max 48hrs Custom

Aire in riverside car park with views of the town and its fortified castle, guided tours can be booked in advance; €5pp, see www.castillodevalderrobres.com Town commerce 2 mins via medieval bridge. Town adj to Puertos de Beceite national park, which has numerous walking/cycling trails. A231 is a pleasant drive. www.valderrobres.es Inspected 2015.

All The Aires Spain And Portugal entry above. All The Aires France map below.

LPG All The Aires Benelux.

TOWN	Grid Ref	Map Ref	GPS	DIRECTIONS
ALLERBORN	F4	A	N50°02.203' E005°53.212'	Esso. 12, east of village.
HOSINGEN	F4	B	N50°00.893' E006°05.507'	Gulf. Haaptstroos, main route through town centre.
ECHTERNACH	G4	C	N49°48.596' E006°26.124'	Total. Off N10/N11 roundabout east of town at German border.
WASSERBILLIG	G5	D	N49°43.615' E006°29.537'	Esso. A1 Junction 15 adj to German border.

The history of ACSI

From duplicated booklet to 571,000 guides

No more closed barriers

Teacher Ed van Reine set off with his family in the summer of 1965. The fervent camper steered his car towards the Spanish sun in good spirits. However the journey ended in disappointment as there was no room for the family at the campsite they had so carefully selected. Situations such as this could surely be prevented? Van Reine brainstormed on the spot with two teacher colleagues about a reservation system for popular European campsites. They called it '**A**uto **C**amper **S**ervice **I**nternational'. ACSI had been born and the basis was formed for the familiar green ACSI campsite guides.

The three pioneers selected 55 campsites, collected information and distributed it in a duplicated booklet for the modest price of one Dutch guilder. No more closed barriers; from now on it was possible to contact the campsite in advance to reserve a pitch. In the Sixties when camping was something of a national sport, demand for the guide grew.

The way to the top

By the third year a number of campsites asked if it was possible to supplement their entry in the guide for a fee to include a piece of text and a photo. Inspectors were recruited (then known as selectors) and so was created the first team to travel around Europe to collect campsite details.

Ed van Reine

At the beginning of the Eighties ACSI set its sights high when the company decided to publish the campsite guide itself. The number of campsites increased to 7,500 and in 1985 the first group of Dutch campers went on holiday with ACSI Camping Tours: group tours offering individual freedom. These tours are now also being organised for German and English speaking campers. ACSI officially became a family business from the moment that Ed van Reine introduced his son Ramon, the current director of ACSI. From that moment things developed rapidly.

ACSI diversifies

In the Nineties ACSI was involved with digitisation, product expansion and internationalisation. In 1999 ACSI was the first in Europe to launch a dynamic campsite search engine on the internet. The information on the www.eurocampings.net website could be accessed in four languages (nowadays www.eurocampings.eu is available in 14 languages) and the visitor could already filter the inspected amenities.

Various new guides with different interests and themes have appeared and these are also published in multiple languages. The introduction of CampingCard ACSI in 2004 put the campsite specialist on the record for good: the incredibly simple, user-friendly discount system for the low season proved to be immensely popular with campers!

Nowadays 135 permanent employees are occupied in optimising existing products and developing new ones. More than 300 enthusiastic inspectors travel throughout Europe in order to ensure that only campsites with the highest standards of quality appear in the ACSI campsite guides. The extensive and objective information that results from these annual inspections has for years been ACSI's strength.

Progressive since 1965

ACSI brings campers and campsites together throughout Europe by publishing campsite information, but ACSI does much more. ACSI Club ID members can go on holiday with a camping carnet (an alternative identity document, accepted at 8,800 campsites).

ACSI continues to listen to the wishes of both campers and campsites and react to them. The result is clear: over the years ACSI has grown to become the most progressive campsite specialist which receives more than 10 million visitors a year on Eurocampings.eu, which has sold more than 180,000 apps and which this year will reach the record circulation of 571,000 campsite guides. You now have one of them. Thanks for your trust! ACSI wishes you lots of enjoyable camping in 2016.

Your off-season discount card

It couldn't be easier. Using your discount card you can enjoy bargain holidays in low season at top-quality campsites throughout Europe. And all that for just one of five fixed rates: 11, 13, 15, 17 or 19 euros per night.

The rates

The fixed rates of 11, 13, 15, 17 and 19 euros are lower than the minimum prices charged by the participating campsites in the low season. You can therefore be certain of big discounts on the overnight price! At least 10% - and in some cases as much as 50%! Some campsites offer an extra discount if you stay for a longer period. Campsites are just as attractive in the low season as in the high season; the owners guarantee the same standards of facilities and service and the main facilities are also available in the low season; you just pay less. You can therefore avoid the busy period and take advantage of your discount in early and late season!

What do you have to do to enjoy your discount?

It couldn't be easier - take the CampingCard ACSI with you and present it to the receptionist when you arrive at one of the participating campsites and take advantage of our preferential rates! Show your discount card again at the reception when you pay and you will be charged the advantageous CampingCard ACSI rate. You can see what is included in the rate in the 'Rate per overnight stay' section on page 18 of this guide, and you can see any supplementary charges there may be in the 'Not included in the overnight rate' section on page 19.

Payment conditions

CampingCard ACSI may seem a bit like a credit or debit card but it is simply a discount card. You show your CampingCard ACSI and you can stay on selected sites at advantageous rates. You don't usually have to pay in advance for a fixed number of nights; just pay when you depart.

However, payment conditions may in some circumstances be determined by the campsite's own policy, including when you should pay or provide a deposit. If for example you announce that you will be staying for just one night or want to reserve, the campsite may ask you to pay in advance or pay a deposit. The campsite reception will inform you of their policy in this matter.

Reservation with CampingCard ACSI

On some campsites you can reserve in advance with CampingCard ACSI. A campsite has

Instructions for use

1. Place name - Postal code - Region

4. Campsite name and star ratings

5. Address

6. Telephone and fax

7. Opening period

8. E-mail address

9. Facilities (see fold-out flap)

Facilities open throughout the campsite's entire opening period

Vilanova i la Geltrú, E-08800 / Cataluña

Vilanova Park Cat.1
Carretera Arboç km 2,5
+34 93-8933402
FAX +34 93-8935528
1/1 - 31/12
@ info@vilanovapark.com

40ha 348**T**(70-100m²) 10A

1 ABCD**F**IJKLM**P**RS
2 FGJLSTUVXY
3 BC**F**GHJK**M**N**Q**RUV
4 **A**(B 23/3-3/11) (F) (G 23/3-3/11) J**KL**N**P** (Q+S+T+U+V) (W 1/7-31/8) (X+Y) Z
5 **AB**DFGIJKLMNOPUWXY
6 ACDEGH**I**J**K**M(N 2,5km)O QRSTVWX

On a hillside, 2 km from Vilanova i la 3.5 km from the beach. Enjoyable stays i late season with adapted facilities includi pool, sauna, jacuzzi and fitness. Bus stop entrance for the beach, village and statio to Barcelona.

Toll road A7, exit 29 direction Vilano Vilanova turn right on roundabout directi C31. After km-marker 153 exit right direc Then follow signs.

CC € 17 *1/1-19/6 27/6-3/7 29/8-31/12* **14=11**

10. Surface area of the campsite in hectares (1 ha = 10,000 m² (square metres) or approximately 2.5 acres)
11. Number of touring pitches (size of the pitches is shown in brackets)
12. Maximum loading available for electrical connections
13. Three pin Euro adaptor required (CEE)
14. Rate and (possible) extra discount
15. Acceptance period
16. Description
17. Route description

2. Three children up to and including the age of 5 included

NEW New CampingCard ACSI campsite in 2016

Dogs not permitted

Campsite totally suitable for naturists

Campsite partially suitable for naturists

Winter sports campsite

Amenities suitable for the disabled

WiFi zone on the campsite

WiFi coverage on at least 80% of the campsite

Recognised by the environmental organisation in that particular country

iD ACSI Club ID accepted as an identity card

3. 2009 Campsite number

18. Match2Camp

19. Sectional map with the exact position of the campsite

20. GPS coordinates

1. Place name, postal code and region

The place name and postal code of the campsite and the region in which it is located.

2. Three children up to and including the age of 5 included (possible)

You will find 714 campsites in this guide where (maximum) three children up to and including the age of 5 are included in the CampingCard ACSI rate. The symbol is shown in the editorial entry for these campsites. Take note: where a campsite displays this symbol they may still require you to pay tourist tax for children, as the campsite has to pay the tourist tax directly to the local authorities. Items such a shower tokens for children are not included.

WiFi zone and/or WiFi 80-100% coverage

If there is a WiFi zone on the campsite, then there is a location on the campsite where you can access wireless Internet. In the editorial entry for these campsites you will see this symbol:

If there is 80-100% WiFi coverage, then you can access wireless internet on most of the campsite. In the editorial entry for these campsites you will see this symbol:

ACSI Club ID

On many campsites you can use the ACSI Club ID Card, this is a substitute identity card. When you can use the ACSI Club ID at a campsite, this is indicated in the facilities with the symbol . You will find more explanation of this Camping Carnet on page 20 of this guide.

3. Campsite number 2669

The number in the blue CC logo refers to the number in the mini-atlas, included with this guide, which gives a good overview of where the campsite is located. See also: 'In the mini-atlas' on page 10.

4. Campsite name and star ratings

Here you can see the campsite name and possibly the number of stars. ACSI does not

give stars or other classifications to campsites. Star ratings or other types of classification are awarded to the campsite by local or national organisations and are shown after the campsite name. Stars do not always indicate the quality but more often the comfort that a campsite offers. The more stars there are, the more amenities. The judgement of whether a campsite is good or not and whether you think it deserves two stars or four is something you must decide for yourself. Some good advice: if things are not what you expect, don't stay for ten days moaning about the unfriendly receptionist. Pack your bags and leave. Who knows what lovely places are just around the corner!

5. Address

The postal address of the campsite. You will find the postal address including the post code in the uppermost block of the editorial entry. Sometimes, in France and Italy for example, you will see that there is no postal address. You will discover that you will usually be able to find the campsite yourself once you have arrived in the town. To make it easier to find the campsite we have included a route description and the GPS coordinates in the editorial entry.

6. Telephone and fax FAX

The telephone and fax numbers in this guide are preceded by a + sign. The + is the international access code (00 in the United Kingdom). The digits after the + denote the country where the campsite is located. For example: the phone number of a German campsite is shown as +49 followed by the area code with the 0 (in brackets) and the subscriber number. In most European countries, you should not dial the first zero of the area code after dialling the international access code. So for Germany you dial 0049 and then the area code, without the zero, followed by the subscriber's number. In general you do need to dial the zero in Italy.

7. Opening period

The periods advised by the campsite management during which the site will be open in 2016. TAKE NOTE: most campsites do not offer the CampingCard ACSI discount for the entire period that they are open. For dates when the CampingCard ACSI discount is available you will need to refer to the acceptance periods in the lower block of the campsite's editorial entry. See also: 'Acceptance period' on page 16.

The opening and acceptance data have been compiled with the greatest care. It is possible that circumstances may cause these dates to change after publication of this guide. Go to www.CAMPINGCARD.com/modifications before you leave to see whether there have been changes at your chosen campsite.

8. E-mail address

The campsite's e-mail address. The e-mail address is especially useful to make a reservation or enquiries in the low season, when the reception may be staffed less frequently.

9. Facilities

CampingCard ACSI is a discount card for the low season. Participating campsites will ensure that the most important facilities will also be available and functioning in the acceptance period of the discount card.
You will find a complete summary of all the facilities that are included in this guide in the fold-out cover at the front of the guide. If you leave the cover folded out you can see precisely which facilities are available at each camp site. By the numbers 1 to 6 you will find six categories with facilities:

1 Regulations
2 Location, ground and shade
3 Sports and play
4 Water recreation / Shops and restaurants
5 Washing up, laundry and cooking / Washing and toilet facilities
6 Miscellaneous

The letters after the numbers relate to the facilities in each category. By some facilities a period is shown in brackets, showing the day and month. These are the dates that you can expect these facilities to be available.
If a small key is shown, this facility can be used at least during the entire opening period of the campsite (amenities such as restaurants may in a few cases stay open longer than the campsite itself).
Take note: if a letter by a campsite name is printed in bold it means that this facility is not included in the overnight rate. More information about this in the fold-out cover.

10. Surface area of the campsite

The surface area of the campsite is given in hectares. 1 ha = 10,000 m^2 (square metres) or approximately 2.5 acres).

11. Number of touring pitches

As a camper on the move, it is interesting to know how many overnight pitches a site offers. The size of the pitches is shown in brackets, in m^2. If it says > 100 m^2, then the pitches are larger than 100 m^2. < 100 m^2 means smaller than 100 m^2. Every campsite makes some of these touring pitches available for campers with CampingCard ACSI. A standard pitch is included in the CampingCard rate. See page 18 for more explanation.

12. Maximum loading available for electrical connections

With your CampingCard ACSI a connection with maximum 6A and/or power consumption to a maximum of 4 kWh per day, including the

connection fee, is included in the overnight rate. If you use more, for example 5 kWh it is quite likely you have to pay a surcharge. You will find the minimum and maximum amperage available for the electrical connection for each campsite in the block with facilities. When the campsite information mentions 6-10A, this means that at this campsite there are pitches with an amperage of minimum 6 and maximum 10. This does not mean that 10A is included in the CampingCard ACSI rate.
State clearly on arrival at the campsite if you want a higher amperage than the included 6A, but be aware that you may have to pay a surcharge. Only when there is no lower amperage than 10A available at the campsite, you will not have to pay extra. Take note: you cannot connect electric equipment or batteries of, for example, 16A to an access point which allows a maximum of 10A.

13. CEE

This indication means that you will need a three pin euro-adapter.

14. Rate and extra discount

A rate of 11, 13, 15, 17 or 19 euros is shown for each campsite. The rates offered by CampingCard ACSI are already low but could be even lower. Some campsites give an extra discount if you stay longer.
If, for example is a campsite is showing '7=6' this means that you pay only 6 nights at the CampingCard ACSI rate for a 7 night stay. Be sure to indicate the number of nights you wish to stay when arriving or reserving. The campsite will make one booking for the entire period and will apply the discount. The discount may not apply if you decide to stay longer during your stay and thereby reach the required number of days.
Take note! If a campsite has several of these discounts you only have the right to one of these offers. For example: the special offers are 4=3, 7=6 and 14=12. If you stay for 13 nights you only have the right to one 7=6 discount and not to multiples of 4=3 or a combination of 4=3 and 7=6.

15. Acceptance period

Each campsite decides its own acceptance period and so defines its own low season. For dates when the CampingCard ACSI discount is available you will need to look at the acceptance periods in the lower blue block of the editorial entry for the campsite. The last date shown is the date on which the discount is no longer valid. For example an acceptance period of 1/1 - 30/6 means that if you arrive at the campsite on 1 January you will already receive a discount for the first night. You can enjoy this discount for the last time on the night of 29-30 June. So for the night of 30 June - 1 July you will pay the normal tariff.

The opening and acceptance periods are compiled with the greatest care.
It is possible that circumstances may cause these dates to change after publication of this guide.
Check www.CAMPINGCARD.com/modifications to see whether we have been informed of any changes at the campsite of your choice.

16. Description

In this section you will get an idea of the layout of the campsite and its characteristics. Some examples: on the coast, by a lake, quiet family campsite, high specification of facilities, pleasant views, plenty of shade, privacy, pitches separated by shrubbery, stony ground, grass, terraced, etc.

17. Route description

The written directions in this route description will assist you in finding your way for the last few miles to the campsite entrance and will advise you which motorway exit to take and which signs to follow.

18. Match2Camp

Match2Camp gives you an extra facility to help you decide which campsite best meets your wishes. You will see a Match2Camp coloured icon next to each campsite. Each colour is based on the amenities that a camper with this colour expects to find at a campsite. To find out which colour suits you best visit page 22.

19. Sectional map

The sectional map shows where the campsite is located in its immediate surroundings. The precise location of the campsite is shown with the blue CampingCard ACSI logo.

20. GPS coordinates

If you make use of a navigation system the GPS coordinates are almost indispensable.

ACSI has therefore noted the GPS coordinates in this guide. Our inspectors have measured the coordinates right next to the campsite barrier, so nothing can go wrong. Take care: not all navigation systems are configured for cars with a caravan so always read the route description that is included with each campsite and don't forget to watch out for the signs. The shortest route is, after all, not always the easiest one. The GPS coordinates are shown in degrees, minutes and seconds. Check when you enter the data into your navigation system that it is also configured in degrees, minutes and seconds. The letter N is shown by the first number. By the second number there is a letter E or W (right or left of the Greenwich meridian). Tip: you can also download the coordinates free of charge into your navigation system via www.CAMPINGCARD.com/gps.

Rate per overnight stay

There are five CampingCard ACSI rates:

€11 €13 €15 €17 €19

At campsites in countries which use currencies other than the euro, you will normally pay in that country's currency. The CampingCard ACSI rates will be converted to that currency. Bear in mind that exchange rates are subject to fluctuation.

Inclusive

Participating campsites offer the following in the CampingCard ACSI rate on touring pitches:

- A camping pitch.*
- Overnight stay for 2 adults.
- Car & caravan & awning, or car & folding caravan, or car & tent, or motor home & awning.
- Electricity. A connection of maximum 6A is included in the CampingCard ACSI rate. When a campsite only has pitches with a lower amperage, this lower amperage will apply. A 6A connection with a maximum of 4 kWh per day is included in the price. If you use excess, for example 5 kWh, it is possible that you might have to pay extra. See also 'Maximum loading available for electrical connections' on page 15.
- Hot showers. In campsites where showers are operated by tokens, CampingCard ACSI holders are entitled to one token per adult per day.**
- Maximum one dog staying on campsites which accept dogs. For a second (or additional) dog you might have to pay extra.
- VAT.

* Some campsites make a distinction between standard, luxury or comfort pitches. Luxury or comfort pitches are in general larger and equipped with their own water supply and drainage. CampingCard ACSI gives you the right to a standard pitch but it may occur that you are able to have a more expensive pitch at the CampingCard ACSI rate. The campsite has the right to decide this; you can NEVER insist on a luxury or comfort pitch.
Be aware also that some campsites have a different policy with regard to twin-axled caravans and mobile homes which are so large that they will not fit on a standard pitch.

** The campsite is required to allow the CampingCard ACSI holder one shower per day in accordance with the CampingCard ACSI conditions. Consequently each CampingCard ACSI holder has the right to one shower token per person per day. Where a campsite operates a different 'shower system' such as tokens, a key or a SEP key, the above conditions still apply but the camper will need to make the necessary arrangements with the campsite.
Hot water in washing up sinks is not included in the price. Unused shower tokens cannot be exchanged for money.

Not included in the overnight rate

In general the CampingCard ACSI rate is sufficient to pay for the overnight charge. The campsite may however make extra charges for a number of items:

- Tourist taxes, environmental taxes, waste disposal charges or local authority requirements are not included in the CampingCard ACSI rate. These taxes can differ greatly by country and region. In Switzerland and Austria in particular, and also in the Netherlands, you should be prepared for high charges for some of these taxes.
- Reservation and administration charges are not included in the CampingCard ACSI rate. You can read more about reserving with CampingCard ACSI on page 8.
- A campsite may make a surcharge for a luxury or comfort pitch (unless the campsite only has comfort pitches).
- The charge for a third adult or child, provided the campsite agrees to more than two people staying on a pitch designated for CampingCard ACSI users.
  However, at campsites which display the following symbol 👫, (a maximum of) three children up to and including the age of 5 are included in the CampingCard ACSI rate.
- Extra services such as facilities for which the campsite makes a charge, such as a tennis court, can be charged to you at the applicable low season rate.
- Electricity, if more is consumed than is specified on page 18. See also 'Maximum loading available for electrical connections' on page 15.

ACSI Club ID

The ACSI Club ID, the leading Camping Carnet for Europe, is indispensable for every camper. You will benefit from it both during your camping holiday and at home! Become a member at once and pay only € 4.95 a year.

Why does ACSI offer the ACSI Club ID?

It is ACSI's aim to offer you, the camper, a stress-free and pleasant holiday in as many different ways as possible.

All the advantages one by one:

- **Alternative identity card**

You can hand in your Camping Carnet, the ACSI Club ID, at participating ACSI Club ID campsites instead of your passport or identity papers. This means you will never have to hand in your identity papers but can always keep them safely in your pocket.*

**Please note: showing your identity papers is still required in some countries.*

- **Liability insurance coverage**

If you are in possession of the ACSI Club ID, you and your travelling companions (max 11 people) are insured against liability during your camping holiday or when staying in a hotel or rented accommodation. This insurance applies when you cause damage for third parties, for example if you accidentally let your bicycle fall onto your neighbour's tent during your holiday.

- **Accepted at more than 8,800 campsites in Europe**

More than 8,800 campsites in the ACSI campsite guides accept the ACSI Club ID. The amenity that shows that a campsite accepts the ACSI Club ID is mentioned in the list of amenities as 1A. You can also recognise these campsites by the 'ID' logo in the orange bar above the campsite's entry.
If you are going camping in Scandinavia, there is a chance that you will need a special card that you must show at reception. You can purchase this card at the relevant campsite.
Take note: the ACSI Club ID does not entitle you to a discount at campsites.

Differences between CampingCard ACSI and ACSI Club ID

There are differences between the ACSI Club ID and CampingCard ACSI. We have put these differences in a table for your benefit.

ACSI Club ID	CampingCard ACSI
The Camping Carnet, a substitute means of identification	The discount card for camping in low season
A membership	A loose product or a subscription
Liability insurance and discounts on ACSI products in the ACSI webshop	Gives you the right to a fixed low overnight rate during low season
Accepted as alternate means of identification at 8,800 campsites in 30 countries	Accepted at 3,142 participating campsites in 20 countries
Valid for 1 year, until the expiration date	Valid for one calendar year, from 1 January until 31 December
€ 4.95 per year	From € 10.95 per year (subscription)
www.ACSIclubID.eu	www.CAMPINGCARD.com

Application

You can apply for the ACSI Club ID via www.ACSIclubID.eu. Your card can be ordered in just a few steps. Be sure to have your identity papers handy when ordering.

The ACSI Club ID can be used by campers with one of the following nationalities: Dutch, Belgian, French, German, Austrian, Swiss, British (English, Scottish, Welsh and Northern Irish), Irish, Spanish, Italian, Norwegian, Swedish, Finnish and Danish.

Take note: campers with the above nationalities but who are not resident in the Netherlands, Germany, France, Belgium, Denmark, Switzerland, Austria, Ireland, United Kingdom, Norway, Sweden, Finland, Portugal, Spain or Italy cannot apply for the ACSI Club ID for insurance-related reasons.

Find the campsite that suits you best!

3,142 CampingCard ACSI campsites have been included in this guide, with extensive information about location and the amenities available. Even so it is not always easy to make a choice quickly. Match2Camp can help in this situation.

Match2Camp is a useful aid which you can use to quickly find a campsite that meets your requirements. ACSI conducted a survey of campers' wishes. Based on this, four lifestyles and nine categories were defined. Each campsite is then assigned to a category.

Decide first which lifestyle appeals to you most. Then choose a description that best describes the way you like to spend your holiday. All campsites in this guide have been assigned a Match2Camp icon with a colour or colour combination which corresponds to the description. So you can see at once which campsite is the right one for you.

The lifestyles and the various categories

Yellow lifestyle

For campers in this lifestyle a holiday is something you can live to the full. It should contain some exertion, either recreational or sportive. The camping holiday is seen as the high point of the year. The travel companions are central. Everyone must have the opportunity to have their own way with fun activities and meeting friendly fellow campers.

MATCH2CAMP

Lifestyles in brief

In the yellow lifestyle we meet campers looking for lively campsites with a large variety of amenities and fun activities.

Relax and enjoy
Complete and comfortable
Sociable

In the green lifestyle we meet campers looking for leisure. Keywords: relaxation and privacy.

Relaxation
Informal

In the blue lifestyle we meet campers looking for a comfortable campsite which can serve as a base for an active and sportive holiday.

Comfortable
Active

In the red lifestyle we meet campers looking for a special camping experience, a campsite that is 'just that bit different'. Keywords: nature, sport and leisure activities.

Unusual
Sportive

Campers in this lifestyle usually go camping twice a year. A long summer holiday and a shorter holiday in the low season. The summer holiday is the more important. Campsites with many amenities and facilities are therefore very appealing. And that may cost a bit extra.

Three categories can be defined within this lifestyle:

Yellow: Relax and enjoy

This category is particularly looking for a relaxing holiday. Using the motto 'you can't always have everything', these people are not necessarily looking for a campsite 'with all mod cons'. Provided there are enough fun activities for a relaxing holiday.

Yellow/blue: Complete and comfortable

This category is looking for a campsite with all mod cons. This is often a larger campsite with large pitches, plenty of amenities and a complete entertainment programme. This campsite may be a bit more expensive, provided this is reflected in the many amenities which are available for use.

Yellow/red: Sociable

This category is mainly looking for a campsite which has plenty of recreational facilities and where social activities are organised for the guests.

Green lifestyle

For campers in this lifestyle the holiday is mostly about 'chilling out' and 'letting yourself relax'. For these campers also, everything revolves around the travel companions they go with.

They are looking for a campsite that is not too big. The human factor and clear scale are most important. If the basic amenities are up to standard the campsite will meet their requirements.

These campers are enthusiastic about the peace and quiet of the surroundings, authentic villages and countryside, rather than large scale entertainment and leisure pools with big adventure slides.

Two categories can be defined within this lifestyle:

Green: Relaxation

This category is looking mainly for their own spot with plenty of privacy, peace and space. A marked out pitch, for example. The absence of entertainment, a large camp shop or a restaurant is not really a problem for these campers.

Green/yellow: Informal

For this category the ambiance of the campsite is also important. These campers want to meet each other and enjoy a pleasant walk or take a relaxing cycle trip in the vicinity of the campsite.

Blue lifestyle

For campers in this lifestyle it is important to relax on holiday. To get away from the hectic everyday life. Time then for the family and for hobbies. The campsite should be designed to facilitate these wishes.

Relaxation for this category certainly does not mean just 'doing nothing'. When it comes to relaxation these campers usually have their own equipment to pursue their hobbies. A bike, for example, or a set of golf clubs or a motor boat. The campsite is chosen to facilitate this hobby.

These campers go on holiday several times a year. They have the budget for it, but the campsite does not need to be the top in luxury.

Provided sufficient comfort is offered and there are (specific) amenities that go with the activity/hobby they want to pursue. It must certainly not be a case of 'roughing it'.

Two categories can be defined within this lifestyle:

Comfortable

For this category it is important that the campsite has some (luxury) extras, such as comfort pitches, a sauna, a beauty centre or a sunbed.

Sportive

This category is looking for a campsite that is primarily geared up for sports activities such as golf, cycling or watersports.

Red lifestyle

Campers in this lifestyle have a clear and established plan for their holiday. A short break to relax, for example, a themed holiday or something to really get involved in (active/sportive). The campsite is selected with this in mind. Campers in this category like to find a campsite that is 'a bit out of the ordinary'.

Two categories can be defined within this lifestyle:

Red: Unusual

This category wants to experience something unique, something a bit out of the ordinary. The camper wants to have a 'story' to take home. Activity is often central to this so they usually look for an 'unusual' location. The campsite should have something special, a tree-house or a tepee for example. These are often smaller campsites with a restricted number of amenities.

Red/green: Sportive

This category is sports-minded and is looking for a campsite that fits in with the programme that has been planned. The campsite is then more of a base camp. It's a bonus if it can offer amenities that are available when returning from an activity. A supermarket, for example, or a restaurant or swimming pool. This category is not really demanding. It's more about the atmosphere that is created. The off-beat is really a fun, fascinating or interesting experience.

Internet

Let your computer do the work!

The www.CAMPINGCARD.com website has been completely redesigned. The website can help you to find a campsite even more quickly and easily. The site has also been adapted for tablets and mobile phones, and is useful as an addition to this guide. If you prefer to make use of our content without having internet access, maybe our app is something for you. You will find more information on page 30.

On the website there are various easy ways to search for a campsite, including:

- **By map**
  You are searching for a campsite in a particular area. Each time you click on the map you reduce the search area. The result is a summary list of campsites from which you can make a choice. By clicking the tent symbol on the map the details of your chosen campsite will be displayed.

- **By place name, region or country**
  Simply type in the name or a part of the town, region or country in the search field. The redesigned site recognises more than 500,000 place names throughout Europe. This way, you will always find a campsite that is located close to you.

- **By campsite number**
  The campsite number of a campsite - that you can find with every campsite in this guide and the mini-atlas - can be used to find your campsite quickly by filling in the number in the search field on the website.

- **By campsite name**
  Simply type in the name of the campsite. You can find this in the CampingCard ACSI guide and in the mini-atlas.

- **By holiday period**
  When you search by holiday period you will see a summary of campsites that (partly) meet the search criteria. You will find more information about a campsite's acceptance period on page 16.

- **By facilities**
  You can also easily filter for particular facilities at the campsite. That way you can quickly find the campsites you require.

- **By theme**
  Here you will find campsites with various themes, such as sites adapted for the disabled, wintersports campsites and naturist campsites.

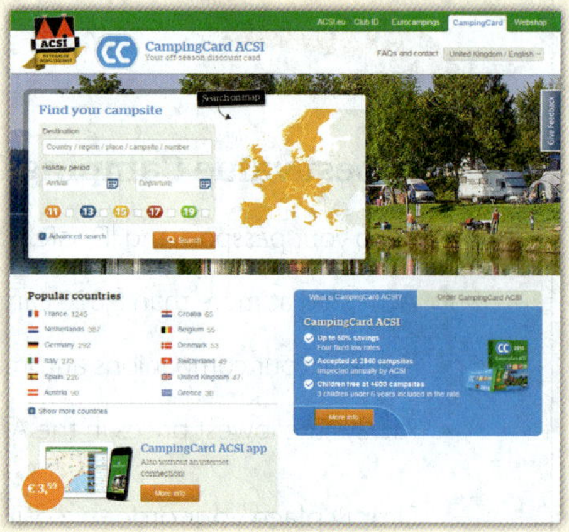

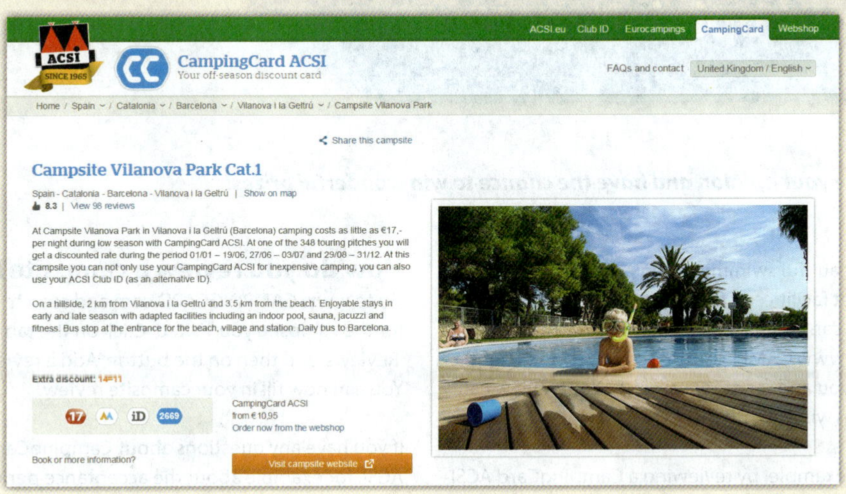

Integrated route planner

When you have found the campsite where you want to go on holiday, you can use the route planner on the campsite page under the 'Address & Route' tab to plan the journey completely from your home address to the CampingCard ACSI campsite via Google Maps. You can also plan out the return journey. Convenient and quick!

Reviews

Would you like to know what other campers think of a campsite? You can read other campers' reviews per campsite on www.CAMPINGCARD.com. These campers have reviewed a campsite for its staff, value for money and the surroundings, among other things. In this way you will get an independent and extensive impression of the campsite. You can also place your own review of a campsite. By leaving a review you will enter a draw for great prizes! See also page 28.

Newsletter

If you sign up to our newsletter you will monthly receive useful tips, special offers and information about CampingCard ACSI! This way you will always be kept up to date on the latest news. You can sign up for this newsletter via www.CAMPINGCARD.com/newsletter.

Modifications

There may be some changes in the information which is displayed about a campsite in the course of a year. So check www.CAMPINGCARD.com/modifications before you leave.

Take the Match2Camp test

With the Match2Camp test you can find out what kind of camper you are and find campsites to suit you. You will find more information about Match2Camp on page 22 and on www.CAMPINGCARD.com/match2camp.

Tips, comments or suggestions?

If you have any tips, comments or suggestions for CampingCard ACSI, go to www.CAMPINGCARD.com/customerservice.

Your opinion matters

Give your opinion and have the chance to win wonderful prizes!

A beautiful swimming pool, well maintained toilet facilities or friendly staff at the campsite: you can submit a review for every campsite on our www.CAMPINGCARD.com website. Useful for you and for other campers. Your review can even win you prizes.

For example, by reviewing a CampingCard ACSI campsite you could win a Suncamp holidays camping cheque worth € 450.
So don't wait any longer and share your opinion!

How do you review a campsite?

Go to www.CAMPINGCARD.com and search for the campsite you visited. Click on the tab 'Reviews' and then on the button 'Add a review'. You can now fill in your campsite review.

If you have any questions about CampingCard ACSI, for example about the acceptance period or the rate of a campsite, you can contact ACSI via www.CAMPINGCARD.com/customerservice.

I want to thank you for the wonderful CampingCard ACSI discount system. We travelled through France and Italy for a few weeks and have had an excellent time with virtually no unpleasant experiences to speak of.
Thank you very much and kind regards,
D. Löttrich

CampingCard ACSI app

Now even more convenience with the CampingCard ACSI app

With the CampingCard ACSI app you have all campsite information at your fingertips! The app contains all CampingCard ACSI campsites and has lots of useful functions and search options. The app is suitable for smartphones and tablets (Android and iOS) and can also be used without an internet connection!

"Easy to use, clear and has handy filters for rate and acceptance period"
B. Jager

- **Search by name**

You can search campsites by country, region, place, campsite number or campsite name. Enter a search term and view the campsite(s) on the map. The database is very extensive and contains more than 500,000 search terms!

- **Search in the area**

Is location awareness activated on your device? If so the app will identify your location and show the CampingCard ACSI campsites that are close to you. If you prefer to search for a specific place on the map you can set your location on the map manually. That way you'll always find a campsite close by. Perfect if you're looking for a place to stay overnight.

- **Search filters**
The app contains really useful search filters. You can filter by more than 150 amenities, the CampingCard ACSI rates, periods of stay, stopover campsites and Match2Camp

- **View the campsite**
You will find comprehensive information about the grounds and the amenities for each campsite. Check if it's suitable by looking at the photos, map resources and campsite reviews from other campers

- **Favourites**
When you have found one or more campsites that meet your requirements, you can add them to your favourites so you can find them again quickly. Your favourites will then also be recognisable on the map.

- **Contact with the campsite**
When you have chosen a campsite you can call the site directly from the app to check availability. You can also send an e-mail from the app.

Campsite reviews

Since 2015 it is also possible to review a campsite in the app. Even when there is no internet connection. The app will save the review and send it automatically when your device connects to the internet at a later time!

Attention:
In order to be able to take advantage of the low, fixed rates you will always need to be able to show a physical, valid discount card at the reception. Showing only the app or campsite guide does not suffice.

Go to www.CAMPINGCARD.com/appinfo for more information and an explanation on how to purchase access to the app.

All CampingCard ACSI campsites in one app!

- Can also be used offline; always have campsite information at hand!
- Read other people's campsite reviews, and write your own
- Free updates with modified campsite information
- Very extensive information per campsite
- Find a campsite near you or use the handy search filters

€ 3.59 per calendar year

Your unique purchase code.

In order to gain access to the CampingCard ACSI app you will need a unique purchase code. With this code, we can verify that you have a valid CampingCard ACSI. You will find the code on the back of your discount card, as pictured below:

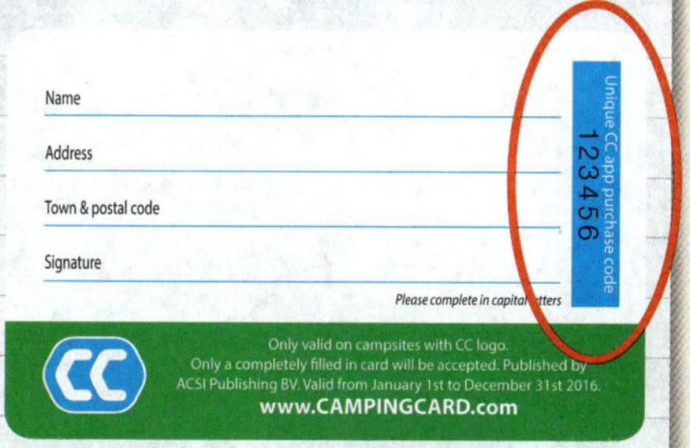

Extra information
Disabled and wintersports lists

♿ Campsites suitable for the disabled
Every year ACSI produces a list showing which campsites are suitable for the disabled. The norms for this are agreed in consultation with the Dutch Council for the Disabled. Campsites that are included in the list are all equipped with a toilet and shower, or a combination of the two, which have been specially adapted for use by disabled people. Furthermore we indicate whether a campsite has any other amenities suitable for the disabled.

Winter sports campsites
ACSI also compiles an extensive list of winter sports campsites and their facilities once a year.

Download/request
We continue to update this unique lists annually. You can download the extensive lists from our website www.CAMPINGCARD.com/disabled and www.CAMPINGCARD.com/wintersports.

The loveliest
family campsites
Suncamp holidays
Book a wonderful, carefree holiday with Suncamp holidays!
• More than 500 campsites in 14 countries
• Never more expensive than when you book directly with the campsite
• All campsites inspected annually by the campsite specialist ACSI
• Service and dependability
Camping pitches
Glamping tents
Mobile homes
Book easy on: www.SUNCAMP.co.uk or call: +44 (0)845-22 50 931
ANVR
SGR

Holiday exhibitions

A chance to meet us! The start of a new year is the perfect time to begin making your holiday plans. And to get yourself into the holiday mood.

We enjoy listening to your experiences of previous holidays, and welcome your ideas and suggestions.

Person to person

We would like to meet you in person at the 2016 Holiday Exhibitions and tell you more about the CampingCard ACSI formula. You can also get to know more about other ACSI products.

You're more than welcome!

In 2016:

Caravan Camping & Motorhome Show, Birmingham
23 - 28 February
www.caravancampingmotorhomeshow.co.uk

Please visit www.CAMPINGCARD.com/fairs for more information about trade fairs.

France

General

France is a member of the EU.

Time

The time in France is the same as Amsterdam, Berlin and Rome and one hour ahead of London.

Language

French. You can also get by in English in tourist areas.

Border formalities

Many formalities and agreements about matters such as necessary travel documents, car papers, requirements relating to your means of transport and accommodation, medical expenses and taking pets with you do not only depend on the country you are travelling to but also on your departure point and nationality. The length of your stay can also play a role here. It is not possible within the confines of this guide to guarantee the correct and most up to date information with regard to these matters.

We advise you to consult the relevant authorities before your departure about:
- which travel documents you will need for yourself and your fellow passengers
- which documents you need for your car
- which regulations your caravan must meet
- which goods you may import and export
- how medical treatment will be arranged and paid for in your holiday destination in cases of accident or illness
- whether you can take pets. Contact your vets well in advance. They can give you information about the necessary vaccinations, proof thereof and obligations on return. It would also make sense to enquire whether any special regulations apply to your pet in public places at your holiday destination. In some countries for example dogs must always be muzzled or transported in a cage.

You will find plenty of general information on ▸ ***www.europa.eu*** ◂ but make certain you select information that is relevant to your specific situation.

For the most recent customs regulations you should get in contact with the authorities of your holiday destination in your country of residence.

Currency

The currency in France is the euro. Approximate exchange rates September 2015: £ 1 = € 1.37.

In general you can pay in France using your debit card.

Credit cards

You can pay almost everywhere by credit card, including motorway tolls. You usually have to validate a purchase with a signature and you may sometimes be asked for identification.

Opening times/Public holidays

Banks

French banks are open from Tuesday to Friday between 9:00 and 18:00. Banks are open on Saturday mornings.

Shops

Shops are open from Tuesday to Saturday until 19:00/20:00. Most shops in country areas are closed between 13:00 and 14:00. Many shops are closed on Monday morning or for the whole day.

Chemists
French chemists are open on weekdays until 19:00.

Public holidays
New Year's Day, Easter, 1 May (Labour Day), 8 May (1945 Armistice), Ascension Day, Pentecost, 14 July (Bastille Day), 15 August (The Assumption), 1 November (All Saints), 11 November (1918 Armistice), Christmas Day.

Communication

(Mobile) phones
The mobile network works well throughout France, except in some areas in the Alps and the Massif Central. There is a 3G network for mobile internet. You can use a credit card or a phone card to pay at telephone boxes. You can buy phone cards at post offices, tobacconists and kiosks.

WiFi, internet
You will find internet cafes everywhere in France, and especially in cities. WiFi is often available and more campsites are now offering it.

Post
Post offices are open from Monday to Friday until 18:00 and on Saturday until 12:00.

Roads and traffic

Road network
You are advised not to drive after dark in rural areas. Along major roads breakdown assistance can be summoned using emergency phones to warn the motorway operators who are in contact with the police.

Traffic regulations
Remember, all traffic in France drives on the right and overtakes on the left! Headlight deflectors are advisable to prevent annoying oncoming drivers. France uses the metric system, so distances are measured in kilometres (km) and speeds in kilometres per hour (km/h). Traffic from the right has priority except on main roads. Uphill traffic on narrow mountain roads has priority over descending traffic. You have priority on a roundabout if this is indicated by a triangular sign showing a roundabout. If there is no such sign drivers entering the roundabout will have priority.

Maximum speed

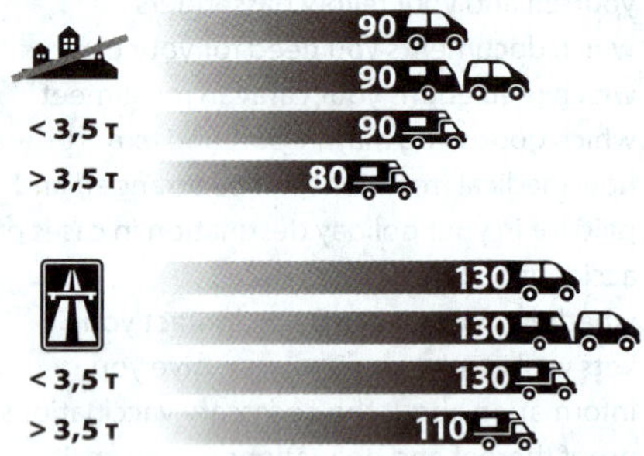

Maximum permitted alcohol level is 0.5‰. You must use dipped headlights in poor visibility. You must phone hands-free.
You are required to wear a high visibility jacket in the event of a breakdown. Children under 10 must always sit in the back. Take note: never cross continuous white road markings, not even with one wheel! Winter tyres are not compulsory but if you have an accident in adverse winter conditions and your vehicle does not have winter tyres, you could be held (jointly) liable.

You are required to carry a breathalyser in your vehicle, but you won't be fined if you don't. You can buy breathalysers at filling stations, supermarkets and chemists.

Navigation
Notification of fixed speed cameras by navigation systems or mobile phones is not permitted. You are advised to remove speed camera locations from your navigation system.

Caravans, motorhomes
If your caravan weighs more than 3.5 tonnes lower speed limits apply. Overnight stays in your caravan or motorhome in built up areas and beside the motorway are prohibited, except in specially designated areas and for a maximum of 24 hours.
Caravans with a twin axle are generally not permitted on municipal campsites.

Permitted dimensions
Height unlimited, width 2.55 metres and maximum length 12 metres.

Fuel
Euro 95 has been replaced almost totally by E10. Check before your holiday whether E10 is suitable for your vehicle. Superplus 98 is a suitable alternative for euro 95. Diesel and LPG are easily available at the pumps.

Filling stations
Most filling stations on motorways are open 24 hours. Some service stations on 'routes nationales' are also open day and night, but many close at 21.00. Take note that an increasing number of service stations away from motorways are closed on Sunday.

Credit cards and most bank cards showing the Maestro logo are accepted at filling stations.

Tolls
Tolls apply to most French motorways. Blue signs indicate a road leading to a motorway. The indication 'péage' shows that it is a toll road. If you don't wish to pay a toll, follow the green signs which show alternative routes. You can pay the toll by credit card. Some of them can only be paid in cash. Take note that your toll ticket is only valid for 24 hours. More information about toll roads in France: ▸ *www.autoroutes.fr* ◂ (also in English)

Black Saturday
The busiest Saturdays in the summer season are known as 'black Saturdays'. Black Saturdays occur in the last week of July and the first week of August every year.

Emergency numbers
- 112: the national emergency number for fire, police and ambulance
- 17: police
- 18: fire
- 15: ambulance

Camping
With more than 10,000 campsites, France is Europe's biggest camping country. Be sure to reserve early if you want to go to the Ardèche or Dordogne in the interior, or to large seaside resorts. Pitches inland are often more spacious, better equipped and better value than on the coast.

It is worth noting that certain amenities such as the swimming pool, restaurant, snack bar, pizzeria and such like may only open in July and August. In all swimming pools, proper swimming trunks/costumes are obligatory and women are often required to wear a bathing cap. For hygienic reasons, boxer shorts, Bermuda shorts and other similar clothing is not allowed. On campsites in France you may come across signs 'Inondation par temps de grosse pluie', meaning that the area is prone to flooding during heavy rainfall.

Practical
- Prices for electrical hook-ups are high and can vary from € 1.50 to € 4.50 per day. (These are included in the CampingCard ACSI rate!)
- Make sure you have a world adaptor for electrical appliances.
- Drink bottled (mineral) water in preference to mains water.

Corsica
Most campsites on Corsica are on the coast and are usually well indicated. The roads, especially in the west, are narrow and sinuous. French is the official language but an accent similar to Italian is also spoken. There are few service stations inland!
Corsica can be reached by various routes.

PROMENADE EN MER
RISTORANTE

Autingues, F-62610 / Nord-Pas-de-Calais (Pas-de-Calais)

1243

St. Louis***
223 rue de Leulène
+33 (0)3-21354683
1/4 - 18/10
camping-saint-louis@sfr.fr

2ha 30T(80-110m²) 10A CEE

1 ACDGIJKLMOPQ
2 FRTVX
3 AGRU
4 (Q 1/5-30/9) (R)
(T+U+X 1/5-15/9) Z
5 **A**FGIJKMN**P**UZ
6 EGJ(N 2km)OTV

A quietly located campsite in the Calais-Boulogne-St. Omer triangle. Spacious marked out pitches. A site with nice new toilet facilities and a lovely bar.

Take the A26 Calais-St. Omer. Exit Ardres/ Nordausque. In Ardres RN43 direction Calais. Campsite signposted.

CC € 17 *1/4-30/6* *1/9-16/10* *15=13*

N 50°50'18'' E 1°58'36''

Boiry-Notre-Dame, F-62156 / Nord-Pas-de-Calais (Pas-de-Calais)

1244

La Paille Haute**
145 rue de Sailly
+33 (0)3-21481540
FAX +33 (0)3-21220724
1/4 - 31/10
lapaillehaute@wanadoo.fr

5ha 60T(80-100m²) 6A CEE

1 ACDGIJKLMPQ
2 FJKLRVWXY
3 BCDGRUW
4 (C+**H** 1/6-15/9) (Q)
(T+U+V 15/6-31/8)
(W+X 15/6-7/9) Z
5 **AB**DFGIJKLMNPUW
6 EG**I**K(N 2km)RTV

Child friendly stopover campsite with swimming pool and various types of play equipment. Rural location with spacious marked out pitches. Ideal for exploring the area around Arras. Free WiFi.

From Lille A1 direction Paris, exit 15, then D939 direction Cambrai. Left after about 3 km to Boiry-Notre-Dame. Campsite signposted.

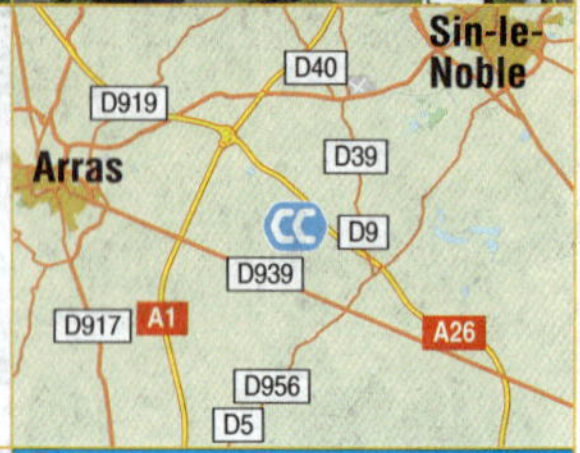

CC € 17 *1/4-25/6* *1/9-31/10* *7=6*

N 50°16'25'' E 2°56'56''

Equihen-Plage, F-62224 / Nord-Pas-de-Calais (Pas-de-Calais)

1245

Mun. La Falaise***
rue Charles Cazin
+33 (0)3-21312261
FAX +33 (0)3-21805401
28/3 - 12/11
camping.equihen.plage@orange.fr

8ha 112T(100-120m²) 10A CEE

1 ACD**G**IJKLMPQ
2 AEFIRSVX
3 BGNRU
5 ABFJKLNPUW
6 CEGJ(N 2km)T

A large municipal campsite with marked out pitches which are positioned only 150m from the sea. There is plenty of shade. A good base for visiting Boulogne-sur-Mer, Le Touquet-Paris-Plage, picturesque Wimereux, Cap Gris-Nez and Cap Blanc-Nez.

N1 Boulogne-Abbeville, exit Le Portel/Hardelot or A16 Boulogne-Paris, exit Neuchâtel.

CC € 17 *28/3-8/7* *25/8-12/11*

N 50°40'15'' E 1°34'18''

Guines, F-62340 / Nord-Pas-de-Calais (Pas-de-Calais)

iD **1246**

La Bien Assise*****
route D231
+33 (0)3-21352077
FAX +33 (0)3-21367920
2/4 - 26/9
@ castels@bien-assise.com

15ha 149**T**(100-200m²) 10A CEE

1 ACD**G**IJKLMOPQ
2 FLRVX
3 ABGH**MNQ**RU
4 (**E**+H 4/4-15/9) J
(Q+S+T+U+X 4/4-15/9)
(Y 4/4-1/10) Z
5 **AB**DEFGIJKLMNOPUVWXY
Z
6 ADEGI**J**(N 1km)ORTV

Lovely, well-maintained castle campsite. Varied surroundings and only 8 km from the coast. The campsite is equipped with modern toilet facilities, a restaurant with an excellent menu, an indoor pool and spacious pitches. Please reserve in advance.

From the centre of Calais follow D127 towards Guines. Follow the signs through the centre of Guines. Campsite located on the D231. From St. Omer take N13 to Ardres. Next, take D231 past Guines. Follow signs to campsite.

CC € 19 *2/4-27/5 6/6-26/6 5/9-26/9 7=6, 14=12, 21=18*

N 50°51'59'' E 1°51'30''

Licques, F-62850 / Nord-Pas-de-Calais (Pas-de-Calais)

iD **1247**

Pommiers des Trois Pays****
273 rue du Breuil
FAX +33 (0)3-21350202
15/3 - 31/10
@ contact@pommiers-3pays.com

2,5ha 36**T**(100-150m²) 16A CEE

1 ACD**G**IJKLMOPRS
2 FRUVWX
3 ABGHJRU
4 (E+F+H 6/4-20/9)
(Q+T+U+V+X 1/4-15/10) Z
5 **AB**DEFGIJKLMNOPUXYZ
6 CDEGK(N 0,8km)TV

The campsite is located in a former apple orchard with spacious marked out pitches. The Parc Natural Régional and the Marais d'Opale invite you for lovely walks while the undulating landscape is a challenge for energetic cyclists. Licques is just 25 km from the sea and is the ideal base to explore the Opal Coast with Cap Gris Nez and Cap Blanc Nez.

From Lille, dir. Saint-Omer via A26/E15. Exit 2 dir. Licques. Campsite signposted.

CC € 17 *15/3-4/7 28/8-31/10 7=6*

N 50°46'47'' E 1°56'52''

Rang-du-Fliers, F-62180 / Nord-Pas-de-Calais (Pas-de-Calais)

iD **1248**

l'Orée du Bois****
chemin Blanc
+33 (0)3-21842851
FAX +33 (0)3-21842856
1/4 - 31/10
@ oree.du.bois@wanadoo.fr

18ha 100**T**(80-110m²) 6A CEE

1 ACD**G**IJKLMPQ
2 ABFGLRVX
3 B**F**GHJMNRUW
4 (C 1/6-15/9) (E 8/4-30/10)
(H 1/6-15/9) **KLN**
(Q+S+T+U+V+X+Y+Z)
5 **AB**CFGJLNPUVW
6 CDEGH**I**JMTUV

This French campsite with a leisure pool is situated in a natural wooded area with marked out pitches and 4 km from the sea. Bar, restaurant (closed Wednesday), heated swimming pools and toilet facilities, jacuzzi and sauna. Some open-air fitness equipment. There is a supermarket next to the campsite.

A16 exit 25. Then D303 direction Rang-du-Fliers. After entering Rang-du-Fliers turn left just past Lidl. Follow signs, not your SatNav for the last section.

CC € 17 *1/4-3/7 22/8-31/10 7=6*

N 50°25'1'' E 1°36'42''

Wacquinghen, F-62250 / Nord-Pas-de-Calais (Pas-de-Calais) — 1249

Camping l'Escale***
15 Route Nationale
+33 (0)3-21320069
FAX +33 (0)3-21337957
1/4 - 15/10
@ camp-escale@wanadoo.fr

11ha 30T(60-100m²) 10A CEE

1 ACDGIJKLMOPQ
2 FGRUWX
3 BGHIMNQRUW
4 (Q 1/5-31/8) (R 1/6-31/8) (U+Y 1/4-30/9) Z
5 **AB**FGJLNPUVWZ
6 CEG**IK**(N 3km)OTV

This 11 hectare parkland campsite invites you to take relaxing walks along the cliffs of Cap Gris Nez and Cap Blanc Nez. Just 5 minutes from the sandy beaches of the Opal Coast. Good connections to the Channel Tunnel and ferries to the UK. Good restaurant at the site.

A16 between Calais and Boulogne-sur-Mer exit 34 direction Wacquinghen.

CC € 17 *1/4-1/7 28/8-15/10 7=6*

N 50°47'2'' E 1°40'9''

Wimereux, F-62930 / Nord-Pas-de-Calais (Pas-de-Calais) — 1250

Mun. L'Olympic***
49 rue de la Libération
+33 (0)3-21324563
FAX +33 (0)3-21836894
21/3 - 16/10
@ camping.wimereux@orange.fr

3,8ha 91T(63-90m²) 6A CEE

1 ACD**G**IJKLMPQ
2 EFGRVWX
3 AB**F**GHN**O**RUY
4 (Q)
5 **AB**DEFGIJKLMNOPUXYZ
6 EG**J**(N 0,8km)TV

An unpretentious campsite marked out by hedges and close to the picturesque seaside village of Wimereux. Located between Cap Gris-Nez, the Opal Coast and Boulogne-sur-Mer. 5 km from Nausicaá, the world-famous sea aquarium in Boulogne-sur-Mer. Easily accessible by bus.

A16, exit Wimereux Sud. Direction Wimereux. Campsite signposted.

CC € 17 *21/3-10/7 29/8-16/10*

N 50°45'40'' E 1°36'28''

Albert, F-80300 / Picardie (Somme) — 1251

Camping Le Vélodrome**
avenue Henry Dunant
+33 (0)3-64622253
1/4 - 11/10
@ campingalbert@laposte.net

1,6ha 75T(72-120m²) 10A CEE

1 ACDFIJKLMOPQ
2 CDGRTVWX
3 AHJR
4 (Q)
5 GIJKLMNOPUWXYZ
6 ACDEGJ(N 0,6km)T

The campsite is located on the River Ancre and by several well-stocked fishing lakes. There is a free practice range for golf with 5 holes next to the site. The area around Albert formed the front line during the attacks of the Somme in 1916. The many graveyards and monuments are a silent witness to this. There is a special area for motorhomes.

Via D929 direction Albert. Then follow signs.

CC € 15 *1/4-26/6 23/8-11/10 7=6*

N 50°0'41'' E 2°39'20''

Berny-Rivière, F-02290 / Picardie (Aisne)

1252

La Croix du Vieux Pont*****
rte de Fontenoy
+33 (0)3-23555002
FAX +33 (0)3-23550513
1/1 - 31/12
info@la-croix-du-vieux-pont.com

34ha 200T(100-450m²) 16A CEE

1 ACDGIJKLMOPRS
2 ACDLRVXY
3 ABCGHJK**M**N**OP**QR**T**U**V** **W**Z
4 (C+E+H 1/4-31/10) IJ**KMN** O**P**(Q)
(S+T+U+V+W+X+Y 1/4-31/10)Z
5 **AB**DEFGIJKLMNOPRUXYZ
6 BEG**IJ**ORTV

A very large, well equipped campsite on the River l'Aisne. All types of pitches. A family campsite suitable mainly for older children including a heated swimming pool and many other sports opportunities. Own bus connection to Paris and Disneyland.

In Vic-sur-Aisne take the D91 in the direction of Soissons. The campsite is located to the right after 1 km in Berny-Rivière.

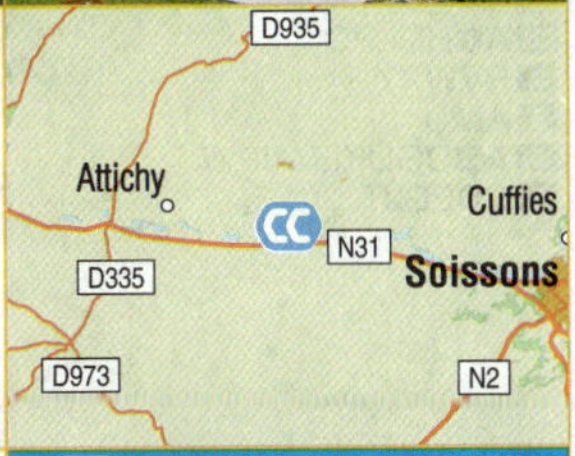

CC € 19 *1/1-30/6 1/9-31/12*

N 49°24'19'' E 3°7'44''

Bresles, F-60510 / Picardie (Oise)

1253

Camping de la Trye
34 rue de Trye
FAX +33 (0)3-44078095
1/1 - 31/12
camping.bresles@sfr.fr

3ha 40T(100-250m²) 6A CEE

1 ACDGIJKLMPQ
2 FGMRVWXY
3 ADGHJK**M**OPR**W**
4 (A 1/7-31/8) (B 1/5-15/10) (Q+T 1/7-31/8)
5 **AB**GIJMNPUXZ
6 ACEGJ(N 1km)O

A congenial campsite near Beauvais in natural surroundings and with plenty of walking and cycling opportunities. You can visit Paris by car or train. Special pony, horse and donkey activities for young and old. The Parc Asterix and Saint Paul theme parks are close by.

N31 from Compiègne to Beauvais, exit Bresles. Then follow Stade or camping signs.

CC € 15 *1/1-15/7 1/9-31/12* *7=6, 14=12*

N 49°24'19'' E 2°15'29''

Brighton-les-Pins, F-80410 / Picardie (Somme)

1254

Le Bois de Pins***
rue Guillaume le Conquérant
+33 (0)3-22267104
FAX +33 (0)3-22266081
1/4 - 30/10
info@campingleboisdepins.com

4ha 60T(82-200m²) 10A CEE

1 ABCD**G**IJKLM**P**Q
2 BENRSVX
3 AGHNR
4 (Q+R)
5 **AB**DEFGJLNPU
6 AEGH**K**(N 3km)

A modest campsite where you will be able to relax. The (pebble) beach is about 500m from the campsite. Cayeux-sur-Mer is about 1 km away and there you can swim in the sea. Reception closed from 12:00 to 14:00 outside high season.

At Abbeville go from the A28 to the D40 then D940. After St. Valéry-sur-Somme to the D3. Right in La Mollière to the D102. Campsite signposted before Brighton.

CC € 17 *1/4-8/7 26/8-30/10*

N 50°11'51'' E 1°31'0''

Charly-sur-Marne, F-02310 / Picardie (Aisne)

1255

Les Illettes***
route de Pavant
+33 (0)3-23821211
+33 (0)3-23821399
1/4 - 30/9
marie.charly@wanadoo.fr

2ha 42T(80-100m²) 5A

1 AGHIJLPQ
2 RVWXY
3 AMU
5 ABDGIJKLMNPW
6 CDEGJT

Discover the Champagne region, visit Paris/ Disneyland in just 1 hour. Peaceful campsite in a friendly village.

Coming from Château-Thierry D969 along the Marne Valley for about 15 km. A4 from Paris exit St. Jean-les-deux-Jumeaux. Another 20 km dir. la Ferté-sous-Jouarre, then dir. Charly. Follow signs from here (next to Super-U).

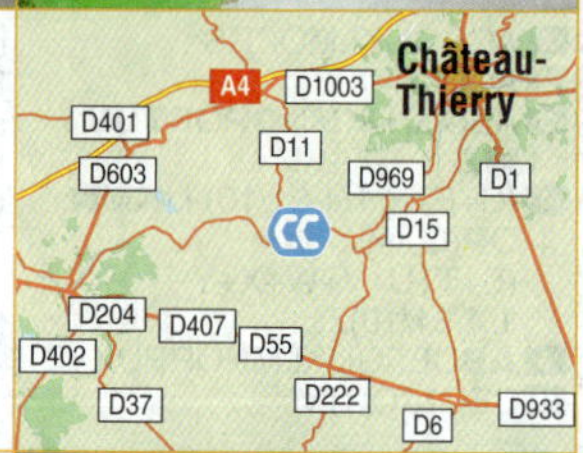

CC € 11 1/4-15/7 1/9-30/9

N 48°58'25'' E 3°16'55''

Feuillères, F-80200 / Picardie (Somme)

1256

Château de l'Oseraie***
10 rue de Château
+33 (0)3-22831759
15/3 - 31/10
jsg-bred@wanadoo.fr

1,5ha 30T(80-120m²) 6-10A

1 ACDGIJKLMPR
2 CFLRTVWXY
3 BGJMNR
4 (C+H 1/4-15/10) (Q 1/6-31/8) (R) (T 1/4-30/9) Z
5 ABDGJLNPSU
6 BDEGIK(N 8km)OV

Welcoming camping grounds in a small village. Many sports options. The area around the river Somme is perfect for nice days out. Fishing is possible nearby. Close to the town of Peronne. The owners are friendly, enthusiastic and young.

Exit Autoroute A1 at 13.1 km, Feuillères 2 km further, road on right by the church goes to the campsite.

CC € 17 1/4-15/6 1/9-31/10

N 49°56'53'' E 2°50'36''

Forest-Montiers, F-80120 / Picardie (Somme)

1257

Camping de la Mottelette**
Ferme de la Mottelette
+33 (0)3-22283233
+33 (0)3-22283497
1/4 - 31/10
fermedelamottelettemanier@ wanadoo.fr

1ha 35T(100-150m²) 6A CEE

1 ADGIJKLMOPRS
2 DFLMRWX
3 AGRW
4 (Q+R) (Z 1/7-31/8)
5 ACGJLNPUXZ
6 ACDEGJ(N 4km)OTV

A small farmyard campsite close to the Bay of the Somme. You will be welcomed in friendly surroundings to spend an enjoyable holiday.

A16, exit 24 direction Rue. Follow signs at roundabout.

CC € 13 1/4-8/7 25/8-31/10

N 50°15'10'' E 1°42'45''

Fort-Mahon-Plage, F-80120 / Picardie (Somme) 1258

Le Royon****
1271 route de Quend
+33 (0)3-22234030
FAX +33 (0)3-22236515
18/3 - 1/11
info@campingleroyon.com

4,5ha 36T(95-130m²) 6A

1 ACD**F**IJL**P**Q
2 GLRVX
3 A**F**GKMNQRU**W**
4 (C 1/7-31/8) (F 16/4-30/10) (G 1/7-31/8) (Q) (R+T+U+X 1/7-31/8) Z
5 **AB**CDEFGIJKLNPUXZ
6 CDEGH**IK**(N 1km)ORTV

A campsite with plenty of amenities and a swimming pool. Pitches on grassland and separated by trees and hedges. 3 km from the resort of Fort-Mahon-Plage with its lovely sandy beach and good fish restaurants.

Motorway A16 take exit Quend. Then, in direction Fort-Mahon-Plage. Campsite is signposted.

CC €17 *18/3-9/7 26/8-31/10*

N 50°19'57'' E 1°34'46''

La Mollière-d'Aval, F-80410 / Picardie (Somme) 1259

Les Galets de la Mollière***
rue Faidherbe
+33 (0)3-22266185
FAX +33 (0)3-22266568
1/4 - 30/10
info@campinglesgaletsdelamolliere.com

6ha 75T(80-120m²) 10A CEE

1 ABCD**G**IJKLM**P**Q
2 BLNRSVX
3 AGHJMRU**W**
4 (C+H 1/5-15/9) K(Q+R) (T 1/7-31/8) Z
5 **AB**CFGJLNPUZ
6 ACEH**K**(N 3km)T

The campsite is located near a lovely shingle and sandy beach (no swimming), close to the dunes and pine forests. The campsite has a heated swimming pool. Kite-surfing possible in the bay when wind is good.

Follow A16 motorway to the A28, then dir. Cayeux-sur-Mer. Turn right at the first village La Molliere. Signs on the right side of the road.

CC €17 *1/4-8/7 26/8-30/10*

N 50°12'10'' E 1°31'34''

Le Crotoy, F-80550 / Picardie (Somme) 1260

Camping le Tarteron***
route de Rue, BP 70034
+33 (0)3-22270675
FAX +33 (0)3-22270249
1/4 - 31/10
contact@letarteron.fr

7ha 50T(100-140m²) 6A

1 ACDGIJKLMPQ
2 AFMRVWX
3 AGHJMNRW
4 (F+H 15/4-15/10) (Q+R+Z 1/7-31/8)
5 **AB**CFGIJKLNPRUWX
6 AGJ**K**(N 1,5km)T

The camping grounds have a peaceful location in the heart of the Bay of Somme. Partly marked out pitches, partly on large grassy fields. Lovely indoor swimming pool. Good cycling options.

From A16, exit 23 route Le Crotoy. In Le Crotoy turn right at first roundabout. Signposted.

CC €17 *1/4-4/7 29/8-31/10*

N 50°13'50'' E 1°38'25''

Le Crotoy, F-80550 / Picardie (Somme)

1261

Les Aubépines****
rue de la Maye - St. Firmin
+33 (0)3-22270134
FAX +33 (0)3-22271366
25/3 - 1/11
@ lesaubepines@
baiedesommepleinair.com

4ha 68**T**(90-180m²) 6A CEE

1 ACD**G**IJKLMO**P**Q
2 AFGLRVX
3 AD**F**GHJKMR
4 (A 1/7-31/8) (C+H 1/5-15/9) (Q+R)
5 **AB**CDEFGIJKLMNPUWXYZ
6 ACEGI**K**(N 3km)ORT

Les Aubépines, a small flowery family campsite is located in the heart of the Somme bay region, in natural surroundings and 1 km from the beach. A paradise for cyclists and walkers.

From A16 exit 23, follow road to Le Crotoy. At Le Crotoy, follow D4 Crotoy/St. Firmin de C. Left at St. Firmin sign. The campsite is signposted. Do not follow SatNav on last section.

CC € 17 *25/3-7/7 24/8-1/11 7=6*

N 50°14'59'' E 1°36'43''

Le Crotoy, F-80550 / Picardie (Somme)

1262

Les Trois Sablières****
1850 rue de la Maye
+33 (0)3-22270133
FAX +33 (0)3-22271006
1/4 - 8/11
@ contact@
camping-les-trois-sablieres.com

2ha 30**T**(100-120m²) 6-10A CEE

1 ACD**G**IJKLMO**P**Q
2 AERUVX
3 AGHJRUV
4 (C+H 1/5-15/9) **KN** (Q+R) (T 1/7-30/8) (U+Z)
5 **AB**CEFGIJKLMNOPRUWXZ
6 ADEGK(N 4km)RTV

The campsite is located in one of the loveliest bays in the world. Sabine and Jean-Michel welcome you to their campsite for a wonderful holiday. The site is located ± 300m from a fine sandy beach (no swimming). Only campers are allowed in the toilet block (with key) and (free) showers. Office closed from 12:30-14:30.

From the A16 exit 24 direction Rue. Follow Le Crotoy road. At Le Crotoy follow D4 Crotoy/St. Firmin de C. Left at St. Firmin sign. Campsite signposted.

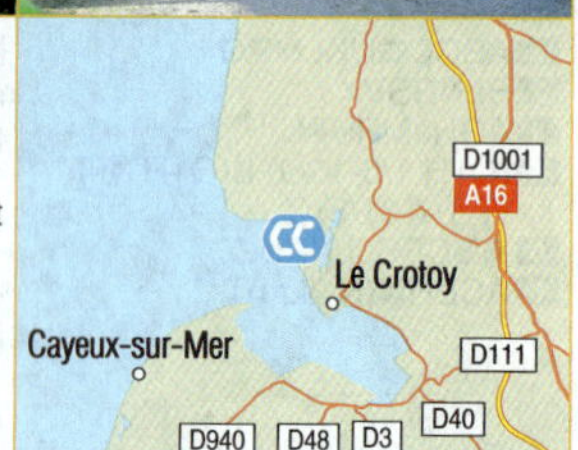

CC € 17 *1/4-4/7 22/8-8/11*

N 50°14'54'' E 1°35'55''

Le Crotoy, F-80550 / Picardie (Somme)

1263

Yelloh! Village Le Ridin****
Lieu Dit Mayocq
+33 (0)3-22270322
FAX +33 (0)3-22277076
25/3 - 30/9
@ leridin@
baiedesommepleinair.com

3ha 40**T**(80-170m²) 6-10A CEE

1 ACD**G**IJKLM**P**Q
2 DFRVXY
3 A**F**GHJKRUV
4 (A 7/7-25/8) (C+H 1/5-15/9) **K**(Q+R+T+U+V+X+Z)
5 **AB**CDEFGIJLMNPRSUWXYZ
6 ABCEG**K**(N 1km)ORTV

Campsite located in the bay of the Somme in authentic surroundings, pitches marked out with flowers and plants.

A16, exit 24 direction Le Crotoy. Follow the D4, signposted.

CC € 17 *25/3-7/7 24/8-30/9 7=6*

N 50°14'21'' E 1°37'55''

Mers-les-Bains, F-80350 / Picardie (Somme) 1264

Le Rompval***
Lieu dit Blengues
+33 (0)2-35844321
FAX +33 (0)826388076
26/3 - 5/11
@ campinglerompval@gmail.com

3ha 79T(100-150m²) 13A CEE

1 ACD**G**IJKLMOPQ
2 RVX
3 AGHKR
4 (E+H+Q+R+T+U+V+Z)
5 **AB**DEFGIJKLMNPUWZ
6 ACEGJ(N 2km)ORTV

A quietly situated Flower campsite for those who appreciate the countryside. Located next to a protected wood less than 1 km from the Falaise.

A28, exit 2 direction Le Tréport. Follow the D940 (Route d'Eu) direction St. Valery-sur-Somme. Left after 3 km. Signposted. Don't go via Mers-les-Bains with a caravan.

CC € 15 *26/3-9/7 26/8-5/11 7=6, 14=11*

N 50°4'39'' E 1°24'52''

Miannay, F-80132 / Picardie (Somme) 1265

Sites & Paysages Le Clos Cacheleux***
rue de Bouillancourt
+33 (0)3-22191747
15/3 - 15/10
@ marie@camping-lecloscacheleux.fr

5ha 83T(200-270m²) 10A CEE

1 ACD**G**IJKLMPQ
2 FLRUVWXY
3 ADGHJK**P**RW
4 (A 1/7-31/8) (E 15/4-30/9) (H 1/6-7/9) K(Q+R) (T+U+X 26/4-31/8) (Z)
5 **AB**CEFGIJKLMNPRUWXZ
6 DEGJ(N 8km)O

A peaceful campsite in the grounds of an old castle located in the natural Trie valley. Campers can make use of the swimming pool at 'Le Val de Trie' right next to the campsite.

From Abbeville D925 direction Eu and Le Tréport, do not go towards Moyenneville. Turn left in Miannay village on the D86 towards Toeufles. Campsite signposted. Significant inclination to reception on campsite.

CC € 17 *15/3-7/7 25/8-15/10 7=6, 14=11*

N 50°5'10'' E 1°42'46''

Moyenneville, F-80870 / Picardie (Somme) 1266

Le Val de Trie****
rue des Sources
+33 (0)3-22314888
1/4 - 4/10
@ raphael@camping-levaldetrie.fr

3ha 76T(100m²) 10A CEE

1 ACD**G**IJKLPQ
2 CFLRTUVXY
3 ABGHIJKN**P**RUW
4 (A 7/7-29/8) (C+E 15/4-1/10) (H 1/6-7/9) IK(Q+R) (T+U+X 26/4-31/8) (Z)
5 ABDEFGIJKLNPUWXYZ
6 CDEGJ(N 8km)OV

Family campsite with a pleasant atmosphere in the green valley of the Trie, near the coast. Green, marked out pitches.

From Abbeville D925 direction Eu and Le Tréport. Don't follow Moyenneville! When leaving the village Miannay turn left D86 direction Toeufles. Campsite signs can be found on the left side of the road.

CC € 15 *1/4-13/7 31/8-4/10 7=6, 14=11*

N 50°5'10'' E 1°42'56''

Nampont-St-Martin, F-80120 / Picardie (Somme)

1267

La Ferme des Aulnes****
Fresne
+33 (0)3-22292269
FAX +33 (0)3-22293943
25/3 - 31/10
@ contact@fermedesaulnes.com

3,5ha 41T(100-120m²) 10A CEE

1 ACD**G**IJKLMO**P**Q
2 FLRTUVX
3 AC**F**GNRUVW
4 (A 2/7-31/8) (E) **KN** (Q+R+T+U+V+Y+Z)
5 **AB**CDEFGJLNPUWXYZ
6 CDEGIK(N 10km)ORTV

The campsite is peacefully located in a rural area 5 km from the motorway, next to a traditional renovated farmhouse. Good cycling options and a golf course at 2 km. At 15 km you will find the Marquenterre nature reserve. A campsite with a lovely ambiance.

A16, exit 25 direction Arras. After ± 2 km direction Abbeville as far as Nampont-Saint-Martin then right towards Villers/Fresne, campsite signposted.

CC € 15 *25/3-1/7 18/8-31/10*

N 50°20'11'' E 1°42'44''

Orvillers/Sorel, F-60490 / Picardie (Oise)

1268

Camping de Sorel***
24 rue St. Claude
+33 (0)3-44850274
FAX +33 (0)3-44421165
1/1 - 31/12
@ contact@aestiva.fr

7ha 124T(110-170m²) 6A CEE

1 ACDGIJKLMOPQ
2 FLRVXY
3 A**F**GHJKNRUV
4 (Q+R+T) U(V+X) Z
5 **A**GIJKLMNOPUVWXYZ
6 EG**K**(N 3km)ORTV

You are welcome from 7.30 to 22.30 hours, every day of the week, in these quiet and green surroundings. 60 minutes from Paris and 90 minutes from Lille. Exit 11 from motorway A1 - E15 - E19, RN17 Orvillers/Sorel.

When approaching from the north: after Roye take the N17. The campsite is located on the left side of the N17, after Orvillers.

CC € 17 *1/4-30/6 1/9-31/10 7=6, 14=12*

N 49°34'2'' E 2°42'29''

Péronne, F-80200 / Picardie (Somme)

1269

Port de Plaisance***
route de Paris
+33 (0)3-22841931
FAX +33 (0)3-22733637
1/3 - 31/10
@ contact@camping-plaisance.com

2ha 82T(80-150m²) 10A CEE

1 ACD**G**IJLMOPQ
2 CFGRVX
3 AGKRU**W**
4 (C+H 1/6-31/8) (Q 1/6-30/9) (R 10/5-15/9) (U 29/6-30/8) Z
5 **AB**DGIJKLMNPUW
6 ACDEG**IJK**(N 1km)OV

This campsite is located a few kilometres from the A1 near a yacht harbour close to Peronne. The grounds are level with a choice of shaded or non-shaded pitches. The area is known for its many historic World War I locations.

The campsite is located south of Péronne, on the N17.

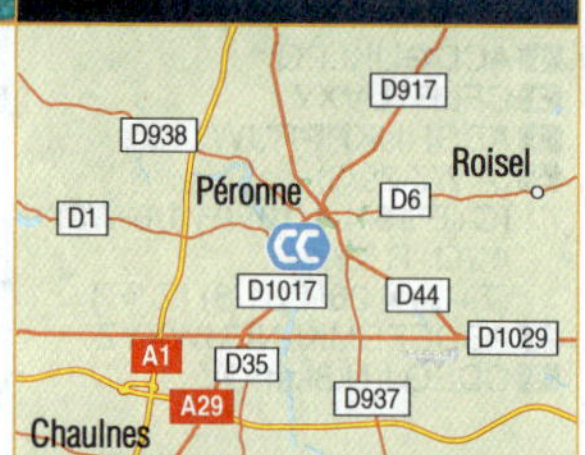

CC € 17 *1/3-6/7 1/9-31/10 7=6*

N 49°55'4'' E 2°55'57''

Poix-de-Picardie, F-80290 / Picardie (Somme)

1270

Le Bois des Pêcheurs***
rue de Verdun
+33 (0)3-22901171
FAX +33 (0)3-22903291
1/4 - 30/9
@ camping@ville-poix-de-picardie.fr

2,4ha 88T(80m²) 6A

1 AGIJLMPRS
2 CFRTVWXY
3 ABGR
5 ABFGIJMNPUWZ
6 CEGK(N 0,3km)V

A very well maintained municipal campsite with marked out pitches. Quiet location, within walking distance of the village with opportunities for shopping. Free WiFi. Stay three nights and pay for two.

D1029. From Amiens turn right at Poix-de-Picardie, town centre. From Rouen in Eplessier head for Poix-de-Picardie to the town centre. Follow camping signs. From Rouen A29/E44 exit 13.

CC € 17 1/4-30/6 1/9-30/9 3=2

N 49°46'34'' E 1°58'28''

Port-le-Grand/Abbeville, F-80132 / Picardie (Somme)

1271

Château des Tilleuls***
rue de la Baie
+33 (0)3-22240775
FAX +33 (0)3-22242380
1/3 - 1/11
@ contact@chateaudestilleuls.com

11ha 40T(120-150m²) 10A CEE

1 ACDGIJKLMPQ
2 FIJLRVX
3 AFGJKNPQRUV
4 (C+H 1/6-15/9) N(Q+S) (T+U 1/4-1/11) (Z)
5 ABDFGIJKLMNOPUWXYZ
6 ACEGHIKL(N 6km)OTV

A campsite set in a park with trees more than a hundred years old. An oasis of peace in natural surroundings. Large pitches for a stopover or for longer stays. The new young owners are renovating the site beautifully.

Located on the D40. From Abbeville after about 6 km, direction St. Valéry/Le Crotoy, before Port-le-Grand. Short incline after barrier.

CC € 17 1/3-2/7 28/8-1/11

N 50°8'29'' E 1°45'48''

Quend, F-80120 / Picardie (Somme)

1272

Des Deux Plages***
15 rue des Maisonnettes
+33 (0)3-22234896
FAX +33 (0)3-22234869
1/4 - 31/10
@ camping@camping2plages.com

2ha 30T(100-120m²) 6A CEE

1 AGIJKLPRS
2 FRTVX
3 AFGJKRUW
4 (E 15/4-15/9) (G 1/7-31/8) (Q+R+T+U+Z)
5 ABFGIJKLMNPUVZ
6 AEGK(N 5km)ORTV

A small, peaceful family campsite with an indoor swimming pool. 5 km from Fort-Mahon-Plage with its fine sandy beaches and good fish restaurants. Suitable for short or longer stays, also with children. 5 km from Marquenterre park. Excellent area for cycling.

A16 exit Quend. In Quend D32 direction Fort-Mahon-Plage. Campsite shown on small signs.

CC € 17 1/4-15/7 1/9-31/10 7=6

N 50°19'25'' E 1°37'28''

Quend-Plage-les-Pins, F-80120 / Picardie (Somme) — 1273

Les Vertes Feuilles****
25 route de la Plage-Monchaux
+33 (0)3-22235512
FAX +33 (0)3-22190752
2/4 - 1/11
@ contact@lesvertesfeuilles.com

3,5ha 45T(70-100m²) 10A

1 ACD**G**IJKLM**P**RS
2 FRVXY
3 A**F**GHJKRU
4 (E) (H 1/6-15/9) (Q+R+T+U+X+Z)
5 **ABC**DEFGIJKLMNOPUWXZ
6 AEG**K**(N 2km)OTV

A small family campsite surrounded by greenery. There is a heated swimming pool for your use. Close to cycle paths, an ornithological park, an extensive beach and the Golf de Belle Dune golf course.

From Calais A16. Exit Quend direction Quend/ Plages Les Pins. Campsite signposted.

CC € 17 2/4-9/7 26/8-1/11 7=6

N 50°19'9'' E 1°36'24''

Ressons-le-Long, F-02290 / Picardie (Aisne) — 1274

La Halte de Mainville***
18 rue du Routy
+33 (0)3-23742669
FAX +33 (0)3-23740360
15/1 - 8/12
@ lahaltedemainville@wanadoo.fr

5ha 74T(120m²) 6A CEE

1 AGIJKLMOPRS
2 RVX
3 AGNRUW
4 (C+H 15/6-15/9) (Q 1/6-1/9)
5 **AB**CEGIJKLMNPUVXZ
6 CDEGIJ(N 1km)RT

Level grounds with marked out, partly shaded pitches. Good facilities. A peaceful family campsite with a swimming pool and tennis court. Close to the completely restored Pierrefonds chateau. Free carp fishing. Disneyland about one hour away, Parc Astérix half an hour's drive.

On the N31 Compiègne-Soissons about 15 km from Soissons follow the D17 southwards to Ressons-le-Long. Follow camping signs.

CC € 17 15/1-30/6 1/9-30/11

N 49°23'34'' E 3°9'6''

Rue, F-80120 / Picardie (Somme) — 1275

Camping de la Maye**
32 rue du Moulin
+33 (0)3-22250955
1/4 - 31/10
@ campingdelamaye@orange.fr

2,5ha 100T(70-150m²) 6-10A CEE

1 ACD**G**IJKLMO**P**Q
2 CDFLRVX
3 AGRW
4 (Q+R)
5 **AB**DEFGJKLMNPQUVZ
6 CDEG**K**(N >30km)OT

This refurbished campsite is close to the historic village of Rue, close to the Bay of Somme and the Marquenterre nature reserve. A stopover campsite, but also suitable for longer stays.

D940 from Berck to Rue. Follow Rue Centre (D175) at roundabout. Campsite entrance opposite Carrefour Market.

CC € 15 1/4-4/7 22/8-31/10

N 50°16'31'' E 1°39'39''

Seraucourt-le-Grand, F-02790 / Picardie (Aisne)

1276

Camping du Vivier aux Carpes***
10 rue Charles Voyeux
+33 (0)3-23605010
20/3 - 20/10
contact@camping-picardie.com

1,8ha 67**T**(100m²) 10A CEE

1 ACD**G**IJKLMPQ
2 DFGKLRTUVX
3 ADGHJKRU**W**
4 (Q+R ⊶)
(T+U+V 15/6-31/8)
5 **AB**DFGJLNPQUWZ
6 CDEG**K**ORTV

The campsite is located on the edge of a village. A perfect site for carp fishing, walking or cycling. You can fish in the natural pond from a number of pitches. A well maintained site with nicely marked out pitches. It has a friendly, amicable ambiance.

Leave A26 at exit 11 St. Quentin-Sud, direction Gauchy. Via D321 to Seraucourt-le-Grand Signposted.

CC € 17 *20/3-2/6 1/9-19/10 7=6*

N 49°46'55'' E 3°12'51''

St. Quentin-en-Tourmont, F-80120 / Picardie (Somme)

1277

Le Champ Neuf****
8 rue du Champ Neuf
+33 (0)3-22250794
FAX +33 (0)3-22250987
1/4 - 31/10
campinglechampneuf@orange.fr

4,3ha 60**T**(100-140m²) 6A CEE

1 ACD**G**IJKLMO**P**RS
2 FLRSTVX
3 A**F**GHJKMNPRUV
4 (F+H 2/4-31/10) IKNP
(Q+R ⊶) (T+U+Z 9/4-17/9)
5 **AB**DEFGJLNPUWXYZ
6 ACEG**K**(N 5km)ORT

This lovely campsite is located in the heart of the Marquenterre close to the Ornithological Park. Marked out pitches in natural surroundings. You can enjoy the indoor leisure pool and the adjacent sun terrace. Your horse is also welcome here.

The campsite is located in Le Bout des Crocs and can be reached via the D204 by following the 'Parc Ornithologique' signs. Follow the campsite signs, not the SatNav for the last section.

CC € 17 *1/4-7/7 26/8-31/10*

N 50°16'13'' E 1°36'4''

St. Valery-sur-Somme, F-80230 / Picardie (Somme)

1278

Domaine de Drancourt*****
BP 80022
+33 (0)3-22269345
FAX +33 (0)3-22268587
15/4 - 11/9
chateau.drancourt@wanadoo.fr

17ha 160**T**(< 120m²) 10A CEE

1 ACD**G**IJKLMO**P**Q
2 LRVX
3 BHJKMN**P**QRU**V**W
4 (C 15/6-11/9) (E+H ⊶) J
(Q+S+T+U+V ⊶)
(X 1/7-31/8) (Z ⊶)
5 **AB**DEFGJLNPUWZ
6 ADEGHJ(N 3km)RV

This large campsite is located in an area with many places of interest. Large, partly marked out pitches on grass. Plenty of amenities are available on the campsite.

From Abbeville D40 and D940 direction St. Valery-sur-Somme. Campsite is signposted.

CC € 17 *15/4-1/7 27/8-10/9 7=6, 14=10*

N 50°9'8'' E 1°38'9''

St. Valery-sur-Somme, F-80230 / Picardie (Somme)

iD **1279**

Le Walric****
345 route d'Eu
+33 (0)3-22268197
FAX +33 (0)3-22607726
1/4 - 30/10
info@campinglewalric.com

5,7ha 50**T**(95m²) 6A CEE

1 ABCD**F**IJKL**P**Q
2 LNRTVX
3 AGHJKMNRU
4 (E+H+Q+R+T+U+Z)
5 **AB**CDEFGJLNPU
6 ACEGH**IK**(N 3km)OT

A campsite with spaciously appointed pitches marked out by natural bushes. The site has a lovely indoor swimming pool. Located close to the bay of Somme and near the medieval district of the village of St.Valery-sur-Somme.

From Abbeville D40, D940 and D3 direction St. Valery-sur-Somme. Campsite well indicated on the right of the D3. Do not use SatNav for last section.

CC €17 *1/4-8/7 26/8-30/10*

N 50°11'0'' E 1°37'4''

Suzy, F-02320 / Picardie (Aisne)

iD **1280**

Les Etangs du Moulin***
+33 (0)3-23809286
1/4 - 30/9
contact@etangsdumoulin.fr

7ha 40**T**(80-200m²) 6A

1 ACD**G**IJKLMOQ
2 BDIRTUWXY
3 ABGHIJPRU**W**
4 (F) H(Q+R+U+X) Z
5 EFGJLNPQRUWZ
6 DEG**K**(N 6km)TV

A spacious, quiet campsite in wild-west style close to Laon. There are marked-out and open pitches which vary in size. Good playing facilities for young and older children. Beautiful places for fishing on the campsite. Toilet facilities are clean and well-maintained.

Exit Chivi from N2. From N44 exit Cerny-lès-Bucy. In Suzy follow campsite signs.

CC €17 *18/5-30/6 1/9-30/9*

N 49°32'58'' E 3°28'5''

Villers-sur-Authie, F-80120 / Picardie (Somme)

iD **1281**

Sites et Paysages
Le Val d'Authi*****
20 route de Vercourt
+33 (0)3-22299247
FAX +33 (0)3-22299330
1/4 - 30/9
camping@valdauthie.fr

7ha 60**T**(100-150m²) 6-10A

1 ACD**G**IJKLM**P**Q
2 FLRVX
3 AFGKMNRUV
4 (E) (H 1/5-15/9) **KLN** (Q+S+T+U+V+X+Z)
5 **AB**CDEFGIJKLNPUWXZ
6 CDEGHI**K**(N 6km)RTV

This five-star campsite with excellent toilets and many facilities is 10 minutes from the coast, with Marquenterre nature reserve, and from the woods at Crécy. The site is an oasis of peace and has a good restaurant, indoor swimming pool and wellness room. Good cycling options.

D901 Boulogne-Abbeville, exit Nampont, direction Villers-sur-Authie.

CC €15 *1/4-10/7 27/8-30/9* 7=6, 14=11

N 50°18'49'' E 1°41'42''

Blangy-sur-Bresle, F-76340 / Haute-Normandie (Seine-Maritime) — 1282

Aux Cygnes d'Opale***
Zône de Loisirs
+33 (0)2-35945565
1/4 - 31/10
contact@auxcygnesdopale.fr

1ha 46**T**(80-120m²) 10A CEE

- **1** ACD**G**IJKLMP
- **2** CDFLRTWX
- **3** ABGHJKM**Q**R**W**
- **4** (E+H 15/4-15/10) (Q+R+T+U+X 🔑) Z
- **5** **AB**CDGHJKLMNPUZ
- **6** ACEGHK(N 1,5km)RT

A quiet family campsite located by a lake with fishing opportunities. Small, indoor pool with movable walls. Marked-out walking and cycling routes. Free WiFi. Pleasant bar/restaurant with a large terrace.

From A28 exit 5. Then D40 to the right. Campsite is signposted (500m).

CC € 15 *1/4-30/6 1/9-30/10* *7=6*

N 49°55'29" E 1°39'27"

Bouafles, F-27700 / Haute-Normandie (Eure) — 1283

Château de Bouafles****
2 rue de Mousseaux
FAX +33 (0)2-32540315
15/1 - 15/12
chateaudebouafles@gmail.com

13ha 25**T**(> 200m²) 15A CEE

- **1** ACD**G**IJKLMPQ
- **2** CGRUVWXY
- **3** B**F**GHJKMNQRU**W**
- **4** (Q+Z 🔑)
- **5** **AB**DEIJKLMNOPUW
- **6** EGJ(N 5km)TV

Ideal campsite for those who love very spacious pitches in natural surroundings.

From A15 to D14 and Les Andelys exit. Via D125 then D313 to Bouafles, then follow camping signs.

CC € 15 *15/3-30/6 27/8-13/11*

N 49°12'47" E 1°23'18"

Breteuil-sur-Iton, F-27160 / Haute-Normandie (Eure) — 1284

Les Berges de l'Iton***
53 rue du Fourneau
+33 (0)2-32627035
1/4 - 30/9
campinglesberges-de-liton@orange.fr

1ha 25**T**(70-110m²) 6A CEE

- **1** ACFIJKLMPQ
- **2** CDGLRTUVWXY
- **3** ABGJUW
- **4** (D 🔑) (Q 15/6-15/9) (T+U+V+Z 🔑)
- **5** **AB**DGIJKLMNOPUWZ
- **6** ACDEGIK(N 0,3km)ORTV

Campsite close to a river and a pond, including special facilities for the disabled and a heated swimming pool. 30 km from Evreux and 11 km from Verneuil sur Avre. You can go for nice walks in the woods close to the campsite and there are museums and other places to visit.

From Evreux on the D830 as far as Conches-en-Ouche. Then on the D840 as far as Breteuil, then follow the camping signs. From Verneuil-sur-Avre on the D840 as far as Breteuil then follow the camping signs.

CC € 17 *1/4-30/6 1/9-27/9*

N 48°49'54" E 0°54'45"

Hautot-sur-Mer, F-76550 / Haute-Normandie (Seine-Maritime) 1285

La Source***
63 rue des Tisserands
+33 (0)2-35842704
FAX +33 (0)2-35822502
15/3 - 15/10
@ info@camping-la-source.fr

2,5ha 70T(80-130m²) 6-10A CEE

1 ACD**G**IJKLMOPRS
2 CLRTUVWX
3 ABGHJKNRU**W**
4 (C 1/6-15/9) (Q+R) Z
5 **AB**DFGIJKLMNPUVZ
6 CDEG**K**(N 1km)TV

This very quiet campsite is located on a small river with fishing opportunities. Heated swimming pool. Ideally located 3 km from the beach and cliffs.

Follow route D925 between Dieppe and Valéry-en-Caux. The campsite is clearly signposted in Petit Appeville.

CC € 17 15/3-5/7 22/8-14/10

N 49°53'55'' E 1°3'25''

Honfleur/Fiquefleur, F-27210 / Haute-Normandie (Eure) 1286

Sites & Paysages Domaine Catinière***
910 route de la Morelle
+33 (0)2-32576351
FAX +33 (0)2-32421257
1/4 - 15/10
@ info@camping-catiniere.com

5,5ha 89T(80-100m²) 4-13A CEE

1 ACD**G**IJKLMPQ
2 CFLRVWXY
3 ABDGHRUW
4 (C+H 1/6-10/9) J (Q+R+T+U+X+Z)
5 **AB**FGIJLMNPUVWXZ
6 ACEG**K**(N 3km)RV

A three star campsite (verging on four stars) with modern sanitation in the middle of the countryside. An ideal base for visiting the picturesque town of Honfleur by bike along a quiet road.

From A13 exit 28 Beuzeville, then D22 direction Honfleur. Or from the Pont de Normandy 3.5 km on the left.

CC € 17 1/4-3/7 27/8-15/10

N 49°24'3'' E 0°18'24''

Jumieges, F-76480 / Haute-Normandie (Seine-Maritime) 1287

de la Forêt****
rue Mainberte
+33 (0)2-35379343
FAX +33 (0)2-35377648
1/4 - 31/10
@ info@campinglaforet.com

3ha 80T(80-150m²) 10A CEE

1 ACDGHIJKLMPQ
2 BRVWXY
3 A**F**GHJK**M**RU
4 (E 15/4-15/10) (H 1/7-31/8) (Q+R) (T+U 1/6-31/8) (Z)
5 **AB**DFGIJKLMNPUWXYZ
6 ACEG**K**(N 0,6km)TV

A campsite in wooded surroundings on one of the lovely meanders of the Seine. The famous Abbey of Jumièges is in the village. Close to the medieval city of Rouen. Sanitary facilities completely new from 2015.

On the A29 exit 5, direction Yvetot, then the D131e and D131 direction Pont-de-Brotonne. Before the bridge via D982 direction Rouen and via D143 to Jumièges. The campsite is signposted.

CC € 17 1/4-8/7 26/8-31/10

N 49°26'5'' E 0°49'40''

Le Bec-Hellouin, F-27800 / Haute-Normandie (Eure) — 1288

Le Clos Saint Nicolas***
15 rue St. Nicolas
+33 (0)2-32448355
15/3 - 15/10
campingstnicolas@orange.fr

2,8ha 61**T**(90-110m²) 10A CEE

1 ACD**G**IJKLMOPQ
2 BFLRVWX
3 A**F**GHJKMNRUV
4 (E 1/4-30/9)
(Q+R+T+U+X+Z)
5 **AB**DEFGIJKLMNPUZ
6 ACEGK(N 2km)ORTV

This three star campsite in idyllic surroundings and surrounded by trees will welcome you for a stay in the countryside in peace and tranquillity. A place to relax. 18 hole golf within 10 km. Indoor pool at the campsite. You can enjoy your holiday here in your caravan, motorhome or tent.

From the A28 exit 13, direction Brionne. Take the D581 towards Malleville sur le Bec. The campsite is signposted.

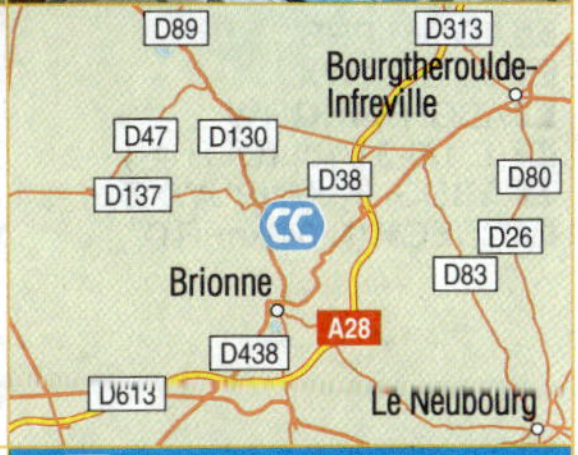

CC €15 15/3-7/7 24/8-15/10 7=6, 14=12

N 49°14'5'' E 0°43'30''

Les Andelys, F-27700 / Haute-Normandie (Eure) — 1289

Camping de l'Ile des Trois Rois***
1 rue Gilles Nicolle
+33 (0)2-32542379
FAX +33 (0)2-32511454
15/3 - 15/11
campingtroisrois@aol.com

10ha 300**T**(100-250m²) 6A CEE

1 ACD**G**IJKLM**P**RS
2 CFGLRTUVWX
3 AB**EF**GHJRUVW
4 (C+H 15/5-30/9)
(Q 1/7-31/8)
(T+U+V+X+Z 15/5-15/9)
5 **AB**DFGIJKLMNPUVWZ
6 ABCEG**K**(N 0,5km)ORTV

Peacefully located campsite on the banks of the Seine. Marked out pitches. Lovely heated swimming pool. New heated toilet facilities. The campsite is 500 metres from the centre. WiFi 100% (charges apply).

In Les Andelys direction Évreux, the campsite is located before the bridge over the Seine; well signposted.

CC €15 15/3-1/7 18/8-14/11 7=6, 14=11

N 49°14'8'' E 1°24'1''

Les Loges, F-76790 / Haute-Normandie (Seine-Maritime) — 1290

L'Aiguille Creuse****
24 residence de L'Aiguille Creuse
+33 (0)2-35295210
FAX +33 (0)2-35108664
2/4 - 18/9
camping@aiguillecreuse.com

3ha 135**T**(110-150m²) 10A CEE

1 ACD**G**IJLMPQ
2 GLRVWX
3 AB**F**GHMR
4 (E+Q) (T 1/7-31/8)
(Z)
5 **AB**DEFGIJLNPQRUZ
6 ACEGJ**K**(N 0,4km)RV

A lovely campsite with marked out pitches; a bar, playground, football field, large tennis court, covered pool with sliding roof.

Les Loges is located along the D940 Fécamp-Le Havre. Campsite well signposted in the town.

CC €15 2/4-3/7 24/8-17/9

N 49°41'56'' E 0°16'33''

1291 Lyons-la-Forêt, F-27480 / Haute-Normandie (Eure)

Municipal Saint-Paul***
2 route St. Paul
+33 (0)2-32494202
1/4 - 31/10
camping-saint-paul@orange.fr

3ha 52T(80-100m²) 6A

1 A**G**IJKLPRS
2 CGLRTVWX
3 ABGHJ**MNQ**R**W**
4 (E 1/6-31/10) (Q+R)
5 **AB**DGIJKLMNPUWXZ
6 CDEG**K**(N 0,6km)RTV

A peacefully located campsite by a small stream (only fish). Municipal swimming pool next to the campsite; this is free for campers.

Campsite well signposted at the entrance to the village.

CC € 15 1/4-30/6 1/9-31/10

N 49°24'12'' E 1°28'47''

1292 Marcilly-sur-Eure, F-27810 / Haute-Normandie (Eure)

Domaine de Marcilly****
rue de Saint André de l'Eure
+33 (0)2-37484542
FAX +33 (0)2-37485111
1/4 - 30/12
domainedemarcilly@wanadoo.fr

15ha 100T(100-200m²) 10A CEE

1 ACGIJKLMPQ
2 BLRTVX
3 GKMNRU
4 (C 1/6-30/9) (Q+R)
5 **AB**GIMNPUVWXYZ
6 ACDEG**K**(N 1km)RTV

A really lovely campsite in the middle of a wood with lovely marked out grounds, a wonderful (heated) swimming pool, 2 tennis courts, a large petanque alley. The reception is open from 09:00 to 12:00 and 14:00 to 18:00.

Coming from Dreux on the D928 turn left after about 15 km towards Marcilly. Then follow camping signs. From Annet on the D928 turn right after about 8 km. Follow route as shown above.

CC € 19 1/4-30/6 1/9-30/12

N 48°49'55'' E 1°19'47''

1293 Martigny, F-76880 / Haute-Normandie (Seine-Maritime)

Municipal Des Deux Rivières***
D154
+33 (0)2-35856082
25/3 - 8/10
martigny.76@orange.fr

6ha 75T(80-100m²) 9A CEE

1 ACD**G**IJKLMPQ
2 CDRTVWX
3 ABGRU**W**
4 (Q 1/7-31/8) (R)
5 **AB**FGIJKLMNPUZ
6 EGHJ(N 2km)RT

A very peacefully located campsite on a 2 hectare lake with fishing opportunities. Located on the Avenue Verte, a 40 km cycling and walking path.

From Dieppe about 8 km along the D154. Very well signposted beside the road.

CC € 17 25/3-30/6 1/9-8/10

N 49°52'14'' E 1°8'39''

Neufchâtel-en-Bray, F-76270 / Haute-Normandie (Seine-Maritime)

iD 1294

Sainte Claire***
19 rue Grande Flandre
+33 (0)2-35930393
1/4 - 15/10
fancelot@wanadoo.fr

2,5ha 87**T**(60-180m²) 6-10A CEE

1 ACDGIJKLMOPQ
2 CFLRUVWX
3 GHJ
4 (Q+R+T+U+X 1/5-30/9) Z
5 **AB**FGIJKLMNPUZ
6 ABCDEG**K**(N 0,2km)

The campsite is located in the grounds of a picturesque old farmstead in the shade of apple trees and a few steps from the 'Avenue Verte'. A dream for cyclists and walkers. Campers are welcome after 13:00.

Well signposted about 1 km from Neufchâtel-en-Bray. Coming from Amiens exit 7 and from Rouen exit 9 on A28/E402 motorway.

CC € 15 *1/4-30/6 1/9-14/10*

N 49°44'16'' E 1°25'41''

Pont-Audemer, F-27500 / Haute-Normandie (Eure)

iD 1295

Risle Seine Les Etangs***
route des Etangs
+33 (0)2-32424665
FAX +33 (0)2-32422417
25/3 - 31/10
camping.etangs@wanadoo.fr

1,5ha 53**T**(85-150m²) 10A CEE

1 ACD**G**HIJKLM**P**Q
2 CDFLRVWX
3 AEGHIJNRU**W**
4 (C 1/5-30/9) (Q+R)
(U+V 1/6-30/9)
5 **AB**FGIJKLMNPUWXYZ
6 AEGK(N 2km)RV

A quiet campsite next to some beautiful small lakes. Pitches separated by beech hedges. Just 2 km from the picturesque town of Pont-Audemer with all its amenities. Close to Honfleur (20 km) and Rouen (46 km). A paradise for anglers. Golf course (9 holes) next to the campsite.

A13 motorway Rouen-Caen, exit 26 direction Pont-Audemer. Then follow the Toutainville signs. Campsite is signposted.

CC € 15 *25/3-8/7 29/8-31/10* *7=6, 14=11*

N 49°22'1'' E 0°29'15''

Pourville-sur-Mer, F-76550 / Haute-Normandie (Seine-Maritime)

iD 1296

Le Marqueval***
1210 rue de la Mer
+33 (0)2-35826646
FAX +33 (0)2-35845503
21/3 - 15/10
contact@campinglemarqueval.com

8,5ha 85**T**(80-120m²) 6A CEE

1 ACD**G**IJKLMO**P**RS
2 CGKLNQRVWX
3 ABGKNRUW
4 (C+H 15/6-15/9) **KN**
(Q 15/4-15/9) (R)
(T+U+V+X 1/5-31/8) Z
5 **AB**DGJLNPUWZ
6 CDEG**K**(N 5km)OR

There are three fishing ponds and a small river on the campsite. 1500m from the beach with its lovely chalkstone cliffs. Heated swimming pool. Plenty of cycle and footpaths from the campsite to the coast.

Coming from Dieppe well signposted on the D75, follow the camping signs. Coming from Veules-les-Roses well signposted on the D75.

CC € 17 *21/3-10/7 27/8-14/10*

N 49°54'32'' E 1°2'26''

St. Aubin-sur-Scie, F-76550 / Haute-Normandie (Seine-Maritime)

1297

Dieppe Vitamín****
865 rue des Vertus
+33 (0)2-35821111
1/4 - 15/10
camping.vitamin@wanadoo.fr

5ha 69T(80-120m²) 10A CEE

1 ACD**G**IJKLMPQ
2 LRTVX
3 ABGNRV
4 (C 15/6-15/9) (F+H) JK**N** **P**(Q) (T 15/6-15/9) Z
5 **AB**EFGIJKLMNPUZ
6 DEGJ**K**(N 0,2km)RTV

A really lovely and well run campsite 3 km from Dieppe centre. The indoor swimming pool is also enjoyable when the weather is not so good. There are various department stores close to the campsite.

Coming from the D925 direction Dieppe water tower. Coming from Rouen N27. Direction water tower.

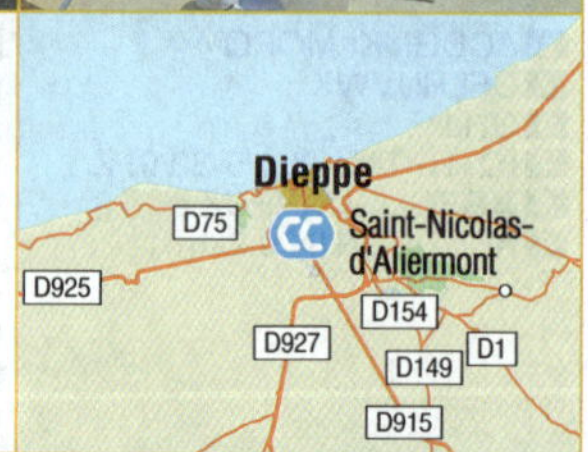

€17 *1/4-5/7 22/8-14/10*

N 49°54'1" E 1°4'28"

St. Martin-en-Campagne, F-76370 / Haute-Normandie (Seine-Maritime)

1298

Les Goélands****
11 rue des Grèbes
+33 (0)2-35838290
FAX +33 (0)2-35832179
15/3 - 30/10
contact@camping-les-goelands.fr

4,5ha 62T(80-100m²) 16A

1 ACD**G**IJKLMOPQ
2 AEGJKNQRTUVWX
3 ABGHMNQRUWY
4 (A 1/7-31/8) (Q 1/6-30/9) (R) (T+U 1/7-31/8) (Y) (Z 1/7-31/8)
5 **AB**DEFGJKLMNOPQRUWXYZ
6 DEGHIK(N 2km)ORTV

A very attractive terraced campsite within walking distance of a large sandy beach and chalk cliffs. The restaurant is open all year.

Follow D925 Dieppe-Le Treport. Turn off towards St. Martin-en-Campagne (D113). Campsite clearly signposted.

€17 *15/3-2/7 20/8-30/10*

N 49°57'59" E 1°12'15"

St. Pierre-en-Port, F-76540 / Haute-Normandie (Seine-Maritime)

1299

Les Falaises**
130 rue du Camping
+33 (0)2-35295158
1/4 - 5/10
lesfalaises@cegetel.net

4,2ha 72T(120-140m²) 10A CEE

1 AGIJKLMPQ
2 EGLNQRVWX
3 ABGHNRUY
4 (A 1/5-30/9) (U+V+Z 1/7-31/8)
5 **A**EGJLNPUVWZ
6 CEG(N 0,3km)T

Extremely well located campsite high up on the cliffs and 300 metres from the beach. Access to beach via cliff path difficult. All the necessary accommodation available.

Take the D79 between Fécamp and St. Valéry. Signposted in St. Pierre-en-Port.

€15 *1/4-6/7 23/8-4/10*

N 49°48'35" E 0°29'38"

St. Valéry-en-Caux, F-76460 / Haute-Normandie (Seine-Maritime)

1300

Seasonova Etennemare***
21 Hameau d'Etennemare
+33 (0)2-35971579
1/4 - 4/11
contact@
camping-etennemare.com

4ha 56T(100m²) 10A

1 ACDGIJLMPRS
2 RTVWX
3 ABGKRU
4 (E) J(Q 1/7-31/8)
5 ADEGIJKLMNPTUZ
6 EGKL(N 2km)RV

A beautiful, quiet campsite with marked out pitches and modern toilet facilities. The city centre is a 15 min walk.

Campsite well signposted coming from Cany-Barville (Fécamp) D925. If coming from Dieppe follow 'Centre Ville'. Campsite well signposted from there.

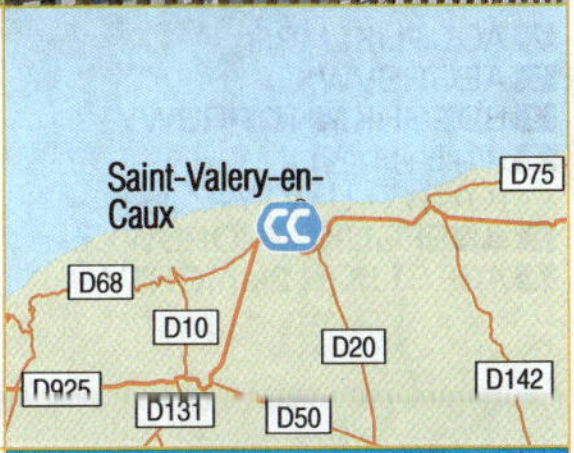

CC € 15 1/4-8/7 26/8-4/11

N 49°51'31" E 0°42'16"

Veules-les-Roses, F-76980 / Haute-Normandie (Seine-Maritime)

1301

Seasonova Les Mouettes***
avenue Jean Moulin
+33 (0)2-35976198
FAX +33 (0)2-35973344
1/4 - 4/11
contact@
camping-lesmouettes-normandie.com

3,6ha 122T(80-150m²) 6A CEE

1 ACGIJKLMPRS
2 EGRTVWX
3 ABGHKNPRU
4 (E+H 15/4-15/10) KN
(Q 1/7-31/8) (R)
(T+Z 1/7-31/8)
5 ABDFGIJKLMNOPUZ
6 CEGIKL(N 0,4km)V

A lovely campsite with marked out pitches, located 300 metres from the beach. A beautiful village with France's shortest river, just 1100 metres long. This is an extremely peaceful campsite with excellent toilet facilities. Heated indoor swimming pool, children's pool and jacuzzi.

Campsite well signposted from the centre.

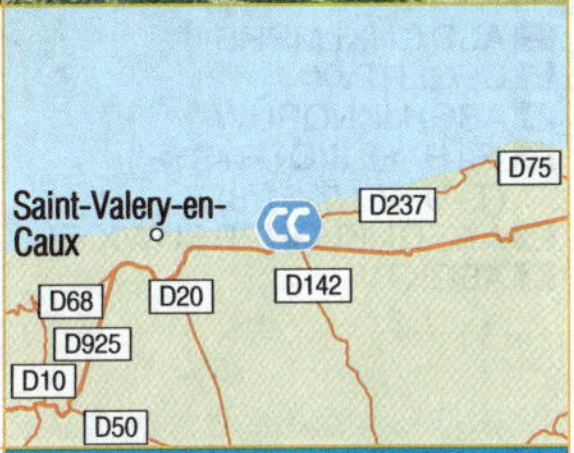

CC € 17 1/4-8/7 26/8-4/11

N 49°52'33" E 0°48'11"

Yport, F-76111 / Haute-Normandie (Seine-Maritime)

1302

La Chênaie***
rue H. Simon / D104
+33 (0)2-35273356
FAX +33 (0)2-22446562
2/4 - 1/10
camping.yport@
flowercampings.com

2,7ha 40T(80-90m²) 6A CEE

1 ACDGIJLPRS
2 BIJRVWX
3 AGHJRU
4 (E+H+Q+R+U+V)
5 ABEFGIJKLMNPQRUWZ
6 ACEGKL(N 0,5km)RV

A natural campsite on the Alabaster coast 800 metres from the beach. The site will tempt you with its large pitches, relaxation and the richness of the surroundings.

On the D940 Fécamp-Le Havre, exit Yport (D211). Campsite on the left just before the village.

CC € 17 2/4-1/7 1/9-1/10 7=6

N 49°43'58" E 0°19'14"

Barneville-Carteret/St.J-d-l-R, F-50270 / Basse-Normandie (Manche)

1303

Yelloh! Village Les Vikings*****
4 rue des Vikings
+33 (0)2-33538413
FAX +33 (0)2-33530819
1/4 - 18/9
@ contact@camping-lesvikings.com

6ha 70T(80-130m²) 10A

1 ACD**F**IJKLMPR
2 AEGRSVWX
3 BD**F**GHK**M**N**OP**RUWY
4 (C+E+H) J (Q+S+T+U+V+Y+Z)
5 **AB**EFGIJKLMNOPUWXZ
6 ACEG**IJK**(N 2km)ORTV

Yelloh! Village Les Vikings is located 400 metres from the sea with a wonderful sandy beach in a natural setting across the sea from Jersey. Plenty of cycling possibilities from here: the picturesque harbour towns of Portbail en Carteret for example. The campsite has a leisure pool with a heated indoor pool and an excellent restaurant.

From Barneville-Carteret, direction Barneville. Signposted further on.

CC € 17 *1/4-30/6 1/9-18/9*

N 49°21'51'' W 1°45'13''

Beauvoir, F-50170 / Basse-Normandie (Manche)

1304

Aux Pommiers***
28 route du Mont-St-Michel
+33 (0)2-33601136
23/3 - 13/11
@ campingauxpommiers@gmail.com

1,8ha 83T(95-105m²) 10A CEE

1 ACD**G**IJKLMPRS
2 CFGLRTVX
3 ABGHJKNQRUW
4 (F+H) J(Q+R+S) (T+U+V 1/7-31/8) Z
5 **AB**FGIJKLMNPR**S**UWXYZ
6 AEGKTV

A family campsite with a heated and covered swimming pool, only 4 km from Mont St. Michel which can easily be reached by bike. Arrival from 12:00.

Via N175 from Avranches direction Pontorson, then via D976 direction Mont-St-Michel. Follow arrows.

CC € 17 *23/3-24/6 30/8-13/11 7=6*

N 48°35'47'' W 1°30'45''

Bénouville, F-14970 / Basse-Normandie (Calvados)

1305

Yelloh! Villages Les Hautes Coutures****
avenue de la Côte de Nacre
+33 (0)2-31447308
25/3 - 25/9
@ info@campinghautescoutures.com

8ha 47T(80-165m²) 10A

1 ACD**G**IJKLMPRS
2 CGIJLRVWXY
3 B**F**GHJKN**P**RUW
4 (C 15/6-15/9) (D) (H 15/6-15/9) IJKP (Q+R+T+U+V+X+Z)
5 **AB**EFGIJKLMNPUWZ
6 ACEGJ**K**(N 1,5km)ORTV

A beautifully landscaped campsite, situated on the Caen-Ouistreham canal. A completely new swimming pool and the proximity to the sea and monuments from World War II make this a holiday for everyone.

From A13 exit Ouistreham. Campsite signposted in centre of Bénouville.

CC € 19 *25/3-9/7 27/8-25/9*

N 49°15'1'' W 0°16'25''

Bernières-sur-Mer, F-14990 / Basse-Normandie (Calvados)

iD **1306**

Le Havre de Bernières****
chemin de Quintefeuille
+33 (0)2-31966709
FAX +33 (0)2-31973106
26/3 - 29/10
@ campingnormandie@sfr.fr

5ha 97**T**(80-110m²) 20A CEE

1 ACD**G**IJKLM**PQ**
2 AEGRVWX
3 AFG**M**NRUWY
4 (C+H 1/5-15/9) **KN**(Q)
(R 1/7-31/8)
(T+U+V+Y+Z)
5 **AB**DEFGIJKLMNPUWZ
6 ACFGIJ(N 0,45km)TV

A lively campsite with a heated swimming pool and a restaurant. There are both shaded and unshaded pitches. The campsite is just 200 metres from the sea, close to the World War Two Landing Beaches.

Coming from Caen on the Periphérique exit CHU/Côte de Nacre. Direction Courseules-sur-Mer then direction Bernières-sur-Mer. Campsite is on the left just outside the village.

CC € **15** *26/3-9/7 26/8-29/10*

N 49°19'56'' W 0°25'41''

Cahagnolles, F-14490 / Basse-Normandie (Calvados)

iD **1307**

L'Escapade****
rue de l'Église
+33 (0)2-31216359
1/4 - 30/9
@ escapadecamping@orange.fr

7ha 43**T**(100-200m²) 10A CEE

1 ACD**G**IJKLMOPRS
2 CDIJLRVWX
3 ADGHJKMN**P**RUW
4 (E 12/4-30/9) (H 15/6-15/9)
J(Q+R+T+U)
(V 1/7-31/8) (Z)
5 **AB**DEFGIJKLMNPUWZ
6 ADEGJ(N 12km)RV

Very spacious park-like site with big pitches in hilly, natural surroundings 25 km from the landing beaches and 15 km from Bayeux. Right next to a lake with plenty of free fishing. Toilet facilities renovated and heated in 2014.

N13, exit Bayeux, direction St. Lo, then direction St. Paul-du-Vernay. Then Cahagnolles. Campsite signposted.

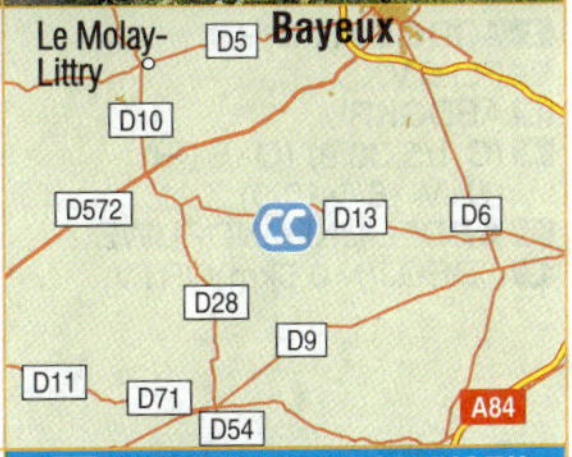

CC € **17** *1/4-3/7 29/8-30/9*

N 49°9'26'' W 0°45'37''

Carentan, F-50500 / Basse-Normandie (Manche)

iD **1308**

Camping Le Haut Dick***
30 chemin de Grand-Bas Pays
+33 (0)2-33421689
FAX +33 (0)970065590
26/3 - 30/9
@ contact@
camping-lehautdick.com

2,5ha 71**T**(100m²) 10A CEE

1 ACD**G**IJKLM**P**RS
2 CFGRVWXY
3 BGHJKN**P**QRUW
4 (C+H 1/6-15/9)
(Q+R+U+Y+Z)
5 **AB**FGIJKLMNPUWXZ
6 ACDEG**K**(N 0,5km)RTV

A friendly, peaceful campsite with naturally separated pitches. Right next to the yacht harbour. About a 15 minute walk to the centre. The campsite has a heated swimming pool. The following sights are within a one hour drive: Mont St. Michel, Cherbourg, Cap de la Hague and le Val de Saire.

First direction Centre Ville. Then the campsite is clearly signposted. Beware the 2 metre height restriction on navigation route.

CC € **17** *26/3-24/6 1/9-30/9*

N 49°18'36'' W 1°14'21''

Colleville-sur-Mer, F-14710 / Basse-Normandie (Calvados) 1309

Le Robinson****
D514
+33 (0)2-31224519
1/4 - 30/9
@ dourthe.le.robinson@wanadoo.fr

2ha 42T(80-120m²) 6A CEE

1 ACD**G**IJKLMPRS
2 AFGLRVWX
3 A**F**GHN**P**RU
4 (E+H) J(Q+R)
(T+U+V+Z 1/6-15/9)
5 **AB**EFGIJLNPRUZ
6 ACEG**K**(N 5km)TV

A small, well maintained family campsite within walking distance (± 1 km) of Omaha Beach. Close to the World War Two Landing Beaches and the big American cemetery. An indoor heated swimming pool with water slide and bar guarantees a pleasant stay.

From A13 Caen-Cherbourg exit Vaucelles, direction Mosles, then D97 dir. Ste Honorine-des-Pertes. Then D514 direction Colleville-sur-Mer.

CC € 17 *1/4-8/7 26/8-30/9*

N 49°21'1'' W 0°50'1''

Courtils, F-50220 / Basse-Normandie (Manche) 1310

St. Michel***
35 route du Mont-Saint-Michel
+33 (0)2-33709690
FAX +33 (0)2-33709909
25/3 - 2/11
@ infos@campingsaintmichel.com

5,2ha 100T(90-100m²) 6A CEE

1 ACD**G**IJKLM**P**RS
2 FLRTVX
3 ABDGKRU
4 (C 1/5-30/9) (Q+S)
(U+V 16/6-10/9) Z
5 **AB**DFGIJKLMNOPUWZ
6 CDEGJ(N 0,5km)ORTV

A beautifully floral family campsite with a heated pool. Close to Mont St. Michel, St. Malo and Dinard.

From Avranches via D43 direction Mont St. Michel. Campsite is located on the left just after Courtils.

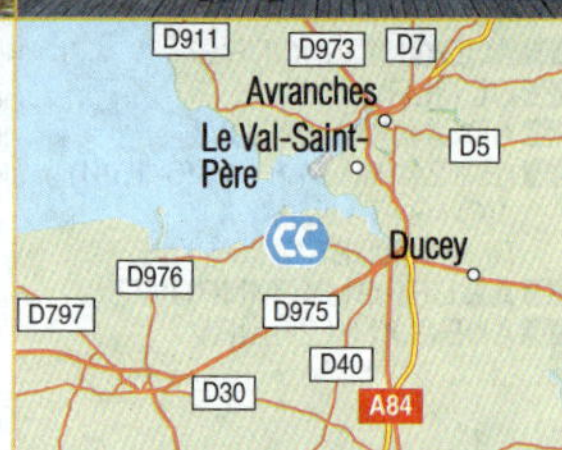

CC € 17 *25/3-24/6 27/8-2/11 7=6, 14=10*

N 48°37'41'' W 1°24'57''

Deauville/St. Arnoult, F-14800 / Basse-Normandie (Calvados) 1311

La Vallée de Deauville*****
rue des Genêts
+33 (0)2-31885817
FAX +33 (0)2-31881157
1/4 - 31/10
@ contact@camping-deauville.com

19ha 105T(80-120m²) 10A CEE

1 ACD**G**HIJKLMPQ
2 CDFGLRVWX
3 AB**F**GKNRUVW
4 (C+H 1/6-15/9) IJ**KLN**
(Q+R+T+U+V+X+Z 1/4-30/9)
5 **AB**DEFGIJKLMNPQRU
6 ACEG**IK**(N 0,8km)**PV**

Large terrain with spacious pitches in a natural environment. The campsite is near the famous seaside resorts of Deauville and Trouville. New heated swimming paradise.

From A13 exit Deauville. Direction Caen at roundabouts. Campsite is near the 3rd roundabout.

CC € 17 *1/4-10/7 27/8-31/10*

N 49°19'44'' E 0°5'11''

Etreham/Bayeux, F-14400 / Basse-Normandie (Calvados) — 1312

Reine Mathilde***
route de Ste Honorine
+33 (0)2-31217655
1/4 - 30/9
campingreinemathilde@gmail.com

6ha 80**T**(100-150m²) 6A CEE

1 ACD**F**IJKLMP**R**S
2 FLRVWXY
3 A**F**GNRU
4 (C+H 15/6-15/9) (Q 1/5-30/9) (R+T+U+X+Z)
5 **AB**DEFGIJKLMNPUWZ
6 ACEQJ(N 1km)V

This peaceful family campsite set in parkland is run by its friendly owners. It has very spacious marked out pitches and is located just 4 km from the renowned Omaha Landing Beach. This is an ideal base for visiting the many World War Two monuments and for trips inland, including Bayeux the regional capital

Leave N13 at exit 38. Take the N2013 direction Tour-en Bessin at the roundabout, then right onto D206. Campsite signposted from here.

CC € 15 *1/4-9/7 27/8-30/9*

N 49°19'53'' W 0°48'9''

Falaise, F-14700 / Basse-Normandie (Calvados) — 1313

Camping du Château**
1 rue du Val d'Ante
+33 (0)2-31901655
FAX +33 (0)2-31905338
1/4 - 30/9
camping@falaise.fr

1,5ha 60**T**(80-100m²) 10A CEE

1 ACD**F**IJKLMPQ
2 CGIJRVX
3 ABG**M**NRUW
5 **AB**DGIJKLMNPUVWZ
6 CEGHJ(N 0,5km)TV

Quiet, flowery campsite, pitches marked out by hedges, beautiful view of castle from 11th century and at 500 metres from medieval town centre.

From Caen N158 dir. Falaise, left on roundabout dir. 'centre ville', right on 2nd roundabout dir. 'Voie Panoramique', see campsite signs.

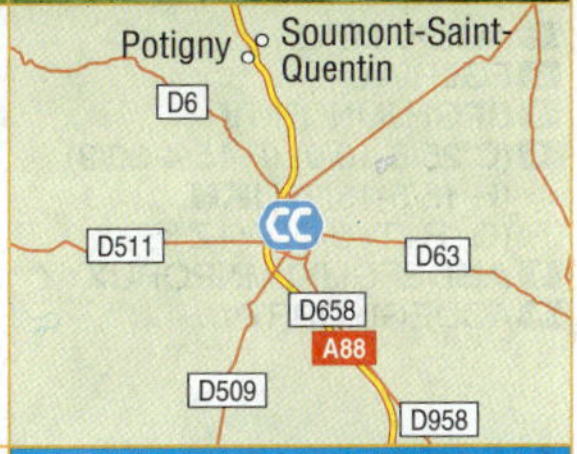

CC € 13 *1/4-3/7 22/8-30/9*

N 48°53'44'' W 0°12'18''

Formigny/Surrain, F-14710 / Basse-Normandie (Calvados) — 1314

La Roseraie d'Omaha****
Le Bourg
+33 (0)2-31211771
FAX +33 (0)2-31510220
25/3 - 30/9
camping.laroseraie@gmail.com

3ha 51**T**(85-120m²) 10A CEE

1 ACD**G**IJKLMP**R**S
2 FLRVWXY
3 B**F**GHJK**MNQ**RU
4 (F) (H 15/6-31/8) J (Q+S) (T 1/6-15/9) (U+Z)
5 **AB**DFGIJKLMNPUWZ
6 EG**K**(N 4km)OTV

A peaceful campsite with marked out pitches and a wide variety of planting 4 km from the sea and close to the American landing beaches from WWII. Beautiful grounds with excellent toilet facilities. 12 km from the medieval town of Bayeux.

N13 from Bayeux direction Cherbourg, exit 38. Follow Tour-en-Bessin/Mosles then Surrain. The campsite is in Surrain village. Signposted.

CC € 15 *25/3-8/7 25/8-30/9*

N 49°19'36'' W 0°51'52''

Grandcamp-Maisy, F-14450 / Basse-Normandie (Calvados)

1315

Camping du Joncal***
Quai du Petit Nice, BP 33
+33 (0)2-31226144
FAX +33 (0)2-31227399
1/4 - 30/9
@ campingdujoncal@hotmail.fr

4ha 300**T**(80-100m²) 10A CEE

1 A**G**IJKLMOPRS
2 AEFGKQRTVX
3 BH**OP**RUWY
4 (A+Q)
5 **AB**EGIJKLMNPUWZ
6 EGH**K**T

The campsite is located near the harbour of Grandcamp-Maisy. Pitches by the sea or more sheltered, marked out pitches in the middle of the grounds. Just a few km from Pointe du Hoc. Perfect base for visiting the many WWII monuments such as Omaha Beach, the American Cemetery at Pointe du Hoc and the German military cemetery at La Cambe.

N13 exit Grandcamp-Maisy. Via D113 towards village centre. Campsite is next to the harbour, follow signs.

€17 *1/4-30/6 1/9-30/9*

N 49°23'17'' W 1°3'5''

Honfleur/Équemauville, F-14600 / Basse-Normandie (Calvados)

1316

La Briquerie*****
D62
+33 (0)2-31892832
FAX +33 (0)2-31890852
1/4 - 30/9
@ info@campinglabriquerie.com

11ha 200**T**(100m²) 5-10A

1 A**G**IJKLMPQ
2 FGLRVWXY
3 B**F**GHJMNQRU**V**
4 (C 25/6-10/9) (F 15/4-30/9) (H 15/5-15/9) IJ**KN** (Q+R+T+U+X+Y+Z)
5 **AB**DEFGIJKLMNPQRUXYZ
6 ACDEGIKOPRTV

In easily accessible woodland with large marked out pitches. Easy access. 3 km from the sea and the picturesque town of Honfleur. 1 km from a large wood for walks. 100m from large supermarket. Since 2011: new toilet facilities. Five stars from 2012.

From A29 exit 1. Go towards Pont-l'Évêque. Right after 2 km on D579 dir. Honfleur. Third exit at Intermarché to D62. Campsite about 150m on the right.

€17 *1/4-10/7 27/8-30/9* *7=6*

N 49°23'53'' E 0°12'31''

Houlgate, F-14510 / Basse-Normandie (Calvados)

1317

Yelloh! Village La Vallée*****
88 rue de la Vallée
+33 (0)2-31244069
FAX +33 (0)2-31244242
1/4 - 1/11
@ camping.lavallee@wanadoo.fr

14ha 151**T**(100-130m²) 6-10A CEE

1 ACD**F**IJKLMPQ
2 AIJKLRVWX
3 BC**F**GK**M**N**OP**RU
4 (C 1/5-15/9) (F 1/4-30/10) (H 1/5-15/9) IJP (Q+S+T+U) (V 1/5-30/9) (X+Z)
5 **AB**FGIJKLMNPUWXYZ
6 CDEG**K**(N 1km)OTV

A spacious campsite with plenty of greenery, a 15 minute walk to the village and beaches. Beautiful views of the surrounding hills. The site offers all amenities and is well maintained. There is also an entertainer in the early season. Renewed sanitary facilities

A13 exit Dozulé, then D400 direction Dives-sur-Mer/Houlgate and then follow the signs.

€17 *1/4-1/7 28/8-1/11*

N 49°17'37'' W 0°4'6''

Isigny-sur-Mer, F-14230 / Basse-Normandie (Calvados) 1318

Le Fanal****
rue du Fanal
+33 (0)2-31213320
FAX +33 (0)2-31221200
1/4 - 30/9
@ info@camping-lefanal.com

8,4ha 93**T**(80-110m²) 16A CEE

1 ACD**F**IJKLMPRS
2 DFLRVWXY
3 BGHJMNRUVW
4 (C 15/6-31/8) (E)
(H 15/6-31/8) IJ
(Q 15/4-15/9)
(T+U+V+Y+Z 15/6-15/9)
5 **AB**DEGIJKMNPUWXZ
6 CEG**IJK**(N 1km)TV

An attractive, peaceful campsite located by a recreational lake. Fishing and surfing are permitted. Indoor swimming pool (sliding roof) and a large outdoor pool with slide and deckchairs. Good toilet facilities. An ideal location for visiting the Landing Beaches, Pointe du Hoc and the American and German war cemeteries.

Isigny-centre exit; then signposted.

CC € 13 1/4-8/7 25/8-30/9 7=6, 14=11

N 49°19'8'' W 1°6'32''

Le Brévedent/Pont-l'Évêque, F-14130 / Basse-Normandie (Calvados) 1319

Castel Camping le Brévedent****
+33 (0)2-31647288
1/5 - 15/9
@ contact@campinglebrevedent.com

6ha 102**T**(60-200m²) 6-10A CEE

1 ACDEHIJKLMPQ
2 BCDIJLRVWXY
3 BGHJK**M**NQRUW
4 (A 1/7-30/8)
(C+H+Q+S 4/5-15/9)
(T 1/7-31/8) (U 15/5-15/9)
(V 4/5-15/9)
(X+Y 15/5-15/9) (Z)
5 **AB**FGIJKLMNPUWZ
6 ACEGJ(N 4km)ORV

Campsite positioned around an old hunting lodge. The small lake and a swimming pool in the grounds provide plenty of fun in the water. Friendly and agreeable atmosphere.

From Pont-l'Évêque take the D579 towards Lisieux. After 5 km turn left over the D51 to Blangy-le-Château. Le Brévedent is about 3 km past this town. Follow signs.

CC € 17 1/5-2/7 27/8-15/9

N 49°13'29'' E 0°18'17''

Le Rozel, F-50340 / Basse-Normandie (Manche) 1320

Le Ranch*****
La Mielle
+33 (0)2-33100710
FAX +33 (0)2-33100711
1/4 - 30/9
@ contact@camping-leranch.com

4ha 32**T**(100-130m²) 10A CEE

1 ACD**G**IJKLMPQ
2 AEJKRSVW
3 BGNRUVWY
4 (C 1/5-30/9) (E)
(H 1/5-30/9) J**N**
(Q 15/4-15/9) (S)
(T+U+V+X+Y 1/5-15/9)
(Z)
5 **AB**CDEFGIJKLMNOPUWXY
6 CEG**IK**(N 5km)ORTV

Camping Le Ranch is located on the west coast of the Cotentin (La Manche) in the middle of a beautiful dune landscape and right on a wide sandy beach. The location and the amenities of this campsite ensure a unique ambiance in spring and autumn.

In Les Pieux follow the D904, direction Barneville-Carteret. Turn right just beyond Les Pieux. Signposted further on.

CC € 17 1/4-1/7 1/9-30/9

N 49°28'49'' W 1°50'32''

Le Vey, F-14570 / Basse-Normandie (Calvados) — 1321

Des Rochers des Parcs***
La Cour, 8 rte du Viaduc
+33 (0)2-31697036
1/4 - 30/9
camping.normandie@gmail.com

1,5ha 60**T**(80-140m²) 10A CEE

1 ACGIJKLMOPQ
2 CJRTUVX
3 ABGHJR**W**X
4 (Q+R+T+Z)
5 **AB**DEFGIJKLMNOPUZ
6 BCDEJ(N 0,8km)T

A green oasis of peace. Terraced campsite located on a river. At walking distance from a small, pretty village with shops and restaurants.

D562 Caen-Flers then D133A Le Vey, then follow signs. Turn right after Orne bridge.

CC € 15 *1/4-7/7 24/8-30/9* *7=6, 14=11*

N 48°54'49'' W 0°28'27''

Maupertus-sur-Mer, F-50330 / Basse-Normandie (Manche) — 1322

L'Anse du Brick*****
+33 (0)2-33543357
FAX +33 (0)2-33544966
9/4 - 19/9
welcome@anse-du-brick.com

17ha 173**T**(90-150m²) 10A CEE

1 ACD**F**IJKLMOPQ
2 ABCEGJKNOQRTVWXY
3 B**F**GH**M**NRUWY
4 (C 1/5-15/9) (F+H) JK
(Q+S+T+U+V+X+Z)
5 **AB**CDEFGIJKLMNOPQUW
XYZ
6 ACEG**IJK**(N 8km)ORTV

A lovely campsite with every comfort close to Cherbourg and by the sea. Large pitches on terraces, heated toilet facilities and two swimming pools. Direct access to footpaths and the beach. Daily 30 minutes free WiFi.

From Cherbourg via the D116 towards Bretteville-Barfleur. Follow the D116. Campsite signposted after about 4 km. Attention: difficult to reach via Maupertus, take D116 via Cherbourg.

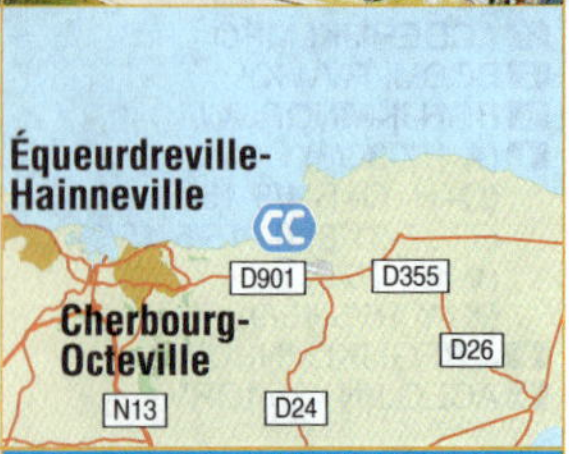

CC € 19 *9/4-1/7 29/8-19/9*

N 49°40'4'' W 1°29'19''

Merville-Franceville-Plage, F-14810 / Basse-Normandie (Calvados) — 1323

Les Peupliers****
allée des Pins
FAX +33 (0)2-31240507
1/4 - 31/10
contact@camping-peupliers.com

4ha 118**T**(80-146m²) 10A CEE

1 ACD**G**IJKLMPST
2 ACEFLRVWX
3 AFGHJNOPRUV**WY**
4 (C+H 1/6-30/9) (Q)
(R 1/7-31/8) (T+U 1/7-30/8)
(Z 1/7-31/8)
5 **AB**DEFGIJLMNPQRUWXYZ
6 ACEGIJ**K**(N 2km)RUV

A peacefully located family campsite with large pitches in an open setting. Grounds with plenty of flowers, close to Cabourg for all your shopping. Heated swimming pool and good heated toilet facilities. 300 metres from the sandy beach. Walking and cycle routes right from the campsite. Your stay will begin with a friendly welcome.

Drive from Cabourg via the D514 in the direction of Merville. The campsite is located on the left of this road and is signposted.

CC € 17 *1/4-4/7 1/9-31/10* *7=6, 14=12*

N 49°17'3'' W 0°10'8''

Merville-Franceville-Plage, F-14810 / Basse-Normandie (Calvados) — 1324

Seasonova Le Point du Jour****
75 route de Cabourg
+33 (0)2-31242334
1/4 - 30/10
contact@
camping-lepointdujour.com

2,7ha 109**T** 10A CEE

1 ACD**G**IJKLMPQ
2 AEFGJKLRSVWX
3 A**F**GHIJKPRUVWY
4 (A 3/4-31/8)
(F+H 10/4-1/11) **KN**P
(Q+R) (T+U+V 1/7-31/8)
(Y) (Z 1/7-31/8)
5 **AB**DEFGJLMNPUWXY
6 ACEG**IK**(N 1,5km)**P**RIV

Located right by the sea with an indoor pool. Close to Caen and Cabourg with plenty of shops. A cycle path leads from the site to Cabourg. The centre of Merville is a 400m walk via the beach.

A13 exit 29B Dozulé, direction Cabourg. Then via D514 towards Ouistreham. Campsite signposted. From the west: A13, exit 29 Dozulé, direction Cabourg. Then D514 direction Ouistreham.

CC € 17 *1/4-8/7 29/8-30/10*

N 49°17'0'' W 0°11'29''

Pontaubault, F-50220 / Basse-Normandie (Manche) — 1325

Vallée de la Sélune**
7 rue Maréchal Leclerc
+33 (0)2-33603900
1/4 - 20/10
campselune@wanadoo.fr

1,6ha 70**T**(100-110m²) 10A CEE

1 ACDGIJKLMPQ
2 FGTVX
3 ABG**M**
4 (R) Z
5 **AB**GIJKLMNPUZ
6 EGK(N 0,2km)O

Small, quiet campsite in a beautiful small village with shops and a restaurant. The campsite is only 15 km from Mont-Saint-Michel.

From N175 direction Mont-St-Michel D43. Exit Pontaubault; turn right over the bridge, then the second street to the left.

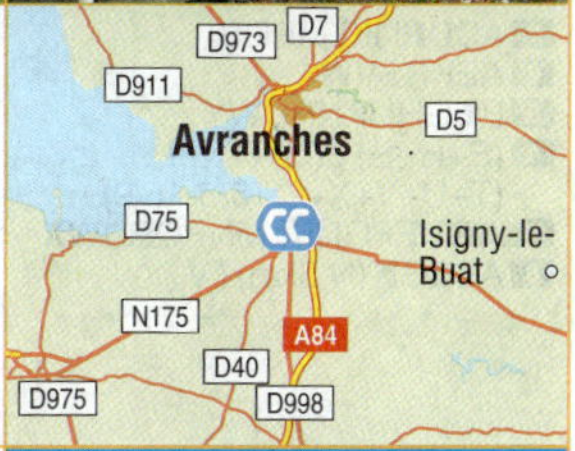

CC € 15 *1/4-7/7 24/8-20/10* *5=4, 14=10*

N 48°37'49'' W 1°21'10''

Pontorson, F-50170 / Basse-Normandie (Manche) — 1326

Haliotis***
boulevard Patton
+33 (0)2-33681159
FAX +33 (0)2-33589536
25/3 - 2/11
camping.haliotis@wanadoo.fr

8ha 150**T**(90-200m²) 16A CEE

1 ACD**G**IJKLM**PQ**
2 CFRTVX
3 ABDGHJKMNRUW
4 (C+H 1/5-30/9) KN
(Q+R) Z
5 **AB**DFGIJKLMNP**S**UWZ
6 CEGIK(N 0,5km)RTV

Beautiful, quiet and floral campsite within walking distance of the centre (market on Wednesday) and within cycling distance of Mont St. Michel.

N175 Avranches direction Pontorson, exit Pontorson. Follow the signs in the town.

CC € 17 *25/3-24/6 27/8-1/11* *7=6, 14=10*

N 48°33'29'' W 1°30'52''

St. Aubin-sur-Mer, F-14750 / Basse-Normandie (Calvados)

1327

Côte de Nacre*****
17 rue du Général Moulton
+33 (0)2-31971445
+33 (0)2-31972211
25/3 - 12/9
cotedenacre@sandaya.fr

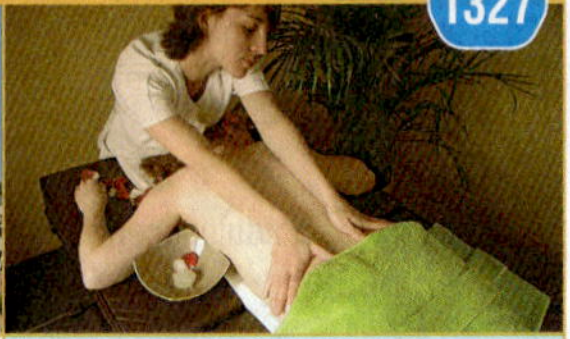

10ha 145**T**(80-120m²) 10A

1 ACD**G**IJKLMPRS
2 GLRVWX
3 B**F**GKNRU
4 (C 15/6-31/8) (D+F+H) IJ **LN**P(Q+S+T)
(U 4/4-12/9) (V+Y+Z)
5 **AB**DEFGIJKLMNOPUWXYZ
6 ACEGH**I**J(N 0,5km)TV

A beautiful parkland campsite with a leisure pool (open air and indoor and heated); sauna, Turkish bath, jacuzzi, restaurant, shopping facilities. Campsite is within walking distance of St. Aubin and 650 metres from the beach. All amenities are also open in the early and late seasons.

On the Caen ring road exit Côte de Nacre, then via the D7 to Langrune-sur-Mer and St. Aubin-sur-Mer. Campsite is on the D7 and is signposted.

CC € 19 *25/3-1/7 29/8-10/9*

N 49°19'33'' W 0°23'26''

St. Jean-de-la-Rivière, F-50270 / Basse-Normandie (Manche)

1328

Camping du Golf****
43 chemin des Mielles
+33 (0)2-33047890
+33 (0)9-70632192
1/4 - 1/11
contact@camping-du-golf.fr

3,2ha 157**T**(110-150m²) 6A CEE

1 ACD**F**IJKLMPRS
2 AEKRSVW
3 B**E**GHIJKNRUWY
4 (E+H) J(Q+R)
(T+U+V+X+Z 15/5-15/9)
5 **AB**DEFGIJKLMNPQRUWX
6 ACEG**K**(N 3km)TV

A family campsite with large pitches, located 500m from the Normandy Beaches, opposite the Channel Islands of Guernsey and Jersey. New covered and heated swimming pool. Bar, restaurant, pizzeria and shop on site. Plenty of activities available.

From Barneville-Carteret towards Barneville/St. Jean-de-la-Rivière. Signposted beyond there.

CC € 17 *1/4-3/7 28/8-1/11*

N 49°21'35'' W 1°44'55''

St. Pair-sur-Mer, F-50380 / Basse-Normandie (Manche)

1329

Lez-Eaux*****
St. Aubin-des-Préaux
+33 (0)2-33516609
+33 (0)2-33519202
1/4 - 11/9
bonjour@lez-eaux.com

11ha 134**T**(100-150m²) 10A CEE

1 ACGIJKLMOPQ
2 DLRVX
3 ABGK**M**NRW
4 (C 15/5-11/9) (F+H) IJ
(Q+S+U) Z
5 **AB**DEFGIJKLMNOPUWXYZ
6 CDEG**IJ**(N 2km)RTV

For an unforgettable holiday: a quiet flowery family campsite in a castle park, with a 1200 m² heated indoor swimming paradise close to Granville.

From Caen via the A84 and D924 towards Granville. Before Granville via the D971 and D973 towards Avranches. The campsite is well signposted on the right. Do not take direction St. Pair-sur-Mer or direction St. Aubin-des-Préaux.

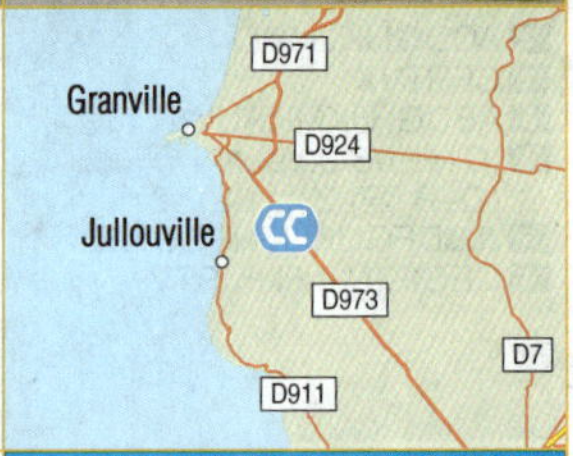

CC € 19 *1/4-30/6 1/9-11/9*

N 48°47'52'' W 1°31'30''

St. Vaast-la-Hougue, F-50550 / Basse-Normandie (Manche) — 1330

La Gallouette****
rue de la Gallouette
+33 (0)2-33542057
FAX +33 (0)2-33541671
1/4 - 30/9
@ contact@camping-lagallouette.fr

3,5ha 110**T**(85-105m²) 10A CEE

1 ACD**G**IJKLMPRS
2 AEQRVWX
3 BGHNRUWY
4 (C+H 15/5-15/9)
(Q+R+T+U+Z 1/7-31/8)
5 **AB**EFGJKLMNOPUWYZ
6 ACDEG**IK**(N 0,3km)OTV

A modern campsite with good toilet facilities and beautiful pool. Spacious pitches. Located in a tourist area, trips out to places such as Tatihou Island and Barfleur are possible.

N13 Caen-Cherbourg, at Valognes D902 direction Quettehou and St. Vaast-la-Hougue. Right at traffic lights, turn right after 300m - Rue de la Galouette.

CC € 17 *1/4-3/7 29/8-30/9*

N 49°35'4'' W 1°16'8''

Ste Marie-du-Mont, F-50480 / Basse-Normandie (Manche) — 1331

UTAH Beach***
La Madeleine
+33 (0)2-33715369
FAX +33 (0)2-33710711
1/4 - 30/9
@ utah.beach@wanadoo.fr

5ha 40**T**(80-100m²) 6A CEE

1 ACD**G**IJKLMOPQ
2 AELRSTVWX
3 BFHJK**MNQ**RUWY
4 (F+H) **KN**(Q+S)
(U 1/6-31/8) (V)
(X 1/6-31/8) (Z)
5 **AB**EFGIJKLMNPUWZ
6 ACEGIJK(N 6km)OTV

A family campsite in Western style 100 metres from the sea. Close to Utah Beach landing beaches. The area is rich in history and architecture. Motorhome site also available, open all year.

From Carentan take the D913 direction Ste Marie-du-Mont (Utah Beach). Follow signs after Utah Beach monument.

CC € 17 *1/4-31/5 10/6-30/6 1/9-30/9 7=6, 14=10*

N 49°25'10'' W 1°10'55''

Torigni-sur-Vire, F-50160 / Basse-Normandie (Manche) — 1332

Le Lac des Charmilles***
route de Vire
+33 (0)2-33569174
FAX +33 (0)2-33559113
1/4 - 30/9
@ contact@
camping-lacdescharmilles.com

2,4ha 40**T**(100-150m²) 16A CEE

1 ACD**G**IJKLM**P**RS
2 DFJLRVWX
3 AG**M**NRU**W**
4 (C 15/5-15/9)
(Q+R+T+U+V+X+Z)
5 **AB**DFGIJKLMNOPUWZ
6 CDEG**K**(N 0,5km)V

A well-located and well-maintained campsite by a lake and within walking distance of the small town of Torigni-sur-Vire. The campsite has a heated outdoor pool. One hour from Mont St. Michel and the Landing Beaches.

From A84 Caen-Rennes exit 40. Then D974 direction Torigni-sur-Vire. Campsite on the right before the town.

CC € 17 *1/4-9/7 26/8-30/9*

N 49°1'43'' W 0°58'20''

Villedieu-les-Poêles, F-50800 / Basse-Normandie (Manche) 1333

Les Chevaliers***
2 impasse Pré de la Rose
+33 (0)2-33610244
FAX +33 (0)2-33494993
1/4 - 30/9
@ contact@camping-deschevaliers.com

1,5ha 53T(90-100m²) 8A CEE

1 ACD**G**IJKLM**P**Q
2 CFRTVX
3 ABGNRU**W**
4 (C 15/6-15/9) (Q+R) (T+U+V+X 15/4-30/9) Z
5 **AB**DEFGIJKLMNPUWZ
6 ACDEGIJ(N 0,3km)OV

A small campsite in the countryside with marked out pitches. Located 300 metres from the centre. Copper works, bell-foundry and a typical weekly market.

From Caen A84 direction Mont St. Michel. In Villedieu take exit 38 towards the centre. Campsite well signposted.

CC € 17 1/4-9/7 26/8-30/9 7=6, 14=10

N 48°50'12'' W 1°13'2''

Villers-sur-Mer, F-14640 / Basse-Normandie (Calvados) 1334

Bellevue****
route de Dives
+33 (0)2-31870521
FAX +33 (0)2-31870967
1/4 - 31/10
@ camping-bellevue@wanadoo.fr

5,5ha 39T(80-110m²) 6-10A CEE

1 ACD**G**HIJKLPRS
2 FGIJRVWX
3 A**F**GHKRUV
4 (E+H 15/4-15/10) (Q+R+T+U+V+X+Z)
5 **AB**FGIJKLMNPUXY
6 AEG**K**(N 1,8km)

Campsite with terraces, high above the sea. Places are marked out with natural growth. Nice swimming pool and a pleasant outdoor café.

On the A13 exit 'La Haye Tondue', on the N175 towards Caen. After 4 km take the D45 (changes into D163) in the direction of Houlgate/Villers-sur-Mer. At the junction with the D513, drive towards Villers-sur-Mer. Campsite is marked with signs.

CC € 15 1/4-8/7 29/8-31/10

N 49°18'34'' W 0°1'9''

Arradon, F-56610 / Bretagne (Morbihan) 1335

Camping de l'Allée***
L'Allée
+33 (0)2-97440198
1/4 - 30/9
@ contact@camping-allee.com

134T(80-140m²) 15A CEE

1 ACD**G**IJKLMOPQ
2 EFIOQRVWXY
3 B**F**GHRUW
4 (C+H 1/5-15/9) (Q+R+U 2/7-30/8)
5 **AB**EFGIJKLPUVZ
6 ACE**K**(N 2km)OTV

A peaceful campsite in the green belt between the town and the sea, a rugged coastline with many coves and islands in the Gulf of Morbihan. Large level pitches between trees and hedges or open pitches with plenty of sun, but not all of these are level. Plans for 2016: covered pool and luxury, heated toilet blocks.

N165/E60 Nantes-Lorient, exit Vannes Ouest/ Arradon. Via D101 and D127 to Arradon just past shopping centre. Follow camping signs on roundabout.

CC € 15 1/4-1/7 29/8-29/9

N 47°37'17'' W 2°50'25''

Arradon, F-56610 / Bretagne (Morbihan)

1336

Sites & Paysages De Penboch****
9 chemin de Penboch
+33 (0)2-97447129
2/4 - 25/9
camping.penboch@wanadoo.fr

3,5ha 117**T**(85-110m²) 10A CEE

1 ACD**G**IJKLMOPQ
2 AEFKOQRVWXY
3 BC**F**GHJKN**Q**RUWY
4 (C 5/5-12/9) (F+H 9/4-25/9) IJK(Q+R) (T+U+Z 5/5-12/9)
5 **AB**CDEFGHIJKLMNOPQR**ST**UWXYZ
6 ACEGH**IK**(N 2km)RTV

Excellently equipped campsite 300m from the north coast of the Golfe Du Morbihan. 300m from Grande Randonnée 34. You can book boat excursions on the Golfe Du Morbihan at the campsite. Nearby Vannes is worth visiting, 8 km by bike. Excellent toilet facilities, a lovely indoor swimming pool and heated outdoor pool with slides.

N165/E60 Vannes-Lorient, exit Vannes-Ouest/ Arradon. Via the D101 direction Arradon, then follow campsite signs or 'Pointe de Penboch'.

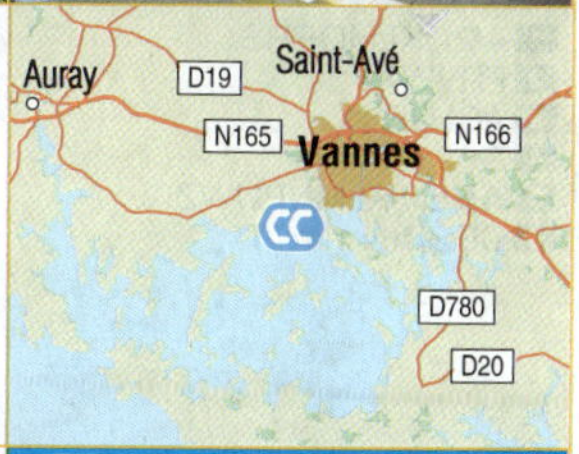

CC € 17 *2/4-9/7 27/8-24/9*

N 47°37'20" W 2°48'4"

Arzano, F-29310 / Bretagne (Finistère)

1337

Le Ty Nadan*****
route d'Arzano
+33 (0)2-98717547
FAX +33 (0)2-98717731
4/5 - 5/9
info@tynadan-vacances.fr

21ha 110**T**(90-160m²) 10A CEE

1 ACD**G**IJKLMOPRS
2 ACKLRVWXY
3 BCDGHJK**MNOP**RUWX
4 (A+C+F+H) IJKMP (Q+S+T+U+V+Y+Z)
5 **AB**DEFGJLMNPQ**ST**UWXYZ
6 CEGH**IK**(N 3km)O**P**RTV

A family campsite in the countryside. Located in the middle of nature. The swimming pools are heated to 28° C. There is an obstacle course in the trees. A few kilometres from the Devil's Rocks, well worth a visit.

North of Lorient via the N165/E60 towards Quimperlé, exit Quimperlé-Est. Take the D22 before Quimperlé-centre to Arzano. Head towards Locunolé just before Arzano-centre, or follow the signs.

CC € 17 *4/5-2/7 27/8-5/9 7=6, 14=11*

N 47°54'17" W 3°28'30"

Baden/Bourgerel, F-56870 / Bretagne (Morbihan)

1338

Campéole Penn Mar***
21 route de Port Blanc
+33 (0)2-97574990
FAX +33 (0)2-97311124
1/4 - 30/9
pennmar@andretriganogroupe.com

6ha 72**T**(100-150m²) 10A CEE

1 ACD**G**IJKLMO**P**ST
2 AEGKOQRVWXY
3 A**F**GHJ**M**NRUW
4 (E+H) M(Q 4/7-26/8) (R) (T+U+Z 4/7-26/8)
5 **AB**CDFGHIJKLMNOPQRUZ
6 CEGHJ(N 4km)ORTV

A family campsite with sufficient, modern toilet facilities close to the 'Golfe du Morbihan' with its hundreds of islands, the most famous of which, Île-aux-Moines, is especially worth a visit. Lovely new indoor pool with a fun open air water playground.

N165/E60 Vannes-Lorient, exit Vannes-Ouest/ Arradon. Via D101 direction Baden/Île-aux-Moines. Then follow Île-aux-Moines via D316, campsite on the left.

CC € 15 *1/5-4/7 22/8-30/9*

N 47°36'25" W 2°52'32"

Bannalec, F-29380 / Bretagne (Finistère) 1339

Les Genets d'Or***
Kermerour, Pont Kereon
+33 (0)2-98395435
21/5 - 30/9
info@campingbannalec.com

2ha 40T(80-140m²) 6A CEE

1 A**G**IJKLMOPRS
2 FRVWXY
3 AGHJR
4 Z
5 **AB**GIJKLMNPUWZ
6 CEG**J**(N 1km)T

A campsite in the countryside with modest but well maintained toilet facilities. Walking, cycling and relaxation are top of the list here. 1500m from a supermarket, village close by. Relaxation is important here. With CampingCard ACSI free WiFi.

N165/E10 Nantes-Quimper. Exit Bannalec/Pont-Aven, then towards Bannalec. Take ring road in town to Quimperle. Follow camping signs.

CC € 15 21/5-10/7 27/8-30/9

N 47°55'30'' W 3°41'23''

Beg-Léguer/Lannion, F-22300 / Bretagne (Côtes-d'Armor) 1340

Les Plages de Beg-Léguer***
route de la Côte
+33 (0)2-96472500
29/4 - 30/9
info@campingdesplages.com

4,7ha 149T(80-120m²) 6A CEE

1 ACGIJKLMOPRS
2 AEFGLQRVXY
3 AB**F**GHJMNRUWY
4 (C+D+G) J(Q+R)
(T+U+V+X+Z 1/7-31/8)
5 A**B**EFGIJKLMNPUVWZ
6 AEGIK(N 4km)RTV

You will be warmly received at this beautiful campsite adorned by many flowers. Spacious pitches with glimpses of the sea. The sandy beach is 400 metres away and Lannion is just 5 km. Ideal base for the Côte de Granit Rose, Les Sept Îles and the Île Grande. A campsite worth going back to.

Lannion-Trébeurden (total 9 km). After about 6 km turn off at Champ Blanc towards Les Plages de Beg-Léguer. (Better not to drive through Servel).

CC € 15 29/4-30/6 1/9-30/9 7=6, 14=12

N 48°44'18'' W 3°32'41''

Bénodet, F-29950 / Bretagne (Finistère) 1341

Camping du Poulquer****
23 rue du Poulquer
+33 (0)2-98570419
FAX +33 (0)2-98662030
1/5 - 30/9
contact@campingdupoulquer.com

3ha 148T(80-100m²) 6-10A

1 CD**G**IJKLOPQ
2 AERVWXY
3 B**F**GHRUWY
4 (C 15/6-10/9) (E 1/5-15/9)
(H 15/6-10/9) IJKLN
(Q+R+T+U 1/7-31/8) Z
5 **AB**EFGIJKLMNOPUZ
6 AEGIJ(N 1km)TV

Family campsite close to the town and located near Bénodet promenade. The beach is also close by. Modern and very neat toilet facilities. It has a lovely heated outdoor pool with jacuzzi and slides, but it also has an indoor pool with sliding roof, free hammam and sauna, a wellness area with jetstream and Balneo. Free internet and WiFi-point.

From Quimper take the D34 to Bénodet. Continue Bénodet-plage. Turn left at the end of the boulevard. Follow the signs!

CC € 17 1/5-10/7 27/8-30/9

N 47°52'4'' W 4°5'54''

Beuzec-Cap-Sizun, F-29790 / Bretagne (Finistère)

iD **1342**

Camping Pors Peron**
+33 (0)2-98704024
1/4 - 30/9
campingporsperon@hotmail.com

3ha 98T(60-120m²) 10A CEE

1 ACD**G**IJKLMPQ
2 AEJQRX
3 BGHJKRWY
4 (Q+S)
5 **AB**FGIJKLMNPUZ
6 AE**I**J(N 5km)OV

Camping Pors Peron is situated in a peaceful, rural location on the lovely headland of Cap Sizun in western Brittany. It has 98 marked out pitches. 200 metres from a remote, sandy bay which can be reached via a footpath. All the ingredients for a relaxing holiday. Free WiFi. Shop. English owners.

From Châteaulin take the D7 direction Douarnenez and then follow Beuzec-Cap-Sizun. Turn right about 5 km before Beuzec-Cap-Sizun, direction Pors Peron, then follow camping signs.

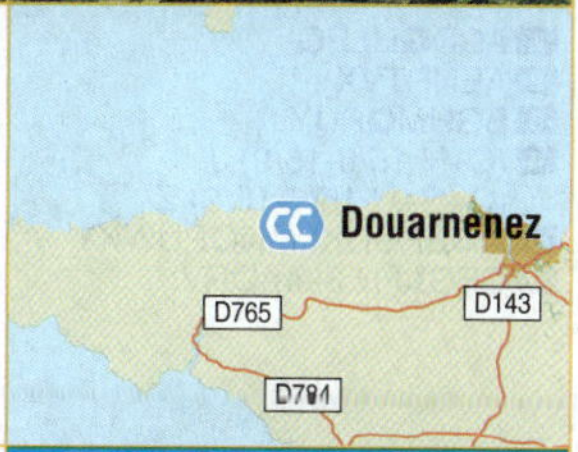

CC € 15 *1/4-10/7 27/8-30/9*

N 48°5'3" W 4°28'56"

Binic, F-22520 / Bretagne (Côtes-d'Armor)

iD **1343**

Le Panoramic***
rue Gasselin
+33 (0)2-96736043
2/4 - 30/9
camping.le.panoramic@wanadoo.fr

5,8ha 66T(80-130m²) 10A CEE

1 ACDFIJKLMOPQ
2 AFGIJKLQRTVWXY
3 AB**F**GHN**OP**RUW
4 (C 1/6-15/9) (F+G) IJ (Q+R) (T 2/7-27/8) (Z)
5 **AB**DEFGJLMNPRUZ
6 ADEGK(N 1km)ORTV

A spacious and attractive campsite close to the harbour town of Binic. Heated, indoor swimming pool and terrace, cafe, bar and the welcome trees all give the place a pleasant feeling. Lovely modern, heated toilet facilities. The pitches are separated by low hedges. Panoramic views of Binic. Free WiFi.

Via the N12 after St. Brieuc, keep in direction Paimpol-par-la-Côte (D786). The campsite is signposted to the right, just before Binic. Turn right immediately.

CC € 17 *2/4-2/7 27/8-30/9*

N 48°35'30" W 2°49'29"

Brest, F-29200 / Bretagne (Finistère)

iD **1344**

du Goulet****
chemin de Lanhouarnec
+33 (0)2-98458684
22/1 - 14/12
campingdugoulet@wanadoo.fr

6ha 155T(< 100m²) 10A CEE

1 ACDFIJKLMPQ
2 EFGLRTUWXY
3 ABCGHQRUWY
4 (C+H 14/5-15/9) JKM (Q 1/7-30/8) (R) (T+U+V+X 1/7-30/8) Z
5 **AB**CDFGIJKLMNOPUVWXYZ
6 CDEGIJ(N 5km)ORTV

Very well maintained campsite with a lovely heated swimming pool, also ideally located for visiting Brest and surroundings.

From Rennes or Morlaix turn right at 1st roundabout (Boulevard de L'Europe) to Plouzané-Le Conquet. Straight ahead ± 8 km. On D789 past Thalès company left at roundabout towards Technopole, Camping du Goulet.

CC € 15 *22/1-30/6 1/9-14/12* 7=6

N 48°21'55" W 4°32'24"

Camaret-sur-Mer, F-29570 / Bretagne (Finistère)

1345

Le Grand Large****
Lambézen
+33 (0)2-98279141
FAX +33 (0)2-98279372
1/4 - 30/9
@ contact@campinglegrandlarge.com

2,8ha 123T(80-130m²) 10A CEE

1 ACD**G**IJLPQ
2 AENRTVX
3 BGHM**Q**RUY
4 (C+H 15/6-15/9) J (Q+S+U 15/6-15/9) Z
5 **AB**EFGIJKLMNOPUWXY
6 CEG**IJ**(N 3km)ORV

A campsite that deserves its star rating; very clean and well-maintained new toilet facilities including showers and washbasins in the same room. 450m to the beach with spectacular panoramas of the sea and rocks.

From Cozon the D8 to Camaret. Just past Camaret the roundabout to the right, direction Roscanvel/D355 (1.8 km). At Lambézen follow signs to the right.

CC € 15 *1/4-6/7 23/8-30/9 7=6, 14=11*

N 48°16'51'' W 4°33'53''

Camaret-sur-Mer/Crozon, F-29160 / Bretagne (Finistère)

1346

Plage de Trez Rouz***
route de Camaret à Roscanvel
+33 (0)2-98279396
15/3 - 15/10
@ contact@trezrouz.com

1,8ha 80T(85-100m²) 16A CEE

1 ACD**G**IJKLMPQ
2 AEKRVWX
3 BGHQRWY
4 (A+Q+R) (T+U+V 14/4-15/10) Z
5 **AB**DFGIJKLMNOPUVWZ
6 CEG**IJ**(N 3km)V

You will be warmly welcomed by Isabelle and Yannick Trouplin on their beach campsite with views of Camaret. Sandy beaches, ochre coloured rocks, abundant greenery and small towns in the area. Guided walks on Thursdays led by the campsite boss. The views of Crozon are unique. Several boat trips possible.

From Crozon take the D8 to Camaret. Just before Camaret turn right at the roundabout direction Pointe des Espagnols. Follow this road (D355) for 2.8 km.

CC € 13 *15/3-6/7 25/8-15/10 15=14*

N 48°17'17'' W 4°33'55''

Carnac, F-56340 / Bretagne (Morbihan)

1347

Les Druides***
55 chemin de Beaumer
+33 (0)2-97520818
FAX +33 (0)9-60538264
23/4 - 10/9
@ contact@camping-les-druides.com

2,5ha 90T(80-130m²) 10A CEE

1 ACD**G**IJKLOPQ
2 AEGQRVWXY
3 B**F**GHJNRUWY
4 (C+H 1/6-10/9) (Q 10/7-28/8)
5 **AB**CEFGHIJKLMNOPQRUVXYZ
6 ACEG**J**(N 0,5km)TV

A peaceful campsite. Well maintained toilet facilities. Pitches between hedges. Close to Carnac. Beach and supermarket 500m. Walking or cycling trips to the coast and the stone Megaliths. Reception open 09:30-12:00 and 14:00-18:30.

N165/E60 Nantes-Quimper exit Carnac/Quiberon, to Carnac Plage as far as roundabout at market place in Carnac centre. Then towards La Trinité as far as the roundabout with restaurant, then right, site entrance ± 1 km on the right.

CC € 19 *23/4-5/7 22/8-10/9*

N 47°34'48'' W 3°3'25''

Carnac/Plouharnel, F-56340 / Bretagne (Morbihan) — 1348

Les Bruyères***
Kerogile
+33 (0)2-97523057
1/4 - 30/9
contact@camping-lesbruyeres.com

4,5ha 71**T**(80-120m²) 10A CEE

1 ACD**G**IJKLMOPQ
2 FGLQRVWXY
3 BD**F**GHJKN**OPR**T**U**
4 (E+H) (Q 1/5-13/9) (S) (T+U+V+X 4/7-31/8) Z
5 **AB**CDEFGHIJKLMNOPUWZ
6 ACEGJ(N 2km)TV

A lovely, quiet campsite divided into shaded fields of six pitches, separated by green hedges. Well maintained toilet facilities. Perfect base for visiting historical remains and the Carnac beaches. Indoor, heated swimming pool open all season.

South of Auray, via D768 to Quiberon-Carnac. Beyond Carnac exit follow road to Quiberon as far as roundabout with blue and white building. Then left dir. Kerogile (C4). 300m to campsite.

CC € 17 1/4-8/7 25/8-30/9 7=6, 14=11

N 47°36'28'' W 3°5'26''

Châteaulin, F-29150 / Bretagne (Finistère) — 1349

de Rodaven***
Rocade de Prat Bihan
+33 (0)2-98863293
1/4 - 30/9
contact@campingderodaven.fr

2ha 82**T**(80-120m²) 10A CEE

1 AC**G**HIJLPRS
2 CFRVWXY
3 AGJR**W**
4 (Q 1/5-30/9) (T 7/4-30/9) (U 1/5-30/9)
5 **AB**GIJKLMNPUWZ
6 CEJ(N 0,8km)O

Located in the heart of Finistère (Brittany) on the banks of the 'Nantes à Brest' canal. The site is well maintained, quiet with plenty of greenery and within walking distance (800m) from the centre. A unique starting point for the many sights in this region. Cycling and walking beside the canal is well worth the effort.

From N125 and N164 intersection follow D887. Left at third roundabout, then first left. Then 1 km to the swimming pool. The campsite is opposite.

CC € 13 1/4-7/7 25/8-30/9 7=6

N 48°11'29'' W 4°5'18''

Châteaulin, F-29150 / Bretagne (Finistère) — 1350

La Pointe***
route de St. Coulitz
+33 (0)2-98865153
15/3 - 15/10
lapointecamping@aol.com

2ha 60**T**(80-120m²) 10A

1 ACD**G**IJKLMPQ
2 BCFRTVWXY
3 AKRU**W**
4 (Q+R)
5 **AB**EFGIJKLMNOPQUWZ
6 CEGK(N 1,5km)

A modest, quiet and well-maintained campsite where kindness, friendliness and hospitality are top of the list. Its central location in Finistére makes this a good campsite for trips out in the region. The centre is within walking distance (1,5 km) along the lovely 'Nantes-Brest' canal which can also be cycled.

In Châteaulin take direction Saint-Coulitz, then follow signs.

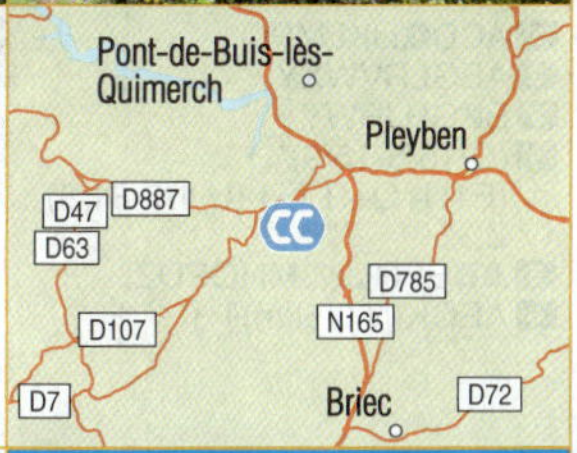

CC € 15 15/3-8/7 25/8-15/10 7=6

N 48°11'15'' W 4°5'5''

Clohars-Carnoët, F-29360 / Bretagne (Finistère) 1351

Le Kergariou***
Kervec
+33 (0)2-98715465
1/4 - 3/9
camping.lekergariou@wanadoo.fr

2,7ha 71**T**(80-150m²) 10A CEE

1 ACD**G**IJKLMOPRS
2 FGQRVWXY
3 BCGHJKNRU
4 (E+H) **N**
(Q+T+U 1/7-31/8) Z
5 **AB**FGIJKLMNPQUXYZ
6 CDEG**K**(N 1,5km)TUV

Peacefully located campsite with pitches between hedges and several mature trees. Well equipped toilet facilities. Cycling to the nearby small harbours is possible but watch out for some steep roads. The owner is a fervent angler and can inform you of the best places to fish. Indoor heated swimming pool open throughout the season.

E60/N165 Lorient-Quimper, exit Kervidanou. Via D16 to Clohars-Carnoët, straight through centre to roundabout. Direction Doëlan.

CC € 11 *1/4-1/7 27/8-2/9* N 47°46'58'' W 3°35'20''

Clohars-Carnoët/Le Pouldu, F-29360 / Bretagne (Finistère) 1352

Les Embruns*****
2 rue de Philosophe Alain
+33 (0)2-98399107
FAX +33 (0)2-98399787
26/3 - 1/10
contact@camping-les-embruns.com

6ha 65**T**(100-120m²) 16A CEE

1 ACD**G**IJKLMOPQ
2 AEFGQRVWXY
3 BDGHJK**MNOP**QRU**V**WY
4 (E 2/4-24/9) (H 8/7-27/8) J
LN(Q)
(S+T+U+V+Y+Z 2/4-24/9)
5 **AB**DEFGIJKLMNOPQRUWXY
6 ACDEGHIJKLOSTUVW

Beautiful family campsite near the beach. Located in the village centre. Lovely indoor swimming pool. Often awarded for being the campsite with the most beautiful planting in Brittany and even in all of France. Supermarket open whenever the campsite is. Excellent toilet facilities.

E60 Lorient towards Quimperlé. Exit Kervidanou or exit Kergostiou/Quimperlé centre. Via D16 to Clohars-Carnoët, straight through centre, D24 to Le Pouldu. Campsite in the town centre.

CC € 17 *26/3-9/7 26/8-30/9* N 47°46'7'' W 3°32'42''

Combrit/Sainte-Marine, F-29120 / Bretagne (Finistère) 1353

Le Helles***
55 rue du Petit Bourg
+33 (0)2-98563146
25/3 - 30/9
contact@le-helles.com

2,7ha 80**T**(90-120m²) 6-10A

1 ACD**G**IJKLMPQ
2 AEGLRVWXY
3 B**F**GHJRWY
4 (C 15/5-15/9)
(E+H+Q+R) (U 1/7-31/8)
Z
5 **AB**EFGIJKLMNOPUZ
6 AEGK(N 0,5km)T

An informal and quiet campsite with a heated outdoor swimming pool and new indoor swimming pool, opposite the renowned resort of Bénodet. 300 metres from a natural beach with fine sand and dunes and lots of opportunities to walk such as GR34. WiFi is free. New enthusiastic owners since 2013.

From Quimper to Bénodet. Then towards Pont-l'Abbé via D44. Over the bridge and 1st left to Ste Marine at roundabout. Then 2nd right and follow signs.

CC € 15 *25/3-7/7 25/8-30/9* N 47°52'10'' W 4°7'42''

Concarneau, F-29900 / Bretagne (Finistère) — 1354

Les Prés Verts aux 4 Sardines**
Kernous-Plage
+33 (0)2-98970974
1/5 - 26/9
info@presverts.com

3ha 111**T**(100-120m²) 10A

1 ACD**G**IJKLMOPRS
2 AEFKQRVWX
3 AB**F**HJQRWY
4 (C+H 12/5-17/9)
5 **AB**EGIJKLMNPUZ
6 ACEGK(N 2km)T

A peaceful, well-equipped campsite with spacious, flat pitches and well maintained toilets. 300m from a sheltered beach with direct sea access. 2,9 km from the famous medieval walled town of Concarneau which can be reached by a footpath along the rocky coast. Shops ± 2 km away.

N165/E60, exit Concarneau, D70 until just before the centre of Concarneau. Then direction Les Sables Blancs as far as the sea. Then direction Fouesnant. Signposted on the fourth street on the left.

CC €13 *1/5-5/7 24/8-26/9*

N 47°53'25'' W 3°56'19''

Concarneau, F-29900 / Bretagne (Finistère) — 1355

Les Sables Blancs****
avenue du Dorlett
FAX +33 (0)2-98971644
1/4 - 31/10
contact@
camping-lessablesblancs.com

2,9ha 105**T**(80-200m²) 16A CEE

1 ACD**G**IJKLMOPQ
2 AEFGJKQRVWXY
3 B**F**GHJKNRVWY
4 (C+H 11/4-13/9) KP (Q+R+T+U+V+X+Y) Z
5 **AB**DEFGIJKLMNOPQRUW XYZ
6 ACEGK(N 1,5km)TV

Small quiet site with pool in the middle of the countryside. 250m from a beach and a 15 min. walk from Concarneau, a lovely medieval walled town. Market twice a week in the town centre. Modern, heated toilet facilities. Some pitches have sea views.

From N165 direction Concarneau, centre via D70, to the roundabout with supermarket, direction Concarneau. Third to the right to Les Sables Blancs, via 2 roundabouts to the sea, as far as the T-junction, then turn right.

CC €15 *1/4-8/7 25/8-31/10* *7=6, 14=12, 21=18*

N 47°52'55'' W 3°55'43''

Crac'h, F-56950 / Bretagne (Morbihan) — 1356

Le Fort Espagnol***
rte du Fort Espagnol
+33 (0)2-97551488
9/4 - 24/9
fort-espagnol@wanadoo.fr

5,5ha 63**T**(75-140m²) 10A

1 ACD**G**IJKLMOPS
2 BFQRVWXY
3 BGHJKM**OP**RUW
4 (C 16/5-18/9) (E+H) IJ (Q+S+T+U+V+Z 1/7-31/8)
5 **AB**DEFGIJKLNPUVXYZ
6 ACEGJ**K**(N 0,6km)TV

Medium-sized campsite with homely atmosphere, large pitches at the back, in a pine forest. The most modern toilet facilities are centrally located next to the indoor pool. Located in a well-known and well-visited region. The campsite is quiet, with all sights within 20 km.

N165/E60 Nantes-Vannes-Lorient, exit Crac'h. Via D28 until roundabout at centre. Left dir. Fort Espagnol, entrance on right after 600m.

CC €13 *9/4-2/7 27/8-24/9* *7=6, 14=12*

N 47°36'56'' W 2°59'24''

Crozon, F-29160 / Bretagne (Finistère)

iD **1357**

L'Aber***
Tal-ar-Groas, 50 rte de l'Aber
+33 (0)2-98270296
1/4 - 8/10
contact@camping-aber.com

2ha 85**T**(100m²) 10A CEE

1 ACD**G**IJKLMPQ
2 ACJKLRTVWXY
3 AGHJRUW
4 (C+H+Q 15/6-15/9)
(R+T+U+V 1/4-1/10) Z
5 **A**EJ**L**MNPUV
6 EG(N 5km)V

A panoramic terraced campsite about 1500m from the sea. The site has a heated swimming pool and a friendly bar. New and refurbished toilet facilities. Fantastic views of the sea, the beautiful coastline and the River l'Aber from anywhere on the site.

Follow the D887 from Chateaulin to Crozon. Follow camping signs in Tal-ar-Groas towards plage de L'Aber.

CC € 15 *1/4-30/6 1/9-8/10*

N 48°14'32" W 4°25'46"

Damgan, F-56750 / Bretagne (Morbihan)

iD **1358**

Grand Air Cadu***
rue de Cadu
+33 (0)2-97411730
FAX +33 (0)2-97412857
2/4 - 9/10
info@campingcadu.com

7,8ha 93**T**(80-200m²) 16A CEE

1 ACD**G**IJKLM**P**ST
2 AEFGRVWX
3 BGHJKL**MNQ**RUWY
4 (C+E 7/5-17/9) (H 7/5-17/7)
J(Q+U+V 8/7-27/8)
5 **AB**CDFGHIJKLMNOPUXYZ
6 ACEG**K**(N 0,8km)OTU

A campsite 300m from the beach with pitches separated by bushes and hedges. Modern and well maintained toilet facilities and a heated indoor swimming pool. Typical beach village with beaches within walking distance. Microclimate due to its proximity to the sea and the many tidal pools in the area. Level area, so good for walking and cycling.

N165/E60 Vannes-Nantes. Exit Damgan or Muzillac, then to Damgan and follow camping signs.

CC € 17 *2/4-5/7 29/8-8/10*

N 47°31'19" W 2°35'34"

Dinard/St.Lunaire, F-35800 / Bretagne (Ille-et-Vilaine)

iD **1359**

La Touesse***
171 rue de la ville Gehan
+33 (0)2-99466113
FAX +33 (0)2-99160258
1/4 - 30/9
camping.la.touesse@wanadoo.fr

3ha 80**T**(90-120m²) 5-10A CEE

1 ACD**G**IJLMPQ
2 AEGQRVWXY
3 AB**F**GHJKRUWY
4 (C 1/6-30/9) (F)
(H 1/6-30/9) IJM**N**
(Q+R+T+U+V+X) Z
5 **AB**DFGHIJKLMNPUXYZ
6 ABCDEG**IK**(N 1km)ORTV

Intimate, sheltered site with leisure and covered pool. Ideal for families. Nice restaurant with garden. 300m from sea, lovely sandy beach. Site is separated by hedges and trees into fields with 2 or 4 pitches. Close to historic town Dinard.

N137 via St. Malo over barrage. 1st rndbt with viaducts dir. Dinard. On dual carriageway after 500 metres 2nd exit left dir. St. Énogat. After 300 metres left at 1st traffic lights dir. St. Lunaire. Stay on D786. Follow signs.

CC € 15 *1/4-5/7 26/8-30/9*

N 48°37'51" W 2°5'3"

Douarnenez, F-29100 / Bretagne (Finistère)

1360

Camping de la Baie de Douarnenez****
30 rue Luc Robet, Poullan-sur-Mer
+33 (0)2-98742639
+33 (0)2-98745597
1/5 - 11/9
info@camping-douarnenez.com

5,5ha 100T(100-150m²) 10A

1 ACD**G**HIJKLMPQ
2 RVX
3 BGMN**Q**RUW
4 (C+F+H) J(Q+S) (T+U+V+Y 4/7-31/8) Z
5 **AB**FGIJKLMNPU
6 CEG**IK**(N 0,8km)ORV

A friendly family campsite with plenty of greenery, spacious pitches and a lovely indoor swimming pool. The restaurant is recommended. Good base for exploring the beautiful surroundings, also by bike. The lovely little harbours and rugged cliffs contrast with sandy beaches and are a unique area for birdwatchers.

From Douarnenez D7 to Poullan-sur-Mer. Just before Poullan-sur-Mer, turn left direction campsite. Signposted further on.

CC € 15 *1/5-10/7 27/8-11/9 7=6*

N 48°4'54" W 4°24'24"

Epiniac/Dol-de-Bretagne, F-35120 / Bretagne (Ille-et-Vilaine)

1361

Domaine des Ormes*****
Domaine des Ormes
+33 (0)2-99735300
+33 (0)2-99735355
2/4 - 24/9
info@lesormes.com

200ha 127T(80-150m²) 6A CEE

1 ACD**G**IJKLMOPRS
2 BDLMRVX
3 ABD**EF**GHJKL**M**N**OPQ**RU**VW**
4 (C 24/5-4/9) (F+H) IJK**N** (Q+S+T+U+V+X+Y) Z
5 **AB**DEFGJKLMNPUWZ
6 ACEGH**IK**M(N 7km)OPTV

A castle campsite in open countryside located in the heart of the Emerald Coast between St. Michel and St. Malo. The indoor heated aqua park (4000 m²) welcomes both young and old. Do not miss the wave pool. Many lodgings within the nature park (woods, forest).

From Dol-de-Bretagne take the D795 in the direction of Combourg. The campsite is located 7 km down the road at the left side.

CC € 19 *2/4-8/7 29/8-24/9 7=6*

N 48°29'15" W 1°44'10"

Erdeven, F-56410 / Bretagne (Morbihan)

1362

Des Mégalithes***
Kerfelicite, chemin des Saules
+33 (0)2-97556876
30/4 - 25/9
campingdesmegalithes@orange.fr

5ha 100T(90-160m²) 10A CEE

1 ACD**G**IJKLMOPQ
2 RVWXY
3 B**F**GHJNR
4 (C+H 1/6-13/9) (Q+R 1/7-31/8) (U 9/7-21/8)
5 **AB**FGIJKLMNOPUWZ
6 ACDEGK(N 1,5km)T

A quiet, well equipped campsite with level pitches set between hedges and separated from the mobile homes. Megalith park within 500m. You can go for peaceful bike rides between the site and the sea, or make a trip to Quiberon via the cycle path. Payment by bank card not possible out of season.

N165/E60 Vannes-Lorient, exit Quiberon/Carnac, D768 direction Quiberon. At the crossroad in Plouharnel turn right to Erdeven via D781. After about 3.5 km turn left.

CC € 17 *30/4-8/7 25/8-25/9*

N 47°37'43" W 3°8'46"

Erquy, F-22430 / Bretagne (Côtes-d'Armor) 1363

Des Hautes Grées***
123 rue St. Michel les Hôpitaux
+33 (0)2-96723478
FAX +33 (0)2-96723015
2/4 - 2/10
@ hautesgrees@wanadoo.fr

3,5ha 177T(80-98m²) 10A CEE

1 ACDGIJKLMOPQ
2 AEGLNQRTUVX
3 ABGHJLRUVWY
4 (A 1/7-31/8)
(C+H 15/5-20/9) LN
(Q+R) (U+V+X 1/7-31/8)
5 ABFGIJKLMNPQRUVW
6 ACDEGIK(N 2,5km)OPRTV

Quiet, well-maintained family campsite. Spaciously appointed, royal pitches, lots of flowers. Heated pool, at 400 metres from the beach. Close to fishing harbour, good base for anglers. Ideal for young families, but also for people seeking some peace and quiet in the low seasons.

Campsite located east of Erquy. At roundabout south-west of Erquy, where the D781 becomes the D34, direction 'Les Hôpitaux'. Then follow signs.

CC €17 2/4-2/7 27/8-2/10

N 48°38'31'' W 2°25'27''

Erquy, F-22430 / Bretagne (Côtes-d'Armor) 1364

La Vallée***
St. Pabu
+33 (0)2-96720622
25/4 - 15/9
@ campinglavalleeerquy@wanadoo.fr

1,5ha 30T(90-110m²) 10A CEE

1 ACDGIJKLMOPQ
2 AEJRTVWX
3 ABFGHJRWY
4 KN(Q+R)
5 ABEFGIJKLMNPUZ
6 ACEGJ(N 2km)ORTV

A campsite located in the lovely, restful countryside of a valley. 700m from the sea and a sandy beach. Terraced campsite with modern toilet facilities. Pitches separated by small hedges. Unique relaxation room in oriental style including a sauna and jacuzzi.

Follow D786 between Val-André and Erquy. When the dual carriageway becomes a two-way road turn left immediately towards St. Pabu. Campsite signposted.

CC €15 25/4-8/7 25/8-15/9

N 48°36'16'' W 2°29'19''

Erquy, F-22430 / Bretagne (Côtes-d'Armor) 1365

Les Roches***
Rue Pierre Vergos
+33 (0)2-96723290
FAX +33 (0)2-96635784
1/4 - 30/9
@ info@camping-les-roches.com

3ha 175T(80-120m²) 6-10A CEE

1 ACDGIJKLMOPQ
2 AGJKLQRTUVWXY
3 ABCFGHLPQRU
4 (Q+R) (U+V 1/7-30/8)
5 ABDEFGIJKLMNPUZ
6 ACEGIK(N 2,5km)ORTV

In the middle of farm land, this peaceful campsite is 900m from the sea. The grounds are surrounded by tall hedges. Plenty of shelter against the wind. Lovely pitches with panoramic views of the sea. Modern toilet facilities provided. Free WiFi.

Campsite located between Erquy and Pléneuf-Val-André, D786. Follow signs, well indicated.

CC €13 1/4-3/7 22/8-30/9

N 48°36'37'' W 2°28'33''

Erquy, F-22430 / Bretagne (Côtes-d'Armor)

1366

Sites & Paysages Bellevue****
route de la Libération
+33 (0)2-96723304
6/4 - 15/9
info@campingbellevue.fr

3ha 128T(90-130m²) 10A CEE

1 ACD**G**IJKLMOPQ
2 KRTVXY
3 B**F**GHJMNRU
4 (E+H+Q ⊶)
(R+T+U+V 15/6-1/9) Z
5 **AB**EFGIJKLMNOPQRUWX
YZ
6 ACDEGIK(N 5km)ORTV

Beautiful grounds with plenty of greenery and a lovely indoor swimming pool, children's pool, modern toilet facilities, playground and small cafe. Hedges provide the spacious camping pitches with plenty of privacy. Free WiFi.

Between Erquy and Val André at the D786 near the village La Couture.

CC € 17 *6/4-8/7 28/8-15/9*

N 48°35'39" W 2°29'4"

Fouesnant, F-29170 / Bretagne (Finistère)

1367

Camping de la Piscine****
Kerleya-Beg Meil, BP 12
+33 (0)2-98565606
FAX +33 (0)2-98565764
10/5 - 11/9
contact@campingdelapiscine.com

5ha 160T(85-110m²) 10A

1 AC**G**IJKLMOPQ
2 ARVWXY
3 BGKMNRU
4 (C 15/6-31/8) (F ⊶)
(H 15/6-31/8,19/4-7/9) IJ**KL**
N(Q+S 1/6-11/9)
(T+U+Z 2/7-31/8)
5 **AB**CDFGIJKLMNPUVWYZ
6 ACEGJ(N 3km)OTV

A lovely quiet campsite with spacious marked out pitches. Wonderful water park with heated pool, bubble bath and jet stream. Wellness area, sauna, hammam and jacuzzi. Access via a footpath (1000m) to a nice fine sandy beach. Ideal starting point for cycle trips and a visit to the region: Quimper, La Pointe du Raz, Locronan.

From Fouesnant take the D45 direction Mousterlin. Then follow camping signs.

CC € 17 *10/5-3/7 27/8-11/9 7=6, 14=11*

N 47°52'1" W 4°0'53"

Fouesnant, F-29170 / Bretagne (Finistère)

1368

Sunêlia L'Atlantique****
Kerbader, BP 11
+33 (0)2-98561444
FAX +33 (0)2-98561867
23/4 - 3/9
sunelia@latlantique.fr

9ha 120T(90-120m²) 6-10A CEE

1 ACDEIJKLMOPRS
2 AELRVWXY
3 BGHJK**MNQ**RU**V**WY
4 (C+E+H ⊶) IJK**LNP**
(Q+S+T+U+V ⊶)
(X 1/7-31/8) (Z ⊶)
5 **AB**EFGIJKLMNOPRSUW
6 CDEG**IK**(N 2km)RTV

A natural and protected water paradise 400m from sandy beach. Three heated pools - one with a sliding roof - with balneo spa and solarium. Wellness area with sauna, hammam, fitness and beauty centre.

In Fouesnant take the D145 direction Kerbader. Follow the camping signs.

CC € 15 *23/4-4/7 21/8-2/9 7=6, 14=11*

N 47°51'23" W 4°1'15"

Fouesnant/Beg-Meil, F-29170 / Bretagne (Finistère)

1369

Le Kervastard***
56 Hent Kervastard
+33 (0)2-98949152
1/4 - 2/11
camping.le.kervastard@wanadoo.fr

2,5ha 59T(90-100m²) 10A CEE

1 ACD**G**IJKLMOPQ
2 AEGQRVWX
3 B**F**GHKRUWY
4 (C+H 15/6-15/9) (Q+R)
5 **AB**FGIJKLMNOPUWYZ
6 CDEG**K**(N 0,15km)TV

Family campsite, located in the centre of the village of Beg-Meil. 150 metres from the shops and 300 metres from the beach. You can forget your car this holiday.

From Fouesnant to Beg-Meil. Left at the centre. See camping signs.

CC € 15 *1/4-7/7 26/8-2/11*

N 47°51'37'' W 3°59'17''

Fouesnant/Cap Coz, F-29170 / Bretagne (Finistère)

1370

Kerscolper***
Hent Kerscolper
+33 (0)2-98560948
2/4 - 2/10
kerscolper@gmail.com

3,5ha 40T(80-120m²) 10A CEE

1 ACD**F**IJKLMOPRS
2 AEGLOQRVWXY
3 B**F**GHKNRUWY
4 (C+H 15/6-15/9) (Q+T+U+V+Z 1/7-31/8)
5 **AB**GI**J**KLMNO**P**UWZ
6 AEGJ**K**(N 2km)TV

This campsite is located opposite the Îles de Glénans and just 400m from the beautiful beaches of Cap Coz, and offers a relaxing and friendly stay. Equipped with swimming pool, bar and a lovely playground.

In Fouesnant take 3rd roundabout to Cap Coz/ Beg Meil. Left at 4th roundabout towards Cap Coz then 400m further on the right.

CC € 17 *2/4-30/6 1/9-2/10 7=6*

N 47°52'49'' W 3°59'34''

Guidel, F-56520 / Bretagne (Morbihan)

1371

Les Jardins de Kergal****
rte des Plages
+33 (0)2-97059818
1/4 - 11/11
jardins.kergal@wanadoo.fr

5ha 76T(90-150m²) 16A CEE

1 ACD**G**IJKLMPQ
2 AFLQRVWXY
3 B**F**GHJKMNQRU
4 (C 1/6-10/9) (E+H) J (Q 2/7-27/8) (R) (T+U+V+Z 2/7-27/8)
5 **AB**EFGIJKLMNPRUWZ
6 ACEGJ**K**(N 1,5km)TUV

A lovely quiet campsite between Guidel and the sea. Lovely heated indoor pool, well maintained toilets, pitches among the trees and hedges. Supermarket 1 km, village 1.2 km with shops and a Sunday market. Lovely walking routes by the sea or the River Laïta.

From N165 Quimper-Lorient exit Guidel. Towards Guidel centre, round the church dir. Guidel-plages via D306, left at roundabout after about 1,8 km, left at next crossroads, campsite entrance 500m on the right.

CC € 15 *1/4-1/7 3/9-11/11*

N 47°46'29'' W 3°30'22''

Huelgoat, F-29690 / Bretagne (Finistère)

1372

La Rivière d'Argent**
La Coudraie
+33 (0)2-98997250
26/3 - 10/10
contact@lariviedargent.com

5ha 84**T**(100m²) 6A CEE

1 ACD**G**IJKLPRS
2 BCGRTVWXY
3 BHMRU**W**
4 (A 1/7-31/8) (E ⊶)
(Q+R 1/6-15/9)
(T+U 1/7-15/9) Z
5 **AB**GIJKLMNPUVZ
6 CE**IK**(N 3km)O

Well maintained, very peaceful campsite set in woods by a lovely little river. You will wake up to the birds. A good starting point for walks through the woods, heathland and by the river. Plenty of opportunities for fishing. The north, south and west coasts can all be reached within an hour by car.

From Guingamp take the N12 to Morlaix. Pass this town via the D785 and the D764 to Huelgoat. From the centre follow the signs 3 km in an eastern direction.

CC € 15 *26/3-7/7 25/8-10/10 7=6*

N 48°21'47" W 3°42'57"

Jugon-les-Lacs, F-22270 / Bretagne (Côtes-d'Armor)

1373

Au Bocage du Lac****
rue du Bocage
+33 (0)2-96316016
FAX +33 (0)2-96317504
1/4 - 15/9
contact@campinglacbretagne.com

7ha 183**T**(100-180m²) 10A CEE

1 ACGIJKLPRS
2 DFLMRVXY
3 ABGHK**M**N**PQ**RUV**W**
4 (**A** 1/7-31/8) (C 1/5-9/9)
(F 10/4-5/10) (H 1/5-9/9) IJ
(Q 1/7-31/8) (S 7/4-9/9)
(T+U+V+X+Z ⊶)
5 **AB**EFGIJKLMNOPUVWZ
6 CDEGH**IJ**(N 0,8km)RTV

A pleasant rural family campsite with safe direct access to a 70 hectare lake. A paradise for anglers. For those who like lazing around there is a heated indoor and outdoor swimming pool with a slide and a toddlers pool.

N176 exit Jugon-les-Lacs. The campsite is clearly signposted and is on the Jugon-les-Lacs to Mégrit road (D52).

CC € 17 *1/4-30/6 1/9-15/9*

N 48°24'6" W 2°19'0"

La Forêt-Fouesnant, F-29940 / Bretagne (Finistère)

1374

De Kéranterec****
route du Petit Manoir-Kerleven
+33 (0)2-98569811
FAX +33 (0)2-98568173
9/4 - 24/9
info@camping-keranterec.com

6,5ha 139**T**(90-150m²) 16A

1 ACD**G**IJKLMOPQ
2 AEFGIJKQRVWXY
3 B**F**GHJKMNRUWY
4 (C 9/5-20/9) (D+H ⊶) JK
(Q+R ⊶)
(T+U+V+X 20/6-5/9) Z
5 **AB**CEFGHIJKLOPRUWXY
6 ACEGIJ(N 3km)TUV

A rural campsite with an informal atmosphere. Right by the sea and direct access to the sandy beach. Excellent base for visiting Quimper-Concarneau and surroundings. Environmentally friendly, peaceful site with good modern toilet facilities and interesting, varied coast.

Between Lorient and Quimper via N165-E60, exit Fouesnant/Concarneau, through D44 direction Fouesnant till signs to Plage de Kerleven or Port la Forêt. Well signposted.

CC € 17 *9/4-9/7 28/8-24/9*

N 47°53'57" W 3°57'19"

La Trinité-sur-Mer, F-56470 / Bretagne (Morbihan)

1375

De Kervilor****
Kervilor
+33 (0)2-97557675
+33 (0)2-97558726
1/4 - 18/9
camping.kervilor@wanadoo.fr

4,7ha 164T(80-120m²) 10A

1 ACD**G**IJKLMOPRS
2 CGQRVWXY
3 BFGHJK**MNOPQ**RUVW
4 (C 4/5-18/9) (E+H) JK (Q+S) (T+U 4/5-4/9) (V 1/7-31/8) (Z 4/5-4/9)
5 **AB**EFGIJKLMNOPRUWXYZ
6 ACEGHIJ(N 1,5km)OTUV

Peaceful campsite in well-visited area. Free choice of pitches out of season. Heated indoor pool. Outdoor pool heated from 4 May. 3 km from the famous prehistoric megalith park at Carnac. The centre of La Trinité is 1.5 km away. Market twice weekly, large yacht harbour. The surroundings are wooded and good for cycling and walking.

South of Auray. D768 dir. Carnac, then D186 dir. La Trinité then via campsite signposts. Turn left before the centre.

CC € 17 *1/4-2/7 22/8-17/9 7=6, 14=12*

N 47°36'8'' W 3°2'12''

Landéda, F-29870 / Bretagne (Finistère)

1376

Des Abers****
Plage de St. Marguerite
+33 (0)2-98049335
1/5 - 30/9
camping-des-abers@wanadoo.fr

5,5ha 158T(90-120m²) 10A

1 ACD**G**IJKLMPQ
2 AEGJKRSTVWX
3 BGHJKNRUWY
4 (A 1/7-31/8) (Q) (S 15/5-15/9) (U 1/7-31/8) (V+Z)
5 **AB**FGIJKLMNO**P**UW
6 ACEGIK(N 2,5km)ORT

Hubert and his team offer you a warm welcome in French, German or English to their lovely campsite positioned right on a sandy beach. Panoramic views of the ocean and countless small islands which are accessible at low tide. A wonderful site for an extended stay. Free WiFi on entire campsite.

From Lannilis follow green 'campings' signs through Landéda. 1.7 km past Landéda follow camping signs.

CC € 17 *1/5-30/6 1/9-30/9 14=12*

N 48°35'36'' W 4°36'9''

Landrellec/Pleumeur-Bodou, F-22560 / Bretagne (Côtes-d'Armor)

1377

Camping Du Port****
3 chemin des Douaniers
+33 (0)2-96238779
26/3 - 29/10
renseignements@
camping-du-port-22.com

3,8ha 44T(100-140m²) 5-15A CEE

1 ACD**G**IJKLMO**P**RS
2 AEIJKORSVWX
3 BFHJKPRWY
4 **KN** (Q+R+T+U+V+X+Z 15/4-15/9)
5 **AB**DEFGIJKLMNPUWXZ
6 ACEG**IK**(N 0,3km)ORUV

This beautiful and spacious campsite is located south of Trégastel-Plage on the Landrellec headland. Spacious pitches on grass, partially divided by low bushes and trees. Some of the pitches have a magnificent view of the sea. Opportunities for sea-fishing with the owner. The 'Fruits de Mer' platter in the restaurant is recommended.

From Trégastel follow coastal route towards Trébeurden D788. Turn right at Landrellec. The road to the campsite is clearly signposted.

CC € 15 *26/3-9/7 27/8-29/10 7=6*

N 48°48'35'' W 3°32'27''

Lanloup/Paimpol, F-22580 / Bretagne (Côtes-d'Armor)

iD **1378**

Le Neptune****
Ker Guistin
+33 (0)2-96223335
1/4 - 10/10
contact@leneptune.com

1,5ha 65T(80-120m²) 10A CEE

1 ACD**G**IJKLMOPQ
2 AGLNQRTVWXY
3 BD**F**GHJKN**P**RU
4 (D) (H 1/7-31/8) (Q+S+T+U+X) Z
5 **AB**DFGIJKLNPUVWXYZ
6 ACDEGIK(N 0,5km)ORTV

A hospitable natural campsite with a heated indoor swimming pool. Pleasantly small-scale. Pitches with plenty of privacy. Free WiFi.

From Plouézac direction Lanloup. Follow signs campsite.

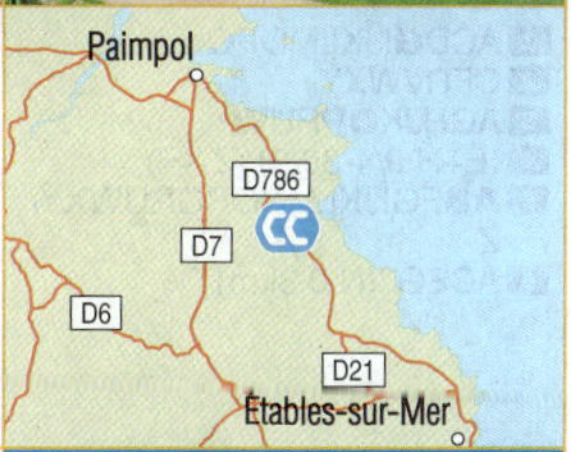

CC € 15 *1/4-4/7 21/8-10/10* *7=6, 14=11*

N 48°42'49'' W 2°58'1''

Lantic, F-22410 / Bretagne (Côtes-d'Armor)

iD **1379**

Les Etangs***
route de Châtelaudren
FAX +33 (0)2-96719547
16/4 - 26/9
contact@campinglesetangs.com

2,1ha 65T(60-108m²) 6-10A CEE

1 ACD**G**IJKLOPQ
2 IJRWXY
3 AB**F**GHJU**W**
4 (C+H) (Q 1/7-28/8) (R 1/6-27/9) (U 1/6-15/9)
5 **AB**FGIJKLNPUV
6 ADEGJ(N 3km)RTV

An attractive, peaceful campsite in lovely countryside. Swimming pool. Slightly sloping campsite. Pitches are sometimes separated by bushes or marked out by trees. Poplars and fruit trees give adequate shade. Free WiFi.

D786, in Binic left direction Lantic. The campsite is located on the left after 3 km and is already signposted in Binic.

CC € 13 *16/4-8/7 25/8-26/9*

N 48°36'23'' W 2°51'42''

Lanvéoc/Crozon, F-29160 / Bretagne (Finistère)

iD **1380**

Gwel Kaër**
40, rue de Pen an Ero
+33 (0)2-98276106
1/4 - 30/9
info@camping-gwel-kaer.com

2ha 98T(70-90m²) 8A CEE

1 ACDEHIJKLPQ
2 EGJKLOQRTUWXY
3 ABGHIJMRWY
4 (Q+R 15/6-15/9)
5 **AB**CEFGIJKLMNOPUVXZ
6 EGIJ(N 0,8km)T

This campsite offers you a relaxing holiday in natural surroundings with a beautiful view over the Brest bay thanks to its 300 metres of coast and the terraced pitches.

D155 Crozon; then D55 towards Fret at roundabout. Follow signs.

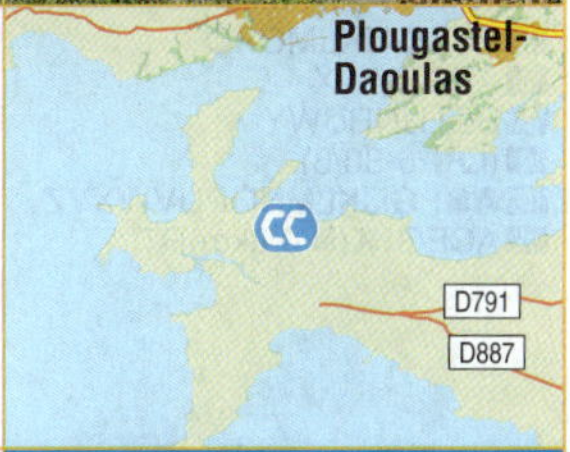

CC € 15 *1/4-30/6 1/9-30/9*

N 48°16'51'' W 4°30'9''

Le Roc-St-André, F-56460 / Bretagne (Morbihan) 1381

Domaine du Roc***
rue Beaurivage
+33 (0)2-97749107
26/3 - 3/11
domaine-du-roc@orange.fr

2,5ha 28T(90-150m²) 10A CEE

1 ACD**G**IJKLMOPQ
2 CFRVWXY
3 AGHJK**OPR**U**W**
4 (E+H 9/4-30/9) (Z)
5 **AB**FGIJKLMNOPQRUWXY Z
6 ACEGJ(N 0,3km)T

A quiet campsite on the banks of the Oust. At the junction of two almost level cycle routes between several historic villages. There are cycle tracks beside the river and on an old railway track. Restored antique caravans, a tree house and a log cabin for rent.

N24 Rennes-Quimper, in Ploërmel towards Vannes via N165. Exit Le Chapelle Caro/Le Roc-St-André, via D4 over the bridge and beyond the church follow camping signs.

CC € 15 *26/3-3/7 29/8-2/11 7=6, 14=12, 21=18*

N 47°51'49" W 2°26'46"

Lesconil, F-29740 / Bretagne (Finistère) 1382

Camping de la Grande Plage***
71 rue Paul Langevin
+33 (0)2-98878827
9/4 - 30/9
campinggrandeplage@hotmail.com

2,5ha 100T(80-120m²) 10A CEE

1 ACD**G**IJKLMOPQ
2 AEGRTVX
3 BGHJKRUWY
4 (C+H 1/5-30/9) IJ (Q+T+U+Z 15/6-15/9)
5 **AB**EFGIJKLMNPUVWZ
6 ACDEG**J**(N 1km)OTV

A campsite with direct access to a large beach with sand and granite rocks. Modern well maintained toilet facilities, water park with slides and bubble bath and a snack bar with takeaway meals.

From Pont-l'Abbé D102 to Lesconil. Turn right past the football stadium and skating park (camping signs). Keep left for 200m, campsite is another 1 km.

CC € 15 *9/4-1/7 27/8-30/9 7=6*

N 47°47'52" W 4°13'44"

Lesconil, F-29740 / Bretagne (Finistère) 1383

Camping des Dunes***
67 rue Paul Langevin
+33 (0)2-98878178
1/4 - 30/9
campingdesdunes@gmail.com

2,8ha 155T(80-100m²) 10-16A CEE

1 ACD**G**IJKLMOPQ
2 AEGRVWX
3 BGHJNRUWY
4 (Q 1/6-30/8)
5 **AB**FGIJKLMNOPUVWXYZ
6 ACEG**IK**(N 0,8km)RT

A well-maintained campsite located behind the dunes. Lovely plants mark out the large pitches. Selected as a natural floral campsite. The charm of outdoor life by the side of the sea.

In Pont-l'Abbé keep on to Lesconil(D102). Right after football stadium (camping sign). After 100m keep left at junction.

CC € 17 *1/4-8/7 25/8-30/9 7=6*

N 47°47'50" W 4°13'43"

Locmariaquer, F-56740 / Bretagne (Morbihan)

1384

Lann Brick***
18 Lieu Dit Lann Brick
+33 (0)2-97573279
26/3 - 23/10
camping.lannbrick@wanadoo.fr

1,5ha 39T(70-90m²) 10A CEE

1 ACD**G**IJKLMOPRS
2 AEGQRVWXY
3 BGHJKRUWY
4 (A 1/7-30/8) (C+H 5/5-23/9) (Q+R+T+U+Z)
5 **AB**CEFGHIJKLMNOPUVZ
6 AEGJ(N 3km)OTV

A small, quiet campsite with well maintained toilet facilities located on a headland between the ocean and the Golfe du Morbihan 300m from the beach. You can walk or cycle on the central pathway which covers the entire length of the headland past many prehistoric sights.

N165/E60 Nantes/Quimper, exit Crach, via D28 direction Locmariaquer. towards La Trinité/Carnac. Via D781 direction Locmariaquer, after + 2 km turn right.

CC € 17 *26/3-5/7 27/8-22/10*

N 47°34'43'' W 2°58'28''

Locronan, F-29180 / Bretagne (Finistère)

1385

Camping Locronan***
rue de la Troménie
+33 (0)2-98918776
2/4 - 30/9
contact@camping-locronan.fr

2ha 103T(90-130m²) 10A CEE

1 ACD**G**IJKLMRS
2 ABJRVX
3 BHJM**O**R
4 (D+H) (Q 1/7-31/8)
5 **AB**FGJKNPRUZ
6 EGJ(N 0,4km)

A rustic and informal campsite in the heart of La Montagne de Locronan, one of France's most beautiful villages. Ideal starting point for visiting Pointe Bretagne. Indoor heated swimming pool. A mecca for walking: GR38 and the Bois du Névet. Lovely views of the Baie de Douarnenez from the site. You can walk to the Montagne for sea views. Free WiFi.

Take Locronan exit on N165 Quimper/Brest then follow camping signs after 15 km when entering Locronan.

CC € 15 *2/4-9/7 26/8-30/9 7=6*

N 48°5'46'' W 4°11'53''

Loctudy, F-29750 / Bretagne (Finistère)

1386

Les Hortensias***
38 rue des Tulipes
+33 (0)2-98874664
1/4 - 30/9
hortensias@camping-loctudy.com

2ha 76T(80-110m²) 3-6-10A CEE

1 ACD**G**IJKLMOPQ
2 AEGQRVXY
3 BGHKNRWY
4 (C+H 15/5-15/9) K (Q 1/7-30/8) (R+T+U+V+Z)
5 **AB**EFGIJKLMNOPQUZ
6 EGK(N 3km)OTV

Quiet family campsite at 300 metres from the sea in the south of the Finistère. This campsite welcomes families to an enormous area where nature is being preserved.

From Pont-L'Abbé dir. Loctudy. Right before the chapel, straight on through traffic lights. 1 km further site is on left.

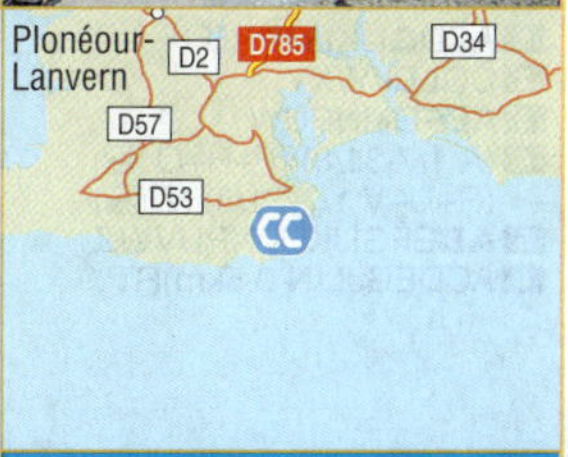

CC € 15 *1/4-8/7 25/8-30/9*

N 47°48'47'' W 4°10'54''

Loudéac, F-22600 / Bretagne (Côtes-d'Armor) — 1387

Seasonova Aquarev***
route de Rennes
+33 (0)2-96262192
1/4 - 4/11
contact@camping-aquarev.com

3,2ha 78T(80-150m²) 10A CEE

1 ACD**G**IJKLMPRS
2 DFKLRUVW
3 BGHIJKMNU**W**
4 (Q 1/4-1/11) (T 3/4-1/10)
5 **AB**CGIJKLMNOPUZ
6 ACDEG**K**(N 2km)TV

A new family campsite since 2012. The site has spacious pitches. You can play tennis and football on the site. You can also go fishing. Or just enjoy yourself with the crazy the water games.

Exit Loudéac centre direction Loudéac, left at roundabout towards Aquarev.

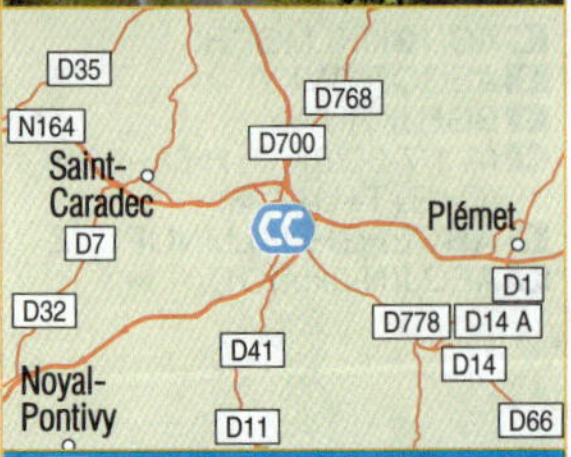

CC € 13 *1/4-8/7 26/8-4/11 7=6, 14=11*

N 48°10'45'' W 2°43'41''

Loyat/Ploërmel, F-56800 / Bretagne (Morbihan) — 1388

Merlin l'enchanteur**
8 rue du Pont
+33 (0)2-97930552
FAX +33 (0)2-97738937
1/1 - 31/12
contact@camelotpark.fr

6ha 65T(70-120m²) 16A

1 ACD**G**IJKLMOPRS
2 CDFRVWXY
3 B**F**GHJKLMR**W**
4 (E+H 1/5-30/9)
5 **AB**DGIJKMNPUWXYZ
6 ACDEGH**K**(N 0,5km)T

A campsite with large pitches, shaded by tall trees. Basic toilet facilities but free hot water. Hydrangea garden with free entry 4.5 km along a lovely cycle path along the lake. 500 metres from a baker, butcher and restaurant with reasonable prices. From 1/10 until 30/4 CampingCard rate is 15 Euros.

N24 Rennes-Quimper, exit Ploërmel/Dinan/St.Malo, ring road via several roundabouts direction Dinan/St.Malo. Via D766 to Loyat, entrance 100m past bridge before Loyat.

CC € 17 *1/1-8/7 26/8-31/12 7=6, 14=12*

N 47°59'6'' W 2°22'52''

Matignon, F-22550 / Bretagne (Côtes-d'Armor) — 1389

Le Vallon aux Merlettes***
43 rue Jobert
+33 (0)2-96803799
1/4 - 30/9
contact@
campingdematignon.com

3,5ha 81T(100-130m²) 10A CEE

1 ACD**G**IJKLM**P**RS
2 CGLRVWXY
3 AB**F**GMNRUW
4 (A 1/7-31/8) (F+H+Q) (R+U+V 1/7-31/8) (Z)
5 **AB**EFGIJKLMNPUVWZ
6 ACDEGJL(N 0,5km)RTV

In green and very quiet surroundings, 400 metres from shops, 4 km from the beaches and many walking paths. Free: heated, indoor pool, WiFi. Service: toilet facilities with all amenities, bread, sweet rolls, ice-cream, grocer, self-service freezer, laundry.

From Dinard: D168, exit D786 towards Matignon, follow camping signs. From Rennes N12 as far as Lamballe. Stay on the D768, then D13. Follow camping signs.

CC € 13 *1/4-1/7 1/9-30/9*

N 48°35'28'' W 2°17'45''

Merdrignac, F-22230 / Bretagne (Côtes-d'Armor) 1390

Val de Landrouët**
14 rue de Gouede
+33 (0)2-96284798
FAX +33 (0)2-96265544
30/4 - 30/9
camping.merdrignac@orange.fr

1ha 43T(83-120m²) 5A CEE

1 ABCGIJKLMPQ
2 CDFGLMRUVWXY
3 ABC**E**GHJ**MNQ**RU**W**
4 (**C+H** 15/6-31/8) JKLN
(Q 5/7-23/8) (T+U 1/7-31/8)
Z
5 **AB**FGIJKLMNOPSTUWXYZ
6 CEG**J**(N 0,2km)V

A level, quiet campsite which is part of a park with sports accommodation. The pitches are partly shaded and are marked out with trees and bushes.

Campsite well signposted in Merdrignac and located north of the centre.

CC € 13 *30/4-30/6 29/8-30/9*

N 48°11'54'' W 2°24'56''

Milizac, F-29290 / Bretagne (Finistère) 1391

Camping de la Récré****
Le Lac des 3 Curés
+33 (0)2-98079217
1/1 - 31/12
campingdelarecre@orange.fr

5,5ha 102T 10A CEE

1 ACD**G**IJKLMNOPQ
2 BDFJLRTUWXY
3 ABCGHJKNQ**W**
4 (F+H 1/5-15/9) JM
(Q 1/5-15/9) (R)
(T+U 1/5-15/9)
5 **AB**CFGHIJKLMNOPQRUV
WZ
6 CDEGHIK(N 4km)ORTV

A very attractive campsite in a peaceful location. Ideal for families as the campsite forms part of a lovely amusement park. Well located for visiting Brest and the surroundings.

From Brest Nord on the D26 exit 'Les Trois Curés'.

CC € 17 *1/1-30/6 1/9-31/12*

N 48°28'32'' W 4°31'37''

Morgat, F-29160 / Bretagne (Finistère) 1392

Les Bruyères***
Le Bouis
+33 (0)2-98261487
FAX +33 (0)2-98261773
15/4 - 30/9
info@
camping-bruyeres-crozon.com

4ha 130T 8A CEE

1 ACD**G**HIJKLPRS
2 ABLQRTUVWXY
3 ABHIJR
4 (C+F+H) IJM
(Q+R 1/7-31/8)
5 **AB**EFGIJKLMNOPUVZ
6 EGJ(N 1,5km)T

A very peaceful campsite in woodland surroundings with a lovely indoor and outdoor swimming pool.

From Crozon towards Morgat. Then via D255 direction Bouis. Follow signs.

CC € 17 *15/4-30/6 1/9-30/9*

N 48°13'15'' W 4°31'21''

Noyal-Muzillac, F-56190 / Bretagne (Morbihan)

iD **1393**

Moulin de Cadillac****
route de Berric
+33 (0)2-97670347
2/4 - 11/9
infos@moulin-cadillac.com

7ha 139**T**(100-150m²) 16A CEE

1 ACD**G**IJKLMOPRS
2 CDFRVWXY
3 BDGHJMN**Q**RUVW
4 (C 15/6-4/9) (F+H) IJM (Q 6/7-27/8) (R) (U+Z 6/7-27/8)
5 **AB**CDEFGHIJKLMNOPQUV WZ
6 ACDEGIJ(N 5km)OTUV

A quiet campsite in natural surroundings. A stream flows through the site that turned the mill wheel, hence the name. Experienced cyclists can enjoy themselves in undulating landscape. In the morning all you can hear are the birds.

Between Nantes and Vannes via N165/E60 exit Muzillac, in the centre D5 towards Noyal-Muzillac. Follow the signs of the campsite. Turn left in the centre of Noyal-Muzillac before you reach the church, 4.5 km. Campsite entrance on the right.

CC € 15 *2/4-4/5 9/5-13/5 17/5-3/7 1/9-10/9*

N 47°36'51'' W 2°30'5''

Pénestin, F-56760 / Bretagne (Morbihan)

iD **1394**

Le Domaine d'Inly****
BP 24, rte de Couarne
+33 (0)2-99903509
2/4 - 30/9
inly-info@wanadoo.fr

16ha 80**T** 10A CEE

1 ACD**F**IJKLMOPQ
2 DGQRVWXY
3 BCDGHJK**M**N**OP**RU**V**W
4 (C 14/5-13/9) (E+F+H) IJ M(Q+S+T+U+V+X+Y+Z)
5 **AB**DEFGIJKLMNOPQRUW Z
6 ACEGHJ**K**(N 1km)TV

Spaciously laid-out campsite. Fields divided into circles with an informal ambiance. Some pitches have views of the lake. All amenities open during the whole period. Wellness centre, open and covered swimming pools. 1 km from a village with twice weekly market and large supermarket. 2 km from the beach and sea.

N165/E60 Nantes-Vannes, take exit Pénestin or exit Barrage d'Arzal towards Pénestin on the D34 or D139. Follow the signs to the campsite before the centre.

CC € 17 *2/4-5/7 28/8-29/9* *7=6, 15=13*

N 47°28'17'' W 2°28'2''

Pénestin-sur-Mer, F-56760 / Bretagne (Morbihan)

iD **1395**

Le Cénic***
rte de la Roche-Bernard
+33 (0)2-99904565
9/4 - 18/9
info@lecenic.com

7ha 225**T**(80-150m²) 10A CEE

1 ACD**G**IJKLMOPRS
2 DEQRVWXY
3 BDGHJN**P**RUWY
4 (C 1/7-31/8) (F+H) IJ**LM** **N**(Q+R+U+Z 1/7-31/8)
5 **AB**EFGIJKLMNOPQUWXYZ
6 ACEGJ**K**(N 1km)OTUV

A campsite with lovely spacious pitches. Indoor tropical swimming pool. 1 km from the village with shops and restaurants. Market day twice a week. The surroundings are undulating with a cycle routes to the coast, the Vilaine and inland. Beach 500m (via path), supermarket 1 km.

N165/E60 Nantes-Vannes. Exit Pénestin or exit Barrage d'Arzal and via D34 or D139 in direction Pénestin. On roundabout, at the church, drive round and return to the entrance of the campsite.

CC € 17 *9/4-3/5 16/5-30/6 1/9-17/9*

N 47°28'43'' W 2°27'18''

Pénestin-sur-Mer, F-56760 / Bretagne (Morbihan)

1396

Les Pins***
Bois de la Lande
+33 (0)2-99903313
1/4 - 30/10
camping.lespins@wanadoo.fr

5ha 71**T**(80-150m²) 10A CEE

1 ACD**G**IJKLMO**PQ**
2 BEQRVWXY
3 BDGHJKN**P**RUW
4 (C 17/6-4/9)
(E+H 6/4-30/10) J
(Q+R+T+U+V+Z 1/7-31/8)
5 **AB**CDEFGHIJKLMNPRUXY
Z
6 ACEGJ(N 1,2km)OTUV

The most attractive pitches are at the back of the grounds among the flowers. Cycle track and footpath to the village, the sea, River Vilaine and the inland at 100 metres. Lightly undulating area with interesting coast. All amenities are open at the weekend and during school holidays. One heated toilet block.

N165/E60 Nantes-Vannes, exit Pénestin or Arzal. Direction Pénestin via the D34 or the D139. Turn left at the first roundabout before Pénestin. Signposted.

CC € 13 *1/4-7/7 26/8-29/10*

N 47°28'36'' W 2°27'7''

Penmarc'h, F-29760 / Bretagne (Finistère)

1397

Flower Camping Les Genêts****
rue Gouesnac'h Nevez
+33 (0)2-98586693
2/4 - 30/9
campinglesgenets29@orange.fr

3,2ha 55**T**(100m²) 10A CEE

1 ACD**G**IJKLMOPQ
2 AGLRVWXY
3 BGHJKNRU
4 (E+H) IJ
(Q+R+T+U+V+X+Z)
5 **AB**DEFGIJKLMNOPUZ
6 ACEGJ(N 1km)T

Brigitte and Pascal welcome you in a calm family atmosphere to Bigouden's loveliest beach with plenty of trees and surrounded by three large fishing harbours. Lovely new toilet facilities, partially heated. New since 2011: swimming pool with sliding roof, slide, a playful toddlers' pool and heated toilets.

From Pont-L'Abbé take direction Plomeur and Penmarc'h. Turn left at roundabout 1 km before the centre; direction Plobannalec. Campsite on the left after about 500 metres.

CC € 15 *2/4-8/7 25/8-30/9*

N 47°49'6'' W 4°18'34''

Penvénan, F-22710 / Bretagne (Côtes-d'Armor)

1398

Les Hauts de Port Blanc***
12 bis rue Keranscouc'h
+33 (0)2-96928672
FAX +33 (0)2-96926197
2/4 - 30/9
contact@portblanc.com

3ha 39**T**(80-200m²) 10A CEE

1 ACD**G**IJKLMOPRT
2 AKLNQRVWX
3 BCGHJNQRU
4 (C+F+H) **KN**(Q)
(U 1/7-31/8) (Z)
5 **AB**FGIJKLMNPUWXZ
6 ACEGIJ(N 0,6km)TUV

Family campsite located on level grounds opposite the 7 islands. Distance to the beach is 2 km. Partially covered swimming pool and wellness. Marked out pitches. Opportunities for watersports and excursions around the beautiful wild coastline. 'Voies Vertes de Bretange' cycle routes close to the campsite. A boat trip to the seabird colonies on Les Sept Îles islands is recommended.

From Tréguier in NW direction towards Plouguil and Penvénan. Follow signs in Penvénan.

CC € 15 *2/4-8/7 26/8-30/9* 7=6

N 48°49'5'' W 3°18'7''

1399 Pléboulle, F-22550 / Bretagne (Côtes-d'Armor)

Le Frèche à l'Âne***
Le Bourg, 6 rue du Champ St. Paul
+33 (0)2-96410872
1/4 - 31/10
info@camping-frechealane.com

2ha 68T(100-200m²) 6-10A CEE

1 AGIJKLMOPRS
2 GJKLRVWXY
3 ABCFHJLRU
4 (Q+R) (U 1/7-31/8)
5 ABFGHIJKLNPQUZ
6 ACEGHJL(N 3km)T

A small, welcoming family campsite in the middle of beautiful surroundings. Lovely beaches between Erquy and Saint-Malo. Located on the edge of a small charming village.

Coming from Matignon. D786 direction Fréhel, turn left onto D16. Follow signs.

CC € 11 1/4-30/6 1/9-31/10

N 48°36'32" W 2°20'13"

1400 Pléneuf-Val-André, F-22370 / Bretagne (Côtes-d'Armor)

Campéole Les Monts Colleux***
26 rue Jean Lebrun
+33 (0)2-96729510
FAX +33 (0)2-96631049
1/4 - 25/9
monts-colleux@andretriganogroupe.com

3,7ha 114T(80-143m²) 10A CEE

1 ACFIJKLMPST
2 AEGJKQRTVW
3 ABFGHJRUWY
4 (F+Q+R)
(T+U 5/7-30/8) Z
5 ABEFGIJKLMNOPQRUZ
6 AEGHJ(N 0,3km)RT

A family campsite positioned on a hill. Lovely views of the Bay of Saint Brieuc. Shops and the beach are just 300m from the site.

In Rennes take the N12/E50, dir. Saint-Brieuc/Brest. Past Lamballe take the Pléneuf-Val-André exit and the D768 to Erquy-Cap Fréhel. In St. Alban take D58 to Pléneuf-Val-André. The campsite is in Val-André. Follow signs.

CC € 15 1/5-4/7 22/8-25/9

N 48°35'23" W 2°33'3"

1401 Pleubian, F-22610 / Bretagne (Côtes-d'Armor)

Port la Chaîne****
+33 (0)2-96229238
16/4 - 17/9
info@portlachaine.com

5ha 150T(100-130m²) 6A CEE

1 ACDGIJKLMOPQ
2 AEJKNQRSVWXY
3 BGHNRWY
4 (C 1/7-31/8) (F+H+Q)
(R+T+U+Z 4/7-27/8)
5 ABFGIJKLMNPQUVWZ
6 AEGIJ(N 1,5km)OV

An agreeable ambiance, floral and peaceful surroundings and a fresh, salty sea breeze all add up to a wonderful stay at this campsite right by the sea. The only sounds are the murmur of the sea and birdsong. The campsite is very well maintained and is ideally located between L'île de Bréhat and the Côte de Granit Rose. New: covered heated swimming pool.

After Pleubian 2 km along the D20 towards Larmor/Pleubian, turn left and follow camping signs.

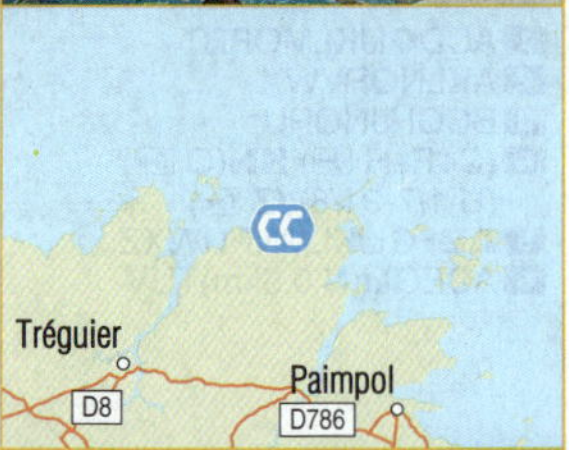

CC € 17 16/4-3/7 20/8-17/9

N 48°51'20" W 3°7'58"

Ploëmel, F-56400 / Bretagne (Morbihan)

1402

Le St. Laurent***
Kergonvo, D186
+33 (0)2-97568590
9/4 - 22/10
contact@camping-saint-laurent.fr

3,5ha 41T(80-130m²) 10A CEE

1 ACD**F**IJKLMOPST
2 BFLQRVWXY
3 A**F**GHJK**OP**RU
4 (E+H) (Q 2/7-26/8) (R) (T+U 1/5-24/10) (Z)
5 **AB**DEFGIJKLMNPUWZ
6 ACDEGJ(N 5km)TV

A lovely campsite with modern heated toilet facilities, located in woods close to Carnac and 800m from a golf course. Relaxation is assured here, the only sound comes from the birds. Although if you are staying on pitches at the back you will hear traffic on the D22 during the day. Trips out by bike, car or on foot are perfectly possible.

N165/E60 Vannes/Lorient, exit Quiberon/Carnac. Via D22 direction Belz/Etel. Left after ± 9 km, campsite 100m on left.

CC € 15 *9/4-8/7 25/8-22/10 14=12*

N 47°39'51" W 3°5'59"

Ploërmel/Taupont, F-56800 / Bretagne (Morbihan)

1403

La Vallée du Ninian***
Le Rocher Ville Bonne
+33 (0)2-97935301
26/3 - 30/9
infos@camping-ninian.fr

2,7ha 83T(100-160m²) 10A CEE

1 ACD**G**IJKLMOPRS
2 CFLRVWXY
3 BD**F**GHJKL**OP**RU**W**
4 (E) (H 1/7-31/8) (Q+R) (T+U+X+Z 9/7-27/8)
5 **AB**FGJKLMNPQUWXYZ
6 ACEGK(N 7km)TV

A lovely site with large 'grand confort' pitches in front, among apple trees. An attractive area for walking and cycling trips. Region with many legends and places of interest. New toilet facilities (2015).

N24 Rennes-Quimper, exit Ploërmel/Dinan/St.Malo, follow ring road to Lac Au Duc, then direction Taupont. D8 towards the north. Follow the road just beyond the village with the camping sign on the left. Site located about 2.5 NW of Taupont.

CC € 15 *26/3-8/7 27/8-29/9*

N 47°58'9" W 2°28'12"

Plonévez-Porzay, F-29550 / Bretagne (Finistère)

1404

Campéole Trezmalaouen***
20 route de la Baie
FAX +33 (0)2-98925424
29/4 - 18/9
trezmalaouen@campeole.com

4ha 33T(80-100m²) 10A

1 ACDFIJKLNPQ
2 AEIJKLQRVWX
3 BGHMRU**W**Y
4 (Q) (T+U 1/7-31/8) Z
5 **AB**FIJKLMNOPWZ
6 CEGH**J**(N 5km)QRTV

Sheltered from the wind with views of Douarnenez bay and the famous Sardines harbour. Direct access to the beach from the campsite.

From Quimper continue to Locronan. Follow signs beyond Plonévez-Porzay.

CC € 15 *1/5-4/7 22/8-18/9*

N 48°6'40" W 4°16'37"

Plonévez-Porzay, F-29550 / Bretagne (Finistère)

1405

La Plage de Tréguer
plage de Ste Anne-la-Palud
+33 (0)2-98925352
FAX +33 (0)2-98925489
9/4 - 24/9
@ camping-treguer-plage@wanadoo.fr

6ha 272T(90-130m²) 10A

1 ACD**F**IJKLMPRS
2 AELQRSVWX
3 BGHNRUWY
4 (C+H 15/6-15/9) K(Q+R) (T+U+V 1/7-31/8) (Y) Z
5 **AB**FGIJKLMNPUVYZ
6 CE**IJ**(N 4km)OV

A family campsite by the sea, right behind the dunes. Gently sloping sandy beach. Suitable for children. Plenty of activities. Toilet facilities are very well maintained. Ideal starting point for visits to Douarnenez, Quimper and Pointe Duraz. The GR34 runs past the site by the dunes. Due to its location a wonderful climate!

From Châteaulin take the D7 in the direction of Douarnenez. Then take the D107 and D61 to Ste Anne-la-Palud. Then follow the camping signs.

CC € 15 *9/4-9/7 27/8-24/9 14=11*

N 48°8'40" W 4°16'8"

Plouézec/Paimpol, F-22470 / Bretagne (Côtes-d'Armor)

1406

Le Cap de Bréhat****
route de Port Lazo
+33 (0)2-96206428
FAX +33 (0)2-96206388
1/4 - 25/9
@ info@cap-de-brehat.com

5ha 97T(80-110m²) 16A CEE

1 ACD**F**HIJKLMPRS
2 EJKLNQRTUVX
3 BC**F**GHIJKMNRUWY
4 (A 1/7-31/8) (E) (H 1/7-30/8) (Q+R+S+T+U+V) (X 1/7-31/8) Z
5 **AB**DEFGHIJKLMNPRUWXYZ
6 ACDEGIJ**K**L(N 2km)TV

Uniquely located terraced campsite with unforgettable views of the sea and the Isle de Bréhat. Oyster beds at low tide. Direct access to the sea and the GR34. The camping pitches are well secluded and offer plenty of privacy. Heated indoor swimming pool.

The campsite is located in Port-Lazo, 2.5 km from the D786. Follow the signs carefully; also the signs for one-way traffic with access only for residents and the campsite. (In other words, ignore the No Entry!)

CC € 17 *1/4-1/7 27/8-25/9*

N 48°45'34" W 2°57'46"

Plouézoc'h, F-29252 / Bretagne (Finistère)

1407

De la Baie de Térénez***
+33 (0)2-98672680
2/4 - 30/9
@ campingbaiedeterenez@wanadoo.fr

2,3ha 75T(100-140m²) 10A

1 ACD**G**IJKLMPQ
2 AEGRVWXY
3 AHJ**Q**RUW
4 (C+G 15/5-15/9) (Q 15/6-15/9) (R+T+U+Z 1/7-31/8)
5 **A**BFGJKLMNPUWZ
6 ACDEG**J**(N 2,5km)TV

Baie de Térénez is located in a bay close to the old harbour town of Morlaix and is suitable for discovering the beautiful beaches and the typical Breton villages and harbours. Located between Perros-Guirrec en Carantec. The burial mounds at Barnénez, the largest in Europe are near the campsite. The spacious grassy pitches are separated by low hedges and trees.

To Plouézoch-centre. Continue following signs to the campsite. The campsite is on the right after about 2.5 km.

CC € 15 *2/4-2/7 27/8-30/9 7=6, 14=11*

N 48°39'35" W 3°50'53"

Plougasnou, F-29630 / Bretagne (Finistère) 1408

Flower! Camping Domaine de Mesqueau***
870 route de Mesqueau
+33 (0)2-98673745
1/5 - 24/9
contact@domaine-de-mesqueau.com

7ha 52T(120-200m²) 10A CEE

1 ACGIJKLMPRS
2 CDLRVWX
3 AGKLMNQRUW
4 (C 1/7-30/8) (F+H+Q+R+Z)
5 IJKLMNPUWX
6 AEGIJ(N 4km)ORT

The campsite near 'la côte de granit rose' (pink granite coast) and the Bay of Morlaix will welcome you on holiday with family or friends in natural surroundings of 7 hectares. A relaxing holiday a short distance from the beach, ideally located for visiting Morlaix, Plougasnou and Roscoff. Also an ideal starting point for the most beautiful towns in Brittany.

From Morlaix direction Plougasnou D46. Follow signs. From Lanmeur direction Plougasnou D78. Follow signs.

CC € 15 1/5-8/7 27/8-24/9 7=6, 14=10

N 48°39'53" W 3°46'51"

Plougastel-Daoulas, F-29470 / Bretagne (Finistère) 1409

Saint Jean****
lieu dit Saint Jean
+33 (0)2-98403290
FAX +33 (0)2-98042311
9/4 - 30/9
info@campingsaintjean.com

2ha 81T(70-120m²) 10A CEE

1 ACDGIJLPR
2 BEFJORVX
3 BGHKLNRUW
4 (C+F+H) JM(Q) (R+T+U+X 2/7-27/8) Z
5 ABDFGJKLNPQUVWZ
6 ACDEGIJ(N 2,5km)V

This green and flowery campsite should not be missed on your tour around Brittany. There is a heated indoor swimming pool and heated toilet buildings. Brest and the Océanopolis are just 10 km away.

Motorway Quimper-Brest. Exit Plougastel/Daoulas (Centre Commercial Leclerc). Then follow the camping signs (2 km).

CC € 15 9/4-9/7 26/8-30/9 7=6

N 48°24'6" W 4°21'13"

Plouguerneau, F-29880 / Bretagne (Finistère) 1410

De la Grève Blanche**
St. Michel
+33 (0)2-98047035
25/3 - 9/10
lroudaut@free.fr

3ha 90T(80-120m²) 10A CEE

1 AGIJLOPQ
2 AEGJKLQRTVW
3 ABGHJNRUWY
4 (Q+R) (T+U 1/7-31/8) (Z)
5 CGIJKMNOPUZ
6 CEGJ(N 3km)ORT

Campsite with very friendly staff and direct access to the beach. Spacious pitches on terrace-shaped grounds with an open view of the sea and of the highest lighthouse in Europe. Beautiful sandy beach, a welcoming bar, fresh bread daily and a free WiFi point. Nature and the environment are important at this campsite (eco-label). The GR 34 runs along this campsite.

Follow camping signs in centre of Plouguerneau.

CC € 15 25/3-3/7 29/8-9/10

N 48°37'49" W 4°31'26"

Plouguerneau, F-29880 / Bretagne (Finistère) — 1411

Du Vougot***
route de Prat Ledan
+33 (0)2-98256151
2/4 - 15/10
campingduvougot@hotmail.fr

2,5ha 38T(100-300m²) 10A CEE

1 ACDGIJKLMPRS
2 AERSVWXY
3 ABHJ**P**RUW
4 (Q 1/6-1/9) (R)
(U 1/7-1/9) (X 15/5-15/9)
(Z 1/5-30/9)
5 **AB**FGIJKLMN**P**UWZ
6 ACEGIK(N 5km)QT

You will receive a warm welcome at this peaceful, small and well run campsite which is sheltered from the wind. New toilet facilities, plenty of greenery, flowers and spacious pitches 250 metres to the beautiful beach at Vougot. A good base for visiting Brest with its Oceanopolis and unique Abers or Meneham.

In Lesneven direction Plouguerneau. Follow signs. Campsite is situated on coastal road.

CC € 15 2/4-8/7 25/8-15/10 7=6, 14=12

N 48°37'53" W 4°26'59"

Plouhinec, F-56680 / Bretagne (Morbihan) — 1412

Le Moténo****
rue du Passage d'Etel
+33 (0)2-97367663
FAX +33 (0)2-97858184
2/4 - 24/9
info@camping-le-moteno.com

5ha 59T(75-110m²) 10A CEE

1 ACD**F**IJKLMPQ
2 AEJRWXY
3 BGHKLNRUVW
4 (C 1/5-24/9) (E)
(H 1/5-24/9) J(Q)
(R 1/7-31/8) (T+U+V+Z)
5 **AB**EFGIJKLMNOPQRUVW
Z
6 FG**K**(N 3km)T

Spaciously appointed campsite with pitches under trees. Indoor and outdoor pool with various slides. Nice toilet facilities.

From N165, exit Port Louis direction Plouhinec. In Plouhinec centre, direction Carnac/Quiberon. Turn right about 1 km after the church and follow campsite signs towards Le Magouër.

CC € 15 2/4-2/7 27/8-24/9 7=6, 14=12

N 47°39'54" W 3°13'16"

Plozévet, F-29710 / Bretagne (Finistère) — 1413

La Corniche***
chemin de la Corniche
+33 (0)2-98913394
21/3 - 30/9
campinglacorniche@
flowercampings.com

2ha 81T(80-120m²) 10A CEE

1 ACD**G**IJKLMOPRS
2 GKLRTVWXY
3 BGHJKNRU
4 (C+H 1/6-15/9)
(Q+S+T+U+V) Z
5 **AB**EFGIJLMNPUVWXYZ
6 CDEGK(N 0,5km)ORTV

This natural campsite offers you every comfort and fun in a family atmosphere. 500m from the centre of Plozévet with sea views. 1.5 km from the beach. Perfectly maintained grounds and toilet facilities. Heated swimming pool from 1/6 - 15/9 and WiFi. Snack bar open every day in high season.

In Plozévet, follow signs to 'Camping de la Corniche'. After the village, about 400 metres on the right.

CC € 15 21/3-10/7 28/8-30/9

N 47°58'50" W 4°25'50"

Plurien/Sables-d'Or-les-Pins, F-22240 / Bretagne (Côtes-d'Armor) — 1414

Les Salines
11 rue de l'Islet
+33 (0)2-96721740
1/4 - 13/11
campinglessalinesplurien@gmail.com

4,2ha 150T 6A CEE

1 ACDGIJKLMPRS
2 AEGJQRTVWXY
3 AB**F**GHJKL**P**RUWY
4 **A**(Q+R)
5 **AB**CEFGHIJKLMNOPQUVYZ
6 ACDEG**J**(N 3km)ORT

Spaciously appointed terraced campsite in natural surroundings. Close to lagoon area. Beautiful walking and cycling trips from the campsite.

From N12 Brest-Rennes exit Erquy, Pléneuf-Val-André. 2 km before Erquy exit Cap Fréhel, Sables d'Or les Pins. Follow campsite signs.

CC € 11 *1/4-30/6 1/9-13/11*

N 48°37'55" W 2°24'49"

Pont-Scorff, F-56620 / Bretagne (Morbihan) — 1415

Ty Nenez***
route de Lorient
+33 (0)2-97325116
1/1 - 31/12
camping-ty-nenez@wanadoo.fr

2,5ha 69**T**(100-200m²) 16A CEE

1 ACD**G**IJKLMOP
2 FGLRVWX
3 AB**F**GHJRU**W**
4 (F+H+Q+R) (T 4/7-31/8) (Z)
5 **AB**DEFGIJKMNPQUXYZ
6 ACDEGHK(N 1km)OQTV

Peacefully located campsite with nice spacious pitches. Indoor pool that is open for the entire season. Shops at 1 km and zoo nearby.

N165 dir. Brest, exit Quéven dir. Pont-Scorff, 600 metres after zoo turn right. Then follow signs.

CC € 13 *1/1-3/7 1/9-31/12*

N 47°49'13" W 3°24'12"

Pordic, F-22590 / Bretagne (Côtes-d'Armor) — 1416

Les Madières***
Le Vau-Madec
+33 (0)2-96790248
9/4 - 30/10
campinglesmadieres@wanadoo.fr

2ha 75**T**(90-300m²) 10A CEE

1 ACD**G**IJKLMPQ
2 AFGKLNQRVWXY
3 ABGHJNRUW
4 (C 15/6-15/9) (Q 1/7-31/8) (R+T+U+V) Z
5 **AB**CDFGIJKLMNPUVZ
6 ACDEGK(N 1,8km)RTV

Beautifully appointed and well maintained campsite. Lovely swimming pool in Spanish style, attractive small restaurant. The natural layout of the grounds makes it possible to go real camping due to the absence of permanent pitches. Most suitable for hikers, 10 minutes from the sea. Free WiFi.

N12, after Plérin exit Les Rampes direction Pordic. D786 direction Pordic centre. Follow 'campings' sign in Pordic. Campsite well signposted.

CC € 15 *9/4-2/7 1/9-30/10*

N 48°34'58" W 2°48'17"

Port-Manech/Névez, F-29920 / Bretagne (Finistère) 1417

Le Saint Nicolas***
8 Kergouliou
+33 (0)2-98068975
1/5 - 18/9
info@campinglesaintnicolas.com

3,5ha 161T(80-130m²) 10A CEE

1 ACDGIJKLMOPQ
2 AEGJQRVWXY
3 BGHJ**M**NRUWY
4 (A 1/7-31/8) (C 26/6-28/8) (E+H) IJKP(Q 10/7-21/8)
5 **AB**CFGIJKLMNOPQRUVXYZ
6 ACEG**K**(N 0,3km)TV

A lovely peaceful campsite within walking distance of the beach and harbour. A small shop (300m) sells fresh bread daily. 3 km from a beautifully restored Breton village. Numerous trips out possible. Indoor heated pool open all season. Outdoor pool open and heated from the end of June.

From Lorient, take N165/E60 direction Quimper, exit Kerampaou via the D24 to Névez, then direction Port-Manech. Do not follow SatNav. On entering Port-Manech follow signs to the left.

CC €17 1/5-8/7 25/8-17/9

N 47°48'18" W 3°44'44"

Quiberon, F-56170 / Bretagne (Morbihan) 1418

Do Mi Si La Mi***
31 rue de la Vierge
+33 (0)2-97502252
FAX +33 (0)2-97502669
1/4 - 30/9
camping@domisilami.com

5ha 184T(80-110m²) 10A CEE

1 ACD**G**IJKLMOPQ
2 AEGKQRVWX
3 BFGHJKNRUWY
4 (Q+S+T+U+V+X 11/4-18/9) Z
5 **AB**CEFGHIJKLMNOPQRUVXYZ
6 ACDEG**K**OTV

Campsite by a sandy beach, natural hedges ensure plenty of shade and privacy. Well maintained toilet facilities. Bar/restaurant and self service-shop (with fresh fruit and vegetables and a meat section). Lightly undulating cycle and footpaths close by. 10% discount after 21/9. You will receive a surprise by using code AC16DO.

N165/E60 Nantes-Quimper exit Carnac/Quiberon, via D768 direction Quiberon. Turn left after St. Pierre/Quiberon. Well signposted.

CC €17 1/4-1/7 28/8-30/9

N 47°29'59" W 3°7'13"

Quiberon, F-56170 / Bretagne (Morbihan) 1419

Le Bois d'Amour***
rue St. Clément
+33 (0)2-97501352
2/4 - 1/10
camping.boisdamour@flowercampings.com

5,5ha 53T(70-120m²) 6A CEE

1 ACD**F**IJKLMO**P**RS
2 AEGQRSVWX
3 B**F**GHJK**MQ**R**T**UWY
4 (E+H+Q+R+T+U+V+Y+Z)
5 **AB**EFGIJKLMNOPUWZ
6 ACEGK(N 1,5km)T

A good campsite with many facilities, 150m from a flat sandy beach. Noisy near the entrance, quieter at the rear. Located in an old dune area, so plenty of sand and long tent pegs are required. Indoor pool.

South of Auray, via the D768 to Quiberon. In Quiberon town direction Thalassotherapie or follow the camping signs.

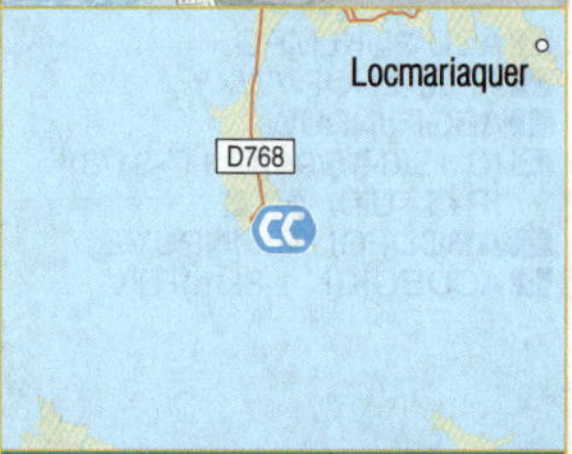

CC €17 2/4-1/7 1/9-1/10 7=6

N 47°28'35" W 3°6'15"

Quiberon, F-56170 / Bretagne (Morbihan)

1420

Les Joncs du Roch***
rue de l'Aérodrome
+33 (0)2-97502437
2/4 - 24/9
camping@lesjoncsduroch.com

2,3ha 107**T**(80-120m²) 10A CEE

1 ACD**G**IJKLMOPRS
2 AEGQRVWX
3 BFGHJK**M**N**OP**RUWY
4 (E+H+Q)
5 **AB**EFGIJKLMNOPQUVXZ
6 ACEG**K**(N 1km)TV

A hospitable campsite close to a lovely beach and town. 800m from a supermarket. Large level pitches and well maintained toilet facilities. You can watch light aircraft take off and land at the nearby airfield (open from 08:00 to 18:00). Indoor swimming pool, always heated to 30°C.

N165/E60 Nantes-Quimper, exit Carnac-Quiberon, via D768 to Quiberon. Left just before railway beyond St. Pierre/Quiberon. Follow Aerodrôme and Port-Haliguen signs.

CC €17 *2/4-8/7 25/8-23/9*

N 47°28'45'' W 3°6'2''

Quimper, F-29000 / Bretagne (Finistère)

1421

Domaine de L'Orangerie
de Lanniron*****
allée/chemin de Lanniron/Chât. de L
+33 (0)2-98906202
FAX +33 (0)2-98521556
26/3 - 2/11
contact@lanniron.com

6,5ha 199**T**(80-150m²) 10A CEE

1 ACD**G**IJKLMOPQ
2 CFGKLRVWXY
3 B**EF**GHJK**M**N**PQ**RUW
4 (A 1/7-31/8)
(C+H 15/5-15/9) IJKMP
(Q) (S 15/5-15/9)
(T+U+V 20/5-20/9)
(X+Y+Z)
5 **AB**DEFGIJKLMNOPUWXYZ
6 ACEGJ**K**(N 2km)ORTV

A unique terraced site with a view of the Odet, the most beautiful river in France. Level pitches, marked out by exotic trees and plants in a 17th century castle park (38 hectares). Restaurant and shop in authentic buildings. Lovely aqua park, 9 hole golf course, 3 fishing locations. Quimper is 2 km away via a woodland path. Superior, comfort or Castel premium pitches for a supplement.

In Quimper continue towards Pont-l'Abbé. Follow Lanniron camping signs.

CC €19 *28/3-30/6 1/9-2/11*

N 47°58'46'' W 4°6'24''

Raguénès/Névez, F-29920 / Bretagne (Finistère)

1422

Airotel Le Raguenès Plage****
19 rue des Îles
+33 (0)2-98068069
FAX +33 (0)2-98068905
9/4 - 26/9
leraguenesplage@orange.fr

7ha 218**T**(90-140m²) 15A CEE

1 ACD**G**IJKLMOPQ
2 AEKQRVWXY
3 BGHJKNRU**V**WY
4 (C 29/5-13/9) (E+H) IJ**N**
(Q+S 4/5-26/9)
(T+U+V 4/5-13/9)
(Y 18/6-11/9) (Z 4/5-13/9)
5 **AB**EFGIJKLOPRUVWXYZ
6 ACEG**K**(N 2,5km)TV

A lovely, luxurious campsite close to the sea. Choose a pitch with plenty or with little shade. There are a couple of nice walking and cycling routes close by. A lovely sandy beach 300m away via a footpath. Indoor pool heated all season, outdoor pool heated from 1 June. Sea views from 15 of the pitches.

N165 Lorient-Quimper, exit Kerampaou and via D24/D77 to Névez. Then direction Raguénès-Plage. Well indicated after 3 km.

CC €17 *9/4-10/7 27/8-25/9* 14=12

N 47°47'36'' W 3°48'3''

Rochefort-en-Terre, F-56220 / Bretagne (Morbihan)

1423

Sites & Paysages Au Gré Des Vents***
2 chemin de Bogeais
+33 (0)2-97433752
1/4 - 25/9
gredesvents@orange.fr

2,5ha 70**T**(85-150m²) 10A CEE

1 ACD**G**IJKLMOPRS
2 GIRVWXY
3 B**F**GHJK**M**NRU**W**
4 (E+H+Q+R) (T+U 30/4-18/9) (Z)
5 **AB**FGIJKLMNPUVW
6 ACEGI**K**(N 1,5km)OTV

Within walking distance of Rochefort-en-Terre, one of the loveliest and most characteristic towns in France, noted for its artists and an old soap industry. Level pitches or rougher ones between old trees, well maintained toilets and indoor pool. At the beginning of walking routes.

N116 Ploermel-Vannes exit D775, 21 km direction Redon, left just after the second level crossing. After 3 km you pass a lake, the campsite is located on the left near the Rochefort sign.

CC € 17 *1/4-8/7 25/8-24/9*

N 47°41'43'' W 2°20'57''

Roz-sur-Couesnon, F-35610 / Bretagne (Ille-et-Vilaine)

1424

Les Couesnons***
l'Hôpital
FAX +33 (0)2-99802686
1/4 - 1/11
courrier@lescouesnons.com

0,9ha 40**T**(80-110m²) 6A CEE

1 ACD**G**IJKLMPRS
2 FGRTVX
3 ABGHJRU
4 (Q+X+Y) Z
5 **AB**DEFGIJKLMNPRUWZ
6 CEJ(N 2km)

Located at the entrance to the polders, 10 minutes from Mont Saint Michel, 20 minutes from Cancale, 30 minutes from Saint Malo. A friendly welcome at this family campsite, relaxing, comfortable, marked out pitches. Beautiful, typical Breton restaurant, closed in the off-season on Tuesday evening and all day Wednesday.

N175 Avranches direction Dol-de-Bretagne, exit Roz-sur-Couesnon, D797 direction St. Malo coastal road. Campsite signposted 7 km on the right.

CC € 15 *1/4-30/6 1/9-1/11*

N 48°35'40'' W 1°35'55''

Sarzeau, F-56370 / Bretagne (Morbihan)

1425

La Ferme de Lann Hoëdic***
rue Jean de la Fontaine
+33 (0)2-97480173
1/4 - 31/10
contact@camping-lannhoedic.fr

3,6ha 108**T**(100-160m²) 10A CEE

1 ACD**G**IJKLMPQ
2 AOQRVWXY
3 BD**F**GHJKRUW
4 **N**(Q+R) (U 6/7-27/8) (Z)
5 **ABC**EFGHIJKLMNOPQUZ
6 ACEGHI**J**(N 2km)TUV

Near the sea, a natural campsite with rural charm and 3 star comfort. Beach 800m, supermarket 2 km, Sarzeau 2.5 km. Coastline with sandy beaches and cliffs. Good walking and cycling. 15 mins. free WiFi per day.

N165 Vannes-Nantes, exit Sarzeau via D20 or D780 (Do not enter Sarzeau). Follow the D20 direction Port Navalo to the roundabout with the Super U supermarket. On the roundabout turn left direction Roaliguen. After 1.5 km follow the sign to the site on the left.

CC € 15 *1/4-10/7 27/8-30/10 14=12*

N 47°30'26'' W 2°45'39''

Sarzeau, F-56370 / Bretagne (Morbihan)

1426

Lodge Club Presqu'île de Rhuys****
rte d'Arzon
+33 (0)2-97412993
FAX +33 (0)2-97417097
25/3 - 30/9
@ info@lodgeclub.fr

15,5ha 266**T**(100-180m²) 15A CEE

1 ACD**G**IJKLMOPRS
2 QRVWXY
3 B**F**GHJKLN**OP**RUV
4 (C 1/5-30/9) (D+H) IJM (Q) (R+T+U+Y+Z 1/7-31/8)
5 **AB**EFGIJKLMNOPQRUWXYZ
6 ACEGIK(N 2km)OTV

On the Presqu'ile de Rhuys headland with lovely sandy beaches. Golfe du Morbihan with small harbours and islands. The site has large pitches between apple trees, extensive modern toilets and an indoor leisure pool. Cycling and walking routes from the entrance.

N165/E60 Vannes-Nantes, exit Sarzeau. Before Sarzeau, take the D20 or D780 dir. Arzon. At the second roundabout from Super U direction Arzon. Go left after 1.5 km. Follow the signposts, Le Bohat/ Le Spernec.

CC € 17 *25/3-5/7 22/8-29/9 21=18*

N 47°31'21'' W 2°47'50''

St. Benoît-des-Ondes, F-35114 / Bretagne (Ille-et-Vilaine)

1427

de l'Ile Verte****
42 rue de l'Ile Verte
+33 (0)2-99586255
1/4 - 1/11
@ bienvenue@campingdelileverte.com

1,8ha 38**T**(100-120m²) 6A CEE

1 ACD**G**IJKLMPRS
2 AEGLMRTVX
3 ABGKRUW
4 (F 1/4-30/9) (Q+T+U 1/7-31/8) Z
5 **AB**EFGIJKLMNOPQUX
6 CEG**K**(N 0,5km)TV

A peaceful and charming family campsite 400m from the sea and shops. The campsite is close to Cancale, between St. Malo and Mont Saint Michel. Spacious marked out wind-free pitches.

At Dol-de-Bretagne take exit Cancale (D155-D4). At La Fresnais take D207 and D7 to Vildé-la-Marine, then to St. Benoît. Turn left at service station in the village.

CC € 15 *1/4-1/7 28/8-1/11*

N 48°36'58'' W 1°51'7''

St. Brieuc, F-22000 / Bretagne (Côtes-d'Armor)

1428

des Vallées***
boulevard Paul Doumer
FAX +33 (0)2-96940505
14/3 - 14/10
@ campingdesvallees@wanadoo.fr

3,2ha 35**T**(80-120m²) 10A CEE

1 ACD**F**IJKLMPR
2 CFGRTUVX
3 BGHJKLN**OP**RU
4 (**C+F+H**) **IJ**KMN (Q+R+S+T+U+V 1/7-31/8) Z
5 **AB**EFGIJKLMNOPQSUWXZ
6 CDEGIKL(N 1km)ORTV

Campsite in natural surroundings, close to the centre of St. Brieuc. Lovely pitches beside a stream. Close to an indoor and outdoor leisure pool. Free WiFi.

Via the N12 exit St. Brieux. Campsite well signposted throughout the town. Follow the Brézillet part of town.

CC € 15 *14/3-30/6 1/9-14/10*

N 48°30'2'' W 2°45'31''

St. Cast-le-Guildo, F-22380 / Bretagne (Côtes-d'Armor)

1429

Château de Galinée*****
La Galinée
+33 (0)2-96411056
FAX +33 (0)2-96410372
7/5 - 9/9
@ contact@chateaudegalinee.com

14ha 272T(120-130m²) 10A CEE

1 ACD**G**IJKLM**P**RS
2 BLRTVXY
3 ABF**G**M**N**Q**R**UW
4 (C 11/5-5/9) (F+H 19/4-5/9) IJ**N**(Q+S 24/5-5/9) (U+V+X 24/5-31/8) Z
5 **AB**DEFGIJLMNPR**ST**UWX YZ
6 AEGH**IK**(N 3km)RTV

Beautiful family grounds in a castle park. Lovely water park with slides, bar and restaurant with views of the pool. Free fishing pond. Ancient trees in the castle park add ambiance. Marked out pitches with small hedges. Excellent heated toilet block. Swimming in the indoor heated pool when the weather is cool. Reception only open in the mornings 7/5-11/5.

From Dinard take the D168, then take the D786 and after leaving Notre Dame, signposted after 3 km on the left.

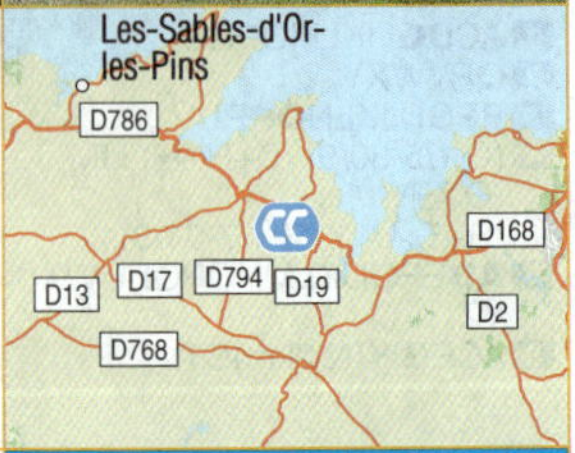

CC € 17 *7/5-8/7 25/8-9/9*

N 48°35'4" W 2°15'26"

St. Cast-le-Guildo, F-22380 / Bretagne (Côtes-d'Armor)

1430

Le Chatelet*****
rue des Nouettes
+33 (0)2-96419633
FAX +33 (0)2-96419799
11/4 - 10/9
@ chateletcp@aol.com

9ha 105T(80-120m²) 8A CEE

1 ACD**G**IJKLM**P**RS
2 AEJKQRTVWXY
3 AB**F**GHJN**OP**RUWY
4 (A 3/7-26/8) (E+H) (Q+S 5/5-4/9) (U+V 13/6-4/9) (Z 5/5-4/9)
5 **AB**CDEFGIJKLMNPQUWX YZ
6 ACEGH**K**L(N 0,8km)ORTV

A lush campsite with beautiful sea views from many of the pitches. 150m from a fine sandy beach. Small lake. The pitches are marked out by trees, hedges and bushes. Indoor heated pool, fishing pond, friendly clubhouse with bar and cafe with sea views.

D786, first drive to Matignon. Then, D13 to St. Cast-le-Guildo. After the supermarket and garage, turn left direction 'le Port'. Site is clearly signposted. Avoid driving through the centre of St. Cast-le-Guildo.

CC € 19 *11/4-7/7 24/8-10/9*

N 48°38'14" W 2°16'10"

St. Coulomb/La Guimorais, F-35350 / Bretagne (Ille-et-Vilaine)

1431

Des Chevrets***
+33 (0)2-99890190
FAX +33 (0)2-99890116
31/3 - 14/10
@ contact@campingdeschevrets.fr

13ha 254T(80-100m²) 6A CEE

1 ACD**G**IJKLMPRS
2 AEJRSVX
3 ABGHNQRUWY
4 (Q+S+T+U+V+X+Y) Z
5 **AB**EFGIJKLNPUYZ
6 CEG**IK**(N 2km)OT

A peaceful, floral campsite with pitches marked out by plants. This site has a unique location: on high dunes with direct access to the beach and lovely views over the bay. There is a good restaurant for gourmets.

From Cancale via the D201 direction St. Malo. In La Guimorais turn right. The campsite is to the right of the D201 and is clearly signposted.

CC € 15 *31/3-3/7 22/8-14/10*

N 48°41'24" W 1°56'30"

St. Gildas-de-Rhuys, F-56730 / Bretagne (Morbihan) 1432

Camping du Menhir****
19 route du clos er bé
+33 (0)2-97452288
29/4 - 18/9
campingmenhir@aol.com

3ha 121**T**(90-100m²) 6A

1 ACD**G**IJKLMPRS
2 AGQRVWXY
3 B**F**GHJ**MQ**RUV
4 (C 15/5-18/9) (H 5/5-18/9) J (Q+R 1/7-31/8) (T+U+V+X+Z 1/7-17/9)
5 **AB**EFGIJKLMNPUWXYZ
6 ACEGJ(N 3km)TUV

Very quiet, comfortable four-star campsite, especially in low season. Surroundings almost level, sea is nearby in three directions, beach 1 km. Free choice of pitches in low season. Cycling routes nearby. In low season it's not possible to pay by card.

N165/E60 Vannes-Nantes, exit direction Sarzeau, then via D20 or D780 direction Port Navalo until the campsite signs direct you to the left.

CC € 17 *29/4-5/7 26/8-17/9* N 47°31'44'' W 2°50'51''

St. Jouan-des-Guérêts, F-35430 / Bretagne (Ille-et-Vilaine) 1433

Le P'tit Bois*****
St. Malo
+33 (0)2-99211430
FAX +33 (0)2-99817414
1/4 - 18/9
contact@ptitbois.com

6ha 96**T**(80-120m²) 10A CEE

1 ACD**F**IJKLMPST
2 FLRTVX
3 ABGKMN**Q**RU
4 (C+F+H) IJKL (Q+S+T+U+V+X) Z
5 **AB**EFGIJKLMNPUVWXYZ
6 CEGHK(N 1km)ORTV

Pleasant, quiet campsite, with plenty of flowers in a green environment. On the edge of the town of St. Malo. Close to Dinand, Mont St. Michel, Cap Frehel, la Pointe de Grouin and the walled town in the city of St. Malo. Heated indoor swimming pool with jacuzzi. Tennis, minigolf and free WiFi in low season.

Leave the N137 between Châteauneuf and St.Malo at the second exit St. Jouan-des-Guérêts and 'Centre Commercial'. Campsite is well marked in the village.

CC € 17 *1/4-2/7 27/8-18/9* N 48°36'36'' W 1°59'13''

St. Lunaire/Dinard, F-35800 / Bretagne (Ille-et-Vilaine) 1434

Longchamp***
773 boulevard de Saint Cast
+33 (0)2-99463398
1/4 - 30/9
contact@camping-longchamp.com

4ha 176**T**(100-120m²) 10A CEE

1 ACD**G**HIJKLMOPQ
2 AEFGLRSWXY
3 AB**F**GHJKNRUWY
4 (C 1/6-6/9) (E 15/4-30/9) (F) (H 15/4-30/9) IJM (Q+R+T+U+V+X+Z)
5 **AB**CFGJKLMNOPUV
6 ACEG**K**(N 0,6km)ORTV

Rural family campsite 150m from the beach. Heated indoor and outdoor pool with spa, slides and toddlers' pool. Spacious pitches. 800m from the centre of St. Lunaire. Ideally situated for St Malo, Dinard, Cap Fréhel, Mont St. Michel, Cancale.

N137 after passing Barrage de la Rance (reservoir) at Dinard take the D168. Turn right before the centre along the coast D786 direction St. Briac. Campsite located just outside the built-up area on the left. Well signposted.

CC € 15 *8/4-1/7 25/8-30/9* N 48°38'4'' W 2°7'14''

St. Malo, F-35400 / Bretagne (Ille-et-Vilaine) — 1435

Domaine de La Ville Huchet****
rte de la Passagère
+33 (0)2-99811183
FAX +33 (0)2-99815189
2/4 - 18/9
@ info@lavillehuchet.com

6,4ha 107**T**(100-120m²) 6A CEE

1 ACD**G**IJKLMPRS
2 FGLRTX
3 ABGKN**Q**RU
4 (C 1/6-18/9) (F+H) IJ
(Q+R+T+U+V+Z)
5 **AB**EFGIJKLMNPUWZ
6 CEG**K**(N 2km)OV

You can discover the Brittany region, the ancient city of Intra Muros, Saint-Malo from this friendly, peaceful family camping with its indoor pool (28°C). You will experience unforgettable, natural, culinary and historical richness.

N137 from Rennes to St. Malo, firstly direction 'centre ville'. At the roundabout exit La Ville Huchet Quelmer, straight ahead at the next roundabout then turn 100 metres to the right under the bridge to the campsite.

CC € 17 *2/4-3/7 28/8-18/9*

N 48°36'54" W 1°59'14"

St. Pol-de-Léon, F-29250 / Bretagne (Finistère) — 1436

Ar Kleguer****
avenue de la Mer
+33 (0)2-98691881
2/4 - 25/9
@ info@camping-ar-kleguer.com

5,5ha 132**T**(90-120m²) 10A

1 ACD**G**IJLMOPRS
2 AEJKLRVWX
3 BCD**F**GHKMNQRUWY
4 (C 20/6-1/9) (F)
(G 20/6-1/9) J(Q 15/4-25/9)
(R) (S+T 1/7-31/8)
(Y) (Z 1/7-31/8)
5 **AB**DFGHIJKLMNPQRUW
6 ACEGK(N 1km)OQRTV

Unique location, luxury 4-star campsite with lovely views of the bay of Morlaix and the many islands near St. Pol-de-Léon. Restaurant within walking distance. Since 2013 spacious modern toilet facilities and a lovely indoor pool. The subtropical plants growing on the site will delight you. Free WiFi on entire campsite.

On the D58, take exit St. Pol-de-Léon and follow 'camping' and 'plage' signs. Don't use SatNav from Roscoff or Landivisian.

CC € 17 *2/4-3/7 29/8-25/9*

N 48°41'26" W 3°58'3"

St. Pol-de-Léon, F-29250 / Bretagne (Finistère) — 1437

De Trologot***
Grève du Man
+33 (0)2-98690626
1/5 - 30/9
@ camping-trologot@wanadoo.fr

2,5ha 85**T**(80-100m²) 10A CEE

1 ACD**G**IJKLOPRS
2 AENQRVX
3 BGHRUWY
4 (C+H 10/6-10/9)
(Q 1/6-15/9) (R+Z 1/7-31/8)
5 **AB**CFGIJKLMNPUVZ
6 EGJ(N 2km)V

A well maintained peaceful campsite with excellent amenities for a pleasant stay on the coast. Close to St. Pol-de-Léon with its cathedral, Île de Batz with exotic gardens and Roscoff with its ferries. Extra service: special pitches outside the campsite for arrival and departure outside reception opening times.

On D58 take exit St. Pol-de-Léon. Turn SatNav off. Follow 'camping' and 'plage' signs. Then follow 'De Trologot'. Campsite is on the north east of the town.

CC € 15 *1/5-10/7 27/8-30/9 7=6, 14=12*

N 48°41'36" W 3°58'10"

Surzur, F-56450 / Bretagne (Morbihan)

1438

Ty-Coët***
38 rue du Bois
+33 (0)2-97420905
1/3 - 15/11
contact@camping-tycoet.com

6ha 58T(90-100m²) 16A CEE

1 ACD**G**IJKLMOP
2 FGRVWX
3 BGHJ**OP**R
4 (Q 1/7-30/8)
(T+U+Z 2/4-30/10)
5 **AB**FGIJKLMNOPUZ
6 EGJ(N 1,5km)OT

Ty-Coët means rest, space, nature and fun. Ideally located for exploring the headland. 1.5 km from a supermarket. Barbecues permitted except in July and August. Many sights in the vicinity. 500m from a swimming complex, discounts for campsite guests. Walking and cycling in the undulating surroundings.

N165/E60 Vannes-Nantes, exit 22 Surzur, direction Surzur as far as roundabout before village, towards centre and follow signs. Do not follow SatNav after centre.

CC € 13 *1/3-3/7 22/8-31/10*

N 47°35'16'' W 2°37'9''

Telgruc-sur-Mer, F-29560 / Bretagne (Finistère)

1439

Armorique****
112 rue de la Plage
+33 (0)2-98277733
1/4 - 30/9
contact@campingarmorique.com

3ha 100T(80-120m²) 10A CEE

1 ACD**G**IJKLPQ
2 AJKLQRVWXY
3 BGHJRU
4 (C 15/5-15/9) (H 15/6-30/9)
J(Q 15/6-30/9) (R)
(T+U 1/7-31/8) Z
5 **AB**FGIJKLMNOPUWZ
6 ACEGIJ(N 0,7km)OTV

Very peaceful terraced campsite with heated swimming pool (± 27°C), children's pool and water slide (12 metres) with unique views over the bay of Douarnenez. Sandy beaches within 700 metres. The campsite is run by an enthusiastic couple with a passion for hygiene (toilets cleaned 3 times a day). Park-like entrance. In the centre of unspoiled scenery. The campsite is easily accessible.

D887 from Châteaulin to Crozon. Campsite is clearly marked in Telgruc.

CC € 15 *1/4-8/7 25/8-30/9 7=6*

N 48°13'32'' W 4°22'17''

Telgruc-sur-Mer, F-29560 / Bretagne (Finistère)

1440

Sites & Paysages Le Panoramic****
130 route de la Plage le Penker
+33 (0)2-98277841
FAX +33 (0)2-98273610
1/5 - 15/9
info@camping-panoramic.com

4ha 180T(100-160m²) 10A CEE

1 ACD**G**IJKLMPQ
2 JKRTVX
3 BGHJK**M**RU
4 (C+H 1/6-15/9) K
(Q 1/7-30/8) (R+T 1/7-31/8)
(U+V+X+Y) Z
5 **AB**FGJLNOPUVWXYZ
6 ACDEGIJ(N 1,5km)ORV

A peaceful family campsite with plenty of privacy. Views of Douarnenez Bay in the middle of the regional nature park of Armorique. 500 metres from a lovely sandy beach. Plenty of opportunities for taking walks. The heated swimming pool is open from 1 June.

From Châteaulin, the D887, direction Crozon. In Telgruc continue straight ahead. The campsite is signposted.

CC € 15 *1/5-8/7 26/8-15/9 7=6*

N 48°13'25'' W 4°22'21''

Tinténiac, F-35190 / Bretagne (Ille-et-Vilaine) 1441

Domaine Les Peupliers***
21, La Besnelais
+33 (0)2-99454975
1/4 - 30/9
contact@domainelespeupliers.fr

5ha 91**T**(100-130m²) 6A CEE

1 AC**G**IJLPQ
2 CFLRVWX
3 BGJMN**O**RUW
4 (C 15/6-15/9) (Q 15/4-15/9) (R+S) (T 15/5-15/9) (Z)
5 **AB**GIJKLMNOPUW
6 CEG**K**(N 2km)TUV

A family campsite in a natural area of 5 hectares in the middle of a 16th century estate. Close to Rennes, St. Malo, Mont St. Michel. Ideal for families and senior citizens. Opportunities for walking (canal d'Ille et Rance), fishing and various trips out. Lake, swimming pool, tennis courts, various games and pitch & putt golf. Large pitches screened by hedges.

N137 Rennes-Dinard/St. Malo, exit Hédé/Tinténiàc. Campsite is south of Tinténiàc.

CC € 17 1/4-8/7 26/8-30/9 7=6, 14=12

N 48°18'34'' W 1°49'19''

Trédrez, F-22300 / Bretagne (Côtes-d'Armor) 1442

Flower camping Les Capucines****
Ancienne Voie Romaine
+33 (0)2-96357228
FAX +33 (0)2-96357898
25/3 - 30/9
les.capucines@wanadoo.fr

4ha 89**T**(90-130m²) 10A CEE

1 ACD**G**IJKLMOPRS
2 AIJKLQRVWXY
3 B**C**D**F**GHJK**M**NQRU
4 (D+H) (Q 15/4-15/9) (R+U) (Z 15/4-15/9)
5 **AB**DEFGHIJKLMNOPUWXY
6 ACEGIJ**K**(N 1km)RTV

A peaceful campsite 1 km from St. Michel-en-Grève beaches. Locquémeau fishing village is worth a visit. Spacious pitches (comfort pitches without supplement) on parkland with beautiful views. On GR 34 walking route. Lovely heated indoor pool with a sliding roof.

From Lannion direction Morlaix D786. At Trédrez-Locquémeau intersection turn right then turn left three times. Follow signs.

CC € 15 25/3-8/7 25/8-30/9

N 48°41'34'' W 3°33'26''

Trélévern, F-22660 / Bretagne (Côtes-d'Armor) 1443

Seasonova du Palud
Port L'epine
+33 (0)296-917311
1/4 - 4/11
camping-trelevern@vacances-seasonova.com

2,8ha 135**T**(80-140m²) 10A CEE

1 ACD**G**IJKLMPQ
2 AEKLNORSTVW
3 AGHLRUWY
4 (Q+R+T+U+X+Z)
5 **AB**GIJKLMNPUVXZ
6 EGHJ**K**(N 3km)V

This long campsite is located directly on the coast and has a beautiful view over the 'Les 7 Îles' island group. The Côte le Granit Rose and Perros Guirec are nearby. The campsite has its own restaurant. The toilet facilities are basic, but clean.

From Lannion dir. Trélèvern via D38. In Trélèvern follow signs Le Palud or Port L' Epine until the beach.

CC € 15 1/4-8/7 26/8-4/11 7=6, 14=11

N 48°48'54'' W 3°22'59''

Trélévern, F-22660 / Bretagne (Côtes-d'Armor) — 1444

RCN Port l'Épine***
10 Venelle de Pors Garo
+33 (0)2-96237194
23/4 - 17/9
portlepine@rcn.fr

3ha 112T(80-150m²) 16A CEE

1 ACD**F**IJKL**P**Q
2 EKNQRSVWX
3 BGHRWY
4 (A 1/5-1/7) (C+H+Q+T+U+X)
5 **AB**FGIJKLMNOPUWXYZ
6 CEG**K**(N 2km)T

A beautiful little campsite, uniquely situated on a promontory. The south side of the campsite has beautiful views over the sea to the resort of Perros-Guirec. On the north side is a beach with views of seven islands. The flat grass pitches are separated by colourful hedges and trees.

From D6, direction Trélévern (± 5 km), then follow campsite and Port l'Epine signs.

€15 23/4-9/7 26/8-17/9

N 48°48'47'' W 3°23'9''

Vannes, F-56000 / Bretagne (Morbihan) — 1445

Le Conleau****
188 avenue Maréchal Juin
+33 (0)2-97631388
FAX +33 (0)2-97403882
2/4 - 1/10
camping.conleau@flowercampings.com

5ha 129T(80-150m²) 10A CEE

1 ACD**G**IJKLMO**P**RS
2 AEFGIKPQRUVWXY
3 B**F**GHJKRUW
4 (E+H+Q+R) (T+U+V+X+Z 1/7-17/9)
5 **AB**CEGHIJKLMNPUVWXYZ
6 ACDEGIK(N 1km)TV

Typical beach campsite near the sea with well equipped toilet facilities. Choice of pitches with plenty of sun or shade. 2 km to historical city centre. 500m from a landscaped swimming pool filled with sea water and a small beach. Cycling and walking routes right by the entrance.

N165/E60 Nantes-Lorient exit Vannes Ouest/Arradon. Then Vannes Centre and follow camping signs, each roundabout has a 'le Conleau' sign.

€17 2/4-1/7 1/9-1/10 7=6

N 47°38'0'' W 2°46'48''

Vannes-Meucon/Monterblanc, F-56250 / Bretagne (Morbihan) — 1446

Du Haras*****
5 rue de Kersimon
+33 (0)2-97446606
FAX +33 (0)2-97444941
15/3 - 12/11
contact@campingvannes.com

14ha 110T(100-200m²) 15A CEE

1 ACD**G**IJKLMO**P**RS
2 BFGLQRUVWXY
3 BDGHJKMN**OP**QRUV
4 (C 1/5-30/9) (F+H 2/4-31/10) IJ**KL**M**NP** (Q 2/7-27/8) (R+T+U+X) Z
5 **AB**CDEFGHIJKLMNOPQRUWXYZ
6 ACDEGIJ**K**(N 3km)TV

In the countryside, ideal for children and for a trip to Vannes, Auray or the Golfe de Morbihan. Spacious pitches, comfortable heated toilet facilities. Heated swimming pool with slides, lovely wellness building separate indoor pool with an unusual shallow section. 12 km to Vannes via a cycle track.

N165/E60 Vannes-Lorient, exit Pontivy/St. Brieuc. From the D767 dir. Josselin, first right dir. Vannes airfield. Third left before the control tower. Follow the signs.

€17 15/3-1/7 27/8-11/11

N 47°43'50'' W 2°43'41''

Allonnes, F-49650 / Pays de la Loire (Maine-et-Loire)

1447

Le Pô Doré****
51 route de Pô
+33 (0)2-41387880
15/3 - 15/11
camping-lepodore@orange.fr

2,5ha 51T(100-120m²) 6-10A CEE

1 ACGIJKLPQ
2 FGLRTVWXY
3 BGNRU**W**
4 (B 15/5-15/9) (Q 1/7-31/8) (R) (U+V 1/7-31/8) Z
5 **AB**FGIJKLMNOPUZ
6 CEGIK(N 2km)TV

A charming and quiet campsite with an unusually landscaped swimming lake and a sandy beach. Located in the countryside yet close to the Loire Valley with all its attractions.

From Saumur drive towards Allonnes, D10. Follow signs 1 km from the centre of Allonnes.

CC € 15 *15/3-15/7 1/9-15/11 7=6*

N 47°17'57" W 0°0'45"

Ambrières-les-Vallées, F-53300 / Pays de la Loire (Mayenne)

1448

Camping Le Parc de Vaux***
35 rue des Colverts
+33 (0)2-43049025
1/4 - 31/10
parcdevaux@camp-in-ouest.com

3,5ha 76T(80-110m²) 10A

1 ACD**F**IJKLMOPQ
2 CDGIJLRVWXY
3 ABGHJ**MNOPQ**RU**W**X
4 (A 1/7-31/8) (C+H 5/6-12/9) J(Q+S) (T+U+V+X+Z 1/7-31/8)
5 **AB**GIJKLMNOPQUWXYZ
6 ACEGIJK(N 0,5km)ORV

A small quiet campsite with pitches marked out by hedges on the banks of a river. The site forms part of a recreational park. Various sports facilities such as kayaking, pedal boats, tennis, swimming and mountain biking.

The campsite is located 2 km south of Ambrières-les-Vallées on the D23 from Domfront to Mayenne.

CC € 13 *1/4-6/7 26/8-31/10 7=6, 14=11*

N 48°23'31" W 0°37'1"

Angers, F-49000 / Pays de la Loire (Maine-et-Loire)

1449

du Lac de Maine****
avenue du Lac de Maine
+33 (0)2-41730503
FAX +33 (0)2-41730220
25/3 - 10/10
camping@lacdemaine.fr

4ha 146T(67-136m²) 10A CEE

1 ACD**G**IJKLPQ
2 ADFGLRTVWXY
3 BGHJMNRUV**WZ**
4 (C+H 15/6-10/9) K (Q 10/6-15/9) (V 15/6-10/9) Z
5 **AB**DEFGIJKLMNOPUWXYZ
6 CEGIJK(N 2km)RTV

In the heart of the Anjou in an unusual location: close to a famous historical town in the heart of 100 hectare area abundant in water. 1 hour from famous tourist towns, surrounded by renowned vineyards. Area of good living, gastronomy, heritage and a lovely climate. Recreation ground. Offers opportunities for sailing, swimming, free tennis, swing golf, fishing. Bus stops 300m from the campsite.

Located in Bouchemaine, clearly signposted in Angers. Via Lac de Maine.

CC € 15 *25/3-4/7 21/8-10/10*

N 47°27'17" W 0°35'47"

Assérac, F-44410 / Pays de la Loire (Loire-Atlantique)

1450

Le Moulin de l'Eclis****
Pinede Treiz Gwen, Pont Mahé
+33 (0)2-40017669
+33 (0)2-40017775
1/4 - 13/11
info@camping-leclis.com

3,8ha 79T(90-140m²) 16A CEE

1 ACD**G**IJKLMPST
2 AEGKQRVWXY
3 AGHJKN**P**RUWY
4 (C 1/6-11/9) (D+H 16/4-30/10) IJ (Q+S) (T+U+V 1/7-28/8) (Y 2/4-31/10) (Z 1/7-28/8)
5 **AB**CDEFGHIJKLMNOPQRUWXYZ
6 ACEGHIJ(N 5km)TV

Pleasant site with covered and open leisure pools. By the beach. A few pitches have sea views. Shellfish can be dug out of the sands and eaten. Good cycling and walking area. Very luxurious toilet facilities with Eco label. Kitesurfing centre. Near good restaurant.

N165/E60 Nantes-Vannes, after La Roche-Bernard dir. Guérande/La Baule as far as Herbignac, then to Assérac. In the centre at roundabout (with houses in the middle) dir. Pont-Mahé and follow signs.

CC € 17 1/4-3/5 9/5-12/5 17/5-30/6 29/8-12/11

N 47°26'41'' W 2°27'2''

Aubigny, F-85430 / Pays de la Loire (Vendée)

1451

Campilô***
L'auroire
+33 (0)2-51316845
1/1 - 31/12
accueil@campilo.com

16ha 42T 16A CEE

1 A**G**IJKLMNOPST
2 DFLMRVXY
3 AGHJKNRW
4 (E 15/4-31/10) (Q+R+T+U+V 1/7-31/8) (Z)
5 **AB**CGIJKLMNOPUX
6 ACDEGKORT

A lovely new campsite in countryside next to two lakes in the heart of the Vendée. Open all year.

From La Roche-sur-Yon take A87 towards Les Sable d'Olonne; exit 32. Follow signs in Aubigny.

CC € 15 1/1-3/7 29/8-31/12

N 46°37'24'' W 1°27'18''

Avrillé, F-85440 / Pays de la Loire (Vendée)

1452

Beauchêne***
avenue de Lattre de Tassigny
+33 (0)2-51223049
1/4 - 10/10
contact@campinglebeauchene.com

2,5ha 53T(80-120m²) 10A CEE

1 ACD**G**IJKL**P**RS
2 DRVWXY
3 BDGHJKNRUW
4 (C+H 15/5-15/9) (Q+R) (T+U+V+Z 1/7-31/8)
5 **A**FGIJKLMNPUVXZ
6 ACEGJ(N 0,5km)RTV

A peaceful, friendly campsite with a homely atmosphere and spacious pitches in natural surroundings. Free fishing lake. A good starting point for cycling and walking tours.

Signposted from Avrillé.

CC € 13 1/4-8/7 26/8-10/10 7=6, 14=12

N 46°28'12'' W 1°29'13''

Barbâtre, F-85630 / Pays de la Loire (Vendée) — 1453

Domaine Le Midi****
rue du Camping
+33 (0)2-51396374
1/4 - 18/9
midi@originalcamping.com

13ha 207**T**(80-200m²) 16A CEE

1 ACD**G**IJKLMOPST
2 ABEIRSVWXY
3 ABGHJKMNQRVW
4 (C+F+H) (Q+R+T+U+V+Z 1/7-31/8)
5 **AB**EFGIJKLMNOPUZ
6 CEGI**K**(N 0,5km)V

This lovely campsite in the dunes has direct access to the beach and has an indoor and an outdoor pool, tennis court and a multi-sports pitch. In the vicinity you will find many beautiful sandy beaches and cycle routes. In the region of Vendée there is plenty of history to see, for example you can visit castles and ancient fortresses.

Dir. Noirmoutier. Left on 3rd roundabout after bridge. Follow signs to 'Du Midi' campsite.

CC € 17 *1/4-1/7 28/8-17/9*

N 46°56'43" W 2°11'7"

Batz-sur-Mer, F-44740 / Pays de la Loire (Loire-Atlantique) — 1454

Les Paludiers***
rue Nicolas Appert
+33 (0)2-40601728
FAX +33 (0)2-40601724
2/4 - 1/10
paludiers@flowercampings.com

8ha 120**T**(80-100m²) 10A CEE

1 ACD**G**IJKLMO**P**RS
2 AEGQRSVWXY
3 B**F**GHJKN**Q**RUWY
4 (A 4/7-26/8) (C+G 1/5-18/9) (Q+S+T+U+V+X+Z)
5 **AB**DEFGJLMNOPQRUVW
6 ACDEGIK(N 1,5km)ORTV

Located on a neck of land about 500m wide on a headland, close to La Baule. Camping pitches separated by hedges and just 100m from a lovely sandy beach. Cycling to La Baule, St. Nazaire or Guerande is perfectly possible. A trip through salt marshes on car-free roads is possible.

Nantes-Lorient N165, via N171 dir. St. Nazaire. Then follow Guérande, before Guérande turn onto the D774 at roundabout to Le Croisic and Batz-sur-Mer, then turn left just past Batz village.

CC € 17 *2/4-1/7 1/9-1/10 7=6*

N 47°16'42" W 2°29'31"

Brain-sur-l'Authion, F-49800 / Pays de la Loire (Maine-et-Loire) — 1455

Du Port Caroline***
rue du Pont Caroline
FAX +33 (0)2-41804218
1/4 - 30/9
info@campingduportcaroline.fr

3,2ha 94**T**(110-200m²) 10A

1 AC**G**IJKLMPST
2 CFGRVWXY
3 ABGHJKRU**W**
4 (C+H 15/5-8/9) (Q+T 15/6-15/9)
5 **A**DEFIJKLMNPUVWZ
6 CEGJTV

Quiet campsite, 3 km from the Loire. Lovely pool. Located between Angers and Saumur. Many walking and cycling paths.

From Angers A87, exit 17, then follow signs.

CC € 15 *1/4-3/7 22/8-30/9 7=6, 14=11*

N 47°26'36" W 0°24'31"

Brem-sur-Mer, F-85470 / Pays de la Loire (Vendée) — 1456

L'Océan***
rue des Gabelous
+33 (0)2-51905916
2/4 - 6/11
contact@campingdelocean.fr

7ha 97**T**(90-120m²) 6A

1 AC**G**IJKLMPQ
2 ARSVX
3 BGHJKNRU**V**W
4 (C+F+H) J**P**
(Q+S+T+U+V+X+Z)
5 **AB**EFGIJKLMNOPUVWXZ
6 EG**K**TV

A large, welcoming family campsite, close to the sea. There is a water park of 1000 m² with slides, wellness and a toddler's pool on the campsite. Many activities in the surroundings such a local markets and a climbing park.

Via D38 from Bretignolles-sur-Mer follow road to Les Sables d'Olonne. In Brem-sur-Mer follow signs.

CC € 15 *2/4-2/7 20/8-6/11 14=11*

N 46°36'4'' W 1°50'39''

Brem-sur-Mer, F-85470 / Pays de la Loire (Vendée) — 1457

Le Chaponnet****
16 rue du Chaponnet
+33 (0)2-51905556
FAX +33 (0)2-51909167
2/4 - 30/9
contact@le-chaponnet.com

6ha 90**T**(100-120m²) 10A CEE

1 ACD**F**IJKLMOPS
2 AGRSVWXY
3 ABGHJKMNRUVW
4 (C 1/5-15/9) (F)
(H 1/5-15/9) JK**NP**
(Q 1/7-31/7)
(T+U+V+X 1/6-31/8) (Z)
5 **AB**EFGIJKLMNOPUZ
6 ACEGI**K**(N 0,2km)TV

An attractive well equipped campsite with an international flavour. Lovely swimming pool (also indoors), excellent restaurant and a favourable position by the ocean. This campsite is most pleasant throughout the season.

D38 from St. Gilles direction Brem, then the one-way street on the right.

CC € 19 *2/4-8/7 27/8-29/9*

N 46°36'15'' W 1°49'57''

Brétignolles-sur-Mer, F-85470 / Pays de la Loire (Vendée) — 1458

La Trévillière****
rue de Bellevue
+33 (0)2-51330505
FAX +33 (0)2-51339404
2/4 - 24/9
info@chadotel.com

3,2ha 69**T**(100-130m²) 10A CEE

1 ACD**F**IJKLMOPQ
2 RTVXY
3 BGHJKN**Q**RU
4 (C+E+G 1/5-15/9) J
(Q 15/5-15/9) (R 1/6-15/9)
(T+U+V+X+Y 17/5-15/9)
(Z)
5 **AB**EFGIJKLMNOPUWYZ
6 ACEG**K**(N 1km)ORTV

A modestly sized campsite with shaded pitches on the edge of the village.

From St. Gilles-Croix-de-Vie take the D38 in the direction of Brétignolles. Overhead camping sign on bend after 8 km, indicating left.

CC € 13 *2/4-9/7 27/8-24/9*

N 46°38'10'' W 1°51'30''

Brissac-Quincé, F-49320 / Pays de la Loire (Maine-et-Loire) 1459

Sites & Paysages de l'Etang****
route de St. Mathurin
+33 (0)2-41917061
FAX +33 (0)2-41917265
23/4 - 11/9
@ info@campingetang.com

8ha 125**T**(120-150m²) 10A CEE

1 ACD**G**IJKLPRS
2 CDFLRTVX
3 ABFGJK**PQ**RUWZ
4 (C+F+G 15/5-13/9) (Q+S) (T+U 15/5-13/9) (X) Z
5 **AB**DEFGIJKLMNOPUWXYZ
6 CEG**K**(N 1km)OQRTV

Pleasantly sized campsite with spacious pitches, just right to find peace and quiet. The campsite offers a warm welcome to campers who are looking for a natural camping spot with the comfort necessary for an unforgettable stay in the Loire Valley. Plenty of amenities are available to you: wine tasting, free fishing lake, heated indoor pool, laundry room, sale of bread...

Take D761 at Brissac-Quincé direction St. Mathurin (D55). Follow signs. Parc de Loisirs.

CC € 17 *23/4-15/7 3/9-11/9*

N 47°21'34'' W 0°26'4''

Brûlon, F-72350 / Pays de la Loire (Sarthe) 1460

Le Septentrion***
chemin de Parcaigneau
+33 (0)2-43956896
FAX +33 (0)2-43926036
1/4 - 30/9
@ le.septentrion@orange.fr

2ha 75**T**(100-120m²) 10A CEE

1 ACFIJLPRS
2 ACDFLMRVWXY
3 BGHJ**MNQ**RU**WZ**
4 (E+G 1/6-30/9) (Q+R+T+U) (X 15/4-30/9) (Z)
5 **A**DEFGIJKLMNPRUZ
6 EG**JK**(N 0,8km)V

A three star campsite situated on the banks of a lake with extensive water recreation. Includes a heated pool, trampoline, tennis, pétanque, WiFi. The toilet facilities are heated, the campsite is peaceful. Eating out: bar and pizzeria/ice cream parlour.

A81 Le Mans-Rennes, exit 1 direction Brûlon, 5 km, follow the signs in the village.

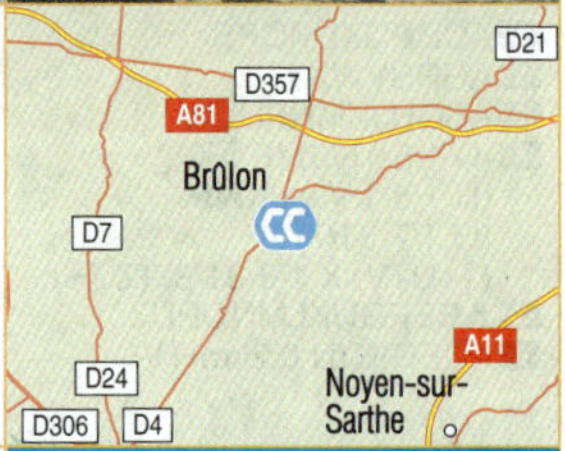

CC € 15 *1/4-7/7 24/8-30/9*

N 47°57'45'' W 0°13'40''

Chaillé-les-Marais, F-85450 / Pays de la Loire (Vendée) 1461

L'Île Cariot***
rue du 8 mai
+33 (0)2-51567527
1/4 - 30/9
@ camping.ilecariot@gmail.com

4,5ha 38**T**(70-120m²) 10A CEE

1 ACD**F**IJKLPRS
2 RVXY
3 AGHJKNRU
4 (C+H 15/6-15/9) (Q+R+T+X+Z)
5 **AB**DGIJKLMNOPUZ
6 CEGJ(N 0,2km)TV

A friendly campsite with spacious pitches in the countryside of the 'Vénise verte'. Explore the Marais Poitevin from the campsite in a canoe (free). All amenities. Bikes for hire.

From the D25, signposted in the village of Chaillé-les-Marais.

CC € 13 *1/4-9/7 26/8-30/9 7=6, 14=11*

N 46°23'31'' W 1°1'10''

Chalonnes-sur-Loire, F-49290 / Pays de la Loire (Maine-et-Loire)

1462

Les Portes de la Loire***
route de Rochefort
+33 (0)2-41780227
1/5 - 30/9
contact@
campinglesportesdelaloire.fr

3ha 203T(< 80m²) 10A CEE

1 BGIJKLRS
2 CRWXY
3 AJR
4 (Q)
5 **A**EFIJMNOPU
6 J(N 1km)

Located in natural surroundings on the banks of the Loire. Close to the cycle routes of La Loire à Vélo and an ideal base to visit the town of Tours. Close to the Loire castles and a wine route. Beautiful area for walking and cycling. Canoe and kayak rental next to the campsite.

From Angers via D751 to Chalonnes-sur Loire. Clearly signposted.

CC € 17 *1/5-30/6 1/9-30/9*

N 47°21'3'' W 0°44'57''

Chemillé, F-49120 / Pays de la Loire (Maine-et-Loire)

1463

de Coulvée***
chemin de Coulvée
+33 (0)2-41303997
FAX +33 (0)2-41303900
1/5 - 15/9
camping-chemille-49@
wanadoo.fr

5ha 40T(100-120m²) 10A CEE

1 AC**G**IJKLOPST
2 ACDFJLMRTVXY
3 BGHJKRU**W**XZ
4 (Q 1/7-31/8) Z
5 **A**GIJKLNPUWXYZ
6 CEGHIK(N 1km)TV

A small, well-kept, friendly campsite located by a reservoir with private patrolled beach on the edge of a charming village. Marked pitches separated by hedges and bushes. There are many facilities, shops and sights in the village. The region is especially suitable for cycle tours and trips out.

A87, exit 25. The campsite is located just outside Chemillé on the N160 in the direction of Cholet. Signposted.

CC € 13 *1/5-2/7 24/8-14/9 7=6, 14=11*

N 47°12'8'' W 0°44'5''

Coëx, F-85220 / Pays de la Loire (Vendée)

1464

RCN La Ferme du Latois****
D40
+33 (0)2-51546730
FAX +33 (0)2-51600214
23/4 - 17/9
ferme@rcn.fr

21ha 176T(110-250m²) 10A CEE

1 ACFIJKLMOPQ
2 DLRVWXY
3 AB**F**GHJKN**P**RUW
4 (A 1/6-31/8) (C+H) J
(Q+S+T+U+V+X+Y+Z)
5 **AB**EFGIJKLMNOPRUWZ
6 ACEGH**KL**(N 1,5km)OTV

A lovely farm campsite with very varied vegetation and a pond. Large pitches and lovely fields with ample privacy.

Coëx, take the D40 in the direction of Brétignolles-sur-Mer. Signposted.

CC € 15 *23/4-9/7 26/8-17/9*

N 46°40'36'' W 1°46'8''

Damvix, F-85420 / Pays de la Loire (Vendée) 1465

Camping des Conches***
route du Grand Port
+33 (0)2-51871706
1/4 - 15/10
campingdesconches@orange.fr

7ha 72**T**(80-120m²) 10A CEE

1 ACD**G**IJKLMPQ
2 CLRVXY
3 BGHIJMR**W**
4 (C 15/5-15/9) (T+U+Z)
5 **A**FGHIJKLMNOPUVZ
6 ACEG**K**L(N 0,3km)T

A friendly campsite, quietly located in 'Marais de Poitevin' in the peaceful village of Damvix. Ideal for cycling and trips out in the surrounding area.

From Fontenay-le-Comte direction Niort. Then direction Maillezais, then to Damvix. Campsite signposted in Damvix village.

CC € 13 *1/4-30/6 1/9-15/10*

N 46°18'46" W 0°43'57"

Durtal, F-49430 / Pays de la Loire (Maine-et-Loire) 1466

Les Portes de l'Anjou***
9 rue du Camping
+33 (0)2-41763180
25/3 - 14/10
contact.camping@lesportesdel'anjou.com

3ha 91**T**(80-120m²) 10A CEE

1 AC**F**IJLPRS
2 CFGLRTVWXY
3 BGHJNRU**W**
4 (C+H+Q 1/7-31/8) (R) (T+U+V 1/6-15/9) (Z)
5 **AB**FGIJKLMNPUWZ
6 CEG**K**(N 0,5km)RV

Small campsite along the Loir and the GR 35. Close to the centre. Shaded pitches marked out by hedges and trees. Beautiful countryside and architectural heritage are there to be discovered from the campsite. New and heated toilet facilities. A paradise for anglers: Fishing directly next to the campsite.

When entering the city (from the A11, exit 11, Durtal), follow the camping signs. The campsite is located south of the town centre on the Loir.

CC € 15 *25/3-8/7 26/8-14/10 7=6*

N 47°40'16" W 0°14'9"

Givrand/St.Gilles-Croix-de-Vie, F-85800 / Pays de la Loire (Vendée) 1467

Le Domaine de Beaulieu****
rue du Parc - Givrand
+33 (0)2-51330505
FAX +33 (0)2-51339404
2/4 - 24/9
info@chadotel.com

8ha 127**T**(100-125m²) 6A CEE

1 AC**G**IJKLMOPRS
2 GRTVWX
3 B**F**GHJK**MNQ**RU**W**
4 (C 10/5-20/9) (F 13/4-20/9) (H 10/5-20/9) J (Q 15/6-31/8) (S+T+U+V+X+Y 1/6-10/9) (Z)
5 **AB**FGIJKLMNOPUZ
6 AEGH**IJK**(N 3km)ORTV

Good campsite on fine, green, maintained level grounds. The swimming pool and restaurant are the main features of this peaceful campsite.

From St. Gilles-Croix-de-Vie: D38 direction Les Sables-d'Olonne. Located to the left after 3 km.

CC € 13 *2/4-9/7 27/8-24/9*

N 46°40'16" W 1°54'13"

Guémené-Penfao, F-44290 / Pays de la Loire (Loire-Atlantique)

iD 1468

L'Hermitage***
46 avenue de Paradis
+33 (0)2-40792348
FAX +33 (0)2-40511187
1/4 - 31/10
@ camping.hermitage@orange.fr

2,8ha 80T(36-70m²) 6A CEE

1 AGIJKLPRS
2 BGRTVXY
3 AGJMNRUW
4 (C 15/6-20/9) (H 1/7-20/9) J (R+T+U 1/7-31/8)
5 AGIJKLMNPUZ
6 CEGJ(N 0,8km)OV

A pleasant and informal campsite in natural surroundings with three rivers.

Redon-Châteaubriant, exit Guémené-Penfao. Campsite signposted.

CC € 15 1/4-9/7 27/8-31/10 7=6

N 47°37'33'' W 1°49'8''

Guérande, F-44350 / Pays de la Loire (Loire-Atlantique)

iD 1469

Camping La Fontaine***
rte de Saint Molf -D233 - Kersavary
+33 (0)2-40249619
2/4 - 15/10
@ lafontaine.guerande@orange.fr

2,5ha 80T(100-150m²) 10A CEE

1 ACDGIJKLMOPQ
2 FGQRVWXY
3 AGHJR
4 (C+H 15/6-15/9) (Q+T+U 1/7-31/8)
5 ABEFGIJKLMNOPQRUXYZ
6 AEK(N 2km)OT

A campsite in the countryside, close to the historic Guérande. Pitches min. 100 m², in the sun or half-shaded. Comfortable, modern toilet facilities but not sheltered from the wind, heated swimming pools 100 m². Well located for visits to Guérande and nearby salt marshes.

Nantes E60 and N171 direction St. Nazaire, N171 direction Guérande. Then past several roundabouts to Vannes, then D233 direction St. Molf, camping signs after 500m.

CC € 13 16/4-8/7 27/8-14/10

N 47°20'57'' W 2°26'3''

Guérande, F-44350 / Pays de la Loire (Loire-Atlantique)

iD 1470

Domaine de Léveno****
Lieu dit Léveno
+33 (0)2-40247930
FAX +33 (0)2-40620123
9/4 - 25/9
@ domaine.leveno@wanadoo.fr

10ha 78T(100-250m²) 10A

1 ACDGIJKLMPR
2 BFQRVWXY
3 BCFGHJKMNQRUV
4 (C 14/5-18/9) (E+H) IJLM (Q+S+T+U+V+X+Y+Z)
5 ABDEFGIJKLMNOPQRST UVXYZ
6 ACEGIJK(N 1,8km)OTV

Large luxury campsite, pitches around toilet block with indian tents, separated from mobile homes by trees and bushes. Well located for visiting medieval Guerande and the salt marshes. Cycle and walking routes near the site. Shops and hypermarket 1800m.

N165 Nantes-Lorient. Exit La Roche-Bernard. Direction Guérande/La Baule via the D774. At the roundabout (near Guérande) with Super Leclerc supermarket follow the signs. Site is located 1 km behind the supermarket.

CC € 17 9/4-2/7 29/8-24/9 7=6, 14=12

N 47°20'0'' W 2°23'26''

Guérande, F-44350 / Pays de la Loire (Loire-Atlantique) 1471

Le Domaine de Bréhadour****
route du Bréhadour
+33 (0)2-40176515
25/3 - 25/9
camping@
domainedebrehadour.com

8ha 124**T**(100-150m²) 10A CEE

1 ACD**F**IJKLMOPST
2 BFIQRVWXY
3 BD**E**GHJLM**OP**RV
4 (E+H) J(Q)
(R 8/7-28/8)
(T+U+V+X+Z)
5 **AB**FGIJKLMNOPUW
6 EG**K**(N 1,5km)OTV

Good, comfortable campsite with a number of sheltered pitches between trees and hedges, a number of other pitches with are more open and have more sun, close to the medieval town of Guérande. About 10 minutes from the beaches of La Turballe or the more crowded La Baule by car.

Nantes-Vannes via N165/E60 exit Guérande/La Baule, at roundabout near Guérande follow signs Bréhadour.

CC € 15 *1/4-1/7 27/8-25/9*

N 47°20'32'' W 2°25'4''

Guérande/Sandun, F-44350 / Pays de la Loire (Loire-Atlantique) 1472

De L'Etang du Pays Blanc***
47 rue des Chênes
+33 (0)2-40619351
1/1 - 31/12
camping-etang@orange.fr

2ha 42**T**(90-120m²) 10A CEE

1 ACD**G**IJKLMOPRS
2 DFGQRVWXY
3 BD**F**GHJK**O**RUV**W**
4 (A 2/7-24/8)
(E+H 26/3-1/11) **KN**
(Q 2/7-24/8) (R)
(T+U+V+Z 2/7-24/8)
5 **AB**FGIJKLPU
6 CDEGHI**K**(N 1,5km)OTV

Peacefully located site close to natural park Le Brière, at 20 minutes from the sophisticated La Boule. The site is planning completely renovated, modern and comfortable toilet facilities and comfort pitches for early 2016. Indoor pool opened and heated from Easter weekend.

N165/E60 Vannes-Nantes, exit Guérande/La Baule. Via D774 to Herbignac via the D47 direction St. Lyphard. Direction St. Nazaire as far as Sandun. Turn right and follow the signs to the campsite.

CC € 15 *1/1-30/6 1/9-31/12*

N 47°20'46'' W 2°20'47''

Héric, F-44810 / Pays de la Loire (Loire-Atlantique) 1473

La Pindière***
La Denais
+33 (0)2-40576541
1/1 - 31/12
contact@
camping-la-pindiere.com

3ha 51**T** 6-10A CEE

1 ABC**G**IJKLMOPR
2 FLRUVX
3 ABGIJR
4 (E+H 1/4-30/9) (Q 1/7-31/8)
(X+Y)
5 **AB**DFGJLNPRUWXYZ
6 DG**I**J(N 0,500km)OR

A friendly campsite with a relaxing atmosphere, heated indoor pool and a 3 hectare garden. The campsite offers space and marked out pitches. Ideally located between Rennes and Nantes and open all year. Close to the Nantes to Brest canal. Explore the Loire Atlantique and its lovely sandy beaches.

From the Nantes/Rennes dual carriageway in Héric continue towards Fay de Bretagne and turn left 500m after the Super 4 petrol station.

CC € 15 *1/1-8/7 25/8-31/12 7=6, 14=12*

N 47°24'48'' W 1°40'14''

Jard-sur-Mer, F-85520 / Pays de la Loire (Vendée) — 1474

L'Oceano d'Or*****
84 rue Georges Clémenceau
+33 (0)2-51330505
FAX +33 (0)2-51339404
2/4 - 24/9
info@chadotel.com

8ha 200T(100m²) 10A

1 ACD**F**IJKLMOPRS
2 AGRTVWXY
3 BGK**M**NRUV
4 (C 15/5-15/9) (E+H) J (Q+S+T+U+V 15/5-15/9) Z
5 **AB**EFGIJKLMNOPUZ
6 CEGI**K**(N 0,4km)RTUV

A family campsite on the edge of the village with spacious pitches separated by hedges and a lovely swimming pool.

When leaving Jard-sur-Mer, located to the right of the road direction La Tranche on the D21.

CC € 17 *2/4-2/7 27/8-24/9*

N 46°25'15'' W 1°34'10''

Jard-sur-Mer, F-85520 / Pays de la Loire (Vendée) — 1475

La Ventouse***
18bis rue Pierre Curie
+33 (0)2-51335865
FAX +33 (0)2-51330369
2/4 - 30/9
campings.parfums.ete@wanadoo.fr

5,5ha 134T(80-100m²) 10A

1 ACD**F**IJKLPS
2 BEGIJRSXY
3 BGKNR
4 (C+H 15/5-30/9) (Q 1/5-28/9) (R 1/5-27/9) (T 1/7-30/8) Z
5 **AB**FGIJKLMNPUVZ
6 CEGJ**K**(N 0,5km)RT

The charm of bush-camping on a campsite. Lovely location in a forest at walking distance from the sea and the touristic Jard-sur-Mer. Basic but good amenities.

In Jard-sur-Mer follow signs 'campings' and then signs 'Parfums d'Eté'.

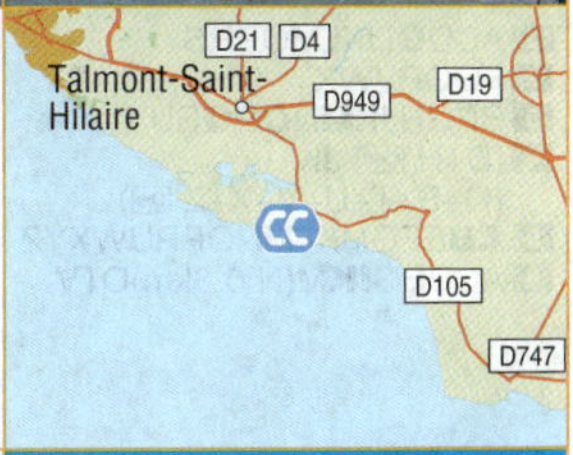

CC € 15 *2/4-6/7 25/8-30/9*

N 46°24'45'' W 1°34'53''

L'Épine, F-85740 / Pays de la Loire (Vendée) — 1476

Camping de la Bosse**
rue du Port
+33 (0)2-53469747
1/4 - 18/9
labosse@originalcamping.com

10,5ha 259T(60-150m²) 4A CEE

1 ACD**G**IJKLOP
2 ABEJKORSTWX
3 BGHJRWY
5 **AB**GJLNPUVZ
6 AEG(N 2km)T

In a beautiful setting, this modest campsite for your holiday in the countryside is located between marshland, woods, the sea and the beach. Pitches in the sun or shade.

Follow L'Épine signs on Noirmoutier headland. Then follow road to stop sign at harbour (Port du Morin). Then left. Campsite is 1 km on the right.

CC € 13 *1/4-1/7 28/8-17/9*

N 46°59'7'' W 2°17'0''

La Barre-de-Monts, F-85550 / Pays de la Loire (Vendée)

iD **1477**

Campéole La Grande Côte***
route de la Grande Côte
+33 (0)2-51685189
FAX +33 (0)2-51492557
29/4 - 18/9
@ grande-cote@andretriganogroupe.com

22ha 481**T**(80-120m²) 10A CEE

1 ACD**G**IJKLMO**P**ST
2 ABEIJSWXY
3 ABCHJKNRUWY
4 (C+H 15/6-20/9)
(Q+S+T+U+V 1/7-31/8) Z
5 **AB**EFGIJLMNOPUVZ
6 ACFGH**K**L(N 1km)ORV

A typical dune campsite in the middle of the countryside, with direct access to the beach. Relatively level pitches. The village of Fromentine is within walking distance.

From Nantes continue towards Noirmoutier as far as La Barre-de-Monts. Then take the Route de la Grande Côte. Follow campsite signs.

CC € 17 *1/5-4/7 22/8-18/9*

N 46°53'8'' W 2°8'51''

La Baule, F-44500 / Pays de la Loire (Loire-Atlantique)

iD **1478**

La Roseraie****
20 avenue Jean Sohier
+33 (0)2-40604666
FAX +33 (0)2-40601184
2/4 - 25/9
@ camping@laroseraie.com

5ha 50**T**(90-120m²) 10A

1 ACD**G**IJKLMOPRS
2 FGQRVWX
3 B**F**GHJK**M**N**OPQ**RUV
4 (D+H) JK
(Q+S+T+U+V+X+Z)
5 **AB**EFGIJKLMNOPRUWXYZ
6 ACDEG**IK**M(N 0,3km)OTV

A luxurious family campsite near La Baule. The site has an indoor swimming pool that can be opened up in hot weather. 2 km from one of France's most beautiful golf courses. Cycling along the beach and on cycle paths and roads with no traffic is recommended.

Between Guérande and St. Nazaire, via the N171 to La Baule Escoublac Golf de La Baule exit. On to Escoublac. At roundabout drive to village as far as the church, then Golf de La Baule, immediate right over the bridge.

CC € 17 *2/4-8/7 29/8-24/9 7=6, 14=11*

N 47°17'54'' W 2°21'27''

La Bernerie-en-Retz, F-44760 / Pays de la Loire (Loire-Atlantique)

iD **1479**

Les Écureuils****
24 ave Gilbert Burlot
+33 (0)2-40827695
FAX +33 (0)2-40647952
4/4 - 17/9
@ camping.les-ecureuils@wanadoo.fr

5,5ha 164**T**(80-110m²) 10A

1 ACD**G**IJKLMOPS
2 AEFGQRVWXY
3 B**F**GHJKLMNRWY
4 (C+H 5/5-17/9) IJM
(Q+T+U+V 1/7-31/8)
(Z 5/5-31/8)
5 **AB**EFGIJKLMNOPUVWXYZ
6 ACEGIJ**K**(N 0,45km)ORTV

350m from the sea and the centre of La Bernerie-en-Retz. A beautiful sandy beach and cycle routes. New toilet facilities. GB/D/NL/FR spoken at the reception during the whole opening period. Pets maximum 10 kg allowed on camping pitches. Attractive village with a lovely beach.

Ring road Nantes-West, exit Noirmoutier/Pornic via D13 dir. Noirmoutier. Exit La Bernerie-en-Retz dir. centre. After 400 metres (50 metres before the railway line) right, then immediately left.

CC € 17 *4/4-5/7 27/8-16/9*

N 47°5'3'' W 2°2'14''

La Chapelle-Hermier, F-85220 / Pays de la Loire (Vendée) 1480

Le Pin Parasol*****
Châteaulong
+33 (0)2-51346472
FAX +33 (0)2-51346462
22/4 - 25/9
@ contact@campingpinparasol.fr

12ha 230T(150-250m²) 10A CEE

1 ACD**G**IJKLMOPQ
2 ADJKMRVWX
3 B**F**GHIJKL**M**N**P**RUV**W**
4 (A 9/6-31/8) (C 1/6-25/9) (F) (H 1/6-25/9) IJKLM (Q+R) (T+U+V 1/6-31/8) (Z)
5 **AB**DEFGJLOPQRUWXY
6 ABCDEGH**IK**(N 4km)ORTV

A beautifully located campsite with excellent toilet facilities. Superb water recreation for children, and internet throughout the site. A lovely terrace with extraordinary views. A campsite for the camper who appreciates the French countryside!

From St. Gilles-Croix-de-Vie take the D6 in the direction of Coëx. Follow the road as far as the D21. Turn right. The campsite is signposted on the right after 2.5 km.

CC € 17 22/4-7/7 1/9-25/9 — N 46°39'56'' W 1°45'21''

La Chartre-sur-le-Loir, F-72340 / Pays de la Loire (Sarthe) 1481

Camping du Vieux Moulin***
chemin des Bergivaux
+33 (0)2-43444118
1/3 - 30/11
@ campingduvieuxmoulin72@gmail.com

2,5ha 82T(80-120m²) 10A CEE

1 A**G**IJKLMPQ
2 CDGLMRVWXY
3 ABGHJKNRU**W**
4 (C+H 15/6-15/9) (Q 1/7-31/8) (R 1/7-30/8) (T 1/7-31/8) (U) (V+X+Z 1/7-30/8)
5 **AB**FGIJKLMNPUWZ
6 CDEG**K**(N 0,5km)TV

On the banks of the Loir. Plenty of options for cycling, walking, fishing and just enjoying the peace and the open air.

Via D305. Dir. Poncé after centre. Left immediately after bridge. Well signposted.

CC € 17 27/3-30/6 1/9-30/11 — N 47°43'58'' E 0°34'17''

La Flèche, F-72200 / Pays de la Loire (Sarthe) 1482

Camping Municipal de la Route d'Or***
allée du Camping
+33 (0)2-43945590
1/3 - 31/10
@ info@camping-laroutedor.com

4ha 190T(80-100m²) 10A CEE

1 ACD**G**IJKLMPQ
2 CRUVXY
3 BG**M**NR**W**
4 (C 15/6-15/9) (Q 1/7-31/8)
5 **AB**DFGIJKLMNOPUVYZ
6 CDEGJ(N 0,5km)QV

Ideal location in the heart of town but still in the green, on the banks of the Loir. Spacious pitches, everything is available for your dream holiday! Cycle routes, canoe/kayak, recreation, archery... See you soon!

The campsite is clearly signposted in the village and is located at the river.

CC € 13 1/3-8/7 28/8-31/10 7=6 — N 47°41'42'' W 0°4'46''

La Plaine-sur-Mer, F-44770 / Pays de la Loire (Loire-Atlantique)

1483

La Guichardière***
2 rue de Mouton
+33 (0)2-40215509
FAX +33 (0)2-40215550
16/4 - 25/9
@ contact@camping-laguichardiere.net

5ha 50**T**(90-120m²) 10A CEE

1 ACD**G**IJKLMOPRS
2 AEFQRVWXY
3 B**F**GHJKMN**P**RWY
4 (C+H) M
(Q+R+T+U+V+Z)
5 **AB**FGIJKLMNOPQUXYZ
6 CEGJ(N 1,5km)OTV

Family campsite on the coast, plenty of greenery for shade and flowers, walking and cycling along the sea which is 300 metres away, or on the marked routes in the lightly undulating interior. Beach at 400 metres.

From D213 St. Nazaire-Pornic to exit La Plaine s/Mer. Then via D96 past Tharon Plage, and via D96 to Port de Gravette. Follow signs.

CC € 15 *16/4-10/7 27/8-24/9 7=6, 14=12*

N 47°9'8'' W 2°12'30''

La Plaine-sur-Mer, F-44770 / Pays de la Loire (Loire-Atlantique)

1484

La Tabardière****
2 rte d.l. Tabardière
+33 (0)2-40215883
FAX +33 (0)2-40210268
2/4 - 24/9
@ info@camping-la-tabardiere.com

6ha 155**T**(90-110m²) 10A CEE

1 ACD**G**IJKLMOPRS
2 FIJQRVWXY
3 B**F**GHJKMN**OP**QRUV
4 (C 1/5-15/9)
(D+H 15/4-24/9) J(Q)
(S 1/6-3/9)
(T+U+V 1/7-31/8)
(Z 1/6-3/9)
5 **AB**EFGIJKLMNOPQUVWZ
6 ACDEGIK(N 3km)OTUV

A pleasant and peaceful campsite with well maintained toilet facilities. There is choice of pitches either on the level terraces or large open pitches higher up the campsite. The swimming pool always heated to 28°C.

D213 St. Nazaire-Pornic, take the exit La Plaine-sur-Mer/Pornic-Ouest. Subsequently, take the D13 towards La Plaine-sur-Mer until you see the signs to the campsite.

CC € 15 *2/4-8/7 25/8-23/9 7=6, 14=11, 21=17*

N 47°8'27'' W 2°9'12''

La Plaine-sur-Mer, F-44770 / Pays de la Loire (Loire-Atlantique)

1485

Le Ranch***
chemin des Hautes Raillères
+33 (0)2-40215262
1/4 - 30/9
@ info@camping-le-ranch.com

3,5ha 83**T**(90-100m²) 10A

1 ACD**G**IJKLMOPRS
2 AFQRVWXY
3 B**F**GHJKMN**P**RU
4 (A 2/7-27/8) (C 1/5-10/9)
(H 1/5-30/9) J
(Q+R+T+U+V+Z 2/7-27/8)
5 **AB**EFGIJKLMNPRUWZ
6 CEGI**J**(N 3km)OTV

Quiet, well maintained campsite with pitches between hedges and shade-giving trees. 800 metres from the beach. 2016 project: new open-air and covered swimming pools. Bread available at weekends on request outside high season. Free WiFi point outside high season.

South of St. Nazaire via D219, La Route Bleu, exit La Plaine-sur-Mer and Tharon-Plage. Via D96 to La Plaine-sur-Mer and follow camping signs. (SatNav unreliable in immediate vicinity.)

CC € 17 *1/4-8/7 25/8-29/9 14=13*

N 47°9'17'' W 2°9'55''

La Tranche-sur-Mer, F-85360 / Pays de la Loire (Vendée) 1486

Du Jard GC****
123 bd Mar. de Lattre de Tassigny
+33 (0)2-51274379
FAX +33 (0)2-51274292
7/5 - 10/9
info@campingdujard.fr

6ha 180T(100-120m²) 10A CEE

1 ACEIJKLMOPRS
2 ARVX
3 BGHK**M**N**Q**RUVW
4 (C 11/6-10/9) (F)
(H 11/6-10/9) JKN(Q)
(S+T+U+V+X+Y 2/7-27/8)
5 **AB**EFGIJKLMNOPQUWZ
6 EGIJ(N 1km)RTV

Very good family campsite in the village with spacious pitches separated by hedges. Indoor and giant outdoor swimming pool. Plenty of sports opportunities. Lovely beach within walking distance.

From La Roche-sur-Yon take the D747 to La Tranche. Follow the signs Grière-Plage, and then follow the camping signs.

CC € 17 *7/5-13/7 30/8-10/9* *7=6, 14=12, 21=17* N 46°20'52" W 1°23'13"

La Tranche-sur-Mer, F-85360 / Pays de la Loire (Vendée) 1487

La Grande Vallée**
145 blvd de Lattre de Tassigny
FAX +33 (0)2-51301282
1/4 - 30/9
c.lagrandevallee@orange.fr

1ha 52T(80-140m²) 10A CEE

1 ACDFIJKLM**PQ**
2 GRWXY
3 BGKR
4 (Q 15/4-15/9)
(T+V+Z 1/5-15/9)
5 **AB**FGIJKLMNPUZ
6 ACEGJ**K**RT

A small, congenial campsite within walking distance of the sea and a beautiful sandy beach. Good cycling options (Vélodyssée). All basic facilities provided and a free WiFi point at the bar.

From La Roche-sur-Yon D747 to La Tranche. Follow La Grière-Plage signs, signposted further.

CC € 13 *1/4-10/7 27/8-30/9* *7=6, 14=12, 21=18* N 46°20'52" W 1°22'59"

La Turballe, F-44420 / Pays de la Loire (Loire-Atlantique) 1488

La Falaise****
1 boulevard de Belmont
+33 (0)2-40233253
25/3 - 29/10
info@camping-de-la-falaise.com

3ha 63T(100-130m²) 10A CEE

1 ACD**G**IJKLMOPQ
2 AEFGKQRSVWXY
3 AC**F**GHJK**M**NWY
4 (E+H+Q+T+U+Z)
5 **ABC**DEFGHIJKLOPQRUW
X
6 ABCDEGK(N 0,4km)OTW

Campsite close to beach with panoramic views of the sea. Luxury new heated toilet facilities. Indoor pool heated to 28 °C. Pitches divided by hedges. Located on edge of the village, 400 metres from a supermarket. 10 pitches with sea views. For a nice pitch in May and June please book.

N165/E60 Vannes-Nantes, exit Guérande/ La Baule. Via D774 as far as Guérande, via D99 to La Turballe, follow camping signs or Super U on the D99 when entering the village.

CC € 17 *25/3-2/7 28/8-29/10* N 47°21'13" W 2°31'4"

Le Château-d'Olonne, F-85180 / Pays de la Loire (Vendée)

1489

Le Petit Paris****
41 rue du Petit Versailles
+33 (0)2-51220444
FAX +33 (0)2-51331704
27/3 - 30/9
@ contact@campingpetitparis.com

3ha 55T(80-130m²) 10A CEE

1 ACDFIJKLOPQ
2 GRVWXY
3 AB**F**GJKNRU
4 (E+H 9/4-30/9) J(Q+R) (T+U 1/7-30/8) Z
5 **AB**EFGIJKLMNPUX
6 AEG**JK**(N 3km)TV

A pleasant child friendly family campsite between the ocean and the countryside. 5 minutes from the fine sandy beaches of Les Sables d'Olonne. Spacious separated pitches. Heated indoor swimming pool. Good basic amenities.

From Les Sables-d'Olonne follow D949 towards Talmont-St. Hilaire. Straight on at traffic lights. Follow camping signs.

CC € 15 *1/4-8/7 25/8-29/9 7=6, 14=12*

N 46°28'25" W 1°43'16"

Le Château-d'Olonne, F-85180 / Pays de la Loire (Vendée)

1490

Le Puits Rochais****
25 rue de Bourdigal
+33 (0)2-51210969
FAX +33 (0)2-51236220
11/4 - 30/9
@ info@puitsrochais.com

3,5ha 60T(100m²) 10A CEE

1 ACD**F**IJKLPS
2 AGRTVX
3 B**F**GJK**M**N**P**RU
4 (C+H 1/5-30/9) J (Q+S+T+U+V+W+Z 15/6-10/9)
5 **AB**DEFGIJKLMNOPUWX
6 ACEGJ**K**(N 0,6km)RTV

Good campsite on the outskirts of the village. Lovely swimming pool and clearly separated, shady pitches. Les Sables-d'Olonne is well worth a visit. The motor museum and amusement park Puy du Fou are also close by. La Rochelle is about one hour away by car.

Take the D949 from Talmont-St-Hilaire to Les Sables. Turn left at the first traffic lights in Le Château-d'Olonne.

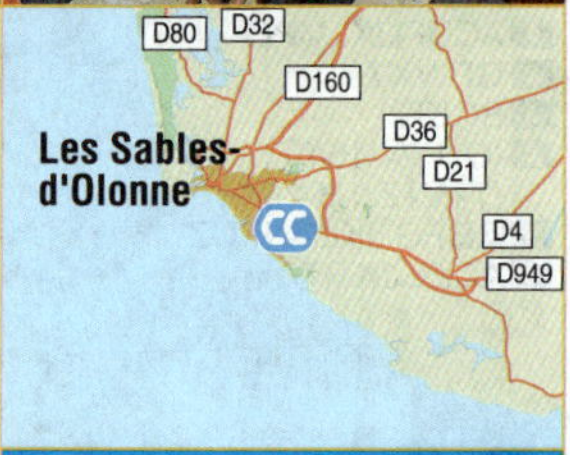

CC € 15 *11/4-12/7 29/8-29/9 7=6, 14=12*

N 46°28'53" W 1°43'53"

Le Château-d'Olonne, F-85180 / Pays de la Loire (Vendée)

1491

Les Fosses Rouges
8 rue des Fosses Rouges
+33 (0)2-51951795
4/4 - 24/9
@ info@camping-lesfossesrouges.com

3,5ha 168T(75-120m²) 10A

1 ACD**G**IJKLMOPQ
2 GRVXY
3 ABGK**MQ**R
4 (E+H+Q) (R+S 8/5-22/9) (U+Z 1/7-31/8)
5 **AB**FGIJKLMNPU
6 ACEGJ(N 1km)OTV

Friendly family campsite close to the fine sandy beaches of Les Sables-d'Olonnes. Indoor swimming pool, bar and entertainment room. Ideal as base for walking and cycling trips. Free WiFi.

From Talmont-St-Hilaire take the D949 direction Les Sables. Follow signs to the left at first traffic lights 7 km further on.

CC € 15 *4/4-9/7 26/8-24/9*

N 46°28'46" W 1°44'28"

Le Croisic, F-44490 / Pays de la Loire (Loire-Atlantique)

1492

de l'Océan Village et Spa*****
route de la Maison Rouge
+33 (0)2-40230769
FAX +33 (0)2-40157063
9/4 - 25/9
@ camping-ocean@wanadoo.fr

7,5ha 60**T**(90-120m²) 10A

1 ACD**G**IJKLMPQ
2 AEFGOQRVWXY
3 BC**E**GHJK**M**N**OP**RUVWY
4 (C 14/5-25/9) (F+H) IJ**K** **LMNP** (Q+S+T+U+V+Y+Z)
5 **AB**DEFGIJKLMNOPQRUWXYZ
6 ACEGIJ**K**(N 1km)OTV

A campsite close to Le Croisic with an outdoor leisure pool and super deluxe indoor pool with wellness centre. Highly recommended! The small town with its attractive harbour is within walking distance. Salt marshes between the headland and the village of Guérande. Just 800m from a supermarket.

N165-E60 to Nantes, and the N171 to Guérande. Before Guérande head towards Le Croisic (D774) at the roundabout. Just before the centre of Le Croisic follow the signs.

CC € 19 *9/4-2/7 28/8-24/9 15=14*

N 47°17'51" W 2°32'7"

Le Givre, F-85540 / Pays de la Loire (Vendée)

1493

La Grisse***
+33 (0)2-51308303
1/1 - 31/12
@ info@campinglagrisse.com

2,4ha 31**T**(120-350m²) 16A CEE

1 ACD**F**IJKLMOPQ
2 RTVXY
3 ABGKR
4 (Q+R 1/7-31/8)
5 **AB**FGJLMNOPUWXYZ
6 AEK(N 6km)

A lovely friendly campsite open all year, ten minutes from the beaches at La Tranche sur Mer. A spectacular natural setting with large shaded pitches. Free WiFi throughout the grounds. Plenty of footpaths from the campsite. A good base for trips out to the Vendée. You will find relaxation, space and comfort at Camping La Grisse.

From Moutiers to La Tranche via the D747. Left about 1 km past the D949 intersection. Campsite clearly signposted.

CC € 13 *1/1-10/7 27/8-31/12*

N 46°26'41" W 1°23'53"

Les Epesses, F-85590 / Pays de la Loire (Vendée)

1494

La Bretèche***
Base de Loisirs de Bretèche
+33 (0)2-51573334
FAX +33 (0)2-51574198
1/4 - 30/9
@ contact@campinglabreteche.com

3,5ha 122**T**(80-110m²) 10A CEE

1 ACD**G**IJKLMOPST
2 DFLRVWXY
3 ABGHJMRU**W**
4 (A 1/7-31/8) (C+H 1/5-5/9) (Q 15/4-15/9) (T+U+X+Z 1/7-31/8)
5 **AB**FGIJKLMNPUWZ
6 ACEGHJL(N 1km)RTV

A well run campsite situated by a lake and a stone's throw from the Puy du Fou theme park. The site has many sports and recreational amenities and is a good base for many excursions in the region. The pitches are spacious, as is the 300 m² heated swimming pool.

Campsite signposted in Les Epesses.

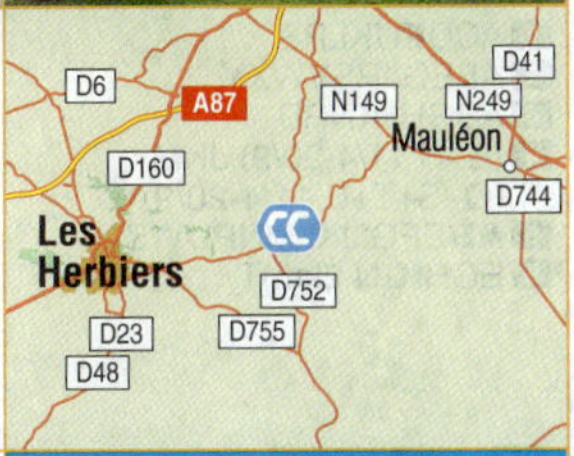

CC € 17 *1/4-3/7 22/8-30/9 7=6, 14=11*

N 46°53'23" W 0°53'57"

Les Moutiers-en-Retz, F-44760 / Pays de la Loire (Loire-Atlantique) — 1495

Les Brillas***
Le Bois des Tréans
+33 (0)2-40827978
FAX +33 (0)2-40647960
1/4 - 30/10
info@campinglesbrillas.com

4,5ha 53**T**(82-278m²) 10A

1 ACD**G**IJKLMOPRS
2 AFGKLQRVWXY
3 BD**F**GHJRUW
4 (C+H 1/5-25/9) (Q)
(R 2/7-28/8)
(T+U+V+X+Z 1/5-25/9)
5 **AB**FGIJKLMNOPUWXYZ
6 ACEGK(N 1km)TV

A campsite with a choice of pitches between hedges or on an open field. Well maintained toilets. All amenities open from the beginning of May. Peaceful and close to a small town and the sea with its unusual coastline. A centre for farming oysters and mussels. All amenities are definitely open at weekends out of season.

From ring Nantes-West, exit Noirmoutier/Pornic, continue towards Noirmoutier/Pornic as far as Les Moutiers-en-Retz village, then follow camping signs.

CC € 17 *1/4-3/7 29/8-29/10*

N 47°4'30'' W 2°0'27''

Les Rosiers-sur-Loire, F-49350 / Pays de la Loire (Maine-et-Loire) — 1496

Les Voiles d'Anjou****
6 rue Sainte Baudruche
+33 (0)2-41519433
FAX +33 (0)2-41518913
1/4 - 30/9
contact@camping-valdeloire.com

4,5ha 111**T**(100-130m²) 10A

1 AC**F**IJKLPQ
2 FRVWXY
3 ABGHJKMN**Q**RU
4 (C+F+H) **N**
(Q+R+T+V) Z
5 **AB**EFGIJKLMNOPRUWXYZ
6 CEGK(N 0,8km)OTV

Located in the UNESCO heritage site of the Loire, with its beautiful chateaux, 500 metres from a lively village. Two swimming pools, one open air and one indoor with a lovely terrace. It also offers a playground, bike hire, an attractively furnished restaurant with room for music and theatre, and many opportunities for cycling and walking trips and excursions.

Via D952. Towards Beaufort at the traffic lights in the village. Follow signs. Campsite well signposted.

CC € 15 *1/4-7/7 24/8-30/9 7=6*

N 47°21'32'' W 0°13'32''

Longeville-sur-Mer, F-85560 / Pays de la Loire (Vendée) — 1497

Le Petit Rocher****
1250 avenue de Docteur Mathevet
+33 (0)2-51204194
FAX +33 (0)2-51221109
2/4 - 24/9
contact@camp-atlantique.com

4,5ha 76**T**(85-120m²) 10A CEE

1 ACD**F**IJKLPS
2 ABEGJRSVWXY
3 ABGHJKNRU
4 (E+H 11/4-20/9) JKM
(Q+S+T+U 11/4-20/9)
5 **AB**EFGIJKLMNPUWZ
6 EGH**K**(N 2km)T

A lovely terraced campsite with spacious pitches under tall deciduous trees. Within walking distance of the sea and a sandy beach. Heated indoor swimming pool, wellness and snack bar.

Follow the D105 as far as Longeville-sur-Mer. At roundabout, take the D91a direction Le Rocher as far as the sea. Campsite signposted.

CC € 17 *2/4-9/7 26/8-24/9*

N 46°24'13'' W 1°30'27''

Marçon, F-72340 / Pays de la Loire (Sarthe)

1498

Du Lac des Varennes***
route du Port Gauthier/Saint Lezin
+33 (0)2-43441372
1/4 - 30/10
contact@lacdesvarennes.com

7ha 250**T**(100-300m²) 10A CEE

1 AC**G**IJKLMPRS
2 ACDLRVWXY
3 AGHK**M**RU**W**XZ
4 (Q+R)
(T+U+V+Z 1/7-31/8)
5 **AB**DEFGJLMNPUWZ
6 EG**K**(N 6km)T

This peaceful and spacious campsite borders both a large lake and the Loir. There is plenty of countryside around with footpaths and fishing on the site.

Drive via the D305 to Marçon. In the centre pass the Post Office/Town Hall (on the left). Follow the road. Signposted.

CC € 15 1/4-7/7 24/8-30/10 7=6, 14=11, 21=16

N 47°42'45'' E 0°29'58''

Montjean-sur-Loire, F-49570 / Pays de la Loire (Maine-et-Loire)

1499

La Promenade***
quai des Mariniers
+33 (0)2-41390268
1/4 - 30/9
contact@
campinglapromenade.com

3ha 162**T**(85-125m²) 10A CEE

1 AC**G**IJKLPQ
2 CGLRVWXY
3 ABGHJKNRU**W**
4 (B+G+Q 1/7-31/8) (R+T)
Z
5 **AB**FGIJKLMNOPUXYZ
6 EGJ**K**(N 1km)TV

Located near a small village in the middle of Anjou or the banks of the Loire. In the area between Angers and Nantes, famous for the unusual Corniche Angevine. Plenty of possibilities for walking and cycling. Wine regions, Puy de Fou and lovely villages invite you for a visit. Spacious marked out pitches, lovely swimming pool, new toilet facilities, snack bar and hospitable owners.

From Angers to the D751. Follow this as far as Montjean-sur-Loire. Campsite well signposted.

CC € 15 1/4-8/7 25/8-30/9 7=6, 14=12

N 47°23'31'' W 0°52'13''

Montreuil-Bellay, F-49260 / Pays de la Loire (Maine-et-Loire)

1500

Les Nobis d'Anjou****
rue Georges Girouy
+33 (0)2-41523366
2/4 - 2/10
contact@campinglesnobis.com

3ha 107**T**(100-145m²) 10A

1 ACD**G**IJKLMOPQ
2 BCLRTVWXY
3 BGHJRUW
4 (C 1/5-30/9) (Q+R+T+Y)
Z
5 ABEFGIJKLMNOPUWXY
6 ACEGHK(N 0,2km)RTV

Located in medieval Montreuil-Bellay at the foot of a castle and on the banks of the River Thouet. Many modern facilities: large pitches, heated swimming pool, lovely new toilet facilities, restaurant, lively bar and entertainment. Plenty of walking and cycling tours, and also the heritage of the Loire region; everything therefore for a wonderful stay in this beautiful region.

Via N147 from either Saumur or Thouars. Follow camping signs once you get to the roundabout.

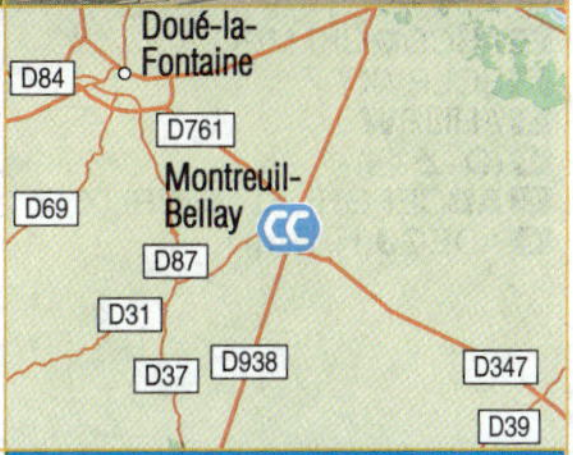

CC € 15 2/4-5/7 22/8-2/10 7=6

N 47°7'54'' W 0°9'33''

Nantes, F-43000 / Pays de la Loire (Loire-Atlantique)

1501

Nantes Camping*****
21 boulevard du Petit Port
+33 (0)2-40744794
FAX +33 (0)2-40742306
1/1 - 31/12
@ nantes-camping@nge-nantes.fr

8,5ha 83**T**(100-200m²) 16A CEE

1 ACD**G**IJKLMPQ
2 BCFGLRTUVXY
3 AB**F**HJKQRU**W**
4 (D+F) **JLM**
(Q+R+T+U+V 1/5-11/9)
(X+Y 1/7-31/8) (Z)
5 BDEFGJLNPUWXYZ
6 BEGHIK(N 0,2km)TV

Nantes Camping is located in grounds covering 8.5 hectares and is a natural campsite, a few minutes from the centre of Nantes.

Take N39 Nantes from the ring road north, exit Porte de la Chapelle. Direction Nantes Centre. Campsite signposted and located on roundabout.

CC € 19 *1/1-10/7 29/8-31/12 7=6, 14=11*

N 47°14'36'' W 1°33'24''

Noirmoutier-en-l'Île, F-85330 / Pays de la Loire (Vendée)

1502

Indigo Noirmoutier***
23, allée des Sableaux/rue des Sabl
+33 (0)2-51390624
FAX +33 (0)2-51359763
14/4 - 3/10
@ noirmoutier@
camping-indigo.com

12ha 386**T**(80-100m²) 10A CEE

1 AC**F**IJKLM**P**ST
2 ABEKNRSWXY
3 ABGHJKRWY
4 (A 1/7-31/8) (Q+R)
(T+U+V+Z 1/5-30/9)
5 **AB**FGIJKMNPRUWZ
6 ABCEGIJ(N 2km)

A campsite by the sea alongside the beach at Les Sableaux in a pine forest. Uniquely situated on the island of Noirmoutier. Direct beach access in several places. Quality amenities. CampingCard ACSI is only valid for standard pitches.

From Nantes direction Noirmoutier. Via the bridge to the island towards Noirmoutier-en-l'Île. Then follow Plage des Sableaux from centre.

CC € 17 *14/4-24/6 1/9-2/10*

N 46°59'49'' W 2°13'14''

Nort-sur-Erdre, F-44390 / Pays de la Loire (Loire-Atlantique)

1503

Seasonova Port Mulon
rue des Mares Noires
+33 (0)2-40722357
1/4 - 4/11
@ contact@
camping-portmulon.com

2ha 100**T**(88-347m²) 10A CEE

1 ABCD**G**IJKLMPQ
2 BCLRVXY
3 AHIJR**W**
4 (Q+Z)
5 **AB**CEFGHIJKLMNPRUXYZ
6 ADEG**J**(N 1km)T

A pleasant, refurbished campsite with many opportunities for the water enthusiast. Modern toilet facilities. Located by a river and close to a marina.

Direction Sucé-sur-Erdre. Follow 'camping' on the left.

CC € 13 *1/4-8/7 26/8-4/11 7=6, 14=11*

N 47°25'42'' W 1°29'51''

Notre-Dame-de-Riez, F-85270 / Pays de la Loire (Vendée)

1504

Domaine des Renardières***
13 chemin du chêne vert
+33 (0)2-51551417
1/4 - 31/10
caroline.raffin@free.fr

3,5ha 67**T**(90-130m²) 6A

1 A**F**IJKLMOPST
2 BRSVXY
3 AB**F**GHJKNRU**W**
4 (C 5/4-2/9) (F)
(H 5/4-2/9) (Q 1/7-31/8)
(R 5/4-2/9)
(T+U+V 1/7-25/8) (Z)
5 **AB**EFGIJKLNOPTUVXZ
6 ACDEGHI**K**(N 1km)OTV

A beautiful campsite for the whole season. Covered saltwater pool, fine toilet facilities, spacious pitches. Excellent motorhome pitches in park-like surroundings. More than worth a visit. Bicycles for hire.

Challans direction Sable d'Olonne (8 km), first intersection after the level crossing (right). In Notre-Dame-de-Riez sharp turn to the right. Signposted.

CC € 15 *1/4-7/7 1/9-31/10*

N 46°45'18'' W 1°53'53''

Olonne-sur-Mer, F-85340 / Pays de la Loire (Vendée)

1505

Le Nid d'Été****
2 rue de la Vigne Verte
+33 (0)2-51953438
+33 (0)2-51953464
1/4 - 30/9
info@leniddete.com

3ha 100**T**(100-160m²) 10A CEE

1 ACD**G**IJKLMOPQ
2 AFRVX
3 A**F**GHJKNRUW
4 (C+D+H 3/4-25/9) JK**P**
(Q+R 1/7-31/8)
(T+U+V 1/6-31/8)
(X 1/7-31/8) (Z)
5 **AB**FGIJKLOPUVWZ
6 AEG**J**(N 2km)QRTV

This family campsite is a nice place to stay in the early and late seasons, just 3 km from a lovely sandy beach. The swimming pool is open from the beginning of April. There is excellent cycling in the lovely area.

From Angers follow the A87 as far as La Roche-sur-Yon. Then take the Les Sables d'Olonne route. Follow the signs in Olonne-sur-Mer.

CC € 17 *1/4-14/7 1/9-30/9*

N 46°32'0'' W 1°47'37''

Piriac-sur-Mer, F-44420 / Pays de la Loire (Loire-Atlantique)

1506

Parc du Guibel***
route de Kerdrien
+33 (0)2-40235267
+33 (0)2-40155024
1/4 - 30/9
camping@parcduguibel.com

14ha 300**T**(100-200m²) 10A CEE

1 ACD**G**IJKLMOPQ
2 ABGQRVWXY
3 BGHJN**OP**QRUW
4 (C+F+H 15/4-30/9) IJ(Q)
(S+T+U+V+Y+Z 2/7-26/8)
5 **AB**EFGIJKLOPUVXYZ
6 CDEGHJ(N 3,5km)TV

Wooded campsite with marked out pitches among pine trees. You will be assigned a quiet pitch if you wish. Comfortable toilet facilities. In the swimming pools, both indoor and outdoor, with indoor pool heated to 28°C you can swim from inside to outside. Peaceful almost level surroundings 1200m from a quiet beach and village.

N165/E60 Nantes-Vannes. Guérande/La Baule exit. Via D774 direction Guérande and via D52 to St. Molf and Piriac-sur-Mer. Campsite located on the D52.

CC € 15 *1/4-15/7 1/9-29/9*

N 47°23'10'' W 2°30'36''

Pornic, F-44210 / Pays de la Loire (Loire-Atlantique)

1507

La Boutinardière****
23 rue de la Plage de la Boutinard
+33 (0)2-40820568
+33 (0)2-40824901
9/4 - 30/9
info@laboutinardiere.com

8ha 100T(80-120m²) 10A CEE

1 ACD**G**IJKLMOPQ
2 AEFGQRVWXY
3 BC**F**GHJK**M**N**PQ**RUVWY
4 (C 5/5-27/9) (F+H) IJ**KL** M**N** (Q+S+T+U+V+X+Y+Z)
5 **AB**DEFGHIJKLMNOPUVW XYZ
6 ACDEGIJ**K**(N 2km)ORTV

Family campsite with well maintained toilet facilities. The pitches are separated by hedges. 200m from the sea with a sheltered sandy beach between two cliffs. Lovely footpath along the coast. Open air swimming pool 400 m², indoor pool 300 m² with sauna, steam bath and beauty centre.

Take the exit La Boutinardière/La Rogére at the D13 between Pornic and Bourgneuf-en-Retz, west of Nantes. Follow the signs to the campsite.

CC € 19 *9/4-1/7 28/8-29/9*

N 47°5'52'' W 2°3'7''

Pornic, F-44210 / Pays de la Loire (Loire-Atlantique)

1508

Le Patisseau****
29 rue du Patisseau
+33 (0)2-40821039
+33 (0)2-40822281
2/4 - 25/9
contact@lepatisseau.com

4,5ha 76T(90-130m²) 10A CEE

1 ACD**F**IJKLMOPRS
2 BFJQRVWXY
3 B**F**GHJKNRUV
4 (C 1/6-25/9) (F+H) IJKM NP(Q) (S 6/7-31/8) (T+U+V+X+Y+Z)
5 **AB**DEFGIJKLMNOPQRUW XYZ
6 ACDEGI**K**L(N 1km)RTV

A lovely campsite with luxurious heated toilet facilities and an indoor swimming pool. 300 m² outdoor pool. Good restaurant on site. The campsite is located in a green belt close to Pornic. Marked out footpaths, a sports complex and gently sloping cycle tracks close to the site. Category 1 and 2 dogs are not permitted.

South of St. Nazaire via the D213 as far as the Pornic/Le Clion-sur-Mer exit. Follow the camping signs at the roundabout towards Le Clion-sur-Mer.

CC € 17 *2/4-5/7 31/8-24/9* *7=6, 14=12, 21=18*

N 47°7'8'' W 2°4'23''

Pornichet, F-44380 / Pays de la Loire (Loire-Atlantique)

1509

Du Bugeau***
33 avenue de Loriettes
+33 (0)2-40610202
29/4 - 2/10
campingdubugeau@wanadoo.fr

2ha 61**T**(70-95m²) 10A

1 ACDGIJKLMPRS
2 AEFGRVWXY
3 B**F**GHJRUWY
4 (E) (G 1/7-31/8) (Q+R+T+U+V+Z 1/6-2/10)
5 **AB**EFGIJKLMNOPUWZ
6 ACEGK(N 0,5km)RTV

Quiet campsite close to the beach. It is divided into small fields separated by hedges, with several trees between the pitches providing shade. The large promenade with its well-known half-moon beach is 1 km away. ± 1 km from supermarket, 500 metres from the beach.

Via the D92 from St. Nazaire direction La Baule and Pornichet. At roundabout with Carrefour supermarket, direction St. Sébastien. Turn left before the church, 400 metres further, entrance on the left.

CC € 17 *29/4-3/7 22/8-1/10*

N 47°15'10'' W 2°19'10''

Puyravault, F-85450 / Pays de la Loire (Vendée) 1510

Flower Camping Le Merval**
chemin de l'Epine
+33 (0)2-51286084
FAX +33 (0)2-51294168
16/4 - 17/9
lemerval@orange.fr

2,5ha 30T(100-120m²) 10A CEE

1 ACD**F**IJKLMOPRS
2 RVX
3 ABDG**P**R
4 (C 1/5-15/9) (Q+R 🔑) (T+Z 1/7-31/8)
5 **A**FGIJKLMNPUZ
6 CEG**J**(N 3,5km)TV

Small family campsite near the 'Venise Verte' with marked-out pitches, modern toilet facilities and good basic amenities.

Follow RN137 dir. La Rochelle until Moreille. Take D10A dir. Puyravault at roundabout. Campsite located 2 km before village.

CC € 13 16/4-15/7 1/9-17/9 7=6

N 46°21'9'' W 1°5'23''

Rochefort-sur-Loire, F-49190 / Pays de la Loire (Maine-et-Loire) 1511

Seasonova Les Plages de Loire***
route de Savennières
+33 (0)2-41685591
1/4 - 4/11
contact@camping-lesplagesdeloire.com

6ha 105T(80-140m²) 10A CEE

1 ABCD**G**IJKLMPQ
2 ACDFGKLRVWXY
3 ABGHJKQRU**W**X
4 (A 🔑) (B+F+G 1/7-31/8) **KL** **N**(Q+R+T+U+X 🔑) Z
5 **AB**DFGIJKLMNOPZ
6 CEGJ**K**(N 0,5km)OT

A new campsite designed by a landscape architect and very attractively laid out. Close to all the amenities in the village and positioned by a small river.

Via the A11 to N160 dir. Les Ponts-de-Cé. Rochefort is indicated here on the D751. A87 exit 23 dir. Denée, D160, D123, D751.

CC € 13 1/4-8/7 26/8-4/11 7=6, 14=11

N 47°21'37'' W 0°39'24''

Saumur, F-49400 / Pays de la Loire (Maine-et-Loire) 1512

Ile d'Offard*****
rue de Verden
+33 (0)2-41403000
FAX +33 (0)2-41673781
12/3 - 30/10
iledoffard@flowercampings.com

4,5ha 187T(100-120m²) 10A CEE

1 ACD**G**IJKLPQ
2 CFGLRTVWX
3 B**F**GHJKMN**P**QRU**W**
4 (A 1/7-31/8) (C 1/4-30/9) (H 1/5-30/9) K(Q 1/4-30/10) (S 🔑) (T 1/4-31/10) (U 1/7-31/8) (X+Y 15/6-15/9) Z
5 **AB**DFGIJKLMNOPUWXYZ
6 CEGIK(N 1km)OV

The campsite is located in a verdant 4.5 hectare park between both banks of the Loire. 15 minute walk from the centre of Saumur, where a number of events are organised throughout the year. An exceptional location. Vineyards, culture and tradition. CampingCard ACSI is valid for comfort pitches, not for privilege pitches.

The campsite is on an island in the Loire opposite Saumur castle. Easily accessible via the N152, D947 or N147.

CC € 17 12/3-1/7 1/9-30/10 7=6

N 47°15'36'' W 0°3'52''

Sillé-le-Guillaume, F-72140 / Pays de la Loire (Sarthe) — 1513

De La Forêt***
Sillé-Plage
+33 (0)2-43201104
FAX +33 (0)2-43208482
1/4 - 31/10
campingsilleplage@wanadoo.fr

4ha 144**T**(100-150m²) 10A

1 AC**G**IJLPT
2 BDLMRVXY
3 ABGHJ**MNPQ**RU**WZ**
4 (**A** 1/7-30/8) (Q 🔑)
5 **AB**FGIJKLMNPUWZ
6 CDEGIJ(N 3km)OTV

A level campsite on the edge of a deciduous forest and by a lake with opportunities for watersports. The campsite has shaded and sundrenched pitches. Country walking possible from the campsite in 3500 hectares of woods.

From Sillé-le-Guillaume direction Le Lac and La Forêt. Follow signs.

CC €13 *1/4-30/6 1/9-31/10*

N 48°12'33'' W 0°8'5''

Sillé-le-Guillaume, F-72140 / Pays de la Loire (Sarthe) — 1514

Indigo Les Molières***
Sillé-Plage
+33 (0)2-43201612
FAX +33 (0)2-43245684
4/5 - 26/9
molieres@camping-indigo.com

9ha 122**T**(100-150m²) 10A CEE

1 ACD**G**IJKLMPST
2 BDRWXY
3 ABGHJK**OP**RU**WZ**
4 (C+Q+R 🔑)
(T+U+V 1/7-31/8) (Z 🔑)
5 **AB**GIJKLMNPTUW
6 CDEIJ(N 1,5km)

A campsite on the shores of Lake Sillé in the middle of municipal woodland. Opportunities for walking and water recreation. Heated swimming pool and recreation facilities. CampingCard ACSI is only valid on standard pitches.

From Sillé-le-Guillaume direction Le Lac and La Forêt. Follow signs as far as La Crêperie du Lac. Turn right just before La Crêperie du Lac. Look out for campsite signs.

CC €13 *4/5-5/7 1/9-25/9*

N 48°12'13'' W 0°7'39''

St. Brévin-les-Pins, F-44250 / Pays de la Loire (Loire-Atlantique) — 1515

Le Fief*****
57 chemin du Fief
+33 (0)2-40272386
FAX +33 (0)2-40644619
26/3 - 24/9
camping@lefief.com

7ha 127**T**(80-130m²) 10A CEE

1 ACD**F**IJKLMOPRS
2 AEFGQRVWXY
3 BGHJKMNRU**V**WY
4 (C 1/5-24/9) (F+H 🔑) IJ**KL**
M**NP**(Q 🔑) (S 1/5-24/9)
(T+U+V+Y+Z 🔑)
5 **AB**DEFGIJKLMNOPQRUW
XYZ
6 ACDEGH**IJK**L(N 0,8km)RT
UV

A family campsite 900m from the beach, between the two village centres of St. Brévin-les-Pins with a market 3 times a week. Own restaurant with very reasonable prices (always open at weekends out of season). Beautiful outdoor and indoor swimming pools. Only CampingCard ACSI for touring pitches, not for seasonal pitches. Larger motorhomes are permitted out of season.

South of St. Nazaire via the D213, exit D5 then Casino. Follow St. Brevin-l'Océan and camping signs.

CC €19 *26/3-3/5 17/5-1/7 31/8-24/9*

N 47°14'7'' W 2°10'3''

St. Christophe-du-Ligneron, F-85670 / Pays de la Loire (Vendée)

1516

Domaine de Bellevue***
Bellevue de Ligneron
+33 (0)2-51933066
1/1 - 31/12
campingdebellevue85@orange.fr

13ha 55**T**(100-200m²) 16A CEE

1 ACD**G**IJKLMOPQ
2 DRVX
3 ABGHJKNRUW
4 (E+H 1/5-30/9)
(Q+R+T+U+V+X 1/7-31/8)
(Z)
5 **AB**EFGIJKLMNOPUXYZ
6 CDEG**K**(N 2km)ORTV

A beautiful, spaciously appointed campsite with fine amenities. Excellent fishing water on the campsite and a lovely indoor pool.

From La Roche-sur-Yon take D948 dir. Challans. In village St. Christophe-du-Ligneron follow signs.

CC € 13 *1/3-10/7 27/8-31/10 7=6*

N 46°48'54" W 1°46'30"

St. Hilaire-de-Riez, F-85270 / Pays de la Loire (Vendée)

1517

La Plage****
106 av. de la Pège
+33 (0)2-51543393
FAX +33 (0)2-51559702
1/4 - 30/9
campinglaplage@
campingscollinet.com

5,5ha 46**T**(100-120m²) 10A

1 AC**G**IJKLMPQ
2 AERSVX
3 AB**F**GJKL**M**NR**T**UWY
4 (C 15/5-15/9) (F 7/4-30/9)
(H 8/4-30/9) JK
(Q+R+T+U+V 8/4-15/9)
(X 15/6-31/8) (Z)
5 **AB**EFGIJKLMNOPUVZ
6 ACEG**J**(N 1,5km)OQRTV

A large campsite with many facilities on a coastal road. Deciduous and conifer trees alternate with bushes, quiet avenues and busier sections at the entrance to the campsite. Cycle tracks in area and lovely swimming pool (also covered).

Take the D38 around St. Hilaire as far as the roundabout (Fina service station). Then take the D123 in the direction of La Pège. Signposted after 4.5 km.

CC € 17 *1/4-8/7 1/9-30/9*

N 46°44'43" W 2°0'36"

St. Hilaire-de-Riez, F-85270 / Pays de la Loire (Vendée)

1518

La Plage de Riez***
avenue des Mimosas
+33 (0)2-51543423
1/4 - 31/10
riez85@free.fr

11ha 289**T**(80-140m²) 6A CEE

1 ACD**F**IJKLMOPT
2 ABERSVXY
3 AGHJKNRUWY
4 (C+H 8/5-15/9)
(Q+R+T+U+V 15/5-15/9)
(X 1/7-31/8) (Z)
5 **AB**EFGIJKLMNOPUXZ
6 CDEG**K**(N 0,2km)OTV

You will be camping 'with your feet in the water' at this friendly and hospitable campsite in the middle of woods and with direct access to the beach. Extensive network of cycle paths, including one to Sion where you can go shopping.

From Nantes: Ri La Roche-sur-Yon via Route Départementale, then Challans, St. Hilaire-de-Riez/ St. Gilles-Croix-de-Vie and dir. Sion-sur-L'Ocean (not towards centre).

CC € 17 *1/4-30/6 1/9-31/10*

N 46°43'22" W 1°58'46"

St. Hilaire-la-Forêt, F-85440 / Pays de la Loire (Vendée)

1519

La Grand' Métairie****
8 rue de la Vineuse en Plaine
+33 (0)2-51333238
FAX +33 (0)2-51332569
2/4 - 25/9
info@
camping-grandmetairie.com
3,8ha 42**T**(80-100m²) 10A

1 ACD**F**IJKLMO**P**RS
2 RTVXY
3 BGJKNRU
4 (C 15/6-8/9) (F+H) **N**
(Q+R+T+U+V+X+Y+Z)
5 **AB**EFGIJKLMNOPUXZ
6 EGHJ**K**ORTV

A lovely family campsite with many amenities within walking distance of the village. Indoor heated swimming pool, bar and restaurant are open all season.

La Roche-sur-Yon D747 as far as Moutiers; D19 via Avrillé to St. Hilaire-la-Forêt. Signposted from here.

CC € 13 *2/4-9/7 27/8-25/9* *7=6, 14=12, 21=18*

N 46°26'55'' W 1°31'35''

St. Hilaire-St-Florent, F-49400 / Pays de la Loire (Maine-et-Loire)

1520

Chantepie*****
+33 (0)2-41679534
FAX +33 (0)2-41679585
4/5 - 26/9
info@campingchantepie.com
12ha 120**T**(100-140m²) 10A CEE

1 ACD**G**IJKLPQ
2 CFRVWXY
3 B**F**GHJKLN**PQ**RU**W**
4 (A 1/7-31/8) (B 25/4-13/9)
(D 13/6-30/8) (G 26/4-13/9)
(Q+S) (T 13/6-30/8)
(U+V+W+X 21/6-31/8) Z
5 **AB**EFGIJKLMNOPUWXYZ
6 CEGIK(N 5km)ORTUV

An unusual location among the vineyards with exceptional views of the Loire. 10 hectares of countryside, spacious marked out pitches, two swimming pools (one of which is heated) grocery shop, bar, take away meals, pizzeria. Quality campsite hallmark. 6 km from Saumur. A place for rest and relaxation.

From Saumur direction Cholet. After the round-about dir. St. Hilaire, turn right at the end of the road. Follow 'Gennes touristiques' (D751). Follow the signs.

CC € 17 *4/5-5/7 1/9-25/9*

N 47°17'38'' W 0°8'33''

St. Jean-de-Monts, F-85160 / Pays de la Loire (Vendée)

1521

Aux Coeurs Vendéens****
251 rte Notre-Dame-de-Monts
+33 (0)2-51588491
23/4 - 18/9
info@coeursvendeens.com
2ha 47**T**(60-120m²) 10A CEE

1 AC**F**IJKLMOPST
2 AGRVXY
3 AB**F**GHJKNRUV
4 (C 15/5-31/8) (E)
(H 15/5-31/8) KLN
(Q 1/6-18/9)
(R+T+U+V+Z 1/7-31/8)
5 **AB**EFGIJKLMNOPUVWXY
6 AEGH**I**K(N 0,4km)ORV

A peaceful family campsite 700m from the sea, with spacious pitches. The campsite has two heated swimming pools, one of which is covered and has a free spa, sauna and hammam. Fitness equipment. Free WiFi throughout the campsite. A paradise for cyclists with cycle routes from the campsite.

Follow the D38 from St. Jean-de-Monts to the north to Noirmoutier. The campsite is situated directly on the D38.

CC € 17 *23/4-1/7 27/8-18/9* *7=6*

N 46°48'35'' W 2°6'35''

St. Jean-de-Monts, F-85164 / Pays de la Loire (Vendée)

1522

Campéole Les Sirénes***
71 avenue des Demoiselles
+33 (0)2-51580131
FAX +33 (0)2-51590367
1/4 - 30/9
@ sirenes@andretriganogroupe.com

15ha 280T(> 90m²) 10A CEE

1 ACGIJKLMOPST
2 ABRSWXY
3 ABFGHJKNR
4 (C+H 1/6-13/9) (Q+R+S+T 1/7-31/8) Z
5 **AB**FGIJKLMNPU
6 CEGH**K**L(N 0,4km)RT

A beautiful dune campsite located in the woods with large open and shaded pitches. Large heated swimming pool. Beach and village nearby. Many cycling and walking opportunities.

Direction Nantes/La Roche-sur-Yon. Follow Challans and St. Jean-de- Monts. Then Le Bourg, La Plage and Palais des congrès. Enter Avenue des Demoiselle at roundabout. Campsite located 500 metres on the left.

CC € 17 *1/5-4/7 22/8-30/9*

N 46°46'49" W 2°3'18"

St. Jean-de-Monts, F-85161 / Pays de la Loire (Vendée)

1523

Campéole Plage des Tonnelles - Dornier****
18 route de la Tonnelle
+33 (0)2-51588116
1/4 - 25/9
@ plage-tonnelles@andretriganogroupe.com

25ha 229T(70-110m²) 6A CEE

1 ACD**G**IJKLMO**P**ST
2 ABEGISWX
3 AB**F**HJKNRUVY
4 (C+H 1/6-13/9) **KN** (Q+S 5/5-5/9) (T+U+W+Z 1/7-31/8)
5 **AB**EFGIJKLMNOPQRUVZ
6 ACEGH**K**L(N 0,2km)RV

A dune campsite with outdoor pool in sheltered surroundings. Access to the beach via a gate and through the dunes; the night guard locks the gate. Shop in immediate vicinity. New: fitness room and sauna with jacuzzi. Walking and cycling.

Coming from Nantes, dir. Noirmoutier/Challans/ St. Jean-de-Monts at the first roundabout in St. Jean-de-Monts, continue towards D38 Notre Dame-de-Monts/Noirmoutier. Turn left at the Tonnelles roundabout and follow camping signs.

CC € 17 *1/5-4/7 22/8-25/9*

N 46°48'37" W 2°7'12"

St. Jean-de-Monts, F-85160 / Pays de la Loire (Vendée)

1524

Camping-Caravaning La Forêt****
190 chemin de la Rive
FAX +33 (0)2-51588463
30/4 - 24/9
@ camping-la-foret@wanadoo.fr

1ha 45T(88-120m²) 10A CEE

1 AC**G**IJKLMOPST
2 AEGRSVX
3 AB**F**GHJKRUWY
4 (**C+H** 1/5-24/9) (Q+R+T+U 1/6-31/8) (V 1/7-31/8)
5 **AB**CFGHIJKLMNOPQUWXYZ
6 CEGH**K**(N 0,8km)RTV

Camping la Forêt is a smaller, quiet family campsite and is geared to its clients. High standards. Heated swimming pool. On the edge of a wood. 400m from the beach which is accessible via a path. Various walking and cycling opportunities opposite the site. 1 km from the centre of Notre-Dame-de-Monts.

In St. Jean-de-Monts take the D38 towards Notre-Dame-de-Monts. Turn left at Notre-Dame-de-Monts sign, Chemin de la Rive. Campsite 300m on the left.

CC € 17 *30/4-8/7 26/8-24/9* *8=7*

N 46°49'6" W 2°7'48"

St. Jean-de-Monts, F-85160 / Pays de la Loire (Vendée)

1525

l'Océan****
67 rue de Notre Dame de Monts
+33 (0)2-51580388
Fax +33 (0)2-51582463
2/4 - 18/9
info@campinglocean.com

4,2ha 94T(80-120m²) 10A

1 ACD**G**IJKLMOPRS
2 AGRSVWXY
3 AB**F**GHJNRU
4 (C+H 15/5-18/9)
(Q+T+U+Z 1/7-31/8)
5 **A**BEFGIJKLMNPUZ
6 AEG**J**(N 1,0km)ORV

Christophe and Valérie welcome you to their friendly campsite with a heated pool (26°C) and lovely, semi-shaded pitches. Located on the edge of the dunes with marked-out cycle tracks, 1 km from the beach and the town centre.

From St. Jean-de-Monts direction Notre-Dame-de-Monts on the D38. At the end of the town it is the 1st campsite on the left, beside the D38.

CC € 15 *2/4-1/7 29/8-17/9 7=6*

N 46°48'1'' W 2°4'42''

St. Jean-de-Monts, F-85160 / Pays de la Loire (Vendée)

1526

La Davière Plage***
197 rte de N.D./
ch. de la Davière
Fax +33 (0)2-51582799
23/4 - 30/9
contact@daviereplage.com

3ha 146T(90-135m²) 10A CEE

1 ACD**G**IJKLMPST
2 AGRSVWXY
3 B**F**HJKRV
4 (C+H 1/5-30/9) K
(Q+R+S+T+U+V+X+Z
1/7-31/8)
5 **AB**FGIJKLMNPRUVZ
6 CEG**K**(N 3km)V

This family campsite welcomes you on the edge of a beautiful wood and the St. Jean-de-Monts dunes and 900 metres from a lovely sandy beach. Spacious pitches, heated swimming pool, sun meadow and jacuzzi. Excellent cycling and walking in the immediate surroundings.

The campsite is located 1.5 km north of St. Jean-de-Monts. Follow D38 direction Notre-Dame-de-Monts. Campsite on the left on Chemin de la Davière.

CC € 15 *23/4-12/7 29/8-30/9*

N 46°48'20'' W 2°6'5''

St. Jean-de-Monts, F-85160 / Pays de la Loire (Vendée)

1527

La Prairie****
146 rue du Moulin Cassé
+33 (0)2-51581604
Fax +33 (0)2-44842695
1/4 - 9/10
contact@campingprairie.com

2ha 37T(85-100m²) 6A

1 ACD**G**IJKLMOPST
2 AGRVWX
3 AB**F**GHJKNRUV
4 (C 1/5-20/9) (F 8/4-30/9)
(H 1/5-20/9) JK(Q 1/7-31/8)
(R+T+U+Z)
5 **AB**EFGIJKLMNPUVXZ
6 CEG**K**(N 2km)OV

A pleasant, peaceful campsite close to dunes and woods with direct access to the beautiful sandy beaches and with walking and cycle paths beside the campsite. Located 2.5 km from the town centre. Heated outdoor swimming pool. New: indoor pool with spa/wellness. Spacious marked out, half-shaded pitches.

From St. Jean-de-Monts take the D38 towards Notre-Dame-de-Monts. Campsite about 1500m north of St. Jean-de-Monts, follow camping signs.

CC € 17 *23/4-2/7 1/9-30/9 15=14*

N 46°48'15'' W 2°5'36''

St. Jean-de-Monts, F-85160 / Pays de la Loire (Vendée) 1528

La Yole****
chemin des Bosses
+33 (0)2-51586717
+33 (0)2-51590535
2/4 - 24/9
contact@la-yole.com

9ha 172T(90-150m²) 10A

1 ACD**F**IJKLMOPS
2 RSVXY
3 B**F**GHIJK**M**NRUVW
4 (C+F+H) JKP (Q+S+T+U+V+X+Y 1/5-15/9) (Z)
5 **AB**DEFGIJKLMNOPQRUWYZ
6 ACEGHI**J**(N 0km)OTV

A well-organised campsite just near the coast with varied landscaping and playgrounds. Playfully designed swimming pool. Extra discount with CampingCard ACSI in April and May, when if you stay for 14 nights, you pay for 10. In June, July and September: stay for 14 nights, pay for 11.

From St. Hilaire take the D38b north-west as far as Le Pissot. Then take the D38, signposted to the left after 4 km. Or from St. Jean-de-Monts direction St. Hilaire 6 km on the right.

CC € 15 2/4-14/7 1/9-24/9 7=6

N 46°45'23" W 2°0'27"

St. Jean-de-Monts, F-85160 / Pays de la Loire (Vendée) 1529

Le Bois Joly****
46 route de Notre Dame
+33 (0)2-51591163
2/4 - 25/9
info@camping-leboisjoly.com

7,5ha 201T(80-110m²) 10A CEE

1 AC**F**IJKLMOPST
2 AGLRVWXY
3 AB**F**GHJKNRUW
4 (C 15/6-15/9) (F+H) IJK (Q+T+U+V+X+Z)
5 **AB**DEFGIJKLMNOPQUVXYZ
6 ACDEGHI**JK**(N 0,9km)ORTV

Pleasant campsite with spacious pitches. Heated toilet facilities, an outdoor and indoor swimming pool and free WiFi point. At walking distance from St. Jean-de-Monts. Beautiful beach nearby. Plenty of options for cycling and walking.

Take the D38 from St. Jean-de-Monts direction Notre-Dame-de-Monts. The campsite is located on the edge of the village, right on the D38.

CC € 17 2/4-30/6 1/9-25/9

N 46°47'59" W 2°4'28"

St. Jean-de-Monts, F-85169 / Pays de la Loire (Vendée) 1530

Les Amiaux****
223 rte Notre Dame de Monts
+33 (0)2-51582222
+33 (0)2-51582609
2/5 - 30/9
accueil@amiaux.fr

16ha 300T(100-120m²) 10A CEE

1 ACD**F**IJKLMO**P**ST
2 AGRVWXY
3 AB**F**GHJK**M**NRUV
4 (C 1/7-31/8) (F+H 5/5-11/9) JKM (Q+S+T+U+V+X+Y+Z 2/5-31/8)
5 **AB**FGIJKLMNOPUVXYZ
6 EGH**K**(N 3,5km)ORUV

A beautiful, large, four-star campsite with many amenities. An own campsite shop will supply you with groceries in the spring season. There is a fitness room and a spacious indoor pool. Not far from the sea. Cycling and walking options nearby.

From St. Jean-de-Monts, the D38 in northerly direction to Noirmoutier. The campsite is directly on the D38.

CC € 17 5/5-30/6 31/8-30/9

N 46°48'28" W 2°6'17"

St. Jean-de-Monts, F-85160 / Pays de la Loire (Vendée) — 1531

Plein Sud****
246 route Notre Dame de Monts
+33 (0)2-51591040
FAX +33 (0)2-51589229
14/5 - 17/9
info@campingpleinsud.com

2ha 30T(90-100m²) 6A CEE

1 ACF**I**JKLMPQ
2 AGRVWX
3 AB**F**GHJKNRU
4 (C+H) M
(Q+U+Z 1/7-31/8)
5 **AB**FGIJKLNPUWXYZ
6 EG**J**L(N 0,3km)OV

Located between St. Jean-de-Monts and Notre-Dame-de-Monts. A quiet, small but, more importantly, neat and well-maintained family campsite with nice toilet facilities. Heated pool with sun loungers open all season.

North of St. Jean-de-Monts on the D38 direction Notre-Dame-de-Monts.

CC € 15 *14/5-30/6 1/9-17/9 7=6*

N 46°48'35" W 2°6'33"

St. Julien-de-Concelles, F-44450 / Pays de la Loire (Loire-Atlantique) — 1532

du Chêne***
1 route du Lac
+33 (0)2-40541200
1/4 - 30/10
contact@campingduchene.fr

2,5ha 70T(70-150m²) 10A CEE

1 ABCD**G**IJKLMPQ
2 DFGLMRUVWXY
3 AB**F**GHJ**MRW**
4 (E+H 1/5-30/9) (Q 1/4-30/9)
(T+U+Z)
5 **AB**EFJLMNPQUVWZ
6 CDEGJRTV

The campsite has a friendly atmosphere and is located between the Loire and several vineyards, on the edge of a lake. This is a lovely natural area for complete relaxation.

Exit 44 Porte du Vignoble direction St. Julien-de-Concelles.

CC € 17 *1/4-8/7 2/9-29/10*

N 47°14'57" W 1°22'17"

St. Julien-des-Landes, F-85150 / Pays de la Loire (Vendée) — 1533

Château La Forêt****
+33 (0)2-51466211
FAX +33 (0)2-51466087
1/5 - 5/9
camping@chateaulaforet.com

50ha 150T(100-140m²) 10A

1 ACD**G**IJKLMOPS
2 BDKLMRVXY
3 ABCDGHJK**MNOPQ**RUW
4 (C 1/7-31/8) (**F**+H) JK**P**
(Q+R)
(T+U+V+Y 13/5-5/9) (Z)
5 **AB**EFGHIJKLNPUWXY
6 ACDEGH**IJK**L(N 0,3km)RT
V

Château La Forêt is a lovely international campsite on a 50 hectare estate. The site opens on 1 May and most amenities, such as the swimming pool, can be used immediately. The campsite is up to full strength from 13 May. Well worth a visit!

D12 La Chaize-Giraud direction St. Julien-des-Landes. Then pass the church and turn left unto the D55. Signposted.

CC € 17 *1/5-30/6 1/9-5/9*

N 46°38'36" W 1°42'41"

St. Julien-des-Landes, F-85150 / Pays de la Loire (Vendée) — 1534

Flower Camping La Bretonnière****
+33 (0)2-51466244
FAX +33 (0)2-51466136
9/4 - 30/9
@ info@la-bretonniere.com

5,5ha 119T(140-200m²) 12A CEE

1 ACD**G**IJKLMOPQ
2 ADRWXY
3 AFGHJK**M**NRUW
4 (**A** 15/6-31/8)
(C 10/5-20/9)
(D+H 10/5-30/9) M
(Q+R+T+U+V 15/6-31/8)
(Z)
5 **AB**EFGIJKLMNPUVWZ
6 ACEGK(N 2km)OTV

A beautiful campsite located in the countryside around a former farmhouse with its own fish pond and large pitches.

From Angers take the A87 in the direction of Cholet, Roche-sur-Yonne. Here continue to Sables d'Olonne. At the exit La Mothe-Achard / St. Julien drive in the direction of St. Gilles.

CC € 15 *9/4-2/7 1/9-30/9*

N 46°38'39'' W 1°43'57''

St. Julien-des-Landes, F-85150 / Pays de la Loire (Vendée) — 1535

La Garangeoire*****
+33 (0)2-51466539
FAX +33 (0)2-51466985
2/5 - 20/9
@ info@garangeoire.com

20ha 174T(120-180m²) 12A CEE

1 ACD**G**IJKLMOPST
2 ADLRSVXY
3 BCDFGHJKL**MNOP**QRUW
4 (A 5/5-20/9) (C+E+H) **JK N**
(Q+S+T+U+V+X+Y 5/5-20/9)
(Z)
5 **AB**DEFGIJKLMNOPRSUW XY
6 ABCEGHIJ(N 3km)OPRTV

A large castle campsite on a beautiful wooded estate. Paths criss-cross woods and fields. An international campsite also for teenagers. Horse and pony riding also in early and late seasons. Sandy beach on campsite.

On the N160 Les Sables d'Olonne - La Roche-sur-Yon, at La Mothe-Achard take the D12 in the direction of St. Julien-des-Landes. Located to the right after 3 km on the D21 in the direction of La Chapelle.

CC € 17 *2/5-30/6 28/8-20/9*

N 46°39'39'' W 1°42'56''

St. Laurent-sur-Sèvre, F-85290 / Pays de la Loire (Vendée) — 1536

Le Rouge Gorge***
route de la Verrie
FAX +33 (0)2-51678639
1/4 - 10/10
@ campinglerougegorge@wanadoo.fr

2ha 57T(100-200m²) 13A CEE

1 ACD**G**IJKLMPST
2 FLRVWXY
3 ABGHJNRU**W**
4 (C+H 8/5-15/9)
(Q+R+T+U+V+Z 1/7-31/8)
5 **AB**DEFGIJKLMNPUVXYZ
6 AEJL(N 0,8km)ORTV

A friendly campsite with 93 grassy pitches set in countryside on the edge of the Barbiniere. Heated swimming pool (May to September), snack bar, free WiFi, good toilet facilities and friendly owners. The area (10 minutes from Puy de Fou, Cholet, the Loire region) is unique, with plenty of opportunities for cycling and walking tours.

Campsite clearly signed in St. Laurent-sur-Sèvre.

CC € 15 *1/4-11/7 28/8-10/10* 7=6

N 46°57'30'' W 0°54'14''

St. Malo-du-Bois, F-85590 / Pays de la Loire (Vendée)

1537

La Vallée de Poupet
+33 (0)2-51923145
FAX +33 (0)2-51923865
1/5 - 15/9
@ camping@valleedepoupet.com

30ha 94T(90-120m²) 8A

1 ACD**G**IJKLMOPQ
2 BCLRVWXY
3 ABGHJRU**W**
4 (A 1/7-31/8) (E+H) (Q 1/7-31/8) (R+U+V+Z)
5 **AB**FGIJKLMNOPQUWXYZ
6 CEGHK(N 3km)ORTV

Welcoming family campsite with own pool and an attractive restaurant in front of the entrance. There is an open air theatre next to the campsite.

From A83 exit Les Herbiers. From Cholet direction St. Malo. From there campsite is clearly signposted.

CC € 17 *1/5-30/6 1/9-15/9*

N 46°55'33'' W 0°52'27''

St. Martin-Lars-en-Ste-Hermine, F-85210 / Pays de la Loire (Vendée)

1538

Le Colombier****
+33 (0)2-51278384
FAX +33 (0)2-51278729
1/4 - 1/10
@ lecolombier.nat@wanadoo.fr

50ha 176T(120-200m²) 6-10A CEE

1 ACD**G**IJKLMOPST
2 BCDILRVWXY
3 ABDGHJNRUVW
4 (C+H) **KLN** (Q+R+T+U+X+Z)
5 **AB**EFGIJKLMNOPUW
6 AEGH**IK**L(N 1,5km)RTUV

A well maintained naturist campsite with excellent toilet facilities. Large swimming pool, spacious pitches and a lively atmosphere in the bar and restaurant.

From Noirt take the N148 to Ste Hermine, D8 through Thiré direction La Caillère, turn left D52 St. Martin-Lars. Signposted from here.

CC € 19 *1/4-11/7 28/8-1/10*

N 46°35'52'' W 0°58'9''

St. Michel-en-l'Herm, F-85580 / Pays de la Loire (Vendée)

1539

La Dive****
12 route de la Mer
+33 (0)2-51302694
1/4 - 30/9
@ camping-la-dive@wanadoo.fr

110T 10A CEE

1 ACD**F**IJKLMOPRS
2 GRVWXY
3 BDGHJKN**OPQ**RV
4 (**A** 1/7-31/8) (C+H) **IJK** **MN**(Q 1/6-31/8) (R) (T+U+V+X 1/7-31/8)
5 **AB**EFGIJKLMNPUWX
6 ACEGH**K**(N 0,5km)TUV

A lovely campsite between land and sea. 5 minutes from the lovely sandy beaches and close to the 'Vénise Verte'. Bar, small shop and a beautiful jacuzzi and sauna. Wonderful atmosphere.

In St. Michel-en-l'Herm direction l'Aiguillon-sur-Mer. Right at end of village and follow camping signs.

CC € 15 *1/4-9/7 26/8-30/9*

N 46°20'57'' W 1°14'53''

St. Vincent-sur-Jard, F-85520 / Pays de la Loire (Vendée)

1540

La Bolée d'Air****
route du Bouil
+33 (0)2-51330505
FAX +33 (0)2-51339404
2/4 - 24/9
info@chadotel.com

6ha 120**T**(80-100m²) 10A CEE

1 ACD**F**IJKLMOPRS
2 ALRVWX
3 AB**F**GK**MNQ**RU
4 (C 15/5-10/9) (F)
(H 15/5-10/9) JK**N**
(Q+R+T+U 15/5-10/9) Z
5 **AB**EFGIJKMNPUZ
6 FG**K**(N 2km)RTV

A large campsite with marked out pitches next to the route Départementale (D21). The site is 1000m from the unguarded beach at Bouil and 1500m from the village. Lovely indoor-outdoor swimming pool with extensive entertainment for young and old.

Les Sables d'Olonne direction La Tranche-sur-Mer, 1500m beyond St. Vincent sur Jard (D21), on the right of the road.

CC € 13 *2/4-9/7 27/8-24/9*

N 46°25'5" W 1°31'38"

Talmont-St-Hilaire, F-85440 / Pays de la Loire (Vendée)

1541

Loyada*****
111 rue de la Source/av. de l'Atl.
+33 (0)2-51212810
FAX +33 (0)2-51203758
1/4 - 8/10
contact@camping-loyada.fr

5ha 28**T**(100-150m²) 16A CEE

1 ACD**F**IJKLMPST
2 RTVWX
3 ABFGKNRU
4 (C 15/6-15/9) (F)
(H 15/6-15/9) IJK**LN**(Q)
(R+S 9/4-30/9)
(T+U 1/7-31/8) (Z 1/6-31/8)
5 **AB**DEFGJLNPUVXYZ
6 AEGHJ**K**(N 2km)ORTUV

A modern campsite with excellent toilets, spacious pitches and a lovely new swimming pool. A good starting point for cycle trips. The automobile museum and Les Sables d'Olonne are worth visiting in the area.

From Talmont-St-Hilaire D949 direction Sables-d'Olonne. Then D4a left towards Bourgenay. Campsite signposted 1 km at the right.

CC € 15 *1/4-9/7 27/8-8/10* *7=6, 14=12*

N 46°27'57" W 1°39'10"

Talmont-St-Hilaire, F-85440 / Pays de la Loire (Vendée)

1542

Sun Océan***
538 av. des Sables
FAX +33 (0)2-51906124
2/4 - 2/10
camping-sunocean@wanadoo.fr

2,2ha 58**T**(100-140m²) 10A CEE

1 ACD**F**IJKLMOPRS
2 GRVWXY
3 BGHJNRU
4 (E+H) (T+Z 1/7-31/8)
5 **A**GIJKLMNPUXYZ
6 EGJRTV

A wonderfully peaceful campsite with a friendly ambiance and spacious marked out pitches. Very well-maintained toilet facilities. A good starting point for walking and cycling tours. Bakery and shops within walking distance.

On the D949 when leaving Talmont-St-Hilaire towards Les Sables. On the right.

CC € 15 *2/4-15/7 1/9-2/10* *7=6, 14=12, 21=18*

N 46°28'14" W 1°38'6"

Talmont-St-Hilaire, F-85440 / Pays de la Loire (Vendée)

1543

Yelloh! Village Le Littoral*****
Le Porteau
+33 (0)2-51220464
FAX +33 (0)2-51220537
15/4 - 30/9
@ info@campinglelittoral.fr

9ha 60**T**(80-100m²) 10A CEE

1 ACD**F**IJKLMOPST
2 BEGNQRSVWXY
3 ABFGHJK**M**N**P**RUW
4 (C 15/4-11/9) (F)
(H 15/4-11/9) IJKM
(Q+R+S+T+U+V+X+Y
15/4-11/9)Z
5 **AB**DEFGIJKLMNOPUVWXY
Z
6 ACDEGHI**JK**(N 3km)ORTV

A lovely family campsite with plenty of comfort and all facilities within walking distance from the ocean. Wonderful heated leisure pool and indoor pool. Bar, restaurant and small supermarket open all season. Walking and cycling routes from the campsite. Five minutes from Sables d'Olonne.

D949 from Talmont-St-Hilaire to Les Sables-d'Olonne, turn left just past the racecourse. Signposted.

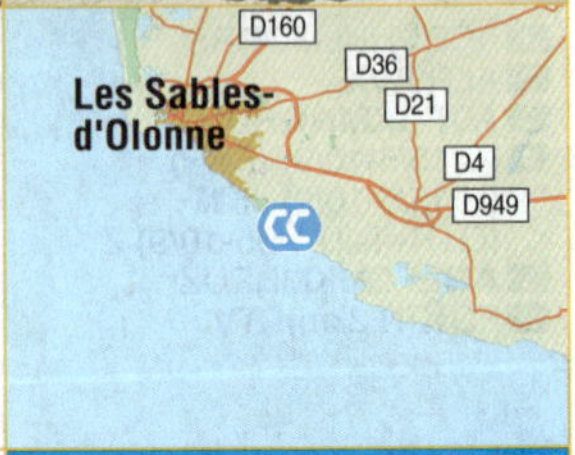

CC € 17 *15/4-2/7 31/8-30/9*

N 46°27'7'' W 1°42'6''

Tuffé, F-72160 / Pays de la Loire (Sarthe)

1544

du Lac****
route de Prévelles
+33 (0)2-43938834
FAX +33 (0)2-43934354
9/4 - 9/10
@ campingdulac.tuffe@orange.fr

4ha 115**T**(85-200m²) 6A CEE

1 ACD**G**IJKLMPRS
2 ACDGLMRTVWXY
3 ABGHJK**MNOPQ**RU**W**Z
4 (C+E+H+Q+R+Z)
5 **AB**DEFGJLMNPQUWZ
6 ACDEG**K**(N 0,7km)RTV

This fine municipal campsite with a swimming pool, fishpond and plenty of recreational opportunities is located in lovely natural surroundings. Well worth a visit!

Follow the D323 to Connerré, then via the D33 to Tuffé and follow the 'Base de Loisirs' camping signs. Camping du Lac is next door.

CC € 15 *9/4-10/7 27/8-9/10* 7=6

N 48°7'6'' E 0°30'36''

Vendrennes, F-85250 / Pays de la Loire (Vendée)

1545

de la Motte***
La Motte
+33 (0)2-51635967
1/1 - 31/12
@ contact@camping-lamotte.com

3ha 43**T**(100-140m²) 16A CEE

1 ACD**G**IJKLMOPQ
2 FGRVXY
3 ADGHJNUW
4 (C+H 1/6-15/9) J
(Q+R 1/6-30/9)
(T+U+V 1/6-15/9) (Z)
5 **AB**DGIJKLMNOPUZ
6 AEG**J**(N 0,5km)ORTV

This friendly campsite with large pitches in the interior of the Vendée is a guarantee for rest and space.

From the A83 or A87 take the Les Essarts exit, then the D160 towards Cholet. Campsite signposted in the village of Vendrennes.

CC € 15 *1/1-7/7 24/8-31/12*

N 46°49'38'' W 1°7'2''

Yvré-l'Evêque, F-72530 / Pays de la Loire (Sarthe) 1546

Camping Le Pont Romain****
allée des Ormeaux
+33 (0)2-43822539
15/3 - 15/11
contact@campinglepontromain.fr

2,5ha 67T(80-150m²) 16A CEE

1 ACD**G**IJKLNPQ
2 FGLRTUVWXY
3 BGHJQRU
4 (C+H 15/6-15/9) (Q 1/5-30/10) (R) (T 1/7-31/8)
5 **AB**DEFGIJKLMNPUWXYZ
6 ACDEGJ(N 0,5km)T

This campsite is located in a natural oasis a few kilometres from the centre of the art and history town of Le Mans. A convenient location for visiting the tourist attractions. The campsite has a swimming pool, toddlers' pool, activity room and snack bar with terrace to guarantee you a pleasant stay.

From E50/A11, at exit 6 head south to the A28. On A28, exit 23 Le Mans-Centre.

CC € 17 *15/3-30/6 1/9-15/11*

N 48°1'9" E 0°16'47"

Airvault, F-79600 / Poitou-Charentes (Deux-Sèvres) 1547

de Courte Vallée***
rue Courte Vallée
+33 (0)5-49647065
FAX +33 (0)5-49941778
1/3 - 15/11
camping@caravanningfrance.com

3,5ha 65T(110-130m²) 13A CEE

1 ACDGIJKLMOPST
2 CLRTVWXY
3 ABGHJNR**W**
4 (C 1/6-20/9) (Q+R+T+U+X+Z)
5 **AB**GIJKLMNPUWZ
6 ABDEG**KL**(N 1,5km)QTV

Campsite is located in the Thouet valley close to medieval town of Airvault and the Loire valley. The campsite is characterized by the high level of maintenance; pitches with electricity, excellent toilets, swimming pool. Wireless internet and nice terrace. The English family is hospitable and will do a lot to offer you a wonderful holiday.

From Thouars take the D938. Then take the D725-bis as far as Airvault. In the village follow the camp signs 'de Courte Vallée'.

CC € 19 *1/4-30/6 1/9-31/10*

N 46°49'59" W 0°8'53"

Avanton, F-86170 / Poitou-Charentes (Vienne) 1548

Du Futur***
9 rue des Bois
+33 (0)5-49540967
1/4 - 30/10
contact@camping-du-futur.com

3ha 55T(100-120m²) 10A

1 AC**G**IJKLMOPRS
2 FLRVWX
3 AB**F**GNQR
4 (C 30/6-15/9) (Q+R) Z
5 **AB**FGIJLMNPUWZ
6 ACDEG**JK**(N 5km)V

The owners of this campsite are extremely hospitable. An ideal place for a relaxing holiday. The surroundings are quiet and there are numerous historic towns to visit in the 'Vienne' region. And only 7 km from Parc Futuroscope. Also a good stop en route to the South of France or Spain.

N10 exit Avanton, follow arrows, on D757 (the road to Poitiers). Or via motorway exit 29.

CC € 17 *1/4-5/7 26/8-30/10 14=12*

N 46°39'22" E 0°18'7"

Aytré/La Rochelle, F-17440 / Poitou-Charentes (Charente-Maritime)

1549

Les Sables****
chemin du Pontreau
+33 (0)5-46454030
1/4 - 15/10
camping_les_sables@yahoo.fr

5,5ha 298**T**(100-140m²) 6A CEE

1 ACD**F**IJLPQ
2 AERTVWX
3 ABGKMN**OP**RUVWY
4 (C 1/5-30/9) (F 1/5-15/9)
(H 1/6-30/9) IJ**LMNO**
(Q+R+T+U 1/7-31/8)
(V 15/6-31/8) (X 1/7-31/8) Z
5 **AB**EFGIJKLMNPRUVZ
6 FG**IK**(N 2km)RTV

A wonderful family campsite with every amenity. Spacious pitches separated by hedges. Sandy beach within walking distance. Close to La Rochelle.

N137 La Rochelle-Rochefort. Exit Aytré (D939). Turn right at the roundabout. At the following roundabout third exit left onto the D937. Turn left at the second traffic lights. Follow the signs 'La Plage'.

CC € 19 *1/4-11/6 20/6-1/7 1/9-15/10*

N 46°6'59'' W 1°7'10''

Bignac, F-16170 / Poitou-Charentes (Charente)

1550

Marco de Bignac***
2 chemin de la Résistance
+33 (0)5-45217841
1/3 - 30/11
info@marcodebignac.com

8ha 85**T**(100m²) 6A

1 ACDGIJKLMPRS
2 DGRVWXY
3 ADGHJMNRW
4 (B 1/7-31/8) (Q+R)
(U+Y 1/5-30/9) Z
5 **A**FGIJKLMNPUWZ
6 EGJ(N 3km)T

The campsite is located by a lake, surrounded by old trees. Campers can fish free for carp. The touring pitches are marked out by trees. These provide welcome shade. An idyllic, relaxing location with a swimming pool. Restaurant with a terrace by the water.

Leave the RN10 at the La Touche D'Anais sign. Follow the 'Vars', 'Bignac' and then 'Camping Marco de Bignac' signs.

CC € 17 *1/3-2/7 20/8-30/11 7=6*

N 45°47'51'' E 0°3'47''

Bois Vert/Com. du Tallud, F-79200 / Poitou-Charentes (Deux-Sèvres)

1551

Le Bois Vert****
14 rue Boisseau
+33 (0)5-49647843
FAX +33 (0)5-49959668
4/4 - 30/10
campingboisvert@orange.fr

3ha 88**T**(70-130m²) 10A CEE

1 ACD**G**IJKLMPST
2 CLRTVWXY
3 ABGHJKMRU**W**
4 (C+G 1/6-15/9)
(Q 1/5-30/9) (R 15/5-15/9)
(T+U+V+X+Z 8/5-15/9)
5 **AB**CDEFGIJKLMNOPQRU
WXYZ
6 ADEG**IK**(N 2km)ORTUV

Medium sized campsite on a lake and a river with opportunities for fishing. Close to the medieval town of Parthenay. Well marked-out cycling and walking paths.

From Niort take the D743 as far as the southwest edge of Parthenay, then turn left onto the D949bis, over the bridge and immediately right.

CC € 17 *4/4-3/7 22/8-30/10 7=6*

N 46°38'30'' W 0°16'3''

Boyardville, F-17190 / Poitou-Charentes (Charente-Maritime)

iD 1552

Les Saumonards**
route des Saumonards
+33 (0)5-46472320
FAX +33 (0)5-46856406
1/4 - 31/10
@ campingmunicipal.
stgeorgesdoleron@wanadoo.fr
267T(60-120m²) 5A CEE

1 ACDGHIJKLMOP
2 ABESXY
3 AFGHJR
4 (Q)
(T+U+V+Z 15/6-15/9)
5 ABFGIJKLMNOPUZ
6 (N 1,2km)

A peaceful campsite in pine woods with access to the beach.

From the viaduct towards Dolus and then Boyardville. Over the bridge in Boyardville. Campsite shown as 'Municipal'.

CC € 13 *1/4-30/6 1/9-31/10*

N 45°58'42'' W 1°14'28''

Chalandray, F-86190 / Poitou-Charentes (Vienne)

iD 1553

Du Bois de St. Hilaire
route de la Gare
FAX +33 (0)5-49602084
1/5 - 30/9
@ accueil@camping-st-hilaire.com
8ha 38T(100-198m²) 10A CEE

1 ACDGIJKLMOPQ
2 BRVWXY
3 ABFHKMNQRU
4 (B 21/6-31/8)
5 ABGIJKLMNOPUW
6 AEKL(N 0,7km)TV

A peaceful campsite in a wood with plenty of tall trees, but 1 km from the local shops. The site has a lovely swimming pool, a tennis court with practice wall and a friendly English owner. You can stand on the prime meridian on the campsite. Plenty of cycling and walking in the immediate surroundings.

From Poitiers take the N149 direction Partenay (or vice versa). In Chalandray take the D24 direction Vauzailles. The campsite is located about 750 metres on the right.

CC € 13 *1/5-30/6 1/9-30/9*

N 46°40'4'' W 0°0'11''

Châtelaillon-Plage, F-17340 / Poitou-Charentes (Charente-Maritime)

iD 1554

Camping Au Port-Punay***
allée Bernard Moreau,Les Boucholeur
+33 (0)5-17810000
FAX +33 (0)5-46568644
2/5 - 24/9
@ contact@
camping-port-punay.com
3ha 116T(100m²) 10A CEE

1 ACDFIJKLMPQ
2 AEGRSTVWXY
3 ABGJKRUWY
4 (C+H) K(Q+R+S)
(T+U+V+X+Z 15/6-11/9)
5 ABEFGJLMNPRUVXYZ
6 ACEGHIK(N 0,2km)OTUV

A friendly campsite, partly under trees and 200m from a sandy beach. Heated swimming pool. Excellent toilet facilities and large pitches. Starting point for visiting the islands Ré and Aix, situated between the towns La Rochelle and Rochefort. Châtelaillon can be visited by bike. WiFi. The site has an Ecolabel.

N137 La Rochelle-Rochefort, exit D109 Châtelaillon-Plage. First left at the second roundabout. Follow 'Les Boucholeurs' then follow campsite signs.

CC € 19 *2/5-2/7 28/8-24/9*

N 46°3'18'' W 1°5'0''

Châtelaillon-Plage, F-17340 / Poitou-Charentes (Charente-Maritime)

iD **1555**

L'Océan***
ave d'Angoulins
+33 (0)5-46568797
21/5 - 25/9
campingocean17@free.fr

1,9ha 97**T**(85-120m²) 10A CEE

1 ACD**F**IJKLMOPST
2 AGRVWXY
3 BGHJKRU
4 (B 1/6-15/9) (Q ⊶) (T+U 1/7-31/8) Z
5 **AB**EFGIJKLMNOPUVZ
6 ACEG**K**(N 1km)TV

Pure camping pleasure (only touring pitches) within walking distance (600m) of the sea. Congenial atmosphere and excellent toilet facilities. Lovely swimming lake. Walking and cycling paradise. A good base for visiting la Rochelle, Fort Boyard, les îles de Ré, Oléron en Aix and le Marais Poitevin.

N137 La Rochelle southwards, exit Angoulins. Then D202 Châtelaillon-Plage. Campsite is signposted on entering Châtelaillon.

CC € 19 *21/5-3/7 22/8-25/9*

N 46°5'12'' W 1°5'39''

Châtelaillon-Plage, F-17340 / Poitou-Charentes (Charente-Maritime)

iD **1556**

Le Village Corsaire des 2 Plages****
av. d'Angoulins
+33 (0)5-46562753
FAX +33 (0)5-46435118
1/5 - 25/9
reception@2plages.com

4,5ha 97**T**(80-150m²) 10A CEE

1 ACD**F**IJKLMOPST
2 AEGPRSTVXY
3 AB**F**GJKMNRUWY
4 (C+H+Q+R+S+T+U+V+X 1/5-15/9)Z
5 **AB**EFGIJKLMNOPUVWZ
6 ACGH**K**(N 1km)ORTV

An attractive campsite with a lovely heated swimming pool. Walking distance from the sea. Spacious partly shaded pitches under high deciduous trees. Good base for cycle and walking tours.

N137 La Rochelle direction south, exit Angoulins. Then the D202 Châtelaillon-Plage. You will see the campsite when entering Châtelaillon.

CC € 19 *1/5-11/6 20/6-3/7 22/8-25/9* ***7=6, 14=11***

N 46°5'3'' W 1°5'36''

Chef-Boutonne, F-79110 / Poitou-Charentes (Deux-Sèvres)

iD **1557**

Le Moulin***
Treneuillet, 1 route de Niort
+33 (0)5-49297346
1/1 - 31/12
info@campingchef.com

11ha 37**T**(40-150m²) 10-16A

1 ACD**G**IJKLM**P**RS
2 CGLRUVWXY
3 AGHJR
4 (C 1/5-30/9) (Q+T 1/7-31/8) (U+Y 1/3-1/12) (Z 1/7-31/8)
5 **A**GIJKLMNPUWZ
6 ACDEG**K**(N 2km)T

A peaceful, family campsite by an old watermill. Level grounds, swimming pool and restaurant. Children's playground. Close to an active silver mine, Chateau de Javarzay, with fishing opportunities and guided tours.

In Chef-Boutonne follow the D740 towards Brioux. Campsite signposted.

CC € 15 *1/1-8/7 26/8-31/12*

N 46°6'28'' W 0°5'38''

Condac, F-16700 / Poitou-Charentes (Charente)

1558

Le Réjallant***
+33 (0)5-45312906
+33 (0)9-70600133
1/1 - 31/12
camping@lerejallant.fr

2ha 50**T**(80-150m²) 10A

1 ACDGIJKLMOPRS
2 CDRTUVWXY
3 BHJR
4 (C+G 1/5-15/9) (Q+R) (T+U 1/7-31/8) Z
5 **AB**DFGIJKLNPUXYZ
6 ACDFGK(N 1,5km)OTV

Located in the Charente, 150m from the river which bears its name, you can enjoy a holiday in the countryside throughout the year. 50 km from Futuroscope and Cognac.

Ruffec is 50 km south of Poitiers, towards Condac village follow 'Aire de Réjallant' signs.

CC € 11 *1/1-30/6 1/9-31/12 7=6*

N 46°0'54" E 0°12'46"

Confolens, F-16500 / Poitou-Charentes (Charente)

1559

des Ribières
route de St Germain de Confolens
+33 (0)5-45853527
1/5 - 30/9
camping-les-ribieres@orange.fr

2,3ha 127**T**(60-250m²) 16A CEE

1 ACD**G**IJKLMPQ
2 CRUVWXY
3 ABR**W**
4 (Q 1/7-30/8)
5 **AB**CIJKLNPUV
6 EGK(N 0,6km)

Quiet campsite on the Vienne (and on the D95), 5 minutes walking distance from Confolens centre. Excellent base for walking and cycling in the peaceful Charente region. The area has many culinary options.

In Confolens dir. St. Germain. Campsite on left of road after 500 metres.

CC € 11 *1/5-30/6 1/9-30/9 7=6, 14=12*

N 46°1'9" E 0°40'31"

Couhé, F-86700 / Poitou-Charentes (Vienne)

1560

Sites & Paysages Les Peupliers****
RN10
+33 (0)5-49592116
+33 (0)5-49379209
2/5 - 30/9
info@lespeupliers.fr

16ha 187**T**(80-140m²) 16A

1 ACGIJKLMOPQ
2 BCFLRVWXY
3 ABGHN**Q**RUW
4 (C+H) J(Q+S) (T+U+V 1/7-31/8) Z
5 **AB**CDEFGIJKNOP**ST**UWXYZ
6 ACEG**K**(N 1km)OTV

A lovely campsite with a relaxed atmosphere. Marked out pitches. On both sides of the river. A campsite with plenty of recreational facilities, heated toilets, located in a rural area. Reception is very customer-friendly.

At the N10, exit Couhé-Nord.

CC € 19 *2/5-9/7 26/8-30/9 7=6, 14=12*

N 46°18'44" E 0°10'55"

Coulon, F-79510 / Poitou-Charentes (Deux-Sèvres)

1561

la Venise Verte****
178 route des Bords de Sèvre
+33 (0)5-49359036
1/4 - 31/10
accueil@camping-laveniseverte.fr

2,2ha 120T(80-187m²) 10A CEE

1 ACD**F**IJKLMOPS
2 BCFRTVWXY
3 ABGHJKLNR**W**
4 (C+G 15/6-15/9) (Q+R ⊶) (T+U+X+Z 1/5-30/9)
5 **AB**EFGIJKLMNOPUWXYZ
6 ACEGHJ(N 2km)OSTV

A campsite 2 km from Coulon, in the heart of the Marais Poitevin. Lovely cycling and walking trips are possible. 120 pitches, large swimming pool (open 15/6 to 15/9), restaurant and many recreational opportunities. The campsite has been awarded the European ECO label, thanks to the sustainable tourism that is practiced here. A lovely campsite for a relaxing stay.

From Niort dir. Coulon (D9), then from Coulon D123 direction Irleau. Site on this road.

CC € 17 *1/4-8/7 1/9-30/10*

N 46°18'54'' W 0°36'33''

Courçon, F-17170 / Poitou-Charentes (Charente-Maritime)

1562

Camping La Garenne
14 rue du Collège
+33 (0)5-46679094
1/4 - 31/10
campinglagarenne17@gmail.com

1ha 38T(80-120m²) 10A

1 ACD**G**IJKLMO**P**Q
2 GKRVWXY
3 ABGHMR
4 (C+H 1/7-31/8) (Q 1/5-31/8) (T+U+Z 1/7-31/8)
5 **AB**DEGIJKLMNOPUZ
6 AEGKL(N 0,5km)T

A quiet campsite very close to the 'Marais Poitevin', La Rochelle and Rochefort. Heated swimming pool. Pitches with plenty of shade. 5 minutes by foot from Courçon where all amenities are available.

Follow 'Complexe Sportif' in Courcon. Campsite right opposite this sports centre.

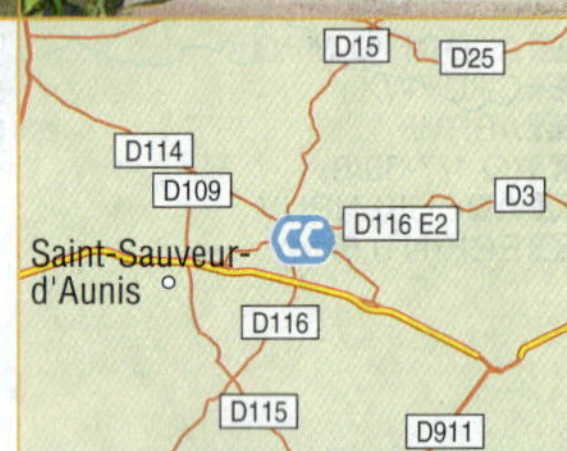

CC € 13 *1/4-4/7 22/8-31/10*

N 46°14'26'' W 0°48'24''

Dolus-d'Oléron, F-17550 / Poitou-Charentes (Charente-Maritime)

1563

La Cailletière***
route de Boyardville
+33 (0)5-46753633
FAX +33 (0)5-46855985
1/4 - 30/9
camping.la.cailletiere@wanadoo.fr

3ha 52T(80-120m²) 10A

1 ACD**G**HIJKLMPST
2 ABQRUVXY
3 B**F**GHJKNR
4 (C ⊶) (G 1/6-30/9) (Q 1/7-30/8) (T+U+V 1/7-31/8) Z
5 **AB**EFGIJKLMNOPUZ
6 E**K**(N 0,8km)OV

An amiable campsite located at the edge of wooded surroundings.

From the viaduct direction St. Pierre. At the roundabout in Dolus (by the Intermarché) direction Boyardville. Signposted thereafter.

CC € 17 *1/4-3/7 27/8-30/9*

N 45°54'59'' W 1°15'10''

Dolus-d'Oléron, F-17550 / Poitou-Charentes (Charente-Maritime)

1564

Ostrea****
route des Huitres
+33 (0)5-46476236
+33 (0)5-46752001
1/4 - 30/9
camping.ostrea@wanadoo.fr

2ha 60T(75-120m²) 6A

1 ACGIJKLMPRS
2 AEKRSTVWX
3 BFGJKNRUWY
4 (E+F+H) K(Q)
(R 15/6-15/9)
(U+V+X 1/7-31/8) Z
5 ABEFGIJKMNOPUVWZ
6 CEGK(N 3,5km)OPUV

A small, peaceful family campsite located right by the sea. Indoor heated swimming pool with jacuzzi. Pontoon for boats provided. Very well maintained toilet facilities.

Turn right over the bridge direction Le Château, through the village right on the coast road. Campsite 3 km further on.

CC € 17 1/4-30/6 1/9-30/9

N 45°54'46'' W 1°13'26''

Eymouthiers/Montbron, F-16220 / Poitou-Charentes (Charente)

1565

Castel Camping Les Gorges du Chambon****
Le Chambon
+33 (0)5-45707170
1/5 - 15/9
info@camping-gorgesduchambon.com

28ha 109T(132-300m²) 10A CEE

1 ACDGIJKLMPRS
2 ACIKLRVWXY
3 BFGHJMPQRUWX
4 (C 1/5-14/9) (H 1/7-31/8)
(Q+R) (T 20/4-14/9)
(U+V+X+Y+Z)
5 ABDEFGHJLMNPUWXZ
6 ACDEGJ(N 7km)ORTV

This castle campsite is located in the middle of unspoilt countryside on the borders of the Dordogne and the Charente. Attractively landscaped with plenty of space. Heated swimming pool and restaurant.

N10 Poitiers-Angoulême, in Mansle turn left on the D6 direction La Rochefoucauld and Montbron. Signposted in Montbron. Turn left in La Tricherie, take the D163 (follow the signs).

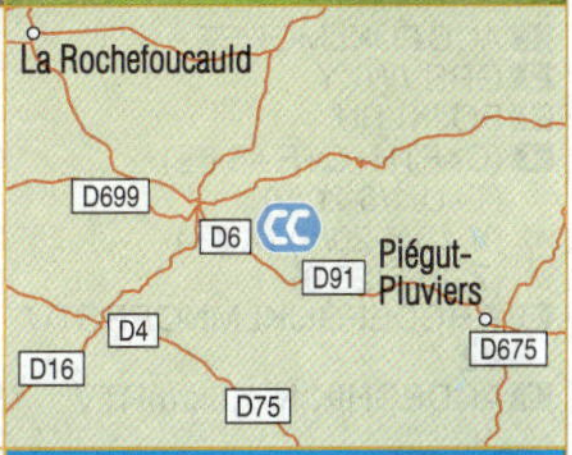

CC € 17 1/5-4/7 25/8-15/9 7=6, 14=11

N 45°38'39'' E 0°32'27''

Ingrandes, F-86220 / Poitou-Charentes (Vienne)

1566

Le Petit Trianon de Saint Ustre****
1 rue du Moulin St. Ustre
+33 (0)5-49026147
+33 (0)5-49026881
16/4 - 8/9
contact@petit-trianon.com

7ha 116T(120-150m²) 10A

1 ACGIJKLMOPRS
2 FIKLRVWXY
3 ABGHJKNQRU
4 (A 4/7-27/8) (C+H) K
(Q+R+T+U+V+Y+Z)
5 ABDEFGIJKLOPUWXYZ
6 CDEGIJK(N 3km)OQRV

This family campsite is located around a castle in a rural setting, and has spacious pitches and a heated swimming pool. Excellent base for visiting Roman churches, castles and the Poitou and Touraine rivers.

N10 Tours-Poitiers, turn left before Ingrandes, follow the signs.

CC € 17 16/4-3/7 26/8-8/9 7=6, 14=12, 21=18

N 46°53'16'' E 0°35'13''

L'Houmeau, F-17137 / Poitou-Charentes (Charente-Maritime)

iD 1567

Au Petit Port de l'Houmeau***
rue des Sartières
+33 (0)5-46509082
+33 (0)5-46500133
1/4 - 30/9
info@aupetitport.com

2,2ha 50**T**(70-110m²) 16A CEE

1 ACD**F**IJKLOPT
2 GNRTVXY
3 B**F**JKRUW
4 (C+H 1/5-30/9) K
(Q+R+T+X+Z)
5 **AB**EFGIJKLMNPUWZ
6 ACEGK(N 0,5km)TV

Peaceful campsite with good services and heated pool. 5 km from La Rochelle and the bridge to Ile de Ré. Good base for cycling and walking tours.

La Rochelle ring road towards Ile de Ré. Exit Lagord. Exit D104 Nieul at roundabout. Then take the D106 towards L'Houmeau.

CC € 19 *1/4-8/7 3/9-30/9 7=6, 14=12*

N 46°11'44" W 1°11'17"

La Couarde-sur-Mer, F-17670 / Poitou-Charentes (Charente-Maritime)

iD 1568

La Tour des Prises****
route d'Ars
+33 (0)5-46298482
+33 (0)5-46298899
25/3 - 29/9
camping@lesprises.com

2,5ha 85**T**(85-120m²) 16A CEE

1 ACD**F**IJKLMOPST
2 GRSVWXY
3 BGJKLRU
4 (C+F+H+Q+R+S)
(T+U 1/6-20/9)
(V 15/5-20/9) (X)
(Z 15/5-20/9)
5 **AB**CDEFGIJKLMNOPRSTU
VZ
6 ACDEGHIK(N 1,5km)RTV

A peaceful family campsite in the middle of Ile de Ré and 600 metres from a fine beach and the sea. Heated indoor swimming pool. A paradise for cyclists and walkers.

Take D735 dir. La Flotte after the bridge, then to St. Martin-de-Ré and past Couarde-sur-Mer dir. Ars-en-Ré. Turn right on roundabout in Couarde. Signposted.

CC € 17 *25/3-9/7 27/8-29/9 14=12, 28=24*

N 46°12'16" W 1°26'47"

La Flotte-en-Ré, F-17630 / Poitou-Charentes (Charente-Maritime)

iD 1569

La Grainetière****
route de St. Martin
+33 (0)5-46096886
+33 (0)5-46095313
1/4 - 2/10
la-grainetiere@orange.fr

2,6ha 60**T**(80-120m²) 10A CEE

1 ACD**F**IJKLMO**P**ST
2 BSVXY
3 AB**F**GHKL**OP**RU
4 (C+F+H) K
(Q+R+S+T+U+Z)
5 **AB**DEFGIJLMNOPUWXYZ
6 ACEGHIK(N 1km)ORTV

A friendly family campsite close to the idyllic town of La Flotte in the middle of wooded surroundings with spacious pitches. Heated in- and outdoor swimming pool, bar, shop, snack bar and bike hire. Free WiFi.

D735 towards La Flotte after the toll bridge. Just past La Flotte take direction St. Martin. Well signposted.

CC € 17 *1/4-7/7 28/8-1/10*

N 46°11'15" W 1°20'37"

La Roche-Posay, F-86270 / Poitou-Charentes (Vienne) 1570

La Roche-Posay Vacances****
route de Lesigny
+33 (0)5-49862123
9/4 - 24/9
info@
larocheposay-vacances.com

8,5ha 200T(80-140m²) 10A CEE

1 ACFIJKLMPQ
2 CGLRVWXY
3 BFGHJKNRUW
4 (B+E+H) IJK
(Q+T+U+V+X) Z
5 ABDEFGIJKLMNOPSUVWZ
6 ADEGIJK(N 0,7km)RV

Family campsite situated on the River Creuse, 1.5 km from the village. Large pitches marked out by trees. Indoor heated swimming pool open all season.

A10 exit 26 Châtellerault-Nord (km 273). Follow La Roche-Posay signs. Then D275 to La Roche-Posay. Follow camping hippodrome signs at roundabout.

CC €17 9/4-30/6 28/8-24/9

N 46°47'57" E 0°48'34"

Le Bois-Plage-en-Ré, F-17580 / Poitou-Charentes (Charente-Maritime) 1571

Campéole Les Amis de la Plage***
68 avenue du Pas des Boeufs
+33 (0)5-46092401
1/4 - 30/9
les-amis-de-la-plage@
andretriganogroupe.com

5ha 136T(80-110m²) 10A CEE

1 ABCDGIJKLOPST
2 AEIJSVWXY
3 BGJKRUWY
4 (Q+R 1/7-31/8)
5 ABEFGIJKLMNOPQUVZ
6 ACEGHK(N 1km)RT

A family campsite with direct access to the beach. Swimming pool (entrance charge) and shops at the site entrance. Most suitable for visiting the beach, fishing from the beach, watersports and cycle trips between saline pools, oyster beds and bird sanctuaries....

Follow La Rochelle then cross the (toll) bridge to Ile de Ré island.

CC €17 1/5-4/7 22/8-30/9

N 46°10'39" W 1°23'12"

Le Bois-Plage-en-Ré, F-17580 / Poitou-Charentes (Charente-Maritime) 1572

Les Varennes****
Raise Maritaise
+33 (0)5-46091543
FAX +33 (0)5-46094727
9/4 - 29/9
info@les-varennes.com

2,5ha 56T(80-100m²) 10A CEE

1 ACDFIJKLPST
2 AERSVWX
3 ABGKRY
4 (C+F+Q+R+S+Z)
5 ABDEFGJLNOPUVWZ
6 ACEGHK(N 0,8km)RTV

A small, happy, family campsite under tall conifers with good amenities. Fairly sheltered pitches. There is a nice sandy beach within walking distance. Free WiFi on the campsite.

From the toll bridge, via the roundabout, onto the D201. In Le Bois-Plage follow the signs 'Les Varennes'.

CC €19 9/4-4/7 1/9-29/9

N 46°10'43" W 1°22'59"

Le Château-d'Oléron, F-17480 / Poitou-Charentes (Charente-Maritime)

1573

Airotel Oléron****
19 avenue de la Libération
+33 (0)5-46476182
FAX +33 (0)5-46477967
1/4 - 30/9
@ info@
camping-airotel-oleron.com

7,4ha 123**T**(80-150m²) 10A CEE

1 AC**G**HIJKLMPQ
2 DRTVWX
3 B**F**GHJK**M**N**OP**RUW
4 (**A** 1/7-30/8) (C+H)
(Q 1/7-31/8) (R 15/6-15/9)
(T+U+V+X+Y 1/6-15/9) Z
5 **AB**DFGIJKLMNOPUVZ
6 EG**IK**(N 1km)ORTV

Campsite close to the centre of Château-d'Oléron. Perfect for horse lovers, with a swimming pool and other sports opportunities.

Direction Le Château beyond bridge, then left towards centre. Follow signs by 'Crédit Agricole'.

CC € 17 *1/4-8/7 25/8-30/9* ***7=6, 14=11***

N 45°52'57'' W 1°12'24''

Le Château-d'Oléron, F-17480 / Poitou-Charentes (Charente-Maritime)

1574

Au Pigeonnier****
73 avenue d'Antioche
+33 (0)5-46476220
FAX +33 (0)5-46474849
25/3 - 30/9
@ campaupigeonnier@gmail.com

1,5ha 22**T**(100-112m²) 10A CEE

1 ACD**F**HIJKLMPST
2 ARVWXY
3 A**F**GHJKLRUW
4 (E) (H 1/7-31/8)
(Q+R) Z
5 **AB**EFGHIJKLMNOPUWXYZ
6 CEGK(N 0,8km)V

Small, homely, easy-going campsite with pool. The large giraffe bouncy castle can be seen from afar.

From viaduct, right on 3rd roundabout, dir. Le Château. Then follow signs.

CC € 17 *25/3-7/7 24/8-30/9*

N 45°53'15'' W 1°12'51''

Le Château-d'Oléron, F-17480 / Poitou-Charentes (Charente-Maritime)

1575

La Brande*****
route des Huîtres
+33 (0)5-46476237
FAX +33 (0)5-46477170
27/3 - 1/11
@ info@camping-labrande.com

5,5ha 109**T**(100-200m²) 10A

1 ACD**F**IJKLMPST
2 AELRSTVWXY
3 BFGHJKL**M**N**Q**R**T**UWY
4 (A 1/7-30/8)
(D+F+H 31/3-11/11) JK**LN**
(Q 5/4-31/10) (R 1/6-31/8)
(T 4/7-31/8)
(U+V+X+Y 1/7-31/8) Z
5 **AB**EFGIJKLMNOPR**ST**UV
WXY
6 CEGJ(N 3km)ORV

A family campsite located in a rural area at 300 metres from the sea. Indoor heated swimming pool with slide. Free WiFi hot spot.

From Le Château take the coastal road Route des Huitres in a north-westerly direction. The campsite is located to the left after about 3 km.

CC € 17 *27/3-3/7 28/8-1/11*

N 45°54'15'' W 1°12'55''

Le Château-d'Oleron/La Gaconn., F-17480 / Poitou-Charentes (Charente-Maritime) 1576

Le Fief Melin***
rue des Alizés
+33 (0)5-46476085
1/5 - 30/9
lefiefmelin@wanadoo.fr

3ha 81**T**(82-130m²) 10A CEE

1 ACDGIJKLMOPQ
2 GRTVX
3 B**F**GHJKNRU
4 (E) (Q+R 1/7-30/8) (T+U+X 1/7-31/8) Z
5 **A**GIJKLMNPUVZ
6 EG**K**(N 1km)R

A peacefully located campsite with a lovely indoor swimming pool. 1 km from the beach.

From the bridge towards Le Château, then direction Dolus to La Gaconnière, follow Rue des Illexés 400m on the right.

CC € 15 *1/5-9/7 26/8-30/9 8=7*

N 45°53'37'' W 1°12'52''

Le Fouilloux, F-17270 / Poitou-Charentes (Charente-Maritime) 1577

La Motte*
D270, Lieu-dit La Motte
+33 (0)5-46042691
4/1 - 16/12
camping-la-motte17@orange.fr

3,5ha 45**T**(125-200m²) 16A CEE

1 AGIJKLMO**P**ST
2 DKLMRTUVWXY
3 AGHJ**O**W
4 T
5 GIJKLMNOPUWZ
6 CDEGK(N 3,6km)O

The campsite owner has deliberately opted for peace and quiet, ideal for walkers and cyclists. Anglers can indulge themselves in the small lake at the campsite. Swimming possible in the nearby lake.

A10 exit Montguyon. At Montguyon dir. St. Aigulin (D730). At Intermarché roundabout continue to St. Aigulin (D730). 2nd left after viaduct (D270). Campsite 1800m. 12 km from exit N10.

CC € 13 *4/1-15/7 1/9-16/12*

N 45°12'45'' W 0°8'16''

Le Grand-Village-Plage, F-17370 / Poitou-Charentes (Charente-Maritime) 1578

Camping-Club Les Pins****
6 allée des Pins
+33 (0)5-46475013
1/4 - 29/9
contact@lespinsdoleron.com

6ha 116**T**(80-100m²) 10A CEE

1 ABCD**G**HIJKLMOPST
2 ABISVWXY
3 A**F**GHJKRUW
4 (B+T+U+V) Z
5 **AB**EFGIJKLMNOPQRUWXY
6 CEG**K**(N 0,2km)OTV

A campsite located in pine woods. Friendly reception, every comfort provided. Swimming lake with sandy beach.

From viaduct straight on at 1st roundabout, 2nd roundabout direction Grand-Village, 3rd roundabout direction Centreville-Plage, 4th roundabout straight on. Campsite then signposted.

CC € 15 *1/4-2/7 28/8-29/9 7=6*

N 45°51'44'' W 1°14'26''

Le Grand-Village-Plage, F-17370 / Poitou-Charentes (Charente-Maritime) — 1579

Le Maine****
24 route du Maine
+33 (0)5-46754276
1/2 - 15/11
camping.lemaine@wanadoo.fr

1,7ha 23T(85-100m²) 10A CEE

1 ABCD**G**HIJKLMO**P**Q
2 ARTUVXY
3 A**F**GHJKLRU
4 (Q 1/7-31/8) (R)
(V 1/4-30/9)
5 **A**DFGIJKLMNOPUZ
6 EGK(N 2,5km)ORV

A small family campsite 1,5 km from the sea. Every comfort. Free WiFi.

From the viaduct towards St. Pierre-d'Oléron, 3rd exit at roundabout after 1st crossroads. Then direction Vert Bois. Left at traffic lights. 100m on the left.

CC € 17 *1/2-30/6 1/9-15/11* *7=6, 14=12*

N 45°52'53" W 1°14'56"

Les Mathes, F-17570 / Poitou-Charentes (Charente-Maritime) — 1580

La Palombière***
1551 route de la Fouasse
+33 (0)5-46226925
FAX +33 (0)5-46224458
1/4 - 15/10
camping.lapalombiere@wanadoo.fr

9,5ha 218T(100-200m²) 6-10A CEE

1 A**G**IJKLMOPS
2 BGRUWXY
3 AB**F**GHJKLN**PR**
4 (C+H 1/6-30/9)
(Q+R 15/6-15/9)
(T+U+V+X+Z 1/7-31/8)
5 **AB**DFGIJKLMNOPQRUZ
6 ACDEG**K**(N 1,5km)TV

A campsite idyllically situated in the woods with luxurious toilet facilities and just 3 km from the sandy beaches of the Côte Sauvage. An ideal base for interesting trips out. Restaurant and free WiFi available.

Take exit 35 on the A10 at Saintes direction Royan N150. Then follow La Palmyre signs. Direction Les Mathes at the large roundabout. Campsite signposted at the next roundabout.

CC € 17 *1/4-3/7 27/8-15/10*

N 45°43'24" W 1°10'27"

Les Mathes, F-17570 / Poitou-Charentes (Charente-Maritime) — 1581

Le Petit Dauphin
1696 route de la Fouasse
+33 (0)5-46063823
1/4 - 2/10
lepetitdauphin2@wanadoo.fr

1,7ha 94T 10A CEE

1 BC**F**IJKLMOP
2 AGRSVWXY
3 **FQ**R
4 (C+H 1/5-30/9)
(Q+T+V+X+Z 1/4-30/9)
5 ADEFGIJKLMNOPQUW
6 ABGK(N 5km)O

Naturist campsite located close to the Atlantic coast. Heated pool from June to September. Surroundings with lots of plantlife and flowers.

CC € 17 *1/5-8/7 25/8-2/10*

N 45°43'27" W 1°10'28"

Les Mathes/La Palmyre, F-17570 / Poitou-Charentes (Charente-Maritime) — 1582

Beausoleil***
20 ave de la Coubre La Palmyre
+33 (0)5-46223003
1/5 - 17/9
camping.beausoleil@wanadoo.fr

3,5ha 120**T**(70-120m²) 10A CEE

1 ACDGIJKLMPS
2 ABEGIJRSVWXY
3 B**F**HRW
4 (C+H 1/6-15/9) (Q 🔑)
(R+T+U+V+X 15/6-15/9) Z
5 **AB**FIJKLMNOPUV
6 AEGI**K**(N 0,2km)ORTV

This ideally located and very peaceful campsite 400m from the beach is a good base for discovering the Charente Maritime.

Drive to La Palmyre then take direction Phare de la Coubre at the large roundabout. Campsite immediately on the right.

CC € 17 *1/5-4/7 25/8-17/9*

N 45°41'32'' W 1°11'0''

Les Mathes/La Palmyre, F-17570 / Poitou-Charentes (Charente-Maritime) — 1583

La Clé des Champs****
1188 route de la Fouasse
+33 (0)5-46224053
FAX +33 (0)5-46225696
1/4 - 16/11
contact@la-cledeschamps.com

7,6ha 119**T**(80-100m²) 10A CEE

1 ACD**G**IJKLMPQ
2 RVWXY
3 B**F**GKLN**Q**RU**V**
4 (C+E 🔑) (H 1/5-15/9) **KN**
(Q+S+T+U+V+X+Z 1/4-30/9)
5 **AB**DEFGIJKLMNPUW
6 ADEGH**IJK**(N 1,5km)ORTV

This campsite, tucked away in the greenery 4 km from the beach, invites you to enjoy a relaxing stay in a friendly and warmhearted atmosphere. Breathe in the healthy open air.

From La Palmyre after the roundabout take route de la Fouasse D141/E4. First campsite on the right.

CC € 17 *1/4-9/7 27/8-16/11* *7=6*

N 45°43'16'' W 1°10'17''

Les Mathes/La Palmyre, F-17570 / Poitou-Charentes (Charente-Maritime) — 1584

La Pinède****
2103 route de la Fouasse
+33 (0)5-46224513
FAX +33 (0)5-46225021
2/4 - 25/9
contact@campinglapinede.com

8ha 80**T**(80-100m²) 10A CEE

1 ACDEIJKLPS
2 BSVWXY
3 BDFGHKNQRU
4 (B 1/7-31/8) (F+H 🔑) IJM
(Q+R+T+U+V+X 🔑)
(Y 1/7-31/8) (Z 🔑)
5 **AB**EFGIJKLMNOP**ST**UWZ
6 AEGH**K**(N 4km)RTV

Family campsite, located in a peaceful area just 5 minutes from the beach, equipped with modern comforts with five water slides, two swimming pools and a variety of activities.

On the A10 near Saintes take exit 35 towards Royan, N150. At Royan towards La Palmyre.
In Palmyre direction Les Mathes and the campsite is signposted from there.

CC € 17 *17/5-5/7 5/9-25/9*

N 45°43'41'' W 1°10'33''

Loix (Île de Ré), F-17111 / Poitou-Charentes (Charente-Maritime) 1585

Les Ilates****
route du Grouin
+33 (0)5-46290543
FAX +33 (0)5-46290679
2/4 - 1/10
camping.les.ilates@flowercampings.com

69T(90-115m²) 10A CEE

1 ACD**F**IJKL**P**Q
2 RVWX
3 BGKMR
4 (C+H 1/5-15/9) K (Q+R+T+U+V+X) Z
5 **AB**EFGIJKLMNOPUWXY
6 CEGIJ**K**(N 2km)RTV

A large campsite with separate camping pitches. Lovely swimming pool and sports opportunities.

Follow the D102 almost to Loix. Then well signposted.

CC € 17 2/4-1/7 1/9-1/10 7=6

N 46°13'35'' W 1°25'34''

Magné, F-79460 / Poitou-Charentes (Deux-Sèvres) 1586

Le Martin-Pêcheur****
155 avenue du Marais Poitevin
+33 (0)5-49357181
1/5 - 18/9
info@camping-le-martin-pecheur.com

2,5ha 57T(100-200m²) 10A CEE

1 ACD**G**IJKLMPQ
2 GLRVWXY
3 AB**F**GHJRU**W**
4 (C+G 15/6-30/8) (R)
5 **AB**DEFGIJKLMNOPQUW
6 ADEGK(N 1km)T

A well-maintained campsite with good facilities. Located 8 km from Niort and 6 km from Coulon. In the middle of the 'Marais de Poitevin'. The campsite is an ideal starting point for walking and cycling tours. Boat trips are also available. Lovely big free swimming pool.

From Niort D9 direction Coulon. Before Coulon direction Magné. Magné and Coulon are about 3 km from each other. Campsite next to the D9.

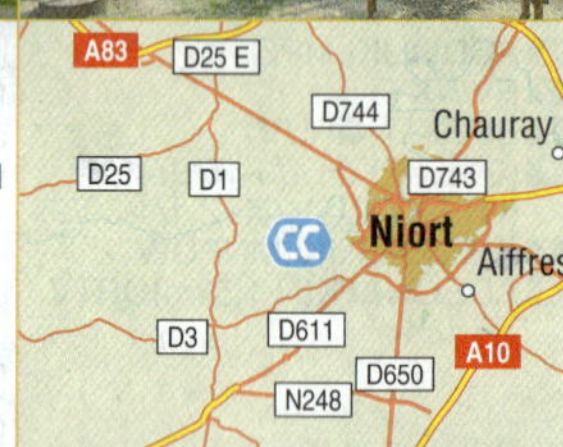

CC € 15 1/5-10/7 28/8-18/9 7=6

N 46°18'49'' W 0°32'6''

Marennes, F-17320 / Poitou-Charentes (Charente-Maritime) 1587

Au Bon Air***
9 avenue Pierre Voyer
+33 (0)5-46850240
FAX +33 (0)5-46362254
1/4 - 30/9
contact@aubonair.com

2,3ha 40T(80-120m²) 16A CEE

1 ACD**F**IJKLM**P**ST
2 AERVXY
3 BGHJRUWY
4 (C+H 1/5-30/9) (Q) (R 1/5-30/9) (T+U+Z 1/7-31/8)
5 **AB**FGIJKLMNOPUVZ
6 AEG**IK**(N 3km)ORTV

A small, quiet and shaded family campsite 150m from the beach. Located at the entrance to l'île d'Oléron and its rugged coast. Swimming pool and a paddling pool open from May to September.

From Saintes direction Ile d'Oléron to Marennes, then direction Marennes (Plages) where the campsite is signposted.

CC € 17 1/5-30/6 1/9-30/9

N 45°49'8'' W 1°8'4''

Meschers, F-17132 / Poitou-Charentes (Charente-Maritime)

iD **1588**

Le Soleil Levant****
33 allée de la Longée
+33 (0)5-46027662
FAX +33 (0)5-46025056
15/4 - 30/9
@ info@camping-soleillevant.com

3ha 132**T**(76-100m²) 10A CEE

1 ACD**F**IJLPQ
2 AGQRTVWXY
3 BGJKN**OP**RUW
4 (B+G 20/6-15/9) J
(Q+R+T+U+V+X 1/7-31/8) Z
5 **AB**FGIJKLMNPUVXY
6 CDEGI**K**(N 1km)TV

A peacefully located campsite with swimming pool and slide, close to a lively harbour and 1 km from the sea. Separate grounds with service point for motorhomes.

In Meschers drive in the direction of the harbour and turn left just before it. The campsite is located here. Clearly signposted.

CC € 17 *15/4-30/6 1/9-30/9*

N 45°33'25'' W 0°56'47''

Port-des-Barques, F-17730 / Poitou-Charentes (Charente-Maritime)

iD **1589**

Municipal de la Garenne***
av. de l'Ile Madame
+33 (0)5-46848066
FAX +33 (0)5-46849833
1/4 - 31/10
@ camping@ville-portdesbarques.fr

7ha 242**T**(83-130m²) 10A CEE

1 ACD**G**IJKLMOPQ
2 AEGRSVWX
3 BG**M**NRUWY
4 (B+G 15/6-15/9) (Q 🔑)
(T+U+V+Z 15/5-15/9)
5 **AB**FGIJKLMNPUVZ
6 EGHIK(N 1km)T

This campsite welcomes you in superb surroundings opposite 'l'Ile Madame' island. On offer: fishing, watersports, visiting special sights and other activities. Ideally situated by the sea between Rochelle and Royan. Amenities include: playground, swimming pool, free WiFi. Motorhome service point.

N137 La Rochelle to the southern edge of Rochefort (becomes the D733). Right after Charente bridge onto D238 and D125. 12 km on the left, just past the small village.

CC € 15 *1/5-30/6 1/9-30/9*

N 45°56'53'' W 1°5'45''

Puilboreau/La Rochelle, F-17138 / Poitou-Charentes (Charente-Maritime)

iD **1590**

Le Beaulieu****
3 rue du Treuil Gras
+33 (0)5-46680438
FAX +33 (0)5-46358595
1/4 - 30/9
@ contact@
camping-la-rochelle.com

5ha 35**T**(85-120m²) 10A CEE

1 ACD**F**IJKLPST
2 RUVWXY
3 BJKMNR
4 (C 15/5-15/9) (E+H 🔑) JK**N**
(Q 🔑) (R 1/7-31/8)
(T+U 🔑) (V 1/7-31/8)
(X+Z 🔑)
5 **AB**DEFGIJKLMNPUWZ
6 ADEGJ**K**TV

A lovely town campsite with new, marked out pitches. Within cycling distance of La Rochelle, cycle track from the campsite and Île de Ré. Heated indoor swimming pool, heated toilets, sauna, jacuzzi. Good starting point for visiting La Rochelle and 'Marais Poitevin'.

From Niort, 2 km before La Rochelle, take 'Centre Commercial Beaulieu' exit. Follow camping signs at first roundabout.

CC € 19 *1/4-7/7 29/8-30/9*

N 46°10'40'' W 1°6'55''

Rivedoux-Plage, F-17940 / Poitou-Charentes (Charente-Maritime) 1591

Campéole Le Platin***
125 avenue Gustave Perreau
+33 (0)5-46098410
FAX +33 (0)5-46356559
1/4 - 25/9
platin@andretriganogroupe.com

3,7ha 139T(60-171m²) 10A CEE

1 ACDFIJKLMOPST
2 AEFGKRSTUWXY
3 ABGJKLRUWY
4 (Z 1/7-31/8)
5 ABEFGIJKLMNOPQRUZ
6 ACDEGHJRTV

Campsite with sea views and modest facilities.

Over the bridge to the Île de Ré direction Rivedoux-Plage. Thereafter signposted.

CC € 17 1/5-4/7 22/8-25/9

N 46°9'35" W 1°15'59"

Royan, F-17200 / Poitou-Charentes (Charente-Maritime) 1592

Campéole Clairefontaine****
16 rue du Colonel Lachaud
+33 (0)5-46390811
FAX +33 (0)5-46381379
1/4 - 30/9
clairefontaine@andretriganogroupe.com

5ha 123T(80-100m²) 10A CEE

1 ACDGIJKLMPST
2 AEGRTWXY
3 BFMNRUWY
4 (C+H 15/5-15/9) (Q+T+U+V+X+Z 1/6-15/9)
5 ABEFGIJKLMNOPQRUVW
6 ACEGHIJ(N 0,3km)TV

A lovely camping ground in natural surroundings yet still close to shops, restaurants, the beach and providing everything you could need for an enjoyable holiday.

A10, near Saintes take exit 35 direction Royan (N150). In Royan drive in the direction of Pontaillac (west of Royan). From there the campsite is clearly signposted.

CC € 17 1/5-4/7 22/8-30/9

N 45°37'52" W 1°3'0"

Saujon, F-17600 / Poitou-Charentes (Charente-Maritime) 1593

Du Lac***
Voie des Tourterelles
+33 (0)5-46068299
1/3 - 31/10
campingdesaujon@gmail.com

3,7ha 150T(120-250m²) 10A CEE

1 ACDGIJLPQ
2 DLRTVWXY
3 AFGHJKMOPRUW
4 (C+F 1/4-30/10) J (Q 1/6-31/8) (R+S+T+U+V+Y 1/7-31/8) Z
5 ABFGIJKLMNOPUVWXY
6 CEGJ(N 1km)TV

A well-maintained campsite. Ideal base for visits to many old towns such as Talmont-sur-Gironde, Mornac-sur-Seudre, Royan, La Rochelle and L'Ile d'Oléron.

On the N50 Royan-Saintes, exit Saujon follow dir. centre. From there follow campsite signs by pool.

CC € 17 1/3-10/7 27/8-31/10

N 45°40'59" W 0°56'16"

St. Augustin-sur-Mer, F-17570 / Poitou-Charentes (Charente-Maritime) 1594

Le Logis du Breuil***
36 rue du Centre
+33 (0)5-46232345
+33 (0)5-46234333
7/5 - 30/9
info@logis-du-breuil.com

9ha 390T(144-280m²) 10A CEE

1 ACD**G**IJKLMOPST
2 BGJRVWXY
3 B**F**GK**M**NRU
4 (E+H) IJ
(Q+S+T+U+V+X+Y+Z)
5 **AB**FGIJKLMNPR**ST**UVWX
YZ
6 CEG**IJ**(N 0,2km)ORTV

Located in the heart of the Arvert peninsula. You can enjoy the friendly, rural atmosphere of our grounds on a spacious pitch (± 200 sq.m.)in a woodland setting. With the ocean close by you can also enjoy the beach and sea. The surroundings are also well worth the effort. A holiday just made for relaxing.

On the A10 at Saintes take exit 35 towards Royan, N150. At Royan follow direction St. Palais as far as the St. Augustin exit. Indicated from there.

CC € 19 *7/5-12/6 1/9-30/9*

N 45°40'32'' W 1°5'42''

St. Christophe, F-16420 / Poitou-Charentes (Charente) 1595

Camping & Gîtes "en Campagne"***
Essubras
+33 (0)5-45316757
1/4 - 1/10
info@encampagne.com

30T(150-240m²) 10A CEE

1 A**G**IJKLM**P**RS
2 KLRTVWX
3 ABGHJKR
4 (C+H 15/5-15/9)
(Q+T+X)
5 **AB**CFGHIJKLMNOPUWXY
6 CDEGIK(N 9km)V

Easy-going and welcoming campsite in Charente-Limousin. Close to the war-time village of Oradour-sur-Glane. Regular communal meals. Free WiFi.

From the D82 in the centre of St. Christophe, take D330 to Nouic. Campsite is indicated.

CC € 13 *1/4-4/7 22/8-1/10*

N 46°0'52'' E 0°52'45''

St. Clément-des-Baleines, F-17590 / Poitou-Charentes (Charente-Maritime) 1596

La Plage****
408 rue du Chaume
+33 (0)5-46294262
+33 (0)5-46290339
1/4 - 25/9
info@la-plage.com

33T 10A CEE

1 ACD**G**IJKLOPST
2 AEGRVX
3 B**F**GJK**M**NRUVWY
4 (C+H) LN
(Q+R+T+U+V+X+Y) Z
5 **AB**DEFGIJKLMNOPQUVW
Z
6 CEGIK(N 4km)QTV

Sunny campsite behind the dunes with an attractive beach. Lovely, heated pool and many amenities. Wellness facility with sauna and hammam.

On Ile de Ré follow D735 past Ars-en-Ré. Follow signs 'Phare des B'. After St. Clément-des-Baleines campsite is clearly indicated.

CC € 19 *1/4-1/7 27/8-24/9*

N 46°14'28'' W 1°33'12''

St. Clément-des-Baleines, F-17590 / Poitou-Charentes (Charente-Maritime) 1597

Les Baleines***
chemin Devaude
+33 (0)5-46294076
+33 (0)5-46296712
16/4 - 24/9
contact@
camping-lesbaleines.com

4,6ha 171**T**(80-140m²) 10A CEE

1 ACD**F**IJKLMOPST
2 AEGJOQRSVWXY
3 ABFGHJKQRWY
4 (Q+R+S) (V 8/7-28/8)
5 **AB**EFGIJKLMNOPUWZ
6 ACEGHJ(N 1km)RTVW

A terraced campsite by the sea, new toilet facilities also for the disabled (including partially sighted). Excellent starting point for walking and cycling trips. Views of the bay and Phare des Baleines. A lovely naturist beach 10 minutes away by bike. Free internet. Eco label.

From the bridge direction 'Phare des Baleines' (± 30 km). Turn left before 'Le Phare' car park (signposted) in the Rue du Chaume and Rue de la Madeleine, then straight ahead to the campsite.

CC € 19 *16/4-1/7 29/8-24/9*

N 46°14'23'' W 1°33'35''

St. Cyr, F-86130 / Poitou-Charentes (Vienne) 1598

Camping du Lac de Saint-Cyr****
+33 (0)5-49625722
+33 (0)5-49522858
25/3 - 30/9
contact@
campinglacdesaintcyr.com

5ha 157**T**(90-120m²) 10A CEE

1 AC**G**IJKLMOPST
2 ADLORTVWXY
3 AB**E**GKMN**P**RUV**WZ**
4 (C+H 1/6-30/9)
(Q+R+T+U+V) Z
5 **AB**GIJKLPUWXYZ
6 EGHJ(N 7km)OV

A campsite with spacious pitches and plenty of vegetation located in an oasis of greenery by a lake and just 10 minutes from Futuroscope. Heated swimming pool (28°C), bird sanctuary and opportunities for fishing, watersports, walking and golf (27 holes).

Left in Beaumont-La Trichérie (after 15 km) and follow signs. Coming from Poitiers, take N10 towards Châtellerault. Right in Baumont-La Trichérie and follow signs.

CC € 15 *25/3-1/7 29/8-30/9* *7=6, 14=11, 21=17*

N 46°43'9'' E 0°27'33''

St. Denis-d'Oléron, F-17650 / Poitou-Charentes (Charente-Maritime) 1599

Les Seulières**
1371 rue des Seulières
+33 (0)5-46479051
1/4 - 31/10
campinglesseulieres@
wanadoo.fr

2,5ha 60**T**(80-100m²) 10A CEE

1 ABCD**G**HIJKLPST
2 AERTUWX
3 **F**GHJKRUWY
4 (Q+R 1/4-30/10)
(V 1/7-31/8) (Z)
5 **AB**EFGIJKLMNOPUZ
6 CE**J**(N 4km)OV

An informal campsite with Dutch owners, 300m from the sea. There are watersports and cycling opportunities in the immediate vicinity. WiFi hotspot. Fully renovated toilet facilities.

Continue towards St. Pierre D734 from the viaduct, direction St. Denis, left just before village, direction Les Seulières. Campsite signposted after ±3 km.

CC € 17 *1/4-8/7 29/8-31/10*

N 46°0'17'' W 1°22'59''

St. Georges-d'Oléron, F-17190 / Poitou-Charentes (Charente-Maritime) — 1600

La Campière****
route des Huttes - Chaucre
+33 (0)5-46767225
9/4 - 2/10
contact@la-campiere.com

1,6ha 48**T**(80-120m²) 10A CEE

1 ACD**G**IJKLMOPT
2 ABERSVWXY
3 B**F**GHJK**M**RU
4 (C 15/5-2/10) (Q+R) (T+U+V+Z 1/5-15/9)
5 **AB**CEFGIJKLMNOPQUVWXYZ
6 CEG**K**(N 3km)RSV

A small family campsite beautifully located at the edge of a wood. Swimming pool. Close to the dunes.

From the viaduct direction St. Pierre-d'Oléron, then direction St. Denis-d'Oléron, exit Chcray. 2nd road on left after football field. Right in Chaucre.

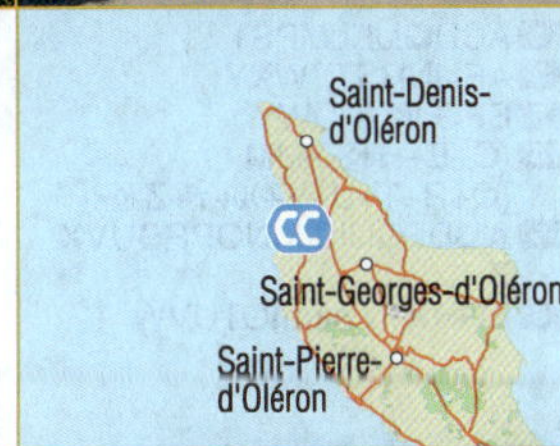

CC € 17 *9/4-2/7 3/9-2/10*

N 45°59'28'' W 1°22'54''

St. Georges-d'Oléron, F-17190 / Poitou-Charentes (Charente-Maritime) — 1601

La Maurie***
La Jousselinière
+33 (0)5-46766169
15/5 - 17/9
camping.lamaurie@wanadoo.fr

1,5ha 40**T** 10A

1 ACD**F**HIJKL**P**Q
2 ABRTVWX
3 A**F**GJKQRU
4 (C+H 1/6-15/9) (Q 1/7-31/8) (R) (T+U+V 1/7-31/8) (Z 1/6-15/9)
5 **AB**EFGIJKLMNOPUZ
6 EGJ(N 2,5km)OT

Homely campsite in the midst of vineyards. 5 minutes from beaches and harbour.

From bridge on Ile d'Oléron, dir. Dolus and Phare de Chassiron. In St. Pierre follow main road. In St.-Gilles turn right dir. La Jousselinière. Keep straight on. Straight on at traffic lights, then left.

CC € 15 *15/5-15/7 1/9-17/9*

N 45°58'2'' W 1°19'4''

St. Georges-d'Oléron, F-17190 / Poitou-Charentes (Charente-Maritime) — 1602

Le Domaine d'Oléron****
La Jousselinière
+33 (0)5-46765497
2/4 - 24/9
info@chadotel.com

3,5ha 56**T**(80-120m²) 10A CEE

1 ABCD**F**IJKLMOPS
2 RTVWXY
3 A**F**GJKNRU
4 (B+**G** 1/5-15/9) J (Q+T+U+V+X 15/5-10/9) Z
5 **AB**CEFGIJKLMNPQUZ
6 CEG**K**(N 1,5km)TV

Peacefully located campsite. Swimming pool with slides.

From the overpass direction St. Pierre. Right at Leclerc supermarket. Left at next roundabout direction Bois Fleurie. Turn right then immediately left after airfield.

CC € 15 *2/4-9/7 27/8-24/9*

N 45°58'4'' W 1°19'7''

St. Georges-d'Oléron, F-17190 / Poitou-Charentes (Charente-Maritime) — 1603

Le Suroit****
1720 rue Ponthézières
☎ +33 (0)5-46470725
FAX +33 (0)5-46750424
🔑 26/3 - 30/9
@ info@camping-lesuroit.com

5ha 226T(80-130m^2) 10A CEE

1 ACD**G**IJKLMPST
2 AEIJNRSTVWXY
3 B**F**GJKNRUWY
4 (C+E+H 🔑) IJM (Q+R+T+U+V+X+Y+Z 🔑)
5 **AB**DFGIJKLMNOPR**S**UVX Z
6 EGH**K**(N 4km)OTUVW

Friendly four-star campsite with an attractive restaurant and an indoor pool with three water slides. Located close to the sea. WiFi.

From the bridge N734 as far as St. Gilles. Campsite on the left 3 km further on.

CC € 17 *26/3-4/7 28/8-30/9*

N 45°56'53'' W 1°22'22''

St. Georges-d'Oléron, F-17190 / Poitou-Charentes (Charente-Maritime) — 1604

Les Gros Joncs GC*****
route de Ponthezières, BP 17
☎ +33 (0)5-46765229
FAX +33 (0)5-46766774
🔑 1/1 - 31/12
@ info@camping-les-gros-joncs.com

5,1ha 50T(94-240m^2) 16A CEE

1 AC**G**IJLMPST
2 AEINRSTVWXY
3 B**F**GJKNRU**V**WY
4 (A 1/7-31/8) (C 1/4-30/9) (**F** 🔑) (H 1/4-30/9) IJK**LP** (Q+S 1/4-30/9) (T 🔑) (U 1/4-30/9) (V 1/7-30/8) (Y 🔑) Z
5 **AB**EFGIJKLMNPUVWXYZ
6 BCDEG**IK**M(N 1,5km)RTV

Family campsite close to the woods and the sea. Heated outdoor pool and WiFi. The site has wellness with a beauty centre, massages and baths.

From the bridge direction St. Pierre. Turn left at Chéray, direction Sables Vigniers left direction La Cotinière.

CC € 17 *1/1-11/7 28/8-31/12*

N 45°57'2'' W 1°22'48''

St. Georges-de-Didonne, F-17110 / Poitou-Charentes (Charente-Maritime) — 1605

Ideal Camping***
16 avenue de Suzac
☎ +33 (0)5-46052904
FAX +33 (0)5-46063236
🔑 2/5 - 11/9
@ info@ideal-camping.com

8ha 400T(90-100m^2) 10A

1 ACDEHIJLPST
2 ABEGRSUVWXY
3 BCGHJRUWY
4 (C+H 10/6-5/9) IJK (Q 2/5-10/9) (S 1/6-1/9) (T+U+V+W+X+Y 2/5-10/9) Z
5 **AB**GIJKLMNOPUVZ
6 CEG**J**(N 2km)OTV

Very well maintained campsite near the sea (300m). Beautiful heated leisure pool. 2 km from St. Georges de Didonne. A peaceful campsite with plenty of sports and games for children.

Drive on the D25 from Royan to St. Georges-de-Didonne. The campsite is signposted before the centre of St. Georges-de-Didonne.

CC € 15 *2/5-3/7 25/8-10/9*

N 45°35'6'' W 0°59'7''

St. Georges-de-Didonne, F-17110 / Poitou-Charentes (Charente-Maritime)

1606

Ocean Vacances****
63 allée des Bruyères
+33 (0)5-46068000
+33 (0)5-46064546
1/4 - 20/10
contact@oceanvacances.com

4,6ha 45**T**(80-142m²) 10A CEE

1 ACD**F**IJKLN**P**ST
2 BEFGVWXY
3 AGHJKQRUVY
4 (B+G 1/6-30/8) J**KLNOP**
(Q 1/4-30/9)
(S+T+U+V+W+Y 1/4-30/8) Z
5 **AB**EFGIJKLMNOPUWXZ
6 AG**K**(N 1km)**P**QTV

A very well-maintained campsite with many opportunities such as massage, sauna etc. 600 metres from the sea and in the woods. Very good restaurant. Free WiFi.

Coast road in St. Georges-de-Didonne dir. Mechers, about 300 metres from roundabout, on left. See signs.

CC € 15 *1/4-30/6 1/9-20/10*

N 45°35'1" W 0°58'42"

St. Hilaire-la-Palud, F-79210 / Poitou-Charentes (Deux-Sèvres)

1607

Le Lidon***
Lieu-dit Lidon
+33 (0)5-49353364
+33 (0)5-49353263
2/4 - 18/9
info@le-lidon.com

4ha 119**T**(90-120m²) 10A

1 ACD**F**IJLMPQ
2 CLRTVWXY
3 ABHJKRU**W**
4 (C+G 1/7-31/8)
(Q+R+T+U+V+X+Z)
5 **AB**DFGIJKLMNOPUWZ
6 AEG**J**(N 4km)

A peaceful, attractive and natural campsite in the rural area of the Marais (= plenty of water). Swimming pool and children's pool. Attractive toilet buildings. Many opportunities for fishing, ideal for cycling. Boats and canoes available for rent.

From Niort N11 continue in direction Rochefort, turn right onto D3, just past St. Hilaire-la-Palud take Lidon exit on the right. Indicated from here.

CC € 15 *2/4-10/7 28/8-18/9 7=6*

N 46°17'3" W 0°44'36"

St. Jean-d'Angely, F-17400 / Poitou-Charentes (Charente-Maritime)

1608

Val de Boutonne***
56 quai Bernouët
+33 (0)5-46322616
1/4 - 30/9
campingvaldeboutonne@gmail.com

1,9ha 99**T**(95-120m²) 10A CEE

1 AC**G**IJKLM**P**Q
2 CDFLRTVWXY
3 AGKNR**W**
4 (B+G 1/7-31/8) (Q+R)
5 **AB**GIJKLMNOPUVXYZ
6 CEG**IK**(N 0,7km)TV

A campsite located in the centre of St. Jean-d'Angly. An old town well worth a visit, also suitable as a base for visiting historic towns.

A10 exit 34 direction St. Jean-d'Angely (Ouest). The campsite is very clearly signposted.

CC € 15 *1/4-3/7 1/9-30/9*

N 45°56'55" W 0°32'11"

St. Palais-sur-Mer, F-17420 / Poitou-Charentes (Charente-Maritime)

1609

Des Deux Plages****
41 avenue des Acacias
+33 (0)5-46231142
1/4 - 30/9
contact@campingdes2plages.fr

3ha 80**T**(80-140m²) 10A CEE

1 ACD**F**IJKLMOST
2 AGIQRVWXY
3 B**F**GKRUW
4 (C 15/4-30/9) **KN** (Q+R+T+U+V+Y+Z 1/7-31/8)
5 **AB**EFGIJKLMNPUZ
6 AEGI**K**(N 0,6km)ORTV

A very peaceful campsite overlooking 2 beaches in the distance (600m). Lovely pitches on an undulating site near the centre of St Palais-sur-Mer.

From the A10 near Saintes, take exit 35 to Royan. At large roundabout near Royan diretion St. Palais. Campsite well signposted in the centre.

CC €17 *1/4-30/6 1/9-30/9*

N 45°38'45'' W 1°4'48''

St. Palais-sur-Mer, F-17420 / Poitou-Charentes (Charente-Maritime)

1610

Puits de l'Auture****
151 av. de la Grande Côte
+33 (0)5-46232031
FAX +33 (0)5-46232638
28/4 - 3/10
contact@camping-puitsdelauture.com

4ha 186**T**(100-200m²) 10A

1 ACD**G**IJKLMOPST
2 AEGKQRTVWXY
3 B**F**GHJRUWY
4 (Q+R+T+V 15/6-15/9)
5 **AB**CDEFGIJKLMNOPUWXYZ
6 ACEGIK(N 0,25km)RTV

A traditional and homely four star campsite conveniently facing the ocean. Cycle path past the site, and 250m from 'la Grande Côte' beach, restaurants, bars and shops. A very quiet campsite with no entertainment. Spacious, level pitches with grass in both sun and shade. New toilet facilities and free WiFi.

From the A10 take exit 35 towards Royan. In Royan direction St. Palais-sur-Mer, then direction La Grande Côte on the boulevard.

CC €17 *1/5-3/7 20/8-30/9*

N 45°38'59'' W 1°7'3''

St. Pierre-d'Oléron, F-17310 / Poitou-Charentes (Charente-Maritime)

1611

La Perroche Plage***
18 rue du Renclos (la Perroche)
+33 (0)5-46753733
26/3 - 2/10
laperroche@oleron-camping.eu

1,8ha 70**T**(80-100m²) 10A CEE

1 AC**G**IJKLMPST
2 AEORSVWXY
3 B**F**GJKLNRWY
4 (Q+R 15/5-15/9)
5 **AB**FGHIJKLMNOPUVZ
6 CEG**K**(N 2,5km)O

A small, peaceful family campsite with direct access to the dunes and the sea. Opportunites for many watersports. 2 minutes from La Cotinière.

After the bridge direction Grand Village Plage, then turn right and follow the coast road. Located to the left after 8 km. 3 km before La Cotinière.

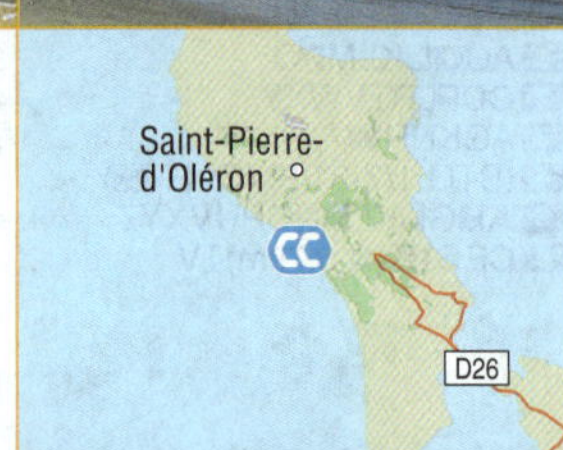

CC €15 *26/3-9/7 27/8-2/10*

N 45°54'6'' W 1°18'9''

St. Pierre-d'Oléron, F-17310 / Poitou-Charentes (Charente-Maritime)

1612

Le Sous Bois***
avenue des Pins, La Cotinière
+33 (0)5-46472246
1/4 - 31/10
resa.lesousbois@orange.fr

2,5ha 110**T**(80-130m²) 10A CEE

1 ABCD**G**HIJKLMPT
2 ABEGNORVWXY
3 AGJKNRUWY
4 **KN**
5 **A**BFGIJKLMNOPUZ
6 EG**K**(N 1km)R

A small, friendly campsite in the countryside. Located next to La Cotinière. The peaceful atmosphere is especially appealing! Sylire offers you half an hour free WiFi during your stay.

From the bridge direction St. Pierre. In St. Pierre direction La Cotinière. In La Cotinière direction L'Ileau. Signposted thereafter.

CC € 17 *1/4-30/6 1/9-31/10*

N 45°55'23" W 1°20'29"

St. Sornin, F-17600 / Poitou-Charentes (Charente-Maritime)

1613

Les Etangs Mina***
D733
+33 (0)5-46228261
FAX +33 (0)5-46069573
1/4 - 30/9
contact@campingmina.com

7ha 55**T**(80-120m²) 10A CEE

1 ACD**F**IJKLMPRS
2 CDLRTUVWXY
3 AGHJK**OP**RUW
4 (B+G 1/6-30/8) (Q) (R 1/4-30/6,1/9-28/9) (S 1/7-31/8) (T+U+V+X) Z
5 **AB**FGIJKLMNOPQUWXZ
6 **IJ**OTV

A beautiful well maintained campsite, ideal for anglers, walkers and cyclists. Located around a lake. Many excursion opportunities.

A10 as far as Saintes. Exit Marennes. Follow camping signs on the D728 in St. Sornin.

CC € 17 *1/4-10/7 27/8-30/9*

N 45°45'35" W 0°56'37"

St. Trojan-les-Bains, F-17370 / Poitou-Charentes (Charente-Maritime)

1614

Indigo Oléron Les Pins***
11 avenue des Bris
+33 (0)5-46760239
4/5 - 12/9
oleron@camping-indigo.com

5ha 163**T**(80-150m²) 10A CEE

1 ACD**F**HIJKLMNO**P**ST
2 ABJKLSXY
3 ABGHJK**OP**R
4 (C+Q+R) (T+U+V 1/7-31/8) Z
5 **AB**FGIJKLMNOPQRUWY
6 CDEGIJ(N 1,5km)O

NEW

In a majestic pine wood, close to the centre of Saint Trojan-les-Bains, this campsite offers you plenty of activities. You can make use of the many services at the campsite and the village: swimming pool, refurbished toilet facilities, leisure products.

From Bordeaux: follow A10. Exit 35 dir. Saintes and then dir. Ile d' Oléron. From Paris/Nantes: follow A10, take exit 33 La Rochelle/Rochefort and then follow Surgères/Rochefort/Ile d' Oléron.

CC € 15 *4/5-5/7 1/9-11/9*

N 45°49'53" W 1°12'49"

St. Trojan-les-Bains, F-17370 / Poitou-Charentes (Charente-Maritime)

1615

St-Tro'Park****
36 avenue des Bris
+33 (0)5-46760047
1/4 - 15/10
info@st-tro-park.com

4ha 105T(80-120m²) 10A CEE

1 ACD**F**HIJKLMOPST
2 ABISVWXY
3 B**F**GHJKNRUVW
4 (A 1/7-30/8)
(C+H 15/5-15/9) **KLN**
(Q 1/5-30/9)
(S+T+U+V 15/6-15/9) Z
5 **AB**EFGIJKLMNOPUVXYZ
6 CEG**K**(N 1,5km)OST

A peaceful campsite in wooded surroundings. The site has a heated swimming pool, jacuzzi, hammam and sauna. Toilet facilities for the disabled. WiFi.

From the bridge, direction St. Pierre 'autres directions', follow St. Trojan as far as the harbour. Straight ahead at harbour roundabout. Turn right at roundabout with fountain. Keep left at junction. Then signposted.

CC € 17 *1/4-2/7 29/8-15/10 7=6, 14=12*

N 45°49'46" W 1°13'1"

Surgères, F-17700 / Poitou-Charentes (Charente-Maritime)

1616

Camping de la Gères***
10 rue de la Gères
+33 (0)5-46077997
11/1 - 16/12
contact@campingdelageres.com

1ha 32T(80-120m²) 6-10-16A CEE

1 ACD**F**IJKLM**P**Q
2 CGRUVXY
3 ABJR**W**
4 (C+H 1/5-30/9)
(Q 1/7-31/8)
(T+U+Z 15/6-15/9)
5 **AB**DFGIJKLMNOPUVZ
6 ACEGK(N 0,2km)T

Close to La Rochelle, Camping de la Gères is located on the shady banks of a river and 30 minutes from the beaches. A traditional family campsite, quiet and hospitable, 5 minutes by foot from Surgères centre and 300m from a supermarket. Many visit La Rochelle, Rochefort, Le Marais Poitevin etc. Free WiFi zone.

Campsite well signposted in Surgères.

CC € 15 *28/2-9/7 28/8-12/11*

N 46°6'5" W 0°45'12"

Vaux-sur-Mer, F-17640 / Poitou-Charentes (Charente-Maritime)

1617

Le Nauzan-Plage****
39 ave de Nauzan Plage
+33 (0)5-46382913
FAX +33 (0)5-46381843
1/5 - 30/9
contact@campinglenauzanplage.com

4,5ha 165T(90-160m²) 10A CEE

1 ACD**G**IJKLMPQ
2 AEGRTVWXY
3 AB**F**K**M**NRUW
4 (C+G+Q+S+T+U+V+X+Z)
5 **AB**EFGIJKLMNOPUWYZ
6 ACEG**K**(N 0,7km)RTV

Located 450 metres from the beach, this 4 star campsite offers you all the ingredients of an enjoyable stay. All amenities are available on site or in the immediate surroundings. Horse riding, golf, sailing, swimming, fishing, walking and cycling are just some of the possibilities. There are also plenty of interesting sights in the vicinity.

From the A10 near Saintes take exit 35 towards Royan, N150. At Royan direction Vaux-sur-Mer. Campsite well signposted in Vaux.

CC € 17 *1/5-15/7 1/9-30/9 7=6*

N 45°38'34" W 1°4'20"

Agen/St. Hilaire-de-Lusignan, F-47450 / Aquitaine (Lot-et-Garonne)

iD **1618**

Le Moulin de Mellet***
D107
+33 (0)5-53875089
1/4 - 15/10
moulin.mellet@wanadoo.fr

5ha 42T(130-200m²) 10A CEE

1 ACD**G**IJKLMPQ
2 BCDLRVWXY
3 BDGKMNRUW
4 (B 15/5-15/9)
(Q+R+T+U+V+X+Z)
5 **A**EFGJKLOPQUZ
6 ACDEGJ(N 3km)OTV

Small scale, peaceful rural family campsite, ideally suited to families with children up to about 14 years old. A good out-of-season base for discovering the area. Fishing possible. Very large swimming pools. Modern, neat and clean toilet facilities. Spacious pitches.

N113. 4 km west of Agen at Colayrac-St-Cirq, take route D107 direction Prayssac. Campsite signposted from here.

CC € 15 *1/4-30/6 29/8-15/10 7=6*

N 44°14'38'' E 0°32'33''

Aire-sur-l'Adour, F-40801 / Aquitaine (Landes)

iD **1619**

Les Ombrages de l'Adour**
rue des Graviers
+33 (0)5-58717510
16/4 - 15/10
hetapsarl@yahoo.fr

2ha 92T(80-115m²) 10A CEE

1 ACD**F**IJKLMPST
2 CFGLRUXY
3 AGHNQU**W**
4 (**C**+R) (T 1/7-31/8)
5 **AB**GIJKLNPUVWZ
6 CDEGI**K**(N 0,3km)T

Level, spaciously appointed campsite on the banks of the river and close to the centre of the little town. Enjoy the peace and quiet under the trees.

Campsite located on river, just over the bridge and next to the arena.

CC € 15 *16/4-8/7 25/8-15/10*

N 43°42'9'' W 0°15'29''

Andernos-les-Bains, F-33510 / Aquitaine (Gironde)

iD **1620**

Fontaine Vieille***
4 bd du Colonel Wurtz
+33 (0)5-56820167
FAX +33 (0)5-56820981
1/4 - 30/9
contact@fontaine-vieille.com

13ha 420T(100-150m²) 10A

1 AC**G**IJKLMO**P**
2 ABDGJKRSVWXY
3 A**F**GJKNRUZ
4 (B 1/7-30/9) (F 1/5-30/9)
(G 1/7-30/9)
(Q+S+T+U+V+X 15/4-30/9)
(Z)
5 **AB**EFGJKLMNPUV
6 CEGHIJ(N 1km)OQRTV

A large, quiet and shaded campsite with spacious pitches and beautiful panoramas of Arcachon Bay. The swimming pool, the bay and the ocean 10 km away guarantee you plenty of fun in the water close to the congenial resort of Andernos.

The campsite is located just past the centre of Andernos direction Biganos (D3). Clearly signposted on the D3.

CC € 17 *1/4-30/6 1/9-30/9*

N 44°43'34'' W 1°4'51''

Antonne/Périgueux, F-24420 / Aquitaine (Dordogne)

1621

Au Fil de l'Eau***
6 allée des Platanes
+33 (0)5-53061788
15/4 - 15/9
campingaufildeleau@wanadoo.fr

2ha 31**T**(90-100m²) 6A CEE

1 A**G**IJKLMOP
2 CFLMRTVWXY
3 ABD**F**GHNRUWX
4 (B+G 1/6-15/9)
(Q+R 1/7-31/8) (T)
(U 1/7-31/8) (Z)
5 **AB**FGIJKLMNOPUZ
6 EGJ(N 4km)RV

Quiet and pleasant small-scale family campsite on the L'Isle river, only 10 km from Périgueux. With a new pool (2014).

N21 Limoges-Périgueux. About 10 km before Périgueux, left in Antonne (350 metres).

CC € 15 *15/4-30/6 29/8-15/9*

N 45°12'46'' E 0°50'16''

Arès, F-33740 / Aquitaine (Gironde)

1622

La Canadienne****
82 rue du Général de Gaulle
+33 (0)5-56602491
FAX +33 (0)5-57704085
1/3 - 31/10
info@lacanadienne.com

2ha 35**T**(80-120m²) 15A

1 AC**G**IJKLMO**P**
2 BRSVXY
3 AGJKR
4 (C+H+Q+R+T+U+V+X+Z
1/6-15/9)
5 **AB**DEFGIJKLMNPUWXZ
6 EGJ(N 2km)ORTV

Shaded campsite with large swimming pool and bike hire, 7 km from the ocean. Ideal for trips out to Bordeaux, Arcachon, the Pilat dunes and Cap Ferret.

La Canadienne is located 1 km from Arès centre in direction Lège-Cap-Feret on the right hand side.

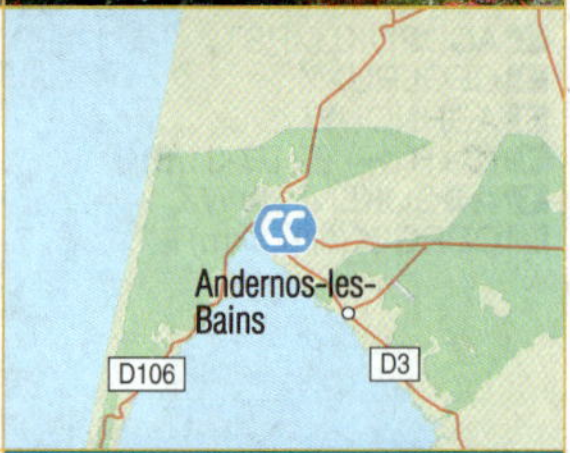

CC € 17 *1/3-9/7 1/9-31/10*

N 44°46'43'' W 1°8'35''

Atur/Périgueux, F-24750 / Aquitaine (Dordogne)

1623

Le Grand Dague****
+33 (0)5-53042101
FAX +33 (0)5-53042201
22/4 - 25/9
info@legranddague.fr

22ha 70**T**(100-120m²) 16A CEE

1 ACD**F**IJKLQ
2 FIKLRVWXY
3 BC**F**GHJKNRU
4 (C+G) IJ
(Q+R+S+T+U+V+X+Y) Z
5 **AB**DEFGIJKLMNOPQUZ
6 EGH**IJ**(N 1km)RTV

A holiday village in the heart of the countryside with beautiful views across a valley. Lovely swimming pool, plenty of play facilities and entertainment throughout the season. Close to the village of Atur and a 10-minute drive from the town of Périgueux. Free WiFi in low season.

Coming from Brive follow Atur signs at 2nd roundabout. Then follow signs on the A89 exit 16 St. Laurent-sur-Manoire and the follow Atur and camping signs.

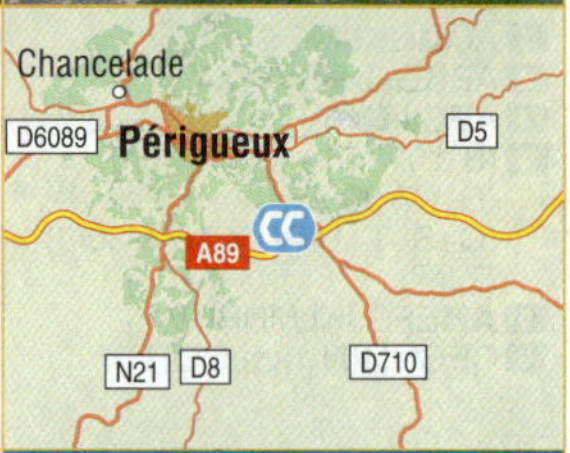

CC € 13 *22/4-2/7 27/8-25/9*

N 45°8'52'' E 0°46'40''

Audenge, F-33980 / Aquitaine (Gironde) — 1624

Le Braou***
26 route de Bordeaux
+33 (0)5-56269003
FAX +33 (0)5-57760366
1/4 - 30/9
info@camping-audenge.com

90**T**(66-180m²) 6A

1 AC**G**IJKLM**P**ST
2 FGRSVWXY
3 A**F**GHJKNRU
4 (B 15/6-15/9)
(Q+T+U+V+X+Z 1/7-31/8)
5 **AB**GIJKLMNOPUVXZ
6 CDEGIJ(N 1km)OQT

A peaceful campsite with very large pitches and a lovely swimming pool. Ideal for cycling and walking tours or trips out to Arcachon, Bordeaux, the ocean or Pilat Dunes.

D3 Biganos-Andernos. In Audenge right at cooond roundabout. Campsite 700m on the right.

CC € 17 *1/4-8/7 28/8-30/9*

N 44°41'3'' W 1°0'15''

Bayas/St. Émilion, F-33230 / Aquitaine (Gironde) — 1625

Le Chêne du Lac***
3 Lieu-dit Châteauneuf
+33 (0)5-57691378
1/1 - 31/12
lechenedulac@orange.fr

4,6ha 54**T**(96-180m²) 10A

1 A**G**IJKLM**P**ST
2 ABCDFLMRSTVWXY
3 AGHJKNRU**V**XZ
4 (Q 1/6-15/9)
(R+T+U+V 1/5-15/10) Z
5 **A**GIJKLMNPUXYZ
6 CEGJK(N 3km)V

A wooded campsite within walking distance of the town of Guitres. After visiting the Benedictine abbey you can board a steam train, rent a canoe / kayak or go fishing in one of the many streams. Close to a lake with a sandy beach and swimming area. Choose a well-shaded or less-shaded pitch. Opportunities for football, basketball and table tennis. Covered terrace.

N10 Bordeaux-Angoulême exit Laruscade/ Guitres. Bayas is on the D247 coming from Guitres.

CC € 13 *1/3-15/7 1/9-30/11*

N 45°4'45'' W 0°12'24''

Beauville, F-47470 / Aquitaine (Lot-et-Garonne) — 1626

Les 2 Lacs***
+33 (0)5-53954541
1/4 - 31/10
camping-les-2-lacs@wanadoo.fr

22ha 50**T**(100m²) 6A CEE

1 ACD**G**IJLPRS
2 ABDLMPRVWXY
3 ABGHJKLMNRUWZ
4 (Q+T+U+Y+Z)
5 **AB**DFGIJKLMNOPRUWX
6 AEGJ(N 1km)RTV

Lovely, spacious campsite with its own woods and walks. Walking and cycling (hilly) in beautiful surrounding countryside. Fishing lake (3 hectares) with carp, pike, perch (no licence required). Swimming lake (0.8 hectares) with A-quality water. In the middle of the old Gascogny region: delicious food, beautiful nature, peace and space. Dutch, English speaking owners.

From Cahors D656 direction Agen. Exit Beauville. Follow signs in the village.

CC € 15 *1/4-30/6 1/9-31/10*

N 44°16'20'' E 0°53'17''

Belvès, F-24170 / Aquitaine (Dordogne)

1627

RCN Le Moulin de la Pique*****
La Pique
+33 (0)5-53290115
+33 (0)5-53282909
23/4 - 24/9
moulin@rcn.fr

10ha 170T(80-140m²) 10A CEE

1 ACD**F**IJKLMOPQ
2 CDLRVXY
3 ABFGH**M**N**OPQ**RUVWXZ
4 (A 1/5-15/9) (C+H) IJ (Q+R+T+U+V+Y+Z)
5 **AB**DEFGIJKLMNPRUWXYZ
6 ACDEGH**K**(N 2km)OTV

A very well maintained, child friendly family campsite, situated on an estate with 18th century buildings. You will notice the 4 pools and 3 water slides as soon as you arrive. Plenty of trips out in the Dordogne Périgord Noir, with its many castles and historic towns. Canoe trips on the Dordogne every week for guests.

The campsite is located on the D710 Fumel-Belvès. About 2 km south of Belvès. Clearly signposted.

CC € 15 *23/4-5/7 26/8-24/9*

N 44°45'43'' E 1°0'51''

Bergerac, F-24100 / Aquitaine (Dordogne)

1628

La Pelouse***
8b rue J.J. Rousseau
+33 (0)5-53570667
1/4 - 31/10
campinglapelouse24@orange.fr

2,5ha 62T 10A CEE

1 ACD**G**IJL**P**Q
2 CMRXY
3 AGQUX
4 (Q)
5 **AB**DGIJKLMNOPUZ
6 CEGJ(N 1km)RT

The campsite is located on the southern banks of the Dordogne just west of the centre. You can walk to the historic town centre in 10 minutes. The campsite is often used as a stopover campsite and favoured by wine lovers (Bergerac-Monbazillac). Plenty of activities in the Dordogne. Tranquility and nature. No big attractions.

Campsite located on the south bank of the Dordogne. Around Bergerac follow signs to Bergerac centre, then the campsite is signposted.

CC € 15 *1/4-1/7 1/9-31/10* *7=6*

N 44°50'57'' E 0°28'35''

Bidart, F-64210 / Aquitaine (Pyrénées-Atlantiques)

1629

Camping + Residence Oyam****
chemin Oyamburua
+33 (0)5-59549161
+33 (0)5-59547687
9/4 - 25/9
accueil@camping-oyam.com

4,5ha 54T(80-100m²) 6A

1 AC**G**HIJKLMPRS
2 FGJRVXY
3 A**F**GNRU
4 (C+H 1/5-19/9) IJ(Q) (T+U+X+Z 1/7-31/8)
5 **AB**EFGIJKLMNOPUWZ
6 CDEGI**K**(N 0,8km)TV

Shaded grounds just 1200 metres from the Atlantic Ocean beaches and from the centre of Bidart. Spacious heated leisure pool with water slide. Biarritz, Bayonne and St. Jean-de-Luz are a short distance away.

A63 Bayonne-St. Sébastian. Exit 4 Biarritz. Then the D810 (formerly the N10) dir. St. Jean-de-Luz. Turn left at supermarket and Jardiland and follow camping signs. Campsite located about 1 km from the D810.

CC € 17 *9/4-25/6 3/9-25/9*

N 43°26'7'' W 1°34'58''

Bidart, F-64210 / Aquitaine (Pyrénées-Atlantiques) — 1630

Ilbarritz****
avenue de Biarritz
+33 (0)5-59230029
FAX +33 (0)5-59412459
9/4 - 24/9
contact@camping-ilbarritz.com

10ha 88T(80-120m²) 10A CEE

1 AC**G**IJKLPQ
2 EFGIJRSVWXY
3 B**F**GHKMN**Q**RU
4 (C 1/6-24/9) (E) (G 1/6-24/9) IJM (Q+S+T+V+Y+Z)
5 **AB**DEFGIJKLMNPUWZ
6 ADEGH**IK**(N 2km)OQRTV

Sloping grounds in walking distance of a beach (across the road). Lovely planting with hydrangeas gives the place a floral ambiance. The centre of Biarritz is about 3 km further on.

A63 Bayonne-St. Sebastián, exit 4 Biarritz. Take the D810 (formerly N10) direction St. Jean-de-Luz. Turn right by the supermarket after about 2.5 km and take D911 towards the coast. Campsite 300 metres on the right.

CC € 17 *9/4-30/6 1/9-24/9*

N 43°27'11" W 1°34'24"

Bidart, F-64210 / Aquitaine (Pyrénées-Atlantiques) — 1631

Sunêlia Berrua****
rue Berrua
+33 (0)5-59549666
FAX +33 (0)5-59547830
19/3 - 16/10
contact@berrua.com

5ha 85T 6A

1 AC**G**IJKLPQ
2 FGJRVWXY
3 B**F**GKL**M**NRU
4 (C+E+G) IJK**L**P (Q+S+T+U+V+Y) Z
5 **AB**EFGJLPUWZ
6 CEGHI**K**(N 1km)OTV

A terraced campsite with plenty of shade and good amenities. About 1 km from a sandy beach and the picturesque village. Extensive swimming pool complex with indoor pool and heated outdoor pool.

A63 Bayonne-St. Sebastián, exit 4 Biarritz. Then D810 direction St. Jean-de-Luz. Campsite signposted on the left of the road in Bidart centre and at the 'Intermarché'. Site about 800m from the D810.

CC € 17 *1/5-10/7 27/8-10/10*

N 43°26'18" W 1°34'55"

Bidart, F-64210 / Aquitaine (Pyrénées-Atlantiques) — 1632

Ur-Onea***
375 rue de la Chapelle
+33 (0)5-59265361
9/4 - 17/9
contact@uronea.com

5ha 155T(80-140m²) 10A

1 AC**G**HIJKLMPRS
2 EFGJRVXY
3 B**F**GNRU
4 (C 15/5-18/9) (E+H) IK**P** (Q+S+T+U+V+X) Z
5 **AB**EFGIJKLNPUVWXYZ
6 ACDEGI**K**(N 0,5km)OQRTU V

Ur-Onea is a well maintained campsite with paved paths with shade for tents and caravans. It has a heated indoor and outdoor pool. Within walking distance of the ocean and the town centre with the white cottages along the hillside.

A63 Bayonne-St. Sebastián, exit 4 Biarritz. Then take the D810 (formerly RN10) direction St. Jean-de-Luz. The campsite is signposted on the left of the road just beyond the centre of Bidart and is located about 400 metres from the D810.

CC € 17 *9/4-3/7 25/8-17/9 7=6, 14=12, 21=18*

N 43°26'1" W 1°35'25"

Biscarrosse, F-40600 / Aquitaine (Landes) — 1633

Bimbo****
176 chemin de Bimbo
+33 (0)5-58098233
FAX +33 (0)5-58098014
16/4 - 30/9
info@campingbimbo.fr

6ha 55**T**(100-150m²) 6A

1 ACD**F**IJKLO**P**ST
2 GRSVXY
3 AB**F**GHJKMNRUV
4 (C+H) **KN**
(Q+R+T+U+V+X+Z 15/6-15/9)
5 **AB**DEFGIJKLMNOP**Q**UX
6 ACEGI**K**(N 2km)ORTV

Family campsite with well-maintained infrastructure. Within walking distance of a lake. Heated swimming pool, sauna, jacuzzi, spa, massage and fitness room. Watersports options and cycling routes nearby. Keywords: lakes, ocean, leisure pool and countryside.

On the Sanguinet-Biscarrosse road (D652), direction Biscarrosse-Plage. Campsite clearly signposted.

CC € 15 *16/4-30/6 1/9-30/9*

N 44°25'37'' W 1°9'36''

Biscarrosse, F-40600 / Aquitaine (Landes) — 1634

Campéole Navarrosse****
712 chemin de Navarrosse
+33 (0)5-58098432
FAX +33 (0)5-58098622
25/3 - 30/9
navarrosse@
andretriganogroupe.com

8ha 162**T**(80-110m²) 10A CEE

1 ACD**G**IJKLMO**P**ST
2 ABDMRSWXY
3 AB**F**GHJKLMRU**W**Z
4 (A+Q 1/7-31/8)
(S 15/6-15/9)
(T+V+Z 1/7-31/8)
5 **AB**DEFGHIJKLMNPQUWZ
6 ACEGH**IK**(N 3km)RTV

An ideal campsite for watersports enthusiasts thanks to its exceptional location on the Biscarosse lake. The shallow water makes it safe for children. New toilets and spacious pitches on wooded grounds.

From Biscarrosse direction Biscarrosse-Plage, Sanguinet and Navarrosse.

CC € 17 *1/5-4/7 22/8-30/9*

N 44°25'54'' W 1°10'10''

Biscarrosse, F-40600 / Aquitaine (Landes) — 1635

Mayotte Vacances*****
368 chemin des Roseaux
+33 (0)5-58780000
FAX +33 (0)5-58788391
2/4 - 25/9
camping@mayottevacances.com

15ha 163**T**(90-140m²) 16A CEE

1 ACD**F**IJKLMO**P**S
2 ABDLMRSVWXY
3 AB**F**GHJKLNQRUV**WZ**
4 (C) (F+H) IJKLNP
(Q+S+T+U+V+X+Y+Z)
5 **AB**DEFGIJKLMNPRUWXY
6 ACEGH**K**(N 5km)ORTV

Five-star campsite with sandy beach on lake. A 600 m² outdoor swimming pool, water slide, jacuzzi, hammam, sauna, hydromassage and heated indoor pool. Multi-sports area with plenty of options, fitness room and outdoor exercise equipment.

The campsite is on Lake Biscarrosse between Sanguinet and Biscarrosse. Clearly signposted.

CC € 17 *2/4-2/7 27/8-24/9*

N 44°26'7'' W 1°9'17''

Biscarrosse-Plage, F-40600 / Aquitaine (Landes)

1636

Campéole Le Vivier***
681 rue du Tit
+33 (0)5-58782576
+33 (0)5-58783523
17/5 - 18/9
vivier@andretriganogroupe.com

25ha 368**T**(100-250m²) 10A CEE

1 ACD**G**IJKLMO**P**
2 ABRSVWXY
3 BFGHJKL**M**NRU
4 (C+G+Q+R+T+U+V+Z)
5 **AB**GIJKLMNOPUZ
6 AEGH**K**(N 10km)RV

A large campsite offering every comfort located in a wood and 800 metres from the sea. Excellent starting point for trips out, cycling and walking.

From Biscarrosse direction Biscarrosse-Plage. Follow camping signs.

CC € 17 *17/5-4/7 22/8-18/9*

N 44°27'31" W 1°14'25"

Biscarrosse-Plage, F-40600 / Aquitaine (Landes)

1637

Campéole Plage Sud***
230 rue des Bécasses
+33 (0)5-58782124
+33 (0)5-58783423
1/4 - 30/9
plagesud@
andretriganogroupe.com

35ha 600**T**(70-110m²) 6A CEE

1 ACD**F**IJKLMO**P**
2 BRSVWXY
3 AB**F**GHJKNRU
4 (C+H 1/5-30/9) JK
(Q+T+U+V+Y+Z 1/7-31/8)
5 **AB**EFGIJKLMNOPUZ
6 ACDEGH**K**(N 0,2km)RTV

A large campsite in a shaded wood. 800 metres from the sea and from the lively resort of Biscarrosse-Plage. Lovely heated swimming pool and water slide. Campsite completely renovated. Plenty of walking and cycling opportunities in the area.

From Biscarrosse direction Biscarrosse-Plage. Follow 'Plage-Sud' camping signs.

CC € 17 *1/5-4/7 22/8-30/9*

N 44°26'29" W 1°14'44"

Brantôme, F-24310 / Aquitaine (Dordogne)

1638

Brantôme Peyrelevade***
46 avenue André Maurois
+33 (0)5-53057524
+33 (0)5-53058730
1/5 - 30/9
info@camping-dordogne.net

4ha 127**T**(100-200m²) 10A CEE

1 ACD**G**IJKLMOPRS
2 ACLMRVWXY
3 ABGHJK**M**NR**WX**
4 (C+G+Q+R)
(T+U 1/7-31/8) Z
5 **AB**DEFGHIJKLMNOPQUW
XYZ
6 ACDEGK(N 1km)TV

A peaceful parkland campsite on the banks of the Dronne river. Large pitches within walking distance of Brantôme. Plenty of walking and cycling opportunities, swimming pool and good toilet facilities. Free WiFi available throughout the campsite, faster internet for a fee.

Continue from Perigueux/Brantôme towards Thiviers. From Angoulême towards centre then direction Thiviers. About 1 km from centre. Follow camping signs.

CC € 15 *1/5-3/7 27/8-30/9* *7=6, 14=12, 21=18*

N 45°21'39" E 0°39'38"

Campagne, F-24260 / Aquitaine (Dordogne)

1639

Le Val de la Marquise****
Le Petit Moulin
+33 (0)5-53547410
1/5 - 30/9
contact@levaldelamarquise.com

4ha 71T(100-180m²) 15A CEE

1 ACDGIJKLMPQ
2 BCDLPRTVY
3 BGHJKPRUW
4 (A 8/7-23/8) (C+G)
(Q+R+T+U+V+X+Z 15/6-15/9)
5 ABDEFGIJKLMNOPUXY
6 CEGK(N 3,5km)QRTV

4-star campsite with beautiful location in the lovely Dordogne forests. Excellent toilet facilities and an attractive pool are available for campers. Peace and quiet, and quality. Good base for the Perigord Noir.

Take the road from Le Bugue to Les Eyzies and the D35 direction St. Cyprien. Signposted

€15 1/5-3/7 29/8-30/9

N 44°54'23" E 0°58'27"

Castelnaud-la-Chapelle, F-24250 / Aquitaine (Dordogne)

1640

Camping Maisonneuve***
+33 (0)5-53295129
FAX +33 (0)5-53302706
1/4 - 30/10
contact@campingmaisonneuve.com

6ha 140T(90-120m²) 6-10A CEE

1 ACDGIJKLMOPQ
2 CMRVWXY
3 ABFGHJKNQRUWX
4 (C+H+Q)
(R+T+U+V+Y 1/7-30/8)
(Z)
5 ABDEFGIJKLMNOPQUWZ
6 ACEGJ(N 1km)ORTV

Typical Dordogne campsite located on the River Céou. The grassland and the peace and quiet both day and night are all you need for good camping. Heated toilet facilities. Ideal for canoeing. Nature all around. Castelnaud is a tourist village.

From the D703 via the D57 in the direction of Daglan. The campsite is signposted after passing Castelnaud. From Daglan take the D57 towards St. Cybranet and Castelnaud. Campsite signposted on the right before Castelnaud.

€17 1/4-4/7 25/8-30/10

N 44°48'18" E 1°9'30"

Castelnaud/Veyrines-de-Domme, F-24250 / Aquitaine (Dordogne)

1641

Sites & Paysages Les Pastourels***
Le Brouillet
+33 (0)5-53294217
14/5 - 15/9
camping@lespastourels.com

12ha 49T(100-250m²) 6-10A

1 ACDGIJKLMOPQ
2 BJKLRTVXY
3 BFGHJNOPRU
4 (C+G 1/6-15/9)
(Q+R 15/6-31/8)
(T+U+V+Z 15/6-15/9)
5 ABEFGIJKLMNOPQUWXYZ
6 AEGJ(N 6km)RT

A 12 hectare campsite located on a hill with extensive views of the Dordogne valley. 6 km from Castelnaud. In the middle of lovely woods. Nice big pitches. Peace, space and compactness are the key words. Lovely swimming pool. Child friendly.

Go to Castelnaud-la-Chapelle, follow Château des Milandes and then camping signs.

€15 14/5-4/7 28/8-15/9

N 44°48'54" E 1°6'2"

Castets, F-40260 / Aquitaine (Landes)

1642

Le Galan**
73 rue du Stade
+33 (0)5-58894352
1/3 - 30/11
@ contact@camping-legalan.com

4ha 161**T**(80-100m²) 10A

1 AC**F**IJKLMO**PT**
2 BCDFGRSVXY
3 BGH**M**NRU**W**
4 (G 1/7-31/8)
(Q+R 15/6-15/9)
5 **AB**DGIJKLMNOPUVWYZ
6 CEGHK(N 0,8km)TV

Campsite is located in a mixed forest at walking distance from the centre of Castets. It is suitable as a stopover campsite for the Spanish interior and/or Portugal because it is close to the N10. Here, you will be a 15-minute drive away from the Atlantic coast in Moliets-Plage and the lake of Léon.

A63 and N10 Bordeaux-Bayonne until exit 12 Castets. In Castets centre, campsite is signposted. Site is located just past roundabout on D42 to Taller.

CC € 13 *1/3-1/7 20/8-30/11*

N 43°52'50" W 1°8'16"

Cénac-et-Saint-Julien, F-24250 / Aquitaine (Dordogne)

1643

Le Pech de Caumont***
+33 (0)5-53282163
1/4 - 30/9
@ info@pech-de-caumont.com

10ha 100**T**(80-120m²) 16A

1 ACDGIJKLMPQ
2 BJKLRTVXY
3 B**F**GHJKRU
4 (B+G 20/4-30/9) (Q+R key)
(T+U+V+X+Z 1/7-30/8)
5 **AB**FGIJKLMNPUVWXZ
6 ACEGJ(N 1,5km)RTV

A large spacious, beautifully laid out terraced campsite with lovely views. The site is located about 1 km outside Domme. Relaxation, space and views are the keywords. Lovely swimming pool.

From the A20, exit 55 Souillac direction Carsac D703. Then Vitrac D703. Then towards Cénac on the D46. Campsite located about 1.5 km south of the Dordogne. Signposted.

CC € 13 *1/4-3/7 26/8-30/9*

N 44°47'12" E 1°12'33"

Coux-et-Bigaroque, F-24220 / Aquitaine (Dordogne)

1644

Le Clou***
Meynard route D703
+33 (0)5-53316332
FAX +33 (0)5-53316933
16/4 - 2/10
@ info@camping-le-clou.com

4ha 66**T**(80-150m²) 10A CEE

1 ACD**G**IJLPRS
2 IKLQRSTVXY
3 A**F**GHJNRU**W**
4 (B+H key) J
(Q+R+T+U+V+X+Z key)
5 **AB**EFGIJKLMNPQRUWZ
6 AEGJ(N 3,5km)TV

A Dutch owned campsite. A wonderful location in the Dordogne with its mild climate and beautiful landscapes, caves, castles, monasteries and medieval villages. You will receive a personal and warm welcome. 'Mediterranean' swimming complex. From early in the season camping guests can enjoy the various facilities. Many walking opportunities in the vicinity. Walking routes available.

Campsite located between Le Bugue and Coux-et-Bigaroque on the D703 and is signposted.

CC € 15 *16/4-9/7 27/8-2/10*

N 44°51'42" E 0°58'53"

Créon, F-33670 / Aquitaine (Gironde)

1645

Bel-Air***
D671 Lorient-Sadirac
+33 (0)5-56230190
+33 (0)5-56230838
16/1 - 15/12
info@camping-bel-air.com

3,5ha 64T(80-90m²) 10A

1 ACD**F**IJKLPQ
2 FGLRVWX
3 BGHJN**OP**QR
4 (B+G 15/6-1/9)
(Q 1/6-31/8)
(T+U+V+Y+Z 15/6-1/9)
5 **AB**DGIJKLNPUVZ
6 EGJ(N 0,8km)TV

Perfectly maintained and quiet family campsite close to Bordeaux with a bus connection to the centre from the campsite. Swimming pool. heated toilet facilities, bar and small restaurant. Free WiFi point.

The campsite is located on the D671 between Bordeaux and Créon, 2 km before Créon.

CC €17 *16/1-8/7 25/8-15/12*

N 44°47'2" W 0°22'16"

Daglan, F-24250 / Aquitaine (Dordogne)

1646

La Peyrugue***
D57
+33 (0)5-53284026
1/4 - 1/10
camping@peyrugue.com

5ha 76T(95-160m²) 6-10A CEE

1 ACD**G**IJKLPQ
2 JKLRTVXY
3 B**F**GHJN**O**RU**W**
4 (B+G 1/5-1/10) (Q)
(R+T+U+V+X+Z 1/5-1/10)
5 **AB**CFGJLNOPQUWX
6 AEGK(N 1km)ORTV

Emmy and Phlip Cappetti have turned this site into one of the nicest low season family sites. The pitches are spacious and well maintained. Walking and cycling routes and canoeing close by. In the middle of the scenic area of the Dordogne.

A20 Limoges-Toulouse, exit 55 Souillac, D820 direction Gourdon, then D673 direction Gourdon, turn right D801 direction Gourdon. Through Gourdon and again the D673 direction Fumel. D6, D46, D60 and D57 through Daglan direction St. Cybranet.

CC €15 *1/4-2/7 19/8-1/10*

N 44°45'9" E 1°11'15"

Daglan, F-24250 / Aquitaine (Dordogne)

1647

Le Moulin de Paulhiac****
D57
+33 (0)5-53282088
+33 (0)5-53293345
1/5 - 17/9
francis.armagnac@wanadoo.fr

5ha 160T(100-120m²) 10A CEE

1 ACDGIJKLMOPQ
2 CLNRVXY
3 AB**F**GHJKLNRU**W**X
4 (C 15/5-15/9) (F)
(H 15/5-15/9) IJP(Q+S)
(T+U+V+Y 15/5-15/9)
(Z)
5 **AB**EFGIJKLMNOPQRUWX
YZ
6 ACEG**J**(N 1,5km)ORTV

This spectacular four star campsite with refreshing and varying swimming opportunities is noted for its spacious marked out pitches. The 'Céou' which borders one side of the site offers a safe descent by boat. Restaurant with competitive prices. Beautiful new toilet facilities

From Souillac, direction Sarlat, Vézac, Castelnaud (D57). Campsite signposted beyond St. Cybranet. Or from Daglan take the D57 direction St. Cybranet. Campsite situated ± 4 km on the right.

CC €17 *1/5-7/7 24/8-17/9*

N 44°46'4" E 1°10'35"

Dévillac/Villeréal, F-47210 / Aquitaine (Lot-et-Garonne) 1648

Sites & Paysages Fontaine du Roc***
Aux Moulaties
+33 (0)5-53360816
1/4 - 1/11
fontaine.du.roc@wanadoo.fr

2ha 60**T**(120-175m²) 10A

1 ACD**G**IJKLMOPST
2 KLRTVWXY
3 BDGHJKN**OP**RUVW
4 (A 1/7-31/8)
(B+G 15/5-30/9) JK**N**
(Q+R) (T+U 15/4-30/9)
(V 15/5-30/9)
(X+Y+Z 15/4-30/9)
5 **AB**EFGIJKLMNPUWZ
6 ACDEGIJ(N 6km)ORTV

Three-star campsite right on the border of the Dordogne/Lot-et-Garonne provinces, well-known for its Southern French climate, rolling hills and friendly villages, rivulets and caves. You will find peace and quiet and have spectacular panoramic views of Chateau Biron. Swimming pool, children's pool, bar, restaurant, shop, new toilet facilities. Dutch owners.

Campsite is located 500 metres from the D255 (Villeréal-Lacapelle-Biron) and the D272 crossroads. Signposted.

CC €15 *1/4-9/7 27/8-1/11*

N 44°36'51" E 0°49'8"

Domme, F-24250 / Aquitaine (Dordogne) 1649

Le Bosquet***
La Rivière
+33 (0)5-53283739
FAX +33 (0)5-53294195
9/4 - 24/9
info@lebosquet.com

1,5ha 36**T**(100-140m²) 10A CEE

1 ACD**F**IJKLMPQ
2 LRTVXY
3 AFGHJRU
4 (A 1/7-30/8) (C+Q+R)
(T+U+V 20/5-15/9)
5 **AB**FGIJKLMNOPUWZ
6 ACEG**K**(N 3km)TV

Beautifully located campsite 300 metres from the Dordogne. Quiet location, lovely countryside and extensive views over the hills, close to Domme. Heated swimming pool, free WiFi. Walking routes from the campsite. Beautiful covered toilet facilities.

From Souillac and Sarlat, direction Vallée-de-la-Dordogne as far as Vitrac Port. Over bridge. Campsite 300m and is signposted.

CC €13 *9/4-2/7 20/8-24/9 8=7*

N 44°49'20" E 1°13'36"

Domme, F-24250 / Aquitaine (Dordogne) 1650

Le Perpetuum***
D50 La Rivière
+33 (0)5-53283518
1/5 - 10/10
luc.parsy@wanadoo.fr

4,5ha 120**T**(80-120m²) 10A

1 A**G**IJKLMOPQ
2 CNRTXY
3 AB**F**GHJKLNRU**W**X
4 (A 1/7-31/8)
(C+G 10/5-30/9) (Q)
(R+T+U+V+X+Z 15/5-30/9)
5 **AB**DEFGIJKLMNOPUZ
6 ACEGJ(N 2,5km)OV

Lovely site on banks of Dordogne. Canoeing and kayaking from the site. The lovely town Domme and the beautiful countryside of the Lot and Dordogne are close by. Walking and cycling trips from the site. Nice swimming pools, one is heated. Free WiFi. New restaurant.

Coming from Sarlat, Souillac, Gourdon or Bergerac, follow direction Vitrac Port on the D703. Cross the Vitrac bridge and follow the signs (turn right towards the D50 at the crossroads). Don't go to Domme.

CC €13 *1/5-5/7 23/8-10/10*

N 44°48'56" E 1°13'14"

Douville, F-24140 / Aquitaine (Dordogne) 1651

Lestaubière***
Pont-St-Mamet
+33 (0)5-53829815
15/4 - 30/9
lestaubiere@gmail.com

24ha 104**T**(160-250m²) 10A

1 ACD**F**IJKLMOPQ
2 ABDFIKLMRTVXY
3 BGHJ**M**NRUWZ
4 (B+G 1/5-15/9) (Q ⊶)
(R 4/7-21/8) (T+U+V ⊶)
(X 1/5-15/9) (Z ⊶)
5 **AB**FGJKLMNPQUWX
6 ACEGJ(N 1km)OTV

A magnificently located campsite with Dutch owners, close to the historic towns of Bergerac and Perigueux. The campsite has modern toilet facilities and very spacious pitches (more than 160 m²). Breathtaking views of the campsite and the surrounding area from the terrace under the plane trees (with free WiFi). Enjoy the peace, space and countryside!

19 km north of Bergerac. Take exit Pont-St-Mamet from the N21. Campsite 2 km further on.

CC € 17 *15/4-9/7 27/8-30/9 7=6, 14=12*

N 44°59'33'' E 0°35'50''

Douville, F-24140 / Aquitaine (Dordogne) 1652

Orphéo Negro
RN21, Les Trois Frères Lieu-dit
+33 (0)5-53829658
FAX +33 (0)5-53806711
1/4 - 30/10
camping@orpheonegro.com

11ha 50**T**(80-150m²) 6A CEE

1 ACDGIJKLMPQ
2 BDLMRTVWXY
3 BGHJMNQTUW
4 (B+G 15/5-30/9) **JKLN**
(Q+R+T+V+X+Y ⊶)
5 **A**FIJKLMNOPUWYZ
6 EG**K**(N 4km)ORTV

A very spacious campsite in naturally wooded surroundings. Recreational lake on the site. Suitable for an active holiday.

From Périgueux follow the RN21 towards Bergerac. On the right after 25 km. Signposted.

CC € 15 *1/4-11/7 30/8-30/10 7=6, 14=12, 21=18*

N 45°1'39'' E 0°37'2''

Duras, F-47120 / Aquitaine (Lot-et-Garonne) 1653

Le Cabri Holiday Village
Malherbe
FAX +33 (0)5-53838103
1/3 - 31/10
holidays@lecabri.eu.com

6ha 40**T**(150m²) 16A CEE

1 ACD**G**IJKLMOPQ
2 DJKRTVWXY
3 AB**F**GHJN**OP**QRUW
4 (B 1/6-30/9) (Q+T 1/4-1/11)
(U ⊶) (X 1/4-1/11) (Y ⊶) Z
5 **AB**DGIJMNOPRUWXY
6 ACDEGJ(N 0,7km)T

This campsite is located 800m from the centre of the lovely town of Duras, famous for its delicious wines. The campsite has an excellent restaurant (closed on Tuesday evening and all day Wednesday). The toilet facilities are heated.

From Duras direction D203. Savignac-de-Duras signposted.

CC € 17 *1/3-7/7 25/8-31/10 7=6, 14=11*

N 44°40'56'' E 0°11'10''

Espelette, F-64250 / Aquitaine (Pyrénées-Atlantiques)

iD **1654**

Biper Gorri****
chemin de Lapitxague
+33 (0)5-59939688
FAX +33 (0)5-59939689
26/3 - 6/11
@ info@camping-biper-gorri.com

2,5ha 56**T**(100-120m²) 10A CEE

1 AC**G**HIJKLM**PQ**
2 CRVWXY
3 BFGN**P**RU**VW**
4 (C+H) **KLN**P (Q+R+T+U+V+Y+Z)
5 **AB**DEFGJLNPUWXY
6 CDEGH**IK**(N 1,5km)TV

The campsite is located 1.5 km from Espelette in a rocky area. The campsite has a typical Basque character. Biper Gorri means 'red pepper' for which Espelette is renowned. Swimming pool heated in early season.

A63 exit 5 Bayonne-Sud. Then D932 direction Ustaritz and via Cambo-les-Bains towards Espelette. Campsite well signposted from there.

CC € 17 *26/3-2/7 27/8-6/11*

N 43°21'12" W 1°26'59"

Fumel, F-47500 / Aquitaine (Lot-et-Garonne)

iD **1655**

Les Catalpas**
La Tour
+33 (0)5-53711199
1/4 - 30/10
@ les-catalpas@wanadoo.fr

2ha 47**T**(70-100m²) 10A CEE

1 ACD**G**IJLMPRS
2 CKLRTUVWXY
3 BFGHJKNRU**W**X
4 (B 1/6-31/8) (Q) (T+U+Z 1/5-30/9)
5 **AB**DFGIJKLMNOPQUYZ
6 CDFG**K**(N 2,5km)TV

Campsite with lovely location on the Lot. Partly directly on the water with many willow trees, other part on slightly higher ground close to the 79 beautiful old catalpa trees. Within walking distance (3.5 km) of the 'Bonaguil' castle. A good base for walking and cycling along the Lot, fishing, exploring the surroundings or just unwinding.

In Fumel follow dir. Puy- l'Évêque, campsite is located 3 km after the village of Fumel and is clearly signposted from Fumel.

CC € 15 *1/4-24/6 3/9-30/10*

N 44°29'18" E 0°59'48"

Groléjac, F-24250 / Aquitaine (Dordogne)

iD **1656**

Les Granges****
+33 (0)5-53281115
FAX +33 (0)5-53285713
23/4 - 10/9
@ contact@lesgranges-fr.com

6ha 80**T**(90-100m²) 6A CEE

1 ACD**F**IJKLMPR
2 BJLRTVXY
3 BFGHJKN**Q**RU**W**
4 (C+G) IJ(Q 1/7-31/8) (T+U+V+Y+Z)
5 **AB**EFGIJKLMNOPUWXYZ
6 AEGI**K**L(N 0,5km)RTV

A modern 4 star campsite 600m from the Dordogne and 1.5 km from a large fishing lake. Lovely terraced campsite with 3 swimming pools and 2 large slides. Attractive restaurant area with bar. All this in the authentic ambiance of the Périgord. Plenty of opportunities for kayaking.

The campsite is clearly signposted from the D704 in Groléjac.

CC € 15 *23/4-9/7 28/8-10/9*

N 44°48'57" E 1°17'28"

Hendaye, F-64700 / Aquitaine (Pyrénées-Atlantiques)

iD **1657**

Ametza****
156 boulevard de l'Empereur
+33 (0)5-59200705
FAX +33 (0)5-59203216
15/4 - 30/9
@ contact@camping-ametza.com

5ha 140**T**(80-100m²) 6A CEE

1 AC**G**IJKLMPRS
2 AFGJKRSVXY
3 BGJMRU
4 (**A** 1/7-31/8)
(C+G 1/5-30/9) (Q+S+T)
(U 1/5-15/9) (V+Y+Z)
5 **AB**EFGJLOPUWZ
6 ACDEGHIK(N 2,5km)OQTV

Close to Hendaye Plage. It has a swimming pool, bar and restaurant (open from 1 May). Spacious marked-out pitches amongst the flowers. 3 specially equipped motorhome pitches with amenities!

Exit A63 in St. Jean-de-Luz (Sud). Then follow the D912 Socoa - Hendaye-Plage over the Corniche Basque. Campsite signposted 4 km on the left.

CC € 19 *15/4-30/6 1/9-30/9*

N 43°22'22" W 1°45'21"

Hourtin-Port, F-33990 / Aquitaine (Gironde)

iD **1658**

Les Ourmes****
90 avenue du Lac
+33 (0)5-56091276
FAX +33 (0)5-56092390
23/4 - 30/9
@ info@lesourmes.com

7ha 300**T**(80-100m²) 10A

1 AC**F**IJKLMPST
2 ADGRSVWXY
3 BGJ**MNOP**RU**W**Z
4 (B+H+Q) (S 1/7-31/8)
(T+U+V+X+Z)
5 **AB**EFGHIJKMNOPUVWZ
6 CDEG**IK**(N 1km)ORTV

Just 400 metres from a lake with a beach and watersports opportunities and 10 km from the ocean beaches, with cycle paths from the campsite, the prestigious Médoc wine chateaux, lively markets and tranquillity: these are just some of the top features of this clean and well equipped campsite.

Drive from the centre of Hourtin direction Hourtin-Port. Located about 1 km outside Hourtin on a corner. Clearly signposted.

CC € 17 *23/4-3/7 29/8-29/9*

N 45°10'55" W 1°4'32"

Itxassou, F-64250 / Aquitaine (Pyrénées-Atlantiques)

iD **1659**

Hiriberria***
D918
+33 (0)5-59299809
FAX +33 (0)5-59292088
1/1 - 31/12
@ hiriberria@wanadoo.fr

4,5ha 189**T**(100-120m²) 10A

1 AC**G**HIJKLMPQ
2 JKRUVXY
3 BGHNRU
4 (E+Q+T+U+V+X 1/4-31/10)
5 **AB**CDEFGIJKLMNPUVWXYZ
6 CDEGK(N 1km)TV

A campsite in two sections. The older part is positioned right by the reception while the newer part is next to the swimming pool. Level, marked out pitches in a rural setting between the hills which mark the beginning of the Pyrenees.

A63 exit 5 Bayonne-Sud. Then D932 via Ustaritz and Cambo-les-Bains direction St. Jean-Pied-de-Port. Campsite located 3 km south of Cambo on the left of the D918. Drive past site entrance to roundabout then back to the entrance.

CC € 17 *1/1-30/6 1/9-31/12*

N 43°20'19" W 1°24'3"

La Roque-Gageac, F-24250 / Aquitaine (Dordogne)

1660

Beau Rivage***
Lieu-dit 'Gaillardou'
+33 (0)5-53283205
FAX +33 (0)5-53296356
23/4 - 10/9
@ camping.beau.rivage@wanadoo.fr

9ha 152T(80-200m²) 6A

1 AC**F**IJKLMPRS
2 CLMNRVXY
3 B**F**GHJ**M**RUWX
4 (C+H 15/5-10/9) (Q+R) (S 1/6-10/9) (T) (U+V+Y 1/6-10/9) Z
5 **AB**EFGIJKLMNOPRUVWXZ
6 DEGJ(N 2km)ORTV

The campsite is located on the Dordogne with direct access to the water facilities. 7 km from Sarlat, close to the village of La Roque Gageac with its old houses, cliffs and meanderings.

A20 exit 55 Souillac, direction Calviac-Carsac-Sarlat-Vitrac, then follow signs (advisable for caravans).

CC € 13 *23/4-2/7 19/8-10/9*

N 44°48'58" E 1°12'53"

Labenne-Océan, F-40530 / Aquitaine (Landes)

1661

Sylvamar*****
avenue de l'Océan
+33 (0)5-59457516
FAX +33 (0)5-59454639
23/3 - 9/10
@ camping@sylvamar.fr

14ha 225T(100-150m²) 10A CEE

1 AC**G**IJKLMPST
2 ABFRSVWXY
3 BC**F**GHJKMN**OPQ**RUV
4 (C+**F**+H) IJ**KLMNP** (Q+S+U+V+Y) Z
5 **AB**DEFGIJKLMNPUWXYZ
6 ACDEGHI**K**M(N 3km)QRTV

A luxurious campsite with a well equipped beauty centre and balneotherapy. Virtually all amenities are also available in low season. 800m from the beach at Labenne.

In Bordeaux continue to Bayonne on the A63 and the N10 as far as exit 8 in Bénesse-Maremne, then the D810 towards Labenne. Turn right in Labenne towards Labenne-Océan on the D126. Campsite about 3 km on the right.

CC € 17 *1/4-26/4 2/5-2/6 5/6-9/6 12/6-16/6 19/6-23/6 11/9-9/10*

N 43°35'44" W 1°27'25"

Lacanau-Lac, F-33680 / Aquitaine (Gironde)

1662

Le Tedey***
route de Longarisse
+33 (0)5-56030015
FAX +33 (0)5-56030190
23/4 - 24/9
@ camping@le-tedey.com

14ha 700T(80-100m²) 10A CEE

1 ACDGIJKLOPST
2 ABDSVXY
3 B**F**GJKNQRU**WZ**
4 (Q+S) (U 15/6-5/9) (V 15/6-15/9) (Z)
5 **AB**EFGIJKLMNPUVXZ
6 CEGHI**K**(N 6km)ORTV

This site offers relaxation and nature in the middle of a 14 hectare pine forest. It has its own access to the shores of Lake Lacanau with plenty of watersport activities. The campsite offers every type of amenity.

From Lacanau towards Lacanau-Océan, D6 direction Le Moutchic. Follow road to the end of Le Moutchic, also to the end of the lake, then turn left.

CC € 17 *23/4-30/6 1/9-23/9*

N 44°58'56" W 1°8'32"

Lacanau-Océan, F-33680 / Aquitaine (Gironde)

1663

Yelloh! Village Les Grands Pins*****
Plage Nord
+33 (0)5-56032077
FAX +33 (0)5-57700389
29/4 - 18/9
@ reception@lesgrandspins.com

14ha 410**T**(100m²) 10A CEE

1 ACD**G**IJKLNOPS
2 ABEGIJRSTVWXY
3 B**F**GJK**M**NR**V**WY
4 (C+F+G) IK**LNP**
(Q+S+T+U+V+W+X+Y) Z
5 **AB**FGJLNPUWZ
6 CG**IK**L(N 1km)OQRTUV

Located near the resort of Lacanau, world-renowned as a surfing centre, the five star Yelloh! Village Les Grands Pins campsite enjoys an ideal location 350m from a lovely beach, in the middle of pine woods. Everything here is geared towards making every camper satisfied.

Take the D6 from Lacanau to Lacanau-Océan. Then direction Plage-Nord. Clearly signposted.

CC € 17 *29/4-18/6 4/9-18/9*

N 45°0'40'' W 1°11'38''

Le Bugue, F-24260 / Aquitaine (Dordogne)

1664

Les Trois Caupain***
725 allée Paul-Jean-Souriau
+33 (0)6-85484425
1/4 - 30/10
@ info@camping-bugue.com

4ha 116**T**(110-170m²) 16A CEE

1 ACD**G**IJKLMPRS
2 BCRVWXY
3 AB**F**GHJNRU**W**
4 (A 3/7-27/8) (C+F+G)
(Q 1/7-30/8)
(T+U 1/5-30/10)
(V 1/7-30/8) (X+Y 1/5-15/9)
(Z)
5 **AB**DEFGIJKLMNOPRUVXY
6 ACDEGJ(N 0,9km)TV

Les Trois Caupain campsite offers shaded pitches with every comfort. There are three swimming pools, one of which is covered. A perfect base for visiting the valley of Vézère. 900 metres from the lively village of Le Bugue with shops and places to eat. Good restaurant on the campsite. Campsite on the Dordogne.

On the right of the D703 from Le Bugue to Les Eyzies and indicated by signs.

CC € 15 *1/4-12/7 29/8-30/10*

N 44°54'33'' E 0°55'55''

Le Bugue, F-24260 / Aquitaine (Dordogne)

1665

Rocher de la Granelle***
La Borie
+33 (0)5-53072432
1/4 - 30/9
@ info@lagranelle.com

7,5ha 102**T**(80-150m²) 10A CEE

1 ACDGIJKLMPRS
2 BCKLMRVXY
3 BGK**M**NRU**W**
4 (B+G 1/5-15/9) J(Q)
(R 1/7-30/8)
(T+U+V 1/5-15/9) (Z)
5 **AB**EFGIJKLNPUZ
6 CEG**K**(N 0,8km)ORTV

Peaceful family campsite with its own typical French ambiance. You can swim in the river or in the swimming pool with slide. The Perigord-Noir region is renowned for its sumptuous gastronomy, caves and castles.

Campsite located on the south side of Le Bugue on the D31e direction Le Buisson and is well signposted.

CC € 13 *1/4-6/7 23/8-30/9 7=6, 18=15*

N 44°54'42'' E 0°55'0''

Le Buisson-de-Cadouin, F-24480 / Aquitaine (Dordogne) — 1666

Du Pont de Vicq En Périgord***
avenue de La Dordogne
+33 (0)5-53220173
FAX +33 (0)5-53220670
1/4 - 30/10
@ le.pont.de.vicq@wanadoo.fr

5,5ha 100**T**(100-110m²) 6A CEE

1 ACDGIJKLMOPRS
2 CSWXY
3 B**F**GHJR**W**
4 (C 1/5-30/9) (H 1/6-30/9) (Q+T+U+V+X 1/7-31/8) (Z 15/6-15/9)
5 **AB**EFGIJKLMNOPUZ
6 CDEGJ(N 1km)V

The campsite borders about 300m of the Dordogne banks. The campsite surrounds a rugby field (not in use in summer).

Fom Le Buisson-de-Cadouin direction Le Bugue. Campsite on the right just before the Dordogne bridge.

CC € 15 1/4-5/7 22/8-30/10 7=6, 14=12

N 44°51'13'' E 0°54'38''

Les Eyzies-de-Tayac, F-24620 / Aquitaine (Dordogne) — 1667

La Rivière****
+33 (0)5-53069714
2/4 - 16/10
@ la-riviere@wanadoo.fr

7ha 109**T** 6-10A

1 ACDGIJKLPRS
2 CLRTVWXY
3 AGHJKMRU**W**
4 (C+G+Q+R+S+T+U+V+X+Y)Z
5 **AB**CDEFGIJKLMNPUWXY
6 EGIJ(N 0,5km)ORUV

A 16th century mansion in Périgord style has been transformed into a lovely campsite-hotel-restaurant. Close to the many sights in the region.

In Les Eyzies continue towards Périgueux, left immediately after the (River Vézère) bridge, 200m to campsite.

CC € 17 2/4-2/7 27/8-16/10 7=6, 14=12, 21=17

N 44°56'12'' E 1°0'22''

Les Eyzies-de-Tayac, F-24620 / Aquitaine (Dordogne) — 1668

Le Pech Charmant***
+33 (0)5-53359708
16/4 - 16/9
@ info@lepech.com

17ha 83**T**(100-180m²) 10A CEE

1 ACD**G**IJKLPS
2 BIJRTVWXY
3 AGHJKN**OP**RU
4 (B+H 30/4-16/9) **KN** (Q+R+T+U+V 23/4-16/9) (X+Y 25/4-12/9) (Z)
5 **AB**FGJLMNOPRUWZ
6 ACDEGJ(N 2km)OV

'Le Pech Charmant' lives up to its name. The original 'camping à la ferme' has developed into a modern campsite but has kept its unique farmhouse atmosphere. The chance to enjoy typical 'communal' French meal, donkey trips and the outdoor life make a stay on this site well worthwhile.

From Sarlat take the D47 towards Les Eyzies. Turn left in Les Eyzies towards Le Bugue, then turn left immediately after the garage. Then follow campsite signs around the one-way system.

CC € 15 16/4-8/7 27/8-16/9 14=12, 21=18

N 44°55'26'' E 1°1'46''

Lestelle-Bétharram, F-64800 / Aquitaine (Pyrénées-Atlantiques) — 1669

Le Saillet***
rue Soum de Castet
+33 (0)5-59719865
1/5 - 30/9
le-saillet@orange.fr

4ha 80**T**(100m²) 10A CEE

1 ACD**G**IJKLMOPQ
2 CGKLRVX
3 BGHJKMNRU**W**X
4 (B 1/6-30/9) (T+U+Z)
5 **AB**CGHIJKLMNPUVZ
6 ACEGJT

Come and relax in these peaceful surroundings where you can hear the water trickle and bubble. Spacious pitches with a view of the river and the Pre-Pyrenees. Shaded and sunny pitches. Easy access to the river. 5 minutes' walk from the village, with shops for the most important groceries and restaurants. Beautiful walking and cycling options from the campsite.

Campsite located between Pau and Lourdes (D937). Signposted in Lestelle-Bétharram.

CC € 13 *1/5-10/7 28/8-30/9* *7=6, 14=10*

N 43°7'46'' W 0°12'24''

Limeuil, F-24510 / Aquitaine (Dordogne) — 1670

La Ferme de Perdigat***
+33 (0)5-53633154
25/3 - 10/10
accueil@perdigat.com

7ha 45**T**(90-220m²) 10A

1 AGIJKLMPRS
2 CDLMRTUVWXY
3 BGHJNRUWX
4 (C+H 1/5-15/9)
(Q+R 1/5-30/9)
(T+U 1/5-15/9) (V 1/7-30/8)
(X 1/5-15/9) (Z 1/5-30/9)
5 **AB**EFGIJKLMNOPQUXZ
6 ACDEGJ(N 3,5km)RT

This relaxing campsite alongside the Vézère is situated in the grounds of an old farmhouse, and has many types of trees, bushes and flowers. The camping pitches are separated by bushes. Beautifully maintained grounds. Excellent toilet facilities. A good base for visiting the caves and the Dordogne.

From Port de Limeuil to Le Bugue. Signposted.

CC € 13 *25/3-8/7 25/8-10/10*

N 44°53'37'' E 0°54'52''

Limeuil/Alles-sur-Dordogne, F-24480 / Aquitaine (Dordogne) — 1671

Le Port de Limeuil****
D31
+33 (0)5-53632976
1/5 - 24/9
leportdelimeuil@orange.fr

7ha 90**T**(100-200m²) 10A CEE

1 ACD**G**IJKLMPRS
2 CLNRSVXY
3 BGHJKMN**O**RU**W**X
4 (C+H) K(Q+S)
(T+U+V+X 15/5-15/9)
(Z)
5 **AB**DFGIJKLMNOPUWXZ
6 ACDEGI**JK**(N 0,5km)ORTV

Port de Limeuil campsite is located where the Dordogne and Vézère rivers converge, and on the other side from Limeuil, one of France's most beautiful villages. The site has its own 400m beach for swimming and fishing and canoes can be rented. The site has a shop, bar and snack bar. WiFi and tennis are free. There is also a lovely swimming pool and a heated jacuzzi.

From Le Bugue follow the D31 direction Limeuil. Campsite is sign posted in plenty of time.

CC € 15 *1/5-6/7 26/8-24/9*

N 44°52'47'' E 0°53'9''

Lisle, F-24350 / Aquitaine (Dordogne)

1672

Camping Le Pont**
+33 (0)6-30533827
1/4 - 15/10
contact@toofyk.fr

2,5ha 49**T**(80-110m²) 16A CEE

1 ACGIJKLMOPQ
2 ACLMRVWXY
3 ABGHJ**MOP**R**W**X
4 (T) Z
5 **A**FGHJKNPUWZ
6 ACDEGK(N 1,5km)

On the edge of the village, yet rural and peaceful. Directly on the banks of the Dronne. Excellent and affordable restaurant with covered terrace and lovely views next to the campsite.

D939 Angoulême-Périgueux. South of Brantôme D78 direction Boudeilles then Lisle, turn right just before village. On the right just before the bridge.

€ 11 *1/4-15/7 1/9-15/10 7=6, 14=11*

N 45°16'52" E 0°32'25"

Louvie-Juzon, F-64260 / Aquitaine (Pyrénées-Atlantiques)

1673

Le Rey***
route de Lourdes
+33 (0)5-59057852
1/2 - 13/11, 5/12 - 18/1
celine@campinglerey.com

2,5ha 38**T**(80-120m²) 10A CEE

1 A**F**IJKLM**P**Q
2 IJLRVXY
3 AGHJKLN**OP**RU**W**
4 (**A** 1/7-31/8)
(C+H 15/6-15/9)
(Q+R+T+U+V+Z)
5 **AB**DGIJKLMNOPUWZ
6 ABDEGK(N 0,9km)

Small, well-maintained campsite on 2.5 hectares, just outside Louvie-Juzon. Part of the site is not suitable for camping pitches, which gives the site a natural character. A central point for the sights of the Pyrenees. Also a stopover campsite en route to Spain (via the Col de Pourtalet). Walkers and cyclists will love it here.

Centre of Louvie-Juzon, road to Lourdes (D35). Drive through village (about 400 metres). Site signposted.

€ 17 *1/1-18/1 1/2-30/6 1/9-13/11 5/12-31/12 7=6*

N 43°5'22" W 0°24'37"

Messanges, F-40660 / Aquitaine (Landes)

1674

Airotel Le Vieux Port*****
route de la Plage Sud
+33 (0)1-76767000
FAX +33 (0)5-58480169
19/3 - 25/9
contact@levieuxport.com

30ha 800**T**(100-120m²) 6A CEE

1 AC**G**IJKLM**PS**
2 ABEIRSTVXY
3 B**F**GHJK**MNOPQ**RU**VWY**
4 (C+F+H) I**JKLMNP**
(Q+S+T+U+V+Y+Z)
5 **AB**EFGIJKLOPUVWXYZ
6 CDFGHI**K**M(N 1km)OQRTV

A large, spaciously planned campsite, but still peaceful as many of the facilities are near the reception. Located in a large pine forest. Divided into coloured zones with a toilet block for each zone. Large leisure pool.

D652 Léon - Vieux-Boucau, 1 km north of Vieux-Boucau. Well signposted.

€ 17 *19/3-18/6 3/9-25/9 7=6, 14=10*

N 43°47'52" W 1°24'4"

Messanges, F-40660 / Aquitaine (Landes) — 1675

Albret-Plage***
100 chemin du Junca
+33 (0)5-58480367
FAX +33 (0)5-58482191
1/4 - 30/9
@ albretplage@wanadoo.fr

6ha 125**T**(80-100m²) 6A

1 ACG**G**IJLMOPST
2 ABEGRSTUVWXY
3 B**F**GHJNRU**W**Y
4 (Q+S+T+U+V+Y+Z 15/6-15/9)
5 **AB**GIJKLMNOPUVZ
6 AEGH**IJK**(N 1km)OTV

Camping grounds 1 km from the centre of Vieux Boucau. The campsite is predominantly level but there is also a slightly sloping section that is set in a pine forest. There is direct access to the Atlantic Ocean (300 metres). The swimming section of the beach has lifeguards.

D652 Léon-Vieux-Boucau, 1 km north of Vieux-Boucau. The campsite is situated next to Le Vieux Port, but has its own access road on the D652.

CC € 15 *1/4-24/6 5/9-30/9*

N 43°47'47'' W 1°24'4''

Messanges, F-40660 / Aquitaine (Landes) — 1676

La Côte****
361 chemin de la Côte BP 37
+33 (0)5-58489494
FAX +33 (0)5-58489444
1/4 - 30/9
@ info@campinglacote.com

3,5ha 113**T**(100-130m²) 10A

1 AC**G**IJKLMPST
2 RVXY
3 B**F**GHJKNRU
4 (B+H 15/5-20/9) K
(Q+R 15/6-15/9)
(U+V 1/7-31/8)
5 **AB**EFGIJKLOPUWXYZ
6 ACEG**IK**(N 2km)OQRTV

A campsite on level ground with spacious shaded pitches. Ideal for families thanks to the playground, lovely swimming pool with toddlers' pool and bubble bath. The swimming complex is open from 15 May. Just 1 km to the Atlantic beaches. Refurbished toilet facilities in 2015.

In Bordeaux follow Bayonne A63 and D810 as far as exit 11 Magescq. In Magescq centre direction Azur and Messanges. Then direction Vieux-Boucau, D652. 2 km past centre of Messanges on the right.

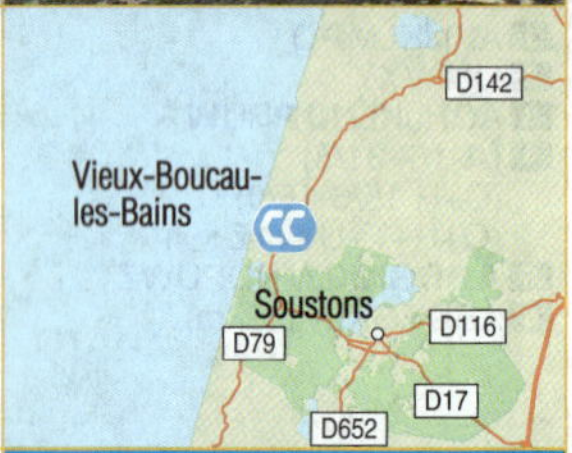

CC € 13 *1/4-3/7 27/8-30/9*

N 43°48'1'' W 1°23'30''

Messanges, F-40660 / Aquitaine (Landes) — 1677

Les Acacias***
101 chemin du Houdin
+33 (0)5-58480178
FAX +33 (0)5-58482312
23/3 - 23/10
@ lesacacias@lesacacias.com

3,4ha 75**T**(90-120m²) 10A CEE

1 ACD**G**IJKLMPST
2 RSUVWXY
3 B**F**GHJKNRU
4 (Q 🔑) (S 15/6-15/9)
(U+V 4/7-31/8)
5 **AB**EFGIJKLMNPUWXYZ
6 ACDEGH**IK**(N 1,5km)OQRT

Friendly family campsite about 2 km from the Atlantic coast. Although you are here in Les Landes you will not be camping among pine trees. There is sufficient shade however. Very well maintained toilet facilities.

A63 and N10 Bordeaux-Bayonne to exit 11 Magescq. Then dir. Azur and Messanges. Then dir. Vieux-Boucau. Left at roundabout 2 km before Messanges centre (Quartier Caliot road). Campsite 1 km further on the left.

CC € 13 *23/3-6/7 24/8-23/10*

N 43°47'54'' W 1°22'33''

Mézos, F-40170 / Aquitaine (Landes)

1678

Le Village Tropical Sen Yan*****
avenue de la Gare
+33 (0)5-58426005
+33 (0)5-58426456
7/5 - 9/9
reception@sen-yan.com

8ha 110**T**(80-150m²) 10-16A CEE

1 ACD**G**IJKLMO**P**S
2 ADLRSVXY
3 ABGHJK**M**N**Q**RU**V**Z
4 (B 6/6-11/9) (E) (G 6/6-11/9) J**KMN** (Q+S 20/6-11/9) (T) (U 4/7-31/8) (V+X) (Y 4/7-31/8) (Z)
5 **AB**DEFGIJLMNPUZ
6 EGH**IK**(N 1km)ORTV

Large campsite with an exotic ambiance in a parkland setting with thousands of tropical plants. A luxurious holiday village with lovely swimming pools and a natural pool, an excellent restaurant and a fairy-tale minigolf course. The campsite is located in an undulating landscape. Not all amenities are available in low season.

N10/E5/E70, exit Laharie. In Onesse-et-Laharie, 5 km from the motorway, signposted.

CC € 19 *7/5-3/7 27/8-9/9*

N 44°4'20" W 1°9'23"

Mimizan-Plage-Sud, F-40200 / Aquitaine (Landes)

1679

Airotel Club Marina-Landes****
rue Marina
+33 (0)5-58091266
+33 (0)5-58091640
29/4 - 18/9
contact@clubmarina.com

9ha 358**T**(80-110m²) 10A CEE

1 ACD**G**IJKLMOPST
2 BERSVWXY
3 B**F**GHJKL**M**NQRUV**WY**
4 (B+E+H) IJK**P** (Q+S+T+U+V+X+Y+Z)
5 **AB**DEFGIJKLMNOPUZ
6 ACEG**IJK**(N 1km)OQRTV

A lovely campsite with all the amenities to ensure a wonderful stay. You will enjoy the heated indoor pool and if the weather is good in the large outdoor pool. The sea and dunes are 500 metres away and back on the site you will find a good restaurant, jeu de boules, minigolf and direct access to Les Landes cycle route network.

In Mimizan drive in the direction of Mimizan-Plage (6 km). The campsite is located on this road.

CC € 17 *29/4-9/7 27/8-17/9*

N 44°12'17" W 1°17'27"

Moliets-Plage, F-40660 / Aquitaine (Landes)

1680

Le Saint Martin****
2655 avenue de l'Océan
+33 (0)5-58485230
+33 (0)5-58485073
23/4 - 30/10
contact@camping-saint-martin.fr

18ha 450**T**(80-150m²) 10A CEE

1 ACGIJKLMOPST
2 AEIJKRSVWXY
3 B**F**GHJKLNRU**WY**
4 (B 1/6-15/9) (**F**+H) **KN** (Q) (S+T 1/4-15/10) (V 20/6-15/9) (Y) Z
5 **AB**DEFGIJKLPUXYZ
6 ACDEGH**IK**M(N 2km)OQRT V

Large beach campsite, partly in woodland and partly in the dunes. Trees have been planted to give shade. Most pitches are bordered by hedges. Terraced swimming pools. There is also a square with catering facilities.

From Bordeaux direction Bayonne over the A63 and N10. Take exit 'Castets' then direction Léon. Turn left just before the centre of Léon towards Messanges. In Moliets take the road to Moliets-Plage. Last campsite before the ocean.

CC € 17 *23/4-2/7 5/9-30/10*

N 43°51'9" W 1°23'13"

Monflanquin, F-47150 / Aquitaine (Lot-et-Garonne)

iD **1681**

Domaine Laborde****
Commune Paulhiac
+33 (0)5-53631488
FAX +33 (0)5-53616023
1/4 - 1/10
@ domainelaborde@wanadoo.fr

20ha 150**T**(120-160m²) 15A

1 ACD**G**IJKLMNOPST
2 CDLRTVWXY
3 ABDGHJMN**OP**RUVWZ
4 (A) (B 1/5-30/9) (F+H) J**KLN** (Q+S+T+U+V+Y+Z)
5 **AB**DEFGIJKLMNOPUVWZ
6 ACDEGIJ(N 7km)ORV

Four-star naturist campsite directly on the border of the Dordogne and Lot et Garonne, famous for its Southern French climate, small villages, castles, creeks and caves. Indoor leisure pool, sauna with hammam, outdoor pool with 2 slides, restaurant, shop, bar and internet. Great campsite.

D255 from Villeréal to Lacapelle-Biron. The road to the campsite is on the left, 10 km from Villeréal. Indicated by Domaine Laborde signs.

CC € 19 *1/4-9/7 27/8-1/10*

N 44°36'50" E 0°50'8"

Monplaisant, F-24170 / Aquitaine (Dordogne)

iD **1682**

La Lénotte***
D710
+33 (0)5-53302580
FAX +33 (0)5-53596123
1/4 - 31/10
@ contact@la-lenotte.com

8ha 39**T**(90-120m²) 10A CEE

1 ACD**F**IJKLMPQ
2 CLMRTVX
3 A**F**GHJQRUW
4 (C 1/6-31/10) (G 1/7-31/10) (Q+R) (T+U+V 1/7-31/8) (Z)
5 **A**FGIJKLMNOPRUX
6 CDEGJ(N 4km)OTV

A spacious, peaceful campsite where you will be welcomed by the young, enthusiastic owners. A lovely brook meanders through the campsite, suitable for fishing. The Dordogne, Sarlat and the fortified towns are close by, as well as castles and caves. Level grounds and easy access, making it suitable as a stopover campsite (Bis-Toulouse).

Bergerac-Sarlat 7 km east of Le Buisson-de-Cadouin. Follow the D710 at Siorac for 5 km (Bis-Toulouse).

CC € 13 *1/4-10/7 27/8-31/10 7=6*

N 44°47'46" E 1°0'29"

Montalivet, F-33930 / Aquitaine (Gironde)

iD **1683**

Centre Helio-Marin (CHM) Montalivet***
46 av. de l'Europe
+33 (0)5-56737373
FAX +33 (0)5-56093215
2/4 - 1/10
@ infos@chm-montalivet.com

200ha 561**T**(100m²) 16A CEE

1 ACD**G**IJKLMPST
2 AEGSVWXY
3 BGHJKL**M**NQRU**VY**
4 (C+H) IJ**KLNP** (Q+S+T+U+V+W+X+Y+Z)
5 **AB**DEGIJKLMNOPUVXYZ
6 CDEGH**IK**M(N 1km)ORTV

This naturist campsite extends over 200 hectares of pine forest with direct access to a two kilometre Atlantic beach. The site has a leisure pool and a thermal complex and offers many sporting opportunities with cycle and walking routes right from the site. Ffurther afield the vineyards of the Médoc and the Pointe du Verdon lure.

Follow D101 from Vendays-Montalivet direction Soulac. After 7 km in l'Hôpital turn left and follow the CHM signs.

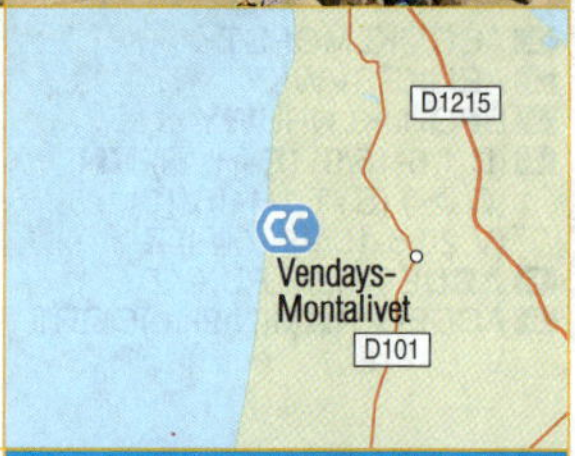

CC € 15 *2/4-9/7 27/8-1/10*

N 45°21'48" W 1°8'44"

Montalivet-les-Bains, F-33930 / Aquitaine (Gironde)

1684

Campéole Médoc Plage****
av. de l'Europe
+33 (0)5-56093345
+33 (0)5-56093312
10/5 - 11/9
montalivet@
andretriganogroupe.com

30ha 393T(100-120m²) 16A CEE

1 ACDGIJKLMOPST
2 GRSVWXY
3 BGJK**M**NRU
4 (C+H 15/5-13/9) **I**J
(Q+R+T+U+V+Z 1/7-31/8)
5 **AB**EFGIJKLMNOPUVZ
6 CEGH**J**L(N 0,5km)RTV

A large well equipped campsite with a number of sporting opportunities 700m from the beach.

In the suburbs of Montalivet-les-Bains (D102) immediate left after filling station on the left of the road. Well indicated.

CC € 17 *10/5-4/7 22/8-11/9*

N 45°22'12'' W 1°8'41''

Montignac, F-24290 / Aquitaine (Dordogne)

1685

Le Moulin du Bleufond***
avenue Aristide Briand
+33 (0)5-53518395
+33 (0)9-82631828
1/4 - 5/10
info@bleufond.com

1,3ha 61T(70-120m²) 10A CEE

1 ACD**G**IJKLMPST
2 CLRTVWXY
3 BGHIJKL**MNQ**RU**W**
4 (**A** 1/7-31/8) (C+H ⊶) **KN**
(Q+R+T+U+V+X ⊶) Z
5 **AB**CDFGJLNPUXYZ
6 ACEGIJ(N 0,5km)RTVW

You will receive a warm welcome on this comfortable rural campsite. Very attractive with heated toilets. The swimming pool is also heated. The campsite is within walking distance of the village where you can do all your shopping. Plenty of sights in the immediate vicinity. An ideal location for visiting the Lascaux caves.

On the A89 exit Thenon, direction Montignac/ Lascaux. In Montignac direction Valojoux Sergeac. Follow the signs.

CC € 17 *1/4-8/7 29/8-5/10*

N 45°3'36'' E 1°9'31''

Montignac/Lascaux, F-24290 / Aquitaine (Dordogne)

1686

La Fage****
la Chapelle-Aubareil
+33 (0)5-53507650
9/4 - 9/10
contact@camping-lafage.com

2,5ha 61T(80-150m²) 10A

1 ACD**G**IJKLPQ
2 BLRVWXY
3 ABCGHJNRU
4 (**A** 1/7-31/8)(E+G 15/5-15/9)
(Q 1/6-31/8)
(R 1/5-30/7,1/9-30/9)
(S 1/7-31/8)
(T+U+V 1/6-15/9)
(X 1/7-31/8) (Z 1/5-30/9)
5 **AB**EFGIJKLMNOPUWZ
6 CEGK(N 2km)ORV

The campsite is located between Montignac and Sarlat, close to the caves at Lascaux and les Eyzies and the many beautiful castles in the Dordogne. Definitely worth a visit.

On the D704 after 8 km between Montignac and Sarlat, south of the Lascaux caves. Then follow camping signs.

CC € 15 *9/4-10/7 27/8-9/10* 7=6, 14=11

N 45°1'4'' E 1°11'17''

Ondres, F-40440 / Aquitaine (Landes) 1687

Du Lac*****
518 rue de Janin
+33 (0)5-59452845
FAX +33 (0)5-59452945
23/3 - 3/10
@ contact@camping-du-lac.fr

3ha 61**T**(100-120m²) 10A CEE

1 AC**F**HIJL**P**ST
2 CDFGIJRSVWX
3 BGJK**M**RU**W**
4 (C+H 1/6-30/9) **IKLN**P
(Q+T+U+Y+Z 1/7-31/8)
5 **AB**DEFGIJKLMNOPQRUW
XYZ
6 ACEGK(N 0,5km)RTV

The touring pitches are between the swimming pool and a lovely little lake. The seasonal pitches are on another part of the campsite. Flemish-French owners.

In Bordeaux follow direction Bayonne A63 as far as exit 7. Then take D810 (formerly known as RN10). Stay on D810 (RN10) till about 1 km before Ondres centre. Take the road to the left to Ondres-Plage. Left at the 1st roundabout and follow the signs.

CC € 17 *23/3-8/7 25/8-3/10*

N 43°33'56" W 1°27'12"

Parentis-en-Born, F-40160 / Aquitaine (Landes) 1688

L'Arbre d'Or****
1037 route du Lac
+33 (0)5-58784156
FAX +33 (0)5-58784962
26/3 - 31/10
@ arbre-dor@hotmail.fr

5ha 109**T**(90-120m²) 10A CEE

1 ACDGIJKLMOPST
2 RSVWXY
3 B**F**GHJKNRU**W**
4 (C 15/5-1/10)
(E 10/4-31/10)
(G 15/5-1/10) KP(Q+R)
(T+U+V+X+Y+Z 15/5-30/9)
5 **AB**EFGIJKLMNOPUWZ
6 ACEGJ**K**(N 0,5km)ORTV

An excellent campsite for exploring parts of Landes in the early or late season by foot, on a bike or in the car. 500 metres from the lake of Biscarrosse. Heated indoor swimming pool with jacuzzi and spacious pitches. Friendly and hospitable management. Highly recommended!

Leave the Bordeaux motorway A63/N10 in Liposthey and drive towards Parentis (D43). The campsite is signposted in Parentis.

CC € 13 *26/3-8/7 27/8-30/10*

N 44°20'46" W 1°5'35"

Pineuilh/Ste Foy-la-Grande, F-33220 / Aquitaine (Gironde) 1689

Camping de la Bastide***
allée de Camping
FAX +33 (0)5-57461384
1/4 - 23/10
@ contact@camping-bastide.com

1,2ha 28**T**(60-100m²) 10A

1 ACD**G**IJKLMPRS
2 CORTVY
3 AGHJRU**WX**
4 (B 15/5-30/9)
5 **AB**GIJKLMNPUWXY
6 ACDEGK(N 0,5km)RTV

Campsite is located right next to the village of St. Foy-la-Grande on the Dordogne. The popular market has a reputation throughout the region. A hospitable, cozy campsite run by a very friendly English family. Internet bookings also possible. Small-scale and tranquil. Beautiful surroundings.

From Bordeaux D936 to Bergerac, at Ste. Foy. Continue via the D936 to the roundabout by Super U. Third exit towards hospital. Signposted after 500m.

CC € 17 *1/4-11/7 1/9-23/10*

N 44°50'39" E 0°13'29"

Plazac, F-24580 / Aquitaine (Dordogne)

iD 1690

Le Lac***
Lieu dit Le Lac
+33 (0)5-53507586
+33 (0)5-53505836
8/5 - 30/9
contact@
campinglelac-dordogne.com

8ha 75T(100-180m²) 10A

1 ACDGIJKLPQ
2 ADLMRTVWXY
3 BGHMN**OP**QRUWZ
4 (C+H 1/6-30/9) (Q) (S 8/5-15/9) (T+U+V+X+Z 15/5-30/9)
5 **AB**CEFGJLNPUVXYZ
6 ACDEGJ(N 1km)TV

For 40 years this top-quality family campsite has been located in the middle of Dordogne with its beautiful countryside, picturesque villages, countless castles and prehistoric caves. Positioned by a lake and with a lovely heated swimming pool which guarantees hours of fun in the water under the French sun.

A20, then A89, exit 17, direction Montignac, Thonac, Plazac. Campsite signposted.

CC € 15 *8/5-7/7 24/8-30/9*

N 45°1'52'' E 1°2'53''

Pujols, F-47300 / Aquitaine (Lot-et-Garonne)

iD 1691

Lot & Bastides à Pujols***
allée de Malbentre
+33 (0)5-53368679
+33 (0)9-70632807
26/3 - 29/10
contact@
camping-lot-et-bastides.fr

12ha 83T(115-140m²) 16A CEE

1 ACD**G**IJKLMO**P**Q
2 GRVWX
3 B**F**GHJKRUW
4 (C+G 15/5-15/9) K (Q 1/5-30/9) (R) (T+U+V+Z 15/5-15/9)
5 **AB**GIJKLMNOPUWXY
6 ACDEGK(N 4km)OTV

The campsite is located at the foot of the medieval village of Pujols; Pujols is listed as one of the most beautiful villages of France and a stone's throw from Villeneuve-sur-Lot. Comfortable camping pitches in a brand new, well designed park.

On the N21 from the north dir. Villeneuve-sur-Lot (D661) at first roundabout. Follow Bordeaux then Pujols signs. Then follow Piscine de Malbentre and/or campsite.

CC € 13 *26/3-2/7 27/8-29/10*

N 44°23'41'' E 0°41'13''

Pyla-sur-Mer, F-33115 / Aquitaine (Gironde)

iD 1692

Panorama du Pyla****
route de Biscarrosse
+33 (0)5-56221044
+33 (0)5-56221012
9/4 - 3/10
mail@camping-panorama.com

15ha 450T(64-150m²) 10A CEE

1 AC**G**IJKLMO**P**ST
2 ABEGIJKSUVXY
3 AB**F**GHJK**M**NQRUVWY
4 (C+H) IJKMN (Q+S+T+U+V+X+Y) Z
5 **AB**EFGHIJKLMNOPQRUW Z
6 CDEG**K**LOQRTUV

Large friendly campsite with private steps up to the Pilat Dunes. Plenty of fun swimming, large choice of activities for everyone (sauna, classical music).

A660, N250 Bordeaux-Arcachon, exit Dune de Pyla. Follow 'campings'. Fourth to the right.

CC € 17 *1/5-19/6 18/9-30/9*

N 44°34'22'' W 1°13'15''

Pyla-sur-Mer, F-33115 / Aquitaine (Gironde) — 1693

Pyla Camping***
rte de Biscarosse
+33 (0)5-56227456
FAX +33 (0)5-56221031
1/4 - 30/9
reception@pylacamping.fr

8,5ha 283T(35-100m²) 10A CEE

1 BCGIJKLMOPS
2 ABEGIJKSUVWXY
3 AFGJKNRUWY
4 (C) (G 15/5-30/9) (Q+S+T+U+V+X+Y+Z 1/5-24/9)
5 ABFGIJLMNPU
6 CEGJ(N 7km)QRTV

Quiet family campsite by the Pilat dune, the largest dune in Europe with options for swimming and parasailing.

A660, N250 Bordeaux-Arcachon, exit Dune de Pyla. Follow 'Campings'. 3rd campsite on the right.

CC € 17 1/4-30/6 1/9-30/9

N 44°34'40'' W 1°12'47''

Rauzan, F-33420 / Aquitaine (Gironde) — 1694

du Vieux Château***
6 Blabot-Bas
+33 (0)5-57841538
1/4 - 15/10
contact@vieuxchateau.fr

2,5ha 47T(110-130m²) 6A

1 ACDFIJKLMPST
2 BRVXY
3 ABGJNRU
4 (C+G 1/6-15/9) (Q+R 1/7-30/8) (T+U+X+Z 15/5-15/9)
5 AFGIJKLMNPUWZ
6 ACDEGJ(N 0,5km)TV

Experience the magic and peace of a castle park with centuries old trees and a feudal castle built on the orders of the English monarchy. Visit a Celestine cave under the village with a subterranean river. You can walk to the shops in the town in minutes.

In Rauzan towards 'gendarmerie' on the D123 opposite and follow signs to 'du Château'. Campsite in 300m.

CC € 15 1/4-8/7 27/8-14/10

N 44°47'6'' W 0°7'32''

Rives/Villeréal, F-47210 / Aquitaine (Lot-et-Garonne) — 1695

Le Château de Fonrives****
D207
+33 (0)5-53366338
FAX +33 (0)5-53360998
9/4 - 9/9
chateau.de.fonrives@wanadoo.fr

20ha 84T(80-150m²) 10A

1 ACDGIJKLPQ
2 DLMRUVWXY
3 BGHJKMNPQRUVW
4 (C+E+F+G) IJKN (Q+S) (T+U+V 1/7-31/8) (X+Y+Z)
5 ABDEFGIJKLMNOPRSUW XYZ
6 CDEGJK(N 3,5km)ORTV

An allround campsite with many own amenities. Park-like design around a château. Walking around the grounds with 2 lakes and a forest takes 45 minutes.

The campsite is on route D207 Issigeac-Villeréal near the village Rives and is signposted.

CC € 17 9/4-1/7 28/8-9/9

N 44°39'26'' E 0°43'54''

Rouffignac-St-Cernin, F-24580 / Aquitaine (Dordogne)

1696

Bleu Soleil***
Domaine Touvent
+33 (0)5-53054830
15/4 - 30/9
infos@camping-bleusoleil.com

42ha 90**T**(80-120m²) 10A CEE

1 ACD**G**IJLPQ
2 JKLRTVWXY
3 ABD**F**GHJMNRU
4 (B+G 15/5-15/9)
(Q 1/6-15/9) (R 🔑)
(T+U+V+Y 1/6-15/9) Z
5 **AB**EFGIJKLMNPRUWZ
6 AEGJ(N 1,3km)OQRV

A charming campsite located in a natural domain in the heart of the Dordogne. Many pitches with panoramic views. Ideally located for the sights. The campsite is easily accessible. Nature and peace set the tone. Tennis court and swimming pool available. Village centre 1 km away. Supermarket close by.

A89/E70 Brive-Bordeaux, exit 17. Then N89 direction Bordeaux. Past Thenon turn left onto D31 direction Rouffignac. Follow signs on left before Rouffignac.

CC € 15 *15/4-10/7 27/8-30/9*

N 45°3'18" E 0°59'14"

Salies-de-Béarn, F-64270 / Aquitaine (Pyrénées-Atlantiques)

1697

Domaine d'Esperbasque**
route de Sauveterrre
FAX +33 (0)5-59382104
1/3 - 31/10
info@esperbasque.com

3ha 94**T**(80-100m²) 6A CEE

1 A**G**IJKLPRS
2 FIJKLRXY
3 A**F**GHJN**OP**RU
4 (B+G 25/4-15/10) (Q 🔑)
(U 1/7-31/8) (Z 🔑)
5 **AB**GJKLMNPU
6 ABDEJ(N 3km)V

Esperbasque Estate (16 hectares) is set on a hillside with splendid views of the pastures where horses graze. Lovely countryside and plenty of space. Home-baked bread, occasional communal meals, gardening, horses and other animals, pétanque, archery, visits to wine growers and the salt town of Salies de Bearn.

Campsite on the east side of the D933 between Salies-de-Béarn and Sauveterre. From the north do not turn left, turn around at next exit. See signs.

CC € 15 *1/3-9/7 1/9-31/10*

N 43°27'11" W 0°55'15"

Sanguinet, F-40460 / Aquitaine (Landes)

1698

Campéole Le Lac Sanguinet***
526 rue de Pinton
+33 (0)5-58827080
FAX +33 (0)5-58821424
1/4 - 18/9
lac-sanguinet@
andretriganogroupe.com

10,6ha 147**T**(80-150m²) 10A CEE

1 ACD**G**IJKLMO**P**
2 ADLMRSVWXY
3 ABGHJNRU**WZ**
4 (C+H 1/5-18/9) P
(Q+T+U+V+X 1/7-31/8) Z
5 **AB**EFGJLNPQUY
6 ACEGH**J**L(N 1km)RTV

Family campsite near the welcoming village of Sanguinet in the heart of the Landes forests. Quiet location on the shore of one of the most beautiful and largest lakes of Europe. Direct access to a sandy beach.

A10, exit Arcachon. Follow d'Arcachon road. Exit Mios/Biscarosse, then direction Sanguinet. Campsite in Sanguinet by the lake. Signposted.

CC € 17 *1/5-4/7 22/8-18/9*

N 44°28'53" W 1°5'36"

Sanguinet, F-40460 / Aquitaine (Landes)

1699

Les Grands Pins****
1039 avenue de Losa
+33 (0)5-58786174
FAX +33 (0)5-58786915
1/4 - 30/9
info@campinglesgrandspins.com

8ha 65T(80-130m²) 10A CEE

1 ACD**G**IJKLM**P**
2 ADMRSVWXY
3 B**F**GHJK**M**NRU**W**Z
4 (A 1/7-30/8) (C+E+H) IJ M(Q) (S 1/7-31/8) (T+U+V+X+Y) Z
5 **AB**CDEFGIJKLMNOPRUZ
6 ACGH**K**(N 1km)TV

Campsite on sandy beach of Lake Sanguinet for a successful holiday in Landes. Outdoor pool and heated indoor pool. Various types of water recreation. Network of cycle paths.

The campsite is located in Sanguinet. Clearly signposted and positioned by a lake.

CC € 17 *1/4-30/6 1/9-30/9*

N 44°29'2'' W 1°5'24''

Sarlat, F-24200 / Aquitaine (Dordogne)

1700

Le Moulin du Roch*****
route des Eyzies
+33 (0)5-53592027
FAX +33 (0)5-53592095
14/5 - 16/9
moulin.du.roch@wanadoo.fr

8ha 195T(100-120m²) 10A CEE

1 ACDEIJKL**P**RS
2 JRTVY
3 BGHN**OP**RUW
4 (A 1/6-31/8) (C+G) (Q 1/7-31/8) (S+U+V) (X 1/7-31/8) (Y) Z
5 ABDEFGIJKLMNOPUXYZ
6 EG**K**(N 10km)OTV

An easily accessible campsite where pets are not allowed. Catering mainly for French and English guests, this Castel campsite has a beautiful swimming pool.

On the D47 Sarlat-Les Eyzies.

CC € 15 *14/5-8/7 25/8-16/9 8=7*

N 44°54'30'' E 1°6'54''

Sarlat-la-Canéda, F-24200 / Aquitaine (Dordogne)

1701

Indigo Sarlat****
rue Jean Gabin
+33 (0)5-53590584
FAX +33 (0)5-53285751
24/3 - 26/9
sarlat@camping-indigo.com

6ha 106T(100-115m²) 6A CEE

1 ACDGIJKLPRS
2 JRVXY
3 ABG**M**NRU
4 (B 2/4-28/9) (F+G) **N** (Q+R) (T 1/7-31/8) UVZ
5 **AB**DFGIJKLMNOPUWXZ
6 CEGJ(N 0,8km)OTUV

The closest campsite to Sarlat, just 10 minutes walk from the historic centre of the capital of the Périgord Noir. Beautiful wooded grounds laid out in terraces. Swimming pools (one of which is indoors), tennis courts, social activities. Camping ACSI valid only on standard pitches.

From Paris and Toulouse: A20, exit Souillac. From Bordeaux: A89, exit Périgueux.

CC € 17 *24/3-5/7 31/8-25/9*

N 44°53'36'' E 1°13'41''

Sarlat-la-Canéda, F-24200 / Aquitaine (Dordogne) — 1702

Les Acacias***
avenue-de-la-Canéda
+33 (0)5-53310850
12/4 - 30/9
@ camping-acacias@wanadoo.fr

4ha 102T(80-150m²) 10A

1 ACDFIJKLPRS
2 BGIJKLRTVXY
3 B**F**GHJKNRU
4 (C+G 10/5-20/9)
(Q+R 12/4-25/9)
(U+V 12/5-15/9) Z
5 **AB**DEFGIJKLMNOPUZ
6 ACEGJ(N 1,3km)V

A friendly compact French campsite in the centre of La Canéda. Located in the heart of the loveliest tourist sights. Within cycling distance of Sarlat for those who prefer to leave the car behind. Even an inexperienced walker can easily make the 2.5 km into the centre. There is a bus stop near the campsite. Modern toilet facilities. Free WiFi-point.

In Sarlat direction Cahors, exit La Canéda. Campsite signposted.

CC € 13 *12/4-6/7 23/8-29/9* 21=20

N 44°51'27'' E 1°14'15''

Sarlat-la-Canéda, F-24200 / Aquitaine (Dordogne) — 1703

Les Terrasses du Périgord***
Pech d'Orange
+33 (0)5-53590225
FAX +33 (0)5-53591648
16/4 - 19/9
@ terrasses-du-perigord@wanadoo.fr

6ha 75T(120m²) 16A CEE

1 ACD**F**IJKLPQ
2 JKLRTVXY
3 B**F**GHJKN**Q**R**T**UV
4 (B+H) **K**(Q 1/7-31/8)
(R) (T+U 1/7-20/9)
(W+X 1/7-10/9) Z
5 **A**FGIJKLMNOPUWXY
6 CEG**IK**(N 2,7km)ORV

The campsite has beautiful panoramic views but is still easy to reach, just 2 km from the medieval village of Sarlat. Central location for exploring the many sights.

When entering Sarlat from the north, direction Ste Nathalène. After 2 km follow signs at the junction to the left.

CC € 17 *16/4-30/6 1/9-19/9*

N 44°54'23'' E 1°14'13''

Sarlat/Carsac, F-24200 / Aquitaine (Dordogne) — 1704

Le Plein Air des Bories***
Les Bories
+33 (0)5-53281567
23/4 - 10/9
@ contact@camping-desbories.com

3ha 80T(100-120m²) 6-16A

1 ACD**G**IJLPRS
2 ACLRSVWXY
3 BGHJMNRUWX
4 (B 25/4-10/9) (E+G)
(Q+R+T+U+V+X 1/7-31/8) Z
5 **A**EFGJKLNPUVZ
6 CEG**J**(N 0,6km)V

A really quietly located campsite. Suitable for families. Hidden away in wooded countryside and located right by the River Dordogne it is an ideal spot to enjoy peace and watersports. The swimming pool can be covered over.

On the A20 exit Souillac, direction Sarlat via D703. Left past Calviac towards 'Vallée de la Dordogne'. Go under the railway bridge in Carsac and take the second left. Follow the signs.

CC € 15 *23/4-2/7 20/8-10/9*

N 44°49'59'' E 1°16'5''

Sarlat/Marcillac, F-24200 / Aquitaine (Dordogne) — 1705

Les Tailladis***
Marcillac/St. Quentin
+33 (0)5-53591095
FAX +33 (0)5-53294756
15/3 - 31/10
@ tailladis@wanadoo.fr

4,5ha 78T(80-110m²) 6A

1 ACD**F**IJLPRS
2 CIJKLRVXY
3 ABGHJNRUW
4 (C+G 1/5-1/10) (Q+S+T+U+V+X+Y 15/4-1/11)Z
5 **AB**DFGIJKLMNOPUZ
6 EG**IK**(N 8km)OQR

In the Beune valley, between Montignac and Sarlat. A 25 hectare site with a brook, natural lake and swimming pool. Heated toilet facilities, excellent cuisine and a special welcome. Ideal starting point for discovering the locality and the many places of interest in all seasons.

In Brive direction Montignac. Then D704 direction Sarlat. After St. Genies name board (± 8 km) right on D48 towards Tamniès. To next junction then left to Marcillac (± 6 km). Follow signs.

CC € 15 *15/3-8/7 25/8-31/10*

N 44°58'29'' E 1°11'16''

Sarlat/Ste Nathalène, F-24200 / Aquitaine (Dordogne) — 1706

La Palombière*****
+33 (0)5-53594234
FAX +33 (0)5-53284540
30/4 - 18/9
@ contact@lapalombiere.fr

6,5ha 68T(100-110m²) 10A CEE

1 ACD**F**IJKLPRS
2 JKLRTVWXY
3 BGHJKMNQRUV
4 (C+H ⊶) IJ**KNP** (Q+T+U+V+Y ⊶) Z
5 **AB**CDEFGIJLNPQUWXY
6 EGH**I**K(N 6km)ORUV

An entrance that gives camping guests a wonderful feeling at this beautiful and enchanting site located on a hillside. The reception and excellent restaurant built in Perigord style offer a warm welcome. The stunning views and beautifully maintained grounds, with sports areas, will please everyone. New in 2016: indoor leisure pool.

A20 exit Souillac, D704 direction Sarlat. Turn right in Rouffiac, D47 Carlux-Sarlat. 8 km from Sarlat in Ste Nathalène.

CC € 17 *30/4-9/7 27/8-18/9*

N 44°54'23'' E 1°17'31''

Sauveterre-la-Lémance, F-47500 / Aquitaine (Lot-et-Garonne) — 1707

Moulin du Périé****
+33 (0)5-53406726
FAX +33 (0)5-53406246
14/5 - 17/9
@ moulinduperie@wanadoo.fr

5ha 125T(80-120m²) 6-10A CEE

1 ACD**G**IJKLMOPQ
2 ACDLRVXY
3 B**F**GHJKNRU**WZ**
4 (B 1/6-17/9) (Q+R+T+U+V+Y+Z ⊶)
5 **AB**EFGIJKLMNOPRUWXYZ
6 ACDEGJ(N 3km)TV

The Baudot family welcomes you in a park around an old mill in the south of the Périgord Noir. Lovely pitches in the sun or in shade, a natural spring lake with a beach, plenty of peace and quiet: an ideal campsite for relaxing. From here you can easily visit the many attractions of the Dordogne and the Lot.

Campsite signposted in Sauveterre-la-Lémance. Follow road over railway to the left. Campsite is located about 3 km past the village towards Loubejac.

CC € 15 *14/5-2/7 20/8-17/9 7=6*

N 44°35'26'' E 1°2'52''

Socoa/Urrugne, F-64122 / Aquitaine (Pyrénées-Atlantiques) — 1708

Juantcho**
875 route de la Corniche
+33 (0)5-59471197
1/5 - 15/10
juantcho64@gmail.com

6ha 215T(80-100m²) 5A

1 AC**G**HIJKLMPRS
2 EFIJKQRUVWXY
3 A**F**GR
4 (Q+U 1/7-31/8)
5 **AB**FGIJKLNPUV
6 CDE(N 0,5km)R

Juantcho is located in a valley at the 'Corniche Basque'. This spectacular route runs along the coast and is one of France's most beautiful. You have wonderful views of the ocean and St.Jean de Luz bay from the Corniche. Hedges between the terraces provide privacy.

Exit the motorway at St. Jean-de-Luz Sud and from there drive in the direction of Socoa. The campsite is situated at the beach road D912, not far from the lighthouse.

CC € 17 *1/5-10/7 29/8-15/10* *7=6, 14=12, 21=18*

N 43°23'38" W 1°41'30"

Soulac-sur-Mer, F-33780 / Aquitaine (Gironde) — 1709

Flower camping des Pins***
213 Passe de Formose l'Amilie
+33 (0)5-56098252
+33 (0)5-56736558
1/5 - 30/9
contact@campingdespins.fr

3,4ha 150T(90-100m²) 6A CEE

1 AFIJLM**P**S
2 ABIJSTVWXY
3 BGKNRW
4 (C+H+Q+R)
(T+U+V+X 1/7-31/8)
5 **AB**IJKLMNOPXZ
6 ADEGIK(N 3km)TV

A campsite located in a quiet natural setting, away from the bustle of everyday life. The 3.4 hectare grounds are 2 minutes from the Atlantic with a wide beach. It has a new swimming pool and modern energy efficient toilet facilities. Environmentally friendly campsite.

On the A10 exit 25 towards Saintes Royan. Take ferry across the Gironde to Le Verdon. In Soulac take the Route des-Lacs southbound. After leaving built-up area 1st right, 2nd left.

CC € 15 *1/5-3/7 28/8-30/9*

N 45°28'58" W 1°7'38"

Soulac-sur-Mer, F-33780 / Aquitaine (Gironde) — 1710

Les Lacs*****
126 route des Lacs
+33 (0)5-56097663
+33 (0)5-56099802
2/4 - 5/11
info@camping-les-lacs.com

5,8ha 98T(102-170m²) 10A

1 ACD**G**IJKLMOPST
2 ARSVWXY
3 ABDGKN**OP**QRUW
4 (A 1/7-31/8) (B 15/6-30/9)
(F) (G 15/6-30/9) IJ
(Q+S+T+U+V)
(X+Y 11/4-30/9) (Z)
5 **AB**DEFGIJKLMNOPUWXYZ
6 ACDEGI**K**(N 4km)OTV

This campsite offers everything you could wish for on holiday near the ocean. In addition you can enjoy two lovely swimming pools, one of them indoors and heated. Ideally located for trips out.

From Bordeaux: Rocade exit 7. Then N215 Le Verdon or D2 Pauillac along the D101. From the boat: first to Soulac then direction L'Amélie. Follow Route des Lacs. On the left outside the built up area.

CC € 17 *2/4-9/7 27/8-5/11* *7=6*

N 45°29'0" W 1°7'8"

Soulac-sur-Mer, F-33780 / Aquitaine (Gironde)

1711

Sandaya Soulac-Plage****
Lieu-dit l'Amélie
+33 (0)5-56098727
FAX +33 (0)5-56736426
1/4 - 10/9
@ soulacplage@sandaya.fr

10ha 182**T**(75-240m²) 10A CEE

1 ACD**G**IJKL**P**ST
2 ABEIKSVWXY
3 BGKNRUWY
4 (B 15/6-13/9) (E 12/4-13/9) (G 15/6-13/9) IJ (Q+S+T+U+V+X+Z)
5 **AB**EFGIJKLMNPUW
6 AEGH**IK**L(N 0,2km)ORTV

This campsite located right by the sea offers you a leisure pool. The surrounding countryside is fine for cycling, walking and horse riding.

In L'Amélie-Plage directly in the direction of the beach.

CC € 17 *1/4-1/7 29/8-10/9*

N 45°28'55'' W 1°9'4''

St. Antoine-d'Auberoche, F-24330 / Aquitaine (Dordogne)

1712

de La Pélonie***
La Pélonie
+33 (0)5-53075578
FAX +33 (0)5-53037427
20/4 - 30/9
@ lapelonie@aol.com

3ha 68**T**(100-120m²) 10A CEE

1 ACDGIJKLMPRS
2 FJLRUVXY
3 BCGHJN**OP**RU
4 (C+G 15/5-30/9) IJ (Q+R) (T+U+V 15/6-31/8) (Y 1/7-31/8) Z
5 **AB**DEFGIJKLMNPRUWYZ
6 ACDEGIK(N 5km)OTV

Nice family campsite, well maintained. Located in the countryside, in the heart of Dordogne, 15 km from Périgueux. Suitable for discovering touristic sights in Dordogne. Two heated pools (1 covered) and various water slides. WiFi free in low season.

On the D6089 (don't take the A road) Brive-Périgueux, 5 km past Fossemagne on the right side, turn in and continue for 200 metres, or coming from Périgueux 5 km past St. Pierre on the left.

CC € 13 *20/4-10/7 27/8-30/9*

N 45°7'54'' E 0°55'43''

St. Avit-de-Vialard, F-24260 / Aquitaine (Dordogne)

1713

Saint Avit Loisirs*****
+33 (0)5-53026400
FAX +33 (0)5-53026439
26/3 - 24/9
@ contact@saint-avit-loisirs.com

52ha 199**T**(100m²) 6A CEE

1 ACD**G**IJKLMOPQ
2 BDJKLMPRTVXY
3 ABC**EF**GHJKL**MNQ**RUVW
4 (C+F+H) IJKMOP (Q+S+T+U+V+Y+Z)
5 **AB**EFGIJKLMNOPRUWXY
6 ACDEGHI**K**(N 4km)OPRTV

A luxurious five-star, 52-hectare campsite surrounded by meadows in a very tranquil area. Every comfort on offer, from swimming pool to jacuzzi, from thermal bath to hydro massage. Beautiful restaurants and shops.

From Le Bugue D710 direction Périgueux. Campsite is signposted.

CC € 17 *26/3-2/7 27/8-24/9*

N 44°57'7'' E 0°51'1''

St. Crépin-Carlucet/Sarlat, F-24590 / Aquitaine (Dordogne)

1714

Les Peneyrals*****
Le Poujol
+33 (0)5-53288571
30/4 - 10/9
camping.peneyrals@wanadoo.fr

13ha 117T(100-120m²) 10A

1 ACD**F**IJL**P**RS
2 JRTVX
3 BGHJK**M**N**Q**RUW
4 (A 5/6-31/8) (C+D+H) J
(Q+S+T+U+V+X+Y) Z
5 **AB**DEFGIJKLMNOPUWZ
6 CEGH**IK**(N 4km)ORTV

The campsite is 12 km from the spectacular medieval town of Sarlat and blends well into the surroundings. The heated pools, 1 indoors, paddling pool and toilet facilities ensure every comfort, even in early and late season. Excellent restaurant and café with Belgian beers. A hospitable welcome and peaceful surroundings. Free WiFi in May, June and September.

A20 exit Brive or Souillac, direction Salignac/ Sarlat. Campsite signposted. Located 12 km north of Sarlat.

CC € 17 *30/4 6/7 25/8-10/9* *14=12, 21=18*

N 44°57'28'' E 1°16'20''

St. Émilion, F-33330 / Aquitaine (Gironde)

1715

Yelloh! Village St. Émilion****
2 lieu dit Les Combes - D122
+33 (0)5-57247580
FAX +33 (0)5-57246968
29/4 - 25/9
info@camping-saint-emilion.com

10ha 125T(80-130m²) 10A CEE

1 ACD**F**IJKLMPS
2 DLMRUVXY
3 BGHJKMNQRW
4 (A+C+H) J
(Q+R+T+U+V+X+Y+Z)
5 **AB**FGJLMNOPUVWZ
6 CDEG**IK**(N 3km)OTV

The only campsite in Saint-Émilion, situated in the middle of vineyards on the edge of a lake. Facilities: a grocer, bakery, wine cellar, restaurant, launderette, free shuttle to Saint-Émilion and bike hire. Also free amenities such as a heated swimming pool, tennis, pedalos and minigolf.

The campsite is on the D122 between St. Émilion and Montagne. Continue till you see the campsite flags. Take the D243, not via the D670.

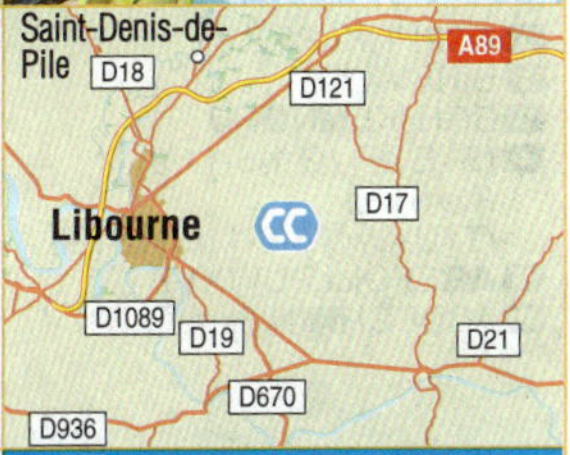

CC € 17 *29/4-1/7 4/9-25/9*

N 44°55'0'' W 0°8'31''

St. Étienne-de-Villeréal, F-47210 / Aquitaine (Lot-et-Garonne)

1716

Les Ormes****
Fauquie-Haut
+33 (0)5-53366026
FAX +33 (0)5-53366990
26/3 - 24/9
info@campinglesormes.com

10ha 140T(150-250m²) 6A CEE

1 ACD**G**IJKLM**P**Q
2 DILRVWXY
3 B**F**GHJKMN**OP**RUW
4 (B+G 25/4-12/9)
(Q+T+U+V+W+X+Y+Z)
5 **AB**EFGIJKLMNOPQUWX
6 EJ(N 4km)ORTV

Large undulating parkland grounds. Everything is very spacious. A very peaceful site with spacious pitches. Centrally located for visiting Monflanquin, Pujols, Monpazier or Bergerac. Not far from canoe trips on the Dordogne. An attractive restaurant with excellent wines. Separate restaurant for children.

Site signposted on the D676 between Villeréal and Monflaquin. Follow this road direction St. Étienne-de-Villeréal for 2 km.

CC € 13 *26/3-8/7 27/8-24/9*

N 44°36'34'' E 0°45'51''

St. Girons-Plage, F-40560 / Aquitaine (Landes)

1717

Campéole Les Tourterelles***
route de la Plage
☎ +33 (0)5-58479312
FAX +33 (0)5-58479203
1/4 - 30/9
@ tourterelles@
andretriganogroupe.com

20ha 516**T**(80-120m²) 10A CEE

1 ACGIJKLMP
2 ABEGIJKRSVWXY
3 BGJKNRY
4 (A 1/7-31/8) (C+H 🔑) IK
(Q 15/5-30/9)
(T+V 1/7-31/8) Z
5 **AB**FGIJKLMNPUZ
6 ACDEGH**IK**(N 0,2km)QRT

Campsite in Les Landes in a pine forest with two direct entrances to the beach. Spacious heated swimming facilities with a large paddling pool. Large camping pitches with space for an extra tent (must be paid for). Ideal location for surfers.

In Bordeaux dir. Bayonne on the A63 and the N10 as far as exit 12 Castets. In Castets centre continue towards Linxe and St. Girons. Then towards St. Girons-Plage till almost at the beach. Campsite on the right.

CC € 17 *1/5-4/7 22/8-18/9*

N 43°57'18" W 1°21'25"

St. Girons-Plage, F-40560 / Aquitaine (Landes)

1718

Eurosol****
4756 route de la Plage
☎ +33 (0)5-58479014
FAX +33 (0)5-58477674
10/5 - 18/9
@ contact@camping-eurosol.com

18ha 322**T**(70-120m²) 10A CEE

1 AC**F**HIJKLPST
2 BIRSVXY
3 BGHJKL**M**N**Q**RU
4 (B+E 🔑) (G 1/6-11/9) I
(Q+S 🔑)
(T+U+V+Y 6/6-11/9) (Z 🔑)
5 **AB**EFGIJLPUWXYZ
6 ACDEGH**K**(N 8km)OQRTV

Located in an area with hills, run by French-Dutch management. At the reception there is a small square with a bar-restaurant and shop and swimming pools, one of which is indoors. You will camp under coniferous trees 600 metres from the ocean.

In Bordeaux take direction Bayonne A63 and N10 as far as exit 12 (Castets); in Castets centre keep in direction Linxe and St. Girons. Then direction St. Girons-Plage. Campsite located 5 km on the left of the road (D42).

CC € 17 *10/5-1/7 27/8-18/9 14=12, 21=17*

N 43°57'6" W 1°21'7"

St. Jean-de-Luz, F-64500 / Aquitaine (Pyrénées-Atlantiques)

1719

Atlantica****
quartier Acotz/chemin
de Miquelenea
☎ +33 (0)5-59477244
FAX +33 (0)5-59547227
1/4 - 30/9
@ info@campingatlantica.com

3,5ha 73**T**(80-120m²) 6A

1 ACGIJKLPRS
2 EFGIJRVWXY
3 B**F**GJKNQRU**V**
4 (C+H 🔑) **IKN**
(Q+R+T+U+V+X+Z 🔑)
5 **AB**FGIJKLPUWXYZ
6 ACEG**IK**(N 1km)QRTV

You could not tell by looking at the entrance how lovely this campsite is. Hidden behind a hedge and a small wall is a lovely, heated swimming pool. An extended reception building houses a games room and a restaurant.

A63 Bayonne-St. Sebastián, exit 3 St. Jean-de-Luz (Nord). D810 (formerly N10) direction Bayonne. Continue 1 km and take exit 'Acotz-plages'.

CC € 15 *1/4-30/6 1/9-30/9*

N 43°24'56" W 1°36'58"

St. Jean-de-Luz, F-64500 / Aquitaine (Pyrénées-Atlantiques) — 1720

Bord de Mer***
71, chemin d'Erromardie
+33 (0)5-59262461
8/4 - 2/11
bord-de-mer64@orange.fr

1ha 78T(90-120m²) 10A

1 AGHIJKLMPQ
2 AEFGKQRTVWX
3 AWY
4 (Q) (X+Z 1/5-15/10)
5 **AB**FGIJLMNPUZ
6 ACEG**K**(N 1km)

A campsite with access to the beach at Erromardie. Borders the beach over a distance of 300m. Stunning views of the ocean and mountains from the campsite. Less than 2 km from the centre of St. Jean-de-Luz.

A63 Bayonne-St. Sébastian, exit St. Jean-de-Luz (Nord). Then dir. St. Jean-de-Luz on the D810 (formerly RN10). Just over 1 km turn right to Plage Erromardie. Follow road ± 2 km to the campsite on the left.

CC € 17 *8/4-7/7 27/8-2/11*

N 43°24'24'' W 1°38'31''

St. Jean-de-Luz, F-64500 / Aquitaine (Pyrénées-Atlantiques) — 1721

Inter-Plages****
305 route des Plages-Acotz
+33 (0)5-59265694
1/4 - 30/9

63T(20-100m²) 10A

1 A**F**IJKL**P**ST
2 AEFJKNQRTUVX
3 B**F**GKRUWY
4 (C+G) (Q+S 15/6-15/9) (T+U+V+X 1/7-31/8) Z
5 **A**DEFGIJKLNOPUVXYZ
6 CEG**J**(N 1,5km)OTV

As its name suggests, the site is located between two beaches. You will have a beautiful panoramic view of the Atlantic ocean. It is 3 km to St. Jean-de-Luz from the campsite. The pool is heated.

Bayonne - St. Jean-de-Luz motorway. Exit 3 St. Jean-de-Luz Nord towards Bayonne on the RD 810 to the Plages 'Acotz'. After entering the quartier Acotz turn left and follow this road to the campsite.

CC € 17 *1/4-23/6 19/9-29/9*

N 43°24'54'' W 1°37'36''

St. Jean-de-Luz, F-64500 / Aquitaine (Pyrénées-Atlantiques) — 1722

International Erromardie****
allée de la Source/
Plage Erromardie
+33 (0)5-59260774
+33 (0)5-59511211
2/4 - 13/11
info@chadotel.com

4ha 70T(80-120m²) 10A CEE

1 AC**F**IKLMPRS
2 AEFGKQRSVWXY
3 B**F**GHJKRUWY
4 (C 15/5-15/9) M (Q+S+T+U+V+X+Z 1/5-30/9)
5 **AB**EFGJLNPUWY
6 ACEG**K**(N 3km)RTV

Campsite at less than 2 km from the centre of St. Jean-de-Luz. Large pitches on level grounds with direct access to the ocean. A stream in the undergrowth divides the site into two parts. It has all the amenities of a four-star campsite.

A63 Bayonne-St. Sébastian, exit St. Jean-de-Luz (Nord). Then dir. St. Jean-de-Luz on D810 (formerly RN10). Right after ± 1 km to Plage Erromardie. Follow road and turn right just past 1st campsite on the left. Site signposted.

CC € 17 *2/4-2/7 3/9-15/10*

N 43°24'26'' W 1°38'19''

St. Jean-de-Luz, F-64500 / Aquitaine (Pyrénées-Atlantiques) — 1723

Itsas Mendi****
115 chemin de Duhartia-Acotz
+33 (0)5-59265650
FAX +33 (0)5-59265444
25/3 - 29/10
@ itsas@wanadoo.fr

9ha 230T(80-100m²) 10A CEE

1 ACD**G**IJKLMOPQ
2 AEFGIJKRVXY
3 B**F**GHJKLMNRUWY
4 (C+E+H) IJ**KMN**
(Q+S+T+U+V+Y+Z)
5 **AB**DEFGIJKLMNOPUWZ
6 CEGH**IK**(N 1km)OQRTV

Come with family and friends and enjoy this campsite with its spacious shaded and half-shaded pitches separated by bushes and trees and 500m from the Basque coast. There is a leisure pool in the middle of the campsite with a toddlers' pool, waterfalls, steam baths, slides, lawns and an indoor heated swimming pool with a jacuzzi.

N10 Bayonne-St. Jean-de-Luz. 3 km north of St. Jean-de-Luz exit 'Acôtz-plages' (A63, exit 3 north).

CC € 15 25/3-2/7 27/8-29/10 7=6

N 43°24'50'' W 1°37'0''

St. Jean-de-Luz, F-64500 / Aquitaine (Pyrénées-Atlantiques) — 1724

La Ferme Erromardie****
40 chemin Erromardie
+33 (0)5-59263426
FAX +33 (0)5-59512602
15/3 - 30/9
@ contact@camping-erromardie.com

2ha 110T(70-120m²) 16A

1 ACDGHIJKLMPRS
2 AEFGNOQRVWXY
3 B**F**GJKLRUWY
4 (**E**+**H**) P
(Q+R+U+V+Y+Z)
5 **AB**EFGIJKLOPUVWZ
6 ACEG**K**(N 2,5km)STV

A campsite in three separate parts on the Plage d'Erromardie. Stretches out along the beach for a length of 300m. The distance from some of the pitches to the sea is sometimes only 20 to 50m. The grounds are about 2 km from the centre of St. Jean-de-Luz.

A63 Bordeaux-Bayonne-San Sébastian, exit 3 St. Jean-de-Luz Nord. Then direction St. Jean-de-Luz centre and after ± 1 km turn right to Plage Erromardie. Campsite then signposted.

CC € 15 15/3-8/7 26/8-30/9 7=6, 14=12, 21=18

N 43°24'20'' W 1°38'30''

St. Jean-de-Luz, F-64500 / Aquitaine (Pyrénées-Atlantiques) — 1725

Tamaris Plage****
720 route des Plage - Acotz
+33 (0)5-59265590
FAX +33 (0)5-59477015
2/4 - 2/11
@ tamaris1@wanadoo.fr

30T(80-120m²) 7A

1 ACD**G**IJKLM**P**Q
2 AEFGKNOQRVXY
3 AJRUV
4 (B+G 15/5-1/11) K(Q)
(T+U+Z 2/4-15/10)
5 **AB**DEFGIJKLMNPUVWZ
6 ACEG**K**(N 1,5km)QTV

A small, friendly campsite on the edge of the Atlantic Ocean with wonderful views of the ocean from the entrance. Toilet facilities in Spanish style.

From Bordeaux direction Bayonne on the A63. Take exit 3 in St. Jean-de-Luz (nord). Then the D810 direction Bayonne. Take 'Acotz-plages' exit on left after about 2 km. Then another 1500m following camping signs.

CC € 17 2/4-11/7 29/8-2/11

N 43°25'3'' W 1°37'26''

St. Jean-Pied-de-Port, F-64220 / Aquitaine (Pyrénées-Atlantiques)

1726

Narbaïtz - Vacances Pyrénées Basques****
route de Bayonne (Ascarat)
+33 (0)5-59371013
FAX +33 (0)5-59372142
23/4 - 24/9
@ camping-narbaitz@wanadoo.fr
2,8ha 101T(80-140m²) 10A

1 ACGIJKLMPQ
2 CKRVXY
3 AGHRU**W**
4 (**A** 1/7-31/8) (C+H+Q)
(R+T+U+X 1/7-31/8)
5 **AB**DEFGJKLOPUWZ
6 ACEGIJ(N 2km)OTV

The campsite is on the route to St. Jean-du-Port, a well-known stop for pilgrims on their way to Santiago del Compostella. Hydrangea bushes are everywhere. The swimming pool is heated to 28°C for the entire season.

A63 exit 5 Bayonne-Sud. Then take the D932 via Ustaritz and Cambo-les-Bains to St. Jean-Pied-du-Port. The campsite is located on the right of a bend on the D918 2.5 km before the town of Ascarat.

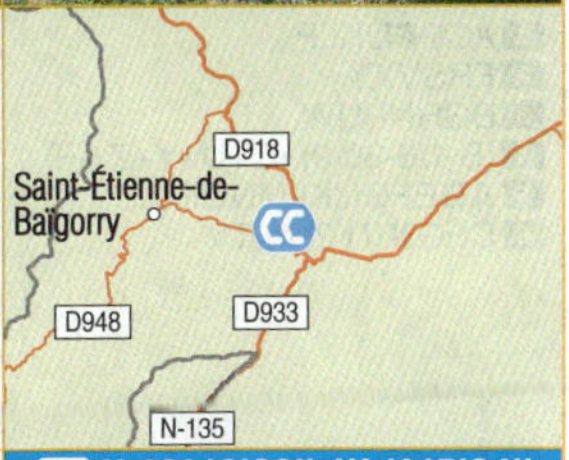

CC € 19 *23/4-9/7 26/8-24/9*

N 43°10'39" W 1°15'34"

St. Jory-de-Chalais, F-24800 / Aquitaine (Dordogne)

1727

Maisonneuve**
1 chemin de Maisonneuve/D98
+33 (0)5-53551063
28/3 - 31/10
@ camping.maisonneuve@wanadoo.fr
10,5ha 40T(100-150m²) 10A CEE

1 A**G**IJKLMPRS
2 CDLRVWXY
3 AGHJMN**OP**RUW
4 (B 1/5-31/10) **N**(T+U+Y)
Z
5 **AB**FGIJKLOPUVWYZ
6 CDEGJ(N 0,4km)V

A peaceful, family-run campsite in the Périgord countrysyide, just 7 km from the N21 between Limoges and Périgueux. Ideal stopover en route to Spain or Portugal. Excellent facilities with 4-star shower block, swimming pool, sauna, fishing lake, on-site bar and restaurant with home-cooked meals 7 nights a week.

N21 south from Limoges. Right at Mavaleix onto D98 to St. Jory de Chalais. Campsite well signposted and on your left just as you enter St. Jory de Chalais.

CC € 17 *28/3-1/7 2/9-31/10*

N 45°29'58" E 0°54'21"

St. Julien-de-Lampon, F-24370 / Aquitaine (Dordogne)

1728

Le Mondou***
Le Colombier
+33 (0)5-53297037
1/4 - 15/10
@ lemondou@camping-dordogne.info
1,7ha 49T(80-130m²) 6A

1 A**G**IJKL**P**RS
2 ILRVXY
3 AGHJNRU
4 (B+G 1/5-15/9)
(Q+T+U 15/4-15/10)
(V 1/5-15/10) (X 1/5-15/9)
(Z)
5 **AB**EFGIJKLMNPUWZ
6 AEG**K**(N 0,6km)TV

John, Lia and Nick Doejaaren have run this pleasant and peaceful campsite in the Dordogne for over 15 years. They provide an informal and friendly atmosphere and are very helpful. The beautiful swimming pool (up to 2 metres deep) is striking. Totally renovated toilet facilities. Good cycling and walking opportunities.

A20 exit 55 Souillac. Then D804 direction Sarlat. Over the bridge at Rouffillac direction St. Julien-de-Lampon. Campsite signposted in the village.

CC € 13 *1/4-3/7 20/8-15/10* 7=6, 14=12, 21=18

N 44°51'48" E 1°22'24"

St. Justin, F-40240 / Aquitaine (Landes)

1729

Le Pin***
route de Roquefort
+33 (0)5-58448891
15/4 - 15/10
camping.lepin@wanadoo.fr

3ha 45T(100-120m²) 10A

1 ACD**F**IJKLP
2 FRSVXY
3 BGHNRUW
4 (B 1/6-30/9) (Q+U+Y+Z)
5 **AB**EFGIJKLMNOPUZ
6 CEG**K**(N 2km)TV

This dream-come-true campsite is located between oak and fir trees and will allow you to relax completely. Here, children can play safely and freely. There is a welcoming little restaurant with an atmospheric terrace next to the swimming pool. Free WiFi (10 minutes a day).

The campsite is situated between Roquefort and St. Justin at the D626.

CC € 15 *15/4-15/7 1/9-15/10* *7=6, 14=12, 21=18*

N 44°0'7" W 0°14'5"

St. Léon-sur-Vézère, F-24290 / Aquitaine (Dordogne)

1730

Le Paradis*****
La Rebeyrolle
+33 (0)5-53507264
FAX +33 (0)5-53507590
25/3 - 20/10
le-paradis@perigord.com

8ha 144T(80-200m²) 10A CEE

1 ACD**G**IJKLMOPQ
2 CLRTVXY
3 BGHKL**M**NRU**W**X
4 (**A**) (C 15/5-15/9) (E) (H 15/5-15/9) KLN (Q+S+T+U+Y+Z)
5 **AB**CDEFGJLNPQUWXYZ
6 ACEGHIK(N 13km)ORTVW

A very luxurious campsite on the banks of the Vézère. Spacious pitches surrounded by lovely vegetation. Many historic sights in the immediate vicinity. Plenty of sports opportunities and entertainment. Very clean and comfortable toilet facilities.

The campsite is located on the D706 Montignac-Les Eyzies (do not turn off towards the village St. Léon). Follow the signs.

CC € 19 *26/3-9/7 1/9-20/10*

N 45°0'6" E 1°4'17"

St. Palais, F-33820 / Aquitaine (Gironde)

1731

Chez Gendron**
2 chez Jandron
FAX +33 (0)5-57329647
1/3 - 15/10
info@chezgendron.com

3,5ha 50T(100-160m²) 10A CEE

1 ACD**G**IJKLPST
2 BFIJLRTUWXY
3 AGHJKNO**P**RU
4 (B 1/5-15/9) (G 1/5-30/9) (Q+T+U+X+Y 1/5-15/9) Z
5 **AB**DFGIJKLMNOPRUWXZ
6 EGK(N 3km)TV

Situated in an undulating landscape with woods, wine and sunflower fields. Sander, Aletta and the kids manage the campsite with a heart for the environment and for their guests. The site has modern toilet blocks with a solar water heater, a bio-uv pool filter, organic restaurant products and extended opening hours at reception.

From the north; A10 exit 37. On the N137 through Mirambeau then follow signs. From the south; exit 38 St. Ciers then follow camping signs.

CC € 15 *1/3-30/6 1/9-15/10*

N 45°18'50" W 0°36'12"

St. Pardoux-la-Riviere, F-24470 / Aquitaine (Dordogne)

1732

La Font Pissotte
Vigne Chave
+33 (0)5-53562218
1/4 - 15/10
@ contact@toofyk.fr

2ha 39**T** 15A CEE

1 AGIJKLMPQ
2 CLRVWX
3 ABHJR**WX**
4 (Q)
5 **A**IJKLMNOPU
6 CDEKT

Municipal campsite that re-opened with a completely new slate in 2014. The plants are still small but the campsite is neat and proper. Located directly on the Dronne with many recreation options (canoeing, kayaking, fishing, swimming). Peaceful and child-friendly. Good base for e.g. Brantôme, the Villais caves, at walking distance from village.

St. Pardoux la Riviere is situated south-east of Nontron (D675) at about 8 km. Campsite is signposted at St. Pardoux church.

CC € 11 *1/4-15/7 1/9-15/10 7=6, 14=11*

N 45°29'52" E 0°44'53"

St. Paul-en-Born, F-40200 / Aquitaine (Landes)

1733

La Clairière***
1151 route de Talucat
+33 (0)5-58048307
26/3 - 30/9
@ contact@camping-laclairiere.fr

3,4ha 80**T**(100-130m²) 10A CEE

1 ACD**G**IJKLMOPST
2 CRSVWXY
3 A**F**GHJK**Q**RU**W**
4 (C+G 1/6-30/9) (Q)
(R+T+U+V+X 1/7-30/8) Z
5 **AB**EFGIJMNPQUZ
6 CEGH**K**(N 1km)RTV

Welcoming, quiet family campsite on a little babbling river. Many options for families that like a 'real' holiday in beautiful surroundings under high oaks. Beautiful new pool. Direct connection to cycling network through the wooded Landes area.

Take the A10 as far as Labouheyre, then take the D626 in the direction of Mimizan as far as St. Paul-en-Born. The campsite is clearly signposted in the centre of St. Paul-en-Born.

CC € 11 *26/3-2/7 27/8-29/9*

N 44°14'3" W 1°9'5"

St. Paul-lès-Dax, F-40990 / Aquitaine (Landes)

1734

Les Pins du Soleil****
route des Minières
+33 (0)5-58913791
1/4 - 31/10
@ pinsdusoleil@gmail.com

6ha 42**T**(100-120m²) 10A

1 AC**G**HIJKLMPST
2 RSVWXY
3 AGRUV
4 (B+G 1/6-15/9) K(Q+R)
(T 1/7-31/8) (U+V+X+Z)
5 **AB**DEFGIJKLOPUWXY
6 CEGIJ(N 2,5km)OTV

Campsite in the heart of Landes not far from the Atlantic Ocean and on the edge of the French Basque Country. The well-known spa Dax is a few kilometres away. Heated toilet facilities in low season. Reasonably spacious pitches. Grounds are slightly undulating. Restaurant/bar open from June to September.

St. Paul is west of Dax in dir. of Bayonne. Take exit on roundabout just outside built-up area. Campsite is signposted.

CC € 15 *1/4-30/6 1/9-31/10*

N 43°43'14" W 1°5'37"

St. Pée-sur-Nivelle, F-64310 / Aquitaine (Pyrénées-Atlantiques)

1735

d'Ibarron***
D918
+33 (0)5-59541043
FAX +33 (0)5-59545195
23/4 - 30/9
camping.dibarron@wanadoo.fr

3ha 119**T**(80-130m²) 6A

1 ACGIJKLPRS
2 CFGRVWXY
3 BGHJKNRU
4 (C 20/5-15/9) (G+Q+R+U+V 1/7-31/8)
5 **AB**DEFGIJKLMNOPUVWZ
6 CDEG**K**(N 0,2km)TV

Large, level and shaded pitches at the foot of the Pyrenees. 8 km from the Spanish border and 10 km from the Atlantic coast in St. Jean-de-Luz. Beautiful swimming pool. Lovely marked out footpaths. Large supermarket close by.

A63 exit 3 St. Jean-de-Luz Nord. Then D810 direction St. Jean-de-Luz. Left just before the centre towards Ascain and St. Pée-sur-Nivelle. Campsite located 2 km before St. Pée by a roundabout and opposite Intermarché.

CC € 15 *23/4-7/7 25/8-30/9*

N 43°21'28'' W 1°34'29''

St. Pée-sur-Nivelle, F-64310 / Aquitaine (Pyrénées-Atlantiques)

1736

Goyetchea****
route d'Ahetze
+33 (0)5-59541959
14/5 - 16/9
info@camping-goyetchea.com

3,5ha 104**T**(80-120m²) 6A

1 ACGIJKLMPRS
2 FRTVWXY
3 BCGRU
4 (C+G) (Q 15/6-15/9) (T+U+V+X+Z 1/7-31/8)
5 **AB**EFGIJKLPUVW
6 EG**K**(N 0,8km)V

Family campsite not far from St. Pée-sur-Nivelle, 10 km from the Atlantic coast and 5 km from St. Pée lake. Spacious sunny and shady pitches. Heated pool (excl. toddler's pool). Outdoor and indoor playground.

Motorway past Biarritz take exit 3 'St. Jean-de-Luz Nord' and drive in dir. of town. Left just before centre, dir. Ascain and St. Pée-sur-Nivelle. Continue to St. Pée. Another 1 km from roundabout and supermarket and then left to campsite. Signposts there.

CC € 15 *14/5-30/6 1/9-16/9*

N 43°21'45'' W 1°33'56''

St. Saud-Lacoussière, F-24470 / Aquitaine (Dordogne)

1737

Wakan Tanka - La Bûcherie**
La Bûcherie
+33 (0)5-24121130
1/4 - 31/10
info@wakantanka.nl

7,5ha 48**T**(80-250m²) 10A CEE

1 A**G**IJKLMNPRS
2 BIRTVWXY
3 ABDHJNU
4 (Q+T+U+X) Z
5 **A**EFGIJKLMNPRUZ
6 AEGJ(N 3,5km)T

Small and natural campsite in the middle of the Périgord Limousin regional park. Spacious, naturally appointed pitches. Good toilet facilities. Recreational lake within walking distance. Suitable for people who love peace, space and nature. Walking options. No cars in high season.

From Limoges follow Périgueux signs (N21). In Châlus D6bis dir. Dournazac as far as Les Trois Cerisiers. Drive towards Nontron. Then follow signs for 4 km to Wakan Tanka/La Bûcherie.

CC € 13 *1/4-9/7 26/8-31/10 7=6, 14=12*

N 45°34'1'' E 0°50'16''

St. Symphorien, F-33113 / Aquitaine (Gironde) — 1738

Vert Bord'Eau**
route de Sore
+33 (0)5-56257954
2/4 - 29/10
camping@vertbordeau.com

4ha 48T(100-200m²) 10A

1 ACD**G**IJKL**P**ST
2 BCLRSVXY
3 BGHJKRW
4 (C 1/6-30/9) (Q) (T+U+X 1/7-31/8) (Z)
5 **AB**GIJKLMNOPUWZ
6 EJ(N 0,2km)T

NEW

Welcoming family campsite in the heart of Parc Régional des Landes. Heated pool and free WiFi point. Many cycling and walking routes and wine tasting events ('route du vin', by bike).

In St. Symphorien follow signs.

€13 *2/4-8/7 25/8-29/10*

N 44°25'5" W 0°29'39"

Ste Eulalie-en-Born, F-40200 / Aquitaine (Landes) — 1739

Municipal Le Camping du Lac***
1590 route du Lac
+33 (0)5-58097010
FAX +33 (0)5-58097421
30/4 - 28/10
contact@lecampingdulac.com

6ha 127T(80-150m²) 10A CEE

1 ACD**G**IJKLMOPST
2 ABDLMRSVWXY
3 AB**F**GHJKR**WZ**
4 (B+G 15/6-15/9) (Q+R+T+U+V+X+Z 1/7-31/8)
5 **AB**EFGIJKLMNOPUVZ
6 ACEGH**K**(N 4km)OT

A peaceful campsite located by the lake. Own harbour close by, perfectly suitable for all watersports. Adjacent to the Les Landes cycle route network.

In Parentis-en-Born on the D652 continue in direction Mimizan. Campsite clearly signposted between Gastes and Ste Eulalie-en-Born.

€13 *30/4-30/6 1/9-27/10*

N 44°18'28" W 1°10'51"

Tamnies-en-Périgord, F-24620 / Aquitaine (Dordogne) — 1740

Le Pont de Mazerat****
+33 (0)5-53291495
9/4 - 30/9
le.pont.de.mazerat@wanadoo.fr

2ha 47T(80-110m²) 10A

1 ACDGIJKLMPRS
2 CJLRVY
3 BGHJN**Q**RUW
4 (C+H+Q+R) (T+U+X 1/7-30/9) Z
5 **AB**FGIJKLPUVWZ
6 EG**K**(N 8km)ORV

NEW

Campsite with a very peaceful location between the picturesque Montignac and the medieval Sarlat. 2 km from Tamnies, a quiet Périgord village with a welcoming restaurant. Close to a small lake. Spacious marked-out pitches.

On D704 from Montignac to Sarlat, take exit to D48 dir. Les Eyzies. Campsite is near Tamnies' lake.

€15 *9/4-9/7 27/8-30/9*

N 44°57'54" E 1°9'54"

Tardets/Abense-de-Haut, F-64470 / Aquitaine (Pyrénées-Atlantiques)

1741

du Pont d'Abense**
Abense-de-Haut
+33 (0)5-59285876
1/1 - 31/12
camping.abense@wanadoo.fr

1,5ha 50T(90-100m²) 10A

1 A**G**IJKLMP
2 CGKNRWXY
3 HJ**WX**
4 (A 1/7-30/8) (Q)
5 GIJKLMNOPUVWZ
6 ABCEK(N 0,5km)O

A friendly campsite in the heart of the French Basqueland with many different types of birds and flowers on the site and where you can fish for trout to your heart's content. Plenty of excursion possibilities within 15 km of the site. Lovely area. Basic toilet facilities.

Follow the D918 as far as Tardets. Just south of the town centre Pont d'Abense is indicated. The campsite is over the bridge on the right.

CC € 17 *10/4-7/7 24/8-11/11 7=6*

N 43°6'42'' W 0°51'49''

Thiviers, F-24800 / Aquitaine (Dordogne)

1742

Le Repaire***
Le Repaire
+33 (0)5-53526975
1/4 - 1/11
contact@camping-le-repaire.fr

10ha 90T(100-150m²) 6A

1 ACD**G**IJKLMPQ
2 DLMRVWXY
3 ABGHJ**M**RUW
4 (B+G 1/7-30/9) (Q+T) Z
5 **AB**GHIJKLOPUWZ
6 ACEGJ(N 0,8km)V

A beautiful, park-like campsite within walking distance of a village. Lovely swimming pool and close to a lake with opportunities for swimming (1 km).

N21 Limoges-Périgueux, at the second traffic lights (large intersection) in Thiviers turn left onto the D707 in the direction of Lanouaille. Follow the signs.

CC € 13 *1/4-15/7 1/9-1/11*

N 45°24'47'' E 0°55'56''

Thonac/Montignac, F-24290 / Aquitaine (Dordogne)

1743

La Castillonderie***
+33 (0)5-53507679
4/4 - 15/9
contact@
dordogne-castillonderie.fr

5ha 57T(80-300m²) 3-10A CEE

1 ACD**G**IJKLPST
2 BDLMRTVWXY
3 ABGHJ**OP**RUW
4 (C+G 15/5-15/9)
(Q+R+T+U+V)
(X 1/7-31/8) (Z)
5 **AB**DFGIJKLMNPQRUWXZ
6 ACDEG**K**(N 2,5km)TV

Comfortable campsite surrounded by woods, in a lovely part of the Dordogne. Family atmosphere. Spacious pitches. Renovated toilet facilities with spacious showers. Swimming and children's pools and a lovely fishing lake. Opportunities for walking and cycling. An excellent base for many places of interest.

Turn right on the D706 Montignac-Les Eyzies and Thonac; at the roundabout towards Fanlac. Turn right after 1 km. Follow the signs.

CC € 15 *4/4-8/7 27/8-15/9 14=13, 21=19*

N 45°2'27'' E 1°7'10''

Urrugne, F-64122 / Aquitaine (Pyrénées-Atlantiques) — 1744

Col d'Ibardin***
220 route d'Olhette
+33 (0)5-59543121
FAX +33 (0)5-59546228
1/4 - 30/9
@ info@col-ibardin.com

8ha 105T(80-100m²) 10A

1 AC**G**IJKLM**P**Q
2 FIJKRSTVXY
3 B**F**GNRU
4 (A 1/7-31/8) (C+G 1/5-30/9) M(Q) (S 15/6-15/9) (T+U+V+Y 1/5-15/9) Z
5 **AB**EFGIJKLMNPUXYZ
6 ACDEHIJ(N 4km)OQTV

Under centuries old oak trees on the Spanish border at the foot of the Col d'Ibardin. Bargain shopping there on te col. Restaurant and swimming pool with a splash pool for children.

A63 Bayonne-St. Sébastian. Exit 2 St. Jean-de-Luz. D810 dir. Urrugne/Hendaye. At roundabout just before Urrugne dir. D4 (Col D'Ibardin). Don't go up the hill, but turn left by the customs house. Campsite 200 metres on the right.

CC € 17 *1/4-30/6 1/9-30/9*

N 43°20'2'' W 1°41'5''

Urrugne, F-64122 / Aquitaine (Pyrénées-Atlantiques) — 1745

Larrouleta***
210 route de Socoa
+33 (0)5-59473784
FAX +33 (0)5-59474254
1/1 - 31/12
@ info@larrouleta.com

10ha 327T(80-100m²) 5A

1 ACD**G**IJKLMPQ
2 ACDFGKLRTUVWXY
3 B**F**GHMNRUWZ
4 (E) (G 15/6-30/9) (Q) (S 15/6-15/9) (T+U+Y+Z 1/3-15/9)
5 **AB**DEFGIJKLMNPUWXYZ
6 CDEG**IK**(N 0,5km)OQRTV

The owner is a real, proud Basque. He can be proud of his campsite. The part in the front is less beautiful than the part in the back. Here are the pleasant pitches by a small lake. There is also a quiet part for swimming, sunbathing and fishing. There is also an indoor swimming pool!

From Bordeaux A63 direction Bayonne-St. Sébastian exit 2 (St. Jean-de-Luz Sud). Then drive towards the coast and the Corniche Basque. Take second on the left after the bridge then follow signs.

CC € 17 *1/1-30/6 1/9-31/12*

N 43°22'13'' W 1°41'10''

Urrugne, F-64122 / Aquitaine (Pyrénées-Atlantiques) — 1746

Suhiberry****
1575 route de Socoa
+33 (0)5-59470623
FAX +33 (0)5-59471893
1/5 - 30/9
@ suhiberry@wanadoo.fr

4ha 119T(80-120m²) 10A

1 ACGIJKLPQ
2 CFJRVY
3 B**F**GHMNRUW
4 (B+G 1/6-30/9) (Q+R+T+U+V 1/7-31/8) (X 1/7-30/9) (Z 1/7-31/8)
5 **AB**EFGIJKLMNPUWXYZ
6 ACEGIK(N 1,8km)OTV

Suhiberry is located between the hills of the Basque coast. Located on a side road between Urrugne and Socoa. It is peaceful here but you can be at a large department store or the lively St. Jean-de-Luz fishing harbour within minutes.

From Bordeaux take A63 dir. Bayonne-St. Sebastián, exit 2 St. Jean-de-Luz Sud. Then towards Socoa-Hendaye. Second left after the bridge. Then follow signs.

CC € 17 *1/5-8/7 28/8-30/9*

N 43°22'46'' W 1°41'28''

Valeuil/Brantôme, F-24310 / Aquitaine (Dordogne)

1747

Du Bas-Meygnaud
D939
+33 (0)5-53055844
1/4 - 30/9
camping-du-bas-meygnaud@wanadoo.fr

1,7ha 50**T**(100-120m²) 6A CEE

1 A**G**IJKL**P**RS
2 BILRWXY
3 BGHJNRU
4 (B+G 15/5-30/9) (Q 1/7-30/8) (R 1/6-30/9) (T 1/7-30/9) (U+V) (X+Z 1/7-31/8)
5 **A**FGJLMNPUZ
6 AEGJ(N 4km)T

A small, peaceful campsite with plenty of shade in the Dronne valley. Child-friendly and very suitable for nature lovers. Good starting point for walkers and cyclists. Campsite located between the idyllic tourist villages of Brantôme and Bourdeilles.

In Brantôme D939 direction Périgueux. Right after about 4 km. Take second Lasserre exit then follow signs. Take note: do not go via Valeuil. From Périgueux 4 km before Brantôme on the left.

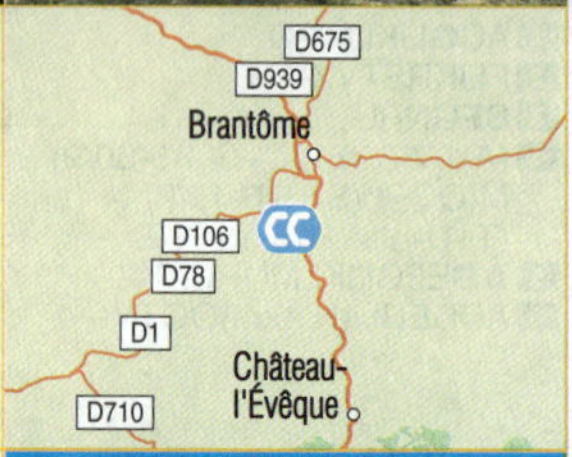

€13 *1/4-1/7 1/9-30/9*

N 45°19'48'' E 0°38'16''

Vensac, F-33590 / Aquitaine (Gironde)

1748

Les Acacias****
44 route St. Vivien
+33 (0)5-56095881
1/5 - 30/9
contact@les-acacias-du-medoc.fr

4ha 100**T**(100-150m²) 10A CEE

1 AC**G**IJKLMOPS
2 BGRSTVWXY
3 BGKN**Q**RU**W**
4 (C+H) K(Q+R 1/7-31/8) (T 1/7-15/9) (U+V+X+Y+Z 1/7-31/8)
5 **AB**EFGJKNPUWXZ
6 EG**IK**L(N 2km)ORTV

Located between Soulac and Bordeaux, between the Médoc and the ocean beaches, Les Acacias du Médoc is the starting point for a relaxing stay with countless walking and cycling opportunities. Combine this with a visit to the Gironde estuary, a drive through the Haut-Médoc vineyards, a famous chateau or a day on the beach.

The campsite is located next to the N215 between Vensac and St. Vivien-de-Médoc on the route St. Vivien 44. Follow the camping signs from N215.

€15 *1/5-3/7 29/8-30/9*

N 45°24'37'' W 1°2'7''

Vézac, F-24220 / Aquitaine (Dordogne)

1749

La Plage***
La Malartrie
+33 (0)5-53295083
15/3 - 20/10
campinglaplage24@orange.fr

3,5ha 83**T**(80-120m²) 10A

1 ACGIJKLMPQ
2 CKLNRWXY
3 ABGHIJKLRU**WX**
4 (B+G 1/5-20/10) (Q+R 1/7-31/8) (T 1/6-31/8) (U 1/7-31/8) (V 1/6-31/8) Z
5 **AB**EFGJLMNPUZ
6 EGJ(N 2km)OV

Located on the Dordogne within walking distance of La Roque-Gageac (1 km) and cycling distance to Domme (4 km). Easily accessible site in the centre of Perigord Noir by the Marqueyssac gardens.

From Sarlat direction Vézac, direction Roque-Gageac, campsite is signposted.

€15 *15/3-6/7 24/8-20/10*

N 44°49'26'' E 1°10'16''

Vézac, F-24220 / Aquitaine (Dordogne) 1750

Les Deux Vallées***
La Gare
+33 (0)5-53295355
14/3 - 18/10
contact@campingles2vallees.com

3,3ha 94**T**(90-160m²) 10A CEE

1 ACD**G**IJKLMPQ
2 RSVWXY
3 AB**F**GHJKNRUW
4 (B+G 1/5-1/10) (Q+R 15/4-1/10) (U+X+Y+Z 1/5-1/10)
5 **AB**DFGIJKLMNPUZ
6 ACEGK(N 0,5km)OV

A beautiful, relaxed campsite in stunning countryside west of Sarlat, with views of Beynac Castle. 'La Roque Gageac', Domme, Castelnau and the river Dordogne are all close by, making it an ideal place for exploring. The region is well known for its excellent cuisine and good wine. Free WiFi. Heated toilet facilities.

On the D57 from Sarlat, turn right just after Vézac sign. Campsite is marked.

CC € 15 *14/3-10/7 27/8-18/10* *8=7, 15=13, 22=18*

N 44°50'8" E 1°9'30"

Vielle-St-Girons, F-40560 / Aquitaine (Landes) 1751

Arnaoutchot (FKK)***
5006 route de Pichelèbe
+33 (0)5-58491111
FAX +33 (0)5-58485712
1/4 - 2/10
contact@arna.com

25ha 250**T**(100-120m²) 6A

1 AC**F**IJLPST
2 ABEIRSVXY
3 B**F**GHJK**M**NQRUV**W**Y
4 (B 1/4-27/9) (F+H) IJ**KL** **NP**(Q) (S+T+U+V+Y+Z 1/5-18/9)
5 **AB**DEFGIJKLMNOPUVWZ
6 CDEGHI**K**(N 8km)OQRTV

Undulating grounds for naturists. Right on a lovely sandy beach. It has swimming pools (one of which can be covered) and many activities are organised.

A63 and N10 Bordeaux-Bayonne. Exit 12 Castets. Towards Léon (14 km) in Castets centre. From Léon centre direction St. Girons as far as Vielle. Left at water tower to Arnaoutchot.

CC € 15 *1/4-8/7 25/8-2/10* *7=6, 14=11, 21=18*

N 43°54'24" W 1°21'42"

Vielle-St-Girons, F-40560 / Aquitaine (Landes) 1752

Le Col Vert****
1548 route de l'Etang
+33 (0)8-90710001
FAX +33 (0)5-58429188
1/4 - 18/9
contact@colvert.com

30ha 270**T**(100-130m²) 6A

1 AC**F**IJKLMPST
2 ABDKLRSVXY
3 BD**F**GHJK**MNOPQ**RU**VW** Z
4 (B+E+H) IJ**KLNP** (Q+S+T+U+V+Y+Z)
5 **AB**DEFGIJKLMNP**ST**UWX YZ
6 ACDEGHI**K**(N 3km)OPQRT UV

A campsite next to the Léon lake in Les Landes. Lovely view of the lake. Most amenities are also available in low season, such as entertainment. CampingCard ACSI holders are entitled to a comfort pitch in low season.

A63 and N10 Bordeaux-Bayonne. Exit 12 Castets. Head for Léon in the centre of Castets (14 km). From Léon centre direction St. Girons as far as Vielle. Campsite indicated along this road.

CC € 15 *1/4-8/7 25/8-18/9* *7=6, 14=11, 21=18*

N 43°54'10" W 1°18'38"

Vieux-Mareuil, F-24340 / Aquitaine (Dordogne) — 1753

Parc Touristique L'Etang Bleu
D93
+33 (0)5-53609270
1/4 - 20/10
letangbleu@orange.fr

10ha 50T(100-160m²) 10A

1 AC**G**IJKLMO**P**Q
2 LRVXY
3 AGHJNRU**V**W
4 (B 15/5-30/9)
(Q+R+T+U+V+Y) Z
5 **AB**FGJLMNPUWX
6 AEG**K**(N 5km)OV

This well run campsite is an excellent base from which you can explore the Dordogne countryside and visit its lovely villages such as Brantôme. Plenty of leisure opportunities in the near vicinity. Large, marked out pitches.

Along the D939, from Angoulême. In Vieux-Mareuil (half way between Angoulême and Périgueux). Turn left (1500 metres). Clearly signposted.

CC € 13 *1/4-5/7 27/8-20/10*

N 45°26'46'' E 0°30'32''

Villefranche-du-Périgord, F-24550 / Aquitaine (Dordogne) — 1754

La Bastide****
route de Cahors
+33 (0)5-53289457
2/4 - 30/9
campinglabastide@wanadoo.fr

2,5ha 66T(80-130m²) 6-10A CEE

1 ACDFIJKLM**P**Q
2 JKLRTUVWXY
3 ABGHJRU**W**
4 (C+G 15/5-15/9)
(Q+R+T+U+V+X+Y 1/7-30/8)
Z
5 **A**DEFGIJKLMNPQUWXY
6 ACDEG**I**K(N 0,3km)RTV

Lovely terraced campsite with panoramic views of the stunning surroundings. The historic medieval centre of Villefranche du Périgord is just 250 metres away with a good selection of shops. Suitable for those who like relaxation. Plenty of excursion opportunities. Free WiFi. Also good as a stopover site.

On the D660. 500 metres from Villefranche-du-Perigord and 45 km from Cahors. Campsite signposted.

CC € 13 *2/4-30/6 1/9-30/9 7=6, 14=12*

N 44°37'40'' E 1°4'57''

Villefranche-du-Queyran, F-47160 / Aquitaine (Lot-et-Garonne) — 1755

Moulin de Campech***
D11
+33 (0)5-53887243
FAX +33 (0)5-53880652
1/4 - 7/10
camping@
moulindecampech.co.uk

5ha 46T(80-150m²) 6A CEE

1 ACD**G**IJKLMOPQ
2 BCFLRUVWXY
3 A**F**GHJR**W**
4 (C 7/5-19/9) (Q 1/5-20/9)
(R)
(T+U+X+Y+Z 1/5-20/9)
5 **AB**GIJKLNPUVWX
6 DEG**J**(N 10km)RTU

An English family runs this campsite in wooded surroundings near an old water mill. Toilet facilities are good. Lovely grounds, alternating well and less shaded level pitches. Swimming pool higher up with panoramic views. Opportunities for trout fishing in the lake.

Exit 6 on autoroute A62. Then towards Montmarsan. After about 3 km direction Casteljaloux (D11). Campsite 5 km on the right.

CC € 17 *1/4-30/6 6/9-7/10*

N 44°16'18'' E 0°11'27''

Vitrac, F-24200 / Aquitaine (Dordogne)

1756

La Bouysse de Caudon***
Caudon/Vitrac
+33 (0)5-53283305
3/4 - 25/9
info@labouysse.com

5ha 142**T**(100m²) 10A CEE

1 ACDGIJLPQ
2 CNORVWXY
3 BGHJK**M**NRUWX
4 (A 1/7-31/8) (B+G 15/5-15/9) (Q+R+T+U 15/6-31/8) Z
5 **AB**FGIJKLMNPUZ
6 ACEGHI**K**(N 4km)ORTV

Located on the banks of the Dordogne with its own canoes for hire. This homely campsite offers the necessary relaxation and opportunities to enjoy the sporting facilities in the vicinity and to explore the many sights. Free WiFi.

Located on the Dordogne. Signposted on the D703 at Vitrac and Montfort.

CC €15 *3/4-3/7 26/8-25/9 14=12, 21=18*

N 44°49'26'' E 1°15'3''

Vitrac/Sarlat, F-24200 / Aquitaine (Dordogne)

1757

La Sagne***
Lieu dit Lassagne
+33 (0)5-53281836
1/4 - 24/9
info@camping-la-sagne.com

3,5ha 100**T**(100-120m²) 16A CEE

1 ACD**F**IJKLMPST
2 CRVWXY
3 A**F**GHJ**W**X
4 (E+H) K (Q+R+T+V 1/7-31/8) Z
5 **AB**EFGIJKLMNOPUWXY
6 E**K**(N 1km)V

A young campsite on the Dordogne, close to the picturesque commune of Vitrac. Excellent base for discovering the many sights.

Situated on the Dordogne. Indicated on D703 near Vitrac and Montfort.

CC €15 *1/4-10/7 28/8-24/9 7=6, 14=12*

N 44°49'31'' E 1°14'32''

Boulancourt, F-77760 / Ile-de-France (Seine-et-Marne)

1758

Ile de Boulancourt***
6 allée des Maronniers
+33 (0)1-64241338
FAX +33 (0)1-64241043
1/1 - 19/12, 26/12 - 31/12
campingiledeboulancourt@orange.fr

5,3ha 32**T**(120m²) 6A

1 AC**G**IJKLMOPQ
2 BCLRSWXY
3 AFHJR**W**
5 **AB**DFGIJKLMNOPUVZ
6 CDEGI**K**(N 0,4km)T

Quiet, environmentally friendly campsite with spacious pitches and high trees (Clef verte, camping qualité). Many options in surroundings: rock climbing (close to Fontainebleau), fishing, walking, cycling. Paris easily accessible by train. Ideal for nature lovers!

A6, exit 14 Ury, direction Malesherbes, then D410 direction Puiseaux, and then Boulancourt. Then follow signs.

CC €15 *1/4-15/7 1/9-31/10*

N 48°15'19'' E 2°26'3''

Champigny-sur-Marne, F-94507 / Ile-de-France (Val-de-Marne)

1759

Paris-Est***
boulevard des Alliés
+33 (0)1-43974397
FAX +33 (0)1-48890794
1/1 - 31/12
@ champigny@campingchampigny.fr

8ha 117T(40-100m²) 16A CEE

1 ACDGIJKLMPQ
2 CFGRTVWXY
3 AFKNRV
4 **KP**
(Q+S+T+V+X+Z 1/4-31/12)
5 **AB**DGIJKLMNPUVWZ
6 ACDG**IJK**(N 1km)TV

Located close to the motorway with public transport from the campsite. Perfectly located for those wishing to visit Paris or Disneyland.

Paris-Est via A86 and A4; exit 5, Nogent/Champigny-sur-Marne. Signposted on the N4 in Joinville-le-Pont. Towards Paris before Marne bridge, right via boulevard Foch. Take note: one-way traffic and narrow streets, small camping signs.

CC € 17 *1/1-8/7 27/8-31/12*

N 48°49'46'' E 2°28'37''

Dourdan, F-91410 / Ile-de-France (Essonne)

1760

Les Petits Prés***
11 ave Mendes France
+33 (0)1-64596483
1/4-2/10,8/10-9/10,15/10-30/10
@ camping@mairie-dourdan.fr

7,5ha 70T(80-110m²) 6A CEE

1 ACDFHIJKLMPQ
2 FGIRVWX
3 AGRU
4 (Q 1/7-15/8)
5 DFGIJKLMNPUVZ
6 EGJ(N 0,5km)TV

A hospitable oasis of peace on your way to and from the south. Department store and leisure pool close by. A 10 minute walk to the centre of Dourdan.

A10 exit Dourdan; D116 Dourdan. Direction Étampes. Signposted, located on the eastern ring road in Dourdan.

CC € 15 *1/4-30/6 1/9-2/10 8/10-9/10 15/10-30/10*

N 48°31'35'' E 2°1'41''

Jablines, F-77450 / Ile-de-France (Seine-et-Marne)

1761

International de Jablines***
Base de Loisirs
+33 (0)1-60260937
FAX +33 (0)1-60264333
26/3 - 30/10
@ welcome@camping-jablines.com

3,5ha 143T(90-100m²) 10A CEE

1 ACD**G**HIJKLMPQ
2 ADFGLMRUVWXY
3 BFGHJK**MNOPQ**RWZ
4 (Q+S)
5 **AB**DEFGIJKLMNPUYZ
6 CEGH**I**KL(N 12km)RT

A lovely, hospitable campsite in natural surroundings of 450 hectares. Marked out pitches, free WiFi, ticket sales and shuttle bus to Disneyland. The largest beach in the Paris region (an enormous lake) for swimming and many types of watersport is next to the campsite. Close to Paris, 9 km from Disneyland and 30 km from Parc Asterix.

A104 exit 8 or N3 exit D404 'Base de Plein Air et de Loisirs-Jablines'. Follow signs. The campsite is along the D45.

CC € 17 *26/3-24/6 27/8-29/10*

N 48°54'49'' E 2°44'4''

Maisons-Laffitte, F-78600 / Ile-de-France (Paris) 1762

International Maisons-Laffitte****
1 rue Johnson
+33 (0)1-39122191
FAX +33 (0)1-39127050
25/3 - 5/11
@ maisonslaffitte@sandaya.fr

6,5ha 336**T**(80-110m²) 15A CEE

1 ABCD**G**IJKLM**P**ST
2 CFRVWXY
3 BGNR**W**
4 (Q+S+V+X+Y+Z)
5 **AB**DGIJKLMNPUZ
6 ABCFG**K**(N 1,5km)ORT

Ideal for a visit to Paris or Disneyland. The campsite is located on an island with views of the Seine. Just a 12 minute walk to the RER station, and 20 minutes later you will be in Paris.

Coming from the north A1 and then A86 as far as Bezons, exit 2 and then D308 direction Houilles to Maisons-Laffitte. Follow camping signs instead of using SatNav.

CC € 19 *25/3-1/7 22/8-5/11*

N 48°56'23" E 2°8'45"

Monnerville, F-91930 / Ile-de-France (Essonne) 1763

Le Bois de la Justice***
chemin de Mennessard
+33 (0)1-64950534
FAX +33 (0)1-64951731
7/2 - 24/11
@ boisdelajustice@gmail.com

5,6ha 30**T**(80-150m²) 6A

1 ACD**G**IJKLM**P**Q
2 BIRTVWXY
3 BGNRU
4 (C 15/6-15/9) (Q 1/5-30/9) (T+U+V 1/7-31/8)
5 **AB**DFGIJKLMNPUW
6 EGJ(N 6km)V

Campsite in a peaceful setting in a wood. Heated pool. Friendly welcome. 2 km from the N20 Paris-Orléans.

N20 Paris-Orléans, exit Monnerville. Follow the signs 'Camping Bois de la Justice'.

CC € 17 *1/3-30/6 1/9-30/10*

N 48°19'56" E 2°2'49"

Pommeuse, F-77515 / Ile-de-France (Seine-et-Marne) 1764

Le Chêne Gris***
24 place de la Gare de Faremoutiers
+33 (0)1-64042180
FAX +33 (0)1-64200589
25/3 - 6/11
@ info@lechenegris.com

7ha 47**T**(75-120m²) 6A CEE

1 ACD**G**IJKLPQ
2 FGIJRTUVWXY
3 BC**F**RU
4 (C) (E 1/4-1/11) (H+Q+S+T+U+V+X+Y+Z)
5 **AB**EFGIJKLNPUZ
6 BFG**J**(N 2km)TV

The campsite is terraced with marked out pitches surrounded by old trees. Modern toilet facilities, restaurant, shop and swimming pool. Something for young families.

A4 exit 13 Serris. D231 direction Provins; left to Faremoutiers 3 km beyond roundabout with obelisk. Opposite Pommeuse/Faremoutiers station.

CC € 17 *25/3-2/7 27/8-6/11*

N 48°48'30" E 2°59'34"

Rambouillet, F-78120 / Ile-de-France (Paris) 1765

Huttopia Rambouillet***
route du Château d'Eau
+33 (0)1-30410734
FAX +33 (0)1-30410017
24/3 - 2/11
@ rambouillet@huttopia.com

4,7ha 149**T**(100-200m²)

1 ABCD**F**IJKLNPST
2 BDLRTUVXY
3 ABGHJKR**W**
4 (A 1/7-31/8) (B 15/6-30/9) (Q+S) (T+U 3/4-30/9) (V+W 1/7-31/8) Z
5 **AB**DEFGIJKLMNOPQRTWX
6 ACDEG**I**(N 3km)TV

In the middle of woods on the banks of the Etang d'Or, this is a campsite with excellent facilities: café-restaurant, natural swimming pool, etc. Ideal for a family holiday in natural surroundings a few kilometres from Paris.

When approaching from the north, take the N10 and then Rambouillet (les Eveuses). Follow the sign 'Laboratoires Garnier'. Pass under the N10 and follow the camping signs.

CC €17 *24/3-30/6 1/9-1/11*

N 48°37'35'' E 1°50'38''

St. Chéron, F-91530 / Ile-de-France (Essonne) 1766

Héliomonde***
La Petite Beauce
+33 (0)1-64566137
FAX +33 (0)1-64565130
12/3 - 16/10
@ reservations@heliomonde.fr

47ha 90**T**(80-100m²) 10A CEE

1 ABCD**G**IJKLMNPQ
2 BLRSXY
3 B**F**GHMNRUV
4 (C+H 15/4-30/9) LN (Q+R 1/5-30/9) (T) (U+V 15/4-15/10) (X 15/4-31/12) (Y 15/4-15/10) Z
5 **AB**EGIJKLMNPUVWZ
6 CEIK(N 3km)OTV

A lovely naturist campsite with spacious pitches located in a 47 hectare wood. Friendly ambiance. Large 400 m² swimming pool, hammam, sauna, relaxation room and WiFi are included in price. 40 km from Paris, but Fontainebleau, Provins and Versailles are all close by. Highly recommended!

N20. At Arpajon take the D116 to Dourdan as far as St. Chéron (centre ville). Campsite signposted from here. Or A10, exit Dourdan then St. Chéron.

CC €17 *12/3-26/6 29/8-16/10 7=6*

N 48°32'39'' E 2°8'16''

Varreddes, F-77910 / Ile-de-France (Seine-et-Marne) 1767

Le Village Parisien Varreddes****
rue des Otages
+33 (0)1-64348080
FAX +33 (0)1-60228984
1/4 - 1/11
@ direction@villageparisien.com

7ha 62**T**(250-300m²) 10A CEE

1 ACDFIJKLMPQ
2 CFGRVWXY
3 AGHJKMNRU**W**
4 (B 1/5-1/9) (F) (G+Q 1/5-1/9) (R 1/5-15/9) (T+U 1/5-30/9) (V 15/6-15/9) (X 15/4-15/9) Z
5 **A**BDGIJKLMNPUWYZ
6 AG**K**(N 0,5km)TV

Large level terrain with plenty of sports and recreational opportunities. Ideal starting point for trips to Paris, Disneyland and Parc Asterix. Bus stop next to campsite entrance.

From Meaux D405 direction Villers-Coterêts. After about 7 km route D97, then D121 direction Congis.

CC €17 *1/4-30/6 1/9-1/11 7=6, 11=14, 30=21*

N 49°0'10'' E 2°56'29''

Veneux-les-Sablons, F-77250 / Ile-de-France (Seine-et-Marne)

1768

Les Courtilles du Lido***
chemin du Passeur
+33 (0)1-60704605
+33 (0)1-64706265
20/3 - 26/9
lescourtilles-dulido@wanadoo.fr

5ha 161T(100-300m²) 10A CEE

1 ACD**G**IJKLMPQ
2 CRTVXY
3 BFG**MQ**R**W**
4 (C 1/5-20/9)
(Q+R+V 20/3-20/9) Z
5 **AB**FGJKNPUWZ
6 CEGJ(N 1km)TV

This is the place to relax. Heated swimming pool, tennis, minigolf. Paris and Fontainebleau within easy reach by train or car. Free internet on the entire campsite. Climbing opportunities in the vicinity.

From Fontainebleau take the N6 in the direction of Sens. After the exit Veneux-les-Sablons and after the bridge take the third street to the left and follow the camping signs.

CC €17 *20/3-30/6 1/9-26/9*

N 48°22'59'' E 2°48'6''

Versailles, F-78000 / Ile-de-France (Paris)

1769

Huttopia Versailles***
31 rue Berthelot
+33 (0)1-39512361
+33 (0)1-39536829
24/3 - 2/11
versailles@huttopia.com

4ha 126T(70-130m²) 10A CEE

1 ACD**F**HIJKLM**P**ST
2 BFGIRSVXY
3 B**F**GHJKRU
4 (C+H 30/4-20/9)
(T+U+V+X 15/4-15/10) Z
5 **AB**DEFGIJKLMNOPRUWZ
6 BCEGIJ(N 0,2km)TV

Huttopia Versailles is a natural campsite close to Paris, just a five minute drive from the Palace of Versailles. The campsite offers very good amenities: an attractive café-restaurant, heated swimming pool, comfortable toilet facilities. The nearby RER C station offers easy access to central Paris.

From Paris: A13 direction Rouen, exit Versailles Centre, then Camping. From A86: N12, then exit Versailles Centre, follow Camping.

CC €19 *24/3-9/6 1/9-1/11*

N 48°47'39'' E 2°9'40''

Andelot-Blancheville, F-52700 / Champagne-Ardennes (Haute-Marne)

1770

Le Moulin***
5 rue du Moulin
+33 (0)3-25306948
10/2 - 28/11
info@lemoulin-andelot.com

2,6ha 57T(80m²) 10A

1 ACDGIJKLMPQ
2 CRTVWXY
3 AGHJ**Q**R**W**
4 (D 1/5-30/9) **K**
(Q+T+U+V+Y) Z
5 **AB**CGIJKLMNPUZ
6 ACEGJ(N 1km)TV

A peaceful, small, dog-friendly campsite by a river with large pitches and a service point for motorhomes. It has a heated swimming pool that can be covered, an 18 hole minigolf course, free WiFi and delicious food in the restaurant/pizzeria. Walking, cycling and fishing in the area. The site is Dutch managed.

Andelot is located on the D674 Neufchâteau-Chaumont. Campsite clearly signposted in the centre of Andelot. Campsite just 500m from the main Route Nationale.

CC €15 *10/2-10/7 29/8-27/11*

N 48°15'8'' E 5°17'56''

Arrigny, F-51290 / Champagne-Ardennes (Marne)

1771

De la Forêt
Presqu'île de Larzicourt
+33 (0)3-26726317
1/4 - 30/9
laforet51@wanadoo.fr

4ha 100**T**(80-130m²) 6A CEE

1 ACD**G**IJLMPQ
2 ABDJLRTVWXY
3 BGHJRU**W**Z
4 (C+H 1/5-5/9) (Q 1/5-30/9) (R 1/7-31/8) (T+V 5/7-25/8)
5 **AB**FGJKLNOPUWXYZ
6 ACEJ(N 15km)OV

A wooded campsite 100m from the sandy beach of Lac-du-Der-Chantecoq. Ideal for families with children. In and around the lake there are plenty of nature and water sports opportunities and cycling. A paradise for ornithologists.

From Vitry-le-François follow 'Lac du Der'. Signposted on the D13. On north side of lake. To avoid city Châlons-en-Champagne follow the N4 direction St. Dizier. Turn south off halfway towards Orconte, Larzicourt, Arrigny. Then follow signs.

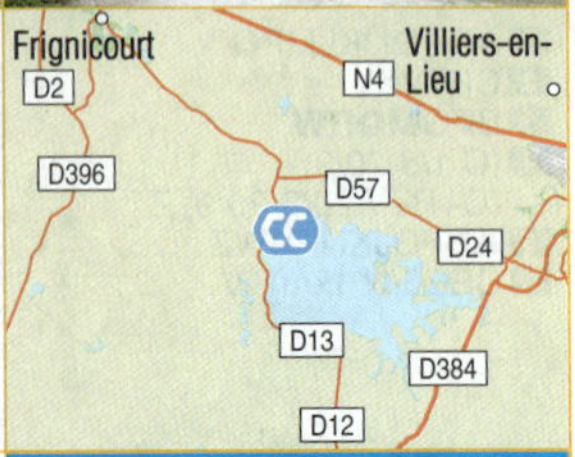

CC € 15 *1/4-3/7 22/8-30/9*

N 48°36'14" E 4°42'55"

Bannes, F-52360 / Champagne-Ardennes (Haute-Marne)

1772

Hautoreille
6 rue Boutonnier
+33 (0)3-25848340
4/1 - 27/11
campinghautoreille@orange.fr

3,5ha 100**T**(100-150m²) 10A CEE

1 ACD**G**IJKLMPQ
2 RTVWXY
3 BGK
4 (Q 🔑) (R 1/4-30/10) (U 🔑) (X+Z 1/4-22/10)
5 **A**DFGIJKLMNPUWZ
6 ACDEGJ(N 6km)T

Peaceful campsite in countryside. Heated toilet facilities. Bar, restaurant and terrace in a courtyard with many flowers. In April, the restaurant is open on Friday, Saturday and Sunday evenings. Take-out meals can always be ordered.

From the south (A31: exit 7), via N19 10 km direction Langres. Turn left at the traffic lights before Langres, direction Neufchâteau. Via D74 to Bannes. From the north (A31: exit 8), via D74. direction Langres. 15 km. Clearly signposted.

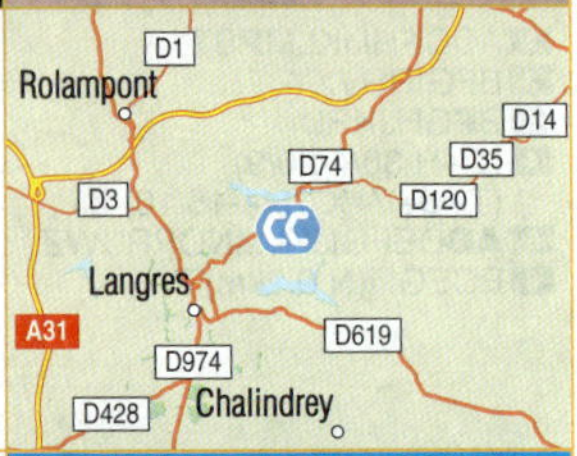

CC € 17 *15/3-30/6 1/9-30/9 7=6, 14=11, 21=17*

N 47°53'42" E 5°23'41"

Bourbonne-les-Bains, F-52400 / Champagne-Ardennes (Haute-Marne)

1773

Montmorency***
rue du Stade / BP 7
+33 (0)3-25900864
FAX +33 (0)9-71701367
20/3 - 30/10
c.montmorency@wanadoo.fr

4ha 75**T**(85-150m²) 6-10A CEE

1 ACD**G**IJKLMPQ
2 IKRTUVWXY
3 AGHJ
4 (Q 15/5-15/9) (R 1/4-31/10) (Z 1/4-30/10)
5 **AB**GIJKLNPUZ
6 CEG**K**(N 0,8km)RT

Homely atmosphere, warm and friendly, for a quiet and relaxing stay in green surroundings. Wonderful walks and cycling tours through the Haut Marnaise forest. This spa resort is called la Petite Provence de l'Est and is situated in Bourbonne les Bains. Montmorency *** campsite offers classic surroundings at the foot of the Vosges mountains.

From the centre of Bourbonne-les-Bains follow the (information)signs Montmorency. Then follow the camping signs.

CC € 15 *20/3-30/6 1/9-29/10*

N 47°57'26" E 5°44'25"

Châlons-en-Champagne, F-51000 / Champagne-Ardennes (Marne) **1774**

Camping de Châlons-en-Champagne****
rue Plaisance
+33 (0)3-26683800
7/3 - 6/11
camping.chalons@orange.fr

7,5ha 140T(100-120m²) 10A

1 ACD**G**IJKLM**P**Q
2 DFGLRUVWXY
3 BGJKMNQRUW
4 (Q 🔑) (T+U+X+Z 1/5-30/9)
5 **AB**EFGIJKLOPUWXYZ
6 ACDEG**K**(N 0,2km)V

A lovely, level, large, peaceful town campsite with pitches marked out by hedges, half of them shaded. Ideal for visiting the town and Champagne region. Recommended as a stopover campsite. Parking and motorhome pitches for the disabled must be booked in advance.

A26, exit 18. When entering the town keep to the right. The campsite is signposted. From the A4, exit 27 to the N44. In Châlons on the ring road exit St. Memmie. Follow the camping signs 'camping Municipal'.

CC € 15 *7/3-3/7 20/8-6/11*

N 48°56'9'' E 4°22'59''

Dienville, F-10500 / Champagne-Ardennes (Aube) **1775**

Du Tertre***
route de Radonvilliers
FAX +33 (0)3-25922650
19/3 - 10/10
campingdutertre@wanadoo.fr

3,5ha 102T(100-120m²) 10A

1 ACD**G**IJKLMOPQ
2 ADRUVX
3 BGHJNRU**W**Z
4 (C+H 15/5-15/9)
(Q+R+T+U+X 1/7-31/8)
(Z 🔑)
5 **A**GIJKLMNOPUWXYZ
6 ACEGJ(N 0,2km)OTV

A lovely level site with sections separated by hedges and bushes and with its own swimming pool, restaurant and snack bar. This and the proximity of the sport harbour and village make it an ideal family campsite.

From Troyes take the D960 as far as Piney. Then take the D11 from Piney to Dienville. From Brienne-le-Chateau take the D443 direction Vendeuvre-sur-Barse as far as Dienville. Located opposite 'Port Dienville'.

CC € 15 *19/3-3/7 22/8-10/10*

N 48°20'56'' E 4°31'39''

Flagey, F-52250 / Champagne-Ardennes (Haute-Marne) **1776**

Ferme de la Croisée
3 route de Auberive
+33 (0)3-25880126
1/3 - 31/10
yannick.durenne52@orange.fr

5ha 106T(90-130m²) 10A CEE

1 ACD**G**IJKLMPRS
2 FRUVWX
3 AG
4 (Q+R 🔑)
(T+X+Z 15/5-15/9)
5 GIJKLMNOPUZ
6 ACDEGK(N 8km)T

An ideal campsite for a stopover. Quiet but close to the motorway. If you reserve you can also join other guests for the chambre d'hôte dinner.

A31 exit 6 direction Langres via D428. Campsite on your left after 1 km.

CC € 15 *1/3-30/6 1/9-31/10*

N 47°47'43'' E 5°13'58''

Géraudot-Plage, F-10220 / Champagne-Ardennes (Aube)

1777

Les Rives du Lac/L'Epine aux Moines**
rue de Fort St. Georges, RD43
+33 (0)3-25412436
1/1 - 31/12
camping.lepineauxmoines@orange.fr

3,5ha 160T(80-150m²) 10A

1 ACDGIJKLMOPRS
2 ADLMRTUVWXY
3 AFGHJKMQRWZ
4 (Q 1/3-31/10) (R)
(T+U+V+Z 1/5-30/9)
5 ABDGIJKLNPUVZ
6 ACDEGK(N 7km)O

Convinial family campsite with pitches more or less separated between the trees. Good toilet facilities. Separate section for teenagers. Close to a lovely (patrolled) beach, also suitable for small children.

From Troyes D960 direction Piney. In or before Piney exit towards Geraudot. From the RN19 Troyes - Bar-sur-Aube direction north, take the D619 in Lusigny or the D79/D43 in Vendeuvre to Geraudot. Located on the north side of Lac d'Orient.

CC € 15 *1/1-3/7 22/8-31/12*

N 48°18'10'' E 4°20'15''

Matton-et-Clemency, F-08110 / Champagne-Ardennes (Ardennes)

1778

Résidence du Banel*
11 rte du Banel
+33 (0)3-24271589
FAX +33 (0)3-24265561
20/3 - 31/10
residence-du-banel-sarl@wanadoo.fr

13ha 32T(< 200m²) 16A CEE

1 ACDGIJKLMPQ
2 BCRTVWXY
3 BGJR
4 KN(Q)
(T+U+X+Y 15/6-15/9) Z
5 ABGJKLMNOPSTUXYZ
6 CEGJK(N 5km)T

Small, green and dog-friendly campsite. Hidden away at the edge of the woods. Separate field for tourists with large pitches and private toilet facilities in a wooden cabin. Tasteful restaurant, open each week in the low seasons. Sights nearby. Countryside for walking and cycling. If reception is closed please choose your own spot. You will be welcomed by Glenn and Wendy.

From Florenville direction Carignan, after Les Deux-Villes follow campsite signs.

CC € 17 *20/3-28/4 9/5-12/5 16/5-7/7 24/8-31/10*

N 49°40'10'' E 5°13'11''

Mesnil-St-Père, F-10140 / Champagne-Ardennes (Aube)

1779

Lac d'Orient
17 route du Lac
+33 (0)3-25406185
FAX +33 (0)3-25709687
9/4 - 23/9
info@camping-lacdorient.com

4ha 164T(80-160m²) 10A CEE

1 ACDGIJKLMOPQ
2 ALRTUVWXY
3 BHJNRUW
4 (C 15/5-15/9) (F 15/4-15/9)
(H 15/5-15/9) J(Q)
(R+U+V 1/5-15/9)
(X 4/4-15/9) (Z 1/5-15/9)
5 ABDEFGIJKLMNOPUWXYZ
6 CDEGIJ(N 10km)V

Large, beautiful campsite on even grounds with parts marked out with hedges and bushes. Restaurant and indoor and outdoor pools. Close to a beautiful beach and little marina. Options and facilities for water freaks, outdoor enthusiasts, anglers and nature lovers.

From the D619 Troyes - Bar-sur-Aube, D43 direction North (between La Villeneuve-au-Chêne and Lusigny-sur-Barce) to Mesnil-St-Père. Located on the south side of the Lac d'Orient, on the D43.

CC € 15 *9/4-5/7 22/8-23/9 7=6*

N 48°15'48'' E 4°20'48''

Montigny-le-Roi, F-52140 / Champagne-Ardennes (Haute-Marne) 1780

Du Chateau***
rue Hubert Collot
+33 (0)3-25873893
15/4 - 30/9
camping@communevaldemeuse.fr

6ha 75T(90-110m²) 6-10A CEE

1 ACDGIJKLMPQ
2 FIJKRTVWXY
3 BGHMR
4 (Q 17/6-4/9) (R) (T 1/6-15/9)
5 GIJKLMNPUW
6 CDEGJKT

This lovely well maintained campsite is an ideal stopover location on your way south and invites you to stay longer. Close to the motorway but still very quiet. Pitches are spacious and marked out, some with extensive panoramas. The village is close by within walking distance.

From the A31 exit 8, Montigny-le-Roi, direction centre. From there on, campsite is clearly signposted.

CC € 15 15/4-30/6 1/9-30/9

N 48°0'3" E 5°29'47"

Pont-Ste-Marie/Troyes, F-10150 / Champagne-Ardennes (Aube) 1781

Municipal de Troyes***
7 rue Roger Salengro (N77)
+33 (0)3-25810264
1/4 - 16/10
info@troyescamping.net

4ha 150T(80-150m²) 10A CEE

1 ACD**G**IJKLMPQ
2 FGRUVWXY
3 BCGJKR
4 (C 15/5-30/9) (Q 15/6-15/9) (R) (V+X 1/6-30/9) (Z)
5 **AB**EFGIJKLNOPUWZ
6 CDEGJV

Atmospheric town campsite. Quiet, many trees and plants, pitches marked out by hedges and bushes and sufficient shade. Public transport nearby. Ideal location for a visit to the old town. Suitable as a stopover campsite or for a longer stay. Heated pool from 15 May. Cycling routes in the area.

A26, exit Troyes/Pont-Ste-Marie. Then follow signs Municipal. Other approach roads direction Pont-Ste-Marie. Follow the signs in the town.

CC € 19 1/4-15/6 10/9-16/10

N 48°18'40" E 4°5'50"

Saints-Geosmes/Langres, F-52200 / Champagne-Ardennes (Haute-Marne) 1782

La Croix d'Arles***
route de Dijon
+33 (0)3-25882402
15/3 - 31/10
croix.arles@yahoo.fr

7ha 100T(85-100m²) 10A CEE

1 ACDGIJKLMPQ
2 BFRTVWXY
3 BGHJQR
4 (B+G 15/5-15/9) **KN** (Q+R) (T+U+X 1/5-30/9) (Z)
5 **AB**FGIJKLMNOPU
6 ACEGJ(N 3km)OT

A busy stopover site. Trees provide adequate shade. The site has a swimming pool and restaurant. The fortified town of Langres is nearby. You can cycle to Langres via the 'Voie Verte' (7 km). The site has quiet pitches further from the road which are recommended for longer stays.

A31 exit 6 Langres-Sud, Dir. Langres via D428, then to Dijon via D974. After 2 km the campsite is clearly signposted on your right.

CC € 15 15/3-7/7 24/8-31/10 7=6, 14=12, 21=18

N 47°48'47" E 5°19'16"

St. Hilaire-sous-Romilly, F-10100 / Champagne-Ardennes (Aube)

iD **1783**

La Noue des Rois
+33 (0)3-25244160
FAX +33 (0)3-25243418
1/1 - 31/12
@ contact@lanouedesrois.com

30ha 70T(120-200m²) 16A

1 ACF**I**JKLM**P**Q
2 DLMRUVX
3 ABGHJMNQRU
4 (C+E+H 1/5-15/10) J
(Q 1/6-30/9) (R)
(T+Z 16/1-15/12)
5 **AB**DGIJKLMNPRUVXY
6 CDEGJ(N 1km)TV

Relaxation by a lake in very natural surroundings (30 hectares). Indoor and outdoor swimming pool heated by solar panels and with slide; minigolf, everything included in the price.

Follow D619 Troyes - Romilly-sur-Seine. Follow St. Hilaire-sous-Romilly. Site is clearly signposted. Or Paris dir. Provins. Then dir. Nogent-sur-Seine. Then dir. St. Hilaire-sous-Romilly and follow signs.

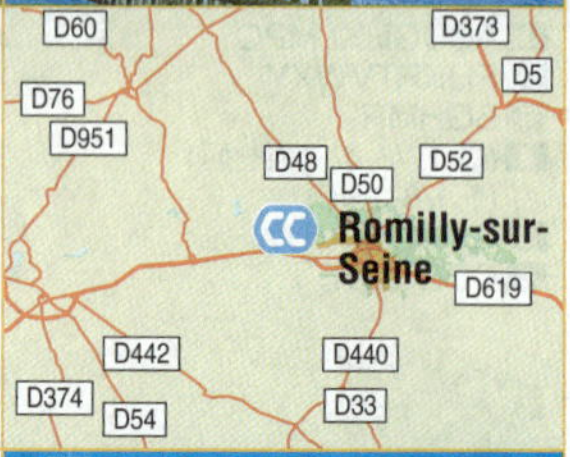

CC € 17 *1/1-30/6 1/9-31/12*

N 48°31'32" E 3°39'53"

Thonnance-les-Moulins, F-52230 / Champagne-Ardennes (Haute-Marne)

iD **1784**

La Forge de Ste Marie*****
D427
+33 (0)3-25944200
FAX +33 (0)3-25944143
22/4 - 9/9
@ info@laforgedesaintemarie.com

11ha 144T(100-200m²) 6-10A CEE

1 ACD**G**IJKLMPQ
2 BCJLRUVWXY
3 BDGHJKN**P**RU**W**
4 (A+F+H) K
(Q+R+T+U+V+Y) Z
5 **AB**DEFGIJKLMNPRUWXYZ
6 ACEG**K**(N 5km)OTV

This luxurious five star campsite is located in wooded surroundings in the heart of the Champagne region. A lovely, peaceful campsite. Enjoy the new jacuzzi and the heated indoor pool with outside its terrace. All facilies open during the opening period. Spacious pitches, trout fishing, 100% WiFi coverage.

From Joinville via the D60 to Thonnance-les-Joinville (2 km), then via the D427 through Poissons and Noncourt in the direction of Thonnance-les-Moulins (10 km).

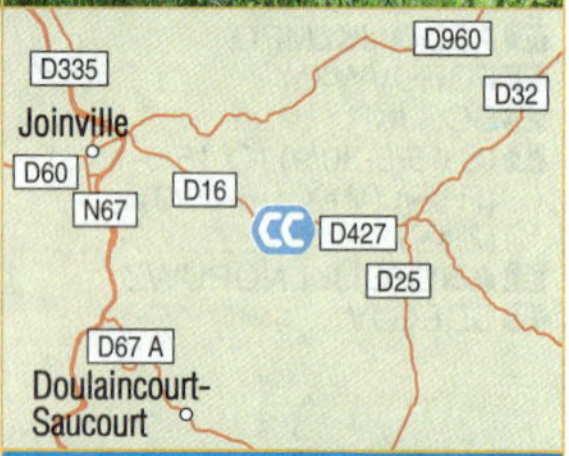

CC € 17 *22/4-1/7 27/8-9/9*

N 48°24'23" E 5°16'16"

Baerenthal, F-57230 / Lorraine (Moselle)

iD **1785**

Ramstein Plage***
+33 (0)3-87065073
FAX +33 (0)3-87066231
1/4 - 30/9
@ camping.ramstein@wanadoo.fr

12ha 100T(100m²) 10A CEE

1 ACD**G**IJKLMPQ
2 ADLRTVX
3 BGHJMNU**W**Z
4 (A+C 1/7-31/8)
(T+U+V+X+Y)
5 **AB**DFGIJKLNPUX
6 ACEGH**J**(N 0,4km)TV

The campsite has an idyllic location next to a small lake which is suitable for swimming. The surrounding area has been designated by UNESCO as a site of ecological world importance.

From Sarreguemines take the D662 direction Haguenau. At Phillipsbourg turn right onto D36 to Baerenthal. Follow signs.

CC € 17 *1/4-30/6 1/9-30/9*

N 48°58'53" E 7°30'53"

Bulgnéville, F-88140 / Lorraine (Vosges)

1786

Porte des Vosges***
rte de Suriauville, La grande Tranc
+33 (0)3-29091200
1/4 - 31/10
contact@
camping-portedesvosges.com

3,5ha 100T(85m²) 6A CEE

1 ACDGIJLMPQ
2 FITWXY
3 AGNR
4 (C 15/5-15/9)
(Q+T+U+Z 🔑)
5 DGIJKLMNPUW
6 CEGJ(N 0,8km)TV

Well-maintained stopover campsite, located near the motorway exit. Restaurants and shops at walking distance. Heated pool. Snackbar also open in both low seasons. The well-known spa resorts Contrexéville and Vittel are only a few minutes drive away.

A31 exit 9, through Bulgnéville via D164 dir. Contrexéville. Follow campsite signs.

CC €17 1/4-6/7 1/9-31/10 7=6

N 48°11'57'' E 5°50'41''

Burtoncourt, F-57220 / Lorraine (Moselle)

1787

La Croix du Bois Sacker**
D53a
+33 (0)3-87357408
1/4 - 17/10
camping.croixsacker@
wanadoo.fr

11ha 49T(80-120m²) 6A

1 ACGIJKLMPRS
2 ABDLMRVWX
3 AGHJNRUWZ
4 (Q 1/6-31/8) (R 🔑) Z
5 AGJMNPUVXYZ
6 ABEGJ(N 8km)ORTV

Not too big a site surrounded by woods on a natural lake where you can fish and swim. Opportunities for sports and games and for walking and cycling in the area. Sunny terrace. The lovely Metz is only 25 minutes away by car. Arrival no later than 8 pm.

A4 (north of Metz) direction Strasbourg, exit 37. D38 Malroy-Chieulles-Vany. Then take the D3 towards Bouzonville. After ± 13 km direction Burtoncourt. Follow camping signs.

CC €17 1/4-30/6 17/8-17/10

N 49°13'25'' E 6°23'59''

Bussang, F-88540 / Lorraine (Vosges)

1788

Le Domaine de Champé*****
14 rue des Champs-Navets
+33 (0)3-29616151
FAX +33 (0)3-29615690
1/1 - 31/12
info@domaine-de-champe.com

5,5ha 110T(90-110m²) 10A CEE

1 ACD**F**IJKLMOPQ
2 CGLRVWXY
3 ABCDGHIJKLMNRUV**W**
4 (A 1/7-31/8) (C 1/5-30/9)
(**F** 🔑) (H 1/5-30/9) IJ**KLM**
NOP(Q 1/6-30/9)
(T 1/7-31/8) (U 🔑)
(V 1/7-31/8) (Y+Z 🔑)
5 **AB**CDFGHIJKLNPQRUWXYZ
6 ACDEGH**K**(N 0,5km)OTVW

A well maintained, sportive campsite, partly divided by hedges. Very relaxed ambiance. The 3.5 km long Old Moselle river flows through the campsite. Paragliding takes place on the hill above the campsite and you can take your maiden flight here.

The campsite is signposted in Bussang from the RN66. At the church follow the camping signs.

CC €15 1/1-15/2 15/3-7/7 24/8-15/12

N 47°53'20'' E 6°51'27''

Celles-sur-Plaine, F-88110 / Lorraine (Vosges) 1789

Camping des Lacs***
6 Place de la Garde, BP3
+33 (0)3-29412800
+33 (0)3-29411869
2/4 - 2/10
camping@paysdeslacs.com

3ha 123**T**(75-140m²) 10A

1 ACD**G**IJKLMPRS
2 ACDLRTVX
3 ABGHJL**MNQ**RU**W**XZ
4 (C+H 1/6-15/9)
(Q+R 1/7-31/8)
(T+U+X+Z 1/6-31/8)
5 **AB**DEFGIJKLNPQUVY
6 EGJTV

A lovely campsite with many activities for young and old. New heated toilet facilities, open air swimming pool and heated indoor pool. Free WiFi.

From Nancy, first the N4, then the N59. In Raon-l'Étape follow Lacs de Pierre Percée. In Celles-sur-Plaine, the campsite is signposted.

CC € 17 *2/4-30/6 1/9-2/10 7=6*

N 48°27'18'' E 6°56'52''

Corcieux, F-88430 / Lorraine (Vosges) 1790

Sites & Paysages Au Clos de la Chaume***
21 rue d'Alsace
+33 (0)3-29507676
27/4 - 20/9
info@camping-closdelachaume.com

5ha 100**T**(80-150m²) 10A

1 ACD**G**IJKLMPQ
2 CLRTVXY
3 BGHJNRU**W**
4 (**A** 1/7-31/8) (E 15/5-30/9)
(Q+R 1/7-30/8)
(U 1/7-31/8)
5 **AB**EFGJLNPRUWXYZ
6 ACDEG**K**(N 0,6km)OT

Pascaline and Michael, an Anglo-French couple, welcome you to their quiet campsite with large pitches, swimming pool and new toilet facilities. Ideal for visiting the Vosges and Alsace. New: the pool is heated and covered.

From St. Dié take the N415 in the directon of Gérardmer/Colmar. In Anould turn right direction Gérardmer. 3 km further on turn right direction Corcieux. Located just before the village on the right side of the road.

CC € 15 *27/4-8/7 25/8-20/9 7=6, 14=12*

N 48°10'5'' E 6°53'24''

Épinal, F-88000 / Lorraine (Vosges) 1791

Parc du Château**
37 chemin du Petit Chaperon Rouge
+33 (0)3-29344365
1/3 - 31/10
camping.parcduchateau@gmail.com

1,7ha 43**T**(60-200m²) 16A CEE

1 ACDGIJKLMOPRS
2 FGRUVWXY
3 AGHJ
4 (B+G 1/6-15/9) (Q)
(T+U+X+Z 1/5-25/9)
5 **AB**DFGIJKLMNOPUWZ
6 ACDEGIK(N 0,5km)OTV

Pleasant, quiet, small campsite. No entertainment. Located on the grounds of a castle park with swimming pool and free WiFi. Restaurant with varied and tasty dishes.

From Nancy take the RN57 exit 'Razimont' or 'Parc des Expositions'. Drive towards the centre. Signposted from here on. The campsite is located 500 metres from the exit, 1st road on right.

CC € 17 *1/3-8/7 27/8-31/10 7=6, 14=12*

N 48°10'47'' E 6°28'5''

Gérardmer, F-88400 / Lorraine (Vosges)

1792

Les Sapins**
18 chemin de Sapois
+33 (0)3-29631501
1/4 - 15/10
les.sapins@camping-gerardmer.com

1,3ha 67**T**(80-120m²) 10A

1 A**G**IJKLMOPQ
2 ADLRVY
3 BHJNRU**W**Z
4 (Q 1/6-15/9) (R) (T 1/7-31/8) (Z)
5 GIJKLMNPUVY
6 EGIJ(N 1,5km)TV

Pleasant, peaceful campsite within walking distance of the tourist town of Gérardmer. Spacious pitches with views of the wooded hills. Gérardmer Lake is 200 metres away from the campsite.

The campsite is located at the start of the southern section of the Gérardmer ring road (chemin du Tour du Lac D69).

CC € 15 *1/4-10/7 28/8-15/10 7=6, 14=12*

N 48°3'48'' E 6°51'21''

Granges-sur-Vologne, F-88640 / Lorraine (Vosges)

1793

Flower Camping La Sténiole***
1 le Haut Rain
+33 (0)3-29514375
9/4 - 16/10
steniole@wanadoo.fr

7ha 119**T**(80-200m²) 10A CEE

1 ACD**G**IJKLPQ
2 CDIJLRTX
3 ABGHJNRUW
4 (E) (Q 1/6-31/8) (R+T 1/7-31/8) (U 1/6-31/8) (V 1/7-31/8) Z
5 **AB**DFGIJKLMNPQRUVWZ
6 CEG**K**(N 3km)OV

A friendly family campsite by a small lake. Large pitches. Campfires permitted on your pitch. New, heated pool with retractable roof.

From Gérardmer take the D423 in the direction of Granges-sur-Vologne. Turn left just before Granges. Follow the signs.

CC € 13 *9/4-3/7 28/8-16/10 14=12*

N 48°7'16'' E 6°49'43''

Herpelmont, F-88600 / Lorraine (Vosges)

1794

Domaine des Messires****
rue des Messires
+33 (0)3-29585629
15/4 - 25/9
mail@domainedesmessires.com

12ha 115**T**(80-100m²) 10A CEE

1 ACD**G**IJKLMPRS
2 ADMRSTVXY
3 AGHJ**Q**RUWZ
4 (Q+R) (T 1/7-31/8)
5 **AB**EFGHIJKLPQRUWXZ
6 AEG**J**(N 1,5km)V

Lovely four-star campsite on a small lake in unspoilt nature. Fishing is free. New toilet facilities. Walking and mountainbiking possible from the campsite.

N57, exit N420 direction St. Dié. After 27 km D423 direction Bruyères/Gérardmer. Turn right after 4 km towards Herpelmont/Lac des Messires.

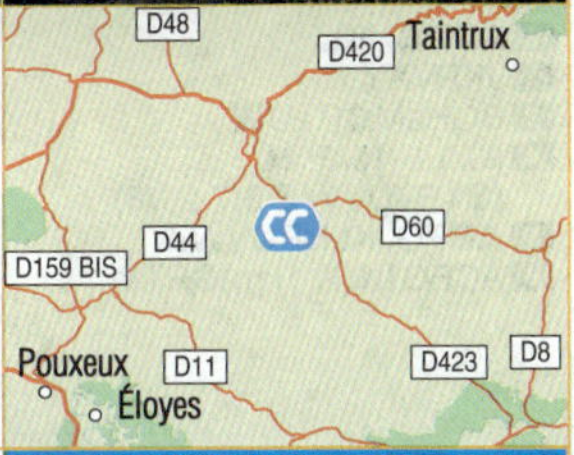

CC € 17 *15/4-8/7 28/8-25/9 14=12*

N 48°10'43'' E 6°44'34''

Jaulny, F-54470 / Lorraine (Meurthe-et-Moselle)

iD **1795**

Camping de la Pelouse**
chemin de Fey
+33 (0)3-83819167
1/4 - 2/10
campingdelapelouse@orange.fr

3ha 87**T**(110-115m²) 6A CEE

1 ACD**F**IJLMPQ
2 CIRTUVWXY
3 AGU**WX**
4 (C 1/6-15/9) (Q+R+T)
(X 1/5-2/10) Z
5 **AB**GIJKMNPU
6 AFGH(N 4km)O

A site with shaded pitches in the old part. Walking, cycling and visits to WW1 Museum. Trains may be heard in the distance. Restaurant is open Sunday and holiday afternoons, closed Monday, open Tuesday to Saturday evenings.

From the A31, exit 31 dir. Ars-sur-Moselle via the D6, Then D91 dir. Arnaville, then D952 dir. Onville. Then D28 to Jaulny, follow camping signs.

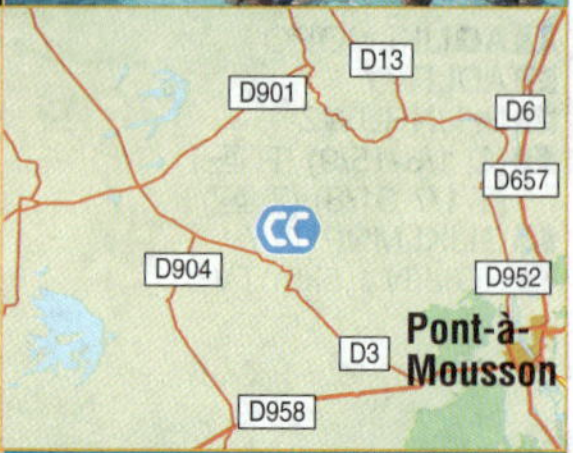

CC € 15 *1/4-10/7 27/8-2/10*

N 48°57'57'' E 5°53'7''

La Bresse, F-88250 / Lorraine (Vosges)

iD **1796**

Domaine du Haut des Bluches***
5 rte des Planches
+33 (0)3-29256480
1/1 - 12/11, 16/12 - 31/12
hautdesbluches@labresse.fr

4,2ha 109**T**(100m²) 13A CEE

1 ACD**G**IJKLMPQ
2 CJKRVX
3 ABHJN**OPRUW**
4 (Q+R+U+X+Z)
5 **AB**DEFGIJKLMNPRU
6 CDEGIJ(N 4km)TV

Campsite in hilly surroundings. A mountain stream runs through the site. During the winter there is a shuttle bus service to the ski area 5 km higher up. Excellent sanitary facilities. Rooms for rent on half or full board basis.

In La Bresse take the D34 direction La Schlucht. Campsite is 4 km further on, on your right.

CC € 13 *1/4-30/6 22/8-12/11* *7=6, 14=12, 21=18*

N 47°59'56'' E 6°55'5''

Le Tholy, F-88530 / Lorraine (Vosges)

iD **1797**

JP Vacances - camping de Noirrupt****
15 chemin de l'Étang
+33 (0)3-29618127
1/5 - 30/9
info@jpvacances.com

3ha 70**T**(90-200m²) 10A CEE

1 ACD**G**IJKLPQ
2 JKRVXY
3 BGHJM**O**RTU**W**
4 (C 1/6-15/9) **N**
(Q+R+U+V+Z 3/7-21/8)
5 **AB**FGJKLNPUVWZ
6 ACEG**IK**(N 1km)ORTV

Attractive and peaceful 4 star campsite set in the heart of upper Vosges. You will receive a warm welcome from the owners. Panoramic views of the surrounding area and excellent toilet facilities. The site has earned the title 'Camping Qualité'.

From Gérardmer take D417 direction Remiremont. Turn right onto D11 at Le Tholy. Turn left 0,5 km after leaving Le Tholy. Follow arrows.

CC € 17 *1/5-2/7 21/8-30/9* *7=6, 14=12*

N 48°5'20'' E 6°43'44''

Liverdun, F-54460 / Lorraine (Meurthe-et-Moselle)

iD **1798**

Les Boucles de la Moselle**
7 avenue Eugène-Lerebourg
+33 (0)3-83244378
1/5 - 30/9
contact@
lesbouclesdelamoselle.com

2,1ha 165**T**(70-90m²) 6A CEE

1 ACD**G**IJKLMOPQ
2 CGLMRTWXY
3 A**F**HJK**M**NR**W**
4 (B 1/6-15/9) (Q+R+T)
(U 1/7-31/8) (Z)
5 AGIJKLMNPUZ
6 CG**J**(N 2,5km)T

A campsite with swimming pool in the natural area between Metz and Nancy. At the foot of medieval Liverdun and the Moselle. Enjoy the untouched countryside by bike, foot or boat.

On A31 take exit 22 dir. Frouard, Liverdun. Left at traffic lights and follow signs.

€ 15 *1/5-30/6 1/9-30/9 7=6*

N 48°44'51'' E 6°3'28''

Lutzelbourg, F-57820 / Lorraine (Moselle)

iD **1799**

Piscine du Plan Incliné***
D98
FAX +33 (0)3-87253013
1/4 - 15/10
campingplanincline@wanadoo.fr

2ha 45**T**(100m²) 6A CEE

1 A**G**IJKLMPRS
2 FGKLRX
3 AGHJNRU**W**
4 (A 1/4-30/6,1/9-18/10)
(B+G 2/7-28/8)
(Q+R+U+X+Y+Z)
5 **AB**DEGIJKMNPUX
6 CDG**J**(N 2km)OR

This campsite is located on the Marne-Rhine Canal in a beautiful, wooded area. WiFi for 1 Euro per day!

From Phalsbourg D38 to Lutzelbourg. Then the D98 direction Dabo. The campsite is located near the boat lift, 2 km outside Lutzelbourg, on the right.

€ 15 *1/4-2/7 22/8-15/10 7=6, 14=12, 21=18*

N 48°43'10'' E 7°13'35''

Nancy/Villers-lès-Nancy, F-54600 / Lorraine (Meurthe-et-Moselle)

iD **1800**

Campéole Le Brabois***
2301 avenue Paul Muller
+33 (0)3-83271828
FAX +33 (0)3-83400643
25/3 - 30/9
brabois@
andretriganogroupe.com

4ha 185**T**(70-100m²) 15A CEE

1 ACD**G**IJKLMOPQ
2 FGRTUVWXY
3 BGNRU
4 (Q+R)
(T+U+X 15/4-15/9) Z
5 **AB**DFGIJKLMNOPUWZ
6 ABCEGH**IK**(N 2km)TV

Easily accessible from the A33 (exit 2B). Parkland setting with spacious, shaded pitches. Excellent bus connections to historic Nancy. Covered picnic area with cooking facilities, modern toilet facilities. Attractive restaurant (also organic), bar and terrace. Internet and WiFi. Reductions for various sights from the reception. Bikes for loan.

A33, exit 2B (Brabois). Keep on the left to turn left at the roundabout. Follow camp signs.

€ 17 *1/5-4/7 22/8-30/9*

N 48°39'26'' E 6°8'25''

Plombières-les-Bains, F-88370 / Lorraine (Vosges)

1801

- de l'Hermitage***
- 54 rue du Boulot
- +33 (0)3-29300187
- 15/4 - 15/10
- camping.lo@wanadoo.fr

1,4ha 48T(77-135m²) 10A CEE

- **1** ACD**G**IJKLM**P**Q
- **2** CJRTVWXY
- **3** ABGHJRU
- **4** (C 15/6-15/9) (Q+R+T+U+V+X)
- **5** **AB**DFGIJKLMNPUWZ
- **6** ACEGJ(N 1,5km)OTV

Located in the 'Ballons des Vosges' nature park. 1.5 km from a thermal centre with a Roman bathhouse, fitness centre and casino. The campsite has over 40 marked out shaded pitches and a swimming pool. Quiet family campsite.

From Épinal take the N57 to Plombières-les-Bains. In built up area follow signs direction Xertigny/Ruaux. Campsite located just in Plombières-les-Bains, on the right of the D20.

CC € 13 *15/4-30/6 17/8-15/10* *7=6, 14=12, 21=18*

N 47°58'2'' E 6°26'48''

Plombières-les-Bains/Ruaux, F-88370 / Lorraine (Vosges)

1802

- Au Fraiteux***
- 81 rue du Camping - Ruaux
- +33 (0)3-29660071
- 1/1 - 31/12
- campingfraiteux@orange.fr

0,8ha 30T(80-120m²) 16A

- **1** A**G**IJKLMOPQ
- **2** IJRTVWX
- **3** AGHJR
- **4** (Q 1/4-30/9) (R+T+U) (V 1/5-15/10) (X+Z)
- **5** **AB**DGIJKLMNPUVWZ
- **6** ADEGK(N 4km)OT

Well maintained; large pitches separated by hedges. Totally peaceful location with lovely views; you can hear the village clock strike the hour (during the day).

From Épinal take the N57 to Plombières-les-Bains. In the outskirts follow sign dir. Route des Chalots. Campsite located in Ruaux (± 4 km). Coming from Luxeuil follow Route Thermale.

CC € 15 *1/1-30/6 17/8-31/12* *7=6, 14=11*

N 47°57'55'' E 6°24'59''

Sanchey, F-88390 / Lorraine (Vosges)

1803

- Club Lac de Bouzey****
- 19 rue du Lac
- +33 (0)3-29824941
- FAX +33 (0)3-29642803
- 1/2 - 31/12
- lacdebouzey@orange.fr

3,5ha 155T(58-100m²) 10A

- **1** ACD**G**IJKLMOPQ
- **2** ADFGJLRTVWXY
- **3** AB**F**GHJKLMNR**T**U**WZ**
- **4** (A 1/7-31/8) (C+H 15/6-15/9) (Q+S) (T+U+V+X+Y+Z 1/4-30/9)
- **5** **AB**DEFGIJKLNPUVXYZ
- **6** CDEGHK(N 0,5km)OPRTV

A lovely family campsite located by a lake, suitable for a longer stay. Extensive recreational opportunities: tennis, carting, golf, rock climbing, kayaking, horse riding, Jorkeyball. Lovely unusually shaped swimming pool. The campsite has the 'Camping Qualité' hallmark.

From Nancy take the N57/E23 in the direction of Épinal. Exit Chavelot direction Uxegney. In Uxegney take the D41 in the direction of Lac de Bouzey. Then follow the signs.

CC € 17 *1/2-10/7 28/8-31/12* *7=6*

N 48°10'1'' E 6°21'35''

Vittel, F-88800 / Lorraine (Vosges) — 1810

Camping de Vittel***
270 rue Claude Bassot
+33 (0)3-29080271
25/3 - 23/10
vittel.camping@orange.fr

2ha 125**T**(85-125m²) 10A CEE

1 ACD**G**IJKLMPQ
2 GRTUVWXY
3 B**F**NRU
4 (Q 🔑)
5 **AB**DEFGIJKLMNOPQRUVZ
6 CDEG**K**(N 0,8km)V

A campsite for those passing through or anyone wanting to visit the chique resort of Vittel. Numbered pitches and surrounded by lovely hedges.

From A31 exit 9, via D165 direction Vittel (new road) or D164 (old road). Campsite signposted in Vittel.

CC € 15 *25/3-3/7 20/8-23/10* *7=6, 14=11*

N 48°12'28'' E 5°57'19''

Xonrupt-Longemer, F-88400 / Lorraine (Vosges) — 1811

Flower Camping Verte Vallée***
4092 route du Lac
+33 (0)3-29632177
1/1 - 31/10, 15/12 - 31/12
contact@campingvertevallee.com

3,5ha 82**T**(80-140m²) 10A

1 ACD**G**IJKLM**P**Q
2 CTVWX
3 ABHJMNRU**W**
4 (**A** 6/7-23/8)
(C+D+H 1/5-30/9)
(Q+R 1/6-15/9)
(U 1/7-31/8) (Z 1/6-30/9)
5 **AB**DFGJLMNOPUWZ
6 AEGIJ(N 8km)TV

A beautiful campsite with a new, heated indoor pool with a sliding roof. The campsite is located 300 metres from the lake.

From Gérardmer take the D417 towards Colmar. Just past Xonrupt, at Hotel du Lac de Longemer turn right onto D67. Campsite at the end of the lake.

CC € 17 *1/1-30/6 1/9-31/10 15/12-31/12* *7=6, 14=12*

N 48°3'45'' E 6°57'53''

Xonrupt-Longemer, F-88400 / Lorraine (Vosges) — 1812

Les Jonquilles**
route du Lac 2586
+33 (0)3-29633401
FAX +33 (0)3-29600928
15/4 - 2/10
info@camping-jonquilles.com

4,5ha 228**T**(80-120m²) 10A

1 ACD**G**IJKLMPQ
2 DIKLORTVX
3 BGHJNRTU**WZ**
4 (Q+S 🔑)
(T+U+V+X 1/6-31/8)
5 **AB**FGIJKLMNOPUV
6 ACDEGJ(N 2,5km)OTV

Beautiful, pleasant family campsite on the shores of the lake of Longemer. Suitable for longer visits. Large pitches, which nearly all have a view over the lake. Many different walking (hiking) routes start from the campsite.

Take the D417 from Gérardmer to Xonrupt-Longemer. Take the D67a in this village to the campsite, which is situated 2.5 km from the church in Xonrupt-Longemer left of the road.

CC € 13 *15/4-1/7 20/8-2/10* *7=6, 14=12, 21=18*

N 48°4'4'' E 6°56'53''

Bassemberg, F-67220 / Alsace (Bas-Rhin)

1813

Campéole Le Giessen****
route de Villé
+33 (0)3-88589814
FAX +33 (0)3-88570233
1/4 - 30/9
@ giessen@andretriganogroupe.com

4ha 70T(80-110m²) 6A CEE

1 ACD**G**IJKLM**P**Q
2 CLRWXY
3 BG**M**NRU**VW**
4 (C 15/6-31/8) (F+H) J**LN** (Q 1/7-31/8) (S) (T+U+V+Z 1/7-31/8)
5 **AB**EFGIJKLMNOPQUVZ
6 CEG**K**(N 1,1km)RTV

A lovely campsite well endowed with trees and bushes and situated by a mountain stream. The adjacent swimming pool (indoors and outdoors) is free of charge for you.

From Sélestat D424 in westerly direction. After 12 km Villé, D39 to Bassemberg. Follow 'Campéole' signs.

CC € 15 *1/5-4/7 22/8-30/9*

N 48°20'11'' E 7°17'20''

Burnhaupt-le-Haut, F-68520 / Alsace (Haut-Rhin)

1814

Les Castors***
4 route de Guewenheim
+33 (0)3-89487858
1/1 - 31/12
@ camping-castors@outlook.com

4ha 120T(100-150m²) 10A CEE

1 ACD**G**IJKLMO**P**
2 ACDFLNRSVWXY
3 BHJRU**W**XZ
4 (Q 1/3-31/10) (R+U+X)
5 **AB**CFHIJKLMNOPU
6 CEGJ(N 1km)OTV

Spacious campsite on the river, with lake for swimming and fishing. Restaurant is open the entire season. New owner is developing new possibilities.

A36 exit 15 'Burnhaupt-le-haut' dir. Cernay. First exit (D484). Then take dir. Maseveaux on roundabout D466.

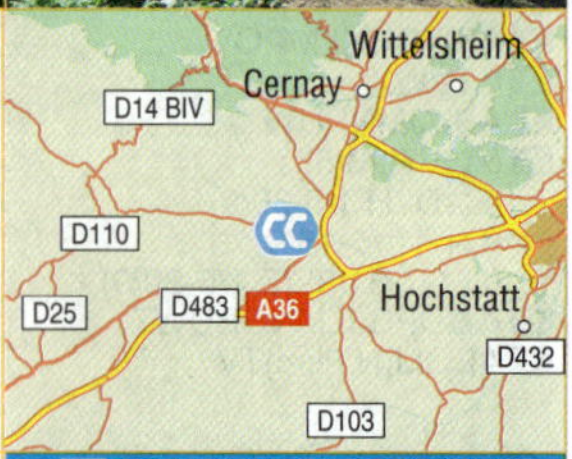

CC € 17 *1/1-10/7 27/8-31/12*

N 47°44'49'' E 7°7'28''

Cernay, F-68700 / Alsace (Haut-Rhin)

1815

Les Cigognes***
16, rue René Guibert
+33 (0)3-89755697
1/4 - 30/9
@ campinglescigognes@wanadoo.fr

4ha 146T(80-100m²) 6A CEE

1 ACD**G**IJKLM**P**Q
2 RVWXY
3 BGHJ**M**NU
4 (C+**F**+H)
5 **AB**DFGIJKLMNPU
6 CEG**K**(N 0,5km)T

A large, spacious and peaceful campsite located in a natural setting, surrounded by storks and the River Thur and close to the town centre of Cernay. Storks fly from their nests and ask to be fed. New heated outdoor swimming pool. 500m from a large shopping centre. Level grounds.

A5 direction Basel, then A36 direction Mulhouse, exit the A36 at Than. Via the N66 direction Cernay and D483 and follow the signs. Left before the bridge in Cernay.

CC € 13 *1/4-10/7 27/8-30/9 7=6, 14=12, 21=18*

N 47°48'16'' E 7°10'12''

1816

Colmar/Horbourg-Wihr, F-68180 / Alsace (Haut-Rhin)

Indigo Colmar***
1 allée du Camping
+33 (0)3-89411594
1/1 - 4/1, 24/3 - 31/12
colmar@camping-indigo.com

4ha 150**T**(80-100m²) 16A CEE

1 ACD**F**IJKLM**P**ST
2 CFGJLRVWXY
3 AGJK**M**RU**W**X
4 (C+H+Q)
(T+U+V+Z 1/5-31/5,1/7-31/8)
5 **AB**DFGIJKLMNOPUXZ
6 BCDGIJ(N 0,3km)TV

Surrounded by countryside, on the banks of the River Ill, this campsite is ideally located for visiting Colmar, a town typical of the Alsace. A piece of countryside close to the city.

Leave the A35 via exit 25, then D415 direction Freiburg. After 3 km on roundabout via D418 to Horbourg-Wihr. Follow campsite signs.

€15 *24/3-3/7 1/9-18/11*

N 48°4'47'' E 7°22'25''

1817

Eguisheim, F-68420 / Alsace (Haut-Rhin)

Les Trois Châteaux***
10 rue du Bassin
+33 (0)3-89231939
21/3 - 3/11, 25/11 - 23/12
camping.eguisheim@orange.fr

1,8ha 133**T**(80-100m²) 10A CEE

1 ACD**G**IJLMPQ
2 FGRTVWXY
3 A**F**GHJRU
4 (A 15/6-15/9) (R)
5 **AB**GIJKLMNOPUW
6 ABCDEGJ(N 0,3km)OTV

A restful campsite in the wine region on the edge of the stunning town of Eguisheim, which is a great place to look around. You can walk into this floral medieval pearl of Alsace from the campsite and get to know the delicious local specialities. Walking and cycling routes from the campsite. Marked pitches, also for motorhomes, shade possible.

E35 exit 28. Then take the D1B dir. Herrlisheim. After ± 7 km direction Eguisheim then follow camping signs.

€17 *21/3-1/7 1/9-3/11*

N 48°2'37'' E 7°18'40''

1818

Erstein, F-67150 / Alsace (Bas-Rhin)

Wagelrott**
rue de la Sucrerie
+33 (0)3-88980988
1/1 - 10/1, 1/4 - 31/12
contact@opale-dmcc.fr

7ha 80**T**(80m²) 16A CEE

1 ACD**G**IJKLMO**P**Q
2 DFGLRTX
3 AGJRUWZ
4 (Q 1/5-15/9) (T 1/4-30/9)
(U+V+Z 1/5-31/8)
5 **AB**DGIJKLMNPU
6 EGH**K**(N 0,5km)T

A peaceful campsite with one part for mobile homes and a separate section for people who are only stopping. There is an indoor municipal swimming pool next to the campsite. Swimming possible in campsite lake. Within walking distance of the village.

From the D1083 exit Erstein. Follow signs in the village

€17 *1/1-10/1 1/4-30/6 1/9-31/12* 7=6

N 48°24'50'' E 7°40'13''

Masevaux, F-68290 / Alsace (Haut-Rhin)

1819

Les Rives de la Doller***
3 rue du Stade
+33 (0)3-89398394
15/3 - 31/10
info@masevaux-camping.com

3,5ha 127T(100m²) 6A CEE

1 ACDGIJKLMPST
2 CGRUVWXY
3 BGHJKLNRU**W**
4 (F) (Q 15/6-31/8) (R) (U+X 15/6-31/8) (Z)
5 **AB**CDEFGHIJKLMNOPUW Z
6 AEGJ(N 0,2km)TV

Lovely, welcoming campsite in the countryside, with spacious pitches. Near the centre of Masevaux, an ideal base for exploring the Doller area on foot or by bike.

From the A36 take exit 15 to Masevaux. Exit N466 Pont d'Aspach and via the N83 to Masevaux. In the town follow 'Centre-Ville' signs, then 'Zone de Sport Loisirs' signs.

CC € 13 *15/3-30/6 1/9-30/10* *7=6, 14=12*

N 47°46'42" E 6°59'27"

Molsheim, F-67120 / Alsace (Bas-Rhin)

1820

Municipal Molsheim**
6 rue des Sports
+33 (0)3-88498245
26/3 - 30/10
camping-molsheim@orange.fr

1,6ha 95T(80-100m²) 10A CEE

1 ACD**G**IJKLPQ
2 CFLRTVWXY
3 BGJ**OP**R**W**
4 (C+G 24/5-7/9) (Q+R)
5 **AB**DGIJKLOPUWZ
6 ABCEGHKT

This site is located on the edge of an attractive craftsmen's village, typical of the Alsace. The municipal swimming complex with a lovely new playground is next to the site and is free for campers. Lovely linden trees. Within walking distance of the Super-U supermarket. Free WiFi.

On the A4 exit Saverne. N4 to Wasselone. Via the D422 to Molsheim. Turn left just past the centre, before the bridge. Follow the signs.

CC € 15 *26/3-8/7 25/8-30/10* *5=4*

N 48°32'29" E 7°29'58"

Mulhouse, F-68200 / Alsace (Haut-Rhin)

1821

Camping de l'Ill***
1 rue P. Coubertin
+33 (0)3-89062066
FAX +33 (0)3-89611834
1/4 - 30/9
campingdelill@wanadoo.fr

5,5ha 185T(90-110m²) 10A CEE

1 AC**G**HIJKLM**P**RS
2 CFLMRTVWXY
3 B**M**N**Q**R
4 (C+H 1/5-30/9) (Q+R) (V 1/7-30/9)
5 **AB**DFGIJKLMNOPUW
6 CDEGH**K**(N 1km)RT

Camping de l'Ill, located in a lovely 5.5 hectare park 1.5 km from the centre and 200m from the bus stop, welcomes you from 1/4 to 30/9. Suitable for the disabled. Free heated swimming pool from 1/4 to 30/9. Sports ground, jeu de boules. Various museums within easy reach.

From the A36 take exit 16a, direction Mulhouse. Then take exit 3 Mulhouse-Centre, keep on going. Then follow camping signs.

CC € 15 *1/4-25/6 27/8-30/9* *7=6, 14=12, 21=18*

N 47°44'4" E 7°19'28"

Neuf-Brisach, F-68600 / Alsace (Haut-Rhin) 1822

Vauban**
Entrée Porte de Bâle
+33 (0)3-89725425
1/4 - 31/10
contact@camping-vauban.fr

4ha 140**T**(< 100m²) 10A CEE

1 ACD**F**IJKLMPQ
2 GRWXY
3 AGJK
4 **N**(Q+R)
5 **AB**DGLMNPUZ
6 CDEGK(N 0,3km)T

A 4 hectare site next to the famous fortress of Neuf Brisach dating from 1699 (UNESCO World Heritage Site) in a striking rural setting. You will be on one of the spacious sunny or shaded places to relax and enjoy woodpeckers, pheasants and the many other birds around you.

Leave the A35 at Colmar (sortie 25), N415 direction Freiburg. Left at roundabout after 15 km to Neuf-Brisach and follow signs.

CC € 15 1/4-7/7 24/8-31/10 11=10

N 48°0'57'' E 7°32'8''

Oberbronn, F-67110 / Alsace (Bas-Rhin) 1823

L'Oasis***
3 rue du Frohret
+33 (0)3-88097196
15/3 - 15/11
contact@opale-dmcc.com

9ha 139**T**(100m²) 10A CEE

1 ACD**F**IJKLPQ
2 IKLRVWXY
3 BGHJ**M**NRU**VW**
4 (B 1/7-31/8) (**F** 1/5-30/9) (G 1/7-31/8) **KLNP** (Q+R+T+U+Y 1/4-30/9) Z
5 **AB**FGIJKLMNPUZ
6 DEG**IK**(N 1,5km)T

A quiet family campsite in unspoilt countryside. Lovely views of the wooded surroundings from most pitches. There is a nice fitness centre with sauna, Turkish bath, jacuzzi and indoor pool.

From Sarreguemines take the N62 via Bitche direction Haguenau. At Niederbronn take the D28 to Oberbronn. Drive through the village and turn left after 400 metres. Signposted.

CC € 17 15/3-30/6 1/9-15/11

N 48°55'46'' E 7°36'15''

Obernai, F-67210 / Alsace (Bas-Rhin) 1824

Mun. Le Vallon de l'Ehn***
1 rue de Berlin
+33 (0)3-88953848
FAX +33 (0)3-88483147
1/1 - 11/1, 13/3 - 31/12
camping@obernai.fr

3ha 150**T**(90-95m²) 16A CEE

1 ACD**G**IJKLMPQ
2 GRVWX
3 BGHIKLRU
4 (**A** 1/7-31/8) (Q 1/5-28/10) (R) (T+U 1/5-31/10)
5 **AB**DFGIJKLMNOPUWYZ
6 CDEGK(N 1km)QRT

A lovely campsite close to a tourist village. Level pitches with some shade. Good modern amenities.

From Molsheim or Strasbourg take Obernai exit. Not to Centre Ville, but follow Le Mont-Ste-Odile at roundabouts. Right at end of ring road then immediate left. Campsite 100m on the left.

CC € 17 1/1-11/1 13/3-30/6 1/9-31/12 11=10

N 48°27'53'' E 7°28'3''

Ranspach, F-68470 / Alsace (Haut-Rhin) 1825

Les Bouleaux****
8 rue des Bouleaux
+33 (0)3-89826470
FAX +33 (0)3-89391417
1/1 - 31/10, 1/12 - 31/12
@ contact@alsace-camping.com

2,8ha 56T(80-100m²) 6-10A CEE

1 ACGIJKLMOPQ
2 CGIKLRVXY
3 BGHJNQRUW
4 (F+H) KLP(Q 1/7-31/8) (R 1/4-30/9) (U+V+X) Z
5 ABCDFGHIJKLMNOPUVW Z
6 DEGJ(N 1km)OTV

This peaceful campsite with marked out pitches, partly under trees, is located in floral surroundings on the route des vins d'Alsace. Views of the wooded hillsides. It has a heated indoor swimming pool, spa-hammam and a daily menu with local produce for a reasonable price.

From Nancy take the N57 to Remiremont, then follow the N66 for about 10 km. Ranspach is beyond Col de Bussang. Follow signs in Ranspach.

CC € 17 1/1-2/7 27/8-31/10 1/12-17/12

N 47°52'48'' E 7°0'37''

Saverne, F-67700 / Alsace (Bas-Rhin) 1826

Seasonova Les Portes d'Alsace***
40, rue du père Liebermann
+33 (0)3-88913565
1/4 - 4/11
@ contact@camping-lesportesdalsace.com

3ha 145T(80-120m²) 12A CEE

1 ACDGIJLPQ
2 FRTXY
3 AGHKLMRU
4 (E+H 1/5-15/9) (Q+U+V)
5 ABDGIJKLMNPUWX
6 EGHK(N 1km)TV

A peaceful campsite with lovely big trees within walking distance of the small town of Saverne. It has a small heated swimming pool with a sliding roof.

From the A4 exit 45 direction Saverne. Campsite signposted from the centre.

CC € 15 1/4-8/7 26/8-4/11 7=6, 14=11

N 48°43'52'' E 7°21'19''

Ste Croix-en-Plaine, F-68127 / Alsace (Haut-Rhin) 1827

ClairVacances****
route de Herrlisheim
+33 (0)3-89492728
20/4 - 10/10
@ reception@clairvacances.com

4ha 135T(90-100m²) 16A CEE

1 ACDEIJKLPST
2 FRTVWY
3 BJRU
4 (C 1/5-15/9) (H 15/6-1/9) (Q+R) (T 1/7-31/8) (U)
5 ABDEFGJLMNPUW
6 ADEGK(N 2km)OT

ClairVacances is located near Colmar and tourist attractions, in a green heart with a large variety of bushes and flowers. The site is known for its excellent amenities which are superbly maintained. Heated swimming pool from 1 May. ClairVacances will enchant you.

Exit 27 on the A35 direction Herrlisheim. Then follow camping signs.

CC € 17 20/4-1/7 24/8-10/10

N 48°0'58'' E 7°21'1''

Ste Marie-aux-Mines, F-68160 / Alsace (Haut-Rhin)

1828

Les Reflets du Val d'Argent***
20 route d'Untergrombach
+33 (0)3-89586431
1/1 - 31/12
camping@les-reflets.com

3ha 110**T**(90-110m²) 16A

1 ACDGIJKLMPQ
2 CGJRTVWXY
3 AB**F**GHJ**M**RU**W**
4 (A 1/7-31/8) (C 1/5-30/9) **N** (Q 15/6-15/9) (R 15/4-1/11) (U+V+Y+Z)
5 **A**GIJKLMNOPUVZ
6 CDEGJ(N 1km)ORTV

Situated among hills and woods in the centre of Alsace and set in a beautiful valley on the edge of an old town close to a silver mine. This family campsite offers many amenities for an enjoyable stay, such as a restaurant, bar and swimming pool.

N59 Sélestat-St. Dié. Follow the signs to the campsite in Ste Marie-aux-Mines.

€17 *1/1-7/7 24/8-31/12* *7=6, 14=11*

N 48°14'7" E 7°10'14"

Strasbourg, F-67200 / Alsace (Bas-Rhin)

1829

Camping Indigo Strasbourg****
2 rue Robert Forrer
+33 (0)3-88301996
1/1 - 31/12
strasbourg@camping-indigo.com

2,2ha 98**T**(80-100m²) 10A CEE

1 ACD**F**IJKLM**P**
2 FGRTWXY
3 BGKRU
4 (B 1/5-30/9) (Q+T+U) (X 1/7-31/8,1/12-31/12) (Z)
5 **AB**EFGIJKLMNOPUWZ
6 CFGK(N 0,5km)TV

Campsite is located in surroundings with lots of plantlife and large trees, a few km away from the touristy centre of town.

From A35, exit 4. Follow signs 'Montagne Verte - camping'.

€17 *2/1-3/7 1/9-25/11*

N 48°34'31" E 7°42'52"

Turckheim, F-68230 / Alsace (Haut-Rhin)

1830

Le Médiéval
5 quai de la Fecht
+33 (0)3-89270200
23/3 - 7/11, 25/11 - 24/12
camping.turckheim@laposte.net

2ha 117**T**(80-100m²) 16A CEE

1 ACD**G**IJKLMPST
2 CRTVWXY
3 A**F**HJKL**M**RU
4 (Q 7/7-31/8)
5 **AB**EFGIJKLMNOPUZ
6 ACDFGK(N 0,4km)TV

Located 300m from intimate medieval Turckheim between vineyards and close to the Route des Vins. You can be in Colmar by bus or train within 10 minutes. Level pitches set back in newly renovated grounds. Come enjoy the Alsatian wines and agreeable restaurants.

Leave the A35 at Colmar, exit 24 to Logelbach. Direction Turckheim at roundabout and turn left immediately after the level crossing to the campsite.

€15 *23/3-1/7 24/8-7/11*

N 48°5'7" E 7°16'21"

Wihr-au-Val, F-68230 / Alsace (Haut-Rhin)

1831

La Route Verte**
13 rue de la Gare
+33 (0)3-89711010
25/4 - 30/9
info@camping-routeverte.com

0,9ha 55T(80-105m²) 10A CEE

1 ACDGIJKLPQ
2 GIRSVWXY
3 AGHJKRU
4 (R+V+Z)
5 AFGIJKLMNPUW
6 CEGKOT

Cosy family campsite on the edge of the village in the colourful valley of Munster. The region with e.g. the wine and cheese route and with charming villages and towns will pleasantly surprise you. Spacious level pitches, some with shade. Walking and cycling through vineyards, but the peace and quiet will also do you good.

Leave D8 west of Colmar and follow D417. After ± 10 km right turn to Wihr-au-Val. After ± 400m La Route Verte is on your left.

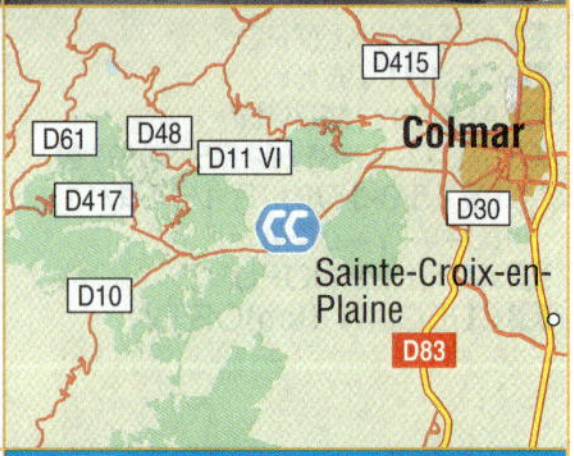

CC € 13 25/4-3/7 28/8-30/9

N 48°3'6'' E 7°12'18''

Argenton-sur-Creuse, F-36200 / Centre-Val de Loire (Indre)

1832

Les Chambons***
37 rue des Chambons
+33 (0)2-54241526
1/5 - 30/9
camping-les-chambons@orange.fr

1,3ha 60T(100m²) 10A CEE

1 ACDGIJKLMPQ
2 CFGLMRTVWXY
3 AHJRUWX
4 (Q)
5 AGIJKLMNPUVZ
6 CEGK(N 1km)T

A friendly campsite with tall trees situated by the River Creuse in the town of Argenton, sometimes called 'the Venice of the Berry', with several medieval and Roman remains (Museum Argentomagus). Close to the centre (a 15 minute walk). The long 'Voie Verte' is close by.

When approaching from the north, take the A20 Orléans-Limoges, exit 17, and follow the camping signs.

CC € 15 1/5-13/7 1/9-30/9

N 46°35'47'' E 1°30'23''

Aubigny-sur-Nère, F-18700 / Centre-Val de Loire (Cher)

1833

Des Étangs***
route de Oizon
+33 (0)2-48580237
1/4 - 30/9
camping.aubigny@orange.fr

2ha 85T(80-200m²) 10A

1 ACDGIJKLMOPQ
2 DLRSTVWXY
3 ABGHJMRUW
4 (C+H 1/6-15/9) (Q 1/7-1/9) (R) (T 15/6-15/9) (Z 1/7-31/8)
5 ABGIJKLMNPUWXZ
6 AEGIK(N 2km)TV

A well maintained campsite with excellent toilet facilities close to a fishing pond. Marked out spacious pitches mostly with shade. An indoor 25 metre swimming pool with toddlers' pool is next to the campsite.

In Aubigny-sur-Nère, east of the town, 200 metres past sports centre. Clearly signposted.

CC € 15 1/4-2/7 29/8-30/9

N 47°29'5'' E 2°27'21''

Ballan-Miré, F-37510 / Centre-Val de Loire (Indre-et-Loire) 1834

La Mignardière****
22 avenue des Aubépines
+33 (0)2-47733100
2/4 - 25/9
info@mignardiere.com

3,5ha 168**T**(80-150m²) 6-10A CEE

1 ACD**G**IJKLMOPQ
2 FGORVXY
3 B**F**GJKMN**Q**RU**W**
4 (C+F+G 4/4-19/9) **KNP**
(Q+S 4/4-19/9)
(T+U 1/4-21/9)
(V+X 4/4-19/9)
5 **AB**EFGIJKLMNOPUWZ
6 ACEG**K**(N 2km)RTV

A lovely family campsite with good toilet facilities. Heated swimming pool (also covered), tennis. Playground opposite. There is a lake close by for surfing. A good base for cycle trips or visiting the chateaux of the Loire.

Via A10 past Tours, take exit 24 Joué-les-Tours, centre direction Ballan-Miré. Right at first traffic lights and follow camping signs.

CC € 17 *2/4-8/7 29/8-25/9 7=6*

N 47°21'19" E 0°38'2"

Blois/Vineuil, F-41350 / Centre-Val de Loire (Loir-et-Cher) 1835

Le Val de Blois***
RD951 Lac de Loire
+33 (0)2-54788205
1/4 - 30/9
contact@campingvaldeblois.fr

10ha 120**T**(> 100m²) 10A

1 A**G**IJLMPST
2 FRSVWX
3 JKU**W**
4 (B 30/5-31/8) (G 28/5-15/9)
(Q)
5 GIJKLMNOPUX
6 EJ(N 3km)T

This ONLYCAMP site welcomes you on the banks of the Loire in privileged surroundings where you can relax. Suitable for visiting Blois, the famous Château Royal and the other Loire castles. The campsite offers amenities for a pleasant stay such as a heated swimming pool and playground. The site is located on the cycle route 'La Loire à Vélo'.

Via A10 exit Blois, then towards Vierzon, turn right over the bridge direction Orléans (D951). 3 km east of Blois.

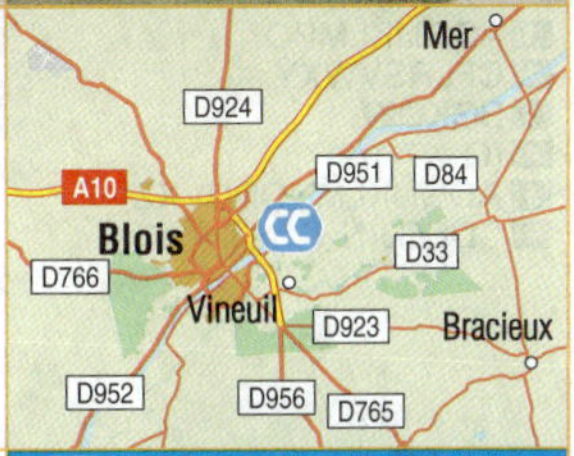

CC € 17 *1/4-30/6 1/9-30/9*

N 47°36'23" E 1°22'35"

Bracieux, F-41250 / Centre-Val de Loire (Loir-et-Cher) 1836

Indigo Les Châteaux***
11 rue Roger Brun
+33 (0)2-54464184
FAX +33 (0)2-54464121
24/3 - 2/11
chateaux@camping-indigo.com

8ha 233**T**(100-120m²) 10A CEE

1 ACD**F**IJLMO**P**Q
2 CGLRSTVWXY
3 B**F**HJK**M**RU**W**
4 (C+E+H+Q+R)
(T+V 3/7-30/8) Z
5 **AB**DFGIJKLMNPRUW
6 ACEGJM(N 0,3km)OTV

Located just 8 km from the chateau of Chambord, this completely renovated campsite offers quality amenities with numerous opportunities for hiking and cycling. The closest camp site to Chambord. CampingCard ACSI is valid only on standard pitches.

From Paris A10, exit 16 Mer. From Tours A10, exit 17 Blois, then D923. In Bracieux cross the bridge and turn right.

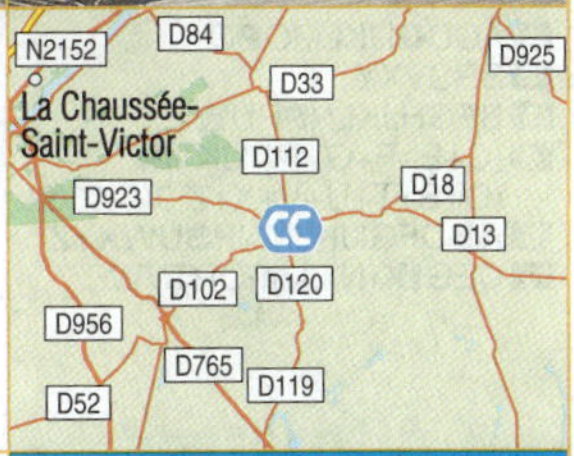

CC € 17 *24/3-5/7 1/9-1/11*

N 47°33'5" E 1°32'21"

Bréhémont, F-37130 / Centre-Val de Loire (Indre-et-Loire) 1837

Loire et Châteaux***
Lieu-dit Le Stade
+33 (0)6-61910142
1/1 - 31/12
camping@loireetchateaux.com

1,5ha 65T(100-150m²) 16A CEE

1 ACD**G**IJKLM**P**Q
2 FRVW
3 AGJKLU**W**
4 (A 15/7-31/8)
(C+H 1/4-30/9) (Q+R)
(T+U+V 1/4-30/9) (Z)
5 **AB**DEFGIJKLMNOPQUWX
YZ
6 ACDEGIJ(N 8km)RTV

A campsite in rural surroundings with a friendly atmosphere. Enjoy the comfort including the brand new (eco) toilet facilities. The campsite is set among castles and in countryside listed as a Unesco World Heritage Site. Heated swimming pool (with facilities for the disabled), snack bar and playground. Close to the 'Loire à vélo' cycle route.

Via D16 direction Bréhémont. Left in village after church. Follow signs. Right at crossroads.

CC € 17 *1/1-15/7 1/9-31/12*

N 47°17'27'' E 0°21'13''

Briare-le-Canal, F-45250 / Centre-Val de Loire (Loiret) 1838

Le Martinet***
Val du Martinet
+33 (0)2-38312450
1/4 - 30/9
contact@campinglemartinet.fr

4,2ha 160T(80-100m²) 10A CEE

1 AC**G**IJKLMPQ
2 CFLRSVWXY
3 BGKQ**W**
4 (Q 1/7-1/9)
5 **A**DGIJKLMNOPUVXZ
6 CDEGJ(N 1km)T

A relaxing campsite beside the Loire, close to the touristy Briare-le-Canal which is famous for its water works and the canal bridge over the Loire. Ideal for cyclists (Loire à vélo cycle route). The campsite has pitches partly marked out by hedges and with some shade.

Via A77 Paris-Nevers. From Montargis drive south on the N7. Near Briare exit towards Briare. In the town keep on towards Nevers, cross the bridge at the marina and turn right. Clearly signposted.

CC € 17 *1/4-30/6 1/9-30/9*

N 47°38'30'' E 2°43'33''

Candé-sur-Beuvron, F-41120 / Centre-Val de Loire (Loir-et-Cher) 1839

La Grande Tortue*****
route de Pontlevoy
+33 (0)2-54441520
9/4 - 20/9
camping@grandetortue.com

6ha 88T(100-200m²) 10A CEE

1 ACD**G**IJKLMO**P**Q
2 BRSVXY
3 B**F**GHJKLN**P**RU**W**
4 (C+E+F+G) IJKM**N**
(Q+S+T+U+V+X+Z 9/4-15/9)
5 **AB**DFGIJKLMNP**S**UWXYZ
6 CEG**IK**(N 6km)ORTVW

Child-friendly five star site in an old oak wood. Surrounded by chateaux in the Loire Valley. An inspiring destination for nature and culture lovers. Heated indoor pool, open air leisure pool with slides and toddlers' pool. 'La Loire à vélo' cycle routes 500m from the site.

From Blois direction Vierzon. Via southern Loire-route (D751) direction Montrichard, Pont-le-Voye. Follow the Loire as far as Candé. Straight ahead at bend in the centre of Candé. Signposted.

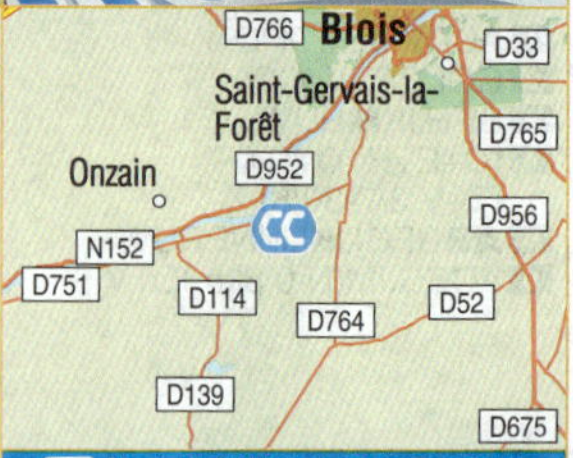

CC € 15 *9/4-3/7 28/8-20/9*

N 47°29'23'' E 1°15'31''

Chartres, F-28000 / Centre-Val de Loire(Eure-et-Loir) 1840

Les Bords de l'Eure***
9 rue de Launay
+33 (0)2-37287943
1/3 - 31/10
camping-roussel-chartres@wanadoo.fr

3,8ha 97T(100-150m²) 6A CEE

1 ACGIJKLO**PQ**
2 CFLRWX
3 BGKNR**W**
4 (R 1/7-31/8) (S+T 1/4-30/9) (U 1/7-31/8) (V+W+X 1/4-30/9)
5 **AB**FGIJKLMNPUV
6 CDEGIKORTV

A lovely overnight campsite in the centre of the town with plenty of trees and greenery all around. A lovely footpath leads from the campsite through the park to the cathedral. The river flows past the campsite. Refurbished playground for the children.

The campsite is located the southeast of the city. Drive via the N10 and take the ring road N123 until the intersection with the N154. Then follow the signs 'Centre Douane' and afterwards follow the camping signs.

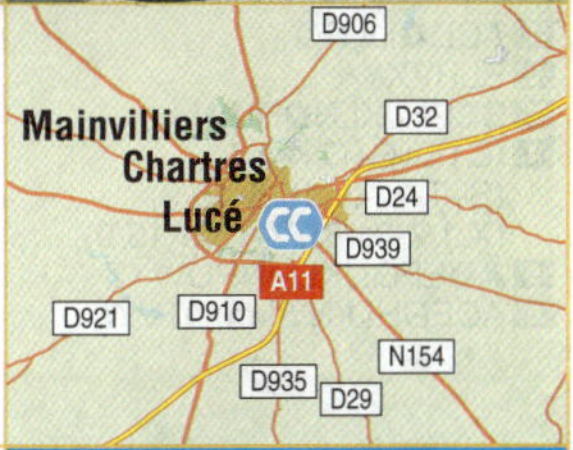

CC € 17 *1/3-15/6 1/9-31/10*

N 48°26'3" E 1°29'57"

Châteauroux, F-36000 / Centre-Val de Loire (Indre) 1841

Le Rochat Belle-Isle***
17 avenue Daniel Bernardet
+33 (0)2-54089629
25/3 - 23/10
camping.lerochat@orange.fr

2,5ha 152T(80-130m²) 10A CEE

1 ACD**G**IJKLM**P**Q
2 ACDFGLMRTVWXY
3 AB**F**GHKR**T**Z
4 (F+G 7/4-26/10) J (Q+R+X+Y 7/4-26/10) Z
5 **AB**DEFIJKLMNOPUZ
6 CDGJ(N 2km)TV

Nice stopover campsite (also for longer stays) located in parkland surroundings near the town centre. Close to recreational lake with playground. Restaurant on the lake. Free pool 100 metres from site. Cycle routes from campsite. Free bus service to centre.

A20 exit 13, dir. Châteauroux centre. Left at 1st traffic lights. Continue on road. Straight on at roundabout. Straight on through traffic lights. Left after green building. Campsite located on left.

CC € 15 *25/3-3/7 20/8-23/10 7=6, 14=11*

N 46°49'26" E 1°41'39"

Chemillé-sur-Indrois, F-37460 / Centre-Val de Loire (Indre-et-Loire) 1842

Les Coteaux du Lac****
+33 (0)2-47927783
26/3 - 8/10
lescoteauxdulac@wanadoo.fr

2,5ha 47T(100-170m²) 16A CEE

1 ACD**G**IJKLMOPQ
2 ADKLRVX
3 BGHJK**Q**RUV**W**Z
4 (C+H 15/4-15/9) (Q 15/6-15/9) (R+T+U) (V 1/7-31/8) (X) (Z 1/7-31/8)
5 **AB**FGIJKLMNOPRUWXZ
6 ACDEGK(N 3km)RTV

Situated on the shore of a lake. Ideal place for family holidays and for discovering the Châteaux of the Loire. Heated swimming pool, children's toilets, shop, television room. Also: paddle boats, canoes, supervised beach, fishing (carp), bar/restaurant.

From St. Aignan via the D675 to Nouans, then D760 direction Montrésor and via the D10 to Chemillé. After passing the village cross the bridge and turn right. Follow the signs.

CC € 17 *26/3-9/7 26/8-8/10 7=6*

N 47°9'28" E 1°9'35"

Cheverny, F-41700 / Centre-Val de Loire (Loir-et-Cher)

1843

Sites & Paysages Les Saules****
les Saules
+33 (0)2-54799001
+33 (0)2-54792834
1/4 - 17/9
contact@camping-cheverny.com

8ha 164T(100-140m²) 10A CEE

1 ACD**G**IJL**P**Q
2 BLRVXY
3 B**EF**HJKLN**Q**RUW
4 (C+E+G+Q)
(S+T+U+V 15/5-15/9)
(X 1/7-31/8) (Z 15/5-15/9)
5 **AB**EFGIJKLMNPUWXZ
6 ACEGHIJ(N 3km)OTVW

The woods around Les Saules offer relaxation. The campsite fits in perfectly with spacious shaded pitches and well maintained toilets. The friendly ambiance provides the rest. Good walking and cycling opportunities such as the 'Loire à vélo' cycle route which can be reached from the site. Golf course 2 km away.

A10, exit 17 Blois direction Vierzon. From centre Cheverny take direction Château. Campsite on the right 1.4 km after castle.

CC € 17 *1/4-3/7 22/8-17/9 7=6, 14=12*

N 47°28'40'' E 1°27'3''

Cloyes-sur-le-Loir, F-28220 / Centre-Val de Loire(Eure-et-Loir)

1844

Parc de Loisirs Le Val Fleuri****
route de Montigny
+33 (0)2-37985053
+33 (0)2-37983384
15/3 - 15/11
info@val-fleuri.fr

5ha 196T(100-150m²) 6A CEE

1 AC**G**IJKLPR
2 CDGLRTVWXY
3 ABGJNPQRU**W**
4 (C+H 1/5-30/9) IJ**K**
(Q+S+T+U+V+X) Z
5 **AB**EFGIJKLMNOPUWYZ
6 CEGHI**K**(N 0,5km)OQRTV

A lovely, large campsite for young and old in a beautiful area close to the chateaux of the Loire and not far from Paris and Versailles. Lovely outdoor heated swimming pool with slide, toddlers' pool and jacuzzi (free). Also minigolf, sailing, pony riding and bouncy castle.

Drive from Châteaudun via the N10 and D35. Turn right before the built up area of Cloyes-sur-le-Loir. Camping signs indicate the route clearly.

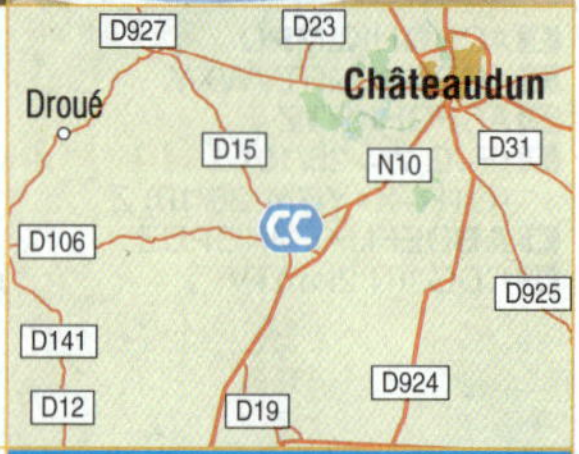

CC € 15 *15/3-30/6 1/9-15/11*

N 48°0'8'' E 1°13'59''

Éguzon, F-36270 / Centre-Val de Loire (Indre)

1845

Éguzon La Garenne***
1 rue Yves Choplin
+33 (0)2-54474485
10/3 - 15/10
info@campinglagarenne.eu

2ha 78T(100-150m²) 6-10A CEE

1 ACDGIJKLMOPQ
2 FIJLRTWXY
3 BGHJNRU
4 **A**(C 22/5-13/9)
(H 13/6-1/9)
(T+V 22/5-13/9) Z
5 **AB**DFGIJKLNPUZ
6 ACDEGK(N 0,3km)V

A Dutch run campsite with heated pool. 3 km from Lac d'Eguzon with all watersports opportunities, 300m from the centre with shopping and small restaurants. Lovely walking and cycling routes (partly hilly, partly level). Privacy, rest and space. Heated toilet facilities in low season.

On A20 exit 20 direction Éguzon. In centre D45 direction Pont des Piles. The campsite is 300m further on. It is located in Éguzon. Follow the Camping 'La Garenne' signs in Éguzon.

CC € 17 *10/3-10/7 27/8-15/10 7=6, 14=11*

N 46°26'46'' E 1°34'56''

Faverolles-sur-Cher, F-41400 / Centre-Val de Loire (Loir-et-Cher) — 1846

Couleurs du Monde****
1 Rond Point de Montparnasse
+33 (0)2-54320608
FAX +33 (0)2-54326135
21/3 - 29/9
@ touraine-vacances@wanadoo.fr

4ha 100**T**(120m²) 6-10A CEE

1 ACD**G**IJKLMOPQ
2 FGLRVXY
3 BDGHJKNRU**W**
4 (C+E+H) **KLN** (S+T+U+V+X+Z)
5 **AB**EFGIJKLMNOPUWZ
6 ACEG**K**MORTV

Surrounded by beautiful castles and vineyards in the Loire Valley. A stone's throw from the historic town of Montrichard. Parkland grounds (4 hectares). Family atmosphere: 'la douce France'. Hospitable, good facilities, peace and space. Heated swimming pool on site, restaurant, bar, bike hire. Supermarket within walking distance.

From Blois D764 direction Montrichard/Loches. From Montrichard direction Faverolles. Campsite on left after second roundabout.

CC € 15 *21/3-15/7 1/9-29/9* *7=6, 14=12* N 47°20'2'' E 1°11'15''

Francueil/Chenonceaux, F-37150 / Centre-Val de Loire (Indre-et-Loire) — 1847

Le Moulin Fort***
+33 (0)2-47238622
1/5 - 30/9
@ lemoulinfort@wanadoo.fr

3ha 137**T**(80-100m²) 6A CEE

1 ACD**G**IJKLMOPRS
2 CLRVX
3 BGHJK**Q**RU**W**
4 (B+G 21/5-20/9) (Q+S) (T+U+X+Z 21/5-20/9)
5 **AB**FGIJKLMNOPUWZ
6 CEG**J**(N 7km)OTV

Well maintained campsite very close to Chenonceaux Castle. Site located on the banks of the River Cher. Good amenities and good leisure opportunities in and around the grounds.

From Bléré via the D976, after 6 km turn left towards Chenonceaux. Before you reach the bridge turn right. Clearly signposted.

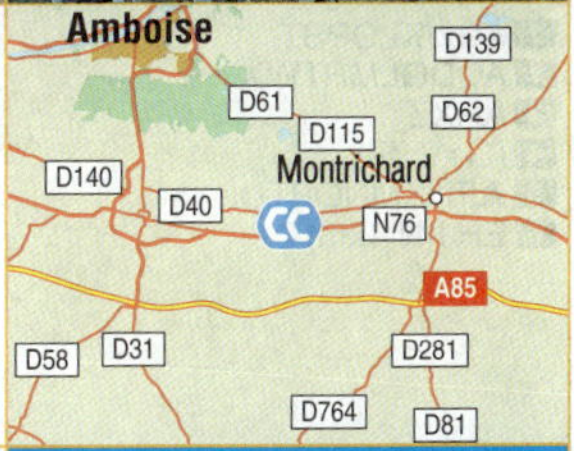

CC € 17 *1/5-9/7 27/8-30/9* N 47°19'35'' E 1°5'1''

Illiers-Combray, F-28120 / Centre-Val de Loire(Eure-et-Loir) — 1848

Le Bois Fleuri***
route de Brou
+33 (0)2-37240304
4/4 - 31/10
@ infos@camping-chartres.com

3,5ha 89**T**(80-190m²) 10A CEE

1 ACFIJLMPQ
2 BCLMRVWXY
3 BGKRW
4 (**C** 3/6-15/9) (**G** 15/6-15/9) J(Q 1/7-31/8) (T) Z
5 **A**DFGIJKLMNPTUWXZ
6 DEGJ(N 2km)OT

A really nice stopover campsite with a lovely swimming pool for young and old. Located near the village of Illiers-Combray a few kilometres from Chartres. Close to the banks of the Loire.

From Brou D921 direction Chartres. Turn right 2 km before Illiers. From Chartres D921 direction Brou. 2 km past Illiers.

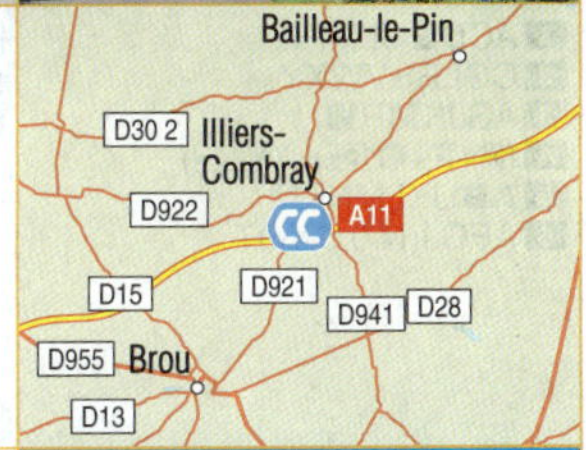

CC € 17 *4/4-30/6 1/9-31/10* N 48°17'10'' E 1°13'39''

Jargeau, F-45150 / Centre-Val de Loire (Loiret)

iD **1849**

L'Isle aux Moulins**
rue du 44ème R.i.
+33 (0)2-38597004
1/4 - 31/10
campingjargeau@orange.fr

7ha 186**T**(110-200m²) 10A CEE

1 AC**G**IJKLM**P**Q
2 ACRSVWXY
3 AG
5 **AB**DEFGIJKLMNOPUVXYZ
6 EGIJ(N 0,3km)T

A peaceful family campsite alongside the Loire with a friendly reception. Varied planting and flowers. Close to Orléans and on the chateaux route of the Loire. 'La Loire à vélo' info available at the reception. Within walking distance of a typical French town with plenty of shopping opportunities.

From Orléans direction Montargis. Half way along the D921 towards Jargeau. Turn right immediately past the bridge over the Loire, then right again.

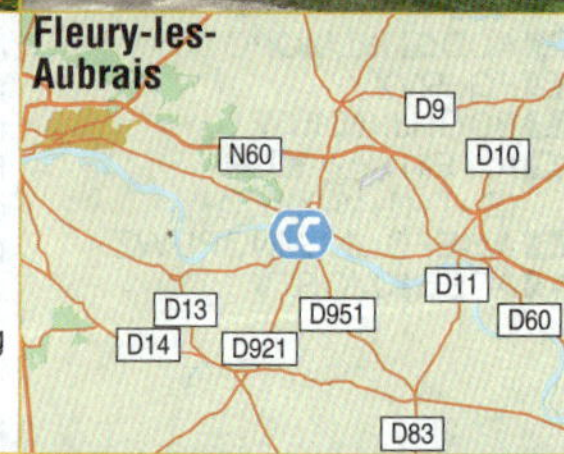

CC € 17 *1/4-30/6* *1/9-31/10* *7=6*

N 47°52'9'' E 2°6'55''

La Chapelle-d'Angillon, F-18380 / Centre-Val de Loire (Cher)

iD **1850**

Paradis Nature**
Les Murailles (route de la Forge)
+33 (0)6-70295200
5/4 - 14/10
info@
camping-paradis-nature.com

0,8ha 54**T**(80-120m²) 10A

1 AGIJKLOPST
2 ACDGLMRTWXY
3 ARXZ
4 (Q+V)
5 **A**FIJKMNOPTU
6 EHJ(N 1km)T

Welcoming, quiet, authentic campsite with spacious pitches, located in green surroundings near a lake and 10 minutes from a picturesque village with shopping. Campsite is close to a 11th century castle. There are excellent cycling routes.

Via D940 Paris-Bourges or D926 Auxerre-Vierzon. Well signposted.

CC € 13 *8/4-7/7* *24/8-14/10*

N 47°21'35'' E 2°26'31''

La Ferté-St-Aubin, F-45240 / Centre-Val de Loire (Loiret)

iD **1851**

du Cosson**
avenue Lowendal
+33 (0)2-38765590
15/4 - 30/9
campingducosson45@outlook.fr

52**T** 10A CEE

1 ACD**G**IJLMPQ
2 CGLRSVWXY
3 AGJK**M**R**W**
4 (**B**+**F**+**G**) J(Y)
5 **AB**IJKLMNPU
6 AEGJ(N 0,5km)T

Situated in parkland grounds on the banks of the Cosson. A stone's throw away from a castle, the centre and a leisure pool.

In centre follow dir. castle via D2020. Campsite is well signposted.

CC € 15 *15/4-30/6* *1/9-30/9* *7=6*

N 47°43'31'' E 1°56'1''

La Ferté-Vidame, F-28340 / Centre-Val de Loire(Eure-et-Loir)

1852

Les Abrias du Perche
route de la Lande
+33 (0)2-37376400
1/4 - 31/10
lesabriasduperche@orange.fr

2ha 48T(70-100m²) 6A CEE

1 AC**F**HIJKLMPST
2 BDLRTUVXY
3 AGHJ**M**R**W**
4 (A 1/7-30/9) (E)
(Q+T 1/4-30/9) (W+X) Z
5 ACDGIJKLMNOPUXYZ
6 ACDEGJK(N 0,8km)OTV

A beautifully located campsite in the middle of a wood with many lakes. Good marked out pitches with plenty of shade. Large playground and heated swimming pool. Modern toilet facilities and WiFi throughout the campsite.

From Verneuil-sur-Avre direction Nogent-le-Rotrou as far as La Ferté-Vidame and then follow camping signs.

CC € 15 *1/4-7/7 1/9-31/10*

N 48°36'28'' E 0°53'23''

La Guerche-sur-l'Aubois, F-18150 / Centre-Val de Loire (Cher)

1853

Robinson
2 rue de Couvache
+33 (0)2-48741886
1/1 - 31/12
camping-laguerche@orange.fr

1,8ha 65T(50-80m²) 10A

1 AC**G**IJKLMOPRS
2 ABDTUVWXY
3 ABGIJKQRU**W**Z
4 (Q+T+U)
5 **A**DFGIJKLMNOPUWX
6 CEG**K**(N 0,5km)RTV

Located in densely wooded, peaceful surroundings with all types of swimming and recreational opportunities. Located by a large lake where you can enjoy kayaks and pedalo boats. Children's playground, minigolf, volleyball, snack bar and a games room, including table tennis.

A77 Montargis-Nervers. After Nevers take the D976 direction Bourges. Campsite on this road. Signposted.

CC € 11 *1/1-5/7 25/8-31/12 7=6, 14=11, 30=22*

N 46°56'24'' E 2°57'32''

La Ville-aux-Dames, F-37700 / Centre-Val de Loire (Indre-et-Loire)

1854

Tours Les Acacias***
rue Berthe Morisot
+33 (0)2-47440816
2/1 - 24/12, 26/12 - 31/12
contact@camplvad.com

3,5ha 88T(100-120m²) 10A CEE

1 ACD**G**IJKLMO**P**Q
2 BCFGLRSUVWXY
3 B**F**GHJKLNRU**W**
4 (Q 1/4-30/9) (R)
(T+V+X 1/4-30/9) Z
5 **AB**DFGIJKLMNOPUZ
6 ABCEGIK(N 1km)TV

A quiet and partly shaded campsite where peace and hospitality are the order of the day all year round. Passers-by and longer stayers can benefit optimally from the many opportunities. Route 'Loire à Velo' from the campsite. Free WiFi.

A10 exit 21. Accessible from Tours. 6 km direction Montlouis. Clearly signposted.

CC € 15 *1/3-30/6 1/9-30/11*

N 47°24'7'' E 0°46'48''

Loches, F-37600 / Centre-Val de Loire (Indre-et-Loire)

1855

La Citadelle****
Aristide Briand
+33 (0)2-47590591
26/3 - 7/10
camping@lacitadelle.com

4ha 115T(50-180m²) 10-20A CEE

1 ACD**G**IJKLMOPQ
2 CGLRVXY
3 B**E**FGHJ**M**RU**W**
4 (C+**G** 10/4-7/10) (Q+R) (T+U+V+X+Z 25/6-2/9)
5 **AB**EFGIJKLMNPUVWXY
6 ACEG**K**(N 0,5km)ORTUV

A hospitable campsite on the edge of the historic town of Loches with its interesting castle. Both the town and the surroundings offer various leisure opportunities. On the site itself a heated swimming pool, bar/snack/restaurant and good toilet facilities. The site has a mobile home adapted for the disabled. Low season opening times: 08:00-12:15 and 14:00-19:30. Discount offered at restaurant and wellness centre in town.

Follow camping signs in the centre.

CC € 17 *26/3-8/7 25/8-7/10*

N 47°7'22" E 1°0'8"

Luynes, F-37230 / Centre-Val de Loire (Indre-et-Loire)

1856

Les Granges***
avenue de l'Europe
+33 (0)2-47557905
FAX +33 (0)2-47409243
1/4 - 2/10
reception@campinglesgranges.fr

1,8ha 29T(> 100m²) 10A CEE

1 ACD**G**IJKLM**P**RS
2 FGRVX
3 BGHJN**P**RUV**W**
4 (C+H+Q+R) (T+U+Z 15/4-15/9)
5 **AB**GIJKMNOPUXZ
6 ACEGHI**K**L(N 0,5km)TV

A peacefully located campsite near the town of Luynes. Good amenities, swimming pool and shop. Improved toilet facilities. Good cycling and walking opportunities in the area.

Easily accessible via the N152, west of Tours direction Saumur. Campsite signposted

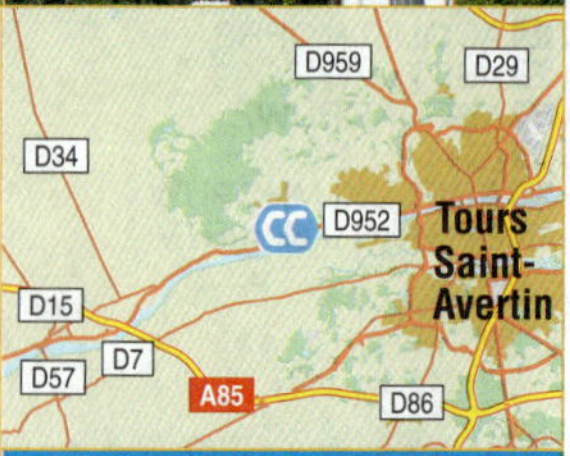

CC € 15 *1/4-2/7 29/8-2/10*

N 47°22'52" E 0°33'31"

Mesland, F-41150 / Centre-Val de Loire (Loir-et-Cher)

1857

Yelloh! Village Parc du Val de Loire*****
155 route de Fleuray
+33 (0)2-54702718
FAX +33 (0)2-54702171
1/4 - 10/9
parcduvaldeloire@wanadoo.fr

14ha 150T(100-170m²) 10A CEE

1 ACD**G**IJKLM**P**RS
2 BFLRVXY
3 BD**F**GHJKL**MNPQ**RU**W**
4 (B 25/4-13/9) (E+F+G) IJ (Q+S+T+U+V+X+Z)
5 **AB**CDEFGHIJKLMNPQRUX YZ
6 ABCEGIJ**K**(N 6km)ORTV

Located between Blois en Amboise (2 hours from Paris) in rural surroundings in the heart of the prestigious castles of the Loire and the vineyards of Touraine. There are 31 castles within a radius of 30 km. Surrounded by woods where clear air and peace await you. Heated sanitary facilities.

A10 motorway, exit 18 (Chateau-Renault / Amboise), follow the 'Parc du Val de Loire' signs, or: N152, through Onzain, towards Mesland, follow the 'Parc du Val de Loire' signs.

CC € 17 *1/4-9/7 27/8-10/9*

N 47°30'38" E 1°6'18"

Montbazon, F-37250 / Centre-Val de Loire (Indre-et-Loire)

iD **1858**

de la Grange Rouge***
D910
+33 (0)2-47260643
1/4 - 15/10
contact@camping-montbazon.com

3ha 110**T**(100-120m²) 10A CEE

1 ACD**G**IJKLMPQ
2 CFGLRVX
3 HJ**M**NR**W**
4 (B 1/5-30/9) (Q+R) (T+U+V+X+Y 1/4-15/9) (Z)
5 **AB**FGIJKLMNOPUV
6 AEJT

Quietly located in the heart of the Touraine, on the banks of the Indre. A good stopover site, close to the N910. Also suitable for longer stays. Restaurant next to site. Shops in town. Within walking distance (2 min.) of the town centre. In the midst of the Azay le Rideau-Amboise-Villandry-Ussé castles and Honoré de Balzac museum (Saché).

From Tours via D910 dir. south A10, exit 23. Before centre turn right. Clearly signposted. Exit is at the Office de Tourisme.

CC € 15 *1/4-9/7 27/8-15/10 7=6*

N 47°17'25'' E 0°42'59''

Montlouis-sur-Loire, F-37270 / Centre-Val de Loire (Indre-et-Loire)

iD **1859**

Les Peupliers***
D751
+33 (0)2-47508190
FAX +33 (0)3-86379583
25/3 - 23/10
camping.lespeupliers@wanadoo.fr

4ha 72**T**(100-120m²) 10A CEE

1 ACD**G**IJKLMPQ
2 CRUVXY
3 BGHJK**M**RU**W**
4 (C 4/7-31/8) (Q+R+T+Z)
5 **A**BFGIJKLMNOPUXYZ
6 DEG**J**(N 0,5km)TV

This municipal campsite has sunny and shaded pitches. Good amenities.

From Tours via the D751 direction Amboise, well signposted.

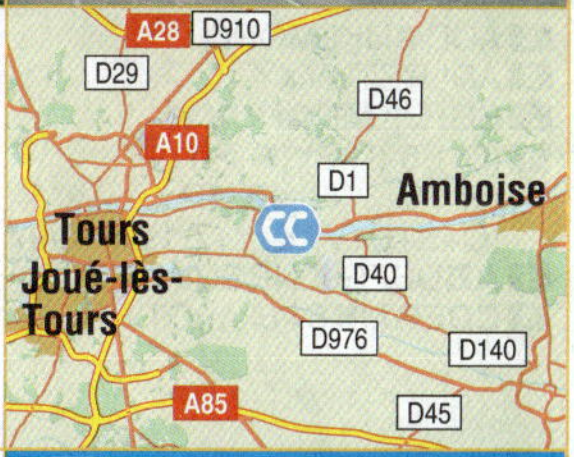

CC € 15 *25/3-3/7 20/8-23/10 7=6, 14=11*

N 47°23'40'' E 0°48'42''

Néret, F-36400 / Centre-Val de Loire (Indre)

iD **1860**

Le Bonhomme**
Mulles
+33 (0)2-54314611
1/4 - 1/10
info@camping-lebonhomme.com

1,5ha 37**T**(100-120m²) 6A CEE

1 A**G**IJL**P**Q
2 ILRTVWXY
3 GIJR
4 (Q+V+X)
5 **A**CGIJKLMNOPUWZ
6 CEG**K**L(N 6km)T

A small, friendly campsite among fruit and nut trees in a very peaceful, undulating landscape. The surroundings are a paradise for walking and cycling. The campsite is Dutch run. Communal meals and bread at your tent.

Exit 12 Chateauroux from Vierzon on the A20. Then D943 direction Montluçon. Left at Néret exit. In Néret follow the 'Aire Naturelle' signs, 2 km beyond Néret sign to 'Le Bonhomme' on the left of the road.

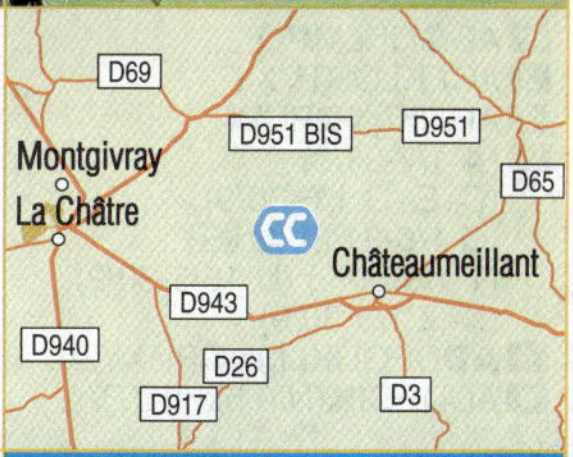

CC € 15 *1/4-30/6 17/8-1/10*

N 46°35'19'' E 2°7'59''

Nouan-le-Fuzelier, F-41600 / Centre-Val de Loire (Loir-et-Cher) — 1861

La Grande Sologne***
rue Cauchoix
+33 (0)2-54887022
1/4 - 15/10
info@campingrandesologne.com

10ha 150T(80-120m²) 10A

1 ACD**G**IJKLPRS
2 BCDFGLRVWXY
3 BGHJK**MNOP**QRTUW
4 (C+H 15/6-31/8) J
(Q 1/7-31/8) (R)
(T+U+X 1/7-23/8)
5 **AB**EFGIJKLMNPUWZ
6 ACDEGJK(N 0,5km)OTV

A friendly family campsite located around a fish pond; spacious shaded pitches, extensive sports facilities including tennis and swimming pool next to the site. Children's playground, free WiFi. Close to the chateaux of the Loire (including Chambord). Various cycling and walking routes.

From the north A71, exit 3 dir. RD2020. From Orléans follow the RD2020 dir. Vierzon until past the town of Nouan-le-Fuzelier. From the south A71 exit 4 dir. Orléans.

CC € 15 *1/4-5/7 22/8-15/10* *7=6, 14=11*

N 47°31'58'' E 2°2'12''

Poilly-lez-Gien/Gien, F-45500 / Centre-Val de Loire (Loiret) — 1862

Les Bois du Bardelet*****
Le Petit Bardelet
+33 (0)2-38674739
FAX +33 (0)2-38382716
9/4 - 25/9
contact@bardelet.com

15ha 120T(100-300m²) 16A CEE

1 ACD**G**IJKLMOPQ
2 ADLRSTUVXY
3 BGHJK**MNQ**RU**VW**
4 (C 1/5-31/8) (**F**)
(**H** 1/5-31/8) **JKNP**
(Q+S+U+V+X+Y+Z 19/4-12/9)
5 **AB**DEFGJLNP**S**UWXYZ
6 CDEG**IJK**(N 6km)OTV

Luxury holiday resort with indoor and outdoor pools, and indoor playing pool 'Robin' for children up to 12. All the amenities you can think of, including for groups. Spacious marked-out pitches, partly with shade. Fishing lake of 1 hectare. Cycling options (Loire á vèlo). Full WiFi coverage. Water slide by pool.

In Gien the D940 direction Bourges. With SatNav: Le Petit Bardelet 45500 Poilly-lez-Gien. Campsite is clearly signposted.

CC € 17 *9/4-23/6 1/9-24/9*

N 47°38'29'' E 2°36'54''

Poilly-lez-Gien/Gien, F-45500 / Centre-Val de Loire (Loiret) — 1863

Sites & Paysages Camping de Gien***
rue des Iris
+33 (0)2-38671250
FAX +33 (0)2-38671218
7/3 - 29/10
camping-gien@wanadoo.fr

6ha 200T(100-120m²) 10A CEE

1 AC**G**IJKLM**P**Q
2 ACFKLORTVXY
3 AHIJKLN**Q**RU**W**
4 (**A** 1/7-31/8)
(C+E+G 1/6-30/9)
(Q 1/6-31/8) (S)
(T 1/5-30/9) (U 15/5-30/9)
(X+Z 1/5-30/9)
5 **AB**DFGIJKLMNOPUXYZ
6 ACDEGI**K**(N 0,5km)OTV

A campsite with shaded but unreserved pitches alongside the banks of the Loire. Views of the town of Gien, famous for its pottery. The swimming pool can be covered. You can make canoe trips from the campsite. This part of the Loire is perfect for walking and cycling trips.

Campsite is located on the Loire, close to the old bridge, opposite the castle. Take first exit Gien-Centre from roundabout, then follow signs 'Bord de Loire'.

CC € 19 *7/3-9/7 27/8-29/10*

N 47°40'56'' E 2°37'23''

Romorantin-Lanthenay, F-41200 / Centre-Val de Loire (Loir-et-Cher)

1864

Le Tournefeuille***
32 Rue des Lices
+33 (0)254761660
1/4 - 30/9
entreprisefrery@orange.fr

NEW

1,9ha 90T(80-130m²) 10A CEE

1 ACD**G**IJKLMPQ
2 CFRVWX
3 AGJKLMRU
4 (**A**+C+E+H+Q+T+U+Z)
5 ABFGIJKLMNOPSUWXY
6 CDEJ(N 0,3km)OTV

On the banks of the Sauldre on the edge of the historic town Romorantin. The possibilities are many: fishing, walking, visiting museums (Matra).

In centre via D922/D922a or D764. Follow signs 'Complexe Sportif'.

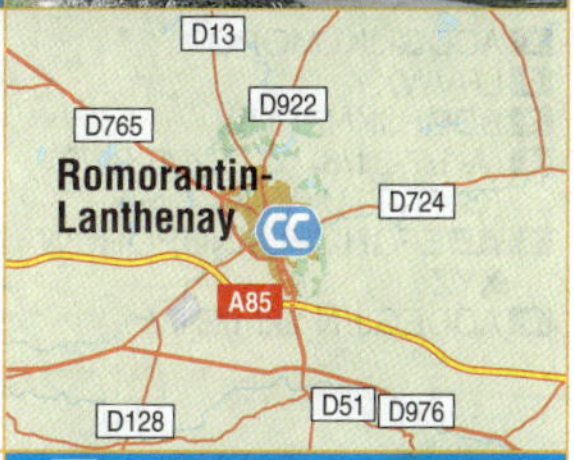

CC €15 *1/4-30/6 1/9-30/9 7=6*

N 47°21'18'' E 1°45'20''

Salbris, F-41300 / Centre-Val de Loire (Loir-et-Cher)

1865

Camping de Sologne***
8 alleé de la Sauldre
+33 (0)2-54970638
1/4 - 30/9
campingdesologne@wanadoo.fr

2ha 85T(60-100m²) 10A CEE

1 AC**G**HIJKLMOP
2 CDFRVWX
3 AGHJ**M**RW
4 (**C** 1/6-15/9) (Q 15/6-15/8) (R) (T+X+Z 1/5-31/8)
5 **A**FGIJKLMNPUXYZ
6 FGI**K**TV

A beautiful, relaxing campsite by a lake. Located 2 km from the motorway. Restaurants and shops within walking distance of the pleasant and quiet Salbris. Close to a swimming pool.

From Orléans via the N20 towards Vierzon, turn left at Salbris onto the D55 to Pierrefitte. Campsite 300m n the right.

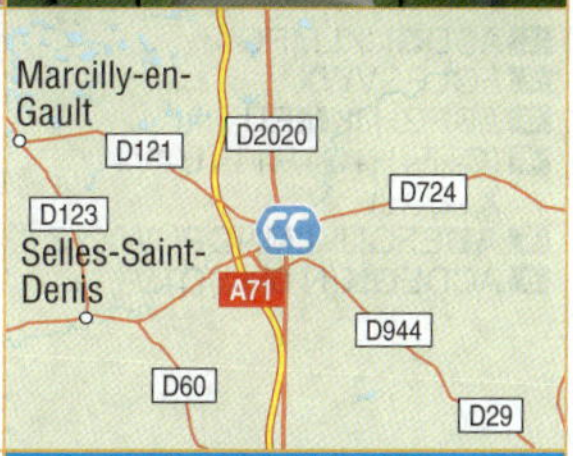

CC €15 *1/4-24/6 29/8-30/9*

N 47°25'49'' E 2°3'16''

Savonnières, F-37550 / Centre-Val de Loire (Indre-et-Loire)

1866

La Confluence***
route du Braye
+33 (0)2-47500025
1/5 - 30/9
contact@campinglaconfluence.fr

NEW

80T(95-100m²) 10A CEE

1 ACD**G**IJKLMPQ
2 CFGMRVWXY
3 BGHJMNR**W**
4 (Q 1/7-31/8)
5 **AB**EFGIJKLMNOPQRUXYZ
6 DEGJ(N 0,6km)T

La Confluence is located on the banks of the Cher with a view of the village. Spacious pitches. The stalactite caves and mushroom farms in the vicinity are worth a visit. Don't forget to visit Ussé castle (Sleeping Beauty castle) and Villandry with its beautiful gardens.

Accessible via A58, exit Villandry. Follow dir. Villandry/Savonnières. Left after centre. Via D37 exit Savonnières. Right before centre. Well signposted.

CC €17 *1/5-30/6 1/9-30/9*

N 47°20'59'' E 0°33'0''

Seillac, F-41150 / Centre-Val de Loire (Loir-et-Cher)

1867

Camping-Ferme de Prunay****
Ferme de Prunay
+33 (0)2-54700201
25/3 - 3/11
contact@prunay.com

3ha 85T(200-400m²) 12A CEE

1 ACD**G**IJKLMOPQ
2 LRVWXY
3 BDGHJKNPRUW
4 (A 1/7-31/8) (C+H 1/5-30/9) (Q+R+T+U+V+X+Z)
5 **AB**EFGHIJKLMNOPQRUWXYZ
6 ACDEGJ(N 2km)RTV

'Le Prunay' is a rural and peaceful campsite with spacious pitches (200 to 400 m²). Heated swimming pool, fishing pond and children's farm. Discounts available for visiting various tourist attractions in the region. Perfect base for exploring the Loire Valley by bike.

A10, exit Blois dir. Angers/Château-Renault. D131 Molineuf - Chambon-sur-Cisse, in Molineuf continue towards Seillac (D135 and D760). Campsite signposted.

€15 *28/3-2/7 19/8-3/11* *10=9, 14=13*

N 47°33'17" E 1°10'50"

Sonzay, F-37360 / Centre-Val de Loire (Indre-et-Loire)

1868

L'Arada Parc****
rue de la Baratiere
+33 (0)2-47247269
26/3 - 8/10
info@laradaparc.com

1,7ha 59T(85-115m²) 10A CEE

1 ACD**G**IJKLMPQ
2 FGLRSVWX
3 AB**F**GHJK**M**RU
4 (C+F+H+Q+R+T+U+V+X+Z)
5 **AB**EFGIJKLMNOPUWXYZ
6 ACDEG**K**(N 6km)OTV

A beautiful campsite in the countryside between the valleys of the Loire and the Loir, close to the chateaux. Indoor and outdoor swimming pools and spa. On presentation of CampingCard ACSI during acceptance period, free WiFi for one device.

From Château-Renault D766 to Neuillé-Pont-Pierre then follow camping signs. From the A28 take exit 27 to Neuillé-Pont-Pierre, then follow camping signs.

€15 *26/3-8/7 25/8-8/10* *11=10, 16=14*

N 47°31'37" E 0°27'11"

St. Amand-Montrond, F-18200 / Centre-Val de Loire (Cher)

1869

La Roche***
chemin de la Roche
FAX +33 (0)2-48960936
1/4 - 30/9
camping-la-roche@wanadoo.fr

4ha 120T(100-120m²) 6A CEE

1 AGIJKLM**P**Q
2 CFGRVWXY
3 ABG**M**NRU**W**
4 (Q)
5 **AB**DGIJKLMNOPUV
6 EGK(N 1km)TV

A well maintained campsite by a canal and near the Cher. Pitches with sufficient shade separated by bushes. The centre is within walking distance and there is a bus stop next to the site. A free bus goes to the centre (where there is a swimming pool).

A71 exit 8, through the centre direction Montluçon. Just before the bridge, when leaving the city, turn right and keep on the side of the river.

€13 *1/4-30/6 1/9-30/9* *7=6*

N 46°43'4" E 2°29'26"

St. Avertin, F-37550 / Centre-Val de Loire (Indre-et-Loire) 1870

Tours Val de Loire****
61 rue de Rochepinard
+33 (0)2-47278747
15/3 - 15/11
contact@campingtoursvaldeloire.fr

2,6ha 90T(80-100m²) 10A CEE

1 ACD**G**IJKLMPQ
2 CDFGLRUVX
3 GJMR**W**
4 (Q+R 1/7-31/8)
5 A**B**FGIJKLMNPUW
6 CEGJ(N 0,2km)OT

Near the centre of the art and history city of Tours, this site is located in shaded, well-maintained surroundings on the banks of the Cher. A convenient location for visiting the tourist attractions. Swimming pool and playground. The site is located on the cycle route 'La Loire à Vélo'.

A10 exit Tours-Sud/St. Avertin. Follow direction Bléré via N76 direction Vierzon. Also A85 exit Bléré (Est) and exit St.Avertin (Ouest). Campsite signposted.

CC € 17 *15/3-30/6 1/9-15/11*

N 47°22'15" E 0°43'25"

St. Satur, F-18300 / Centre-Val de Loire (Cher) 1871

Les Portes de Sancerre***
Quai de Loire
+33 (0)2-48721088
2/4 - 16/10
camping.sancerre@flowercampings.com

2,5ha 85T(80-120m²) 6A CEE

1 AC**G**IJKLMPQ
2 ACLRSVXY
3 A**F**GHJK**MQ**R**W**
4 (**B**+**G** 1/7-31/8)
(Q 1/5-31/8) (R 5/4-30/9)
5 **AB**IJKLMNPUWXZ
6 AEGIK(N 1km)TV

Well maintained campsite on the Loire. Spacious marked out pitches with sufficient shade. Opportunities for tennis, golf and canoeing on site. Outdoor pool next to the site. Very close to Sancerre, famous for its wine.

From Cosne take the D955 in the direction of Bourges. In St. Satur drive in the direction of St. Thibault (D2). The campsite is located on the left of the road by the river, just before the bridge over the Loire.

CC € 13 *2/4-1/7 1/9-16/10 7=6*

N 47°20'32" E 2°51'58"

Ste Catherine-de-Fierbois, F-37800 / Centre-Val de Loire (Indre-et-Loire) 1872

Parc de Fierbois*****
+33 (0)2-47654335
2/5 - 4/9
contact@fierbois.com

30ha 189T(130-150m²) 10A CEE

1 ACDFIJKLMOPQ
2 ADFLRVXY
3 BGHJKMN**PQ**RUVW
4 (C+F+G) IJ
(Q+S+T+U) (V 1/7-31/8)
(X+Z)
5 **AB**EFGJLNPUWXYZ
6 CEGI**J**(N 1km)RTV

This Castel campsite is located in 30 hectare grounds around a lake that is surrounded by an old wood. The facilities include an indoor heated swimming pool, aquatic park with slides, skate park, bar and restaurant. Many castles and vineyards in the area.

Can be reached via the A10 exit St. Maure (25) and Sorigny (24.1), then Tours. Via the N10, located 16 km south of Montbazon.

CC € 19 *2/5-30/6 1/9-4/9 7=6*

N 47°8'49" E 0°39'10"

Suèvres, F-41500 / Centre-Val de Loire (Loir-et-Cher)

1873

Camping La Grenouillère*****
La Grenouillère RN152
+33 (0)2-54878037
FAX +33 (0)2-54878421
16/4 - 11/9
@ la.grenouillere@wanadoo.fr

12ha 79T(90-150m²) 10A CEE

1 ACDFIJKLMOPRS
2 BFLRVXY
3 B**F**GJK**M**NRU**V**W
4 (C+F+H) IJKM**N**
(Q+S+T+U+V+X+Y+Z)
5 **AB**DEFGIJKLMNOPSTUWX
Z
6 ACEG**K**(N 2,5km)TV

This chateau campsite is located between Orléans and Blois and can be reached via the RN152 (via A10 exit Mer). Rural location. Good facilities such as well maintained toilets, heated indoor swimming pool. Bar restaurant, pizzeria, spacious shop. A good base for exploring further in the Loire Valley. Dogs not allowed.

From Blois via RN152 direction Orléans. 3 km beyond Suèvres on the left.

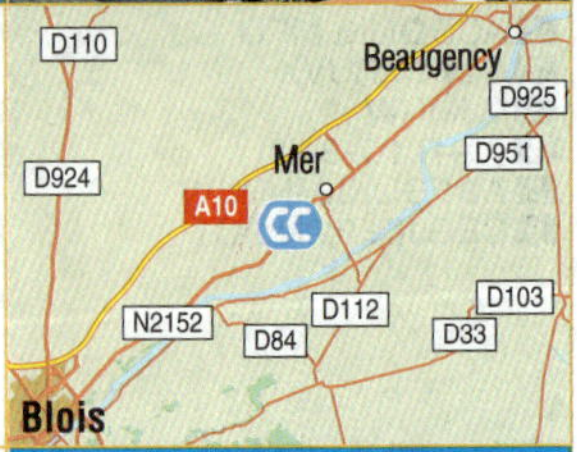

CC € 15 *16/4-13/7 30/8-11/9*

N 47°41'8'' E 1°29'14''

Sully/St. Père-sur-Loire, F-45600 / Centre-Val de Loire (Loiret)

1874

Le Jardin de Sully***
1 rue d'Orleans
+33 (0)2-38671084
FAX +33 (0)9-71706705
1/1 - 31/12
@ info-camping-lejardindesully@orange.fr

5ha 80T(90-120m²) 10A CEE

1 AC**G**IJKLMOQ
2 ACGLMRSUVXY
3 AB**F**GHJKMQRU**W**
4 (C 1/7-1/9) (H 1/7-10/9)
(Q+R 1/7-1/10)
(T+U+V+Z 1/7-1/9)
5 **AB**DFGIJKLMNPSUWXYZ
6 CEGHI**K**(N 1,5km)TV

A very peaceful campsite with spacious pitches and attention to planting. An area rich in nature, right by the Loire. An excellent starting point for light walking and cycling in level surroundings. Various castles, towns and villages with plenty of sights close by. Sully has an attractive centre.

Approaching from Lorris or Bellegarde towards Sully, turn right at the roundabout before the Loire bridge. Campsite indicated.

CC € 17 *1/1-8/7 29/8-31/12 7=6*

N 47°46'16'' E 2°21'44''

Trogues, F-37220 / Centre-Val de Loire (Indre-et-Loire)

1875

Château de la Rolandière****
+33 (0)2-47585371
1/5 - 18/9
@ contact@larolandiere.com

4ha 50T(90-110m²) 10A CEE

1 ACD**G**IJKLM**P**Q
2 FLRVXY
3 BHJN**Q**RU**V**
4 (B+G+Q+R)
(T+U 15/7-15/8) (Z)
5 **AB**FGIJKLMNOPUWZ
6 AEG**K**(N 6km)RTV

The elegant château is the centre of this rural campsite. Next to the castle are shaded camping pitches, a park, swimming pool, minigolf, restaurant and clubhouse. Hospitality and relaxation are high on the list here. Good starting point for walking and cycle trips.

A10 exit 25. Or via RD910. Follow D760 for 6 km direction Chinon/l'Ile Bouchard. After Noyant-de-Touraine straight ahead at roundabout towards Chinon/l'Ile Bouchard. Site located about 3 km on the left.

CC € 19 *1/5-9/7 26/8-18/9*

N 47°6'42'' E 0°30'58''

Velles, F-36330 / Centre-Val de Loire (Indre) — 1876

Les Grands Pins***
D920 Les Maisons-Neuves
+33 (0)2-54366193
19/3 - 9/10
contact@les-grands-pins.fr

5ha 46T(120-140m²) 10A CEE

1 ACD**G**IJKL**P**
2 BFLRVWXY
3 BG**MQ**R
4 (B+Q 1/7-31/8) (X+Y) Z
5 **A**GIJKLMNPRUVXYZ
6 CEGJ(N 7km)TV

A spacious campsite with partially shaded pitches. Suitable as a stopover campsite and as a starting point for trips out. Ideal for an overnight stop on your way south (A20). The restaurant has been completely refurbished. New interior and new chef.

7 km south of Châteauroux. Located 5 min. from the A20 between exit 14 and 15. On the D920 direction 'Les Maisons Neuves'.

CC € 17 *19/3-30/6 17/8-9/10*

N 46°44'30" E 1°37'16"

Vendôme, F-41100 / Centre-Val de Loire (Loir-et-Cher) — 1877

Au Coeur de Vendôme***
rue Geoffroy Martel
+33 (0)2-54770027
FAX +33 (0)2-54894101
17/4 - 2/11
aucoeurdevendome@camp-in-ouest.com

2,5ha 140T(80-100m²) 10A CEE

1 ACD**G**IJKLM**P**Q
2 CGLRVWXY
3 BGHJK**M**R**W**
4 (C+H 1/6-31/8) (Q) (R 15/6-2/11) (V 1/7-31/8)
5 **AB**DGIJKLMNPUYZ
6 ACEG**K**(N 0,4km)TV

Close to the historic and cultural town of Vendôme. Next to (free) swimming pool. Suitable for those passing through or staying. Located next to the N10.

Via N10 from north. In Vendôme, turn right at third traffic light Quartier des Grands Prés, then first left and left again. Follow signs to swimming pool and sports centre.

CC € 15 *17/4-11/7 28/8-2/11 7=6*

N 47°47'28" E 1°4'19"

Villiers-le-Morhier, F-28130 / Centre-Val de Loire(Eure-et-Loir) — 1878

Les Ilots de St. Val***
Les Ilots
+33 (0)2-37827130
FAX +33 (0)2-37827767
1/2 - 22/12
lesilots@campinglesilotsdestval.com

10ha 50T(125-400m²) 10A CEE

1 ACGIJKLM**P**Q
2 IRTUVWX
3 ABC**F**GH**M**RU
5 ACDGIJKLMNOPUWXYZ
6 DEG**J**(N 3km)OT

5 km from Chateau de Maintenon, 25 km from Chartres cathedral and 1 hour from Paris by train or car. Attractive, natural surroundings, every comfort.

On the D983 coming from either Nogent-le-Roi or from Maintenon follow the camping signs about halfway along.

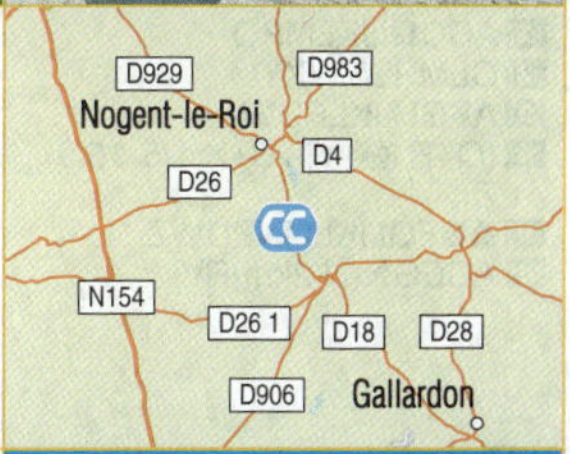

CC € 17 *1/4-15/6 1/9-30/9*

N 48°36'39" E 1°32'53"

Andryes, F-89480 / Bourgogne (Yonne) — 1879

Sites & Paysages Au Bois Joli***
2 route de Villeprenoy
+33 (0)3-86817048
1/4 - 31/10
info@campingauboisjoli.com

4,5ha 89**T**(100-250m²) 10A CEE

1 ACD**F**IJKLPQ
2 BIKRTXY
3 ABGHJKMNR
4 (C+H 1/6-15/9) (Q+R+S 🔑) (T 1/7-1/9) (V 🔑)
5 **AB**DEFGIJKLMNOPQRUW XYZ
6 ACDEG**I**J(N 5km)ORT

On the edge of the Morvan natural park, near a cycle track along the Canal du Nivernais. Wonderfully peaceful, pleasant natural campsite, with orchids in spring. Heated swimming pool and view over the hills. Located close to Vézelay and Guédelon. Many options for cultural and sportive days out.

From Auxerre or Clamecy follow N151. In Coulanges-sur-Yonne take D39 dir. Andryes. From there follow signs to campsite.

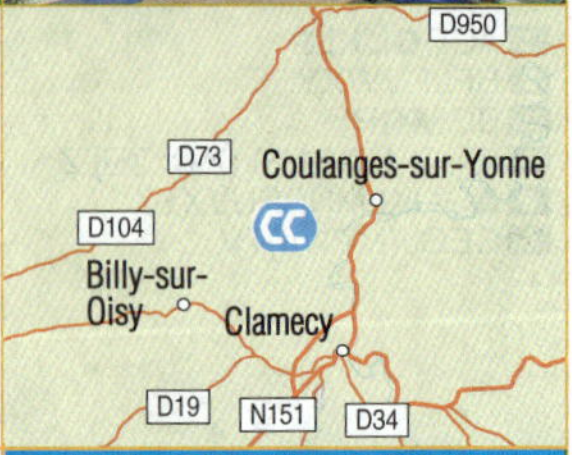

CC €17 1/4-30/6 26/8-31/10

N 47°31'0'' E 3°28'48''

Arnay-le-Duc, F-21230 / Bourgogne (Côte-d'Or) — 1880

de l'Étang de Fouché****
rue du 8 Mai 1945
+33 (0)3-80900223
14/4 - 10/10
info@campingfouche.com

8ha 209**T**(80-140m²) 10A CEE

1 ACD**G**IJKLM**P**RS
2 ADLMRVWXY
3 ABGHJK**M**N**P**RU**WZ**
4 (C+H 15/5-30/9) J (Q+R 15/4-30/9) (T 1/7-31/8) (U+V+X 15/4-30/9) (Z 🔑)
5 **AB**DEFGIJKLMNPQUWZ
6 CEGJ(N 1km)TV

A campsite situated by a lake with large marked out pitches offering sufficient shade. Plenty of watersports opportunities at the lake.

Follow camping signs in Arnay-le-Duc. The campsite is located 1.2 km east of the N6.

CC €17 14/4-5/7 1/9-10/10

N 47°8'5'' E 4°29'49''

Autun, F-71400 / Bourgogne (Saône-et-Loire) — 1881

de la Porte d'Arroux***
rue du Traité d'Anvers
+33 (0)3-85521082
7/3 - 6/11
camping.autun@orange.fr

2,5ha 79**T**(50-100m²) 10A CEE

1 ACD**G**IJKLMPQ
2 CLMRUVWXY
3 AFGHJKLRU**W**
4 (Q+R 🔑) (T+U+X 1/5-15/9) Z
5 **AB**FGIJKLMNPUWZ
6 ACEG**K**(N 2km)RV

A peaceful campsite with a restaurant, conveniently located for visiting the historic town of Autun. Shaded pitches some of which are marked out by tall hedges.

A6 afslag 24.1 Beaune-Centre. D973 to Autun. Leave Autun via the D980 towards Saulieu/ St. Forgeot. Signposted.

CC €15 7/3-3/7 20/8-6/11 7=6, 14=11

N 46°57'53'' E 4°17'34''

Auxonne, F-21130 / Bourgogne (Côte-d'Or)

iD **1882**

De l'Arquebuse***
route d'Athée
+33 (0)3-80310689
FAX +33 (0)3-80311362
5/3 - 18/12
camping.arquebuse@wanadoo.fr

4,5ha 100T(100m²) 10A CEE

1 ACD**G**IJKLMPQ
2 CFLRTVWXY
3 BGR**W**
4 (**C**+**G** 15/5-31/8) (Q)
(R 15/5-15/10)
(U+V+Y+Z)
5 **AB**DGIJKLMNPUV
6 AEGI**K**(N 1km)OTV

A peaceful campsite right next to the River Saône. Bar/restaurant with big screen TV. Large open air swimming pool next to the site and all sorts of watersports in the river. Restaurant closed Sunday and Monday in low season. You can walk along the Saône to Auxonne with its various shops and restaurants.

From Dijon take the N5 in the direction of Auxonne. Before Auxonne exit D24, direction Athée. The campsite is located on the right after about 500 metres.

CC € 17 *1/5-20/6 12/9-30/9*

N 47°11'56'' E 5°22'57''

Bourbon/Lancy, F-71140 / Bourgogne (Saône-et-Loire)

iD **1883**

Camping et Village-chalets du Breuil***
11 rue des Eurimants
+33 (0)3-85892098
25/3 - 31/10
camping.chaletsdubreuil@orange.fr

2ha 42T(80-105m²) 10A CEE

1 ACD**G**IJKLMPQ
2 DLRTVWXY
3 A**F**GHJRU**WZ**
4 (B+G 1/6-15/9) (Q+R)
5 **AB**DFGIJKLMNPUZ
6 CEG**K**(N 0,4km)O

Campsite close to the centre of Bourbon/Lancy. Pitches marked out by hedges.

Campsite on edge of town, towards Decize.

CC € 15 *25/3-3/7 20/8-31/10 7=6, 14=11*

N 46°37'9'' E 3°45'13''

Chagny, F-71150 / Bourgogne (Saône-et-Loire)

iD **1884**

Pâquier Fané***
20 rue du Pâquier Fané
+33 (0)3-85872142
1/4 - 31/10
camping-chagny@orange.fr

1,8ha 91T(80-100m²) 16A CEE

1 ACD**G**IJKLMPQ
2 CLRVWXY
3 AGHJMNRU**W**
4 (**C**+**H** 1/5-31/8) (Q)
(T+U+V+X 1/5-31/8) Z
5 **AB**EFGIJKLMNOPU
6 ACDEGK(N 0,3km)R

Lovely camping pitches (on grass) with some shade from a few tall trees. Close to the centre of Chagny. Lovely cycle routes.

A6 exit 24.1 Beaune-Centre, D974 direction Chalon-sur-Saône. After 13 km head for Chagny. In Chagny follow 'complexe sportif'/'camping' signs.

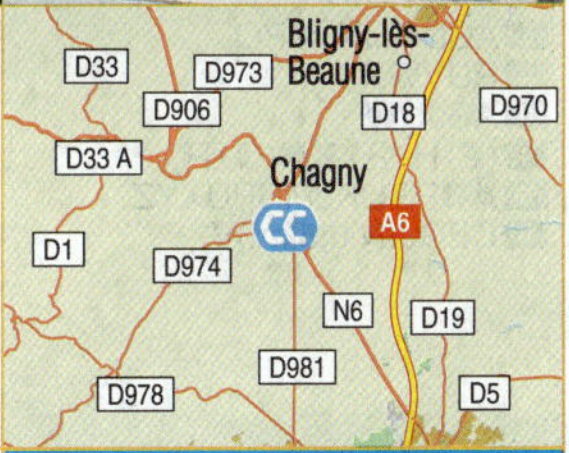

CC € 15 *1/4-3/7 20/8-31/10 7=6, 14=12*

N 46°54'43'' E 4°44'44''

Chalon-sur-Saône/St. Marcel, F-71380 / Bourgogne (Saône-et-Loire)

iD 1885

Du Pont de Bourgogne***
12 rue Julien Leneveu
+33 (0)3-85482686
FAX +33 (0)3-85485063
1/4 - 30/9
@ campingchalon71@wanadoo.fr

3ha 91T(50-100m²) 10A CEE

1 ACD**G**IJKLMOPQ
2 CLRTUVWXY
3 A**F**JR**W**
4 (Q+R) (T+U+V 15/4-30/9) Z
5 **AB**EFGIJKLMNOPQUWZ
6 ACFGHJ(N 1,5km)OV

A campsite located along the Saône with shaded pitches. Near exit 26 Chalon Sud on the A6. Within walking distance (15 min) from the centre of Chalon-sur-Saône. Starting point for cycling: Voie Verte. New modern toilet facilities.

In Chalon-sur-Saône follow campsite and Roseraie St. Nicolas signs.

CC € 17 1/4-4/7 25/8-30/9 7=6, 14=12

N 46°47'3'' E 4°52'21''

Charny, F-89120 / Bourgogne (Yonne)

iD 1886

Les Platanes***
41 route de la Mothe
FAX +33 (0)3-86918360
1/4 - 30/10
@ info@campinglesplatanes.fr

2ha 91T(100-120m²) 16A CEE

1 ACD**G**IJLMPQ
2 CGRVXY
3 AGHJK**M**RUW
4 (C) (Q 1/7-31/8) (R+Z)
5 **AB**DGIJKLMNOPUVWXYZ
6 DEGK(N 0,5km)TV

Located between Auxerre, Sens and Montargis. Campsite with plenty of plantlife and flowers, with level motorhome pitches, partly partitioned camping pitches. Guests can use a heated pool. WiFi everywhere. A multi-lingual reception offers comfort and quality.

A6 exit 18. Follow the recommended route to the campsite.

CC € 13 1/4-30/6 1/9-30/10

N 47°53'29'' E 3°5'39''

Châtillon-sur-Seine, F-21400 / Bourgogne (Côte-d'Or)

iD 1887

Municipal Louis Rigoly**
Esplan. St. Vorles
+33 (0)3-80910305
1/4 - 2/10
@ camping-chatillon-sur-seine@ orange.fr

0,8ha 43T(80-120m²) 6A CEE

1 ACDGIJKLMPQ
2 RUVWXY
3 AGJU**W**
4 (**F**+H) **KN**(Q)
5 **AB**FGIJKLMNPUXYZ
6 CEGJ(N 0,5km)V

Located in the Côte d'Or on the edge of the Champagne region, the Louis Rigoly campsite welcomes you in natural surroundings 2 km from a large wood. Intimate and shaded, close to the town centre and next to a swimming pool (free for long-stay campers). Free WiFi and TV room. Suitable for a sporting and cultural holiday.

From Paris A5 direction Troyes, exit 21. Then D971 direction Bar-sur-Seine, then Châtillon-sur-Seine. Follow signs.

CC € 15 1/4-3/7 22/8-2/10

N 47°51'34'' E 4°34'47''

Chaumot, F-58800 / Bourgogne (Nièvre)

1888

de l'Ardan
Route de Germenay
+33 (0)3-86200770
1/4 - 1/10
@ delardan@bbox.fr

1,1ha 40T(70-100m²) 10A CEE

1 AGIJKLMPQ
2 CGRTWXY
3 GHJKW
4 (Q+Y+Z)
5 AGJKMNPUZ
6 DEGIJ(N 3km)

The campsite is positioned on an island between River l'Ardan and Canal du Nivernais. Shaded pitches, intimate character and good amenities. Treat yourself to a meal in the restaurant. Regional specialities and various suggestions from the chef are on offer. Dutch owners.

From Clamecy to Corbigny. Follow camping signs there to Chitry-les-Mines.

CC € 15 1/4-30/6 1/9-1/10

N 47°15'31'' E 3°38'29''

Crux-la-Ville, F-58330 / Bourgogne (Nièvre)

1889

de l'Etang du Merle***
Le Merle
FAX +33 (0)3-86583842
25/3 - 16/10
@ etangdumerle@orange.fr

6ha 43T(80-100m²)

1 ACDGIJLPQ
2 ABDLRSXY
3 ABGHJNRUWZ
4 (B+G 15/5-30/9) (Q+R)
(T+U+Z 1/5-30/9)
5 ABFGIJKLMNPSTUZ
6 EGJ(N 5km)ORTV

A shaded family campsite by a lake with plenty of water sports such as pedal boats, surfing and fishing. Spacious pitches among the trees. In the middle of the Parc du Morvan; a good starting point for cyclists and walkers.

Located on the D34, 6.8 km from St. Révérien.

CC € 15 25/3-3/7 20/8-16/10 7=6, 14=11

N 47°8'13'' E 3°29'35''

Decize, F-58300 / Bourgogne (Nièvre)

1890

Des Halles***
rue Marcel Merle
+33 (0)3-86251405
25/3 - 23/10
@ camping.decize@orange.fr

3,5ha 79T(80-100m²) 10A

1 ACDGIJKLMPQ
2 CLRTVWXY
3 AGKMNQRW
4 (C+F) J(Q 1/5-1/10)
(R 1/5-12/10) (T 1/5-31/8) Z
5 ABFGIJKLMNPU
6 CDEGK(N 0,8km)OV

The campsite is located right beside the Loire, water sports are possible. Within walking distance of the centre of Decize. The pitches are shaded by tall trees.

In Decize head towards Moulins. Keep to the right after the Loire bridge; follow signs.

CC € 15 25/3-3/7 20/8-23/10 7=6, 14=11

N 46°50'7'' E 3°27'21''

Digoin, F-71160 / Bourgogne (Saône-et-Loire)

1891

La Chevrette***
41 rue de la Chevrette
☎ +33 (0)3-85531149
FAX +33 (0)3-85885970
1/4 - 8/10
@ info@lachevrette.com

1,6ha 85T(60-100m²) 10A CEE

1 ACD**G**IJKLMPQ
2 CGRTVY
3 BGHJQRU**W**
4 (C 1/5-7/9) (Q+R) (T+U+X 1/7-31/8) Z
5 **AB**DFGJLNPUWX
6 ACEGK(N 0,5km)RV

The campsite is located on the banks of the Loire with opportunities for cycle trips over the Voie Verte and canoe trips. The campsite has free WiFi internet.

The campsite is signposted in Digoin by the side of the D979 from Moulin to Paray-le-Monial.

CC € 17 *1/4-8/7 27/8-8/10*

N 46°28'47'' E 3°58'3''

Dompierre-les-Ormes, F-71520 / Bourgogne (Saône-et-Loire)

1892

Le Village des Meuniers****
344 rue du Stade
☎ +33 (0)3-85503660
1/4 - 31/10
@ contact@villagedesmeuniers.com

4ha 80T(80-300m²) 16A CEE

1 ACD**G**IJKLM**P**Q
2 IJLMRVWXY
3 ABGHJKLMN**Q**RUW
4 (C+H 1/5-30/9) J(Q+R) (T+U+V+Y 1/5-30/9) Z
5 **AB**DEFGIJKLMNOPUWXYZ
6 ACEGJ(N 0,3km)OV

Friendly campsite with spacious pitches in the sun or shade. Heated pool. Walking and cycling trips through the area possible. Restaurant with extensive menu.

A6 Mâcon-Sud direction Charolles N79. Dompierre-les-Ormes is signposted via D41. Follow camping signs in Dompierre.

CC € 19 *1/4-1/7 29/8-31/10*

N 46°21'50'' E 4°28'29''

Epinac, F-71360 / Bourgogne (Saône-et-Loire)

1893

Du Pont Vert***
rue de la Piscine
☎ +33 (0)3-85542983
25/4 - 2/10
@ camping.epinac@orange.fr

3,8ha 68T(80-120m²) 10A CEE

1 ACDGIJKLMPQ
2 CLRVX
3 AGHJNQRU**W**
4 (Q 1/7-31/8) (T+U+X 1/5-15/9) Z
5 **AB**GIJKLMNOPU
6 CEGK(N 0,5km)V

Peacefully located campsite on the La Drée rivulet. Pitches with shade from high trees.

A6 exit 24.1 Beaune-Centre. D973 direction Autun. At La Drée D43 direction Epinac. In the location, follow the camping signs.

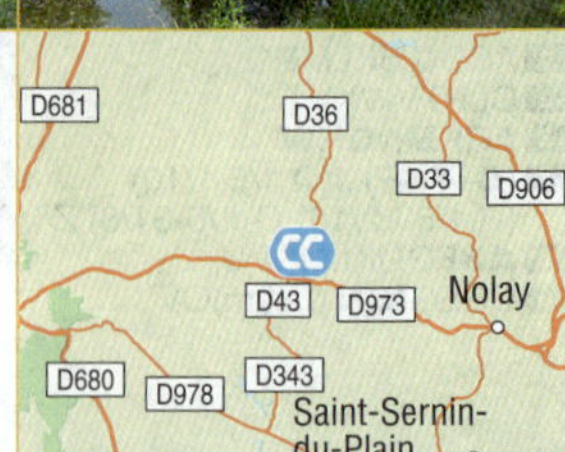

CC € 15 *25/4-3/7 20/8-2/10 7=6, 14=11*

N 46°59'9'' E 4°30'22''

Étang-sur-Arroux, F-71190 / Bourgogne (Saône-et-Loire) — 1894

Des 2 Rives**
26-28 rue de Toulon
+33 (0)3-85823973
1/1 - 31/12
camping@des2rives.com

2,5ha 100T(85-150m²) 6A CEE

1 ACD**G**IJKL**P**Q
2 CGLMRSVWXY
3 AGHJNRU**W**X
4 (Q+T 1/7-31/8)
5 **A**DFGIJKLMNPUZ
6 AEGHK(N 0,3km)OV

The camping terrain is peacefully located in parkland between two rivers: the Mesvrin and the Arroux. The pitches are separated by tall trees. The toilet block is heated in early and late season. Dutch owners. Free WiFi.

From Autun to Étang-sur-Arroux on D681 direction Moulins-Luzy. Via D994 to Étang. In 'centre ville' direction Toulon-sur-Arroux. Campsite just outside Étang-sur-Arroux at the D994.

CC € 15 *1/1-9/7 28/8-31/12*

N 46°51'42'' E 4°11'31''

Fourchambault, F-58600 / Bourgogne (Nièvre) — 1895

De la Loire
2 rue de la Folie
+33 (0)9-78978978
21/3 - 2/11
campingdelaloire@bbox.fr

3,3ha 70T(150m²) 10A CEE

1 AC**F**IJKLM**P**Q
2 CFGRXY
3 FGHJ**M**W
4 (Q+T 1/6-30/9)
5 **AB**GJKNPUVY
6 CEGJ(N 0,5km)T

A campsite right on the Loire. Spacious grounds with many large trees. Unmarked pitches, basic toilet facilities. The campsite has a bar and bakery service. You can cycle along the Loire. There are also opportunities for fishing.

Campsite well signposted from Fourchambault.

CC € 11 *21/3-14/7 31/8-2/11 7=6, 14=11, 21=16*

N 47°0'43'' E 3°4'41''

La Celle-en-Morvan, F-71400 / Bourgogne (Saône-et-Loire) — 1896

Les Deux Rivières***
Le Pré Bouché
+33 (0)3-45740138
14/5 - 17/9
info@les2rivieres.com

1,8ha 41T(80-220m²) 10A CEE

1 A**G**IJLMPQ
2 CLRVWXY
3 ABFGHIJRU**W**
4 (**C**+**H** 15/5-15/9)
(Q+R+T+U)
5 **AB**FGIJKLMNPQRUWZ
6 ABCEGI**K**(N 7km)O

The campsite is located by two rivers on the edge of the Morvan nature reserve. Starting point for hikers and cyclists. Many antiquities in the area; Autun, Vezelay, Bibracte, the Burgundy wine route and routes through the Morvan lakes. Heated swimming pool. Dutch owners. Open pitches in the sun, enclosed pitches with shade.

In La Celle-en-Morvan D978, follow camping signs from Autun-Château-Chinon. Campsite is 300m from the D978.

CC € 17 *14/5-7/7 29/8-17/9*

N 47°0'44'' E 4°11'30''

La Clayette, F-71800 / Bourgogne (Saône-et-Loire)

1897

Les Bruyères***
9 route de Gibles, D79
+33 (0)3-85280915
1/4 - 6/11
contact@campingbruyeres.com

2ha 90**T**(90-150m²) 16A CEE

1 ACD**G**IJKLMO**P**Q
2 DILRSTUVWXY
3 BGHJ**MNQ**R**W**
4 (C+G 1/6-31/8) J(Q) (T+U+V+X 1/7-31/8) Z
5 **AB**DFGIJKLMNPUWZ
6 CDEGJ(N 0,6km)V

A spacious family campsite next to a municipal swimming pool (free) overlooking a lake and castle, within walking distance of the centre with restaurants, bars etc. A good base for exploring Charolais by bike. For experienced cyclists there are many opportunities: various villages with artists with their own studios, Beaujolais wine route.

Leave the town in the direction of Mâcon/Lyon. At the edge of the town take the D79, where the campsite is located on the left.

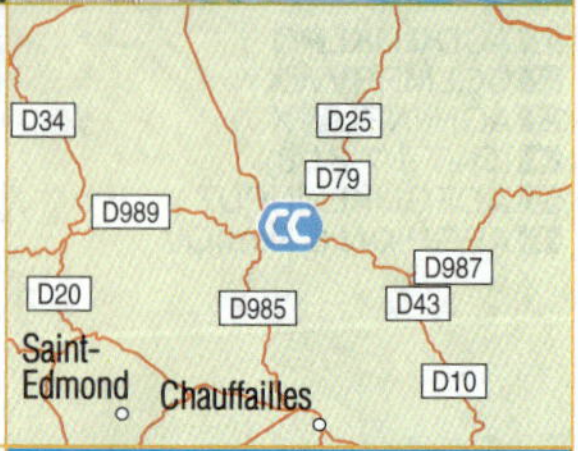

CC € 15 *1/4-1/7 1/9-6/11*

N 46°17'30" E 4°19'10"

La Tagnière, F-71190 / Bourgogne (Saône-et-Loire)

1898

Le Paroy
+33 (0)3-85545927
1/4 - 30/9
info@campingleparoy.com

1,2ha 34**T**(100-250m²) 10A CEE

1 A**G**IJKLMO**P**Q
2 DJKRTVWXY
3 ADGHJKLNRUW
4 (Q+R)
5 **A**FGIJKLMNPUXYZ
6 AEGK(N 2km)OV

A very quiet campsite in the Morvan, a paradise for nature lovers and birdwatchers. Lovely walking routes from the campsite. Table d'hôte, free WiFi. Dutch owner. Modern toilet facilities.

From Autun via N81 richting Moulin/Luzy. After 10 km left through Étang-sur-Arroux direction Toulon. 3 km after Etang left to La Tagnière (D224). Follow camping signs in Tagnière.

CC € 13 *1/4-9/7 26/8-30/9*

N 46°46'38" E 4°12'20"

Laives, F-71240 / Bourgogne (Saône-et-Loire)

1899

La Héronnière***
route de la Ferté
+33 (0)3-85449885
19/3 - 2/11
camping.laives@wanadoo.fr

2ha 80**T**(100m²) 10A CEE

1 ACD**G**IJKLMOPRS
2 ACDLRVXY
3 ABGJKNRU**WZ**
4 (C+H 1/5-13/10) (Q+R) (T+U 1/5-31/8) (Y 1/5-30/9) Z
5 **AB**DFGIJKLMNPUVWZ
6 ACDEGK(N 6km)ORV

Peaceful campsite 200 metres from large recreational lake, plenty of fishing opportunities, swimming pool on campsite. Suitable for cycle trips.

From North: A6 exit 26 Chalon-sur-Saône. D906 dir. Mâcon. At Varennes-le-Grand: D6 to Ferté. D18 dir. Lacs-des-Laives. From South: A6 exit 27 Tournus. In Sennecy-le-Grand: D18 dir. Lacs-des-Laives.

CC € 17 *19/3-30/6 1/9-2/11* *7=6, 14=12, 21=18*

N 46°40'19" E 4°49'58"

Lormes, F-58140 / Bourgogne (Nièvre)

1900

de l'Etang du Goulot***
rue des Campeurs
+33 (0)3-86228237
15/4 - 30/9
campingetangdugoulot@gmail.com

2,7ha 64T(75-300m²) 16A CEE

1 AGIJKLMPQ
2 ADKLRTVWXY
3 ABGHJKNP**Q**RU**W**Z
4 (T+U+X 1/7-30/8)
5 **A**GIJKLMNOPQRUWXZ
6 ACDEGHIJ(N 0,4km)OT

In the heart of the Morvan (an area of large lakes). A shady and peaceful campsite with a friendly family atmosphere located on the Lac du Goulot. Offers 64 spacious pitches. Supermarket and shops within walking distance (400 metres).

The campsite is located on the southern edge of Lormes. Well signposted.

CC € 15 *15/4-30/6 1/9-30/9*

N 47°16'57" E 3°49'21"

Louhans, F-71500 / Bourgogne (Saône-et-Loire)

1901

Municipal Les Trios Rivières***
10 chemin de la Chapellerie
+33 (0)3-85751902
FAX +33 (0)3-85767511
1/4 - 30/9
camping@louhans-chateaurenaud.fr

1,2ha 53T(100-140m²) 10A CEE

1 A**G**IJKLMOPQ
2 CLRUVWXY
3 AGRU**W**
5 **A**GIJKLMNPUVY
6 DEGK(N 1km)T

A well maintained campsite on the edge of town. Large traditional weekly market on Monday (extra big on first Monday of the month). Louhans is also known for its arcades and its 15th century facades. Within walking distance of the baker (500m).

D996 as far as Louhans then follow signs to the campsite or swimming pool.

CC € 11 *1/4-10/7 27/8-30/9 7=6, 14=11*

N 46°37'51" E 5°13'1"

Louvarel/Champagnat, F-71480 / Bourgogne (Saône-et-Loire)

1902

Le Domaine de Louvarel****
+33 (0)3-85766271
9/4 - 24/9
info@louvarel.com

8ha 110T(80-110m²) 10A CEE

1 ACD**G**IJKLMOPQ
2 ADFJLRVWX
3 BGHJR**W**Z
4 (E+H+Q)
(T+U+V 23/4-24/9)
(Y 18/4-26/9) (Z 23/4-24/9)
5 **AB**EFGIJKLMNPUWXYZ
6 ACDEGJ**K**(N 4km)TV

A campsite with excellent toilet facilities and young landscaping on Lake Louvarel. Since 2011 there has been a heated indoor swimming pool. There is a swimming lake with a sandy beach and a swimming zone that is patrolled in high season. There is also a fishing pond.

A39 exit 9, then follow signs. Campsite is signposted. Or exit Champagnat on the N83 and follow Louvarel or camping signs. Campsite located on the 'Base de Loisirs Louvarel'.

CC € 17 *9/4-4/7 21/8-24/9*

N 46°29'50" E 5°19'30"

Luzy, F-58170 / Bourgogne (Nièvre)

1903

Domaine de la Gagère****
+33 (0)3-86304811
1/4 - 30/9
info@la-gagere.com

5ha 120T(100-120m²) 6A CEE

1 ACD**G**IJKLMNPST
2 KLMRSTVWXY
3 AGHINR
4 (A 1/5-14/9) (C+H) **N** (Q) (R 1/5-30/9) (S 15/5-15/9) (T+U 1/5-15/9) (X) Z
5 **AB**DEFGIJKLMNOPUWZ
6 CDEGIK(N 9km)RV

A lovely naturist campsite high up in the middle of the countryside with extensive views of the Morvan. Guided walking tours to Mont Dône.

From Autun take D981 to Luzy. La Gagère is signposted about 6 km before Luzy on the left. Campsite 3 km uphill on narrow road.

CC € 19 *1/4-2/7 27/8-30/9*

N 46°49'0'' E 4°3'23''

Luzy/Tazilly, F-58170 / Bourgogne (Nièvre)

1904

Airotel Château de Chigy****
route Moulins
+33 (0)3-86301080
23/4 - 30/9
reception@chateaudechigy.com.fr

10ha 100T(100-150m²) 6A CEE

1 ACDGIJKLPQ
2 DIJLRSTVWXY
3 AGHJNQRUW
4 (B 15/6-30/9) (D+Q+R) (T+U+X+Z 4/7-31/8)
5 ABDFGIJKLOP**S**UWZ
6 AEI(N 4,5km)V

Large grounds with very spacious pitches, heated swimming pool, shaded by tall trees. Apartments and chalets for rent, 25 hectare fishing lake, indoor swimming pool in 70 hectares of grounds. Fresh bread available.

In Luzy D973 direction Moulins. Campsite signposted.

CC € 17 *23/4-8/7 25/8-30/9*

N 46°45'28'' E 3°56'39''

Marcenay, F-21330 / Bourgogne (Côte-d'Or)

1905

Camping Les Grèbes du Lac de Marcenay***
5 rue du Lac
+33 (0)3-80816172
1/5 - 30/9
info@campingmarcenaylac.com

3,6ha 90T(80-120m²) 10A

1 ACD**G**IJKLMPQ
2 ADLMRVWXY
3 BGHJKNRU**W**Z
4 (B+G 15/5-30/9) (Q) (X 1/7-25/8)
5 **AB**EGIJKLPUWZ
6 EGJ(N 4,8km)V

Surprisingly complete and natural campsite. Avoid tolls, enjoy back roads! Discover Burgundy: delicious dining, outings, walking, cycling, boating, fishing, good toilet facilities, sheltered, solar pool, play castle, campfires and free WiFi. Call manager Dirk in FR, NL, EN, DE on +33(0)380816172, open 24h.

From Châtillon-sur-Seine follow D965 dir. Tonnerre. After 12 km right to Marcenay. Signposted. From Laignes 4.8 km via D102 to Marcenay. Follow 'Lac' signs here.

CC € 15 *1/5-7/7 29/8-30/9*

N 47°52'12'' E 4°24'17''

Matour, F-71520 / Bourgogne (Saône-et-Loire) 1906

Le Paluet***
2 rue de la Piscine
+33 (0)3-85597092
22/4 - 30/9
lepaluet@matour.fr

3ha 63**T**(80-120m²) 10A CEE

1 ACD**G**IJKLMOPQ
2 DLRTVWXY
3 ABGHJ**M**N**Q**RU**W**
4 (C+H 23/5-31/8) JKN (T+Z 1/7-31/8)
5 **AB**FGIJKLOPUWZ
6 AEGHJ**K**(N 0,3km)V

A family campsite with sunny and shaded places next to a free municipal swimming pool. Located in the beautiful area known as 'Little Switzerland'. Hiking trails in the area. Within walking distance of the centre and all shops. 30 minutes free WiFi close to the campsite reception. Free sauna.

Follow the camping signs in the town.

€15 *22/4-1/7 1/9-30/9 7=6, 14=10*

N 46°18'16'' E 4°28'43''

Meursault, F-21190 / Bourgogne (Côte-d'Or) 1907

La Grappe d'Or***
2 route de Volnay
+33 (0)3-80212248
6/4 - 15/10
info@camping-meursault.com

3,5ha 131**T**(80-100m²) 12A CEE

1 ACD**G**IJKLM**P**Q
2 FIJKRVWXY
3 AB**F**GHJK**M**R
4 (B+G 15/6-15/9) J(Q) (R 16/5-15/9) (T+U+Y 15/4-30/9) Z
5 **AB**DEFGJLNOPUW
6 CDFGH**K**(N 0,5km)OR

A quiet terraced campsite with wonderful views of the Meursault vineyards. Also suitable as a stopover campsite.

A6 exit Beaune. In Beaune-Centre take the D974 in the direction of Chalon-sur-Saône. Follow the camping signs in Meursault.

€17 *6/4-30/6 1/9-15/10*

N 46°59'8'' E 4°46'6''

Montbard, F-21500 / Bourgogne (Côte-d'Or) 1908

Municipal de Montbard 'Les Treilles'***
Michel Servet
+33 (0)3-80926950
26/3 - 30/10
camping.lestreilles@montbard.com

2,5ha 78**T**(100-150m²) 16A CEE

1 ACD**G**IJKLM**P**Q
2 KRUVWXY
3 ABGHJMRU**W**
4 (A 1/7-31/8) (C+F+H 26/3-31/8,15/9-30/10) J**KLN**(Q+R+T 1/6-30/9) (Z)
5 **AB**DFGIJKLMNPUWXYZ
6 ACDEGHK(N 1km)V

A campsite with large, shaded pitches in a region that is rich in historical heritage and gastronomy. Located near a swimming pool complex (free entry for campers, closed from 1/9-15/9), this is an ideal place to stay by the Canal de Bourgogne. Bakery service, bar, WiFi, tennis, volleyball, billiards.

Follow D980 around Montbard town. Turn off to the north at sharp bend between the Canal de Bourgogne and the D5 to Laignes. Signposted 'Camping/Piscine'.

€15 *26/3-3/7 22/8-30/10*

N 47°37'52'' E 4°19'56''

Montsauche-les-Settons, F-58230 / Bourgogne (Nièvre)

1909

Les Mésanges***
Rive Gauche
+33 (0)3-86845577
14/5 - 15/9
campinglesmesanges@orange.fr

5ha 100T(100-200m²) 16A

1 ACD**G**IJKLMOPQ
2 ADKLMRTVWXY
3 BGHJNRWZ
4 (Q+R) (U+V 1/7-1/9)
5 **AB**EFGIJKLPUVXYZ
6 EGK(N 3km)T

A peaceful campsite with large, fenced, well maintained pitches, opposite Lac des Settons in the heart of the Morvan. Plenty of walking and cycling routes in the rural surroundings. You will find relaxation here. Clean toilet facilities, large fishing lake.

Take the D977 bis from Saulieu to Montsauche-les-Settons. In Montsauche follow the direction of Lac des Settons, then Rive Gauche. Then follow camping signs.

CC € 15 *14/5-7/7 24/8-15/9*

N 47°10'54'' E 4°3'10''

Nevers, F-58000 / Bourgogne (Nièvre)

1910

Camping De Nevers
rue de la Jonction
+33 (0)3-86364075
7/3 - 6/11
campingdenevers@orange.fr

1,6ha 73T(85-110m²) 10A CEE

1 ACD**G**IJKL**P**Q
2 CFMRSTUVWXY
3 AGJ**W**
4 (Q) (T 1/7-31/8) (Z)
5 **AB**DFGIJKLMNPUXYZ
6 ACEGJ(N 1km)

A campsite with spacious shaded pitches on the banks of the Loire opposite the town centre. The town is within walking distance and is suitable for cyclists, anglers and canoeists.

A77 exit 37 direction Nevers. Campsite is in Nevers on the right before the bridge. Signposted. In Nevers follow Moulins signs.

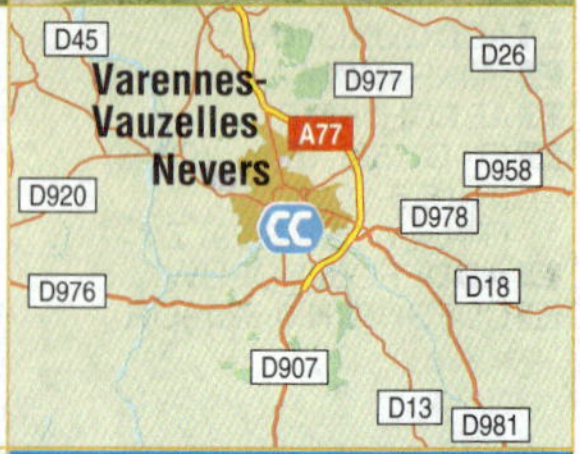

CC € 17 *7/3-3/7 20/8-6/11 7=6, 14=11*

N 46°58'56'' E 3°9'39''

Ouroux-en-Morvan, F-58230 / Bourgogne (Nièvre)

1911

Les Genêts du Morvan***
9 route de Lormes
+33 (0)3-86782288
15/4 - 30/9
camping.ouroux@orange.fr

1,7ha 43T(80-120m²) 10A CEE

1 ACDGIJKLMPQ
2 KRVWXY
3 AGR
4 (B 15/5-15/9) (Q) (T+U+Z 1/7-31/8)
5 **AB**EFGJLNPUWZ
6 EG**I**JM(N 0,6km)RT

A rurally located campsite with lovely panoramic views. Good spacious pitches with dividing hedges.

Take the D37 from the D978 Château-Chinon then follow D17. From Lormes follow the D17. Campsite signposted in Ouroux.

CC € 13 *15/4-1/7 28/8-30/9 14=12*

N 47°11'19'' E 3°56'21''

Paray-le-Monial, F-71600 / Bourgogne (Saône-et-Loire)

1912

de Mambré****
19 rue du Gué Léger
+33 (0)3-85888920
7/5 - 1/10
camping.plm@gmail.com

6ha 141**T**(80-100m²) 10A CEE

1 ACD**G**IJLPQ
2 FRTVWXY
3 ABGJKNR
4 (B 15/5-1/10) (G 1/6-1/10) (Q) (R 1/7-31/8) Z
5 **AB**DFGIJKLMPUW
6 AEG**JK**(N 1km)V

A shaded campsite in a parkland setting at the edge of the historical town of Paray-le-Monial. Shaded and sunny pitches. Car and cycle trips possible in the surrounding area. Good cycling opportunities along the canal (Voie verte). Dutch owner.

Leave the N70 and N79 at Paray-le Monial-Sud. The campsite is signposted along Canal-du-Centre on the D979 on the edge of Paray-le-Monial.

CC € 15 *7/5-3/7 22/8-1/10*

N 46°27'26'' E 4°6'18''

Pouilly-en-Auxois, F-21320 / Bourgogne (Côte-d'Or)

1913

Camping Vert Auxois***
15 rue du Vert Auxois
+33 (0)3-80907189
26/3 - 2/10
contact@camping-vert-auxois.fr

1,5ha 66**T**(80-100m²) 16A CEE

1 ACD**G**IJKLM**P**Q
2 CFGKLMRUVWXY
3 **F**HIJU**W**
4 (Q 15/6-15/9) (T 25/5-15/9) (U+X) Z
5 **AB**DGIJKLMNOPUXYZ
6 AEGIJ(N 0,5km)ORT

A small, peaceful campsite in the countryside next to a canal and a stone's throw from the town. The pitches are separated by high hedges.

Campsite located in Pouilly-en-Auxois and signposted.

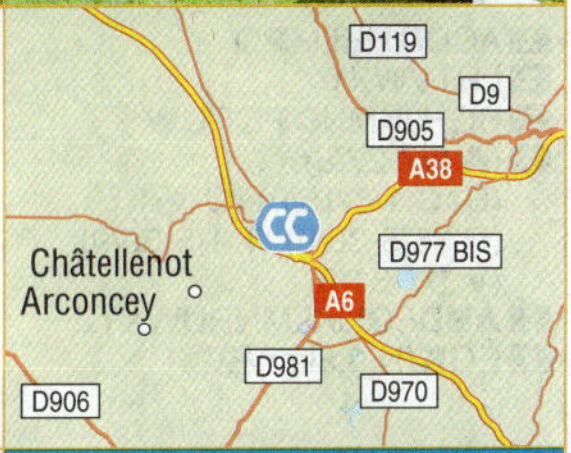

CC € 17 *1/5-8/7 25/8-2/10*

N 47°15'55'' E 4°32'56''

Prémeaux/Prissey, F-21700 / Bourgogne (Côte-d'Or)

1914

Du Moulin de Prissey
14, rue du Moulin de Prissey
+33 (0)3-80623115
FAX +33 (0)3-80613729
4/4 - 15/10
cpg.moulin.prissey@free.fr

1,1ha 64**T**(83-120m²) 6-10A CEE

1 AC**G**HIJKLMOPST
2 DFILRVWXY
3 AGHIJR**W**
4 (Q+T+U 15/5-15/9)
5 **A**GIJKLMNOPUVXYZ
6 CEG(N 4km)T

A very peacefully located level campsite among the vineyards. The pitches are reasonably shaded. Snacks and a small restaurant. Ideal starting point for visiting the wine region.

On A31 motorway between Dijon and Beaune take the Nuits-St-Georges exit. Take the D974 from here to Prémeaux/Prissey. Then follow camping signs.

CC € 15 *4/4-3/7 22/8-30/9*

N 47°6'13'' E 4°56'29''

Santenay, F-21590 / Bourgogne (Côte-d'Or)

1915

Camping des Sources Santenay***
avenue des Sources
+33 (0)3-80206655
25/3 - 23/10
camping-de-santenay@orange.fr

3,1ha 150T(90-120m²) 6A CEE

1 ACGIJKLMOPQ
2 LRTVWX
3 BGHJMR
4 (C+H 1/6-1/9) (Q+R 1/5-15/10)
5 ABGIJKLMNPU
6 ACEGK(N 1,5km)

A family campsite in the middle of the Côte de Beaune vineyards. Next to the municipal swimming pool. Large pitches in the shade of several trees.

A6 exit 24.1 Beaune-Centre. In Beaune D974 direction Chalon-sur-Saône to Santenay. Follow camping signs in Santenay.

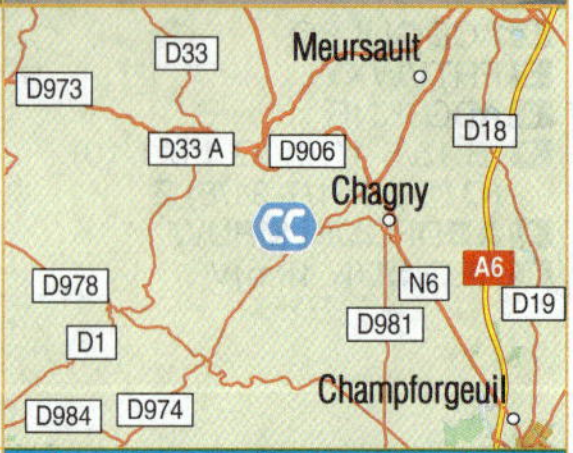

CC € 15 25/3-3/7 20/8-23/10 7=6, 14=11

N 46°54'26" E 4°41'8"

Saulieu, F-21210 / Bourgogne (Côte-d'Or)

1916

Camping de Saulieu***
Route Nationale
+33 (0)3-80641619
7/3 - 6/11
camping.saulieu@wanadoo.fr

6ha 68T(100-110m²) 10A CEE

1 ACDGIJKLMPQ
2 LRTVWXY
3 BGHJKMNOPQRUW
4 (A 9/7-27/8) (B+G 1/6-15/9) (Q) (R 15/5-30/9) (T 1/5-30/9) (V 1/7-31/8)
5 ABDFGIJKLMNPUWXYZ
6 EGK(N 0,8km)RV

A campsite located near the town with large, sunny camping pitches and a swimming pool. Countless recreational possibilities in the immediate vicinity.

Campsite located near the north exit of the town on the N6.

CC € 15 7/3-3/7 20/8-6/11 7=6, 14=11

N 47°17'22" E 4°13'26"

St. Boil, F-71390 / Bourgogne (Saône-et-Loire)

1917

Moulin de Collonge****
+33 (0)3-85440032
FAX +33 (0)3-85440040
1/4 - 30/9
millofcollonge@wanadoo.fr

1ha 50T(80-100m²) 6A CEE

1 ACDGIJKLMPQ
2 ADLMRVWX
3 AGHJKNRUWZ
4 (E+H+Q+R+U+V+X) Z
5 ABDEFGIJKLNPUWZ
6 AEGJ(N 1,5km)OV

A small, flower-filled campsite with an indoor heated swimming pool, a lake for swimming, a small fish pond and pizzeria. Ideal departure point for cyclists (voie verte) to discover the Route des Vins from Beaune to Cluny.

On the D981 at the southern end of St. Boil take the small V5 road and follow the camping signs.

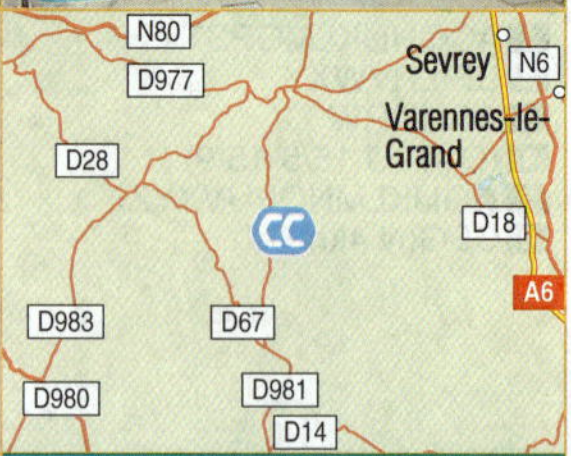

CC € 17 1/4-10/7 27/8-30/9 7=6, 14=12, 21=18

N 46°38'47" E 4°41'41"

St. Honoré-les-Bains, F-58360 / Bourgogne (Nièvre)

1918

Camping et gîtes des Bains***
15 ave Jean Mermoz
+33 (0)3-86307344
1/4 - 31/10
campinglesbains@gmail.com

4,5ha 130T(80-100m²) 10A CEE

1 ACD**G**IJKLMPQ
2 CLRTVWXY
3 BGHJ**MNQ**RUV**W**
4 (B+G 8/6-15/9) J**OP**
(Q+R+T+U+X) Z
5 **AB**DEFGIJKLMNPUVWZ
6 AEG**K**(N 0,8km)ORV

The campsite is located in St. Honoré village. The site has pitches marked out by trees and bushes. The area offers plenty of chance to take in the nature: rest and space.

In St. Honoré-Les-Bains direction Vandenesse, follow signs to Des Bains. The campsite is 200 metres to the left after the park.

CC € 15 *1/4-2/7 27/8-31/10*

N 46°54'23'' E 3°49'42''

St. Léger-de-Fougeret, F-58120 / Bourgogne (Nièvre)

1919

Sites & Paysages Etang de la Fougeraie****
Hameau du Champs
+33 (0)3-86851185
2/4 - 1/10
info@campingfougeraie.fr

10ha 71T(90-600m²) 10A CEE

1 ACD**G**IJKLMPRS
2 BCDIJKLMORTVWXY
3 ABHJR**WZ**
4 (C+H) K
(Q+R+S+U+V+X+Z)
5 **AB**CEFGHJKLNPUWZ
6 CEGIJ(N 11km)ORTV

A friendly family campsite at an altitude of 440 metres in the Morvan regional nature reserve, located by a small lake with a beach for swimming and fishing. Space, rest, nature, calm, walking tours, table tennis, jeu de boules. Bar, restaurant and terrace with splendid views.

From Château-Chinon D27 direction Onlay. After about 4 km turn right onto the D157 towards St. Léger-de-Fougeret. Follow the camping signs for 2 km in St. Léger.

CC € 17 *2/4-1/7 28/8-1/10*

N 47°0'23'' E 3°54'18''

St. Léger-sous-Beuvray, F-71990 / Bourgogne (Saône-et-Loire)

1920

De La Boutière
La Boutière
+33 (0)6-80408128
15/4 - 15/10
camping@la-boutiere.com

2ha 36T(100-150m²) 10A CEE

1 A**G**IJKLM**P**Q
2 RSVWX
3 GHJNR**W**
5 **A**DGIJKLMNOPUXYZ
6 ADEGK(N 0,6km)O

You will experience the nostalgia of camping on this small, rural campsite. Within walking distance of a village, in the Morvan regional park. A paradise for walkers. More than 30 marked out routes. Plenty of opportunities close by for anglers. Free WiFi.

From Autun to St. Léger-sous-Beuvray on the D681 direction Moulins-Luzy. After 4 km turn right towards St. Léger (D3) and continue until the campsite is signposted.

CC € 15 *15/4-8/7 25/8-15/10*

N 46°55'54'' E 4°6'4''

St. Sauveur-en-Puisaye, F-89520 / Bourgogne (Yonne) — 1921

Parc des Joumiers***
+33 (0)3-86456628
FAX +33 (0)3-86456027
1/4 - 15/10
@ campinglesjoumiers@laposte.net

23ha 100**T**(150m²) 16A

1 ACD**G**IJKLM**P**Q
2 ADKLRVWXY
3 AB**F**GHJNRU**W**
4 (C 1/6-30/9) (Q+T+U+X) Z
5 **A**DGIJKLMNOPUXYZ
6 CEGK(N 1,5km)OT

Quiet, customer-friendly family campsite located on a fishing lake. Swimming pool and playground, as well as a restaurant with a basic menu will complete your holiday. A visit to Château Fort 'Guédelon' (16/3 - 1/11) is one of the possibilities.

Take the D965 from Auxerre. In Mezilles follow the D7 towards St. Sauveur. The campsite is located just before the village.

CC €15 *1/4-5/7 29/8-15/10*

N 47°37'51'' E 3°11'33''

Tonnerre, F-89700 / Bourgogne (Yonne) — 1922

La Cascade*
8 avenue Aristide Briand
+33 (0)3-86551544
2/4 - 13/11
@ contact@revea-vacances.com

2ha 54**T**(100m²) 6A CEE

1 ACD**G**IJKL**P**Q
2 BCLRTWXY
3 ABGHJNRU
4 (C) (Q 1/7-30/8) (R+T)
5 **A**DGIJKLMNPUWZ
6 CDEGJ(N 1km)TV

Spacious campsite with large, non-marked-out pitches along a river, close to the centre of Tonnerre. There's a railway line (TGV) next to the campsite.

Located between the towns of Troyes and Auxerre. In Tonnerre the campsite is signposted.

CC €13 *2/4-1/7 1/9-13/11 7=6*

N 47°51'36'' E 3°59'3''

Tournus, F-71700 / Bourgogne (Saône-et-Loire) — 1923

Camping de Tournus***
14 rue des Canes
+33 (0)3-85511658
1/4 - 30/9
@ camping-tournus@orange.fr

1,5ha 94**T**(80-100m²) 10A CEE

1 ACDFIJKLMOPST
2 CFRUVWX
3 AJKR**W**
4 (**B**+**G** 1/7-31/8) **J** (Q+T+U) Z
5 **AB**FGIJKLMNOPUVWZ
6 CDEGK(N 1km)OV

A campsite with spacious pitches, close to the centre of the historic town of Tournus, famous for its many restaurants, 1000 year old abbey and the starting point of the Voie Bleue cycle path along the Saône. Most suitable as a stopover campsite.

A6 exit 27 Tournus. Follow D906 towards Tournus. Turn off opposite the station. Campsite signposted.

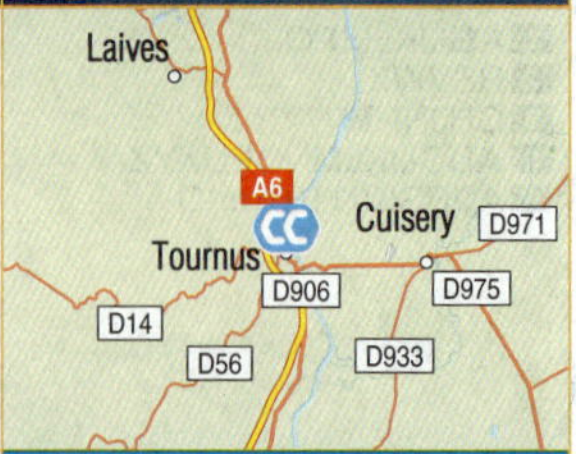

CC €17 *1/4-3/7 22/8-30/9 7=6, 14=12*

N 46°34'25'' E 4°54'34''

Uchizy, F-71700 / Bourgogne (Saône-et-Loire)

1924

Le National 6**
Port d'Uchizy
+33 (0)3-85405390
1/4 - 30/9
camping.uchizylen6@wanadoo.fr

6ha 95**T**(100m²) 6A CEE

1 A**G**IJKLMPQ
2 CLRVWXY
3 AGJRU**WX**
4 (B+G 15/5-15/9)
(Q+S+T+U 15/4-15/9)
(V 1/7-31/8) (X 15/4-15/9) Z
5 **A**EFGIJKLMNPUV
6 EJ(N 5km)V

A quiet campsite located on the banks of the Saône with shaded pitches, swimming pool and restaurant.

Campsite on left of the D906, near Uchizy (on the banks of the Saône) when arriving from the north. Follow camping signs.

CC €17 *1/4-15/6 1/9-30/9*

N 46°29'16'' E 4°54'45''

Vandenesse-en-Auxois, F-21320 / Bourgogne (Côte-d'Or)

1925

Du Lac de Panthier****
1 chemin du Lac
+33 (0)3-80492194
FAX +33 (0)3-80492580
8/4 - 9/10
info@lac-de-panthier.com

7ha 210**T**(110-150m²) 6A CEE

1 ACD**G**IJKLM**P**RS
2 ADFJKLPRTVWXY
3 ABC**F**GHIJK**P**RUV**W**Z
4 (B 15/6-15/9) (F)
(G 15/6-15/9) JMN
(Q+R+T+U+V+X+Y+Z)
5 **AB**DEFGIJKLMNOPQUWX
YZ
6 ABCDEGH**IK**(N 4km)ORTV

A campsite located between a lake and the edge of a wood. Pitches marked out by hedges with sufficient shade, some of which have a view of the lake. There is also an indoor swimming pool and a panoramic bar.

Leave motorway at A6 and A38 intersection near Pouilly-en-Auxois. Then follow Dijon, Créancey and camping signs.

CC €17 *8/4-8/7 25/8-30/9*

N 47°14'13'' E 4°37'41''

Vermenton, F-89270 / Bourgogne (Yonne)

1926

Les Coullemières***
route de Coullemières
FAX +33 (0)3-86815302
1/4 - 30/9
contact@
camping-vermenton.com

1ha 47**T**(80-120m²) 6A CEE

1 ACD**G**IJKLPQ
2 ACGLRTUVWXY
3 BGMNRU**WX**
4 (Q+R)
5 **AB**DGIJKLMNOPUVW
6 CDEGK(N 1km)TV

Marked-out pitches with bushes and many trees and therefore plenty of shade. Takes part in a competition for campsite with the most flowers every year. Within walking distance from the old town Vermenton with sights such as a 12th century church.

On the N6 Auxerre-Avalon the campsite is clearly signposted before Vermenton. Pay attention to the name. Site is located behind a small train station.

CC €13 *2/4-24/6 27/8-30/9*

N 47°39'31'' E 3°43'51''

Vincelles, F-89290 / Bourgogne (Yonne) — 1927

Les Ceriselles****
route de Vincelottes
+33 (0)3-86425047
1/4 - 30/9
camping@cc-payscoulangeois.fr

2,5ha 76T(90-150m²) 10A CEE

1 ACD**G**IJKLPQ
2 CGRTVWX
3 BGHJKL**M**N**Q**RU**W**
4 (**E**+Q+R+T+U+X) Z
5 **AB**DFGIJKLMNOPUXYZ
6 ACDEGIK(N 0,2km)TV

Les Ceriselles is a lovely quiet 4 star campsite full of flowers in the heart of the Burgundy vineyards and among cherry trees. Hallmarks:'Camping Qualité' and 'Tourisme et Handicap'. The site is located alongside the Yonne, Canal du Nivernais with its cycle routes, not far from lake (4 ha) offering plenty of opportunities for anglers. You can visit the lovely countryside of Sud de l'Yonne.

South of Auxerre, 10 km from the D606. Campsite signposted from Vincelles.

CC € 15 *1/4-10/7 27/8-30/9*

N 47°42'25'' E 3°38'8''

Arbois, F-39600 / Franche-Comté (Jura) — 1928

Les Vignes**
5 rue de la piscine
+33 (0)3-84661412
15/3 - 15/10
campinglesvignes@hotmail.fr

5,2ha 121T(100-120m²) 10A CEE

1 ACD**G**IJKLPQ
2 IJRTUVWX
3 AGHJNRU
4 (**C**+**G** 1/6-7/9)
(Q+R+T+X+Z)
5 FGIJKLMNPUXYZ
6 CDEG**JK**(N 0,8km)

At walking distance from the welcoming village Arbois. Large pitches (paved if required), marked out with hedges and bushes. Restaurant and bar. From 1 June to mid-September you can use the heated 50-metre pool for a one-time payment p.p. per stay of 2 Euros. Many options for cycling and walking, fishing and swimming in the rivulets and Jura lakes at a short distance.

Arbois is located on the N83 between Besançon and Poligny. Campsite signposted in the town.

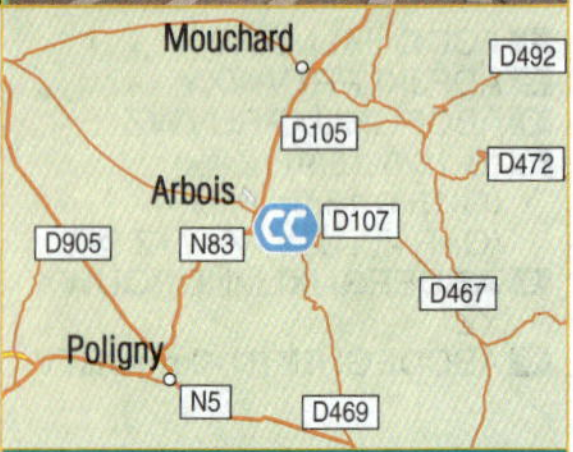

CC € 13 *15/3-30/6 27/8-15/10*

N 46°54'13'' E 5°47'11''

Bonlieu, F-39130 / Franche-Comté (Jura) — 1929

Camping L'Abbaye***
2 route du Lac
+33 (0)3-84255704
1/5 - 30/9
camping.abbaye@wanadoo.fr

4ha 80T(100-120m²) 10A CEE

1 ACD**G**IJKLMOPQ
2 CJRUVWXY
3 BGHJN**OP**R**W**
4 (Q+R+T+U+V+X+Y+Z)
5 **AB**FGJKLNPUZ
6 ACDEGK(N 5km)V

A terraced campsite with spacious pitches marked out by bushes and hedges. Lovely views of the cliffs. Ideal starting point for walks and cycle trips. The campsite is only a few minutes from the Herrisson waterfalls and has an excellent restaurant with the 'Tourisme' and 'Maître-restaurateur' hallmarks.

From Clairvaux-les-Lacs continue on to Geneva on the N78 through Bonlieu. Turn right at end of built up area about 1 km further to 'Lac de Bonlieu' and the campsite.

CC € 15 *1/5-8/7 1/9-30/9*

N 46°35'48'' E 5°52'17''

Chalezeule/Besançon, F-25220 / Franche-Comté (Doubs)

1930

Camping de Besançon - La Plage***
12 route de Belfort
+33 (0)3-81880426
15/3 - 31/10
@ contact@campingdebesancon.com

2,5ha 100**T**(75-120m²) 16A CEE

1 ACD**G**IJKLMPQ
2 FGRUWXY
3 A**F**GHJN**Q**R**W**
4 (C+H 1/7-30/8) (Q+T 20/6-30/8)
5 **AB**CDEFGHIJKLMNOPUVWZ
6 ACDFGIK(N 0,2km)TV

A campsite with a good location for visiting the World Heritage Site of Besançon. There are many opportunities for sports in and around the campsite. Renovated toilet facilities. Fast connection to centre of Besançon with new tram.

RD683, Belfort-Besançon. Campsite signposted from there.

CC € 17 *15/3-5/7 22/8-31/10 7=6*

N 47°15'57'' E 6°4'18''

Champagnole, F-39300 / Franche-Comté (Jura)

1931

Camping de Boyse***
20 rue Georges Vallerey
+33 (0)3-84520032
FAX +33 (0)3-84520116
1/4 - 30/9
@ camping.boyse@wanadoo.fr

7ha 156**T**(100-150m²) 10A CEE

1 ACD**G**IJKLMPQ
2 CJLORVWXY
3 ABFGHJ**M**NQRU**WX**
4 (C+H 1/6-30/9) (Q) (T+U+V+X+Z 1/4-31/8)
5 **AB**FGIJKLMNOPRU
6 CEGHJ(N 0,3km)TV

A slightly undulating campsite on the edge of town. Mostly shaded pitches which are spacious and marked out. Within walking distance of a large department store. 15 km from some waterfalls and caves. Swimming pool and very good restaurant with local dishes near the campsite.

From Poligny N5 to Champagnole. Now take the D5 towards Lons-le-Saunier and follow camping signs.

CC € 15 *1/4-8/7 27/8-30/9*

N 46°44'48'' E 5°53'57''

Clairvaux-les-Lacs, F-39130 / Franche-Comté (Jura)

1932

Le Grand Lac***
chemin du Langard
+33 (0)3-84252214
FAX +33 (0)3-84252620
14/5 - 25/9
@ grandlac@odesia.eu

6ha 147**T**(80-100m²) 10A CEE

1 ACD**F**IJKLMO**P**Q
2 ADJLMRTVWXY
3 AGHJNRU**WZ**
4 (C+H 1/7-31/8) (Q+R 23/5-26/9)
5 **AB**EFGIJK**L**MNPRUVZ
6 ACEGJ(N 0,6km)RT

A quiet family campsite with direct access to the lake and the public beach (patrolled in high season). Within walking distance of the centre. Gently sloping grounds with mostly shaded pitches. The grounds are fenced and access to the beach is via a gate with an entry code (safe for small children). There is a pool on the campsite.

Enter Clairvaux-les-Lacs via the D678. Follow the D118 then the campsite signs.

CC € 13 *14/5-8/7 26/8-25/9*

N 46°34'6'' E 5°45'19''

Clairvaux-les-Lacs, F-39130 / Franche-Comté (Jura) **1933**

Yelloh! Village Fayolan****
BP 52
☎ +33 (0)3-84258852
FAX +33 (0)3-84252620
4/5 - 11/9
@ lefayolan@odesia.eu

17ha 308**T**(80-140m²) 10A CEE

1 ACD**F**IJKLMO**P**Q
2 ADJLRTVWXY
3 ABGHJNRU**WZ**
4 (**A**+C+F+H) JLNP
(Q+S+T+U+V+X+Y+Z)
5 **AB**EFGIJKLNPRUWXYZ
6 CEGIK(N 0,8km)ORTV

An open terraced zone, a shaded woodland zone and a beach zone in the heart of the Jura. Swimming in a lovely open air pool with a slide, in the indoor pool (with hydromassage, hammam and sauna) or in the lake with its own beach. There is an adventure park next to the site.

Drive into Clairvaux-les-Lacs on the N78. Follow D118 the follow 'campings' sign.

CC € 17 *4/5-8/7 25/8-11/9*

N 46°33'51" E 5°45'23"

Cromary, F-70190 / Franche-Comté (Haute-Saône) **1934**

l'Esplanade**
rue du Pont
☎ +33 (0)3-84918200
1/4 - 30/9
@ lesplanade@ymail.com

2,2ha 37**T**(100-180m²) 4-8A

1 A**G**IJKLMP**P**Q
2 CKLMNRVWXY
3 AGN**OP**RX
4 (A 15/7-20/8)
(Q+R+T+Z)
5 **AB**GJKMNPU
6 EGJ(N 8km)TV

Campsite is located in a rural area with views of the Jurassic mountains. Spacious pitches with shade. You can fish, canoe, walk and cycle or swim in the river. Cafeteria and shop on site. 1 Euro surcharge for 8 Amps. Free WiFi.

On the N57 between Vesoul and Besançon, about 9 km beyond Rioz, take the exit right to Voray and Cromary in the opposite direction on the N57 (about 5 km). Then take D276 to They and Cromary. Campsite signposted from the N57. Near Cromary center.

CC € 15 *1/4-30/6 1/9-30/9*

N 47°21'32" E 6°4'43"

Dole, F-39100 / Franche-Comté (Jura) **1935**

Du Pasquier***
18 chemin Thévenot
☎ +33 (0)3-84720261
FAX +33 (0)3-84792344
15/3 - 25/10
@ lola@camping-le-pasquier.com

2ha 120**T**(80-110m²) 10A

1 ACD**G**IJLMPQ
2 CFLORVWXY
3 BGKR**W**
4 (C 1/6-15/9) (Q 15/4-25/10)
(R) (T+U+Z 1/7-31/8)
5 **AB**FGIJKLMNOPUW
6 CDEGK(N 1,0km)OQT

A friendly and attractive campsite 15 minutes' walk from the town centre. The town of Dole is a well-preserved historic town, the birthplace of Louis Pasteur.

From the A36 take the Dole exit. In Dole follow 'camping' or 'stade-camping' signs.

CC € 15 *15/3-3/7 27/8-24/10*

N 47°5'22" E 5°30'11"

Doucier, F-39130 / Franche-Comté (Jura) — 1936

Domaine de Chalain****
+33 (0)3-84257878
FAX +33 (0)3-84257006
29/4 - 19/9
chalain@chalain.com

30ha 417T(90-120m²) 10A CEE

1 ACDGIJKLOPQ
2 ADJLORVWXY
3 ABEGHJMNQRUWZ
4 (B 1/6-15/9) (F 21/4-13/9) (H 25/4-15/9) IJKLNP (Q+S+T+U+V+X+Z)
5 ABDEFGJLNPU
6 ACDEGHIKM(N 3km)OQRTV

A campsite located by a lake and surrounded by a richly wooded and hilly landscape. An excellent departure point for discovering the area: rivers, panoramas, waterfalls. Swimming pool.

From Champagnole via the D471 direction Lons-le-Saunier. Via the D27 direction Clairvaux-les-Lacs. Follow the camping signs in the village of Doucier.

CC € 17 29/4-4/7 1/9-19/9

N 46°39'51'' E 5°48'50''

Doucier, F-39130 / Franche-Comté (Jura) — 1937

Les Merilles***
rue des 3 Lacs
+33 (0)3-84257306
1/4 - 30/9
camping.lesmerilles@wanadoo.fr

2ha 96T(80-140m²) 10A CEE

1 ACDGIJKLPQ
2 CLRVWXY
3 BGHJLNOPRUW
4 (A 1/7-30/8) (C+H 15/5-30/9) (Q 1/7-15/9) (R 15/6-30/9) (T+U+Z 15/6-15/9)
5 ABDEFGIJKLMNOPRSUVZ
6 ACEGK(N 0,5km)OTV

A friendly campsite close to lakes and waterfalls. The village with various restaurants and shops is within walking distance. You can walk and cycle in beautiful and surprising countryside. You will find information about numerous trips out in the Jura at the reception.

In Doucier via the D27 follow signs to Clairvaux-les-Lacs. Campsite located 150 metres from the outskirts of Doucier.

CC € 15 1/4-3/7 28/8-30/9

N 46°39'6'' E 5°46'29''

Ecrille, F-39270 / Franche-Comté (Jura) — 1938

La Faz***
4 Pont de Vaux
+33 (0)3-84254027
1/5 - 30/9
camping.la.faz@sfr.fr

6ha 99T(100-150m²) 6A CEE

1 AFIJKLMOPRS
2 CLRVXY
3 BGHNRUW
4 (B 1/6-30/9) (Q+R) (T+U+Z 15/6-31/8)
5 AGIJKNPUZ
6 CEJ(N 1,5km)RTV

A campsite located in extensive grounds by a river and a stone's throw from Lake Vouglans. The area is perfect for rest, relaxation and nature walks. Pitches marked out by hedges. Swimming pool on the campsite.

From Lons-le-Saunier D52 direction Orgelet via the D678 and then D52e and D52 as far as Orgelet. Take the D470 and turn immediately right to Ecrille. Follow camping signs.

CC € 13 1/5-6/7 29/8-30/9

N 46°30'35'' E 5°37'14''

Huanne-Montmartin, F-25680 / Franche-Comté (Doubs)

1939

Du Bois de Reveuge****
route de Rougemont
+33 (0)3-81843860
FAX +33 (0)3-81844404
30/4 - 3/9
@ info@campingduboisdereveuge.com

24ha 168T(80-180m²) 6-16A CEE

1 ACD**G**IJKLMPRS
2 ABDFIJKLMRTUVWXY
3 BC**F**GHJKN**OP**QRUVW
4 (C+F+H) IJM (Q+R+T+U) (V 1/7-27/8) Z
5 **AB**FGIJKLMNPUVWXYZ
6 CDEG**IK**M(N 5km)ORTV

A lovely rural 4 star campsite with an indoor swimming pool. You can go fishing, cycling, play minigolf or visit towns (Belfort, Mont Beliard, Besançon) and caves or castles.

From A36 exit Baume-les-Dames, follow route Villersexel. Follow signs to the Huanne campsite.

CC € 17 *30/4-1/7 28/8-3/9*

N 47°26'26'' E 6°20'36''

La Tour-du-Meix, F-39270 / Franche-Comté (Jura)

1940

Domaine du Surchauffant***
Le Pont de la Pyle
+33 (0)3-84254108
FAX +33 (0)3-84355688
29/4 - 19/9
@ info@camping-surchauffant.fr

3ha 156T(80-110m²) 10A CEE

1 ACD**G**IJKLMOPQ
2 ADJLRVWXY
3 ABGHIJRU**W**Z
4 (C+G+Q+R+T+U+V+X+Y+Z)
5 **AB**EFGIJKLMNPUXZ
6 CEGH**K**(N 5km)QRTV

An extensive campsite sloping down to the lake. Marked out pitches, some with shade. Various watersports possibilities in the swimming pool and in the lake.

From Lons-le-Saunier take the N78 then the D52. In Orgelet take D470 towards St. Claude. Follow camping signs.

CC € 13 *29/4-4/7 24/8-19/9*

N 46°31'24'' E 5°40'27''

Leval, F-90110 / Franche-Comté (Territoire-de-Belfort)

1941

Flower Camping du Lac de la Seigneurie***
3 rue de la Seigneurie
+33 (0)3-84230013
1/4 - 31/10
@ camping-du-lac-de-la-seigneurie@orange.fr

3,8ha 77T(90-360m²) 6-10A

1 ACD**G**IJKLMPQ
2 BDFMRTUVXY
3 B**F**GHJNR**W**
4 (C+H 1/6-30/9) (Q+R+U+X) Z
5 **AB**IJKLMNOPUVWZ
6 CDEG**J**(N 5km)

A peaceful campsite on the shores of 'Lac de la Seigneurie'. 20 minutes from Belfort and Mulhouse and 25 minutes from Ballon d'Alsace. A natural domain with plenty of outdoor activities 20 minutes away. The restaurant next to the campsite is open every day except Monday. New heated outdoor swimming pool.

E36 exit 14.1 'Fontaine', third exit on roundabout D60A. Next roundabout 1st exit D12, turn right onto the D83. Campsite signposted from there, located on the D11.

CC € 15 *1/4-30/6 17/8-31/10* 7=6, 14=12

N 47°44'9'' E 7°0'58''

Levier, F-25270 / Franche-Comté (Doubs) — 1942

Camping de la Forêt***
route de Septfontaine
+33 (0)3-81895346
25/4 - 18/9
camping@camping-dela-foret.com

2ha 67T(100-120m²) 6-10A CEE

1 ACD**G**IJKLMO**P**RS
2 LRVWXY
3 BGHJNRU
4 (A 8/7-31/8) (C 1/6-15/9) (Q+R+U+Z 1/7-31/8)
5 **AB**EFGIJKLMNPUWZ
6 EGJ**K**(N 0,5km)ORT

Family friendly, very well-maintained campsite located on a plateau with direct access to a wooded walking area. 500 metres from a supermarket. Cycling opportunities from the campsite. Mushroom picking in September in the woods around the campsite. Lovely heated pool.

Levier is located on the D72 between Salins-les-Bains and Pontarlier. The campsite is located just 1 km northeast from the towncentre. Along the D41 direction Septfontaine.

CC € 15 *25/4-8/7 27/8-18/9*

N 46°57'35'' E 6°7'58''

Lons-le-Saunier, F-39000 / Franche-Comté (Jura) — 1943

La Marjorie****
640 boulevard de l'Europe
+33 (0)3-84242694
FAX +33 (0)3-84240840
1/4 - 15/10
info@camping-marjorie.com

7,5ha 192T(100-120m²) 10A CEE

1 ACD**G**IJKLMOPQ
2 CFGLRUVWXY
3 AB**F**GHJNRU
4 (A 1/7-21/8) (Q+R+T+U+Z)
5 **AB**DEFGIJKLMNPUWXYZ
6 CDEG**IJK**(N 0,5km)ORTV

A neat campsite with pitches marked out by hedges. Near the town of Lons with its health resort. Free swimming in the municipal indoor heated swimming pool (200m) if staying a minimum of 5 days.

A39, exit 7 from the north, 23 km on the dual carriageway (N83). Exit 8 from the south, 9 km op N78. Follow campsite signs.

CC € 15 *1/4-5/7 1/9-15/10*

N 46°41'3'' E 5°34'7''

Malbuisson, F-25160 / Franche-Comté (Doubs) — 1944

Les Fuvettes***
24 route de la Plage des Perrières
+33 (0)3-81693150
1/4 - 30/9
les-fuvettes@wanadoo.fr

6ha 200T(80-140m²) 6A CEE

1 ACD**G**IJKLMOPRS
2 ADORVWXY
3 ABDGHJN**Q**RU**W**Z
4 (C 1/6-31/8) (H 1/6-30/9) IJ (Q+S+T+U+V+X 1/6-31/8) Z
5 **AB**EFGJKLMNPUWZ
6 ACEG**K**(N 1km)OT

Campsite on the St. Point Lac with opportunities for watersports recreational and fishing. Ideal base for long and short walks and for trips out in the ever-changing countryside of the 'Haut-Jura'.

After Pontarlier (on the N57) turn right and follow route D437 to Malbuisson direction Lac St. Point-Rive Droite. In the village turn right and follow signs to the campsite.

CC € 17 *1/4-30/6 1/9-30/9*

N 46°47'31'' E 6°17'36''

Marnay, F-70150 / Franche-Comté (Haute-Saône) — 1945

- Vert Lagon****
- route de Besancon
- +33 (0)3-84317316
- 1/5 - 30/9
- contact@camping-vertlagon.com

3ha 77**T**(100-120m²) 10A CEE

1 ACD**G**IJKLMPQ
2 CRVWXY
3 AGHJQRU**W**
4 (B+G) (Q 1/7-31/8) (T 1/5-30/8) (U+Z 1/5-31/8)
5 **AB**DFGJMNPU
6 CDFGKT

Located at walking distance from the old village of Marnay. This campsite is an ideal place for sportive campers. Kayaking, mountain biking and other activities.

From A36 exit 3. Dir. Graz via D67. Then D29 to Marnay. Entrance is left of road, just before centre.

CC € 15 *1/5-30/6 1/9-30/9*

N 47°17'20'' E 5°46'38''

Mesnois/Clairvaux-les-Lacs, F-39130 / Franche-Comté (Jura) — 1946

- Sites & Paysages Beauregard****
- 2 Grande rue Mesnois
- +33 (0)3-84483251
- 25/3 - 30/9
- reception@juracampingbeauregard.com

6ha 195**T**(100-120m²) 6A

1 ACD**G**IJKLMOPRS
2 RVXY
3 BGHJMNQRU**W**
4 (B 1/6-15/9) (F+H) JKLN P(Q 1/6-31/8) (R) (U 1/5-30/9) (V 25/6-31/8) (X+Y 1/5-30/9) (Z 25/6-31/8)
5 **AB**DEFGJLNPUVYZ
6 ACDEG**K**(N 1km)T

A well maintained, friendly family campsite with fitness apparatus, playground and bouncy castle in rustic surroundings. An ideal location for exploring this surprising region. Excellent restaurant! New indoor pool with water slide.

From Lons-le-Saunier via the D52 direction Clairvaux-les-Lacs. Caravans go via the D678 (D52 prohibited for caravans). Follow the camping signs.

CC € 15 *25/3-8/7 28/8-30/9*

N 46°35'59'' E 5°41'18''

Montbarrey, F-39380 / Franche-Comté (Jura) — 1947

- Les 3 Ours***
- 28 rue du Pont
- +33 (0)3-84815045
- 15/4 - 26/9
- h.rabbe@orange.fr

3,5ha 68**T**(100-140m²) 10A

1 ACD**G**IJKLMPQ
2 CLORSVWXY
3 BGHJNR**WX**
4 (B+G 1/6-15/9) (Q 1/5-30/9) (R 1/5-15/9) (U+Y+Z)
5 **A**EFGIJKLMNPUWZ
6 CEGIJ(N 3km)TV

A delightfully quiet campsite by the River Loue. Perfect fishing. Enjoy the flora and fauna. Excellent cycling and many marked out walks in the area. The campsite has an excellent restaurant with local dishes.

South of Dole via N5 or D405, go through Parcey. Then keep on towards Pontarlier-Lausanne via D472. Follow campsite signs.

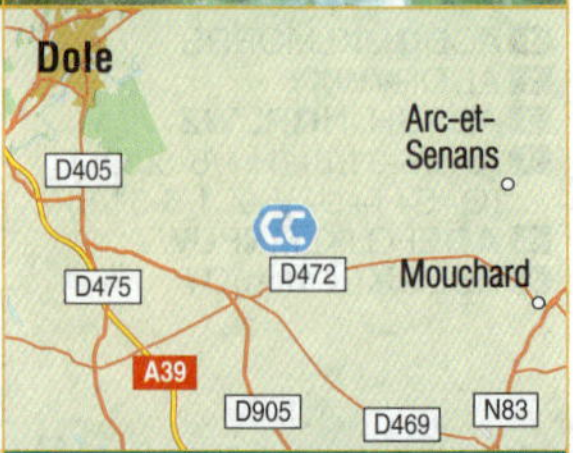

CC € 15 *15/4-3/7 27/8-26/9*

N 47°0'44'' E 5°37'50''

Ornans, F-25290 / Franche-Comté (Doubs) — 1948

Le Chanet***
9 chemin du Chanet
+33 (0)3-81622344
1/4 - 5/10
contact@lechanet.com

2,5ha 68T(80-120m²) 10A CEE

1 ACD**G**IJLPQ
2 JKLRUVWXY
3 BGHJK**M**RU**VW**
4 (C+H [key]) **N**(Q+S [key]) (T+U+V+X+Z 1/7-31/8)
5 **AB**DEFGIJKLMNPUWZ
6 ACDEGJ(N 2km)ORTV

Good campsite for short or long stays, located between Besançon and Pontarlier. Perfect for anglers, walkers and cyclists. Eco-friendly swimming. The area is noted for its gastronomy in the historic picturesque town of Ornans.

Leave the D67 in Ornans and follow D241 direction Chassagne-St-Denis. Turn right over the bridge and follow the signs.

CC € 15 *1/4-4/7 22/8-5/10 7=6, 14=11*

N 47°6'1'' E 6°7'40''

Ounans, F-39380 / Franche-Comté (Jura) — 1949

La Plage Blanche***
3 rue de la Plage
+33 (0)3-84376963
4/5 - 26/9
plageblanche@camping-indigo.com

22ha 220T(120-200m²) 10A CEE

1 ACD**G**IJKLMPQ
2 CLMNRVWXY
3 ABGHJNRU**W**X
4 (B 15/5-15/9) (F [key]) (G 15/5-15/9) KN(Q+R [key]) (T+U+V+Y+Z 1/7-31/8)
5 **AB**DEFGIJKLMNOPUWZ
6 ACDEGIJ(N 1km)RTV

An extensive grassy campsite, partly shaded and located next to a river. Countless opportunities for walking and cycling in the wooded surroundings. The Jura with its waterfalls, lakes, villages and towns is not far away. Free WiFi. Also enjoy the free whirlpool and infra-red sauna.

N5 Dole-Poligny. After about 18 km from Dole at Mont-sous-Vaudrey take the D472 in the direction of Pontarlier. Then follow the camping signs.

CC € 17 *4/5-5/7 1/9-25/9*

N 47°0'9'' E 5°39'49''

Parcey, F-39100 / Franche-Comté (Jura) — 1950

Les Bords de Loue***
chemin du Camping
+33 (0)3-84710382
FAX +33 (0)3-84710342
2/4 - 9/10
contact@jura-camping.fr

17ha 264T(100-200m²) 10A

1 ACD**G**IJKLMPQ
2 CFLORTVWXY
3 B**E**HKMN**P**RU**W**X
4 (C+H 1/5-11/9) J (Q 1/5-25/9) (R 26/6-11/9) (T+U+V 7/5-29/5,26/6-4/9) (Z 7/5-11/9)
5 **AB**DEFGIJKLMNPUWZ
6 ACDEGJ**K**(N 7km)OTV

An attractively located campsite on the river Loue, ideal for trout fishing. Archery and golf close to the site. Shops and good restaurants are within walking distance in the village. The area invites you to go walking or cycling. New: heated toilet facilities in low season.

Follow the N5 south of Dole in the direction of Genève up to Parcey. Campsite is well marked in both directions.

CC € 15 *2/4-3/7 28/8-8/10 7=6, 14=10*

N 47°0'59'' E 5°28'53''

Patornay, F-39130 / Franche-Comté (Jura)

iD **1951**

Le Moulin****
chemin du Camping
+33 (0)3-84483121
FAX +33 (0)3-84447121
4/5 - 11/9
contact@camping-moulin.com

5ha 227**T**(80-100m²) 6A CEE

1 ACD**F**IJKLPRS
2 CLORVXY
3 ABGJNRU**WX**
4 (C 1/6-11/9) (E) (H 1/6-11/9) JKLN (Q+R+T+U+V+Z 15/6-5/9)
5 **AB**EFGIJKLNPUWZ
6 ACEG**IJK**(N 0,8km)ORTV

A campsite with plenty of greenery and shade. Outdoor swimming pool with slide and indoor pool with sauna by means of a sliding roof. Located by a river with a beach and plenty of water sports opportunities.

From Lons-le-Saunier via the D52 direction Clairvaux-les-Lacs. Caravans via the D678. D52 is prohibited for caravans. Follow camping signs in Patornay.

CC € 17 *4/5-5/7 1/9-11/9 7=6*

N 46°35'14'' E 5°42'3''

Pont-les-Moulins, F-25110 / Franche-Comté (Doubs)

iD **1952**

de L'Île*
1 rue Pontarlier
+33 (0)3-81841523
29/4 - 3/9
info@campingdelile.fr

1,5ha 35**T**(120-200m²) 6A

1 AGIJKLPQ
2 CFRWX
3 AHJKNRU**W**X
4 (T) Z
5 **AB**GIJKMOPUV
6 FG**J**(N 0,5km)

A modest campsite by a small river with spacious (unmarked) pitches in beautiful natural surroundings.

Take the N83. In Beaume-les-Dames exit Pont-les-Moulins. The campsite is located in the beginning of Pont-les-Moulins, on the left side of the road.

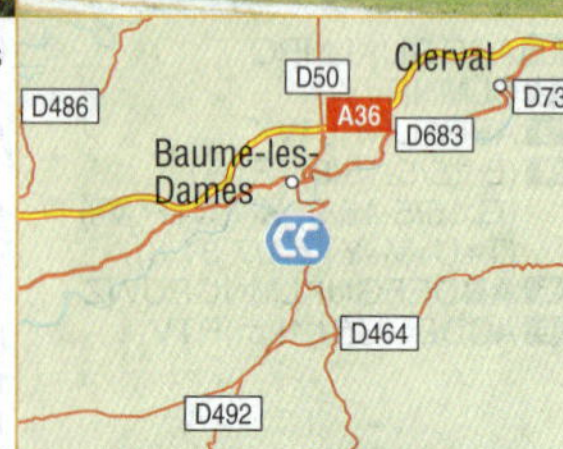

CC € 11 *29/4-15/7 1/9-3/9*

N 47°19'30'' E 6°21'41''

Port-Lesney, F-39600 / Franche-Comté (Jura)

iD **1953**

Les Radeliers***
1 rue Edgar Faure
+33 (0)3-84738144
1/5 - 30/9
lesradeliers@woka.fr

3,5ha 100**T**(< 80m²) 8A CEE

1 ACD**G**IJKLMO**P**Q
2 CNORTVWXY
3 BGHJ**M**RU**WX**
5 **A**EFGIJKLMNPU
6 CEGK

Neat campsite along the Loue with pebble beach and located just beside the church in the village. Shops for groceries and restaurants beside the campsite.

Campsite located on D48 in Port-Lesney between the church and the river Loue.

CC € 17 *1/5-30/6 1/9-30/9*

N 47°0'12'' E 5°49'25''

Villard-Saint-Sauveur, F-39200 / Franche-Comté (Jura)

1954

Flower Camping Le Martinet***
12 le Martinet
+33 (0)3-84450040
1/4 - 30/9
contact@camping-saint-claude.fr

3ha 111**T**(50-100m²) 10A CEE

1 ACDGIJKLMPQ
2 CIJLRTUVWXY
3 A**FGHJM**RU**W**
4 (C+H 1/6-1/9) (Q+R 🔑)
(T+U+V+X 15/5-15/9) Z
5 **AB**DEFGIJKLMNPUWXYZ
6 CDEGK(N 3km)RV

A very large and completely renovated municipal campsite on the River Tacon. It has a large swimming pool complex. St. Claude is a picturesque village in the south of the high Jura with views of the beautiful rock formations.

On entering St. Claude from the west, cross the bridge over the Bienne via de D436. Immediately right at the cathedral. Follow campsite signs.

CC € 13 *1/4-2/7 29/8-30/9*

N 46°22'18'' E 5°52'21''

Ambazac, F-87240 / Limousin (Haute-Vienne)

1955

L'Ecrin Nature***
Etang de Jonas
+33 (0)6-52927165
2/4 - 15/10
contact@
campinglecrinature.com

3,5ha 54**T**(80-100m²) 6A CEE

1 ABCD**G**IJKLMPR
2 BDJKLRUVWXY
3 ABHIJR**W**
4 (**A** 1/7-31/8) (C 🔑)
(Q 1/7-31/8) (R 🔑)
5 **AB**FIJKLMNPQUVZ
6 DEG**IK**(N 2km)R

Quiet campsite in the countryside. Near a lake. With a security gate, stop there and ring the bell. Stéphanie will be happy to let you in. Enjoy your stay!

A20 exit 26 dir. Ambazac. In Ambazac follow signs Camping L'Ecrin Nature or Plan d'eau de Jonars.

CC € 15 *2/4-8/7 27/8-15/10*

N 45°58'17'' E 1°24'48''

Argentat, F-19400 / Limousin (Corrèze)

1956

Au Soleil d'Oc****
Monceaux-sur-Dordogne
+33 (0)5-55288484
+33 (0)5-55281212
23/4 - 30/10
info@dordogne-soleil.com

3,5ha 99**T**(120-140m²) 6-10A CEE

1 ACD**F**IJKLMPQ
2 CGJLNRTVWXY
3 BGHJN**OPQ**RUV**W**X
4 (B 1/7-30/9) (F 🔑)
(G 1/7-30/9) (Q 1/5-15/9)
(R 1/7-31/8)
(T+U+V+X+Z 15/6-30/9)
5 **AB**DEFGJLMNOPRUVZ
6 ACEG**K**(N 4,5km)RTV

A campsite on the Dordogne with pitches by the water. Plenty to see in the area in terms of nature and culture. Also well suited in low season for lovers of peace and tranquillity. 4 km from picturesque Argentat. The indoor swimming pool is in use from the opening date of the campsite.

A20 exit 45. D1120 Uzerche-Tulle-Argentat. In Argentat D12 direction Beaulieu, in Laygues (after 3.5 km) left, over the bridge, direct left.

CC € 15 *23/4-10/7 27/8-30/10* *7=6, 14=11*

N 45°4'31'' E 1°55'2''

Argentat, F-19400 / Limousin (Corrèze)

1957

Le Vaurette****
Monceaux-sur-Dordogne
+33 (0)5-55280967
1/5 - 21/9
info@vaurette.com

4ha 120T(90-140m²) 6A CEE

1 ACD**F**IJKLMOPRS
2 CJKLNRTVWXY
3 BGHK**M**NRUV**W**X
4 (A 1/7-31/8) (C+G+Q+R) (S+T+U+V 1/7-31/8) Z
5 **AB**CEFGJLNPUWZ
6 ACEGJ(N 9km)OTV

Comfortable campsite located on the Dordogne. All major sports events are shown on big-screen television and there is a wide diversity of sport fields including a football pitch and fitness apparatus. The lovely heated swimming pool is open from 1 May. Plenty of walking and excursion programmes. Dutch-French management.

A20 exit 45 direction Tulle. Then take the D1120 to Argentat. At the roundabout take the D12 towards Beaulieu. Then follow the signs and the river.

CC € 17 *1/5-5/7 25/8-21/9*

N 45°2'44'' E 1°53'2''

Aubazine, F-19190 / Limousin (Corrèze)

1958

Campéole Le Coiroux****
Centre Touristique
+33 (0)5-55272196
FAX +33 (0)5-55271916
29/4 - 30/9
coiroux@andretriganogroupe.com

7ha 62T(100-200m²) 10A CEE

1 ACD**G**IJKLPQ
2 ABDLMRTVWXY
3 B**E**GHMN**Q**RU**W**Z
4 (A 1/7-31/8) (C+H 1/5-28/9) K(Q) (S+T+U+V+X+Y+Z 1/7-31/8)
5 **AB**CEFGHJLNPQRUWZ
6 ACEGHI**K**L(N 5km)RTV

Very peacefully located campsite with spacious pitches. Walking and cycling routes in the wooded surroundings. Swimming and fishing possible in the lake. Heated swimming pool. Golf course with 27 holes. Day trips to historic sights or picturesque villages.

A89 exit Tulle direction Beaulieu-Figeac. 2 km after St. Fortunade turn right towards Centre Touristique Coiroux. Or take A20 exit 49 towards Tulle. Right at Gare d'Aubazine village. Follow Centre touristique de Coiroux.

CC € 15 *1/5-4/7 22/8-30/9*

N 45°11'10'' E 1°42'26''

Beaulieu-sur-Dordogne, F-19120 / Limousin (Corrèze)

1959

des Iles Beaulieu***
bd Rodolphe de Turenne
+33 (0)5-55910265
FAX +33 (0)5-55910519
4/5 - 26/9
beaulieu@camping-indigo.com

5ha 145T(80-120m²) 10A CEE

1 ACD**G**IJKLMPRS
2 CNRTVWXY
3 ABGHKRU**WX**
4 (A 1/7-31/8) (C+H+Q+R) (T+U+V+Z 1/7-31/8)
5 **AB**DFGIJKLMNPUVWZ
6 ACEGIK(N 0,2km)TV

The campsite is situated on an island making it ideal for water sports enthusiasts. Only a bridge separates it from the friendly medieval town of Beaulieu with its many pavement cafes and restaurants. During May there is a 'strawberry festival' and as well as visiting the many places of interest locally you can also relax on the site.

Direction to the campsite is marked in the centre of Beaulieu.

CC € 15 *4/5-5/7 1/9-25/9*

N 44°58'46'' E 1°50'25''

Beynat, F-19190 / Limousin (Corrèze) 1960

Camping du Lac de Miel****
Centre Touristique de Miel
+33 (0)5-55855066
1/5 - 30/9
@ info@camping-miel.com

7ha 61T(150-300m²) 6-10A CEE

1 ACDFIJKLMPQ
2 ADGIKLMRTWXY
3 BFGHJ**M**N**Q**RUWZ
4 (E+H) J(Q+R 1/7-31/8) (T+U+V+X) Z
5 **AB**EFGJLNPUVZ
6 CEGJ(N 4km)V

Comfortable, child-friendly campsite on a lake with a sandy beach. Spacious pitches with views of the lake. Swimming possible in the swimming pool with sliding roof or in the lake (Pavillon Bleu) with a water slide.

Take the N120 as far as Tulle, then N940 direction Beaulieu/Figeac to Beynat. The campsite is signposted. Or take the A20 as far as Brive, D921 direction Argentat.

CC € 15 *1/5-10/7 27/8-30/9* *7=6, 14=11*   N 45°7'54'' E 1°45'47''

Bonnac-la-Côte, F-87270 / Limousin (Haute-Vienne) 1961

Du Château de Leychoisier*****
route de Leychoisier
FAX +33 (0)5-55399343
15/4 - 20/9
@ contact@leychoisier.com

4ha 80T(80-200m²) 10A CEE

1 A**G**IJKLM**P**RS
2 DFLRTVWXY
3 AGHMRUWZ
4 (B+Q+R) (U+X 22/4-20/9) Z
5 **AB**FGJLNPRUWXYZ
6 AEG**J**(N 2,5km)RV

This castle campsite is located close to the Bonnac-la-Côte turning. A private park with a lake, next to a listed 9th century castle ensures a unique setting. Here you will have every comfort for a successful holiday: spacious pitches, peaceful surroundings, comfortable toilets, swimming pool, restaurant. Golf course in the immediate vicinity.

A20 Châteauroux-Limoges, ca. 10 km before Limoges turn right (exit 27) direction Bonnac-la-Côte. Clearly signposted.

CC € 19 *15/4-6/7 25/8-20/9*   N 45°56'0'' E 1°17'23''

Boussac, F-23600 / Limousin (Creuse) 1962

Creuse Nature Naturiste***
route de Bétête, D15
+33 (0)5-55651801
2/4 - 29/10
@ creuse.nature@wanadoo.fr

19ha 100T(80-160m²) 10A

1 ACD**G**HIJKLMNOPS
2 BDLRTUVXY
3 AFGHJNRUW
4 (A 1/5-30/9) (B 1/6-15/9) (F 5/9-1/11) (G 1/6-15/9) K **N**(Q) (R 1/7-30/8) (T+U+V+X+Z)
5 **AB**GIJKLMNOPUWXYZ
6 ACDEGHI**K**(N 2km)ORTUV

A lovely naturist campsite in a woodland setting. Heated indoor pool and sauna. Good facilities and spacious pitches. A lovely area for walking and cycling. There is a restaurant and fresh bread daily.

Boussac is located in the La Châtre-Montluçon-Guéret triangle. In Boussac via the D15 direction Bétête. Campsite is beside this road, well signposted.

CC € 19 *2/4-4/7 22/8-29/10*   N 46°20'57'' E 2°11'11''

Boussac/Bourg, F-23600 / Limousin (Creuse)

1963

Le Château de Poinsouze/les Castels****
route de la Châtre
+33 (0)5-55650221
13/5 - 14/9
info.camping-de.poinsouze@orange.fr

23ha 123T(110-250m²) 25A CEE

1 ACD**G**HIJKLM**P**Q
2 DILRTVX
3 ABGHJNRUW
4 (B+G) J
(Q+R+T+U+X) Z
5 **AB**FGIJKLMNPUWXYZ
6 CDEGJ**K**(N 2,5km)ORV

A beautiful castle campsite with very spacious and grassy level pitches. The toilet facilities are excellent. There is a lovely small lake, with possibilities for canoeing and suitable for the novice surfer. There is also a swimming pool with water slide. There are many trips out possible nearby in 'La Creuse'.

From La Châtre, drive via the D917 in the direction of Boussac. Signposted on the right side of the road 2 km before Boussac.

CC € 17 13/5-5/7 27/8-14/9

N 46°22'20'' E 2°12'4''

Bugeat, F-19170 / Limousin (Corrèze)

1964

Camping Aux Portes des Mille Sources
16, rue des 3 Ponts
+33 (0)5-55943212
2/4 - 29/10
auxportesdesmillesources@orange.fr

8,5ha 83T(100-300m²) 6-16A CEE

1 ABDFIJKLMPR
2 BCGKLRTUVWXY
3 ACGHMQRUW
4 (Q+R 1/7-31/8)
(T+U+V+Z 1/5-30/9)
5 ABDGJLNPUWZ
6 CDEK(N 0,7km)T

Very spacious, green, quiet campsite with large pitches. Spacious sports room. Plenty of cycling and walking options in the surroundings.

From Paris A20 dir. Toulouse. Exit Eymoutiers and follow Bugeat. In Bugeat D97 and follow signs.

CC € 11 2/4-7/7 25/8-29/10 7=6, 14=11

N 45°36'20'' E 1°55'22''

Châteauneuf-la-Forêt, F-87130 / Limousin (Haute-Vienne)

1965

Le Cheyenne***
avenue Michel Sinibaldi
+33 (0)5-55693929
1/4 - 30/9
campinglecheyenne@neuf.fr

1,4ha 49T(90-120m²) 6A CEE

1 ACD**G**IJKLMPRS
2 ADKLMRTVWXY
3 AGHJ**M**RU**WZ**
4 (Q+T+U+V+X+Y+Z)
5 **AB**EGJKLNPUVZ
6 CEGJ(N 0,5km)RTV

Quiet campsite on a lake with a sandy beach. Walking, cycling, swimming. Have a drink afterwards or head to the restaurant.

A20, exit 35 dir. Eymoutiers.
D979 Châteauneuf-la-Forêt follow signs 'Le Lac'.

CC € 15 1/4-6/7 26/8-30/9 7=6

N 45°42'59'' E 1°36'5''

Cognac-la-Forêt, F-87310 / Limousin (Haute-Vienne) 1966

Camping des Alouettes***
1 les Alouettes
+33 (0)5-55032693
1/4 - 30/9
info@camping-des-alouettes.com

4ha 68T(150m²) 10A CEE

1 ACD**G**IJKLPS
2 FKLRTVWXY
3 ABGHJRU
4 (C+H 1/5-30/9) (Q+X) Z
5 **A**FGIJKLMNOPQRUZ
6 AEG**IK**(N 1km)TV

Very spacious pitches on the edge of a wood at 25 km from Limoges. Dutch owners. An ideal area for relaxation, walking and exploring this beautiful region. Heated pool. Unlimited WiFi for 1 Euro per day. Table d'hôtes on Monday and Friday.

A20, exit 28 direction Périgueux (N520). Continue towards Périgueux (D2000) as far the roundabout with Cognac-la-Fôret turning (D10). Follow signs beyond Cognac-la-Fôret to the campsite. Parking near the entrance of the camping.

CC € 15 *1/4-2/7 20/8-30/9*

N 45°49'30'' E 0°59'48''

Fourneaux, F-23200 / Limousin (Creuse) 1967

La Perle***
Commune de St. Médard-la-Rochette
+33 (0)5-55830125
1/4 - 30/9
info@camping-laperle.nl

3ha 33T(50-120m²) 10A

1 A**G**IJKLMPST
2 IJKLRUVWXY
3 ABD**F**GHJNPR**W**
4 (B+G 1/6-30/8) (Q+X+Y) Z
5 **A**FGIJKLMNPQUWXZ
6 DEG**K**(N 0,5km)V

A homely campsite with friendly Dutch owners. Countryside, hospitality, breathtaking views, lovely sights and the River Creuse within walking distance. Plenty of walking, cycling, golf and fishing opportunities. Restaurant/bar/terrace, swimming pool, spacious camping pitches and well maintained toilet facilities. WiFi and bakery service.

A20 exit 23 direction Guéret, then D942 direction Aubusson. Campsite well signposted.

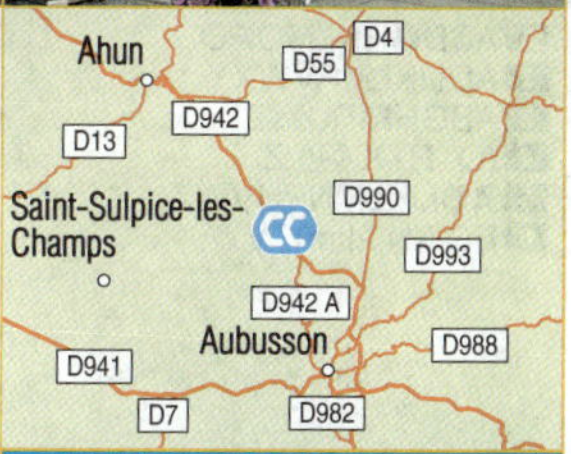

CC € 13 *1/4-30/6 1/9-30/9 7=6, 14=12*

N 46°1'18'' E 2°8'22''

Guéret, F-23000 / Limousin (Creuse) 1968

de Courtille***
rue Georges Aulong
+33 (0)5-55819224
1/4 - 30/9
contact@camping-courtille.com

2,7ha 60T(80-100m²) 10A CEE

1 A**G**IJLPST
2 ADFKLMRVWXY
3 AHJR**WZ**
4 (Q+R)
5 **AB**GIJKLMNPUVWZ
6 ACEG**K**(N 3km)TV

Well maintained campsite in a parkland setting, spaciously positioned next to a small lake with watersports activities (20 hectares). Marked out pitches.

From the A20 exit 23 direction Guéret (N145). Then exit 49 and follow signs.

CC € 13 *1/4-8/7 25/8-30/9*

N 46°9'45'' E 1°51'31''

Limoges, F-87280 / Limousin (Haute-Vienne)

iD **1969**

Camping d'Uzurat***
40 avenue d'Uzurat
+33 (0)5-55384943
15/3 - 31/10
contact@campinglimoges.fr

2,5ha 155T(70-80m²) 10A CEE

1 ACD**G**HIJKLMOPR
2 BCDFKLMNRTUVWXY
3 ABCGHJMQRUW
4 B(Q) V
5 ABDEFJLMNPUVZ
6 CEK(N 0,3km)TV

Less than 2 km from motorway exit. Site is clearly signposted. Ideal stopover site with neat and new toilet facilities. Also ideally suited for visiting Limoges and its green surroundings. Walking, cycling, sports and recreation options close by. Friendly welcome.

From north along the A20, take exit 30. From south exit 31 and follow Zone Industriël (ZIN) Lac Uzurat.

CC € 15 *15/3-7/7 27/8-31/10*

N 45°52'14'' E 1°16'32''

Marcillac-la-Croisille, F-19320 / Limousin (Corrèze)

iD **1970**

Camping du Lac***
28 route du Viaduc
+33 (0)5-55278138
25/3 - 23/10
campingdulac19@wanadoo.fr

3,5ha 100T(80-120m²) 6A

1 ACD**G**IJKLMO**PQ**
2 ADIJKLMRVWXY
3 ABGH**M**RU**WZ**
4 (Q+R+X) Z
5 **AB**IJKLMNPUVWZ
6 EGJ(N 2km)TV

A beautifully located campsite with plenty of parking space; lovely touring pitches with reasonable privacy; plenty of shade. Ideal for water sports enthusiasts. The campsite is located 2 km from the centre of the village.

D978 Tulle-Mauriac. Follow signs in the village. Or D18 Egleton-Argentat, follow 'Complexe Touristique du Lac la Valette' in the village.

CC € 15 *25/3-3/7 20/8-23/10 7=6, 14=11*

N 45°16'9'' E 2°0'33''

Neuvic, F-19160 / Limousin (Corrèze)

iD **1971**

Domaine de Mialaret****
route d'Egletons
+33 (0)5-55460250
FAX +33 (0)5-55460265
22/4 - 21/10
info@lemialaret.com

45ha 160T(150-160m²) 10A CEE

1 ACDGIJKLMOPQ
2 BDIKLRSUVWXY
3 ABD**F**GHJLMN**OP**RUW
4 (A 7/7-25/8) (B 15/6-15/9) (Q+R) (T 1/7-31/8) (U 1/5-30/9) (V+X 1/7-31/8) (Y) (Z 1/7-31/8)
5 **AB**DEFGIJKLMNOPUWZ
6 CEGHIK(N 4km)PTV

Beautiful campsite located in a 44 hectares natural castle park with a unique Art Deco pool. Natural pitches available in woods at 150 metres from campsite.

A89 as far as exit 23 Ussel Ouest, then follow signs to Neuvic D979 and D982. After Neuvic direction Egletons. Via D991 ± 4 km after Neuvic, take narrow road to the right. Campsite signposted. Nearest crossroads: D991 and D89.

CC € 17 *22/4-9/7 26/8-21/10 14=11*

N 45°22'56'' E 2°13'45''

St. Germain-les-Belles, F-87380 / Limousin (Haute-Vienne)

iD **1972**

de Montréal***
rue du Petit Moulin
+33 (0)5-55718620
1/1 - 31/12
contact@campingdemontreal.com

2ha 47**T**(80-130m²) 10A

1 ACD**G**IJKLMPRS
2 ADFJLRTVWXY
3 ABGH**M**NRU**W**Z
4 (C+Q+T+U+V+X 1/4-31/10) Z
5 **AB**DEFGJLNPUWZ
6 AEGK(N 1km)RTV

A quietly located campsite by a lake with a sandy beach. Clean comfortable toilet facilities. Plenty of opportunities for sports. Within walking distance of an attractive village.

A20, exit 42. Direction St. Germain-les-Belles. Then follow signs (Plan d'eau de Montréal).

CC € 15 *1/1-2/7* *22/8-31/12* *7=6*

N 45°36'42'' E 1°30'5''

St. Pardoux, F-87250 / Limousin (Haute-Vienne)

iD **1973**

Fréaudour****
Site de Freaudour
+33 (0)5-55765722
7/3 - 6/11
camping.freaudour@orange.fr

4,5ha 103**T**(80-150m²) 10A CEE

1 ACD**G**IJKLM**P**Q
2 ABDFGIKLMRVWXY
3 AGHJKN**P**RU**W**Z
4 (B 5/6-11/9) (Q 1/5-30/9) (R 1/4-30/9) (T+U 1/7-31/8) Z
5 **AB**EFGIJKLMNPUZ
6 EGJ(N 7km)RTV

By the lake (Lac de Saint-Pardouxin) in wooded surroundings with First Aid post and a supervised swimming area. Lovely outdoor swimming pool on the grounds.

Take the A20 in the direction of Limoges. Exit 25 Lac de St. Pardoux, then 'Site de Fréaudour'.

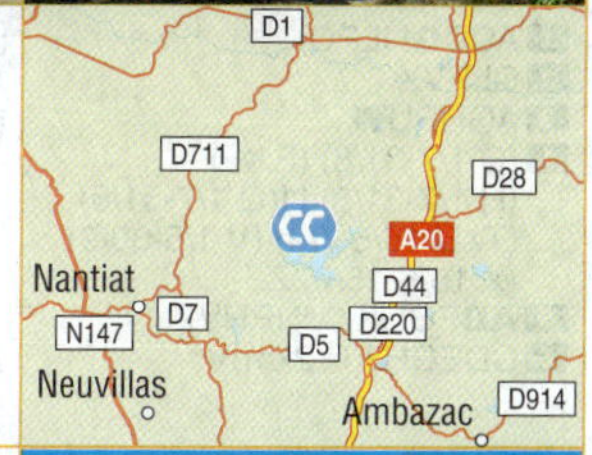

CC € 15 *7/3-3/7* *20/8-6/11* *7=6, 14=11*

N 46°2'59'' E 1°16'44''

Treignac-sur-Vézère, F-19260 / Limousin (Corrèze)

iD **1974**

La Plage***
Lac des Barriousses
+33 (0)5-55980854
2/4 - 1/10
camping.laplage@flowercampings.com

3,7ha 94**T**(80-150m²) 6A

1 ACD**G**IJL**P**RS
2 ABDJKLRTVWXY
3 AGHJNQRUWZ
4 (**A** 1/7-31/8) (E+H) (Q+R 1/7-31/8)
5 **AB**CEFGJLNPUVW
6 CEGJ(N 3,5km)RTV

A comfortable campsite by a lake with a sandy beach. Quiet location and close to a lively village. Spacious pitches marked out by bushes.

A20 exit 43 towards Treignac. Treignac direction Gueret via D970.

CC € 13 *2/4-1/7* *1/9-1/10* *7=6*

N 45°33'35'' E 1°48'48''

Abrest/Vichy, F-03200 / Auvergne (Allier)

1975

La Croix St-Martin***
99 avenue des Graviers/ allée du cp
+33 (0)4-70326774
2/4 - 2/10
camping-vichy@orange.fr

3ha 72T(100-200m²) 10A CEE

1 ACGHIJKLMPQ
2 CGRVWXY
3 BGHJNRUW
4 (C 1/5-30/9) (Q+R 10/4-10/10) (U 15/5-15/9)
5 ABFGIJKLMNPRUWZ
6 CEGK(N 1,5km)

A peaceful campsite on the banks of the Allier, within walking distance of the spa resort of Vichy. An ideal location for trips out into the Auvergne. Heated swimming pool and free WiFi. Reception open 08:30 to 12:00 and 13:30 to 20:00.

In Vichy keep in direction Thiers. The campsite is signposted and is located along this road.

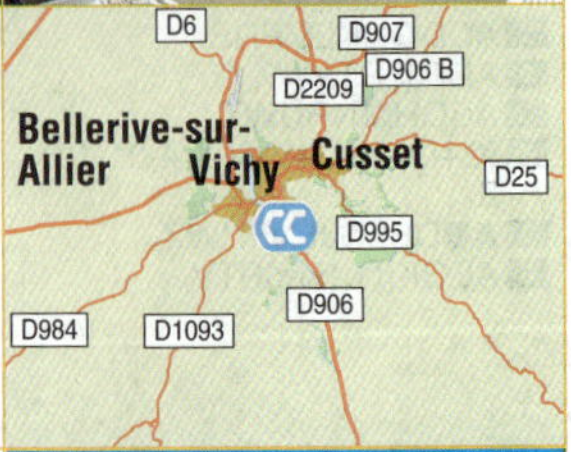

CC € 13 *2/4-7/7 26/8-2/10*

N 46°6'28'' E 3°26'12''

Ambert, F-63600 / Auvergne (Puy-de-Dôme)

1976

Les Trois Chênes***
route du Puy
+33 (0)4-73823468
29/4 - 30/9
tourisme@ville-ambert.fr

5ha 94T(100-150m²) 10A CEE

1 ACDGIJLPQ
2 CLRVX
3 AGHRUW
4 (C 1/7-31/8) (F) (H 1/7-31/8) IJ(Q 1/7-31/8) (T+U 15/5-7/9) (V 1/5-30/9) (X 15/6-15/9) Z
5 ABFGIJKLMNPUVZ
6 CDEGHJ(N 2km)V

Spacious campsite located in the south of the Auvergne. Very spacious shady pitches, marked out by hedges.

Take the D906 south of Ambert. The campsite is located on the left 3 km down the road.

CC € 15 *29/4-30/6 1/9-30/9*

N 45°32'22'' E 3°43'43''

Bellerive-sur-Allier/Vichy, F-03700 / Auvergne (Allier)

1977

Beau Rivage sur les berges de l'Allier****
rue Claude Decloître 15 - 17
+33 (0)4-70322685
1/4 - 8/10
camping-beaurivage@wanadoo.fr

2ha 37T(100m²) 10A CEE

1 ACGIJKLOPQ
2 CRVXY
3 BGKNRUW
4 (E+H 15/5-15/9) J (Q 1/5-15/9) (R) (T 1/5-15/9) Z
5 ABDFGIJKLMNOPUVWZ
6 CEGK(N 1km)OUV

Located on the edge of the Allier, opposite the Vichy parks. 2 km from the city centre, in a quiet and natural area. Indoor heated swimming pool.

In Bellerive continue towards Hauterive and follow the green 'Berges de l'Allier' signs. At Allier enter 'rue Claude Decloitre'. Beau Rivage is on the left at the end of the road.

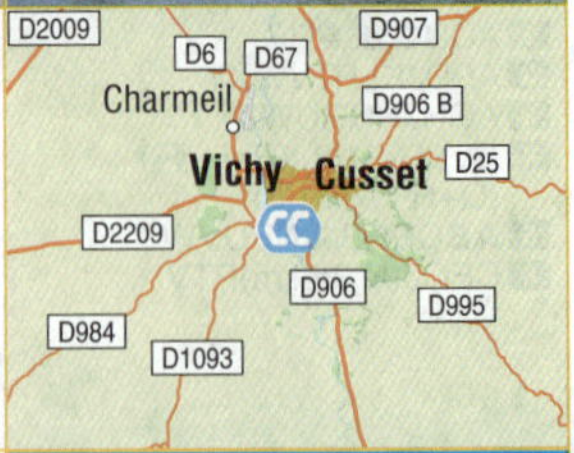

CC € 15 *1/4-3/7 29/8-8/10*

N 46°6'56'' E 3°25'49''

Blot-L'Église, F-63440 / Auvergne (Puy-de-Dôme)

iD **1978**

La Coccinelle**
Le Bourg
+33 (0)4-73649315
1/3 - 31/10
info@campingcoccinelle.com

1,6ha 41**T**(80-110m²) 6A CEE

1 ACD**G**IJKLMPST
2 KRTVWXY
3 ABGHJ**M**NRU
4 (B 15/6-15/9) (T+U) Z
5 **AB**CDFGJKMPUW
6 ADEGK(N 0,5km)T

A peacefully located family campsite on the edge of the village of Blot. In beautiful natural surroundings with many places of interest. This is the place for people who like walking, (electrically rechargeable) cycling, fishing, countryside and relaxation. Free WiFi. Dutch owners.

From A71 toll road exit 12.1 continue to St. Pardoux. Then follow camping signs. From Montluçon D2144, follow camping signs in Pouzol.

CC € 11 *1/3-3/7 20/8-31/10*

N 46°1'56'' E 2°57'23''

Brioude, F-43100 / Auvergne (Haute-Loire)

iD **1979**

Camping de la Bageasse***
avenue Bageasse
+33 (0)4-71500770
7/3 - 6/11
aquadis1@wanadoo.fr

2ha 49**T**(80-160m²) 10A CEE

1 ACD**G**IJKL**P**
2 CJMRTVWXY
3 AGHJRU**WX**
4 (B+G 1/7-31/8)
(Q+R 1/6-15/9)
(T+X+Z 1/6-30/9)
5 **AB**GIJKLMNPUVZ
6 EGJ(N 3km)RTV

Campsite along the Allier river with swimming pool and paddling pool. Marked-out, shady pitches.

A75 exit 20 to Brioude. Then follow campsite signs. About 3 km from town centre.

CC € 15 *7/3-3/7 20/8-6/11 7=6, 14=11*

N 45°16'53'' E 3°24'16''

Buxières-sous-Montaigut, F-63700 / Auvergne (Puy-de-Dôme)

iD **1980**

Les Suchères**
Les Suchères
+33 (0)4-73859266
1/4 - 30/9
contact@campinglessucheres.com

7,5ha 35**T**(100-140m²) 6A

1 ACD**G**IJKLPRS
2 IRVX
3 AD**F**GJKNRU
4 (A 1/5-31/8) (B 1/6-15/9)
(Q+R+T+U+X) Z
5 **A**BFGIJKLMNPUVW
6 EGJ(N 1,5km)V

A small family campsite with a friendly pavement cafe and restaurant. It is located in peaceful surroundings with plenty of opportunities for walking. The swimming pool is open from June.

From Montmarault direction St. Eloy-les-Mines and keep on D13 as far as the camping signs.

CC € 15 *1/4-30/6 17/8-30/9 7=6*

N 46°11'36'' E 2°49'10''

Chambon-sur-Lac, F-63790 / Auvergne (Puy-de-Dôme) — 1981

De Serrette***
+33 (0)4-73886767
23/4 - 11/9
camping.de.serrette@wanadoo.fr

3ha 75T(80-130m²) 10A CEE

1 AGIJKLPRS
2 CJKRVX
3 ABHJRUW
4 (A) (E+H 1/6-11/9) N
(Q+R) (T+U 1/6-11/9) Z
5 ABFGIJKLMNPUVZ
6 AEGJ(N 5km)ORTV

A quiet family campsite at an altitude of 1000m with wonderful views of Lac Chambon and Murol Castle. The heated swimming pool has a sliding roof and there is also a sauna. Restaurant with panoramic views. Free WiFi. Plenty of sights in the immediate vicinity.

A75 exit 6 direction Le Mont Doré. Follow camping signs past Murol.

CC € 15 23/4-2/7 27/8-11/9 14=12

N 45°34'16'' E 2°53'28''

Chambon-sur-Lac, F-63790 / Auvergne (Puy-de-Dôme) — 1982

Les Bombes***
chemin de Pétary
+33 (0)4-73886403
25/4 - 18/9
lesbombes@orange.fr

5ha 132T(100-130m²) 10A

1 AGIJKLMPQ
2 CKLRVXY
3 ABHJKNRW
4 (C+H 1/6-15/9)
(Q 15/6-30/8) (R 1/7-31/8)
(T+U+V 15/6-31/8) Z
5 ABFGIJKLMNOPUVXYZ
6 EGJ(N 3km)V

This lovely and well run campsite with swimming pool and beautiful mountain views is close to the village of Chambon-sur-Lac and 1 km from Lac Chambon. Plenty of walking and cycling trips possible in the beautiful Parc Naturel des Volcans.

From exit 6 on the A75 to the 996 direction Le Mont Doré. Follow camping signs after Muro.

CC € 15 25/4-1/7 29/8-18/9

N 45°34'11'' E 2°54'8''

Châtel-de-Neuvre, F-03500 / Auvergne (Allier) — 1983

Deneuvre***
route de Moulins
+33 (0)4-70420451
FAX +33 (0)9-72256263
1/4 - 30/9
campingdeneuvre@wanadoo.fr

1,2ha 70T(70-115m²) 4A

1 ACDGIJKLPQ
2 CNORVWXY
3 AGRWX
4 (Q+R+T+U+X) Z
5 ABFGJKMNPRUZ
6 ACDEGK(N 0,8km)ORV

A friendly family campsite located in the Allier valley. A peaceful open and level region. Attractive restaurant with a snack menu.

Direction Clermont-Ferrand/St. Pourçain. On the RD2009 (RN9) turn left before the small town Châtel-de-Neuvre. Signposted.

CC € 15 1/4-30/6 1/9-30/9

N 46°24'47'' E 3°19'8''

Châtel-Guyon, F-63140 / Auvergne (Puy-de-Dôme)

1984

Le Ranch des Volcans***
route de la Piscine
+33 (0)4-73860247
FAX +33 (0)4-73860564
19/3 - 5/11
contact@ranchdesvolcans.com

5ha 278**T**(80-200m²) 6A

1 ACD**G**IJKLMO**P**Q
2 FGRSVXY
3 ABGHJMNQRU
4 (B+G 15/5-30/9)
(Q+R+T+U+X+Y) Z
5 **AB**DFGIJKLMNPUV
6 ACDEGJL(N 0,5km)OV

The three star Le Ranch des Volcans campsite is located in Châtel-Guyon, a resort in the regional park of the volcanoes of the Auvergne. Near the towns of Volvic en Clermont-Ferrand. Lakes and volcanoes are close at hand. The campsite has a swimming complex with three pools, a playground, mini-golf and other sports activities. The campsite restaurant serves regional specialities.

A71, exit Riom. Then direction Châtel-Guyon. Signposted.

CC €15 *19/3-1/7 28/8-5/11*

N 45°54'54'' E 3°4'38''

Dallet, F-63111 / Auvergne (Puy-de-Dôme)

1985

Les Ombrages***
rue de pont du Chateau
FAX +33 (0)4-73831097
14/5 - 15/9
lesombrages@hotmail.com

3ha 90**T**(120-250m²) 6A CEE

1 ACDEIJKLPST
2 CFLNORSTVY
3 AHJNRU**WX**
4 (B+G+Q+T+U+X+Z)
5 **A**GIJKLMNPQUZ
6 AE**J**(N 0,5km)V

A friendly campsite on the banks of the Allier in the middle of the Auvergne plains. Numerous deciduous trees give the pitches plenty of shade. Dutch owners. Dogs not allowed. A 5-minute walk to the village. Cycle and walking route maps available. Baby and children's toilet facilities.

From Pont-du-Château via the D1 direction Cournon. Signposted.

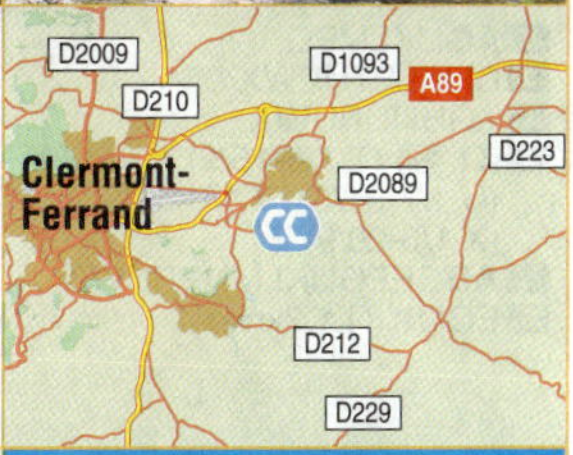

CC €13 *14/5-7/7 27/8-15/9*

N 45°46'31'' E 3°14'31''

Ebreuil, F-03450 / Auvergne (Allier)

1986

Camping de la Filature****
route de Chouvigny
+33 (0)4-70907201
15/4 - 1/10
camping.filature@gmail.com

3,5ha 70**T**(100-150m²) 6A CEE

1 ACGIJKLMOPQ
2 CFLORSVWXY
3 BGHN**OQ**RU**WX**
4 (Q 1/5-1/10) (S)
(U 1/6-30/9) Z
5 **A**FGIJKLMNOPUVZ
6 EGJ(N 1km)OV

An attractive campsite on the banks of the Sioule. Hedges separate most of the pitches from each other and trees offer sufficient shade to a large part of the grounds.

A71, exit 12 Vichy/Gannat to A719. After tollbooth exit 13 dir. Ebreuil. Then dir. 'Gorges de la Sioule'. Site is located beside the D915.

CC €17 *15/4-12/7 29/8-1/10*

N 46°6'30'' E 3°4'25''

La Bourboule/Murat-le-Quaire, F-63150 / Auvergne (Puy-de-Dôme)

iD 1987

Le Panoramique***
Le Pessy
+33 (0)4-73811879
15/2 - 15/3, 12/4 - 30/9
info@campingpanoramique.fr

2,7ha 50**T**(70-100m²) 10A

1 ACGIJKLMPST
2 FJKLRTVX
3 ABDFGHJNRU
4 (C+H+Q 1/7-31/8)
(R 15/2-15/3,1/7-31/8)
(T+U+V 1/7-31/8) Z
5 **AB**DEFGIJKLNPUVWXYZ
6 CEGJ(N 2km)OV

The campsite lives up to its name: all pitches have spectacular views of the nearby Auvergne mountains. You can enjoy sunny days and fresh nights, especially in early and late season (1000 metres altitude). Perfect if you like walking, sports cycling or simply fresh mountain air. Excellent sanitation. La Bourboule (2 km) and Mont-Dore (6 km) are popular mountain areas.

A89, exit 25. Then the 219 to Murat-le-Quaire. Then follow camping signs.

CC € 15 *15/2-15/3 12/4-10/7 27/8-30/9 14=13*

N 45°35'49'' E 2°45'4''

La Tour-d'Auvergne, F-63680 / Auvergne (Puy-de-Dôme)

iD 1988

La Chauderie***
route de Besse
+ 31 06-33785345
7/5 - 18/9
info@la-chauderie.com

NEW

4,2ha 73**T**(90-150m²) 6A

1 AGIJKLMPQ
2 CIJKLRTUVWXY
3 AGHIJNRU**W**X
4 (Q) (T 1/6-15/9)
(U 1/7-31/8) (V 1/6-31/8)
(X 1/6-20/9) Z
5 **AB**CEFGIJKLMNPRUWZ
6 EGIJ**K**(N 1,3km)V

Nice family campsite, less than half an hour on foot from the welcoming town of La Tour d'Auvergne. Very well-maintained, spacious pitches, some with a beautiful view. Lake for swimming (guarded) at a less than 15 minutes walk. There is a waterfall of about 6 metres next to the campsite. Bar, terrace and free WiFi.

On the Besse-en-Chandesse to La Tour-d'Auvergne road, 1300m before La Tour-d'Auvergne. Campsite clearly signposted.

CC € 15 *7/5-8/7 25/8-18/9*

N 45°31'40'' E 2°42'2''

Le Chambon-sur-Lignon, F-43400 / Auvergne (Haute-Loire)

iD 1989

Camping Le Lignon
7 route du Stade
+33 (0)4-71597286
15/4 - 30/9
contact@campingdulignon.com

2,3ha 76**T**(82-100m²) 10A CEE

1 ACDGIJKLMPQ
2 CRTWXY
3 BFGHIJU**W**
4 (Q+T+U+V+X) Z
5 **AB**DGIJKLMNOPUVW
6 AEGJ(N 0,3km)TV

A pleasant, hospitable campsite 300m from the centre on the banks of the Lignon. Level pitches, TV room, restaurant, take-away service, WiFi point and heated toilet facilities.

From Valence-Le Puy on the D15 take the D103 to Le Chambon. Follow camping signs in the centre. Campsite is past the fire station and sports centre.

CC € 11 *15/4-5/7 22/8-30/9*

N 45°3'34'' E 4°17'49''

Lempdes-sur-Allagnon, F-43410 / Auvergne (Haute-Loire)

1990

Le Pont d'Allagnon***
rue René Filiol
+33 (0)4-71765369
27/2 - 5/11
centre.auvergne.camping@orange.fr

1,7ha 60**T**(80-140m^2) 10A CEE

1 ACFIJKLMPQ
2 CFLMRTVXY
3 BDGHJMNQRU**W**
4 (C+H 15/6-15/9) (T) Z
5 **AB**FGIJKLMNOPUVWZ
6 ACDEGHIJ(N 0,5km)RTV

A well maintained, quiet campsite on the edge of a village, with heated swimming pool and toddlers' pool. Modern sports complex including tennis courts. About 500 metres from the A75, suitable for stopovers or longer stays. Base for walks in the surrounding area.

From Clermont-Ferrand follow the A75/E11. Exit 19 Lempdes direction Lempdes. Follow signs. From St. Flour follow the A75 as far as exit 20 direction 'Centre Ville'. Then follow camping signs.

CC € 13 27/2-9/7 26/8-5/11 7=6

N 45°23'13'' E 3°15'57''

Les Pradeaux, F-63500 / Auvergne (Puy-de-Dôme)

1991

Château de Grange Fort***
La Grange Fort
+33 (0)4-73710243
FAX +33 (0)4-73710769
5/4 - 31/10
chateau@lagrangefort.eu

7ha 120**T**(80-120m^2) 6A CEE

1 ACD**G**IJKL**P**Q
2 BCFIKLORTVWXY
3 BGHJ**MNOP**RU**W**X
4 (A 1/5-31/10) (B 15/6-15/9)
(F 15/4-1/7,31/8-15/10)
(G 15/6-15/9) **N**
(Q+R 1/5-15/9)
(T+U+V+X 15/4-30/9) Z
5 **AB**EFGIJKLMOPUZ
6 CDEG**IJ**(N 1km)OV

This castle campsite located in the heart of the Auvergne offers peace, ambiance and numerous leisure activities. You can enjoy the heated indoor swimming pool and a delicious meal in the castle in early and late seasons. Dutch owners.

On A75 exit 13 direction Parentignat. 1st turn to the right at roundabout after 1.5 km, direction St. Rémy-de-Chargnat via D999. Then right again at the 2nd roundabout after 1.5 km, direction Les Pradeaux (D34). Campsite 1 km on the right.

CC € 17 5/4-4/7 25/8-31/10

N 45°30'31'' E 3°17'5''

Murol, F-63790 / Auvergne (Puy-de-Dôme)

1992

Le Pré Bas****
Lac Chambon
+33 (0)4-73886304
FAX +33 (0)4-73886593
23/4 - 17/9
prebas@campingauvergne.com

3,5ha 71**T**(90-130m^2) 6A CEE

1 ACD**F**IJKLPQ
2 ACDLMRUVXY
3 BCGJNRU**VW**Z
4 (A 1/7-30/8) (C 20/5-9/9)
(E 4/5-17/9) (H 20/5-9/9) J
KLMN(Q 1/5-20/9)
(R 1/6-10/9) (T+U 1/5-20/9)
(V 25/6-31/8)
(X+Y 1/5-20/9) Z
5 **AB**EFGIJKLMNOPRUV
6 CDEGH**IK**(N 2km)PRV

Located in the volcanic heart of the Auvergne, right on the shores of the beautiful Lac Chambon. The campsite offers excellent facilities including high quality toilet facilities. It has a heated indoor pool. Family Centre with sauna, hammam, jacuzzi and massage.

Take the D996 from Murol to Le Mont-Dore. Campsite is marked with green signs.

CC € 17 23/4-30/6 29/8-17/9 14=12

N 45°34'31'' E 2°54'51''

Murol, F-63790 / Auvergne (Puy-de-Dôme)

1993

Le Repos du Baladin***
Groire
+33 (0)4-73886193
23/4 - 17/9
reposbaladin@free.fr

2,4ha 67**T**(80-120m²) 10A CEE

1 A**G**IJL**PQ**
2 CJKLRVWXY
3 BGHJNRU**W**
4 (C 15/6-12/9)
(Q+R+T+U+V 15/6-31/8) Z
5 **AB**DEFGIJLMNPQRUVXYZ
6 AEGIJ(N 1km)RV

A peaceful campsite with sheltered pitches in a very natural setting. Small family campsite about 2 km from the really attractive town of Murol. This is absolutely the place for anyone who enjoys a restful holiday. Fine marked out pitches with plenty of shade, excellent sanitary facilities and a lovely swimming pool. The surroundings are perfectly wonderful for walks and excursions.

In Murol direction Syndicat d'Initiative. Then follow the signs 'Le Repos du Baladin'.

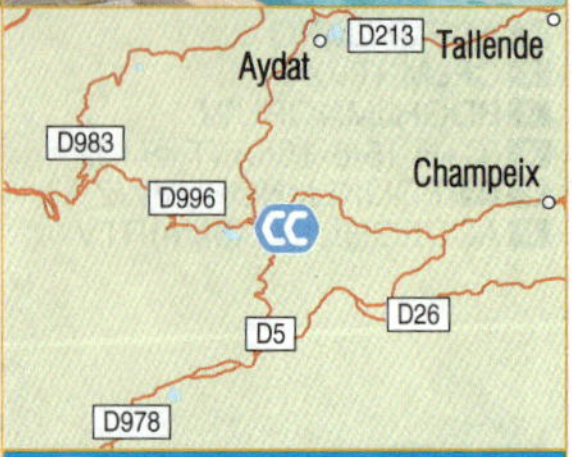

CC €15 *23/4-30/6 28/8-17/9 8=7, 14=12*

N 45°34'25'' E 2°57'27''

Nêbouzat, F-63210 / Auvergne (Puy-de-Dôme)

1994

Les Dômes***
Les 4 routes de Nêbouzat
+33 (0)4-73871406
23/4 - 3/10
contact@les-domes.com

1ha 43**T**(80-100m²) 10A CEE

1 ACDGIJKLMPQ
2 GLRTUVX
3 A**F**GJRU
4 (**A** 10/7-25/8)
(E+Q+R+T+U+V+X 1/5-15/9)
(Y)
5 **AB**DEFGHIJKLMNOPUVW
YZ
6 ACDEGIJ(N 1,3km)ORTV

A fine family campsite with facilities for motorhomes. Level rectangular grounds with plenty of flowers and well maintained camping pitches. Indoor heated swimming pool in early and late seasons. The largest number of volcanoes in the Auvergne are in this region. Close to Vulcania and Le Puy de Dôme.

From the A75 exit 5 direction Aydat. Take the Col de la Ventouse D2089 in the direction of Ussel and pass Nêbouzat. Signposted.

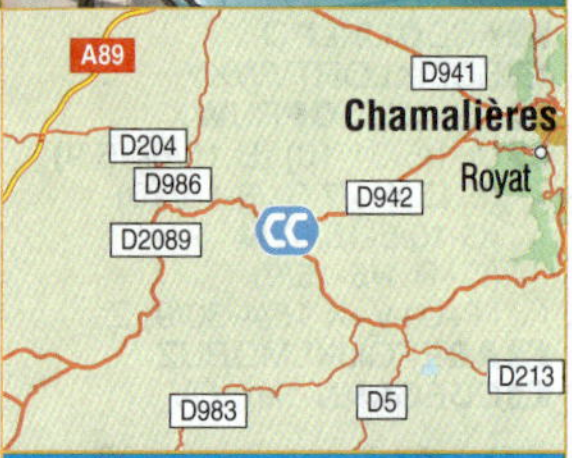

CC €15 *23/4-3/7 28/8-3/10*

N 45°43'33'' E 2°53'25''

Neuvéglise, F-15260 / Auvergne (Cantal)

1995

Flower Camping Le
Belvédère****
Lanau
+33 (0)4-71235050
9/4 - 8/10
belvedere.cantal@orange.fr

3,5ha 80**T**(80-100m²) 15A

1 ACDGIJLMPRS
2 JKRTVX
3 ABGHNRU**VW**
4 (**A** 1/7-31/8) (E 1/5-25/9)
(G 1/7-15/9) **N**(Q)
(R 1/7-8/10)
(T+U+V+X+Z)
5 **AB**CFGIJKLMNOPUWYZ
6 ACEGJ(N 6km)ORTV

This terraced campsite is located on a south-facing slope with beautiful views of the valley, some pitches have a view of Lanau Lake. Snacks available, indoor and heated pool. Sportive as well as cultural outings are possible. The health spa Chaudes-Aigues is 5 km away with a hot water spring of 82 °C.

On D921 take exit St. Flour/Chaudes-Aigues. Pass Neuvéglise on right. Dir. Lanau, 1st right when you have reached the dam (signposted).

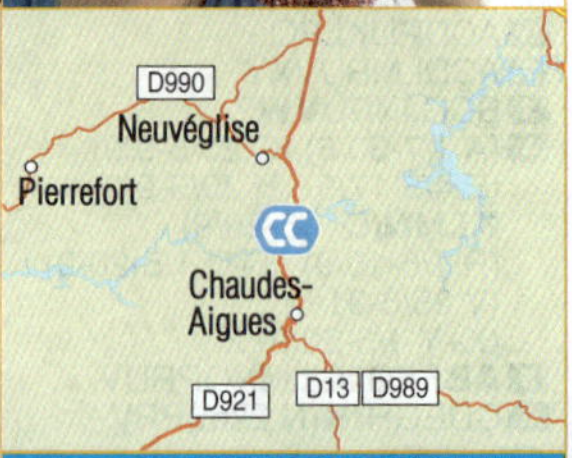

CC €15 *9/4-24/6 3/9-8/10*

N 44°53'42'' E 3°0'5''

Nonette, F-63340 / Auvergne (Puy-de-Dôme)

iD 1996

Les Loges***
+33 (0)4-73716582
30/4 - 11/9
@ les.loges.nonette@wanadoo.fr

3ha 143T(80-130m²) 6A CEE

1 ACD**F**IJKLMPR
2 CFNORSTVXY
3 ABGRU**WX**
4 (C 20/6-15/9) (H 1/6-15/9) J **N**(Q 1/7-31/8) (R 1/6-15/9) (T+U+V+X+Z 1/7-31/8)
5 **AB**FGIJKLMNPUZ
6 ACEG**JK**(N 5km)TV

Peaceful campsite on the Allier. Shaded pitches. Walking and cycling tours possible. An ideal overnight site just a few kilometres from the A75, with static caravans for rent. With swimmingpool in June and September.

A75, from Clermont-Ferrand exit 17 Nonette, then turn left. Follow campsite signs (± 5 km).

CC € 15 *30/4-8/7 25/8-11/9*

N 45°28'10'' E 3°16'20''

Olliergues, F-63880 / Auvergne (Puy-de-Dôme)

iD 1997

Les Chelles***
+33 (0)4-73955434
1/4 - 31/10
@ info@camping-les-chelles.com

3,5ha 43T(80-180m²) 10A CEE

1 ACD**G**IJKLMPQ
2 BIJKRTVXY
3 AGHJMRUW
4 (C+G 1/6-31/8) (Q+R+T+U+X ⊶) Z
5 **AB**FIJKLMNOPQUVZ
6 CDEGIJ(N 5km)V

Peaceful family campsite with plenty of ambiance and lovely pitches on various terraces. The campsite has a swimming pool. Located in the Livradois-Forez nature reserve. English, French, Dutch and German spoken at the reception.

Take the D906 from Thiers to Ambert. Campsite clearly marked by arrows in Olliergues village.

CC € 15 *1/4-9/7 28/8-31/10*

N 45°41'25'' E 3°37'59''

Orcet, F-63670 / Auvergne (Puy-de-Dôme)

iD 1998

Le Clos Auroy****
rue de la Narse
FAX +33 (0)4-73842697
1/1 - 31/12
@ orcet@wanadoo.fr

2,5ha 82T(100-120m²) 5-10A CEE

1 ACD**G**IJKLPQ
2 CFGJLRTVX
3 ABGHN**O**RU**W**
4 (C 15/5-15/9) (**G** 1/7-31/8) I J(Q ⊶) (T+U 1/7-31/8) Z
5 **AB**FGIJKLMNOPUVWZ
6 ACEG**K**L(N 0,2km)OV

Open all year. Reception open from 14:00-19:00. When not available you can check at the automatic check-in machine. WiFi. Heated swimming pool, bubble bath, children's pool and slides. 5A connection in early and late seasons. 10A also possible. Close to all amenities.

At 2.5 km from autoroute A75 Clermont-Ferrand/ Issoire. Take exit 5 direction Orcet/Cournon. Then follow camping signs.

CC € 17 *1/4-3/7 20/8-31/10*

N 45°42'1'' E 3°10'9''

Pers, F-15290 / Auvergne (Cantal)

1999

- Du Viaduc***
- Le Ribeyrès Village
- +33 (0)4-71647008
- 23/4 - 15/10
- campingduviaduc@wanadoo.fr

1,3ha 45**T**(80-110m²) 10A CEE

1 ACD**G**IJLMPQ
2 DJKMRTVWXY
3 B**F**GRU**W**Z
4 (B 15/6-15/9) (Q 21/6-31/8) (R ⊶) (T+U+V+Z 1/6-30/9)
5 **AB**CDFGIJKLMNOPUWZ
6 ACGJ(N 7km)

The large lake on which all types of water sports are permitted is directly accessible from this small, well maintained terraced campsite. Every pitch has wide views of this lake. Anglers are of course very welcome. You can swim in the swimming pool and in the lake a reasonable distance away. Delicious pizzas are also made to order.

From Aurillac take the N122 towards Figeac. After Sansac keep right D61 direction Pers. The campsite is signposted from here.

CC € 15 *23/4-30/6 29/8-15/10 7=6*

N 44°54'21" E 2°15'14"

Royat, F-63130 / Auvergne (Puy-de-Dôme)

2000

- Indigo Royat****
- route de Gravenoire
- +33 (0)4-73359705
- FAX +33 (0)4-73356769
- 24/3 - 2/11
- royat@camping-indigo.com

8ha 136**T**(80-120m²) 10A

1 ACD**F**IJKLMOPS
2 FGJKRSVX
3 BGHJMNRU
4 (C+H 30/4-15/9) K (Q 29/4-2/11) (R 29/4-3/11) (T+X 1/7-31/8) Z
5 **AB**DFGJKLNPUWZ
6 CEGIJ(N 1,5km)V

In the spa town of Royat, at the foot of the Puy de Dôme. This terraced campsite is located in beautiful natural surroundings. Various top-quality amenities: heated swimming pool, tennis courts, central facilities, playground.

On the A71 continue to A75. Take exit Le Mont Dore/La Bourboule just after Clermont-Ferrand. Follow N89 until you are in Ceyrat. Take the exit and follow signs to Royat.

CC € 17 *24/3-5/7 1/9-1/11*

N 45°45'31" E 3°3'16"

Singles, F-63690 / Auvergne (Puy-de-Dôme)

2001

- Hôtel de Plein Air Le Moulin de Serre***
- D73, Vallée de La Burande
- +33 (0)4-73211606
- 9/4 - 18/9
- moulindeserre@orange.fr

7ha 64**T**(90-150m²) 10A

1 ACD**G**IJKLM**P**Q
2 CRVWXY
3 BGH**M**NRU**W**
4 (A 4/7-1/9) (C 26/5-15/9) **K** (Q+R+T+U ⊶) (X 5/7-30/8) (Z ⊶)
5 **AB**DFGIJKLMNOPUWXZ
6 CEGJ**K**(N 9km)OTV

Friendly well run campsite with heated pool in beautiful surroundings. Fishing and sailing in the Bort lake, trout fishing in the Dordogne and the Burande, where you can pan for gold under supervision. Close to many sights.

A89 exit 25. D922 in direction of Bort-les-Orgues. Turn right 1 km south of Tauves D29. Follow camping signs.

CC € 13 *9/4-30/6 26/8-18/9*

N 45°32'35" E 2°32'34"

St. Constant, F-15600 / Auvergne (Cantal)

2002

Moulin de Chaules***
D28, route de Calvinette
+33 (0)4-71491102
30/4 - 16/10
camping@
moulin-de-chaules.com

3,5ha 50T(60-110m²) 10A

1 ACDFIJKLNPRS
2 BCJKLMNRTVXY
3 BGHJRU**WX**
4 (C 15/6-15/9) (Q+R+T+U+V+X) Z
5 **AB**EFGIJKLMOPUWZ
6 ACEG**I**J(N 3km)TV

Friendly, green, south facing terraced campsite. The grounds, the river and the buildings are in perfect harmony with the surrounding Chaules country estate. Swimming pool, bar, small shop and restaurant. Internet and free WiFi. The campsite is traffic-free in July and August.

A20 exit 56 direction Figeac and then towards Aurillac. In Maurs take the D663 direction St. Constant. After St. Constant left on the D28 towards Mourjou. Campsite signposted.

CC € 15 *30/4-1/7 28/8-16/10*

N 44°40'54" E 2°15'38"

St. Didier-en-Velay, F-43140 / Auvergne (Haute-Loire)

2003

La Fressange***
Camping Municipal
+33 (0)4-71662528
22/4 - 30/9
camping.lafressange@orange.fr

2ha 65T 15A CEE

1 ACD**G**IJKLMPQ
2 GIJRTVXY
3 AGHJNR**W**
4 (**C**+Q 1/7-31/8) Z
5 **A**IJKLMNOPUVW
6 DEGJ(N 0,8km)T

An attractive terraced campsite by a lovely municipal swimming pool. The campsite is located in a beautiful, peaceful area.

Leave St. Étienne N88 at exit St. Didier-en-Velay. At La Séauve-sur-Semène turn left towards St. Didier-en-Velay. Follow the signs in the village.

CC € 13 *22/4-30/6 1/9-30/9*

N 45°18'4" E 4°16'59"

St. Maurice-de-Lignon, F-43200 / Auvergne (Haute-Loire)

2004

Camping du Sabot
813 route du Stade
+33 (0)4-71653268
16/4 - 15/10
contact@campingdusabot.fr

3,5ha 29T(80-120m²) 6-10A

1 AGIJKLMOPQ
2 BJKLRTUWXY
3 AGR
4 (Q)
5 **A**GIJKLMNPUV
6 DEGJ(N 1,5km)T

Lovers of the outdoors, nature and relaxation will enjoy staying in these extraordinary surroundings. Located between the Loire Gorges and Lignon at 30 minutes from Puy-en-Velay. There are fishing and walking options in this country of old volcanoes. Village within walking distance, jeu de boules, table football, table tennis and a weekly market.

RN88 St. Etienne - Le Puy-en-Velay, exit St. Maurice-de-Lignon. Left at entrance to village and follow signs.

CC € 15 *16/4-3/7 22/8-15/10*

N 45°13'23" E 4°9'6"

St. Nectaire, F-63710 / Auvergne (Puy-de-Dôme)

2005

La Clé des Champs***
route des Granges
+33 (0)4-73885233
8/4 - 25/9
campingcledeschamps@free.fr

2ha 63**T**(75-150m²) 6A

1 AC**F**IJKLMOPQ
2 CRVXY
3 BGHJRU**W**
4 (C+G 1/6-15/9) J
(Q+R 1/7-31/8) (T)
(U+X 1/7-31/8) Z
5 **AB**FGIJKLMNOPUV
6 CDEGJ(N 0,3km)OV

This campsite in the spa resort of St. Nectaire offers plenty of opportunities for relaxation. Walking, cycling, historical visits. Located in wooded surroundings with a babbling brook running through the site.

From Murol to Issoire via the D996. The campsite is located directly after St. Nectaire-Bas village. Or from A75 exit 6 dir. Champaix. In Champaix dir. St. Nectaire. Campsite indicated just before St. Nectaire.

CC € 13 *8/4-2/7 29/8-25/9*

N 45°34'31" E 3°0'7"

St. Nectaire, F-63710 / Auvergne (Puy-de-Dôme)

2006

La Vallée Verte***
route des Granges
+33 (0)4-73885268
16/4 - 18/9
contact@valleeverte.com

2,5ha 74**T**(80-100m²) 8A

1 ACDGIJKLMPQ
2 CRVWXY
3 BGHNRU**W**
4 (E+H+Q+R)
(T+U+Z 1/7-31/8)
5 **AB**DFGJLMNOPUWZ
6 CEGJ(N 0,5km)RV

A quiet, green campsite of 2.5 hectares. Pitches are marked out by plants. Covered pool, snack bar, fresh bread, ice cream, etc. In the heart of the Massif du Sancy and the Parc des Volcans d'Auvergne, at a height of 700 metres and close to St. Nectaire. Lakes and waterfalls nearby.

From Murol via D996 to Issoire. Campsite is indicated directly after St. Nectaire-Bas. Or from A75 exit 6 dir. Champaix and then to St. Nectaire. Indicated just before St. Nectaire.

CC € 13 *16/4-5/7 22/8-18/9*

N 45°34'31" E 2°59'58"

St. Nectaire, F-63710 / Auvergne (Puy-de-Dôme)

2007

Le Viginet***
2 chemin du Manoir
+33 (0)4-73885380
9/4 - 30/9
info@camping-viginet.com

3,5ha 59**T**(90-140m²) 10A CEE

1 ACD**G**IJKLMPST
2 KLRUVWXY
3 ABGHNRU
4 (C+H 1/6-15/9)
(Q 15/5-10/9) (R 1/6-31/8)
(T+U+V 1/7-30/8) Z
5 **AB**EFGIJKLMNOPQ**R**UVW
XYZ
6 ACDEGJ(N 2km)RV

Set in the beautiful Auvergne countryside, a true paradise for walkers and nature lovers, you can choose from the spacious marked out pitches in this beautifully maintained parkland campsite. Snack bar, pizzeria, small shop, library, free WiFi and freshly baked bread. In just 5 minutes you can walk to St. Nectaire with its various restaurants and sights.

A75 exit 6 to St. Nectaire. First road right in the village.

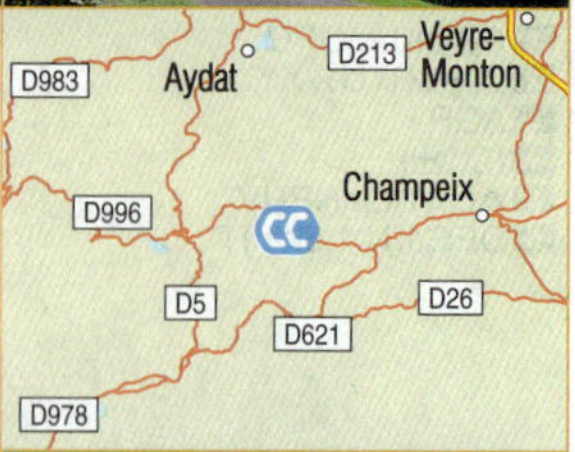

CC € 13 *9/4-3/7 27/8-30/9* 7=6, 14=11

N 45°34'46" E 3°0'10"

St. Paulien, F-43350 / Auvergne (Haute-Loire) — 2008

La Rochelambert***
route de Lanthenas
+33 (0)4-71005402
1/4 - 30/9
infos@
camping-rochelambert.com

4ha 80T(18-61m²) 16A CEE

1 ACD**G**IJKLMPQ
2 CIJLMRTVWX
3 BGHJMNRU**W**
4 (C+H 20/5-15/9) **N**
(Q 1/5-30/9) (R)
(T+U+V+X 26/6-26/8)
(Z)
5 **AB**DEFGIJKLMNPUWXYZ
6 ACEGHJ(N 3km)TV

Well maintained, quite campsite with an informal ambiance in the undiscovered east of the Auvergne, 15 km from Le Puy. Starting point for walks. The site is located by a river in natural surroundings with a heated pool and toddlers' pool. Own tennis court.

The campsite is signposted from the N102 Le Puy - Clermont-Ferrand in the direction of St. Paulien. Follow camp signs (3 km) from St. Paulien centre (D906).

CC € 15 *1/4-5/7 1/9-30/9*

N 45°7'13'' E 3°47'38''

St. Rémy-sur-Durolle, F-63550 / Auvergne (Puy-de-Dôme) — 2009

Camping Les Chanterelles***
Chapon
+33 (0)4-73943171
9/4 - 8/10
campingleschanterelles@yahoo.fr

4ha 140T(100-120m²) 8A CEE

1 ACD**G**IJKLMPRS
2 DFIJKLRSVXY
3 AGHNRU**WZ**
4 (**A** 1/7-31/8) (Q+R+Z)
5 **A**GIJKLMNOPUVW
6 CDEJ(N 2km)RV

A campsite located within walking distance of a recreational lake at St. Rémy-sur-Durolle. This terraced campsite has large trees which provide sufficient shade.

A72, exit 3 St. Rémy-sur-Durolle. In St. Rémy, the Parc de Loisirs with campsites are clearly signposted.

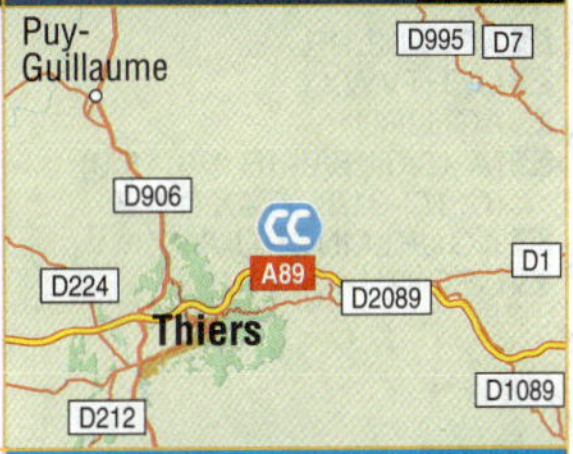

CC € 15 *9/4-10/7 27/8-8/10 7=6*

N 45°54'11'' E 3°35'56''

Ste Sigolène, F-43600 / Auvergne (Haute-Loire) — 2010

de Vaubarlet****
+33 (0)4-71666495
FAX +33 (0)4-71661198
29/4 - 30/9
camping@vaubarlet.com

3,5ha 100T(80-120m²) 16A CEE

1 ACD**G**IJKLMPQ
2 CLRTVWX
3 AGHJNRU**W**
4 (A 1/7-31/8)
(C+H 15/5-15/9) (Q+R)
(T+U 15/5-15/9) Z
5 **AB**FGIJKLMNP**S**UVW
6 EGJ(N 6km)OTV

A family campsite with character and a heated swimming pool, bar and restaurant in the south of the Auvergne. Fourteen hectares of unspoilt countryside in a valley, surrounded by rolling hills. On the banks of the river Dunière.

Leave the N88 at Monistrol-sur-Loire/Ste Sigolène exit. Direction Ste Sigolène at roundabout. Towards Grazac at roundabout before village and follow camping signs.

CC € 15 *29/4-8/7 25/8-30/9 7=6, 14=11*

N 45°12'59'' E 4°12'45''

Vic-sur-Cère, F-15800 / Auvergne (Cantal) 2011

La Pommeraie****
+33 (0)4-71475418
FAX +33 (0)4-71496330
1/5 - 2/9
@ pommeraie@wanadoo.fr

4ha 40T(60-110m²) 10A

1 ACF**I**JLPQ
2 HJRTVWXY
3 BCGHMNRU
4 (A 1/7-31/8) (B 1/5-30/8) (F+H) **I**JP (Q+R+T+U+V+Y+Z)
5 **AB**DEFGIJKLMNPQUVWXY
6 EGI**J**(N 2km)OTV

A view of the hilltops of the Cantal, the peace and quiet of the surroundings, and the fact that there is a village nearby make La Pommeraire an ideal spot for a holiday. Luxury indoor and heated pool with water slide. The owner organises surprising entertainment and the cook organises excellent meals.

In Vic-sur-Cère leave the N122. In village follow signs dir. municipal sports field/ swimming pool. Stay on road for about 3 km. Follow 'la Pommeraie'.

CC € 15 *1/5-1/7 29/8-2/9*

N 44°58'17" E 2°37'59"

Vollore-Ville, F-63120 / Auvergne (Puy-de-Dôme) 2012

Le Montbartoux**
Chemin de Montbartoux
+33 (0)4-73537005
1/1 - 31/12
@ contact@camping-montbartoux.com

1,8ha 35T(90-250m²) 10A CEE

1 ADF**I**JKLPR
2 IJKRTVWXY
3 AGHJRU
4 (A 15/5-15/9) (B 1/6-15/9) (Q 1/7-31/8) (T+X) Z
5 **A**GIJKLMNOPUVWZ
6 CEGK(N 10km)V

A small and attractive campsite with beautiful views of the Auvergne valley and of the volcanoes of the Puy de Dôme. Located in the Monts du Forez Livadois nature park.

From A72 Clermont-Ferrand-St. Etienne. Exit 2 in Thiers direction Courpière. Just past Courpière direction Vollore-Ville. From Vollore-Ville direction Vollore-Montagne. Campsite signposted.

CC € 15 *1/1-30/6 1/9-31/12*

N 45°47'59" E 3°36'59"

Vorey-sur-Arzon, F-43800 / Auvergne (Haute-Loire) 2013

Les Moulettes****
chemin de Félines
+33 (0)4-71037048
1/5 - 15/9
@ contact@camping-les-moulettes.fr

2ha 55T(90-150m²) 10A

1 **A**F**I**JKLMPQ
2 CGLRTVX
3 BGHJNRU**W**
4 (A 1/7-31/8) (C+H 1/6-5/9) I J(T+U+V+X+Z 1/7-31/8)
5 **AB**EFGIJKLMNPUXYZ
6 ACDEGJK(N 0,2km)TV

A hospitable campsite in the beautiful valley of the Haute Loire, 22 km from Le Puy-en-Velay and close to the village of Vorey. The pitches are sheltered and are mostly semi-shaded. The site is near a small river with a lovely pool with three slides on the opposite side. Free for camping guests. Free WiFi.

From Puy-en-Velay follow the D103. Campsite signposted in Vorey village.

CC € 17 *1/5-30/6 1/9-15/9*

N 45°11'11" E 3°54'23"

Aigueblanche, F-73260 / Rhône-Alpes (Savoie)

iD **2014**

Eliana***
176 rue des Pommiers
+33 (0)4-79242387
15/3 - 31/10
campingeliana@hotmail.com

1ha 35**T**(120-220m²) 15A CEE

1 A**G**IJKLMOPQ
2 GKRUVXY
3 AHJRUV**W**
4 (C+H+Q 15/6-15/9)
5 **AB**CDGHIJKLMNOPU
6 CEGJ(N 0,8km)T

Small, peacefully located campsite with very large marked-out pitches located in an old orchard. A free shuttle bus will take you to the spa resort Léchère-les-Bains.

N90 Albertville-Moutiers, exit 38. Follow campsite signs. Campsite located in dead-end street opposite swimming pool car park (Base de Loisir du Morel).

CC € 11 *15/3-8/7 25/8-31/10*

N 45°30'25'' E 6°29'29''

Albertville, F-73200 / Rhône-Alpes (Savoie)

iD **2015**

Les Adoubes
24 avenue du Camping
+33 (0)4-79320662
1/1 - 31/12
hello@camping-albertville.fr

3ha 90**T**(80-120m²) 10A CEE

1 ACDGIJKLMOPRS
2 CFGKRTWXY
3 AGN
4 (Q ⚿) Z
5 **AB**DGJKLMNPUVWZ
6 FG**K**(N 0,2km)ORTV

Campsite located in a green area, yet still also close to Albertville centre. Suitable for longer stays or as a stopover campsite, especially for winter sports. In spring and autumn there is great cycling over a secured cycle path of about 40 km up to Annecy. Albertville and the medieval area of Conflans are worth a visit.

Take exit Albertville centre and follow campsite signs or Médiévale de Conflans.

CC € 15 *1/1-8/7 27/8-31/12* **14=11**

N 45°40'41'' E 6°23'43''

Allevard-les-Bains, F-38580 / Rhône-Alpes (Isère)

iD **2016**

Clair Matin***
20 rue de Pommiers
+33 (0)4-76975519
FAX +33 (0)4-76458715
16/4 - 16/10
contact@camping-clair-matin.com

5,5ha 195**T**(100-110m²) 2-10A

1 ACD**G**IJKLMO**P**Q
2 BGJKRVXY
3 BGHJNRU
4 (**A** 1/7-31/8)
(B+G 1/6-15/9)
(Q+T+U+X+Z ⚿)
5 **AB**FGIJKLMNPRUVZ
6 ABCDEG**K**(N 0,5km)ORV

Clair Matin is located 500 metres from the Allevard-les-Bains spa. Thanks to its sheltered location in the Belledonne-Massif it enjoys pleasant temperatures, even in spring and autumn. Recommended for both sportive and not-so-sportive campers. Camping Qualité.

A41, exit 23 Le Touvet. Then via D29 towards Goncelin. Then D525 direction Allevard. Campsite is on the left before the roundabout.

CC € 15 *16/4-9/7 27/8-16/10*

N 45°23'19'' E 6°3'53''

Anneyron, F-26140 / Rhône-Alpes (Drôme)

iD

2017

Flower camping La Châtaigneraie****
50 route de Font-Flacher
+33 (0)4-75314333
+33 (0)4-75038467
9/4 - 25/9
contact@chataigneraie.com

2ha 30**T**(90-120m²) 10A

1 ACD**G**IJKLPS
2 IJKLRTVWXY
3 B**F**GHJMN**O**RU**W**
4 (C+H 15/5-15/9) **KN** (Q+S+T+U+V+Y) Z
5 **AB**EFGIJKLMNOPQUWYZ
6 AEG**IJ**K(N 3km)ORTV

Peaceful, beautifully located campsite on the Anneyron hills. Views of the Rhône valley and the Ardèche mountains. You can also treat yourself to gastronomic delights. Enquire about restaurant opening times in the low season.

From the A7 exit 12 Chanas. N7 direction Valence, before Le Creux-de-la-Tine take the D1 towards Anneyron. Follow the camping signs in Anneyron.

CC € 15 *9/4-8/7 25/8-25/9* *7=6, 14=12, 21=18*

N 45°15'18" E 4°54'13"

Anse, F-69480 / Rhône-Alpes (Rhône)

iD

2018

Les Portes du Beaujolais****
495 avenue Jean Vacher
+33 (0)4-74671287
1/3 - 31/10
contact@camping-beaujolais.com

10ha 198**T**(100m²) 10A CEE

1 ACD**G**IJKLM**P**Q
2 CFLRTVWXY
3 BGJ**MNQ**RU**W**
4 (B+G 1/5-30/9) J(Q+R) (T+U+V+X 20/6-31/8) Z
5 **A**DEFGIJKLMNPUXYZ
6 CFG**K**(N 0,5km)TV

A very well maintained campsite on the edge of the village of Anse. A tourist train takes you from the campsite to the village. You will enjoy the countryside.

From the north A6 exit 31.2 Anse then N6 direction Anse/Villefranche. Turn right after Saône bridge and follow signs. Exit 33.1 from the south.

CC € 17 *1/3-5/7 25/8-31/10* *7=6, 14=11*

N 45°56'26" E 4°43'36"

Ars-sur-Formans, F-01480 / Rhône-Alpes (Ain)

2019

Du Bois de la Dame**
590 chemin du Bois de la Dame
+33 (0)4-74007723
1/4 - 30/9
camping.boisdeladame@orange.fr

103**T**(80m²)

1 GIJKLPQ
2 BJRTXY
3 ABHJMRW
6 DEG**J**(N 0,5km)T

Peaceful campsite, spacious pitches, flowers and lots of plantlife all around. Ideal location, close to a (fishing) lake and a historic village centre. Close to Beaujolais, Lyon and the beautiful Dombes with its iconic Parc des Oiseaux. The campsite is the perfect base and offers excellent value for money. Accessible for disabled people.

A6 exit Villefranche-sur-Saône. D904 direction Bourg/Ars-sur-Formans. Campsite signposted.

CC € 15 *1/5-30/6 1/9-30/9*

N 45°59'27" E 4°49'1"

Artemare, F-01510 / Rhône-Alpes (Ain)

2020

Sites & Paysages Le Vaugrais***
2 chemin le Vaugrais
+33 (0)4-79873734
1/3 - 1/12
contact@camping-le-vaugrais.fr

1,6ha 50T(80-120m²) 10A CEE

1 AC**G**IJLM**P**R
2 CRUVWX
3 AHJKRU**W**
4 (C 1/6-30/9) (Q 1/5-31/8) (T+U 1/6-31/8)
5 **A**FGIJKLMNPUVWXYZ
6 AGJ(N 0,2km)

A small family campsite on the edge of the Savoie, 10 km from Lake Bourget. It has 48 level, shaded pitches. The heated swimming pool and snack bar with takeaway meals are open from 1 June. Free WiFi. Lovely walking and cycle routes from the campsite.

From Belley N504 dir. Ambérieu and Bugey, right after Pugieu onto D904 as far as Artemare. From Ambérieu and Bugey N504 dir. Belley, left before Pugieu, follow D904 as far as Artemare. Follow camping signs.

CC € 13 *1/3-30/6 1/9-1/12*

N 45°52'28" E 5°41'2"

Auberives-sur-Varèze, F-38550 / Rhône-Alpes (Isère)

2021

Camping des Nations***
RN7, 8 Bis
+33 (0)4-74849513
1/3 - 31/10
contact@campingdesnations.com

1,5ha 60T(100m²) 8A

1 ACDGIJKLMOPQ
2 FGRVXY
3 BGR
4 (B 1/6-15/9) (Q+U+X) Z
5 ABDGIJKLMNOPZ
6 EJ(N 2km)TV

A small, pleasant stopover campsite on the RN7 between Vienne and Chanas. Shaded, marked out pitches. Suitable for day trips to the Ardèche and the Vercors. Friendly, helpful reception. Free WiFi.

A7 exit Vienne, follow the N7 as far as Auberives-s-V. Campsite on the right of the road south of the village.

CC € 17 *1/3-30/6 1/9-31/10*

N 45°24'46" E 4°48'48"

Baix, F-07210 / Rhône-Alpes (Ardèche)

2022

Domaine du Merle Roux - FranceLoc****
Le Roux Est
+33 (0)4-75858414
FAX +33 (0)4-75858307
9/4 - 18/9
merle-roux@franceloc.fr

15,8ha 105T(80-250m²) 10A CEE

1 ACD**G**IJKLM**P**ST
2 FJKRTVWXY
3 BGHJNQRU
4 (C+H) IJ(Q+R+T+U) (V 1/7-31/8) (Y+Z)
5 **A**DEFGIJKLMNOPRUWXYZ
6 AEGHJ**K**L(N 5km)OV

This terraced campsite has a lovely swimming complex with water slides. There is a special pool for small children. Wonderful views over the Rhône valley in good weather. Plenty of activities. The restaurant is open regularly in early and late seasons. New French owners.

Campsite located 6 km NW of Baix. A7 exit 16 Loriol. Via Le Pouzin N86 dir. Le Teil. At the level crossing left D22a. Left after a few kilometres. Continue to campsite.

CC € 15 *9/4-13/7 30/8-18/9*

N 44°42'18" E 4°44'17"

Balbigny, F-42510 / Rhône-Alpes (Loire) — 2023

La Route Bleue***
Pralery, D56
+33 (0)4-77272497
15/3 - 31/10
camping.balbigny@wanadoo.fr

2ha 100T(100m²) 10A

1 ACDGIJKLMPQ
2 CFLRTVWXY
3 GJU**W**
4 (B+G 1/6-30/9)
(Q 1/5-15/9)
(T+U+V+Z 1/4-15/10)
5 **AB**GIJKLMNOPUVWZ
6 CEG**K**(N 2km)OTV

A peaceful campsite with a friendly atmosphere. Direct access to the Fleuve Loire coast. Easy access. Tourist region. Ideal for a holiday in the open air. You can go fishing and walking here. The site has a bar, snack bar, take away meals. Swimming pool and toddlers' pool.

On the north side of Balbigny. From the N82 take the D56. Campsite signposted.

CC € 15 *15/3-3/7 20/8-31/10*

N 45°49'51" E 4°9'43"

Barbières, F-26300 / Rhône-Alpes (Drôme) — 2024

Le Gallo-Romain****
1090 route du Col de Tourniol
+33 (0)4-75474407
18/4 - 18/9
info@legalloromain.net

3ha 75T(80-100m²) 6A CEE

1 ACD**F**IJKLMPT
2 CFJKLRTVXY
3 AB**F**GHJKN**OP**RU**W**
4 (A+B+G+Q+R+T+U+V+Y+Z)
5 **AB**DEFGIJLMNOPRUWXZ
6 AEG**I**J(N 1km)RTV

This beautiful campsite, proclaimed to be one of the loveliest in France is located close to the imposing Vercours. Various sporting activities are possible from the campsite, such as walking, cycling, kayaking and golf. Free WiFi.

A7 exit 14, dir. A49 Grenoble exit 5 towards Alixan. In Alixan D101 to Barbières, via Besayes and follow the camping signs. You will find the campsite beyond the village of Barbières on the right.

CC € 17 *18/4-8/7 25/8-18/9 7=6, 14=12*

N 44°56'40" E 5°9'4"

Belmont-Tramonet, F-73330 / Rhône-Alpes (Savoie) — 2025

Des Trois Lacs****
+33 (0)4-76370403
+33 (0)4-69962736
22/4 - 23/9
info@les3lacs.com

5ha 65T(100-250m²) 10A

1 ACD**G**IJKLM**P**RS
2 CFRVXY
3 BGH**M**NRU**W**X
4 (C+G) I(Q+S)
(T+U+V+Y 10/6-30/8) Z
5 **AB**EFGIJKLMNOPUWZ
6 AEGJ(N 3km)OV

A campsite in a lovely park with 2 small rivers (trout fishing and canoeing). Very spacious pitches, camp shop. Plenty of walking opportunities. Lovely swimming pool with water slide and toddlers' pool. Restaurant only open at weekends in low season.

A43 Lyon-Chambéry. Exit 11: St. Génix/Belmont-Tramonet. Left at the end of the exit road towards Belmont-Tramonet and Pont de Beauvoisin. Located beyond the small bridge on the right of the D916a.

CC € 15 *22/4-3/7 26/8-23/9*

N 45°33'33" E 5°40'33"

Bourdeaux, F-26460 / Rhône-Alpes (Drôme)

2026

Yelloh! Village Les Bois du Châtelas*****
route de Dieulefit
+33 (0)4-75006080
FAX +33 (0)4-75006081
8/4 - 11/9
@ reservation@chatelas.com

17ha 52T(90-120m²) 10A CEE

1 ACD**G**IJKLMOPST
2 IJKRTVWX
3 BGHJN**OP**RUV
4 (A+C+F+G) IJK**LMN** (Q+S+T+U+V+X+Y) Z
5 **AB**DEFGIJKLMNOPQRUW XYZ
6 ACEGH**JK**L(N 1km)ORTV

Terraced campsite with beautiful panoramic views of the nearby mountains from every pitch. The swimming pool and the terrace with a panoramic restaurant make it especially appealing in the evenings to enjoy the sunset. Heated indoor pool, wellness centre, free fitness hall.

From the north: A7 exit 15 Valence-Sud. dir. Gap and Crest. In Crest dir. Bourdeaux/Dieulefit. Campsite just south of Bourdeaux, on a bend to the left.

CC € 17 8/4-5/7 26/8-11/9 28=21

N 44°34'42'' E 5°7'39''

Bourg-St-Andéol, F-07700 / Rhône-Alpes (Ardèche)

2027

Le Lion***
Quartier Ile Chenevier
+33 (0)4-75545320
FAX +33 (0)9-74445570
1/4 - 30/9
@ contact@campingdulion.com

5ha 119T(100-250m²) 6A CEE

1 ACD**G**IJKLMPST
2 BCFGLMORTVXY
3 AGHJLNQRU**W**X
4 (B+G 1/6-30/9) (Q) (T+U+V+X 14/5-30/9) (Z)
5 **AB**EFGIJKLMNPUVZ
6 AEGJ(N 0,6km)RV

The camping pitches at Le Lion are set under tall trees, giving it a typical French ambiance. The pitches are spacious, between 100 and 250 m². There are opportunities for watersports on the Rhône. There is a supermarket 600m from the campsite.

Site located north of Bourg-St-Andéol 800m from centre. From the north: N86 dir. village, left after supermarket. Follow signs. From the south: N86 to village, dir. Viviers. Right before supermarket. Follow signs.

CC € 17 1/4-3/7 27/8-30/9 7=6, 14=12, 21=18

N 44°22'53'' E 4°38'55''

Bramans-en-Vanoise, F-73500 / Rhône-Alpes (Savoie)

2028

Val d'Ambin Bramans-Vanoise**
602 route de l'Église
+33 (0)4-79050305
FAX +33 (0)4-79052316
20/4 - 31/10
@ campingbramans@gmail.com

4ha 155T(100-115m²) 6A CEE

1 ACD**F**IJKLMO**P**Q
2 FGJKRTVWXY
3 BGHJL**M**NRU**W**
4 (**A** 1/7-31/8) (Q 1/7-30/8)
5 **AB**DFGIJKLMNPUVZ
6 ACEGK(N 12km)

The campsite is set on undulating ground 500 metres from Bramans. The pitches are marked out with stakes. The views of the surrounding mountains are an invitation to go walking.

D1006 St. Jean-de-Maurienne - Col du Mt. Cenis. You will find the site just across town centre behind the church of Bramans and at a distance of only 200 metres from N6.

CC € 15 20/4-30/6 25/8-31/10

N 45°13'44'' E 6°46'51''

Buis-les-Baronnies, F-26170 / Rhône-Alpes (Drôme) 2029

Domaine La Gautière***
La Penne-sur-Ouvèze
+33 (0)4-75280268
+33 (0)4-75282411
26/3 - 31/10
accueil@camping-lagautiere.com

3,5ha 20T(100-120m²) 6A

1 ACGIJKLMPST
2 IJKTVWX
3 BDGHJNU**W**
4 (B+G 15/5-30/9)
(Q+R 1/5-15/9)
(T+U 1/4-30/9)
(V+X 1/5-30/9) Z
5 AEFGIJKLMNOPUZ
6 CDEGK(N 3km)OTV

Charming rural campsite set among olive groves and the vineyards of warm Provence. Located in a large valley with rustic wooded mountains. Restaurant, terrace and swimming pool protected from the mistral. Close to the historic holiday resort of Buis-les-Baronnies.

Vaison-la-Romaine direction Buis-les Baronnies, left before village and follow the signs.

CC € 17 26/3-10/7 27/8-31/10

N 44°15'8'' E 5°14'35''

Buis-les-Baronnies, F-26170 / Rhône-Alpes (Drôme) 2030

La Fontaine d'Annibal***
Quai de l'Ouvèze
+33 (0)4-75280312
+33 (0)4-75275541
2/4 - 10/10
contact@
vacances-baronnies.com

2ha 42T(70-120m²) 10A CEE

1 ACD**G**IJKLP
2 CKRTVWX
3 BGJNRU
4 (B 1/6-1/9)
(Q+R+X 1/7-31/8) Z
5 **A**FIJKLMNOPUZ
6 AEGJ(N 0,8km)PT

The campsite is 800m from Buis-les-Baronnies with shops, restaurants and a large weekly market. Protected countryside and a starting point for walking and cycle routes. Here you will smell the flowers and the aromatic herbs of Provence.

From Vaison-la-Romaine/Nyons direction Buis-les-Baronnies and towards Séderon in centre. Left 300m further on at Quai du Pont Neuf towards site.

CC € 17 2/4-2/7 28/8-10/10

N 44°17'3'' E 5°16'55''

Challes-les-Eaux, F-73190 / Rhône-Alpes (Savoie) 2031

Municipal Le Savoy***
av. du Parc
+33 (0)4-79729731
1/4 - 15/10
contact@
camping-challesleseaux.com

2,8ha 70T(80-150m²) 6-10A CEE

1 ACD**G**IJLM**P**ST
2 DFGNRUVWX
3 AGHJ**M**RU**W**
4 (Q) (T+U 15/6-15/9) Z
5 **AB**DFGIJKLMNOPUWXYZ
6 CDEG**JK**(N 0,2km)OTV

A quiet, well-maintained campsite with spacious, partly marked out pitches and paved roads. Heated toilet facilities by the entrance. Walking, cycling, swimming and fishing close by. Many tourist sights in the vicinity. Close to Chambèry. Snack bar is only open at weekends in low season.

A43 Lyon-Chambéry. In Chambéry direction Grenoble as far as Challes-les-Eaux exit. Then N6 Albertville-Grenoble. Campsite located just before the centre on the left of the road.

CC € 15 1/4-8/7 25/8-15/10

N 45°33'5'' E 5°59'3''

Châteauneuf-de-Galaure, F-26330 / Rhône-Alpes (Drôme) 2032

Château de Galaure****
D51
+33 (0)4-75686522
22/4 - 25/9
info@chateaudegalaure.com

12ha 165T(100-120m²) 10A

1 ACD**G**IJKLMPQ
2 CRVWXY
3 BCGHNORW
4 (B+G 1/5-31/8) J**NP**
(Q+R)
(T+U+V+X 1/5-31/8) Z
5 **AB**GIJKMNPUZ
6 CEGH**IJ**(N 0,2km)TV

A peaceful, friendly family campsite. This is an ideal campsite to relax in a pleasant way, where children can develop and where you can enjoy real camping.

Exit Chanas, then take the N7 direction Valence, until just past St. Vallier. Then take the D51 to St. Uze and Hauterives. The campsite is located about 10 km behind St. Uze on the D51, before Châteauneuf-de-Galaure.

CC € 13 *22/4-2/7 27/8-25/9* N 45°13'26'' E 4°57'3''

Châteauneuf-sur-Isère, F-26300 / Rhône-Alpes (Drôme) 2033

Le Soleil Fruité****
Les Pêches
+33 (0)4-75841970
FAX +33 (0)4-75780585
26/4 - 15/9
contact@lesoleilfruite.com

3,5ha 138T(140m²) 6A CEE

1 C**F**IJKLM**P**ST
2 FKRTVWX
3 B**F**GRU
4 (B+E) (H 28/4-15/9) J
(Q+R+T+U+V) Z
5 **AB**EFJKLMNOPQUZ
6 CEGIJ(N 8km)TV

A family campsite located in an orchard and with magnificent views of the Drôme valley. Modern toilet facilities. Sports lovers will find everything to their satisfaction. Cycle trips and canoeing/kayaking make everything complete. The campsite has an indoor heated swimming pool.

Exit Valence North A7. Direction Lyon N7. Direction Pont d'Isère. Follow camping signs.

CC € 19 *26/4-8/7 25/8-14/9* N 45°0'7'' E 4°53'42''

Châtillon-en-Diois, F-26410 / Rhône-Alpes (Drôme) 2034

Municipal Les Chaussières
Les Chaussières
+33 (0)6-43002500
1/4 - 16/10
camping.chatillonendiois@wanadoo.fr

2ha 159T(60-110m²) 10A CEE

1 ACD**G**IJKLMOPST
2 CGKRTVWXY
3 ABGHJ**M**NQ**W**
4 (C+H 15/6-19/9) J
(T+X 1/5-15/9) Z
5 **A**FGIJKMNPUVZ
6 EGH**IJ**(N 0,5km)

Camp in the Drôme, at the foot of the Vercors in the medieval wine village of Châtillon-en-Diois. Plenty of shade, along the river, surrounded by mountains. Many options for walking, cycling and mountain-biking. 3 swimming pools and 1 slide. Snack bar, tennis, games for children.

From Valence D93 to Die. After Die D539 dir. Châtillon-en-Diois. Drive into village. After 1 km turn right after bridge. Site is then after 500 metres.

CC € 15 *1/4-15/7 1/9-16/10* N 44°41'38'' E 5°29'1''

Châtillon-en-Diois, F-26410 / Rhône-Alpes (Drôme)

2035

VivaCamp Le Lac Bleu***
Quartier la Touche
+33 (0)4-75218530
16/4 - 24/9
info@lacbleu-diois.com

6,5ha 75T(100-130m²) 6A CEE

1 ACD**G**IJKLMPST
2 ACDKLMRTVWXY
3 ABGHJKRU**W**XZ
4 (A 12/7-22/8) (E+H) K (Q+R+T) (U+V 15/5-15/9) (X) Z
5 **A**EFGIJKLMNOPUWZ
6 AEGIJ(N 3km)OTV

Located on the shores of a lake where swimming is possible from early in the season. Wonderful views of the lake and the surrounding mountains from the terrace. The valley is wide and flat. An excellent location for making lovely trips out. Restaurant and shop are open for the whole season. Lovely indoor pool with jacuzzi.

From Loriol direction Die; then D539 direction Châtillon-en-Diois. Right 1 km beyond St. Roman. The campsite is well signposted.

CC € 17 *16/4-5/7 24/8-23/9*

N 44°40'59" E 5°26'56"

Chauzon, F-07120 / Rhône-Alpes (Ardèche)

2036

La Digue****
chemin des Digues
+33 (0)4-75396357
27/3 - 30/9
info@camping-la-digue.fr

2,5ha 69T(80-130m²) 6-10A CEE

1 ACDGIJKLMOPST
2 ABCNORTVXY
3 AGHJMNRU**WX**
4 (C+H 1/4-30/9) (Q+S+T+U) (V 1/7-29/8) (Y 1/5-15/9) (Z)
5 **AB**DEFGIJKLMNOPQRUW Z
6 AEGJ**K**(N 3km)OTV

Attractive site, good toilet facilities, enthusiastic French owner speaks English and will do all she can.

A7 exit Montélimar-Nord. N7 to Le Teil. N102 to Aubenas. Past Villeneuve-de-Berg left at rndbt, D103. Left D579 to Vallon. In Pradons right to Chauzon at supermarket. Left before village, keep right at end of road (route d. Gras). Right at end of road, then keep left (route d'Uzer). Left before village, keep right, then left (route d. Digues). Site on right.

CC € 13 *5/4-6/7 23/8-30/9*

N 44°29'15" E 4°22'14"

Cordelle, F-42123 / Rhône-Alpes (Loire)

2037

Mars****
RD56,
route du Château de la Roche
+33 (0)4-77649442
1/4 - 15/10
campingdemars@gmail.com

1,8ha 46T(5-41m²) 10A CEE

1 ACD**G**IJKLPQ
2 JKRVX
3 A**F**GHJR**W**
4 (A 1/7-31/8) (C+G 1/5-30/9) (Q+S+T+U+V+X+Z)
5 **AB**DFGIJKLMNPUVWXY
6 EGJ(N 5km)OT

Quiet, beautifully located terraced campsite. You will have a view of the nearby reservoir of Villerest. Great for surfing and sailing. The campsite has a restaurant.

From Roanne follow D43 and then D56. After Cordelle campsite is on right side of road. Follow signs.

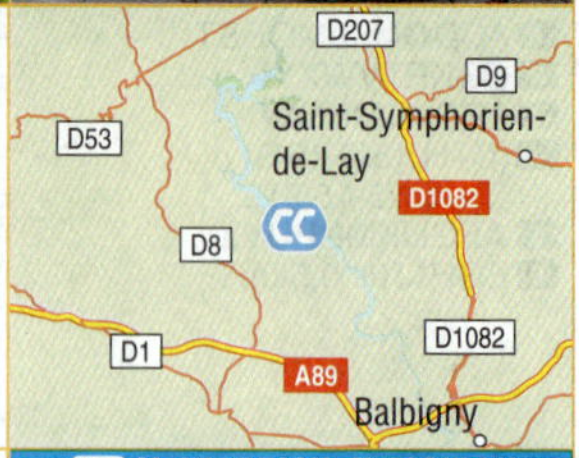

CC € 15 *1/4-8/7 25/8-15/10* 7=6

N 45°55'8" E 4°3'53"

Cormoranche-sur-Saône, F-01290 / Rhône-Alpes (Ain)

2038

du Lac****
Base de Loisirs,
365 chemin du Lac
+33 (0)3-85239710
1/5 - 30/9
contact@lac-cormoranche.com

4ha 93T(80-100m²) 10A CEE

1 ACD**G**IJKLMPQ
2 ADFLMRSVWXY
3 B**F**GHJKNRU**W**Z
4 (A 1/7-31/8)
(Q+R+T+U+V+X+Z)
5 **AB**EFGIJKLPUWXY
6 ACFGHIJ**K**(N 5km)RTV

The campsite is situated in a large natural area on a big swimming and fishing lake. Good base for cycling tours and visiting wine cellars in Mâcon, Beaujolais and Bourgogne. Good food in Bresse. The site has sunny pitches with several trees and bushes.

In Mâcon-centre D906 dir. Lyon. In Crêches left (D51) over the Saône. In Cormoranche follow Base de Loisirs signs. A40 dir. Bourg. Exit 3 Mâcon-Sud via Pont-de-Veyle to Cormoranche.

CC € 15 1/5-11/7 28/8-30/9 7=6, 14=12, 21=18

N 46°15'5'' E 4°49'33''

Crest, F-26400 / Rhône-Alpes (Drôme)

2039

Les Clorinthes***
Quai Soubeyran
+33 (0)4-75250528
FAX +33 (0)4-75767509
24/4 - 18/9
clorinthes@wanadoo.fr

4ha 154T(90-120m²) 6A CEE

1 AC**G**IJKLM**P**ST
2 CLORTVWXY
3 AB**F**GHJK**MOP**RU**WX**
4 (**A** 1/7-31/8)
(B+G 1/5-10/9) (Q)
(T+U+V 1/7-1/8) Z
5 **AB**FGIJKLMNPUZ
6 ACEG**JK**(N 0,8km)TV

Nice park with shade-giving trees. Modern toilet facilities. Swimming in swimming pool or in the Drôme, the river that flows past the campsite. Good start for cycling, walking or car trips. Medieval Crest within walking distance. Free WiFi for CCA-owners.

Leave the A7 at Loriol. D104 direction Crest. Left at 2nd traffic lights toards centre. Over the railway line. Turn right at the large roundabout with monument. Continue for another 600m beside the river to the campsite.

CC € 17 24/4-5/7 22/8-18/9

N 44°43'27'' E 5°1'40''

Cublize/Amplepuis, F-69550 / Rhône-Alpes (Rhône)

2040

Campéole Lac des Sapins****
+33 (0)4-74895283
FAX +33 (0)4-74895890
1/4 - 25/9
lacdessapins@
andretriganogroupe.com

8ha 85T(50-100m²) 16A CEE

1 ACD**G**IJKLM**P**
2 ACDLMRTUVWXY
3 BGHJMN**OPQ**RWZ
4 (B 1/7-31/8) (Q 1/5-25/9)
(R+T 1/7-31/8) Z
5 **AB**EFGIJKLMNOPUVXYZ
6 ACEGHK(N 0,5km)R

Family campsite located close to the lake with plenty of water sports. It has a bar and restaurant.

Follow the camping signs in the village. Drive past the village campsite. The entrance to the campsite 'Du Lac des Sapins' is located after about 600 metres.

CC € 17 1/5-4/7 22/8-25/9

N 46°0'47'' E 4°22'54''

Culoz, F-01350 / Rhône-Alpes (Ain)

2041

VivaCamp Le Colombier***
Ile de Verbaou
+33 (0)4-79871900
23/4 - 24/9
info@camping-alpes.net

1,5ha 54T(70-100m²) 10A

1 ACGIJKLMPQ
2 ADLMRTVWXY
3 BGHJMNQRUZ
4 (Q)
(T+U+X+Z 15/5-26/9)
5 ABDFGIJKLMNPUVWXYZ
6 DEGJ(N 0,3km)OV

This campsite lies between the Rhône and the Grand Colombier (1534m) in an oasis of green. Within walking distance of a large department store and centre. Swimming in the lake by the entrance. The extensive grounds offer plenty of shade. Various sports facilities available in the vicinity.

A40 dir. Genève. Exit 11: Éloise. RN508 as far as Frangy. In Frangy dir. Seyssel. Via D992 dir. Culoz. Campsite is located on the right of the road by the roundabout in Culoz.

CC € 13 23/4-5/7 24/8-23/9 7=6, 14=11

N 45°51'6'' E 5°47'38''

Darbres, F-07170 / Rhône-Alpes (Ardèche)

2042

Camping Les Charmilles***
Le Clapas, D258
+33 (0)4-75885627
30/4 - 30/9
info@campinglescharmilles.fr

5ha 56T(80-135m²) 10A CEE

1 BGIJKLPST
2 JKRTVWXY
3 ABDGHJMNRU
4 (A+C+G+Q+R+T+U+V+
Y+Z)
5 ABCEFGIJKLMNOPQRUW
Z
6 AEGHJ(N 8km)OV

Playfully designed, well-maintained and with a beautiful view. Friendly, helpful Dutch owners. Heated pool, bar/restaurant and a little shop (fresh bread daily) which is open all season. You can borrow cycle, walking and car tours. Free WiFi.

A7 exit Montélimar-Nord dir. Le Teil. Then dir. Aubenas and via Villeneuve-de-Berg N102 to Lavilledieu. Exit (D224) towards Lussas, then D224 dir. Darbres. After Darbres, 3 km dir. Mirabel. Follow this route, not SatNav.

CC € 17 30/4-9/7 27/8-30/9 14=12, 21=18

N 44°38'0'' E 4°30'30''

Die, F-26150 / Rhône-Alpes (Drôme)

2043

Chamarges**
route de Valence
+33 (0)4-75221413
26/3 - 2/10
campingchamarges@orange.fr

3,5ha 150T(80-110m²) 6A CEE

1 ACDFIJKLMPST
2 CKLORWXY
3 AGHJNRW
4 (B 4/4-5/10) (Q)
(T+U+V+X+Y 28/4-4/10)
5 GIJKLMNOPUVWZ
6 EJ(N 1,5km)TV

Level, sunny and shaded grounds. Beautiful views. Canoeing and kayaking on the Drôme right from the campsite. Swimming pool. Good restaurant with nice terrace. Lovely trips into the beautiful countryside and picturesque villages. Free WiFi.

From Valence take the D93. Campsite just before Die. Take campsite exit at roundabout. Camping sign on the right.

CC € 13 26/3-8/7 25/8-2/10

N 44°45'44'' E 5°20'47''

Die, F-26150 / Rhône-Alpes (Drôme)

2044

Le Glandasse***
Quartier de la Maladrerie
+33 (0)4-75220250
10/4 - 30/9
camping-glandasse@wanadoo.fr

3,5ha 120**T**(80-120m²) 10A CEE

1 ACD**G**IJKLOPQ
2 BCKLNRSTVWXY
3 ABGHJN**Q**RU**W**X
4 (C+H 25/4-30/9) K
(Q+R+T+U 15/4-30/9)
(V 1/5-30/9) (X 15/4-30/9) Z
5 **AB**EFGIJKMNOPUZ
6 EGK(N 1km)ORTV

The campsite is located right by the river in a wide valley. Lovely pitches with shady trees. Discover the natural area of the Vercors on foot, by bike or in your car. Good restaurant, lovely swimming pool, minigolf, fitness. 1 km from Die.

Exit Valence, then dir. Crest/Die. After the centre of Die, 1 km south of town continue towards Gap. Campsite clearly signposted. You reach the campsite via a tunnel (max. height 2.80m).

CC €13 *10/4-6/7 23/8-30/9*

N 44°44'41'' E 5°23'7''

Die, F-26150 / Rhône-Alpes (Drôme)

2045

Le Riou-Merle***
route de Romeyer
+33 (0)4-75222131
1/4 - 15/10
lerioumerle@gmail.com

2,5ha 97**T**(70-300m²) 6A CEE

1 AFIJKLMPST
2 KRTVWXY
3 BGHJR
4 (B 15/5-30/9) (U+X+Y) Z
5 **A**FGIJKLMNPUVZ
6 CEG**K**(N 0,4km)

Quiet campsite close to the medieval town of Die. Modern toilet facilities. Swimming pool. Mountain views. Tall trees give necessary shade and the small trees do not obstruct the sun. A base for making excursions through the countryside. Lovely new restaurant with excellent cuisine. WiFi on entire campsite.

From Crest take direction Gap before Die centre. Drive round the centre. Towards the centre again at the large roundabout. Just before the centre on the right.

CC €15 *1/4-8/7 26/8-15/10*

N 44°45'16'' E 5°22'40''

Dieulefit, F-26220 / Rhône-Alpes (Drôme)

2046

Huttopia Dieulefit***
Quartier d'Espeluche
+33 (0)4-75546394
FAX +33 (0)4-75904276
14/4 - 3/10
dieulefit@huttopia.com

20ha 90**T**(120-300m²) 10A CEE

1 ACD**F**IJKLN**P**ST
2 BDKLRTWXY
3 BGH**P**RUZ
4 (C 25/4-30/9) (Q+S)
(T+U+V+X 1/7-31/8) Z
5 **AB**DFGIJKLMNOPQUWZ
6 EGI(N 2km)V

A campsite in a wooded area of 20 hectares surrounded by countryside. Very spacious pitches with stunning mountain views. Modern, large centre with restaurant and recreation room. Two swimming pools, one of them heated, swimming possible in the pond, natural activity programme. Everything very modern and clean.

A7, exit Montélimar Nord. Direction Dieulefit (D540). In Dieulefit direction hospital (Santé). Left at hospital and follow signs. Another 1 km along a lane.

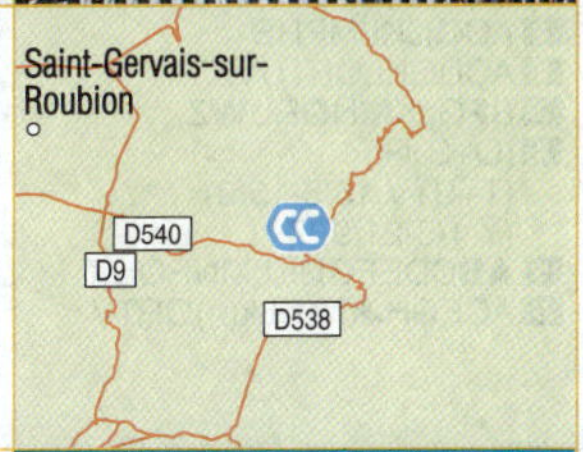

CC €17 *14/4-5/7 1/9-2/10*

N 44°32'24'' E 5°3'29''

Dieulefit, F-26220 / Rhône-Alpes (Drôme)

2047

Le Domaine des Grands Prés***
Les Grands Prés
+33 (0)4-75499436
20/3 - 1/11
info@
lesgrandspres-dromeprovencale.com

1,9ha 50T(80-100m²) 10A CEE

1 ACD**F**IJKLMPST
2 CGRTVWXY
3 AGHJL**M**RU
4 (B 1/6-20/9) (G 15/6-15/9) **KN**
5 **AB**DEFGIJKLMNOPUVZ
6 EGJ**K**(N 0,3km)RTV

A lovely campsite with plenty of shade near the picturesque village of Dieulefit, where you will find many artists. All shops are within walking distance. The fresh air invites you to go walking and cycling in the unique countryside.

A7 exit Montélimar-Nord, direction Dieulefit (D540). At the entrance to the town on the south side of the road, right. Follow signs.

CC € 15 20/3-8/7 25/8-1/11

N 44°31'18'' E 5°3'41''

Divonne-les-Bains, F-01220 / Rhône-Alpes (Ain)

2048

Indigo Divonne***
Quart. Villard, 2465 Vie de l'Etraz
+33 (0)4-50200195
+33 (0)4-50200035
22/2 - 18/11
divonne@camping-indigo.com

8ha 175T(80-150m²) 10A CEE

1 AC**F**IJKLM**P**ST
2 CFIJKRVWXY
3 B**F**GHJ**M**NRU**W**
4 (**A** 5/7-30/8)
(C+G 1/5-13/10) (Q+R)
(T+U+V+X 1/7-31/8) Z
5 **AB**DFGIJKLMNOPUW
6 CEGIJ(N 3km)TV

A lovely wooded campsite laid out in terraces. Pitches delightfully set among trees. A large swimming pool, plenty of amenities for children, fun activities. Switzerland, Geneva and Lake Geneva are close by.

From Gex D984 direction Divonne. Take the road to St. Gixet before Divonne and follow the camping signs.

CC € 15 22/2-5/7 1/9-17/11

N 46°22'29'' E 6°7'16''

Doussard, F-74210 / Rhône-Alpes (Haute-Savoie)

2049

Campéole La Nublière***
30 allée de la Nublière
+33 (0)4-50443344
+33 (0)4-50443178
28/4 - 25/9
nubliere@
andretriganogroupe.com

11ha 350T(100-110m²) 6A CEE

1 AC**G**IJKLMPRS
2 ACDGKLORTUVXY
3 BFGJK**M**N**Q**RU**W**Z
4 (Q+S)
(T+U+V 15/6-15/9)
(Y 1/5-21/9) Z
5 **AB**CDEFGIJKLMNPQUZ
6 ACEGH**J**(N 1,5km)ORTV

Quite a big campsite with a beach and a meadow by a lake. Interesting for water sports enthusiasts. Shade present everywhere and a separate area with bungalows. A nice view from the beach on the surrounding mountains and the lake.

D1508 Annecy-Albertville. The campsite is located near this road. Well signposted on the southwest shore of the lake, follow the camping signs in the community of Doussard.

CC € 17 1/5-4/7 22/8-25/9

N 45°47'24'' E 6°13'4''

Doussard, F-74210 / Rhône-Alpes (Haute-Savoie)

2050

La Ferme de la Serraz*****
rue de la Poste
+33 (0)4-50443068
1/5 - 17/9
info@campinglaserraz.com

3,5ha 79**T**(80-120m²) 16A CEE

1 A**G**IJKLPRS
2 GRVWXY
3 B**F**HJKRU**W**
4 (**C**+**H**)
(Q+T+U+V+X 1/7-31/8) Z
5 **AB**EFGIJKLMNPUWXYZ
6 ACEGHI**K**(N 0,3km)TV

There is a lovely swimming pool and a paddling pool here. There is a bar and a restaurant. Good impression as you drive onto the site. Sunny grassland or shade provided by trees.

Route D1508 Annecy-Albertville. The campsite is signposted on the south side of the lake at the roundabout which leads to Doussard centre.

CC € 15 *1/5-15/7 1/9-17/9*

N 45°46'31'' E 6°13'34''

Duingt, F-74410 / Rhône-Alpes (Haute-Savoie)

2051

Mun. Les Champs Fleuris**
631 voie Romaine
+33 (0)4-50685731
FAX +33 (0)4-50770317
16/4 - 25/9
camping@duingt.fr

1,5ha 111**T**(80-120m²) 6A

1 A**G**IJKLMPQ
2 GJKRVWXY
3 BFGHJR
4 (Q+T)
5 **AB**FGIJKLMNPUVZ
6 ACEG**IJ**(N 1km)T

Grounds with wide terraces from which some pitches have views of Lake Annecy. The Annecy-Faverges-Marlens cycle route goes right past the campsite. For shopping, Duingt centre is 1 km away. It is 10 km to Annecy and about 25 km to Albertville.

D1508 Annecy-Albertville. The campsite is on the right of the D1508 between St. Jorioz and Duingt, exit Entrevernes. Clearly signposted.

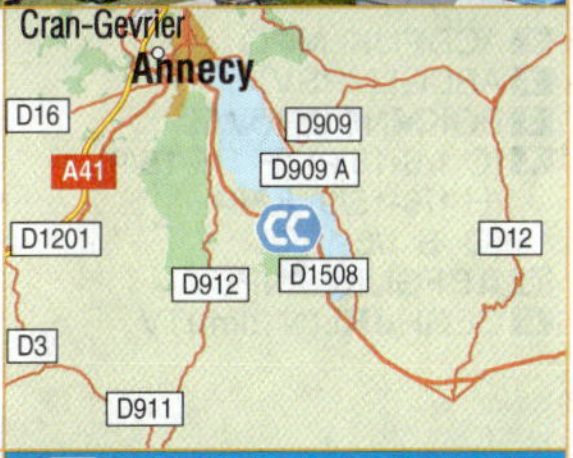

CC € 17 *16/4-8/7 25/8-25/9*

N 45°49'36'' E 6°11'19''

Eclassan, F-07370 / Rhône-Alpes (Ardèche)

2052

l'Oasis****
Le Petit Chaléat
+33 (0)4-75345623
1/5 - 5/9
info@oasisardeche.com

5ha 38**T**(90-250m²) 6A CEE

1 ACD**F**IJLPST
2 CJKLMRVWXY
3 BGHJLN**Q**RU**W**
4 (C 8/5-6/9)
(H+Q+T+U+V+X) Z
5 **A**DEFGIJKLMNPQRUWZ
6 AEGJ**K**(N 4km)ORTV

Terraced campsite in beautiful country, a small paradise on earth with attention and care for nature, a real oasis. The swimming pool is heated from 2 May. Walking and cycling maps are available. You can get a delicious dish of the day and home made pizzas. Call them, and they will pitch your caravan for you.

A7, exit 12 Chanas. Then N7 dir. Valence as far as St. Vallier. D86 over the Rhône to Sarras. Then D6 dir. Eclassan and then following the camping signs.

CC € 15 *1/5-3/7 21/8-5/9* *14=12*

N 45°10'45'' E 4°44'22''

Entre-deux-Guiers, F-38380 / Rhône-Alpes (Isère)

2053

L'Arc en Ciel***
chemin des Berges
+33 (0)4-76660697
1/3 - 15/10
info@camping-arc-en-ciel.com

1,3ha 60T(100-110m²) 2-6A CEE

1 AC**G**IJKLMOPQ
2 CGORSVXY
3 BGHJ**MRW**
4 (C 15/5-15/9) (G 15/5-25/9) (V)
5 **AB**GJKLNOPUVZ
6 ACDEG**IK**OV

Peaceful grounds situated in a village. Pitches are shaded by tall trees. The low altitude makes it ideal for exploring the Chartreuse highlands and surrounding district in spring and autumn. The mountain stream with its pebble beach next to the site is an added attraction.

D1006 from Chambéry towards Les Echelle. Then take the D520 direction St. Laurent-du-Pont. On the roundabout follow campsite signs.

CC € 15 *1/3-14/7 31/8-15/10*

N 45°26'5'' E 5°45'22''

Excenevex-Plage, F-74140 / Rhône-Alpes (Haute-Savoie)

2054

Campéole La Pinède***
10 avenue de la Plage
+33 (0)4-50728505
FAX +33 (0)4-50729300
28/4 - 30/9
pinede@andretriganogroupe.com

12ha 246**T** 16A CEE

1 ACD**F**IJKLM**P**Q
2 ABDGLMRSVXY
3 BGK**MNOQ**RUWZ
4 (C 1/6-15/9) (E 1/5-15/9) (H 1/6-15/9) K**NP** (Q+S 1/6-15/9)
5 **AB**FGIJKLMNPUV
6 CEGH**JK**L(N 2km)TV

A large family campsite set in a wood right next to Lake Geneva with its sandy beaches. Quite secluded but with all amenities next to the entrance. Pitches spread out among the permanent camp facilities.

N5 Genève direction Thonon-les-Bains. Before Bonnatrait turn left to Yvoire/Excenevex. The campsite is 500 metres to the right after the roundabout.

CC € 17 *1/5-4/7 22/8-30/9*

N 46°20'45'' E 6°21'29''

Fleurie, F-69820 / Rhône-Alpes (Rhône)

2055

VivaCamp La Grappe Fleurie****
rue de la Grappe Fleurie
+33 (0)4-74698007
9/4 - 16/10
info@beaujolais-camping.com

3,5ha 59**T**(70-150m²) 16A CEE

1 ACD**G**IJKLMO**P**ST
2 JKRVWXY
3 BGHJK**M**RU
4 (A 1/7-31/8) (B 15/5-15/9) (Q+R) (T+U+V 1/5-30/9) Z
5 **AB**DFGHJLMNOPQUWXYZ
6 ACEGKL(N 0,8km)RV

A quiet campsite with pitches on terraces, surrounded by the Beaujolais vineyards. Marked out pitches separated by hedges, spaciously appointed and shaded.

A6 exit Mâcon-Sud. D906 (N6) direction Villefranche. Right after La Maison Blanche on D32 to Fleurie. Follow campsigns.

CC € 17 *9/4-1/7 31/8-15/10* *7=6, 14=11*

N 46°11'16'' E 4°41'56''

Grâne, F-26400 / Rhône-Alpes (Drôme)

2056

Les 4 Saisons***
495 route de Roche-sur-Grâne
+33 (0)4-75626417
1/4 - 30/9
contact@
camping-4-saisons.com

3ha 61**T**(80-130m²) 6A CEE

1 ACD**G**IJKLMOPST
2 FIJKRSTVWXY
3 AGHJRU
4 (C+G 1/5-30/9) (Q 🔑) Z
5 **A**EFGIJKLMNOPUWZ
6 EG**K**(N 0,8km)TV

A friendly terraced family campsite with views of the mountains. 10 minutes from the A7. Suitable as a stopover campsite. Starting point for unforgettable trips in the countryside and picturesque villages. Heated swimming pool.

A7 exit 16 direction Loriol, then towards Crest. Take Grâne exit. Continue to roundabout with Grâne exit and campsite.

CC € 15 *1/4-8/7 25/8-30/9 7=6, 14=12*

N 44°43'37'' E 4°55'37''

Gresse-en-Vercors, F-38650 / Rhône-Alpes (Isère)

2057

Les 4 Saisons***
La Rivoire
+33 (0)4-76343027
1/5 - 15/10, 20/12 - 31/3
camping-les4saisons@orange.fr

2,2ha 85**T**(75-100m²) 10A CEE

1 ACD**F**IJKLMO**P**Q
2 CGJKLRUVX
3 B**E**GHJ**MOP**RU**W**
4 (C 1/7-31/8)
(Q+R 1/5-15/10,20/12-31/12)
(T+U+V+Z 1/7-31/8)
5 **AB**DFGIJKLMNPUVZ
6 ACEG**JK**(N 1km)O**P**TV

This campsite is located in a natural park with exceptionally lovely views. Pretty mountain flowers (gentian, orchids and edelweiss) abound in the spring. Walking routes from the campsite. Cold nights may occur. Bakery a 2 minute walk away.

Follow signs to Gresse-en-Vercors to the north of Monestier-de-Clermont. Keep right at the church; then left at the first roundabout, then left after 400 metres. Don't take the difficult route south of Monestier-de-Clermont!

CC € 17 *1/5-3/7 29/8-15/10*

N 44°53'48'' E 5°33'20''

Hauterives, F-26390 / Rhône-Alpes (Drôme)

2058

Le Château***
5 route de Romans (D538)
+33 (0)4-75688019
FAX +33 (0)4-75689094
2/4 - 25/9
contact@
camping-hauterives.com

4ha 73**T**(80-120m²) 10A CEE

1 ACD**G**IJKLMPST
2 CGRTUVWXY
3 BGHJKN**P**RU**W**
4 (A 1/7-31/8)
(C+H 15/6-31/8)
(Q+S+T+U 🔑)
(X+Y 1/5-31/8) (Z 🔑)
5 **AB**EFGIJKLMNOPQUVWZ
6 ACDE**IK**(N 0,2km)OTV

A campsite with marked out pitches, mostly in the shade. No chlorine in the swimming pool, just salt. The town of Hauterives and its Palais Ideal which is a World Heritage Site is just 200 metres away.

A7, exit 12. Via D519 and D538 towards Hauterives. Well signposted.

CC € 13 *2/4-3/7 21/8-25/9 7=6, 14=12, 21=18*

N 45°15'10'' E 5°1'37''

Hauteville-Lompnès, F-01110 / Rhône-Alpes (Ain)

2059

Les 12 Cols***
chemin de Cormaranche
+33 (0)4-37865587
1/1 - 9/10, 17/12 - 31/12
contact@camping-les12cols.fr

100T(85-135m²) 10A CEE

1 ACD**F**IJKLP
2 JLRVWXY
3 AD**F**GHJK**M**NR**SUW**
4 (B 1/6-30/9) (Q 1/7-30/8) Z
5 **AB**DGIJKLMNOPUWXZ
6 CDEG**IK**(N 1km)

A peaceful campsite at an altitude of 800m with terraced pitches on flowery and well landscaped grounds with clean, modern facilities. Perfect for nature lovers. Various sports activities are possible on the Plateau d'Hauteville, an ideal location for cycling or exploring the waterfalls.

A40, exit St. Martin-du-Fresne. Then follow signs to Hauteville-Lompnes. A42, exit Ambérieu-en-Bugey direction Belley RN504 Tenay. Direction Hauteville-Lompnes.

CC € 15 *1/4-30/6 1/9-9/10 7=6*

N 45°58'15" E 5°35'44"

Joyeuse, F-07260 / Rhône-Alpes (Ardèche)

2060

La Nouzarède***
chemin d'Orival
+33 (0)4-75399201
9/4 - 17/9
campingnouzarede@wanadoo.fr

2ha 58T(80-120m²) 10A

1 ACD**G**IJKLMOPST
2 ABCLNRTVXY
3 AGMNR**WX**
4 (C+H) K
(Q+R+T+U+V+Y+Z)
5 **A**CDEFGIJKLMNPQUXYZ
6 AEGK(N 0,8km)TV

All the charm of the Ardèche at La Nouzarède, 5 min. from the centre of the village and 100m from the river. Walking, swimming and excursions, that's the joy of life! All you need on holiday at this site. Swimming pool and jacuzzi heated in late season.

A7 exit Montélimar-Nord dir. Le Teil/Aubenas. In Le Teil N102 to Aubenas. Then D104 direction Alès. From roundabout at Joyeuse to the village. After 1 km, after garage, turn right. Left at stop sign. 2nd left after bridge.

CC € 15 *9/4-9/7 26/8-17/9 7=6, 14=11*

N 44°29'2" E 4°14'8"

La Motte-Chalancon, F-26470 / Rhône-Alpes (Drôme)

2061

La Ferme de Clareau***
route de Die (RD 61)
+33 (0)4-75272603
15/4 - 16/10
campingfermeclareau@wanadoo.fr

9ha 42T(100-500m²) 10A CEE

1 AGIJKLM**P**ST
2 BCIKRWXY
3 AGHJRU**W**
4 (**A** 1/7-31/8) (B 1/6-1/9)
(Q+U+V+X) Z
5 **A**IJKMNOPUV
6 AEJ(N 1,5km)

Christine and Olivier welcome you to this undulating campsite with 42 pitches on 9 hectares of grounds. Plenty of space, lovely views, also from the swimming pool. You can swim and fish in the river, go cycling and walking. There are Provençal markets in the area at Nyons, Die and Vaison la Romaine.

A7, exit Montélimar south. D94 direction Nyons and Gap. At Rémuzat take the D61 towards La Motte-Chalancon. Follow signs on the D61, through the centre and follow camping signs.

CC € 15 *15/4-1/7 20/8-16/10*

N 44°28'43" E 5°23'43"

Lalley, F-38930 / Rhône-Alpes (Isère)

2062

Sites & Paysages Belle Roche***
+33 (0)6-32613882
26/3 - 10/10
camping.belleroche@gmail.com

2,5ha 57T(100-250m²) 10A CEE

1 ACD**G**IJKLMOPST
2 CGKLRTVWX
3 BGHJMNRUVW
4 (A 1/6-31/8) (B 1/6-15/9) (Q+T+U+V+Y+Z)
5 **A**DFGIJKLMNOPUWXZ
6 ACEG**I**J(N 0,5km)TV

A sunny campsite at an altitude of 900 metres in mountainous surroundings. Swimming pool. Plenty of walking and cycling tours possible. The surrounding mountains form a beautiful panorama. Restaurant and terrace with mountain views.

N57 Grenoble-Sisteron. Indicated before the Col de la Croix-Haute by signs at Lalley.

€ 17 *1/4-3/7 22/8-30/9*

N 44°45'17" E 5°40'44"

Lamastre, F-07270 / Rhône-Alpes (Ardèche)

2063

Camping de Retourtour***
1 rue de Retourtour
+33 (0)4-75064071
11/4 - 25/9
campingderetourtour@wanadoo.fr

2,9ha 85T(90-120m²) 13A CEE

1 A**G**IJKLMPST
2 ACDLMNRTUVWXY
3 BGHJN**P**QRUV**W**XZ
4 (Q+R+T+U+V+X) Z
5 **A**FGIJKLMNOPUVZ
6 CEG**JK**(N 1,5km)OTV

A quiet family campsite in the heart of the Ardèche just 1.5 km from Lamartre. Ideal for a holiday with family or friends. Less than 100m from Le Doux river.

From Tournon take the D534 to Lamastre, then towards St. Agreve. Camping sign after 1.5 km, then turn right and go downhill.

€ 15 *11/4-7/7 24/8-25/9*

N 44°59'30" E 4°33'55"

Lanslevillard, F-73480 / Rhône-Alpes (Savoie)

2064

Camping Caravaneige de Val Cenis***
+33 (0)4-79059052
FAX +33 (0)4-79052685
28/5 - 30/9, 19/12 - 16/4
campoland@orange.fr

2,5ha 86T(100-140m²) 10A CEE

1 ACDFHIJKLMOPQ
2 CGKRTVW
3 AGHJ**M**NRU
4 (**A** 1/7-31/8) **N** (T+U+V+X+Z)
5 **AB**DEFGIJKLMNOPQUZ
6 ACEGJ(N 0,5km)OV

A spacious level campsite with 360° panorama views of the mountain range and village. All pitches are marked out. 200m from the ski lifts.

A43 exit Modané. Then D1006 direction Mont-Cenis. Campsite located on the left of the village.

€ 15 *4/1-5/2 7/3-1/4 28/5-15/7 1/9-30/9*

N 45°17'28" E 6°54'32"

Lathuile, F-74210 / Rhône-Alpes (Haute-Savoie) — 2065

l'Idéal****
715 route de Chaparon
+33 (0)4-50443297
+33 (0)4-50443659
1/5 - 18/9
contact@campingideal.com

3ha 180**T**(80-110m²) 6A

1 AC**G**IJKLPRS
2 IJKRVWXY
3 B**F**GHJKMNQRUV
4 (B 1/6-4/9) (E)
(H 1/5-10/9) IJ**K**MP
(Q+R)
(T+U+V+Y+Z 15/5-4/9)
5 **AB**EFGIJKLPUWZ
6 CDEG**J**(N 2km)OTV

A beautifully located campsite with lovely swimming pools, of which the indoor pool is heated. The restaurant is open from the middle of May. Open-air fitness equipment for all ages.

Route Annecy-Albertville D1508. The campsites are signposted on green signs at the lights in Brédannaz (Lathuile).

CC € 17 *1/5-1/7 27/8-18/9*

N 45°47'43'' E 6°12'21''

Laurac-en-Vivarais, F-07110 / Rhône-Alpes (Ardèche) — 2066

Les Châtaigniers Camping***
Le Mas de Peyrot
+33 (0)4-75368626
1/4 - 30/9
chataigniers07@orange.fr

1,2ha 57**T**(90-100m²) 10A CEE

1 ACD**F**IJKLPST
2 JKRTVWXY
3 AGHJRU
4 (B+G 1/5-30/9)
(Q 1/7-31/8) (Z)
5 **A**FGJKMNPUXYZ
6 AEGJ(N 0,3km)RT

Wonderfully peaceful here by the chestnut trees. A small campsite with good toilet facilities close to the owner's vineyards. You can walk to the village of Laurac-en-Vivarais for your shopping. No entertainment, therefore quiet.

A7 exit Montélimar-Nord direction Le Teil/ Aubenas. At Le Teil N102 to Aubenas. Follow the D104 direction Alès from there. The campsite is beyond Prends-Toi-Gardes to the right.

CC € 15 *1/4-30/6 1/9-30/9*

N 44°30'14'' E 4°17'40''

Le Bourg-d'Oisans, F-38520 / Rhône-Alpes (Isère) — 2067

La Cascade****
route de l'Alpe d'Huez
+33 (0)4-76800242
+33 (0)4-76802263
1/1 - 30/9, 15/12 - 31/12
lacascade@wanadoo.fr

2,5ha 128**T**(90-100m²) 16A

1 ACDGIJKLMPQ
2 CGKRSTVWXY
3 BGHJNRU**W**
4 (**A** 1/7-31/8)
(C+H 15/5-15/9)
(Q+T+V 1/7-31/8) Z
5 **AB**DFGIJKLMNOPUVWZ
6 ABEGIK(N 1,2km)OTV

A campsite on the first bend of the climb up l'Alpe d'Huez, well known from the Tour de France. The pitches are separated by hedges. Le Bourg d'Oisans just a stroll away. The l'Alpe d'Huez ski bus stops in front of the site.

Route D1091 Grenoble-Briançon. Turn left as you leave Le Bourg-d'Oisans via ring road direction l'Alpe d'Huez, the campsite 500 metres on the right.

CC € 17 *1/1-27/5 6/6-24/6 22/8-30/9*

N 45°3'51'' E 6°2'21''

Le Bourg-d'Oisans, F-38520 / Rhône-Alpes (Isère)

2068

RCN Belledonne****
Rochetailleé
+33 (0)4-76800718
FAX +33 (0)4-76791295
1/4 - 10/10
@ belledonne@rcn.fr

4ha 175**T**(80-140m²) 10A

1 ACD**F**IJKLMPQ
2 GRSVXY
3 BGHJ**M**NRU
4 (A 1/7-30/8)
(C+H 15/5-31/8) **N**
(Q+R 🔑) (T 1/7-31/8)
(U+V+X 🔑) Z
5 **AB**CEFGIJKLMNOPRUVWZ
6 ABEG**IK**(N 8km)OV

A spacious campsite with extensive facilities. Lovely views from the marked out pitches. The site is located in a mountainous landscape. Thanks to its location at the beginning of a valley (l'Eau d'Olle), the park-like grounds are level and easy accessible. A large number of trees provide plenty of shaded areas.

D1091 Grenoble-Briançon. In Rochetaillée turn right towards Allemont (D526). Campsite is on the right after 500 metres and is signposted.

CC € 15 *1/4-28/5 4/6-25/6 3/7-9/7 26/8-10/10*

N 45°6'53'' E 6°0'32''

Le Bourg-d'Oisans, F-38520 / Rhône-Alpes (Isère)

2069

Sites & Pays. A la Rencontre du Soleil*****
route de l'Alpe d'Huez
+33 (0)4-76791222
FAX +33 (0)4-76802637
1/5 - 30/9
@ contact@rencontresoleil.fr

1,5ha 48**T**(80-120m²) 10A CEE

1 ACDFIJKLMPQ
2 CGKRSTVXY
3 BGHIJMNR
4 (C+D 1/5-20/9)
(Q 20/5-31/8)
(T+U+V+X 15/5-15/9)
(Y 20/5-3/9) (Z 15/5-15/9)
5 **AB**DEFGIJKLMNPUVWY
6 AEG**IK**(N 0,8km)OV

Well maintained grounds 1.3 km from le Bourg d'Oisans. The many flower borders and views of the surrounding mountain ranges make this a suitable base for your holiday.

D1091 Grenoble-Briançon. After leaving the Le Bourg-d'Oisans ring road, take direction L'Alpe-d'Huez on roundabout. Well signposted.

CC € 19 *1/5-27/5 5/6-25/6 17/8-30/9*

N 45°3'54'' E 6°2'24''

Le Crestet, F-07270 / Rhône-Alpes (Ardèche)

2070

Les Roches****
+33 (0)4-75062020
FAX +33 (0)4-75062623
1/4 - 30/9
@ camproches@nordnet.fr

4ha 50**T**(100m²) 6A CEE

1 ACD**G**IJKLMPS
2 ABJKLMNRTVXY
3 BCHJNRU**W**
4 (C+H+Q+R 🔑) (T 1/7-30/8)
(U+V 1/6-30/8)
(X+Y 1/7-30/8) (Z 1/6-30/8)
5 **AB**EFGJLNPUVXZ
6 DEG(N 5km)RTV

A quiet family campsite in the heart of the rural Ardèche with wonderful views of the Doux valley. You can play and fish in the river.

From Tournon D534 direction Lamastre. Do not drive to village of Le Crestet but stay on the road till you see the Les Roches camping or restaurant sign on the right, then follow signs.

CC € 13 *1/4-7/7 24/8-30/9*

N 45°0'38'' E 4°37'25''

Le Grand-Bornand, F-74450 / Rhône-Alpes (Haute-Savoie)

2071

l'Escale***
33 chemin du Plein Air
+33 (0)4-50022069
FAX +33 (0)4-50023604
20/5 - 25/9, 16/12 - 10/4
@ contact@campinglescale.com

3,2ha 142**T**(80-100m²) 10A CEE

1 AC**G**HIJKLMOPQ
2 CGJKRTVWX
3 B**F**GHJKLM**Q**RU**W**
4 (C 1/7-31/8) (F+H) K
(Q 9/7-30/8,17/12-3/1)
(U+Y+Z)
5 **AB**DEFGIJKLOPRUWXYZ
6 ACDEGHIJ(N 0,2km)O**P**TV

Campsite 150 metres from the centre of Le Grand-Bornand. 240 m² indoor and outdoor swimming pool. Restaurant is in an old farmhouse in Savoy style. Also good wintersports opportunities. Télécabines just outside the village.

9A41 exit Annecy-Nord, then direction Thônes. In Thônes head for St. Jean-de-Sixt. Go towards Le Grand-Bornand at the roundabout. Turn right before the centre towards 'Vallée du Bouchet'. Campsite 1 km on the right.

CC € 19 *20/5-5/7 30/8-25/9*

N 45°56'26'' E 6°25'40''

Le Grand-Serre, F-26530 / Rhône-Alpes (Drôme)

2072

Le Grand Cerf****
+33 (0)4-75688614
26/3 - 2/10
@ contact@campingdrome.fr

2ha 60**T**(80-160m²) 10A

1 ACD**G**IJKLMPST
2 AGIJKLRVWXY
3 BDGHJKMNR
4 (C 30/4-2/10) (G 29/5-11/9)
J(Q 1/7-31/8)
(T+U+V+X+Y+Z)
5 **A**FGIJKLMNPUWZ
6 ACEGJ(N 1km)V

A peaceful campsite with marked out pitches, partly shaded. As a guest of the campsite you can enjoy free swimming, play tennis or borrow a mountain bike (6 available).

N7 Valence-Vienne. In Sablon take D519 direction Beaurepaire. Right here towards Hauterive. Then D51 to Le Grand-Serre. Well signposted.

CC € 11 *26/3-9/7 26/8-2/10*

N 45°16'17'' E 5°6'6''

Le Poët-Célard, F-26460 / Rhône-Alpes (Drôme)

2073

Le Couspeau****
Quartier Bellevue
+33 (0)4-75533014
16/4 - 15/9
@ info@couspeau.fr

8ha 100**T**(100-180m²) 6A CEE

1 ACD**G**IJKLMPST
2 IJKRTVWXY
3 BGHJNRU
4 (C 1/6-15/9) (E)
(H 1/6-15/9) JM
(Q+R+T+U+V+X+Y) Z
5 **AB**EFGIJKLMNOPQRUWX
YZ
6 CEGHK(N 4km)OT

In 2016 this beautiful terraced campsite will celebrate its 40-year anniversary. For this reason prices are being kept extra low so campers can enjoy the festivities. Le Couspeau is very child friendly because of the watery playground with unexpected fountains.

A7 exit 15 in Valence-Sud. D111 Valence-Crest. In Crest direction Dieulefit, Bourdeaux. In Bourdeaux dir. Dieulefit. Signposted south of Bourdeaux.

CC € 11 *1/5-8/7 25/8-15/9*

N 44°35'47'' E 5°6'40''

Lépin-le-Lac, F-73610 / Rhône-Alpes (Savoie)

2074

Le Curtelet***
Lac d'Aiguebelette
+33 (0)4-79441122
15/5 - 20/9
lecurtelet@orange.fr

1,3ha 91T(90-110m²) 4-6-10A

1 AGIJKLPQ
2 DFLMRVWXY
3 BMNQRWZ
4 (Q 1/6-15/9) Z
5 ABFGJLNPUWZ
6 EGK(N 1km)T

A peaceful family campsite with direct access to Lake Aiguebelette, the warmest lake in France, with views of the mountains. Reliable toilet facilities.

A43 Lyon-Chambéry, exit Lac d'Aiguebelette. After péage turn right at roundabout, after 300 metres left at roundabout direction St. Alban-de-Montbel. Via south bank towards Lépin-le-Lac. Campsite on the left of the road on D921d.

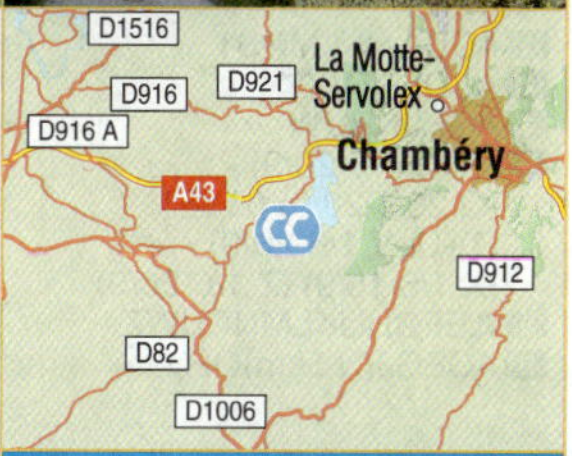

CC € 15 *15/5-30/6 1/9-20/9*

N 45°32'23" E 5°46'45"

Lépin-le-Lac, F-73610 / Rhône-Alpes (Savoie)

2075

Les Peupliers**
D921d / Lac d'Aiguebelette
+33 (0)4-79360048
1/4 - 31/10
info@camping-lespeupliers.net

3ha 114T(70-100m²) 6A CEE

1 ACDGIJKLMPRS
2 ADFLMRVWXY
3 AGNRUWZ
4 (Q+T) Z
5 ABFGIJKLMNPUVZ
6 ACEIK(N 3km)O

Extended grounds that slope gently down to Lake Aiguebelette. Swimming and fishing permitted via a direct access. The pitches are large, shaded and marked out by hedges. In the vicinity: paragliding, rock climbing, canoeing, kayaking, mountain biking and cycling. WiFi (not free).

A43 Lyon-Chambéry. Exit 'Lac Aiguebelette'. After the toll station left at the roundabout towards Aiguebelette and Lépin-le-Lac. Campsite about 9 or 10 km on the right.

CC € 15 *1/4-1/7 29/8-31/10 7=6*

N 45°32'19" E 5°47'57"

Les Contamines-Montjoie, F-74170 / Rhône-Alpes (Haute-Savoie)

2076

Le Pontet***
2485 rte de Notre Dame de la Gorge
+33 (0)4-50470404
1/1 - 25/9, 17/12 - 31/12
campinglepontet74@orange.fr

2,8ha 150T(90-120m²) 10A

1 ACGIJKLMOPQ
2 ACDGKLMRTVWXY
3 AGHMNOPQRUWZ
4 (Q+R) (T 28/6-30/8) (V 1/7-31/8)
5 ABDFGIJKLMNPUVWZ
6 CEGJ(N 2,5km)OTV

Partly rocky but also grassy grounds (1200 metres). Easily accessible. Ideal base for beautiful walking tours in the surrounding mountains. There are not many trees which means open views.

A40 exit St. Gervais, direction St. Gervais-centre. Another 9 km past the centre to Les Contamines. Site is located 3 km beyond the centre on the left of the D902, the Route de Notre Dame de la Gorge.

CC € 17 *16/5-3/7 21/8-25/9*

N 45°48'9" E 6°43'19"

Les Ollières-sur-Eyrieux, F-07360 / Rhône-Alpes (Ardèche)

2077

Le Chambourlas***
Chambon de Bavas, D2
+33 (0)4-75662431
20/4 - 20/9
info@chambourlas.com

2,5ha 62T(100-200m²) 10A CEE

1 ACDGIJKLM**P**ST
2 ACDLRTVXY
3 AGHJNRU**W**
4 (C+G 1/5-20/9)
(Q 20/5-20/9) (R)
(T+U+V 1/6-20/9)
(X 1/6-15/9) (Z 1/6-20/9)
5 **A**EFGHIJKLMNPUWZ
6 ACEGJ(N 5km)ORV

The campsite is located in the Ardèche in the Eyrieux valley, and welcomes you on spacious, shaded pitches. Discover old villages with local markets, canoe on the Eyrieux. Numerous walking trails from the campsite. The owners speak German and English. For anglers: the lake and the river flow past the campsite.

Take Autoroute exit Loriol, the D304 direction Privas. In Privas turn right on the D2 to Les Ollières/Le Cheylard. Campsite located about 13 km on the right.

CC €15 *20/4-5/7 23/8-20/9 7=6, 14=11*

N 44°46'53" E 4°37'5"

Les Ollières-sur-Eyrieux, F-07360 / Rhône-Alpes (Ardèche)

2078

VivaCamp Le Mas de Champel****
quartier Champel
+33 (0)4-75662323
16/4 - 17/9
masdechampel@wanadoo.fr

4ha 56T(100-130m²) 10A CEE

1 ACD**F**IJKLMPS
2 ACGJKRSTVWX
3 AGHJKNRU**WX**
4 (C+G 1/5-15/9) **KN**
(Q 1/5-15/9) (R)
(T+U+V+Y 1/5-15/9) (Z)
5 **AB**DEFGIJKLMNOPUVWXZ
6 ACEGJ(N 0,4km)V

Located along the River l'Eyrieux. Includes terraces with magnificent views over the mountains. Facilities are housed in a beautiful old farmhouse. Wellness room with jacuzzi and sauna. Restaurant with panorama terrace.

From the A7, exit Valence-Sud. Then D86 to La Voulte. Past La Voulte take the D120 to Les Ollières-sur-Eyrieux. From the south, A7 exit Loriol. Then N304 to Privas. Then the D2 and D120 to Les Ollières-sur-Eyrieux.

CC €17 *16/4-5/7 24/8-16/9 7=6, 14=11*

N 44°48'26" E 4°36'54"

Les Vans, F-07140 / Rhône-Alpes (Ardèche)

2079

Lou Rouchetou***
Chassagnes
+33 (0)4-75373313
1/4 - 30/9
info@rouchetou.com

5ha 100T(80-100m²) 10A CEE

1 A**G**IJKLMPST
2 ACNORTVXY
3 AGHNRU**WX**
4 (B 1/5-20/9) (G 1/5-15/9)
(Q+R+U+V+Y+Z 1/4-20/9)
5 **A**DEFGIJKLMNOPQUZ
6 ACDEG**K**(N 4km)OQTV

A campsite in attractive surroundings, 3 km from Les Vans. Plenty of space in the grounds and by the river. Swim and sail in the Chassezac. Lovely swimmingpool. The restaurant is open all season.

A7, exit 17 Montélimar-Nord. Then dir. Le Teil/Aubenas. In Le Teil Nioz dir. Aubenas. Then N104 dir. Alès. ± 3 km past Joyeuse turn right dir. Les Vans/Chambonas, D104A. Then D295 dir. Chassagnes. Follow road and in big bend turn right then left. Best to use SatNav coordinates.

CC €17 *1/4-4/7 22/8-30/9*

N 44°24'38" E 4°10'16"

Luc-en-Diois, F-26310 / Rhône-Alpes (Drôme)

iD **2080**

Les Foulons***
rue de la Piscine
+33 (0)4-75213614
10/4 - 31/10
contact@
camping-luc-en-diois.com

1,8ha 100T(80-130m²) 10A CEE

1 ACDGIJKLMO**P**ST
2 CGKLRVWXY
3 ABGHJKL**M**NRU**W**X
4 (**C**+H 15/6-15/9) (Q)
(T+U+V+X 1/7-31/8) Z
5 **A**GIJKLMNPUXZ
6 ADEG**J**(N 0,6km)OTV

A campsite with sun and shade on the Drôme. Good toilet facilities. Tennis court. Wonderful trips out from the campsite in the beautiful mountains and old villages. Recharging point for electric bikes. (E-)bikes for rent.

On the D93 from Die to Gap, in Luc-en-Diois on the west side of the road. Drive to the centre then follow signs.

CC €15 *10/4-8/7 25/8-30/10*

N 44°36'56'' E 5°26'46''

Lugrin, F-74500 / Rhône-Alpes (Haute-Savoie)

iD **2081**

La Vieille-Eglise***
53 route des Prés Parrau
+33 (0)4-50760195
FAX +33 (0)4-50761312
10/4 - 20/10
campingvieilleeglise@wanadoo.fr

2ha 73**T**(100-120m²) 10A CEE

1 ACD**G**IJKLPQ
2 JKLRVWX
3 AGQRU
4 (C+H 14/5-20/9)
(**Q**+R 15/6-30/8)
(Z 1/7-30/8)
5 **AB**FGIJKMNPUWXYZ
6 AEGH**K**(N 0,8km)

A friendly, peaceful, shaded campsite with a heated swimming pool. Water supply, drainage and electricity on all pitches. Close to a supermarket, shops, Lake Geneva and Evian-les-Bains. Ideal for visiting the Swiss side of the lake.

From Evian-les-Bains on D1005 by the lake to the east. The campsite is clearly signposted near Lugrin.

CC €17 *10/4-5/7 22/8-20/10* *7=6, 14=12, 21=18*

N 46°24'2'' E 6°38'48''

Lus-la-Croix-Haute, F-26620 / Rhône-Alpes (Drôme)

iD **2082**

Champ la Chèvre***
Le Village
+33 (0)4-92585014
24/4 - 30/9
champlachevre@orange.fr

3,7ha 85T(80-150m²) 6A CEE

1 ABCD**G**IJKLM**P**RS
2 IJKLRXY
3 ABGHJRU**W**
4 (C+E+H) K(T+U+V)
(X 24/4-15/9) (Y)
(Z 24/4-15/9)
5 **A**DEFGIJLMNOPQRUWZ
6 CDEIJK(N 0,2km)OTV

Beautiful peaceful campsite, with a spacious feel. All around you are mountains, you can do your shopping 200m from the campsite. Lovely restaurant. A site for campers on their way south or returning home. The perfect resting place. About 500 metres from the N1075 but you don't hear it. Also very suitable for longer stays.

From Grenoble N75 direction Sisteron. Past Col de la Croix-Haute, enter the town of Lus-la-Croix-Haute, then follow the campsite signs.

CC €15 *24/4-10/7 27/8-30/9*

N 44°39'52'' E 5°42'26''

Lussas, F-07170 / Rhône-Alpes (Ardèche) — 2083

VivaCamp Ludo Camping***
route de Lavilledieu
+33 (0)4-75942122
23/4 - 25/9
info@ludocamping.com

6ha 115T(100-160m²) 10A CEE

1 ACD**G**IJKLMPST
2 CNORTVWXY
3 ABGHJKNRU**W**
4 (A 16/5-24/9)
(C+H+Q+R 🔑)
(T+U+V+X 15/5-15/9)
(Z 🔑)
5 **AB**DEFGIJKLMNPUWZ
6 ACEGJ(N 2km)V

This campsite is located by a stream. The level part of the site is pleasantly shaded. The terraced section still has young trees but the pitches here are bigger. Toilet facilities in the lower grounds are new.

Via the A7, exit Montelimar-Nord dir. Le Teil. Then via Villeneuve-de-Berg (dir. Aubenas) to Lavilledieu. Via D224 to Lussas/Darbres. Turn right before the village.

CC € 15 *23/4-5/7 24/8-24/9*

N 44°36'18'' E 4°28'17''

Lyon/Dardilly, F-69570 / Rhône-Alpes (Rhône) — 2084

Camping Indigo International de Lyon****
allée du Camping International
+33 (0)4-78356455
FAX +33 (0)4-72170426
1/1 - 31/12
lyon@camping-indigo.com

6ha 165T(80m²) 10A CEE

1 AC**G**IJKLMP
2 FGIJRTVXY
3 AGNRU
4 (B+G 30/4-20/9) (Q 🔑)
(U+X 1/7-31/8) (Z 🔑)
5 **AB**DFGIJKLMNOPUZ
6 CFG(N 0,5km)V

A municipal campsite located in a landscaped park on the outskirts of Lyon. Ideal for a stopover on the way to your holiday destination or to visit the city of Lyon, included on the UNESCO World Heritage List. Tourist information centre, swimming pool, TV room on the site.

From Paris: A6 Lyon - Villefranche-sur-Saône. Exit 33. Follow the 'Complexe Touristique' and/or 'Camping Porte de Lyon' signs.

CC € 17 *1/1-11/6 1/9-1/12 11/12-31/12*

N 45°49'11'' E 4°45'42''

Marlens, F-74210 / Rhône-Alpes (Haute-Savoie) — 2085

Champ Tillet***
D1508
+33 (0)4-50443374
FAX +33 (0)4-50662344
1/4 - 31/10
duchamptillet@wanadoo.fr

3ha 104T(80-110m²) 10A CEE

1 AC**G**HIJKLMPRS
2 GRSTVWXY
3 B**F**GJKR
4 (C+H 15/5-15/9) (Q+U 🔑)
(V 1/7-30/8) (Y 🔑) Z
5 **AB**DEFGIJKLMNPUWZ
6 ACFGIJ(N 4km)TV

Level, open grounds. Many campers choose this campsite to avoid the busy campsites around the lake. Shopping centre 4 km away. The campsite has a good restaurant.

D1508 Annecy-Albertville. The campsite is located along the D1508, 4 km past Faverges on the right side. Clearly signposted.

CC € 15 *1/4-9/7 27/8-31/10*

N 45°45'43'' E 6°20'12''

Marsanne, F-26740 / Rhône-Alpes (Drôme) — 2086

Les Bastets****
Quartier les Bastets
+33 (0)4-75903503
FAX +33 (0)4-75903505
1/4 - 30/9
@ contact@campinglesbastets.com

3,5ha 61**T**(80-120m²) 10A CEE

1 ACDGIJKLMO**P**ST
2 FIJKRSTVWXY
3 ABFGHJN**Q**RU
4 (A 1/7-31/8)
(B+G 23/4-30/9) (Q 🔑)
(R 1/6-30/9)
(T+U+V+Y 1/7-31/8) Z
5 **AB**DEFGIJKLMNOPUWXYZ
6 ACEGJ(N 2km)OTV

A terraced campsite with stunning views of the Plaine de la Valdaine. Infinity swimming pool where you can look over the side into the valley. Lovely trips from the campsite. A level section with 30 pitches since 2013.

A7, exit 17 Montélimar-Nord. Direction Tourette then towards La Coucourde. Left in centre towards Sauzet. Then direction Condillac/Marsanne.

CC € 15 *1/4-3/7 22/8-30/9*

N 44°39'29" E 4°53'28"

Massignieu-de-Rives, F-01300 / Rhône-Alpes (Ain) — 2087

VivaCamp Lac du Lit du Roi****
La Tuillière
+33 (0)4-79421203
16/4 - 17/9
@ info@camping-savoie.com

2,5ha 90**T**(80-120m²) 10A

1 ACD**G**IJLM**P**R
2 DJLMRTVWXY
3 AGHJKMRU**W**Z
4 (A 1/7-31/8)
(B+G 15/5-19/9) M
(Q+R 🔑) (U+V+X 1/5-15/9)
Z
5 **AB**FGIJKLMNPUVWXYZ
6 EGJ(N 7km)OV

Extensive grounds with three toilet blocks. Almost all pitches have views of the lake that is connected to the Rhône. There is also a small swimming pool. 300m from a small harbour with a slipway.

A40 direction Genève. Exit 11 Eloise. RN508 direction Frangy. D992 direction Culoz. Continue on D992 for a further 12 km past Culoz. Over the bridge to Massignieu-de-Rives. Well signposted.

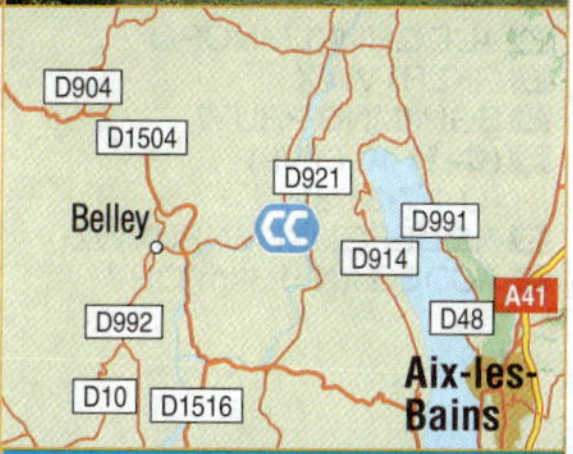

CC € 17 *16/4-5/7 24/8-16/9 7=6, 14=11*

N 45°46'7" E 5°46'11"

Matafelon-Granges, F-01580 / Rhône-Alpes (Ain) — 2088

Les Gorges de l'Oignin***
rue du Lac
+33 (0)4-74768097
15/4 - 20/9
@ camping.lesgorgesdeloignin@
orange.fr

2,6ha 128**T** 10A CEE

1 ACD**G**IJLPQ
2 DJKLMRTUVWXY
3 ABD**F**GHNRU**W**Z
4 (C+G 1/6-20/9)
(Q+R+T+U+V+X 1/5-20/9) Z
5 **AB**DFGIJKLMNOPUXZ
6 AEGJ(N 3km)ORTV

A lovely modern and spacious terraced campsite with heated swimming pools by a small reservoir. The campsite has wonderful views. The Gorges de l'Ain are close by. For a day out, Geneva or Lyon, the Jura or the bird park at Villars-les-Dombes.

From Bourg-en-Bresse in the direction of Nantua, turn left at roundabout and take D18 as far as Matafelon, follow the signs. Matafelon is not signposted coming from Oyonax.

CC € 17 *15/4-6/7 23/8-20/9 7=6, 14=12*

N 46°15'19" E 5°33'26"

Mayres-Savel, F-38350 / Rhône-Alpes (Isère)

iD **2089**

Camping de Savel**
D116
+33 (0)4-76811479 (tel/fax)
1/4 - 30/10
@ contact@camping-savel.com

7ha 100T(100-120m²) 12A CEE

1 ACD**G**IJKLMPST
2 DJKLMNORTVWXY
3 ACGHJNRU**VWZ**
4 (B 1/5-30/9) **LN**(Q 🔑)
(R 1/4-15/10)
(T+U 1/5-15/9) (V 1/7-31/8)
(X 🔑) (Z 1/5-15/9)
5 **A**EFGIJKLMNPUXZ
6 ACDEGHIJ(N 13km)TV

The campsite is located right by a lake. Swimming pool. Ample trees which give necessary shade. Large restaurant with spacious terrace with views of the mountains and lake. 3 km from the campsite is one of Europe's most beautiful footpaths, La Passerelle du Drac with a footbridge over the lake. Beautiful countryside.

Grenoble N85 dir. Vizille-La Mure. In La Mure, at the roundabout drive Mayres-Savel and 'Camping de Savel', then another 15 km to the campsite.

CC € 13 *1/4-30/6 30/8-30/10*

N 44°52'56" E 5°41'16"

Méaudre, F-38112 / Rhône-Alpes (Isère)

iD **2090**

Les Buissonnets***
Les Grangeons
+33 (0)4-76952104
1/1 - 31/10, 12/12 - 31/12
@ camping-les-buissonnets@wanadoo.fr

2,3ha 109T(100-110m²) 2-10A CEE

1 ACD**G**HIJKLMNOPQ
2 GKLRTVWX
3 BGHJMN**OP**RU**W**
4 (**C+H** 10/6-5/9)
(Q 1/7-31/8)
5 **AB**DEFGIJKLMNPUVWZ
6 ACDEGJ(N 0,3km)ORV

Les Buissonnets is a level terrain with marked out pitches, partly in the shade. Beautiful views of the surrounding area. The large open air swimming pool is 100m away. Perfect location for trips out.

In Grenoble (Sassenage) direction Villard-de-Lans. Continue towards Méaudre. Campsite is located near the swimming pool, 300 metres north of the village centre.

CC € 15 *1/4-30/6 1/9-31/10*

N 45°7'46" E 5°31'57"

Menglon, F-26410 / Rhône-Alpes (Drôme)

iD **2091**

L'Hirondelle****
Bois de St. Ferréol
+33 (0)4-75218208
FAX +33 (0)4-75218285
9/4 - 25/9
@ contact@campinghirondelle.com

14ha 123T(80-300m²) 6A CEE

1 ACDGIJKLMOPST
2 BCKLNRSTXY
3 BGHJKN**OP**QRU**WX**
4 (**A** 1/7-28/8)
(C+H 1/5-25/9) IJ
(Q+R+T 🔑) (U 25/4-12/9)
(V+X+Y 🔑) Z
5 **AB**EFGIJKLMNOPQRUVW
Z
6 EHI**K**(N 3km)ORTV

The campsite forms part of the countryside (10 hectares of forest, river and open views of the fields). There is a lake nearby. Plenty to do for young and old. Lovely leisure pool. Plenty of pitches at the edge of the woods with views over fields and the mountains.

From Die D93 towards the south, road beside the Drôme, then left onto D539 direction Châtillon-en-Diois. D140 after St. Roman. Cross bridge. Campsite on the right.

CC € 17 *9/4-8/7 25/8-25/9*

N 44°40'53" E 5°26'49"

Meyras, F-07380 / Rhône-Alpes (Ardèche) 2092

Le Ventadour***
Pont de Rolandy
+33 (0)4-75941815
16/4 - 2/10
info@leventadour.com

3,5ha 115**T**(70-150m²) 10A

1 ACD**G**IJKLM**P**ST
2 ACORTVWXY
3 AGHJNRU**WX**
4 (Q 1/6-13/9) (R 25/6-28/8) (T+U+V+X 2/7-28/8) (Z 25/6-28/8)
5 **AB**DFGJLMNPRUVZ
6 ACFGJ(N 2km)OV

A perfect location with a hospitable family. Ideal for sports or trips to cultural and natural surroundings. Between mountains and volcanoes, on the River Ardèche. Private beach. Spacious, shaded, level pitches. Heated toilets in spring. Free WiFi-zone.

A7 exit Montélimar-Nord dir. Le Teil-Aubenas. N102 to Aubenas. In Aubenas N102. After Pont de Labeaume campsite on your left. From Le Puy first follow N88, before Pradelles N102 dir. Aubenas. Campsite on the right.

CC € 17 16/4-5/7 22/8-2/10 14=13, 21=19

N 44°40'6'' E 4°17'0''

Mirabel-et-Blacons, F-26400 / Rhône-Alpes (Drôme) 2093

Gervanne Camping****
Bellevue
+33 (0)4-75400020
FAX +33 (0)4-75400397
1/4 - 30/9
info@gervanne-camping.com

3,8ha 150**T**(90-157m²) 6A CEE

1 ACD**G**IJKLMOPST
2 CGORTVWXY
3 ABGHJKLNRUWX
4 (**A** 15/5-30/9) (C+H 1/5-30/9) (Q+S) (T+U+V+X+Y 1/5-30/9) Z
5 **AB**DEFGIJKLMNOPRUVWXYZ
6 CEGH**IJK**ORTV

There are pitches: around the swimming pool and beside the Drôme. Abundant with beautiful trees. Nice walks along the Drôme. You can also go kayaking and swimming. A good starting point for exploring the Vercors and the Drôme Provençale. Picturesque villages (including Crest) a short distance away. Good restaurant.

A7 exit Valence dir. Crest D111. Before Crest dir. Die D164. 6 km past Crest left and continue to Mirabel-et-Blacons. Campsite signposted.

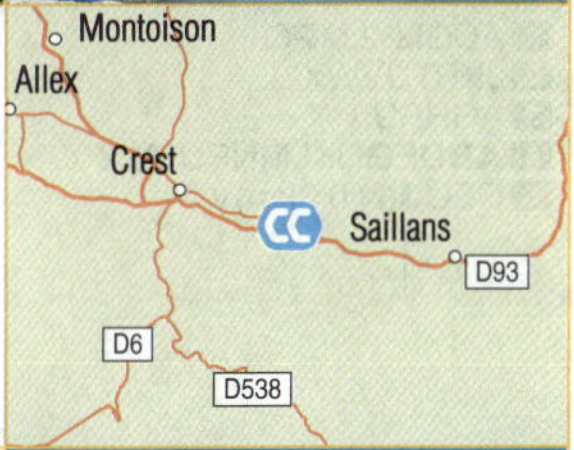

CC € 17 1/4-8/7 25/8-30/9

N 44°42'39'' E 5°5'23''

Mirmande, F-26270 / Rhône-Alpes (Drôme) 2094

La Poche***
Quartier la Poche
+33 (0)4-75630288
25/3 - 2/10
camping@la-poche.com

3,5ha 72**T**(80-140m²) 6A CEE

1 ACDGIJKLMPST
2 BCFJKLRTVWXY
3 AGHJN**O**RU
4 (A 1/7-1/9) (C+G 1/5-1/10) (Q+R 15/5-15/9) (T 15/6-31/8) (Y 1/7-31/8) (Z 15/6-31/8)
5 **A**EFGIJKMNOPUVWZ
6 EG**I**J(N 6km)OV

A little way from the motorway (7 km from the Route du Soleil), La Poche offers an oasis of peace in the countryside with, among other things, a beautiful swimming pool. Mirmande is at walking distance (3 km) and has been voted one of the most beautiful villages in Europe.

From north: A7 exit 16 Loriol, left dir. Loriol/ Montélimar. After ± 2 km left dir. Mirmande. From south: A7 exit 17 Montélimar-Nord dir. Valence. After 2 km right dir. Mirmande and follow signs.

CC € 13 25/3-8/7 25/8-2/10

N 44°41'13'' E 4°51'16''

Montbrison/Moingt, F-42600 / Rhône-Alpes (Loire)

iD **2095**

Municipal du Surizet***
31 rue du Surizet
+33 (0)4-77580830
15/4 - 15/10
campingmunicipal@ville-montbrison.fr

2,5ha 96T(100m²) 10A

1 AGIJKLMPQ
2 CGRVXY
3 AR**W**
4 (B)
5 **AB**DGHIJKMNPUVWZ
6 CEG(N 3km)T

Small, but welcoming municipal campsite. Located on the edge of Montbrison. Options for horseback riding in the surroundings and a great place for anglers.

In Montbrison direction St. Anthème, St. Étienne via D496. Follow signs on left. In the south side of Montbrison.

CC € 11 *15/4-30/6 1/9-15/10*

N 45°35'29'' E 4°4'41''

Montchavin-les-C/Bellentre, F-73210 / Rhône-Alpes (Savoie)

iD **2096**

de Montchavin-les-Coches**
D225
+33 (0)4-79078323
1/1 - 30/9, 1/11 - 31/12
campingmontchavin@orange.fr

1,3ha 45T(80-100m²) 10A

1 ACGIJKLM**PQ**
2 JKRTUVWX
3 AGHRU
5 **AB**DEGIJKLMNPUVWZ
6 CEG**J**(N 0,3km)V

High-altitude terraced campsite with extensive view over the valley from every pitch. Very welcoming village with good restaurants at 5 minutes from the campsite on foot. Ideal for skiing in winter.

From Moutiers take the N90. After Bellentre drive in the direction of Montchavin-les-Coches. Signposted from here on. The campsite is located on the left of the village centre.

CC € 13 *1/5-9/7 26/8-30/9*

N 45°33'38'' E 6°44'22''

Montferrat, F-38620 / Rhône-Alpes (Isère)

iD **2097**

Détente et Clapotis**
1578 rue des Chevaliers de l'An Mil
+33 (0)4-76553394
15/4 - 15/9
campingmontferrat@gmail.com

2,5ha 100T(70-110m²) 10A

1 AGIJKLM**P**RS
2 DGKLNRVX
3 BHJNR**WZ**
4 (Q+T+U+V) Z
5 **A**FGIJKMPUZ
6 EGJ**K**(N 3km)

Come and enjoy the services of a 4-star campsite for the price of 2 stars. On the Paladru lake with its blue water and beach. New on the campsite: a swimming pool and a small spa to relax, and sports grounds. There is a restaurant on the campsite where you can dine with a view over the lake and where you can enjoy musical nights.

From Voiron take the D1075 as far as Montferrat. Left in the village towards Lac de Paladru/camping D50/D50c. Well signposted.

CC € 15 *15/4-8/7 28/8-15/9*

N 45°28'4'' E 5°33'31''

Montrevel-en-Bresse, F-01340 / Rhône-Alpes (Ain)

2098

La Plaine Tonique****
599 route d'Etrez
+33 (0)4-74308052
FAX +33 (0)4-74308800
21/4 - 16/9
@ plaine.tonique@wanadoo.fr

15ha 380**T**(100m²) 10A CEE

1 ACD**G**IJKLMPQ
2 ACDFGLRVY
3 BGHJ**MNPQ**RU**WZ**
4 (B 18/6-28/8) (E 1/7-16/9) (F) (G 18/6-28/8) IJM**N** (Q+T+U 4/7-28/8) (X) Z
5 **AB**EFGIJKLMNOPUWZ
6 CDEG**IJ**(N 0,5km)RTV

A very large, lovely family campsite with a big leisure pool. Located by a large lake with plenty of watersports opportunities. Suitable for older children. Located in fairly level countryside, therefore suitable for cycle trips. Swimming shorts not allowed in the pool.

In Montrevel-en-Bresse take the D28 in the direction of Etrez/Marboz. Campsite on the left of the road.

CC € 17 *1/5-30/6 1/9-15/9*

N 46°20'21'' E 5°8'12''

Montrigaud, F-26350 / Rhône-Alpes (Drôme)

2099

La Grivelière****
2980 route de la Verne
+33 (0)4-75717071
1/4 - 30/9
@ courrier@lagriveliere.com

2,5ha 35**T**(60-120m²) 6A CEE

1 ACD**F**IJKLMPST
2 CLRTUVXY
3 BGHJN**OP**RU
4 (C+H 1/5-30/9) (Q+R+T+V+X+Z)
5 **A**EFGIJKLMNOPQUZ
6 AEGHJ(N 3km)OV

A small 4 star campsite with 4 star service and first class toilet facilities. Located in a picturesque area of the Drôme. Swimming pool heated from 1/5. Perfectly accessible along easy, quiet roads. An ideal base for exploring the surrounding area.

D538 Beaurepaire - Romans-sur-Isére. In Le Cabaret-Neuf D67 direction Montrigaud. At roundabout follow the signs.

CC € 13 *1/4-8/7 25/8-30/9 7=6*

N 45°13'18'' E 5°10'1''

Murs-et-Gélignieux, F-01300 / Rhône-Alpes (Ain)

2100

L'Île de la Comtesse****
route des Abrets
+33 (0)4-79872333
30/4 - 25/9
@ camping.comtesse@wanadoo.fr

3ha 60**T**(100-120m²) 6A CEE

1 ACD**G**IJLM**P**RS
2 CDFRSVWX
3 AGJKNRU**W**
4 (A 5/7-27/8) (C+H) JM (Q+S+T+U) (V 1/7-31/8) (X) Z
5 **AB**FGJKLNPUWXYZ
6 CEGIK(N 1km)OV

A friendly four star campsite located between a lake and mountain, close to Chambéry and Lyon. It has a swimming pool, children's pool and slide. The campsite is located on the unique 'Via Rhôna' cycle route. Many kilometres of cycling beside the Rhône. The snack bar, pizzeria and restaurant are only open at weekends in low season.

A43 Lyon-Chambéry, exit 10 Chimilin/Aoste, then on the B592 direction Belley. Campsite located on the right after the 2nd bridge.

CC € 17 *30/4-2/7 27/8-25/9*

N 45°38'23'' E 5°38'56''

Neydens, F-74160 / Rhône-Alpes (Haute-Savoie) — 2101

Sites & Paysages La Colombière****
166 chemin Neuf
+33 (0)4-50351314
FAX +33 (0)4-50351340
23/3 - 31/10
@ la.colombiere@wanadoo.fr

2,3ha 113T(80-120m²) 16A

1. ACD**G**IJKLMPQ
2. FGKRUVWX
3. ABCGHIJKL**M**NRU
4. (A 1/6-30/9) (C 15/6-15/9) (F 1/4-31/10) (G 15/6-15/9) **KLN**(Q (key)) (R 15/6-15/9) (U (key)) (V 1/7-31/8) (Y (key)) Z
5. **AB**DEFGIJKLMNOPUWXYZ
6. ACDEGHK(N 0,3km)OQRT VW

Pitches marked out by overgrowth. Peaceful location but close to Geneva. The warden organises guided visits to Geneva, also in low season (min. 6 participants). Indoor pool and excellent restaurant (open all year). Heated outdoor pool refurbished with children's section with slide and jacuzzi, also sauna and hammam.

From Lausanne follow signs to France. From Macon the A40. Exit St. Julien. Follow the green signs to Annecy, D1201 to the village Neydens/campsite.

CC € 19 *23/3-7/7 24/8-31/10*

N 46°7'11'' E 6°6'19''

Nyons/Venterol/Novézan, F-26110 / Rhône-Alpes (Drôme) — 2102

Les Terrasses Provençales****
450 route de Rousset
+33 (0)4-75279236
1/4 - 30/9
@ lesterrassesprovencales@gmail.com

2,5ha 69T(80-100m²) 10A CEE

1. AC**G**IJKLPST
2. JKRTUVWXY
3. BGHJKLRU
4. (C 15/4-30/9) (Q+R+T+U+V+X (key)) Z
5. **A**BDFGIJKLMNPUWZ
6. CEGIJ(N 3km)OTV

A terraced campsite with beautiful views of the mountains, vineyards, apricot and olive trees. The toilet facilities and swimming pool, with terrace and bar, are heated. Close to Mont Ventoux, Nyons, Vaison la Romaine and Orange.

Campsite located between Valréas and Nyons D538. From Valréas 3 km before Venterol.

CC € 15 *2/4-9/7 27/8-30/9*

N 44°24'30'' E 5°4'48''

Pelussin, F-42410 / Rhône-Alpes (Loire) — 2103

Sites & Paysages Bel'Epoque du Pilat***
2 rte de la Vialle
+33 (0)4-74876660
1/4 - 30/9
@ contact@camping-belepoque.fr

3,5ha 55T(50-150m²) 6A CEE

1. ACD**G**IJKLMPQ
2. BCIJKRTVXY
3. ABCGHJMRU**W**
4. (C+Q 1/5-15/9) (T+U 1/7-31/8) Z
5. **A**EFGJLNOPUW
6. EG**JK**(N 1,5km)ORT

A peaceful campsite 45 km south of Lyon. There are many marked out footpaths and mountain bike trails in the Côte du Rhône wine area and the Pilat nature reserve. Heated pool from 1 May. Tennis courts.

A7, exit 10, Ampuis. On N86 direction Serrières, in Chavanay D7 to Pelussin. At roundabout follow D79 and signs. Do not follow GPS, use these directions.

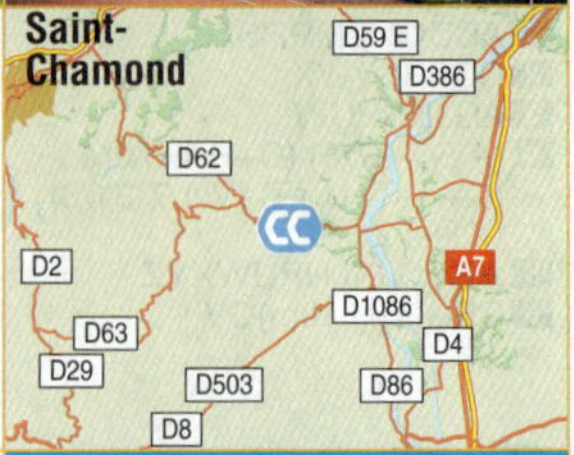

CC € 15 *1/4-1/7 22/8-30/9* 14=13, 21=19

N 45°24'50'' E 4°41'29''

Petichet/St. Théoffrey, F-38119 / Rhône-Alpes (Isère) — 2104

Ser Sirant***
Lac de Laffrey
+33 (0)4-76839197
24/4 - 2/10
info@campingsersirant.com

2ha 87**T**(90-110m²) 10A

1 AC**G**IJKLMPQ
2 DJKLMNRVWXY
3 ABCGHJN**OP**RU**W**Z
4 (A 1/7-15/8) (Q+R+T+U+V+X+Y+Z 1/5-30/9)
5 **AB**DEFGIJKLNPQUZ
6 ACDEGIJ**K**(N 8km)TV

A campsite right by a large lake where you can go rowing, surfing and sailing. It has the French quality hallmark 'Camping Qualité'. An active family campsite: activities during the day and relaxation in the evening. A wonderful area for (mountain) hiking, cycling and mountain biking.

N85 dir. Napoléon, 30 km south of Grenoble towards Gap. Turn left at traffic lights in village of Petichet. Follow signs.

CC € 15 *24/4-2/7 27/8-2/10*

N 45°0'0'' E 5°46'39''

Pont-de-Vaux, F-01190 / Rhône-Alpes (Ain) — 2105

Aux Rives du Soleil***
D933A
+33 (0)3-85303365
FAX +33 (0)3-85303123
15/4 - 17/10
info@rivesdusoleil.com

7ha 160**T**(100m²) 6A

1 ACD**G**IJKLMOPQ
2 CFLMRTVWXY
3 AD**F**GHJKLNRU**W**X
4 (B+G 14/5-11/9) (Q+R) (T 1/5-30/9) (U+V 1/7-31/8) (X+Y) Z
5 **AB**EFGIJKMNOPUWZ
6 ACEGJ(N 3km)OV

Spacious natural campsite on the banks of the Saône, suitable for cycling, walking and fishing. Separate overnight terrain.

From the north: A6, exit 27 Tournus. From the south: A6, exit Mâcon. Mâcon-Nord. Then the D906 direction Pont-de-Vaux. At roundabout Fleurville over the Saône. Campsite located on the Saône.

CC € 17 *15/4-3/7 22/8-17/10*

N 46°26'49'' E 4°53'56''

Pont-de-Vaux, F-01190 / Rhône-Alpes (Ain) — 2106

Champ d'Été****
Champ d'Été
+33 (0)3-85239610
1/4 - 15/10
info@camping-champ-dete.com

3,5ha 130**T**(80-100m²) 10A CEE

1 ACD**G**IJLM**P**Q
2 DLMRUVXY
3 AGHJKRU**VW**
4 (C 1/7-31/8) (F+H) IJ**KL** **N**(Q) (R 1/7-31/8) (T+Z 15/6-15/9)
5 **AB**GIJKLPUWZ
6 ACDEGJ(N 1km)

This quiet campsite is located in park-like surroundings, at walking distance from the vibrant village of Pont-de-Vaux, on a large fishing lake, beside the municipal pool (free entrance). The campsite is not far from the A6.

At Fleurville (D906) over the Saône to Pont-de-Vaux (D933). In Pont-de-Vaux follow base-de-loisirs and camping signs.

CC € 15 *1/4-9/7 26/8-15/10*

N 46°25'46'' E 4°56'0''

Pont-de-Vaux, F-01190 / Rhône-Alpes (Ain) 2107

Les Ripettes***
+33 (0)3-85306658
1/4 - 30/9
@ info@camping-les-ripettes.com

2,5ha 55T(150-400m²) 10A CEE

1 ACDGIJKLOPQ
2 RUVXY
3 AGHJR
4 (B 15/5-15/9) (Q)
(T 1/6-15/9)
5 ABGIJKLMNPUVWX
6 ADEGJ(N 2,5km)

A lovely, quiet and friendly campsite with very spacious pitches just 4 km from the town of Pont-de-Vaux. The campsite is expertly run and is always kept perfectly clean. Cycle routes close by.

At Fleureville D906 cross the Saône to Pont-de-Vaux (D933). In Pont-de-Vaux dir. St. Trivier-de-Courtes. (D2). Campsite on the left 4 km past St. Bénigne next to the water tower.

CC € 15 *1/4-3/7 21/8-30/9*

N 46°26'40'' E 4°58'50''

Pradons/Ruoms, F-07120 / Rhône-Alpes (Ardèche) 2108

Camping de Laborie***
780 route de Ruoms
+33 (0)4-75891837
9/4 - 25/9
@ camping-de-laborie@wanadoo.fr

3ha 68T(100-150m²) 6-10A CEE

1 ACDGIJKLMOPST
2 BCNOPRTVXY
3 AGHJNRUWX
4 (C+H) K(Q)
(R+T 1/5-31/8) (V 4/7-25/8)
(Z 1/5-31/8)
5 ABEFGJKMNOPQUWZ
6 EGJ(N 1,5km)OV

Campsite located on the Ardèche with a beach. De Laborie is situated along the road to Ruoms and Vallon-Pont-d'Arc, two tourist villages with country markets. Nature and environment are held in high esteem. Very well-maintained.

A7, exit Montélimar-Nord. Then dir. Le Teil. Then N102 dir. Aubenas. After Villeneuve-de-Berg left D103. At Vogüé left on roundabout D579. Follow road to site left of road.

CC € 15 *16/4-2/7 22/8-24/9*

N 44°28'47'' E 4°22'41''

Pradons/Ruoms, F-07120 / Rhône-Alpes (Ardèche) 2109

Du Pont****
225A, route du Cirque de Gens
+33 (0)4-75939398
18/3 - 18/9
@ campingdupont07@wanadoo.fr

1,5ha 52T(80-110m²) 10A CEE

1 ACDFIJKLMPST
2 ABCGRTVXY
3 AGHJRUWX
4 (A 1/7-20/8)
(C+H+Q+T+U+V+X+Z)
5 AEFGIJKLMNOPUWZ
6 ACEGHKL(N 0,3km)RTV

Du Pont is close to Pradons and just 300m from a supermarket. You have wonderful views of the Cirque de Gens rocks which are on the other side of the river. A small-scale campsite with personal attention.

A7 exit Montelimar Nord, N7 to Le Teil, then N102 dir. Aubenas. Left at roundabout after Villeneuve-de-Berg, D103. Then left D579 dir. Vallon. Right in Pradons at supermarket. Campsite on left.

CC € 15 *18/3-1/7 26/8-17/9*

N 44°28'29'' E 4°21'7''

Pradons/Ruoms, F-07120 / Rhône-Alpes (Ardèche) 2110

Les Coudoulets****
125 chemin de l'Ardèche
+33 (0)4-75939495
FAX +33 (0)4-75396589
16/4 - 17/9
@ camping@coudoulets.com

2,5ha 120T(80-160m²) 16A

1 ACD**F**IJKLMPST
2 ACGJNORTVWXY
3 AGHJKLNRU**WX**
4 (A 1/7-31/8) (C+E+H) K (Q+T+U+V) (X 14/5-11/9) (Z)
5 **AB**DEFGIJKLMNOPQ**S**UV WXYZ
6 ACDEG**K**RTUV

A real family campsite with a lively atmosphere. The river with its large rocks flows past the site. Aquapark with, among other things, an indoor pool with jacuzzi and aqua-bikes. Pitches with private toilet facilities for extra fee.

A7, exit Montélimar-Nord direction Le Teil. In Le Teil N102 in the direction of Aubenas. Past Montfleury, turn left onto the D103. At Vogüé turn left onto the D579. The campsite is located on the right, before the village of Pradons.

CC €17 16/4-30/6 26/8-17/9 14=13, 21=19 N 44°28'36'' E 4°21'30''

Recoubeau-Jansac, F-26310 / Rhône-Alpes (Drôme) 2111

Domaine du Couriou****
D93
+33 (0)4-75213323
1/5 - 15/9
@ contact@lecouriou.fr

7ha 90T(80-150m²) 10A CEE

1 ACD**G**IJKLMPST
2 JKRTVWXY
3 BGHJN**OP**RU**W**
4 (C+G) IJ (Q+R+T+U+V+X 1/7-31/8)
5 **AB**FGIJKLMNPUWZ
6 EGI**J**(N 1km)ORTV

Camping Le Couriou is a lovely terraced campsite with panoramic views. The campsite is located in a wide valley that invites you to explore the mountains. The swimming pool is one of the largest in the area. Good restaurant with terrace offering stunning views of the mountains.

Exit Valence-Sud direction Gap/Crest/Die. After Die direction Gap. Campsite on the right before Recoubeau.

CC €13 1/5-8/7 25/8-15/9 7=6 N 44°39'31'' E 5°24'26''

Rosières, F-07260 / Rhône-Alpes (Ardèche) 2112

Domaine Arleblanc Camping****
Domaine Arleblanc
+33 (0)4-75395311
FAX +33 (0)4-75399398
20/3 - 30/10
@ info@arleblanc.com

7ha 127T(100-150m²) 6-10A CEE

1 ACDGIJKLMOPST
2 ACNRTVWXY
3 AGHJL**MNQ**RU**WX**
4 (A 1/7-31/8) (C+G 15/4-15/10) (Q+S) (T+U+V+Y+Z 20/3-15/9)
5 **AB**DEFGIJKLMNOPQUVXY Z
6 ACEGHIJK(N 2,5km)ORTV

Domaine Arleblanc has an excellent restaurant in a historic building. Excellent toilet facilities. It is heated in low season. The campsite has a typical French ambiance. It has extended grounds along the River Beaume with its lovely cliffs. There is free WiFi on the grounds.

A7, exit 17, 2nd right on roundabout, follow route N7 to Le Teil. Take the N102 to Aubenas, then the D104 towards Alès. Left before Rosières at the supermarket. Site on right of road.

CC €17 20/3-3/7 28/8-30/10 7=6, 14=12 N 44°27'51'' E 4°16'22''

Rosières, F-07260 / Rhône-Alpes (Ardèche) — 2113

La Plaine****
Les Plaines
+33 (0)4-75395135
1/4 - 20/9
campinglaplaine@orange.fr

3ha 60T(80-150m²) 10A CEE

1 ACD**G**IJKLPST
2 BRTVXY
3 AGHMNQRUVW
4 (C+H) KP(Q 7/7-29/8) (V 1/7-31/8) (Z)
5 **A**DEFGIJKLMNPUZ
6 EGJ**K**(N 0,8km)V

Very well-maintained campsite, 900 metres from La Beaume river. Friendly, homely atmosphere. There's a lake for anglers. At walking distance from Lidl and Intermarché supermarkets. Large swimming pool with jacuzzi.

A7, exit 17. N7 to le Teil. There N102 to Aubenas, there D104 dir. Alès. At Rosières roundabout turn directly right at the Pépiniéres. Continue to campsite.

CC € 15 *1/4-9/7 27/8-20/9 14=12, 21=18*

N 44°29'9'' E 4°15'59''

Roybon, F-38940 / Rhône-Alpes (Isère) — 2114

Camping de Roybon***
D20
+33 (0)4-76362367
1/5 - 30/9
info@campingroybon.com

2,5ha 85T(80-110m²) 10A CEE

1 ACD**G**IJKLMPRS
2 CDGLNRVWXY
3 AGHJN**O**RU**WZ**
4 (C 1/5-15/9) (Q) (T+U+X 1/5-15/9) (Z)
5 **A**FGJKMPUVZ
6 ACEGJ(N 1km)OTV

Located on the shores of a lake 800 metres from Roybon. The Tuscan-like surroundings have not yet been discovered by mass tourism. Plenty of sightseeing within a radius of 25 km (Drôme, Vercors, St. Antoine, outlets in Romans and Anneyron). Enjoy Martine's delicious cooking.

A7/E15 exit 12, D519 direction Voiron. Turn right D71 Bressieux/Roybon. Campsite located 1 km out of the village and is indicated.

CC € 13 *1/5-15/7 1/9-30/9 6=5, 12=10*

N 45°14'49'' E 5°14'53''

Ruoms, F-07120 / Rhône-Alpes (Ardèche) — 2115

Sites & Paysages
Le Petit Bois***
87 rue du Petit Bois
+33 (0)4-75396072
1/4 - 30/9
vacances@campinglepetitbois.fr

3,7ha 48T(100-120m²) 10A CEE

1 ACD**G**IJKLMPST
2 JRTVXY
3 ADGHJNRU**W**
4 (A) (C 3/4-26/9) (E 3/4-15/6) (H 3/4-26/9) J **LN**(Q+T+U+V+X+Z)
5 **A**BEFGIJKLMNOPQRUVWZ
6 ACDEGHJ**K**(N 0,8km)ORTV

This well equipped campsite is located on the edge of Ruoms. The heated swimming pool can also be covered over, when it gets a bit colder. Usually not the case, the Ardèche has a good climate. There is a sauna and Turkish bath.

A7 exit Montélimar-Nord, dir. Le Teil. D102 towards Aubenas. At Villeneuve-de-Berg turn left on the roundabout, D103. At Vogüé take D579 towards Vallon. In Ruoms turn right at 1st roundabout. Right at Gamm Vert. Follow road, site on right.

CC € 15 *1/4-2/7 26/8-30/9 14=13, 21=19*

N 44°27'41'' E 4°20'15''

Ruoms, F-07120 / Rhône-Alpes (Ardèche) 2116

Sunêlia Aluna Vacances*****
route de Lagorce
+33 (0)4-75939315
FAX +33 (0)4-75939090
9/4 - 3/11
contact@alunavacances.fr

15ha 60**T**(120m²) 10A CEE

1 ACD**F**IJKLMT
2 BJSTVXY
3 AGH**M**NOPRU
4 (**A** 1/7-31/8) (C+F+H) IJ **KLMP** (Q+S+T+U+V+Y+Z)
5 **AB**DEFGIJKLMNOPQUWZ
6 ACEGH**K**(N 1km)ORTV

Campsite set in woodland with many naturally laid out pitches on a somewhat rugged terrain. Many sports opportunities. An Oriental style covered and heated 1000 m² leisure pool.

From Ruoms take the D559 direction Lagorce. After 1.5 miles you'll find the campsite on the right side.

CC € 19 *9/4-24/6 27/8-2/11* N 44°26'49" E 4°21'55"

Sahune, F-26510 / Rhône-Alpes (Drôme) 2117

Les Ramières****
+33 (0)4-75274045
FAX +33 (0)4-75260027
8/4 - 9/9
contact@lesramieres.com

10ha 40**T**(100-150m²) 10A

1 ACD**G**IJLMPST
2 CIJKLMNRTVWX
3 ABGRWX
4 (C+H+Q+R+S+T+U+V+X) Z
5 **A**EFGJLNPQRUWXYZ
6 AEGIJ**K**(N 2km)TV

A beautiful location in France with a panoramic and enchanting view from your pitch over mountains and a mountain river. The perfect spot to unwind. Sportive challenges such as walking, cycling and swimming. A unique holiday experience.

Exit motorway Montélimar Sud dir. Grignan, Valréas, Nyons. Road to Gap as far as Sahune. In Sahune turn right, then right after crossing bridge and follow signs to the right. Asphalt road to the campsite, final km is narrow.

CC € 15 *8/4-7/7 24/8-9/9* N 44°23'57" E 5°15'0"

Saillans, F-26340 / Rhône-Alpes (Drôme) 2118

Les Chapelains***
RD493
+33 (0)4-75215547
16/4 - 15/9
camping@chapelains.fr

1ha 40**T**(80-115m²) 10A

1 ACD**G**IJKLPST
2 CKNRTVXY
3 AHJNRU**WX**
4 (Q+R+X+Y)
5 AEFGIJKLMNOPRUWZ
6 EGJ(N 0,5km)R

A friendly campsite located directly on the Drôme on flat ground with marked out pitches. Run by Dutch owners. Many opportunities for hiking, cycling, culture and city visits. Weekly tour of local wine producer. Daily bakery service and an extensive daily menu several times a week. Free WiFi.

D104/D164 as far as roundabout before Saillans. Then turn onto D493, the campsite is just before the village on the right.

CC € 15 *16/4-8/7 25/8-15/9* N 44°41'44" E 5°10'53"

Samoëns, F-74340 / Rhône-Alpes (Haute-Savoie) 2119

Camping Caravaneige Le Giffre***
1064 route du Lac aux Dames
+33 (0)4-50344192
FAX +33 (0)4-50349884
1/1 - 31/12
camping.samoens@wanadoo.fr
6,9ha 212T(80-110m²) 6-10A CEE

1 ACD**G**IJKLM**P**Q
2 CDGKLRTVWXY
3 BCGJMN**OQ**RW
4 (C 1/6-15/9) J(V) (X 15/6-15/9)
5 **AB**DFGIJKLMNPUVWXYZ
6 CDFGH**I**K(N 0,7km)T

A beautiful campsite on level ground beside a river. Marked out pitches. Separate area for small tents. Several trees. Municipal swimming pool and tennis courts right beside the site (free for campsite guests). Small lake near the site with all types of sports facilities. Ice rink in winter also free. Village of Samoëns with its alpine garden within walking distance. Very suitable for wintersports.

Towards Samoëns via D907. Then follow camping signs.

CC € 17 9/1-29/1 30/4-17/6 27/8-11/12

N 46°4'38'' E 6°43'7''

Sampzon, F-07120 / Rhône-Alpes (Ardèche) 2120

Flower camping Le Rivièra****
3319 route du Rocher, D161
+33 (0)4-75396757
FAX +33 (0)4-75939557
16/4 - 28/9
leriviera@wanadoo.fr
6,5ha 135T(85-100m²) 10A

1 ACD**G**IJKLMPS
2 ACGORSTVWXY
3 AGHJNRU**WX**
4 (A 1/7-31/8) (C+H+Q+R) (T+U+V+Y 1/5-15/9) (Z)
5 **AB**DEFGIJKLMNOPQUZ
6 AFGKL(N 4km)RTUV

Site on the Ardèche river with private sandy beach. Pitches under acacia trees. Excellent toilet facilities with much comfort. Close to the Pont d'Arc and La Caverne du Pont d'Arc (Grotte Chauvet).

A7, exit Montélimar-Nord dir. Le Teil. In Le Teil N102 dir. Aubenas. Go down into Villeneuve-de-Berg and left at the roundabout, D103. At Vogüé left D579 towards Vallon. About 3 km past Ruoms right over the bridge.

CC € 17 16/4-1/7 28/8-28/9 21=18

N 44°25'45'' E 4°21'19''

Sampzon/Ruoms, F-07120 / Rhône-Alpes (Ardèche) 2121

RCN La Bastide en Ardèche****
D111, 1 route d'Alès
+33 (0)4-75396472
19/3 - 17/9
bastide@rcn.fr
7,8ha 200T(100-140m²) 6A CEE

1 ACD**F**IJKLPST
2 ACNRTVWXY
3 AGHJKL**MNOP**RUV**WX**
4 (A 1/5-15/9) (C+H+Q+S+T+U+V+Y+Z)
5 **AB**CDEFGIJKLMNOPQRU WXYZ
6 ACFGH**K**(N 4km)ORTV

A family campsite with views of Mount Sampzon. Many activities make it great for young and old. The site has excellent toilet facilities. The weather in low season is usually very agreeable.

A7, exit Montélimar-Nord, dir. Le Teil. Then N102 dir. Aubenas. Downhill at Villeneuve-de-Berg and left onto D103 at roundabout. Then left on D579 direction Vallon. Dir. Alès after Ruoms, D111. Campsite on the left 1 km past the bridge.

CC € 15 26/3-5/7 26/8-17/9

N 44°25'23'' E 4°19'18''

Serrières-de-Briord, F-01470 / Rhône-Alpes (Ain)

2122

du Point Vert***
chemin du Point Vert
+33 (0)4-74361345
FAX +33 (0)9-72413709
2/4 - 2/10
@ campingdupointvert@wibox.fr

3ha 50T(80-120m²) 10A

1 ACD**G**IJKLM**P**Q
2 ACDLMRVWXY
3 AHJMNRUV**WX**
4 (B+G 1/6-30/9) (Q+R+Y) Z
5 **AB**GIJKLMNPUWZ
6 EGK(N 1,5km)OV

Peacefully located family campsite with a pool, on the banks of a wide arm of the Rhône, with an unhindered view of the lake and its wealth of birds. Ideal for all water sports and cycling along the Rhône.

From Bourg-en-Bresse dir. Lyon, exit Ambérieu; N75 dir. Langnieu. From roundabout dir. St. Sorlim - Sault Brénaz - Serrières-de-Briord, through village, then follow signs.

CC € 15 *2/4-8/7 29/8-2/10*

N 45°48'57'' E 5°25'37''

Sévrier, F-74320 / Rhône-Alpes (Haute-Savoie)

2123

Au Coeur du Lac***
3233 route d'Albertville
+33 (0)4-50524645
FAX +33 (0)4-50190145
1/4 - 30/9
@ info@aucoeurdulac.com

1,7ha 73T(70-100m²) 13A CEE

1 ACGHIJKLMPRS
2 DFGIJKLRVWXY
3 AGHJK**MRT**U**W**Z
4 (A 1/7-25/8) (Q+R) (T+U+V 20/6-5/9)
5 **AB**DFGIJKLMNOPUVXYZ
6 CDG**IK**(N 1km)OTV

Located right by the lake 4 km from Annecy in the small village of Sevrier, 40 km from Geneva. Camping pitches on terraces. Some have views of the lake and the mountains. The campsite has direct access to a 24 km paved, traffic-free cycle path. This is also the best way to arrive in Annecy without traffic tailbacks (approx. 15 minutes by bike).

Route Annecy-Albertville. From Annecy; when leaving Sévrier left of the D1508, 500 metres past McDonalds.

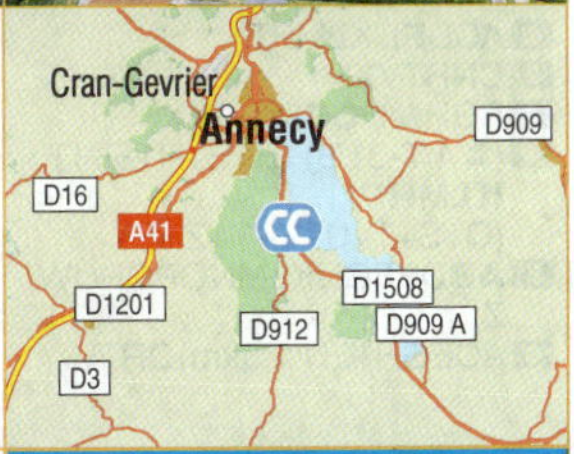

CC € 17 *1/4-4/7 21/8-30/9*

N 45°51'17'' E 6°8'39''

Sévrier, F-74320 / Rhône-Alpes (Haute-Savoie)

2124

l'Aloua**
492 route de Piron
+33 (0)4-50526006
16/4 - 24/9
@ camping-de-l-aloua@orange.fr

2,3ha 173T(90-130m²) 10A

1 AC**F**HIJKLPRS
2 FGRTVWXY
3 A**F**GJKLRU
4 (Q) (T+U+V+Z 1/7-30/8)
5 **AB**FGIJKNPUWZ
6 CFGJ(N 0,2km)TV

Grassland under birch trees and close to a supermarket. The campsite is located between the main road and the lake. There is a beach 250m away.

D1508 Annecy-Albertville. The campsite is located between Sévrier and St. Jorioz, behind the Carrefour supermarket. Turn off at the roundabout.

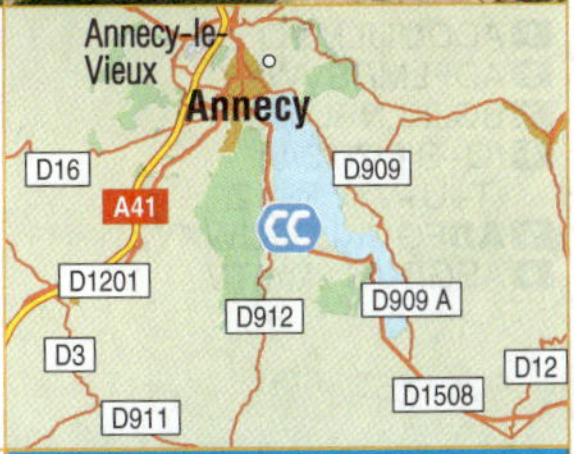

CC € 17 *16/4-4/7 21/8-24/9*

N 45°50'38'' E 6°9'13''

Sévrier, F-74320 / Rhône-Alpes (Haute-Savoie)

iD **2125**

Le Panoramic***
1011 route de Cessenaz
+33 (0)4-50524309
16/4 - 30/9
info@camping-le-panoramic.com

2ha 145T(80-110m²) 10A CEE

1 ACFHIJKLPQ
2 FIJKRVWXY
3 AGHRU
4 (C+H 1/6-18/9)
(Q 1/6-11/9)
(S+T+U+V+Y+Z 1/6-3/9)
5 **AB**EFGIJKLMNPUVZ
6 ACEGJ(N 1,5km)TV

Campsite overlooking the lake of Annecy. Some pitches have panoramic views over the lake and the surrounding villages; hence the campsite's name. Swimming pool is open from 1 June. The restaurant is open from June to the beginning of September. Renovated toilet facilities.

In Annecy continue to Albertville on the D1508. Just past Sévrier take first exit right at the first roundabout to the Col de Leschaux. Small bridge after about 3 km. Campsite is 300m further on the left.

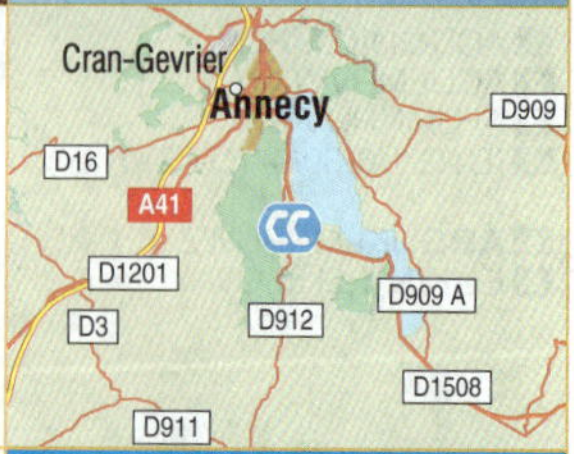

CC € 17 *16/4-9/7 26/8-30/9*

N 45°50'35'' E 6°8'30''

St. Alban-Auriolles/Ruoms, F-07120 / Rhône-Alpes (Ardèche)

iD **2126**

Sunêlia Le Ranc Davaine*****
500 chemin du Ranc Davaine
+33 (0)4-75396055
FAX +33 (0)4-75393850
9/4 - 11/9
contact@rancdavaine.fr

13ha 52T(80-150m²) 10A CEE

1 ACD**F**IJKLMPT
2 CNRTVXY
3 BGH**MNOP**RUV**W**X
4 (**A** 1/7-31/8) (B+E+H) IJ **KLMNP**
(Q+S+T+U+V+Y+Z)
5 **AB**DEFGIJKLMNOPQRUW Z
6 ACEGH**K**(N 1,5km)ORTV

A large campsite. The small river is not very deep. Plenty of amusement, but still set peacefully under oak trees. There is a lovely leisure pool with an indoor pool for those who like swimming. Wellness facilities.

From Ruoms on the D579 turn onto the D111 towards Alès. Right after 5 km onto the D246 (at Grospierres). Left at end of road towards Chandolas. Campsite on your left.

CC € 19 *9/4-24/6 27/8-10/9*

N 44°24'49'' E 4°16'18''

St. Alban-de-Montbel, F-73610 / Rhône-Alpes (Savoie)

iD **2127**

Le Sougey****
Lac Rive Ouest
+33 (0)4-79360144
1/5 - 18/9
info@camping-sougey.com

4ha 148T(85-150m²) 6-10A CEE

1 ACD**G**IJLM**P**Q
2 ADFLMRSVWXY
3 BGJKLNRU**WZ**
4 (Q+S 6/7-23/8)
(T+U+V+Y) Z
5 **AB**FGIJKLOPUWXYZ
6 AEGI**K**(N 3km)TV

Relatively large pitches, separated by hedges. Several sanitary buildings are spread over the hilly site. A few trees provide shade. Within 100 metres is a beautiful meadow at the lake of Aiguebelette (550 hectare).

A43 Lyon-Chambéry, exit Lac d'Aiguebelette. After péage turn right at the roundabout then after 300 metres left at next roundabout direction St. Alban-de-Montbel. Campsite indicated after 2 km on the left.

CC € 15 *1/5-1/7 22/8-18/9*

N 45°33'21'' E 5°47'27''

St. Avit, F-26330 / Rhône-Alpes (Drôme) — 2128

Domaine La Garenne****
156 chemin de Chablezin
+33 (0)4-75686226
FAX +33 (0)4-75686002
15/4 - 30/9
garenne.drome@wanadoo.fr

14ha 50**T**(150-300m²) 6A

1 ACD**G**IJKLMP
2 JRSVXY
3 BGJNRU
4 (C+G 15/5-14/9)
(Q+T 1/7-31/8) (Z)
5 **A**EFGIJKLMNOPUVZ
6 CEJ(N 3km)T

A terraced campsite beside a hill with pine trees. The pitches are spread out in natural surroundings with fir and oak trees. The hedges and the height differences in the grounds offer you pitches with privacy between the hills of the Drôme.

Chanas exit, N7 towards Valence until just past St. Vallier. D51 direction St. Uze and Hauterives. Right in Châteauneuf-de-Galaure towards St. Donat (D53). Campsite 4 km on the left.

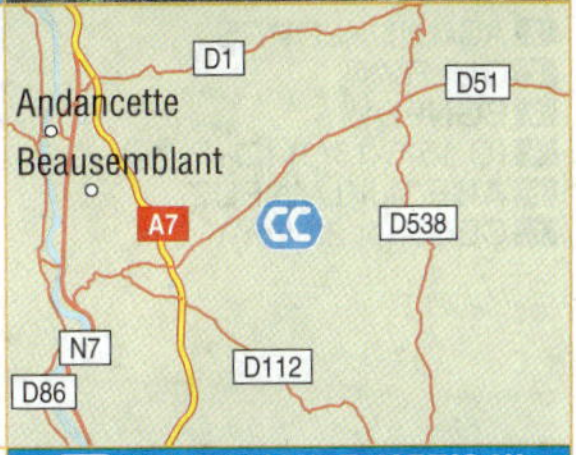

CC € 15 *15/4-4/7 25/8-30/9*

N 45°12'7" E 4°57'24"

St. Clair-du-Rhône, F-38370 / Rhône-Alpes (Isère) — 2129

Le Daxia****
route de Péage de Roussillon D4
+33 (0)4-74563920
1/4 - 30/9
info@campingledaxia.com

7,5ha 116**T**(100-150m²) 6A

1 ACD**G**IJKLMOPQ
2 CRTVXY
3 BGHJN**Q**RU**W**
4 (B+G 1/6-30/9) JM
(Q 15/6-15/9) (T 1/6-30/9)
(U+V+X 1/7-31/8) Z
5 **AB**EFGIJKLMNPUZ
6 CE**J**(N 3km)

A very friendly and attractive campsite in northern Isère. This site, which according to the French is one of the better ones in the area, can indulge tourists for long or short periods. Located in a rural and peaceful setting in Provence and close to Lyon.

A7 exit Vienne. Follow the N7 as far as D4 right direction St. Claire-du-Rhône. Follow camping signs in the village.

CC € 17 *1/4-5/7 22/8-30/9*

N 45°25'27" E 4°46'56"

St. Donat-sur-Herbasse, F-26260 / Rhône-Alpes (Drôme) — 2130

Les Ulèzes****
route de Romans
+33 (0)4-75478320
1/4 - 31/10
contact@domaine-des-ulezes.com

3,5ha 85**T**(100m²) 10A CEE

1 ACD**G**IJKLMPST
2 CRSVWXY
3 BGHJN**Q**RU**W**
4 (B 15/5-30/9)
(Q+R+T+U+V)
(X 15/4-15/9) Z
5 **AB**EFGIJKLMNPRUWXYZ
6 CEG**IJK**(N 0,6km)V

Small but very well-maintained, private campsite. This campsite is ideal as a base for the many sights in the area such as the Tain l'Hermitage wine region.

A7 exit Tain-l'Hermitage, dir. Romans. At Curron D67 dir. St. Donat. Follow signs. Campsite is on right of D53.

CC € 17 *1/4-30/6 1/9-31/10*

N 45°7'9" E 4°59'34"

St. Galmier, F-42330 / Rhône-Alpes (Loire)

2131

Campéole Le Val de Coise****
route de la Thiery
+33 (0)4-77541482
FAX +33 (0)4-77540245
1/4 - 25/9
@ val-de-coise@andretriganogroupe.com
3,5ha 92**T**(80-100m²) 16A CEE

1 ACGHIJKLOPRS
2 CIJLRVX
3 BGNRUW
4 (C 15/6-15/9) (Q+R)
5 ABFGIJKLMNPUZ
6 CEGK(N 2,5km)V

A small but friendly terraced campsite with views of the river, just outside the centre of the flower-filled town of St. Galmier. Nature lovers will certainly find this campsite to their liking.

Past Lyon via the A7 and the A47 direction St. Étienne. Then follow the A72 as far as St. Galmier exit. Follow the signs in St. Galmier.

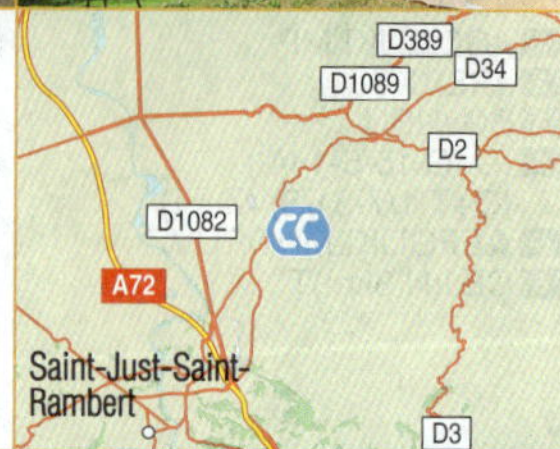

CC € 15 *1/5-4/7 22/8-25/9*

N 45°35'34'' E 4°20'8''

St. Genix-sur-Guiers, F-73240 / Rhône-Alpes (Savoie)

2132

Les Bords du Guiers**
640 route de la Glière
+33 (0)4-76317140
16/4 - 25/9
@ lesbordsduguiers@orange.fr
1,5ha 55**T**(120-160m²) 6-10A CEE

1 ACDGIJLMPQ
2 CFLRTVWXY
3 AGHJKMRWX
4 (B 15/5-10/9) (Q+T+U+X)
5 ABCGIJLMNPUVWZ
6 AFHJOV

Family campsite with quiet location. Pool. The campsite is located 200 metres from the centre, in the middle of a network of walking and cycling routes. Supermarket at 150 metres from the campsite. Dutch owners.

From A43 exit 11 towards St. Genix-sur-Guiers. From D1075 Evrien, D1516 to Aoste, then St. Genix-sur-Guiers. In St. Genix take first exit right on the roundabout then follow camping signs.

CC € 13 *16/4-1/7 18/8-25/9 16=14*

N 45°35'45'' E 5°38'5''

St. Gervais-les-Bains, F-74170 / Rhône-Alpes (Haute-Savoie)

2133

Nature & Lodge Les Dômes de Miage****
197 route des Contamines
+33 (0)4-50934596
FAX +33 (0)4-50781075
14/5 - 15/9
@ info@camping-mont-blanc.com
2,5ha 150**T**(90-200m²) 12A CEE

1 ACGIJKLMOPQ
2 FGKRVWXY
3 BGHNRU
4 (Q+S 1/6-31/8) (U+Y+Z)
5 ABDEFGIJKLMNPUWZ
6 ACDFGHIJ(N 2km)ORTV

Level grassy base with excellent toilet facilities. Lovely views of the snowy mountain tops. A stream divides the ground in two. St. Gervais is a pretty tourist village.

A40 exit St. Gervais (no. 21). To St. Gervais centre then Les Contamines. Campsite on the left after 2 km.

CC € 19 *14/5-8/7 25/8-15/9*

N 45°52'25'' E 6°43'13''

St. Jean-de-Chevelu, F-73170 / Rhône-Alpes (Savoie)

2134

Camping des Lacs***
+33 (0)6-59498394
15/4 - 15/9
campingdeslacs73@gmail.com

4ha 105**T**(100-150m²) 16A CEE

1 ACD**G**IJKLM**P**Q
2 ACDFGKLMRVWXY
3 AGHJRU**W**XZ
4 (A 5/7-30/8) (Q 1/7-31/8) (T+U+X 27/6-31/8) Z
5 **AB**EFGIJKLMNOPRUWZ
6 CDEGJ(N 6km)OV

A comfortable family campsite on the Saint-Jean-de-Chevelu lake, with large, shady pitches, guarded beach, playground.

A41 as far as Chambéry exit 13, N504 direction Aix-les-Bains tunnel direction Yenne, then D210 direction St. Jean-de-Chevelu; campsite signposted from there.

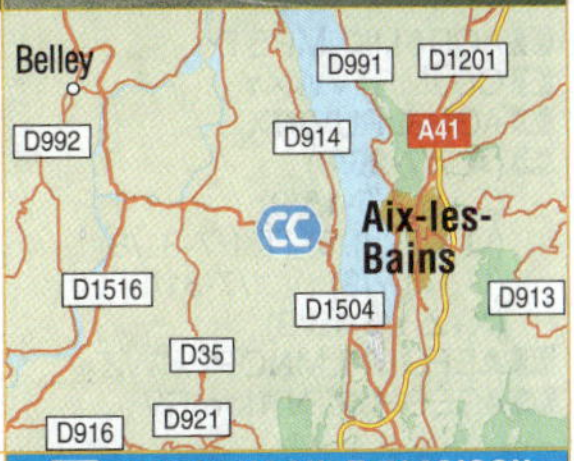

CC € 15 *15/4-1/7 20/8-15/9*

N 45°41'38" E 5°49'29"

St. Jean-de-Maurienne, F-73300 / Rhône-Alpes (Savoie)

2135

Des Grands Cols***
422 ave du Mont-Cenis
+33 (0)4-79642802
14/5 - 23/9
info@campingdesgrandscols.com

2ha 92**T**(80-100m²) 16A CEE

1 ACD**G**HIJKLMOPQ
2 FGKRTUVWXY
3 BGHJLNRUV
4 (Q+R 1/6-31/8) (T 1/7-31/8) (Z 1/6-31/8)
5 **AB**EFGIJKMNOPUVWXYZ
6 ACDEG**J**(N 1km)OV

Located in the heart of the Maurienne valley at the foot of the prestigious 'cols' such as the Glandon, Croix de Fer and Madeleine. The warden will be pleased to help you plan your bike rides, walks or cultural trips out. Cycle repairs and cycle storage on the campsite. Easy to reach via the D1006. 500m from town centre.

D1006 Chambéry - St. Jean-de-Maurienne. In St. Jean direction centre, then follow 'Toutes directions' and 'camping' signs.

CC € 17 *14/5-8/7 25/8-23/9*

N 45°16'15" E 6°21'2"

St. Jean-de-Muzols/Tournon-s-R, F-07300 / Rhône-Alpes (Ardèche)

2136

Le Castelet***
113 route du Grand Pont
+33 (0)4-75080948
23/4 - 7/9
courrier@camping-lecastelet.com

3ha 59**T**(88-110m²) 10A CEE

1 A**G**IJKLPST
2 CFGJLMORTVXY
3 BGHJN**PRW**X
4 (B+G 1/5-7/9) (Q) Z
5 **A**EFGJLNPUW
6 ACEGJ(N 3km)OTV

A well maintained campsite on the river, just 3 km from a village. Lovely swimming pool. Lively bar with terrace and views of the pool. Free WiFi point. Spacious toilet facilities. Also facilities for motorhomes. Walking and cycling routes from the campsite. Fresh bread every morning.

A7, exit 13 Tournon. Over the Rhône D86, first follow direction Tournon, then St. Jean-de-Muzols. When entering St. Jean-de-Muzols go left onto D238. Campsite indicated on the left after 4 km.

CC € 15 *23/4-3/7 22/8-7/9 7=6, 14=12, 21=18*

N 45°4'4" E 4°47'6"

St. Jean-le-Centenier, F-07580 / Rhône-Alpes (Ardèche)

iD **2137**

Les Arches****
Le Cluzel, route de Mirabel, D458
+33 (0)4-75367519
22/4 - 18/9
info@camping-les-arches.com

10ha 133**T**(70-200m²) 10A CEE

1 ACD**F**IJKLMPST
2 CGJMRTVWXY
3 AGHJLRUV**W**X
4 (**A** 7/7-26/8)
(C+H 1/5-15/9)
(Q 1/5-11/9) (T 1/7-31/8)
(U 1/6-7/9) (V 1/7-31/8)
(X+Z 1/6-15/9)
5 **A**EFGIJKLMNOPRUWZ
6 ACEGHJ**K**(N 1km)RV

Parkland campsite with plenty of trees and bushes. Pick your own cherries, enjoy the view, the quiet, the birds and the river. Walking and cycling area. Sightseeing close by, shops, doctors. EN, NL, DE and SP spoken. Heated swimming pool. Restaurant open often.

A7 exit Montélimar-Nord. Then towards Le Teil. Then the N102 direction Aubenas. Drive past St. Jean-le-Centenier exit. Towards Mirabel (D458) before the service station. Continue on road. Don't use SatNav.

CC € 17 *29/4-4/7 21/8-18/9* *14=13, 21=19, 28=25*

N 44°35'15'' E 4°31'33''

St. Jorioz, F-74410 / Rhône-Alpes (Haute-Savoie)

iD **2138**

Europa****
1444 route d'Albertville
+33 (0)4-50685101
FAX +33 (0)4-50685520
30/4 - 17/9
info@camping-europa.com

3,2ha 141**T**(80-100m²) 6A CEE

1 AC**F**IJKLPS
2 FGKRVXY
3 BFGHJKNRU
4 (**C**) (**H** 14/5-4/9) IJKMP
(Q 15/6-31/8)
(V+Y+Z 1/6-31/8)
5 **AB**EFGIJKLMNPUWXYZ
6 AG**IK**(N 1,5km)TV

An excellent site 400 metres from the lake, 9 km from Annecy, with excellent toilets. The lovely leisure pool has 3 open-air pools with additional facilities (deckchairs with water massage), slides and child-friendly water games. Excellent restaurant. Direct access to a cycle path beside the lake. Comfort pitches for extra fee.

D1508 Annecy-Albertville. The campsite is located along this road, just past St. Jorioz it is the second site on the right hand side.

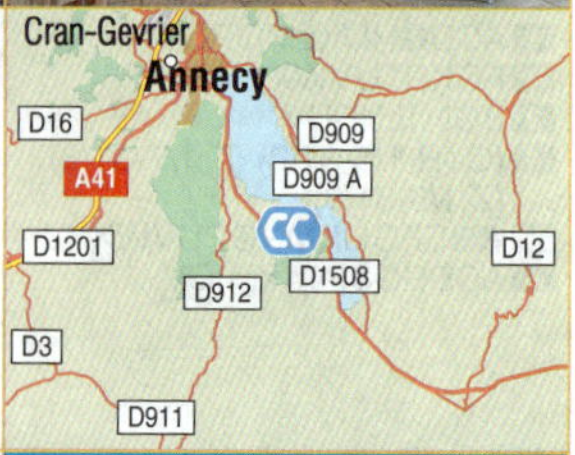

CC € 17 *30/4-1/7 25/8-16/9*

N 45°49'48'' E 6°10'54''

St. Jorioz, F-74410 / Rhône-Alpes (Haute-Savoie)

iD **2139**

International du Lac d'Annecy****
1184 route d'Albertville (D1508)
+33 (0)4-50686793
23/4 - 17/9
contact@camping-lac-annecy.com

2ha 140**T**(80-95m²) 10A CEE

1 AC**G**IJKLPQ
2 FGKRVWXY
3 AFGJKNRU
4 (C+H) IJP
(Q+T+U+V+X+Z 1/6-31/8)
5 **AB**EFGIJKMNPUWXYZ
6 AG**K**(N 1,5km)RTV

Campsite with shaded pitches 400m from Lake Annecy and 1km from the beach. Heated, child-friendly and tropical leisure pool with slide. Direct access to a secure cycle path. Excellent toilet facilities in a building with attractive lighting.

D1508 Annecy-Albertville. Campsite located on this road, just past the centre of St. Jorioz.

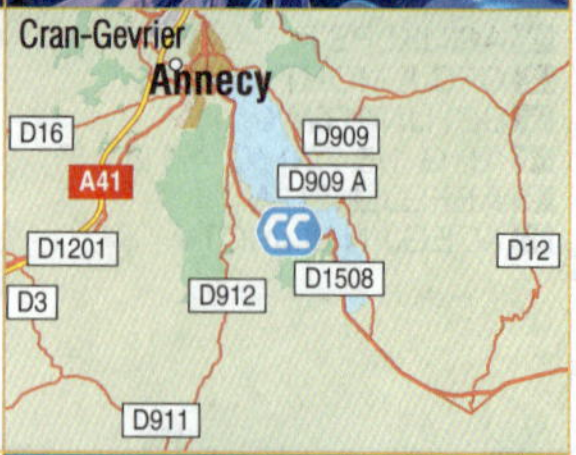

CC € 19 *23/4-1/7 27/8-17/9*

N 45°49'51'' E 6°10'42''

St. Jorioz, F-74410 / Rhône-Alpes (Haute-Savoie) — 2140

Le Crêtoux***
1059 route d'Entredozon
+33 (0)4-50686194
1/4 - 15/11
info@campinglecretoux.com

6ha 75T(100-120m²) 10A

1 AC**G**IJLPRS
2 HIJKRVWXY
3 B**F**RU**W**
4 (Q 1/7-31/8)
5 **AB**DEFGIJKLMNPUVZ
6 ACDEGIJ(N 2km)V

A basic campsite in natural surroundings on a hill just outside the centre of St. Jorioz. You have views over Annecy Lake from certain pitches. The site is recommended for anyone who appreciates peace and nature. The steep access road is short, but that need not be a problem.

D1508 Annecy-Albertville. At traffic lights in St. Jorioz D10a direction St. Eustache. Signposted (about 2 km). Short, steep access road.

CC € 17 *1/4-5/7 22/8-15/11*

N 45°49'9" E 6°8'54"

St. Jorioz, F-74410 / Rhône-Alpes (Haute-Savoie) — 2141

Le Solitaire du Lac***
615 route de Sales
FAX +33 (0)4-50685930
2/4 - 24/9
campinglesolitaire@wanadoo.fr

4,5ha 185T(80-120m²) 6A

1 AC**G**IJKLMPRS
2 ADFLRTVWXY
3 B**F**GJKRU**WZ**
4 (Q+R 1/5-25/9)
(U 1/7-31/8)
5 **AB**EFGIJKLMNPUWZ
6 ACEG**IJK**(N 1km)OV

Well-cared-for campsite divided in parallel avenues. The pitches are under the trees. The pitches are separated from the lake by a playing field. On the shore is a narrow passage to the water.

D1508 Annecy-Albertville. Just before you reach St. Jorioz centre drive to the lake. Follow the camping signs.

CC € 17 *2/4-2/7 20/8-24/9*

N 45°50'27" E 6°9'53"

St. Julien-en-St-Alban, F-07000 / Rhône-Alpes (Ardèche) — 2142

L'Albanou***
chemin de Pampelonne
+33 (0)4-75660097
FAX +33 (0)9-60112471
15/4 - 30/9
campingalbanou@orange.fr

2ha 84T(100-110m²) 10A CEE

1 ACD**G**IJKLMO**P**ST
2 CFGLORTVWXY
3 AGHJNRU**WX**
4 (C+G) K
(Q+R+T+U+V+Z)
5 **AB**GIJKLMNOPUZ
6 ACDEGJ(N 1km)

Ideal springboard to your holiday destination, but also suitable for longer stays. Excellent toilet facilities. Swimming pool with jacuzzi. Free WiFi point. There is well maintained landscaping on this level terrain. Nearly all pitches are marked out by hedges. Easily reached from the A7 autoroute.

A7 exit 16 Loriol, then towards Le Pouzin. Then dir. Aubenas via D104. Site is signposted on left before village (at small industrial site). Then left again and 2nd site on right.

CC € 17 *15/4-3/7 21/8-30/9* *14=12, 21=18, 28=24*

N 44°45'26" E 4°42'46"

St. Laurent-du-Pape, F-07800 / Rhône-Alpes (Ardèche) 2143

La Garenne***
Montée de la Garenne
+33 (0)4-75622462
1/4 - 1/10
info@campinglagarenne-ardeche.fr

6ha 117T(80-125m²) 6A CEE

1 A**G**IJKLP
2 FGJRSTVWXY
3 BGHJKRU
4 (A 19/5-14/9)
(B+G 30/4-18/9)
(Q 1/4-30/9) (R)
(T+U+V 30/4-12/9)
(Y 1/5-14/9) (Z 1/5-30/9)
5 **AB**EFGIJKLMNOPRUWZ
6 AEGJ(N 0,4km)OV

On the edge of a wood, close to the village centre. A friendly and relaxed atmosphere. Plenty of walking and cycling opportunities. A wide range of daily menus. Jeu de boules. Helpful and friendly Dutch wardens. Close to motorway. Dutch, French, English and German spoken.

A7, exit Loriol, dir. Privas. Across the Rhône River in Le Pouzin take D86 to La Voulte. Then follow signs St. Laurent-du-Pape. Turn right at post office. Turn left after bridge.

CC € 19 *1/4-7/7 24/8-1/10*

N 44°49'34'' E 4°45'44''

St. Martin-d'Ardèche, F-07700 / Rhône-Alpes (Ardèche) 2144

Des Gorges****
Sauze
+33 (0)4-75046109
1/5 - 15/9
info@camping-des-gorges.com

3ha 115T(80-120m²) 10A CEE

1 ACDGIJKLMPST
2 ACJORTVWXY
3 ADGHKLNRU**WX**
4 (C+H) K
(Q+S+T+U+V+Y+Z)
5 **AB**DEFGIJKLMNOPQUVW
Z
6 ACEG**K**(N 1km)RTV

Des Gorges has a lovely pool with a wall of bubbles. Lovely views from the terraces. Pitches under tall trees and the Ardèche flows past the grounds. St. Martin d'Ardèche is a lovely tourist village. Toilets partially renovated. New family shower.

Route A7, exit Bollène dir. Pont-St-Esprit. Then N86 to St. Just. Then follow St. Martin-d'Ardèche and Sauze débarcadère. Campsite on left.

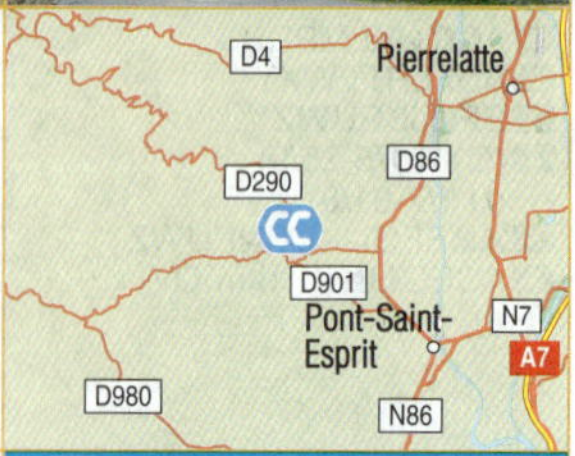

CC € 17 *1/5-30/6 1/9-15/9*

N 44°18'40'' E 4°33'22''

St. Martin-d'Ardèche, F-07700 / Rhône-Alpes (Ardèche) 2145

Indigo Le Moulin***
Le Moulin
+33 (0)4-75046620
28/4 - 26/9
moulin@camping-indigo.com

7ha 121T(100-200m²) 10A CEE

1 ACD**F**IJKLMPST
2 CKLNORTVWXY
3 BGHNRU**WX**
4 (C+G+Q+R)
(T+U+V+X 1/7-31/8) (Z)
5 **AB**FGIJKLMNOPQRUVWZ
6 ACEGI(N 0,2km)V

The campsite is located near the Gorges de l'Ardèche in natural surroundings with quality amenities. An ideal location for taking trips out. Located at the end of the famous descent of the Ardèche by canoe. Lovely pitches on the banks of the river. 300 metres from the village. No WiFi.

A7 exit Bollène. From there towards Pont Saint Esprit. Then follow 'Gorges de l'Ardeche' signs as far as Saint Martin-d'Ardèche.

CC € 17 *28/4-9/6 1/9-25/9*

N 44°18'2'' E 4°34'17''

St. Maurice-de-Gourdans, F-01800 / Rhône-Alpes (Ain)

2146

Les Plages de l'Ain**
11 chemin du Stade
+33 (0)4-74358293
1/4 - 1/11
contact@camping-plage-ain.fr

3ha 100T(150-200m²) 10-16A

1 ACD**F**IJKLMO**P**Q
2 CFNRTVWXY
3 AGHRU**WX**
4 (B+G 1/6-30/9)
(Q 1/7-31/8)
(T+U+V+Z 1/5-30/9)
5 **AB**GIJKLNO**P**UVYZ
6 CDEGJ(N 2km)OTV

A campsite positioned by the River Ain with a pebble beach. The pitches are spacious and the many lovely old trees offer plenty of shade. A perfect place for kayaking, cycling, walking or just enjoying yourself. Swim safely in the two pools.

A42 exit 7 Pérouges/Meximieux, D65B direction St. Maurice-de- Gourdans and follow signs to Stade and the campsite.

CC € 15 *1/4-8/7 29/8-1/11*

N 45°48'31'' E 5°11'4''

St. Nizier-le-Bouchoux, F-01560 / Rhône-Alpes (Ain)

2147

Domaine de Mépillat***
Le Petit Mépillat
+33 (0)4-74529724
17/4 - 9/10
contact@camping-mepillat.fr

5ha 82T(75-100m²) 10A CEE

1 ACD**G**IJKL**P**Q
2 DFJLMRVWXY
3 AGHKNRUW
4 (A 15/5-15/9) (B 15/5-30/9)
(G 15/6-30/8)
(Q+R+T+U+V+X 1/5-30/9) Z
5 **A**EFGIJKLMNPUVWXYZ
6 EGIJ(N 3km)TV

Terraced campsite in very rural area with spacious pitches and options for fishing. Close to the A39, so also suitable as stopover campsite.

A39 exit 10 to St. Trivier-de-Courtes (D56). On left of road after 7 km.

CC € 13 *17/4-6/7 23/8-9/10* *7=6, 14=12, 21=18*

N 46°27'6'' E 5°11'22''

St. Paul-de-Varax, F-01240 / Rhône-Alpes (Ain)

2148

Domaine de la Dombes****
Etang du Moulin,
chemin de Verfey
+33 (0)9-52263384
1/3 - 31/10
contact@
domainedeladombes.com

34ha 100T(100-200m²) 10A CEE

1 AC**G**IJKLMO**P**RS
2 ABCDLRTUVWXY
3 ABD**F**GHJK**M**N**Q**RU**W**
4 (B 15/6-15/9) (Q+R)
(T 1/7-30/8) (U)
(V+X+Z 1/7-30/8)
5 **AB**GIJKLMNOP**R**UVZ
6 ACDEG**IJ**(N 3km)ORTV

This campsite is in an extensive nature reserve with many lakes, the Dombes. It has a very large swimming pool with a sandy beach and a forest adventure trail, one of the largest in Europe.

From Lyon or Bourg-en-Bresse take the N83. In St. Paul-de-Varax take the D70a direction St. Nizier-le-Desert. Follow signs.

CC € 15 *5/3-30/6 27/7-10/8 1/9-31/10* *7=6, 14=11*

N 46°5'11'' E 5°9'7''

St. Paul-de-Vézelin, F-42590 / Rhône-Alpes (Loire)

2149

D'Arpheuilles***
+33 (0)4-77634343
12/4 - 30/9
arpheuilles.camp@gmail.com

3,5ha 66**T**(120m²) 6-10A

1 ACDGIJLPRS
2 ACDJLRVWXY
3 ACGNQRU**W**Z
4 (B+G 1/5-4/9) (Q+R) (T+U+X+Z 1/7-31/8)
5 **AB**GJKLNPUVZ
6 EGJ(N 4km)OT

A lovely well-run campsite on the shores of a reservoir. This campsite offers some type of water recreation for every camper. The nature lover will enjoy exploring the hilly surroundings.

From St. Paul-de-Vézelin follow the D8 direction Dancé. Campsite located a few km outside village. Campsite signposted.

CC € 15 *12/4-8/7 25/8-30/9*

N 45°54'42'' E 4°3'57''

St. Pierre-d'Albigny, F-73250 / Rhône-Alpes (Savoie)

2150

Lac de Carouge***
Base de Loisirs
+33 (0)6-25913831
15/4 - 30/9
contact@lacdecarouge.com

1,9ha 64**T**(100-120m²) 10A CEE

1 AC**G**IJKLM**P**Q
2 ADFKMNRVWXY
3 BGHKN**P**RU**W**Z
4 (Q+R+T+U+V)
5 **AB**EFGIJKLMNOPQUWZ
6 ACGJ(N 1km)OTV

Campsite is at a lake. The camping pitches are minimum 100 m² in size and nearly all of them marked out by hedges. Swimming in the lake is permitted in the patrolled area. The Arbin vineyards and Miolans castle are in the neighbourhood. Good toilet facilities.

From Chambéry A43, exit 23 St. Pierre-d'Albigny which is well signposted 3.5 km from the campsite. From Albertville A43, exit 24 drive to St. Pierre-d'Albigny then follow the camping signs.

CC € 15 *15/4-9/7 27/8-30/9 7=6, 14=12, 21=18*

N 45°33'24'' E 6°9'59''

St. Pierre-de-Chartreuse, F-38380 / Rhône-Alpes (Isère)

2151

Sites & Paysages De Martinière***
route du Col de Porte
+33 (0)4-76886036
5/5 - 15/9
camping-de-martiniere@orange.fr

2,5ha 85**T**(80-110m²) 6-10A

1 ACD**G**IJKLMO**P**ST
2 GKRTVWXY
3 AGHJNRU
4 (C+H 15/5-15/9) (Q 1/7-31/8) (R 1/6-15/9) (T+X+Z 1/7-31/8)
5 **A**GIJKLMNPUVZ
6 ACEGJ(N 3km)OT

Peacefully located campsite within the walls of a Cartusienne farm with a magnificent view on the Chartreuse range. Well maintained area with a lovely swimming pool. Separated pitches, partially with the help of hedges.

Driving with a caravan we advise the route via St. Laurent-du-Pont, direction St. Pierre-de-Chartreuse. 1 km before St. Pierre in the town of Diat turn right direction Col de Porte. From there, it's only 2 km to the campsite.

CC € 17 *5/5-8/7 25/8-14/9 7=6*

N 45°19'32'' E 5°47'51''

St. Priest-la-Prugne, F-42830 / Rhône-Alpes (Loire) — 2152

Le Paradou
Le Moulin Poyet
+33 (0)4-77649032
24/3 - 1/10
info@le-paradou.com

9ha 45**T**(80-130m²) 10A CEE

1 A**G**IJKLOPRS
2 BCDFIKRTVWXY
3 ADGHJR**W**XZ
4 (B 1/6-15/9)
(Q+R+U+Y+Z)
5 **A**FGIJMNOPUWZ
6 EGJ(N 2km)V

An idyllic spot by the river. The ideal campsite for those seeking rest and relaxation. Own fishing pool, swimming lake and swimming pool.

N7 until Lapalisse. There, dir. Le Mayet de Montagne. Then continue on D7 dir. La Prugne.

CC € 13 *24/3-9/7 27/8-1/10* *7=6, 14=11, 21=16*

N 45°57'49'' E 3°44'28''

St. Privat, F-07200 / Rhône-Alpes (Ardèche) — 2153

Le Plan d'Eau***
route de Lussas
+33 (0)4-75354498
30/4 - 24/9
info@campingleplandeau.fr

3ha 75**T**(80-150m²) 8A CEE

1 ACD**G**IJKLMOPRS
2 CLORTVXY
3 AGHIJNRU**W**X
4 (C+H+Q+R+T+U+V+X+Z)
5 **A**DEFGIJKLMNOPUZ
6 ACEGHJ**K**(N 2km)OTV

A campsite with direct access to the Ardèche. Lovely views of the surrounding rock formations. Not far from Aubenas. Pitches often surrounded by hedges. You pay extra for XL pitches. Site has EU eco-label.

A7 exit Montélimar-Nord, dir. Le Teil/Aubenas. Right onto D304 towards St. Privat/Privas before Aubenas. Dir. Lussas on roundabout. Campsite on the right. Do not use SatNav!

CC € 15 *30/4-4/7 22/8-24/9* *27=24*

N 44°37'8'' E 4°25'56''

St. Romans (Isère), F-38160 / Rhône-Alpes (Isère) — 2154

Le Lac du Marandan***
657 route des Marandans
+33 (0)4-76644177
29/4 - 11/9
contact@camping-lac-marandan.com

3ha 100**T**(80-130m²) 6-10A CEE

1 AC**G**IJKLMO**P**Q
2 ABDFKLRTVXY
3 BGHJKMNRUWZ
4 (Q+R+T+U+V+X+Z 1/7-31/8)
5 **AB**EFGIJKLMNOPUVWZ
6 ACEGHJ**K**(N 2km)OT

A family campsite by a shallow lake with a sandy beach. Also suitable for exploring Vercors (altitude 200m) among other places. Restaurant with views of the lake.

Take the D1532 between Grenoble and Valence. Clearly signposted in St. Romans. Through Base de Loisirs to Lac du Marandan campsite. Or take motorway A49, exit 9 St. Marcellin.

CC € 15 *29/4-9/7 29/8-11/9*

N 45°6'11'' E 5°17'30''

St. Sauveur-de-Cruzières, F-07460 / Rhône-Alpes (Ardèche) — 2155

Camping de la Claysse****
La Digue
+33 (0)4-75354065
FAX +33 (0)4-75366865
1/4 - 30/9
camping.claysse@wanadoo.fr

1ha 45T(70-90m²) 10A CEE

1 AGIJKLPST
2 CJMRTVXY
3 AGHJNRUV**W**X
4 (A) (B 15/5-30/9) (Q 1/7-31/8) (T+U+V+X+Z)
5 **A**DEFGIJKLMNOPQUWZ
6 AEG**K**(N 0,2km)TV

Located by the small River Claysse. Views of the mountains and the village. There is a working olive mill on the campsite, great for souvenirs! The Gorges de L' Ardèche and Vallon Pont d'Arc are 20 km away and Barjac with its lively market is 8 km.

A7, exit 19 Bolléne. N86 to Pont St. Esprit. Then D6086 towards Bourg St. Andéol. Left after 2.5 km on D901. In Barjac continue to St. Sauveur. Don't turn off in the village, turn left a bit further by the car park.

€15 1/4-6/7 23/8-30/9

N 44°18'2" E 4°14'57"

St. Sauveur-de-Montagut, F-07190 / Rhône-Alpes (Ardèche) — 2156

l'Ardéchois*****
Le Chambon Gluiras, D102
+33 (0)4-75666187
FAX +33 (0)4-75666367
1/5 - 23/9
ardechois.camping@wanadoo.fr

6,5ha 78T(90-160m²) 10A CEE

1 ACD**G**IJKLMOPST
2 ACJKLMORTVWXY
3 AGHJN**P**RU**W**X
4 (**A**+C+H+Q+R) (T 4/7-29/8) (U+Y+Z)
5 **AB**DEFGIJKLMNOPQRUWZ
6 ACEGI**K**(N 8km)OUV

By a narrow river, suitable for fishing and where you can cool off when it gets hot. The grounds have wonderful views of the mountains that surround the campsite. You can relax far away from everyday pressure. Lovely renovated swimming pool.

A7 exit 15 Valence-Sud. Dir. Le Puy-en-Velay. N7 Montélimar. Right on D111a to Carmes-sur-Rhone. D86 to Privas. In Beauchastel D21. D120 dir. Le Cheylard to St. Sauveur. Then D102 to. Mezilhac. Campsite on right after 8 km.

€15 1/5-2/7 20/8-23/9

N 44°49'44" E 4°31'23"

St. Theoffrey/Petichet, F-38119 / Rhône-Alpes (Isère) — 2157

Au Pré du Lac***
+33 (0)4-76839134
5/3 - 29/10
aupredulac@aupredulac.eu

3,5ha 80T(60-120m²) 10A CEE

1 ACD**G**IJKLMPST
2 DGJKLMRWXY
3 ABGHJNRU**W**Z
4 (Q+X+Y+Z)
5 **A**DEFGJKLMNPU
6 ACEGJ(N 10km)RV

The campsite is located directly next to a beautiful lake with wonderful views of the mountains all around. Plenty of sports opportunities and well positioned for trips out in the area. Both sunny and shaded pitches available. Restaurant with terrace overlooking the lake and the mountains. Private beach.

Grenoble direction Gap. A480, exit 8 direction Vizille. In Vizille direction Gap via the N85. Through Laffrey. Then follow camping signs.

€15 5/3-30/6 27/8-29/10

N 45°0'5" E 5°46'21"

Thonon-les-Bains, F-74200 / Rhône-Alpes (Haute-Savoie)

iD **2158**

Saint Disdille***
117 avenue de Saint-Disdille
+33 (0)4-50711411
FAX +33 (0)4-50719367
1/4 - 30/9
camping@disdille.com

12ha 300**T**(90-120m²) 10A

1 ACD**G**IJKLM**P**Q
2 BDGLNRTVWXY
3 BGKMNR**WZ**
4 (Q+S+T+U+V+X 🔑)
(Y 1/5-15/9) (Z 🔑)
5 **AB**FGIJKLMNPUWYZ
6 ACDEGH**IJK**(N 3km)QRT

Large family campsite with spacious pitches in wooded surroundings. The banks of Lake Geneva are in a park 150 metres from the entrance. Public transport, restaurant, supermarket, newspaper kiosk. Nature reserve next to the campsite. Excellent cycling in the mountainous area around the lake. Bike rental.

N5 Genève-Evian, exit Vongy-Lac, then direction St. Disdille. Campsite signposted.

CC € 17 *1/4-9/7 27/8-30/9*

N 46°23'58'' E 6°30'14''

Tournon-sur-Rhône, F-07300 / Rhône-Alpes (Ardèche)

iD **2159**

Camping de Tournon HPA***
1 prom. Roche Defrance
+33 (0)4-75080528
1/1 - 31/12
camping@camping-tournon.com

1,1ha 56**T**(60-100m²) 6A CEE

1 AC**G**IJKLMPST
2 CFGKRVWXY
3 AHJRU**W**
5 **AB**DEFGIJKMNPUVWZ
6 CDEGKOT

A pleasant campsite near the town centre on the banks of the Rhone, overlooking the vineyards of L'Hermitage. This shaded campsite with heated toilet facilities is open all year round.

A7 exit 13 Tain l'Hermitage. Over the bridge to Tournon and turn right by the water. Follow camping signs.

CC € 17 *1/1-5/7 27/8-31/12*

N 45°4'18'' E 4°49'40''

Tournon-sur-Rhône, F-07300 / Rhône-Alpes (Ardèche)

iD **2160**

Les Acacias***
190, route de Lamastre
+33 (0)4-75088390
1/4 - 30/9
info@acacias-camping.com

2,4ha 44**T**(80-200m²) 6-10A CEE

1 AC**G**IJKLMOPST
2 CFGNRWXY
3 BGHIJNQRU**W**X
4 (B+G 15/5-15/9)
(Q+T+U+V+X 1/7-31/8) Z
5 **A**GIJKLMNOPUW
6 EG**J**(N 3km)ORV

A quiet, attractive family campsite in the heart of the Ardèche and close to Tournon. Spacious shaded pitches, swimming pool. Opportunities for walking from the campsite.

A7, exit 13 Tournon. Over the Rhône turn right. Direction Lamastre at roundabout.

CC € 13 *1/5-8/7 25/8-30/9*

N 45°3'57'' E 4°47'41''

Treffort, F-38650 / Rhône-Alpes (Isère) — 2161

Camping d'Herbelon***
Lac de Monteynard
+33 (0)4-76340547
FAX +33 (0)4-76340599
15/4 - 2/10
info@camping-dherbelon.com

0,6ha 52T(75-150m²) 10A CEE

1 ACDGIJKLMPQ
2 ADFKLNORVWX
3 ABGHJKNRUW
4 (C+H 30/4-15/10) (Q+R) (T 15/6-15/9) (U) (V 15/6-15/9) (Y+Z)
5 **AB**FGIJKLMNOPUWY
6 CEGJK(N 6km)ORT

A campsite for the sportive camper. Located on Lake Monteynard. Lovely walking area, close to the Himalaya suspension bridge. Good restaurant on the site.

Via Grenoble A51 exit 13. Direction Lac de Monteynard/Avignonet. Then Sinard/Treffort. Follow signs. Do not take Treffort exit but keep right.

CC € 13 *1/5-30/6 31/8-2/10*

N 44°53'55'' E 5°40'25''

Treffort, F-38650 / Rhône-Alpes (Isère) — 2162

Camping de la Plage**
Sous Jullières
FAX +33 (0)4-76340631
2/4 - 14/10
contact@camping2laplage.com

2ha 75T(80-150m²) 10A CEE

1 ACD**G**IJLPST
2 DFJKMNOTVWXY
3 BGHJKNR**WZ**
4 (G 1/7-31/8) J(Q+R+T) (U+V 1/7-31/8) (X+Z)
5 **AB**GIJKLMNPUWXYZ
6 AEGL(N 12km)TV

A campsite located by the lake. Plenty of facilities for the sportive camper. Good restaurant. Convenient for a boat trip on the lake and a walk across the Himalaya suspension bridge.

Via Grenoble A51, exit 13 direction Lac de Monteynard. Then Sinard/Treffort. Campsite signposted at lake. Keep left.

CC € 11 *2/4-1/7 1/9-14/10*

N 44°54'34'' E 5°40'13''

Trept, F-38460 / Rhône-Alpes (Isère) — 2163

Les 3 Lacs du Soleil****
La Plaine de Serrières
+33 (0)4-74929206
FAX +33 (0)4-74834381
30/4 - 11/9
les3lacsdusoleil@hotmail.fr

2,6ha 160T(100-120m²) 6A

1 ACD**G**IJLM**P**RS
2 ADGLMORVWXY
3 BGHJKMNQRU**VWZ**
4 (B 1/5-11/9) (G) J (Q+R) (T 1/7-31/8) (V+X 1/6-11/9) Z
5 **AB**FGIJKLMNOPUWZ
6 EGHIK(N 2,5km)OV

A family campsite in the middle of the countryside on 26 hectare grounds between Lyon and Grenoble. A suitable area for anglers, walkers, cyclists and lovers of sites, landscape and architecture. Large, level pitches in the shade. Restaurant on site.

Bourg-en-Bresse direction Lyon. Exit Ambérieu. N75 direction Lagnieu. Then direction Lancin. Follow D522 and D517 towards Trept and Crémieu. Campsite located 3 km before Trept. Well signposted.

CC € 15 *30/4-9/7 27/8-11/9* 7=6

N 45°41'21'' E 5°21'6''

Trévoux, F-01600 / Rhône-Alpes (Ain)

2164

- Sites & Paysages Kanopee Village***
- rue Robert Baltié
- +33 (0)4-74084483
- 1/4 - 30/9
- contact@kanopee-village.com

2,5ha 164**T**(100-140m²) 10A CEE

1 ACDGIJKLMOPS
2 CRVXY
3 A
4 (C 1/6-31/8) (H 1/7-31/8) IJ **LN**(Q+R 1/7-31/8)
5 CIJKLMNPUVZ
6 E**J**(N 1km)T

This campsite on the edge of the River Saône is just 30 km from Lyon. Camping pitches for tents, caravans and motorhomes in natural surroundings. For no additional charge you can use the aqua complex des Cascades on weekdays.

From the north A46 exit 2 (Trévoux). Follow signs to town. Campsite signposted. From the south A6 take exit 32.

CC € 17 *1/4-5/7 25/8-30/9 7=6, 14=11*

N 45°56'21" E 4°46'6"

Tulette, F-26790 / Rhône-Alpes (Drôme)

2165

- Les Rives de l'Aygues***
- route de Cairanne
- +33 (0)4-75983750
- FAX +33 (0)4-75983670
- 1/5 - 25/9
- camping.aygues@wanadoo.fr

3,5ha 100**T**(80-300m²) 6-10A CEE

1 AC**F**IJKLM**P**S
2 BCRSTUVWXY
3 ABGHJNRUX
4 (C+G+Q+R 🔑) (T+U+V 1/7-31/8) Z
5 **A**FGIJKMNOPUXZ
6 EG**K**(N 2,5km)OTV

A campsite located in the middle of the countryside on the edge of extensive vineyards and in a wood by a river. Plenty of privacy provided by the hedges which screen the pitches, a very basic shop (with bread each morning) and a well-heated pool from May to October. Free WiFi on entire site in low season.

Motorway exit Bollène direction Vaison-la-Romaine, in Tulette turn right and follow signs.

CC € 17 *1/5-8/7 25/8-25/9*

N 44°15'53" E 4°55'54"

Ucel/Aubenas, F-07200 / Rhône-Alpes (Ardèche)

2166

- Domaine de Gil****
- 91 route de Vals
- +33 (0)4-75946363
- 29/4 - 18/9
- resa@domaine-de-gil.com

4,5ha 28**T**(80-130m²) 10A CEE

1 ACD**F**IJKLM**P**ST
2 ACLNORTVXY
3 AGHJ**M**N**Q**RU**W**X
4 (C+H 🔑) K(Q+R 🔑) (T+U+V 12/5-18/9) (Y 18/6-28/8) (Z 🔑)
5 **AB**EFGIJKLMNOPUVWXYZ
6 ACEG**IJK**(N 2km)OTV

A campsite with ambiance and beautiful landscaping. Several natural springs in the area including Vals-les-Bains. Heated swimming pool (27°C). Not far from Aubenas which has plenty of shops. Outdoor fitness by the river.

A7 exit Montélimar-Nord direction Le Teil/Aubenas. Just before Aubenas turn right D304 to St. Privat/Privas. Exit St. Privat, follow St. Privat/Ucel. In Pont d'Ucel, direction Vals-les-Bains/Ucel at roundabout. Campsite on left after 2 km. Don't use SatNav!

CC € 17 *29/4-30/6 20/8-18/9 14=13, 21=19*

N 44°38'33" E 4°22'47"

Vagnas, F-07150 / Rhône-Alpes (Ardèche)

iD **2167**

Huttopia Sud Ardèche***
RD217
+33 (0)4-75387727
14/4 - 17/10

14ha 120T 10A CEE

1 ACD**G**IJKLMNOPQ
2 BCJKLRSTVWXY
3 AGHJKLRU
4 **A**(C+G+Q+R+T+U+V+Z)
5 **AB**DEFGIJKLMNOPQUWZ
6 ACEGHI(N 4km)V

Large, new campsite in an existing natural area in the south of the Ardèche. Lots of attention for nature and ecology. Pitches are marked out with trees and bushes which were already there. No WiFi.

A7 exit 18. Follow Pierrelatte, then Bourg St. Andéol. Then to Vallon Pont d' Arc via D4. In Vallon Toutes directions, then to Salavas. 3.5 km towards Barjac, D579. Left at crossing, right Orgnac l'Aven, D217. Site on left.

CC € 17 *14/4-30/6 1/9-16/10*

N 44°22'6" E 4°22'15"

Vallières, F-74150 / Rhône-Alpes (Haute-Savoie)

iD **2168**

Les Charmilles***
625 route du Val de Fier
+33 (0)4-50621060
FAX +33 (0)4-50621945
1/4 - 31/10
les.charmilles.camping@wanadoo.fr

2ha 76**T**(100-120m²) 8A

1 ACD**G**IJKLM**P**RS
2 FKLRVWXY
3 AGHJNRU
4 (A 1/7-25/8) (C+H 1/5-30/9) (Q 6/7-30/8) (T+U+V+X+Y 15/6-15/9) Z
5 **AB**DFGIJKLMNPQUZ
6 EGJ(N 0,5km)OV

Family campsite with quiet location. Many shady pitches in rural surroundings at the foot of the mountains with a heated pool and good toilet facilities. Local food available. Touristic day trip options in vicinity.

In Mâcon take the A40 direction Genève. Exit 11 Eloise. Then take the N508 as far as Frangy. D910 direction Rumilly. Turn off in Vallières towards Seyssel. Campsite located 500 metres left of the D14.

CC € 15 *1/4-30/6 1/9-31/10*

N 45°54'8" E 5°55'41"

Vallon-Pont-d'Arc, F-07150 / Rhône-Alpes (Ardèche)

iD **2169**

Beau Rivage****
quartier les Mazes
+33 (0)4-75880354
FAX +33 (0)4-75880762
29/4 - 10/9
campingbeaurivage@wanadoo.fr

2,2ha 86**T**(100-110m²) 10A CEE

1 ACD**G**IJKLMPST
2 ACRTVXY
3 BGNRU**WX**
4 (C+H+Q+R) (T+U+V+Y 30/5-31/8) (Z)
5 **A**DEFGIJKLMNOPUVWZ
6 AEGJ(N 2km)RTV

4 star campsite Beau Rivage is located among the vineyards by the river. It has a wide beach and there is enough water in the Ardèche for swimming and sailing. The lovely heated swimming pool has a wall of bubbles. Plenty of shaded pitches. Heated toilet facilities. The owners are very friendly and hospitable.

From Ruoms take D579 dir. Vallon-Pont-d'Arc. Turn right at Les Mazes, left at end of road, campsite on right. Don't use SatNav but this route description.

CC € 17 *30/4-5/7 22/8-10/9* **14=13, 21=19**

N 44°24'23" E 4°21'51"

Vallon-Pont-d'Arc, F-07150 / Rhône-Alpes (Ardèche) 2170

Camping de L'Ardèche - Vallon Pont d'Arc**
chemin de la Plage 100
+33 (0)475880473
25/3 - 25/9
campingvallonpontdarc@gmail.com

150T(75-120m²) 6A CEE

1 ACD**G**IJKLMOP
2 ACGRTUVX
3 AGJR**WX**
4 (B+G+Q+T+U+V+Z)
5 **A**DEFGIJKLMPXZ
6 AEGHJ**K**TV

Easy-going and quiet campsite. Direct access from the campsite to the beach and the river. Close to the centre of Vallon-Pont-d'Arc. New owner who is making changes.

A7, exit 17 N86 dir. Le Teil, then N102 dir. Aubenas. After Villeneuve de Berg left on roundabout dir Vallon Pont d'Arc, D103. Then 579 to Vallon Pont d'Arc. Follow road to Salavas. 3rd exit left on roundabout past Le Chauvieux follow road. Campsite on right.

CC € 13 *25/3-9/7 27/8-25/9*

N 44°23'50" E 4°23'1"

Vallon-Pont-d'Arc, F-07150 / Rhône-Alpes (Ardèche) 2171

Domaine de L'Esquiras****
1280 chemin du Fez
+33 (0)4-75880416
25/3 - 30/9
esquiras@orange.fr

3ha 49T(80-120m²) 10A CEE

1 ACD**G**IJKLMPST
2 KRTVWXY
3 AGHJRU
4 (**A** 1/7-31/8) (B+E+H) IJ (Q 1/5-30/9) (R) (T+U+V+Y 22/4-15/9) (Z)
5 **A**EFGIJKLMNPQUWZ
6 ACDEGK(N 1,5km)TV

This campsite is located near Vallon in the middle of hills and vineyards. Plenty of sports opportunities. A special area for motorhomes. The village is quite touristy and there are supermarkets, including Lidl, close by. Free WiFi throughout the grounds. Indoor, heated pool.

From Ruoms D579 continue towards Vallon-Pont-d'Arc. Left at the roundabout just before the village (3rd exit) and follow camping signs.

CC € 17 *25/3-8/7 25/8-30/9*

N 44°24'55" E 4°22'41"

Vallon-Pont-d'Arc, F-07150 / Rhône-Alpes (Ardèche) 2172

International Camping****
65 Impasse de la Plaine
+33 (0)4-75880099
30/4 - 30/9
inter.camp@wanadoo.fr

3ha 105T(90-130m²) 10A

1 ACD**G**IJKLMPST
2 CGNORTVXY
3 AGHJNRUV**WX**
4 (C+H) K (Q+R+T+U+V+W+Y+Z)
5 **A**EFGIJLMNPUZ
6 ACFGK(N 1km)TUV

Four-star campsite with green zone for sports and games. Cool down in the swimming pool. Good toilet facilities. Restaurant. Pitches with panoramic views by the river. Close to the centre of Vallon and 5 km from the Caverne du Pont d'Arc.

A7 exit 17. N86 dir. Le Teil, then N102 dir. Aubenas. After Villeneuve-de-Berg left at the roundabout D103 dir. Vallon-Pont-d'Arc. Then D579 to Vallon-Pont-d'Arc. Follow road dir. Salavas. Campsite on right after the bridge.

CC € 17 *30/4-10/7 27/8-30/9* 15=14, 23=20

N 44°23'52" E 4°22'59"

Vallon-Pont-d'Arc, F-07150 / Rhône-Alpes (Ardèche)

2173

Mondial Camping****
route des Gorges, D290
+33 (0)4-75880044
+33 (0)4-75371373
19/3 - 25/9
reserv-info@mondial-camping.com

4,2ha 209T(90-110m²) 10A CEE

1 ACD**G**IJKLMOPST
2 ACGNORTVXY
3 AGHMN**OPQ**RU**W**X
4 (C+H) J (Q+S+T+U+V+Y+Z)
5 **AB**DEFGIJKLMNOPRUVWXYZ
6 ACEGIK(N 1km)ORTUV

This lovely campsite is close to Vallon-Pont-d'Arc. The varying greenery provides plenty of shade. There are also luxury pitches with water supply and drainage, for which you pay extra. You can sunbathe beside the pool. Canoeing on the River Ardèche from the campsite. New toilet facilities (2016). Friendly owners.

From Vallon-Pont-d'Arc follow the D290 (Route des Gorges). After 1 km, the campsite is the third on the right.

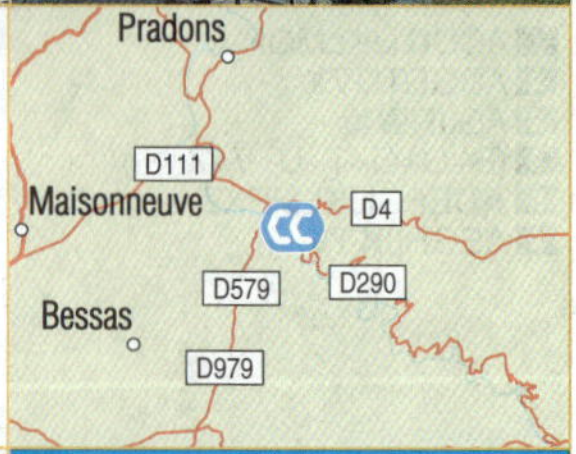

CC € 19 *19/3-3/7 27/8-25/9*

N 44°23'50" E 4°24'4"

Vallon-Pont-d'Arc/Lagorce, F-07150 / Rhône-Alpes (Ardèche)

2174

Domaine de Chadeyron****
Quartier de Chadeyron, D1
+33 (0)4-75880481
25/3 - 15/10
infos@campingchadeyron.com

3ha 30T(100-150m²) 16A CEE

1 ACD**G**IJKLM**P**ST
2 JKRTVWXY
3 AGHJRU
4 (C+H 1/5-30/9) (Q+R+T+U+V+Z)
5 **A**BCDEFGHIJKLMNOPQRUWXYZ
6 ACDEGIK(N 2,5km)V

Terraced site on 43 hectares of grounds with nice views. Peaceful homely ambiance. Free WiFi. Good base for lovely walks and cycle rides. Extra fee for grand comfort pitches. Luxury, new toilet facilities. EN, NL, FR and DE spoken.

A7 exit Montélimar-Nord. N7 dir. Le Teil, then N102 to Aubenas. After Villeneuve-de-Berg left at roundabout onto D103. At Vogüé left towards Vallon on roundabout. Then left and follow D1. Site on right. Ok to use SatNav.

CC € 17 *25/3-8/7 25/8-15/10* *21=19*

N 44°28'13" E 4°25'1"

Vercheny, F-26340 / Rhône-Alpes (Drôme)

2175

Les Acacias***
Les Tours
+33 (0)4-75217251
+33 (0)4-75217398
1/4 - 30/9
infos@campinglesacacias.com

3,6ha 90T(80-120m²) 6A CEE

1 ACD**G**IJKLPST
2 BCKNTVXY
3 BHJKRU**WX**
4 (Q) (R 1/6-30/9) (T+U+X 1/5-15/9) Z
5 **A**GIJKLMNOPUVWZ
6 EGJ(N 1,5km)OTV

Well shaded campsite on the Drôme, ideal as a starting point for exploring the beautiful surroundings by bike (in a large flat area with small towns) or by car (lovely mountains close by). Basic but good and inexpensive restaurant. You can hire canoes and kayaks for sailing on the Drôme. Free WiFi.

A7 exit Valence, direction Crest (D111). After Crest direction Die (D93). Campsite located between Crest and Die on the D93, 2 km before Vercheny on the south of the road.

CC € 15 *1/4-8/7 25/8-30/9*

N 44°41'44" E 5°14'29"

Vernioz, F-38150 / Rhône-Alpes (Isère) 2176

Le Bontemps****
5, Impasse du Bontemps
+33 (0)4-74578352
FAX +33 (0)4-74578370
9/4 - 24/9
@ info@camping-lebontemps.com

8ha 120T(100-150m²) 10A

1 ACD**G**IJKLMOPRS
2 CLMRUVWXY
3 BGHJ**MNQ**RUVW
4 (C 1/5-30/9) (H 15/5-30/9) J (Q 1/5-30/9) (T) (U+Y 15/4-30/9) Z
5 **AB**EFGIJKLMNOPUVWXYZ
6 CDEG**JK**(N 2km)ORTUV

High-class campsite in beautiful park with a rich variety of trees. Many activities: fitness and fishing for free. Located in the Rhône, a few kilometres from Vienne.

A7 exit 10 Condrieu, N7 dir. Valence. In Reventin-Vaugris D31 and follow signs, well signposted.

CC € 15 9/4-5/7 22/8-23/9 7=6

N 45°25'42'' E 4°55'42''

Villars-les-Dombes, F-01330 / Rhône-Alpes (Ain) 2177

Le Nid du Parc****
164 avenue des Nations
+33 (0)4-74980021
9/4 - 2/11
@ camping@parcdesoiseaux.com

4,5ha 160T(80-100m²) 6A CEE

1 ACD**G**IJKLM**P**ST
2 CLMRTUVWXY
3 AB**F**GHJKL**M**NRU**W**
4 (**A** 25/4-20/9) (C+H 1/6-31/8) J(Q) (T 1/5-5/9) (U+X 1/6-31/8)
5 **AB**EFGIJKLMNOPUWXYZ
6 CDEGJTV

A pleasant, friendly campsite located in a beautiful natural area with many lakes and ponds. The campsite has a lovely swimming pool. Plenty of opportunities for (nature) excursions, including the Jura, Gorges de l'Ain and les Dombes. Close to a large bird park. An ideal area for cycle trips. The campsite has new toilet facilities.

From Bourg-en-Bresse follow the RD1083, then follow signs in the village.

CC € 17 9/4-30/6 1/9-2/11

N 45°59'49'' E 5°1'51''

Villefranche-sur-Saône, F-69400 / Rhône-Alpes (Rhône) 2178

Camping Parc Beaujolais*
2788 route de Riottier
+33 (0)4-74653348
15/5 - 16/9
@ contact@campingparc-beaujolais.com

4ha 128T(100m²) 10A CEE

1 ACD**G**IJKLP
2 CDFRVXY
3 AGR**WZ**
4 (X+Y) Z
5 **AB**EFGIJKLMNPUVYZ
6 EG**J**(N 1km)TV

This campsite is located beside the Saône River. Large pitches under the trees. Very suitable as a stopover campsite. Just 1 min drive from exit 31.2 of the A6 motorway. A nice break in the Beaujolais. Free access to lake with small beach for campers. Suitable for groups. When not open, this campsite is a motorhome site.

Exit Villefranche-sur-Saône toll road. Campsite signposted.

CC € 13 15/5-10/7 27/8-16/9 7=6, 14=11

N 45°58'21'' E 4°45'7''

Villeneuve-de-Berg, F-07170 / Rhône-Alpes (Ardèche)

2179

Domaine le Pommier*****
N102
+33 (0)4-75948281
FAX +33 (0)4-75948390
8/4 - 9/9
@ info@campinglepommier.com

30ha 204T(80-120m²) 6A CEE

1 ACDGIJKLM**P**ST
2 CGJKNORTVWXY
3 BGHJ**M**N**Q**RU
4 (A+C+H) IJK
(Q+S+T+U) (W 1/7-31/8)
(Y+Z)
5 **AB**DEFGIJKLMNOPQRUW
Z
6 ACDEGH**K**L(N 1,5km)OTU
V

For those who like to have lots of fun, this place will suit them perfectly. There is always something fun to do. There is a level part and there are terraces with wonderful views of Mirabel. There is a stone grill restaurant. Lovely swimming pools.

A7 exit Montélimar-Nord direction Le Teil/ Aubenas. In Le Teil take the N102 to Villeneuve-de-Berg. Just before the village and the roundabout you'll find the campsite on the right hand side.

CC € 19 *8/4-25/6 3/9-9/9*

N 44°34'21'' E 4°30'40''

Vizille, F-38220 / Rhône-Alpes (Isère)

2180

Le Bois de Cornage***
110 chemin du Camping
+33 (0)4-76681239
1/4 - 31/10
@ campingvizille@orange.fr

3,6ha 115T 16A CEE

1 AC**G**IJKLMOPST
2 BGKRVY
3 BGHJNR
4 (B+G 1/6-15/10)
(Q 1/6-15/9)
(T+U+V+X+Z 1/6-31/8)
5 **AB**FGIJKLMPUVWY
6 ACEJ**K**(N 1km)TV

A campsite with spacious marked pitches under large trees. The centre and historic castle are 1 km from the campsite. An ideal location to explore the Alpine Cols from here in spring or autumn (280m).

D1085 Grenoble-Sisteron. Follow signs from roundabout in Vizille (14 km). Campsite clearly signposted.

CC € 17 *1/4-30/6 29/8-31/10*

N 45°5'11'' E 5°46'12''

Vonnas, F-01540 / Rhône-Alpes (Ain)

2181

Le Renom***
240 avenue des Sports
+33 (0)4-74500275
2/4 - 2/10
@ campingvonnas@wanadoo.fr

2,6ha 82T(80-100m²) 10A CEE

1 ACD**G**IJKLMOPQ
2 CRVWX
3 AGJ**M**NRU**W**
4 (C+H 1/7-31/8) J
(T+X+Z 15/5-15/9)
5 **AB**FGIJKLMNPUZ
6 CDEGK(N 0,3km)

The campsite is located 300m from the centre of Vonnas with many amenities in the Bresse region, which is known for its good food. The site is located beside two rivers, has spacious pitches marked out by hedges which are about 2m high and is filled with flowers. Free WiFi.

Campsite is located in the town of Vonnas and is signposted.

CC € 15 *2/4-30/6 17/8-2/10*

N 46°13'15'' E 4°59'15''

Agos-Vidalos, F-65400 / Midi-Pyrénées (Hautes-Pyrénées)

iD 2182

La Châtaigneraie***
46 avenue du Lavedan
+33 (0)5-62970740
1/1 - 15/10, 1/12 - 31/12
camping.chataigneraie@wanadoo.fr

1,8ha 60**T**(80-100m²) 10A

1 ACD**G**IJKLMOPQ
2 GJKLRVXY
3 BGHJRU
4 (C+H 1/5-30/9) J (Q 1/7-31/8)
5 **AB**CDEFGHIJKLMNPQRUW
6 ACEG**K**(N 2km)TV

A peaceful family campsite with lovely new toilet facilities in a fine wooden building. Shaded pitches on the edge of a chestnut wood with lovely views of the mountains. Heated swimming pool. A good base for all types of excursions and for enjoying some relaxation. WiFi everywhere.

In Lourdes take D821/N21 to Argelès-Gazost. Then exit Agos-Vidalos. In Agos village centre. Signposted.

CC € 13 *1/4-30/6 22/8-15/10* *7=6, 14=13, 21=19, 30=27*

N 43°1'55'' W 0°4'31''

Aguessac, F-12520 / Midi-Pyrénées (Aveyron)

iD 2183

Camping la Belle Etoile***
chemin des Prades
+33 (0)5-65729107
25/4 - 30/9
contact@camping-labelleetoile.fr

2,5ha 69**T**(150-300m²) 6A CEE

1 ACDGIJKLMOPQ
2 CFGKLNRVWXY
3 BGHIJQRU**WX**
4 (T+U+V+Y) Z
5 **A**EFGIJKLMNOPUZ
6 ACDEGJ(N 0,3km)RTV

This charming campsite with lovely views is on the river Tarn. The site is within walking distance of the village. Large pitches and new toilet facilities. The owners are very helpful, friendly and speak English.

From the north: A75, exit 44.1 Aguessac. Left at chemists. From the south: A75, exit 47 Millau. Direction Aguessac. Right after railway line.

CC € 13 *25/4-7/7 25/8-30/9* *30=25*

N 44°9'13'' E 3°5'53''

Aignan, F-32290 / Midi-Pyrénées (Gers)

iD 2184

Le Domaine du Castex***
+33 (0)5-62092513
20/3 - 23/10
info@domaine-castex.com

2,6ha 37**T**(90-150m²) 10A CEE

1 ACD**G**IJKLMPQ
2 RTVWXY
3 AGHL**M**NRU
4 (B 1/6-1/10) (Q 15/6-15/9) (T+U+X) Z
5 **A**GIJKLMNPUYZ
6 CDEG**K**(N 1km)V

On the edge of the medieval village of Aignan: a rural family campsite with plenty of atmosphere. Sufficient shade, small restaurant, giant swimming pool and children's play equipment. In an area with local produce from the Gers, such as Côte de Saint-Mont, Armagnac and duck and goose specialities. Three star campsite.

Direction Bordeaux, A65 direction Pau. Exit Aire-sur-l'Adour. Or direction Toulouse, then Auch (Mont-de-Marsan). At Dému direction Aignan.

CC € 17 *20/3-15/7 1/9-23/10*

N 43°41'34'' E 0°4'32''

Aigues-Vives, F-09600 / Midi-Pyrénées (Ariège)

2185

- Sites & Paysages La Serre***
- 5 chemin de la Serre
- +33 (0)5-61030616
- 19/3 - 31/10
- contact@camping-la-serre.com

10,5ha 48T(200-500m²) 5A CEE

1 AGIJKLMPQ
2 BGJKLRVWXY
3 ABCGHJRU
4 (A+B+Q+R+T+U+Z 1/7-31/8)
5 AEFGIJKMNPQRUVZ
6 ACDEGJ(N 5km)T

Beautiful natural campsite. Lovely flora and fauna. Woods, perfect for walking, with more than 25 different kinds of orchids. Lots of information about this, e.g. a video on a large screen. Nice, big pitches, partly shady.

D625 from Mirepoix to Lavelanet. In Aigues-Vives follow camping signs.

CC € 17 *19/3-9/7 27/8-30/10*

N 42°59'52'' E 1°52'19''

Alliat/Niaux, F-09400 / Midi-Pyrénées (Ariège)

2186

- Des Grottes***
- +33 (0)5-61058821
- FAX +33 (0)5-61038991
- 1/3 - 15/10
- info@campingdesgrottes.com

7ha 120T(90-110m²) 16A CEE

1 ACGIJKLMOPQ
2 CKLRVX
3 BGHJNORUVW
4 (C+G 1/6-15/9) IJKN (Q 1/5-30/9) (S 1/7-31/8) (T+U+V+X 1/6-31/8) Z
5 ABCDEFGHIJKLMNOPUW Z
6 ACEGK(N 3km)OV

A lovely campsite with plenty of atmosphere. Attractive separated pitches in avenues. Now with a heated toilet block. Good starting point for cultural trips and mountain hiking. Good views of the Niaux cave.

From Foix N20 direction Andorra. Turn right just past Tarascon towards Niaux/Vicdessos. Campsite 2 km on the right.

CC € 15 *1/3-4/7 21/8-15/10* *7=6, 14=11*

N 42°48'47'' E 1°35'21''

Arcizans-Avant, F-65400 / Midi-Pyrénées (Hautes-Pyrénées)

2187

- Les Châtaigniers***
- 11 rue Deth Bas
- +33 (0)5-62979477
- 1/5 - 30/9
- contact@camping-les-chataigniers.com

5ha 45T(80-150m²) 6A CEE

1 AGIJKLMPQ
2 JKLRTVWXY
3 BFGHJRUW
4 (A 1/7-30/8) (E+Q ⊶)
5 ABCFGHIJKLMNPRUVZ
6 ABEGJ(N 2km)RV

Small, quiet, in the green countryside, beautiful view of the valley and the Pyrenees. Peaceful and easy-going. There is no ongoing traffic near the campsite. Helpful, jovial owner (also speaks English). Heated pool, very clean toilet facilities. Free WiFi. Fresh bread, many options for excursions and good little restaurants nearby.

From Lourdes the D821: 1st roundabout: Argelès D821a, 2nd roundabout: final exit, 3rd roundabout: Arcizans-Avant. Then follow signs.

CC € 15 *1/5-30/6 1/9-30/9*

N 42°59'8'' W 0°6'19''

Argelès-Gazost, F-65400 / Midi-Pyrénées (Hautes-Pyrénées)

2188

Les Trois Vallées****
avenue des Pyrenées
+33 (0)5-62903547
FAX +33 (0)5-62903548
1/4 - 16/10
@ 3-vallees@wanadoo.fr

15ha 200**T**(100-170m²) 6A

1 ACD**G**IJKLMPQ
2 CGKLRTVXY
3 BCGHJKLNRU**W**
4 (**A** 1/7-31/8) (C 1/6-30/9) (E) (H 1/6-30/9) IJKMP (Q+T+U+V+W 15/6-11/9) (Z)
5 **AB**CDEFGHIJKLMNPQRUV XYZ
6 ABCFGH**IK**L(N 0,5km)TUV

A modern campsite with large indoor and outdoor leisure pools with water slides and jacuzzis. Restaurant and snack bar with garden. New indoor club room for all ages. Beautiful modern toilet facilities. WiFi free in low season. Centre at 300 metres. Excursions: Gavarnie, Tourmalet, zoo, Lourdes, bird of prey show etc. Campsite is easily accessible.

D821 from Lourdes. 1st roundabout turn right. Next roundabout 1st exit.

CC € 17 *1/4-2/7 27/8-16/10*

N 43°0'44'' W 0°5'50''

Argelès-Gazost/Ayzac-Ost, F-65400 / Midi-Pyrénées (Hautes-Pyrénées)

2189

La Bergerie***
8 chemin de la Bergerie
+33 (0)5-62975999
FAX +33 (0)5-62975189
1/5 - 30/9
@ sarl.campingdelabergerie@aliceadsl.fr

3,5ha 51**T**(100-130m²) 6A

1 ACD**G**IJKLMOPQ
2 GKRVWY
3 BGHJRU
4 (C+H 1/6-15/9) JKMP (Q 1/7-30/8) (V) (Z 1/7-31/8)
5 **A**CEFGHIJKLMNOPUZ
6 ACEG**K**(N 0,2km)OV

Level, centrally located campsite with nice large shaded pitches, close to a supermarket and within walking distance of the centre of Argelès-Gazost. New, modern and clean toilet facilities. Heated swimming pool. WiFi

From Lourdes take the D921 as far as the roundabout. 1st turn right. 2nd exit at following roundabout. Then 1st exit at the next roundabout towards Ayzac-Ost. Campsite about 400 metres on the right.

CC € 15 *1/5-5/7 22/8-30/9 14=13, 21=19, 30=27*

N 43°1'9'' W 0°5'44''

Argelès-Gazost/Lau-Balagnas, F-65400 / Midi-Pyrénées (Hautes-Pyrénées)

2190

Le Lavedan****
44 route des Vallées
+33 (0)5-62971884
FAX +33 (0)5-62972068
15/3 - 30/10
@ contact@lavedan.com

2ha 58**T**(80-100m²) 10A

1 ACD**G**IJKLMPQ
2 KRVXY
3 BGHJRU
4 (**A** 1/7-30/8) (E+G 1/5-15/9) K (Q 15/5-15/9) (R) (T+U+V+Z 15/5-15/9)
5 **AB**CDEFGHIJKLMNOPUW XYZ
6 CFGIJ**K**(N 2km)ORTV

Sabine, Michel and Thomas welcome you to the Pyrenees. After a warm greeting you will be staying in green and extraordinary surroundings. You can discover a number of special places here, such as Gavarnie, de Pic du Midi, Lourdes, Cauterets and the Pont d'Espagne.

From Lourdes follow D921. On 1st roundabout take 1st exit (D921b). Next roundabout last exit. Then through south of Argelès-Gazost. Site is signposted.

CC € 17 *15/3-9/7 26/8-30/10 7=6, 14=12*

N 42°59'17'' W 0°5'22''

Ascou, F-09110 / Midi-Pyrénées (Ariège)

2191

Ascou la Forge***
Ascou la Forge
+33 (0)5-61646003
1/1 - 31/12
info@ascou-la-forge.fr

1,5ha 55T(100-120m²) 10A CEE

1 A**G**IJKLMO**PQ**
2 CDKRX
3 AGHNRU**W**
4 (**A** 1/4-31/10) (Q+R)
(S 1/7-31/8) (T 1/7-30/8)
(Y 1/1-12/11,14/12-31/12) Z
5 **AB**FGIJKLMNPQRUZ
6 E**K**(N 7km)OV

Small campsite, located in a beautiful natural area with plenty of options for walking. Many outside sports are organised, such as rafting and rock climbing. The campsite is run by a Dutch couple.

From the roundabout at Ax-les-Thermes follow the signs Ascou/Pailhères. The campsite is located 3 km past the town of Ascou.

CC € 15 *1/1-8/7 27/8-31/12*

N 42°43'28'' E 1°53'35''

Ax-les-Thermes, F-09110 / Midi-Pyrénées (Ariège)

2192

Le Malazéou****
RN20
+33 (0)5-61646914
FAX +33 (0)5-61640560
15/4 - 13/11, 17/12 - 3/4
contact@campingmalazeou.com

6ha 151T(90-100m²) 10A

1 ACDGIJKLMO**PQ**
2 CRTVWXY
3 BGRUV**W**
4 (C 1/6-30/9) N
(T+U+X 1/7-31/8) Z
5 **AB**DEFGJLMNPUVW
6 AFGH**IK**(N 0,8km)TV

Campsite situated by a fast-flowing river within walking distance of the town centre. Lovely swimming pool and lovely new cafeteria.

Campsite is located on the N20, 1 km north of Ax-les-Thermes.

CC € 17 *1/1-5/2 7/3-3/4 15/4-1/7 1/9-13/11 17/12-31/12* *7=6, 14=11, 21=17*

N 42°43'43'' E 1°49'32''

Bagnères-de-Bigorre, F-65200 / Midi-Pyrénées (Hautes-Pyrénées)

2193

Le Monlôo****
6 route de la Plaine
FAX +33 (0)5-62951965
1/1 - 31/12
campingmonloo@yahoo.com

3,5ha 199T(100-120m²) 10A

1 ACD**G**IJKLMPQ
2 ACDGIKLRTVXY
3 AB**F**GJ**M**NRUZ
4 (F+H 15/5-30/9) J
(Q+R+T 1/7-15/9)
(U 5/7-23/8)
5 **AB**DFGIJKLMNOPQU
6 CDE**K**(N 2km)V

Spacious, quiet, shady campsite, centrally located for visiting the sights of the Pyrenees. Heated indoor pool (15/5-30/9) and a constructed swimming lake with a sandy beach and deckchairs. Free tennis in low season.

From Tarbes take the D935 as far as Bagnères-de-Bigorre. Left at the first roundabout, left again at the next roundabout. Then follow camping signs.

CC € 15 *1/1-30/6 1/9-30/10* *21=20*

N 43°4'51'' E 0°8'57''

Bagnères-de-Luchon, F-31110 / Midi-Pyrénées (Haute-Garonne) 2194

Camping Au Fil de l'Oô**
37 avenue de Vénasque
+33 (0)5-61793074
12/3 - 6/11
campingaufildeloo@gmail.com

2,5ha 104T(80-120m²) 2-10A

1 ACDGIJKLMPQ
2 CKLRVWXY
3 AFGHJKRUW
4 (Q) (R 1/7-31/8) (U+V 15/6-30/9)
5 ABDGIJKLMNOPUV
6 CEGK(N 0,7km)TV

Very structured, maintained campsite with majestic mountains visible. The owners made a conscious choice not to have a pool, but a large communal barbecue and a large dining table under an awning.

In Bagnères-de-Luchon follow road to Superbagnères, second campsite on left.

CC € 13 *12/3-9/7 26/8-6/11*   N 42°46'40'' E 0°36'1''

Boô-Silhen, F-65400 / Midi-Pyrénées (Hautes-Pyrénées) 2195

Deth-Potz**
40 route de Silhen
+33 (0)5-62903723
1/1 - 10/10, 10/12 - 31/12
contact@deth-potz.fr

4ha 76T(85-110m²) 3-10A

1 ACDGIJLPQ
2 IJKRTVWXY
3 AGHJNQRU
4 (B+G 15/6-15/9) (Q 1/7-31/8) (R)
5 ACDEFGHIJKMNOPQUV
6 ABCEJ(N 2km)OTV

This campsite is located in an oasis of greenery and relaxation at the foot of a 16th century chapel, two kilometres from Argelès-Gazost in the heart of the Pyrenees. Modern toilet facilities, motorhome service point, playing field. Ideally located for countless sports activities and discovery trips in the countryside.

From Lourdes towards Luz-St-Sauveur, Gavarnie. Last exit on 2nd roundabout, over bridge, immediate left. Campsite 1500m on the left.

CC € 13 *1/1-1/7 1/9-10/10 10/12-31/12*   N 43°0'40'' W 0°4'39''

Boyne/Rivière-sur-Tarn, F-12640 / Midi-Pyrénées (Aveyron) 2196

Camping Moulin de la Galinière**
chemin des Condamines
+33 (0)5-65626560
1/5 - 10/9
info@moulindelagaliniere.fr

2ha 57T(90-150m²) 6-10A CEE

1 ABGIJKLPRS
2 BCFKLMNORSTVWXY
3 AGHJRUWX
4 (Q+T+U+V+X+Z)
5 ACEFGHIJKLMNOPQUVZ
6 AEGJ(N 2km)T

Close to the Gorges du Tarn in the heart of the 'Parc des Grands Causses'. A homely campsite where you can go kayaking and canoeing. Friendly restaurant. Special flora (wild orchids) and fauna (more than 50 species of birds). English, German and Dutch also spoken.

A75 Clermont-Ferrand, exit 44.1 Aguessac. Follow signs to 'Gorges du Tarn'. Go to Boyne, campsite just outside Boyne village on the right by the Tarn.

CC € 15 *1/5-2/7 22/8-10/9*   N 44°12'4'' E 3°9'34''

Camon, F-09500 / Midi-Pyrénées (Ariège)

2197

Camping de la Besse***
+33 (0)5-61688463
30/4 - 29/10
contact@camping-labesse.com

200ha 50T(150-250m²) 16A CEE

1 ACDGIJKLMPQ
2 AKLMRVWXY
3 ADGHJMRU
4 (B 15/6-15/9)
(Q+R+T+U+V+X+Z 1/7-31/8)
5 **A**EFGIJKLMNOPRUVWZ
6 AEJ(N 1km)V

A very spacious farmhouse campsite with large, spacious pitches (150-250 m²) in the sun, the shade or in the woods. Beautiful views of the Pyrenees. Ideal for exploring the surroundings.

From Toulouse take A66 direction Andorra. Exit 6 Mirepoix (D119). Then D625. At the settlement follow D7 to Camon. Follow signs 1 km past Camon.

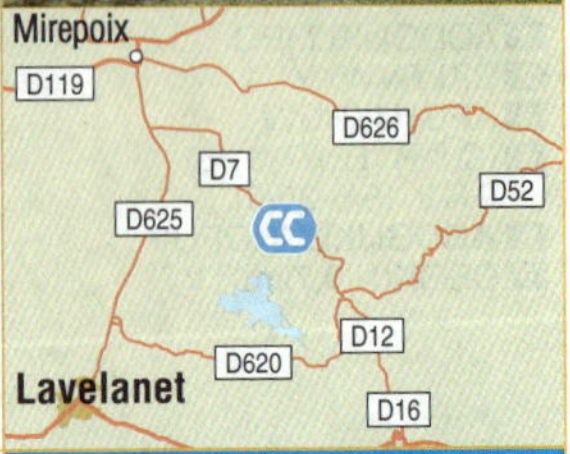

CC € 15 *30/4-8/7 26/8-28/10*

N 43°0'55" E 1°57'56"

Canet-de-Salars, F-12290 / Midi-Pyrénées (Aveyron)

2198

Soleil Levant***
Lac de Pareloup / D993
+33 (0)5-65460365
1/5 - 30/9
contact@
camping-soleil-levant.com

7ha 165T(100-110m²) 6A CEE

1 AC**G**IJKLMPRS
2 ADIJRVWXY
3 BGHJNRU**W**Z
4 (Q 🔑) (T+U+V 1/7-31/8)
(Z 🔑)
5 **AB**EFGJLNPRUVZ
6 AEGJ(N 4km)OUV

Slightly sloping wooded grounds. Large pitches directly on the shores of Lake Pareloup. The shores are like beaches. The large area lends itself to strolling or walking the dog. Free WiFi-spot.

A75 exit 44.1 in the direction of Pont-de-Salars. Follow D911 (27 km) till just before Pont-de-Salars, turn left onto the D993 towards Salles-Curan. Campsite about 8 km on the left just before the bridge.

CC € 13 *1/5-10/7 27/8-30/9* *14=12, 21=18*

N 44°12'55" E 2°46'41"

Carennac, F-46110 / Midi-Pyrénées (Lot)

2199

L'Eau Vive****
Prés Nabots
+33 (0)5-65109739
FAX +33 (0)5-55281212
1/5 - 15/10
info@dordogne-soleil.com

3ha 90T(80-120m²) 6A CEE

1 A**G**IJKLMPRS
2 CRVWXY
3 BFGHJNQRU**WX**
4 (B+G 1/6-30/9)
(Q 1/6-31/8)
(R+T+U+V+Z 1/7-31/8)
5 **AB**FGIJKLMNOPUZ
6 CEGJ(N 1km)RTV

A campsite just outside Carennac, one of France's most beautiful villages but still in the middle of the countryside on the Dordogne. Plenty of opportunities for tourist trips out: culture (villages, markets, caves) and nature (walking, cycling, canoeing). Lovely in summer but also in the early and late seasons. Pitches with sun or shade. Family atmosphere.

From Martel to Carennac via Vayrac (D703), then via Bétaille and via the D20 to Carennac. Campsite signposted.

CC € 15 *1/5-10/7 27/8-15/10* *7=6, 14=11*

N 44°54'36" E 1°44'27"

Carlucet, F-46500 / Midi-Pyrénées (Lot) 2200

Château de Lacomté****
Lacomté
+33 (0)5-65387546
1/5 - 15/9
chateaulacomte@wanadoo.fr

12ha 86T(110-140m²) 10A CEE

1 AFIJKLMOPQ
2 FIJLRTVWXY
3 GHJ**M**NRU
4 (B+Q+R+U+V+Y+Z)
5 **AB**DGIJKLMPUXY
6 DEGJ(N 12km)TV

Beautiful grounds around a lovely castle. Rest is assured, this campsite is geared to adult campers. You can imagine you are the lord of the manor on the spacious grassy pitches. Very many excursion possibilities in the Dordogne, Quercy and Périgord.

A20, exit 56 direction Figeac (D802). Direction Gramat at roundabout (D807). Left after ± 3 km onto D32 towards Carlucet. Campsite signposted

CC € 19 *1/5-10/7 27/8-15/9*

N 44°43'42'' E 1°35'49''

Cassagnabère, F-31420 / Midi-Pyrénées (Haute-Garonne) 2201

Pré Fixe***
route de St. Gaudens
+33 (0)5-61987100
1/5 - 30/9
contact@camping-pre-fixe.com

1,2ha 32T(80-110m²) 16A

1 ACD**F**IJKLPQ
2 JKLRTVWXY
3 AGMRU
4 (C+H+Q+R+T+X) Z
5 **A**FGIJKLMNOPUW
6 AEGJ(N 5km)V

This campsite is a real pearl in rolling countryside. Pleasant atmosphere. Heated swimming pool from the first to the last day of the season. Free tennis within 300m. Bistro wine bar with a high quality daily menu using organic vegetables and local produce. Exceptional wines can be ordered by the glass.

From Toulouse A64 exit 21 and D817 direction Tarbes. After 2 km D635 at roundabout direction Aurignac, then 8 km to Cassagnabère and follow camping signs.

CC € 17 *1/5-2/7 28/8-30/9*

N 43°13'33'' E 0°47'21''

Castelnau-Magnoac, F-65230 / Midi-Pyrénées (Hautes-Pyrénées) 2202

l'Eglantière***
Ariès-Espenan
+33 (0)5-62398800
FAX +33 (0)5-62398144
23/4 - 2/10
infos@leglantiere.com

50ha 80T(90-200m²) 16A CEE

1 AC**G**IJKLMPQ
2 CLMNRVWXY
3 AGHJKNRU**WX**
4 (A 1/6-15/9) (C+H) N
(Q) (R+S 15/6-15/9)
(T) (U 15/5-15/9)
(V 1/6-15/9) (X 15/5-30/9)
(Y 1/6-15/9) Z
5 **AB**EFGIJKLMNOPQUWZ
6 DEG**I**J(N 5km)OV

Naturist campsite located between Gascony and the Pyrenees in a 50 hectare biological agricultural area. The River Gers passes through the campsite. A good spot for lovers of nature, walking and fishing. Heated swimming pool, nice cafe, good restaurant, free WiFi. Welcoming atmosphere and French Dutch staff. Ideal stopover site on way to Spain.

Follow the D929 from Lannemezan to Castelnau-Magnoac. Campsite signposted about 2 km before Castelnau-Magnoac.

CC € 17 *23/4-1/7 31/8-2/10 21=15*

N 43°15'49'' E 0°31'15''

Castres, F-81100 / Midi-Pyrénées (Tarn) — 2203

Camping de Gourjade***
Av. de Roquecourbe/
Parc de Gourjade
+33 (0)5-63593351
1/4 - 30/9
contact@campingdegourjade.net

4ha 100T(80-200m²) 16A CEE

1 ACGIJKLMPQ
2 BCGJLRVWXY
3 AFHJNPQRU
4 (A 1/7-31/8) (B 15/6-15/9) M (Q+R) (T+X+Y 1/4-15/9) Z
5 ABEFGIJKLMNOPUVZ
6 CEGIJ(N 2km)

Beautiful campsite located between the banks of a river and a large park on the edge of Castres with a large sports and water complex. There is a golf course next to the campsite. Public transport is free.

In Castres follow dir. Brassac and then follow campsite signs and signs Parc de Loisirs de Gourjade.

CC € 13 1/4-30/6 1/9-30/9

N 43°37'14'' E 2°15'14''

Cauterets, F-65110 / Midi-Pyrénées (Hautes-Pyrénées) — 2204

Cabaliros**
93 avenue du Mamelon Vert
+33 (0)5-62925536
20/5 - 30/9
info@camping-cabaliros.com

2ha 94T(85-130m²) 6A

1 ACDGIJKLMOPQ
2 CGIJKLRVWX
3 AHJRUW
4 (Q)
5 ABCEFGHIJKLMNOPUVX
6 ACEJKL(N 0,3km)TV

An attractive campsite by a mountain stream close to Cauterets and the National Park with its lakes and waterfalls (including the Pont d' Espagne). Spacious pitches with lovely views of the mountains. Free shuttle buses for most of the year. Good explanation of the various sights and fantastic walks at the reception. WiFi on entire campsite and bread service.

D920. After Carrefour supermarkt 1st road right over bridge.

CC € 15 20/5-3/7 22/8-30/9

N 42°54'11'' W 0°6'26''

Caylus, F-82160 / Midi-Pyrénées (Tarn-et-Garonne) — 2205

De la Bonnette***
672 route de la Bonnette
+33 (0)5-63657020
26/3 - 1/10
info@campingbonnette.com

1,5ha 50T(100m²) 10A CEE

1 AGIJKLMPQ
2 CGKLRVXY
3 AGHJNRW
4 (B 15/4-30/9) (Q 1/5-30/9) (T+U+X+Y+Z)
5 ABCFGIJKLMNOPUWXZ
6 CEGK(N 0,5km)T

An extremely friendly campsite run by a friendly Dutch couple, with good facilities, a swimming pool, bar, restaurant and snacks, large camping pitches, and all this in a charming and rural setting with old villages. Also good for cyclists.

Until Caussade A20. Exit 59 dir. Rodez (D926). Drive through village of Caylus as far as garage on left. Turn right here and follow the camping signs.

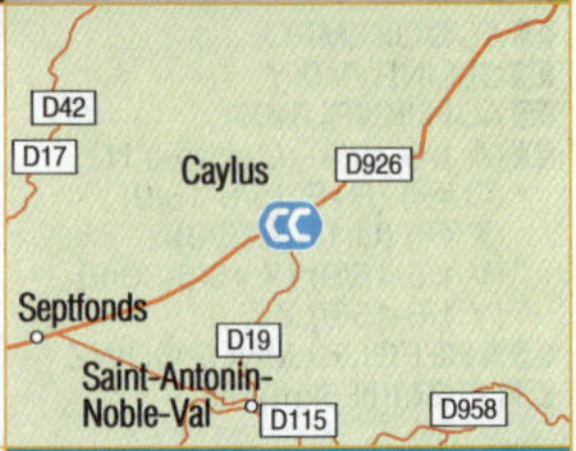

CC € 17 26/3-8/7 27/8-1/10 14=13

N 44°14'2'' E 1°46'31''

Cayriech, F-82240 / Midi-Pyrénées (Tarn-et-Garonne) — 2206

Le Clos de la Lère***
Lieu dit Clergue
+33 (0)5-63312041
1/3 - 15/11
le-clos-de-la-lere@wanadoo.fr

1,5ha 40T(80-130m²) 10A

1 ACFIJLPQ
2 CLRVX
3 BGHJMNRUW
4 (C 1/5-31/10) (Q+S+T+U+X) Z
5 ABDEFGIJKLMNPUWZ
6 ACDEGJK(N 5km)ORTV

A family campsite in a picturesque village in a quiet, natural and rural setting. Heated swimming pool and WiFi. Interesting for groups and cyclists. Small restaurant with local produce, breakfast service.

D820 from Cahors to Caussade. After 30 km turn off to Lapenche (D103), then to Cayriech and follow signs.

CC € 15 1/3-3/7 21/8-15/11 10=9

N 44°13'3'' E 1°36'47''

Conques/Sénergues, F-12320 / Midi-Pyrénées (Aveyron) — 2207

Etang du Camp***
+33 (0)5-65460195
1/4 - 30/9
info@etangducamp.fr

5ha 60T(100-200m²) 6A

1 AGIJKLMPQ
2 DKLRUVWXY
3 AGHJKNRUW
4 (Q+R 1/5-30/9)
5 ACDEFGIJKLMNOPQUVW X
6 EGJ(N 3km)T

Beautiful, peaceful campsite in the heart of nature near a fishing lake. English/German family owned. Welcoming atmosphere. Spacious, partly semi-shaded pitches. Ideally situated for exploring the charming Aveyron. The celebrated medieval village of Conques is nearby. Bread, evening meals and campfire nights. Bicycle hire.

From Rodez dir. Conques (D901). In St. Cyprien follow D46 to Peyrelebade. Left D242 dir. Sénergues. From there campsite is signposted.

CC € 15 1/4-10/7 27/8-30/9 7=6

N 44°33'34'' E 2°27'43''

Cordes-sur-Ciel, F-81170 / Midi-Pyrénées (Tarn) — 2208

Camping Camp Redon***
D107
+33 (0)5-63561464
1/5 - 29/10
info@campredon.com

2ha 49T(100-120m²) 10A CEE

1 ACDGIJKLPQ
2 KLRTVWXY
3 AGHJNRU
4 (B 28/3-18/10) (G+Q+R+U+V+X) Z
5 ABCFGIJKLMNOPUWZ
6 AEGHJL(N 5km)OTV

Between the bastide Cordes-sur-Ciel (France's favourite village) and the lovely town of Albi (UNESCO Heritage Site) you will find Camp Redon campsite in lovely hilly surroundings. In addition to the good amenities (including free WiFi) at this small and friendly campsite, you will find camping pitches with lovely views and sunsets.

Signposted on the D107 Cordes-Albi, 5 km direction Albi.

CC € 17 1/5-9/7 27/8-29/10

N 44°2'30'' E 2°1'1''

Cordes-sur-Ciel, F-81170 / Midi-Pyrénées (Tarn)

2209

Le Moulin de Julien***
D922
+33 (0)5-63561110
1/5 - 24/9
contact@campingmoulindejulien.com

8ha 82T(100-120m²) 5A CEE

1 ACGIJLMPRS
2 CJLRTVWXY
3 BGNQRW
4 (B) J(Q 1/7-31/8) (Z)
5 AEFGIJKLMNPUW
6 EGK(N 0,8km)OTV

An extensive campsite set in parkland and located at the foot of the Cordes sur Ciel. Excellent toilet facilities, lovely swimming pool and large pitches. An ideal base for trips out in the surrounding area and for gastronomic delights.

Leave Cordes via D600 in direction of Albi. Take the D922 after 500 metres towards Gaillac. The entranceway is after 300 metres on the left.

CC € 17 1/5-9/7 26/8-24/9

N 44°3'14'' E 1°58'19''

Crayssac, F-46150 / Midi-Pyrénées (Lot)

2210

Campéole Les Reflets du Quercy****
Mas de Bastide
+33 (0)5-65300027
29/4 - 18/9
reflets-du-quercy@andretriganogroupe.com

8ha 41T(80-100m²) 10A CEE

1 ABCGIJKLMPQ
2 BIJKTUVWXY
3 BGHMNORU
4 (A 1/7-31/8) (B+G 1/6-15/9) M(Q+R+T+U+V+X 1/7-31/8) Z
5 ABCEFGIJKLMNOPUWZ
6 ACEGHIJK(N 5km)TV

Spaciously laid out terraced campsite situated high up overlooking the Lot on the rocky plateau of Quercy. Plenty of sun, swimming pool with solarium and sports facilities. You can taste the Cahor wines and regional products(foie gras, truffles, gastronomy) at the local producers.

On the D811 (Cahors-Puy-l'Évèque) signposted at Crayssac, from the D911 about another 3 km.

CC € 15 1/5-4/7 22/8-18/9

N 44°30'37'' E 1°19'22''

Creysse, F-46600 / Midi-Pyrénées (Lot)

2211

Du Port***
+33 (0)5-65322082
FAX +33 (0)5-65410532
23/4 - 30/9
contact@campingduport.com

5ha 86T(100-300m²) 10A CEE

1 ACDGIJKLPRS
2 CLNRVWXY
3 ABGHJKRUWX
4 (B 1/5-30/9) (Q 1/5-10/9) (R) (S+T+U 1/7-31/8) (Z)
5 AEFGIJKLMNOPUWZ
6 EGJ(N 5km)OV

Direct access to the Dordogne. Close to the historic village of Creysse. The restaurant/brasserie is open during the CampingCard ACSI validity period. You can book canoeing, climbing and potholing trips at the campsite. Beautiful pool. Free WiFi.

A20 exit Rocamadour/Martel. Via the N140 as far as Martel. In Martel via the D23 towards Creysse. Then follow the camping signs.

CC € 13 23/4-2/7 27/8-30/9 10=8

N 44°53'7'' E 1°35'58''

Estaing, F-65400 / Midi-Pyrénées (Hautes-Pyrénées) 2212

Pyrénées Natura****
route du Lac
+33 (0)5-62974544
6/5 - 9/10
info@
camping-pyrenees-natura.com

2ha 47T(90-150m²) 10A CEE

1 ACD**G**IJKLOPQ
2 CIKMRUX
3 AGHJRU**W**
4 N(Q+R+T+U+Z)
5 **AB**CEFGHJLNPUWZ
6 ACDEGHJ**K**(N 11km)ORTV

A four star campsite set in parkland near the village of Estaing. Set in a beautiful valley in the Pyrenees next to the National Park. A campsite to 'crash out' with food and drink at cheap prices. Walking and cycle trips at all levels.

From Argeles-Gazost follow the D918 (direction Col d'Aubisque) as far as the D13 direction Bun. Then follow Lac d'Estaing signs. Do not take the earlier exit to Estaing on the D918 with a caravan!

CC € 17 *6/5-15/7 1/9-9/10* N 42°56'29'' W 0°10'41''

Flagnac, F-12300 / Midi-Pyrénées (Aveyron) 2213

Le Port de Lacombe****
+33 (0)5-65641008
1/4 - 30/9
accueil@
campingleportdelacombe.fr

2,5ha 51T(80-120m²) 6A CEE

1 ACD**G**IJKLMPQ
2 CDLMRVWXY
3 AGHMNRU**W**
4 (A 1/7-30/8) (C+H 15/6-5/9) IJ(Q+R) (T+V+X 1/7-30/8) Z
5 **AB**CGIJKLMNPUWXY
6 AEGK(N 2km)OTV

Our level campsite is located in a wide part of the slow-flowing Lot valley. The spacious, shaded camping pitches are separated by one metre high trimmed bay leaf hedges. A large heated swimming pool with a slide and a lawn provides recreation in the water.

Follow the camping signs from the D963 between Aurillac and Decazeville close to Flagnac.

CC € 15 *1/4-4/7 28/8-30/9* N 44°36'34'' E 2°14'9''

Foix, F-09000 / Midi-Pyrénées (Ariège) 2214

Du Lac***
Quartier Labarre
+33 (0)5-61651158
1/1 - 31/12
camping-du-lac@wanadoo.fr

NEW

5ha 135T(90-110m²) 13A CEE

1 ACD**G**IJKLMPQ
2 CDLRVX
3 AGMNRU**W**
4 (B+G 1/6-30/9) (Q 1/6-5/9) (T+V 15/6-15/9)
5 **AB**DFGIJKLMNPUVZ
6 CFGJ(N 0,2km)RTV

Comfortable campsite with nice pool and renovated toilet facilities (2015). Located on the northern edge of the town. Very easily accessible. Cycling and walking options from the campsite.

The campsite is located on the north side of Foix, dir. Touolouse, on the N20.

CC € 15 *1/1-8/7 25/8-31/12* *7=6, 14=11* N 42°59'22'' E 1°36'56''

Gourdon, F-46300 / Midi-Pyrénées (Lot) 2215

Domaine Le Quercy****
Ecoute s'il pleut
+33 (0)5-65410619
FAX +33 (0)5-65413162
16/4 - 17/9
@ domainequercy@orange.fr

5ha 90**T**(80-120m²) 10A CEE

1 ACDFIJKLMOPRS
2 BDJLRTUVXY
3 BGHJK**M**NRU**W**Z
4 (C+G) J(Q 1/7-31/8) (R 25/6-15/9) (T+U+V+X+Z 4/6-10/9)
5 **AB**EFGIJKLMNOPUWXYZ
6 ACEGHJ(N 2km)RTV

A peaceful terraced campsite in early and late seasons and close to an artificial lake. Lovely swimming pool with slides. Completely renewed toilet facilities. The town of Gourdon is close by and the site is ideally located for exploring the lovely surroundings.

A20, exit 55 or 56 direction Gourdon. In Gourdon centre take the D704 Sarlat. Follow 'Domaine Le Quercy'.

CC € 13 *16/4-1/7 27/8-17/9*

N 44°44'57'' E 1°22'31''

La Bastide-de-Sérou, F-09240 / Midi-Pyrénées (Ariège) 2216

L'Arize****
Bourtol
+33 (0)5-61658151
8/4 - 30/10
@ mail@camping-arize.com

3ha 71**T**(95-200m²) 10A CEE

1 ACD**G**IJKLMO**PQ**
2 CLRVWXY
3 B**F**GHJKN**OP**RU**W**
4 (B 1/6-30/9) (Q+R) (T+U+Z 1/7-27/8)
5 **AB**EFGIJKLOPUWXYZ
6 ACDEGI**K**(N 2km)RTV

The campsite is positioned at the foot of the Pyrenees by a babbling brook in the Pyrénées Ariegeoises. nature area. Excellent starting point for mountain walks, historical and cultural trips out. Restaurant 400 metres from the campsite. Walking and cycling on the 'Voie Verte'. Excellent golf course close by.

La Bastide-de-Sérou is located by the main road from Foix to St. Girons (D117). Campsite signposted.

CC € 15 *8/4-15/7 1/9-29/10 8=7, 14=11*

N 43°0'7'' E 1°26'44''

La Cresse, F-12640 / Midi-Pyrénées (Aveyron) 2217

Le Papillon***
Les Canals
+33 (0)5-65590842
23/4 - 1/10
@ info@campinglepapillon.com

1,5ha 41**T**(80-123m²) 10A CEE

1 A**G**IJKLMPQ
2 ACFJKLMNRTVWXY
3 AGHIJRU**WX**
4 (Q 15/5-15/9) (T+U+V+X 1/5-27/9) Z
5 **A**CEFGHIJLNPRUZ
6 AEGK(N 3km)ORTV

Terraced campsite with magnificent views of Tarn Valley. Friendly owners, Hans and Annette offer you sunny, spacious pitches, modern clean toilet facilities and a lively restaurant. Weekly pizza evenings. Fresh bread daily in the season.

A75, exit 44.1 Aguessac/Rivière-sur-Tarn (SatNav off!). Left at the mini-roundabout towards Gorges-du-Tarn. Turn right over the bridge at La Cresse. Left in village at the church D187 dir. Peyreleau. After 1500m first site on the right.

CC € 13 *23/4-1/7 25/8-1/10*

N 44°11'12'' E 3°8'11''

La Romieu, F-32480 / Midi-Pyrénées (Gers)

2218

Le Camp de Florence****
+33 (0)5-62281558
1/4 - 10/10
info@lecampdeflorence.com

15ha 95T(100-250m²) 10A CEE

1 ACDGIJKLMOPQ
2 LRUVWXY
3 BGHJKMNRU
4 (A 1/6-15/9) (C+G 1/5-30/9) K(Q+T+U+V+Y 1/5-30/9) Z
5 ABEFGIJKLMNOPRUWXYZ
6 CDEGHIJKM(N 0,5km)TV

A gently undulating campsite near a 19th century farmhouse. 500 metres from the fortified village of La Romieu with its magnificent collegiate church, cloister and tower. Armagnac, Floc, Madiran and local wines are in close proximity and there are plenty of opportunities for walking. Discount 7=6 in April and October.

From Agen D931 to Condom. D36 at Ligarde then D166 direction Collegiale de la Romieu. Left in village and follow signs.

CC € 17 1/4-10/7 27/8-9/10

N 43°59'0" E 0°30'7"

Larnagol, F-46160 / Midi-Pyrénées (Lot)

2219

Camping Ruisseau du Treil**
+33 (0)5-65312339
7/5 - 10/9
contact@lotcamping.com

3,2ha 46T(100-350m²) 6A CEE

1 AGIJKLPRS
2 CGLMRVXY
3 BGHJKNRUWX
4 (B+G 20/6-30/8) (Q 1/6-31/8) (R) (T 1/6-31/8) (U) (V 1/6-31/8) (Z)
5 ACEFGIJKLMNOPUWZ
6 EJ(N 5km)V

A very enthusiastic English owner runs this rural campsite which exudes tranquillity. Beautifully situated on a river, the very large pitches invite you to have a restful stay.

Camping du Ruisseau du Treil is located on the D662 between Cahors and Cajarc, on the double bend 300 metres outside Larnagol village in the direction of Cajarc.

CC € 17 7/5-9/7 27/8-10/9

N 44°28'24" E 1°47'1"

Le Mas-d'Azil, F-09290 / Midi-Pyrénées (Ariège)

2220

Le Petit Pyrénéen***
route de Sabarat, Castagnès
+33 (0)5-61697137
26/3 - 3/10
contact@campinglepetitpyreneen.com

1,6ha 46T(80-140m²) 16A CEE

1 ACDGIJKLMPQ
2 CLMRVWXY
3 AGHMRX
4 (B 1/6-30/9) (Q+R 1/7-31/8) (T+U+Z)
5 AFGIJKLMNPUVZ
6 ACEK(N 1km)OT

A small, friendly family campsite with lovely sheltered pitches 1500m from the centre with all its shopping opportunities. Ideal for visiting the caves or one of the surrounding lakes. Service station for motorhomes.

A64 exit 27 Carbonne/Montesquieu /Volvestre. Take the D628 as far as Sabarat. Then follow Le Mas-d'Azil signs.

CC € 15 26/3-8/7 27/8-3/10

N 43°4'44" E 1°22'41"

Lelin-Lapujolle, F-32400 / Midi-Pyrénées (Gers)

2221

La Solanilla***
Lieu-dit Lahount
+33 (0)5-62696409
1/1 - 31/12
info@campinglasolanilla.com

3,5ha 86T 10A CEE

1 ACDGIJKLOPST
2 JRVXY
3 ADGRUW
4 (B+G 1/5-30/9) (Q+R+T+V+X+Z)
5 GJKLNOPUVWZ
6 J(N 7km)OV

Welcoming campsite in a rural area with many amenities such as: croissants, a little shop, snack bar and bar. Wine tasting sessions in the vicinity and all through the year. Free WiFi.

From A65, exit 6 dir. Tarbes. In Saint-Germé dir. Lelin-Lapujolle. Then follow signs.

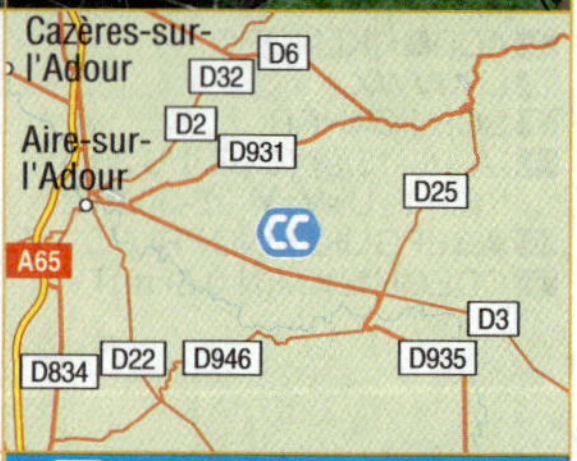

€15 1/1-8/7 25/8-31/12 7=6, 14=12, 21=18

N 43°41'49'' W 0°8'17''

Léran, F-09600 / Midi-Pyrénées (Ariège)

2222

La Régate***
avenue Montjean - route du Lac
+33 (0)5-61030917
1/4 - 30/10
contact@campinglaregate.com

2ha 38T(90-110m²) 10A CEE

1 ACGIJKLPR
2 BDJRTVY
3 BGHJKNRUWZ
4 (A 1/4-30/9) (B 15/6-31/8) (Q+R+U 30/3-30/9) (W 30/3-30/8) (X 30/3-30/9) Z
5 AEFGJLNPUWZ
6 EGJ(N 6km)OTV

The reservoir is one of La Régate's attractions. The campsite has homely, attractive pitches with plenty of peace. Lovely views of the lake from the restaurant. Many activities are organised. Only electric boats/jet skis are permitted (no motor boats).

From the D625 Lavelanet-Mirepoix, take the Léran exit at Aiges-Vives. Follow camping signs or lake in Léran. Do not follow SatNav.

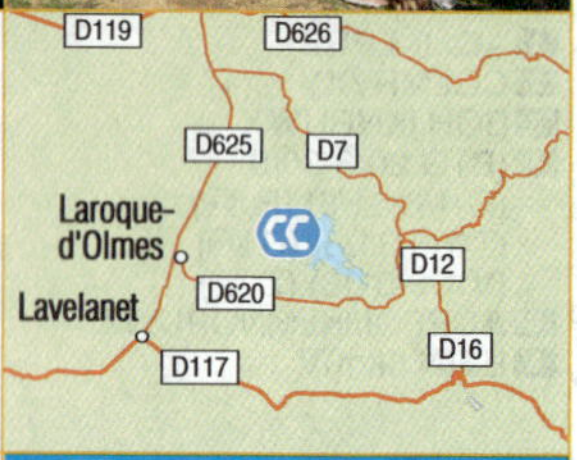

€15 1/4-10/7 27/8-30/10 7=6, 10=8

N 42°59'2'' E 1°56'8''

Loudenvielle, F-65510 / Midi-Pyrénées (Hautes-Pyrénées)

2223

La Vacance Pène Blanche**
+33 (0)5-62996885
1/1 - 3/11, 23/12 - 31/12
info@peneblanche.com

3,5ha 76T(80-120m²) 10A CEE

1 ACDGIJKLMPQ
2 CJKLRUWX
3 BHJLR
4 (Q 1/7-31/8)
5 ABDGIJKLMNPUZ
6 AEGJ(N 0,2km)

A lovely well maintained terraced campsite in an open and sunny valley by a large lake where you can try or watch paragliding or delta flying. The starting point for 30 walking and mountain tours. Well maintained toilet facilities and a friendly atmosphere.

Follow the D929 as far as Arreau then continue left on the D618. At the junction with the D25 continue to Loudenvielle. Campsite 50m before the town.

€15 10/4-24/6 3/9-3/11

N 42°47'48'' E 0°24'23''

Lourdes, F-65100 / Midi-Pyrénées (Hautes-Pyrénées) — 2224

Camping de Sarsan***
4 avenue Jean Moulin
+33 (0)5-62944309
1/4 - 15/10
camping.sarsan@wanadoo.fr

1,8ha 67T(100-150m²) 10A

1 AGIJKLMOPQ
2 CKLRTVXY
3 AFHJRU
4 (D 1/5-30/9) (Q 1/4-30/9) (R 1/7-31/8)
5 **A**CGHIJKLMNOPUZ
6 ABCEGK(N 1km)RT

Level campsite with rural location but close to the town of Lourdes. Spacious sunny or shaded pitches under old trees. The centre of the town can be easily reached from the campsite (1 km). Bus stop in front of the site. Supermarket within walking distance. Free WiFi everywhere.

From Tarbes as you enter Lourdes take the first on the left, zône industrielle du Monge, and keep following this road. Campsite is signposted.

CC € 13 *1/4-6/7 23/8-15/10*

N 43°6'9" W 0°1'39"

Lourdes, F-65100 / Midi-Pyrénées (Hautes-Pyrénées) — 2225

D'Arrouach***
9 rue des Trois Archanges
+33 (0)5-62421143
15/3 - 31/10
contact@camping-arrouach.com

13ha 48T(90-130m²) 10A CEE

1 ACD**G**IJKLMOPQ
2 BGJKRVWY
3 BFGHJRUV**W**
4 (**A**) **N**(Q+R+U+Z)
5 **AB**CFGHIJKLMNOPUW
6 CDEGK(N 1km)ORTV

From the campsite it is a 15-minute walk to the lake and the entrance of Lourdes golf course. Sanctuary is 2 km away (bus stop at entrance of campsite). In 2014 new toilet facilities, also for the disabled. Free WiFi, shop, fitness room and sauna.

From Pau RD940 after entering Lourdes (sign) 2nd road right La Rue des Trois Archanges. Follow signs.

CC € 11 *1/4-6/7 26/8-31/10* *7=6, 14=12*

N 43°6'13" W 0°4'4"

Lourdes, F-65100 / Midi-Pyrénées (Hautes-Pyrénées) — 2226

Le Moulin du Monge***
28 avenue Jean Moulin
+33 (0)5-62942815
FAX +33 (0)5-62422054
1/4 - 10/10
camping.moulin.monge@wanadoo.fr

1,3ha 55T(100-140m²) 6A CEE

1 ACDGIJKLMOPQ
2 FGKRVXY
3 BFGHJNRU
4 (**A** 1/6-30/9) (E+G 21/5-16/9) **N**(Q) (R 1/5-10/10) (S 15/6-15/9)
5 **AB**CDEFGHIJKLMNOPUWZ
6 ACDGK(N 0,4km)RTV

A three-star campsite located on the edge of Lourdes. Good amenities. Spacious pitches and reasonable shade. Camp shop, sauna and heated swimming pool. Basic, clean toilets. 5 minutes from the centre. Supermarket close by. Bus stop by the entrance to the campsite. Free WiFi on entire campsite.

From Tarbes turn left just before Lourdes (Zône industriele de Monge). Campsite 100 metres on the left.

CC € 11 *1/4-6/7 23/8-10/10*

N 43°6'56" W 0°1'53"

Lourdes, F-65100 / Midi-Pyrénées (Hautes-Pyrénées)

2227

Sites et Paysages la Forêt***
route de la Forêt
+33 (0)5-62940438
26/3 - 31/10
hello@camping-hautes-pyrenees.com

3ha 80T(85-120m²) 6A

1 ACD**G**IJKLMOPQ
2 BCGKLRTVWXY
3 B**F**GHJNRU**W**
4 (C+H 1/6-30/9)
(Q+R+T+U+Y+Z)
5 **AB**CEFGHIJKLMNOPUZ
6 ABCEG**K**(N 2km)OTV

Stylish campsite at 800 metres from the Sanctuary, easily accessible on foot or by bus. All amenities present, heated pool, easy-going restaurant and WiFi. Peaceful and natural surroundings. Service station for motorhomes.

In Lourdes direction Pau. Direction St. Pé/Bétharram after 1.5 km. Cross railway left after 1 km. Right over the bridge before sanctuary then signposted direction Ségus.

CC € 13 *26/3-9/7 26/8-31/10 14=12, 21=18*

N 43°5'44'' W 0°4'29''

Luchon/Moustajon, F-31110 / Midi-Pyrénées (Haute-Garonne)

2228

Pradelongue***
D125
+33 (0)5-61798644
FAX +33 (0)5-61791864
1/4 - 30/9
camping.pradelongue@wanadoo.fr

4,1ha 117T(100-150m²) 2-10A

1 ACD**G**IJKLMPQ
2 CKLRSTVWXY
3 BC**F**GHJNRU
4 (**A** 1/7-1/9) (C+G 1/6-30/9)
(Q 1/7-1/9)
5 **AB**DFGIJKLMNOPRUWXYZ
6 ACDEG**K**MTV

Beautiful campsite with spacious, shaded pitches separated by a variety of trees and bushes. Level terrain. Nearby Luchon is a lively town, well known as a spa and winter sports resort.

Follow the D125 and take the exit Antignac and Moustajon approximately 2 km before Luchon. Campsite is next to the supermarket.

CC € 15 *1/4-30/6 1/9-30/9*

N 42°48'31'' E 0°35'50''

Luz-St-Sauveur, F-65120 / Midi-Pyrénées (Hautes-Pyrénées)

2229

International****
B.P. 4
+33 (0)5-62928202
FAX +33 (0)5-62929687
21/5 - 30/9
camping.international.luz@wanadoo.fr

4,5ha 130T(75-120m²) 10A CEE

1 ACDGIJKLMPQ
2 IKRVX
3 BGHJN**Q**R**W**
4 (E+H) JK(Q 1/6-15/9)
(R 1/6-30/9) (S 1/7-20/9)
(U+Z 15/7-15/9)
5 **AB**CDFGHJKLNPUW
6 ACEGK(N 1km)T

A family campsite with 4 stars, 1 km from the lovely mountain village of Luz-St.-Saveur. Shaded, spacious pitches. Shop and heated, indoor swimming pool with 2 jacuzzis. Centrally located for trips out to Gavarnie, Tourmalet, Cirque de Troumouse and the National Parc des Pyrénées. Free WiFi (1 connection per pitch). The campsite is easily accessible.

D921 direction Luz-St-Saveur. Campsite 1 km before Luz-St-Sauveur.

CC € 15 *21/5-7/7 24/8-30/9 7=6, 14=12*

N 42°52'58'' W 0°0'49''

Luz-St-Sauveur, F-65120 / Midi-Pyrénées (Hautes-Pyrénées)

2230

Sites & Paysages Pyrénévasion****
route de Luz-Ardiden/Sazos
+33 (0)5-62929154
1/1 - 20/10, 20/11 - 31/12
camping-pyrenevasion@wanadoo.fr

2,5ha 68T(80-130m²) 10A

1 ACD**G**IJKLMOPQ
2 IJKRTVX
3 BGHJMNRU**VW**
4 (C 1/6-15/9) (F) (H 1/6-15/9) K**N**P (Q 1/6-15/9) (R) (T+U+V 1/7-30/8) (Z)
5 **AB**CDFGHIJKLMNPUWXYZ
6 ABCEG**K**(N 3km)OV

Terraced campsite with modern toilet facilities. Located in the mountains around Luz-St.-Saveur valley. Heated outdoor pool with sundeck and free jacuzzi. Lovely new indoor pool and hydromassage. Bar and terrace. Excursions possible to Col de Tourmalet, Cirque de Gavarnie and Cirque de Troumouse. An excellent area for walking. WiFi.

Take the road to Luz-Ardiden in Luz-St-Sauveur and follow this road for 3 km up to the village of Sazos. Campsite is signposted here.

CC € 15 *1/4-11/7 28/8-20/10 7=6, 14=12, 21=18, 30=25*

N 42°52'56'' W 0°1'20''

Luz-St-Sauveur/Esquièze-Sère, F-65120 / Midi-Pyrénées (Hautes-Pyrénées)

2231

Airotel Pyrénées*****
46 avenue du Barège
+33 (0)5-62928918
FAX +33 (0)9-70065956
2/5 - 25/9
airotel.pyrenees@wanadoo.fr

2,8ha 75T(80-100m²) 10A

1 ACD**G**IJKLOPQ
2 IJKLRVX
3 BGHJNRUV
4 (**A** 1/7-30/8) (C 15/6-15/9) (F) (G 15/6-15/9) **JKLN** (Q 15/5-15/9) (R+U 1/7-30/8)
5 **AB**CDEFGHIJKLNPUVW
6 ACEGK(N 0,8km)OV

A challenging campsite. Plenty of fitness equipment, a sauna, indoor and outdoor swimming pools on site. Guided excursions and walks in the mountains, rafting and cycling. Sports ground for multi-sports. WiFi on entire campsite.

D921 to Luz-St-Sauveur. Located ca. 1 km before Luz-St-Sauveur left of the D921. Clearly signposted.

CC € 15 *2/5-1/7 29/8-25/9*

N 42°52'49'' W 0°0'40''

Marciac, F-32230 / Midi-Pyrénées (Gers)

2232

Du Lac***
FAX +33 (0)5-62082119
25/3 - 8/10
info@camping-marciac.com

4,5ha 72T(100-120m²) 10A CEE

1 ACD**G**IJKLMPQ
2 IJLRUVWXY
3 BFGHJNRU
4 (C 1/5-30/9) (Q+R+T) Z
5 **A**FGJKLMNOPUVWZ
6 CDEG**IK**(N 0,7km)O

Located by a lake suitable for water recreation, 800m from a 'bastide' fortified town with a jazz museum. With the exception of the annual jazz festival, peace and quiet are the order of the day.

Follow the D943 in Marciac direction Bassoues, after about 300m over the bridge turn left. From the lake; follow signs. From Plaisance; turn left on D3.

CC € 15 *25/3-8/7 25/8-8/10*

N 43°31'56'' E 0°10'0''

Martres-Tolosane, F-31220 / Midi-Pyrénées (Haute-Garonne) 2233

Sites & Paysages Le Moulin****
avenue de Saint Vidian
+33 (0)5-61988640
21/3 - 1/10
info@campinglemoulin.com

10ha 61T(80-200m²) 10A

1 ACD**G**IJKLMPQ
2 CFLMRVXY
3 ABCDGHJKMNRUV**W**
4 (C+H 1/6-15/9) JK
(Q 1/5-30/9)
(R+T+U 1/6-15/9)
(V+X 2/7-20/8) (Z 1/6-15/9)
5 **AB**DEFGIJKLMNOPUWXYZ
6 ACEG**IK**(N 2km)ORTVW

The campsite is located on the banks of the Garonne at the edge of the Pyrenees. Ideal for a relaxing stay in open countryside for discovering the immediate vicinity. You can swim, fish, play tennis and relax here. Lovely shaded pitches, comfortable toilet facilities.

Martres-Tolosane is located on the A64 Toulouse-Tarbes, exit 22 or 21 if coming from the south. The campsite is signposted.

CC € 17 21/3-30/6 23/8-30/9 7=6

N 43°11'29" E 1°1'0"

Mercus-Garrabet, F-09400 / Midi-Pyrénées (Ariège) 2234

Du Lac Mercus***
1 Promenade du Camping
+33 (0)5-61059061
1/4 - 22/9
info@campingdulacmercus.com

1,4ha 41T(80-150m²) 10A CEE

1 ACDGIJLPQ
2 DFHJKLMRTVWXY
3 AGHRUW
4 (C+G 15/5-15/9)
(Q+R 1/7-31/8)
5 **A**EFGJKLMNOPRUVWZ
6 EGK(N 2km)T

Quiet, welcoming campsite with heated pool. Everything very well maintained. Friendly owners. Not too far from the motorway between Foix and Tarascon.

N20 from Foix dir. Andorra. Exit 14 Mercus. In Mercus follow signs Camping du Lac.

CC € 13 15/4-7/7 24/8-22/9 7=6, 14=11

N 42°52'18" E 1°37'20"

Millau, F-12100 / Midi-Pyrénées (Aveyron) 2235

Camping des Deux Rivières***
61 avenue de l'Aigoual
+33 (0)5-65600027
1/4 - 24/10
camp2rivieres@yahoo.fr

62T(80-100m²) 10A CEE

1 AGIJKLMPQ
2 CFGKLMRVXY
3 BGHJKR**WX**
4 (Q+T+U) Z
5 **AB**DGIJKLMNPQRUVWZ
6 ACEGK(N 0,5km)T

500m from centre of Millau. Quiet, child friendly, clean, on the banks of the Tarn with private beach; shaded marked-out pitches, beautiful views. Catering: breakfast, snacks and bar. Free WiFi. Friendly welcome. Completely new toilet facilities.

Southwards A75 exit 45 Millau. Northwards A75 exit 47 (toll-free) La Cavalerie-Millau or toll on Viaduc de Millau, exit 45. In Millau follow 'Campings' signs as far as Cureplat bridge, over the bridge, 1st site on the left.

CC € 13 1/4-30/6 25/8-30/9

N 44°6'10" E 3°5'14"

Millau, F-12100 / Midi-Pyrénées (Aveyron) 2236

Camping Indigo Millau***
455 avenue de l'Aigoual
+33 (0)5-65611883
4/5 - 26/9
millau@camping-indigo.com

3,5ha 119T(100-190m²) 6-10A CEE

1 ACD**G**IJKLMO**P**S
2 CFGKLMNRVWXY
3 BGHIJKRU**W**X
4 (C+H+Q+R)
(T+U+V+X 1/7-31/8)
5 **AB**DEGJKLNPUVWXZ
6 ACEGIJ(N 0,5km)TV

A peaceful, natural campsite close to the centre of Millau. Plenty of activities for sport and leisure possible close by. A friendly family site. Spacious pitches, both shaded and sunny. Heated toilet facilities.

From Clermont-Ferrand take the A75, exit 45 (turn off SatNav). From Montpellier A75, exit 47. Then follow camping signs to 'Pont de Cureplat', take D991 at roundabout then 1st site on the right.

CC € 15 *4/5-29/6 1/9-25/9*

N 44°6'9'' E 3°5'27''

Millau, F-12100 / Midi-Pyrénées (Aveyron) 2237

Du Viaduc****
121 avenue de Millau-Plage
+33 (0)5-65601575
8/4 - 26/9
info@camping-du-viaduc.com

5ha 185T(80-130m²) 6A CEE

1 ACD**F**IJKLMOPQ
2 ABCFGKLORSVWXY
3 BGHIJKNRU**W**X
4 (C+H 15/4-15/9) IJP
(Q+S+T+U+V+X+Z)
5 **AB**DEFGIJKLMNOPQRUW
XYZ
6 ACEG**IJK**(N 0,8km)OTV

Good service and quality. All amenities open whole season, restaurant is closed one day a week in low season. New, spacious, clean and modern toilet blocks. Large swimming complex (15/4/ - 15/9), usually heated. Very hospitable welcome. Unlimited WiFi for 1 Euro.

From Clermont-Ferrand A75, exit 45 (turn off Sat-Nav). From Montpellier A75, exit 47. Then follow camping signs as far as 'Pont de Cureplat', towards Paulhe D187 at the roundabout, 1st campsite on the left.

CC € 15 *8/4-1/7 29/8-26/9 7=6, 14=12, 21=18*

N 44°6'18'' E 3°5'18''

Millau, F-12100 / Midi-Pyrénées (Aveyron) 2238

Larribal***
avenue de Millau-Plage
+33 (0)5-65590804
1/4 - 31/10
camping.larribal@wanadoo.fr

1,7ha 72T(80-110m²) 6A CEE

1 ACDGIJKLMOPQ
2 BCFGKLMNRSVXY
3 AGHJ**OPU**W**X**
4 (B+G 1/5-30/9)
(Q 1/4-30/9) (R 1/5-30/9) Z
5 **A**EFGIJKLMNPQUWZ
6 ACEGK(N 1,5km)ORTV

A campsite right on the banks of the Tarn. Shaded and quiet, nice swimming pool with bar. Free WiFi throughout the site. You can be in Millau by bike in 5 minutes for sports opportunities, restaurants and various markets.

From Clermont-Ferrand (A75) take exit 45 (turn SatNav off!), or from Montpellier (A75), exit 47. Then follow 'Campings' sign to the 'Pont de Cureplat' bridge. Over the bridge and towards Paulhe D187 at roundabout, 3rd site on the left.

CC € 11 *1/4-2/7 26/8-31/10*

N 44°6'37'' E 3°5'13''

Millau, F-12100 / Midi-Pyrénées (Aveyron)

2239

Les Erables***
avenue de Millau-Plage
+33 (0)5-65591513
1/4 - 30/9
camping-les-erables@orange.fr

1,5ha 72**T**(100m²) 10A CEE

1 ACDGIJKLMOPQ
2 BCFGKLMRVWXY
3 ABGHIJKNRU**WX**
4 (Q+R+T+U+Z)
5 **AB**CDGHJLNOPUWXY
6 AEGK(N 2km)ORTV

Quiet grounds close to a river and near the town centre, the Millau bridge and leisure activities. Spacious marked out pitches; shaded or sunny. Everything you need for an agreeable holiday in a friendly atmosphere. Free WiFi. Friendly new owners.

Over the bridge in Cureplat, 3rd exit at roundabout direction Paulhe. In Millau follow camping signs, second campsite on the left. Or take the A75, exit 45 Millau centre. Look out for camping signs (turn SatNav off).

CC € 13 1/4-5/7 22/8-30/9

N 44°6'20'' E 3°5'16''

Millau, F-12100 / Midi-Pyrénées (Aveyron)

2240

Les Rivages****
860 avenue de l'Aigoual
+33 (0)5-65610107
9/4 - 30/9
info@campinglesrivages.com

7,5ha 277**T**(100-160m²) 10A CEE

1 ACD**G**IJKLMOPQ
2 CFKLMNRVWXY
3 BCGHIJK**MNOPQ**R**SUW** X
4 (**A** 1/7-30/8) (C+H 1/5-30/9) K (Q 13/4-30/9) (S 15/6-15/9) (T+U+V+Y+Z)
5 **AB**DEFGIJKLMNPQRUXYZ
6 ACDEGIJ**K**(N 0,8km)OTV

Enormous pitches, indoor tennis/ squash hall, magnificent restaurant, heated pools, private beach on the river Dourbie. Only campsite in Millau with a view of the famous viaduct. The site is really peaceful, you cannot hear any noise from traffic.

A75 from north, exit 45 Millau. Exit 47 from south (SatNav off!). Follow 'campings' signs up to Cureplat bridge. 1st exit D991 on roundabout after bridge. Campsite 800m further at next small roundabout.

CC € 15 9/4-5/7 22/8-30/9 7=6, 14=11

N 44°6'3'' E 3°5'45''

Millau, F-12100 / Midi-Pyrénées (Aveyron)

2241

St. Lambert***
2050 avenue de l'Aigoual
+33 (0)5-65600048
30/4 - 26/9
contact@campingsaintlambert.fr

3,5ha 106**T**(80-160m²) 6A

1 ACDGIJKLMPRS
2 ABCFKLMNORSVWXY
3 BGHJKNQRU**WX**
4 (B 1/5-30/9) (Q+S) (T+U+V+X+Z 1/7-31/8)
5 **AB**FGIJKLMNPQUZ
6 ACDEGJ**K**(N 2,5km)ORTV

A campsite quietly located at the entrance to the Gorges du Tarn, between the Grands Causses and the Cévennes, 2,5 km from the centre of Millau. It has a lovely big private pebble beach on the River Dourbie. Friendly atmosphere.

From Millau take the D991 direction La Roque-Sainte-Marguerite. Right after Cureplat bridge. Follow camping signs.

CC € 11 30/4-7/7 28/8-26/9 7=6, 14=11, 21=16

N 44°5'59'' E 3°6'42''

Moissac, F-82200 / Midi-Pyrénées (Tarn-et-Garonne)

2242

Le Moulin du Bidounet***
Saint Benoit
+33 (0)5-63325252
1/4 - 30/9
info@camping-moissac.com

2,5ha 100**T**(70-90m²) 6A CEE

1 AC**G**IJKLMPRS
2 CFKLRTVXY
3 AGHNRU**W**
4 (A 1/7-31/8)
(B+G 15/6-15/9)
(Q+R 1/7-31/8) Z
5 ABFGIJKLMNPUVZ
6 ACDEGIJ(N 0,5km)TV

An attractive stopover campsite with swimming pool. Enjoy the peace of a shaded island in the River Tarn on the pilgrims' route to Compostella. Close to the historic village of Moissac.

Castelsarrasin to Moissac RD813. Follow camping signs just before Moissac.

CC € 15 *1/4-2/7 20/8-30/9*

N 44°5'47'' E 1°5'21''

Molières (Tarn-et-Gar.), F-82220 / Midi-Pyrénées (Tarn-et-Garonne)

2243

Domaine de Merlanes****
Merlanes
+33 (0)6-11524247
23/4 - 1/10
simone.merlanes@gmail.com

6ha 51**T**(200-300m²) 8A CEE

1 ACD**G**IJKLMPQ
2 ADIKLRVWXY
3 BDGN**OP**RUW
4 (C+H+Q+T+U) Z
5 **AB**EFGIJKLMNPRUWZ
6 AEGHJ(N 3,5km)TV

Site (35 hectares) with large pitches in a valley, ideal for those seeking peace and quiet. Excellent amenities: heated pool, terrace, bread, farm animals and stables. A good base for Moissac, Montauban, St. Antonin-Noble-Val.

D820 Cahors-Montauban. Exit Montpezat-de-Q (D20). Just before Molières turn left towards St. Christophe. Follow camping signs. From Toulouse exit 60 (Montauban-Nord). RN20 as far as Réalville then dir. Molières, then follow camping signs.

CC € 17 *23/4-8/7 27/8-1/10* *10=9*

N 44°11'6'' E 1°23'17''

Montcabrier, F-46700 / Midi-Pyrénées (Lot)

2244

Moulin de Laborde***
Laborde
+33 (0)5-65246206
7/5 - 9/9
moulindelaborde@wanadoo.fr

12ha 90**T**(100-150m²) 6-10A

1 AEIJKLPQ
2 CLRTVXY
3 B**F**GHJMNRUW
4 (B 8/5-8/9) (G 1/7-31/8)
(Q+R)
(T+U+V+X+Z 8/5-8/9)
5 **AB**FGIJKLNOPUWZ
6 AEGJ(N 8km)ORTV

The Van Bommel family welcome you to their peaceful, child-friendly campsite with spacious pitches. The attractive interior of a 17th century water mill has a terrace, bar and restaurant. The site has a brook and a small lake. Unique walking area. Close to castles, bastides and the Cahors vineyards. Free WiFi.

A20 direction Cahors, exit 56. Then via the D1 towards Gourdon. Then the D673 direction Fumel. Signposted 11 km before Fumel.

CC € 17 *7/5-3/7 25/8-8/9* *7=6, 14=11, 21=16*

N 44°32'52'' E 1°5'1''

Montgailhard, F-09330 / Midi-Pyrénées (Ariège)

2245

La Roucateille***
15 rue du Pradal
+33 (0)5-61640592
15/4 - 30/9
info@roucateille.com

2ha 71T(90-130m²) 10A CEE

1 ACD**G**IJKLMPQ
2 BCFGLMRSVY
3 AGHJLRU**W**
4 (Q On) (U 1/7-30/8)
5 **A**FGIJKLMNPUVWZ
6 EGIJ(N 2km)V

Peaceful, high-quality campsite with friendly welcome. Everything is in great order with new, clean toilet facilities (2013). Recommended! Electric bicycles for rent. Only 4 km from Foix, which has a beautiful medieval castle.

From Toulouse road 61, exit 11, Montgailhard. 1st right on roundabout (Montgailhard centre). Arrow to camps. onleft after 2 km. From Andorra, exit 12 dir. Lowanalet. 3rd right on roundabout dir. Montgailhard. Camps. sign on right after 2 km.

CC € 11 *15/4-3/7 29/8-30/9*

N 42°55'51'' E 1°38'19''

Montgeard/Nailloux, F-31560 / Midi-Pyrénées (Haute-Garonne)

2246

Camping du Lac de la Thésauque***
Lac de la Thésauque
+33 (0)5-61813467
FAX +33 (0)5-61810012
1/1 - 31/12
camping@thesauque.com

5ha 57T(75-90m²) 6A CEE

1 ACDGIJLPST
2 DFJLRVXY
3 BGHQR**W**
4 (B 1/6-30/9) (Q 11/6-10/9) (R On) (T 1/5-30/9) (X+Y 1/6-30/9) (Z 1/5-30/9)
5 **A**DGIJKLMNPUWZ
6 EG**K**(N 4km)OTV

Terraced campsite with many trees. Located beside the Thésauque lake. Ideal for walking or for outings to Toulouse or Carcassonne.

The campsite is located on the D622 Auterive-Villefranche. The lake at Thésauque is signposted from Nailloux and the A61.

CC € 13 *1/1-8/7 25/8-31/12*

N 43°21'18'' E 1°38'55''

Montréjeau, F-31210 / Midi-Pyrénées (Haute-Garonne)

2247

Midi Pyrénées***
chemin de Loubet
+33 (0)5-61958679
1/1 - 31/12
camping.midi-pyrenees@wanadoo.fr

10ha 110T(100-120m²) 10A CEE

1 AFIJLPQ
2 FIJKRUXY
3 AGN**Q**RU
4 (C 1/6-1/9) P (T+U+V 1/6-1/9) Z
5 **AB**DFGIJKLMNOPUV
6 CDEGK(N 0,6km)OV

The campsite has the most wonderful view of the Pyrenees imaginable. Heated swimming pool from 1/6 to 1/9. An ideal base for exploring the Pyrenees. Open all year, it has heated toilet facilities and summer toilet facilities. 500m from a supermarket. There is a lively town within walking distance.

A65/E80 exit 17 and N117 direction Montréjeau, then follow avenue du Nord/ Z.I. (Zone Industrielle). Campsite signposted.

CC € 13 *1/1-8/7 25/8-31/12*

N 43°5'31'' E 0°33'14''

Montricoux, F-82800 / Midi-Pyrénées (Tarn-et-Garonne)

iD **2248**

Le Clos Lalande***
359 route de Bioule
+33 (0)5-63241889
2/4 - 30/9
contact@camping-lecloslalande.com

3ha 58T(100-150m²) 6A CEE

1 A**G**IJKLMPQ
2 CGLRVWXY
3 BDGHJMN**OP**RU**W**
4 (B+G 1/5-15/9) (Q+T+U+V 15/5-15/9) Z
5 **AB**EFGIJKLMNOPQRUVW Z
6 ACEGJ(N 0,5km)RTV

A peaceful campsite with swimming pool, toddlers' pool, tennis, children's farm and many amenities. Large pitches, new toilets and motorhome facilities. At the entrance to the Gorges de l'Aveyron and 500m from the village and shopping. Close to some of the most beautiful villages in France: Cordes, St.-Cirq-Lapopie, Bruniquel, Puycelci, Penne, Najac...

A20 to Montauban, exit 21. Then D115 direction St. Antonin. Signposted in Montricoux.

CC € 15 *2/4-9/7 26/8-30/9 7=6, 14=12*

N 44°4'39'' E 1°36'40''

Nant, F-12230 / Midi-Pyrénées (Aveyron)

iD **2249**

Sites & Paysages Les 2 Vallées***
route de l'Estrade Basse
+33 (0)5-65622689
15/4 - 17/10
contact@lesdeuxvallees.com

2ha 64T(80-140m²) 6A CEE

1 ACD**G**IJKLMPST
2 BCFGKLRVWXY
3 BGHJK**MNOP**RU**W**
4 (**A** 14/7-20/8) (C 30/5-26/9) (Q+R 1/7-31/8) (T+U+X 15/6-15/9) Z
5 **AB**DFGIJKLMNPUVWXYZ
6 ACEG**I**K(N 0,8km)OTV

A comfortable campsite in beautiful countryside. Friendly welcome. Located 800 metres from the village (including shops). Close to the Gorges du Tarn canyon and the Cevennes mountains. Free WiFi.

A75, exit 47 La Cavalerie. D999 direction Nant. Then follow camping signs 1km from 1st sign.

CC € 11 *15/4-15/7 1/9-16/10*

N 44°1'2'' E 3°18'5''

Nant-d'Aveyron, F-12230 / Midi-Pyrénées (Aveyron)

iD **2250**

RCN Val de Cantobre****
+33 (0)5-65584300
16/4 - 10/10
cantobre@rcn.fr

6,5ha 115T(60-150m²) 6A CEE

1 ACD**G**IJKLMOPQ
2 BCFIJKLMNRTUVWX
3 BGHJMN**Q**RU**W**
4 (A 1/5-1/7) (C+H) IJK (Q+S+T+U+V+Y) Z
5 **ABC**EFGHIJKLMNOPUWZ
6 ACEG**IK**(N 4km)ORTV

A terraced, luxury campsite with stunning views of the beautiful Vale of Dourbie. Lovely touring pitches. Good catering facilities. The service and customer focus is a strong asset here!

After Clermont-Ferrand take the A75 over the Millau Bridge (toll) exit 47 direction Nant/La Cavalerie. Through La Cavalerie towards Nant. Campsite signposted in Nant. Turn left immediately to D991.

CC € 15 *16/4-9/7 26/8-10/10*

N 44°2'44'' E 3°18'8''

Naucelle, F-12800 / Midi-Pyrénées (Aveyron) — 2251

Camping du Lac de Bonnefon***
route de Bonnefon
+33 (0)5-65693320
1/4 - 15/10
info@
camping-du-lac-de-bonnefon.com

4,5ha 67T(80-165m²) 10A CEE

1 ACD**F**IJKL**P**RS
2 DIJRVWXY
3 BCGHJ**Q**RUW
4 (A 7/7-27/8) (C 1/6-30/9) (G 1/7-30/9) K(Q) (T 1/5-30/9) (U+V 1/7-15/9) (Z)
5 **AB**EGIJKLMPUVWXYZ
6 CDEGJ**K**(N 1km)RV

Open from the beginning of April till mid October. Close to a lake abundant with fish (free fishing) in peaceful, richly planted surroundings. Campsite with swimming pool and 1.2 km from the town of Naucelle.

N88 Rodez-Albi, in Naucelle-Gare direction Naucelle; then follow signs.

CC € 15 1/4-1/7 27/8-15/10 7=6

N 44°11'17'' E 2°20'54''

Payrac, F-46350 / Midi-Pyrénées (Lot) — 2252

Yelloh! Village Payrac Les Pins****
avenue de Toulouse
+33 (0)5-65379632
FAX +33 (0)5-65379108
9/4 - 11/9
info@les-pins-camping.com

4ha 49T(80-120m²) 10A CEE

1 ACD**G**IJKLPRS
2 BIJLRTVWXY
3 BGHJMNRU
4 (A 1/7-31/8) (C+F+H) **JK** **N**(Q+R+T+U+V+X+Y+Z)
5 **AB**DFGIJKLMNPUWYZ
6 ACFGIK(N 1km)RTV

Les Pins is located close to the centre of Payrac on the D820. There are plenty of water amusements. The toilet facilities are also heated in the spring. The Lot invites you to experience its beautiful countryside. The restaurant is open from 9/4 to 11/9. The outdoor and indoor swimming pools are heated for the entire season. Free WiFi.

The campsite is located in Payrac and signposted from the D820. From Souillac past Payrac on the right.

CC € 15 9/4-30/6 1/9-11/9 7=6

N 44°47'22'' E 1°28'20''

Pont-de-Salars, F-12290 / Midi-Pyrénées (Aveyron) — 2253

Les Terrasses du Lac****
route du Vibal/La Souquette
+33 (0)5-65468818
FAX +33 (0)5-65468538
1/4 - 30/9
campinglesterrasses@orange.fr

6ha 180T(80-100m²) 10A CEE

1 ACD**G**IJKLMPRS
2 DIJKORTVWXY
3 AGRU**WZ**
4 (A 1/7-31/8) (C+G 1/6-15/9) JK (Q+R+T+U+V+X 1/7-31/8) Z
5 **AB**FGIJKLMNOPUWXYZ
6 ADEGJ(N 4km)ORV

An attractive terraced campsite by a reservoir. The differences in height give optimal privacy to the pitches which are quite a distance from each other. Most of the pitches have fine views of the lake.

A75 exit 44.1 Pont-de-Salars. D911 direction Rodez. Turn right after Pont-de-Salars village onto the D523. Campsite well signposted.

CC € 17 1/4-9/7 26/8-30/9 7=6

N 44°18'17'' E 2°44'7''

Pouylebon, F-32320 / Midi-Pyrénées (Gers)

2254

Camping Pouylebon
Lieu dit "Haouré" D216
+33 (0)5-62667210
15/4 - 15/10
campingpouylebon2@wanadoo.fr

1ha 30T(120m²) 6A CEE

1 ABGIJLPRS
2 KLRXY
3 A**F**GHJRU
4 (B 15/5-15/9) (Q+T+X) Z
5 **AB**GIJKLMPRUWZ
6 AEJ(N 6km)

Campsite with its own swimming pool, very peacefully located around a Gascony farmhouse on grass with trees and lovely views of the Gers countryside. Sunflowers and corn are grown all around. There are 25 spacious pitches with good toilet facilities on 1 hectare of grounds at the end of a no through road.

Follow the D159 to the west from the D34 at Monclar. Then continue to Pouylebon D216 in northerly direction, take track to campsite 500 metres on the left.

CC €15 *15/4-30/6 29/8-15/10*

N 43°33'13" E 0°18'11"

Rieux-de-Pelleport/Varilhes, F-09120 / Midi-Pyrénées (Ariège)

2255

Les Mijeannes***
D311
+33 (0)5-61608223
1/1 - 31/12
lesmijeannes@orange.fr

10ha 152T(100-240m²) 10A CEE

1 ACD**G**IJKLMPQ
2 CFLMNRSVWXY
3 ABGHJNQRU**W**
4 (C 10/6-10/9) (Q 1/7-31/8)
(R 1/6-31/8) (T 15/6-31/8)
(U 15/6-2/9) (Z 15/6-31/8)
5 **AB**DFGIJKLMNOPUWZ
6 ACEGIJ(N 0,9km)ORTV

An attractive, rural campsite with nice landscaping. Animated evening events led by the owner. A real family campsite. 900 metres from an excellent restaurant. Tourist and historical sights in the immediate vicinity: Cathar, Roman and prehistoric remains! Contact by phone in low season.

Toll road from Toulouse, exit 7 Varilhes. In Varilhes, at the town hall (Hotel de Ville) turn onto the road towards Rieux. Campsite signposted.

CC €17 *1/1-8/7 25/8-31/12*

N 43°3'45" E 1°37'17"

Rivière-sur-Tarn, F-12640 / Midi-Pyrénées (Aveyron)

2256

De Peyrelade****
rte des Gorges du Tarn
+33 (0)5-65626254
4/5 - 15/9
contact@campingpeyrelade.com

4ha 137T(90-130m²) 10A CEE

1 ACD**G**IJKLMPQ
2 ABCFJKLNRVXY
3 BGHIJ**MQ**RU**W**X
4 (C+H) IKMOP(Q)
(S 1/7-31/8)
(T+U+V+Y+Z)
5 **AB**EFGIJKLMNOPQRUWZ
6 ACEGJ**K**(N 1km)OTUV

A beautiful site in every way: nature, toilet facilities, pitches, beach, entertainment! And the longest pebble beach on the Tarn. New leisure pool including a Balnéo room and children's play area. Relaxation on holiday with all facilities imaginable: restaurant, supermarket, etc.

A75 exit 44.1.Turn left in Aguessac to get on the D907. The first campsite after the village Rivière-sur-Tarn. The campsite is situated exactly at the entrance of the Gorges du Tarn.

CC €17 *4/5-1/7 27/8-15/9*

N 44°11'27" E 3°9'25"

Rivières, F-81600 / Midi-Pyrénées (Tarn)

2257

Les Pommiers d'Aiguelèze***
Espace Loisirs d'Aiguelèze
+33 (0)5-63330249
1/4 - 30/9
info@camping-lespommiers.com

2,7ha 53T(80-120m²) 13A CEE

1 ACD**G**IJKLMPST
2 CFLRTUVWXY
3 AB**F**GJK**MN**Q**R**W**X**
4 (C+H 1/5-30/9)
(Q+R+X+Z)
5 **A**FGIJKLMNPUWZ
6 ACEG**K**(N 5km)TV

A peaceful and informal campsite located next to the watersports centre in the Tarn. There are plenty of vineyards in the area and you will encounter the culture and history of the UNESCO Heritage Sites like Albi, the 'Route des Bastides' and beautiful panoramas.

A68, exit 10 Lagrave. Then follow Espace Loisirs d'Aiguelèze.

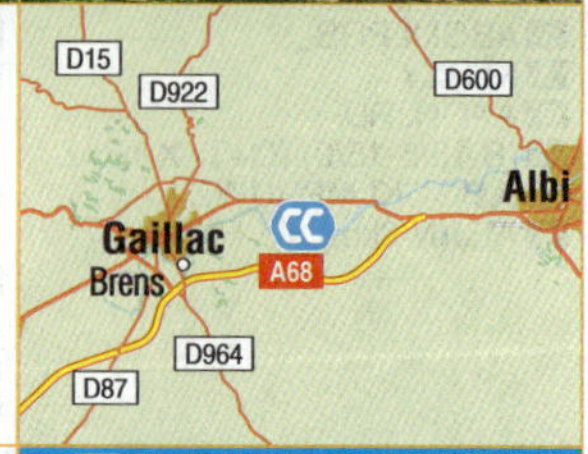

€17 *1/4-5/7 23/8-29/9*

N 43°54'32'' E 1°59'0''

Rocamadour, F-46500 / Midi-Pyrénées (Lot)

2258

Padimadour****
La Châtaigneraie-Varagnes
+33 (0)5-65337211
29/4 - 2/10
camping@padimadour.fr

3ha 25T(120-180m²) 10A CEE

1 ACD**G**IJKLMP
2 ILRVWXY
3 ACGHRU
4 (C 15/6-15/9)
(Q+R+T+U+V 1/6-30/9)
(X 1/7-31/8) (Z 1/6-30/9)
5 **AB**DFGIJKLMNOPQUWZ
6 ACDEGK(N 1,5km)RTV

A peacefully located family campsite in the middle of the countryside. Park-like grounds with very spacious pitches. Ideally situated for visiting the Lot and the Dordogne or for walking. Extremely pleasant heated toilet facilities. The swimming pool is heated from 15/6 to 15/9. Free WiFi. Very friendly welcome.

From A20, exit 54 (from north) dir. Gramat D840, exit 56 (from south) dir. Brive D840; follow Padimadour camping signs in Rocamadour.

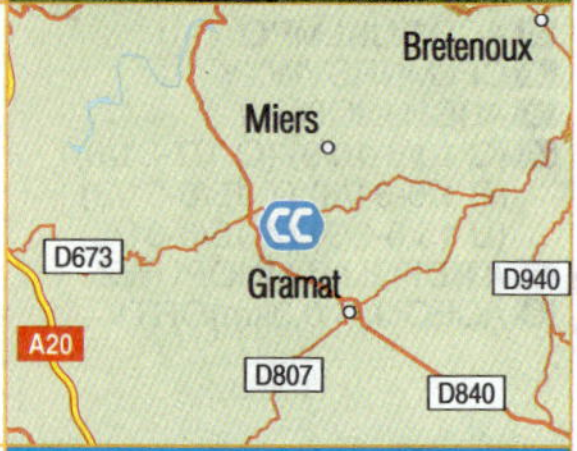

€17 *29/4-5/7 22/8-2/10* *7=6*

N 44°49'5'' E 1°41'11''

Roquelaure/Auch, F-32810 / Midi-Pyrénées (Gers)

2259

Yelloh! Village Le Talouch****
Ragegat
+33 (0)5-62655243
8/4 - 18/9
info@camping-talouch.com

9ha 104T(120-200m²) 10A

1 ACD**F**IJKLPQ
2 CLRVWXY
3 BFGHIJ**M**NRU
4 (A) (C 15/5-15/9) (E)
(G 15/5-15/9) **KLN**
(Q+R+S+T+V)
(X 1/7-30/8) Z
5 **AB**EFGIJKLMNPUWZ
6 CDEG**IK**(N 7km)V

In a valley with a babbling brook, within walking distance of the old Roquelaure fortress, this holiday village has something for everyone. The leisure pool is a popular attraction in the summer.

A20 to Montauban. Direction Auch via D928. Then N124 to Auch, exit to Duran. About 5 km via the D148 to the campsite.

€17 *8/4-1/7 28/8-17/9*

N 43°42'46'' E 0°33'53''

2260 Salles-Curan, F-12410 / Midi-Pyrénées (Aveyron)

Les Genêts****
Lac de Pareloup
+33 (0)5-65463534
10/5 - 11/9
contact@camping-les-genets.fr

3ha 163T(80-100m²) 10A CEE

1 ACD**G**IJKLPST
2 ADMRSVWXY
3 BGKNQRU**WZ**
4 (C+H) K(Q)
(S 1/6-11/9) (T 1/7-6/9)
(U+V 23/6-7/9) (Z 1/7-31/8)
5 **AB**EFGIJLMNOPRUWXYZ
6 CEG**K**(N 6km)OV

Pleasant family campsite on a peninsula with many spacious pitches on the water. Many amenities for children.

To the east of Pont-de-Salars D993 direction Salles-Curan. Take the D577 from Salles-Curan. Campsite signposted.

CC €15 10/5-5/7 22/8-11/9 7=6, 14=11

N 44°11'21'' E 2°46'0''

2261 Salles-Curan, F-12410 / Midi-Pyrénées (Aveyron)

Sites & Paysages Beau Rivage****
route de Vernhes
+33 (0)5-65463332
1/5 - 25/9
camping@beau-rivage.fr

2ha 54T(80-120m²) 6A CEE

1 AC**G**IJLPRS
2 ADIJKRVWXY
3 AGRU**WZ**
4 (A 1/7-30/8) (C 10/6-15/9)
M(Q) (S 15/6-15/9)
(T+U+V+X+Z 1/7-30/8)
5 **AB**FGIJKLMNOPUVWZ
6 CEG**JK**(N 3km)OV

Peaceful terraced campsite on Lake Pareloup. 3 km from the small town of Salles-Curan and its shops. Heated pool (from 10 June). Water sports, fishing, walking. Lovely surroundings.

A75, exit 44.1. Towards Salles-Curan/Lac de Pareloup.

CC €15 1/5-10/7 27/8-25/9

N 44°12'9'' E 2°46'38''

2262 Salles-et-Pratviel, F-31110 / Midi-Pyrénées (Haute-Garonne)

Le Pyrénéen***
7 Molles
+33 (0)5-61795919
15/1 - 17/10, 1/12 - 31/12
campinglepyreneen@orange.fr

1,6ha 36T(70-100m²) 4-10A CEE

1 ACD**F**IJKL**P**R
2 CKLRVWX
3 A**F**GHIJNRU**W**
4 (C 15/6-15/9)
(Q+R+X 1/7-31/8)
5 ABDFGIJKLMNPUVW
6 CEGK(N 4km)T

Pleasant, level, well-maintained campsite in the sunny valley of Luchon at 4 km from a golf course. There are many signposted mountain walks and tours. Heated pool from 1/6 to 30/9. Hospitable welcome, free WiFi. In the skiing season there is a free shuttle bus to the Superbagnères pistes.

From Montréjeau N125 then D125. Then take D27 from there the campsite is signposted.

CC €13 15/1-7/7 25/8-17/10

N 42°49'47'' E 0°36'40''

Seissan, F-32260 / Midi-Pyrénées (Gers)

2263

Camping Domaine Lacs de Gascogne
route du Lac
+33 (0)5-62662794
1/3 - 30/10
info@domainelacsdegascogne.eu

14ha 50T(90-120m²) 16A CEE

1 ACD**F**IJKLMPQ
2 ABDJKLMRWXY
3 AB**F**GHJKMRUVW
4 (A 1/7-31/8) (B+G 1/5-30/9) N(Q+T+U+X+Y+Z)
5 **AB**GIJKLMNOPUWZ
6 AEGJ(N 2km)TV

Enjoy the tranquility between the century-old oak trees that are reflected by the lakes of this domain. Pool heated from 1/5-30/9. Fine restaurant with nice garden. Quiet fishing lake. New dynamic Dutch owners.

Follow the D929 as far as Seissan centre, then follow camping signs.

€15 *1/3-8/7 27/8-30/10 7=6, 14=11, 21=17*

N 43°29'38'' E 0°34'47''

Séniergues, F-46240 / Midi-Pyrénées (Lot)

2264

Domaine de la Faurie****
la Faurie
+33 (0)5-65211436
FAX +33 (0)5-65311117
2/4 - 30/9
contact@camping-lafaurie.com

27ha 56T(100-160m²) 6A CEE

1 ACD**F**IJKLMOPS
2 FIJKLRTUVWXY
3 A**F**GHJRU
4 (A 1/7-31/8) (C+H+Q+R+T+U+V+X+Y+Z)
5 **AB**DFGIJKLMNOPUWZ
6 ACDEGJ(N 3km)TV

Campsite located in the lovely Lot countryside on 27 hectares of grounds in the 'Parc Naturel Régional des Causses du Quercy'. Big, spacious pitches, tranquil location and a good base for days out. Recommended for nature lovers and gastronomy lovers!

A20, exit 56 Gourdon, at roundabout turn right exit St. Germain du Belair and continue for 5 km. Follow camping signs. Or from Souillac dir. Cahors via D820. Exit Montfaucon. Campsite signposted.

€15 *2/4-5/7 22/8-30/9 7=6*

N 44°41'32'' E 1°32'5''

Septfonds, F-82240 / Midi-Pyrénées (Tarn-et-Garonne)

2265

De Bois-Redon***
10 chemin de Bonnet
+33 (0)5-63649249
1/1 - 31/12
info@campingdeboisredon.com

2,5ha 34T(100-150m²) 10A CEE

1 A**F**IJKL**P**ST
2 BFRTXY
3 BGHJKNRU
4 (A 1/7-31/8) (B 1/6-15/9) (Q 1/4-1/11) (T+U 15/6-31/8) Z
5 **A**DFGIJMNPUZ
6 AEGJ(N 1km)TV

A very peaceful and child-friendly campsite with large pitches in a parkland setting in Septfonds. Excellent amenities in an area with plenty of opportunities. Open all year. Free WiFi.

A20 exit 59, through Caussade dir. Caylus, Villefrance via D926. At Caussade switch off SatNav. In Septfonds 3rd left after roundabout and follow signs.

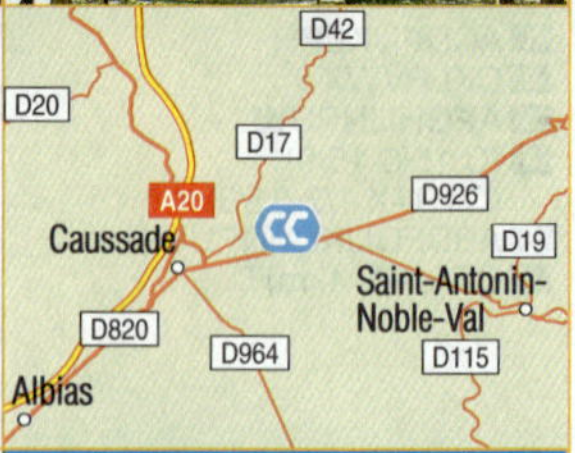

€17 *1/1-1/7 20/8-31/12*

N 44°10'58'' E 1°36'13''

Sévérac-l'Église, F-12310 / Midi-Pyrénées (Aveyron)

2266

La Grange de Monteillac****
chemin de Monteillac
+33 (0)5-65702100
4/5 - 15/9
info@
la-grange-de-monteillac.com

4,5ha 54T(90-276m²) 6-10-20A CEE

1 ACD**G**HIJKLPQ
2 GIRVWXY
3 BGHJK**M**NRU**W**
4 (A 6/7-27/8) (C+H ⊶) K
(Q ⊶) (S 22/5-15/9)
(U+V 6/7-31/8)
(X 15/5-2/7,31/8-15/9)
(Y 2/7-31/8) (Z 15/5-31/8)
5 **AB**EFGIJKLMNOPUWXZ
6 EGJ**K**(N 3km)ORV

Spacious quiet campsite in the centre of an area of interest: the Lot, the Tarn, Viaduc de Millau. Heated pool, tennis, bar, restaurant. A modern campsite with all amenities.

The campsite is located between Rodez and Sévérac-le-Château on the N88. Exit Sévérac-l'Église, then well signposted.

CC € 17 *14/5-9/7 27/8-15/9*

N 44°21'55'' E 2°51'5''

Sévérac-le-Château, F-12150 / Midi-Pyrénées (Aveyron)

2267

Les Calquières****
17 av. Jean Moulin
FAX +33 (0)5-65476482
1/4 - 15/10
contact@
camping-calquieres.com

2,4ha 88T(100-120m²) 6-10-16A CEE

1 ACD**G**IJKLMOPQ
2 FJKLRUVWXY
3 B**E**GHIJLMN**OP**RU**W**
4 (C+E 15/4-30/9)
(Q+R+T+U+V+X+Y ⊶) Z
5 **AB**EFGHIJKLMNOPQRUW
Z
6 ACDEG**K**L(N 0,5km)RTV

Ideal for exploring the Gorges du Tarn and La Jonte. Many excursions in the area. In early and late season you can enjoy sunny days and fresh nights. Perfect stopover campsite on your way south and the last campsite before the breathtaking new viaduct at Millau. Heated indoor swimming pool and restaurant.

Fro north A75 exit 42 or from south 43 Sévérac-le-Château. Follow signs. Campsite located next to municipal swimming pool.

CC € 17 *1/4-30/6 1/9-15/10* *7=6*

N 44°19'11'' E 3°3'51''

Sorèze, F-81540 / Midi-Pyrénées (Tarn)

2268

St. Martin***
rue du 19 mars 1962
+33 (0)5-63502019
1/4 - 30/9
campingsaintmartin@gmail.com

1,2ha 39T(100-120m²) 10A CEE

1 ACD**G**IJKLPQ
2 GLRVWXY
3 AGHJ**M**NR
4 (B 1/5-30/9) (Q 4/7-21/8)
(R ⊶) (T+U+Z 1/5-30/9)
5 **AB**FGJLNPUWZ
6 ACDEGJ(N 0,5km)TV

A village campsite in the heart of the Sorèze with shaded pitches and a swimming pool. Sorèze's heritage: half-timbered houses, the Saint Martin clock tower, Abbaye-école, protected historic monuments. Sorèze's culture: theatre, music festivals, braderies, festivities. Sorèze's natural setting: Rigole de la Plaine and Saint Ferréol lake, protected world heritage monuments.

In Revel follow the D85 towards Sorèze. Campsite signposted in village.

CC € 15 *1/4-8/7 25/8-29/9*

N 43°27'16'' E 2°4'10''

Souillac, F-46200 / Midi-Pyrénées (Lot) — 2269

Beter-uit Vakantiepark 'La Draille'****
+33 (0)5-65326501
23/4 - 1/10
la.draille@wanadoo.fr

35ha 146T(100-120m²) 10A CEE

1 ACD**F**IJLPRS
2 ACFJLRTVY
3 BFGHJK**MNOPQ**RUW
4 (A 1/7-31/8) (C+G) J (Q+S+T+U+V+X) Z
5 **AB**FGIJKLMNOPUZ
6 EGHJ**K**(N 6km)OPRTUV

A beautiful fourstar campsite: perfectly maintained pitches, toilet facilities and amenities. Set among the hills on the River Borrèze. Ideal as stopover campsite and/or starting point for many places of interest. Beautiful woodland walks in the 35 hectare park. Limited services on Sundays.

A20 exit Soulliac. When entering Soulliac turn right to the D15 and then the D62.

CC € 17 *23/4-9/7 27/8-1/10 7=6, 14=12, 21=17*

N 44°56'9" E 1°26'14"

Souillac, F-46200 / Midi-Pyrénées (Lot) — 2270

Castels Domaine de la Paille Basse*****
+33 (0)5-65378548
Fax +33 (0)5-65370958
14/5 - 17/9
info@lapaillebasse.com

12ha 120T(100-110m²) 16A

1 ABCD**G**IJKLMPQ
2 FJKRTUVXY
3 BFGHJ**M**NRU
4 (**A** 1/7-31/8) (B+G) J (Q+R+S) (T+U+X+Y 20/5-10/9) Z
5 **AB**FGJLNPUW
6 EGH**J**(N 9km)OQTV

A medieval village (3 farmhouses) restored and reconstructed into an 80 hectare campsite, all of this without losing its authenticity. Positioned on a hill with lovely views and romantic sunsets. This, with all the facilities you would expect, means this Castels campsite deserves its five stars.

Don't use SatNav. Take exit 55 on A20. At 2nd roundabout dir. Salignac. Follow signs 'La Paille Basse'. Site is 8 km from Souillac.

CC € 17 *14/5-10/7 27/8-17/9 7=6, 14=12, 21=18*

N 44°56'44" E 1°26'29"

Souillac, F-46200 / Midi-Pyrénées (Lot) — 2271

Les Ondines***
rue des Ondines
+33 (0)5-65378644
Fax +33 (0)5-65320504
1/5 - 1/10
camping.les.ondines@flowercampings.com

4ha 135T(90-110m²) 6A CEE

1 ACD**G**IJLPRS
2 CFRVWXY
3 ABFGHJKOPR**WX**
4 (A 1/7-31/8) (C+H+Q) (T 25/5-31/8) Z
5 **AB**CEFGHIJKLMNOPUWZ
6 AEGK(N 0,5km)RW

A campsite located on the banks of the Dordogne, a five minute walk from the centre of Souillac. You can swim in the heated pool on the campsite or from the natural river beach 200m away. The campsite is located between Sarlat and Rocamadour.

A20, exit 55 Souillac and follow camping signs.

CC € 15 *1/5-1/7 1/9-1/10 7=6*

N 44°53'20" E 1°28'29"

St. Antonin-Noble-Val, F-82140 / Midi-Pyrénées (Tarn-et-Garonne)

iD **2272**

Les Gorges de l'Aveyron***
Lieu dit Marsac Bas
+33 (0)5-63306976
29/4 - 25/9
info@
camping-gorges-aveyron.com

3,8ha 80**T**(100-120m²) 10A

1 ABCD**G**IJKLPRS
2 CMRVWXY
3 AGHJNR**W**X
4 (C) (H 1/7-31/8) (Q+S+T+U+V 1/6-15/9) (Z 1/6-25/9)
5 **AB**FGIJKLMNPUZ
6 CEGJ**K**(N 1,5km)V

A peaceful campsite right by the river in the Gorges de l'Aveyron with lovely level grounds and views of the 'Gorges'. It has a beautiful new swimming pool. Beautifully refurbished toilet facilities. Especially friendly wardens. The village of St Antonin is worth a visit.

From Caussade on the N20 take the D5 to St. Antonin. Cross the bridge and enter tunnel to the left. Campsite about 1 km on the left.

CC € 15 *29/4-2/7 1/9-25/9*

N 44°9'5" E 1°46'18"

St. Antonin-Noble-Val, F-82140 / Midi-Pyrénées (Tarn-et-Garonne)

iD **2273**

Sites & Paysages Les 3 Cantons****
+33 (0)5-63319857
1/5 - 15/9
info@3cantons.fr

15ha 80**T**(80-150m²) 6-10A

1 ACD**F**IJL**P**Q
2 BFTXY
3 BGHJMN**OP**RU
4 (C+H 1/6-15/9) (Q+R+T+U) (X 1/6-15/9) (Z)
5 **A**CDFGIJLMNPRUWZ
6 ACDEGJKM(N 6km)TV

A friendly campsite in the middle of woods and in a lovely walking area with orchid displays in the spring. Pleasant bar/terrace, heated refurbished swimming pool, climbing wall and sports on offer. Close to authentic villages, markets and gastronomic opportunities. Dutch owners.

From Caussade D926 direction Caylus, Villefranche-de-Rouergue. Past Septfonds do not take St. Antonin exit, but stay on main road for about 5 km. Turning on the right. Signposted.

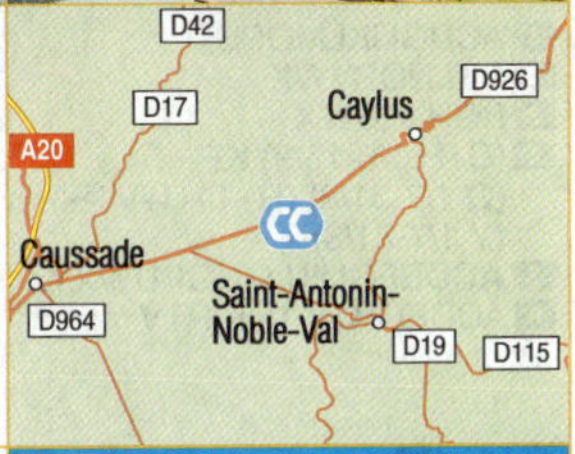

CC € 15 *1/5-3/7 22/8-15/9*

N 44°11'37" E 1°41'47"

St. Cirq-Lapopie, F-46330 / Midi-Pyrénées (Lot)

iD **2274**

Camping Restaurant De la Plage****
Porte Roques
+33 (0)5-65302951
4/4 - 30/9
camping-laplage@wanadoo.fr

3ha 93**T**(100-120m²) 10A

1 ACD**G**IJKLMPST
2 ACGKLMORTUVWXY
3 BGHJKNRU**WX**
4 (**A** 1/7-30/8) (Q 1/5-30/9) (R) (T+U 5/5-25/9) (V 15/6-25/9) (Y 5/5-25/9) Z
5 **AB**CDEFGIJKLMNOPQRUWXYZ
6 ACDEGIJ(N 0,5km)ORTV

Superbly located at the foot of St. Cirq-Lapopie and the banks of the Lot, in the middle of Les Causses du Quercy regional park. Good amenities and plenty of sports (with discounts). Good restaurant with local products and an attractive terrace. St. Cirq is a popular village with the French.

Follow the D653 from Cahors direction Figeac. At Vers take the D662 direction St. Cirq. At Tour-de-Faure cross the bridge over the Lot. Campsite 500 metres right on the D40.

CC € 17 *4/4-4/7 1/9-30/9*

N 44°28'8" E 1°40'51"

St. Cirq-Lapopie, F-46330 / Midi-Pyrénées (Lot)

2275

La Truffière***
D42
+33 (0)5-65302022
9/4 - 30/9
contact@camping-truffiere.com

4ha 83T(100-120m²) 6A CEE

1 ACFIJKLPST
2 BIJKLRTVWXY
3 BGHJNRU
4 (A 1/7-31/8) (C+G 1/5-20/9)
(Q 1/5-15/9) (R)
(T+U 1/6-31/8) (V 1/6-15/9)
(X 1/6-31/8) Z
5 ABDEFGIJLMNOPUWXZ
6 CDEGJ(N 2,5km)OTV

Spaciously laid out yet intimate terraced campsite in a parkland setting with lovely views. Ideal for those who love nature and relaxation. 3 km from the lovely village of St. Cirq (with free shuttle service).

Campsite is signposted in St. Cirq-Lapopie. Approximately 3 km from the village.

CC € 15 9/4-8/7 25/8-30/9

N 44°26'53" E 1°40'29"

St. Jean-du-Bruel, F-12230 / Midi-Pyrénées (Aveyron)

2276

La Dourbie****
route de Nant
+33 (0)5-65460640
FAX +33 (0)5-65460650
15/4 - 30/9
campingladourbie@orange.fr

2,3ha 65T(100-163m²) 10A CEE

1 ACDGIJKLMOPST
2 CKLNORVWX
3 BGHJRUWX
4 (C+H 1/6-15/9) KP
(Q 1/7-31/8) (R+T+U+V)
(Y 1/7-31/8) Z
5 ACDEFGIJKLMNOPUWXYZ
6 ACDEGK(N 1km)RTV

This new, modernly equipped campsite with a heated swimming pool, bar, à la carte restaurant and all amenities for motorhomes is located between the Gorges du Tarn and the Cévennes. Located on the River Dourbie (trout) with beautiful views. You will be warmly received. Restaurant open at weekends in low season.

A75, exit 47 La Cavalerie. Campsite between Nant and St. Jean-du-Bruel. 1 km before St. Jean-du-Bruel, well signposted along the route de Nant.

CC € 13 15/4-7/7 24/8-30/9 7=6, 14=12

N 44°1'11" E 3°20'46"

St. Lary-Soulan, F-65170 / Midi-Pyrénées (Hautes-Pyrénées)

2277

Le Rioumajou****
chemin du Bernet/Bourisp
+33 (0)5-62394832
FAX +33 (0)5-62395827
1/1 - 31/12
lerioumajou@wanadoo.fr

5ha 192T(100-130m²) 2-10A

1 ACDGIJKLMPQ
2 CLRTUVXY
3 ABGHNRUW
4 (A 1/7-31/8)
(C+G 15/6-15/9) KN
(Q+R 1/1-30/12)
(T+U+V+Z 15/6-15/9)
5 ABDEFGIJKLMNOPUWZ
6 CEGHI(N 2,5km)OV

The campsite is located in the Aure valley on the river, close to the mountain village of St. Lary. You can explore the Néouvielle National Nature Park with its 70 lakes and while taking lovely trips, you can discover many rare plants and animals. Also an excellent site for an overnight stop on your journey to Spain (via the Bielsa tunnel).

In Arreau take the D929 to St. Lary-Soulan. About 1500m past the bridge at Bazus-Aure follow camping signs.

CC € 15 1/1-30/6 1/9-31/12

N 42°50'19" E 0°20'20"

St. Pantaléon, F-46800 / Midi-Pyrénées (Lot) — 2278

des Arcades***
Moulin de St. Martial
+33 (0)9-61677498
15/5 - 17/9
info@des-arcades.com

12ha 80T(70-140m²) 6A

1 AC**F**IJKLPQ
2 CDLRTVX
3 BFGHJN**OP**RUW
4 (A) (B 31/5-17/9) (G)
J(Q+T+U+V+Y+Z)
5 **A**GIJKLMNPUWX
6 AEG**JK**(N 8km)V

Set in 12 hectares of grounds with spacious pitches. A 13th century water mill forms its centre point. Outstanding amenities, you can swim or fish and the surroundings lend themselves to cycling. French restaurant right by the entrance. Dutch management.

A20 exit 57. D820 direction Cahors, then direction Montauban. South of Cahors turn right at the 2nd roundabout (through a short tunnel). D653 direction Montcuq. Campsite located on the left, about 3 km before St. Pantaléon.

CC € 17 *15/5-30/6 1/9-17/9*

N 44°22'15'' E 1°18'28''

St. Pierre-Lafeuille, F-46090 / Midi-Pyrénées (Lot) — 2279

Quercy Vacances****
Le Mas de Lacombe
+33 (0)5-65368715
25/3 - 30/9
quercyvacances@wanadoo.fr

5ha 80T(100-130m²) 10A CEE

1 ACDGIJKLMOPQ
2 FRTXY
3 BGHJNRU
4 (B+G 15/6-15/9) **KN**
(Q 1/5-30/9) (R 1/7-31/8)
(T+U+V+Y+Z 15/6-15/9)
5 **A**EFGIJKLMNPUWZ
6 AEGIJ(N 9km)ORT

The campsite is located on the N20/D820 and is suitable as a stopover site. Lovely sauna and jacuzzi close to an enormous swimming pool. Attractive bar and restaurant. The surroundings are very beautiful and the tourist town of Cahors is close by. Relaxation is assured!

RN20/D820 Brive-Cahors, campsite well indicated 800m before St. Pierre-Lafeuille, turn right. Site ± 700m on right. Or: A20 exit 57 dir. Cahors. Onto D820 from roundabout. Then follow route above.

CC € 15 *25/3-3/7 29/8-30/9*

N 44°31'53'' E 1°27'33''

St. Rome-de-Tarn, F-12490 / Midi-Pyrénées (Aveyron) — 2280

de la Cascade****
+33 (0)5-65625659
FAX +33 (0)5-65625862
1/1 - 31/12
contact@camping-cascade-aveyron.com

4ha 99T(80-120m²) 6A CEE

1 AC**F**IJKLPRS
2 CIJKMRTVWXY
3 BGHJKMNRU**WX**
4 (A 1/7-31/8)
(B+G 15/6-15/9)
(Q 1/7-31/8) (R 1/7-30/8)
(T+U+V+X+Z 1/7-31/8)
5 **AB**DEFGIJKLMNPUWZ
6 CDEG**K**(N 0,5km)OPQRV

An attractive campsite with terraces and excellent facilities situated right on the Tarn.

In Millau take the D992 direction Albi.
In St. Georges-de-Luzençan take the D73 direction St. Rome-de-Tarn. Well signposted in the village.

CC € 15 *1/4-9/7 28/8-30/10*

N 44°3'11'' E 2°53'59''

Surba, F-09400 / Midi-Pyrénées (Ariège)

2281

Le Sédour**
Florac
+33 (0)7-82939772
1/1 - 31/12
campinglesedour@orange.fr

1,5ha 50T(90-130m²) 10A

1 AC**G**IJKLMOPQ
2 FRXY
3 AR**W**
4 (Q) Z
5 **AB**DGIJKLPUWZ
6 EGJ(N 2km)OV

A peaceful campsite in the vicinity of Tarascon-sur-Ariège, prehistoric park and the Niaux caves. The Foix and Montségur castles are worth a visit. Just 200m from the road connecting France and Andorra. Somewhat outdated, but perfectly functioning toilet facilities.

From Foix take the dual carriageway to Tarascon-sur-Ariège. At the end by the roundabout take 1st exit St-Girons (D618). Campsite signposted 100m on the right.

CC € 13 *1/1-30/6 1/9-31/12 7=6*

N 42°51'21'' E 1°35'20''

Tarascon-sur-Ariège, F-09400 / Midi-Pyrénées (Ariège)

2282

Le Pré Lombard****
route d'Ussat
+33 (0)5-61056194
FAX +33 (0)5-61057893
2/3 - 5/11
leprelombard@wanadoo.fr

3,5ha 100T(80-110m²) 10A

1 ACD**G**IJKLMOPQ
2 CLRTVY
3 BGHKLNRU**W**
4 (**A** 15/5-15/9)
(C+H 15/5-30/9) K
(Q 18/4-30/9)
(R+T 30/4-4/10)
(U+V+X 15/5-30/9) Z
5 **AB**DFGHIJKLMNOPUWZ
6 EG**IJK**(N 0,3km)O**P**RTV

A well equipped campsite with plenty of cultural and sportive activities. Located in the Ariège-Pyrenees: mountains, nature, culture and history. Walking excursions from the campsite twice a week, for example a walk to a plateau (altitude 2000m). Facilities such as the restaurant, cafeteria and swimming pool are available from 15 May to 30 September.

From Foix N20 towards Tarascon. Follow signs from 2nd roundabout. Take care with SatNav from Tarascon!

CC € 17 *2/3-1/7 28/8-5/11 7=6, 14=11*

N 42°50'24'' E 1°36'41''

Thégra, F-46500 / Midi-Pyrénées (Lot)

2283

Sites & Paysages Le Ventoulou****
Ventoulou
+33 (0)5-65336701
1/4 - 30/10
contact@leventoulou.com

2ha 32T(100-120m²) 10A CEE

1 ACD**F**IJKLMPRS
2 JRTVWXY
3 B**F**GHJNRU
4 (C+E) (G 1/7-31/8)
(Q 1/6-31/8) (R)
(T+U+V+X 1/7-31/8) (Z)
5 **AB**DEFGIJKLMNOPQUWY
Z
6 ACEG**IK**(N 8km)RTV

A lovely campsite, calm and peaceful, situated in protected countryside. Three minutes from Padirac and ten minutes from the medieval district of Rocamadour in the heart of the Vallée region of the Dordogne Lotoise. Ideal for discovering various nearby towns less than 15 kilometres away as the crow flies. Campsite guests can enjoy discounts at many sights in the surroundings.

Campsite signposted on D673 near Padirac. Site located on the D60.

CC € 17 *1/4-10/7 27/8-30/10 7=6, 14=11, 21=16, 28=21*

N 44°49'32'' E 1°46'42''

Toulouse, F-31200 / Midi-Pyrénées (Haute-Garonne) 2284

Camping Toulouse Le Rupé***
21 chemin du Pont de Rupé
+33 (0)5-61700735
FAX +33 (0)5-61709717
1/1 - 31/12
@ campinglerupe31@wanadoo.fr

4ha 84**T**(80-120m²) 10A CEE

1 ACD**G**IJKLMOPQ
2 DFGRUVWXY
3 ABG**MR**V**W**
4 **KN**(Q+R)
(T+U+V+X+Z 15/6-15/9)
5 **AB**DEFGIJKLMNOPUXYZ
6 ACDEGI**K**(N 3km)OTV

A beautifully laid out town campsite. Ideal as a stopover campsite or as a starting point to visit Toulouse.

Toulouse ringroad (A620), exit Sesquieres (33). Campsite signposted. Located north of the town.

CC € 17 *1/1-8/7 26/8-31/12 7=6*

N 43°39'21'' E 1°24'56''

Touzac, F-46700 / Midi-Pyrénées (Lot) 2285

Le Ch'timi***
La Roque
+33 (0)5-65365236
1/4 - 30/9
@ info@campinglechtimi.com

3,5ha 77**T**(100-120m²) 6A CEE

1 ACD**G**IJKLPQ
2 CKLRTVXY
3 B**F**GHJKMNRU**WX**
4 (B 15/5-30/9) (G 1/7-1/9)
(Q 1/5-15/9) (R)
(T+U+V+X 1/5-30/9) (Z)
5 **A**CFGIJKLMNPUWZ
6 ACEGHIJ(N 5km)OTV

This campsite, laid out in the style of an old country estate offers spacious pitches and first rate amenities. Located in a charming valley of the Lot. It is a good base for cyclists and anglers.

A20 exit 57, D820 to Cahors. Sharp right just before Cahors roundabout follow D811 till Duravel, left on the D58 to Port de Vire. Right at the roundabout to Touzac. Campsite signposted from here.

CC € 15 *1/4-4/7 21/8-30/9*

N 44°29'53'' E 1°3'59''

Touzac, F-46700 / Midi-Pyrénées (Lot) 2286

Le Clos Bouyssac***
+33 (0)5-65365221
FAX +33 (0)5-65246851
1/4 - 30/9
@ camping.leclosbouyssac@wanadoo.fr

1,5ha 85**T**(80-190m²) 10A CEE

1 AC**F**IJLMPQ
2 BCJLORVY
3 A**E**GHJNRU**WX**
4 (A 1/7-31/8)
(B+G 15/5-15/9)
(Q 1/6-30/9)
(R+T+U 1/7-31/8) Z
5 **AB**FGIJKLMNPUZ
6 CEJ(N 4km)V

Le Clos Bouyssac is a terraced campsite of 1½ hectares on the banks of the Lot, perfect for fishing. In natural hilly surroundings with beautiful views of the river. The region is unique: gastronomy, culture and architecture in Quercy. On the Cahors wine route.

A20, exit 57 direction Cahors. Sharp right at the roundabout just before Cahors towards Fumel. Left at Duravel via the D58 to Port de Vire. Turn right at the roundabout to Touzac. Campsite signposted

CC € 15 *1/4-30/6 1/9-30/9*

N 44°28'49'' E 1°3'7''

Villefranche-de-Rouergue, F-12200 / Midi-Pyrénées (Aveyron)

2287

Le Rouergue***
35 avenue de Fondies
+33 (0)5-65451624
9/4 - 30/9
campingrouergue@wanadoo.fr

2ha 93T(100-175m²) 16A CEE

1 ACDGHIJKLMPQ
2 CRUVWXY
3 AFGHKRU
4 (A 12/4-30/9)
(B 15/6-15/9) K(Q+R)
(T 1/7-31/8) Z
5 ACFGIJKLMNOPUVWXYZ
6 ACEGHJ(N 2km)RTUV

Camping du Rouergue is situated close to the Villefranche-de-Rouergue royal fortified town with its lovely market square. The site offers you rest and comfort in shady natural surroundings. This campsite has spacious pitches with water and electricity (grand comfort), the toilet facilities meet modern expectations completely.

The campsite is located 2 km from the centre of Villefranche-de-Rouergue. Follow 'Stade' signs towards Monteils-Najac.

CC € 13 9/4-9/7 26/8-30/9

N 44°20'33'' E 2°1'35''

Agde, F-34300 / Languedoc-Roussillon (Hérault)

2288

Camping Le Neptune****
46 blvd du St. Christ
+33 (0)4-67942394
FAX +33 (0)467944877
3/4 - 2/10
info@campingleneptune.com

2,7ha 100T(70-120m²) 10A CEE

1 ACDFIJKLMPST
2 AFRVWXY
3 BFGJKNRUVW
4 (C+G) K(Q)
(R 10/5-15/9)
(T+U+V 27/6-21/8)
(Z 15/5-15/9)
5 ABEFGIJKLNOPUVWZ
6 ABEGHK(N 0,8km)ORTV

A well maintained campsite with plenty of greenery and flowers, located on the banks of the River Herault. If you are sporty you can go for bike rides on lovely cycle tracks in the area, or enjoy the gym or swim a few lengths in a spacious, heated pool. WiFi is free throughout the grounds.

A9 exit Agde direction Agde. Then exit Le Grau-d'Agde. Campsite about 3 km on the left.

CC € 17 3/4-7/7 24/8-2/10

N 43°17'53'' E 3°27'23''

Agde, F-34300 / Languedoc-Roussillon (Hérault)

2289

L'Escale***
route de la Tamarissière
+33 (0)4-67212109
FAX +33 (0)4-67211024
25/3 - 30/9
camping-lescale@hotmail.fr

2,5ha 50T(80-90m²) 6A

1 ACGIJKLMPS
2 ACFRVY
3 BFGKLORUW
4 (B+G 15/5-30/9)
(Q+R+T) (U 1/7-31/8)
(V+X+Y+Z)
5 ABFGJLNPUVZ
6 AEGHIK(N 2,5km)OT

Attractive, shaded family campsite located on the Hérault. River or sea fishing. Wonderful cycling to Cap d'Agde or inland. Bridge competitions for enthusiasts on the campsite. Free WiFi.

A9 exit Agde. At the roundabout N312, direction Agde exit Tamarissière. Campsite about 3 km on the right.

CC € 17 25/3-8/7 27/8-30/9

N 43°17'49'' E 3°26'57''

Agde, F-34300 / Languedoc-Roussillon (Hérault) — 2290

La Pepinière***
3 route du Grau d'Agde
+33 (0)4-67941094
15/3 - 16/10
reception@lapepiniere.com

1,9ha 35**T**(80-100m²) 10A CEE

- **1** ACDGIJKLM**P**ST
- **2** CGTVWXY
- **3** B**F**GJKLNRUW
- **4** (C+H 15/4-30/9) **N** (T+Z 15/6-15/9)
- **5** **AB**GI**J**KLMNPUZ
- **6** ABEGK(N 2km)RT

This quiet family campsite is located near an old fishing harbour in the Mediterranean on the banks of the Hérault. Lovely cycle path to the beach (1200m) and shops. Very good fishing. Free heated swimming pool, bubble bath and sauna. Free WiFi throughout the campsite.

From the A9: exit Cap d'Agde. On D612 exit Grau d'Agde. Then follow 'Campings des Berges de L'Hérault' signs. Campsite signposted.

CC € 13 *15/3-5/7 22/8-30/9 7=6, 14=12, 21=18, 28=24*

N 43°17'47'' E 3°27'8''

Agde, F-34300 / Languedoc-Roussillon (Hérault) — 2291

Le Cap Agathois***
11, rue des Entrepreneurs
FAX +33 (0)4-67940221
15/4 - 15/9
info@campingcapagathois.com

5,5ha 79**T**(60-100m²) 10A CEE

- **1** ACD**G**IJKLPST
- **2** RVWXY
- **3** B**F**GJKLNRU
- **4** (C+H 1/5-15/9) IJKM (Q+R+T+U+V+Z 1/5-15/9)
- **5** **AB**EFGIJKLMNPUZ
- **6** AEGHJ(N 0,8km)TUV

A lovely family campsite a few kilometres from the sandy beaches at Agde and Marseillan-Plage. Spacious, separated pitches and good amenities, bar and recreation room.

On D612 follow dir. Agde centre. Before the roundabout, just past the viaduct, site is indicated on the right.

CC € 15 *15/4-10/7 27/8-14/9 7=6, 14=12*

N 43°18'39'' E 3°30'42''

Agde, F-34300 / Languedoc-Roussillon (Hérault) — 2292

Les Champs Blancs****
76 route de Rochelongue
+33 (0)4-67942342
FAX +33 (0)4-67948781
1/4 - 15/10
contact@campingleschampsblancs.com

6,5ha 160**T**(80-130m²) 10A CEE

- **1** ACD**G**IJKLMOPST
- **2** AFGRTVWXY
- **3** B**F**GJKMNRU**W**
- **4** (C+H) IJM(Q+S) (T+U+V 1/5-30/9) (Y 20/5-15/9) (Z 1/5-30/9)
- **5** **AB**GIJKLMNOPSTUWXZ
- **6** BCEGH**I**J**K**L(N 1km)TUV

Quiet family campsite, 2 km from the sea. Large, heated aquapark and large pitches, marked out by oleander hedges, a few even have private toilet facilities. WiFi on the grounds and many activities for everybody.

A9 exit 34 dir. Bezierz/Agde. On D1612 dir. Grau d'Agde-Rochelongue. At roundabout (with statue) left dir. Grau d'Agde. Next rndbt 2nd exit right. Next rndbt 1st exit right. After bridge 1st right.

CC € 15 *1/4-7/7 24/8-15/10*

N 43°17'47'' E 3°28'37''

Agde, F-34300 / Languedoc-Roussillon (Hérault) — 2293

Les Mimosas****
98 route de Guiraudette
+33 (0)4-67016736
FAX +33 (0)4-67316406
14/3 - 15/10
@ contact@campingmimosas.com

1,6ha 28T(80-110m²) 16A

1 ACDGIJLMPST
2 GSVWXY
3 BFGJKRUW
4 (C+H 9/4-2/10) (Q)
(T+U+V+Z 1/4-15/10)
5 AEFGIJKLMNOPUXZ
6 AEGIK(N 0,6km)RT

Small family campsite with agreeable ambiance and well maintained toilet facilities. Many options for cycling and for cultural trips to Cap d'Agde. Heated pool and free WiFi on entire site. Baker, restaurant and supermarket next to the campsite.

A9 exit Cap d'Agde. (D112). Then exit Le Grau d'Agde turning. 2nd exit on the right at the roundabout with the statue. Follow camping signs.

CC € 13 14/3-8/7 29/8-30/9 7=6, 12=10, 14=11, 20=16

N 43°17'17'' E 3°28'14''

Agde, F-34300 / Languedoc-Roussillon (Hérault) — 2294

Les Romarins****
6 route du Grau
+33 (0)4-67941859
FAX +33 (0)4-67265880
26/3 - 1/10
@ contact@romarins.com

2,5ha 120T(80-115m²) 10A CEE

1 ACDGIJKLMOPST
2 ACFGRVWXY
3 BFGJKNRUW
4 (C+Q+R+T+U+V+X+Z)
5 AEFGJKLMNPUZ
6 ABEGIJK(N 0,6km)RTV

A friendly campsite on the River Hérault 900m from the sea. A friendly couple who will do anything they can to help you. A good base for trips out, also by bike. Multifunctional sports field and some fitness apparatus. Heated swimming pool and free WiFi on the terrace. Fishing on the campsite.

A9 exit Agde. Direction Agde. At Agde exit Le Grau d'Agde. Turn left after about 3 km.

CC € 15 26/3-2/7 27/8-30/9 12=10, 21=17

N 43°17'40'' E 3°27'0''

Alénya, F-66200 / Languedoc-Roussillon (Pyrénées-Orientales) — 2295

Cap Sud***
avenue de la Mer
+33 (0)4-68221726
1/4 - 31/10
@ info@camping-capsud.com

1,5ha 64T 10A CEE

1 ACGIJKLPST
2 VXY
3 AFU
4 (B 1/4-30/9)
5 EFGIJKLNOPU
6 EGIJ(N 0,2km)TV

Cap Sud campsite is located in an authentic Catalan village. It is 5 minutes from the largest sandy beach at Cyprien-Plage and the inland sea of l' Étang de Canet.

A9 Perpignan Sud, exit 42, direction Argelès, exit 7 Alénya. Campsite signposted.

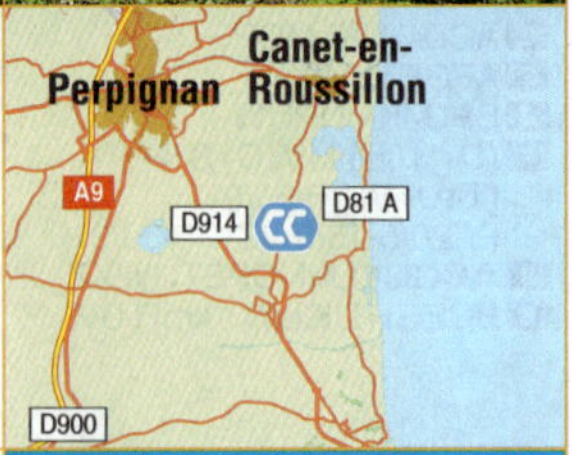

CC € 17 1/4-5/7 27/8-31/10 7=6

N 42°38'18'' E 2°59'3''

Allègre-les-Fumades, F-30500 / Languedoc-Roussillon (Gard) — 2296

Château de Boisson*****
Boisson
+33 (0)4-66248561
FAX +33 (0)4-66248014
2/4 - 24/9
reception@chateaudeboisson.com

7,5ha 178T(85-120m²) 6A CEE

1 ACDGIJKLMOPS
2 IJRTVXY
3 ABG**M**NRU
4 (B 1/5-24/9) (F+H) IJ (Q+R+T+U+V+X+Y+Z)
5 **AB**DEFGIJKLMNOPR**S**UWYZ
6 DEGJ**K**L(N 6km)TV

The site offers all-season service: two restaurants (with take-away meals), a sandwich bar and a heated indoor pool. Ideal base for exploring places in the beautiful area such as the Cevennes, the Ardèche, the Pont du Gard, Barjac, Nîmes, the duchy of Uzès and Avignon.

Campsite in the middle of the Alès-St. Ambroix-Lussan triangle. At the crossing of the D37 and the D7 take the D16. Campsite ± 500 metres by the mountainside and the village of Boisson.

CC € 19 *6/5-25/6 10/9-24/9*

N 44°12'34'' E 4°15'24''

Anduze, F-30140 / Languedoc-Roussillon (Gard) — 2297

Le Castel Rose***
610 chemin Recoulin
+33 (0)4-66618015
1/4 - 25/9
castelrose@wanadoo.fr

7ha 205T(100-260m²) 10A CEE

1 A**G**IJKLMPST
2 ABCGKLMNORSVWXY
3 B**F**GHJKN**P**RUV**WX**
4 (C+H) IJ**KLMN**(Q) (R 15/4-15/9) (S 1/7-31/8) (T+U+V+X+Y 15/4-15/9) Z
5 **AB**CDEFGHIJKLMNOPQRUVWXY
6 ACEGIK(N 0,5km)ORTUV

Family campsite on the banks of the Gardon with private beaches and views of the bamboo plantation. Large shaded pitches, level grounds with heated 1800 m² water park. Wellness, bowling, table tennis, trampoline and playgrounds. Bar, snack bar, supermarket and restaurant. Free WiFi. Pitches by the river and larger than 130 m²: 0.50 Euros per day extra.

From Anduze the D907 dir. St. Jean-du-Gard. Turn right after the bend and continue to the end of the road.

CC € 17 *1/4-3/7 22/8-25/9*

N 44°3'52'' E 3°58'37''

Anduze, F-30140 / Languedoc-Roussillon (Gard) — 2298

Le Pradal***
rte de Générargues
+33 (0)4-66617981
26/3 - 1/10
camping-le-pradal@orange.fr

3,5ha 106T(80-100m²) 10A CEE

1 ACD**G**IJKLMPST
2 BCKLNORSVWXY
3 BGHJMRU**WX**
4 (B+G 15/5-30/9) (Q) (R 1/7-31/8) (T+U 1/6-30/9) (V+X 1/7-30/9) Z
5 **AB**DEFGIJKLMNOPQRUXYZ
6 ACEGJ(N 1km)ORTUV

A ten-minute walk from Anduze and the bamboo garden, close to many interesting places. A pleasant campsite with a private beach on the River Gardon and a large swimming pool. Peaceful and agreeable atmosphere. Large, level shaded pitches. Bar, restaurant with terrace, fresh bread. Free tennis, jeu de boules, trampolines and table tennis, playground. Free WiFi.

A7 Bollène. Then take Bagnols-Alès-Anduze road, turn right before the bridge, follow signs (500 metres).

CC € 17 *26/3-5/7 22/8-1/10*

N 44°3'44'' E 3°58'58''

Anduze, F-30140 / Languedoc-Roussillon (Gard) — 2299

Les Fauvettes***
rte de St. Jean-du-Gard
+33 (0)4-66617223
25/4 - 30/9
camping-les-fauvettes@wanadoo.fr

4ha 102T(90-140m²) 10A CEE

1 ACDGIJKLMOPS
2 BGJKLRVXY
3 BFGHIKNPRUW
4 (B+G 15/5-15/9) JK
(Q 1/6-15/9)
(T+U+V+X 1/7-31/8)
(Z 15/6-1/9)
5 AFGIJKLMNOPQRUVWZ
6 CEGJ(N 0,4km)TV

A 10 minute walk from the centre. Access to the river within 500m and the amenities are close by. Friendly campsite, marked out pitches with shade, swimming pool, toddlers' pool, water slides, jeu de boules, table tennis. Free WiFi.

Campsite on the D907 Anduze - St. Jean-du-Gard. Signposted.

CC € 13 25/4-4/7 22/8-30/9

N 44°3'37" E 3°58'26"

Argelès-sur-Mer, F-66701 / Languedoc-Roussillon (Pyrénées-Orientales) — 2300

Comangès***
avenue du Général de Gaulle
+33 (0)4-68811562
FAX +33 (0)4-68958774
30/4 - 26/9
infos@campingcomanges.com

1ha 71T(70-90m²) 10A CEE

1 ACGIJKLMOPST
2 EGRTVX
3 AFNRUY
5 ABFGJLMNOPUVZ
6 ACGK(N 0,2km)RT

Comangès, located between the sea and the mountains, is an ideal starting point for trips to the Pyrenees or Spain. Walk to the centre of Argelès-Plage, the lovely beach, the lively promenade, the little bars, the shops or the restaurants from the campsite.

A9, exit Perpignan-Sud, D914 direction Argelès-sur-Mer to exit 10, direction Argelès. At the second roundabout direction Argelès, Les Plages. In the village, follow signs to 'Centre Plage'.

CC € 15 30/4-7/7 26/8-25/9

N 42°33'5" E 3°2'40"

Argelès-sur-Mer, F-66700 / Languedoc-Roussillon (Pyrénées-Orientales) — 2301

de Pujol****
avenue de la Retirada 1939
+33 (0)4-68810025
FAX +33 (0)4-68812121
20/4 - 12/10
postmaster@campingdepujol.com

6,3ha 220T(80-120m²) 6A

1 ACDFIJKLMOPST
2 GLRTVWXY
3 ABFGJKNQRU
4 (B+G 1/5-12/10) K
(Q+R+T+U+V+X+Z)
5 ABEFGJKLMNOPSTUVZ
6 ACDEGJ(N 1,5km)OTV

De Pujol is located between the sea and the 'Pyrénées Orientales' and has shaded and sunny pitches. There are lovely swimming pools and it is 1.2 km away from the beautiful beach and the welcoming village of Argelès. Take a trip to Spain or the Pyrenees.

A9 exit Perpignan-Sud, RN114 direction Argelès-sur-Mer as far as exit 10. Drive in the direction of Argelès at the 1st roundabout, at the 2nd roundabout direction Pujols. At the 3rd roundabout direction Plage Nord.

CC € 13 20/4-29/6 25/8-11/10

N 42°33'25" E 3°1'46"

Argelès-sur-Mer, F-66701 / Languedoc-Roussillon (Pyrénées-Orientales)

2302

La Chapelle****
Place de L'Europe - avenue du Tech
+33 (0)4-68812814
FAX +33 (0)4-68958382
23/4 - 1/10
@ contactlc@
camping-la-chapelle.com

9,7ha 299T(80-120m²) 6-10A CEE

1 ACDGIJKLMOPS
2 ACEGVY
3 BFGMNQRVY
4 (C+E+H) J
(Q+R+U+V+Z)
5 ABEFGIJKLMNOPQUVZ
6 ACDEGJK(N 0,2km)RTV

Campsite La Chapelle is ideally located in the centre of Argelès-Plage and 200m from the beautiful beach. Enjoy the peace, the shaded pitches, and the heated, partly covered pools and slides. The boulevard with its small shops, bars and restaurants is close by.

A9 exit 42 Perpignan-Sud, then D914 direction Argelès-sur-Mer. Take exit 10 direction Chemin de Pujol and Plage Centre. Campsite located opposite the 'Office du Tourisme'.

CC €19 23/4-15/6 3/9-1/10

N 42°33'10'' E 3°2'35''

Argelès-sur-Mer, F-66702 / Languedoc-Roussillon (Pyrénées-Orientales)

2303

La Marende****
avenue du Littoral
+33 (0)4-68811209
FAX +33 (0)4-68818852
29/4 - 24/9
@ info@marende.com

2,5ha 137T(90-120m²) 6-10A CEE

1 ACGIJKLMPST
2 AEGRVXY
3 BFGHKLNRUWY
4 (C+H) KP
(Q+S+T+U+V+X+Z)
5 ABCDEFGHIJKLMNOPQRU
VWXYZ
6 ACGIJ(N 0,5km)ORTV

The friendly La Marende campsite with its lovely heated swimming pool, restaurant and new luxurious heated toilet facilities is just 100m from the beach. Close to Spain and the Pyrenees. An ideal starting point for many day trip possibilities.

A9, exit Perpignan-Sud, D914 direction Argelès-sur-Mer, as far as exit 10 direction Taxo-d'Avall. Left at the 2nd roundabout direction Plage Nord and continue on this road until the campsite is signposted.

CC €17 29/4-2/7 3/9-24/9

N 42°34'20'' E 3°2'28''

Argelès-sur-Mer, F-66701 / Languedoc-Roussillon (Pyrénées-Orientales)

2304

Le Dauphin****
route de Taxo à la Mer
+33 (0)4-68811754
FAX +33 (0)4-68958260
16/4 - 25/9
@ info@campingledauphin.com

7,5ha 144T(100-120m²) 10A

1 ACGIJKLOPST
2 GLRTVX
3 BFGKMNRU
4 (C+H) IJKP
(Q+S+T+U+V+X+Z)
5 ABFGIJKLMNOPSUWXYZ
6 AEGIJK(N 3km)TV

Campsite with 87 spacious, marked-out pitches. 7000 m² aqua park with heated swimming pools and a toddler's pool. Bar/restaurant, supermarket and entertainment from April to September. For a small extra fee you can enjoy a pitch with private toilet facilities: shower, toilet and washing basin. In Argelès-sur-Mer!

A9 exit Perpignan-Sud, D914 dir. Argelès-sur-Mer as far as exit 10 Taxo-d'Avall. Left at 2nd roundabout dir. Taxo-d'Avall, Plage Nord. Follow signs.

CC €17 16/4-30/6 1/9-25/9

N 42°34'21'' E 3°1'18''

Argelès-sur-Mer, F-66700 / Languedoc-Roussillon (Pyrénées-Orientales) — 2305

Le Rancho**
route de Sorede
+33 (0)468810488
9/4 - 30/9
info@campinglerancho.com

4ha 65T(70-100m²) 6A CEE

1 ACDFIJKLPS
2 BCJTVXY
3 BGHJRU
4 (B)
(Q+R+T+U+V+X+Z 1/7-31/8)
5 **A**EGJKLMNPUV
6 AEJ**K**(N 3km)V

Le Rancho, a quiet terraced campsite, is located in a forest along the Massane river at the foot of the Pyrenees and 6 km from the bathing resort of Argelès. Cool down in the pool, walk in the surroundings or take a trip to the Pyrenees or Spain.

Via A9 dir. Perpignan to exit 42 Perpignan Sud. Then via RD114 dir. Argelès-sur-Mer to exit 11. After 300 metres on roundabout dir. St. André. After 500 metres follow signs Le Rancho left.

CC € 15 *9/4-30/6 30/8-30/9*

N 42°31'46'' E 2°59'14''

Argelès-sur-Mer, F-66700 / Languedoc-Roussillon (Pyrénées-Orientales) — 2306

Le Romarin***
route de Sorède,
chemin des Vignes
+33 (0)4-68810263
9/4 - 30/9
contact@camping-romarin.com

2,5ha 39T(80-140m²) 6-10A CEE

1 ACD**F**IJKL**P**ST
2 BFRSVWXY
3 ABGHKRU
4 (C+**G**+Q+R+T+U+V+X+Z)
5 **AB**GIJKLMNPUZ
6 ACEG**J**(N 2km)OTV

This welcoming family campsite is surrounded by farmlands with olive trees, is shaded with beautiful landscaping and has a nice heated pool. The sea is close by (4 km) and there are many options for outings to the Pyrenees or Spain.

A9, exit Perpignan-Sud, D914 direction Argelès-sur-Mer as far as exit 11. At the roundabout diretion 'Les Olivettes'. After 1300 metres right at roundabout. Right at next roundabout. Campsite after 200m

CC € 17 *9/4-1/7 27/8-29/9*

N 42°32'24'' E 2°59'43''

Argelès-sur-Mer, F-66702 / Languedoc-Roussillon (Pyrénées-Orientales) — 2307

Le Soleil*****
route du Littoral
+33 (0)4-68811448
+33 (0)4-68814434
4/5 - 24/9
camping.lesoleil@wanadoo.fr

12ha 434T(90-120m²) 6-10A CEE

1 ACD**G**IJKLPST
2 ACEGRSVXY
3 BFGKNRUVWY
4 (C+H) IJKP
(Q+S+T+U+V+X+Y+Z)
5 **AB**DFGIJKLMNOPUWXYZ
6 ACEGHKM(N 1km)ORTUV

All luxury amenities and activities are at your disposal for the entire season. Heated toilet facilities, heated pools and several direct access points to the sea. An ideal base for outings to the Pyrenees or Spain.

A9 exit Perpignan-Sud, D914 direction Argelès-sur-Mer as far as exit 10 direction Taxo-d'Avall. Turn left at the 2nd roundabout in the direction of Plage Nord, continue on this road and follow the camping signs.

CC € 17 *4/5-2/7 27/8-23/9*

N 42°34'33'' E 3°2'33''

Argelès-sur-Mer, F-66701 / Languedoc-Roussillon (Pyrénées-Orientales)

2308

Les Criques de Porteils*****
RD114 - Corniche de Collioure
+33 (0)4-68811273
FAX +33 (0)4-68958576
26/3 - 29/10
@ contactcdp@lescriques.com

5ha 179T(80-100m²) 10A CEE

1 ACDGIJKL**P**S
2 EIJKNOQRSTVXY
3 ABGHMNRY
4 (A+C+H) JKP
(Q+S+U+V+X+Z)
5 **AB**DEFGIJKLMNPUVW
6 ACDEGIJ**K**(N 2km)RTV

Beautiful terraced campsite close to Collioure in an exceptional area with endless views of the sea and on the mountains of Roussillon. Private access to the sublime little creeks on the Mediterranean sea and all kinds of options for trips out.

A9 direction Perpignan. Exit 42 Perpignan-Sud direction Argelès-sur-Mer. D914 towards Collioure, take exit 13. 'Collioure par la corniche' till l'Hotel du Golfe, turn right in direction of campsite.

CC € 19 *26/3-30/4 9/5-12/6 3/9-29/10*

N 42°32'2'' E 3°4'4''

Argelès-sur-Mer, F-66702 / Languedoc-Roussillon (Pyrénées-Orientales)

2309

Les Marsouins****
avenue de la Retirada
+33 (0)4-68811481
FAX +33 (0)4-68959358
30/4 - 8/10
@ lesmarsouins@cielavillage.com

12ha 372T(90-120m²) 5A CEE

1 ACFIJKLMOPS
2 GLRVXY
3 B**F**GKN**OP**RU
4 (C+H) J
(Q+S+T+U+V+X+Y+Z)
5 **AB**EFGIJKLOPUWXYZ
6 ACDEGHIK(N 1,5km)ORTV

Welcoming campsite with a beautiful heated pool, spacious pitches and paved motorhome pitches. All amenities are available throughout the season. Located 800 metres from the sea and close to the Pyrenees and Spain.

A9, exit Perpignan-Sud, D914 direction Argelès-sur-Mer as far as exit 10. First roundabout direction Argelès, second roundabout direction Pujols. At the third roundabout direction Plage Nord.

CC € 15 *30/4-24/6 3/9-8/10*

N 42°33'49'' E 3°2'5''

Argelès-sur-Mer, F-66702 / Languedoc-Roussillon (Pyrénées-Orientales)

2310

Les Pins***
avenue du Tech
+33 (0)4-68811046
FAX +33 (0)4-68813506
9/4 - 7/10
@ camping@les-pins.com

4ha 216T(85-95m²) 10A CEE

1 AC**G**IJKLOPST
2 AEGQRVY
3 AB**F**GRUWY
4 (C+H) J(Q 1/7-31/8)
(T+U+V+X 15/5-15/9)
(Z 1/5-15/9)
5 **AB**DEFGIJKLMNOPUZ
6 AEGHJ**K**RTV

A restful and shaded campsite close to the centre of Argelès-Plage. Enjoy the walks along the magnificent beaches or a dive in the heated swimming pool. The Pyrenees and Spain are close by and invite you for a stunning day trip.

A9, exit Perpignan-Sud, D914 direction Argelès-sur-Mer as far as exit 10 direction Argelès. At the second roundabout direction Argelès, les Plages. In the village follow the signs 'Centre Plage' and 'Plage des Pins'.

CC € 17 *9/4-5/7 28/8-7/10*

N 42°33'21'' E 3°2'32''

Attuech/Anduze, F-30140 / Languedoc-Roussillon (Gard)

2311

Le Fief d'Anduze***
195 chemin du Plan d'Eau
+33 (0)4-66618171
1/4 - 30/9
lefiefdanduze@wanadoo.fr

6ha 90**T**(80-100m²) 10A

1 AC**G**IJKLMOPS
2 ABCDKNORTVWXY
3 A**F**GHJNOPRU**WX**
4 (C+G) **KLN**
(Q+R+T+U+V+X+Z)
5 **A**EFGIJKLMPUVWZ
6 AEGIK(N 5km)OTV

You will enjoy your stay here at the start of the Cévennes and a 5 minute drive from Anduze. Plenty of opportunities for visiting beautiful towns, cultural and sports activities. Free WiFi point on entire camp site.

Exit Bollène dir. Alès, then to Montpellier. In St. Christol-les-Alès dir. Anduze. Past Intermarché left to Lézan. After Gardon bridge to Anduze at roundabout. 2nd site on right.

CC € 15 *1/4-7/7 26/8-30/9 7=6*

N 44°1'37'' E 4°1'40''

Bagnols-les-Bains, F-48190 / Languedoc-Roussillon (Lozère)

2312

Le Tivoli
rte Mende Tivoli
+33 (0)4-66476593
2/4 - 13/11
contact@revea-vacances.com

1,5ha 100**T**(50-100m²) 10A CEE

1 ABC**G**IJKLMPST
2 CGLRVWXY
3 AGM**W**
5 **AB**CDIJKLMNPUVWXZ
6 CEGJ(N 0,5km)

A somewhat older but well maintained campsite which is used mainly for visiting the spa facilities in the village and for fishing in the river.

From the A75 take exit 39 to Mende then towards Langogne on the N88. D901 3 km beyond Bedaroux. Campsite is on the road just before the village.

CC € 11 *2/4-10/7 27/8-13/11 7=6*

N 44°30'30'' E 3°39'38''

Bagnols-sur-Cèze, F-30200 / Languedoc-Roussillon (Gard)

2313

La Coquille***
route de Carmignan
+33 (0)4-66890305
FAX +33 (0)4-66895986
25/4 - 16/9
campinglacoquille@wanadoo.fr

1,5ha 30**T**(90-110m²) 6-10A CEE

1 ACD**F**IJKLPST
2 CTVY
3 AGJQRWX
4 (A) (B 15/6-15/9)
(G 10/7-15/8) (Q)
(T+U+V 10/6-10/9)
(Z 1/6-16/9)
5 **AB**FGJLNPUX
6 AEGK(N 2km)TV

Small, idyllic child-friendly campsite on the banks of the Cèze with pitches in the sun or in the shade. The Ardèche, Provence and Camargue are all close by. Bread available on the site. Genuine campers will feel immediately at home here after a friendly welcome from José and Fifi Gimeno.

A7, exit 19 Bollène direction Pont-St-Esprit and Bagnols-sur-Cèze. The campsite is 1 km from the village at the D360.

CC € 19 *25/4-30/6 20/8-16/9*

N 44°10'34'' E 4°38'9''

Bagnols-sur-Cèze, F-30200 / Languedoc-Roussillon (Gard) — 2314

Les Genêts d'Or****
1840 chemin de Carmignan
Tel/Fax +33 (0)4-66895867
20/4 - 20/9
@ info@camping-genets-dor.com

8ha 120T(90-100m²) 6-10A

1 ACD**F**IJKLPST
2 CNORTVWXY
3 ABGJN**P**RUWX
4 (C 1/5-20/9) (G 15/5-20/9)
(Q+R+T+U+V+Y 10/5-15/9)
(Z key)
5 **AB**DEFGIJKLMNOPUZ
6 ACEGK(N 2km)OTV

On the banks of the river Cèze, you'll find this ambient family campsite surrounded by vineyards. Excellent service, Dutch owners. Bridge games on Monday and Thursday from mid-May to mid-June. Centrally located between Provence, Cévennes and Ardèche. Very suitable for seniors and families. Free WiFi.

A7 exit Bollène. D994 dir. Pont-St-Esprit. There N86 dir. Bagnols-sur-Cèze. About 500 m. past the city limits sign, just before service station turn left. Follow signs.

CC € 19 *20/4-4/7 21/8-20/9*

N 44°10'25" E 4°38'13"

Barjac, F-30430 / Languedoc-Roussillon (Gard) — 2315

Domaine de la Sablière****
St. Privat-de-Champclos
Tel +33 (0)4-66245116
Fax +33 (0)4-66245869
26/3 - 2/10
@ contact@villagesabliere.com

62ha 204T(100-120m²) 10A CEE

1 ACD**G**IJKLMNOPST
2 ABCIJKNORSTVWXY
3 ABGHJMNQRUV**W**X
4 (A 15/6-1/9) (C key)
(E 1/7-31/8) (G 1/5-15/9) **L**
N(Q key)
(S+T+U+V+X+Y 26/3-25/9)
Z
5 **AB**EFGIJKLMNOPUWXYZ
6 CEGHJ(N 6km)OQRTV

This naturist site on the wooded slopes of the Cèze gorge includes: 2 swimming pools, 1 of which is covered, 2 saunas, a beauty centre, sports and other activities and a mini club. Shop, bar and restaurant (partly open, partly sheltered) contribute to your comfort in this dream paradise.

From Pont-Saint-Esprit take the D901, then the D266 on the left. Follow signs.

CC € 15 *26/3-30/6 1/9-1/10*

N 44°16'1" E 4°21'7"

Barjac, F-48000 / Languedoc-Roussillon (Lozère) — 2316

Le Clos des Peupliers**
RN88
Tel +33 (0)4-66470116
1/4 - 30/9
@ leclosdespeupliers@wanadoo.fr

3,2ha 61T(90-240m²) 10A CEE

1 ACD**G**IJLP
2 CGKRTVWXY
3 AGHJRU**WX**
4 (C+H+Q 1/6-30/8)
(T+U+V 1/6-30/9) Z
5 **AB**GIJKLMNOPUVWXY
6 CEGJ(N 0,5km)T

A homely, sunny and shady campsite in the heart of the beautiful Lozère, on the banks of the Lot. The heated pool and the trout in the Lot await you. The village is not far and the surrounding hills offer a beautiful panoramic view. It is a good base for exploring the Tarn and a number of typical French, active villages.

From A75 take exit 39. Follow RN88 dir. Mende until Barjac. Campsite is indicated.

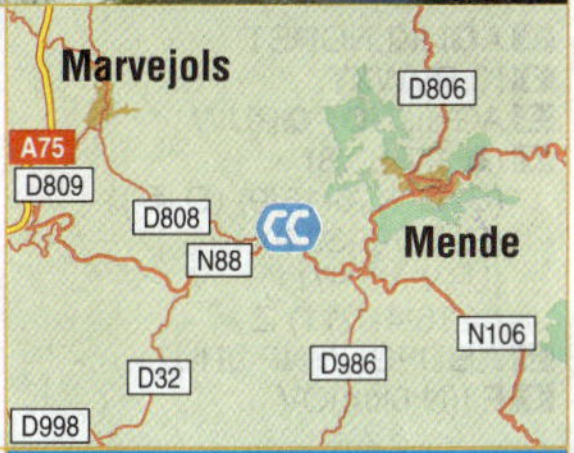

CC € 15 *1/4-30/6 1/9-30/9*

N 44°30'3" E 3°24'26"

Bédouès/Florac, F-48400 / Languedoc-Roussillon (Lozère)

2317

Camping Chantemerle**
La Pontèze
+33 (0)4-66451966
1/4 - 2/11
chante-merle@wanadoo.fr

2,5ha 66T(150-200m²) 10A CEE

1 ACD**G**IJKLMOPST
2 ABCJKLNORVXY
3 BGHIJKLRU**W**X
4 (Q+R+T+U+V+Y+Z)
5 **A**FGIJKLMNPUVZ
6 ACEGIJ(N 5km)OTV

Discover the tranquillity of Chantemerle.
The campsite is situated in the unspoilt countryside of the Cevennes on the banks of the Tarn where beavers swim in the evening. Eat home-made meals in the restaurant by the water and enjoy peace and quiet. Languages spoken: French, English, German, Italian. Free WiFi.

A75 exit 39.1 via N109 direction Mende to Florac. 2.5 km before Florac left at roundabout to Bedoues. Left at Roman bridge past village. Follow camping signs.

CC € 15 *1/4-9/7 26/8-2/11*

N 44°20'43'' E 3°36'38''

Boisseron, F-34160 / Languedoc-Roussillon (Hérault)

2318

Domaine de Gajan****
rue de Pie Bouquet
+33 (0)4-66809430
2/4 - 30/9
info@
campingdomainedegajan.com

3ha 46**T**(80-120m²) 16A CEE

1 ACD**G**IJKL**P**S
2 BCFSTVWXY
3 AGHJRU**W**
4 (C+G)
(Q+R+T+U+V+X+Z 1/5-30/9)
5 **A**BEFGJLMPUZ
6 ACEGJ(N 2,5km)OTV

A spacious campsite with combined swimming pool, terrace and cafe. Central location. Plenty of shade under oak trees. Not far from the River Bénovie for fishing and within walking distance of Boisseron with its small old centre. Between the mountains and the sea. Great for walking.

A9, exit Lunel. Then about 7 km towards Boisseron. Follow signs in Boisseron and turn right before the bridge. 250m to the campsite.

CC € 15 *2/4-5/7 27/8-30/9*

N 43°46'1'' E 4°4'28''

Camurac, F-11340 / Languedoc-Roussillon (Aude)

2319

Les Sapins**
+33 (0)4-68203811
1/1 - 1/11, 15/12 - 31/12
info@lessapins-camurac.com

3,5ha 72**T**(80-100m²) 10A CEE

1 A**G**IJKLNO**P**ST
2 KLRVWXY
3 AGHIJN**OPQ**RUW
4 (**A** 1/7-30/8)
(B+G 15/6-15/9) (Q)
(R+T 1/5-30/9)
(U+V 1/5-1/11)
(X 15/4-1/11) Z
5 **AB**DFGIJMNPQRUZ
6 EJ(N 6km)OV

Welcoming campsite in beautiful countryside with lovely views. The Cathar Ruin of Montaillou is visible. Various walks through pretty flower meadows and small villages. Nearby skiing area (altitude 1625m).

From Quillon follow Ax and Belcaire. Via Ax from dir. Quillon in Camurac follow 'Piste de ski' signs. Right after 1 km. Route for large vehicles via Fax-Lavelanet (D117). Then D117 dir. Belesta and D16/D29 and D613 until the 'Piste de ski' signs.

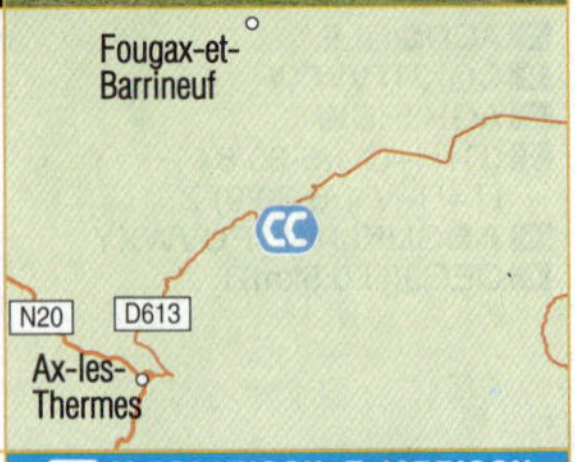

CC € 13 *1/1-3/7 29/8-1/11*

N 42°47'30'' E 1°55'30''

Canet-en-Roussillon, F-66140 / Languedoc-Roussillon (Pyrénées-Orientales) 2320

Ma Prairie****
avenue des Coteaux
+33 (0)4-68732617
+33 (0)4-68732882
16/4 - 24/9
contact@maprairie.com

4,5ha 153T(65-100m²) 10A CEE

1 ACDFIJKLOPST
2 GRVXY
3 BFGKNRUV
4 (C+G 15/5-15/9) JK (Q 1/6-15/9) (T+U 1/7-31/8) (X+Z 1/5-15/9)
5 ABFGIJKLMNOPUWXYZ
6 AEGHK(N 0,2km)ORTV

A friendly family campsite 3 km from the beach with many amenities, some of which are located on the other side of a small road, such as the lovely heated swimming pool, restaurant, playground and fitness room. Ma Prairie is perfect for day trips out to the Pyrenees and Spain.

A9, exit 41 Perpignan-Centre direction Le Barcarès/Canet via the D83 and D81. Then D617 direction St. Nazaire. Right at roundabout after the St. Nazaire exit on the D11.

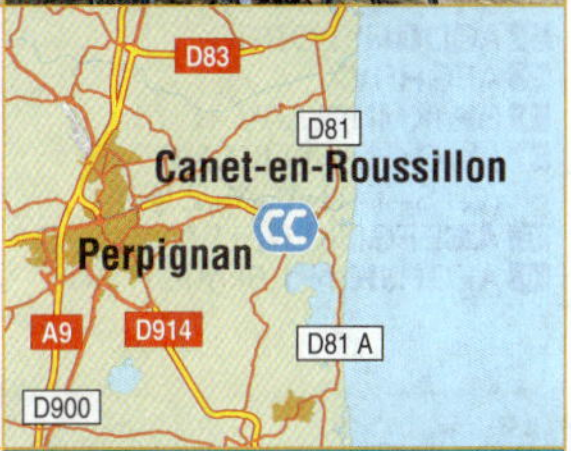

CC €17 16/4-8/7 27/8-23/9 7=6

N 42°42'4'' E 2°59'54''

Canet-en-Roussillon, F-66140 / Languedoc-Roussillon (Pyrénées-Orientales) 2321

Mar Estang****
Voie des Flamants Roses
+33 (0)4-68803553
+33 (0)4-68733294
16/4 - 18/9
contactme@marestang.com

13ha 150T(60-100m²) 6A CEE

1 ACDGIJKLMOPS
2 ADEFGRSUVX
3 ABFGKMNRUVY
4 (C+F+H) IJK (Q+S+T+U+V+X+Y+Z)
5 ABEFGIJKLMNOPU
6 ACDEGHKM(N 2km)RTV

Large campsite located between the Canet-en-Roussillon nature reserve and a beautiful beach, accessible via a tunnel (100m) directly from the campsite. Ample amenities including lovely heated swimming pools. Close to the centre of Canet and close to the Pyrenees and Spain.

A9, exit 41 dir. Le Barcarès and Canet-en-Roussillon. Continue towards St. Cyprien or Plage Sud from Canet. Campsite located south of Canet on the right.

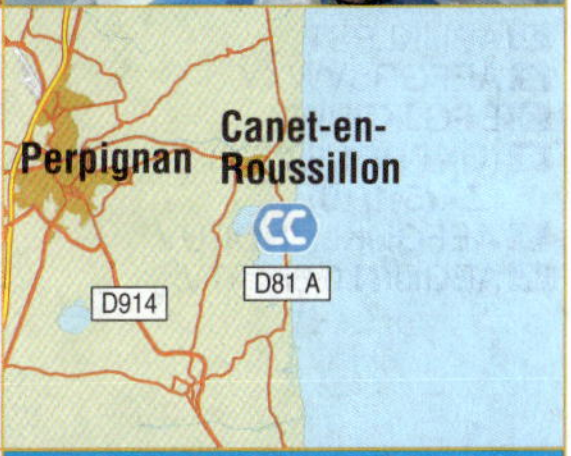

CC €17 16/4-9/7 29/8-18/9

N 42°40'31'' E 3°1'52''

Canet-Plage, F-66140 / Languedoc-Roussillon (Pyrénées-Orientales) 2322

Le Bosquet***
av. des Anneaux du Roussillon
+33 (0)4-68802380
+33 (0)4-68806953
2/4 - 9/10
campinglebosquet@club-internet.fr

1,5ha 71T(70-100m²) 10A

1 ACGIJKLOPST
2 CEGRSTVWXY
3 ABFGKNRUWY
4 (B+G) K (Q+R+T+U+V+Z)
5 ABEFGJLMNPUV
6 AEGJK(N 1,5km)RTV

A small, modest, intimate campsite with sunny and shaded pitches, with a snack bar and a lovely swimming pool. 400m to the beach via an entrance directly from the campsite. A 5 minute walk to the pleasure boat harbour and a ferry to the centre of Canet-Plage.

A9 exit 41 Perpignan-Centre dir. Barcarès/Canet via D83 and D81. In Canet dir. Ste Marie at first roundabout then immediately right direction 'Zone Artisanale las Bigues' and follow camping signs.

CC €15 2/4-1/7 27/8-9/10 7=6

N 42°42'33'' E 3°1'59''

Cap-d'Agde, F-34300 / Languedoc-Roussillon (Hérault)

2323

Camping Mer et Soleil****
88 chemin de Notre Dame-St. Martin
+33 (0)4-67942114
FAX +33 (0)4-67948194
16/4 - 2/10
@ contact@camping-mer-soleil.com

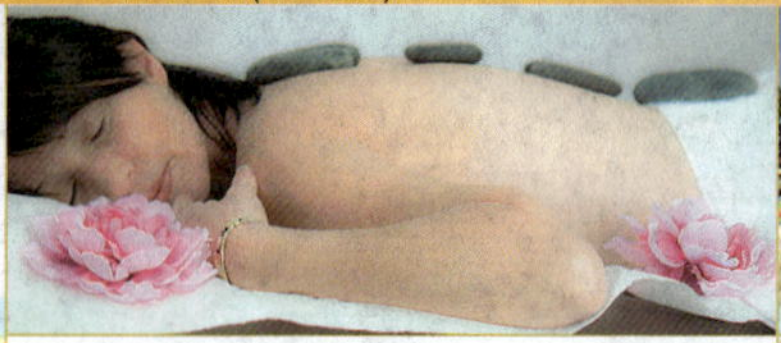

9ha 83**T**(60-100m²) 6A CEE

1 ACD**G**IJKLO**P**RS
2 AFGRSVX
3 B**F**JKMNRUVW
4 (A+C+H) IJK**LNP** (Q+S+T+U+V+Y+Z)
5 **AB**EFGIJKLNPUVWZ
6 AFGHJ**K**(N 1,5km)ORTV

A comfortable campsite in the tourist resort of Cap d'Agde. There is an extensive leisure pool complex, also suitable for small children. Moreover the site has a spa/wellness centre for which all campers receive a 10% discount. All facilities are available for campers right from the opening date until the closing date.

From the A9 (or N312) exit 34 Cap d'Agde, then Rochelongue. Turn right after bridge over Hérault, Rochelongue. Follow camping signs.

€ 17 16/4-2/7 1/9-2/10

N 43°17'11'' E 3°28'41''

Cap-d'Agde, F-34300 / Languedoc-Roussillon (Hérault)

2324

La Mer***
route de Rochelongue
+33 (0)4-67947221
FAX +33 (0)4-67947207
9/4 - 8/10
@ camping-la-mer@wanadoo.fr

3ha 93**T**(60-90m²) 6A

1 A**F**IJKLPST
2 AEFGRSVWXY
3 B**F**GJKRUWY
4 (Q+T+V 1/5-25/9) (Z 1/5-1/10)
5 **A**EFGIJKLMNOPUV
6 AEGIJ(N 0,8km)TV

Very peaceful family campsite where the camper is well taken care of. A paved footpath leads from the campsite right to the sea. The spacious beach is 100 metres away. Free WiFi on the terrace.

A9 exit Agde N312, leads into D112, exit Agde/Rochelongue. Direction Rochelongue at roundabout. Left at 2nd roundabout. At T junction turn right, about 500 metres.

€ 15 9/4-6/7 1/9-8/10

N 43°16'43'' E 3°28'43''

Cap-d'Agde, F-34300 / Languedoc-Roussillon (Hérault)

2325

Le Rochelongue****
route de Rochelongue
+33 (0)4-67212551
9/4 - 9/10
@ le.rochelongue@wanadoo.fr

2,5ha 46**T**(80-90m²) 10A CEE

1 ACD**G**IJKLM**P**ST
2 AEFGRSVWX
3 B**F**JRUWY
4 (C+H 1/5-30/9) (Q+R+T+U+V 15/5-15/9) (X 1/5-30/9) (Z 15/5-15/9)
5 **AB**EFGIJKLMNOPUVWXYZ
6 AEGK(N 0,4km)ORTV

Located on the edge of Cap d'Agde, close to the shopping centre and 500m from the sea. Perfectly suitable for children with its 'safe beach' (a wide stretch of shallow water). Lovely swimming pool with children's pool. 800m from a large water park (Aqualand), a lovely golf course with 24 holes and a disco. Entertainment for all ages!

On the A9 take the Cap d'Agde exit lane. 800m from Cap d'Agde follow camping signs showing Le Rochelongue.

€ 15 9/4-10/7 1/9-9/10 7=6, 14=12, 21=17

N 43°16'45'' E 3°28'53''

Cardet, F-30350 / Languedoc-Roussillon (Gard) — 2326

Beau Rivage**
22 chemin du Bosquet
+33 (0)4-66830248
1/4 - 1/10
receptie@
campingbeaurivage.com

5ha 124**T**(85-125m²) 6A

1 ACD**G**IJKLOPQ
2 ABCLMNRSTWXY
3 B**F**GHJK**MNOP**RU**WX**
4 (C+G+Q 1/5-1/10) (R)
(T+U+V+X 1/5-1/10) Z
5 **A**CDEFGIJKLMNPQRUZ
6 ACEGHJ**K**(N 0,5km)OV

A lovely campsite right by the river. Spacious pitches, heated swimming pool, pleasant pizzeria and modern heated toilet facilities. The river is suitable for prospecting (searching for gold). The area is perfect for walks, cycling tours or visiting medieval villages and small markets. Good WiFi throughout the campsite.

From Alès follow signs to Nîmes, 2nd exit direction Ledignan/Ners, then direction Anduze. After intersection with D6110, 4rd exit in Cardet.

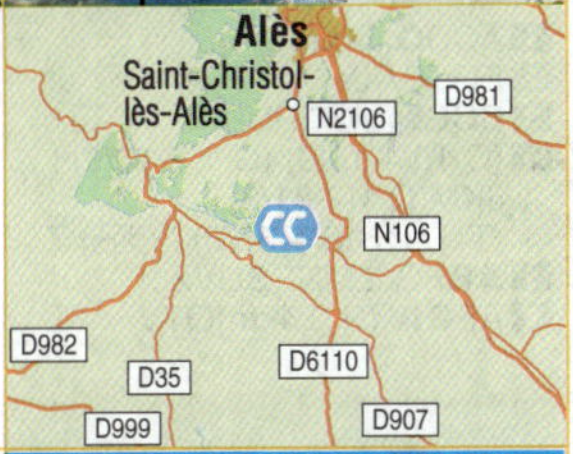

CC € 15 *1/4-8/7 25/8-1/10*

N 44°1'40'' E 4°4'27''

Castries, F-34160 / Languedoc-Roussillon (Hérault) — 2327

de Fondespierre***
277 chemin Pioch Viala
+33 (0)4-67912003
4/1 - 19/12
accueil@campingfondespierre.fr

2,1ha 59**T**(60-120m²) 16A

1 ACD**F**IJLP
2 FIJKTVWXY
3 BG**M**NRU
4 (C 1/5-15/10) (Q+R) Z
5 **AB**FGJLNPUVZ
6 ACEG**K**(N 2km)ORT

The campsite has an exceptional location just 3 km from the motorway. Breathe the tranquillity and enjoy the many attractions: Montpellier's historic centre, wine regions, the Camargue, many cycling and hiking routes around the aqueduct and the castle near the campsite.

A9, exit 28 direction Vendargues, turn right and follow signs to Castries. Take D610 from Castries and 800 metres past the village turn left towards 'Domaine de Fondespierre' and follow the signs.

CC € 17 *4/1-9/7 27/8-18/12*

N 43°41'38'' E 3°59'46''

Chastanier, F-48300 / Languedoc-Roussillon (Lozère) — 2328

Du Pont de Braye***
Lieu dit de Braye
+33 (0)4-66695304
FAX +33 (0)5-31600523
1/5 - 20/9
accueil@
camping-lozere-naussac.fr

1,5ha 28**T**(80-100m²) 6A

1 ACD**G**IJKLMP
2 CJKLRVWXY
3 AB**F**GHKRU**WX**
4 (A 7/7-24/8)
(Q+R+T+U+V) Z
5 **AB**CDFGIJKLMNPUVWZ
6 ACEG**K**(N 10km)TV

It's great to camp on the banks of the Chapeauroux, a little river in the Margueride which can be tumultuous at times. Very quiet roads lead to this secluded, but easily accessible spot. You will be welcomed by a very enthusiastic and helpful owner.

N88 southwards from Langogne towards Naussac, left at the crossroads. Along the D34 past Chastanier. Campsite signposted.

CC € 11 *1/5-8/7 27/8-19/9*

N 44°43'32'' E 3°44'52''

Clapiers, F-34830 / Languedoc-Roussillon (Hérault)

2329

Le Plein Air des Chênes****
avenue Georges Frêche
+33 (0)4-67020253
FAX +33 (0)4-67594219
1/4 - 8/10
pleinairdeschenes@sandaya.fr

8ha 75T(50-80m²) 10A

1 ACD**G**IJKLMOP
2 FGJTVXY
3 BCG**MNOQ**RU
4 (C 10/4-10/9) (G 1/6-10/9) I JKM(Q 1/7-31/8) (T+U+X 13/4-30/9) (Y) Z
5 **AB**FGJLMNP**S**UVZ
6 AEG**IK**(N 0,4km)QTV

Quiet family campsite. On level grounds under the shade of trees. A good starting point for visiting Montpellier. CampingCard ACSI campers are received on comfort pitches.

A9, exit Vendargues. Continue towards Jacou/ Clapiers via D21. Campsite on the D112 in Clapiers, signposted.

CC € 17 *1/4-1/7 29/8-8/10*

N 43°39'6'' E 3°53'46''

Collioure, F-66190 / Languedoc-Roussillon (Pyrénées-Orientales)

2330

Camping Les Amandiers**
route des Campings
+33 (0)4-68811469
1/4 - 9/10
contact@
camping-les-amandiers.com

1,8ha 58T(60-90m²) 10A CEE

1 ACD**G**IJKL**P**ST
2 BEHJNQRVWXY
3 AGHRWY
4 (Q+R+T+U+V+X+Y+Z)
5 **AB**GIJKLMNOPUVZ
6 ACDEGJ(N 1,5km)OTV

Les Amandiers ** campsite is a natural, quiet and shady departure point for trips to Spain or the Pyrenees. The beautiful village of Collioure is at walking distance and the 'La Crique de l'Ouille' beach is 200 metres from the campsite.

A9 to Perpignan, exit 42 Perpignan Sud to Argelès-sur-Mer. D914 to Collioure as far as exit 13 Collioure par la corniche. Follow camping signs to Collioure then turn left.

CC € 17 *1/4-10/7 1/9-8/10*

N 42°31'53'' E 3°4'18''

Colombiers, F-34440 / Languedoc-Roussillon (Hérault)

2331

Les Peupliers***
7 promenade de l'Ancien Stade
FAX +33 (0)4-67370526
1/1 - 31/12
contact@
camping-colombiers.com

1ha 50T(75-100m²) 10A CEE

1 ACD**G**IJKLMOPST
2 FRTVWXY
3 BHJR
4 (B+G 1/6-30/9) (Q 1/4-30/10) (T+U+V+X+Z 1/6-30/9)
5 **AB**DEFGJLNPQRUZ
6 ACEGJ**K**(N 0,6km)OTV

A small attractive campsite within walking distance of the lovely village of Colombiers and the Canal du Midi. Open all year. Perfect for trips in the area and the Mediterranean beaches around Béziers. Heated toilets in winter. 20 minutes free WiFi per day.

A9, exit 36 Béziers-West. Then towards D64 Castres/Mazamet at the roundabout, third road on right towards D11 Capastang/Montady. In Montady at the Colombiers-Les Peupliers roundabout, do not follow your SatNav!

CC € 15 *1/1-1/7 29/8-31/12*

N 43°19'6'' E 3°8'35''

Corbès/Anduze, F-30140 / Languedoc-Roussillon (Gard) — 2332

Cévennes-Provence***
Corbès-Thoiras
+33 (0)4-66617310
FAX +33 (0)4-66616074
20/3 - 1/10
@ info@campingcp.com

30ha 226T(80-200m²) 10A CEE

1 ACDGIJKLPST
2 ABCGJKLMNORSVWXY
3 BGHJKMNPQRUWX
4 (A) (Q+S 1/4-1/10)
(T+U+V+X+Y+Z 1/5-5/9)
5 ABCDEFGHIJKLMNOPQRU
VZ
6 CEGHIJ(N 2km)OPRTUV

Simply stunning, very peaceful natural campsite located between two branches of the Gardon river. Swimming in the clear water of the river. Because of the micro-climate there are more than 120 kinds of trees and many different plants. New toilet block since 2014.

Leave the A7 at Bollène. At Alès drive in the direction of Montpellier. In Anduze take the D907 direction St. Jean-du-Gard. 3 km after Anduze turn to the right at the bus stop (D284 Rte de Corbes).

CC €17 20/3-30/6 1/9-30/9

N 44°4'41'' E 3°57'53''

Elne/St. Cyprien, F-66200 / Languedoc-Roussillon (Pyrénées-Orientales) — 2333

Le Florida****
route Latour Bas Elne
+33 (0)4-68378088
FAX +33 (0)4-68378076
1/1 - 31/12
@ info@campingleflorida.com

7ha 70T(100-135m²) 5A CEE

1 ACDFIJKLMPS
2 GRTVXY
3 BFGMNPRU
4 (B+G 4/4-30/10) J
(Q 1/4-30/9)
(T+U+V 1/5-15/9)
(Z 1/4-30/9)
5 ABDFGIJKLMNOPUWZ
6 ACDEGHK(N 0,2km)TUV

Le Florida campsite, between the sea and the mountains, offers plenty of leisure options and is great for tourist trips out in the area: Cathar castles, Le Perthus on the Spanish border, Carcassonne or Barcelona. The camping part is open all year and one of the toilet blocks is heated.

A9, exit Perpignan-Sud direction Argelès-sur-Mer. Take exit 7 from th N114 to Latour-Bas-Elne via D11 direction Elne-centre. Then via D40 direction St. Cyprien.

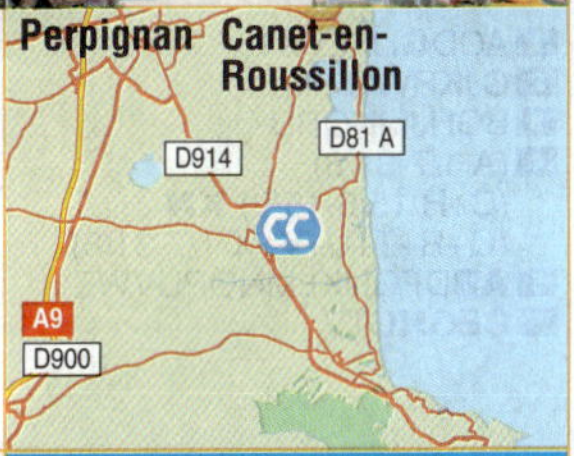

CC €17 1/1-2/7 27/8-31/12 7=6, 14=12, 21=18

N 42°36'26'' E 2°59'28''

Err, F-66800 / Languedoc-Roussillon (Pyrénées-Orientales) — 2334

Las Closas***
1 place St. Genis
+33 (0)4-68047142
1/1 - 25/9, 22/10 - 31/12
@ reception@
camping-las-closas.com

2ha 114T(< 100m²) 6A

1 ACDFIJKLOPQ
2 KRVY
3 BGRW
4 (A 15/7-31/8)
(B 15/6-15/9) J(V 1/6-1/9)
5 ACGIJKLMNPUV
6 EGKRT

Las Closas campsite is located in the village of Err with views of Pic Carlit and Puigmal. 100m from the heated municipal swimming pool. Enjoy the natural surroundings and the extensive walking trails in this mountainous area. A visit to the El Segre Gorge at Llo is a must.

The campsite is signposted at the exit Err on the N116 from Mont-Louis to Bourg-Madame.

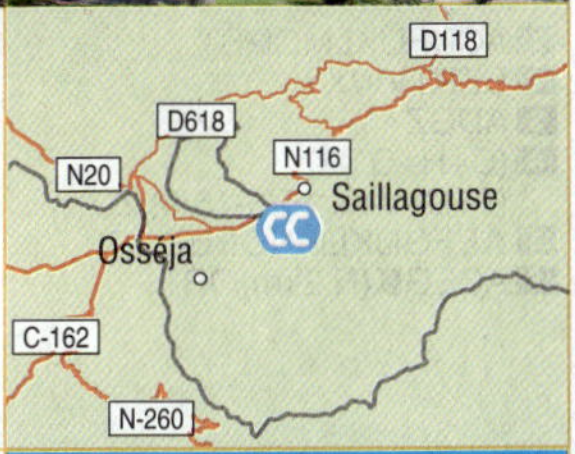

CC €15 1/5-3/7 27/8-25/9

N 42°26'26'' E 2°1'55''

Espira-de-Conflent, F-66320 / Languedoc-Roussillon (Pyrénées-Orientales)

2335

Le Canigou***
+33 (0)4-68058540
25/3 - 30/10
canigou@yahoo.com

4ha 115T(100m²) 10A

1 ACD**G**IJKLMOPS
2 CIORTVXY
3 AGINRUWX
4 (A 1/7-31/8) (Q+R+T+U)
(V 1/7-1/10) (X)
(Z 1/7-1/10)
5 **AB**CFGIJKMNOPU
6 CEGJ(N 10km)OV

The campsite is set in an area where a whole new landscape opens up beyond every mountain, offering numerous walking routes. Adventurous excursions to Canigou Peak, visit the Gorges du Llech in a 4x4 Jeep. Dutch owner.

At Perpignan N116 direction Prades. Turn left about 2.5 km after Vinça. Espira-de-Conflent is signposted.

CC € 15 *25/3-4/7 22/8-30/10*

N 42°37'0" E 2°30'5"

Estavar/Cerdagne, F-66800 / Languedoc-Roussillon (Pyrénées-Orientales)

2336

L'Enclave***
2 rue des Vynials
+33 (0)4-68047227
+33 (0)4-68040715
1/1 - 5/10, 1/12 - 31/12
contact@camping-lenclave.com

4ha 175T(80-130m²) 10A

1 ACD**G**IJKLPST
2 CJKRVXY
3 BGHJMNQRU
4 (A 1/7-31/8)
(C+H 15/6-15/9) **KN**
(Q+R+T+U+V+X 1/7-31/8)
5 **AB**DFGIJKLMNOPUVWZ
6 CEG**K**OTV

This peacefully located campsite is not far from Font Romeu (15 minutes) and the Spanish enclave of Llívia (5 minutes). Marked out and unchallenging walking routes, fishing opportunities and plenty of nature make this campsite an ideal place to stay. Swimming pool.

From Puigcerda/Saillagouse N154 direction Llivia. Then follow the Estavar and camping signs. Campsite located on the D33.

CC € 15 *1/4-5/7 22/8-5/10 7=6, 14=12*

N 42°28'8" E 1°59'55"

Fabrègues, F-34690 / Languedoc-Roussillon (Hérault)

2337

Le Botanic***
Launac-le-Vieux
+33 (0)4-67855318
1/4 - 10/10
contact@
camping-le-botanic.com

2ha 62T(90-180m²) 10A CEE

1 ACDFIJKLMO**P**ST
2 DFRTVWXY
3 ADGZ
4 (C+H+Q)
(T+U+V+X 15/6-15/9) Z
5 **A**EFGIJKLMNOPUZ
6 ACEG**K**(N 2km)ORT

Very well-maintained ecological campsite with exceptional advantages such as its location near Montpellier, the sea and the interior. The campsite has a unique natural lagoon with fine sandy beach.

A9, exit 32 or 33. Between Fabrègues and Gigean on the D613 towards Cournonterral. Campsite 800m on the left.

CC € 15 *1/4-5/7 25/8-10/10*

N 43°32'28" E 3°44'51"

Fitou, F-11510 / Languedoc-Roussillon (Aude) 2338

Le Fun***
Domaine des Bergeries
+33 (0)4-68457197
26/3 - 31/10
contact@lefun-camping.com

10ha 100T(80-180m²) 6A CEE

1 ACD**F**IJKLMP
2 DFIKLRTUVWXY
3 BGMNUW
4 (C+H 1/5-30/9) (Q+R 🔑) (T+U 1/7-31/8) (Z 🔑)
5 AEGJLNPUV
6 CDEGJ**K**(N 2km)TV

This campsite, located on the Leucate lagoon offers watersports opportunities such as surfing and kite surfing. The site also has lovely views.

A9 exit 40 direction Perpignan via D6009. Campsite signposted.

CC € 17 *26/3-3/7 1/9-31/10*

N 42°54'51'' E 2°59'56''

Fleury-d'Aude, F-11560 / Languedoc-Roussillon (Aude) 2339

Yelloh! Naturiste La Grande Cosse****
Saint-Pierre-la-Mer
+33 (0)4-68336187
FAX +33 (0)4-68333223
16/4 - 16/10
contact@grandecosse.com

15ha 325T(100-130m²) 10A CEE

1 ACD**G**IJKLMPST
2 AELRSTVWX
3 BGJKMRUVY
4 (C+G+Q+S+U+V+X+Y+Z 🔑)
5 **AB**FGIJLMNOPUWZ
6 ACEGHI**K**(N 5km)ORV

This site is located between Béziers and the Pyrenees in a large sheltered naturist area by the sea. A campsite with a fine, friendly atmosphere. An attentive reception in various languages and an infrastructure of the highest category. Well appointed toilets spread over these large, well maintained grounds. Renovated, heated pool.

A9 exit Béziers-Ouest direction Béziers. Then to Lespignan/Fleury. Straight ahead at roundabout towards Les Cabanes. Camping sign after ± 3 km.

CC € 17 *16/4-8/7 1/9-16/10*

N 43°12'21'' E 3°12'39''

Florac, F-48400 / Languedoc-Roussillon (Lozère) 2340

Pont du Tarn***
route de Pont de Montvert, D998
+33 (0)4-66451826
1/4 - 1/11
contact@camping-florac.com

5,5ha 153T(80-150m²) 10A CEE

1 ACD**G**IJKLMOPS
2 ACKLMNORTVWXY
3 BGHIJNRU**W**X
4 (C+H 8/5-15/9) (Q 🔑) (T+U+X 9/5-31/8) Z
5 **AB**DFGIJKLMNOPRUVXYZ
6 ABCEGK(N 1,5km)ORTV

With direct access to the natural beaches of the Tarn, the wooded location, the wonderful countryside and just 5 minutes from the centre of Florac and its shops; this campsite is a quiet spot to enjoy the water, sun and nature. Ideal for staying with the family. Excellent services and amenities.

A75, exit 39 direction Florac. Then take the N106 and D998.

CC € 15 *1/4-3/7 28/8-31/10* 7=6

N 44°20'7'' E 3°35'26''

Fontès, F-34320 / Languedoc-Roussillon (Hérault)

iD **2341**

L'Evasion***
route de Cabrières
+33 (0)4-67253200
14/3 - 2/11
cordierseverine@hotmail.fr

2,7ha 35**T**(80-120m²) 10A CEE

1 ACD**G**IJL**P**ST
2 FJKRSTVWX
3 BDHU
4 (B 1/5-15/9)
(Q+R+T+U+V+X+Z)
5 ABEFGIJLMNPUVXZ
6 AEGK(N 0,4km)OTV

Fontès offers an unusual mediterranean micro climate. Magical landscapes and beautiful cultural towns close by.

A75, from north exit 58, from south exit 59 towards Adissan. After Adissan direction Fontès. In Fontès D124 towards Cabrières. Site is located on this road.

CC € 15 *14/3-9/7 26/8-2/11*

N 43°32'51'' E 3°22'48''

Frontignan-Plage, F-34110 / Languedoc-Roussillon (Hérault)

iD **2342**

Camping les Tamaris*****
140 avenue d'Ingril
+33 (0)4-67434477
FAX +33 (0)4-67189790
25/3 - 8/10
lestamaris@sandaya.fr

4ha 121**T**(65-110m²) 10A CEE

1 ACD**G**IJKLMOPQ
2 ADEGRSTUVWXY
3 BGJK**P**RUVWY
4 (C+H+Q+S+T+U+V+X+Z)
5 **AB**DEFGIJKLMNOPUWXYZ
6 AEGHJ**K**(N 6km)ORTV

Your guarantee of a peaceful holiday just outside the lively Frontignan-Plage. Very comfortable campsite right on a lovely sandy beach with a beautiful wetland nature and bird sanctuary on the other side. Fairylike sunrise and sunsets! All facilities available from the opening date till the closing date! Suitable for excursions in the region.

The campsite is located on the D50. At the sign showing campsites follow the sign to the left. Well signposted from then on.

CC € 19 *25/3-1/7 29/8-8/10*

N 43°27'0'' E 3°48'21''

Fuilla, F-66820 / Languedoc-Roussillon (Pyrénées-Orientales)

iD **2343**

Le Rotja***
avenue de la Rotja
+33 (0)4-68965275
2/4 - 15/10
camping@camping-lerotja.com

1,6ha 75**T**(80-100m²) 6A

1 ACD**G**IJKLMPST
2 BFKRTUVXY
3 BGHJR**W**
4 (A 15/6-15/9)
(B+G 1/5-15/10)
(Q+R+T) (X 1/5-12/10) Z
5 **A**CEFGIJKLMNPRUWY
6 EGHJK(N 3km)OTV

Peacefully located attractive campsite in the Apple Valley of La Rotja river. Plenty of walking opportunities with many places of historical interest. Mild climate in the early and late seasons. The Dutch owner also speaks English, French and German. The campsite is positioned exactly on the Green Meridian and this is marked by a post on the site.

Take the N116 to Villefranche direction Mont-Louis. After about 500 metres, past Villefranche, take the exit to Fuilla.

CC € 17 *2/4-2/7 27/8-15/10*

N 42°33'45'' E 2°21'34''

Gallargues-le-Montueux, F-30660 / Languedoc-Roussillon (Gard)

2344

Les Amandiers****
20 rue des Stades
+33 (0)4-66352802
FAX +33 (0)4-66514857
26/3 - 25/9
@ camping-lesamandiers@orange.fr

3ha 87T(70-120m²) 16A CEE

1 AC**G**IJKLMOPST
2 FGRSTVWXY
3 BGHJKMN**OP**RUV**W**
4 (C+H 1/5-30/9) KLNO
(Q 1/6-31/8)
(T+U+V+X+Z 1/6-27/8)
5 **A**BEFJKLMNPUZ
6 ACEG**K**(N 4km)OTV

The campsite is located 2 km from the A9 motorway (exit 26) within walking distance of an old village on a hill. Several types of (heated) pools, spa, fitness room, sun terrace and large camping pitches. Valerie offers you a warm welcome.

A9, exit 26 to Gallargues. Well signposted from there.

CC € 17 26/3-25/6 29/8-25/9 7=6

N 43°43'0'' E 4°10'1''

Grau-d'Agde, F-34300 / Languedoc-Roussillon (Hérault)

2345

Les Sablettes***
55 chemin de Baluffe
+33 (0)4-67943665
1/4 - 30/9
@ lessablettes@hotmail.fr

2,5ha 84T(60-100m²) 10A CEE

1 ACD**F**IJKLMPST
2 AFGSVWXY
3 B**F**GJKRUW
4 (B+G) J
(Q+T+U+V+X+Z)
5 **A**FGJLMNPQUXZ
6 ACEGJ**K**L(N 1,5km)TV

A peaceful family campsite 800 metres from Agde beach. The site has a large swimming pool with slide. Free WiFi at the bar in the restaurant. Trips out from the campsite to Agde or Sète. An afternoon sailing on the Canal du Midi is most enjoyable.

A9 exit Cap d'Agde (D112). Then take Grau d'Agde exit and 2nd exit at the roundabout with statue. 1st exit at next roundabout and follow camping signs.

CC € 13 1/4-10/7 27/8-30/9 7=6, 14=11, 17=13

N 43°17'17'' E 3°27'46''

Junas, F-30250 / Languedoc-Roussillon (Gard)

2346

L'Olivier***
route de Congénies
+33 (0)4-66803952
25/3 - 14/10
@ camping.lolivier@wanadoo.fr

1ha 29T(50-70m²) 10A CEE

1 ACD**G**IJKL**P**S
2 BGSTVWXY
3 AGHJMQR**W**
4 (B 1/5-30/9) (G 1/6-31/8)
(Q 1/7-31/8) (R+T+V+Z)
5 **A**EFGIJKLMNPUVZ
6 AEG**K**(N 2km)ORT

Intimate campsite with differences in altitude, plenty of shade from e.g. 100-year-old olive trees. There's a medieval village nearby. Beautiful for cycling and walking.

A9, exit 26 dir. Sommières. Then D22 to Junas. Follow signs.

CC € 15 25/3-8/7 27/8-14/10

N 43°46'12'' E 4°7'33''

Junas, F-30250 / Languedoc-Roussillon (Gard) — 2347

Les Chênes**
95 chemin des Tuileries Basses
+33 (0)4-66809907
FAX +33 (0)4-66513323
9/4 - 16/10
@ chenes@wanadoo.fr

1,7ha 69**T**(80-100m²) 10A CEE

1 ACD**G**IJKL**P**ST
2 BFIRTVWXY
3 AGHJNR**W**
4 (B+G 15/5-16/10) (Q+R+T+U)
5 **A**EFGJKNPUVZ
6 AEGH**K**(N 5km)OT

Gilles and Nathalie will welcome you on holiday in the south of France in calm and informal surroundings, with a lovely swimming pool under the Languedoc sun in the shade of its own oak trees. Located 5 km from Sommières and 2 km from the 'voie verte' (lovely cycle route), and 30 minutes from the beaches at Nîmes and Montpellier at the foot of the Cévennes.

On the A9 take the Gallargues exit, continue through village towards Sommières (6 km). Campsite signposted from there.

CC € 15 9/4-9/7 27/8-16/10

N 43°45'41'' E 4°7'16''

La Franqui/Leucate, F-11370 / Languedoc-Roussillon (Aude) — 2348

La Franqui**
chemin des Coussoules
+33 (0)4-68457493
FAX +33 (0)4-68453688
1/4 - 18/9
@ franqui@originalcamping.com

3,5ha 256**T**(60-80m²) 6A CEE

1 ACD**G**IJKLMOPST
2 AEFSTVWX
3 AWY
4 (Q+R+U 1/7-31/8)
5 **A**FGIJKLMNOPUZ
6 AEG(N 2km)T

La Franqui is an unpretentious but attractive campsite with direct access to the wide flat beach and the sea. Beach surfing is a fun activity on the wide flat beach. The pitches are not all that big, but reasonably well shaded and marked out by beautiful planting.

A9 direction Perpignan, exit 40 Leucate. Stay on D627 to La Franqui exit. Follow camping signs at La Franqui.

CC € 13 1/4-1/7 28/8-17/9

N 42°56'37'' E 3°1'50''

La Roque-sur-Cèze, F-30200 / Languedoc-Roussillon (Gard) — 2349

La Vallée Verte****
route De Donnat
+33 (0)4-66790889
23/4 - 24/9
@ info@la-vallee-verte.com

36ha 80**T**(75-100m²) 6A CEE

1 ACDGIJKLPST
2 ABCIJKMNORSTVXY
3 ABGMNRUWX
4 (A) (B 25/4-19/9) (G) J(Q+R+U+V+Y+Z)
5 **A**FGJLNPUV
6 AEGHJ(N 2km)V

Terraced campsite set in natural surroundings. Spacious pitches with privacy and beautiful views. New sanitation. Attractive restaurant. Swimming and fishing in the Cèze. Terrace with views of the swimming pool, tennis court and petanque.

A7 exit Bollène/Pont-St-Esprit. Take D994 direction Pont-St-Esprit. Then N86 direction Bagnols-sur-Cèze. D6 to Alès. After 3.5 km D143 direction La Roque-sur-Cèze. 1.5 km past Donnat turn right. At fork turn right to La Roque. After 1.5 km site on the right.

CC € 17 23/4-1/7 27/8-18/9

N 44°10'53'' E 4°32'7''

La Roque-sur-Cèze, F-30200 / Languedoc-Roussillon (Gard)

2350

Les Cascades****
+33 (0)4-66827297
+33 (0)4-66826851
9/4 - 2/10
infos@campinglescascades.com

6ha 76T(90-120m²) 10A CEE

1 ACD**G**IJKL**P**ST
2 BCDIJLNQRTVXY
3 AGHNRWXZ
4 (C+G+Q+S) (T 1/6-31/8) (U+V) (X 24/4-30/9) (Z)
5 **AB**EFGIJKLMNOPUWYZ
6 DEGH**IK**(N 5km)RTV

A particularly friendly family campsite on predominantly level and shaded grounds on the banks of the River Cèze. Lovely beaches and wonderful swimming waters. The lovely waterfalls are an added attraction.

Accessible for caravans and large cars only, but easily, via the D6 Bagnols-Alès, exit Donnat (D143). Then 3 km further.

CC € 15 24/4-2/7 20/8-2/10 7=6, 14=11

N 44°11'19" E 4°31'31"

Langogne/Naussac, F-48300 / Languedoc-Roussillon (Lozère)

2351

Les Terrasses du Lac***
Lac de Naussac - D26
+33 (0)4-66692962
+33 (0)4-66692478
15/4 - 30/9
info@naussac.com

6ha 180T(80-140m²) 10A

1 AC**G**IJKLMPST
2 DIKLTUWXY
3 A**F**GHJ**M**NRU**W**Z
4 (C+H 15/6-15/9) (Q+R+T+U+Y) Z
5 **AB**CDFGIJKLMNPQUVWZ
6 CEG**I**K(N 2km)QTV

You can camp peacefully on the shores of a beautiful lake, not far from Langogne and with lovely views. You can enjoy endless walking and cycling in the Margueride, where typical villages lie scattered. Roman architecture and the Ardèche are not far away. You can enjoy delicious meals in the restaurant, which forms part of the campsite hotel.

N88, southwards from Langogne towards Naussac. Campsite indicated.

CC € 15 15/4-8/7 26/8-30/9

N 44°44'2" E 3°50'8"

Lansargues/Mauguio, F-34130 / Languedoc-Roussillon (Hérault)

2352

Le Fou du Roi***
chemin des Codoniers
+33 (0)4-67867808
1/4 - 15/10
campinglefouduroi@free.fr

1,9ha 36T(< 120m²) 10A CEE

1 ACDGIJKLMO**P**S
2 GRSTVWXY
3 A**F**GJRU**W**
4 (B+G 1/5-30/9) (Q 1/5-31/8) (R) (T+U 1/7-31/8) (Z 1/5-30/9)
5 **A**EFGJLMNPUWZ
6 ACEGJ**K**(N 0,5km)TV

A very modest campsite just 9.5 km from the Mediterranean, in a rural location and within walking distance of an old village.

From Lunel take the D24 to Lansargues/Mauguio. The campsite is signposted along the D24.

CC € 15 1/4-1/7 27/8-15/10

N 43°39'6" E 4°3'59"

Laroque-des-Albères, F-66740 / Languedoc-Roussillon (Pyrénées-Orientales)

2353

Les Albères***
route Moulin de Cassagnes
+33 (0)4-68892364
FAX +33 (0)4-68891430
19/3 - 24/9
lesalberes@cybelevacances.com

7ha 124**T**(50-90m²) 16A CEE

1 BCDEIJLST
2 GIJKRTVWX
3 ABGHKNU
4 (B+D+G) IJM
(Q+R 1/7-31/8)
(T+U+X+Z)
5 **A**FGIJKLMNPU
6 AEG**J**(N 0,9km)T

Homely campsite at the foot of the Eastern Pyrenees, located in a forest of cork oaks and mimosas. Leisure pool with many recreation amenities and wellness: a heated indoor pool, an outdoor pool, a slide and a whirlpool.

A9 exit 43 Le Boulou. Dir. Argelès-sur-Mer (D618). Exit Laroque-des-Albères. Follow this road for 3 km. Left at village dir. Sorède. Right at next roundabout. Then 500 metres.

CC € 15 19/3-2/7 28/8-24/9 14=11

N 42°31'26'' E 2°56'39''

Lasalle/Anduze, F-30460 / Languedoc-Roussillon (Gard)

2354

La Salendrinque***
route de St. Hippolyte-du-Fort
+33 (0)4-66852457
1/5 - 15/9
info@campinglasalendrinque.fr

2,5ha 77**T**(80-140m²) 10A CEE

1 ACD**G**IJKL**P**ST
2 ABCIJKLMRVWXY
3 BGHJRU**WX**
4 (C+H 15/5-15/9) (Q)
(T+U+V 15/6-15/9) Z
5 **A**CDEFGHIJKLMNOPQUXY
6 ACEGJ(N 1km)ORTV

Lovely, friendly campsite on a river with cascades. Pitches on a level section and on the hill. Good toilet facilities. Very friendly and welcoming reception. Free WiFi on terrace. Heated pool.

From Lyon-Bollène-Alès-Anduze-Lasalle-Rte. follow St. Hippolyte-du-Fort to the campsite left of the road. From Clermont-Ferrand, after the Millau bridge take exit 48 'Cornus-La Couvertoirade-Alzon-Le Vigan' Follow Alzon, Le Vigan , Ganges, Saint Hippolyte du Fort and Lasalle.

CC € 15 1/5-8/7 27/8-15/9

N 44°2'19'' E 3°51'42''

Latour-de-France, F-66720 / Languedoc-Roussillon (Pyrénées-Orientales)

2355

La Tour de France***
ave du Général de Gaulle
+33 (0)6-15142346
4/4 - 18/10
contact@camping-latourdefrance.fr

1,5ha 70**T**(50-120m²) 6A CEE

1 AB**F**IJLMP
2 CRTVXY
3 ABGJMRU
4 (B 15/6-15/9) (Q+R)
(T+V+W 1/7-31/8) Z
5 **A**FGJKMNPRUZ
6 DEGH(N 1km)TU

The campsite is located in the Catalan hinterland between the Mediterranean and the Pyrenees. Centrally located for trips out to the many Cathar sites and the wide beaches on the coast, including 'Le Barcarès'. Also the rocky coast towards Spain with beautiful Collioure is not far away.

Millas direction Estnagel. In Estnagel direction Latour-de-France. Campsite signposted on the D17.

CC € 13 4/4-4/7 30/8-18/10

N 42°45'57'' E 2°39'56''

Laurens, F-34480 / Languedoc-Roussillon (Hérault) 2356

Sites & Paysages L'Oliveraie****
chemin de Bédarieux
+33 (0)4-67902436
FAX +33 (0)4-67901120
1/3 - 31/10
@ oliveraie@free.fr

7ha 78T(85-150m²) 10A CEE

1 ACDFIJKLPST
2 JTVXY
3 BGHJMN**OP**QRU
4 (B+G+Q 1/6-30/9)
(S+T+U+V+X+Z 1/7-31/8)
5 **A**DEFGIJLNOPUVWXZ
6 ACEGI**K**(N 1,5km)ORT

The campsite is located at the entrance to the Parc Natural Regional du Haut Languedoc. Being only 30 km from the Mediterranean yet protected by the hills, this is an ideal place to stay in early and late seasons.

Campsite is located on a side-road of the D909. About 1.5 km north of Laurens. Along the D909 signs say 'Centre de Loisirs de l'Oliveraie'.

CC € 17 *1/3-9/7 27/8-31/10*

N 43°32'10" E 3°11'10"

Le Barcarès, F-66423 / Languedoc-Roussillon (Pyrénées-Orientales) 2357

California****
route de St. Laurent
+33 (0)4-68861608
FAX +33 (0)4-68861820
1/5 - 25/9
@ camping-california@wanadoo.fr

6ha 86T(70-100m²) 10A CEE

1 ACD**G**IJKLO**P**ST
2 FGLRTVWXY
3 ABGK**M**NRU
4 (C+G) J(Q+R+T+U)
(V 1/6-31/8) (X+Z)
5 **AB**EFGIJKLMNOPUW
6 ACGH**IJK**(N 1km)RTV

The attractive and well equipped California campsite is close to the extensive sandy beaches of the Mediterranean and lively Port-Barcarès. Lovely excursions can be made from here to the Pyrenees and/or Spain.

A9 exit Perpignan-Centre. Take the D83 in the direction of Le Barcarès as far as exit 9. Then drive via the D81 in the direction of Canet as far as the first exit St. Laurent, direction Le Barcarès-Village.

CC € 15 *1/5-10/7 28/8-25/9* *7=6, 14=12*

N 42°46'33" E 3°1'22"

Le Barcarès, F-66420 / Languedoc-Roussillon (Pyrénées-Orientales) 2358

Le Floride & l'Embouchure****
route de St. Laurent
+33 (0)4-68861175
FAX +33 (0)4-68860750
1/4 - 30/10
@ contact@floride.fr

12ha 186T(80-130m²) 10A

1 ACD**F**IJKL**P**ST
2 ACEFGTVXY
3 ABGNRUVWXY
4 (C+F+H) IJKM(Q)
(R 1/4-20/9) (T 1/7-31/8)
(U+V+X+Y 1/4-20/9) Z
5 **AB**EFGIJKLMNP**ST**UVXYZ
6 AGHKL(N 0,6km)O**P**RTV

The friendly site of Le Floride l'Embouchure is located between Lake Leucate and the Mediterranean. It has heated swimming pools, its own entrance to the beach and for an extra charge pitches with individual sanitary facilities.

A9 exit Perpignan-Centre. D83 direction Le Barcarès. Continue to exit 9 via D81 direction Canet. First exit St. Laurent direction Le Barcarès-Village.

CC € 15 *1/4-3/7 29/8-30/10*

N 42°46'44" E 3°1'47"

Le Barcarès, F-66420 / Languedoc-Roussillon (Pyrénées-Orientales)

2359

Le Pré Catalan****
route de St. Laurent
+33 (0)4-68861260
FAX +33 (0)4-68864017
29/4 - 19/9
info@precatalan.com

3ha 76T(80-100m²) 10A CEE

1 ACFIJKLPST
2 FRTVX
3 BGKMNRU
4 (C+H) M
(Q+R+T+U+V+X+Z)
5 **AB**FGIJKLMNOPUW
6 AG**IK**L(N 1,5km)OTV

An ideally located family campsite a 900m walk to the sandy Mediterranean beach and a few kilometres from the lakes at Leucate and Salses with countless watersports opportunities. You can enjoy the campsite swimming pool, but trips out to Spain and the Pyrenees are also recommended.

A9, exit 9 Perpignan-Centre. D83 direction Le Barcarès as far as exit 9. Via D81 direction Canet to the first exit St. Laurent-de la-Salanque, direction Le Barcarès-Village.

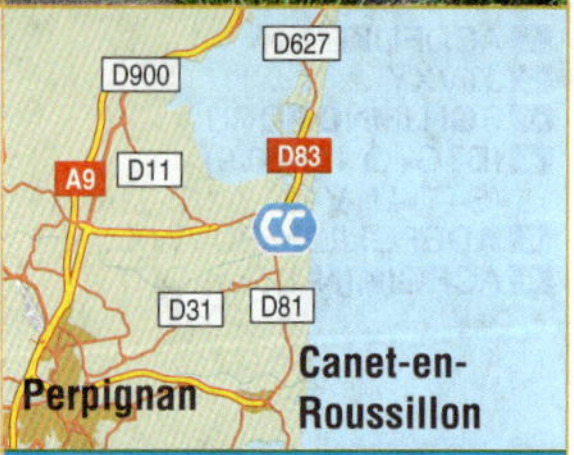

CC € 17 *29/4-1/7 28/8-18/9*

N 42°46'52'' E 3°1'22''

Le Rozier, F-48150 / Languedoc-Roussillon (Lozère)

2360

Municipal de Brouillet***
chemin de Brouillet
+33 (0)5-65626398
FAX +33 (0)5-65626083
1/4 - 30/9
contact@campinglerozier.com

5ha 159T(100-120m²) 6A CEE

1 ACDGIJKLMOPST
2 CGKLMNORSVWXY
3 BGHJNRU**WX**
4 (**A** 1/7-31/8)
(C+H 1/6-13/9)
5 **A**FGIJKLMNOPUYZ
6 ACEGJKMRTV

A very attractive campsite in the picturesque village of Le Rozier. Here you will find good shops and a restaurant. An ideal base for trips out in the area. Reservation is only possible between 1 January and 30 September.

In Augessac A75, take exit 44.1. (Turn off SatNav!) Follow the signs 'Gorges du Tarn' as far as Le Rozier. The campsite is located in the heart of Le Rozier.

CC € 15 *1/4-30/6 1/9-30/9*

N 44°11'29'' E 3°12'16''

Le Rozier/Peyreleau, F-12720 / Languedoc-Roussillon (Lozère)

2361

Les Prades****
D187
FAX +33 (0)5-65626209
1/5 - 15/9
lesprades@orange.fr

5ha 178T(100-120m²) 6A CEE

1 ACDGIJKLOPRS
2 CFKLNORSVWXY
3 BGHIJMNRU**WX**
4 (**A** 1/7-31/8) (C+H) JKN
P(Q) (S 1/7-31/8)
(T+U+V+Y) Z
5 **A**EFGIJKLMNOPQRUVWX
YZ
6 ACDEGIJ(N 4km)OTV

A lovely campsite on the River Tarn. Clean toilet facilities, sauna, jacuzzi, bubble bath, the largest heated leisure pool in the area. Free tennis and 1 hour free use of canoe per family for use near campsite. The à la carte restaurant is open all season.

A75, exit 44.1 (navigation off!). N9 as far as Aguessac. Left onto the D907 Gorges du Tarn. Dir. La Cresse. In La Cresse turn left D187. Campsite on the left after 4 km.

CC € 15 *1/5-3/7 21/8-15/9*

N 44°11'59'' E 3°10'24''

Le Vigan, F-30120 / Languedoc-Roussillon (Gard) 2362

Le Val de l'Arre***
route Du Pont de la Croix
+33 (0)4-67810277
1/4 - 30/9
valdelarre@wanadoo.fr

8ha 135T(80-120m²) 10A

1 ACD**F**IJLPST
2 CLRTVXY
3 BGHJLN**OP**RU**W**X
4 (B 1/6-15/9) (G 15/6-10/9)
(Q) (S 1/6-31/8)
(T+U+X+Z 1/6-15/9)
5 **AB**FGIJKLNPUVWZ
6 ACEG**K**(N 2km)ORTV

This campsite, where a family atmosphere predominates, is located in the south of the Cévennes amid the calm and the shade of the woods. Comfort in the middle of nature.

Via A75 take exit 48 Le Vignan D999. Right 2.5 km past Le Vignan on roundabout. Or via A6/A7/A9 exit Nîmes West. Ring round Nîmes dir. Alès. Then D999 and left at roundabout 2.5 km before Le Vignan.

CC € 15 *1/4-7/7 24/8-30/9*

N 43°59'29'' E 3°38'14''

Les Vignes, F-48210 / Languedoc-Roussillon (Lozère) 2363

La Blaquière***
RD 907 bis
+33 (0)4-66485493
22/4 - 25/9
contact@campingblaquiere.fr

1,5ha 66T(80-120m²) 6A CEE

1 ACDGIJKLPST
2 BCJKLNORSVWXY
3 BGHIJKLNRU**W**X
4 (Q+S)
(T+U+V+X 1/7-31/8) (Z)
5 **AB**EFGIJKLMNPUVWZ
6 ADEGJ(N 6km)OTV

A small, peaceful campsite with a lovely beach on the Tarn. Beautiful surroundings with plenty to see. Helpful warden.

Take A75 from Sévérac-le-Château to Les Vignes, exit 44 Le Massegros to Les Vignes. After Les Vignes 6 km direction Ste Enimie and follow signs.

CC € 15 *22/4-8/7 29/8-25/9*

N 44°18'17'' E 3°16'5''

Llauro, F-66300 / Languedoc-Roussillon (Pyrénées-Orientales) 2364

Al Comu
route Fourques
+33 (0)4-68394208
26/3 - 16/10
alcomu@wanadoo.fr

2,5ha 35T(90-110m²) 16A

1 AGIJKLMOPST
2 ITUVXY
3 AGHJNR
4 (Q+R)
5 **A**CGIJKLMNOPUZ
6 EGJ(N 0,8km)T

A perfect site for those who love tranquillity and nature. Walks directly from the campsite. A few pitches with lovely views of the Mediterranean and Perpignan. French/Dutch wardens.

D615 Thuir direction Llauro. Campsite located about 800 metres before Llauro on the right.

CC € 15 *26/3-8/7 25/8-16/10*

N 42°32'55'' E 2°45'13''

Lodève, F-34700 / Languedoc-Roussillon (Hérault)

2365

Les Vals***
2000 route du Puech
+33 (0)4-30401780
15/4 - 30/10
campinglesvals@yahoo.fr

3,5ha 65T(80-180m²) 6A CEE

1 ACDGIJLN**P**T
2 CFJRSTVXY
3 ABGHIKMNQRU**WX**
4 (B 15/5-15/9) (Q)
(R+T 6/7-24/8) (U+V)
(X 6/7-24/8) Z
5 **AB**EGJLNPUZ
6 AEG**K**(N 2km)OV

The site is 5 minutes from Lake Salagou in the middle of the vineyards on the banks of a river. The camp pool, activities such as tennis, mini golf and table tennis and the region's vast cultural heritage ensure a successful holiday.

From the north: A75 exit 52 dir. Lodève. Follow av. Fumel, not the centre. Right over Vinas bridge dir. Puech. 2 km on the D148. From the south: A75 exit 53 dir. Lodève centre. Dir. Puech on Vinas bridge. 2 km on the D148.

CC € 17 15/4-9/7 30/8-30/10

N 43°42'43" E 3°19'19"

Loupian, F-34140 / Languedoc-Roussillon (Hérault)

2366

Municipal de Loupian***
route de Mèze
+33 (0)4-67435767
FAX +33 (0)4-67437316
8/4 - 16/10
camping@loupian.fr

1,7ha 90T(60-100m²) 6A CEE

1 ACD**G**IJKLMOPST
2 FGRTVWXY
3 AGJ**M**RU
4 (Q+T+U+X 1/5-30/9) Z
5 **A**FGIJKLMNPUZ
6 AEGK(N 2km)T

Lovely clean municipal campsite with spacious pitches in a beautiful rural setting. New toilet facilities. A well cared for campsite. Quietly located but ideal for visiting Sète and Agde

A9 exit 33 (Sète) D613 Mèze. In Loupian follow signs.

CC € 13 8/4-26/6 24/8-16/10

N 43°26'42" E 3°36'55"

Lunel, F-34400 / Languedoc-Roussillon (Hérault)

2367

Bon Port****
383 chemin du Mas St. Ange
+33 (0)4-67711565
FAX +33 (0)4-67836027
2/4 - 24/9
contact@campingbonport.com

5ha 185T(80-100m²) 6A

1 ACD**G**HIJKLMOPS
2 FGRTVXY
3 B**F**GHJKN**OP**RU**W**
4 (C+H 20/4-15/9) IJK(Q)
(S+T+U+V+X+Z 1/7-31/8)
5 **AB**EFGIJKLMNPRUZ
6 AEGH**K**L(N 2km)O

A quiet, friendly campsite with plenty of shade located between Lunel and La Grande Motte. WiFi free before 1 July and after 31 August.

Located on the D61 from Lunel to La Grande Motte. Signposted 2 km outside Lunel on the left side of the road.

CC € 15 2/4-8/7 25/8-23/9

N 43°39'20" E 4°8'31"

Marseillan-Plage, F-34340 / Languedoc-Roussillon (Hérault)

2368

Beauregard Plage***
250 chemin de l'Airette
+33 (0)4-67771545
26/3 - 15/10
reception@
camping-beauregard-plage.com

3,3ha 200**T**(80-155m²) 6A CEE

1 ACD**G**IJKLMPST
2 AEGRSVWXY
3 AB**F**GJRUWY
4 (Q) (T+U+X+Z 1/5-30/9)
5 **A**CFGIJKLNOPUZ
6 ABCEG**K**TV

An authentic and lovely campsite, where respect for nature is tangible. There are only tents, caravans and motorhomes. Genuine campers will feel at home. From 2013 a new restaurant and bar overlooking the sea and beach. If you walk out of the campsite there are the shops and cafes on Marseillan-Plage.

D112 from Agde direction Sète, right at first roundabout direction Plage du Rieu. Left at next roundabout. Straight ahead at next roundabout. Campsite on the right.

CC € 17 *26/3-30/6 1/9-30/9*

N 43°18'54'' E 3°32'56''

Marseillan-Plage, F-34340 / Languedoc-Roussillon (Hérault)

2369

Camping Robinson***
Quai de Plaisance
+33 (0)4-67219007
23/4 - 23/9
reception@
camping-robinson.com

2,5ha 129**T**(60-120m²) 10A CEE

1 ACD**G**IJKLMOPST
2 AEGRSVWXY
3 B**F**GJKNRUWY
4 (Q+R 1/5-10/9)
(T+U+V+Z 1/5-15/9)
5 **A**EFGIJLMNPUVZ
6 ABGHIKL(N 1km)OTV

Located between the Mediterranean and the Bassin de Thau lake which is renowned for its shellfish. The campsite is located on the canal that flows out into the harbour of Marseillan-Plage and has direct access to the beach. Anyone who likes being beside the sea and enjoys a quiet campsite has found the right place. Plenty of fishing opportunities and many other forms of sports and games.

A9 exit Agde or Sète, then direction Marseillan-Plage. Follow camping signs.

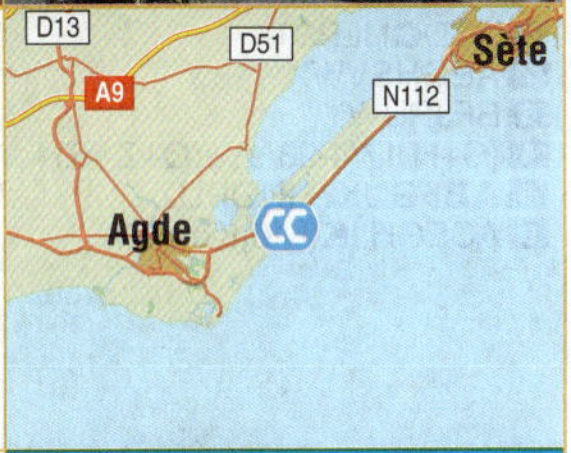

CC € 15 *23/4-3/7 27/8-23/9*

N 43°19'9'' E 3°33'24''

Marseillan-Plage, F-34340 / Languedoc-Roussillon (Hérault)

2370

Dunes et Soleil****
380 chemin de l'Airette
+33 (0)4-67771868
FAX +33 (0)4-67012080
2/4 - 28/9
campingdunesetsoleil@
homair.com

3ha 37**T**(70-130m²) 6A CEE

1 ACD**F**IJKLMOPS
2 AEFGRSVWXY
3 B**F**GJKRUWY
4 (G) IJ(Q+T+U+V+Z)
5 **AB**EFGIJKLMNPUZ
6 ACEGHJ**K**TV

The second site on your left in the centre of the lively Marseillan-Plage. Camping pitches with direct private access to the sandy beach. Enjoy a blissful holiday here on the Mediterranean which is a great place to be in both early and late seasons.

D112 from Agde direction Sète. Right at first roundabout direction Plage du Rieu. Left at next roundabout. Straight ahead at next roundabout. Campsite on the right.

CC € 17 *2/4-2/7 3/9-28/9*

N 43°18'50'' E 3°32'52''

Marseillan-Plage, F-34340 / Languedoc-Roussillon (Hérault) — 2371

La Créole***
74 av. des Campings
+33 (0)4-67219269
FAX +33 (0)4-67265816
26/3 - 15/10
campinglacreole@orange.fr

1,5ha 94T(80-95m²) 6A CEE

1 ACD**G**IJKLMPS
2 AEFGRSTVWXY
3 B**F**GJNRUVWY
4 (T+Z 1/7-31/8)
5 **A**EFGIJKLMNOPUZ
6 ACDEG**K**MT

Third campsite on your left in the centre of lively Marseillan-Plage. The campsite offers shaded pitches, new toilet facilities and a private entrance directly to the lovely sandy beach. Multilingual receptionist. Suitable for a beach holiday and for promenading around the lively resorts.

D112 from Agde to Sète. Turn right at the second roundabout, direction Marseillan-Plage. Then follow the signs.

CC € 17 *26/3-25/6 4/9-15/10*

N 43°18'46" E 3°32'47"

Marseillan-Plage, F-34340 / Languedoc-Roussillon (Hérault) — 2372

Le Galet***
avenue des Campings
+33 (0)4-67219561
FAX +33 (0)4-67218723
1/4 - 30/9
reception@camping-galet.com

2,9ha 136T(50-80m²) 10A

1 ACD**G**IJLPST
2 AEGHSVWXY
3 BFJRUWY
4 (C+H 17/4-28/9) J(Q+Z)
5 **AB**FGIJKLMNOPUZ
6 ACEGHJ**K**(N 0,8km)RT

A quiet, well-maintained campsite with a swimming pool with slides and a children's pool. 300m from the beach. Well maintained sanitary facilities. A site in the centre of Marseillan-Plage with good shopping. A large supermarket, greengrocer and various places to eat are next to the site. 1 hour free WiFi by the heated swimming pool.

A9 exit Agde, from here towards Sète. Right at first roundabout (Ranch la Camargue) then left at second roundabout.

CC € 15 *1/4-5/7 24/8-30/9*

N 43°18'41" E 3°32'40"

Marseillan-Plage, F-34340 / Languedoc-Roussillon (Hérault) — 2373

Les Méditerranées Beach Club Charlemagne*****
avenue des Campings
+33 (0)4-67219249
9/4 - 25/9
info@beach-club-charlemagne.com

7ha 153T(70-100m²) 10A CEE

1 ACD**G**IJKLMPST
2 AEFGRSVWXY
3 B**F**JKRWY
4 (C+H 11/4-27/9) IJKP
(Q+S+T)
(U+V+Y 1/5-1/9) (Z)
5 **AB**EFGIJKLMNOPUVWXYZ
6 AEGHKMORTV

A comfortable campsite with spacious and well maintained pitches. Lovely flowers and plants. Connected directly to Camping Nouvelle Floride, through which you can get to the sandy beach. All facilities at both campsites are available to campers, from the day it opens to the day it closes!

From Agde via D112, right at first roundabout, Plage de Rieu. Campsite on right after last roundabout in Marseillan-Plage.

CC € 17 *9/4-2/7 27/8-25/9*

N 43°18'37" E 3°32'36"

Marseillan-Plage, F-34340 / Languedoc-Roussillon (Hérault) — 2374

Les Méditerranées Beach Garden****
avenue des Campings
+33 (0)4-67219283
9/4 - 25/9
info@beach-garden-camping.com

15ha 617T(80-100m²) 6A CEE

1 ACD**G**IJKLMOPST
2 AEFGRSTUVWXY
3 B**F**GJKNRUWY
4 (C 11/4-27/9) (F) (H 11/4-27/9) IJK**L**M**N**P (Q+S+T+V+X+Y+Z)
5 **AB**EFGJLNOPUW
6 AEGHJ(N 0,2km)ORTV

Shaded campsite by a nature reserve and the Mediterranean. Marseillan-Plage is in walking distance. Spacious touring pitches, two new restaurants, supermarket and good toilets. Swimming pool with 1000 m² of fun in the water! Free WiFi at the bar.

A9 exit Agde and via the D112 to the roundabout, turn right here (Plage de Rieu). Turn right at junction with the main road of Marseillan-Plage. Beach Garden campsite is located at the end of the street. This is a dead end.

CC € 17 *9/4-2/7 27/8-25/9*

N 43°18'21'' E 3°32'16''

Maureillas-Las-Illas, F-66480 / Languedoc-Roussillon (Pyrénées-Orientales) — 2375

Les Bruyères***
route de Céret
+33 (0)4-68832664
FAX +33 (0)4-68831475
10/3 - 15/11
campinglesbruyeres@live.fr

4ha 95T(80-180m²) 6A CEE

1 A**G**IJKLPST
2 BFIRTVY
3 AGQRU
4 (B+G 1/5-30/9) (Q+T 1/5-30/10) Z
5 AGJLNPUVXZ
6 EGIJ**K**(N 0,3km)O**P**TV

A quiet campsite in the lower Pyrenees. The area is ideal for making trips out to the Mediterranean or Argelès Sur Mer. Beautiful view of the south side of the Pic du Canigou.

A9 exit 43. Follow Gerona (D900). Then D618. Through Maureillas. Campsite signposted.

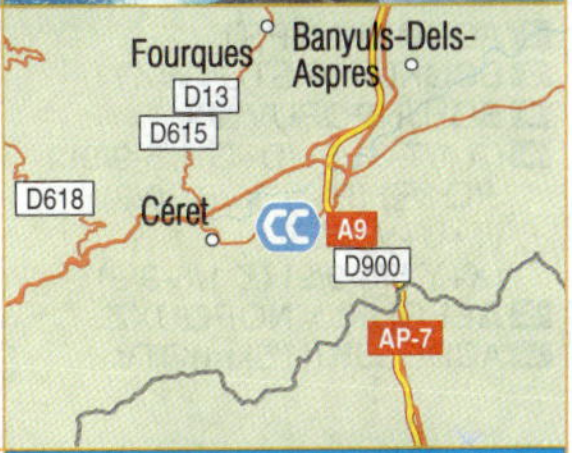

CC € 15 *10/3-1/7 28/8-15/11*

N 42°29'32'' E 2°47'42''

Méjannes-le-Clap, F-30430 / Languedoc-Roussillon (Gard) — 2376

La Genèse***
route de la Genèse
+33 (0)5-56737373
FAX +33 (0)4-66245038
2/4 - 1/10
info@lagenese.com

50ha 458T(90-130m²) 6A CEE

1 ACDGIJL**P**ST
2 ABCINORSTVXY
3 ABGMNQRWX
4 (A 1/7-31/8) (C+G) N (Q+S+T+U+V+X+Y+Z)
5 **AB**GIJKMNOPRUV
6 EG**IJ**(N 7km)OQTV

Located in the Gorges de la Cèze this family naturist campsite extends over 26 hectares of lush and rugged countryside. The river at the campsite offers opportunities for swimming and canoeing.

From the A7 exit Bollène, D994 direction Pont-St-Esprit. From there N86 direction Bagnols-sur-Cèze, then D6 direction Alès. Turn off to Lussan (D979) after 23.5 km. Follow signs in Méjannes.

CC € 15 *2/4-9/7 27/8-1/10*

N 44°16'3'' E 4°22'13''

Meyrueis, F-48150 / Languedoc-Roussillon (Lozère) — 2377

La Cascade***
Salvinsac
+33 (0)4-66454545
9/4 - 2/10
contact@camping-la-cascade.com

1,7ha 41**T**(100-300m²) 16A CEE

1 ACD**G**IJKLMOPQ
2 CJKLNORVWXY
3 BGHIJNPRUV**W**X
4 (A 9/4-1/7,31/8-2/10) (Q+R+T+U+V+X+Z)
5 **A**CDEFGHIJKLMNPUVZ
6 ACEGJ(N 3km)ORTV

Far away from the motorway, in a grand and well-maintained natural area. The ideal place to enjoy pure nature. Wonderful views of the surrounding Causse Méjean mountains, the tranquility of a splashing stream and a diversity of flora and fauna. Because of its small size, this is a great campsite.

This site is located on the Route de Florac, the road connecting Meyrueis and Florac. It is the second campsite after Meyrueis and is signposted.

CC € 13 *9/4-3/7 29/8-2/10*

N 44°11'43'' E 3°27'20''

Mialet, F-30140 / Languedoc-Roussillon (Gard) — 2378

Les Plans***
D50
+33 (0)4-66850246
15/4 - 11/9
info@camping-les-plans.fr

6,5ha 133**T**(80-110m²) 10A CEE

1 ACD**G**IJKLMPST
2 BCGKLNORSTUVWXY
3 BGHJN**P**QRUV**W**X
4 (A 1/7-31/8) (B+G 1/6-9/9) I J(Q) (R+S 30/6-30/8) (T+U+V 1/5-9/9) (X+Y 5/5-9/9) (Z 1/5-9/9)
5 **A**EFGIJKLMNOPQUXZ
6 ACDEGJ**K**(N 5km)OTV

Campsite on the edge of Parc National des Cévennes, in Mialet, in the Gard. Ideal location on a river, with a private beach. Leisure pool, sports grounds, kids club, minigolf, many activities and entertainment. 'La Bambouseraie de Prafance' and the Trabuc caves can be reached by steam train. Good for visiting the Cévennes and surrounding spots.

Route du Soleil - Bollène - Pt. St. Esprit-Bagnols - Alès - Anduze - Generargues - Mialet - Signs - Campsite left.

CC € 13 *15/4-24/6 28/8-11/9*

N 44°7'30'' E 3°55'7''

Montblanc, F-34290 / Languedoc-Roussillon (Hérault) — 2379

Le Rebau***
rue du Rebau
+33 (0)4-67985078
12/3 - 15/10
gilbert@camping-lerebau.fr

3ha 117**T**(80-120m²) 6A

1 A**G**IJKLMPT
2 FGRVXY
3 B**F**GNR
4 (B 1/7-15/9) (Q 1/7-31/8) (T+Z 10/7-26/8)
5 **A**EFGIJKMNPUV
6 EGHJOV

A very hospitable campsite set among vineyards. Walking distance from the village. The campsite is shaded without becoming a wood. A very good base for visiting the area. Free WiFi.

A75 exit 62 Montblanc. Or A9 exit 34 direction Pézenas via D13. After 4 km D18 direction Montblanc.

CC € 17 *12/3-30/6 1/9-15/10*

N 43°23'54'' E 3°22'24''

Montolieu, F-11170 / Languedoc-Roussillon (Aude)

iD **2380**

Camping de Montolieu
D629
+33 (0)4-68769501
26/3 - 31/10
campingdemontolieu@gmail.com

1ha 43T(80-120m²) 10A CEE

1 ACGIJLMPST
2 RTUVWXY
3 AGHNRUW
4 (A [key]) (Q 1/7-31/8) (R [key]) Z
5 AGIJKLMNPUWZ
6 EGIJK(N 1,2km)RT

[speech] A campsite marked out by hedges with spacious pitches. Attractive reception building with a lively terrace and recreation room. Modern and well-placed toilet building. Near the literary town of Montolieu.

[car] From Carcassonne ring road to D6113 direction Castelnaudary. Exit Montolieu D629 until 1 km before the village, indicated on the right.

CC € 13 *26/3-10/6 1/9-31/10*

N 43°17'52" E 2°13'20"

Montoulieu, F-34190 / Languedoc-Roussillon (Hérault)

iD **2381**

Le Grillon***
Place de l'Église
+33 (0)4-67737931
1/1 - 31/12
camping@montoulieu.fr

2ha 30T(80-140m²) 10A

1 ACDGIJKLMNOPST
2 JKRVWXY
3 ABHJLR
4 (B+G 1/5-20/9)
(Q+R+T+U 1/5-30/9) (Y [key])
5 AEFGJLNPU
6 AEGJ(N 7km)RTV

[speech] Montoulieu is a small village between the hills and the Mediterranean, surrounded by vineyards and 'garrigue' scrubland. Quiet but close to fantastic towns: De Grot, Des Demoiselles, Ganges with its weekly market, Montpellier, Cirque de Navacelles, the Mont Aigoual.

[car] D986 Ganges-Montpellier, take the D108 towards Montoulieu at St. Bauzille-de-Putois. Campsite indicated in the village.

CC € 13 *1/1-2/7 27/8-31/12*

N 43°55'36" E 3°47'22"

Narbonne, F-11100 / Languedoc-Roussillon (Aude)

iD **2382**

Camping La Nautique****
La Nautique
+33 (0)4-68904819
FAX +33 (0)4-68907339
1/3 - 31/10
info@campinglanautique.com

16ha 250T(130-140m²) 10A

1 ACDGIJKLMPST
2 DFIKLRTVWXY
3 ABGHIJKMNQRUW
4 (A 1/7-31/8)
(C+H 1/5-1/10) J
(Q 1/4-1/10) (S 15/4-30/9)
(T+U+V 1/7-31/8)
(Y+Z 1/5-30/9)
5 ABGIJKLSWXYZ
6 ACEGHK(N 4,5km)RTV

[speech] Exceptional location on the beautiful Bages bay - lovely panoramic views - and just a few kilometres from the Mediterranean beaches and the historic centre of Narbonne - a friendly welcome, private toilet facilities at your camping pitch - most suitable for excursions. Fully equipped for the disabled.

[car] A9 exit 38 Narbonne-Sud. At the roundabout turn left, follow the signs La Nautique. After about 2.5 km the campsite is on the right hand side.

CC € 19 *1/3-30/6 1/9-31/10*

N 43°8'50" E 3°0'14"

Narbonne, F-11100 / Languedoc-Roussillon (Aude)

2383

- Yelloh! Village Les Mimosas****
- chaussée de Mandirac
- +33 (0)4-68490372
- FAX +33 (0)4-68493945
- 21/3 - 31/10
- info@lesmimosas.com

9ha 140T(80-130m²) 10A CEE

1 ACD**F**IJKLM**P**S
2 CDFLRTVX
3 BGHJK**MNOP**QRUVW
4 (C+H 1/4-15/10) IJKN
(Q+S 1/4-15/10)(T 1/7-31/8)
(U+V+X+Y 1/4-15/10)
(Z 1/7-31/8)
5 **AB**EFGIJKLNOPUW
6 ABCEGH**I**J**K**L(N 6km)OQR
TV

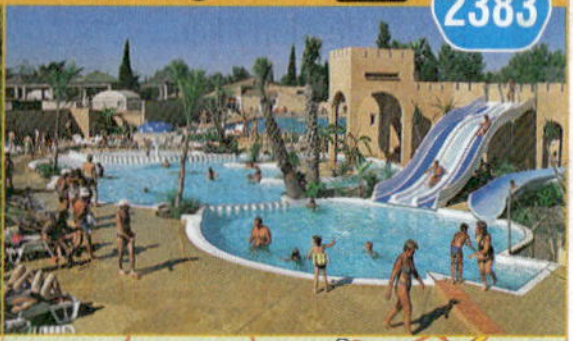

Good, four-star campsite with amiable ambiance. Sauna, fitness room and lovely aqua park with play area for young children and toddler playhouse. Located in the Étangs with rice paddies. Ideal for visiting the lovely surroundings. Narbonne, Gruissan and St. Pierre La Mer. Attention paid to eco-tourism. Most facilities are available from opening to closing.

From the A9 exit Narbonne-Sud. In Narbonne follow the signs La Nautique. Then follow the camping signs Mandirac.

CC € 17 21/3-25/6 1/9-31/10

N 43°8'12'' E 3°1'32''

Narbonne-Plage, F-11100 / Languedoc-Roussillon (Aude)

2384

- Campéole La Côte des Roses***
- route de Gruissan
- +33 (0)4-68498365
- FAX +33 (0)4-68494044
- 1/4 - 30/9
- cote-des-roses@andretriganogroupe.com

16ha 470T(80-100m²) 6A

1 AC**G**IJKLMO**P**ST
2 ADEFGRSTVWXY
3 BGJKN**OQ**RUWY
4 (B+H 1/6-7/9) IM
(Q+S 1/5-7/9)
(T+U+V+X+Y 1/7-31/8) Z
5 **AB**EFGJKLMNOPQRUVZ
6 CEGH**J**(N 2km)ORTUV

A well equipped and very spacious campsite close to the beach, 2 km outside the centre of Narbonne-Plage. Ideally located for walking or cycling trips in the La Clape nature reserve. Swimming pool with large slides and a watery playground for young children.

The campsite is located 2 km south of Narbonne-Plage on the road connecting Narbonne-Plage to Gruissan.

CC € 17 1/5-4/7 22/8-30/9

N 43°8'37'' E 3°8'39''

Néfiach, F-66170 / Languedoc-Roussillon (Pyrénées-Orientales)

2385

- La Garenne***
- D916
- +33 (0)4-68571576
- FAX +33 (0)4-68573742
- 1/3 - 30/11
- contact@camping-lagarenne.fr

3,5ha 73T(80-130m²) 10A CEE

1 ACGIJKLMOPST
2 FGRTVXY
3 AGHJNR
4 (A+B 1/7-31/8)
(D 1/1-30/6,1/9-31/10)
(G 1/6-30/9) (Q 1/7-31/8)
(T+U+V+X+Z 1/5-31/10)
5 **A**DFGIJKMNOPUVZ
6 ACDEGIK(N 2km)TV

Ambiance between orchards and vineyards of Roussillon. Views of the mighty Canigou. Being small is our biggest asset. Peace is guaranteed. Many excursions through the Pyrénées-Orientales with its castles, churches, abbeys and picturesque villages. The Mediterranean beaches are 30 km away. And the tax haven of Andorra is within 120 km.

Green signs in Perpignan towards Andorra la Vella/Prades (N116, toll-free road). After 11 km exit Néfiach. D916 at roundabout towards Néfiach.

CC € 13 1/3-8/7 29/8-30/11 7=6, 21=17

N 42°41'26'' E 2°39'28''

Palau-del-Vidre, F-66690 / Languedoc-Roussillon (Pyrénées-Orientales) 2386

Le Haras***
Domaine St. Galdric
+33 (0)4-68221450
FAX +33 (0)4-68379893
1/4 - 30/9
@ contact@camping-le-haras.com

4ha 99**T**(80-100m²) 10A CEE

1 ACFIJKLOPST
2 GRTVXY
3 BDGNRU
4 (B 15/4-20/9) (Q) (T+U+X+Z 15/4-20/9)
5 **AB**GIJKLMNOPUWZ
6 ACE**K**(N 0,5km)TV

Just before Palau del Vidre is the park-like campsite of Le Haras with its varied flora. The attractive bar next to the swimming pool is surrounded by greenery and beaches of Argeles are 7 km away. Many excursions in the immediate vicinity or to the Pyrenees and Barcelona are possible.

A9, exit Perpignan-Sud, RD914 direction Argelès-sur-Mer. Exit 9 Palau-del-Vidre. Campsite on the left before the village.

CC € 15 *1/4-1/7 27/8-30/9*

N 42°34'33'' E 2°57'53''

Peyremale-sur-Cèze, F-30160 / Languedoc-Roussillon (Gard) 2387

des Drouilhèdes***
+33 (0)4-66250480
FAX +33 (0)4-66251095
1/5 - 15/9
@ info@campingcevennes.com

2,5ha 90**T**(60-100m²) 6A CEE

1 ACGIJKLPS
2 CLNORSVXY
3 BGHJKNQR**W**X
4 (Q+R+U+X+Z)
5 **A**CFGIJKMNOPQUWZ
6 AEGHJ(N 4km)OTV

This friendly family campsite, especially suitable for older people and families with children, is located right on the banks of the River Cèze with natural swimming. English, French, Dutch and German are spoken. Enjoy delicious meals at reasonable prices in the friendly bar and restaurant. Plenty of trips out! A relaxing holiday is assured.

D51 St. Ambroix-Bessèges. In Bessèges take D17 direction Peyremale. Turn right after several kilometres; 3 km west of Bessèges.

CC € 19 *1/5-7/7 25/8-15/9*

N 44°17'27'' E 4°4'3''

Pont-d'Hérault, F-30440 / Languedoc-Roussillon (Gard) 2388

Les Gorges de l'Hérault**
route de Pont d'Hérault
+33 (0)4-67824223
1/4 - 30/9
@ contact@camping-lesgorgesdelherault.com

2,5ha 50**T**(70-190m²) 10A CEE

1 ACD**F**IJKLMO**P**ST
2 CGNRSVXY
3 ABGHRW
4 (B+G 15/5-30/9) (Q 1/7-30/8) (S) (T+X+Z 1/7-30/8)
5 **A**FJKLNPUV
6 EGK(N 4km)OQTV

For anyone wishing to explore the Cevennes and still enjoy the mild southern climate, this campsite is an excellent base and a peaceful oasis beside the River Hérault.

The campsite is located on the D999 between Ganges and Le Vignan close to the Pont-d'Hérault.

CC € 17 *1/4-30/6 1/9-30/9*

N 43°59'32'' E 3°40'59''

Port-Leucate, F-11370 / Languedoc-Roussillon (Aude)

2389

Rives des Corbières***
avenue du Languedoc
+33 (0)4-68409031
FAX +33 (0)4-68408784
1/4 - 2/10
rivescamping@wanadoo.fr

6ha 192**T**(80-100m²) 6A

1 AC**G**IJKLOPST
2 AESTVWXY
3 AGKNRUWY
4 (B+G+Q+R+T+U+V+Y) Z
5 **AB**GIJKLMNPUVZ
6 AEG**K**(N 0,8km)RTV

Situated between the sea and the Étang de Salses, this spacious family campsite offers plenty of watersports opportunities. Equipped with a lovely swimming pool and within walking distance of the sea and the delightful harbour of Leucate.

A9 direction Perpignan. Exit Leucate. Follow D627 as far as exit Port-Leucate. Then second roundabout right. Campsite after about 700 metres.

CC €13 *1/4-7/7 24/8-2/10*

N 42°50'57'' E 3°2'26''

Portiragnes-Plage, F-34420 / Languedoc-Roussillon (Hérault)

2390

Les Sablons*****
av. des Muriers/Plage Est
+33 (0)4-67909055
FAX +33 (0)4-67908291
1/4 - 25/9
contact@les-sablons.com

15ha 223**T**(85-120m²) 10A CEE

1 ACD**G**IJKLMPR
2 ADEFGRSTVXY
3 BC**F**GHJKMN**OP**RUVWY
4 (A+C+H) IJKMP (Q+S+T+U+V+W+X+Y+Z)
5 **AB**DEFGIJKLMNPRUWYZ
6 ACGH**IJK**M(N 0,2km)ORT V

Large friendly campsite by the sea with swimming pools heated to 26°C from 1 April. Plenty of entertainment for young and old. There is a lovely sandy beach. WiFi point, free for one hour per day. The new spa is accessible from the age of 18.

A9 exit Béziers-Est, direction Valras-Plage. At the roundabout left direction Portiragnes. Then direction Portiragnes-Plage. Left past the roundabout.

CC €19 *1/4-3/7 1/9-25/9*

N 43°16'48'' E 3°21'51''

Preixan, F-11250 / Languedoc-Roussillon (Aude)

2391

Camping Village Grand Sud***
Le Breil-d'Aude / D118
+33 (0)4-68268818
1/4 - 30/9
accueil@camping-grandsud.com

11ha 50**T**(100-120m²) 6A CEE

1 AC**G**IJKLMPST
2 CDFLRTVXY
3 AGMRUWX
4 (B) J(Q+R) (U 1/7-30/8) (V+X) Z
5 **AB**DEFGIJKLNPU
6 CF**J**(N 10km)RTV

Campsite 10 km from the 'Canal du Midi' and the legendary town of Carcassonne. Just 1 hour from the Mediterranean and 2 hours from the Andorran mountains. In the heart of Catharen country with opportunities for taking lovely walks and visiting picturesque markets. Shaded floral grounds on a lake.

A61, exit 23 Carcassonne-Ouest, then direction Limoux (7 km) the D118.

CC €15 *1/4-10/7 28/8-30/9*

N 43°9'31'' E 2°17'36''

Rennes-les-Bains, F-11190 / Languedoc-Roussillon (Aude) — 2392

La Bernède***
19, chemin de la Bernède
+33 (0)6-37272234
1/4 - 15/10
infos@labernede.fr

1ha 80T(80-100m²) 16A CEE

1 ADGIJKLMOPST
2 BCGKTUVX
3 A**F**GHNUWX
4 (Q+R) (X 16/6-15/10) (Z)
5 **A**ILMNPUVWXYZ
6 DEGIJ(N 0,5km)RTUV

Camping La Bernède is located on the banks of the small River La Sals, close to the picturesque village of Rennes-les-Bains with its thermal spa.

Carcassonne dir. Quillan D118. In Couiza turn off onto D813. After 5.5 km turn off to Rennes-les-Bains D14.

CC € 15 *1/4-30/6 1/9-15/10*

N 42°54'54'' E 2°19'5''

Salses, F-66600 / Languedoc-Roussillon (Pyrénées-Orientales) — 2393

International du Roussillon**
+33 (0)4-68386072
1/1 - 31/12
camping-roussillon@wanadoo.fr

2,5ha 80T 10A CEE

1 ACDFIJKLMNPT
2 DFTVXY
3 ABR
4 (B+G 1/6-15/9) (Q+T+X+Z 1/7-31/8)
5 AEGIJKLMNOPZ
6 EGI**K**(N 0,5km)OTV

In a tourist region where a whole range of activities is at your disposal, this campsite is 500m from the village and castle of Salses, 5 km from a lake, 10 km from Perpignan and 40 km from Spain, where you can go shopping.

From Montpellier A9, exit 40 direction D900 Fitou/Salses le Château. From L'Espagne A9, exit 41 direction D900 Salses le Château.

CC € 15 *1/1-30/6 25/8-31/12 8=6*

N 42°50'37'' E 2°55'34''

Sérignan-Plage, F-34410 / Languedoc-Roussillon (Hérault) — 2394

Aloha*****
allée des dunes
+33 (0)4-67397130
FAX +33 (0)4-67325815
4/5 - 18/9
info@alohacamping.com

6ha 155T(80-100m²) 10A CEE

1 ACD**G**IJKLM**PQ**
2 AEFRSVXY
3 ABGK**M**N**OPQ**RUVWY
4 (C+H) IJKMP (Q+S+T+U+V+X+Y+Z)
5 **AB**DEFGJLNPQUWZ
6 CDEGH**KM**(N 6km)ORTV

A well-run, pleasant campsite on the beach with a lovely, heated leisure pool. Shaded, well marked out pitches. Plenty of leisure activities right from the opening date for people of all ages.

A9 exit Béziers-Est direction Sérignan. Then D37e direction Sérignan-Plage. Campsite is located right by the sea.

CC € 17 *4/5-14/5 26/5-3/7 3/9-18/9*

N 43°16'2'' E 3°20'6''

Sérignan-Plage, F-34410 / Languedoc-Roussillon (Hérault)

2395

Beauséjour****
Domaine de Beauséjour
+33 (0)4-67395093
FAX +33 (0)4-67320196
1/4 - 30/9
info@camping-beausejour.com

9ha 170T(100m²) 10A CEE

1 ACD**F**IJKLMPQ
2 AEFLRSVXY
3 BGN**OP**RUVWY
4 (C+H) **KLMN**P (Q+S+T+U+V+X+Y+Z)
5 **AB**EFGJLNPR**ST**UVWZ
6 EGHJM(N 4km)ORTV

This campsite, located by a lovey sandy beach, exudes a lively family atmosphere. The water park is heated from 1 April! Free beach club by the sea: canoes, paddle boats, catamaran with skipper. Free, unlimited WiFi.

A9 exit Béziers-Est direction Sérignan. Then direction Sérignan-Plage. At the road junction turn right and follow the signs.

CC € 15 1/4-1/7 1/9-30/9

N 43°16'1'' E 3°19'49''

Sérignan-Plage, F-34410 / Languedoc-Roussillon (Hérault)

2396

Le Clos Virgile****
CD37
+33 (0)4-67322064
FAX +33 (0)4-67320542
7/5 - 17/9
contact@leclosvirgile.fr

5ha 300T(80-90m²) 10A

1 A**G**IJLPST
2 AEFRTVY
3 ABGKN**OPQ**RUWY
4 (B+F+G) JKP(Q+S) (T 15/6-5/9) (U+V+X+Y+Z)
5 **AB**EFGJKLMNPUVWZ
6 ACEG**K**M(N 4km)ORTV

A fine, shaded and well equipped campsite. The campsite is located 400 metres from the beach and has a heated indoor swimming pool and two jacuzzis.

A9 exit Béziers-Est direction Sérignan. Then take the D37e to Sérignan-Plage. The campsite is the second on the left.

CC € 17 7/5-30/6 1/9-17/9

N 43°16'12'' E 3°19'52''

Sommières, F-30250 / Languedoc-Roussillon (Gard)

2397

Domaine de Massereau*****
1990 route d'Aubais
+33 (0)4-66531120
2/4 - 29/10
camping@massereau.com

8ha 90T(100-200m²) 16A CEE

1 ACD**G**IJKLMO**P**S
2 BFLSVWXY
3 ABGHJK**MNOP**QRU**W**
4 (**A** 1/7-31/8) (C+H) **JKL N**(Q+S+T+U 2/4-30/9) (V 1/7-31/8) (Y+Z 2/4-30/9)
5 **A**BDEFGHIJKLOPQR**ST**U WXY
6 ACEGH**IJK**LM(N 2km)RTV

Located in the heart of the wine country, between the Cevennes and the Mediterranean. Quiet and child-friendly. Pitches with a lot of comfort. Heated pool, recreational pool with slide, restaurant, pizzeria, bar, food, adventure park. Private beach, SUP (stand up paddle).

A9, exit 26 direction Gallargues, then direction Sommières, in Sommières direction Aubais, is indicated.

CC € 19 2/4-4/6 1/9-29/10

N 43°45'58'' E 4°5'50''

Sorède, F-66690 / Languedoc-Roussillon (Pyrénées-Orientales)

2398

La Coscolleda***
27 rue de la Coscolleda
+33 (0)4-68891665
+33 (0)4-68898536
1/4 - 1/10
camping-la-coscolleda@wanadoo.fr

1,3ha 35T(80-120m²) 10A CEE

1 ACD**G**IJKLOPST
2 BCGJRTVXY
3 AGHJRU
4 (C+H)
(Q+T+U+Z 1/7-31/8)
5 **A**GIJKLMNOPZ
6 AEGK(N 0,5km)OR

La Coscolleda campsite is located alongside the La Taxo river at the foot of the Pyrenees and 7 km from the Mediterranean Sea. Peace and quiet in the countryside in low season. Heated swimming pool on site, walking, cycling in the area or trips to Collioure, to the Pyrenees or Barcelona.

A9 exit 43 Le Boulou. Follow Argelès-sur-Mer (D618) as far as St. André/Sorède exit. Direction Sorède (D11) at first roundabout and turn left before Sorède.

CC € 13 *1/4-9/7 27/8-1/10*

N 42°32'5" E 2°57'36"

Sorède, F-66690 / Languedoc-Roussillon (Pyrénées-Orientales)

2399

Les Micocouliers***
rte de Palau del Vidre
+33 (0)4-68892027
1/4 - 30/9
contact@camping-les-micocouliers.com

4ha 200T(80-160m²) 6A

1 A**G**HIJKLMPS
2 BCKTVXY
3 ABGRU
4 (B 15/5-15/9) (G 15/6-15/9)
(Q+S+T+U+V+X 1/7-31/8) Z
5 **AB**EFIKMNPZ
6 DEG**I**J(N 2km)OTV

Located in natural, peaceful Sorède, a pleasant village with the charm and authenticity of an old Catalan village. Here you will find art, culture, sea and nature. Located at the foot of the Massif des Albères, close to the beaches at Argeles-sur-Mer (about 11 km). This makes it the ideal spot for an enjoyable and relaxing holiday.

D618 Le Boulou direction Argeles. Exit D11 towards Sorède, campsite entrance at first roundabout.

CC € 17 *1/4-1/7 23/8-30/9*

N 42°32'5" E 2°57'21"

St. Alban-sur-Limagnole, F-48120 / Languedoc-Roussillon (Lozère)

2400

Camping Le Galier**
route de Saint Chély
+33 (0)4-66315880
1/3 - 30/9
accueil@campinglegalier.fr

4ha 66T(100-200m²) 6A

1 ABCGIJKLMPS
2 BCLRWXY
3 AGH**M**RU**WX**
4 (A 1/7-30/8) (B+G 1/7-31/8)
(Q 1/6-31/8) (T 1/5-30/9)
(V 15/6-30/8) (Z)
5 **A**CGIJKLMNOPUVZ
6 EGJ(N 1km)OT

The campsite is located not far from the A75 in the rugged Margeride at the foot of a typical French village. Spacious pitches on the edge of a wood and on both banks of the Limagnole, it is wonderfully healthy. Free bikes for children. Fishing in the Limagnole. Walks with a local guide.

Take the A75 as far as St. Alban, exit 34, then take the N106 in the direction of St. Alban-sur-Limagnole. The campsite is located about 800 metres before the village, on the D987.

CC € 15 *1/3-8/7 29/8-30/9*

N 44°46'31" E 3°22'20"

St. Cyprien-Plage, F-66750 / Languedoc-Roussillon (Pyrénées-Orientales) — 2401

Cala Gogo*****
Les Capellans, av. Armand Lanoux
+33 (0)4-68210712
FAX +33 (0)4-68210219
2/5 - 1/10
@ contact@camping-le-calagogo.fr

12ha 383**T**(80-125m²) 6-10A CEE

1 ACD**G**IJKLPS
2 AEGRTVX
3 B**F**GK**M**NRUWY
4 (C+H+Q+S+T+U+V+X+Y+Z)
5 **AB**DFGIJKLMNOPUVWXYZ
6 ACEGH**K**M(N 2km)ORTV

A beautiful campsite with private access to the beach. One of the toilet blocks is heated and all the amenities are available throughout the season. Enjoy the heated swimming pools and explore the beautiful area with many excursions to the Pyrenees or to Spain.

A9 exit 42 Perpignan-Sud, dir. Argelès-sur-Mer. Follow D914 as far as exit 7 dir St. Cyprien and Elne. Via Latour-Bas-Elne follow St. Cyprien-Plage. Then follow 'Grand Stade' and camping signs.

CC €17 2/5-2/7 27/8-30/9

N 42°35'58" E 3°2'18"

St. Jean-du-Gard, F-30270 / Languedoc-Roussillon (Gard) — 2402

Les Sources***
route de Mialet
+33 (0)4-66853803
FAX +33 (0)4-66851609
1/4 - 30/9
@ camping-des-sources@wanadoo.fr

2,4ha 69**T**(80-120m²) 6-10A CEE

1 ACD**G**IJKLM**P**ST
2 BGJKLRSVWXY
3 BGHIJRU
4 (**A** 17/5-30/9) (C+H+Q+S+T+U+V+X+Y) Z
5 **AB**DEFGIJKLMNOPSTUVWXYZ
6 CDEG**I**J(N 1,3km)TUV

Magnificent campsite, quiet and family-friendly, in the heart of the southern Cévennes. 1.3 km from the village and very close to a river with crystal clear water. In the surroundings: well-known bamboo forest, steam train to Anduze, Nimes, Pont du Gard, Uzès. A ten-minute walk to St. Jean-du-Gard.

A7 Bollène - Pont-St-Esprit - Bagnols-sur-Cèze - Alès - Anduze - St. Jean-du-Gard. After traffic lights right 1.3 km.

CC €13 1/4-28/6 24/8-30/9 7=6, 10=7

N 44°6'48" E 3°53'31"

St. Jean-du-Gard, F-30270 / Languedoc-Roussillon (Gard) — 2403

Mas de la Cam****
route de St. André-de-Valborgne
+33 (0)4-66851202
FAX +33 (0)4-66853207
30/4 - 20/9
@ camping@masdelacam.fr

8ha 200**T**(80-140m²) 6-10A CEE

1 ACD**F**IJKLOPST
2 BCKLMNRVWXY
3 BGHJ**MNP**RU**W**X
4 (C+H 15/5-10/9) MP(Q) (S 15/5-10/9) (T+U 1/6-10/9) (V 1/7-31/8) (X+Y 1/6-10/9) Z
5 **AB**CEFGIJKLMNOPUVWXZ
6 AEGJ(N 3km)OTV

Peaceful floral campsite located on the river. Beautiful views of the Cevennes mountains. Heated swimming pool (500 m²), free tennis (low season), ideal starting point for cycling and walking. Plenty of entertainment in spring: pétanque, painting, bridge. Maximum 20 pitches available for dog owners. 10A power 1 Euro extra.

A7 Bollène, Pont-St-Esprit, Bagnols-sur-Cèze, Alès, direction Montpellier, St. Christol, Anduze, St. Jean-du-Gard direction St. André-de-Valbogne.

CC €17 30/4-3/7 21/8-20/9

N 44°6'45" E 3°51'16"

St. Jean-Pla-de-Corts, F-66490 / Languedoc-Roussillon (Pyrénées-Orientales)

2404

de la Vallée***
route de Maureillas
+33 (0)4-68832320
FAX +33 (0)4-68830794
1/4 - 31/10
campingdelavallee@yahoo.fr

10ha 100T 6A CEE

1 ACFIJLMOPST
2 ACFLMQRTVY
3 ABNRUW
4 (C 1/4-30/10)(G 5/5-9/9) (Q)(R+T+U+V 1/6-30/9) Z
5 AEFGJLNPTUVZ
6 CEGKOTV

At the foot of the Pyrenees, an excellent area for walking with an abundance of marked out routes. Opportunities also for off-road trips in the mountains: les Albères, le Vallespir and the Massif du Canigou (2784m). Heated swimmingpool.

Le Boulou dir. Céret D115. At the roundabout in St. Jean Pla de Corts go towards village centre left over the bridge. Campsite signposted.

CC € 15 *1/4-2/7 20/8-31/10*

N 42°30'24'' E 2°47'40''

St. Julien-de-Peyrolas, F-30760 / Languedoc-Roussillon (Gard)

2405

Le Peyrolais***
821 chemin du Camping
+33 (0)4-66821494
9/4 - 24/9
lepeyrolais@orange.fr

5ha 100T 10A CEE

1 ACDFIJKLMOPST
2 CMRVWXY
3 BGHQRUWX
4 (Q+R+T+U+V+X+Y+Z)
5 AFGIJKLMNOPUZ
6 EGK(N 5km)TV

This campsite has very level grounds and plenty of shade. Just next to the Ardèche river.

Exit Bollène dir. Pont-St-Esprit. Then D6086. Then left onto D901 dir. Barjac. Campsite after 5 km.

CC € 17 *9/4-1/7 20/8-24/9*

N 44°17'23'' E 4°35'22''

St. Pons-de-Thomières, F-34220 / Languedoc-Roussillon (Hérault)

2406

Les Cerisiers du Jaur***
route de Bédarieux
+33 (0)4-67953033
26/3 - 23/10
info@cerisierdujaur.com

2ha 106T(100-170m²) 16A CEE

1 ACDGIJKLMPST
2 ACGIJLRTVWXY
3 ABGHJKNRW
4 (B+G+Q+R) (T 1/7-30/9) (U+V)
5 ACEFGIJKLMNOPQRSTU WXYZ
6 CDEGJ(N 1km)V

The campsite is in an old cherry orchard, alongside which the River Jaur flows. Peaceful climate, plenty of greenery in the area and excellent cycling and walking routes.

Exit at Beziers on A9 motorway. Continue towards St. Pons-de-Thomières on the N112 or D612. At St. Pons D908 direction Bédarieux. 500 metres on the right.

CC € 17 *26/3-1/7 27/8-23/10 7=6, 14=11, 30=20*

N 43°29'25'' E 2°47'6''

Ste Marie-la-Mer, F-66470 / Languedoc-Roussillon (Pyrénées-Orientales)

2407

Le Palais de la Mer****
av. de Las-Illes
+33 (0)4-68730794
FAX +33 (0)4-68735783
14/5 - 24/9
contact@palaisdelamer.com

3ha 122**T**(80-100m²) 10A

1 AC**G**IJKLMOPST
2 AERTVY
3 BDGJMNQRUVWY
4 (C+H) KL
(Q+S+T+U+V+X+Y+Z)
5 **AB**EFGIJKLMNOPUVWXZ
6 AEGJ**K**(N 1km)ORTV

You can discover the charms of the Catalan coastline from Le Palais de la Mer and visit the picturesque hinterland. Among the things to enjoy on the campsite are the swimming pool near the lively restaurant or the various sports options. The site has its own entrance to a lovely beach.

On coastal road D81 take exit Ste Marie-Plage. Then drive straight at the roundabout and turn left at the third intersection. Signposted.

CC € 17 *14/5-30/6 1/9-24/9*

N 42°44'26" E 3°2'1"

Ste Marie-la-Mer, F-66470 / Languedoc-Roussillon (Pyrénées-Orientales)

2408

Le Sainte Marie****
rue des Clauses
+33 (0)4-68804810
2/4 - 4/11
camping@lesaintemarie.com

15ha 150**T**(80-110m²) 10A CEE

1 ACD**G**IJLPST
2 RVY
3 ABDGJN**P**QRUW
4 (B+G 11/6-10/9) JK
(Q+R+T+U+V+X+Z 11/6-10/9)
5 **A**EFGIJKLMNOPUVZ
6 AEGI**K**(N 2km)RTV

A shaded campsite in a quiet nature park with lovely swimming pool, restaurant and plenty of sports and games facilities. 1 km from a rugged, unpatrolled beach which can be reached by a footpath. 2 km from a beautiful beach at Sainte Marie.

Coastal road D81, turn towards Ste Marie-Village at the roundabout. Follow the camping signs through the village and through the tunnel (maximum vehicle height 2.30 metres), or turn to the right and drive around instead.

CC € 13 *2/4-8/7 25/8-4/11* *14=12, 21=16*

N 42°42'51" E 3°1'53"

Ste Marie-Plage, F-66470 / Languedoc-Roussillon (Pyrénées-Orientales)

2409

De la Plage***
av. de las-Illes
+33 (0)4-68806859
FAX +33 (0)4-68731470
1/3 - 31/10
contact@
camping-municipal-de-la-plage.com

7ha 288**T**(90-100m²) 6A CEE

1 ACD**G**IJKLMOPST
2 AEGRTVXY
3 GJ**M**NQRU**V**WY
4 (B+G 20/5-29/9) **KLN**
(Q+S+T+U+V 1/6-15/9)
(X+Y 15/5-15/9)
(Z 1/6-15/9)
5 **AB**DFGIJKLMNPUZ
6 ACEG**K**(N 0,3km)OTV

Spacious friendly campsite with floral landscaping, lovely big swimming pool and extensive sports accommodation. Heated toilet facilities in early and late seasons. Right on the sea with its own access to the supervised sandy beach. Naturist beach in the area.

On the coastal road D81 take exit Ste Marie-Plage. Drive straight over the roundabout and turn left at the third road. Follow the camping signs.

CC € 15 *1/3-30/6 1/9-31/10*

N 42°44'22" E 3°2'2"

Torreilles-Plage, F-66440 / Languedoc-Roussillon (Pyrénées-Orientales)

2410

Le Trivoly****
boulevard des Plages
+33 (0)2-51330505
+33 (0)2-51339404
2/4 - 24/9
info@chadotel.com

5ha 44T(80-120m²) 16A CEE

1 ACD**F**IJKLOPS
2 FGRTVWX
3 BGKMNRU
4 (C+G 1/5-15/9) J
(Q+R+T+U+Z 1/6-8/9)
5 **AB**FGIJKLMNPUZ
6 ACEG**K**(N 3km)RTV

This campsite, equipped with a heated swimming pool with slides, is located 800m from a patrolled clean beach and close to a shopping centre. The site is an ideal location for lovely day trips along the coast to the Pyrenees or Spain.

A9 exit Perpignan-Centre. Direction Le Barcarès via the D83, then direction Canet/St. Cyprien as far as the exit Torreilles-Plage.

CC € 15 *2/4-2/7 3/9-24/9*

N 42°45'57" E 3°1'37"

Torreilles-Plage, F-66440 / Languedoc-Roussillon (Pyrénées-Orientales)

2411

Les Tropiques****
boulevard de la Plage
+33 (0)4-68280509
+33 (0)4-68284890
9/4 - 30/9
contact@
campinglestropiques.com

8ha 88T(100-115m²) 10A CEE

1 AC**G**IJKLMO**P**ST
2 AEFGRTVWXY
3 ABGKMNRUVWY
4 (C+H) **JKLP**(Q+S+T)
(U 1/5-15/9) (V 1/6-15/9)
(X+Y 1/5-15/9) (Z)
5 **AB**EFGIJKLMNPUVWZ
6 ACEGH**I**J**K**LM(N 3km)RTV

This friendly family campsite is located 400m from the lovely Torreilles Plage beach, where you can enjoy the heated swimming pool, the various wellness facilities or a delicious meal in the restaurant.
The campsite is also a perfect starting point for many day trips possible along the coast to the Pyrenees and Spain.

A9 exit Perpignan-Centre. Direction Le Barcarès via the D83, then direction Canet/St. Cyprien as far as the exit Torreilles-Plage.

CC € 17 *9/4-5/7 28/8-30/9*

N 42°46'3" E 3°1'47"

Trèbes, F-11800 / Languedoc-Roussillon (Aude)

2412

A l'Ombre des Micocouliers****
chemin de la Lande
+33 (0)4-68786175
+33 (0)4-68788877
1/4 - 30/9
infos@campingmicocouliers.com

2ha 70T(90-120m²) 16A CEE

1 ACD**G**HIJKLMPQ
2 CFGRSVY
3 AB**F**GHJQRUW
4 (E+F+G+Q)
(T+U+X+Y 15/6-31/8) Z
5 **A**EFGJLNPUVYZ
6 EGIJ(N 0,3km)OTV

Excellent location for visiting nearby Carcassonne from a peaceful campsite. Cycling along the Canal du Midi and all types of sport available. A central point for Cathar country with its typical villages and fortresses. Renovated toilet facilities in 2016.

A61/E80 exit 24 direction Trèbes via the RN113. Campsite well signposted in village.

CC € 13 *1/4-15/6 14/9-30/9*

N 43°12'24" E 2°26'31"

Valras-Plage, F-34350 / Languedoc-Roussillon (Hérault) 2413

Blue Bayou*****
Vendres Plage Ouest
+33 (0)4-67374197
23/4 - 17/9
infobluebayou@orange.fr

6ha 120T(80-100m²) 10A CEE

1 AC**G**IJKLMOPST
2 AEFGRSVWXY
3 BG**M**N**O**PU**V**WY
4 (C+H) IJM(Q) (S 15/6-15/9) (T+U+V+X+Y) Z
5 **AB**DEFGIJKLMNP**ST**UZ
6 EGJ**K**(N 2,5km)ORTV

A large campsite with pitches for touring guests. Some have private toilet facilities. Refurbished leisure pool with water playpark for small children. Lovely swimming pool. 300m from a sandy beach in a beautiful nature reserve. Attractive location, close to the sea and 5 km from the centre of Valras-Plage.

Campsite located on the Valras-Plage Ouest-Vendres-Plage D37E9. Campsite south west of Vendre-Plage.

CC € 15 *30/4-7/7 25/8-17/9*

N 43°13'38'' E 3°14'38''

Valras-Plage, F-34350 / Languedoc-Roussillon (Hérault) 2414

Lou Village****
Chemin des Montilles
+33 (0)4-67373379
FAX +33 (0)4-67375356
1/5 - 11/9
info@louvillage.com

7ha 100T(80-100m²) 10A CEE

1 ACDGIJKLOPRS
2 AEFGLRTVXY
3 BG**M**N**O**PRUWY
4 (C+H) IJ (Q+S+T+U+V+X+Y+Z)
5 **AB**EFGIJKLMNPUZ
6 CFGJM(N 1km)ORTVWX

A good friendly campsite with plenty to do. Direct access to the sea with a lovely beach. There is also a fabulous leisure pool. The owners do all they can to satisfy everyone. Communal fun, for those who want it, is high on the list. 2.5 km from centre of Valras-Plage and the delightful harbour at Port-Vendres.

From Valras the campsite is located by the sea just before La Yole, path on your left, about 200 metres left. Follow signs campsite Valras Plage Ouest.

CC € 15 *1/5-5/7 24/8-11/9*

N 43°14'1'' E 3°15'38''

Valras-Plage/Vendres-Plage, F-34350 / Languedoc-Roussillon (Hérault) 2415

Le Palmira Beach***
avenue du port de Vendres
+33 (0)4-67942900
2/4 - 30/10
contact@palmirabeach.fr

4ha 102T(> 100m²) 10A CEE

1 ACD**F**IJKLMPST
2 AEFGSVW
3 BGHN**O**PRUWY
4 (C+H 15/5-15/9) **JKMN** (Q) (R 1/6-30/9) (T+U+V+X 1/5-30/9) Z
5 **AB**EFGJLMNPQUX
6 CEG**K**(N 5km)OTV

New (2014) campsite 300m from the beach. Lovely large pitches without shade.

From Valras follow Vendres-Plage signs. Then follow camping signs.

CC € 15 *2/4-4/7 24/8-30/10*

N 43°13'44'' E 3°14'44''

Vauvert, F-30600 / Languedoc-Roussillon (Gard) **2416**

Le Mas de Mourgues**
Gallician
+33 (0)4-66733088
15/3 - 15/10
info@masdemourgues.com

2ha 62**T**(50-100m²) 10A CEE

1 ACD**G**IJKLMPST
2 STWXY
3 AGHJR
4 (C 1/4-15/10)
(Q+R+U+V+X+Z)
5 AFGIJKLMNPQUWZ
6 ACDEG**K**(N 5km)T

Welcome to Camping Le Mas de Mourgues, located in an open area of the Camargue, in the Gard between Nimes and Saintes Maries de la Mer. A family campsite with 62 pitches. La Camargue is also known for the sun, its beaches and for doing nothing. Great for cycling.

A9, exit 26 direction Gallargues. Then N313 direction Aimargues. Then N572. Campsite on the left just beyond Vauvert, dir. St. Jilles.

CC € 15 *15/3-15/7 1/9-15/10*

N 43°39'16'' E 4°17'44''

Vendres, F-34350 / Languedoc-Roussillon (Hérault) **2417**

La Plage et du Bord de Mer**
Av. de la Mediterranee
+33 (0)4-67373438
FAX +33 (0)4-67373374
23/4 - 18/9
reservation@
camping-plage-mediterranee.com

13ha 510**T**(80-100m²) 10A

1 ACDEIJKLMOPST
2 AEFGLRSVWXY
3 ABGK**M**N**Q**RUWY
4 (C+G) IJK
(Q+S+T+U+V+X+Y+Z)
5 **AB**EFGIJKLMNOPUVZ
6 CDEG**IJK**ORSTV

A peaceful, spacious campsite with a lovely sandy beach. Refurbished toilet facilities. Nice play equipment also for young children. 1.5 km from the lively centre of Valras-Plage. Also suitable for excursions in a wider area. Lovely water park.

The campsite is located on the boulevard Valras-Plage Ouest. Follow the signs when entering Valras-Plage.

CC € 17 *23/4-2/7 22/8-18/9* *14=13*

N 43°14'7'' E 3°16'8''

Vendres-Plage/Valras-Plage, F-34350 / Languedoc-Roussillon (Hérault) **2418**

Les Vagues****
chemin de Montilles
+33 (0)4-67373312
FAX +33 (0)4-67375036
1/4 - 10/9
t.hannier@sandaya.fr

8ha 107**T**(85-100m²) 6A

1 ACD**F**IJKLMOP
2 AEFGLSTVXY
3 ABGKN**OP**QRUVWY
4 (C+H) IJK
(Q+S+T+U+V+W+X)
(Y 1/7-31/8) (Z)
5 **AB**EFGIJKLMNOPUXYZ
6 AEGJ**K**M(N 5km)ORTVX

Located 500 metres from the Languedoc beaches. The shaded campsite comprises three separate sections. Lovely heated swimming pool with wave pool and slide. Many sights, activities and watersports opportunities in the area.

From Valras follow Valras-Plage Ouest signs. Then follow camping signs.

CC € 17 *1/4-1/7 29/8-10/9*

N 43°13'51'' E 3°15'13''

Vias, F-34450 / Languedoc-Roussillon (Hérault)

2419

Domaine de la Dragonnière*****
RD612
+33 (0)4-67010310
FAX +33 (0)4-67217339
25/3 - 6/11
contact@dragonniere.com

20ha 60T(100-120m²) 10A CEE

1 ACD**F**IJKLM**P**S
2 AFGRVX
3 BC**F**GJKNRU
4 (C+F+H) IJ**LMNP** (Q+S+T+U+V+X+Y) Z
5 **AB**CDEFGHJLNPSTUXYZ
6 ABEGHJ**K**LM(N 4km)O**P**R TVWX

Lovely campsite with extensive leisure activities. A leisure pool including an indoor pool, fully heated from the opening date. Individual heated toilet facilities. All amenities open for entire opening period.

From A9 between exits 34 and 36, dir. A75 Beziers-centre. After toll station, exit 64 dir. Beziers/Cap d'Agde. Turn right at crossing near airport. Follow signs.

CC € 19 *25/3-25/6 27/8-5/11*

N 43°18'45'' E 3°21'48''

Vias-Plage, F-34450 / Languedoc-Roussillon (Hérault)

2420

Beach Farret*****
Chemin des Rosses
+33 (0)467216445
FAX +33 (0)467217049
9/4 - 30/9
farret@wanadoo.fr

63T(100-110m²) 10A

1 ACD**F**IJKLO**P**RS
2 AEFSVWX
3 AB**F**GJKMNQRUVWY
4 (C+H) **KLMNP** (Q+S+T+U+V+W+X+Y+Z)
5 **AB**DEFGIJKLMNOPUWZ
6 CEG**IK**LM(N 0,3km)ORTV

This 4-star campsite is so close to the beach you can almost touch the sand from your bed. All amenities of the campsite next door, Le Club Farret, can be used. The large pitches are marked-out by hedges. The 11 pitches on the first line, immediately by the beach, do not fall under the CampingCard ACSI rate.

A9, exit Agde/Pézenas dir. Agde. Then N112 exit Vias-Plage. Then follow 'campings Sud'. Left at end of road.

CC € 17 *9/4-11/6 9/9-30/9*

N 43°17'29'' E 3°25'8''

Vias-Plage, F-34450 / Languedoc-Roussillon (Hérault)

2421

Camping Club Californie-Plage****
Côte Ouest
+33 (0)4-67216469
FAX +33 (0)4-67215462
1/4 - 30/9
info@californie-plage.fr

5,5ha 273T(80-100m²) 10A CEE

1 ACD**G**IJKLM**P**Q
2 AEFQRSVWXY
3 B**F**GKMNRUWY
4 (C+E+H) IJKP (Q+S+T+U+V+W+X+Y+Z)
5 **AB**EFGIJKLNOPUWZ
6 ACDEGHJ**K**L(N 2,5km)RTV

A well equipped campsite with a beautiful leisure pool, positioned by the sea in a poplar wood. The pitches are marked out by hedges including oleanders. The heated indoor swimming pool has a roof that can be opened.

A9 exit Agde/Pézenas direction Agde, then N112 exit Vias-Plage, then over the Côte Ouest bridge and follow the signs.

CC € 15 *1/4-30/6 1/9-30/9*

N 43°17'26'' E 3°23'55''

Vias-Plage, F-34450 / Languedoc-Roussillon (Hérault) — 2422

Camping Club Le Napoléon****

1171 av. de la Méditerranée
+33 (0)4-67010780
FAX +33 (0)4-67010785
8/4 - 30/9
@ reception@camping-napoleon.fr

3,4ha 120**T**(80-100m²) 10A CEE

1 AC**G**IJKLM**P**ST
2 AEFRSVY
3 AB**F**GJKMN**OPQ**RUVWY
4 (C+H 🔑) KL**NP** (Q+S+T+U+V+W+X+Y+Z 🔑)
5 **AB**FGIJKLMNOPUVWXYZ
6 CEGH**IK**LM(N 1,5km)OQRT VX

A fine campsite with extensive amenities and entertainment for all ages. Tall poplars offer plenty of shade. 150 metres from the sea and a lovely beach with fine sand. Many boutiques, terraces, restaurants and shops are next to the campsite. The swimming pool is heated from the opening day.

D612 exit Vias-Plage, then campings Sud, at the end of the road to the right.

CC € 17 *8/4-10/7 27/8-24/9*

N 43°17'31'' E 3°24'58''

Vias-Plage, F-34450 / Languedoc-Roussillon (Hérault) — 2423

Helios***

avenue des Pêcheurs
FAX +33 (0)4-67216366
23/4 - 30/9
@ contact@camping-helios.com

3ha 108**T**(80-90m²) 6A CEE

1 ACD**G**IJKLMPS
2 ACEFSVY
3 BGNRUWY
4 (C+E+H 🔑) **KLNP** (Q+S+T+U+X+Z 🔑)
5 **A**FGIJKLMNOPSUVZ
6 AEGH**K**(N 4km)OTV

A quiet, natural campsite with a homely ambiance. 200 metres from the beach on the small River Libron and within walking distance from the lively centre of Vias-Plage. The toilet facilities have been renovated and there is a new wellness amenity. From 2015 there is a beautiful new heated leisure pool, partly covered.

A9 exit Agde/Pézenas. D612 direction Agde; exit Vias-Plage. Then 'campings sud' and follow the signs at the roundabout.

CC € 15 *23/4-1/7 27/8-30/9*

N 43°17'33'' E 3°24'26''

Vias-Plage, F-34450 / Languedoc-Roussillon (Hérault) — 2424

L'Air Marin****

+33 (0)4-67216490
FAX +33 (0)4-67217679
1/5 - 17/9
@ info@camping-air-marin.fr

8ha 150**T**(70-120m²) 6A

1 A**G**IJLM**P**S
2 ACFRTVXY
3 ABGJ**M**NRUVW
4 (B+F+G 🔑) JKP(Q+S 🔑) (T+U 1/7-12/9) (V+X+Y+Z 🔑)
5 **AB**FGIJKLMOPUVWX
6 CEG**K**(N 1km)ORTV

A large, peaceful campsite in the shade of plane trees on the Canal du Midi, 10 minute walk from the sandy beach of Vias-Plage. Free indoor heated swimming pool.

A9 exit Agde/Pézenas direction Agde, then N112 direction Vias-Plage, then campsites Côte Est and follow signs.

CC € 19 *1/5-8/7 25/8-17/9*

N 43°18'8'' E 3°25'19''

Vias-Plage, F-34450 / Languedoc-Roussillon (Hérault) — 2425

Le Méditerranée Plage****
D137
+33 (0)4-67909907
FAX +33 (0)4-67909917
26/3 - 25/9
@ contact@
mediterranee-plage.com

7ha 160T(80-90m²) 10A CEE

1 ACD**G**IJKLMPQ
2 AEFRSTVXY
3 ABDGJKMN**OP**QRUWY
4 (A+C+H) J
(Q+S+T+U+V+X+Y+Z)
5 **AB**DEFGIJKLMNPUVWZ
6 CEGH**I**JM(N 5km)ORTV

A well-run four-star campsite by a nice sandy beach. The swimming pools are heated from the opening date. Free WiFi.

A9/A75 exit 63 Béziers-centre, dir. Agde/Sète. After 3.5 km to Agde/Sète at roundabout. Right after 1.5 km dir. Portiragnes-Plage. Over the Canal du Midi bridge, turn left and follow signs.

CC € 17 26/3-2/7 27/8-25/9

N 43°16'55" E 3°22'15"

Vias-Plage, F-34450 / Languedoc-Roussillon (Hérault) — 2426

Le Roucan West***
Côte Ouest
+33 (0)4-67216464
FAX +33 (0)4-67216479
15/5 - 17/9
@ info@campingleroucan.com

3ha 70T(75-100m²) 10A CEE

1 ACD**G**IJKLMPS
2 AEFSVWXY
3 BGJPRWY
4 (C+H+Q+R+T)
(U+V 1/6-15/9) (Y) Z
5 **A**FGJLNPUX
6 EG**K**(N 6km)OTV

An informal and family-friendly campsite by the Mediterranean, with a swimming pool. Only the pitches with sea views have no shade. Very modern security.

A9 exit Agde/Pézenas direction Agde. Then N112 Vias-Plage, over the bridge Côte Ouest. Then follow signs.

CC € 13 15/5-8/7 25/8-17/9

N 43°17'13" E 3°23'30"

Villegly-en-Minervois, F-11600 / Languedoc-Roussillon (Aude) — 2427

Sites & Paysages Le
Moulin de Ste Anne****
chemin de Ste Anne
+33 (0)4-68722080
1/4 - 31/10
@ contact@
moulindesainteanne.com

1,6ha 43T(< 120m²) 10A CEE

1 AC**F**IJLPST
2 CGIJRTVX
3 ABHJNRU
4 (C+G 1/6-30/9) K
(Q+T+U+V+X 15/6-25/8)
5 **A**DGIJKLMNOPUXYZ
6 CEGK(N 0,2km)

This small, peacefully situated campsite is positioned on the edge of the village of Villegly in the Minervois region. Trips out to Carcassonne are possible. Walking routes are conducted in July and August which take you past archaeological discoveries.

A61 exit 23 direction Mazamet. At the roundabout direction Villegly (signposted).

CC € 17 1/4-1/7 3/9-30/9

N 43°16'59" E 2°26'29"

Villeneuve-lès-Béziers, F-34420 / Languedoc-Roussillon (Hérault)

2428

Les Berges du Canal***
promenade des Vernets
+33 (0)4-67393609
FAX +33 (0)4-67398207
12/3 - 15/10
@ contact@lesbergesducanal.fr

1,5ha 30T(80-90m²) 16A CEE

1 BCD**G**IJKLM**P**ST
2 CFGRTVY
3 ABCGJKNRUW
4 (B+G 1/5-15/9) **N**
(Q 16/4-17/9)
(T+U+V+X+Y+Z)
5 **AB**DEFGIJLNPRSUVWZ
6 CDEG**K**ORTV

A quiet, well positioned, friendly family campsite next to the Canal du Midi. Perfectly suited for trips out, also by bike. 7 km from the beach.

The campsite is located in the village on the Canal du Midi. When approaching from Béziers: before the bridge to the left.

CC € 15 12/3-8/7 27/8-15/10 7=6, 14=12, 21=18

N 43°19'0'' E 3°17'4''

Villeneuve-lez-Avignon/Avignon, F-30400 / Languedoc-Roussillon (Gard)

2429

Campéole L'ile des Papes****
1497, D780
+33 (0)4-90151590
FAX +33 (0)4-90151591
25/3 - 2/11
@ ile-des-papes@
andretriganogroupe.com

20ha 176T(100m²) 10A CEE

1 ACD**G**IJKLM**P**ST
2 CFGKLRSTVWXY
3 B**F**GHJKN**Q**RU**W**
4 (C+G 1/5-30/9) I
(Q+R+U+Y) Z
5 **AB**EFGIJLMNPUWZ
6 CDEGHI**J**(N 5km)RTV

Spaciously appointed, luxurious campsite with very many amenities, located on an island in the Rhône. 6 km from Avignon.

A9, exit Roquemaure, dir. Roquemaure-centre, then direction Sauveterre, and Barrage-de-Villeneuve. Campsite signposted

CC € 17 1/5-4/7 22/8-30/9

N 43°59'37'' E 4°49'4''

Aiguines, F-83630 / Provence-Alpes-Côte d'Azur (Var)

2430

L'Aigle***
Quartier Saint Pierre
+33 (0)4-94842375
25/4 - 14/9
@ aigle@campasun.eu

5ha 80T(80-120m²) 6A CEE

1 ACD**G**IJKL**P**
2 BIJKRVWXY
3 BHJRT
4 (Q+U+V+X+Y+Z)
5 **A**CFGHIJKLMNPUVZ
6 ACDEGJ(N 0,4km)TV

A very nicely located campsite with breathtaking panoramas of Lac Sainte Croix. Relatively modest amenities but very well maintained. A few minutes' walk from the picturesque village of Aiguines.

Campsite located 600m east of Aiguines (D19).

CC € 15 25/4-10/7 27/8-14/9

N 43°46'35'' E 6°14'43''

Albaron/Arles, F-13123 / Provence-Alpes-Côte d'Azur (Bouches-du-Rhône)

iD **2431**

Le Domaine du Crin Blanc***
CD37 - Hameau de Saliers
+33 (0)4-66874878
FAX +33 (0)4-66871866
1/4 - 30/9
camping-crin.blanc@wanadoo.fr

4,5ha 50**T**(90-160m²) 10A CEE

1 ACD**G**HIJKLMPST
2 KRSTVX
3 B**F**GHJKMN**OP**RU**W**
4 (C+H) IJ(Q)
(R+T+U+V+Z 1/4-15/9)
5 **AB**EFGIJKLMNPUVZ
6 ACEGJ**K**(N 3km)TUV

Spacious campsite located in the Carmargue National Park, with three heated swimming pools and a water slide. 20 km from Arles, Provence and the Mediterranean Sea.

From Arles D570 direction Stes Maries-de-la-Mer. In Albaron turn right onto CD37 direction St. Gilles. After 7 km on the left.

CC € 15 *1/4-9/7 26/8-30/9*

N 43°39'44'' E 4°28'26''

Annot, F-04240 / Provence-Alpes-Côte d'Azur (Alpes-de-Haute-Prov)

iD **2432**

La Ribière**
route du Fugeret
+33 (0)4-92832144
19/3 - 31/10
info@la-ribiere.com

1ha 64**T**(70-100m²) 6-10A CEE

1 A**G**IJKLM**P**ST
2 CKRTVWXY
3 AGHJN**OP**RU**W**
4 (Q+T+V 1/4-15/10) (Z)
5 **A**DEFGIJKLMNOPUZ
6 ACEGIJTV

La Ribière is situated at an altitude of 700 metres between Mercantour, Verdon and the Mediterranean. It is located on the edge of the picturesque village of Annot. Whether you are a sports or nature lover, you will be charmed by 'Le pays d'Annot'.

Campsite 700 metres north of Annot (D908).

CC € 15 *19/3-15/7 1/9-31/10*

N 43°58'18'' E 6°39'28''

Apt, F-84400 / Provence-Alpes-Côte d'Azur (Vaucluse)

iD **2433**

Le Luberon***
avenue de Saignon
+33 (0)4-90048540
8/4 - 30/9
leluberon@wanadoo.fr

4ha 75**T**(80-150m²) 6A

1 ACD**F**HIJL**P**S
2 IJRTVY
3 AFGHRU
4 (C+H 26/4-26/9) (Q)
(T 1/5-30/8) (X 4/7-25/8) Z
5 **AB**DFGIJKLNOPRUZ
6 CDEGJ**K**(N 1,5km)TV

A campsite in the Apt, the perfect starting point for visiting Lubéron and the typical villages of Roussillon, Gordes, Saignon and Bonnieux. A quiet location in a wood with lovely views of the Saignon cliffs. Heated swimming pool.

Take the N100. At the roundabout on the east side of Apt take the D48 direction Saignon 'village'.

CC € 17 *8/4-20/6 1/9-30/9*

N 43°51'58'' E 5°24'47''

Arles/Pont-de-Crau, F-13200 / Provence-Alpes-Côte d'Azur (Bouches-du-Rhône)

2434

L'Arlesienne***
145 Draille Marseillaise
+33 (0)4-90960212
1/4 - 1/11
camping@larlesienne.com

2,2ha 74T(80-90m²) 6-10A CEE

1 ABCD**G**IJKLMOPST
2 FGRSTVWX
3 A**F**GHJNRU**W**
4 (C+H 15/5-15/9)
(Q+T+U+V+X+Z 1/4-30/9)
5 **A**FGIJKLMNPUZ
6 ACDEG**K**(N 0,5km)V

A campsite located 2 km from the old centre of Arles. Attractive pitches, the campsite has lovely modernised swimming pools. There is a bus stop 200m from the site. Many activities in the vicinity, famous for Van Gogh and the Romans, among others.

The campsite is located in Pont-de-Crau on the south-eastern edge of Arles, direction St. Martin-de-Crau. Signposted.

CC € 17 1/4-10/7 27/8-1/11 7=6

N 43°39'34'' E 4°39'15''

Artignosc-sur-Verdon, F-83630 / Provence-Alpes-Côte d'Azur (Var)

2435

L'Avelanède***
route de Baudinard
+33 (0)4-94807157
1/4 - 15/11
bonjour@
camping-l-avelanede.com

12ha 50T(80-200m²) 6A CEE

1 A**G**IJKLMPST
2 BGRTWXY
3 BGHJKNR
4 (C+H 15/5-15/10)
(Q 19/5-15/6)
(T+U+V+X 1/7-31/8) (Z)
5 **A**GJKLMNPUVZ
6 AEJ(N 2km)

A hospitable campsite in the middle of the countryside, in the heart of the 'Parc Naturel Régional du Verdon' and surrounded by the loveliest lakes in the Verdon. Its location in the centre of the characteristic Provence landscape makes this campsite a unique spot for relaxing and enjoying various activities, and for countless discoveries.

Campsite entrance directly on the D71 and D471 intersection 2.9 km from Artignosc-sur-Verdon.

CC € 15 1/4-30/6 1/9-15/11

N 43°41'22'' E 6°6'35''

Aups, F-83630 / Provence-Alpes-Côte d'Azur (Var)

2436

Les Prés***
181, Carraire n°1, rte de Tourtour
+33 (0)4-94700093
FAX +33 (0)4-94701441
15/3 - 31/10
contact@camping-lespres.com

2ha 80T(70-137m²) 6A

1 ACD**G**IJKL**P**S
2 GKRVWXY
3 BG**M**R
4 (B+G 15/6-15/9)
(Q 1/5-30/9) (T 1/7-31/8)
(Z)
5 **A**DFGIJKLMNOPUZ
6 ADEG**K**(N 0,3km)ORTV

The campsite is located a few minutes' walk from the lively Provençale village of Aups. An ideal campsite for a relaxing stay. Central location in a very interesting region: Lac du Verdon, Gorges du Verdon, Salernes, Ampus, Tourtour, etc. Very friendly welcome.

Campsite located 300m from Aups centre. From centre direction Tourtour. Campsite signposted. Final 150m on a private (gravel) road.

CC € 19 15/3-2/7 27/8-31/10

N 43°37'26'' E 6°13'44''

Avignon, F-84000 / Provence-Alpes-Côte d'Azur (Vaucluse)

2437

Bagatelle***
Île de la Barthelasse
+33 (0)4-90863039
+33 (0)4-90271623
1/1 - 31/12
camping.bagatelle@wanadoo.fr

4ha 227**T**(80-130m²) 10A CEE

1 ACD**F**IJKLMOPST
2 CFGKLMSTVWXY
3 A**F**GHJNU**W**
4 (Q+S+T+U+V+W+X+Y) Z
5 **A**BDFGIJKLMNOPRUVWXYZ
6 ACDGH**IJK**(N 1km)OTV

Camping Bagatelle is located close to the old centre of Avignon, just 7 minutes on foot. Lovely views of the Palais des Papes from the terraces.

From the A9 to Avignon. Campsite located on l'Île de la Barthelasse, opposite the Papal Palace. Campsite indicated on the bridge.

CC € 17 *1/1-30/6 17/8-31/12 7=6, 14=11, 28=21*

N 43°57'10'' E 4°47'59''

Avignon, F-84000 / Provence-Alpes-Côte d'Azur (Vaucluse)

2438

du Pont d'Avignon****
10 chemin de la Barthelasse
+33 (0)4-90806350
+33 (0)4-90852212
29/2 - 20/11
camping.lepontdavignon@orange.fr

7,6ha 276**T**(60-100m²) 10A

1 ACD**G**IJKLMO**P**Q
2 CFGRSTVXY
3 AB**F**GHJKMNRU**W**
4 (B+G 10/5-1/10) (Q+S+T+U+V+X+Z)
5 **AB**GIJKLMNOPUVW
6 ACFGI**K**(N 2km)RTV

A campsite in an attractive parkland setting, located opposite the Pont d'Avignon with views of the Palais des Papes.

From Remoulins and A9 turn right beyond the bridge. Follow 'Île de la Barthelasse' signs.

CC € 15 *29/2-3/7 20/8-20/11 7=6, 14=11*

N 43°57'24'' E 4°48'7''

Banon, F-04150 / Provence-Alpes-Côte d'Azur (Alpes-de-Haute-Prov)

2439

L'Epi Bleu***
Les Gravières
+33 (0)4-92733030
16/4 - 15/10
campingepibleu@aol.com

2ha 40**T**(65-130m²) 10A CEE

1 ACFIJKLM**P**ST
2 BJKTUVWXY
3 ABGHJOPRU
4 (**A** 1/7-31/8) (C 15/5-15/9) (H 1/7-31/8) (Q 18/4-15/10) (R 1/7-31/8) (T 15/6-31/8) (U 1/7-31/8) (V+X 15/6-31/8) Z
5 **A**DFGIJKLMNOPUVWZ
6 AEGHK(N 1km)TV

A hospitable and quiet family campsite located 1.5 km from Banon and close to lavender fields. Alternating touring pitches and mobile homes. Genuinely rural, little tourism. Heated swimming pool from mid June to mid September.

A7, exit Avignon-Sud. Drive in the direction of Apt, then Banon. In Banon follow the signs.

CC € 15 *16/4-2/7 27/8-15/10 7=6*

N 44°1'36'' E 5°37'52''

Baratier, F-05200 / Provence-Alpes-Côte d'Azur (Hautes-Alpes) 2440

Le Petit Liou**
ancienne route de Baratier
+33 (0)4-92431910
FAX +33 (0)4-92436928
1/5 - 21/9
@ info@camping-lepetitliou.com

4,5ha 280**T**(85-120m²) 10A CEE

1 ACD**F**IJKLMPQ
2 BGKRTVWXY
3 BGHJLRU
4 (C+H 15/6-15/9) (Q)
(R 1/7-31/8)
(T+U+V+X 20/6-1/9) Z
5 **A**EFGHIJKLMNOPUVWZ
6 CEGJ**K**L(N 0,5km)OV

A family campsite in rural surroundings and with spacious shaded pitches. Located between Embrun and Barratier.

On the N94 from Gap to Briançon, right at the first roundabout just before Embrun. First left after 150m then first right. Clearly signposted.

CC € 15 *1/5-7/7 24/8-21/9*

N 44°32'50" E 6°29'31"

Baratier/Embrun, F-05200 / Provence-Alpes-Côte d'Azur (Hautes-Alpes) 2441

Les Deux Bois***
route de Pra Fouran
+33 (0)4-92435414
14/5 - 25/9
@ info@camping-les2bois.com

2,5ha 104**T**(70-110m²) 10A CEE

1 ACD**G**IJLPQ
2 CGJKLRTVWXY
3 BGHJRU**W**
4 (B 22/5-25/9) (Q)
(T+U+V+X+Z 30/5-6/9)
5 **A**BEFGIJKLMNOPUVWZ
6 EGJ(N 0,2km)RT

Homely atmosphere in rural surroundings. Well marked-out, shady pitches. Good bar and restaurant. Nice toilet blocks.

Turn off the N94 at the Crots-Embrun roundabout to Baratier.

CC € 15 *14/5-4/7 28/8-25/9*

N 44°32'18" E 6°29'32"

Beaurecueil, F-13100 / Provence-Alpes-Côte d'Azur (Bouches-du-Rhône) 2442

Sainte Victoire**
Quartier Paradou 613 av J. Gautier
+33 (0)4-42669131
FAX +33 (0)4-42669643
8/2 - 14/11
@ campingstevictoire@orange.fr

2ha 85**T**(80-170m²) 6A CEE

1 A**G**IJKLMPST
2 BCFGKLMTVWXY
3 AR
4 (Q+R+V+Z)
5 **A**DGIJKLMNOPRUVZ
6 ACE**I**J(N 7km)OV

A modest campsite, picturesquely located at the foot of Sainte Victoire. Marked out, shaded pitches, an oasis of peace. Starting point for lovely walks or for visiting Aix-en-Provence just 8 km away. Bus to Aix-en-Provence 13 times a day.

In Aix follow the A8 towards Nice/Toulon. Exit 31. Then 2x right towards Palette/Beaurecueil. Then follow arrows.

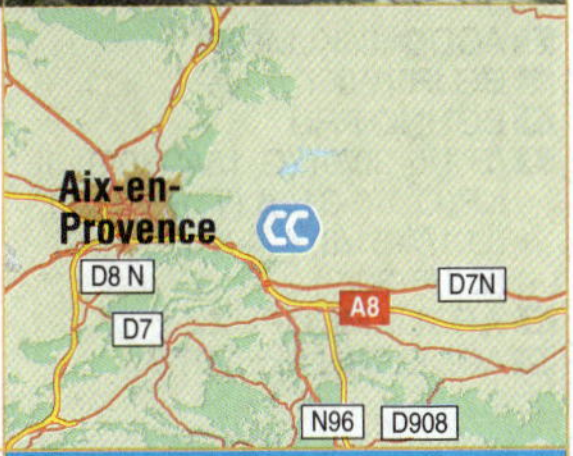

CC € 17 *1/4-4/7 22/8-14/10*

N 43°31'2" E 5°32'26"

Bédoin, F-84410 / Provence-Alpes-Côte d'Azur (Vaucluse)

2443

Camping Le Pastory**
1105 route de Malaucène
+33 (0)4-90128583
1/4 - 1/10
info@camping-le-pastory.com

1,6ha 90T(100-130m²) 10A CEE

1 ABCD**G**IJKLM**P**
2 KRTUVWXY
3 AGR
4 (Q 1/7-31/8) (R 1/5-1/10)
5 AGIJKLMNOPUXY
6 EG**K**(N 0,9km)

Ideal location at the foot of Mont Ventoux, at 900 metres from the Provence village of Bédoin. Le Pastory offers spacious, shaded pitches with a breathtaking view of Mont Ventaux. There is nature all around. Typical Provence market in Bédoin on Monday mornings. Swimming is possible in the surrounding lakes and the local swimming pool near the campsite.

A7 exit Orange-Sud to Carpentras direction Bédoin. In centre of Bédoin follow signs.

CC € 15 *1/4-30/6 1/9-1/10 14=12, 30=24*

N 44°7'54" E 5°10'15"

Bollène, F-84500 / Provence-Alpes-Côte d'Azur (Vaucluse)

2444

La Simioune**
route de l'embisque
+33 (0)4-90631791
1/3 - 30/11
camping@la-simioune.fr

3ha 80T(100-200m²) 10A CEE

1 ACD**G**IJKLMOPS
2 BFJKSTUVWXY
3 BDGHINPRU
4 (B+G 1/5-10/10)
(Q 1/4-30/9) (R)
(T 1/6-31/8) (U)
(V 1/4-30/9) (X+Z 1/6-31/8)
5 **A**EFGIJKLMNOPUXZ
6 EGKOQTV

A typically French, hospitable and natural campsite with spacious pitches. Located just outside the town of Bollène in a wood with tall pine trees.

Leave A7 at Bollène. To roundabout direction Carpentras and follow signs from there (direction Suze la Rousse).

CC € 15 *1/3-3/7 20/8-30/11*

N 44°17'50" E 4°47'15"

Callas, F-83830 / Provence-Alpes-Côte d'Azur (Var)

2445

Les Blimouses**
Quartier Les Blimouses RD225
+33 (0)4-94478341
7/3 - 17/12
camping.les.blimouses@orange.fr

6ha 72T(70-150m²) 16A CEE

1 ACD**G**HIJKLM**P**ST
2 BGJRVWXY
3 BGHN**OP**RU
4 (B 1/5-30/9) (G 15/4-30/9) J KP(Q 1/6-31/8) (T 1/6-30/9) (U 1/7-31/8) (V+X 1/4-15/9) (Z 1/6-30/9)
5 **A**FGIJKMNOPUXZ
6 ACDEGJ(N 3km)OTV

Ideal location in the heart of the Haut Var. Near Callas, the Pennafort gorges and the Provence countryside. You can take a walk, go mountainbiking, enjoy the water activities in the Gorges du Verdon or relax on the beautiful French Riviera beaches. Large pool with slides, toddlers' pool, sun loungers and parasols. Spacious, well marked-out pitches.

A8 exit Le Muy, direction Callas and follow route RD562, then route RD225.

CC € 17 *7/3-30/6 3/9-17/12*

N 43°34'28" E 6°31'55"

Caromb (Vaucluse), F-84330 / Provence-Alpes-Côte d'Azur (Vaucluse)

2446

Le Bouquier**
route de Malaucène
+33 (0)4-90623013
9/4 - 1/10
campinglebouquier@gmail.com

NEW

1,5ha 50**T**(80-100m²) 10A CEE

1 AGIJLPST
2 JKSTVWXY
3 AGHJRV
4 (B) KN(Q+T+U+W+X) Z
5 **A**DGIJKLMNPUWZ
6 EGJ(N 2km)TV

Small, well-maintained terraced campsite with separate location for tents. Beautiful view, among vineyards, olive trees and fig trees. Swimming pool with spa, jacuzzi and there is a fitness room.

A7, exit Bollène/Cairanne/Vacqueyras/Beaurnes de Venise/Caromb. Follow arrows.

CC € 15 *9/4-9/7 27/8-1/10*

N 44°7'25'' E 5°6'35''

Carpentras, F-84200 / Provence-Alpes-Côte d'Azur (Vaucluse)

2447

Lou Comtadou***
881 av. Pierre de Coubertin
+33 (0)4-90670316
+33 (0)4-90460181
15/3 - 15/10
info@campingloucomtadou.com

2ha 97**T**(100-110m²) 6A CEE

1 AC**G**IJKLMPST
2 LRVXY
3 ABGU
4 (C+**G** 23/5-31/8) **J**
(Q 15/5-30/9)
(R+T+U+X 15/6-15/9) Z
5 **A**FGIJKLMNPUX
6 CEGK(N 1,2km)TV

A campsite with lovely marked-out pitches and plenty of sun and shade. Good amenities and simple restaurant. Bus stop next to the site. Close to town centre with a large market on Fridays. Good paved roads.

Follow ring road before Carpentras, then dir. St. Didier. Right at second lights and follow signs. Left at sports complex on leaving the town.

CC € 15 *15/3-8/7 25/8-15/10 7=6*

N 44°2'39'' E 5°3'16''

Carqueiranne, F-83320 / Provence-Alpes-Côte d'Azur (Var)

2448

Le Beau Vezé****
route de la Moutonne
+33 (0)4-94576530
1/5 - 15/9
info@camping-beauveze.com

5ha 118**T**(80-130m²) 10A

1 ACDGIJKL**P**ST
2 BFIJKRTVXY
3 B**F**GMQR
4 (**A** 1/7-31/8) (B+G) J
(Q) (R 1/7-31/8)
(T+U 10/5-5/9) (V 1/7-31/8)
(X+Y+Z 10/5-5/9)
5 **A**EFGIJKLMNPUV
6 AEG**IK**(N 2km)RTV

A peacefully located campsite in a wood with mostly pine and olive trees. The beaches at Hyères are about 3.5 km away. Trips to e.g. Giens, Hyères, Le Pradet are recommended.

Campsite signposted on the RD559.

CC € 15 *1/5-8/7 25/8-15/9 7=6*

N 43°6'52'' E 6°3'22''

Castellane, F-04120 / Provence-Alpes-Côte d'Azur (Alpes-de-Haute-Prov)

iD **2449**

La Ferme de Castellane***
Quartier La Lagne,
route de Grasse
+33 (0)4-92836777
FAX +33 (0)4-92837592
25/3 - 18/9
accueil@camping-la-ferme.com

1,3ha 33**T**(80-100m²) 6A CEE

1 ACD**G**IJKLMOPST
2 CIJKRVWXY
3 BGHJ**OP**RU
4 (Q+R)
5 **A**BCEFGHIJKLMNOPUVWZ
6 ACDEGIJ(N 2,3km)TV

An ideal campsite for relaxing, situated among natural beauty. An agreeable, well kept and well maintained site. Highly recommended. Special attention on arrival. The main building is a restored 18th century water mill.

From Castellane centre continue towards Grasse. Campsite signposted, on the right, 1 km further.

CC € 13 *25/3-12/7 29/8-18/9*

N 43°50'18'' E 6°32'31''

Castellane, F-04120 / Provence-Alpes-Côte d'Azur (Alpes-de-Haute-Prov)

iD **2450**

Provençal***
route de Digne
FAX +33 (0)4-92836550
6/5 - 11/9
camping-provencal@orange.fr

40**T**(80m²) 6A CEE

1 A**G**IJKLM**P**S
2 KRVWXY
3 AGHJNRU
4 (Q+R 1/6-11/9)
(V 15/6-11/9)
5 **A**FGIJKLMNOPUW
6 ACEGJ(N 0,8km)

A small, extremely well maintained campsite with panoramic views (of the Notre-Dame de Castellane chapel). 1 km from the historic centre of Castellane.

Campsite is on the D4085 (Digne-Castellane) just over 1 km from Castellane.

CC € 13 *6/5-5/7 22/8-11/9*

N 43°51'21'' E 6°29'43''

Cavaillon, F-84300 / Provence-Alpes-Côte d'Azur (Vaucluse)

iD **2451**

de la Durance***
495 avenue Boscodomini
+33 (0)4-90711178
FAX +33 (0)4-90719877
1/4 - 30/9
contact@camping-durance.com

4ha 104**T**(80-120m²) 4-10A CEE

1 ACD**G**IJKLMPQ
2 FRSTVWXY
3 AMNR
4 (Q+T 1/7-30/8)
5 **AB**CDFGIJKLMNPUVXYZ
6 ACGJ(N 0,8km)T

A campsite on the edge of the village of Cavaillon in the heart of Provence, between Alpilles and Luberon. In a park with plane trees.

Take exit 25 to Cavaillon on the A7. Cross the River Durance. Right at the roundabout. Then follow camping signs.

CC € 15 *1/4-8/7 25/8-30/9*

N 43°49'18'' E 5°2'12''

Cavalaire-sur-Mer, F-83240 / Provence-Alpes-Côte d'Azur (Var)

2452

Bonporteau****
208 chemin Train des Pignes
+33 (0)4-94640324
FAX +33 (0)4-94641862
15/3 - 15/10
contact@bonporteau.fr

3ha 110T(80-120m²) 10A CEE

1 A**G**IJKLPST
2 AEGIJKQRSVWXY
3 BGKLRUWY
4 (C+H) K (Q+S+T+U+V+X+Y+Z 1/4-30/9)
5 **A**CDEFGHIJKLMNOPUVWXYZ
6 DEG**IK**(N 0,3km)RTV

A really lovely location, a well maintained campsite with good facilities and a genuine Mediterranean landscape. 200 metres from the beach and 800 metres from the centre of the popular seaside resort of Cavalaire-sur-Mer.

The campsite is clearly signposted in the centre of Cavalaire.

CC € 19 *15/3-2/7 3/9-15/10*

N 43°10'2'' E 6°31'9''

Cavalaire-sur-Mer, F-83240 / Provence-Alpes-Côte d'Azur (Var)

2453

Camping Cros de Mouton****
chemin du Cros de Mouton
+33 (0)4-94641087
FAX +33 (0)4-94646312
21/3 - 31/10
campingcrosdemouton@wanadoo.fr

6ha 125T(60-200m²) 10A

1 ACDGIJKLMOPST
2 ABGIJKQTVWXY
3 BGKLNRU
4 (A 1/7-31/8) (C+H) K (Q+R 1/4-30/10) (T+U+V+X+Y+Z 1/4-30/9)
5 **A**CDEFGHIJKLMNOPUWXYZ
6 ABEGH**IK**L(N 1,5km)ORTV

A very attractive campsite with plenty of shade and fantastic views of the Mediterranean Sea and a beautiful nature reserve in the distant surroundings. 1.5 km from a lively seaside resort with beautiful sandy beaches. Restaurant and swimming pool with panoramic views.

A8, exit Le Muy direction Ste Maxime. Direction St. Tropez then direction Cavalaire. Follow signs.

CC € 17 *21/3-30/6 26/8-31/10*

N 43°10'56'' E 6°31'0''

Cavalaire-sur-Mer, F-83240 / Provence-Alpes-Côte d'Azur (Var)

2454

de la Baie****
bd Pasteur
+33 (0)4-94640815
FAX +33 (0)4-94646610
15/3 - 15/11
contact@camping-baie.com

6,5ha 150T(80-120m²) 10A CEE

1 ACDGIJKLPST
2 AEGIJKRSVWXY
3 BGKL**M**NRUWY
4 (C+H) K (Q+S+T+U+V+X+Y+Z)
5 **AB**CDEFGHIJKLMNOPUWZ
6 CEGHIJ**K**ORTVWX

Close to the centre of a lively resort, yet still quiet. 400 metres from wonderful sandy beaches. A campsite with an excellent atmosphere.

A8, exit Le Muy, direction Ste Maxime. From there to La Croix Valmer. Cavalaire centre (harbour). Follow the arrows in the centre.

CC € 19 *15/3-2/7 27/8-15/11*

N 43°10'10'' E 6°31'47''

Ceyreste, F-13600 / Provence-Alpes-Côte d'Azur (Bouches-du-Rhône)

iD 2455

Camping de Ceyreste****
av. Eugène Julien
+33 (0)4-42830768
25/3 - 13/11
campingceyreste@yahoo.fr

3ha 56T(60-100m²) 6A

1 AGHIJLST
2 FJKTVXY
3 AGNQR
4 (C+G 1/5-30/9) J
(Q 15/4-30/9) (R 15/6-15/9)
(T+Z 1/5-30/9)
5 AFGIJKLMNPUVZ
6 ACEGIK(N 1km)OQRT

A quiet terraced campsite located completely under pine trees. Some pitches have wonderful views of the Mediterranean and the harbour of Ciotat. The campsite is located 3 km from the sea.

Take the A50 as far as exit 9 La Ciotat. Then follow the signs 'Ceyreste'.

CC € 19 25/3-1/7 1/9-13/11

N 43°13'13'' E 5°37'43''

Chasteuil/Castellane, F-04120 / Provence-Alpes-Côte d'Azur (Alpes-de-Haute-Prov)

iD 2456

Indigo Gorges du Verdon****
Clos d'Arémus
+33 (0)4-92836364
FAX +33 (0)4-92837472
14/4 - 26/9
aremus@
camping-gorgesduverdon.com

7ha 188T(80-120m²) 6A

1 AGIJKLOPST
2 CGKORVXY
3 BHNRUW
4 (A 1/7-26/8)
(C+Q+S+T+U+V)
(X+Y 8/5-15/9) (Z)
5 ABCEFGHIJKLMNOPUVZ
6 CEGHIJ(N 10km)OQRTV

Very pleasant campsite, located along the Verdon. Very impressive scenery: among other things the famous Gorges du Verdon and the Lac Ste Croix. Great family campsite.

The campsite is located about 10 km south of Castellane, on road D952 to Draguignan.

CC € 17 14/4-23/6 1/9-25/9

N 43°49'22'' E 6°25'53''

Châteauneuf-de-Gadagne, F-84470 / Provence-Alpes-Côte d'Azur (Vaucluse)

iD 2457

Fontisson***
1125 route d'Avignon
FAX +33 (0)4-90225977
2/4 - 1/10
info@campingfontisson.com

2ha 30T(80-100m²) 10A CEE

1 ACDGIJKLPST
2 FISTWX
3 AFGHJMNOQRTW
4 (B+G 15/5-15/9) (Q+R)
(V 2/7-20/8) (Z 1/7-31/8)
5 AFGIJKLMNOPUZ
6 AEGIK(N 5km)RTV

15 minutes from Avignon and l'Isle-sur-la-Sorgue. An ideally located campsite for visiting Provence, choosing the villages of Lubéron, spending a day by the sea, walking up Mont Ventoux or sauntering through the Provençal markets. The campsite is surrounded by vineyards.

In Avignon exit Nord, direction Carpentras. Then via Vedène, direction Saint-Saturnin. In Châteauneuf take the RN100 to Avignon.

CC € 15 2/4-2/7 20/8-1/10

N 43°55'44'' E 4°56'1''

Châteauneuf-du-Pape, F-84230 / Provence-Alpes-Côte d'Azur (Vaucluse) 2458

L'Art de Vivre***
960 Chemin de l'Islon Saint Luc
+33 (0)4-90026543
16/4 - 2/10
contact@
camping-artdevivre.com

3,5ha 82T(80-120m²) 10A

1 AC**G**IJKLMPST
2 BCFGRTUVXY
3 BGHJK**M**RU
4 (B 15/5-2/10) (G 1/7-31/8) (Q+R) (T 1/5-2/10) (U+V 1/6-31/8) (X 10/6-15/9) (Z 1/5-2/10)
5 **AB**GIJKLMNPUZ
6 EGIJ**K**(N 1,5km)T

A campsite in an open wood containing ancient trees, 1.5 km from Châteauneuf-du-Pape. In the middle of the wine growing region with quality wines. Lively covered terrace with restaurant and bar. Close to Orange, Avignon and Mont Ventoux. Very rural and a quiet place to relax.

From the north take exit 22 on the A7 or A9. Then direction Courthézon/Châteauneuf-du-Pape and follow camping signs in the centre. From the south exit Roquemaure/Châteauneuf-du-Pape. Follow arrows.

CC € 17 *16/4-8/7 25/8-2/10*

N 44°2'29'' E 4°49'28''

Châteaurenard, F-13160 / Provence-Alpes-Côte d'Azur (Bouches-du-Rhône) 2459

La Roquette***
745 ave Jean Mermoz
+33 (0)4-90944681
FAX +33 (0)9-72140153
1/4 - 26/10
contact@
camping-la-roquette.com

1,4ha 61T(85-100m²) 10A

1 ACD**G**IJKLMO**P**ST
2 FRSTVWXY
3 A**F**GHJ**M**NRU**W**
4 (C+H+Q+T+U+V+X+Z)
5 **A**FGIJKLNPUVWZ
6 ABEGK(N 1,5km)V

A modest hospitable campsite where a friendly French couple create a pleasant ambiance. Centrally located for lovely trips in Provence. Pitches under the mulberry trees without fruit. Nice for cycling and walking. The campsite displays the 'Camping Qualité' logo. The swimming pool is heated and free WiFi throughout the camp site.

A7, exit Avignon-Sud, direction Châteaurenard. The campsite is signposted.

CC € 17 *1/4-8/7 25/8-26/10 7=6*

N 43°53'1'' E 4°52'13''

Cogolin, F-83310 / Provence-Alpes-Côte d'Azur (Var) 2460

De l'Argentière****
avenue Saint Maur
+33 (0)4-94546363
FAX +33 (0)4-94540615
26/3 - 9/10
camping-largentiere@wanadoo.fr

5ha 100T(80-120m²) 6-10A

1 A**F**IJKLP
2 BKRVWXY
3 BFGK**M**NRU
4 (C+G 15/4-9/10) JK (Q 1/7-31/8) (R) (T+U+V+X+Y+Z 1/7-31/8)
5 **AB**EFGIJKLMNOPUZ
6 AEGH**K**(N 1km)OTV

Lovely, comfortable campsite with an excellent ambiance. Very central location for trips, e.g. to St. Tropez, Sainte Maxime, Port Grimaud, the world-famous beaches of Pampelonne and Ramatuelle, Grimaud, Gassin. Campsite is located in a nature reserve.

In Cogolin keep dir. Collobrières. Campsite entrance is next to Château Saint Maur.

CC € 15 *26/3-3/7 26/8-9/10*

N 43°15'23'' E 6°30'45''

Cotignac, F-83570 / Provence-Alpes-Côte d'Azur (Var) — 2461

Camping des Pouverels
3070 chemin des Pouverels
+33 (0)4-94047191
1/4 - 31/10
@ campingcotignac@orange.fr

3ha 40T(60-100m²) 13A

1 ACD**G**HIJKLM**P**ST
2 BJVWXY
3 AHJ
4 (Q)
5 **A**EJKMNPU
6 J(N 2km)T

The campsite is small and charming and is located in the countryside. Being a small campsite (40 pitches) it has a peaceful and friendly character. Its location in the heart of the Var makes this campsite an ideal starting point for many excursions and walks.

D22, campsite located 2 km outside Cotignac.

CC € 15 *1/4-30/6 1/9-31/10*

N 43°32'16'' E 6°8'55''

Dauphin/Forcalquier, F-04300 / Provence-Alpes-Côte d'Azur (Alpes-de-Haute-Prov) — 2462

L'Eau Vive***
RD13
FAX +33 (0)4-92795191
1/4 - 30/9
@ camping.leauvive04@gmail.com

6ha 90T(100-200m²) 6A CEE

1 ACD**G**IJKLMPST
2 BCFGRTVWXY
3 ABGMN**Q**RU**W**
4 (**A** 1/7-31/8) (C 1/5-30/9)
(G 30/6-1/9) **K**(Q)
(R 1/5-30/9) (T 1/5-15/9)
(U 1/7-31/8) (X+Y 1/5-15/9)
Z
5 **A**FGIJKLMNPU
6 CEG**IJ**(N 2,5km)TUV

This campsite is peacefully located on a small river. Both shaded and sunny pitches. A pleasant terrace and restaurant with traditional cuisine next to the swimming pool.

Take exit 19 on the A51 then D4096 as far as Volx. In Volx follow the D13 till just past Dauphin.

CC € 15 *1/4-2/7 21/8-30/9*

N 43°54'40'' E 5°46'53''

Digne-les-Bains, F-04000 / Provence-Alpes-Côte d'Azur (Alpes-de-Haute-Prov) — 2463

Les Eaux Chaudes***
32 avenue des Thermes
+33 (0)4-92323104
FAX +33 (0)4-92345980
15/4 - 15/10
@ info@
campingleseauxchaudes.com

0,5ha 100T(100-110m²) 6A

1 AC**F**IJKLMPST
2 CGRVX
3 B**F**GHJNR
4 (B+G 1/6-30/9)
(Q 1/5-30/9) (R+Z)
5 **AB**EFGIJKLMNOPUVWZ
6 CEG**K**(N 2km)TV

Campsite with plenty of shade. Close to town. Good base for trips.

From the centre of Digne drive in the direction of 'Les Thermes'. Signposted.

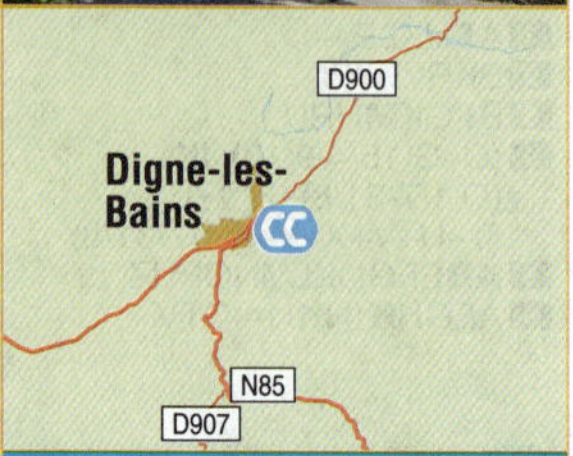

CC € 17 *15/4-9/7 28/8-15/10*

N 44°5'12'' E 6°15'3''

Embrun, F-05200 / Provence-Alpes-Côte d'Azur (Hautes-Alpes) — 2464

La Vieille Ferme****
La Clapière
+33 (0)4-92430408
1/5 - 1/10
info@campingembrun.com

2,6ha 100T(112-140m²) 10A CEE

1 A**G**IJKLMPQ
2 CGRSVY
3 AGHJNRU**W**
4 (A 1/6-30/9)
(Q+T+U+V+X+Z)
5 **A**EFGHIJKLMNPQRUWXYZ
6 EG**IJK**(N 1km)QTV

You will camp on level wooded grounds near a lake and close to Embrun, with an inviting Provençal terrace. Perfect for sportive campers. Dutch owner.

N94 from Gap to Briançon. At the roundabout go towards Embrun, then over the bridge and first turning on the right, then immediately left.

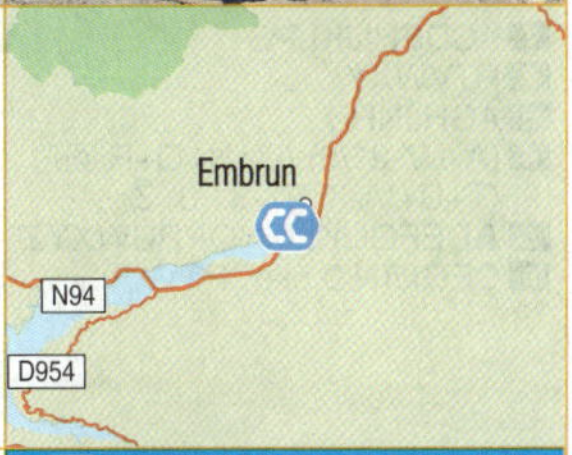

CC € 19 *1/5-2/7 3/9-1/10 21=19*

N 44°33'15" E 6°29'10"

Entrevaux, F-04320 / Provence-Alpes-Côte d'Azur (Alpes-de-Haute-Prov) — 2465

du Brec**
+33 (0)4-93054245
15/3 - 15/10
info@camping-dubrec.com

3,8ha 76T(80-140m²) 10A CEE

1 ACD**G**HIJKLM**P**ST
2 CDKNRTVWXY
3 AGHNRWZ
4 (Q 1/6-15/9) (T+U 1/6-30/9)
(V 1/7-31/8) (Z 1/6-30/9)
5 **AB**DEFGIJKLMNOPUWZ
6 AEGH**K**(N 2km)TV

The campsite is fairly basic, but good. Perfect for the active camper who feels at home in an area of natural beauty which has not yet been discovered by tourists. The nearby medieval town of Entrevaux is worth a visit. Set next to a 4 hectare lake with free use of canoes and kayaks. Top quality swimming water. Perfectly suited to families with children. No entertainment, so quiet.

N202, 2.5 miles (4 km) west of Entrevaux. Follow the signs.

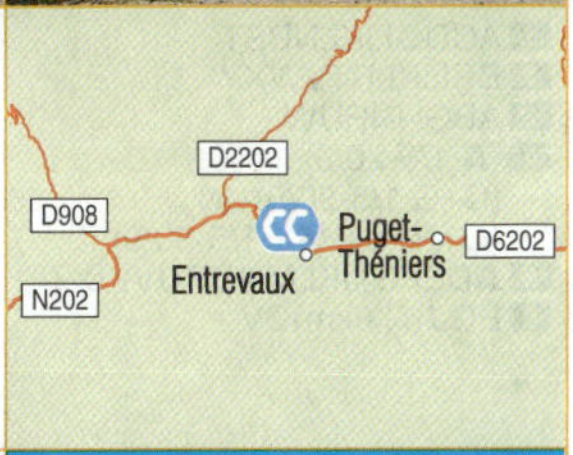

CC € 15 *15/3-30/6 17/8-15/10*

N 43°57'42" E 6°47'56"

Esparron-de-Verdon, F-04800 / Provence-Alpes-Côte d'Azur (Alpes-de-Haute-Prov) — 2466

La Beaume***
route d'Albiosc
+33 (0)4-92771528
+33 (0)4-92771141
26/3 - 31/10
camping.labeaume@free.fr

6ha 34T 6A CEE

1 ACD**G**IJKLST
2 CKRX
3 ABGHN**OP**R
4 E(Q+T+U+V+X 20/6-31/8)
(Z)
5 **A**DJNPZ
6 EGJ(N 2km)O

Very peacefully located campsite in the middle of the countryside, a few kilometres from the lake of Esparron-de-Verdon.

On A51 take exit Gréoux-les-Bains dir. Esparron-de-Verdon. In village follow arrows.

CC € 17 *26/3-5/7 22/8-31/10*

N 43°44'36" E 5°59'41"

Forcalquier, F-04300 / Provence-Alpes-Côte d'Azur (Alpes-de-Haute-Prov) 2467

Indigo Forcalquier***
route de Sigonce
+33 (0)4-92752794
FAX +33 (0)4-92751810
4/5 - 26/9
forcalquier@camping-indigo.com

4ha 80T(80-110m²) 10A CEE

1 ACD**F**HIJKL**P**S
2 RTVWXY
3 AGHJNRU
4 (A 1/7-31/8) (C+H+Q+R) (T+U+V+X 1/7-31/8) Z
5 **A**DEFGIJKLMNOPRUWXYZ
6 CEGIJ(N 0,5km)PTV

A small, intimate campsite close to the centre of the village. Quality amenities such as a heated swimming pool, recreational facilities and cafe-restaurant. CampingCard ACSI is only valid for standard pitches.

A51 Sisteron - Aix-en-Provence to exit 19. Then take the N100 in the direction of Forcalquier. In the centre follow the arrows 'Indigo Camping'.

CC € 15 *4/5-5/7 1/9-25/9*

N 43°57'43'' E 5°47'14''

Forcalquier, F-04300 / Provence-Alpes-Côte d'Azur (Alpes-de-Haute-Prov) 2468

Naturistencamping Les Lauzons****
Limans
+33 (0)4-92730060
17/4 - 16/10
leslauzons@wanadoo.fr

60ha 163T(40-250m²) 10A CEE

1 ACD**G**IJKLNPST
2 BCIJKLRTVWXY
3 ABGHNRUW
4 (**A** 1/6-20/9) (C+G 1/5-30/9) JN (Q+R+U+V+X 1/5-30/9) Z
5 **A**DEFGIJKLMNOPUVWXZ
6 EG**J**(N 6km)OV

Very attractive naturist campsite positioned up in the hills. Both shaded and sunny pitches.

A51 Sisteron - Aix-en-Provence, exit 19. Then follow N100 till past Forcalquier. Follow D950 at roundabout direction Limans.

CC € 19 *17/4-10/7 27/8-16/10*

N 43°58'22'' E 5°44'15''

Freissinières, F-05310 / Provence-Alpes-Côte d'Azur (Hautes-Alpes) 2469

Les Allouviers*
+33 (0)4-92209324
1/5 - 30/9
info@camping-freissinieres.fr

3,9ha 155T(60-130m²) 10A CEE

1 ACDFIJKLM**P**Q
2 BCDGHKLRTVWXY
3 BGHIJMNRUW
4 (Q 1/7-31/8) (R) (T+U+V 1/7-31/8) Z
5 **AB**EFGIJKLMNPUVWZ
6 EGIJ(N 3km)RTV

Campsite on 1000 metres altitude with pine trees and bordering on a little lake in the heart of amazing mountain scenery. Plenty of options for walking and water recreation.

From Gap to Briançon over N94, just past La Roche-de-Rame, take left D38. Steep incline.

CC € 15 *1/5-30/6 20/8-30/9*

N 44°44'30'' E 6°33'42''

Fréjus, F-83600 / Provence-Alpes-Côte d'Azur (Var)

iD 2470

Camping Caravaning Le Fréjus***
3401 rue des Combatt. d'Afr.du Nord
+33 (0)4-94199460
+33 (0)4-94199469
15/1 - 15/12
contact@lefrejus.com
8ha 90T(80-100m²) 6A CEE

1 ACD**G**IJKLMPST
2 FGKRVXY
3 BGKMNRU
4 (A 15/4-15/9) (C+H 15/4-15/10) J (Q+R+T+U+V+X+Y+Z 15/4-15/10)
5 **AB**CDEFGHIJKLMNOPUVXZ
6 ABCEG**IK**(N 4km)RTV

Pleasant, child friendly family campsite with many amenities. The site was originally a farm campsite and it has kept many of these characteristics.

Leave motorway A8 at Fréjus, exit 38. Then turn to the right twice. Campsite is on the left side of the road.

CC € 15 *15/1-3/7 27/8-15/12* *7=6, 12=10*

N 43°27'50'' E 6°43'28''

Fréjus, F-83618 / Provence-Alpes-Côte d'Azur (Var)

iD 2471

La Baume/La Palmeraie*****
3775 rue des Comb. d'Afr. du Nord
+33 (0)4-94198888
+33 (0)4-94198350
26/3 - 30/9
reception@labaume-lapalmeraie.com
27ha 230T(90-130m²) 6A

1 ACD**G**IJKLMP
2 FGKRTVWXY
3 B**F**GKMNRUV
4 (**A**+C+F+H) IJKL (Q+S+T+U+V+X+Y+Z)
5 **AB**CDEFGHIJKLMNOPUVWXYZ
6 AEGH**IJ**(N 3km)ORTV

A lovely campsite with fantastic swimming facilities and very professionally organised entertainment.

A8, exit 38 Fréjus. Then twice right, campsite is on the left.

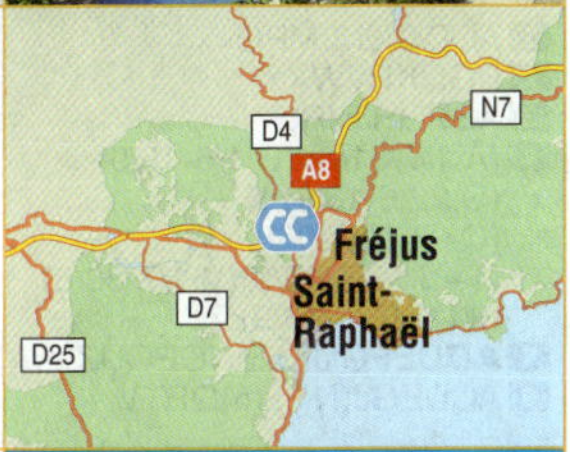

CC € 19 *26/3-17/6 29/8-30/9*

N 43°27'59'' E 6°43'23''

Fréjus, F-83600 / Provence-Alpes-Côte d'Azur (Var)

iD 2472

La Pierre Verte****
1880 route Départementale 4
+33 (0)4-94408830
+33 (0)4-94407541
2/4 - 25/9
info@campinglapierreverte.com
28ha 150T(80-120m²) 6-10A CEE

1 ACD**G**IJKLPST
2 BFGJKRVWXY
3 BGKMN**PQ**RU
4 (C+H) JK (Q+S+T+U+V+X+Y+Z)
5 **AB**CEFGHIJKLMNOPUVXYZ
6 ACEGH**IK**(N 6km)OTV

A campsite set in extensive woodland and natural parkland. The site gets its name from the natural green stone which can be seen everywhere.

Leave autoroute A8 at exit 38 Fréjus. Then direction Bagnols-en-Forêt. Campsite located about 3 km on the right.

CC € 17 *2/4-1/7 27/8-25/9*

N 43°29'3'' E 6°43'13''

Fréjus, F-83600 / Provence-Alpes-Côte d'Azur (Var) 2473

Les Pins Parasols****
3360 rue des Combatt. d'Afr.du Nord
+33 (0)4-94408843
FAX +33 (0)4-94408199
2/4 - 24/9
@ lespinsparasols@wanadoo.fr

4,5ha 144**T**(80-100m²) 6A

1 A**G**IJLP
2 FGJKLRVXY
3 B**F**GKMNRU
4 (C+H) J (Q+S+T+U+V+X+Y+Z)
5 **A**DEFGIJKLMNOP**S**UZ
6 ABEGH**J**(N 2,5km)RTV

Well maintained, comfortable campsite. Centrally located for the Côte d'Azur and Provençal interior.

A8, exit 38 Fréjus. Then turn to the right twice and the campsite is on the right of the road.

CC € 17 *2/4-1/7 22/8-23/9*

N 43°27'50'' E 6°43'32''

Gap, F-05000 / Provence-Alpes-Côte d'Azur (Hautes-Alpes) 2474

Alpes Dauphiné****
route Napoléon / N85
+33 (0)4-92512995
FAX +33 (0)4-92535842
15/4 - 20/10
@ info@alpesdauphine.com

10ha 150**T**(70-120m²) 10A CEE

1 ACD**G**IJKLMPQ
2 BGIJKRVWXY
3 AB**F**GHJNRU
4 (A 1/7-31/8) (C 1/6-16/9) (G 22/6-15/9) K (Q+R 1/5-20/9) (T+U 10/5-15/9)(V 1/7-30/8) (X+Y 10/5-16/9) Z
5 **AB**DEFGIJKLMNOPQUZ
6 ACDEGJ(N 3km)ORTV

Right next to the 'Route Napoléon' on the N85. Shaded pitches. Good restaurant. Heated swimming pool from 1/6 to 15/9. Panoramic views.

Located 3 km north of Gap on 'Route Napoléon', direction Grenoble. Clearly signposted.

CC € 17 *15/4-4/7 25/8-20/10*

N 44°34'49'' E 6°4'57''

Giens/Hyères, F-83400 / Provence-Alpes-Côte d'Azur (Var) 2475

La Tour Fondue
1700 avenue des Arbanais
+33 (0)4-94582286
FAX +33 (0)4-94581163
26/3 - 2/11
@ info@camping-latourfondue.com

2,3ha 119**T**(50-120m²) 10A

1 ACD**G**IJKLPT
2 AEGIKNQRTVWX
3 HKLRWY
4 (Q+R+T+U+V+X+Z)
5 **A**FGIJKLMNOPU
6 CEG**IK**(N 2km)RTV

Ideal for fans of water sports. Diving club is present on site. The campsite is situated by the sea opposite the 'Golden Islands'.

On the peninsula camping signs are posted.

CC € 17 *26/3-25/6 5/9-2/11*

N 43°1'47'' E 6°9'22''

Giens/Hyères, F-83400 / Provence-Alpes-Côte d'Azur (Var)

2476

Olbia***
545 ave René de Knyff,
La Madrague
+33 (0)4-94582196
FAX +33 (0)4-94581163
2/4 - 2/10
@ info@camping-olbia.com

110T 15A CEE

1 ACD**F**IJLPT
2 ABEGIJQRTVXY
3 BHKLRWY
4 (Q+R+T+U+V+X+Z)
5 **A**CEFGHIJKLMNOPUV
6 ACEG**IK**(N 5km)ORTV

Grounds set in an attractive park in one of the loveliest parts of the Giens headland, rich in natural beauty. Trips to the Golden Islands and especially Porquerolles, to picturesque Giens and historically interesting Hyères are all highly recommended.

Campsite located ± 500m east of the harbour at Madrague on the Giens headland.

CC € 17 *2/4-25/6 5/9-2/10*

N 43°2'23'' E 6°6'12''

Gordes, F-84220 / Provence-Alpes-Côte d'Azur (Vaucluse)

2477

Camping des Sources***
route de Murs
+33 (0)4-90721248
9/4 - 30/9
@ campingdessources@wanadoo.fr

3,5ha 40T(80-120m²) 6A CEE

1 ABCD**G**HIJKL**P**S
2 JKTVWXY
3 AGHJLN**Q**RUV
4 (C) (H 1/6-31/8)
(Q+R) (U 1/7-31/8) Z
5 **A**DFGIJKLMNPUZ
6 ACEGJ(N 1,8km)TV

Located close to the centre of Gordes, known as being one of the most beautiful villages in France. In the heart of the Lubéron with panoramic views of the mountains. Typical Provençal vegetation (thyme, green oak etc.) and a heated swimming pool.

Avignon-South direction Apt, then follow N100. Towards Gordes till in the centre. Site signposted.

CC € 19 *9/4-2/7 29/8-30/9*

N 43°55'37'' E 5°12'8''

Graveson, F-13690 / Provence-Alpes-Côte d'Azur (Bouches-du-Rhône)

2478

Les Micocouliers***
445 rte de Cassoulen / D5
+33 (0)4-90958149
15/3 - 15/10
@ micocou@orange.fr

2ha 115**T**(100m²) 6A CEE

1 ACD**G**IJKLMOPST
2 FLRTVWXY
3 A**F**GHJ**OP**RV
4 (B+G 15/5-15/9) (Q+R)
5 **A**CEGIJKLPUVZ
6 ACEG**J**(N 1km)

The campsite is in a rural setting. In the middle of Provence, very quiet and natural with large camping pitches. 12 km from Avignon and 7 km from St. Rémy-de-Provence. The centre of Graveson is 1 km from the campsite. Great for cycling.

A7, exit Avignon-sud, direction Châteaurenard (D28), direction Graveson, between Graveson and Maillane.

CC € 17 *15/3-2/7 22/8-15/10* 14=13

N 43°50'39'' E 4°46'53''

Gréoux-les-Bains, F-04800 / Provence-Alpes-Côte d'Azur (Alpes-de-Haute-Prov) — 2479

Verdon Parc****
Domaine de la Paludette
+33 (0)4-92780808
+33 (0)4-92780017
25/3 - 5/11
info@campingverdonparc.fr

12ha 120T(80-180m²) 10A CEE

1 ACD**F**IJKLPST
2 CFNRTUVX
3 BGHJKLMNRUW
4 (B 10/4-1/11)
(F+G+Q+R+T+U+V+X) Z
5 **AB**DFGIJKLMNOPRUVXYZ
6 CFGH**IJK**(N 1km)RTV

A shaded 11 hectare park in the Haute Provence. Located on the River Verdon the campsite offers you a peaceful and relaxing stay. Close to Lake Esparron (8 km). A spacious campsite with extensive facilities.

In Gréoux-les-Bains follow the road to Varages (D8) at the roundabout. Campsite well signposted.

CC € 17 *25/3-3/7 28/8-5/11*

N 43°45'6'' E 5°53'39''

Grillon, F-84600 / Provence-Alpes-Côte d'Azur (Vaucluse) — 2480

Le Garrigon****
chemin de Visan
+33 (0)4-90287294
14/3 - 13/11
contact@camping-garrigon.com

1,4ha 120T(80-160m²) 16A CEE

1 ACD**G**IJKLM**PT**
2 KRTVWX
3 AGJRU
4 (C+H 10/5-30/9) J
(Q+R 1/4-30/10)
(T 1/7-31/8) (U 1/5-30/10) Z
5 ADEFGIJKLMNOPRXYZ
6 ACEGIK(N 1km)TV

Opened in 2011 with new, spacious toilet facilities and a swimming pool with slide. In a wine and truffle area. Visit Grignan chateau and the towns of Orange, Avignon, Valréas and Nyons. Here you will find relaxation in the sun or shade in rural surroundings. WiFi is free.

A7 exit Montelimar-Sud towards Gap between Grignan and Valréas. Follow signs in Grillon.

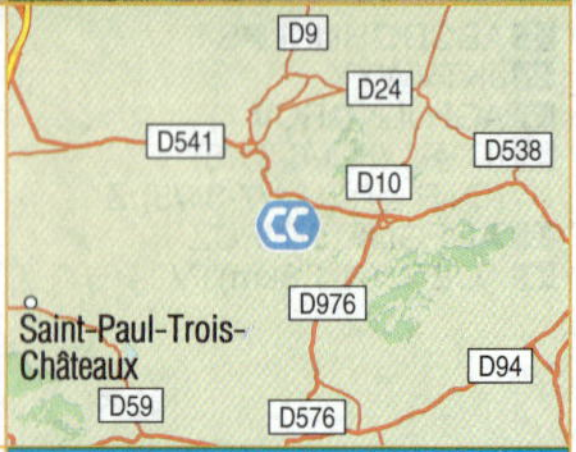

CC € 15 *14/3-9/7 27/8-13/11*

N 44°22'59'' E 4°55'51''

Grimaud, F-83310 / Provence-Alpes-Côte d'Azur (Var) — 2481

Les Mûres****
2721 route du Littoral
+33 (0)4-94561697
+33 (0)4-94563791
19/3 - 8/10
info@camping-des-mures.com

7ha 593T(80-130m²) 6A CEE

1 ACD**G**IJKLPST
2 AEGJKRSVWXY
3 BE**F**GKNRUVWY
4 (Q+S) (T 1/6-30/9)
(U+V+X+Y+Z)
5 **A**EFGIJKLMNOPUXZ
6 ABCEGH**IK**(N 3km)ORTV

Campsite located right on the sea (St.Tropez Bay) with a friendly ambiance. Site is surrounded by vineyards. CampingCard ACSI is valid for the whole of the campsite except for the first row by the beach.

From the centre of St. Maxime take the coastal road in the direction of St. Tropez. The entrance to the campsite is located to the right after about 5 km.

CC € 19 *19/3-30/6 1/9-8/10*

N 43°17'2'' E 6°35'30''

Guillestre, F-05600 / Provence-Alpes-Côte d'Azur (Hautes-Alpes)

iD 2482

Mun. La Rochette***
route des Campings
+33 (0)4-92450215
15/5 - 30/9
guillestre@aol.com

4,4ha 190**T**(70-130m²) 10A CEE

1 ACD**G**IJKLMPST
2 CIKLRTVX
3 AGHIJL**M**RU**W**
4 (**C**+**H** 21/6-30/8)
(Q 1/6-10/9) (R 1/7-31/8)
(S 25/6-10/9)
(T+U+V+X 21/6-30/8) Z
5 **AB**FGIJKLMNOPUVZ
6 AEGH**IJK**(N 0,8km)TV

A peaceful, informal campsite within walking distance of Guillestre and at the entrance to the 'Queyras' nature reserve.

Via the N94 about 30 km south of Briançon take the D902a to Guillestre. Turn right after about 1 km. Follow the camping signs to the end of the road.

CC € 15 *15/5-6/7 26/8-30/9*

N 44°39'30" E 6°38'17"

Guillestre, F-05600 / Provence-Alpes-Côte d'Azur (Hautes-Alpes)

iD 2483

St-James-les-Pins***
+33 (0)4-92450824
FAX +33 (0)4-92451865
1/1 - 30/10, 15/12 - 31/12
camping@lesaintjames.com

3ha 90**T**(80-120m²) 10A CEE

1 ACD**G**IJKLMPST
2 BCRTVXY
3 BGHJNRU
4 (Q) (R+U 1/7-31/8)
5 **AB**DGIJKLMNPUZ
6 EG**IJ**(N 1,2km)ORTV

Campsite located in a pine forest on a fast flowing river. Naturally marked out pitches. The sanitation is heated.

Via N94 about 30 km south of Briançon take the D902a to Guillestre. After ± 1 km take a right turn. Follow camping signs.

CC € 13 *1/5-8/7 25/8-30/9*

N 44°39'26" E 6°37'58"

Istres, F-13800 / Provence-Alpes-Côte d'Azur (Bouches-du-Rhône)

iD 2484

Le Vallon des Cigales**
31 route de St. Chamas
+33 (0)4-42565157
1/1 - 31/12
levallondescigales-camping@orange.fr

6ha 43**T**(100-120m²) 16A CEE

1 AC**G**JKLMPST
2 ABDGKNOQRSWXY
3 AFHJRUWZ
4 (B 1/6-30/9)
(Q+T+U+V+X 1/7-31/8)
(Z)
5 ABFGIJKLMNPQUZ
6 AEGHJ**K**(N 3km)OTV

The campsite is located in a small valley between two lakes. Anglers, hikers, those seeking rest and enthusiasts of the 'cigales' can enjoy the pleasant ambiance here.

Campsite is on the D16 on the shores of Lake Berre between Istres and St. Chamas.

CC € 17 *1/1-10/7 27/8-31/12 7=6*

N 43°31'23" E 5°0'19"

L'Isle-sur-la-Sorgue, F-84800 / Provence-Alpes-Côte d'Azur (Vaucluse)

2485

Airotel La Sorguette***
route d'Apt
+33 (0)4-90380571
FAX +33 (0)4-90208461
15/3 - 15/10
info@camping-sorguette.com

5ha 116T(100-110m²) 10A CEE

1 ACDGIJKLPQ
2 CFLRVX
3 A**F**GKNRU**W**X
4 (Q) (R 1/7-28/8) (T+U 10/7-24/8) Z
5 **AB**EFGIJKLMNOPUVW
6 ACEG**IJK**(N 1,5km)OQTV

Quiet campsite located along the Sorgues. A pleasant and refreshing stay on the river. The campsite is divided in small fields of 4 pitches surrounded by growth. Large accommodation.

A7 exit Avignon Sud - l'Isle-sur-la-Sorge. Follow N100 at the southeast of l'Isle-sur-la-Sorge.

CC € 17 *15/3-9/7 27/8-15/10*

N 43°54'52'' E 5°4'17''

La Couronne, F-13500 / Provence-Alpes-Côte d'Azur (Bouches-du-Rhône)

2486

Pascalounet**
route de la Saulce
+33 (0)4-42807156
1/4 - 31/10
contact@camping-pascalounet.com

2ha 35T(70-80m²) 6A CEE

1 ABC**G**HIJLPST
2 AEFGQTVWXY
3 AGHJRWY
4 (Q)
5 **A**IJKNPUWX
6 EGJ**K**(N 3km)OT

A small, friendly campsite within walking distance of a sandy beach. Level marked out pitches. Attention: reception closes in early afternoon (from 12:00 to 14:30).

Take the A7 towards Marseille to the intersection to Fos-sur-Mer (A55). Take exit 8 then the D9 as far as La Couronne.

CC € 15 *1/4-9/7 27/8-31/10*

N 43°20'4'' E 5°4'11''

La Croix-Valmer, F-83420 / Provence-Alpes-Côte d'Azur (Var)

2487

Sélection Camping****
310 boulevard de la Mer
+33 (0)4-94551030
FAX +33 (0)4-94551039
15/3 - 15/10
camping-selection@wanadoo.fr

4ha 117T(65-80m²) 10A

1 ACD**G**IJKLPST
2 AEGIJKRSVXY
3 BGHJKLNQRUW
4 (C+H 1/4-15/10) K (Q+S+T+U+V+X+Y+Z 1/4-15/10)
5 **ABC**DEFGHIJKLMNOPUV WZ
6 ABCEG**IK**(N 3km)ORTV

The campsite has a magnificent location in an extensive Provençal park (pines, mimosa, etc.). Very good atmosphere. A few minutes walk to beach.

In La Croix-Valmer drive in the direction of Le Lavandou. Signposted at the roundabout 2 km down the road.

CC € 19 *15/3-30/6 22/8-15/10*

N 43°11'40'' E 6°33'18''

Castellane/La Garde, F-04120 / Provence-Alpes-Côte d'Azur (Alpes-de-Haute-Prov) — 2488

RCN Les Collines de Castellane****
route de Grasse
+33 (0)4-92836896
FAX +33 (0)4-92837540
23/4 - 17/9
@ collines@rcn.fr

10ha 160T(80-150m²) 8-12A

1 ACD**F**IJKLOPST
2 BIJKLRSTVWXY
3 BGHJ**M**NRU
4 (A 1/5-31/8) (C+H) J (Q+R+T+U+V+X+Y+Z)
5 **AB**CEFGHIJKLMNPUWXYZ
6 AEG**K**(N 6km)TV

A lovely terraced campsite in unspoilt, breathtaking natural scenery. Located at an altitude of 1000m in the Haute Provence which is characterised by the clean air and the strong sun. Views of the hills and mountains. Informally laid out swimming pool. Characteristic old villages and historic towns in beautiful countryside with purple lavender fields and olive trees.

The campsite is located on the N85 direction Grasse, 6 km south-east of Castellane.

CC € 15 *23/4-9/7 26/8-17/9*

N 43°49'27" E 6°34'12"

La Roche-de-Rame, F-05310 / Provence-Alpes-Côte d'Azur (Hautes-Alpes) — 2489

Camping du Lac**
N94
+33 (0)4-92209031
1/5 - 30/9
@ campingdulacrochederame@orange.fr

1,3ha 81T(70-120m²) 10A CEE

1 ACGIJKLM**P**Q
2 ACDGKLRTVWXY
3 AGHIJNRWZ
4 (Q 1/7-31/8) (T+U) (V 1/7-31/8) (X+Y)
5 **A**FGIJKMNPUZ
6 CEIJ(N 0,3km)T

A peaceful and friendly campsite by a lovely natural lake. Located in the wide Durance valley. Very clean toilet facilities.

Via the N94, 20 km south of Briançon in the centre of La Roche-de-Rame, left at the lake. From Gap on the right of N94.

CC € 15 *1/5-3/7 29/8-30/9* *7=6*

N 44°44'49" E 6°34'53"

La Roche-des-Arnauds, F-05400 / Provence-Alpes-Côte d'Azur (Hautes-Alpes) — 2490

Le Parc des Sérigons***
+33 (0)4-92578177
1/4 - 31/10
@ contact@camping-serigons.com

15ha 130T(130-200m²) 10A CEE

NEW

1 ACD**G**IJKLMPST
2 BCKLRSTXY
3 ABGHJMN**OP**RU
4 (A 5/7-17/8) (B+G 20/6-15/9) (Q 1/6-30/9) (R 1/7-31/8) (T+U+V+X+Z 15/6-15/9)
5 **A**DEFGIJKLMNOPUZ
6 CEGJ(N 3km)OTV

You will be enjoying the peace and quiet of nature from a large pitch. Camp in the forest where you will enjoy a lot of privacy. The trees aren't high so there is plenty of light. Mountains surround the site. Family campsite. Friendly welcome.

N75 Grenoble-Sisteron, dir. Veynes. In Veynes dir. Gap - La Roche-des-Arnands. Big campsite signs on left. For safety reasons bear right and then cross road.

CC € 13 *1/4-9/7 27/8-31/10*

N 44°33'52" E 5°55'3"

Lagnes, F-84800 / Provence-Alpes-Côte d'Azur (Vaucluse) — 2491

La Coutelière***
2765 route de Fontaine de Vaucluse
+33 (0)4-90203397
18/3 - 7/10
info@camping-lacouteliere.com

2,8ha 78**T**(80-142m²) 10A CEE

1 ACG**I**JKL**P**ST
2 CGMRVXY
3 A**F**GHJMNRU**WX**
4 (C+H 1/5-30/9) (Q) (R 1/7-31/8) (T 1/6-15/9) (V 1/6-30/9) (X 1/6-31/8) Z
5 **A**DEFGIJKLMNOPQUWZ
6 ACEG**K**(N 4km)OR

A quiet campsite with level, shaded pitches. Located between Fontaine de Vaucluse and Isle sur la Sorgue. Heated swimming pool with children's pool and tennis. Modern toilet facilities, spacious and heated in the low season.

Follow A7 motorway as far as exit 24. Take turning towards Apt via the D973 and the D22. Turn left after about 12 km onto the D24 direction Lagnes and Fontaine de Vaucluse. Campsite signposted from here.

CC € 17 *18/3-23/6 22/8-7/10*

N 43°54'39'' E 5°6'24''

Lambesc, F-13410 / Provence-Alpes-Côte d'Azur (Bouches-du-Rhône) — 2492

Provence Camping**
avenue d'Aix
+33 (0)4-42570578
FAX +33 (0)4-42929802
1/4 - 30/9
provence.camping@wanadoo.fr

2,3ha 54**T**(72-143m²) 10A CEE

1 ACD**G**HIJL**P**ST
2 BIJTUVXY
3 BGNRU
4 (B+Q+R+T 1/6-30/9) (U 1/7-31/8) (X 1/7-30/9) Z
5 ABFGJLMNOPUZ
6 AEG**K**(N 1,4km)T

Campsite located 1 km from the town in natural surroundings. Central location for visiting places such as the Salon de Provence and Aix-en-Provence.

From Aix-en-Provence follow D7n towards Salon-de-Provence. Left past St-Cannat after entering Lambesc (D917).

CC € 15 *1/4-4/7 22/8-30/9*

N 43°38'23'' E 5°16'31''

Le Lavandou, F-83980 / Provence-Alpes-Côte d'Azur (Var) — 2493

Parc Camping de Pramousquier**
chemin de la Faveirolle
+33 (0)4-94058395
FAX +33 (0)4-94057504
16/4 - 2/10
camping-lavandou@wanadoo.fr

4,5ha 147**T**(70-100m²) 4-6-10A

1 ACD**G**IJLPST
2 AEGIJKRTVWXY
3 B**F**GJR**W**Y
4 (Q+R) (T+U+V+X+Y+Z 1/6-15/9)
5 **AB**GHIJKLMNOPUVZ
6 CFGH**IJ**(N 1,5km)ORTV

A pleasant terraced campsite close to the Mediterranean and a few kilometres from the popular seaside resort of Le Lavandou. Very central location with regard to tourist attractions such as the Golden Islands and St. Tropez. Naturist beach close by.

The campsite is located on the coastal road, right at the front of the town Pramousquier (east side).

CC € 17 *16/4-3/7 29/8-2/10*

N 43°9'23'' E 6°26'53''

Le Muy, F-83490 / Provence-Alpes-Côte d'Azur (Var) 2494

RCN Domaine de la Noguière***
RN7, 1617 route de Fréjus
+33 (0)4-94451378
+33 (0)4-94459295
19/3 - 29/10
noguiere@rcn.fr

14ha 173**T**(50-120m²) 6A

1 ACD**F**IJKLPST
2 FGKLRTVWXY
3 B**F**G**M**NRUW
4 (A+B+G) J (Q+R+T+U+V+X+Y+Z)
5 **AB**CEFGHIJKLMNOPUWZ
6 EGH**IK**(N 1km)ORTV

A lovely well maintained campsite in beautiful natural surroundings. The campsite offers two magnificent swimming pools with slides. There are views of the Roquebrune from the campsite. The Mediterranean beaches are 20 minutes away. Close to the seaside resorts of St. Raphael, Fréjus and St Tropez.

Campsite is located by the N7, about 1 km to the east of Le Muy.

CC € 15 *19/3-5/7 26/8-29/10*

N 43°28'5" E 6°35'31"

Le Pradet, F-83220 / Provence-Alpes-Côte d'Azur (Var) 2495

L'Artaudois***
657 chemin de l'artaude
+33 (0)4-94217261
+33 (0)4-94217594
26/3 - 9/10
info@artaudois.fr

3,5ha 47**T**(80-100m²) 10A

1 ACD**G**IJL**P**T
2 ABJKNRTVXY
3 B**F**GNRUW
4 (**A** 1/7-31/8) (B+G 15/5-30/9) (Q 15/6-15/9) (T+V 1/7-31/8) (Z 15/6-15/9)
5 **AB**CEFGHIJKLMNOPUXYZ
6 AEG**IK**(N 1,2km)OTV

A terraced campsite in a mediterranean wood with beautiful panoramas. Just over 1 km from the Mediterranean Sea and very central for many places including Toulon, Hyères, Les Îles d'Or and Le Lavandou. Well organised, friendly atmosphere.

From centre of Le Pradet follow orange arrows with name of campsite.

CC € 15 *26/3-1/7 24/8-9/10*

N 43°5'58" E 6°1'51"

Le Vernet, F-04140 / Provence-Alpes-Côte d'Azur (Alpes-de-Haute-Prov) 2496

Lou Passavous***
+33 (0)4-92351467
1/5 - 15/9
loupassavous@orange.fr

1,5ha 55**T**(80-120m²) 6A CEE

1 A**G**IJKLNPST
2 GKRTVX
3 AGHJMNRU**W**
4 (A) (C 15/6-31/8) (Q+T+U+V+X+Y+Z 15/5-15/9)
5 **A**EFGIJKLMNPUZ
6 AEGJ**K**(N 8km)TV

Beautifully located campsite with stunning views of the mountains. A good base for mountain walks and car trips through magnificent countryside. Good amenities and a Dutch owner.

From Gap towards Barcelonette, then the D900 towards Digne-les-Bains. Signposted at Le Vernet. Do not take the D900c from Gap.

CC € 17 *1/5-30/6 1/9-15/9* 14=13

N 44°16'55" E 6°23'29"

Les Adrets-de-l'Estérel, F-83600 / Provence-Alpes-Côte d'Azur (Var)

iD **2497**

Les Philippons***
D237, 378 route de l'Argentière
+33 (0)4-94409067
FAX +33 (0)4-94193592
1/4 - 30/9
@ info@lesphilippons.com

5,2ha 101**T**(80-160m²) 10A CEE

1 ACD**G**IJKLMPST
2 BFJKRSTVWXY
3 B**F**GR
4 (B 11/4-3/10) (G+Q+R+T+U+V+X+Z)
5 **A**CGHIJKMNPUVZ
6 AEG**IK**(N 3km)ORTV

A beautifully located, quiet family campsite. Well cared for and well supervised. Recommended. Favourable location with regard to the Mediterranean Sea and the Provençal hinterland.

A8 exit 39, direction Les Adrets-de-l'Estérel, campsite signposted on roundabout.

CC €17 *1/4-8/7 25/8-30/9*

N 43°31'44'' E 6°50'23''

Les Issambres, F-83380 / Provence-Alpes-Côte d'Azur (Var)

iD **2498**

Au Paradis des Campeurs****
La Gaillarde-Plage
+33 (0)4-94969355
FAX +33 (0)4-94496299
1/4 - 3/10
@ campingauparadisdescampeurs@gmail.com

2,7ha 180**T**(60-120m²) 6A CEE

1 ACDGIJKLM**P**S
2 AEGIJKQRVWXY
3 B**EF**GHJNRUWY
4 (Q+S+T+U+V+X+Y+Z)
5 **AB**CEFGHIJKLMNOPUXYZ
6 CEG**IK**(N 2km)ORTUV

Direct access to the sandy beach from the campsite. A congenial family campsite. CampingCard ACSI is only valid for standard pitches. The discount card is not valid for comfort pitches.

On the N98 between St. Aygulf and Les Issambres.

CC €17 *1/4-3/7 1/9-3/10*

N 43°21'58'' E 6°42'43''

Les Vigneaux, F-05120 / Provence-Alpes-Côte d'Azur (Hautes-Alpes)

iD **2499**

Campéole Le Courounba***
Le Pont Du Rif
+33 (0)4-92230209
13/5 - 18/9
@ courounba@andretriganogroupe.com

12ha 250**T**(70-130m²) 10A CEE

1 ABCD**G**IJKLM**PR**
2 BCGKLMRTVWXY
3 ABGHJMNR**W**
4 (C+H 15/6-17/9) J**KN** (Q 1/7-30/8) (R 1/7-31/8) (T+U+V 13/6-13/9) (X 15/6-13/9) Z
5 **AB**DEFGIJKLMNOPRUZ
6 ACEGH**IJ**(N 4km)RTV

A peaceful family campsite in the countryside, at the foot of Mont Brison. Spacious shaded pitches. A completely refurbished ecological swimming pool with a slide and toddlers' pool, BMX area, sauna, jacuzzi, multisports field, tennis.

In L'Argentière-la-Bessée N94 follow the signs to Les Vigneaux, then turn right over the bridge.

CC €17 *13/5-4/7 22/8-18/9*

N 44°49'30'' E 6°31'33''

Lourmarin, F-84160 / Provence-Alpes-Côte d'Azur (Vaucluse) **2500**

Les Hautes Prairies***
route de Vaugines
+33 (0)4-90680289
4/4 - 2/10
leshautesprairies@campasun.eu

3,7ha 135T(80-120m²) 10A CEE

1 ACDGIJKLMOPT
2 RTVXY
3 AGNRU
4 (C 15/4-10/10) (Q+R)
(T+U 5/4-30/9)
(V 1/7-31/10)
(X+Z 5/4-30/9)
5 ADEFGJLNPQUWXYZ
6 CEGHK(N 0,7km)OTV

A campsite located on the south side of the Luberon within walking distance of the historic town of Lourmarin. Quiet location. New luxurious toilet facilities. Reasonably level, marked-out pitches. Privacy.

A7, exit 25 as far as Cavaillon. Then D973 in the direction of Pertuis. Follow the signs in Lourmarin.

CC € 17 4/4-10/7 27/8-2/10

N 43°46'4'' E 5°22'23''

Malemort-du-Comtat, F-84570 / Provence-Alpes-Côte d'Azur (Vaucluse) **2501**

Font Neuve***
660 chemin de l'Annonciade
+33 (0)4-90699000
15/4 - 30/9
campingfontneuve@orange.fr

1,5ha 66T(80-120m²) 10A CEE

1 AGIJKLMPS
2 IJRTVWXY
3 BGHJMRU
4 (A 1/7-31/8) (B 1/5-30/9)
(Q) (U+X 1/5-30/9) Z
5 AEFGIJKLMNOPUVWXY
6 EGJ(N 1km)RTV

NEW

Pleasant, quiet surroundings with fruit and wine fields. Walking distance from village and 20 km from the Mont Ventoux. Welcoming restaurant with a bar by the swimming pool.

From Carpentras dir. Mazan D4 and D5 dir. Malemort. Follow arrows.

CC € 17 15/4-30/6 1/9-30/9

N 44°0'50'' E 5°10'16''

Mallemort, F-13370 / Provence-Alpes-Côte d'Azur (Bouches-du-Rhône) **2502**

Durance Luberon****
Domaine du Vergon
+33 (0)4-90591336
1/4 - 30/9
duranceluberon@orange.fr

4ha 100T(100-150m²) 6-10A CEE

1 AGIJKLMPST
2 FLRVWXY
3 BFGNOPR
4 (B 1/5-30/9) (Q 14/4-30/9)
(T 1/7-23/8) (Z 1/7-28/8)
5 ADEFGIJKLMNOPRUZ
6 AEGJK(N 2km)T

Lovely campsite with large marked out pitches on level grounds, located in the Durance valley. Large swimming pool and modern toilet facilities. Quiet location. Ideal for tents and caravans.

Leave the A7 at exit 26. Then take the N7 in the direction of Aix-en-Provence. After 6 km turn in the direction of Mallemort. The campsite is located just before Charleval, on the D561.

CC € 17 1/4-30/6 23/8-30/9

N 43°43'16'' E 5°12'18''

Manosque, F-04100 / Provence-Alpes-Côte d'Azur (Alpes-de-Haute-Prov)

2503

Camping Provence Vallée***
1138 avenue de la Repasse
+33 (0)4-92722808
1/4 - 31/10
contact@provence-vallee.fr

3,2ha 86T(80-110m²) 10A

1 ACD**G**HIJKLPST
2 FGRVWXY
3 A**F**GR
4 (B+G 1/5-15/9)
(Q 1/5-30/9) (R)
(T+U+V 1/7-31/8) Z
5 **AB**GJLMNPUVYZ
6 CFGHI**K**(N 2km)RV

Spacious marked out pitches on sloping ground. A varied selection of trees provide plenty of shade. Large new swimming pool. At a few kilometres from Manosque, accessible via public transport.

A51, exit 18 direction Manosque. Follow Apt before town centre. Campsite well signposted.

CC € 13 *1/4-1/7 22/8-31/10*

N 43°49'48'' E 5°45'49''

Maussane-les-Alpilles, F-13520 / Provence-Alpes-Côte d'Azur (Bouches-du-Rhône)

2504

Municipal Les Romarins***
+33 (0)4-90543360
15/3 - 1/11
camping-municipal-maussane@wanadoo.fr

3ha 145T(70-100m²) 10A CEE

1 ACD**G**IJKLOPQ
2 RTVY
3 A**F**GHJMRU**W**
4 (B+G 6/6-6/9) (Q+R)
5 **A**EGIJKLMNPUVWZ
6 EGHKM(N 0,3km)OTV

Quiet, green campsite close to a beautiful Provence village south of Les Alpilles.

The campsite is located on the D5. From Maussane via D17 direction Arles, then the D5. Located near the centre on the St. Rémy side.

CC € 17 *15/3-30/6 28/8-1/10*

N 43°43'16'' E 4°48'34''

Mazan, F-84380 / Provence-Alpes-Côte d'Azur (Vaucluse)

2505

Le Ventoux***
1348 chemin de la Combe
+33 (0)4-90697094
15/3 - 31/10
info@camping-le-ventoux.com

1,5ha 46T(90-120m²) 10A CEE

1 ACD**G**IJKLM**P**Q
2 KSTUVWXY
3 BGHJNRU
4 (B 1/5-31/10) (G 1/5-15/10)
(Q+R+U 1/4-31/10)
(X+Y) Z
5 **AB**DEFGIJKLMNOPRUZ
6 AEG**K**(N 3km)TV

A campsite located amid the vineyards with lovely views mostly of Mont Ventoux. A modernised swimming pool in Roman style. Satisfied guests who come back again and again. 3 km from Mazan. Good toilet facilities and a surprisingly good restaurant.

A7, exit Orange-Sud, D974 direction Carpentras. After Carpentras direction Bédoin/Mont Ventoux, then follow signs towards campsite.

CC € 17 *15/3-9/7 27/8-31/10*

N 44°4'50'' E 5°6'50''

Méolans-Revel, F-04340 / Provence-Alpes-Côte d'Azur (Alpes-de-Haute-Prov)

iD **2506**

Camping River***
+33 (0)4-92855713
FAX +33 (0)6-37360909
1/5 - 25/9
@ info@camping-river.eu

1ha 40**T**(80-130m²) 6A CEE

1 ACDGIJKLMNOPST
2 ACDGNRTVXY
3 BFGHJRU**W**Z
4 (**A** 1/7-31/8) (C 1/6-30/9)
(Q+R+T+U+V+X)
(Y 1/7-30/8) (Z)
5 ACFGHJLMNPQRUZ
6 ADEGIJ(N 8km)OTV

A small friendly campsite, situated right by the river. In particular a campsite for nature lovers, walkers and cyclists. Almost all sports activities are possible here.

Located on the D900 Gap-Barcelonnette. In Le Martinet turn right at the bridge. Campsite signposted.

CC € 17 *1/5-9/7 28/8-25/9*

N 44°23'47'' E 6°29'20''

Méolans-Revel, F-04340 / Provence-Alpes-Côte d'Azur (Alpes-de-Haute-Prov)

iD **2507**

Dom. Loisirs de l'Ubaye****
D900
+33 (0)4-92810196
15/5 - 15/10
@ info@loisirsubaye.com

10ha 268**T**(100-120m²) 6A

1 ACD**G**IJL**P**ST
2 CGIJLORTVXY
3 BGHJKMNRU**W**X
4 (A 1/7-30/8)
(C+H 15/6-15/9)
(Q+S+T 1/7-10/9) (U)
(V 1/7-15/9) (X 15/6-15/9)
(Y 25/6-10/9) (Z 1/7-15/9)
5 **AB**EFGIJKLMNPUWYZ
6 CEG**I**J(N 2km)OPRTUV

The only four star campsite in the region. Located by the river in Vallée de l'Ubaye. A spacious campsite with a tennis court and swimming pool. Dutch-run with plenty of activities and entertainment and a homely atmosphere bringing back many campers year after year.

At the side of the main road Gap-Barcelonnette. 8 km west of Barcelonnette, at the right side of the road, you'll find the camping signs.

CC € 15 *15/5-5/7 25/8-15/10 8=7, 14=12, 30=25, 60=45*

N 44°23'49'' E 6°32'44''

Mondragon, F-84430 / Provence-Alpes-Côte d'Azur (Vaucluse)

iD **2508**

Camping La Pinède en Provence***
La Maresque
+33 (0)4-90408298
1/1 - 31/12
@ contact@camping-pinede-provence.com

3,5ha 109**T** 13A CEE

1 ACDGIJKLM**P**ST
2 BFIJRSTXY
3 ABGHJNRU
4 (C+H 30/4-30/9) J(Q+R)
(S 1/3-15/11)
(T 15/6-15/11)
(U+V 1/3-15/11)
(X 15/6-15/9) Z
5 ABDFGIJKLMNOPUXYZ
6 ACEGIK(N 2km)TV

A charming campsite in the middle of pine forests in the heart of Provence. There is a new swimming pool and a reception area with bar. Close to the motorway and near Orange and Avignon.

Exit 19 Bollène, towards town centre at roundabout then direction Mondragon. Follow camping signs.

CC € 17 *1/1-30/6 18/8-31/12 7=6*

N 44°14'37'' E 4°43'45''

Montmeyan, F-83670 / Provence-Alpes-Côte d'Azur (Var)

2509

Château de l'Eouvière****
route de Tavernes
+33 (0)4-94807554
13/5 - 15/9
contact@leouviere.com

30ha 80**T**(100-170m²) 10A CEE

1 A**G**IJKLMO**P**ST
2 BGJKLRVWXY
3 BGHJ**M**NRU**W**
4 (B) (Q 15/6-15/9) (R 15/5-15/9) (T+U+X+Z 1/6-15/9)
5 **A**CEFGHIJKLMNPUWZ
6 ACEG**J**(N 0,5km)TV

A beautifully appointed castle campsite where peace and quiet are the order of the day. It couldn't be more Provençal. Perfect starting point for exploring the Gorges du Verdon and surrounding area. A noticeable effort by the owner to make all guests feel welcome.

Drive out of Montmeyan and follow signs to Barjols. The campsite is clearly signposted from the nearby roundabout.

CC € 17 *13/5-30/6 6/7-20/7 1/9-15/9*

N 43°38'20'' E 6°3'38''

Moustiers-Ste-Marie, F-04360/Provence-Alpes-Côte d'Azur (Alpes-de-Haute-Prov)

2510

Saint Clair***
D952
+33 (0)4-92746715
FAX +33 (0)4-84508074
24/4 - 29/9
direction@camping-st-clair.com

3ha 100**T**(88-136m²) 6A CEE

1 ACDGIJKLPST
2 BCGJKRVWXY
3 BGHR
4 (Q+R) (T+U+V 1/7-31/8)
5 **A**CDEFGHIJKLMNOPUV
6 ACEGK(N 3km)OQRT

A congenial, shaded campsite, located on a river with magnificent panoramas of the very impressive scenery. The very touristy village of Moustiers Ste Marie, with its numerous china shops is just 3 km away. A few minutes drive from Lac Ste Croix.

Campsite entrance on roundabout 3km south of Moustiers-Ste-Marie.

CC € 17 *24/4-8/7 25/8-24/9*

N 43°49'41'' E 6°13'28''

Moustiers-Ste-Marie, F-04360 / Provence-Alpes-Côte d'Azur (Alpes-de-Haute-Prov)

2511

Saint Jean***
Quartier Saint Jean
FAX +33 (0)4-92746685
26/3 - 9/10
contact@camping-st-jean.fr

1,7ha 108**T**(80-150m²) 6-10A

1 ACD**G**IJKLMPST
2 CGKRVWXY
3 BGHJKNQR**W**
4 (Q+R) (T+U+V+Z 11/5-15/9)
5 **A**CDEFGHIJKLMNOPUVWYZ
6 ACEG**I**K(N 0,7km)ORTV

Exceptionally nicely situated campsite in the heart of the impressive Gorges du Verdon region and 700m away from the famous porcelain town of Moustiers Ste. Marie. A lovely well maintained campsite with considerate reception.

D592, campsite located on left of road past the roundabout towards Riez.

CC € 17 *26/3-3/7 21/8-9/10*

N 43°50'37'' E 6°12'54''

Neffes/Gap, F-05000 / Provence-Alpes-Côte d'Azur (Hautes-Alpes)

2512

Les Bonnets***
Quartier Les Bonnets
+33 (0)6-88731359
17/5 - 1/10
camping.les.bonnets@wanadoo.fr

5,8ha 120T(90-130m²) 10A

1 ACD**G**IJKLM**P**Q
2 BFRTWXY
3 BGHJN**P**RUW
4 (B+G 1/6-15/9) (Q 15/6-15/9) (R 1/7-31/8) (T+U+V+X 1/6-30/9) Z
5 **AB**DFGHIJKLMNPUVZ
6 EG**J**(N 5km)ORTV

A peaceful, friendly campsite with a lovely swimming pool. Large shaded pitches. Close to the 'Route Napoleon'.

Follow the N85 south of Gap, then about 3 km on the right take the D46 to Neffes. Turn left beyond the town. Follow the camping signs.

CC € 17 *17/5-4/7 21/8-1/10 7=6*

N 44°29'57'' E 6°1'44''

Niozelles, F-04300 / Provence-Alpes-Côte d'Azur (Alpes-de-Haute-Prov)

2513

Sites & Paysages Moulin de Ventre****
N100
+33 (0)4-92786331
FAX +33 (0)4-92798692
9/4 - 30/9
moulindeventre@gmail.com

28ha 104T(100m²) 10A CEE

1 AC**G**IJKL**PS**
2 ACDFGLMRTVX
3 ABGHJNRU**WZ**
4 (B+G 15/5-30/9) **LN**(Q) (R+T+U 1/7-31/8) (V) (X 1/7-31/8) Z
5 **AB**DEFGJLNPUWXYZ
6 ACEGJ(N 2,5km)OTV

A pleasant family campsite in the heart of nature, peacefully located between two streams on a 1.5 hectare lake. Peaceful, cool nights.

On the A51 exit Brillane. In Brillane take the N100. The campsite is located on the N100. The campsite is 2.5 km further on, to the left.

CC € 17 *9/4-8/7 25/8-30/9*

N 43°56'1'' E 5°52'4''

Oraison, F-04700 / Provence-Alpes-Côte d'Azur (Alpes-de-Haute-Prov)

2514

Les Oliviers****
chemin St. Sauveur
+33 (0)4-92782000
1/1 - 31/12
camping-oraison@wanadoo.fr

2ha 33T(25-110m²) 10A CEE

1 A**G**IJKLNPST
2 FGKRTUVWXY
3 AC**G**HJNRU
4 (B 15/4-30/9) (Q 1/4-30/9) (R 15/4-30/9) (T+U+X 1/7-31/8) Z
5 **A**GJLMNPUXZ
6 ACEGJ(N 2km)TV

A lovely, agreeable campsite with sweeping views of the Lubéron oriental and the 'Montagne de Lurs'. The campsite is set among olive groves. A 5 minute walk to the village and close to the Gorges du Verdon, Lubéron, Forcalquier and Manosque.

On the A51 take exit 19. Then take the N96 towards Oraison. Follow signs in the centre.

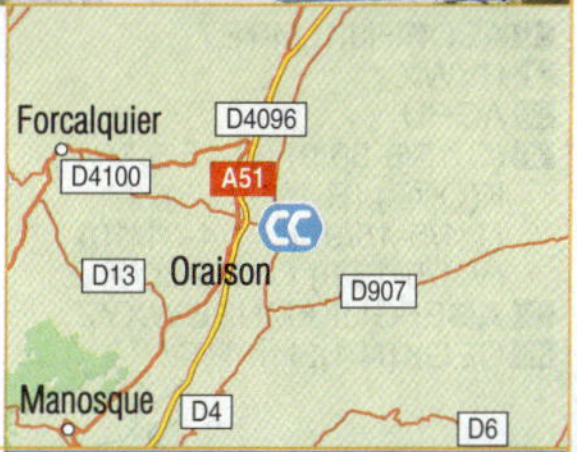

CC € 15 *1/1-2/7 29/8-31/12*

N 43°55'23'' E 5°55'25''

Orgon, F-13660 / Provence-Alpes-Côte d'Azur (Bouches-du-Rhône)

iD **2515**

La Vallée Heureuse***
Impasse Lavau
+33 (0)4-90441713
25/3 - 31/10
contact@valleeheureuse.com

9ha 180T(70-200m²) 10A CEE

1 ACD**G**IJKLPST
2 DFJKLRTUVXY
3 AGHKQRUW
4 (B+G 1/5-30/9)
(Q+R+V+Z)
5 **AB**EFGHJLNPUWZ
6 AEGIK(N 1km)QUV

The campsite is situated in natural surroundings by a lake in a valley encircled by high cliffs. Well known to mountaineers (Massif des Alpilles). Located close to Cavaillon, but still wonderfully peaceful. Dutch owners.

Take A7 as far as Cavaillon exit 25. Direction St. Rémy-de-Provence. Direction Sénas as far as Orgon. Campsite signposted.

CC € 15 *25/3-9/7 26/8-31/10*

N 43°46'55" E 5°2'22"

Orpierre, F-05700 / Provence-Alpes-Côte d'Azur (Hautes-Alpes)

iD **2516**

Les Princes d'Orange****
Flonsaine
+33 (0)4-92662253
FAX +33 (0)4-92663108
1/4 - 31/10
campingorpierre@wanadoo.fr

20ha 89T(80-110m²) 10A CEE

1 A**G**IJKLM**P**ST
2 DJKRTVXY
3 BGN**Q**RU**W**
4 (A 1/7-31/8)
(C+H 15/6-15/9) J
(Q 1/7-31/8) (T+U+V)
(X+Z 15/6-15/9)
5 **AB**EFGIJKLMNPUW
6 AEG**K**(N 0,5km)TV

A very hospitable and personal welcome awaits you at this smart family campsite with stunning views of the charming village of Orpierre. Lovely swimming pool. Renovated toilet facilities and playground. Plenty of activities in the mountains including climbing and walking. Indoor climbing wall at the campsite.

N75 Serres-Sisteron. Turn off at Eyquians. Campsite in the town of Orpierre.

CC € 19 *1/4-2/7 27/8-31/10*

N 44°18'39" E 5°41'41"

Pernes-les-Fontaines, F-84210 / Provence-Alpes-Côte d'Azur (Vaucluse)

iD **2517**

Les Fontaines****
125 chemin de la Chapelette
+33 (0)4-90468255
FAX +33 (0)4-90634291
25/3 - 9/10
contact@campingfontaines.com

2,1ha 65T(100-115m²) 6A CEE

1 ACD**F**HIJKLM**P**ST
2 RVWX
3 AGRU
4 (C 15/5-30/9) (G 15/5-15/9)
K(Q) (R 1/7-31/8)
(T 1/5-15/9) (U 1/4-31/10)
(V 1/5-15/9) (Y 1/5-30/9) Z
5 **AB**EFGIJKLMNPUWXYZ
6 CEGK(N 1,3km)RTV

An attractive new campsite among fields located 1 km from the village. Marked out pitches located around a central brand new toilet block. Overlooking Mont Ventoux. New: pitches with extra comfort at additional fee.

On the A7 exit Le Pontet (Avignon Nord). Direction Carpentras. Follow signs in Pernes-les-Fontaines.

CC € 17 *25/3-5/7 23/8-9/10*

N 44°0'23" E 5°2'18"

Peynier, F-13790 / Provence-Alpes-Côte d'Azur (Bouches-du-Rhône)

2518

Le Devançon***
chemin de Pourrachon
+33 (0)4-42531006
+33 (0)4-42530479
5/3 - 5/11
ledevancon@orange.fr

1,4ha 53T(85-150m²) 6-10A

1 ACD**G**HIJKLMP
2 BJTUVXY
3 BGHRU
4 (B+G 10/6-15/9)
(Q 1/4-1/10)
5 **AB**DFGIJKLMNOPZ
6 ACDEJ(N 0,5km)RTV

A quiet campsite with spacious pitches, close to the village. Excellent toilet facilities and a lovely pool. Excellent starting point for a visit to Aix-en-Provence, Marseille and the Camargue.

Follow A7, then A8 dir. Nice. Exit 32. Follow D6 dir. Trets. At crossing with D56b, right towards Peynier. In village dir. 'centre-ville'. Then D908 dir. Marseille. Right after bridge and follow Chemin de Pourrachon to the campsite.

CC € 17 *5/3-8/7 26/8-5/11*

N 43°26'32'' E 5°37'46''

Pierrefeu-du-Var, F-83390 / Provence-Alpes-Côte d'Azur (Var)

2519

Le Deffends***
109 route des Maures
+33 (0)4-94282062
1/3 - 15/10
camping.ledeffends@free.fr

50T(60-100m²) 6-16A

1 ACD**F**IJKLT
2 BFIJKRTVWX
3 BGNQRU
4 (B+G 15/6-15/9)
(Q 1/7-31/8)
(T+U+V+Z 15/6-15/9)
5 **A**FGIJKLMNPVWXZ
6 E**K**(N 2km)OTV

Pleasant campsite located in a vast pine forest and in the Massif des Maures, with a beautiful view of unspoilt nature. The famous palm tree town of Hyères-les-Palmiers is 14 km away. From there, a boat trip to the 'Golden Islands' is very recommended.

A8, then A57 dir. Toulon. The D14 before Cuers dir. Pierrefeu-du-Var.

CC € 17 *1/3-7/7 24/8-15/10*

N 43°14'3'' E 6°10'0''

Prunières, F-05230 / Provence-Alpes-Côte d'Azur (Hautes-Alpes)

2520

Le Nautic***
N94
+33 (0)4-92506249
+33 (0)4-92535842
14/5 - 15/9
campinglenautic@wanadoo.fr

3ha 100T(60-120m²) 6A CEE

1 ACDGIJKLM**PQ**
2 DJKLMOQTUVWXY
3 AGHJRU**WZ**
4 (C+H 15/6-15/9) K(Q)
(R 1/6-15/9)
(T+U+V 1/7-30/8)
(Z 1/6-15/9)
5 **A**FGIJLMNOPUZ
6 ABCEG**J**(N 5km)ORTV

A panoramic setting by the lake. Heated swimming pool from 15/6 to 15/9. Landing stage for boats.

About 22 km east of Gap on the N94. Just before bridge over the road turn right immediately. Campsite well signposted.

CC € 17 *14/5-5/7 25/8-15/9*

N 44°31'39'' E 6°21'31''

Prunières, F-05230 / Provence-Alpes-Côte d'Azur (Hautes-Alpes) — 2521

Le Roustou***
RN94
+33 (0)4-92506263
14/5 - 30/9
info@campingleroustou.com

9ha 227**T**(80-150m²) 6A

1 AC**G**IJKLMPQ
2 DJKLMRTVX
3 BG**M**NRU**W**Z
4 (B+G 15/6-15/9)
(Q 15/6-31/8)
(T+U+V+X+Z 20/6-31/8)
5 **A**FGIJKLMNPUVXZ
6 EGK(N 4km)RTV

Located on a peninsula on the lake. Private beach and landing stage. Pitches marked out by trees and bushes.

Campsite is located on Serre-Ponçon Lake, halfway between Chorges and Savines-le-Lac. Stay on the N94.

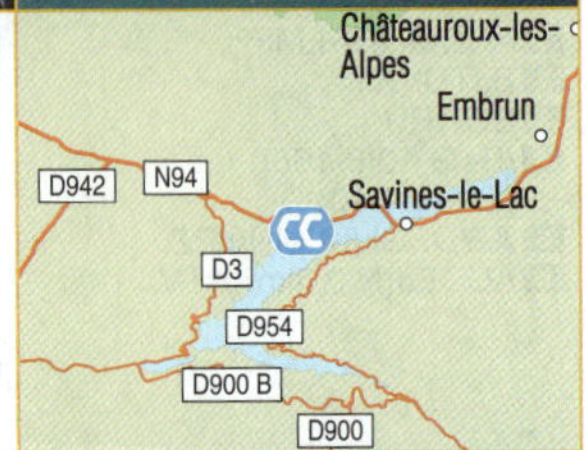

CC € 17 *14/5-2/7 20/8-30/9*
N 44°31'28'' E 6°20'27''

Puget-sur-Argens, F-83480 / Provence-Alpes-Côte d'Azur (Var) — 2522

La Bastiane*****
1056 chemin des Suvières
+33 (0)4-94555594
FAX +33 (0)4-94555593
16/4 - 12/10
info@labastiane.com

3,5ha 60**T**(80-100m²) 10A

1 ACD**F**IJKL**P**T
2 BFLRTVWXY
3 B**F**GHJK**M**N**OP**RU
4 (C+H) K
(Q+S+T+U+V+X+Y+Z)
5 **AB**CDEFGHIJKLMNOPUW
Z
6 ABEGH**IK**(N 2km)ORTV

Nice, well-cared-for, well managed campsite. Beautifully located in the wide Provençal forest and park. Only a few minutes by car from the beaches of Fréjus. It's certainly worth taking a day trip inland and going for a drive along the well-known wine route.

Signs are posted on the N7, west of Puget-sur-Argens.

CC € 17 *16/4-2/7 28/8-12/10*
N 43°28'11'' E 6°40'44''

Roquebrune-sur-Argens, F-83520 / Provence-Alpes-Côte d'Azur (Var) — 2523

Domaine de la Bergerie*****
route du Col du Bougnon
+33 (0)4-98114545
FAX +33 (0)4-98114546
24/4 - 30/9
info@domainelabergerie.com

60ha 200**T**(80-200m²) 6-10A CEE

1 ACDGIJKLPST
2 BCDFGIJKRTVWXY
3 BD**F**GHJKMNP**Q**RUVW
4 (**A** 24/4-15/9) (B+F+G) I
JK**LMN**P
(Q+S+T+U+V+W+X+Y+Z)
5 **AB**CDEFGHIJKLMNOPUV
WXYZ
6 AFGH**IK**(N 7km)OPRTV

Well positioned campsite set in a 60 hectare wood full of oak, fir and mimosa trees. Hedges separate the pitches. Excellent (swimming) facilities including an indoor pool with jacuzzi, sauna and Turkish bath.

From St. Aygulf to Roquebrune-sur-Argens. After about 3 miles (5 km) there's a roundabout. Turn left to Col du Bougnon. After 1 km follow the signs.

CC € 19 *24/4-3/7 26/8-30/9*
N 43°23'55'' E 6°40'30''

Roquebrune-sur-Argens, F-83520 / Provence-Alpes-Côte d'Azur (Var) — 2524

Le Vaudois***
D7
+33 (0)4-94813770
FAX +33 (0)9-72431189
23/4 - 30/9
@ camping.vaudois@wanadoo.fr

3ha 44**T**(80-110m²) 10A CEE

1 ACDGIJKL**P**ST
2 FGRTVWXY
3 B**F**GRU**W**
4 (B+G 15/5-30/9)
(Q+R+T+V 15/5-15/9)
5 **A**CFGHIJKLMNOPUZ
6 AEGIJ(N 4km)TV

A lovely, well run and shaded campsite just 4 km from the beaches at St. Aygulf. Homely atmosphere. No entertainment, so very peaceful.

Campsite located on Départementale D7, 4 km north of St. Aygulf.

CC € 13 *23/4-6/7 24/8-30/9*

N 43°24'39'' E 6°41'31''

Roquebrune-sur-Argens, F-83520 / Provence-Alpes-Côte d'Azur (Var) — 2525

Leï Suves****
route de Marchandise,
bd Ric Hochet
+33 (0)4-94454395
FAX +33 (0)4-94816313
2/4 - 15/10
@ camping.lei.suves@wanadoo.fr

7,5ha 160**T**(80-120m²) 6A CEE

1 ACD**G**IJKLPS
2 BFGJKRTVWXY
3 B**F**GHJMN**OP**RU**W**
4 (A+C+H+Q+S+T+U+V+X+
Y+Z)
5 **AB**CDEFGHIJKLMNOPUXY
Z
6 ACEG**IK**(N 4km)ORTV

In every respect an excellently maintained and well organised campsite in the middle of the Provençal landscape. The site has a very appropriate name: 'Leï Suves', this means cork trees. The campsite was once a cork plantation.

A8, exit Le Muy, direction Fréjus via the N7. Turn left at the roundabout at Roquebrune-sur-Argens, direction La Bouverie.

CC € 17 *2/4-3/7 27/8-15/10 7=6*

N 43°28'40'' E 6°38'19''

Roquebrune-sur-Argens, F-83520 / Provence-Alpes-Côte d'Azur (Var) — 2526

Les Pêcheurs****
+33 (0)4-94457125
FAX +33 (0)4-94816513
1/4 - 29/9
@ info@camping-les-pecheurs.com

5ha 103**T**(80-100m²) 10A CEE

1 ACD**G**IJKLPST
2 CDFGKRVWXY
3 B**F**GKNQRUWZ
4 (A+C+H) **KNP**
(Q+R+T+U+V+X+Y+Z)
5 **AB**CDEFGHIJKLMNOPUZ
6 ACEGH**IK**(N 0,7km)ORTV

A lovely, well-run campsite located by a river 10km from the sandy beaches of Fréjus and St. Raphaël. There is a lake opposite the hotel offering countless watersports opportunities. Lovely swimming pool with wellness facilities.

A8, exit Le Muy, direction Roquebrune. The campsite is located just before the village, opposite the lake.

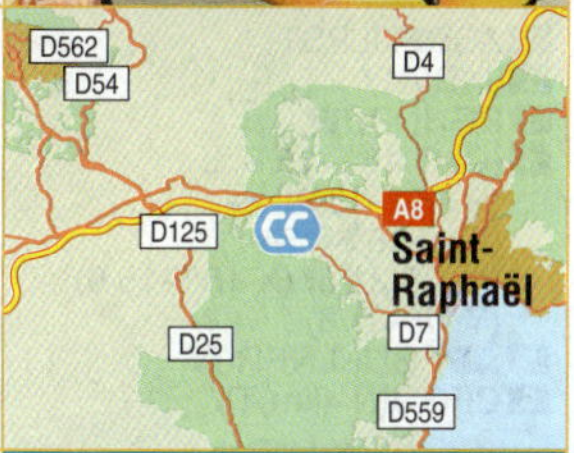

CC € 17 *1/4-3/7 27/8-29/9 7=6*

N 43°27'4'' E 6°38'2''

Roquebrune-sur-Argens, F-83520 / Provence-Alpes-Côte d'Azur (Var) — iD 2527

Moulin des Iscles***
chemin du Moulin des Iscles
+33 (0)4-94457074
FAX +33 (0)4-94454609
1/4 - 30/9
@ moulin.iscles@wanadoo.fr

1,3ha 79**T**(70-100m²) 6A

1 ACD**G**IJLPST
2 CFKRVWXY
3 B**F**GKNQRU**W**
4 (Q+S)
(T+U+V+X 7/4-25/9)
5 **AB**CDEFGHIJKLMNOPUVXYZ
6 AEGHI**K**(N 3km)ORTV

A pleasant, quiet campsite on the banks of the Argens. The 'patronne' cooks wonderful meals for the guests in the restaurant, often using recipes from grandmother's times.

A8 exit Le Muy, then N7 direction Fréjus. After about 10 km right, Roquebrune. Campsite is located just to the south of the village, direction St. Aygulf.

CC € 17 *1/4-3/7 27/8-30/9 7=6*

N 43°26'43'' E 6°39'28''

Rosans, F-05150 / Provence-Alpes-Côte d'Azur (Hautes-Alpes) — iD 2528

Les Hauts de Rosans****
rte du Col de Pomerol
+33 (0)4-92666155
15/4 - 15/10
@ contact@
camping-hautsderosans.com

7ha 57**T**(80-140m²) 10A CEE

1 ACD**G**IJKLMPT
2 DIJKRTVWXY
3 ABGHJU
4 (C+Q+T+V+X 1/5-30/9) Z
5 **A**EFGHIJKLMNOPUWZ
6 ABEGK(N 1km)TV

Chantal and Henri offer a hospitable welcome to their campsite. You can appreciate the beauty of this landscaped park from every terrace, and this gives a feeling of calm. 1 km from Rosans with shops and restaurants. On the road to the Col de Pommerol, a unique walking area. Henri will bring the caravans to the camping pitches because there are height differences because the campsite is terraced.

Nyons-Gap D94, left in Rosans centre. Follow 'Col de Pommerol' signs.

CC € 17 *15/4-5/7 28/8-15/10*

N 44°23'44'' E 5°27'40''

Rousset/Serre-Ponçon, F-05190 / Provence-Alpes-Côte d'Azur (Hautes-Alpes) — iD 2529

La Viste****
Serre-Ponçon
+33 (0)4-92544339
14/5 - 15/9
@ camping@laviste.fr

6ha 160**T**(90-120m²) 5A CEE

1 ACD**F**IJLPST
2 JKRVXY
3 BGHNRU**W**
4 (C+G 15/5-15/9) J
(R 15/5-15/9)
(T+U 15/6-15/9)
(V 1/6-31/8) (X 15/5-15/9)
(Y 1/6-31/8)
5 **AB**FGIJKLNPRUV
6 CEGIJ(N 4km)TV

A high altitude campsite with good toilet facilities and spacious pitches. Lovely views from the terrace and from several of the pitches. The restaurant is certainly worth a visit.

D900 Gap-Barcelonette, exit D3. Then take the route to Rousset, or N94 Gap-Briançon exit D3 for caravans.

CC € 17 *14/5-30/6 1/9-15/9*

N 44°28'33'' E 6°15'48''

2530 Salon-de-Provence, F-2837 / Provence-Alpes-Côte d'Azur (Bouches-du-Rhône)

Nostradamus***
route d'Eyguières RD 17
+33 (0)4-90560836
1/3 - 31/10
camping.nostradamus@gmail.com

2,7ha 65**T**(80-120m²) 6A CEE

1 AC**G**IJKLPRS
2 CFGRVXY
3 A**F**GJNRUWX
4 (B+G 15/5-20/9) (Q) (R+T+U+V+X 1/5-30/9) Z
5 **AB**EFGIJKNPRUZ
6 CEG**J**(N 3km)TV

The campsite is located in a 40 hectare farm, hidden away in an orchard. In a rural location on level grounds. Located in the heart of Provence. Excellent starting point for walks, bike rides and trips out and for visiting places such as Les Baux de Provence, Saint Rémy, Lubéron, Arles, Marseille, Aix-en-Provence and Avignon.

Stay on A7 as far as exit 27 Salon-de-Provence. Continue towards Eyguières (D17) from Salon-de-Provence. Signposted after a few kilometres.

CC € 17 *1/3-8/7 26/8-31/10*

N 43°40'41'' E 5°3'52''

2531 Sanary-sur-Mer, F-83110 / Provence-Alpes-Côte d'Azur (Var)

Campasun Mas de Pierredon****
652 chemin Raoul Coletta
+33 (0)4-94742502
FAX +33 (0)4-94746142
29/4 - 25/9
pierredon@campasun.eu

4ha 60**T**(80-100m²) 10A CEE

1 ACD**G**HIJKL**P**S
2 FIJRTVX
3 A**F**GKMNQRU
4 (C+G) JK (Q+R+T+U+V+X+Y) Z
5 **A**DEFGIJKLMNOPRSUW
6 ACGJ**K**(N 1km)RTV

Lovely campsite 3 km from the beaches at Sanary and Bandol. Renovated, heated pool with slides, aquapark. Multi sports grounds and excellent restaurant with traditional cuisine.

A50 exit 12 Sanary direction Jardin Exotique. Direction Ollioules after the Mercedes garage, then follow signs.

CC € 17 *29/4-7/7 24/8-25/9*

N 43°7'54'' E 5°48'53''

2532 Sanary-sur-Mer, F-83110 / Provence-Alpes-Côte d'Azur (Var)

Campasun Parc Mogador****
167 chemin de Beaucours
+33 (0)4-94745316
FAX +33 (0)4-94741058
15/3 - 6/11
mogador@campasun.eu

3ha 80**T**(80-100m²) 10A CEE

1 ACD**G**HIJKLPST
2 BFGNRTVX
3 AB**F**GKRTU
4 (C+G+Q+R+T+U+V+Z 1/4-30/9)
5 **A**BDEFGIJKLMNOPRUWXYZ
6 ACDEGJ**K**(N 0,8km)ORTV

A quiet campsite located 800 metres from the sea. Very conveniently located a few kilometres from Sanary and Bandol. Pitches with sufficient shade. Luxury toilet block (new) and restaurant.

A50, exit 12 Bandol. Follow D559 direction Sanary. Campsite on the right about 2 km before the village.

CC € 19 *15/3-7/7 24/8-6/11*

N 43°7'26'' E 5°47'16''

Serres, F-05700 / Provence-Alpes-Côte d'Azur (Hautes-Alpes) — 2533

Domaine des 2 Soleils****
D1075
+33 (0)4-92670133
9/4 - 1/10
dom.2.soleils@orange.fr

12ha 114**T**(80-200m²) 6A CEE

1 ACD**G**IJKLMO**P**S
2 BIJKRTUVWXY
3 BGHNPRU
4 (B+G 15/6-15/9) **J**
(Q+T+U+X+Z 1/7-31/8)
5 **A**FIJKLMNOPQUVZ
6 DEGJORV

Family campsite with many terraces and a beautiful view from the pitches. Many options for cycling, walking, horse riding, canyoning and swimming. Caravans are brought to the pitch by tractor if necessary.

N75, from Serres direction Sisteron, after 1.5 km turn left.

CC € 15 *9/4-1/7 27/8-1/10*

N 44°25'21'' E 5°43'46''

Seyne-les-Alpes, F-04140 / Provence-Alpes-Côte d'Azur (Alpes-de-Haute-Prov) — 2534

Les Prairies***
Haute Greyere
+33 (0)4-92351021
6/5 - 10/9
info@campinglesprairies.com

3,9ha 100**T**(100-140m²) 10A CEE

1 ACD**F**IJLPS
2 CLRTVXY
3 ABGHJRU**W**
4 (C 1/6-14/9) (Q)
(R 1/6-1/9)
(T+U+V+X 10/6-30/8)
(Z)
5 **AB**DEFGIJLMNPUVWXYZ
6 CEGJ(N 0,8km)RTV

This exceptionally beautiful campsite offers peace, comfort and relaxation. Besides good sanitary facilities this site has the advantage of being within walking distance of a typical Montagnard (mountain) village. The friendly owners will always have time for you.

From Gap direction Barcelonette. Then D900 direction Digne. Signposted at Seyne.

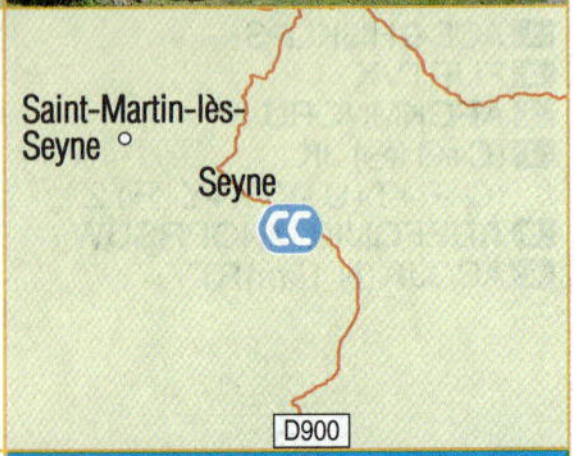

CC € 17 *6/5-3/7 25/8-10/9 8=7, 16=14*

N 44°20'34'' E 6°21'37''

Six-Fours-les-Plages, F-83140 / Provence-Alpes-Côte d'Azur (Var) — 2535

Hôtellerie de Plein Air
Les Playes****
419 rue Grand
+33 (0)4-94255757
FAX +33 (0)4-94071990
1/1 - 31/12
camplayes@wanadoo.fr

1,5ha 47**T**(50-80m²) 10A CEE

1 AC**G**HIJKLPT
2 BFGJTVWXY
3 R
4 (C+H 28/3-1/11)
(Q+R+T+U 1/7-31/8) Z
5 **A**DFGIJKLMNPRUWXYZ
6 ACDEGIJ(N 1,5km)V

Peacefully located campsite on the edge of a wood, 1.5 km from the sea. Numbered pitches laid out in terraces. Lovely heated swimming pool. Modest but clean toilet facilities. A warm welcome throughout the year.

Follow the signs in Six-Fours-les-Plages to Les Playes. Campsite signposted.

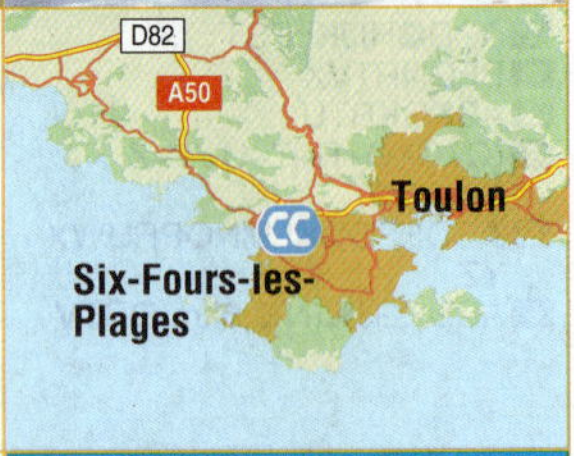

CC € 17 *1/1-1/7 28/8-31/12*

N 43°6'47'' E 5°49'50''

Sorgues, F-84700 / Provence-Alpes-Côte d'Azur (Vaucluse)

2536

La Montagne***
944 chemin de la Montagne
+33 (0)4-90833666
1/1 - 31/12
camping.lamontagne@wanadoo.fr

1,8ha 31**T**(70-90m²) 16A CEE

1 ACD**G**IJKLO**P**ST
2 BFISTVXY
3 AGHJKNRU**W**
4 (C+H 1/4-30/9) J**K**
(Q 1/7-31/8) (R 15/3-30/9)
(T+U+V+X 1/7-31/8)
(Z 1/5-30/9)
5 **AB**DFGIJKLMNPUXY
6 ACDEGK(N 3,5km)RTV

Located a 10 minute drive from Avignon in 2 hectares of pine woods and with a lovely (heated) swimming pool and pleasant catering facilities.

On the A7 take exit 23 Avignon Nord, direction Carpentras, right after 800m direction Sorgues. Campsite signposted from there.

CC € 15 *1/1-5/7 22/8-31/12* *10=9*

N 44°1'15" E 4°53'30"

St. Apollinaire, F-05160 / Provence-Alpes-Côte d'Azur (Hautes-Alpes)

2537

Campéole Le Clos du Lac***
route des Lacs
+33 (0)4-92442743
10/5 - 18/9
clos-du-lac@andretriganogroupe.com

2ha 46**T**(50-100m²) 15A CEE

1 ACD**G**IJKLM**P**S
2 DHIJKLORVWX
3 BGHJQRWZ
4 **KN**(Q) (R 1/7-31/8)
5 **A**CFGIJKLMNOPUZ
6 EGHJ(N 10km)T

An exceptional campsite surrounded by a magnificent mountain range and situated not far from an extensive 5 hectare lake. Angles and swimmers can live life to the full here.

From the north: Grenoble, Gap, Chorges, D9 St. Apollinaire. From the south: A51 as far as La Saulce, Tallard, Chorges, St. Apollinaire.

CC € 15 *10/5-4/7 22/8-18/9*

N 44°33'42" E 6°20'46"

St. Aygulf, F-83370 / Provence-Alpes-Côte d'Azur (Var)

2538

La Barque***
Quartier les Fourgerettes D8
+33 (0)4-94813186
FAX +33 (0)4-94814922
26/3 - 29/10
lecamping-labarque@club-internet.fr

3ha 42**T**(100-150m²) 16A CEE

1 ACD**G**IJKLM**P**ST
2 CFGRSVXY
3 B**F**GHJKLNRW
4 (B 1/4-12/10) (G 1/4-12/9) K
(Q+T+U+V+X+Y+Z 1/4-12/10)
5 **AB**CEFGHIJKLMNPUXZ
6 ACEGH**IK**(N 0,5km)ORTV WX

A friendly, quietly located family campsite with plenty of shade and a really good atmosphere. There is a direct connection to the Mediterranean Sea via the harbour at Argens. The seaside resorts of Fréjus and St. Raphael are just a few hundred metres away. New in 2015: beautiful swimming pool and whirlpool.

From the centre of St. Aygulf towards Roquebrune. Right at roundabout after 4 km. 500m to campsite.

CC € 17 *26/3-2/7 27/8-29/10*

N 43°25'3" E 6°42'12"

St. Aygulf, F-83370 / Provence-Alpes-Côte d'Azur (Var) — 2539

La Plage d'Argens***
541, RD559
+33 (0)4-94511497
FAX +33 (0)4-94512944
2/4 - 16/10
info@laplagedargens.fr

7ha 250**T**(80-100m²) 5A CEE

1 ACD**G**IJL**P**S
2 ACFGLRTVXY
3 B**F**GKLNRUW
4 (**A**+C+H+Q+S+T+U+V+X+ Y+Z)
5 **AB**EFGHIJKLMNOPRUVWZ
6 ACEGH**IK**(N 3km)RTV

A new team, new recreational facilities and beautiful touring pitches. Shaded grounds in a privileged location, on the banks of the Argens, in the heart of the protected coastal area. Easy access to the beaches (600m walk). Leisurely atmosphere. A campsite to discover or rediscover.

On N98, 3 km east of St. Aygulf.

CC € 17 *2/4-6/7 25/8-16/10*

N 43°24'32'' E 6°43'30''

St. Aygulf, F-83370 / Provence-Alpes-Côte d'Azur (Var) — 2540

Les Jardins du Maï Taï***
99 route de Roquebrune
+33 (0)4-94454893
16/4 - 8/10
lesjardinsdumaitai@gmail.com

1,5ha 34**T**(90-120m²) 16A

1 ACD**G**IJL**P**T
2 AFGRWXY
3 B**F**GKNRU
4 (A 1/7-31/8)
(C+H 18/4-3/10) (Q)
(T 15/6-15/9) (U 1/7-31/8)
(V+X 15/6-15/9)
(Z 1/6-15/9)
5 **A**CEFGHIJKLMNPUXYZ
6 AEGI**K**OTV

A recently fully renovated campsite with well maintained amenities and an excellent ambiance. About 2 km to the sandy beaches of the lively seaside resort of Saint-Aygulf. Highly recommended!

Towards Roquebrune-sur-Argens from the centre of St. Aygulf. Just over 2 km, campsite on the right.

CC € 17 *16/4-10/7 27/8-8/10* *14=13, 21=19, 28=25*

N 43°24'37'' E 6°42'29''

St. Aygulf, F-83370 / Provence-Alpes-Côte d'Azur (Var) — 2541

Sandaya Riviera d'Azur*****
189 Les Grands Chât.
de Villepey/RD7
+33 (0)4-94810159
FAX +33 (0)4-94810164
1/4 - 10/10
riv@sandaya.fr

10ha 131**T**(100m²) 10A CEE

1 ACD**G**IJKLM**P**ST
2 ACFGLRTVWXY
3 B**F**GHJK**M**N**Q**RUW
4 (**A** 1/7-31/8) (C+H) J
(Q+S+T+U+V+X+Y+Z)
5 **AB**CEGHIJKLMNOPSUXYZ
6 AEGH**IK**L(N 2,5km)ORTV

Be charmed by the natural resources of the Var and the Mediterranean. Become acquainted with our Provencal villages, our characteristic markets, our festivals and local events. 2.5 km from beaches with fine sand and watersports activities.

The campsite is located on the RD7, 2 km north of St. Aygulf.

CC € 19 *1/4-1/7 29/8-9/10*

N 43°24'33'' E 6°42'32''

St. Cyr-sur-Mer, F-83270 / Provence-Alpes-Côte d'Azur (Var)

2542

Le Clos Sainte Thérèse***
route de Bandol
+33 (0)4-94321221
FAX +33 (0)4-94322962
2/4 - 30/9
@ camping@clos-therese.com

4ha 80**T**(65-150m²) 6-10A CEE

1 AC**F**IJL**PT**
2 FGJKTVX
3 A**F**GHRU
4 (B 4/4-30/9) (G 1/7-1/10) K
(Q+R)
(T+U+V+X+Z 15/6-15/9)
5 **A**DFGIJKLMNPUVWZ
6 CDFG**K**(N 1km)RTUV

A small, well shaded family campsite protruding high above the sea and the Gulf of Frégate 4 km from a sandy beach. Two swimming pools, one of which is heated. 15 km from the medieval village of Castellet and 25 km from Cassis and its magnificent bays.

Follow A50 as far as St. Cyr-sur-Mer exit, then continue towards Bandol. Site is located 3.5 km from the village, on the left.

CC €17 *2/4-30/6 1/9-30/9*

N 43°9'35" E 5°43'46"

St. Maime, F-04300 / Provence-Alpes-Côte d'Azur (Alpes-de-Haute-Prov)

2543

La Rivière***
Lieu-dit 'Les Côtes'
+33 (0)4-92795466
FAX +33 (0)4-92795103
9/4 - 24/9
@ camping-lariviere@orange.fr

3,5ha 44**T**(50-100m²) 6A

1 AD**G**HIJKLPS
2 CDFKLOPRTVX
3 A**F**GNRUW
4 (A 1/7-31/8) (B+G 1/6-15/9)
(Q) (R+T 6/6-31/8)
(U+V+X 1/7-31/8)
(Z 15/6-31/8)
5 **A**DFGIJKLMNOPU
6 EGJ**K**(N 10km)UV

A peacefully located campsite in a valley by a stream with the chance to go fishing. One section of the toilet facilities is heated in low season. Ideal starting point for walks and for visiting the Gorges du Verdon, Valensole and its lavender fields.

A51, exit 19 La Brillanne. Then N96 towards Manosque. After 7 km take the D13. Campsite on the right of the road.

CC €13 *9/4-1/7 22/8-24/9*

N 43°53'52" E 5°48'23"

St. Martin-de-Crau, F-13310 / Provence-Alpes-Côte d'Azur (Bouches-du-Rhône)

2544

De La Crau***
ave de Saint Roch
+33 (0)4-90471709
FAX +33 (0)4-90470992
19/3 - 29/10
@ contact@campingdelacrau.com

3ha 35**T**(> 80m²) 10A CEE

1 ACDGIJKLMPQ
2 FGRSTVXY
3 A**F**GJNRU**W**
4 (B 1/6-15/9)
(Q+S+T+U+X+Y+Z)
5 **A**EFGIJKLMNOPRUZ
6 ACDEGKMQV

A natural campsite located behind a hotel-café-restaurant in the centre of a Provençe village. An ideal starting point for visiting towns in Provence, such as Les Beaux, St. Rémy and Arles, as well as the Camargue, Avignon and Nîmes.

Take D27 from St. Rèmy-de-Provence to the centre of St. Martin. Then N113 direction Arles. The campsite is on your right.

CC €15 *19/3-4/7 21/8-29/10* 7=6

N 43°38'16" E 4°48'21"

St. Maurice-en-Valgodemard, F-05800 / Provence-Alpes-Côte d'Azur (Hautes-Alpes)

2545

Le Bocage**
Hameau le Roux
+33 (0)4-92218648
25/4 - 5/10
campinglebocage@orange.fr

1,3ha 41T(70-150m²) 10A CEE

1 ACD**G**IJKLPST
2 BCGKRTVWXY
3 AGHR**W**
4 (C 25/6-5/9) (Q+R) Z
5 **AB**EFGIJKMNPUV
6 BCEG**K**(N 8km)T

A lovely, well maintained and friendly campsite with a swimming pool. Located on the River Séveraisse. If you are following the 'Route Napoleon' this is the perfect stopover campsite. Unique 300 m² miniature train network.

From Grenoble to Gap via the N85. Take D985a in Saint-Firmin. Campsite 8 km further on.

CC € 15 25/4-3/7 29/8-5/10 7=6

N 44°48'43'' E 6°6'45''

St. Mitre-les-Remparts, F-13920 / Provence-Alpes-Côte d'Azur (Bouches-du-Rhône)

2546

Félix de la Bastide**
Massane Est
+33 (0)4-42809935
15/4 - 15/10
info@campingfelix.com

8ha 100T(100-200m²) 10A CEE

1 ABCD**G**IJLPST
2 DGORWX
3 AHJRWZ
4 (B 1/5-30/9) (G 15/6-15/9) (Q+R+V+X+Z)
5 **AB**GIJKLMNOPU
6 CEHIK(N 6km)V

Quiet, homely campsite located between the hills on the shore of l'Etang de Berre, a salty lake with open access to the sea. Two beaches at walking distance. Warm welcome at campsite. Level grounds, protected by woods and reeds.

In Istres take the D5 Martigues, St. Mitre-les-Remparts. At the end of Istres, after about 2 km, exit D52: Varage, Massane (Les plages). Drive past the campsite Neptune and turn left towards the campsite.

CC € 17 15/4-8/7 25/8-14/10

N 43°28'8'' E 5°1'20''

St. Mitre-les-Remparts, F-13920 / Provence-Alpes-Côte d'Azur (Bouches-du-Rhône)

2547

Le Neptune***
4 allée Gustave Eiffel
+33 (0)4-42440660
1/1 - 31/12
campingneptune@wanadoo.fr

3,2ha 60T(100m²) 16A CEE

1 C**G**IJKLMOPST
2 DFGKLRUVWXY
3 AGHJRWZ
4 (B+G 1/6-30/9) (Q)
5 **AB**DGIJKLMNOPUVXYZ
6 EGI**K**(N 7km)

The campsite has lovely views of l'étang de Berre, good for plenty of water activities. Large marked out pitches. Ideal for people seeking some peace and quiet in the low season.

In Istres follow D5 towards Martigues. At end of town towards Varage Massane (les plages) at roundabout.

CC € 15 1/1-8/7 26/8-31/12

N 43°28'6'' E 5°1'6''

St. Rémy-de-Provence, F-13210/Provence-Alpes-Côte d'Azur (Bouches-du-Rhône) — 2548

Le Parc de la Bastide***
12 avenue Jean Moulin
+33 (0)4-32619486
3/3 - 3/11
auberthonore@orange.fr

70T(80-140m²) 6-10A CEE

1 AGIJKLMOPST
2 RTVWX
3 **F**GHJN
4 (B 15/4-10/10)
(Q 15/4-30/9) (R)
5 ADEFGIJKLOPUZ
6 ACEGK(N 0,5km)OTV

A campsite in Provence, in the heart of the Alpilles. A campsite landscaped with bamboo and mediterranean varieties of trees. 15 minutes walk from the centre of Saint Rémy de Provence. The pitches are easily accessible, level, shaded and bordered by bamboo hedges.

A7 exit 5 Avignon-Sud, from Noves D30 to St. Rémy. In St. Rémy second roundabout left towards town centre. Campsite 50m further on the left.

€17 *3/3-10/7 27/8-3/11 14=13*

N 43°47'24'' E 4°50'39''

St. Saturnin-les-Apt, F-84490 / Provence-Alpes-Côte d'Azur (Vaucluse) — 2549

Domaine des Chênes Blancs***
route de Gargas
+33 (0)4-90740920
25/3 - 15/10
contact@leschenesblancs.com

4ha 122T(80-100m²) 10A CEE

1 ACD**G**HIJKL**P**T
2 BTVWXY
3 BGJNR
4 (B 28/3-17/10) (G+Q+R)
(T+U+V+X 1/7-31/8) (Z)
5 **A**EFGIJKLMNOPUZ
6 ACDEGI**K**(N 3km)O

A shaded campsite peacefully located in an oak forest. Basic toilet facilities but all amenities are available. Spacious pitches on level ground. Restaurant open: May (weekend), June (Wednesday to Saturday).

From A7 exit 24 continue towards Apt (D900). Just before Apt take the D943 then the D2.

€15 *25/3-9/7 27/8-15/10 7=6, 14=11*

N 43°55'15'' E 5°20'28''

St. Vincent-les-Forts, F-04340 / Provence-Alpes-Côte d'Azur (Alpes-de-Haute-Prov) — 2550

Campéole Le Lac***
Le Fein
+33 (0)4-92855157
FAX +33 (0)4-92855763
17/5 - 18/9
lac@andretriganogroupe.com

14ha 300T(100-110m²) 6A CEE

1 AC**G**IJLPS
2 DIJLMRTVWXY
3 ABGHNRU**W**Z
4 (B+G 1/6-31/8) (Q)
(S+T+U+V 15/6-10/9)
(X 1/6-10/9) (Z 15/6-10/9)
5 **AB**FGIJKLMNOPUZ
6 AEGH**IJ**(N 5km)T

A spacious campsite adjoining a lake with beautiful views and a quiet location.

D900 Gap-Barcelonnette, signposted between La Bréole and Le Lauzet-Ubaye.

€17 *17/5-4/7 22/8-18/9*

N 44°27'25'' E 6°21'49''

St.Marcellin/Vaison-la-Romaine, F-84110/Provence-Alpes-Côte d'Azur (Vaucluse)

2551

Le Voconce***
route de St. Marcellin
+33 (0)4-90362810
FAX +33 (0)4-90362035
1/4 - 15/10
contact@camping-voconce.com

96T(70-100m²) 10A

1 ACGIJLMPST
2 COTVXY
3 ABGNRUWX
4 (B+G 15/5-15/9) (Q+R) (T 15/6-15/9) Z
5 AFGIJKLMOPU
6 EGJ(N 2,5km)OTV

A quietly located campsite on the banks of a river, with plenty of regular guests and a friendly couple who manage the site. Wonderful views over many mountains, including Mont Ventoux. Lovely swimming pool. Informal family events are organised.

A7/E15, exit Bollène. Direction Vaison-la-Romaine. In Vaison-la-Romaine drive in the direction of St. Marcellin and then follow the signs.

CC € 17 *1/4-9/7 27/8-15/10*

N 44°13'29'' E 5°6'17''

Ste Maxime, F-83120 / Provence-Alpes-Côte d'Azur (Var)

2552

Les Cigalons**
34 ave du Croiseur Léger Le Malin
+33 (0)4-94960551
FAX +33 (0)4-94967962
20/3 - 16/10
campingcigalon@wanadoo.fr

30T(70-100m²) 10A CEE

1 ACDGIJKLPST
2 AEGJKRSVWXY
3 AFGWY
4 (Q+T+V+Z)
5 ACGHIJKLMNOPUVZ
6 ABEGIK(N 0,2km)TV

Pleasant, quiet, well maintained terraced campsite in a park with centuries-old trees. There is a magnificent sandy beach 50 metres away. Sainte Maxime is just 5 km away and is a very animated resort with countless facilities for sport and recreation.

A8, exit 36 to Le Muy. Once on the coast turn left towards Fréjus. Campsite about 5 km on the left.

CC € 17 *20/3-30/6 1/9-16/10*

N 43°19'50'' E 6°40'1''

Stes Maries-de-la-Mer, F-13460/Provence-Alpes-Côte d'Azur (Bouches-du-Rhône)

2553

Le Clos du Rhône****
route d'Aigues-Mortes, CD38
+33 (0)4-90978599
FAX +33 (0)4-90977885
25/3 - 3/11
info@camping-leclos.fr

7ha 257T(60-100m²) 16A CEE

1 ACDGIJKLOPST
2 AEGKSVWXY
3 BGHJKNOPRUVWY
4 (C+H) JKLP (Q+S+T+U+V+W+X+Z)
5 ABDEFGIJKLMNPUWXYZ
6 ACEGIKL(N 2km)QRTV

A spacious campsite in traditional Camargue style. Positioned directly on a fine sandy beach 800m from Saintes Maries de la Mer. Views of the Camargue opposite the campsite.

From Arles beyond Chateau d'Avignon right onto D38c. Left after a few km on D38. Turn right before Stes Maries-de-la-Mer. Campsite signposted.

CC € 17 *25/3-15/7 1/9-3/11*

N 43°27'0'' E 4°24'6''

Tarascon-sur-Rhône, F-13150 / Provence-Alpes-Côte d'Azur (Bouches-du-Rhône) — 2554

Saint-Gabriel***
D33
+33 (0)4-90911983
14/3 - 14/11
contact@campingsaintgabriel.com

1,2ha 45T(70-110m²) 6A

1 ACD**F**IJKLOPQ
2 RTVXY
3 A**F**GHJRUV**W**
4 (C+H 10/4-10/10) (Q 27/3-31/10) (R) (T+U+V+X 1/6-15/9) (Z)
5 **A**EFGIJKLMNOPUVWXYZ
6 ABEG**K**(N 3km)TV

The heart of the campsite is an old Mas (grange farm). The new swimming pool is in the courtyard. Next to it, outdoors but covered, is the fitness equipment. The bar, shop and reception are in the old farmhouse. Close to Alpilles, Les Beaux and St. Remy-de-Provence. Very centrally located.

The campsite is located on the intersection N570/ D33. From Tarascon follow the main road Arles N570. Direction Maussane.

CC € 15 *14/3-8/7 25/8-13/11*

N 43°46'0" E 4°41'32"

Vaison-la-Romaine/Faucon, F-84110 / Provence-Alpes-Côte d'Azur (Vaucluse) — 2555

de l'Ayguette***
Quartier de l'Ayguette, CD86
+33 (0)4-90464035
FAX +33 (0)4-90464617
17/4 - 25/9
info@ayguette.com

3ha 75T(80-200m²) 10A

1 AC**G**IJLPST
2 JRTVXY
3 ABGNRU
4 (C+Q+R) (T+U+V+X 1/7-23/8) Z
5 **A**FGJKLNPUV
6 CEG**J**(N 1km)OTV

A well kept terraced campsite in a changing landscape of mountains, woods and vineyards close to Vaison-la-Romaine.

Follow Vaison-la-Romaine - Nyons - Gap road. After a few km north follow signs to Faucon from the Intermarché intersection. From the north from Nyons-Vaison-la-Romaine to Mirabel. Left at crossroads to Faucon. Right before Faucon. Look for camping signs.

CC € 15 *17/4-3/7 21/8-25/9*

N 44°15'44" E 5°7'45"

Vallouise, F-05290 / Provence-Alpes-Côte d'Azur (Hautes-Alpes) — 2556

Camping Indigo Vallouise***
chemin des Chambonnettes
+33 (0)4-92233026
FAX +33 (0)4-92223403
26/5 - 3/10
vallouise@camping-indigo.com

6,5ha 136T(80-100m²) 10A CEE

1 ACD**G**IJKL**P**Q
2 CGKRTVWXY
3 BGHIMNRU**W**
4 (**A** 9/7-30/8) (C) (Q+R 1/6-15/9) (T+V 15/6-15/9) Z
5 **AB**DFGIJKLMNOPQUWZ
6 ACEGIJK(N 0,2km)TV

A campsite with lovely views of 'Les Ecrins' mountains. Spacious pitches in sun or shade. Parapente landing area!

Take the D994 in L'Argentière-la-Bessée. Left over the river in Vallouise.

CC € 15 *26/5-5/7 1/9-2/10*

N 44°50'39" E 6°29'25"

Valréas, F-84600 / Provence-Alpes-Côte d'Azur (Vaucluse)

2557

La Coronne***
route du Pegue
+33 (0)4-90350378
1/4 - 21/10
contact@lacoronne.com

2ha 50T(80-130m²) 8A CEE

1 A**G**IJKLM**P**ST
2 CRTUVWXY
3 BGHJRU
4 (B+G+Q+T+U+V+X 1/4-30/9) Z
5 **A**FGIJKLMNOPU
6 AEGJ(N 1,5km)T

A family campsite with plenty of pitches in the shade or in the sun. Lovely swimming pool and many fun activities in the field of sport and leisure. Good opportunities for cycling and walking. Many facilities in the town of Valréas and close by in Vaison, Orange and Avignon.

Exit Montélimar south. Direction Nyons. Turn left just before Valréas and follow the signs.

€15 *1/4-3/7 20/8-15/10*

N 44°23'34'' E 4°59'32''

Vedène, F-84270 / Provence-Alpes-Côte d'Azur (Vaucluse)

2558

Le Flory***
385 route d'Entraigues
+33 (0)4-90310051
30/3 - 30/9
infos@campingflory.com

6,5ha 138T(80-200m²) 10A

1 ACD**G**IJKLM**P**S
2 FIKRSVWXY
3 A**F**GHJNOPRU**W**
4 (B 15/5-15/9) (G 25/6-15/9) (Q+R) (T+Z 9/7-20/8)
5 **AB**EFGIJKLMNPUVWZ
6 ACEGK(N 2km)OTV

Ten minutes drive from Avignon and located around a wooded hillside west of Mont Ventoux. Plenty to see around the campsite: Avignon, l'Isle sur Sorgues, Carpentras, le Mont Ventoux, St. Rémy.

A7, 3 km from the Avignon Nord exit, direction Carpentras, follow the second sign to Vedène (right).

€15 *30/3-2/7 20/8-30/9*

N 43°59'25'' E 4°54'49''

Veynes, F-05400 / Provence-Alpes-Côte d'Azur (Hautes-Alpes)

2559

Camping Solaire****
Quartier des Iscles
FAX +33 (0)4-92581234
1/1 - 31/12
info@camping-solaire.com

6,5ha 158T(150-200m²) 6A CEE

1 A**F**IJKLMPST
2 KRVWXY
3 BGHIJKLN**OPQ**RU**W**
4 (B+G 15/6-30/9) K (Q+R+T+U+V+X+Z 1/7-31/8)
5 **AB**DEFGIJKLMNOPUVWZ
6 EG**IK**(N 2km)OQRTV

A family campsite with a swimming pool, restaurant with terrace and views of the mountains. It has a shaded section but you can also choose a sunny pitch. Pitches of 150 m² or even more. Well maintained grass.

From Grenoble N75 direction Sisteron. Then D994 towards Veynes. Follow Plan d'Eau and camping signs.

€17 *1/4-1/7 18/8-30/9*

N 44°31'14'' E 5°48'15''

Veynes, F-05400 / Provence-Alpes-Côte d'Azur (Hautes-Alpes) 2560

Les Rives du Lac***
Plan d'eau Les Iscles
+33 (0)4-92572090
23/4 - 23/9
booking@camping-lac.com

2,7ha 111**T**(80-190m²) 10A CEE

1 ACD**G**IJKLMOPST
2 CDKMNRVWXY
3 ABCGHIJKLN**OPQ**RU**W**XZ
4 (**A** 1/7-30/8) (C 15/6-15/9) (E 1/5-30/9) (Q 1/5-20/9) (S 1/7-31/8) (T+U+V 15/6-31/8) (X+Z)
5 **A**DEFGIJKLMNPUZ
6 AEGIJ(N 2km)TV

A lovely family campsite with a swimming pool, by a lake where you can swim from May to September. Countless opportunities for walking, cycling and mountain biking from the site up into the surrounding mountains. Fishing in the lake or river. Sports and sports ground for the children. Restaurant with terrace.

From Grenoble N75 direction Sisteron. Then D994 direction Veynes. Follow Plan d'Eau and camping signs.

CC € 15 *23/4-6/7 24/8-23/9*

N 44°31'8" E 5°47'56"

Villes-sur-Auzon, F-84570 / Provence-Alpes-Côte d'Azur (Vaucluse) 2561

Les Verguettes****
119 bis route de Carpentras
+33 (0)4-90618818
7/4 - 2/10
info@provence-camping.com

2ha 70**T**(80-110m²) 10A CEE

1 AC**G**IJKLPST
2 JKRTVWXY
3 BGHJ**Q**RU
4 (B+G 15/5-15/9) (Q 1/6-30/9) (U 1/6-15/9) (X 15/6-15/9) Z
5 **A**DFGIJKLMNPQUYZ
6 ACEG**IK**QRTV

The campsite is located near the village centre with its cafes and restaurants and wonderful views of Mont Ventoux. A lovely swimming pool blends in with the bar and reception area. Good base for walking and cycling tours, also through lavender fields. Romantic mountain villages and the Gorges de la Nesque close by.

Campsite on the D942 Carpentras-Mazan- Villes-sur-Auzon - Sault. Follow the signs in the town.

CC € 19 *7/4-8/7 25/8-2/10*

N 44°3'26" E 5°13'42"

Visan, F-84820 / Provence-Alpes-Côte d'Azur (Vaucluse) 2562

Camping de L'Hérein***
879 route de Bouchet
+33 (0)4-90419599
1/4 - 15/10
accueil@campingvisan.com

3ha 75**T**(80-300m²) 6A CEE

1 ACGIJKLM**P**ST
2 LRTVXY
3 BGNU
4 (A 1/7-31/8) (B 10/5-15/10) (G 20/5-15/9) (Q+R+T+U) (X 1/5-15/9) Z
5 **A**EFGIJKLMNPUV
6 EGJ(N 1km)TV

A quiet family campsite with new toilet facilities, a lovely swimming pool, bar, restaurant and a small shop including fresh fruit from the orchard. Plenty of cycling opportunities also towards Avignon, Mont Ventoux, Orange, Carpentras and Valréas. Plenty of shade or sun, whichever you prefer.

Leave the A7 at Bollène, direction Suze-la-Rousse. At Tulette to Visan, then via signposts to Valreas, direction Bouchet on the route Visan-Bouche on the D161.

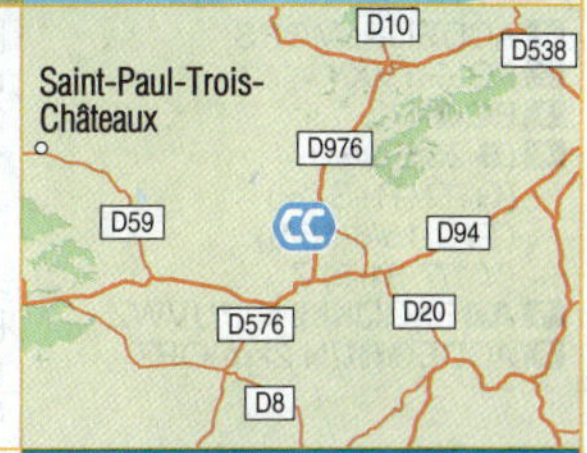

CC € 15 *1/4-5/7 22/8-15/10*

N 44°18'44" E 4°56'9"

Volonne, F-04290 / Provence-Alpes-Côte d'Azur (Alpes-de-Haute-Prov) — 2563

l'Hippocampe****
route Napoleon
+33 (0)4-92335000
FAX +33 (0)4-92335049
9/4 - 30/9
camping@l-hippocampe.com

11ha 447**T**(100-130m²) 10A CEE

1 ACD**F**IJKLMPST
2 DFLMRTVY
3 B**F**GHJKL**MNOPR**U**W**
4 (**A** 1/7-31/8)
(C+H 26/4-30/9) IJK
(Q 26/4-30/9) (R 30/6-9/9)
(T+U+V+X+Z 26/4-15/9)
5 **AB**FGHJLNPUWXYZ
6 ACDEGH**IJK**(N 0,6km)OTV

A campsite that offers plenty of possibilities for relaxing in early and late seasons. Lovely swimming pool, good restaurant and countless opportunities for going on excursions. Within walking distance of a pleasant village. CampingCard ACSI users will also be given comfort pitches.

From Sisteron take the N85, southerly direction. Then exit Volonne. The campsite is located south of Volonne.

CC € 17 *9/4-2/7 22/8-30/9*

N 44°6'16'' E 6°1'1''

Antibes, F-06600 / Rivièra-Côte d'Azur (Alpes-Maritimes) — 2564

Le Rossignol***
2074 av. M. Pellissier/av. J. Grec
+33 (0)4-93335698
FAX +33 (0)4-92919899
27/3 - 30/9
campinglerossignol@wanadoo.fr

1,8ha 111**T**(90-110m²) 10A CEE

1 AC**F**IJKL**P**ST
2 FGJNRTVY
3 A**F**GRU
4 (C 20/4-26/9) (G 1/6-26/9)
(Q+R 1/7-31/8) Z
5 **AB**EFGIJKLMNOPUWXYZ
6 ACEG**IK**(N 0,3km)RTV

Located 1200m from the beach and close to Antibes and Juan les Pins in a natural, quiet and pleasant location, Le Rossignol offers you shaded pitches marked out by hedges and a heated swimming pool. The reception is also open between 12:00 and 14:00.

A8, exit Antibes; direction Marineland. Campsite is signposted.

CC € 17 *27/3-9/7 27/8-29/9*

N 43°36'23'' E 7°6'43''

Antibes, F-06600 / Rivièra-Côte d'Azur (Alpes-Maritimes) — 2565

Les Frênes***
avenue du Pylône
+33 (0)4-93333652
FAX +33 (0)4-93746600
21/5 - 24/9
contact@camping-lesfrenes.com

2,5ha 200**T**(80-100m²) 8A CEE

1 ACD**F**IJKLMOPS
2 FGLRTVXY
3 BG**Q**R
4 (**B** 23/5-26/9)
(**G**+Q+R+S)
(T+U 15/6-15/9)
(V 1/7-31/8) Z
5 **AB**EFGIJKMNOPUVWZ
6 ACDEG**IK**(N 2km)ORT

A peaceful and shaded camping 500m from the beach. Swimming pool and children's pool. Close to Marineland.

A8, exit 44 Antibes/Juan les Pins, then direction Sophia Antipolis/Marineland/Biot. Follow camping signs.

CC € 17 *21/5-11/7 28/8-24/9*

N 43°36'45'' E 7°7'4''

Cagnes-sur-Mer, F-06800 / Rivièra-Côte d'Azur (Alpes-Maritimes) — 2566

Le Colombier***
35 chemin Sainte Colombe
+33 (0)4-93731277
1/4 - 30/9
campinglecolombier06@gmail.com

1,1ha 34**T**(80-110m²) 6A CEE

1 A**F**IJKL**P**ST
2 FGTVXY
3 ABCGR
4 (B 20/5-30/9) (T 1/6-20/9)
5 **AB**DEGIJKLMNOPUVZ
6 CEG**J**(N 0,5km)QTV

Small, homely campsite, peaceful location in green surroundings. Level and shaded grounds. Swimming pool and solarium. WiFi on entire campsite, table football, mini-billiards. 10 minutes to sea, 15 minutes to medieval village, 400 metres to shops and 1 km to town centre.

On the A8 take exit 47. Continue towards Cagnes-sur-Mer centre, follow Colline de la Route de Vence as far as the Durante roundabout. Follow camping signs then Le Colombier campsite sign.

CC € 19 *1/4-10/7 1/9-30/9*

N 43°40'17'' E 7°8'20''

Cagnes-sur-Mer, F-06800 / Rivièra-Côte d'Azur (Alpes-Maritimes) — 2567

Le Val Fleuri***
139 chemin Vallon des Vaux
+33 (0)4-93312174
2/4 - 30/9
valfleur2@wanadoo.fr

1,5ha 86**T**(80-100m²) 6A CEE

1 AC**F**IJKLMPST
2 FGJLNRTVXY
3 ABGR
4 (C+H 15/4-26/9) (Q 🔑)
(R+T 1/7-31/8)
5 **A**DGHIJKLMNOPUZ
6 AFG**K**(N 3,5km)TV

The campsite comprises two sections. The part on the right side of the road has lovely shaded pitches. Away from the bustle of the coast. A very friendly lady owner. Bread ordered in advance is delivered to your caravan in the early and late seasons. Reception closed between 12:00 and 14:00.

A8 exit Cagnes-sur-Mer. Then N7 direction Nice. Signposted through Cagnes-sur-Mer.

CC € 17 *2/4-8/7 27/8-30/9*

N 43°41'14'' E 7°9'21''

La Colle-sur-Loup, F-06480 / Rivièra-Côte d'Azur (Alpes-Maritimes) — 2568

Le Vallon Rouge***
route de Roquefort / D6
+33 (0)4-93328612
+33 (0)4-93328009
9/4 - 28/9
info@auvallonrouge.com

3ha 80**T**(70-100m²) 10A

1 ACD**F**IJKLMPST
2 BCFGLNRTVY
3 ABGHN**OQ**RU**W**X
4 (B+G+Q 🔑)
(R+T+U+V+X+Y 1/7-31/8) Z
5 **AB**EFGIJKLMNPUWZ
6 AEGI**J**(N 3km)OQRTV

Set in lush and shaded surroundings, bordered by a river, you will be welcomed in an oasis of tranquillity.

A8, exit 47 direction Villeneuve-Loubet, after that D6 direction Grasse. Signposted.

CC € 17 *9/4-7/7 24/8-28/9* 14=11

N 43°41'4'' E 7°4'24''

La Colle-sur-Loup, F-06480 / Rivièra-Côte d'Azur (Alpes-Maritimes) 2569

Sites & Paysages
Les Pinèdes****
route du Pont de Pierre
+33 (0)4-93329894
FAX +33 (0)4-93325020
24/3 - 30/9
info@lespinedes.com

4ha 106**T**(80-110m²) 10A

1 AC**F**IJKLPST
2 BCFGJRUVXY
3 B**F**GHN**O**RUV**WX**
4 (C+H 7/4-30/9)
(Q 1/5-30/9) (S 15/5-30/9)
(T+U+V+X+Y) Z
5 **AB**DEFGIJKLMNPUVWXYZ
6 ACEG**IK**(N 1km)QRTV

Close to the sea (7 km) and St. Paul de Vence, ideally located in the centre of the Rivièra/Côte d'Azur. This lovely quiet terraced campsite offers campers spacious pitches, good toilet facilities and a restaurant for culinary indulgence. Heated swimming pool with space for sunbathing open from 11 April.

A8, exit 47 direction Villeneuve-Loubet. Exit La Colle and take route D6 in the direction of Grasse.

CC € 17 *24/3-7/7 24/8-30/9* N 43°40'54'' E 7°5'0''

Le Bar-sur-Loup, F-06620 / Rivièra-Côte d'Azur (Alpes-Maritimes) 2570

Les Gorges du Loup***
965 chemin des Vergers
FAX +33 (0)4-93424506
16/4 - 24/9
info@lesgorgesduloup.com

1,6ha 65**T**(80-160m²) 6-10A CEE

1 A**G**HIJKL**P**ST
2 GJKRTVXY
3 B**F**GNRU
4 (C+Q+R)
(T+U+V+X 1/5-15/9) (Z)
5 **A**CEGHIJKLMNOPUVZ
6 AEG**IK**(N 1km)ORTV

A campsite for early and late seasons, as the surrounding area is one big magnificent natural paradise which will be even more attractive at that time. A convenient location for Cannes, Nice and the perfume city of Grasse. Attentive welcome. Pleasant ambiance. A visit to the Gorges du Loup is highly recommended.

A8 exit 47, directions Roquefort-les-Pins, Le Rouret, Châteauneuf and finally Bar-sur-Loup. Campsite signposted just outside village (about 1,5 km).

CC € 17 *16/4-4/7 24/8-24/9* N 43°42'6'' E 6°59'43''

Le Cannet/Cannes, F-06110 / Rivièra-Côte d'Azur (Alpes-Maritimes) 2571

Le Ranch***
chemin Saint Joseph, l'Aubarède
+33 (0)4-93460011
FAX +33 (0)4-93464430
15/4 - 15/10
info@leranchcamping.fr

2ha 71**T**(80-150m²) 6A CEE

1 ACD**G**IJKLMOST
2 AGIJKTVXY
3 AB**F**GHJNRUV
4 (D 15/5-15/10)
(F 24/4-16/10)
(Q+R+T+U+V+Z)
5 **AB**EFGIJKLMNPQUXZ
6 ACE**K**(N 1km)RV

Located on a wooded hillside with views of Grasse and Mandelieu. Plenty of shade and a swimming pool with a sliding roof are a big advantage. 2 km from Cannes beach (inexpensive bus connection).

A8 exit Le Cannet. Follow direction La Bocca D809. Campsite well signposted.

CC € 19 *15/4-30/6 1/9-15/10* N 43°33'52'' E 6°58'40''

Mandelieu-la-Napoule, F-06210 / Rivièra-Côte d'Azur (Alpes-Maritimes)

2572

Camping Côté Mer***
630 boulevard du Bon Puits
+33 (0)4-93499419
9/4 - 24/9
info@campingcotemer.fr

81T(70-100m²) 6-10A

1 ACFHIJKLPST
2 GKRTVXY
3 BFGHJR
4 (C 11/4-26/9) (Q 15/6-15/9) (T) (U 1/6-16/9) (V 1/6-15/9) (X 15/6-15/9) (Y 1/6-15/9) (Z 1/6-16/9)
5 ABCGHIJKLMNPUZ
6 CEGIJ(N 0,9km)T

A lovely quiet, attractive campsite 700m from the Mediterranean. The campsite is in set a park, so plenty of shade. A friendly welcome. Cannes is close by, but Monaco, Nice and the Italian Floral Riviera are also within easy reach.

Exit 40, A8 Mandelieu Centre, left to La Napoule (av. de Cannes) over the bridge. Over 3 roundabouts and straight on. Campsite signposted.

CC € 19 *9/4-3/7 28/8-24/9*

N 43°31'21'' E 6°55'55''

Mandelieu-la-Napoule, F-06210 / Rivièra-Côte d'Azur (Alpes-Maritimes)

2573

Camping de l'Argentière***
264 boulevard du Bon Puits
+33 (0)4-93499504
1/1 - 31/12
contact@campingdelargentiere.com

30T(80-110m²) 10A

1 ACDGIJKLMOPST
2 CGKRTVX
3 BFHMRW
4 (Q 1/7-31/8) (T+U+V+X)
5 ABCDEFGHIJKLMNOPUXYZ
6 CEGK(N 0,5km)OTV

Quiet campsite with a good location. Lots of plantlife and at 1 km from the Mediterranean Sea. Campsite is situated on the Argentiène river, hence its name. Site has marked-out pitches and plenty of shade. 1 km from a beach promenade. Friendly, homely atmosphere.

A8 exit 40 Mandelieu-Centre. Left dir. La Napoule (Avenue de Cannes). Over the bridge, then straight on over three roundabouts. Site is well signposted.

CC € 19 *1/1-17/6 15/9-31/12*

N 43°31'32'' E 6°56'0''

Mandelieu-la-Napoule, F-06210 / Rivièra-Côte d'Azur (Alpes-Maritimes)

2574

Les Cigales****
505 av. de la Mer
+33 (0)4-93492353
FAX +33 (0)4-93493045
1/1 - 10/1, 6/2 - 31/12
campingcigales@wanadoo.fr

2ha 31T(60-120m²) 6A

1 ACDGIJKLMPST
2 ACFGKRSVWXY
3 BFGKRUW
4 (A 1/6-30/9) (B+G 1/5-30/9) (Q+Y 1/5-31/10) Z
5 ABCDEFGHIJKLMNOPRUXYZ
6 CDEGIJ(N 0,25km)TV

Beautiful and well kept, an ideally located campsite 800m from the Mediterranean. The fashionable and lively resort of Cannes is nearby. Excellent starting point for trips to Nice and the Italian flower riviera or to Monaco and Menton.

A8, exit 40. Then first road right, second traffic lights left. Or N98, between La Napoule and Cannes follow in the direction of Mandelieu-Centre.

CC € 19 *1/1-10/1 6/2-1/7 24/9-14/11*

N 43°32'20'' E 6°56'33''

Puget-Théniers, F-06260 / Rivièra-Côte d'Azur (Alpes-Maritimes)

iD **2575**

Origan****
+33 (0)4-93050600
+33 (0)4-93050934
23/4 - 2/10
origan@orange.fr

35ha 60**T**(50-100m²) 6A

1 ACD**G**IJKLMPST
2 BCIJKLTVWY
3 BHMNRV**W**
4 (A 1/7-31/8) (C+G) JK**L**
N(Q+R+T+U+V+X+Y+Z)
5 **A**EFGIJKLMNOPUVWZ
6 ADEGHIJ(N 3km)ORV

A very well maintained, beautifully situated naturist campsite in impressive surroundings. Nestling on a hillside near a typical village in Haute Provence. 30 km from the Mediterranean Sea.

About 500 metres west of the village Puget-Théniers (by the level crossing) an arrow shows the way.

CC € 17 *23/4-3/7 20/8-2/10*

N 43°57'26'' E 6°51'35''

Aléria, F-20270 / Corse

iD **2576**

Marina d'Aléria****
route de la Mer
+33 (0)4-95570142
+33 (0)4-95570429
23/4 - 8/10
info@marina-aleria.com

9ha 130**T**(80-120m²) 9A CEE

1 ACD**F**IJKLPQ
2 ABEKRSVY
3 BGHK**M**RUVWY
4 (C+H) K
(Q+S+T+U+V+Y+Z)
5 **AB**EFGIJKLMNOPU
6 AEHK(N 3km)OQTV

A lovely family campsite on a long sandy beach. Plenty of comfort and shaded pitches.

Located in Aléria itself, on the intersection in the direction of the coast. Clearly signposted. Coastal road about 3 km.

CC € 19 *23/4-18/6 1/9-8/10*

N 42°6'41'' E 9°33'5''

Aléria, F-20270 / Corse

iD **2577**

Riva Bella Thalasso & Spa Resort****
B.P. 21
+33 (0)4-95388110
+33 (0)4-95389129
20/1 - 20/12
riva-bella@orange.fr

78ha 200**T**(100-120m²) 10A CEE

1 ACD**F**IJKLMNOPST
2 ABDEIKSTXY
3 BDGKLMNRUWY
4 (**A** 1/7-31/8) **KLNOP**
(Q 15/5-30/9) (S 1/5-30/9)
(T) (U 1/6-15/9)
(V+Y) Z
5 **AB**EFGIJKLMNOPUWZ
6 AEG**IK**L(N 7km)OQRTV

Large naturist campsite right by the sea. Fitness, Thalasso, sauna, hammam and thermal bath. Beauty Farm 450 metres away. This naturist site is open before 15 May and after 29 September for non-naturists only.

Located near the N198, 9 km north of Aléria, then 3 km on a private country road to the coast.

CC € 19 *20/1-12/6 10/9-20/12*

N 42°9'55'' E 9°32'39''

Bonifacio, F-20169 / Corse

2578

Pian del Fosse***
route de Santa Manza
+33 (0)4-95731634
20/4 - 15/10
pian.del.fosse@wanadoo.fr

5ha 100**T**(40-80m²) 4-6-10A CEE

1 ACD**G**IJL**P**
2 JRVY
3 B**FGOP**R
4 (Q 1/6-30/9) (R+T 1/7-31/8) Z
5 **AB**EFGIJKLMNOPUVZ
6 ACDEG**J**(N 3,5km)OTV

Very well maintained campsite with a friendly welcome and plenty of shade. The perfect starting point for visiting bays, beaches and towns. A quiet campsite.

At 3.5 km from Bonifacio on the D58 direction Golfe de Sant'Amanza. Clearly signposted, to the right of the road.

CC € 17 *20/4-15/7 1/9-15/10*

N 41°23'59" E 9°12'4"

Bravone, F-20230 / Corse

2579

Bagheera****
N198
+33 (0)4-95388030
FAX +33 (0)4-95388347
15/1 - 15/12
bagheera@bagheera.fr

100ha 250**T**(80-120m²) 10A

1 ABCD**G**IJKLM**P**S
2 ABEKRSXY
3 BDGHJK**M**NRUWY
4 N(Q 1/4-31/10) (S 1/5-30/9) (T+U+V+Y 15/5-30/9) Z
5 **AB**DFGIJKLMNOPUZ
6 ACEGI**K**L(N 6km)OPQRTV

The site has modern heated toilet facilities, restaurants and a mini-market, all of it in a eucalyptus forest by the sea and clear water. You can indulge in many sports: swimming, aqua-gym, yoga, diving, fishing, pedalos, cycling or windsurfing. Or relax in a chaise longue in the shade of the eucalyptus trees.

The campsite is located on the San Nicolao/ Bravone N198, about 18 km south of San Moriani-Plage, and about 12 km north of Aléria, about 3 km from the N198.

CC € 17 *15/1-2/6 1/9-15/12*

N 42°12'53" E 9°33'19"

Ghisonaccia, F-20240 / Corse

2580

Arinella Bianca*****
route de la Mer
+33 (0)4-95560478
FAX +33 (0)4-95561254
16/4 - 30/9
arinella@arinellabianca.com

10ha 140**T**(80-100m²) 10A CEE

1 ACD**F**IJKLMPST
2 ACEGKRSVY
3 BGMN**OP**RUWY
4 (**A** 15/6-31/8) (C+G 1/5-30/9) **KLP** (Q 15/5-30/9) (S 15/5-15/9) (T+U+V+X+Y+Z 15/5-30/9)
5 **AB**FGIJKLMNOPUWZ
6 ACEGHK(N 1km)ORTU

A beautiful family campsite on the beach with a swimming pool and plenty of entertainment. Separated, well shaded pitches.

From the N198 roundabout after Ghisonaccia centre, take route de la Mer 5 km, and turn right at the roundabout. Follow camping signs.

CC € 19 *16/4-2/7 20/8-30/9*

N 41°59'56" E 9°26'32"

Ghisonaccia, F-20240 / Corse

2581

Marina d'Erba Rossa****
route de la Mer
+33 (0)4-95562514
+33 (0)4-95562723
2/4 - 16/10
erbarossa@wanadoo.fr

20ha 80T(80-120m²) 10A CEE

1 ACD**F**IJKLMPRS
2 ABEKRSTVWXY
3 ABDGJMNQRUWY
4 (B) **KNP**(Q 3/5-27/9)
(S) (T+U+V 15/5-30/9)
(Y) Z
5 **AB**EFGIJKLMNOPUW
6 AEGH**IJK**(N 1km)QRTV

A beautiful family campsite located on the beach, with every comfort, shady pitches and lots of entertainment.

From N198 at roundabout after Ghisonaccia centre. Route de la Mer 5 km.

CC € 19 *2/4-3/7 27/8-16/10*

N 42°0'2'' E 9°26'49''

Lecci, F-20137 / Corse

2582

Mulinacciu***
+33 (0)4-95714748
+33 (0)4-95214093
20/5 - 30/9
infos@mulinacciu.com

14ha 160**T**(40-100m²) 6A CEE

1 A**G**IJKL**P**
2 BCSTXY
3 BG**M**NRTUWX
4 (C+H 1/6-30/9) J
(Q 15/6-31/8)
(T+U+V+X 1/6-31/8) Z
5 **A**FGIJLMNPU
6 CEG**K**(N 1km)QV

A quiet campsite next to a river in the woods. The campsite has a heated swimming pool and there is also a bowling alley. Unmarked pitches. Good starting point for walking, 5 km from the sea.

From Lecci N198 towards Porto Vecchio, indicated beyond the village with large signs. On the right of the road.

CC € 19 *20/5-30/6 1/9-25/9*

N 41°40'35'' E 9°18'5''

Lumio, F-20260 / Corse

2583

Le Panoramic**
route de Lavatoggio
+33 (0)4-95607313
1/5 - 30/9
info@le-panoramic.com

100T 6A CEE

1 A**G**IJKL**P**S
2 IJKSTVXY
3 AGHJR
4 (B) (Q 1/6-30/9) (R)
(T+U+V+X+Z 1/6-30/9)
5 **A**FGIJKLMNPQUZ
6 AEGJ(N 1,5km)OQTV

Camping Panoramic is located 1,5 km from Lumio between Calvi and L'Ile Rousse and just 5 minutes from the beaches. The campsite has lovely views of Sant'Ambroggio bay. Its hallmarks are the friendly atmosphere, relaxation and shade. The campsite has a swimming pool and shaded pitches which are marked out by eucalyptus and mimosa trees.

Follow the N197 and take the D71 towards Lavatoggio. Campsite 1500m north of Lumio.

CC € 15 *1/5-30/6 20/8-30/9*

N 42°35'24'' E 8°50'55''

Olmeto, F-20113 / Corse

2584

Vigna Maggiore***
RN196/RD157
+33 (0)4-95746202
1/5 - 30/9
@ vignamaggiore@gmail.com

5,5ha 140T(70-180m²) 6A CEE

1 AFIJKLMOPRS
2 IKLSTWXY
3 ABGHR
4 (C) (Q+R+S 15/5-20/9) (T+U+V 1/7-15/9) (X 1/6-30/9) Z
5 AEIJKLMNOPUZ
6 EGIJ(N 3km)OT

A peaceful campsite on the west coast close to Propiano with its lovely beaches above the Golfe de Valinco. Free choice of pitches with or without shade. Lovely swimming pool with bar. A very good base for visiting Filitosa.

From Propriano direction Olmeto, campsite on a bend on the left just after the D157 intersection.

CC € 17 *1/5-8/7 25/8-30/9*

N 41°41'53'' E 8°53'47''

Pietracorbara, F-20233 / Corse

2585

La Pietra***
Marine de Pietracorbara
+33 (0)4-95352749
FAX +33 (0)4-95352857
20/3 - 4/11
@ lapietra@wanadoo.fr

5ha 170T(95-120m²) 10A CEE

1 ACDGIJKLMOPST
2 AGKLQSVWXY
3 BGU
4 (B 1/6-15/9) K(Q) (R 15/6-30/9) (T+X 15/6-15/9) (Z)
5 AFGIJKLMNOPUVW
6 CDEGHJ(N 3km)TV

Quietly located campsite with excellent sanitary facilities on Cap Corse, a unique part of Corsica. New swimming pool. There is a lovely beach 600 metres away via a footpath.

On the D80 from Bastia to Cap Corse, turn left after 20 km, well signposted.

CC € 17 *20/3-30/6 11/9-4/11*

N 42°50'20'' E 9°28'25''

Porticcio, F-20166 / Corse

2586

Benista****
Pisciatello / D55
+33 (0)4-95251930
FAX +33 (0)4-95259370
1/4 - 15/10
@ camping.benista@orange.fr

5ha 170T(90-110m²) 5A CEE

1 ACDGIJKLMPST
2 CGRSTVY
3 ABEFGMNRU
4 (B+G 15/5-15/9) (Q+R+S+T+U) (V 1/7-31/8) (X 1/6-31/8) Z
5 ABEFGIJKLMNPUW
6 ACGKOQRTV

A friendly, shaded family campsite with a lovely swimming pool. 9 hole golf course next to the site, as well as shops and a restaurant. Lovely sandy beaches 1.5 km away. 10 km from Ajaccio.

Coming from the N196 drive up the D55. The campsite is on the right, after about 600 metres.

CC € 19 *1/4-30/6 1/9-15/10*

N 41°54'25'' E 8°49'21''

Sagone, F-20118 / Corse

2587

Le Sagone Camping****
route de Vico
+33 (0)4-95280415
FAX +33 (0)4-95280828
21/4 - 15/10
sagone.camping@wanadoo.fr

9ha 270**T**(80-120m²) 10A

1 ACD**F**IJKLM**P**RS
2 ABCGRSVY
3 B**E**G**M**NRU**V**W
4 (A 1/7-31/8) (B+G+Q+S+T+U+V+Y) Z
5 **AB**EFGIJKLMNPUWZ
6 ABCEGH**JK**OTUV

Le Sagone is surrounded by miracles: white sandy beaches, the 'Greek' Cargèse, the Piana Calanques, the Scandola nature reserve, the tower of Porto and Genoese Ajaccio. The coast is home to seabirds that nest here peacefully. Le Sagone is also a wild water paradise. Spectacular waterfalls and natural pools give the countryside a special appeal.

Located on the D70, 2 km along the Sagone-Vico road. Signposted in Sagone.

CC € 15 *21/4-29/6 20/9-15/10*

N 42°7'51" E 8°42'18"

Spain

General

Spain is a member of the EU.

Time

The time in Spain is the same as Amsterdam, Paris and Rome and one hour ahead of London. Time on the Canary Islands is the same as London.

Languages

Spanish.

Border formalities

Many formalities and agreements about matters such as necessary travel documents, car papers, requirements relating to your means of transport and accommodation, medical expenses and taking pets with you do not only

depend on the country you are travelling to but also on your departure point and nationality. The length of your stay can also play a role here. It is not possible within the confines of this guide to guarantee the correct and most up to date information with regard to these matters.

We advise you to consult the relevant authorities before your departure about:
- which travel documents you will need for yourself and your fellow passengers
- which documents you need for your car
- which regulations your caravan must meet
- which goods you may import and export
- how medical treatment will be arranged and paid for in your holiday destination in cases of accident or illness
- whether you can take pets. Contact your vets well in advance. They can give you information about the necessary vaccinations, proof thereof and obligations on return. It would also make sense to enquire whether any special regulations apply to your pet in public places at your holiday destination. In some countries for example dogs must always be muzzled or transported in a cage.

You will find plenty of general information on ▸ ***www.europa.eu*** ◂ but make certain you select information that is relevant to your specific situation.

For the most recent customs regulations you should get in contact with the authorities of your holiday destination in your country of residence.

Currency

The currency in Spain is the euro. Approximate exchange rates September 2015: £1 = € 1.37.

Credit cards

Credit cards can be used in most places, including toll roads.

Opening times /Public holidays

Banks

Banks are open Monday to Friday until 14:00, Saturday until 13:00. Banks are closed on Saturdays in June, July and August. Spanish banks adhere strictly to closing times. It may happen that if you arrive at a bank at 13:55, the security guard will not allow you to enter!

Shops

Open from Monday to Friday until 13:30 and from 16:30 to 20:00, on Saturdays between 09:30 and 13:30. During the tourist season shops in the coastal areas are often open until after 22:00.

Chemists

Spanish chemists, which can be recognised by a green cross, are open from Monday to Friday until 13:30 and from 16:30 to 20:00.

Public holidays

New Year's Day, 6 January (Epiphany), Maundy Thursday, Good Friday, Easter, 1 May (Labour Day), Whitsunday, 26 May (Corpus Christi), 15 August (The Assumption), 12 October (National Day), All Saints Day, 6 December (Constitution Day), 8 December (Immaculate Conception), Christmas Day.

In the week before Easter (the 'Semana Santa') the shops open for half the day.

Communication

(Mobile) phones

The mobile network works well throughout Spain. There is a 3G network for mobile internet. You can pay for payphones with coins, credit cards and phone cards which you can buy at tobacconists and kiosks.

WiFi, internet

The best quality cybercafes are the larger cafes with more than 20 seats. Buy a multi-hour pass or 'bono' (valid for 5 to 10 hours) if you want to make longer use of internet. Campsites are increasingly offering WiFi, sometimes upon payment.

Post

In general post offices are open on weekdays until 14:30 and from 17:00 to 20:00, on Saturdays until 13:00.

Roads and traffic

Road network

You are not advised to drive in the dark except on main roads. If you break down you can contact the Spanish motoring organisation RACE (in Catalonia the RACC) using the emergency phones.

Traffic regulations

Remember, all traffic in Spain drives on the right and overtakes on the left! Headlight deflectors are advisable to prevent annoying oncoming drivers. Spain uses the metric system,

so distances are measured in kilometres (km) and speeds in kilometres per hour (km/h). You must give way to traffic from the right, except on priority routes. This also applies to slow traffic. When driving on a roundabout you have priority over drivers entering it. Trams always have priority.

Maximum speed

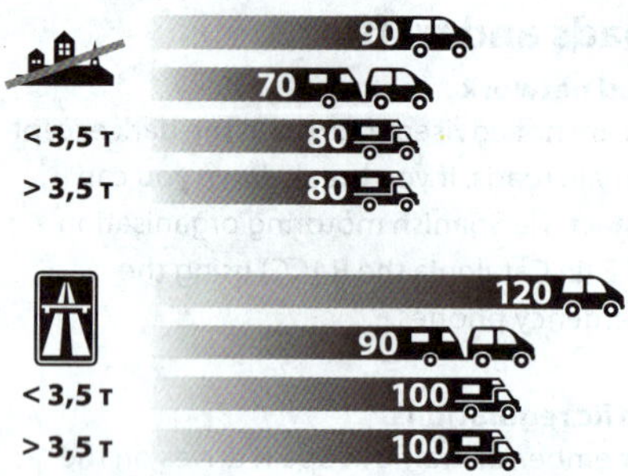

The maximum permitted alcohol level is 0.5‰. Dipped headlights are compulsory in tunnels. Phones may only be used hands-free. Drivers who wear spectacles must carry a spare pair. Use of the horn is compulsory on blind corners in mountain areas. Carrying a spare set of lamps is mandatory. Radios and mobile phones must be switched off when refuelling your vehicle. Use of a head set in cars is not permitted. Winter tyres are not compulsory in winter conditions but are very much advised, especially in areas such as the Pyrenees and the Sierra Nevada.

Navigation
Notification of fixed speed cameras by navigation systems or mobile phones is permitted.

Caravans, motorhomes
If your caravan is longer than 12 metres, the so called ECE 70 is mandatory. You must then have two small or one large, yellow and red reflective sticker on the back of your caravan.
If your caravan is longer than 12 metres you must keep a distance of at least 50 metres from another vehicle outside built up areas.

Permitted dimensions
Height 4 metres, width 2.55 metres and length with a caravan 18.75 metres.

Fuel
Lead-free petrol and diesel are widely available. LPG is available to a very limited extent.

Filling stations
Most filling stations along motorways are open between 06:00 and 24:00. Elsewhere they are open between 07:00 and 22:00. Pay attention when filling up: 'gasolina' means petrol and 'gasoleo' means diesel! You can pay by credit card at all service stations on motorways.

Tolls
Most motorways in Spain charge a toll. You can pay in cash, by credit card or automatically with an electronic (ETC) box.
Toll roads are indicated by the letters AP, while toll free motorways are indicated by the letter A.
More information: ▸ ***www.aseta.es*** ◂

Mountain passes with caravans
The Bonaigua Pass: is not prohibited for caravans but snow chains must be used in the winter months when there is snow on the ground, and the pass may sometimes be closed.
The Portillón Pass: is not prohibited for caravans but the road is not very wide and going in the direction of France is even narrower; driving with a large(r) caravan may then be difficult.

Emergency number
112: the national emergency number for fire, police or ambulance.

Camping

Spain has more than 1000 campsites, of which the sites on the northern Mediterranean coast are the busiest. Reservations here are recommended! Trees, bushes and flowers ensure beautiful campsites, and also provide marked out pitches which increases privacy.

Campsites in Spain are classified by category. Category 1 is the most luxurious. Free camping is not allowed. If you still want to camp where there is no campsite, permission from the landowner must be sought.

Practical

- The Spanish are renowned for eating late; quite often people eat at home and in catering establishments between 20:30 and 22:30.
- Blue camping gas bottles cannot be refilled in Spain. You are advised to buy a Spanish container which can be returned when you leave the country.
- Make sure you have a world adaptor for electrical appliances.
- You are advised to drink bottled (mineral) water in preference to mains water.

Amposta, E-43870 / Cataluña

2588

Eucaliptus Cat.2
Platja Eucaliptus
+34 977-479046
11/3 - 25/9
eucaliptus@campingeucaliptus.com

4,5ha 240**T**(60-90m²) 6A

1 BCDGIJKLM**P**RS
2 AEGLRVXY
3 BJKNRVWY
4 (B+G 1/5-18/9) (Q+S+T+U+X+Y) Z
5 **AB**EFGIJKLMNOPUWX
6 ACEG**J**(N 2km)ORTUV

A campsite located in the Ebro delta with excellent toilet facilities, outdoor swimming pool from the beginning of June. Good opportunities for windsurfing and cycle trips in the 'Delta del Ebre' nature reserve. A paradise for bird enthusiasts.

On the A7 take exit 41 to Amposta and Deltebre. On the N340 take the Amposta exit, turn right at Amposta. Take the TV3405 to Platja dels Eucaliptus, then follow the camping signs.

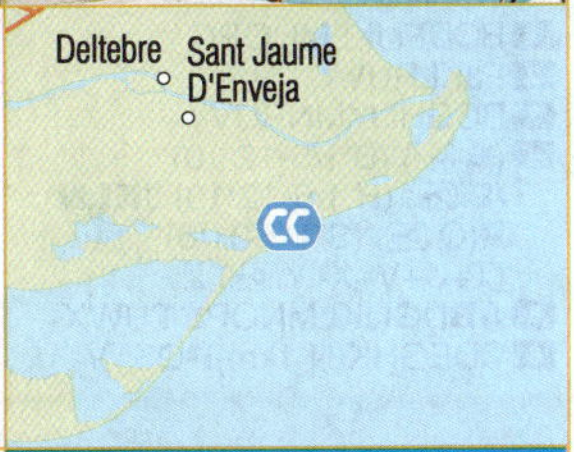

€17 *11/3-23/3 28/3-7/7 24/8-18/9* *7=6, 14=12, 21=18*

N 40°39'24" E 0°46'47"

Arnes, E-43597 / Cataluña

2589

Els Ports Cat. 2
Carretera T-330, km 12
+34 977-435560
1/1 - 31/12
info@camping-elsports.com

3,5ha 81**T**(50-85m²) 6A

1 ACDGIJKLMPQ
2 LRTXY
3 ABHJN
4 (B+G 15/6-30/9) (Q+R+T+V+X) Z
5 **A**DGIJKLMNOPUWX
6 AEG(N 1km)TV

Located in the protected nature reserve of Els Ports. A lovely campsite in a valley near the mountains. Authentic Spanish villages close by. Sportive walking routes. Very peaceful location. Lovely cycle routes on the Via Verde on old railway lines.

AP7 Barcelona-Valencia, exit 40 direction Tortosa, continue towards Lleida as far as Horta/Sant Joan exit. Then left towards Arnes T330 (40 km from AP7) After 3 km on the right.

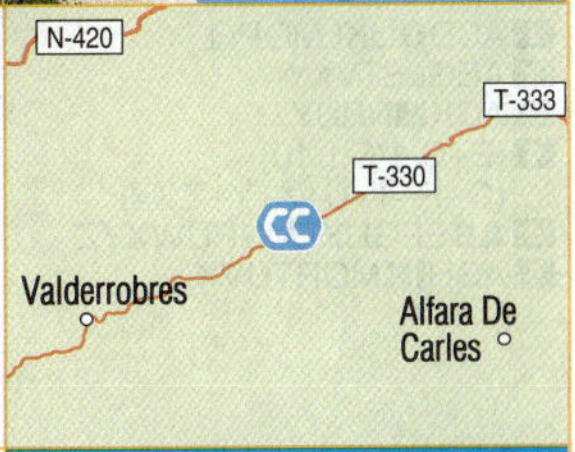

€19 *1/1-23/3 29/3-22/6 1/9-31/12* *7=6, 14=11*

N 40°55'10" E 0°16'6"

Batet de la Serra/Olot, E-17800 / Cataluña

2590

La Fageda Cat.2
Ctra Olot-Sta Pau, km 3,8
+34 972-271239
1/1 - 31/12
info@campinglafageda.com

7ha 109**T**(70-120m²) 10A

1 ACGIJKLM**P**R
2 BJLRVY
3 ABHJNR
4 (A 1/7-31/8) (B 24/6-9/9) (Q+R+T+U+X 1/3-31/12) Z
5 **AB**DEFGIJKLMNOPUW
6 CEGHK(N 4km)TV

The campsite is located in a volcanic region including the Croscat and the Santa Margarida, 4 km from Olot, capital of Garrotxa. Close to the beech woods at La Fageda d'en Jorda. Caravans and tents each have their own level field.

From Olot direction Santa Pau. Campsite on left of road at 3.8km sign.

€17 *1/1-30/6 1/9-31/12*

N 42°9'27" E 2°31'0"

Berga, E-08600 / Cataluña

2591

Berga Resort Cat.1
E-9/C-16 km 96,3, Exit 95
+34 938-211250
+34 938-222388
1/1 - 31/12
bergaresort@bergaresort.com

5,5ha 345T(70-90m²) 10A CEE

1 BCDFIJKLMNOPQ
2 FJKLRUVY
3 BCGHIJKMNRUV
4 (**A**) (B 1/5-12/10) (**F**) (H 1/5-12/10) **JKLN** **P**(Q) (S 1/7-31/8) (T+U+V+X+Y) Z
5 **AB**DGIJKLMNOP**ST**UWX
6 CDEGHK(N 1km)**P**QSTV

A shaded terraced campsite with extensive amenities for fitness and health, such as hydro massage, sauna, Turkish Bath, hot and cold water pools, ice fountain etc. Campsite with one hour a day free use of the indoor pool. Located on the edge of the Pyrenees. CCA guests who stay at least 7 nights can get a pitch with private toilet facilities for EUR 5 extra.

Campsite is located on the E9/C16 from Puigcerdà to Barcelona. 1 km south of Berga.

CC € 19 *1/1-23/3 28/3-29/4 1/5-22/6 4/9-27/10 2/11-2/12 11/12-23/12* ***7=6, 10=8, 14=12, 30=24***

N 42°5'29'' E 1°51'22''

Blanes, E-17300 / Cataluña

2592

Bella Terra
Av. Villa de Madrid 35-40
+34 972-348017
+34 972-348275
19/3 - 2/10
info@campingbellaterra.com

12ha 644T(70-90m²) 6A

1 ACD**G**IJKLMOPQ
2 AEGLSTVXY
3 AGK**M**NRUY
4 (B+G 1/5-1/10) (Q+R+T+U+X+Y+Z)
5 **AB**EFGIJKLMNPUWXYZ
6 AGH**IK**MORTUVX

A friendly campsite within walking distance of the local nightlife, with excellent toilet facilities and plenty of trees. The campsite is partly located right next to the beach/boulevard.

Exit 10 in Blanes, follow the camping signs. Bella Terra is located at the end of the campsite road.

CC € 19 *19/3-19/6 28/8-2/10*

N 41°39'31'' E 2°46'44''

Blanes, E-17300 / Cataluña

2593

Camping El Pinar
Av. Villa de Madrid, 39
+34 972-331083
+34 972-331100
25/3 - 2/10
camping@elpinarbeach.com

6,8ha 449T(60-80m²) 6A

1 ACD**G**IJKLO**P**Q
2 AEGLRSVWXY
3 ADKNRUY
4 (B 1/5-1/9) (G 1/5-15/9) (Q+S+T+U+X+Z)
5 ABFGIJKLMNOPUW
6 EG**K**ORTV

Welcoming beach campsite half under a pine forest, with basic toilet facilities.

Follow the camping signs from the outskirts of Blanes. This brings you to Av. Villa de Madrid. El Pinar is the very last campsite.

CC € 19 *25/3-23/6 1/9-2/10* ***30=27, 45=39***

N 41°39'18'' E 2°46'44''

Blanes, E-17300 / Cataluña

2594

Solmar
Colom 48
+34 972-348034
+34 972-348283
19/3 - 12/10
campingsolmar@campingsolmar.com

6ha 200T(65-85m²) 6A

1 ACDGIJKLOPRS
2 AEGRTVXY
3 BGMNRY
4 (B+G 1/5-30/9) (Q+S) (T+U+V 1/5-1/10) (X) Z
5 ABFIJKLMNOP
6 AGKORTV

Campsite in the centre of the nightlife area with reasonably good sanitary facilities and plenty of shade.

From the edge of Blanes follow signs 'camping'. Arrive in Av. Villa de Madrid. Sign to the right 'Solmar'.

CC € 17 *28/3-22/6 1/9-12/10*

N 41°39'43'' E 2°46'50''

Calella, E-08370 / Cataluña

2595

Roca Grossa Cat.2
Ctra NII km 665
+34 93-7691297
+34 93-7661556
1/4 - 5/10
rocagrossa@rocagrossa.com

7ha 280T(60-90m²) 6A

1 ACDGIJKLMOPQ
2 AEFIJKSVY
3 BFGKLMNRUVWY
4 (B+G 1/5-1/10) (Q+S+T+U+X+Z)
5 AFGIJKMNOPUWZ
6 AEGIJKM(N 0,5km)OQRV WX

A terraced campsite with beautiful sea views. A little 'train' takes you to the swimming pool.

Coastal road NII Malgrat-Barcelona. Between Calella and Sant Pol, 300 metres after 'el Faro' (lighthouse) turn right. Take care! Turn right directly after the bend. Caravan will be placed.

CC € 17 *1/4-30/6 1/9-5/10 7=6, 21=16, 31=25*

N 41°36'23'' E 2°38'19''

Calonge, E-17251 / Cataluña

2596

Camping & Bungalowpark Cala Gogo Cat.1
Av. Andorra 13
+34 972-651564
+34 972-650553
23/4 - 18/9
calagogo@calagogo.es

20ha 670T(60-115m²) 10A

1 ACDGIJKLMOPQ
2 AEGIJKRSTVXY
3 BFHKLMNRUWY
4 (C+H+Q+S+T+U+X+Y+Z)
5 ABEFGIJKLMNOPSTUWX YZ
6 ACEGHIJKM(N 1km)ORTV WX

A friendly family campsite backing onto a hillside with plenty of shade. Designer toilet facilities, a lively swimming pool and plenty of free entertainment.

Exit 6 Palafrugell-Palamós. Direction San Feliu, then Palamós-est. Then Platja d'Aro. Campsite on the right side of the road. Campsite clearly signposted.

CC € 19 *23/4-30/6 28/8-18/9*

N 41°49'49'' E 3°5'2''

Cambrils, E-43850 / Cataluña

2597

Joan Cat.2
N340, km 1141 /
Passeig Marítim 88
+34 977-364604
FAX +34 977-794214
11/1 - 10/12
@ info@campingjoan.com

4,5ha 218**T**(< 90m²) 5A

1 BC**G**IJKLMOPQ
2 AEFGRSTVY
3 AB**F**GKRUWY
4 (B+G 1/5-15/9)
(Q+S+T+U+X+Y 1/3-15/10)
Z
5 **AB**DFGIJKLMNOPUWX
6 ABCDEGH**IK**M(N 2km)ORT
VW

A peacefully located site, not all that big, right by the beach. Close to a holiday homes development on the southern edge of Cambrils.

Motorway AP7, exit 37, dir. Cambrils. At traffic lights right N340 dir. Hospitalet. Directly after Shell service station right and take flyover over the N340. Follow camping signs.

CC € 17 *11/1-22/6* *28/8-10/12* *7=6, 15=12, 30=23, 60=45*

N 41°3'28'' E 1°1'35''

Cambrils, E-43850 / Cataluña

iD **2598**

La Llosa Cat.3
C/ Camí de les Lloses 1
+34 977-362615
FAX +34 977-362604
1/1 - 31/12
@ info@camping-lallosa.com

4,5ha 400**T**(50-75m²) 6A

1 AC**G**IJKLMPQ
2 AEFSVY
3 AB**F**GKNRUWY
4 (B+G 15/5-8/10)
(Q+S 1/6-30/9)
(T+U+X+Y 15/5-30/9)
5 **A**EGIJKLMNOPUWXYZ
6 ACDEG**IK**M(N 0,5km)ORTX

Small shaded campsite 500 metres from the friendly town of Cambrils and within walking distance of the beach. The site works jointly with Club Nautico.

Toll motorway A7, exit 37, follow direction Cambrils. Right at traffic lights (N340) direction Hospitalet. Then bear left and turn left at the blue Camping & Bungalows sign. Follow the signs from here.

CC € 17 *1/1-30/6* *1/9-31/12* *7=6, 15=12*

N 41°3'55'' E 1°2'41''

Cambrils, E-43850 / Cataluña

2599

Platja Cambrils Cat.2
Av. Oleastrum 12
+34 977-361490
FAX +34 977-364988
11/3 - 16/10
@ info@playacambrils.com

8ha 400**T**(60-80m²) 5A

1 BC**G**IJKLMO**P**Q
2 AEFGSTVY
3 BGK**M**NRUWY
4 (B+G) (Q 15/6-15/9)
(S+T+U+W+X+Y) Z
5 **AB**FGIJKLMNOPUW
6 GH**I**JOQRTUV

The campsite is located on the outskirts of Cambrils near Salou at 250 metres from the beach. The pitches are shaded (mulberry trees) and measure 60, 80 or 90 square metres. Solarium and large swimming pool. In 2013 they renewed the sanitary facilities. Close to railway line.

Toll motorway AP7, exit 35 Salou. N340 or AP7 to Cambrils. At the roundabout in the direction of Vilafortuny, at the end of the road at traffic lights to the right. Then follow signs to the campsite.

CC € 15 *11/3-19/6* *22/8-16/10* *7=6*

N 41°4'1'' E 1°4'59''

Campdevànol, E-17530 / Cataluña

2600

Moli Serradell Cat.3
Ctra Campdevanol a Gomb.
+34 972-730927
1/5 - 16/10
info@campingmoliserradell.com

1,2ha 40T(60-80m²) 7A

1 AGIJKLMPQ
2 BCJKLRTVY
3 ABHJKR
4 (B+G 20/6-30/8) (Q+R+T+U+X) Z
5 **AB**DGIJKLMNOPUW
6 AEGIJ(N 4km)OTV

A small but idyllic campsite with shaded pitches under tall trees. It has a swimming pool and a restaurant where you can enjoy locally butchered meat and home baked bread. Impressive sanitary facilities.

Route N152 Puigcerdà-Barcelona. In Campdevànol route GI-401 direction Gombren. Campsite about 4.5 km on the left (take note; it is the 2nd campsite).

CC € 17 *1/5-8/7 26/8-16/10*

N 42°14'8'' E 2°7'7''

Camprodon, E-17867 / Cataluña

2601

Vall de Camprodon Cat.1
Ctra 38, km 7,5
+34 972-740507
1/1 - 31/12
info@valldecamprodon.net

4,8ha 106T(80m²) 10A

1 BC**G**IJKLMOPQ
2 CGKLRUX
3 ABDEGHJMNOPRUWX
4 (A) (B+G 15/6-20/9) (Q+R+S+T+U+V+X+Y+Z)
5 **AB**DEFGIJKLMNOPUWZ
6 ACDEGK(N 2km)ORTV

A spacious campsite with level pitches. Separate field for tents, plenty of sports facilities, animal park and children's playground. Modern toilet facilities and a good restaurant. Established walks, for example to Camprodon. Open only at weekends from January-May and October-December,

From Ripoll direction Camprodon. Campsite located on the C38, km 7.5. From Figueres take A26 which becomes the N260. Campsite 2 km next to Camprodon roundabout and signposted.

CC € 17 *29/4-1/5 6/5-8/5 13/5-15/5 20/5-22/5 27/5-10/7 1/9-30/9*

N 42°17'22'' E 2°21'50''

Canet de Mar, E-08360 / Cataluña

2602

Globo Rojo Cat. 1
Ctra Nac. II km 660,9
+34 93-7941143
11/4 - 30/9
camping@globo-rojo.com

2ha 155T(60-90m²) 10A

1 A**G**IJKLO**P**Q
2 AERVXY
3 A**F**GHJKLMNRY
4 (C+G+Q+R+U+X+Y+Z)
5 AFGIJKMNOPUWZ
6 GJ(N 0,5km)OQRTVW

A family campsite close to the beach with good facilities and plenty of shade. Ideally located for visiting Barcelona by bus, train or car. 5 minutes' walk from Canet de Mar. It also has three lovely swimming pools, one of them with jacuzzi. Free WiFi provided.

Coast road 11 Malgrat-Barcelona on the right after Sant Pol.

CC € 17 *11/4-30/6 31/8-30/9*

N 41°35'27'' E 2°35'30''

Capmany, E-17750 / Cataluña

2603

L'Albera
C/ Ventador s/n
+34 972-549192
1/1 - 31/12
info@campingalbera.com

7,5ha 150**T**(100m²) 6A CEE

1 AC**F**IJKLPST
2 FLRSUVWX
3 **F**GRU
4 (B 1/5-15/10) (Q 1/7-31/8) (R) Z
5 **A**DGIJKLMNOPUXYZ
6 CEG**IK**(N 0,5km)V

The views are a 'delight' to the eye. Highly recommended for a 'relaxing' holiday. Dutch-Spanish management. A combination of 'modern' and the peace and quiet of an old-fashioned campsite.

Exit 2 after Jonquera; direction Figueres; exit Capmany. Follow the camping signs. Coming from Barcelona (A7) exit 4 (salida) to the NII, direction Francia. Turn right before the border towards Capmany.

€17 *1/1-9/7 26/8-31/12*

N 42°22'22'' E 2°54'47''

Coma-Ruga/El Vendrell, E-43880 / Cataluña

2604

Vendrell Platja Cat.1
Av. Sanatori, s/n
+34 977-694009
FAX +34 977-694106
18/3 - 16/10
vendrell@camping-vendrellplatja.com

7ha 421**T**(70-105m²) 6A

1 ABCDGIJKLMO**P**Q
2 AEFGLRSTVX
3 AB**F**GKNRUWY
4 (B 27/3-1/11) (G) J (Q+R+S+T+U+W+X+Y) Z
5 **AB**EFGIJKLMNOP**T**UWZ
6 ACEG**IK**M(N 0,5km)OQRT UV

The campsite is 50 metres from the beach and has various swimming pools and lawns. You can make trips out to Barcelona (70 km), Tarragona (30 km) or to the Port Aventura theme park. Entertainment at weekends in low season. Shaded pitches. Additional facilities on the campsite: modern toilet facilities, bar, restaurant and supermarket. Close to railway line.

Toll motorway sortida (exit) 31. Then take direction Coma-Ruga. Continue to the coast, turn left and follow the signs.

€17 *18/3-1/7 28/8-16/10 7=6*

N 41°11'8'' E 1°33'19''

El Pont de Suert (Lérida), E-25520 / Cataluña

2605

Alta Ribagorça
Ctra Les Bordes s/n km 131
+34 973-690521
14/3 - 20/11
ana.uma@hotmail.com

3ha 50**T**(100m²) 5A

1 ACD**G**IJKLMO**P**RS
2 GJLRTVXY
3 A
4 (B 24/6-15/9) (Q+R 1/7-31/8) (X+Z 15/6-15/9)
5 **A**DFGIJKLMNOPUW
6 EGJ(N 3km)TV

Campsite is close to the beautiful countryside in the valleys of Isabena, Fosca, Aran, Boi and Benasque, for discovering the national parks, the culture and the tradition. More information available at reception. A free meal is offered for stays of ten nights.

Coming from Vielha N230 in the direction of Pont de Suert. About 4 km past the town of Vilaller, the campsite is on the left side of the road.

€13 *14/3-15/7 1/9-19/11 4=3, 7=6*

N 42°26'54'' E 0°42'38''

Esponellà (Girona), E-17832 / Cataluña

2606

Esponellà Cat.2
Ctra de Banyoles a Figueres, km 8
+34 972-597074
FAX +34 972-597132
1/1 - 31/12
informa@campingesponella.com

4,5ha 130T(60m²) 5A

1 ABCFIJLP
2 CRSTVXY
3 BFGMNQRUWX
4 (C+E+G) (S 1/4-30/9) (T+U+X+Y) Z
5 ADGIJKLMOPU
6 EGIJ(N 8km)OTV

Located in hinterland of Figueres on River Fluviá. Marked-out walks and mountain bike routes. Trips out in the area, e.g. Nuria (cog railway to an altitude of 2 km). River close to the campsite for fishing, canoeing or kayaking. Special birds for spotting. Covered heated swimming pool.

A7 exit 3, dir. Figueres N260 Figueres-Besalu. After Navata past service station turn left dir. Banyoles. At hairpin bend after bridge over Fluvia turn right. Signposted.

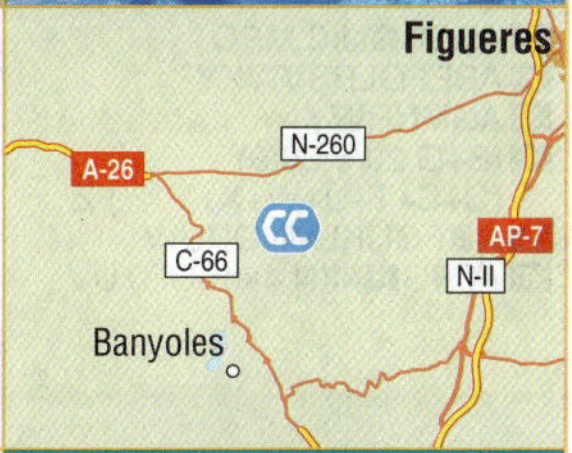

CC € 19 1/1-30/6 1/9-31/12 7=6

N 42°10'54'' E 2°47'42''

Fornells de la Selva, E-17458 / Cataluña

2607

Can Toni Manescal Cat.3
Forn. a Llambil, km 2 (B9)
+34 972-476117
1/5 - 31/10
campinggirona@campinggirona.com

1,1ha 45T(200m²) 5A

1 ACDGIJKLMOP
2 RVWX
3 ADF
4 (B 1/6-31/10) (Q+X+Z)
5 AGIJKMOPUW
6 EJ(N 2km)

Campsite on an estate with animals. Large pitches (200 m²), basic toilet facilities. Beautiful surroundings, lovely pool and at cycling distance from Girona and the airport.

Toll road A7, exit 7 Girona Sud. Dir. San Feliu. Follow until Llambilles (7 km). Turn right after leaving village. When using SatNav, from that point (traffic lights) it's 2 more km and follow campsite signs.

CC € 11 1/5-6/7 25/8-31/10

N 41°55'20'' E 2°49'42''

Garriguella, E-17780 / Cataluña

2608

Vell Empordà Cat.2
Ctra Roses-La Jonquera s/n
+34 972-530200
FAX +34 972-552343
1/4 - 16/10
vellemporda@vellemporda.com

7ha 230T(80-100m²) 6A

1 ACFIJLPQ
2 IJLRTVY
3 ABNRU
4 (A 1/5-1/9) (B+G 15/5-30/9) (Q 15/5-15/9) (S+T+U+V+X+Y) Z
5 AEGIJKLMOPUX
6 CEGIK(N 0,5km)ORTUV

A quiet campsite not quite on the coast. You can visit it close by. In just 10 km you can be on the beach or in the mountains. A family business where mother takes care of the kitchen. Spanish, friendly atmosphere. Beautiful large swimming pool with a separate children's pool.

A7, exit 3, N260 Figueres Llançà. After 9 km, the campsite is signposted. Turn right, C252, turn left under the viaduct direction La Jonquera. Then another 2 km.

CC € 17 1/4-30/6 1/9-16/10

N 42°20'21'' E 3°4'4''

Gavà (Barcelona), E-08850 / Cataluña

2609

3 Estrellas Cat.1
C-31, km 186,2/
Aptdo de Correos 238
+34 936-330637
FAX +34 936-331525
15/3 - 15/10
info@camping3estrellas.com

8ha 316T(70-100m²) 5A

1 ABCD**G**IJKLMPQ
2 ABEFGLRSVWXY
3 AGMNR**W**Y
4 (B+G 20/6-30/9)
(Q+S+T+U+W+X+Y) Z
5 **AB**FGIJKLMNOPUW
6 ACFG**IJ**M(N 4km)ORTUV

A perfect campsite for visiting Barcelona with a bus stop right by the campsite, a lovely swimming pool and good toilet facilities. Not far from the airport, right by a sandy beach. A 10% CampingCard ACSI discount outside low season.

In Barcelona follow 'Ronda de Dalt' (B20), direction airport. C-31 direction Castelldefels, exit Gavà Mar (on the left along the beach), with viaduct over C-31, then three times to the right and back direction Barcelona to the campsite.

CC € 19 *15/3-30/6 1/9-15/10*

N 41°16'21'' E 2°2'35''

Guardiola de Berguedà, E-08694 / Cataluña

2610

El Berguedà Cat.2
Ctra B400 a Saldes, km 3,5
+34 938-227432
23/3 - 1/11
info@campingbergueda.com

2ha 40T(70-110m²) 6A CEE

1 ACDGIJKLMP
2 BCIJKLRTVWXY
3 ABGHJNR
4 (**A** 1/7-31/8)
(B+G 24/6-1/9) (Q)
(R+S 24/6-31/8)
(T+U+V+X+Z 10/7-1/9)
5 **AB**DFGIJKLMNOPUWZ
6 EGJ**K**(N 5km)OTV

A campsite with spacious pitches separated by trees and bushes. Simple meals available out of season at weekends or on special occasions. Nice area for mountain walks. The reception staff gladly provide you with maps of the area.

From Berga C16 in the direction of Cadi Tunnel. Just before Guardiola de Berguedà turn left (Saldes). After about 3.5 km you'll reach the campsite.

CC € 17 *29/3-8/7 28/8-1/11*

N 42°12'59'' E 1°50'13''

Hospitalet del Infante, E-43890 / Cataluña

2611

La Masia
Ctra N340, km 1121
+34 977-820588
FAX +34 977-823354
1/2 - 30/11
info@camping-lamasia.com

2,6ha 264T(60-90m²) 6A

1 BCDGIJKLMPQ
2 AEFGKLSTVWXY
3 B**F**GHJMNRUVWY
4 (B+G 1/5-30/10) K
(Q+R+T+V+X+Y) Z
5 **AB**FGIJKLMNOPUWZ
6 ACEG**K**(N 10km)OTV

A campsite on the Playa de l'Almadrava, a beautiful sandy beach. New swimming pool and jacuzzi, lawn and tennis court. Very good toilet facilities. Very peaceful location.

On the N340 (Tarragona-Valencia) at the 1120,5 km post direction Platja de l'Almadrava. Coming via Autopista Salida 38. Take note: new road under construction.

CC € 15 *1/2-30/6 1/9-30/11*

N 40°56'25'' E 0°51'25''

L'Ametlla de Mar, E-43860 / Cataluña

2612

Camping Ametlla Cat.1
Paratje de Santes Creus
+34 977-267784
FAX +34 977-267868
1/1 - 31/12
info@campingametlla.com

8ha 301**T**(70-100m²) 10A

1 BCDGIJLMPQ
2 EFLNTVWXY
3 BGH**M**NRUVWY
4 (B+G 1/4-30/9) (Q)
(S+T+U+V+X+Y 1/4-30/9) Z
5 **AB**EFGIJKLMNOPRUWXZ
6 ACEG**IK**(N 2km)ORTV

Attractive campsite. Set in a nature reserve 100 metres from the beach, excellent for walking. Lovely, new swimming pools and a very good restaurant. Pitches separated by hedges. Entertainment in July and August.

A7/E15, exit 39. Take the N340 and turn at km-marker 1113 to L'Ametlla de Mar. Follow the signs, just before reaching the town turn right. After 2.5 km you reach the campsite.

CC € 15 *1/1-30/6 22/8-31/12* *7=6, 14=11, 30=21*

N 40°51'54" E 0°46'44"

L'Ametlla de Mar, E-43860 / Cataluña

2613

Nautic Cat.1
Calle Llibertat s/n
FAX +34 977-456110
15/3 - 15/10
info@campingnautic.com

6ha 215**T**(60-75m²) 10A

1 ABCDGIJKLMPQ
2 AEFGJLNTUVXY
3 BGHKMRUWY
4 (**A** 1/7-31/8)
(B 24/3-15/10) (G)
(Q+R 1/4-30/9) (X+Y+Z)
5 **A**GIJKMNOPUXZ
6 CEGK(N 0,2km)ORTV

A lovely peaceful site right on the beach in a bay and near an attractive fishing village. Excellent toilet facilities. Pitches in the sun or shade. Lovely outdoor pools, tennis and a good restaurant. Free WiFi. Reception closed from 14:00-17:15, in that period press the button opposite reception.

Take exit 39 on the A7, cross the railway bridge then follow signs in L'Ametlla. On N340 at the 1113 km marker to L'Ametlla then follow camping signs.

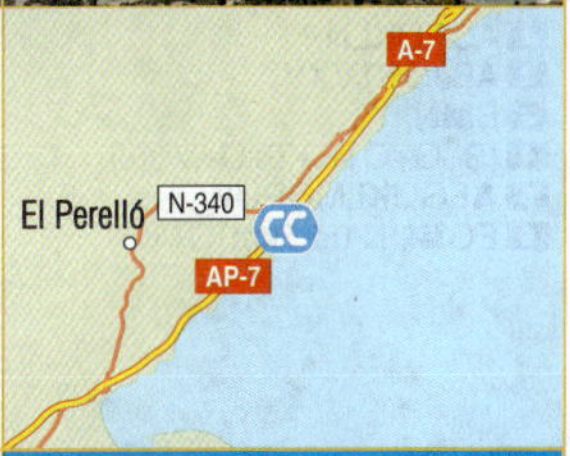

CC € 17 *15/3-12/7 29/8-15/10* *14=11, 30=24*

N 40°53'12" E 0°48'17"

L'Ampolla, E-43895 / Cataluña

2614

Camping Ampolla Playa Cat. 2
Playa Arenal s/n
FAX +34 977-460535
7/3 - 1/11
reservas@campingampolla.es

5ha 65**T**(60-80m²) 10A

1 BCDGIJKLMPQ
2 AEFGLNRSVWXY
3 ABGHJKN**O**RVWY
4 (**A**+Q+R) (S 1/4-30/9)
(T+U+V+X)
(Y 1/3-31/10) (Z)
5 **A**FGIKMOPUWXZ
6 ADEG**K**(N 1km)OSTVW

A campsite on a bay right next to a lovely sandy beach near a fishing village. Close to the Ebro delta with its unusual flora and fauna, including flamingos. Lovely cycle routes. Watersports. Close to the N340 so suitable as a stopover site.

On A7 exit 39a. From N340 1096 km marker. Keep south in L'Ampolla. Follow camping signs on beach road.

CC € 15 *7/3-15/7 1/9-1/11* *5=4, 7=5, 15=10, 30=20*

N 40°47'58" E 0°41'59"

L'Escala, E-17130 / Cataluña

2615

Illa Mateua Cat.1
Avda. de Montgó, 260
+34 972-770200
FAX +34 972-772031
19/3 - 21/10
@ info@campingillamateua.com

6,4ha 318T(80-90m²) 6A

1 ABFIJLPQ
2 ABEGJLORSVY
3 BGHJMNRUWY
4 (C+H+S+T+U+X+Y) Z
5 ABDFGIJKLMNOPUW
6 EGIKM(N 3km)ORTV

A family site, spectacularly located on the sandy beach at Montgó and bordering the Montgri nature park and the rocky beach at Illa Mateua which has excellent snorkelling. Breathtaking views of Roses Bay. Picturesque villages inland. A friendly welcome in various languages.

Toll road exit 5 direction L'Escala. Before L'Escala direction Escala Riells. Then follow camping signs and Montgó. Clearly signposted.

CC € 19 19/3-1/7 29/8-21/10 7=6, 14=11, 21=17, 30=25 | N 42°6'37'' E 3°9'56''

L'Escala, E-17130 / Cataluña

2616

Neus
Cala Montgo
+34 638-652712
FAX +34 972-222409
14/5 - 18/9
@ info@campingneus.com

3,8ha 243T(40-120m²) 6A CEE

1 ACFIJKLNP
2 ABJQSTVXY
3 BMN
4 (B+G+Q+R+T+U+V)
5 AFGIJKLMOPUW
6 EGIK(N 0,25km)OTV

Located in a pine forest and equipped with a swimming pool, where silence and tranquillity prevail. There is a friendly and spontaneous interaction among the campers. The attractive seaside town of L'Escala is easily accessible by car.

From exit 5 continue in the direction of the centre of L'Escala, then direction Cala Montgo and then follow the signs (Neus).

CC € 19 14/5-7/7 26/8-18/9 | N 42°6'18'' E 3°9'30''

L'Estartit, E-17258 / Cataluña

2617

Emporda
Ctra Torroella-l'Estartit, km 4,8
+34 972-750649
FAX +34 972-751430
19/3 - 9/10
@ info@campingemporda.com

3,5ha 230T(70-100m²) 6A

1 AGIJKLMPQ
2 SWX
3 AFJKLN
4 (B+G+Q+R)
(U 28/5-11/9) (X 4/6-4/9)
(Z 28/5-11/9)
5 ABFIKMNOPUW
6 FIK(N 1km)ORTVW

A small, peaceful campsite. Close to the beach and the village of Estartit and next to the Montgri nature reserve, the Medes islands and the Baix Ter. The area around River Ter is perfect for cycle rides and there are fantastic walking routes in the Montgri mountains.

Exit direction Torroella de Montgri, to L'Estartit, right.

CC € 17 19/3-15/6 1/9-9/10 | N 42°2'57'' E 3°11'2''

L'Estartit, E-17258 / Cataluña

2618

La Sirena
C/ Riu Ter s/n
+34 972-751542
9/4 - 9/10
info@camping-lasirena.com

4,8ha 275T(50-200m²) 6A CEE

1 B**G**IJKLOPQ
2 AFRSVWXY
3 A**F**
4 (B+G) (X+Z 15/6-12/9)
5 **A**FGIJKLMOPU
6 FG**K**RT

Located in the heart of the Costa Brava: L'Estartit. Close to natural parks 'Parque Natural Montgri' and 'Islas Medes'. Sandy beach, including a part for disabled people, signaled by a blue flag. Small homely campsite with 272 pitches, sunny as well as shaded. Playground, large and small pool, canteen, bar, restaurant and mini club. Beach and centre within walking distance. Car can remain parked.

Before Jocs turn right into L'Estartit.

CC € 17 *9/4-30/6 1/9-9/10*

N 42°2'57'' E 3°11'17''

L'Estartit, E-17258 / Cataluña

2619

Les Medes Cat.1
Paratge Camp de l'Arbre
+34 972-751805
+34 972-750413
1/1 - 31/12
info@campinglesmedes.com

2,6ha 170T(70-80m²) 16A CEE

1 ACD**G**IJKLPQ
2 GLRVXY
3 B**F**GHJK**M**NRU
4 (B 1/5-15/9)
(F 1/1-15/6,15/9-31/12)
(G 1/5-15/9) **N**
(Q+S+T+U) (Y 1/4-1/11)
(Z)
5 ABDEFGIJKLMNOPUWXYZ
6 ABCEGH**IK**(N 2km)ORTVWX

A top class campsite, open all year. Indoor swimming pool in early and late seasons. An excellent campsite for overwintering.

A7, exit 5. On the road from Torroella de Montgri to Estartit turn right before 'Jocs' and follow signs. Another 2 km to the campsite.

CC € 19 *1/1-19/3 28/3-16/6 12/9-31/12*

N 42°2'33'' E 3°11'6''

L'Estartit, E-17258 / Cataluña

2620

Ter Cat. 2
Ctra Torroella-l'Estartit km 4,3
+34 972-751110
+34 972-750609
19/3 - 18/9
ter@campingter.com

2,2ha 191T(60-80m²) 6A

1 ACD**G**IJKLMOPST
2 GRVWXY
3 A**F**HJKLR
4 (B+G 1/5-18/9) (R+T+Z)
5 **AB**GIJKMNOPU
6 AFG**IK**(N 0,8km)QRTWX

A small campsite near a pleasant village with sunny and shaded pitches. Good toilet facilities. Bar and swimming pool. Near a Lidl supermarket and a restaurant.

Salida (exit) 6 direction Torroella de Montgri, towards L'Estartit. Turn right past Lidl.

CC € 17 *19/3-3/7 20/8-18/9*

N 42°2'55'' E 3°10'45''

La Guingueta d'Àneu, E-25597 / Cataluña

2621

Nou Camping Cat.2
C13, km 156
+34 973-626261
FAX +34 973-626706
1/1 - 2/11, 1/12 - 31/12
noucamping@noucamping.com

1,5ha 150**T**(75m²) 10A

1 ACD**G**IJKLM**P**
2 CDGIJLRVWXY
3 ABHJNRU**W**
4 (A 1/7-31/8)
(C+H 15/6-15/9)
(Q+R+T+U+V+W+X+Y) Z
5 **AB**DFGIJKLMNOPUWZ
6 EG**IK**OTV

Easily accessible luxury campsite close to the Aigüestortes national park and the Saint Mauricie lake. Also suitable as a base for sports: cycling, walking and rafting.

From France take N125 as far as Viella. There the C13 direction Sort. Campsite is located first thing in the village, on the right.

CC € 19 *1/1-10/7 27/8-2/11* ***7=6, 14=11***

N 42°35'33'' E 1°7'54''

Les Cases d'Alcanar, E-43569 / Cataluña

2622

Estanyet
Paseig del Marjal s/n
FAX +34 977-737268
1/1 - 31/12
info@estanyet.com

1,5ha 120**T**(55-100m²) 10A

1 BCDGIJLMPQ
2 EFNRTUVWXY
3 BFHJKWY
4 (B+G+Q+R+T+U+V+X+Y)
Z
5 **AB**DEFGIJKLMNOPUWXYZ
6 ADEGIK(N 1km)ORTV

An attractive, quietly situated campsite with excellent toilet facilities located right on a pebble beach. Lovely swimming pool and very good restaurant.

From the north A7 take exit 41, from the south take exit 43, then on N340 (there is a campsite sign on the right), turn right and after ±300 metres is campsite Estanyet.

CC € 17 *1/1-24/3 29/3-30/6 1/9-31/12*

N 40°32'25'' E 0°31'11''

Llagostera, E-17240 / Cataluña

2623

Ridaura
Ctra Girona-Platja d'Aro,
C-65 km 6
+34 972-830265
4/3 - 12/10
info@campingridaura.com

4ha 202**T**(60-110m²) 10A

1 ACDEIJKLMOPST
2 BITXY
3 B**EF**HJKN
4 (B+G 1/6-15/9)
(Q+R+T+V+X+Z)
5 **A**FGIJKLMNOPUX
6 ABFGJ**K**(N 3km)ORTV

A campsite located in woods alongside the C35. Close to Sant Feliu and Playa d'Aro. It has good toilet facilities and a very attractive swimming pool with a chair lift.

On the AP7 direction Platja d'Aro, then 10 km towards Barcelona.

CC € 15 *29/4-30/6 17/8-11/9* ***7=6***

N 41°49'40'' E 2°57'29''

Lloret de Mar, E-17310 / Cataluña

2624

Lloret Blau
C/ Aiguaviva s/n
+34 972-365483
25/4 - 28/9
info@campinglloretblau.com

2,4ha 300**T**(50-90m²) 5-10A

1 ACDGIJKLMO**PQ**
2 XY
3 **F**
4 (B 30/4-27/9) (R 1/7-30/8) (T+X+Z 24/6-30/8)
5 IJKMOP
6 AD**IK**RTV

Located in the heart of the Costa Brava. In the proximity you will find beautiful sandy beaches and lovely bays. The campsite has a swimming pool and basic toilet facilities. You will find a variety of shops a short distance from the campsite in Lloret de Mar.

E15, exit 9 to Lloret. Left at lights past 'Water World'. Straight on, campsite on left after traffic lights.

CC € 17 *25/4-8/7 25/8-28/9 7=6*

N 41°42'20'' E 2°50'35''

Lloret de Mar, E-17310 / Cataluña

2625

Tucan**
Ctra de Blanes a Lloret
+34 972-369965
+34 972-360079
24/3 - 25/9
info@campingtucan.com

4,2ha 324**T**(65-100m²) 10A

1 ACD**F**IJKLMO**PQ**
2 AGJLSVXY
3 AD**F**GKN**Q**RU
4 (A 1/7-31/8) (B+G) JM (Q) (R 20/6-31/8) (T+U+X+Y+Z)
5 **A**FGIJKLMNOPUXYZ
6 AFG**K**MOQRTVWX

Campsite with good amenities on the outskirts of Lloret de Mar.

The last campsite on the right from Lloret de Mar to Blanes.

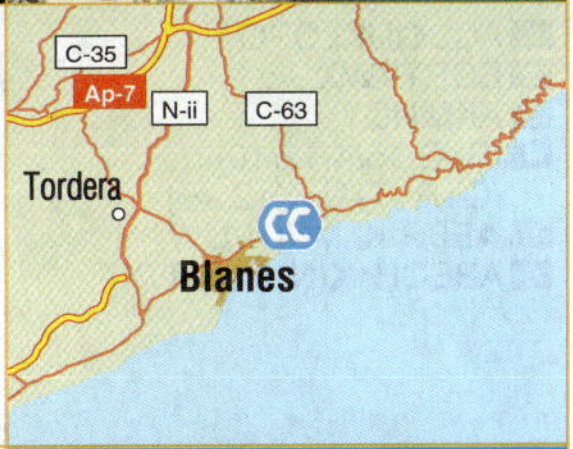

CC € 19 *24/3-30/6 28/8-25/9*

N 41°41'50'' E 2°49'19''

Maçanet de Cabrenys, E-17720 / Cataluña

2626

Camping Maçanet de Cabrenys
+34 667-776648
1/3 - 31/12
campingmassanet@gmail.com

4,5ha 50**T**(80-150m²) 10A

1 ABCD**G**IJKLM**P**
2 BIJKLRVWXY
3 AHJKR
4 (B 1/6-30/9) (Q+R+T+U+X) Z
5 **A**GIJKLMNOPUWXZ
6 AEGJK(N 2km)OTV

A campsite with an outdoor swimming pool in wooded surroundings with mountain panoramas. Excellent for nature lovers who appreciate relaxation and spectacular walks.

Through France on the E15, exit 2 (La Jonquera) to Agullana, then Darnius, past Maçanet de Cabrenys, another 2 km on the left (from Figueres Nord, dir. Darnius).

CC € 17 *1/3-30/6 1/9-31/12*

N 42°22'23'' E 2°45'15''

Malgrat de Mar, E-08380 / Cataluña — 2627

Camping Resort Els Pins
Avda Pomareda s/n
+34 937-653173
FAX +34 937-653280
21/3 - 12/11
@ pinsresort@campingelspins.es

3,2ha 220T(70-110m²) 6A CEE

1 ACDEIJKLOPQ
2 AEGSWX
3 AKNR
4 (B+G 🔑) **N**(Q+R+U 🔑) (X 1/4-30/9) (Z 🔑)
5 ABFGIJKLMNO**P**UWXYZ
6 E**K**(N 1,5km)ORTVX

Malgrat de Mar is a town with more than 5 km of paradisiacal beaches. 1.5 km from the market, shopping and touristic areas. Nearby the Tordera river with its natural diversity of animals and nature. 40 km from Gerona and 60 km from Barcelona. 50 metres from the beaches. Pitches (± 80 m²) limited by trees. Good toilet facilities.

Past Blanes-sud towards centre of Malgrat de Mar. Cross river, left at roundabout, left again at beach. Campsite on the left.

CC €17 *21/3-21/6 27/6-30/6 1/9-12/11 7=6*

N 41°38'54'' E 2°46'12''

Malgrat de Mar, E-08380 / Cataluña — 2628

del Mar
Av. Pomareda s/n
+34 937-653767
FAX +34 937-619121
18/3 - 9/10
@ info@campingdelmar.com

3ha 124T(20-64m²) 6A

1 ACD**G**IJKLOPQ
2 EORTVWX
3 AK**M**NQY
4 (B+G 15/4-12/10) (Q+R+T+U+X+Z 🔑)
5 **A**EFGIKLMNOPUW
6 ABEGHI**K**(N 1km)RVX

A lovely pre-season beach campsite with good facilities and within walking distance of the beach.

Exit Blanes Sud, then direction Malgrat de Mar, over the bridge, left at roundabout, as far as the sea, then right after ± 100m.

CC €17 *18/3-1/7 20/8-9/10*

N 41°38'51'' E 2°45'50''

Malgrat de Mar, E-08380 / Cataluña — 2629

La Tordera
Camí de la Tordera, sn-Ap. 58
+34 937-612778
FAX +34 937-655551
19/3 - 6/11
@ camping@latordera.com

2,2ha 400T(60-80m²) 10A CEE

1 ACD**F**IJKLMOPQ
2 ACESVWXY
3 BFGKNRUWY
4 (B 22/5-25/9) (G 22/5-15/9) (Q 🔑) (R 1/5-25/9) (T+U+V 🔑) (X 1/6-25/9) (Z 🔑)
5 **A**CFGIKMOPQU
6 DE**I**J**K**M(N 4km)QRV

Beautiful beach campsite with large pitches close to the sea, good toilet facilities and parking next to your caravan. Until 1 May and after 25 September only open at weekends.

Blanes-Sud exit, then towards Malgrat de Mar. Over bridge, immediate left. Campsite at end of road, signposted.

CC €19 *19/3-3/7 1/9-25/9*

N 41°38'57'' E 2°46'39''

Mataró, E-08304 / Cataluña

2630

- Barcelona Cat.2
- Ctra N-II, km 650
- ☎ +34 93-7904720
- FAX +34 93-7410282
- 1/3 - 1/11
- @ info@campingbarcelona.com

7ha 312T(60-120m²) 16A CEE

1 ACD**G**IJKLMOPQ
2 AEFGKLQRVWXY
3 ADFGHJKNRU**W**
4 (B+G 16/5-27/9) (Q+S) (T 17/5-28/9) (U+V+X+Y) Z
5 **AB**FGIJKLMNOPUWXY
6 ACFGHI**K**(N 2km)ORSTV

The campsite is located on a rocky coastline and is 1 km from the nearest sandy beach. Free bus service to the beach, the beach club, the centre of Mataró, the railway station and the heated pool. The campsite also offers a (daily) bus service to Barcelona (free except from 4/7 to 26/8). Wine tasting in low season.

C32, exits 103 or 104. AP-7 at km 126 exit to Mataró via C60.

CC € 19 *1/3-30/6 1/9-1/11*

N 41°33'2" E 2°29'0"

Miami-Platja (Tarragona), E-43892 / Cataluña

2631

- Els Prats Village Cat.1
- Ctra N340, km 1137
- ☎ +34 977-810027
- FAX +34 977-170901
- 11/3 - 1/11
- @ info@campingelsprats.com

8,5ha 415T(80-115m²) 5-10A

1 AC**G**IJKLMOPQ
2 AEFGLRTVY
3 B**F**GHJK**M**NQRUVWY
4 (B+G 1/4-20/10) IJ (Q+S+T+U+V+W+X+Y) Z
5 **AB**EFGIJKLMNOPQRUWZ
6 DEGH**IJK**M(N 5km)OPQRT UVWX

This campsite, which has many trees and plants is located right on the beach and has plenty of facilities including a bar, restaurant, supermarket, swimming pool and massage. Local and tourist information is available at the reception. The campsite is next to a railway line. Large new swimming pool in use in 2014.

AP7 toll road, exit 37, then N340, right at 1.137 km marker under the N340. Follow camping signs.

CC € 17 *11/3-22/6 28/8-1/11* *21=20, 28=25*

N 41°2'24" E 0°58'50"

Mont-roig (Tarragona), E-43300 / Cataluña

2632

- Playa Montroig Camping Resort Cat.1
- Apartado de Correos 3
- ☎ +34 977-810637
- FAX +34 977-818419
- 11/3 - 23/10
- @ info@playamontroig.com

35ha 1200T(80-110m²) 10A CEE

1 BCDEIJKLMOPQ
2 AEFGLRTVY
3 AB**F**GJKL**MNQ**RUVWY
4 (C+H) IJM (Q+S+T+U+V+X+Y) Z
5 **AB**DEFGIJKLMNOPUWXYZ
6 ACDEGH**IJK**M(N 3km)OR TVW

A luxuriously laid out, well maintained campsite with a lovely swimming pool. On the Costa Dorada with beaches of fine golden sand and an ideal climate for most of the year. Partly between the N340 and a railway line. New salt water swimming pool with 6 slides and a new toddlers' play pool in 2013.

AP7, exit 37 Cambrils. Follow direction Cambrils to the traffic lights then turn right N340 direction Hospitalet. After km 1136 turn right and follow signs under the N340.

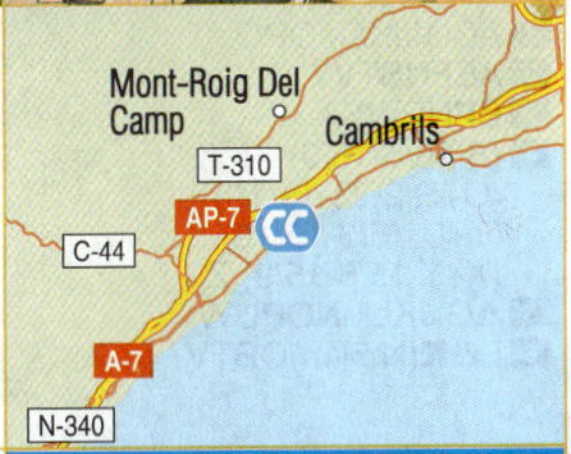

CC € 17 *11/3-22/3 28/3-22/6 28/8-23/10* *21=20, 30=27, 45=36*

N 41°2'1" E 0°58'5"

Mont-roig del Camp, E-43300 / Cataluña

2633

La Torre del Sol Cat.1
Ctra N340 km 1136
+34 977-810486
FAX +34 977-811306
15/3 - 31/10
info@latorredelsol.com

24ha 600**T**(70-100m²) 6-10A

1 ACDEIJKLO**P**Q
2 AEFGLNRTVWY
3 AB**F**GHJK**M**N**Q**R**S**UVWY
4 (C+H) K**LNO**
(Q+S+T+U+V+X+Y) Z
5 **AB**EFGIJKLMNOPQRUWX
Y
6 CEGH**IJK**M(N 6km)OPRTV
W

Beach campsite located between Cambrils and Miami Platja. Good swimming facilities, plenty of opportunities for sports. Close to railway line.

Toll road exit 37 Cambrils direction Cambrils as far as traffic lights, then turn right N340. Bear right just after Els Prat campsite and 1137 km-marker and follow signs.

CC € 17 *15/3-24/3 28/3-22/6 28/8-31/10 21=20, 28=25*

N 41°2'15'' E 0°58'29''

Mont-roig del Camp, E-43892 / Cataluña

2634

Miramar Cat.2
Ctra N340, km 1134
FAX +34 977-811203
1/1 - 30/11
recepcio@camping-miramar.com

3,7ha 50**T**(80-100m²) 6A

1 ACGIJKLMOPRS
2 AEFGSVX
3 AGWY
4 Z
5 **A**GIKMOPUWZ
6 ADEG**IJK**(N 2km)TV

A Spanish campsite with many permanent pitches, 50 touring pitches on the beach and a few pitches in avenues.

Toll road AP 7 exit 37, then N340 left at km 1.134 to the campsite.

CC € 13 *1/1-30/6 1/9-30/11 7=6, 14=12, 30=21*

N 41°1'31'' E 0°57'33''

Mont-roig del Camp, E-43300 / Cataluña

2635

Oasis Mar Cat.2
Ctra N340, km 1139
+34 977-179595
FAX +34 977-179516
1/3 - 31/10
info@oasismar.com

2,5ha 252**T**(60-100m²) 5A

1 AC**G**IJKLMOPQ
2 AEFNSTVY
3 B**F**NRWY
4 (B 15/6-15/9)
(Q+R 20/3-15/10)
(T+U 15/3-15/10)
(X+Y 15/6-15/9) Z
5 **A**GIJKLMNOPUW
6 EG**K**(N 5km)ORTV

This campsite right on the beach, with spacious pitches, with or without shade under mulberry and olive trees, is an oasis of peace between Cambrils and Miami Platja, equipped with a nice swimming pool.

AP7 exit 37, A7 exit 1138. Then N340 direction Hospitalet. At Montroig/Falset crossroads, 3rd exit right on roundabout. From A7 2nd right. Follow 'platja' and 'camping' signs.

CC € 15 *1/3-30/6 1/9-31/10*

N 41°2'49'' E 1°0'15''

Montagut, E-17855 / Cataluña

2636

Montagut
Ctra Montagut a Sadernes km 2
+34 972-287202
15/4 - 16/10
info@campingmontagut.com

2ha 93**T**(65-110m²) 6A

1 ACD**F**IJKLM**PQ**
2 JKLRTVXY
3 BGNRU
4 (B+G 1/5-30/9) (Q+R) (T+U+V+X+Y+Z 1/7-31/8)
5 **AB**DFGIJKLMNOPUW
6 CEGJK(N 2km)OTV

A beautiful swimming pool, carefully maintained grounds with camping pitches varying from sunny to shaded. Suitable for fascinating walking and cycle trips in the surroundings. The restaurant is only open at the weekend in early and late season.

A7, exit Figueras-Norte. C260 direction Besalú. From Besalú A26 exit 75 to Montagut. Then follow the signs.

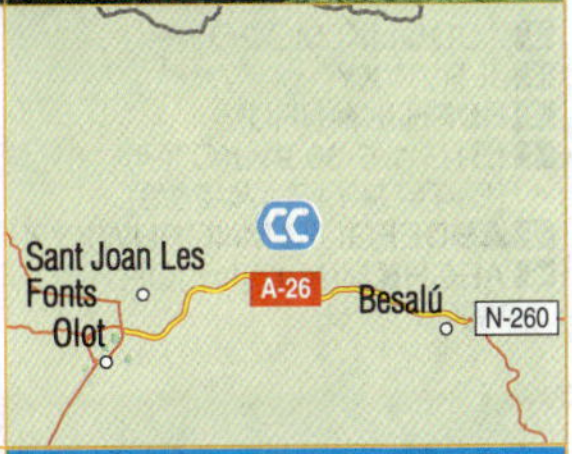

CC € 17 *15/4-7/7 24/8-16/10*

N 42°14'43'' E 2°35'58''

Montferrer, E-25711 / Cataluña

2637

Gran Sol Cat.2
N260, km 230
+34 973-351332
25/3 - 31/10
info@campinggransol.com

1,7ha 160**T**(70-140m²) 10A

1 ACD**G**IJKLM**P**Q
2 LRVWXY
3 ABC**F**HJNRUW
4 (B+G 20/6-11/9) (Q+R+U+X+Y+Z)
5 **A**DFGIJKLMNOPUWZ
6 EGIK(N 1km)OTV

A level campsite with spacious pitches between trees. Lovely swimming pool, good restaurant. Most suitable as a starting point for visiting Seu d'Urgell/ Seo de Urgel, Puigcerdá and Andorra. Also excellent for visiting the mountains.

Coming from Bourg Madame (F) until 3 km beyond La Seu d'Urgell on the N260.

CC € 17 *29/3-10/7 27/8-16/10 7=6*

N 42°20'52'' E 1°25'51''

Palamós, E-17230 / Cataluña

2638

Benelux
Apt. de Correos 270
+34 972-315575
FAX +34 972-601901
27/3 - 25/9
cbenelux@cbenelux.com

4,6ha 250**T**(50-80m²) 6A

1 ACDGIJLMPQ
2 AILSTVY
3 AGKL
4 (B+G 1/6-11/9) (Q+R) (X 1/5-15/9) (Z)
5 AFGIJKLMNOPU
6 AEGH**I**JM(N 2,5km)OQRTV X

An attractive campsite, located in a protected nature reserve in one of the loveliest locations on the Costa Brava. Perfect walking and cycling opportunities. Within walking distance of the sea: Platja Castell. Lovely swimming pool, shop, bar, good restaurant and free WiFi. Diving school.

C31 Palafrugell-Palamós take exit 328. Then follow camping signs.

CC € 19 *27/3-5/7 22/8-25/9*

N 41°52'21'' E 3°9'4''

Pals, E-17256 / Cataluña

2639

Mas Patoxas Cat.1
Ctra de Palafrugell a Pals, km 339
+34 972-636928
FAX +34 972-667349
15/1 - 18/12
@ info@campingmaspatoxas.com

11ha 400T(72-100m²) 6A

1 ACD**G**IJKLMO**P**Q
2 JLRVWXY
3 BD**F**HJK**M**NRUV
4 (B+G 1/5-30/9) J(Q)
(S+T+U+Y+Z 1/4-28/9)
5 **AB**DEFGIJKLMNOPUWXYZ
6 AEGH**K**M(N 1,5km)ORTUV
WX

A family campsite around a large swimming pool on a hilly grounds with trees.

Motorway exit 6 direction Bisbal. From Pals follow direction Begur/Palamos. At roundabout direction Begur. About 1 km after, Pals campsite is located on the left of the road.

CC € 17 *15/1-4/7 22/8-18/12 7=6, 14=10*

N 41°57'19'' E 3°9'26''

Pineda de Mar, E-08397 / Cataluña

2640

Bellsol Cat.2
Passeig Marítim 46
+34 937-671778
FAX +34 937-655551
19/3 - 31/12
@ info@campingbellsol.com

3ha 240T(60m²) 5A

1 ABCD**G**IJKLOPRS
2 AEFGSVXY
3 A**F**GKRY
4 (B+G 1/6-15/9)
(Q+R+T+U+Y+Z)
5 **A**FGIJKMNOPUW
6 AGJ**K**(N 0,2km)ORTV

A small family campsite with good toilet facilities, close to a beach and plenty of greenery.

Toll E15, exit 9 Malgrat. Take the NII to Barcelona. On the southern outskirts of Pineda de Mar, on the NII, take the 1st road to the left (after sign indicating end of built-up area). Continue as far as the Boulev. Turn right towards the campsite.

CC € 17 *19/3-3/7 1/9-31/12*

N 41°37'6'' E 2°40'44''

Pineda de Mar, E-08397 / Cataluña

2641

Caballo de Mar
Passeig Marítim, s/n
Apdo Correos 3
+34 937-671706
FAX +34 937-671615
24/3 - 25/9
@ info@caballodemar.com

3ha 310T(60-70m²) 6A

1 ACD**F**IJL**P**R
2 AEFTVXY
3 AGKNR**V**WY
4 (B+G) K(Q)
(R 1/6-31/8) (T+U+X+Z)
5 **A**EFGIJKLMNOPRSUXYZ
6 ABFG**IJK**MORTV

A family campsite with sufficient shade and within walking distance of Calella. The site is located by the beach. The toilet facilities include individual shower cabins, baby baths and disabled toilets. Located 50 km north of Barcelona. Good train connections.

Take the NII in the direction of Calella, south of Pineda de Mar. Follow the camping signs.

CC € 17 *24/3-30/6 28/8-25/9*

N 41°37'2'' E 2°40'39''

Pineda de Mar, E-08397 / Cataluña

2642

Enmar Cat.2
Av. de la Mercè s/n
+34 937-671730
FAX +34 937-670763
19/3 - 30/10
@ info@campingenmar.com

2,4ha 240T(75-90m²) 6A

1 ACDGIJKLMOPQ
2 AEFGSTVXY
3 AKNRUY
4 (B+G 19/4-30/10) IJ
(Q+R+T+U+X+Z)
5 **A**BFGIJKLMNOPU
6 ABCEGJ**K**ORTVWX

Small friendly campsite with plenty of palm trees, new toilet facilities and close to the beach and a small town.

Follow campsite signs on the Promenada in Pineda de Mar.

CC € 17 19/3-5/7 29/8-30/10

N 41°37'19" E 2°41'10"

Platja d'Aro, E-17250 / Cataluña

2643

Pinell
Punta Prima, 14 - Apartat 110
+34 972-818123
FAX +34 972-826271
25/3 - 2/10
@ info@campingpinell.com

2ha 270T(60-70m²) 6A

1 ACDGIJKLMNO**P**Q
2 AJSTVXY
3 A**F**KR
4 (B+G+Q+U+X+Z)
5 AGIKMOPUW
6 EG**K**(N 0,4km)RTV

A municipal campsite with modest but good toilet facilities. Plenty of shade and hilly grounds. Located 300m from the beach and in the countryside.

Platja d'Aro Centre to S'Agaró. Campsite to the south of Platja d'Aro, and signposted.

CC € 15 25/3-8/7 25/8-2/10

N 41°48'14" E 3°3'21"

Platja d'Aro, E-17250 / Cataluña

2644

Riembau Cat.1
Santiago Rusinyol s/n
+34 972-817123
FAX +34 972-825210
19/3 - 25/9
@ camping@riembau.com

19,7ha 1114T(100m²) 5A

1 CDGIJKLMOPQ
2 LRVXY
3 B**F**GK**M**N**Q**RUV
4 (B)
(**F** 19/3-1/8,1/9-25/9)
(G) **KLN**
(Q+S+T+U+X+Z)
5 **AB**FGIJKLMNOPUWZ
6 CGH**I**KM(N 2km)ORTVW

A large level campsite located in natural surroundings close to golden sandy beaches. Culture, gastronomy, relaxation, countryside and fun at your fingertips. The campsite is located on the Costa Brava, in Platja d'Aro.

Exit 6 direction Palamós, then centre of Playa d'Aro. Drive straight over the roundabout. The campsite is located on the right 600 metres down the road.

CC € 19 19/3-19/6 29/8-25/9

N 41°48'35" E 3°2'48"

Platja d'Aro, E-17250 / Cataluña

2645

Valldaro Cat.1
Cami Vell 63
+34 972-817515
+34 972-816662
18/3 - 25/9
info@valldaro.com

18,3ha 600**T**(70-90m²) 10A

1 AC**G**IJKLMOPQ
2 ALRVXY
3 B**F**GHJK**M**N**Q**RU
4 (B+G) K
(Q+S+T+U+X+Y) Z
5 **AB**DEFGIJKLMNOPUWZ
6 ABCEGH**IJK**M(N 0,5km)O
QRTUVW

A campsite with a jacuzzi, plenty of greenery and trees, located on the edge of a town with plenty of opportunties for going out. For stays longer than a week: one week's free WiFi, after that it must be paid for.

Exit 7 Palafrugell/Palamós direction San Feliu. On C31 exit 314 Castell d'Aro, three quarters round first roundabout direction Platja d'Aro. The campsite is 200m on the right.

CC € 15 *18/3-8/7 26/8-25/9 7=6*

N 41°48'54'' E 3°2'42''

Platja de Pals, E-17256 / Cataluña

2646

Camping Interpals
Av. Mediterrània, km 4,5
+34 972-636179
+34 972-667476
18/3 - 18/9
info@interpals.com

7ha 560**T**(60-200m²) 5A

1 ACD**G**IJKLMPQ
2 ABHIJLSVY
3 A**F**K**M**NR
4 (B+G) K
(Q+S+T+U+X+Z)
5 **AB**FGIJKLMNOPUW
6 AEGH**IK**M(N 5km)ORTUV
WX

A campsite located on hilly wooded grounds with good toilet facilities.

Motorway, exit 6 direction La Bisbal. From Pals direction Platja de Pals. At roundabout after 'Aparthotel Golf Beach' straight ahead. After a few hundred metres campsite on the right.

CC € 15 *18/3-8/7 26/8-18/9 7=6*

N 41°58'52'' E 3°12'4''

Platja de Pals, E-17256 / Cataluña

2647

Cypsela Cat. de Luxe
Rodors 7
+34 972-667696
+34 972-667300
4/5 - 10/9
info@cypsela.com

20ha 912**T**(80-140m²) 6A CEE

1 ACEIJKLMO**P**Q
2 BLSVY
3 B**F**GHJKN**Q**R**T**UV
4 (B+G) J
(Q+S+T+U+V+X+Y+Z)
5 **AB**EFGIJKLMNOPR**S**UWX
YZ
6 CFGH**IK**M(N 3km)OQRTV
WX

A first class campsite with perfect amenities. Located in a wood on level ground.

Motorway exit 6. From Pals direction Platja de Pals. Follow signs. Clearly signposted. Campsite is located on the left of the road.

CC € 19 *4/5-1/7 29/8-10/9*

N 41°59'8'' E 3°10'58''

Pont d'Arros, E-25537 / Cataluña

iD 2648

Verneda
N230, km 171
+34 973-641024
FAX +34 973-643218
24/3 - 9/10
@ info@campingverneda.com

180**T**(40-80m²) 5A

1 ABCD**G**IJKLMO**P**S
2 CGLRVWXY
3 ABHJKNPRU**W**
4 (A+C+H+Q 24/6-11/9)
(R) (T 21/6-13/9)
(U+V+X+Y+Z 24/6-11/9)
5 **AB**EFGIJKLMNPUWZ
6 EG**K**(N 7km)OTV

A lovely, well-maintained campsite by the river. Ideal area for walking and cycling. Wild-water activities, canoeing and rafting. Free WiFi during opening times at the bar. Val d'Aran offers unforgettable locations with challenges and activities for the whole family. Also great as stopover campsite.

From Bossost (N230) the campsite is clearly signposted on the right.

CC € 17 *1/4-23/6 31/8-8/10*

N 42°44'12'' E 0°44'47''

Prades (Tarragona), E-43364 / Cataluña

iD 2649

Prades Park
Ctra T-701, km 6.850
+34 977-868270
FAX +34 977-868279
1/1 - 31/12
@ camping@campingprades.com

3ha 70**T**(70-100m²) 8-10A CEE

1 ABCD**G**IJKLMO**P**Q
2 BCGKLRWXY
3 ABGHIJKLN**O**RU
4 (**A**) (C+H 15/6-15/9)
(Q+R)
(T+U+V+X+Y+Z 1/2-31/12)
5 **A**DEFGIJKLMNOPQRUWZ
6 ACEGHK(N 0,5km)OTV

A peaceful site in fields of hazelnut trees. Lovely walking area. Be sure to visit the towns of Poblet, Reus and Montblanc. You can enjoy affordable, traditional Spanish meals in the restaurant.

From motorway AP-2 (Lleida-Barcelona): exit 9 Montblanc, follow N-240 dir. Lleida past Espluga de Francoli, Vimbodí, Vallclara, Vilanova de Prades and Prades. From motorway AP-7: exit 34 Reus, follow N-240 dir. Falset past Les Borges del Camp, Alforja, Cornudella and Prades.

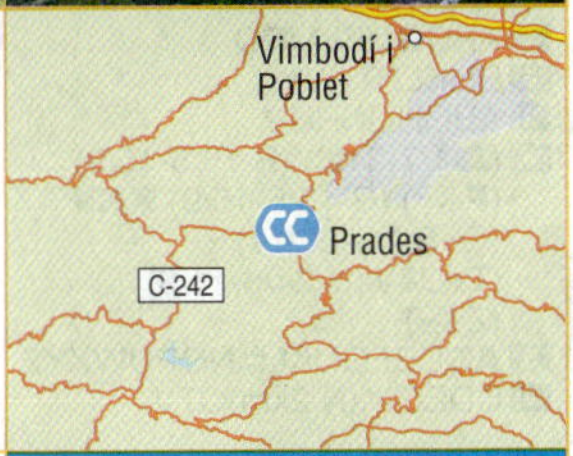

CC € 17 *1/1-15/7 1/9-31/12*

N 41°18'44'' E 0°58'47''

Ribera de Cardós, E-25570 / Cataluña

iD 2650

Del Cardós Cat.2
Av/Hug Roger III s/n
+34 973-623112
FAX +34 973-623183
21/3 - 30/9
@ info@campingdelcardos.com

3ha 190**T**(60-100m²) 6A

1 AGIJKLMPQ
2 BCKLRVXY
3 ABGHJNR**W**
4 (C+H 15/6-15/9)
(Q+R+T+V+Z)
5 **AB**EFGIJKLMNOPUWZ
6 AEGJ(N 0,5km)OTV

Located right in the centre of Cardos valley. You camp under huge trees on separated pitches, on the banks of a small river. Sanitairy facilities of excellent quality. Swimming pool. The snackbar/kiosk offers freshly baked bread each morning.

Take the exit at the electricity works in Llavorsí on the road C13 Sort-Esterri d'Àneu. Then follow this road for about 9 km. The campsite is located just before the village.

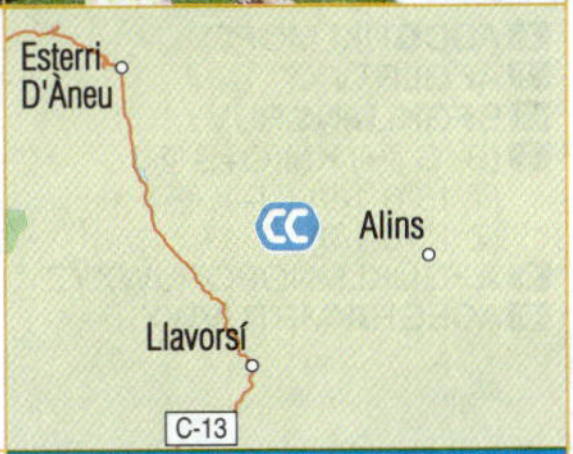

CC € 17 *21/3-15/7 1/9-30/9*

N 42°33'35'' E 1°13'46''

Roses, E-17480 / Cataluña

2651

Salatà
Port Reig 44
+34 972-256086
FAX +34 972-150233
12/3 - 31/10
info@campingsalata.com

4ha 180**T**(60-180m²) 10A

1 BCFIJLP
2 AERSVX
3 AK**M**RWY
4 (B 1/5-31/10) KNP(S 🔑)
(T 14/3-31/10) (U+V 🔑)
(X 14/3-31/10) (Y 1/6-1/10)
Z
5 **AB**EGIJKLMNOPSUVXY
6 EG**IJ**(N 1km)ORTV

Situated in the old fishing village of Roses which has a very old centre. You can spend a lovely time in the beautiful bays. Swimming, snorkeling, water skiing.

A7, exit 3. C260 Figures-Roses, straight on on roundabout B4 Empuria Brava. From roundabout, before Roses well-signposted.

CC € 19 *12/3-30/6* *18/9-31/10*

N 42°15'59'' E 3°9'22''

Saldes, E-08697 / Cataluña

2652

Repòs del Pedraforca Cat.1
B400, km 13,5
+34 938-258044
1/1 - 31/12
pedra@campingpedraforca.com

4ha 70**T**(70-100m²) 10A

1 ABC**G**IJKLM**P**Q
2 BIJKLRTUVY
3 ABGHIJNRU**V**
4 (**A** 1/7-31/8) (B 15/5-15/9)
(**F** 🔑) (G 15/5-15/9) **KNP**
(Q+S 1/4-30/11)
(T+U+V+Y 24/6-11/9)
(Z 🔑)
5 **AB**DEFGIJKLMNOPUWXYZ
6 CDEGIK(N 2km)OTV

A real mountain campsite with marked out pitches under spruce trees. The campsite has a sauna, gym and indoor swimming pool. The campsite also has a bar and a restaurant.

From the C16 to the south of the Caditunnel at Guardiola de Bergueda take the B400 to Salades. The campsite is located on the left after 13.5 km.

CC € 17 *1/1-20/3 29/3-22/6 27/6-15/7 1/9-30/10 4/11-18/12 26/12-31/12* *7=6, 14=11, 20=15*

N 42°13'45'' E 1°45'33''

Sant Antoni de Calonge, E-17252 / Cataluña

2653

Eurocamping
Avinguda Catalunya 15
+34 972-650879
FAX +34 972-661987
23/4 - 18/9
info@euro-camping.com

13ha 561**T**(60-80m²) 5A

1 ACD**G**IJKLMOPQ
2 AEGLRTVXY
3 BFGKL**M**N**Q**RUVY
4 (B+G 🔑) KM(Q+S 🔑)
(T 15/6-1/9) (U+X 🔑)
(Z 15/6-1/9)
5 **A**FGIJKLMNOPQRUWXYZ
6 ACEGH**I**KMRTUVWX

First-class campsite on the edge of a pretty little town with an attractive boulevard. All within walking distance. Free WiFi. Campers who stay for 14 nights or longer within the CampingCard validity period, can also stay for the CampingCard ACSI rate during the Spanish holiday of 21/6-25/6.

Exit 6, Palafrugell-Palamós, direction San Feliu, then Palamós-est and then Platja d'Aro. The campsite is located on the right side of the road at Sant Antoni. Clearly signposted.

CC € 19 *24/4-21/6* *25/6-30/6* *22/8-18/9*

N 41°50'49'' E 3°5'55''

Sant Carles de la Ràpita, E-43530 / Cataluña

2654

Alfacs Cat.2
Ctra Alcanar Platja
+34 977-740561
FAX +34 977-742595
18/3 - 2/10
info@alfacs.com

2,5ha 155T(45-70m²) 10A

1 BCGIJKLPRS
2 BEFGOQTVXY
3 AGJMNRWY
4 (B 15/6-15/9)
(G 15/6-13/9) (Q)
(S 10/4-3/11) (T)
(U 10/4-3/11) (X+Y) Z
5 AGIJKMNOPUZ
6 ACEGK(N 2km)OTV

Right by the Mediterranean coast. 6 km from Ebro Delta nature reserve past the rice fields with unusual flora and fauna. Excellent walking, cycling and fishing in the Delta.

North: on the A7 exit 41 dir. Sant Carles de la Ràpita. N340 at the 1072 km marker, exit to Sant Carles de la Ràpita. Turn right at 2nd roundabout to Calle Sant/Sidre. South: exit 43 on A7, N340 between 1066 and 1065 km markers dir. Sant Carles de la Ràpita. Campsite 2 km on the right.

CC € 15 18/3-23/3 29/3-23/6 1/9-2/10

N 40°35'43'' E 0°34'13''

Sant Feliu de Guixols, E-17220 / Cataluña

2655

Sant Pol
Doctor Fleming 118-130
+34 682-627900
18/3 - 12/10
info@campingsantpol.cat

1,7ha 77T(50-80m²) 10A

1 ACDGIJKLPQ
2 EGHJRTY
3 BFHJKLR
4 (C+G+Q+R+U+X+Z)
5 ABFGIJKLMNOPUWXYZ
6 ACEGIK(N 0,5km)RTVX

A real town campsite with excellent facilities on a main thoroughfare. Swimming pool with flowers and palms.

A7 exit 7 direction Sant Feliu/s'Agaro. Turn right at roundabout, past service station and Red Cross. Site located on the left after 200 metres. Short bend with slight slope.

CC € 19 28/3-28/4 1/5-13/5 16/5-16/6 12/9-12/10

N 41°47'12'' E 3°2'29''

Sant Pere Pescador, E-17470 / Cataluña

2656

Aquarius Cat.2
+34 972-520101
FAX +34 972-550216
15/3 - 31/10
reservas@aquarius.es

8ha 450T(80-100m²) 6A CEE

1 BGIJKLPQ
2 AERVWXY
3 BCGHJKNQRUVWY
4 AG(S+T+U+Y)QZ
5 ABDEFGIJKLMNOPQRUW
6 ACEGHIKM(N 2,5km)OPQR TVWX

Located on the beach where the sea water provides the ultimate relaxation. Many trips out are possible in the area. This is a peaceful campsite. Top of the range toilet facilities. The campsite only offers standard pitches. For an extra car in addition to your motorhome there's a surcharge.

Exit 3, after 12 km dir. Sant Pere Pescador, or exit 5 dir. L'Escala at St. Marti-Empuries via coast road to Sant Pere Pescador.

CC € 19 15/3-23/3 29/3-14/5 19/5-19/6 12/9-10/10 15/10-31/10

N 42°10'38'' E 3°6'29''

Sant Pere Pescador, E-17470 / Cataluña

2657

La Gaviota
Ctra Platja s/n
+34 972-520569
FAX +34 972-550348
19/3 - 23/10
info@lagaviota.com

2ha 153T(70m²) 5A CEE

1 AB**G**IJLPQ
2 ACEKLRVY
3 ABHJKNRWXY
4 (C+G) P
(Q+R+S+T+U+V+X+Y) Z
5 **AB**EFGIJKLMNOPRUW
6 DEG**IK**M(N 2km)ORTV

This campsite is positioned by the beach. The surroundings offer opportunities for various trips out. A quiet campsite with friendly, attentive staff and lovely landscaping. This site has added value as it is actually connected to the beach.

Exit 3 after La Jonquera, direction Roses, after 12 km direction Sant Pere Pescador. After the bridge follow signs.

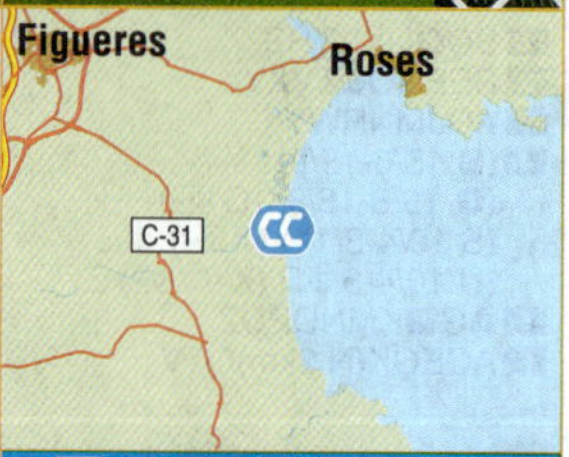

CC € 19 *29/3-14/5 19/5-9/6 12/6-16/6 19/6-22/6 12/9-23/10*

N 42°11'21'' E 3°6'30''

Sant Pere Pescador, E-17470 / Cataluña

2658

Riu**
Ctra de la Platja s/n
+34 972-520216
FAX +34 972-550469
1/4 - 25/9
info@campingriu.com

4ha 159T(100m²) 5A CEE

1 AFIJLPQ
2 ACGLRVY
3 ABGHJKMNRUVW
4 (B+G) K
(R+T+U+V+W+X) Z
5 **A**FGIJKLMNOPUWXY
6 CEG**IJ**MORTV

A family campsite 2 km from the beach set in a pine forest. Opportunities for trips out to Figueres, the Dali Museum and Barcelona. The open pitches ensure a continuous welcome cool breeze. The site is located directly next to a connecting channel to the sea with landing stages.

Take exit 3 towards Rosas. After 12 km direction Sant Pere Pescador. Signposted after the bridge. Or exit 5 direction L'Escala then direction Sant Pere Pescador.

CC € 19 *1/4-30/6 1/9-25/9*

N 42°11'15'' E 3°5'21''

Sitges, E-08870 / Cataluña

2659

El Garrofer Cat.2
Ctra C246a, km 39
+34 93-8941780
FAX +34 93-8110623
27/2 - 11/12
info@garroferpark.com

8ha 526T(70-90m²) 20A CEE

1 ABCD**G**IJKLMO**P**Q
2 AFGOSVWXY
3 AB**F**GHIJKNRUW
4 (B+G 1/4-30/9)
(Q+S+T+U+V 1/3-11/12)
(X+Y 1/3-13/12) Z
5 **AB**EFGIJKLMNPUWXYZ
6 ACDFG**K**(N 2km)ORTUVW
X

A campsite 2 km south of Sitges, 900m by footpath to the beach. You will pitch on gravel under the pine trees. Bus service to Barcelona.

Road C32, exit 26 direction Sitges, road C246a.

CC € 19 *27/2-10/7 1/9-11/12* *7=6, 14=12, 21=18, 28=24*

N 41°14'2'' E 1°46'51''

Solsona (Lleida), E-25280 / Cataluña

2660

El Solsonès Cat.1
Ctra St. Llorenç km 2
+34 973-482861
FAX +34 973-481300
8/1 - 11/12
info@campingsolsones.com

6,3ha 268T(70-100m²) 6-10A

1. ABCDEIJKLMOPQ
2. JKLRUVXY
3. AFGHJ**M**N**O**Q**R**S**U**
4. (A) (B+G+Q+S+T+U+V+X+Y 21/6-14/9)Z
5. **AB**DEFGIJKLMNOPUWZ
6. ACEGKL(N 2km)ORTV

A shaded campsite with a separate area for touring pitches. Various walks from the campsite. 2 km from the town of Solsona with its medieval centre. Many sports facilities. Excellent toilet facilities. Ecological restaurant and shop which are also open every weekend outside the stated periods.

From La Seo de Urgel follow the C1313. Turn left at Basella. In Solsona direction S. Llorenç de Morunys via Coll de Jou, follow signs.

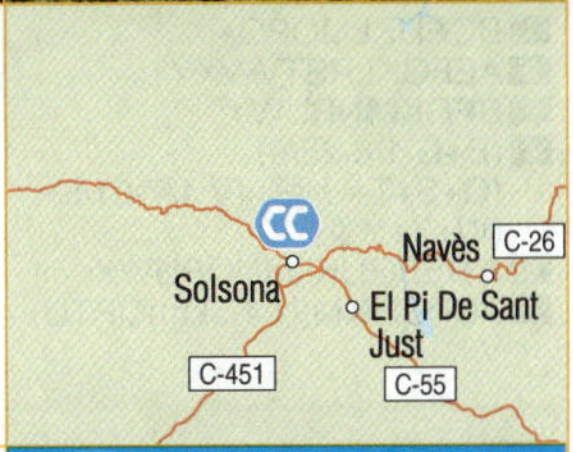

CC € 19 *8/1-24/3 29/3-15/7 1/9-30/11 7=6*

N 42°0'43'' E 1°31'0''

Tamarit/Tarragona, E-43008 / Cataluña

2661

Tamarit Park Resort Cat.1
Platja de Tamarit, N340a km 1172
+34 977-650128
FAX +34 977-650451
14/3 - 16/10
resort@tamarit.com

17ha 476T(66-200m²) 10-16A CEE

1. ACD**G**IJKLMO**P**Q
2. ABCEFGKLQRSTVWXY
3. AB**F**GHJK**M**NQRU**V**WY
4. (B 27/3-12/10) (G) JK (Q+S+T+U+V+X+Y) Z
5. **A**BDEFGIJKLMNOPQR**ST** UWXYZ
6. CDEGH**I**JKM(N 1km)ORST UV

The campsite is beautifully located at the foot of Tamarit castle, right on the beach and some distance from the coast road and railway line. Lively restaurant/bar with roof garden and sea views where the sandy beach meets the rocky coast.

AP7 exit 32, dir. Altafulla/Torredembarra/Tamarit. N340a dir. Tarragona, 1st exit at roundabout, 4th exit next roundabout dir. Tamarit/Altafulla. Right after 250m, follow green and yellow 'Tamarit Park' signs. Campsite on the left.

CC € 19 *28/3-18/6 12/9-16/10*

N 41°7'57'' E 1°21'37''

Taradell/Osona, E-08552 / Cataluña

2662

La Vall Cat.1
Camí de la Vallmitjana s/n
+34 93-8126336
FAX +34 93-8126027
7/1 - 15/12
lavallpark@campinglavallpark.cat

9ha 59T(80-100m²) 10A

1. ABCDGIJKLMOPQ
2. CIJKLRUVXY
3. A**F**HJMNRU
4. (B 21/6-14/9) (G 12/6-14/9) (Q) (R 7/1-21/6,14/9-17/12) (S+T+U+V+X 21/6-14/9) Z
5. **AB**DEFGHIJLMNPUWXYZ
6. CEGHK(N 1km)OTUV

Located in a lovely valley where the natural surroundings have remained unspoilt. Ideal area for walking, mountain biking and participating in other sports activities. Not far from the town of Vic with many cultural events on offer. Campsite is close to 'Parc Naturel del Montseny'.

C17 Vic-Barcelona, exit Taradell, continue to T junction in Taradell, turn right then follow signs. Attention!! On SatNav choose Urbanització de Goitallops. Then follow signs.

CC € 19 *7/1-23/3 29/3-30/6 1/9-15/12*

N 41°51'54'' E 2°17'42''

Tarragona, E-43080 / Cataluña

2663

Las Palmeras Cat.1
Ctra N340, km 1168
+34 977-208081
FAX +34 977-207817
19/3 - 12/10
@ laspalmeras@laspalmeras.com

17ha 700T(70-110m²) 5-10A

1 BC**F**IJKLMOPQ
2 AEFGKLRSTVWXY
3 B**F**GK**M**NRUWY
4 (B+G 1/6-25/9) (Q+S+T+U) (V 1/7-31/8) (W+X+Y) Z
5 **AB**EFGIJKLMNOPUWX
6 ACFGH**K**M(N 4,5km)ORTU V

Paradise for the beach lover. You can camp beside or up to 50m from the beautiful sandy beach. At the end of the campsite is the Punta de la Mora walking area. 4 km from the historic city of Tarragona. All this compensates for the sound of the railway.

Toll road A7, exit 32, roundabout direction Tarragona N340. After a few kilometres on the left restaurant 'El Trull'. Then beyond km-marker 1168 turn left through the tunnel under the railway track to the campsite.

CC € 15 *29/3-16/6 12/9-12/10*

N 41°7'49'' E 1°18'43''

Tarragona, E-43008 / Cataluña

2664

Torre de la Mora S.A. Cat.1
Ctra N340 km 1171
+34 977-650277
FAX +34 977-652858
21/3 - 16/10
@ info@torredelamora.com

16ha 450T(50-70m²) 6A

1 BC**G**IJLMST
2 ABEFGIJQSTVY
3 BFGN**Q**RUWY
4 (B+G 1/5-30/9) (Q+S+T+U+X+Y) Z
5 **AB**EFGIJKLMNOPUW
6 EGH**IJ**M(N 2km)ORTV

A terraced campsite with a lovely beach. Enormous water park. Terrace with free WiFi. 2 km from the N340 and railway line.

Toll road A7 exit 32 Torredembarra/Altafulla, on roundabout direction N340 Tarragona, at the next roundabout direction La Mora and follow signs to campsite further on.

CC € 17 *21/3-17/6 11/9-16/10*

N 41°7'44'' E 1°20'39''

Torredembarra, E-43830 / Cataluña

2665

Clara Cat.2
Passeig Miramar, 276
+34 977-643480
FAX +34 977-646076
1/4 - 16/10
@ info@campingclara.es

1,4ha 125T(60-90m²) 6-10A

1 BCDGIJKLMOPQ
2 AEFGSTVWXY
3 AB**F**GHKNRWY
4 (Q+S+T+U+V+X+Y+Z)
5 ABCFGHIJKLMNOPUWXY
6 ACDEGIK(N 0,2km)OQRTU V

Not such a big campsite, near the village and 50m from the beach. Naturist recreation allowed on the left side of the beach. Free WiFi. Close to railway line.

AP7 exit 31 or 32 to N340 direction Torredembarra. Exit Torredembarra Est. 2nd exit at roundabout. On the left after 500m.

CC € 15 *1/4-7/7 28/8-16/10* *7=6, 15=12, 30=23*

N 41°9'3'' E 1°25'16''

Torredembarra, E-43830 / Cataluña

2666

- La Noria Cat.2
- Passeig Miramar 278
- +34 977-640453
- FAX +34 977-645272
- 19/3 - 2/10
- @ info@camping-lanoria.com

5ha 440T(60m²) 6A

- **1** BCDGIJKLOPQ
- **2** AEFGTVXY
- **3** ABGHJKNRW
- **4** (Q+S+T+U+X+Y+Z)
- **5** ABFGIJKLMNOPUVWZ
- **6** CFGHIK(N 0,5km)ORTVW

A well maintained campsite. Close to a village and beach. Naturist recreation is permitted on the left side. Free WiFi. Attractive terrace and a good restaurant. There is a railway track next to the campsite.

AP7 exit 31 or 32 to N340 direction Torredembarra Est. 2nd exit on roundabout and campsite 400m on the left of the road.

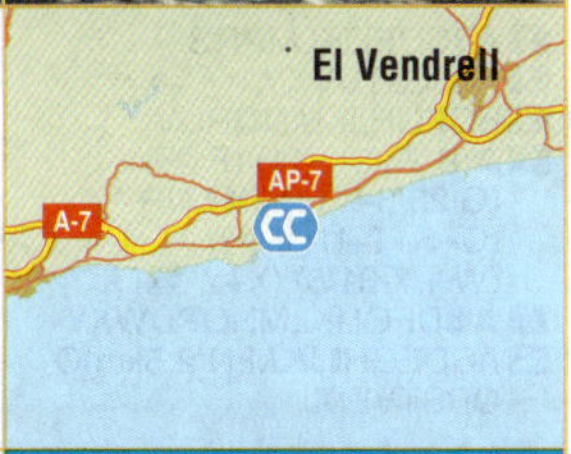

CC € 15 *19/3-30/6 1/9-2/10 7=6, 14=12, 30=23*

N 41°9'0" E 1°25'16"

Tossa de Mar, E-17320 / Cataluña

2667

- Cala Llevadó Cat.1
- Ctra GI-682 Lloret a Tossa km 18,9
- +34 972-340314
- FAX +34 972-341187
- 23/3 - 30/9
- @ comunicado@calallevado.com

17ha 612T(40-100m²) 10A CEE

- **1** ACD**G**IJKLPST
- **2** ABEGIJKOQSTVXY
- **3** BHJNRUWY
- **4** (A 1/7-30/8) (B+G 1/5-30/9) (Q+S) (T+U+V+X+Y 1/5-30/9) Z
- **5** **AB**FGIJKLMNOPUWXYZ
- **6** ACEGH**IJK**MOQRTUV

A fantastic location in the loveliest part of the Costa Brava. Quiet, four beaches, swimming pool, bar, restaurant, supermarket and excellent toilet facilities.

Toll road E15 exit 9. In Lloret drive in the direction of Tossa. Turn to the right after 8 km (clearly signposted). Then continue another 800 metres to the campsite on the private road.

CC € 19 *23/3-30/6 29/8-30/9*

N 41°42'47" E 2°54'23"

Vilanova de Prades, E-43459 / Cataluña

2668

- Serra de Prades Cat.1
- Sant Antonio s/n
- FAX +34 977-869050
- 1/1 - 31/12
- @ info@serradeprades.com

5ha 215T(92-100m²) 6A

- **1** BCD**G**IJKLMOPQ
- **2** JKLRSTVWXY
- **3** BCDGHJ**MN**P**R**UV
- **4** (**A**+C+H 24/6-15/9) **KN** (Q+S+T+U+V+X+Y+Z)
- **5** **AB**DFGIJKMNOPUWZ
- **6** CEGH**I**J**K**LOPTV

Campsite with beautiful and quiet location with heated pool, own wine productions, wellness and restaurant. Surroundings: museums, wine cellars, walking, sports activities. Organised theme options such as photography, plants, nature, animals etc.

From Barcelona AP-7 to Tarragona, AP-2 to Lleida, exit 9 Montblanc, N240 Lleida, Vimbodi, Vilanova de Prades. From Lleida N240, Vimbodi, Vilanova de Prades. From Vimbodi dir. Vallclara. Don't use SatNav but follow directions.

CC € 17 *1/1-22/3 29/3-22/6 26/6-15/7 11/9-6/10 13/10-27/10 2/11-23/12*

N 41°20'59" E 0°57'30"

Vilanova i la Geltrú, E-08800 / Cataluña

iD 2669

Vilanova Park Cat.1
Carretera Arboç km 2,5
+34 93-8933402
FAX +34 93-8935528
1/1 - 31/12
info@vilanovapark.com

40ha 348T(70-100m²) 10A

1 ABCD**F**IJKLM**P**RS
2 FGJLSTUVXY
3 BC**F**GHJK**MNQ**RUV
4 **A**(B 23/3-3/11) (F (key))
(G 23/3-3/11) **JKLNP**
(Q+S+T+U+V (key))
(W 1/7-31/8) (X+Y (key)) Z
5 **AB**DFGIJKLMNOPUWXY
6 ACDEGH**IJK**M(N 2,5km)O
QRSTVWX

On a hillside, 2 km from Vilanova i la Geltrú and 3.5 km from the beach. Enjoyable stays in early and late season with adapted facilities including an indoor pool, sauna, jacuzzi and fitness. Bus stop at the entrance for the beach, village and station. Daily bus to Barcelona.

Toll road A7, exit 29 direction Vilanova. Before Vilanova turn right on roundabout direction Cubelles C31. After km-marker 153 exit right direction Arboç. Then follow signs.

CC € 17 *1/1-19/6 27/6-3/7 29/8-31/12 14=11*

N 41°13'54'' E 1°41'28''

Alcossebre (Castellón), E-12579 / Comunidad Valenciana

iD 2670

Playa Tropicana Cat.1
Camino de l'Atall s/n
+34 964-412463
FAX +34 964-412805
1/1 - 31/12
info@playatropicana.com

3ha 380T(50-100m²) 10A

1 ACDGIJKLOPQ
2 AEFGNTUVXY
3 BGKRUWY
4 (B (key))
(E 1/1-15/5,30/10-31/12)
(G (key)) JK
(Q+S+T+U+V+X+Y (key)) Z
5 **AB**DEFGIJKLMNOPUWZ
6 ACEG**IK**(N 2,5km)ORTV

A large campsite on a sandy beach. New toilet facilities. Pitches separated by hedges. Lovely swimming pool, covered and heated in winter and a good restaurant and large supermarket. 4 km from the town of Alcossebre. Good cycling and challenging walks.

On A7 take exit 44; on N340 at km-marker 1018 to Alcossebre. Follow signs. Take 1st exit at roundabout. Enter village, turn right at 2nd traffic lights. Left at the T junction, then follow coast road to the campsite.

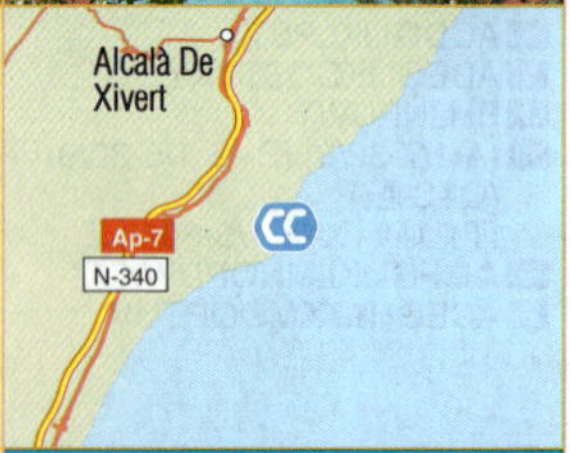

CC € 19 *1/1-23/3 29/3-30/6 1/9-31/12 14=12, 21=18, 30=26*

N 40°13'13'' E 0°16'6''

Alcossebre (Castellón), E-12579 / Comunidad Valenciana

iD 2671

Ribamar Cat.1
Partida Ribamar s/n
+34 964-761163
FAX +34 964-994085
1/1 - 31/12
info@campingribamar.com

2,2ha 71T(40-100m²) 10A CEE

1 ACD**G**IJKLM**P**ST
2 EINOQTUVX
3 BGHJ**M**NRUWY
4 (B+G 1/4-30/10)
(Q+R+Y+Z (key))
5 **AB**DEFGIJKLMNOPUWXYZ
6 ADEG**IK**(N 2,5km)ORTV

Excellent amenities. Very quiet and 150 m from the beach in the 'Sierra de Irta' nature reserve with excellent walking and cycling. Lovely swimming pool, tennis and basketball. Pitches with water tap. Heated toilet facilities. Campsite only accessible along a 1 km unsurfaced road, but worth the effort to stay at this lovely site!

A7, exit 44. Via the N340 to Alcoceber at the 1018 km sign along Las Fuentes. Follow camping signs. The final km is unsurfaced road.

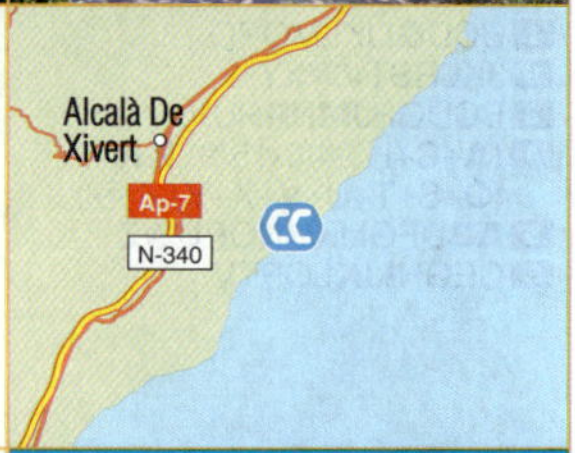

CC € 17 *1/1-23/3 28/3-30/6 1/9-31/12*

N 40°16'13'' E 0°18'24''

Altea/Alicante, E-03590 / Comunidad Valenciana

2672

Cap-Blanch
Playa de Cap-Blanch 25
+34 96-5845946
FAX +34 96-5844556
1/1 - 31/12
info@camping-capblanch.com

4ha 288**T**(80-120m²) 10A

1 ABCD**F**IJKLMOPQ
2 EFGKNOSTUVWXY
3 B**F**GK**M**NRU**V**WY
5 **AB**CDEFGHIJKLMNOPUZ
6 CGK(N 2km)ORT

Attractive grounds with plenty of palms and plants. Located in a bay with a lovely white pebble beach. A lively boulevard with views of Altea. Free WiFi and webcam. Heated toilet facilities.

AP7, exit 64 dir. Altea. Then N332 Valencia-Alicante south of Altea take exit Port Plaja at the traffic lights. Down to the sea. Turn right on boulevard. Campsite at the end of boulevard on the right.

CC € 19 *1/1-20/3 28/3-15/7 1/9-31/12*

N 38°34'40'' W 0°3'54''

Benicarlo, E-12580 / Comunidad Valenciana

2673

Alegria del Mar Cat.2
Ctra Nacional 340 km 1046
+34 964-470871
1/1 - 31/12
info@campingalegria.com

0,8ha 145**T**(60-135m²) 16A CEE

1 ACDGIJKLMOPQ
2 AEFNTUVWX
3 BGWY
4 (B+G 1/4-31/10)
(Q+R+T+U+V+X+Y+Z)
5 **AB**DEFGIJKLMNOPUWXZ
6 CDEG**K**(N 2km)OSTV

A medium sized campsite right by the sea, good facilities, swimming pool, restaurant. Very peaceful location, close to Benicarlo. Good walking and cycling opportunities.

Take exit 42 on the A7. On the N340 (Tarragona-Valencia) exit at km 1046 towards the sea. Then about 1 km on a minor road.

CC € 17 *1/1-4/7 21/8-31/12 7=6, 14=12, 21=18, 30=26*

N 40°25'36'' E 0°26'17''

Benicasim, E-12560 / Comunidad Valenciana

2674

Azahar Cat.1
Partida Vilarroig s/n
+34 964-303551
1/1 - 31/12
info@campingazahar.es

4ha 150**T**(70-95m²) 4A

1 BCD**G**IJLPQ
2 AEFRTVXY
3 B**F**G**M**UWY
4 (B+G+Q) (S 1/7-31/8)
(T+U+X+Y) Z
5 **AB**DEFGIJKLMNOPUWZ
6 EG**K**(N 1km)ORV

A campsite in a pleasant little town 100m from a lovely boulevard and a beautiful sandy beach. The inland area lends itself to trips out. Suitable for longer stays in the low season. Excellent cycling and walking opportunities on 'Via Verde', an old railway track through the lovely countryside to the north and south.

A7, exit 45 or 46. Take exit Benicasim on N340 at km-marker 987 or 989. Follow signs in Benicasim.

CC € 17 *1/1-22/3 29/3-30/6 1/9-31/12*

N 40°3'32'' E 0°5'7''

Benicasim, E-12560 / Comunidad Valenciana — 2675

Bonterra Park Cat.1
Avda de Barcelona 47
+34 964-300007
+34 964-100669
1/1 - 31/12
info@bonterrapark.com

5ha 320T(65-102m²) 6A

1 BCD**G**IJKLMPQ
2 AEFGTUVXY
3 B**F**GK**M**NRU**VW**Y
4 (A+B+E+G+Q+R+T+U+X+Y)Z
5 **AB**DFGIJKLMNOPUWXYZ
6 ACEG**IK**ORTUV

Beautiful, spacious campsite 300m from a sandy beach and a small town. Excellent heated toilet facilities. Swimming pools, one of which is covered and heated. Fitness room, tennis court, Spanish lessons. Sunny marked out pitches. Cycling and walking opportunities on 'Via Verde' from north to south on an old railway track. Suitable for longer stays in the low season.

A7, exit 46, take the N340. At km-marker 987 or 989 turn to Benicasim. Follow the signs.

CC € 19 1/1-22/3 28/3-3/7 29/8-31/12

N 40°3'25'' E 0°4'28''

Benidorm/Alicante, E-03503 / Comunidad Valenciana — 2676

Arena Blanca Cat.2
Avda Doctor Severa Ochoa 44
+34 96-5861889
+34 96-5861107
1/1 - 31/12
info@camping-arenablanca.es

2,5ha 95T(60-80m²) 16A

1 ABCGIJLO**P**ST
2 FGJLSTUVWXY
3 A**F**
4 (B 1/5-15/10) (E 1/1-1/5,15/10-31/12) (Q+R+T+U+V+X+Z)
5 **AB**DFGIJKLMNOPUWXY
6 ABCFG**I**K(N 0,8km)ORSTV

A charming campsite. Small-scale. Swimming all year. Wonderful sunbathing on real lawns when the weather is nice. Pool covered and heated in winter. Very clean toilet facilities. Free WiFi.

On the N332 Valencia-Alicante take Benidorm/Playa de Levante exit between 151 and 152 km markers. Then follow camping signs.

CC € 17 1/1-23/3 28/3-30/6 1/9-31/12

N 38°33'4'' W 0°5'47''

Benidorm/Alicante, E-03503 / Comunidad Valenciana — 2677

Armanello
Avda Com. Valenciana
+34 96-5853190
+34 96-5853100
1/1 - 31/12
info@campingarmanello.com

2,2ha 100T(60-100m²) 16A CEE

1 ABCDGIJKLMOPQ
2 FGLSUVWXY
3 B**F**KU
4 (B+G+Q+R+T+U+V+X+Z)
5 **AB**DFGIJKLMNOPUWXYZ
6 ABCGHIK(N 1,5km)ORSTUV

A lovely new rear part of the campsite with views of Benidorm and of the mountains in the background. New heated toilet facilities. Pleasant ambiance. Many interesting trips out into the hinterland. Free WiFi.

AP7, exit 65 to the N332. Straight on at 1st roundabout. 3rd exit at 2nd roundabout. Then follow camping signs.

CC € 17 1/1-15/7 1/9-31/12 7=6

N 38°32'52'' W 0°6'39''

Benidorm/Alicante, E-03503 / Comunidad Valenciana

2678

Benisol
Av. Com. Valenciana s/n
+34 96-5851673
FAX +34 96-5863616
1/1 - 31/12
info@campingbenisol.com

7ha 100**T**(60-80m²) 10A CEE

1 ABCDGIJLO**P**Q
2 FGJSTUVWXY
3 **F**G**M**RU
4 (B 1/6-31/10)
(F 1/1-31/5,1/11-31/12)
(G 1/6-31/10) JK
(Q+R+T+U+V+X+Y) Z
5 **AB**DFGIJKLMNOPUVXY
6 ABDEG**I**KM(N 3km)ORSTV

A campsite with friendly management and reception (many languages). Ideally located for visiting Benidorm and the beautiful inland region. Swimming all year (outdoor or indoor pools). Terrace next to the pool.

AP7, exit 65. Turn right twice after toll booth. Then keep right again(= exit). The campsite is located on the left a few hundred metres down the road.

CC € 17 *1/1-15/7 1/9-31/12 7=6*

N 38°33'36'' W 0°5'54''

Bétera, E-46117 / Comunidad Valenciana

2679

Valencia Camper Park***
Calle Universo s/n
+34 960-718095
1/1 - 31/12
valcampark@gmail.com

64**T**(40-80m²) 6A CEE

1 ACDGIJKLMOPQ
2 FGHLTUVWX
3 B**F**GHJU
4 (B+G+Q+R+T+U+Y) Z
5 **AB**DGHIJKLMNOPQUW
6 CEGK(N 2km)TV

New campsite with good amenities for motorhomes but also for caravans, situated on the north-west side. If you arrive with your caravan, you can park your car on the car park not far from the touring pitch. The campsite is also very suitable as a stopover campsite for people headed to the south of Spain. Ask reception about the extra discounts for a longer stay.

On A7 exit Bétera, then follow signs.

CC € 15 *15/4-30/6 5/9-25/10*

N 39°34'46'' W 0°26'44''

Bigastro/Alicante, E-03380 / Comunidad Valenciana

2680

La Pedrera*
Cañada de Andrea 100
+34 966-183020
1/1 - 31/12
info@campinglapedrera.com

4,4ha 46**T**(50-185m²) 16A

1 ABCDGIJKLMOPST
2 BJKLSUVW
3 AB**F**GHJR
4 (B+G) KP
(Q+R+T+U+V+X+Y+Z)
5 **AB**DFGIJKLMNOPUWXY
6 ABDEGJK(N 2km)OTV

A small campsite, spacious pitches with plenty of sun and lovely views across the valley. A pleasant friendly atmosphere and a brand new swimming pool with lawn (2014).

AP7, exit 740. 1st roundabout dir. Orihuela (CV921). 2nd roundabout dir. Benejúzar. 3rd roundabout dir. Jacarilla. In Jacarilla dir. Bigastro. Follow camping signs in Biagastro.

CC € 17 *1/1-7/7 24/8-31/12 7=6*

N 38°3'4'' W 0°53'54''

Càlig/Castellon, E-12589 / Comunidad Valenciana

2681

L'Orangeraie Cat. 2
Camino Peniscola-Calig
+34 964-765059
1/2 - 30/11
info@camping-lorangeraie.es

1,8ha 62**T**(70-140m²) 6A CEE

1 BCFIJKLMPST
2 FJKLRTVX
3 BFGR
4 (B+G+Q+R+T+U) Z
5 **A**FGIJKLMNOPUZ
6 AEGK(N 1km)T

A top quality campsite in a lovely setting 10 km from the beach. Perfect amenities. Set among orange and olive groves in a botanical garden. Free WiFi, lovely swimming pool/jacuzzi. Run by Patricia and Laurent, a hospitable French couple. Wonderfully peaceful.

AP7 exit 43 Benicarlo-Peniscola. 1st right at roundabout to Càlig, then follow signs. From N340 dir. Peñiscola, 1st roundabout 1st exit and follow campsite signs. On N340 at Benicarlo exit St. Mateu-Calig.

CC € 15 *1/2-6/7 23/8-30/11* ***10=9, 30=24***

N 40°27'7" E 0°21'8"

Calpe/Alicante, E-03710 / Comunidad Valenciana

2682

CalpeMar Cat. 1
C/ Eslovenia, 3
+34 965-875576
1/1 - 31/12
info@campingcalpemar.com

1ha 107**T**(54-125m²) 10A CEE

1 ABCDGIJKLMO**PQ**
2 AEFGUVWXY
3 AFGNRUWY
4 (A 1/1-30/4,1/10-31/12) (B+Q+T+X+Z)
5 **AB**DFGIJKLMNOPUWXY
6 AEG**IK**(N 0,45km)OTV

A modern, small-scale campsite on the edge of Calpe within walking distance of the sea, beaches, restaurants and supermarket. Perfect for sun worshippers. Views of Calpe and the famous (Peñon Ifach) rocks.

AP7, exit 64 to N332 dir. Calpe. Exit Calpe Norte 800m. Straight on. Turn left at Mercadona to large roundabout with artwork. Then straight on through 2nd roundabout with artwork. Then left and follow camping signs.

CC € 19 *1/1-30/6 1/9-31/12*

N 38°38'42" E 0°3'22"

Crevillente/Alicante, E-03330 / Comunidad Valenciana

2683

Camping Internacional
Las Palmeras****
Partida Deula 75
+34 96-6680630
1/1 - 31/12
laspalmeras@
laspalmeras-sl.com

1ha 51**T**(70-120m²) 10A CEE

1 ABCGIJLO
2 FSUVWX
4 (B+G+Q+T+X+Y+Z)
5 **AB**DFGIJKLMNOPUWXYZ
6 EGIJ(N 0,3km)ORT

Small campsite behind a hotel, lots of flowers. Excellent and very clean toilet facilities. Beautiful pool with sun loungers under palms. Bar and restaurant are good and affordable. Also ideal as a stopover campsite. Register at hotel reception.

AP7, exit 77 direction Crevillente. Then towards N340. Campsite on this road at 708 km marker. Behind hotel Las Palmeras.

CC € 15 *1/1-8/7 25/8-31/12* ***7=6***

N 38°14'26" W 0°48'42"

Crevillente/Alicante, E-03330 / Comunidad Valenciana

2684

Marjal Costa Blanca Camping & Resort****
Partida de las Casicas, 5
+34 965-484945
1/1 - 31/12
camping@marjalcostablanca.com

35ha 1200T(90-180m²) 16A

1 ABCD**G**IJKLMOPQ
2 FGLSTUVWX
3 BC**F**GHJKL**M**N**Q**RU**V**
4 (A 1/7-31/8) (B+**F**+H) IJ **KLNOP**(Q+S+T+U+V) (W 18/6-4/9) (X+Y+Z)
5 **AB**CDEFGHIJKLMNOPQRUWXYZ
6 ABCDGH**IJK**M(N 1km)ORSTUVWX

A very complete, luxurious campsite for long or short stays. Comfortable pitches with all amenities. The most important towns are not far away. Friendly ambiance in the main square with terraces and fountains. Seeing is believing. You will come again.

AP-7 Alicante-Cartagena, exit 730. Follow camping signs.

CC € 17 *1/1-23/3 28/3-30/6 5/9-31/12 7=6*

N 38°10'44'' W 0°48'30''

Cullera/Valencia, E-46400 / Comunidad Valenciana

2685

Santa Marta Cat.1
Avinguda Raço, 25
+34 96-1721440
FAX +34 96-1730820
16/1 - 14/12
info@santamartacamping.com

4ha 151**T**(25-80m²) 10A

1 AC**G**IJL
2 ABEGIJLTUVWXY
3 AKNRUY
4 (B+G 18/6-11/9) (Q+R+T+V+X 18/6-4/9)
5 **AB**DFGIJKLMNOPUWXYZ
6 AEG**K**(N 1km)RTV

An attractive campsite at the foot of a mountain slope with the scent of pine trees. The beach is 300 metres away. There are sunny pitches for those staying through the winter. Campsite is close to the town.

AP7, exit 59 N332 after km post 252 towards Cullera. Follow Cullera platges far signs, then far or faro (lighthouse) signs. Campsite on small roundabout on the right.

CC € 15 *16/1-23/3 28/3-17/6 12/9-14/12*

N 39°10'37'' W 0°14'31''

El Campello/Alicante, E-03560 / Comunidad Valenciana

2686

Costa Blanca Cat.2
C./Convento 143, N332 km 120,5
+34 965-630670
1/1 - 31/12
info@campingcostablanca.com

1,1ha 66**T**(40-80m²) 6A CEE

1 ABCDGIJLOP
2 FGUVXY
3 AFGUV
4 (B+Q) (R 1/7-31/8) (T+U+V+X+Y+Z)
5 **AB**DFGIJKLMNOPUWXY
6 ACEG**K**(N 0,3km)ORTV

Small-scale campsite. Spotlessly clean toilets, very tidy grounds. Agreeable ambiance and friendly staff who will be happy to help you get your caravan onto the pitch (can be difficult for larger caravans). Conveniently located between Benidorm and Alicante. Close to beach (800 metres), swimming in lovely pool (open all year).

AP7 exit 67. Right at 1st roundabout after toll booths, 2nd right, 3rd roundabout straight on, turn right at 4th roundabout. Then follow camping signs.

CC € 17 *1/1-25/3 28/3-10/7 29/8-31/12*

N 38°26'10'' W 0°23'17''

El Campello/Alicante, E-03560 / Comunidad Valenciana

2687

El Jardin
Doctor Severo Ochoa 39
+34 965-657580
1/1 - 31/12
info@campingeljardin.com

1ha 120T(70-80m²) 10A

1 ABCDGIJKLMOPST
2 FGSUVX
3 A**F**GL
4 (B+G 1/6-30/9) (Q)
(T+X+Z 24/4-27/4,1/7-31/8)
5 **AB**FGIJKLMNOPUWXY
6 ADEGJ**K**(N 0,6km)OSTV

A small-scale campsite in a quiet location close to the sea (600m). Located on the Costa Blanca. The very friendly wardens are at the service of campers throughout the year.

A7, then A70 exit 67 to N332 dir. San Joan. Dir. playas/platges at first roundabout to the beach. Then left. Left again at camping sign and straight on. Campsite on dead end road.

CC € 17 *1/1-10/7 27/8-31/12 10=9*

N 38°23'35'' W 0°24'55''

El Saler/Valencia, E-46012 / Comunidad Valenciana

2688

Devesa Gardens Resort
Ctra de El Saler KM 13
+34 961-611136
FAX +34 679-819614
1/1 - 31/12
contact@devesagardens.com

6,9ha 87T(84-96m²) 16A

1 ABCDGIJLOPQ
2 EGLSUVWXY
3 **CDFKMNO**RU
4 (B+G 19/3-12/10)
(Q+R+S+T+V+X+Y+Z)
5 **AB**DGIKMNOPUWZ
6 ABEGK(N 5km)OTV

Very well-maintained grounds with two completely renovated toilet blocks. Surprisingly large meadows for relaxing by a beautiful pool with little groups of trees. Very suitable for a visit to Valencia. Bus stop in front of the campsite with a bus every half hour.

A7 dir. Valencia. In town dir. El Saler (CV500). Campsite is located 7 km south of El Saler.

CC € 17 *1/1-21/3 29/3-10/7 29/8-31/12 7=6*

N 39°19'23'' W 0°18'35''

Grau de Gandía, E-46730 / Comunidad Valenciana

2689

L'Alquería
Avda del Grau, 142
+34 96-2840470
FAX +34 96-2841063
1/1 - 31/12
lalqueria@lalqueria.com

4,4ha 123T(70-80m²) 10A

1 ABCDGIJKLPQ
2 AFGSUVXY
3 AR**V**
4 (B 1/5-30/9)
(D 1/1-30/5,1/10-31/12)
(G 1/5-30/9) K**LNP**
(Q+R)
(T+V+X+Z 1/6-30/9,14/3-28/3)
5 **AB**FGIJKLMNOPUWXYZ
6 AGK(N 0,3km)ORT

Campsite under various types of trees. Lovely swimming pool with plenty of deck chairs, covered and heated out of season. Cycle routes to the beach, the town and the surroundings and also guided cycle tours in the winter months. No dogs on the dangerous breeds list and no dogs weighing more than 15 kg.

AP7, exit 60 to N332. After 3.1 km turn onto N337. Then take the first right on each of the four roundabouts. Campsite 300m on the left.

CC € 17 *1/1-23/3 29/3-30/6 1/9-22/12 7=6, 14=11*

N 38°59'10'' W 0°9'49''

Guardamar del Segura/Alicante, E-03140 / Comunidad Valenciana

2690

Marjal Guardamar Camping & Resort*****
Ctra N332 km 73,4
+34 96-6727070
FAX +34 96-6726695
1/1 - 31/12
camping@marjal.com

4ha 162T(90m²) 16A

1 ABCD**G**IJKLMOP
2 CFLSTUVWX
3 B**CF**GJK**MNQ**RUV
4 (**A**+B+E) IJKMNP (Q+S+T+U+V) (W 18/6-4/9) (X+Y+Z)
5 **AB**CDFGHIJKLMNOPUWXYZ
6 BGH**I**J**K**M(N 2km)ORSTUVW

A spacious campsite with large pitches. Sunny in winter and in the early and late seasons. Large outdoor swimming pool and heated indoor pool. Lovely sunny terrace. WiFi and fitness included in the price. Excursions to Elche (palm gardens), Alicante and Guardamar.

A70, exit 72. From the N332 turn off at roundabout between the villages of La Marina and Guardamar. Campsite clearly signposted.

CC € 19 *1/1-23/3 28/3-30/6 5/9-31/12*

N 38°6'36'' W 0°39'18''

Jávea/Alicante, E-03730 / Comunidad Valenciana

2691

El Naranjal
Cami dels Morers 15
+34 96-5792989
FAX +34 96-6460256
1/1 - 31/12
info@campingelnaranjal.com

2,3ha 164**T**(30-60m²) 10A

1 ACDGIJKLOPQ
2 SUVXY
3 A**F**G**MQ**RUV
4 (B) (Q+T+U+V+X+Y+Z 1/4-11/9)
5 **AB**DFGIJKLMNOPUZ
6 ACEG**IK**(N 1km)ORTV

Very well maintained campsite with excellent and clean toilet facilities. 3 km from the centre of Jávea, but just 600 metres from a shopping area with small restaurants, bars, beach and promenade. Modern amenities for campers.

AP7, exit 62 to the N332. Exit Jávea. Enter Jávea. Drive straight on at roundabout. At Arenal-Platges and Cap de la Nao signs turn right. Then follow signs.

CC € 17 *1/1-20/3 28/3-10/7 28/8-31/12*

N 38°46'14'' E 0°10'55''

Jávea/Alicante, E-03730 / Comunidad Valenciana

2692

Jávea Cat.1
Camino de la Fontana, 10
+34 96-5791070
FAX +34 96-6460507
1/1 - 31/12
info@campingjavea.es

2,5ha 193T(40-80m²) 8A

1 ABCDGIJKLOPQ
2 LSTUVWXY
3 A**F**GK**M**NRU
4 (B+G 15/4-12/10) (Q+R+T+U+V+X+Z)
5 **AB**DEFGIJKLMNOPUWXYZ
6 AEGH**K**(N 0,8km)ORTV

Situated next to an orange tree plantation. View of the Montgo Mountain and the historic town centre of Jávea. Very helpful staff at the reception. Cycling to the local supermarket, village or beach (El Arenal about 2.5 km).

AP7, exit 62 naar N332. Exit Jávea. Drive into Jávea. Straight on at roundabout. Follow signs Arenal/Platges and Cap de la Nao. After McDonalds, Euromarkt take bridge across (dried up) river. Sharp right onto side road. Follow camping signs.

CC € 17 *1/1-22/3 28/3-30/6 1/9-31/12*

N 38°47'1'' E 0°10'20''

La Vall de Laguar/Alicante, E-03791 / Comunidad Valenciana

2693

Vall de Laguar
Carrer Sant Antoni, 24
+34 96-5584590
1/1 - 31/12
info@campinglaguar.com

1,7ha 39T(50-120m²) 5A

1 ACDGIJKLNOPQ
2 GJKSTUVX
3 H
4 (B+G 15/5-31/10)
(U+X+Z 1/7-31/8)
5 ABDFGJLMNOPUWXYZ
6 AEGIK(N 0,3km)ORTV

A small, peacefully located terraced campsite with lovely views of the village, the Montgo mountain and the sea (about 10 km as the crow flies). A place to relax and stay for a long time. A good base for walking in the mountains. Very friendly, helpful management.

AP7, exit 62 to the N332 direction Valencia then direction Orba and then Vall de Laguar. In Campell follow camping signs.

CC €17 1/1-15/7 1/9-31/12

N 38°46'36'' W 0°6'19''

Mareny de Barraquetes/Sueca, E-46410 / Comunidad Valenciana

2694

Barraquetes
Ctra Nazaret-Oliva KM 25
+34 961-760723
+34 961-760130
15/1 - 15/12
info@barraquetes.com

3,7ha 113T(40-65m²) 20A

1 ABCDGIJKLMOPR
2 BGSXY
3 AMNU
4 (B+G 12/6-6/9) J
(Q+R+V+X 15/6-15/9) Z
5 ABFGIJKLMNOPUVXZ
6 CDEGK(N 0,4km)OTVW

Relaxation and space. For nature lovers: the beach and Albufera nature reserve with a wide variety of native trees and plants. Rice fields and picturesque villages in the area.

A7 exit Sueca N332. Then exit to Perelló/Mareny de Barraquetes. Then follow camping signs.

CC €15 15/1-24/3 29/3-16/6 12/9-15/12 7=5, 14=10

N 39°14'31'' W 0°15'50''

Moncofa, E-12593 / Comunidad Valenciana

2695

Los Naranjos
Cami de Cabres
+34 964-580337
1/1 - 31/12
info@campinglosnaranjos.com

185T(60-130m²) 10A CEE

1 BCDGIJKLMOPST
2 AEFNTUVY
3 BCGHJKNRWY
4 (B+G 23/6-8/9)
(Q+R+T+U+V+X+Y+Z)
5 ABDEFGIJKLMNOPRSTUX
YZ
6 DEGJK(N 2km)OQRTV

Medium-sized campsite, 300 metres from a sandy and pebble beach. 2 km from Moncofa.

N340 exit Moncofa. AP-7 exit 49 Moncofa, A7 exit Vall d'Uxo and then Moncofa, in Moncofa right onto ring road and follow signs.

CC €15 1/1-24/3 29/3-19/6 1/9-31/12 11=10

N 39°46'53'' W 0°8'56''

Moncofa/Castellón, E-12593 / Comunidad Valenciana

2696

Camping Mon Mar Cat.2
Camino Serratelles s/n
+34 964-588592
1/1 - 31/12
monmarcamping@gmail.com

2ha 110T(70m²) 6A

1 BCDEIJKLMPQ
2 AEFGNUVXY
3 BGJKNRUWY
4 (B+G) I
(Q+R+T+U+X+Y) Z
5 **AB**DFGIJKLMNOPUWXYZ
6 ACDEGJ**K**(N 0,5km)ORTV

Ideal for Valencia (45 km) with monuments, science park, modern architecture, aquarium, museums, botanical garden, festivals, opera! Cycling. Orange plantations and vineyards. Visit the underwater caves at San Josep.

A7 exit 49 dir. Moncofa. In Moncofa follow 'Camping Mon Mar' signs. A7 exit 283 Moncofa. Then follow 'Camping Mon Mar' signs. On the N340 exit Moncofa between 950 and 953 km markers. In Moncofa follow 'Camping Mon Mar' signs.

CC € 17 *1/1-3/7 29/8-31/12 7=6, 10=8, 20=15, 30=22*

N 39°48'31'' W 0°7'40''

Moraira/Alicante, E-03724 / Comunidad Valenciana

2697

Moraira Cat.1
Camíno Paellero 50, Teulada
+34 96-5745249
+34 96-5745315
1/1 - 31/12
campingmoraira@campingmoraira.com

1,1ha 105T(50-90m²) 10A

1 ABCDGIJL**P**
2 FJKSTUVXY
3 **FU**
4 (B+Q)
(T+V+X+Z 1/1-30/11)
5 **AB**DFGIJKLMNOPUWXYZ
6 AEG**K**(N 1,2km)ORT

Small terraced campsite with a pleasant ambiance by a hill under fir trees. Lovely views of the swimming pool and sea from some of the pitches and certainly from the terrace. Close to the town (shops) and the beach. Possibility for trips out into the area.

From the N332 exit towards Moraira. In Moraira turn right at the roundabout. Follow the camping signs. Clearly signposted. Take care: turn right towards the campsite immediately after passing the restaurant, not before.

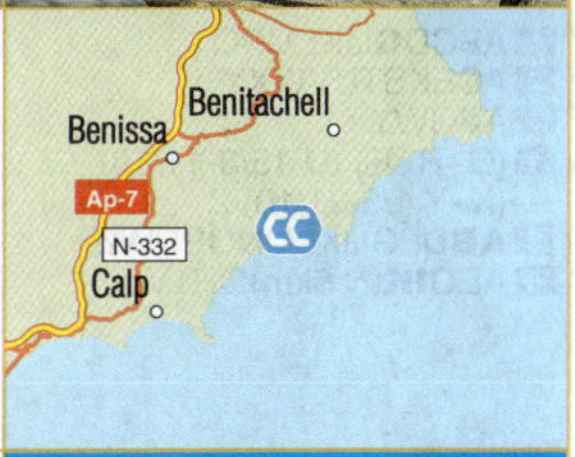

CC € 17 *1/1-17/3 28/3-30/6 1/9-31/12*

N 38°41'9'' E 0°7'10''

Navajas (Castellón), E-12470 / Comunidad Valenciana

2698

Altomira Cat.1
CV-213 Navajas, km 1
+34 964-713211
+34 964-713512
1/1 - 31/12
reservas@campingaltomira.com

2,5ha 50T(70-80m²) 6A

1 BCDGIJKLMO**P**Q
2 FGJKTUVWX
3 BGHJ**M**NRUW
4 (**A** 1/7-31/8)
(B+G 15/6-15/9)
(Q+R+U+X+Y) Z
5 **AB**DFGIJKLMNOPUWXYZ
6 AEGJ**K**(N 0,3km)PTV

A beautiful campsite located in the hills with panoramic views. Just 20 km from the Mediterranean. Good for walking and cycling. A direct train connection to the beautiful city of Valencia. Natural, mineral springs with health-giving water in the area. Good swimming pool and restaurant. Lovely cycling opportunities along a former narrow-gauge railway line.

On the A23 Sagunto-Teruel, at the exit 33 Navajas. Then follow the campingsigns.

CC € 17 *1/1-20/3 4/4-30/6 1/9-31/12*

N 39°52'29'' W 0°30'38''

Oliva/Valencia, E-46780 / Comunidad Valenciana

2699

Azul
Playa Rabdells
+34 96-2854106
FAX +34 96-2854096
10/3 - 31/10
info@campingazul.com

2,5ha 109T(60-100m²) 15A

1 ACDGIJKLPQ
2 AEKSVWXY
3 A**F**GKRWY
4 (Q+R+T+U+V+X) Z
5 **AB**DFGIJKLMNOPUWZ
6 CEG**IK**(N 5km)ORT

Among flowering oleanders right next to a beach. A natural campsite with a chance to cycle through orange groves. An agreeable atmosphere. Lovely new showers and washbasins (2013).

North: on the N332, exit at the 213 km marker. Left under viaduct at 1st roundabout. Right at 2nd roundabout then 3rd road on left (Playa Rabdells). South: on the N332 at the 209 km marker exit at service station (go under viaduct). Keep right after the service station and follow camping signs.

CC € 17 10/3-23/3 28/3-30/6 1/9-31/10

N 38°54'27" W 0°4'4"

Oliva/Valencia, E-46780 / Comunidad Valenciana

2700

Eurocamping
Partida Rabdells s/n
+34 96-2854098
FAX +34 96-2851753
1/1 - 31/12
info@eurocamping-es.com

4,5ha 299T(70-120m²) 10A

1 ABCD**G**IJKLMPQ
2 ACEKSTUVWXY
3 A**F**GWY
4 (Q+R) (U 15/3-11/10)
(X+Y 1/3-31/10) Z
5 **AB**DFGIJKLMNOPUWZ
6 AEG**IK**(N 5km)ORTV

A campsite right on sandy beach. Ideal for beach lovers. Very clean grounds and excellent toilet facilities. Very accessible for caravans and motorhomes. Reception closed between 14:00 and 16:00. Normal camping rate applies to pitches in the dunes.

From the north: on the N332, at the km-marker 210, turn towards the sea (across the viaduct). From the south: on the N332, at the km-marker 209, turn right. Signposted before and at the roundabout. Follow camping signs.

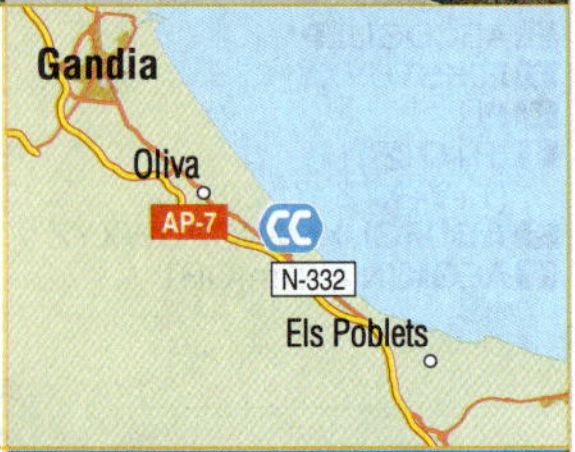

CC € 15 1/1-23/3 28/3-30/6 1/9-31/12

N 38°54'22" W 0°4'2"

Oliva/Valencia, E-46780 / Comunidad Valenciana

2701

Kiko Park Cat.1
C/. Assagador de Carro, 2
+34 96-2850905
FAX +34 96-2854320
1/1 - 31/12
kikopark@kikopark.com

2,9ha 171T(60-110m²) 16A CEE

1 ACD**G**IJKLMOPQ
2 AEFGSTUVWXY
3 **F**K**V**WY
4 (C+H) **KLNP**
(Q+S+U+V+Y) Z
5 **AB**DFGIJKLMNOPUWXYZ
6 ACEG**IK**M(N 0,5km)ORTV

An international, floral campsite situated right next to the sea with a lovely sandy beach, perfect restaurant, large terrace and a tropical bar with sea views. Cycling and walking opportunities in the area. Enlarged with a lovely swimming pool and wellness centre. Also take away meals. Gran Comfort pitches for a surcharge.

Motorway AP7, exit 61. Take the N332 to Oliva. Turn left at the first roundabout/traffic lights. Then follow 'Platges' and campsite signs.

CC € 19 1/1-23/3 29/3-30/6 16/9-31/12

N 38°55'58" W 0°5'51"

Oliva/Valencia, E-46780 / Comunidad Valenciana

2702

Olé Cat.1
Pda. Aigua Morta s/n
+34 96-2857517
+34 96-2857516
1/1 - 31/12
campingole@hotmail.com

4,2ha 314T(50-90m²) 6A

1 ACD**G**IJKLM**P**Q
2 AEKSUVWXY
3 A**F**GNUWY
4 (B 1/7-15/9) (Q)
(S 24/4-28/4,1/7-31/8)
(U+V+X+Y 15/3-15/12) Z
5 **AB**DFGIJKLMNOPUWXYZ
6 CEG**K**(N 5km)ORTV

A campsite right on the beach with fine white sand. Extensive views of the sea and beach. Great for beach walkers. Cycling opportunities. Excursions to Denia and inland. CampingCard ACSI not accepted for pitches on the beach.

When approaching from the north: on the N332 at km-marker 210 turn towards the sea (over the viaduct). When approaching from the south: on the N332 at the km-marker 209 turn right. Signposted before and at the roundabout. Follow camping signs.

CC € 17 *1/1-23/3 29/3-30/6 1/9-31/12*

N 38°53'40" W 0°3'13"

Oliva/Valencia, E-46780 / Comunidad Valenciana

2703

Rio-Mar Cat.2
N332 km 207
+34 96-2854097
+34 96-2839132
1/1 - 31/12
riomar@campingriomar.com

0,8ha 64T(50-80m²) 10A

1 ACD**G**IJKLPQ
2 ACEFKSTUVWXY
3 **F**WY
4 (Q+S+T+U+X+Z)
5 **AB**DFGIJKLMNOPUWZ
6 EGK(N 7km)ORTV

A small campsite right by the sea with a fine sandy beach, convenient boardwalks and foot showers. Free WiFi. Connection to parabolic (TV/ Astro) is possible. Separate kitesurfing zone.
Bus service to Denia six times a day and once a week to the market in Oliva. Also easy to cycle there.

AP7, exit 61 direction Oliva or N332 Valencia-Alicante at km marker 207 direction beach and sea, follow signs to the campsite.

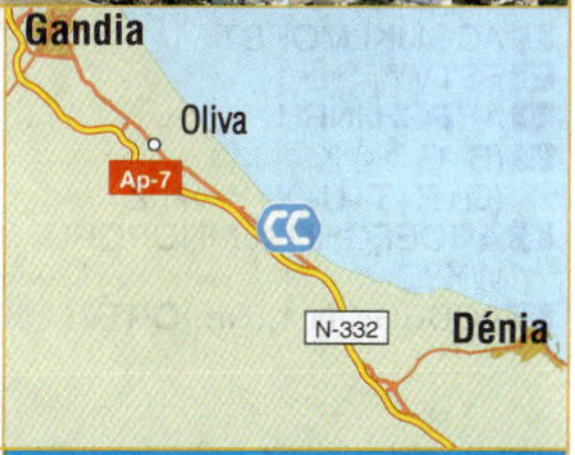

CC € 15 *1/1-8/7 25/8-31/12*

N 38°53'10" W 0°2'20"

Oropesa del Mar (Castellón), E-12594 / Comunidad Valenciana

2704

Didota S.L. Cat.1
Avda Barcelona /
Vereda Didota s/n
+34 964-319551
+34 964-319847
1/1 - 31/12
info@campingdidota.es

1,6ha 144T(90-120m²) 10A

1 BCDGIJKLMPQ
2 AEFGSTUVXY
3 BCGHJKRUVWY
4 (B+F+H) **K**P
(Q+R+T+U+X+Y)
5 **AB**DEFGIJKLMNOPQRUW
Z
6 ACEGHIK(N 0,5km)ORTUV

A beautiful campsite by the beach. Lovely outdoor swimming pools, heated indoor pool with bubble bath and jacuzzi. Pitches with plenty of sun, pitches in summer with shade. Good restaurant and renovated toilet facilities. Plenty of opportunities in low season for dance evenings with live music, flamenco, Spanish lessons, bingo and tennis.

A7, exit 45. Or on the N340 Tarragona-Valencia turn off at 999,2 km sign towards the sea. Follow camping signs (about 1 km).

CC € 15 *1/1-12/7 29/8-31/12 7=6, 15=12, 30=22, 45=30*

N 40°7'16" E 0°9'30"

Peñíscola, E-12598 / Comunidad Valenciana

iD 2705

El Edén Cat.1
Calle Madrid 6
+34 964-480562
FAX +34 964-489828
1/1 - 31/12
camping@camping-eden.com

3,3ha 254T(60-100m²) 10A

1 ACD**G**IJKLMPQ
2 AEFGLSTVXY
3 BGHJKRUVWY
4 (B+G 1/4-15/10) JK(Q) (S 15/6-15/9) (T+U+X+Y 20/1-31/12) Z
5 **AB**DEFGIJKLMNOPUWXYZ
6 ACEG**IK**M(N 0,8km)OQRT V

An attractive large campsite 50 metres from the boulevard and Peñiscola beach with a lovely swimming pool and a good restaurant. Good walking, cycling and watersports opportunities.

A7 exit 43 to Peñiscola. Campsite signposted on the boulevard. Take Peñiscola exit on the N340. Continue on boulevard to Benicarlo. Campsite located 6 km on Avenida Papa Luna. There is a sign before the El Edén restaurant/campsite.

CC €19 *1/1-24/3 27/3-23/6 11/9-31/12 8=7*

N 40°22'16'' E 0°24'10''

Peñíscola, E-12598 / Comunidad Valenciana

iD 2706

Los Pinos SL Cat.1
Camino Abellers, s/n
FAX +34 964-480379
1/1 - 31/12
campinglospinos@hotmail.com

1,2ha 120T(80-100m²) 10A

1 ACGIJKLMOPST
2 FSTVY
3 AB**F**GHJNRU
4 (B+G) K (Q+R+T+U+X+Y) Z
5 **AB**DEFGHIJKLMNOPQRU WXYZ
6 ACDEGK(N 1,5km)ORTV

A medium sized family campsite with a nice swimming pool, jacuzzi, good restaurant and free WiFi. 1.5 km from Peñiscola with a lovely long promenade and a beautiful sandy beach. The former castle of pope 'Papa Luna' can also be viewed here.

A7, exit 43 Peñiscola, drive for 4 km towards Peñiscola then the campsite is signposted.

CC €13 *1/1-23/3 29/3-15/6 14/9-31/12*

N 40°22'45'' E 0°23'18''

Peñíscola, E-12598 / Comunidad Valenciana

2707

Sol d'Or
Avenida de la Estación, 137
+34 964-480653
FAX +34 964-467583
1/1 - 31/12
info@campingsoldor.com

194T(60-100m²) 10A

1 BCDGIJKLMOPQ
2 AFGRVWXY
3 B**F**GRUW
4 (B+G 1/4-31/10) (Q+T+U+V+X+Y+Z)
5 **AB**DFGHIJKLMNOPUZ
6 EGJ**K**(N 1km)ORTVX

Campsite Sol d'Or is 1.5 km from the sandy beach of Peñiscola, has good toilet facilities, spacious camping pitches and a good restaurant.

AP1 exit 43 to N340 dir. Peñiscola, campsite located on right of this road before town.

CC €13 *1/1-23/3 29/3-15/6 14/9-31/12 7=6*

N 40°22'50'' E 0°23'9''

Peñíscola, E-12598 / Comunidad Valenciana — 2708

Vizmar Cat. 2
Ctra Vieja Peñíscola-Benicarló s/n
+34 964-473439
1/1 - 31/12
campingvizmar@hotmail.com

1,6ha 118T(60-70m²) 7A

1 ACGIJLMPQ
2 EFGTUVXY
3 BGRWY
4 (B+G 1/4-30/9) (Q+R+T) (U+X+Y+Z 1/6-30/9)
5 **AB**FGIJKLMNOPUZ
6 ACEG**K**(N 1km)OTV

A campsite with reasonable toilet facilities. Plenty of shaded pitches, but sunny pitches also available. Campsite about 400m from the lovely beach and boulevard at Peñiscola, famous for the Papa Luna castle.

On N340 exit at Peñiscola sign. Towards Benicarlo at roundabout. Campsite ± 2 km on the left.

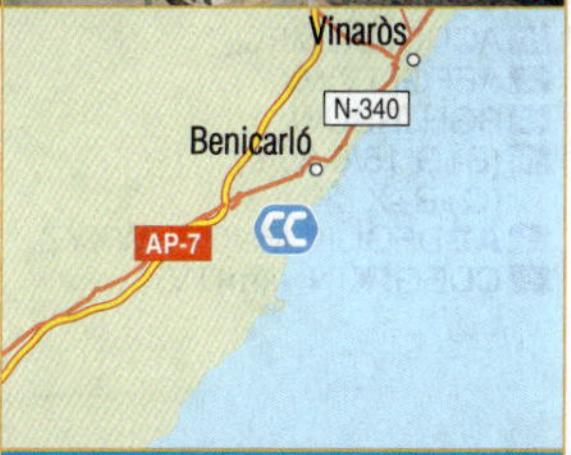

CC € 13 *1/1-20/3 28/3-30/6 15/9-31/12 7=6, 30=26*

N 40°23'32'' E 0°24'25''

Pilar de la Horadada/Alicante, E-03191 / Comunidad Valenciana — 2709

Lo Monte Cat.1
Avda Comunidad Valenciana, 157
+34 966-766782
+34 966-746536
1/1 - 31/12
info@campinglomonte-alicante.es

127T(60-125m²) 16A CEE

1 ABCD**G**IJKLMOP
2 FGLTUVW
3 A**F**GHJKUV
4 (B 1/6-30/9) (F) (G 1/6-30/9) KP (Q+R+T+U+V+X+Y+Z)
5 **AB**DFGIJKLMNOPUWXY
6 ACEGJ**K**(N 0,5km)ORTUV

New (2011) and spacious campsite. Beautifully stylish building including a spa and fitness. Attractive terrace overlooking the swimming pools. Recommended for the whole year.

AP7, exit 770 to N332 direction Pilar de la Horadada. Towards Pueblo Latino at 2nd roundabout. Left at 1st traffic lights.

CC € 17 *1/4-30/6 1/9-31/10*

N 37°52'45'' W 0°45'56''

Pinedo/Valencia, E-46012 / Comunidad Valenciana — 2710

Coll Vert Cat. 2
Ctra del Riu, nr. 486 Pinedo
+34 96-1830036
+34 96-1830040
16/1 - 15/12
info@collvertcamping.com

2,4ha 80T(40-80m²) 10A

1 ACDGIJKLMPQ
2 AEFGRTVXY
3 B**F**GHJKNRWY
4 (B+G 1/6-30/9) (Q+R) (T+U+V+X 1/4-30/9) Z
5 **AB**DFGIJKLMNOPUWZ
6 ACDG**IJK**(N 1km)STV

6 km from Valencia and 300m from a wide sandy beach and l'Albufera nature park. You can get to Valencia by cycle path or by bus. If you don't mind some surrounding noise you will not be disappointed.

N: A7 and V21 dir. Valencia, follow El Saler signs in town. On CV500 1. roundabout go 3/4 of the way roundand exit on CV5010. Campsite 300m on le.
S: A7 before Valencia dir. Albufera and El Saler on the CV500, turn off at El Saler roundabout, campsite 200m on le.

CC € 17 *16/1-15/7 1/9-15/12 7=6, 14=12, 30=25*

N 39°23'47'' W 0°19'58''

Puçol/Valencia, E-46530 / Comunidad Valenciana

2711

Puzol Cat.2
Playa de Puçol
+34 961-421527
+34 961-465586
16/1 - 15/12
campingpuzol@gmail.com

3ha 70T(60-70m²) 10A

1 ACDGIJKLMPQ
2 AEFGLTVWXY
3 BGHJRSUW
4 (B+G 15/6-30/9) (Q+R+X)
5 **AB**DFGIJKLMNOPUWXYZ
6 CDEG**IK**(N 4km)TV

A campsite 20 km from Valencia; little by little being reorganised and renovated for touring campers. There is a separate section with adequate amenities for these tourists. Lovely swimming pool from the end of May. About 150m from the Mediterranean with a fine sandy beach.

On the A7 exit Puçol; on N340 exit Puçol then follow signs to Playa and campsite.

CC € 15 *16/1-15/7 1/9-15/12 7=6, 14=12, 30=25*

N 39°36'20'' W 0°16'8''

Ribera de Cabanes, E-12595 / Comunidad Valenciana

2712

Torre La Sal Cat.1
Camino l'Atall s/n
+34 964-319596
+34 964-319629
1/1 - 31/12
info@campingtorrelasal.com

2ha 177T(60-120m²) 15A

1 BCDEIJKLMNOPQ
2 AEFTUVWY
3 BCGHIJKMNRUWY
4 (A 1/1-1/5,1/10-31/12) (C+H) K(Q+S+T)
5 **AB**DEFGIJKLMNOPUWZ
6 AEGK(N 1km)OQRTVW

A peaceful family campsite right on a sandy beach. With a heated, covered swimming pool and recreation room. Pitches with plenty of shade and sunny pitches in winter. Library with books in Dutch, English, German and French. Free WiFi!

E15 exit 44 or 45. Leave N340 Tarragona-Valencia at 1000 km marker. Then follow signs. Campsite beyond Torre La Sal 2 campsite.

CC € 15 *1/1-23/3 29/3-30/6 1/9-31/12 15=14, 30=28*

N 40°7'42'' E 0°9'34''

Ribera de Cabanes, E-12595 / Comunidad Valenciana

2713

Torre la Sal 2 Cat.1
Avda l'Atall 44
+34 964-319567
+34 964-319744
1/1 - 31/12
camping@torrelasal2.com

9ha 517T(60-140m²) 10A

1 ACDGIJKLMPQ
2 AEFNTUVXY
3 BC**F**GLMNQR**S**TUVWY
4 (B 1/4-31/10) (F+H) IJKM **N**P(Q+S+U+X+Y) Z
5 **AB**DEFGIJKLMNOPRUWXZ
6 CEGHKM(N 3km)OPTUVW

A large residential campsite with beautiful, new toilet facilities and many other amenities: indoor and outdoor swimming pools, heated in winter. Covered car park, tennis and multisports ground. Good cycling opportunities. Free WiFi. Also well equipped for the people with a disability.

On the A7 Barcelona-Valencia take exit 45. On the N340 km-marker 998 or 1000. Signposted.

CC € 19 *1/1-22/3 28/3-17/6 11/9-31/12 15=13, 30=26*

N 40°7'40'' E 0°9'32''

Santa Pola/Alicante, E-03130 / Comunidad Valenciana

2714

- Bahia de Santa Pola Cat.2
- Ctra Elche-Snta Pola km 11
- +34 96-5411012
- FAX +34 96-5416790
- 1/1 - 31/12
- campingbahia@gmail.com

6ha 362T(65-70m²) 10A

1 ABCDGIJKLMOPQ
2 IJTUVXY
3 AG
4 (B+G 15/6-15/9) (Q) (R 1/7-31/8) (Z)
5 **AB**DFGIJKLMNOPUXYZ
6 ACG**J**(N 1km)ORTV

Rather large terraced site with artificial shade in summer. On the slopes of a hill, with a nice cooling breeze on hot days and a great view of the city.

A70, exit 72 Santa Pola. On the N332 turn right at the roundabout to Elche after the 88 km marker. Campsite 100m on the right.

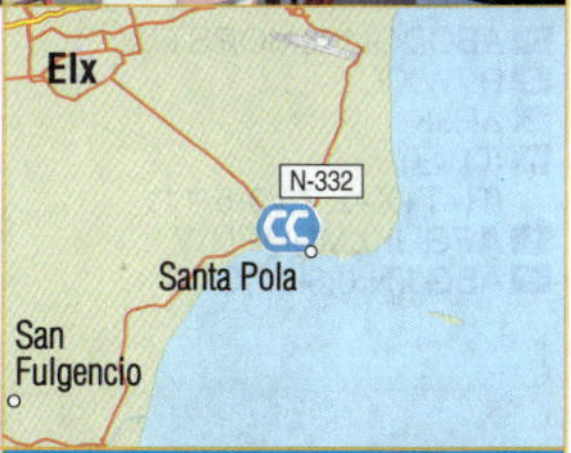

CC € 17 *1/1-7/7 24/8-31/12*

N 38°12'3" W 0°34'13"

Villargordo del Cabriel, E-46317 / Comunidad Valenciana

2715

- Kiko Park Rural
- Ctra Embalse de Contreras km 3
- +34 96-2139082
- FAX +34 96-2139337
- 1/1 - 31/12
- rural@kikopark.com

2ha 76T(70-90m²) 10A CEE

1 BCD**G**IJKLMOPQ
2 DFJLSTUVXY
3 BGHJUW
4 (B+G+Q+R+T+U+X+Y) Z
5 **AB**DFGIJKLMNOPUWXYZ
6 AEG**J**(N 3km)TV

A campsite for peace and quiet. Views of the mountains and close to a large reservoir. Situated in a nature area with opportunities for walking, water sports, rafting, fishing, canoeing, hiking and mountain biking.

A3, exit 255 towards Villargordo. Enter the village, turn right at T junction, campsite clearly signposted there. Another 3 km towards campsite.

CC € 17 *1/1-23/3 29/3-15/7 1/9-31/12*

N 39°33'8" W 1°28'28"

Xeraco, E-46770 / Comunidad Valenciana

2716

- San Vicente
- Avenda de la Mota 24
- +34 962888188
- FAX +34 962888147
- 1/1 - 31/12
- info@campingsanvicente.com

0,5ha 42T(50-60m²) 10A

1 ABCDFIJL
2 AESUXY
3 UY
4 (Q+X+Z)
5 **AB**GIJKLMNOPUWZ
6 ABEGKTV

Small campsite with small fields. Only suitable for tents, small caravans and small motorhomes. Right by the beach. Very easy-going atmosphere.

AP7, exit 59 Favara to N332 dir. Tavernes. On roundabout take CV603 and then CV605. Left after the bridge. Right on roundabout. Campsite is on left.

CC € 15 *1/1-20/3 29/3-19/6 18/9-31/12*

N 39°3'12" W 0°11'53"

Albarracín/Teruel, E-44100 / Aragón

2717

Ciudad de Albarracín**
Camino de Gea s/n
+34 978-710197
4/3 - 27/11, 5/12 - 11/12
campingalbarracin5@hotmail.com

1,5ha 100T(70m²) 10A

1 ABCDGIJKLMOPST
2 RVWXY
3 AHJN
4 (Q)
(R+T+X+Z 20/3-5/11)
5 **A**FGIJKLMNOPUW
6 AEGJ(N 0,8km)OTV

A quiet campsite on the edge of the 'most beautiful city in Spain' (classified historical heritage including Islam) and near an area with prehistoric rock paintings. Abundant fauna and flora. In July and August you pay 1 Euro per person per day in the municipal open air swimming pool.

From Teruel to Albarracín. Follow camping signs in Albarracín .

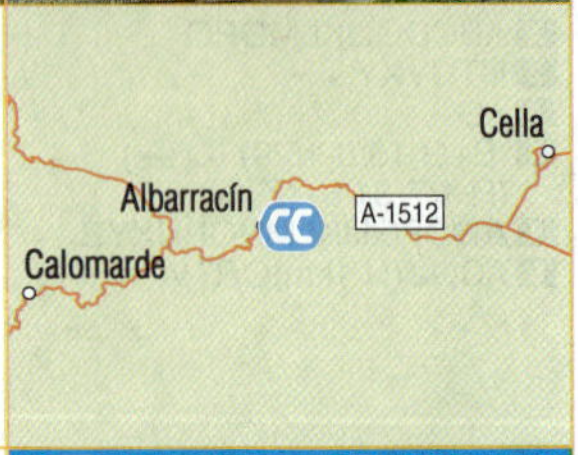

CC € 17 *4/3-23/3 28/3-11/7 28/8-27/11 5/12-10/12*

N 40°24'43'' W 1°25'39''

Alquézar, E-22145 / Aragón

2718

Alquézar
Ctra Barbastro s/n
+34 974-318300
FAX +34 974-318434
1/1 - 31/12
camping@alquezar.com

1,5ha 120T(70-100m²) 10A

1 BCD**G**IJKLMO**P**
2 JKLRVWXY
3 BHJR
4 (**A**+Q+R+T+U+X)
(Y 1/4-30/9) (Z)
5 **AB**CFGIJKLMNOPUWZ
6 CDEGK(N 0,8km)OQTV

A campsite for families and those who love walking, rafting, canoeing, canyoning, escalade (rock climbing), etc. Located in the beautiful Sierra de Guara. ± 1 km from the medieval town of Alquézar with its castle (Christian and Moorish influences). UNESCO World Heritage Site (century-old rock drawings) and typical fauna.

A22 Huesca-Barbastro. Take N240 west of Barbastro direction Barbastro. Then A1232 and A1233 to Alquézar. Follow camping signs.

CC € 17 *1/1-30/6 1/9-31/12*

N 42°9'53'' E 0°0'55''

Alquézar, E-22145 / Aragón

2719

Rio Vero
Puente de Colungo s/n
+34 974-318350
15/3 - 31/10
info@campingriovero.com

3ha 187T(70-100m²) 5A

1 ABCD**G**IJKLMO**P**
2 CJORVWXY
3 AHJ**WX**
4 (Q+S+T+U+V+X+Y+Z)
5 **A**GIJKLMNO**P**UZ
6 CEGJ(N 21km)OTV

A small campsite in a wooded area of the Sierra Ljuera nature reserve and close to the Gvera canyons. Canyoning equipment can be hired at the campsite.

From Barbastro A1233 direction Alquézar. Right A2205 direction Colungo. Follow camping signs.

CC € 15 *15/3-23/3 28/3-6/7 25/8-31/10*

N 42°9'7'' E 0°1'45''

Benasque (Huesca), E-22440 / Aragón

2720

Aneto Cat.1
Ctra Barbastro Francia, km 100
+34 974-551141
FAX +34 974-551663
1/1 - 31/10, 1/12 - 31/12
@ info@campinganeto.com

6ha 200T(40-100m²) 10A

1 ABCDFIJKLMOP
2 CJLRVWXY
3 BHJUW
4 (A)
(C+Q+S+T+U+X+Y
15/6-15/9)Z
5 ABDFGIJKLMNOPUW
6 AEGIJ(N 3,5km)OTV

This family campsite offers relaxation, tranquillity and fresh mountain air. Starting point for various (mountain) walks, also in the rugged countryside. It has a swimming pool. The restaurant is open in the week before Easter and during Holy Week.

From Castejón take the Sos A139 direction Benasque. The campsite is on the left 3 km beyond Benasque.

CC € 17 *1/1-30/6 1/9-30/10 1/12-31/12*

N 42°37'27" E 0°32'39"

Boltaña (Huesca), E-22349 / Aragón

2721

Boltaña
Ctra N260,km 442/
Ctra de Margudgued
+34 974-502347
FAX +34 974-502023
1/1 - 31/12
@ info@campingboltana.com

6ha 204T(75-130m²) 10A CEE

1 ABCDFIJKLMOPST
2 JLRTVWXY
3 BGHJKNOPRUW
4 (A 22/6-31/8)
(B+G 1/6-30/9) (Q+R)
(T+U+X+Y+Z 1/4-30/10)
5 ABDEFGIJKLMNOPUWZ
6 ACDEGIJ(N 1km)ORTUV

This quiet family campsite is located in an area with an agreeable climate in all seasons. An excellent base for trips out to the various National Nature Parks and historic centres in the Pyrenees. It offers a wide variety of activities including the Guara canyons and rock climbing. Excellent restaurant. There is a thermal bath within walking distance of the site.

From Ainsa continue to Boltaña. After ± 7 km take Boltaña exit. Then follow camping signs.

CC € 17 *1/1-19/3 28/3-28/4 2/5-7/7 29/8-31/12*

N 42°25'49" E 0°4'44"

Bonansa (Huesca), E-22486 / Aragón

2722

Camping Baliera Cat.2
N260, km 355,5
+34 974-554016
FAX +34 974-554099
1/12 - 18/12, 26/12 - 30/10
@ info@baliera.com

5ha 173T(80-130m²) 10A

1 ABCDGIJKLMOPS
2 CLRVWXY
3 BGHJNRUVWX
4 (B+G 15/6-25/9) (Q)
(R+V 1/7-31/8)
5 ABCDEFGIJKLMNOPUWZ
6 CEGIK(N 4km)OTUV

Camping Baliera is located in the centre of the Isabena, Benasque, Aran and Boi valleys. It offers access to unusual and beautiful landscapes. You can sample a mix of tradition and culture. Various activities all year: mountain sports, fishing, mushroom collecting in the autumn, skiing.

From Viella N230 direction Pont de Suert. After about 3 km from Vilaller turn right direction Castejón de Sos. After 2.5 km turn left at the forked road. Campsite immediately on the left.

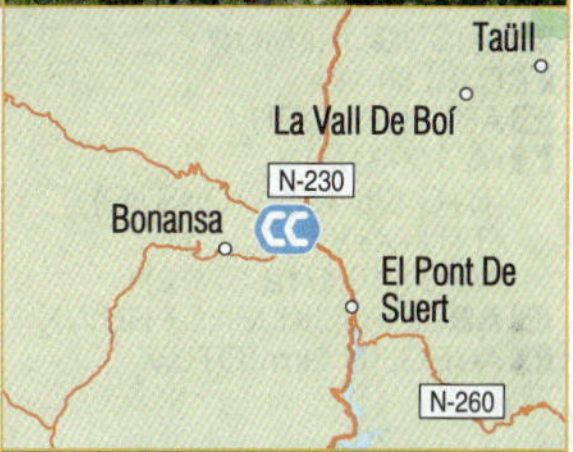

CC € 15 *1/1-15/7 1/9-29/10 1/12-17/12 26/12-31/12 7=6, 10=8, 15=12, 18=14*

N 42°26'22" E 0°41'56"

Bronchales/Teruel, E-44367 / Aragón

2723

Las Corralizas 1727M
Ctra Fuenta del Canto, km 1,5
+34 978-721050
18/3 - 1/11
reservas@lascorralizas.com

8,5ha 112T(70-100m²) 16A

1 ABCDGIJKLMOPST
2 BIKLRVWXY
3 ABGHJU
4 (Q) (T+U+X+Z 1/7-31/8)
5 **AB**DFGIJKLMNOPUW
6 ACEGK(N 1,5km)OSTV

The highest campsite in Spain (altitude 1727m) in the shaded pine woods of the Montes Universales. The village is within walking distance via a woodland path. Pitches are not marked out. Restaurant and bakery service every weekend from Easter.

Motorway A23 Zaragoza-Teruel: exit 144 (Santa Eulalia) or exit 131 (Cella) dir. Bronchales. Drive through centre and then turn right into the forest and follow signs.

CC € 15 18/3-23/3 28/3-15/7 1/9-7/10 12/10-1/11 7=6, 14=11

N 40°30'0" W 1°35'42"

Caspe, E-50700 / Aragón

2724

Lake Caspe Camping***
Ctra N211 km 286,7
+34 976-634174
FAX +34 976-634187
1/3 - 6/11
lakecaspe@lakecaspe.com

10ha 140T(70-140m²) 5-10A

1 ABCD**G**IJKLMOPST
2 DKLNPRTVXY
3 BHJKR**W**Z
4 (B 1/5-30/9) (Q+S+T+U) (Y+Z)
5 **A**EFGIJKLMNOPUW
6 ACEGJ(N 14km)OTUV

Campsite on the Mequinenza Reservoir, ideal for nature and watersports lovers. Kayaks, fishing boats, archery, mountain bikes for rent. Excursions: with guide, kayak and motor boat. Water skiing, windsurfing and sailing courses. Located in lovely Aragón with an agreeable climate. Zaragoza, Lleida and Barcelona are easy to reach.

A2 Lleida-Fraga. After Fraga exit 433, take N211 as far as Caspe. Campsite on right (286,7 km marker).

CC € 17 1/3-20/3 28/3-15/7 1/9-5/11 7=6, 14=11, 21=18, 30=24

N 41°17'38" E 0°3'45"

Gavín, E-22639 / Aragón

2725

Camping Gavín S.L. Cat.1
Ctra N260 km 503
+34 974-485090
FAX +34 974-485017
1/1 - 31/12
info@campinggavin.com

7ha 150T(80m²) 10A

1 ABCD**G**IJKLMO**P**
2 CJKLRVWX
3 ABCHJKL**M**RU
4 (**A** 1/7-31/8) (B+G 5/6-15/9) (Q+S) (T+U+X+Y+Z 1/1-31/10,1/12-31/12)
5 **AB**DEFGIJKLMNOPRUWX
6 ACEGJ(N 2km)OTUV

An attractive terraced campsite, modernly appointed with an excellent restaurant. Beautiful natural surroundings and close to walking and skiing areas and national parks. From a relaxing stroll to a tour lasting several days, wild water recreation, mountain and adventure sports, trips out with a cultural and historical flavour.

From France at Col de Portalet A136 direction Biescas. At Biescas N260 direction Broto (left at the service station). Campsite 3 km on the right.

CC € 17 1/1-10/7 1/9-31/12 7=6

N 42°37'10" W 0°18'12"

La Puebla de Castro, E-22435 / Aragón

2726

Lago Barasona Cat. 1
Ctra Barbastro-Graus/ N123a, km 25
+34 974-545148
1/3 - 10/12
info@lagobarasona.com

30ha 180T(70-120m²) 6A CEE

1 ABCDGIJKLMOPST
2 DJKLMORVWXY
3 BHJKMN**Q**R**VW**Z
4 (B+G 25/5-30/9) **KLN** (Q 1/4-30/10) (R 1/6-30/9) (T 1/5-30/8) (U+V+Y+Z 1/4-15/9)
5 **AB**DEFGIJKLMNOPRUWX
6 ACEG**I**J(N 6km)OTV

A friendly family campsite on several levels. The site has a good restaurant and is a good base for many sights, such as the Guara River gorge (the largest centre for canyoning in Europe); a rich heritage in the footsteps of various cultures.

From Aínsa A138 direction Barbastro. About 8 km before Barbastro turn left towards N123 Benabara/Graus. Take the 123a to Graus at intersection. Campsite 2.4 km on the left. Follow the loop.

CC € 17 *1/3-30/6 1/9-9/12*

N 42°8'32'' E 0°18'51''

La Puebla de Castro (Huesca), E-22435 / Aragón

2727

Bellavista & Subenuix Cat.1
Ctra Barbastro en Benasque
+34 974-545113
1/1 - 31/12
info@hotelcampingbellavista.com

22,5ha 133T(80-100m²) 7,5A

1 ABCD**G**IJKL**P**RS
2 DJKLMRVXY
3 ABHJNRU**WZ**
4 (B+G 15/6-5/9) (Q+R+T) (U 1/1-24/12,26/12-31/12) (V)(X+Y+Z 1/1-24/12,26/12-31/12)
5 **A**DFGIJKLMNOPUWZ
6 EG**I**J(N 6km)OTV

Friendly campsite with lawns by the lake. The best restaurant in the area (according to the Tourist Office). Boats, pedal boats and water skis can be rented. Only at weekends during May and June. Daily in July and August. The area is fascinating with churches, chapels and monasteries next to vineyards. Fishing licence applications only by mail.

From Barbastro to Benasque, campsite on left 6 km before Graus. Take note: take the right hand loop to the site.

CC € 17 *1/1-15/7 1/9-31/12*

N 42°7'48'' E 0°18'36''

La Puebla de Roda, E-22482 / Aragón

2728

Isábena
Ctra Graus a Viella km 27
+34 974-544530
30/3 - 30/11
info@isabena.eu

3ha 85T(100m²) 6A CEE

1 BCD**G**IJKLM**P**S
2 CGLRVXY
3 BHJN**OP**RU**W**
4 (**A** 1/7-15/8) (B 15/5-15/10) **KLN** (Q+T+U+X+Z)
5 **AB**DFGIJKLMNOPUWZ
6 CEGIJ(N 2km)OTV

Welcoming campsite, located in a rough and beautiful mountain area. Walking enthusiasts can enjoy peaceful signposted walks.

From Veilla N230 dir. Lerida, exit Graus (A1605). After 28 km campsite is on right. Or from Graus on the A1605. Site is on left after 28 km.

CC € 17 *30/3-7/7 24/8-30/11*

N 42°18'27'' E 0°32'43''

Labuerda/Ainsa (Huesca), E-22360 / Aragón

2729

Peña Montañesa
Ctra Ainsa-Francia, km 2
+34 974-500032
+34 974-500991
1/1 - 31/12
info@penamontanesa.com

10ha 330T(64-100m²) 6-10A

1 ABCD**F**IJKLMO**P**ST
2 CLRVWXY
3 ABGHJKMNRU**WX**
4 (**A**) (B 20/6-15/9) (F) (G 20/6-15/9) K**N**P (Q+S+T+U+V+X+Y+Z)
5 **AB**DFGIJKMNOPSUWZ
6 ACEG**I**J(N 2km)OQRTV

Something for everyone, including an outdoor swimming pool, heated indoor pool, sauna, jacuzzi, playground, supermarket, bar, restaurant with democratic pricing, multifunctional sportsground, horse riding, squash, canyoning, rafting, good toilet facilities. Close to the National Parks of Ordesa and Monte Perdido.

Ainsa direction French border (Escalona). The campsite is 2 km beyond Ainsa indicated by flags.

CC € 19 *1/1-30/6 1/9-31/12*

N 42°26'6'' E 0°8'7''

Morillo de Tou/Ainsa, E-22395 / Aragón

2730

Morillo de Tou
Ctra A138 Barbastro-Ainsa, km 41,8
+34 974-500793
+34 974-500529
1/3 - 31/12
info@morillodetou.com

54T(60-70m²) 6A

1 ABCD**G**IJKLMOPS
2 DGJRTVWXY
3 BDGHJNRU**W**
4 (**A**) (B 24/6-7/9) (Q) (R 1/7-31/8) (T+U+X+Y+Z)
5 **A**GIJKLMNOPUWX
6 DEGK(N 4km)TV

The campsite is located in the Morillo de Tou holiday centre, a reconstructed village in the Aragon Pyrenees and close to national parks and centres full of art, culture and history.

Campsite on the A138 between Barbastro and Ainsa in Morillo de Tou.

CC € 17 *1/3-7/7 25/8-31/12* *7=6, 14=11*

N 42°22'31'' E 0°9'11''

Nuévalos (Zaragoza), E-50210 / Aragón

2731

Lago Resort***
Ctra Alhama de Aragón-Nuevalos,s/n
+34 976-849038
18/2 - 10/12
lagoresort@gmail.com

10ha 120T(70-90m²) 6A

1 ABCDGIJKLMOP
2 JLTVXY
3 ABCHJKRU
4 (**A**) (B 15/6-10/9) (Q+R+T+U+V+X+Z)
5 **A**FGIJKLMNOPUWZ
6 ACEGJ(N 0,4km)OTV

A terraced campsite close to the Monasterio de Piedra (1194) and the nature park and thermal baths of Jaraba and Alhama. Near the Tranquera reservoir (water sports recreation).

From Calatayud to Nuevalos. Follow camping signs in Nuevalos. Campsite on the left of the road to Alhama opposite the lake.

CC € 17 *18/2-23/3 28/3-12/7 29/8-5/12*

N 41°13'5'' W 1°47'32''

Vera de Moncayo, E-50580 / Aragón

iD **2732**

Veruela Moncayo
Ctra Vera a Veruela s/n.
+34 976-649034
25/3 - 28/3, 27/5 - 12/10
campingveruelamoncayo@gmail.com

1,8ha 80**T**(60-100m²) 6A

1 ABCD**G**IJKLMOP
2 RVWX
3 AHJR
4 (Q+R+T+U+X+Y+Z)
5 **A**GIKMNOPUW
6 EGJ(N 0,15km)TUV

Basic campsite with a good restaurant on the edge of the village and at 500m from the Monasterio de Veruela (13th century). Located on the Parque Natural de Moncayo and at 150m from the centre (shops, municipal outdoor swimming pool). Nature reserve for cycling and walking. Zaragoza is an hour's drive away.

Take the AP68 or the N232 between Zaragoza and Tudela. Then follow the N122 to Vera de Moncayo (direction Tarazona). Then follow the signs.

CC € 15 *25/3-28/3 27/5-15/7 1/9-11/10*

N 41°49'9" W 1°41'32"

Haro, E-26200 / La Rioja

iD **2733**

De Haro Cat.2
Avenida de Miranda 1
+34 941-312737
FAX +34 941-312068
30/1 - 8/12
campingdeharo@fer.es

5ha 125**T**(72-80m²) 6A

1 ABCD**G**IJKLMOP
2 CFKLRTVWXY
3 BHJNRU**W**
4 (B+G 1/6-15/9) (Q+R)
(T+X+Z 1/6-15/9)
5 **AB**DFGIJKLMNOPUWZ
6 CEGJ**K**(N 0,6km)OTV

The lovely small town of Haro (capital of the Rioja Alta wine region) is within walking distance. Also within walking distance is the bus stop and railway station. The annual Haro wine festival (end of June) is famous throughout the whole of Spain.

N232 Logroño-Miranda de Ebro. Follow the camping signs in Haro.

CC € 19 *30/1-30/6 1/9-8/12 7=6, 14=11*

N 42°34'41" W 2°51'16"

Navarrete, E-26370 / La Rioja

iD **2734**

Navarrete Cat.1
Ctra de Entrena s/n
+34 941-440169
15/1 - 18/12
campingnavarrete@fer.es

3ha 50**T**(30-70m²) 6A

1 ACDGIJKLMOPST
2 FKLRVX
3 B**F**MNRU
4 (**A** 1/8-31/8)
(B+G 15/6-15/9)
(Q+R+T+U+X+Z)
5 **AB**DFGIJKLMNOPUWZ
6 ACEGJ(N 1,5km)ORTV

A good campsite in the Rioja region, 10 km from Logroño. A base for trips out in the area, but also suitable as a stopover campsite. Naturally a visit to one of the many Rioja bodegas is 'compulsory'. A very well maintained campsite with top class toilet facilities.

From Miranda to Logroño via the N232, exit Navarrete. The campsite is clearly signposted. Located just outside the village, on the N120.

CC € 17 *15/1-22/3 28/3-15/7 1/9-18/12 7=6, 14=11*

N 42°24'58" W 2°33'6"

Santo Domingo de la Calzada, E-26257 / La Rioja

iD 2735

Bañares****
Ctra N120, km 42,2
+34 941-340131
1/1 - 31/12
info@campingbanares.es

20ha 250T(70m²) 5-10A

1 ABCDGIJKLMNO**P**S
2 FKLRTVWXY
3 B**F**GJ**M**NRU
4 (**A** 1/7-31/8)
(B+G 24/6-11/9)
(Q+S+T+U+X+Y+Z)
5 **AB**DFGIJKLMNOPUWXYZ
6 CDEGH**I**J(N 3km)ORTV

A large campsite with many permanent pitches, a lovely swimming pool and plenty of play equipment. Located near the beautiful village of Santo Domingo de la Calzada on the pilgrims route to Santiago.

Campsite located on N120 at 42.2 km marker near Santo Domingo de la Calzada.

CC € 19 *1/1-30/6 1/9-31/12 7=6*

N 42°26'28'' W 2°54'55''

Etxarri Aranatz, E-31820 / Navarra

iD 2736

Camping Etxarri S.L.
+34 948-460537
+34 948-461509
1/3 - 12/10
info@campingetxarri.com

2,3ha 100T(50-80m²) 6A

1 AC**G**IJKLMOPQ
2 BCFLRSVWXY
3 BHJMNRSU
4 (B+G 1/6-15/9)
(Q+R+T+U+V+X+Y+Z)
5 **A**EFGIJKLMNOPUWXYZ
6 AEG**I**K(N 2km)OTV

A lovely campsite located in the natural area of the Urbasa and Aralar ranges. It has a good swimming pool (open from June). A perfect starting point for visiting the towns of Pamplona, Logrono, Vitoria, San Sebastian and other historical places.

AP10 Pamplona-Victoria, exit Etxarri/Aranatz. Campsite signposted in the village.

CC € 19 *1/3-3/7 28/8-12/10 7=6, 14=11*

N 42°54'46'' W 2°4'46''

Eusa/Oricain/Pamplona, E-31194 / Navarra

iD 2737

Ezcaba Cat.1
Ctra a Francia, km 2,5
+34 948-330315
+34 948-331316
1/1 - 31/12
info@campingezcaba.com

4ha 539T(40-70m²) 10A

1 AC**G**IJKLMO**P**Q
2 CFKLRTVWXY
3 B**F**HJ**W**
4 (B+G 15/6-15/9) (Q)
(R 15/6-15/9)
(T+U+X 15/4-12/10) (Z)
5 **AB**EFGIJKLMNOPUWXZ
6 EG**IK**(N 3km)OTV

Peacefully located campsite with a swimming pool. Mountain bikes can be rented on the campsite for visiting Pamplona (9 km away) among other places. Positioned on the pilgrimage route to Santiago de Compostela.

N121A from Irua to Pamplona. Turn right before Oricain. Campsite signposted.

CC € 19 *1/1-30/6 1/9-31/12 7=6, 14=12, 21=18, 30=25*

N 42°51'26'' W 1°37'25''

Mendigorria, E-31150 / Navarra

2738

Errota - El Molino Cat.1
Ctra Larraga s/n
+34 948-340604
+34 948-340082
1/2 - 15/12
info@campingelmolino.com

10ha 150**T**(60-80m²) 6A

1 ACDGIJKLMOPQ
2 CKLRVWXY
3 BGHJK**M**N**Q**RSUW
4 (**A** 1/7-31/8) (B 1/6-15/9) (**E** 1/2-1/6,1/10-15/12) (G 1/6-15/9) JK (Q+R+T+U+V+X+Y) (Z 15/6-15/9)
5 **AB**FGIJKLMNOPQRSTUW YZ
6 ACEGH**I**KM(N 5km)OTUV

A lovely campsite about 25 km from Pamplona. Conveniently located for visits to Logrono and San Sebastian. The pilgrims' route to Santiago passes nearby through the lovely village of Puente La Reina. Indoor heated winter pool and squash and tennis on the campsite. The area invites you to go walking, mountain biking or canoeing and to take cultural trips out.

A12 Pamplona-Logroño, exit 23 Mendigorria, west of the city centre (ca. 0,5 km). Signposted from the A12.

CC € 19 *1/2-30/6 1/9-15/12 7=6, 14=11*

N 42°37'28'' W 1°50'35''

Villafranca, E-31330 / Navarra

2739

Bardenas
Ctra NA-660 PK 13.4
+34 948-846191
1/1 - 31/12
info@campingbardenas.com

3ha 65**T**(70-105m²) 12A

1 ABCD**G**IJKLMOPR
2 FKLRVWX
3 BGHJMNRUV
4 (**A**) (B 15/6-15/9) (Q) (R 1/4-31/10) (T+U+X+Y+Z)
5 **A**FGIJKLMNOPUWXYZ
6 ACEGJ(N 1,5km)OTV

A new campsite with excellent toilet facilities. Bardenas nature reserve (walking, cycling) is 18 km away. Bodegas, gastronomy and plenty of culture in the area, including the castles of Olite and Marcilla.

From AP15 Pamplona-Zaragoza, take exit 29. Then towards Villafranca, campsite 1500m south of Villafranca.

CC € 19 *1/1-19/3 28/3-15/7 1/9-31/12 7=6, 14=12*

N 42°15'48'' W 1°44'19''

Itziar, E-20829 / Pais Vasco

2740

Itxaspe Cat.1
CN634, km 38,2
+34 943-199377
+34 943-199081
18/3 - 25/9
info@campingitxaspe.com

1,9ha 110**T**(35-100m²) 6A

1 ABCDGIJLPQ
2 FJKLOQRTVWXY
3 BHJNRUW
4 (**A** 1/7-31/8) (B 1/6-15/9) (Q+S+T+U+X+Y+Z)
5 **AB**FGIJKLMNOPUWXYZ
6 ACEGJ(N 2km)OTV

Situated in beautiful surroundings with lovely views of the sea, in a protected nature reserve of great ecological and biological value. About 8 km from the magnificent beaches at Deba and Zumaia. Bilbao (Guggenheim museum) is 50 min by car, San Sebastian just 30 min. Plenty of opportunities for walking and trips out.

N634 Zumia direction Deba. At km 37,5 marker, campsite signposted on the right. Via A8 exit 54, then direction Zumaia, left after 100m, site signposted.

CC € 19 *18/3-30/6 1/9-25/9*

N 43°16'42'' W 2°19'46''

Orio, E-20810 / Pais Vasco

2741

Camping Orio/Orio Kanpina Cat. 1
Playa de Orio
+34 943-834801
1/3 - 1/11
info@oriokanpina.com

3,2ha 122T(60-80m²) 10A

1 ABCDEIJKLMOPQ
2 AEFKLMRVWX
3 BFHRWY
4 (B+G 15/6-15/9) (Q+S+T+U+V+X+Y+Z)
5 ABEGIJKLMNOPUWZ
6 CEGHK(N 1km)ORTV

A family campsite 200m from the sea. It has a sandy beach and you can swim in the sea. There is a harbour for pleasure craft 50m from the campsite. The site has a swimming pool and a good restaurant. Located 20 km from San Sebastian.

On the A8 San Sebastian-Bilbao take the Orio exit. In the village follow beach road, campsite signposted.

CC €17 1/3-13/6 1/9-1/11

N 43°17'12'' W 2°7'34''

San Sebastián, E-20008 / Pais Vasco

2742

Igueldo Cat.1
P. Padre Orkolaga 69
+34 943-214502
FAX +34 943-280411
1/1 - 31/12
info@campingigueldo.com

5ha 236T(20-70m²) 6-10A

1 ACDGIJKLMOPQ
2 FGJKLRTVWXY
3 BFHJR
4 (Q+R+T+U+X+Y+Z)
5 ABEFGIJKLMNOPUWXYZ
6 ACEGHIK(N 1,5km)ORTV

Large, well-maintained campsite, excellent toilet facilities. Bus to San Sebastián stops in front of the campsite. Campsite has a welcoming bar and an excellent restaurant. Beautiful view of the surroundings and the sea.

From border follow A8. Exit Ondarreta, dir. San Sebastián centre. On coast follow Monte Igueldo to campsite. Attention: SatNav chooses route unsuitable for caravans and motorhomes. Ignore this route and follow campsite signs.

CC €17 1/1-30/6 15/9-31/12 7=6

N 43°18'48'' W 2°1'45''

Villanañe, E-01425 / Pais Vasco

2743

Angosto
Ctra. Villanane - Angosto No. 2
+34 945-353271
26/2 - 11/12
info@camping-angosto.com

1,8ha 68T(70-80m²) 6A

1 ABCDGIJKLOPQ
2 CGLRWXY
3 AHIJRUWX
4 (E 1/4-1/11) N (Q+R+T+U+V+X+Y+Z)
5 ABDFGIJKLMNOPQRUWZ
6 BCEGHIJ(N 3km)OTV

Quiet family campsite close to two natural parks, ideal for walkers and mountain bikers. There is a good restaurant. Bilbao, Vitoria and the Rioja are close by.

From Bilbao follow N625 to exit Villanañe. Site is then signposted.

CC €17 4/4-30/6 5/9-31/10

N 42°50'32'' W 3°4'8''

Zarautz, E-20800 / Pais Vasco

2744

Gran Camping Zarautz Cat.2
Monte Talai-Mendi
+34 943-831238
FAX +34 943-132486
1/1 - 31/12
info@grancampingzarautz.com

5ha 440**T**(60-90m²) 6-10A

1 ABCDGIJKLMO**P**Q
2 FJKLRTVWXY
3 A**F**H
4 (Q+S+T+U+V+Y+Z)
5 **AB**DFGIJKLMNOPUWZ
6 ACDEG**I**J(N 1,5km)ORTV

A beautifully located campsite with lovely views of Zarautz Bay. An ideal starting point for trips out to San Sebastian, Bilbao and Pamplona. Many opportunities for walking and mountain biking in the area.

Coming from France take A8 San Sebastian-Bilbao, exit 38 Zarautz. Straight ahead at first roundabout, campsite signposted.

CC € 17 *1/1-30/6 15/9-31/12 7=6*

N 43°17'22'' W 2°8'45''

Zumaia, E-20750 / Pais Vasco

2745

Camping & Bungalows Zumaia
Basusta bidea, 16
+34 943-860475
15/1 - 15/12
info@campingzumaia.com

2,2ha 100**T**(35-70m²) 10A

1 ABCD**G**IJKLMO**P**Q
2 FGJRSUVW
3 AU
4 (B+G 15/6-15/9)
(Q+R+T+U+X+Z)
5 **AB**EFGIJKLMNOPUWXZ
6 CEGJ**K**(N 1,5km)TV

New campsite on the edge of the beautiful coastal town of Zumaia. Many options for walking nearby, good connection by bus and train to Zarautz and San Sebastián.

From N634, on edge of Zumaia, follow dir. station. Site is then signposted.

CC € 17 *15/1-18/3 4/4-15/6 4/9-15/12*

N 43°17'23'' W 2°14'51''

Islares, E-39798 / Cantabria

2746

Playa Arenillas Cat.2
Cu 634 km 156
FAX +34 942-863152
24/3 - 30/9
luis.cueva62@gmail.com

1,7ha 120**T**(50-70m²) 6A

1 ABCDEIJKLMOPQ
2 AEFGKLRVWX
3 BHJKNRWY
4 (Q+R+T+U+X+Y+Z)
5 **AB**FGIJKLMOPUWZ
6 AEG**K**(N 7km)OTV

A friendly and appropriate welcome. Close to a sandy beach. 100m from the bus to Bilbao. Watersports opportunities. Ideal for enjoyable trips out into the surroundings. All information about Bilbao (35 km away) is available at the campsite.

A8 Bilbao to Santander exit 156 in the direction of Islares. Signposted here.

CC € 17 *24/3-7/7 24/8-30/9*

N 43°24'13'' W 3°18'37''

Laredo, E-39770 / Cantabria

2747

Camping Laredo Cat.2
Camino el Regaton 2
+34 942-605035
FAX +34 942-613180
1/5 - 14/9
info@campinglaredo.com

5,5ha 315T(60-90m²) 6-10A

1 ABCDEIJKLMOPQ
2 AEFGLRVWXY
3 ABH**OP**RU**W**
4 (B+G 1/7-31/8) (Q+S+T+X+Z)
5 **AB**FGIJKLMNOPUWZ
6 ACEGJ(N 3km)ORTV

A large campsite with good clean toilet facilities. 400m from a sandy beach. Opportunities for horse riding within 100m. Bilbao and Santander are both about 50 km from the campsite.

A8 from Bilbao to Santander. Take the second exit towards Laredo and drive in the direction of the hospital. Signposted after 1 km.

CC € 15 *1/5-30/6 1/9-14/9*

N 43°24'51'' W 3°26'53''

Potes, E-39570 / Cantabria

2748

La Viorna Cat.1
Car. Santo Toribio
FAX +34 942-732021
1/4 - 1/11
info@campinglaviorna.com

1,9ha 110T(70m²) 6A

1 ABCDFIJKLO**PQ**
2 JKRVXY
3 ABGHJ
4 (A 1/7-15/9) (B+G 25/5-15/10) (Q+R+X) (Y 1/7-20/9) (Z)
5 **AB**EFGIJKLMNOPUW
6 ACEGJ(N 1km)ORTV

Lovely campsite with excellent amenities. The pitches at this terraced campsite have grass and shade. Large swimming pool. Most suitable as starting point for various walks and excursions. Plenty of information about the region available at the reception. Excellent restaurant, appetizing menus of the day. You can be assured of a pleasant stay. Magnificent views of the mountain peaks of the Picos.

1 km past Potes, direction Fuente Dé, turn left to Santo Toribio.

CC € 17 *1/4-30/6 1/9-1/11*

N 43°9'16'' W 4°38'37''

Potes/Turieno, E-39570 / Cantabria

2749

La Isla-Picos de Europa Cat.2
Ctra Potes-Fuente Dé km 2
FAX +34 942-730896
1/4 - 15/10
campinglaislapicosdeeuropa@gmail.com

1,5ha 140T(60-70m²) 6A

1 ABCDGIJKLMO**P**ST
2 CGRVWXY
3 BHJN**P**RX
4 (A) (B 1/6-30/9) (Q+R+T+U+X+Z)
5 **AB**GIJKLMOPUWZ
6 AEGK(N 2km)OTV

This beautiful campsite 2500m from Potes is located on the Rio de Deva River. The grassy field has plenty of shade from the countless fruit trees. Lively restaurant and terrace. Excellent climate at the foot of the majestic Picos de Europa. Departure point for various excursions, walks and mountain sports. Plenty of information at the reception. Excellent toilet facilities. You are most welcome here.

Past Potes direction Fuente Dé. Turn right after about 2.5 km.

CC € 15 *1/4-15/7 1/9-15/10*

N 43°9'27'' W 4°39'22''

Ruiloba, E-39527 / Cantabria

2750

Camping El Helguero
Barrio de la Iglesia
+34 942-722124
FAX +34 942-721020
1/4 - 30/9
@ reservas@campingelhelguero.com

6,5ha 240**T**(70-120m²) 6A

1 BCDGIJKLMO**PQ**
2 FGJRVWXY
3 BHJR
4 (B+G+Q+S+T+U+X+Y+Z)
5 **AB**DFGIJKLMNOPUW
6 EG**K**(N 3km)OTV

A conveniently located campsite for visits to Comillas and Santillana del Mar. Close to the Picos de Europa National Park. Lively terrace and restaurant.

E70/A8, exit 249 dir. Comillas. After 7 km take the CA 359 dir. Ruiloba. Through La Iglesia village and turn right onto CA 358. Campsite 300 metres on the right.

CC € 15 *1/4-15/7 1/9-30/9*

N 43°22'59'' W 4°14'47''

S. Vicente de la Barquera, E-39540 / Cantabria

2751

Caravaning Oyambre Cat.1
Finca Peña Gerra
+34 942-711461
FAX +34 942-711530
4/3 - 30/10
@ camping@oyambre.com

4ha 128**T**(20-120m²) 10A

1 ABCDGIJKLMOPQ
2 AGJLRVWX
3 BF**N**
4 (B+G 1/4-28/9)
(Q+R+T+U+X+Y)
5 **AB**FGIJKMNOPUWZ
6 EGK(N 5km)OTV

A luxury campsite in one of the nature parks of Cantabria. You can go on lovely excursions from the campsite in all weather conditions. Culture (Gaudi in Comillas), nature (dunes, sea, Picos de Europa), history (caves of Altamira in Santillana del Mar).

E70/A8 Santander-Oviedo, exit km post 264 S. Vicente de la Barquera, then N634 for 3 km to Comillas exit on the Ctra La Revilla-Comillas (CA 131) between km posts 27 and 28.

CC € 19 *4/3-30/6 1/9-30/10*

N 43°23'7'' W 4°20'18''

Barreiros, E-27792 / Galicia

2752

Gaivota Camping Cat.2
Playa de Barreiros
+34 982-124451
21/3 - 15/10
@ campinggaivota@gmail.com

1ha 70**T**(50-70m²) 10A

1 AFIJLPST
2 AEFRVWXY
3 ABKWY
4 (Q+R 18/4-30/9) (Z)
5 **AB**FGIJKMNOPUW
6 CEGIK(N 1km)OTV

Attractive campsite with a restaurant built in traditional Gallego style. Situated right by the sea. Family atmosphere.

In Barreiros on the N634 km 567 between Ribadeo and Foz. The campsite is signposted.

CC € 17 *21/3-8/7 25/8-15/10* 7=6, 14=12

N 43°33'44'' W 7°12'28''

Louro, E-15291 / Galicia

2753

A' Vouga
Ctra Mouros-Finisterre, km 3
+34 981-826115
1/3 - 15/11
info@avouga.com

1,5ha 70T 10A

1 ACDGIJLPST
2 AEGOQRVWX
3 HWY
4 (A+Q+R+U+X+Y) Z
5 **AB**IJKMNOPUWX
6 CEGIK(N 0,5km)TV

A small, level campsite on the beach. Easy entrance 500m from the village centre. Bus stop in front of the campsite, which gets you to Santiago in 45 minutes. Very spacious, excellent and pleasant restaurant with typical Galician dishes and panoramic views of the sea. Dolphins can be seen from the terrace. Motorbike riders welcome.

Campsite on the Santiago-Noia-Mouros-Louro road. 3 km beyond Mouros. Well signposted.

CC € 17 1/3-2/6 18/7-31/7 1/9-15/11 10=8

N 42°45'39" W 9°3'44"

Mougas/Oia, E-36309 / Galicia

2754

O Muiño Cat.1
C550 km 158
+34 986-361600
+34 986-361620
18/3 - 2/10
info@campingmuino.com

2,2ha 65T(50-80m²) 5A CEE

1 ACDFIJL**P**Q
2 EFGJLQRVW
3 ABGHJ**M**NUWY
4 (A 1/7-31/8)
(B+G 15/6-30/9)
(Q 18/4-25/4,15/6-30/9)
(S 20/6-15/9)
(T+U+W+X+Y 1/6-15/9) Z
5 **A**EFGIJKLMNOPTUWX
6 CEGK(N 8km)ORTV

A really beautiful, well run, level campsite by the sea with a lovely swimming pool. Hardly ever busy and every comfort is provided. The campsite is only open at the weekend (including Friday) from 1/10 to 28/3.

C550 Baiona-La Guardia as far as km-marker 26. Motorway Vigo-Baiona-a, Guardia. Campsite well signposted.

CC € 19 19/3-10/7 1/9-2/10

N 42°3'50" W 8°53'29"

Portonovo/Sanxenxo, E-36960 / Galicia

2755

Paxariña Cat.2
C550 km 2
+34 986-723055
+34 986-721356
17/3 - 15/10
info@campingpaxarinas.com

2ha 250T(60-80m²) 10A

1 ACFIJLPST
2 AEFGIJQRVX
3 AKRWY
4 (Q+S)
(T+U+X 1/6-25/10) Z
5 **AB**FGIJKLMNOPUV
6 CDEGK(N 1,5km)OTV

A beautifully located campsite on two large bays with beautiful sandy beaches, easily accessible for motorhomes. Reaches down to the sea with all amenities at the hotel complex. A convenient starting point for visits in the area and the special bathing resort Sanxenxo.

Hotel and campsite complex face the sea. (C550). The entrance is on the bend. Clearly signposted.

CC € 17 20/3-30/6 1/9-15/10 8=7, 14=12

N 42°23'32" W 8°50'39"

Ribeira, E-15993 / Galicia

2756

Ria de Arosa 2 Rural
Balteiro-Oleiros
+34 981-865911
FAX +34 981-865555
1/1 - 31/12
@ rural@campingriadearosa.com

10ha 245T(60-90m²) 10A

1 ABCD**G**IJLMPQ
2 BCFJRVXY
3 BHJKMNRU
4 (B+H 15/5-30/9) (Q ⊶)
(S 15/6-15/9)
(T+U+X+Y ⊶) Z
5 **AB**FGIJKLMNOPUWX
6 ACDEG**K**(N 8km)OTV

Close to the Corubedo Nature Park. Lovely views over the Ria de Arosa. Environmentally aware site (ISO norm) and adapted for the disabled. 8 km from the autovia (free) and just 35 minutes from Santiago de Compostella.

Motorway Santiago-Padrón. Freeway Padrón-Ribeira, exit Ribeira. Well signposted.

CC € 19 1/1-15/7 1/9-31/12 5=3, 7=4

N 42°37'15" W 8°59'14"

Valdoviño, E-15552 / Galicia

2757

Valdoviño Cat.1
Ferrol-Cedeira km 13
+34 981-487076
21/3 - 28/3, 15/4 - 15/10
@ campingvaldovino@yahoo.es

1,7ha 80T(60-80m²) 15A

1 AFIJLPQ
2 AEGJRVWXY
3 AKNRWY
4 (Q 1/6-30/9) (S 15/6-30/9)
(U+V+X+Y 5/5-10/10)
(Z ⊶)
5 **AB**FGIJKLMNOPUWZ
6 EG**K**(N 0,7km)ORTV

This quiet campsite has well maintained toilet facilities and is within walking distance of a beautiful bay; surfers are quite in their element here. Restaurant serves traditional, tasty dishes.

A9, exit 34 (8 km). Valdovino is located on the C646 Ferrol-Ortiguera coast road. The site is well signposted.

CC € 17 21/3-28/3 15/4-15/7 1/9-15/10 7=6, 10=8

N 43°36'46" W 8°8'57"

Avin, E-33556 / Asturias

2758

Picos de Europa Cat.2
Carratera Cangas, km 16
+34 985-844070
1/1 - 31/12
@ info@picos-europa.com

4ha 150T(30-100m²) 6A

1 BCDFIJKLMO**P**Q
2 CGJRVWXY
3 AHJ
4 (A+B+G 1/7-31/8)
(Q+S+U+X+Y+Z ⊶)
5 **AB**FGIJKMOPUWZ
6 EGJ(N 2km)ORTV

The campsite is located on the northern side of the Picos de Europa. Include a visit to the pilgrimage centre of Covadonga with its high lakes or follow the course of the River Cares. Centrally located for the sea and mountains. Open all year.

A8-E70 exit 306 direction Naves. Then direction Posada A263. Then A5-115 to end. Then follow camping signs.

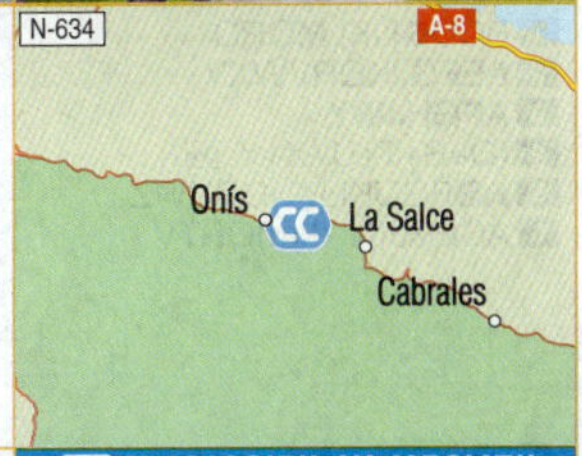

CC € 17 1/1-15/7 1/9-31/12

N 43°20'5" W 4°56'47"

Caravia/Prado, E-33344 / Asturias

2759

Arenal de Moris Cat.1
El Ponton
+34 985-853097
FAX +34 985-853137
23/3 - 15/9
@ camoris@desdeasturias.com

6ha 260**T**(50-150m²) 5A

1 ABCD**G**IJKLMO**P**Q
2 AEFIJORTVW
3 BMR**W**Y
4 (B+Q+S+T+U+W 4/6-15/9) (X 1/6-15/9) Z
5 **AB**GIKMOPUWXY
6 DEGJ(N 6km)OTV

An attractive, spacious campsite 200m from the sea. Swimming pool and tennis court. The restaurant is also open in June and September. Great views of the sea and mountains from the lovely terrace. This coast is known for its many fossil discoveries and original dinosaur tracks. Go back in time millions of years in the new Jurassic Museum in Colunga (10 km).

E70/A8 Santander-Oviedo. Exit 330. Direction Caravia, then N632 between 16 and 15 km posts direction Playa.

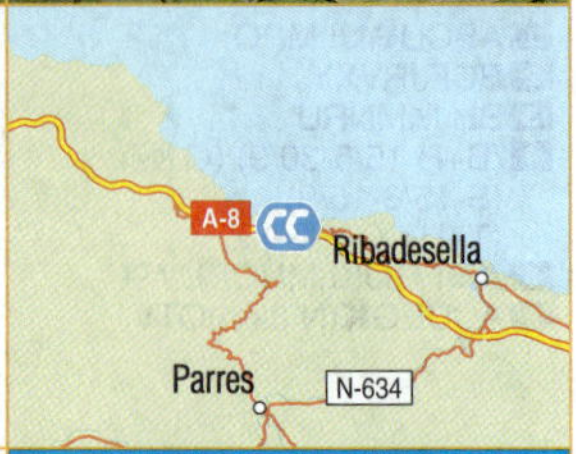

CC € 19 *23/3-30/6 1/9-15/9*

N 43°28'22'' W 5°10'59''

Cudillero, E-33154 / Asturias

2760

Cudillero Cat.2
Playa de Aguilar
+34 985-590663
18/3 - 27/3, 30/4 - 15/9
@ info@campingcudillero.com

2ha 141**T**(30-80m²) 6A CEE

1 AB**F**IJKLMO**P**RS
2 FRVWXY
3 BR
4 (B+G 15/6-6/9) (Q+R 1/5-7/9) (X+Z 26/6-28/8)
5 **AB**EFGIJKLMNOPUW
6 CEG**K**(N 2km)OTV

This well cared for and flower filled campsite is located 1 km from the sea. Lovely sandy beach, and a picturesque fishing village renowned for its authentic fish restaurants. Well worth a visit. The campsite has a lovely swimming pool with deckchairs. Nice level pitches. Excellent toilet facilities.

Motorway A8, exit 425 Muros de Nalon, then 3rd exit on roundabout N632. After 3 km turn right towards El Pito Cudillero. Follow camping signs (AS-317).

CC € 17 *18/3-27/3 30/4-10/7 27/8-15/9*

N 43°33'15'' W 6°7'45''

Llanes/Vidiago, E-33597 / Asturias

2761

La Paz Cat.1
Playa de Vidiago
+34 985-411012
18/3 - 12/10
@ delfin@campinglapaz.com

1,1ha 432**T**(40-90m²) 15A

1 BCD**G**IJKLMOPQ
2 AEFGJKQRVWXY
3 A**F**GHJ**WY**
4 (Q+S+T+U+X+Y)
5 **AB**FGIJKLMNOPUWZ
6 ACEGJ(N 7km)ORTV

A terraced site with fine views of the sea. Picos de Europa (30 mins). Caravans will be towed to and from the pitch by 4WD. Not much shade on the side facing the sea. Enjoy a beautiful sunset in the campsite's restaurant. Due to the big difference in high and low tides you have wonderful wide beaches.

Motorway A8 exit 285, then from Ovieda roundabout dir. N634 Unguera, 2nd roundabout Playa de Vidiago from Santander exit Playa de Vidiago, camping.

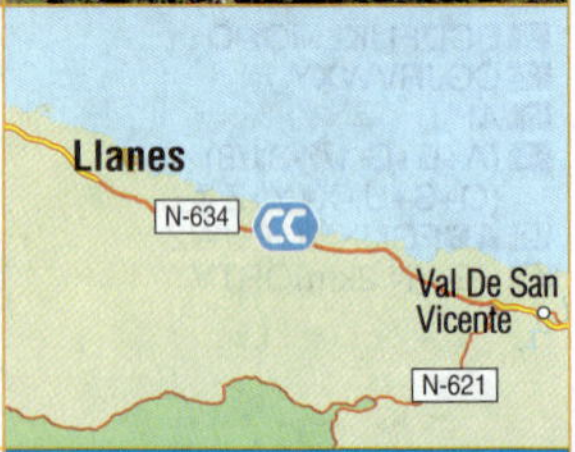

CC € 19 *18/3-30/6 1/9-12/10*

N 43°23'59'' W 4°39'11''

Ribadedeva, E-33590 / Asturias

iD 2762

Camping Colombres Cat.1
Ctra El Peral a Noriega, km 1
+34 985-412244
18/3 - 25/9
info@campingcolombres.com

22ha 89**T**(86-100m²) 6A

1 ABCDGIJKLMOPST
2 FKLRVWX
3 AHJNR
4 (B 18/4-12/9) (G 18/4-14/9)
(Q+R)
(U+X+Y 20/6-12/9) Z
5 **AB**FGIJKLMNOPUWX
6 CEGJ(N 3km)OTV

A campsite with completely renovated amenities. Panoramic views of the Picos de Europa mountain range. Spacious pitches with plenty of vegetation. The enthusiastic owners will do all they can to make your holiday a success. Beautiful, new swimming pool. Also new: special room for children to play and be creative.

E70/A8 Santander-Ovièdo exit 277 direction El Peral N634. Right at petrol station towards Norièga. Follow campsite signs.

CC € 17 *18/3-7/7 24/8-25/9*

N 43°22'31" W 4°33'51"

Ribadesella, E-33560 / Asturias

2763

Ribadesella Cat.1
Ctra de C. Sebreño
+34 985-857721
FAX +34 985-858293
18/3 - 24/9
info@camping-ribadesella.com

4ha 200**T**(40-120m²) 10A CEE

1 BCDGIJKLMO**P**Q
2 FJKLRVXY
3 BGHJ**M**N**O**QRV
4 (B 15/5-20/9) (E)
(G 15/5-20/9) KP
(Q 16/4-18/9) (S)
(T+X+Y+Z 19/3-27/3,
18/6-18/9)
5 **AB**EFGIJKMNOPUWZ
6 ACEGH**I**K(N 0,5km)ORTV

High above the charming town of Ribadesella. A natural campsite with a pleasant restaurant and a large covered terrace offering views of the Picos de Europa mountains. New indoor swimming pool. Enjoy a snack and a drink in the stylish new lounge with TV and panoramic views.

From E70/A8 Santander-Oviedo, exit 326 direction Pando. Turn left past Pando on the AS341. Campsite signposted 1.5 km further on. Key in ctra de Sebreño into SatNav.

CC € 19 *18/3-23/3 27/3-9/7 29/8-24/9*

N 43°27'42" W 5°5'13"

Abejar, E-42146 / Castilla y León

iD 2764

Urbion
Ctra Soria-Burgos, N234
+34 646-243349
FAX +34 975-090330
18/3 - 2/11
info@campingurbion.com

15ha 500**T**(120m²) 10A

1 ACD**G**IJKLMO**P**
2 BDIKLMRXY
3 BHJMNRU**W**
4 (B+G 20/6-31/8)
(Q+R+T+U 20/6-6/9)
(X+Y+Z 5/6-4/9)
5 **A**DFGIJKLMNOPUWZ
6 CEGJ(N 4km)OTV

A spacious campsite for a wonderful, relaxing stay in beautiful natural surroundings. The campsite has good amenities: bar-restaurant, tennis court, football pitch, swimming pool, supermarket etc. The campsite is located close to a recreational area where you can sunbathe or enjoy watersports. The surroundings are rich in art, history, flora and fauna.

From Soria take the N234 direction Burgos, in Abejar towards Molinos on the CL117, campsite 4 km on the right.

CC € 17 *4/4-10/7 1/9-2/11 7=6*

N 41°50'8" W 2°47'13"

Burgos, E-09193 / Castilla y León

2765

Fuentes Blancas Cat.1
Cartuja Miraflores
+34 947-486016
1/1 - 31/12
info@campingburgos.com

4,6ha 300T(50-70m²) 6A

1 ABCD**G**IJKLMOPQ
2 FGRVXY
3 A**F**GJKN**Q**RU
4 (B+G 30/6-31/8) (Q)
(R 1/5-30/9)
(T+U+X+Y+Z)
5 **AB**DFGIJKLMNOPUWZ
6 CEG**IK**(N 3km)ORTV

Ideally located for visiting Burgos. The bus to the town stops in front of the campsite and the centre is only 15 minutes away by bike. Burgos cathedral is world-famous and is a must for any visitor to the city.

A1 Madrid-Burgos. At Burgos follow N623 to Santander. Campsite then signposted.

CC € 17 1/1-20/3 27/3-30/6 1/9-31/12 7=6

N 42°20'30" W 3°39'28"

Cabrerizos/Salamanca, E-37193 / Castilla y León

2766

Don Quijote Cat.2
Ctra Aldealengua km 1,930
+34 923-209052
+34 923-209787
27/2 - 31/10
info@campingdonquijote.com

6ha 86T(70-100m²) 10A

1 ABCDFIJKLMO**P**
2 ACRSTVXY
3 BJWX
4 (B+G 1/6-30/9)
(Q+R+S+T+U+X+Y+Z)
5 **A**GIJKLMNOPU
6 ACEGK(N 2km)ORTV

Campsite close to the river and Salamanca, a town with plenty of sights. Friendly family campsite with different types of pitches available. A beautiful cycling/walking path runs along the river to the town.

When entering Salamanca from any direction: follow the signs to Plaza de España, then follow the signs to Aldealengua village. The campsite is 2 km on the right from Plaza de España.

CC € 15 27/2-11/7 28/8-31/10 7=6

N 40°58'30" W 5°36'11"

Castrojeriz, E-09110 / Castilla y León

2767

Camino de Santiago
Virgen del Manzano s/n
+34 947-377255
+34 947-377236
15/3 - 10/11
info@campingcamino.com

2ha 40T(30-60m²) 5A CEE

1 ACD**F**IJKLO**P**RS
2 FKRVXY
3 HJK
4 (Q+R+U+X+Z)
5 **AB**GIJKLMOPUW
6 AEGJK(N 1km)ORTV

Family campsite on the Santiago de Compostela pilgrim route, 20 min. from Burgos, lovely in the shade of trees. Panoramic views of a Templars' Castle. History, walking and cycling. Birds of prey excursion led by the owner. Photograph the hop and bee eater. Traditional dishes from outdoor oven. Free WiFi.

A231 Leon-Burgos, exit 132, on BU 404 9 km or A62/E80 Valladolid-Burgos, exit 32 on BU 400 16 km to Castrojeriz. Right past petrol station on roundabout. Campsite signposted.

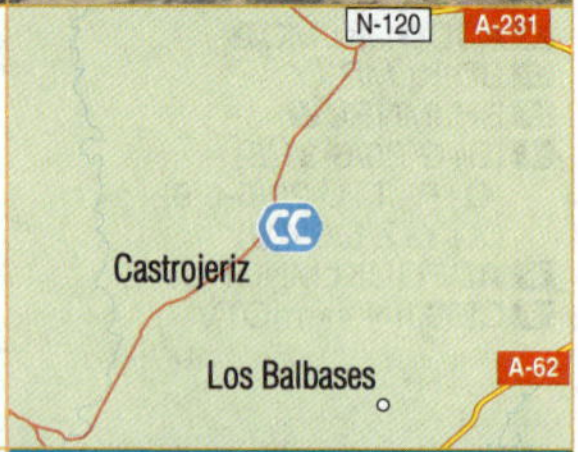

CC € 17 15/3-1/7 1/9-10/11

N 42°17'28" W 4°7'54"

Figueruela de Arriba, E-49520 / Castilla y León

2768

Sierra de la Culebra*
Carretera de Riomanzanas s/n
+34 980-683020
5/3 - 2/11
info@campingsierradelaculebra.com

4,2ha 64T(< 110m²) 7A CEE

1 ACDGIJKLMO**PQ**
2 BKLRVWXY
3 JM
4 (B+G 25/6-4/9) **N** (T+U+V+X+Z)
5 **A**FGIKMNOPUW
6 ADEGJ(N 20km)TV

You will be given a warm welcome on this site surrounded by nature. Especially in spring there is an abundance of wild flowers. Peace and quiet. Spacious pitches. The Iberian wolf lives here and may be observed. Restaurant with home-made traditional specialities. Pool open 25/6 - 4/9.

A52 Benavente-Ourene exit 49 N631. After 4 km ZA912 dir. Alcañices 20 km after Mahide ZAP2438 dir. Figueruela, site after 3 km. Or E82 Zamora-Bragana at Alcañices N631 after Mahide.

€15 *5/3-15/7 1/9-2/11*

N 41°51'52'' W 6°24'52''

Galende/Zamora/Castilla y Leon, E-49361 / Castilla y León

2769

El Folgoso Cat.2
Ctra Galende-S.M. de Casten. km 2,2
+34 980-626774
1/3 - 31/10
info@campingelfolgoso.com

13ha 500T 6A

1 ABCGIJKLMOP
2 ABDGIJORSTY
3 AHWZ
4 (Q) (R 1/7-30/9) (T+U+X+Y+Z)
5 **A**GHIJKLMNOPUWZ
6 CEGJ(N 1,5km)TV

A campsite located in the woods of a nature park and beside the Lago de Sanabria. The campsite has good quality clean toilet facilities, a beach for sunbathing and a lake for non motorised water recreation.

Via A52 exit Benavente/Puebla 79. Towards Ribadeolago via ZA104. Follow arrows to El Folgoso.

€17 *1/3-14/7 1/9-31/10 7=6, 14=12, 21=18, 28=24*

N 42°7'52'' W 6°42'7''

Riaza/Segovia, E-40500 / Castilla y León

2770

Riaza
Ctra de la Estación s/n
FAX +34 921-550580
1/1 - 31/12
info@camping-riaza.com

12ha 185T(96-144m²) 10A

1 ABCDGIJKLMOPQ
2 BFLRSVWX
3 AGH**M**NR**S**U
4 (B+G 15/6-31/8) (Q+R+S+T+U+V+W+X+Y+Z)
5 **AB**DFGIJKLMNOPUWXY
6 AEGJ**K**(N 2km)OTV

Campsite close to the delightful village of Riaza. The villages offer many possibilities for trips out. The province of Segovia is renowned for its excellent food and wine. Restaurant on the campsite is closed on Wednesdays. Wintersports possible in La Pinilla (9 km) from December to March.

From Burgos A1, exit 104. From Madrid A1, exit 103, N110 direction Riaza and Soria. Right at roundabout after 12 km. Campsite on the left, next to the 'Campo de Futbol'.

€19 *1/1-30/6 29/8-31/12 7=6*

N 41°16'10'' W 3°29'50''

Sta Marta de Tormes/Salamanca, E-37900 / Castilla y León

iD **2771**

Regio Cat.1
Ctra Salamanca-Madrid, km 4
+34 923-138888
FAX +34 923-138044
1/1 - 31/12
recepcion@campingregio.com

3ha 129**T**(50-80m²) 10A

1 ABCDFIJLMO**PQ**
2 FGLRTVXY
3 BK**MN**
4 (B+**G** 1/6-15/9) (Q+S+T+U+V+X+Y+Z)
5 **AB**CEFGHIJKLMNOPUWXYZ
6 ACDEGHIJK(N 1km)ORTVW

Spacious, shaded site with large swimming pool. Direct bus to central Salamanca, which can also be reached by foot or bike along level back roads. Adjacent hotel has an excellent restaurant.

Campsite about 4 km outside Salamanca, on N501 to Avila. First drive through Sta Marta de Tormes, hotel on right with the same name. Campsite behind the hotel. From Salamanca: drive to the roundabout and continue to Santa Marta de Tormes, site on the right. From Madrid: site on the left.

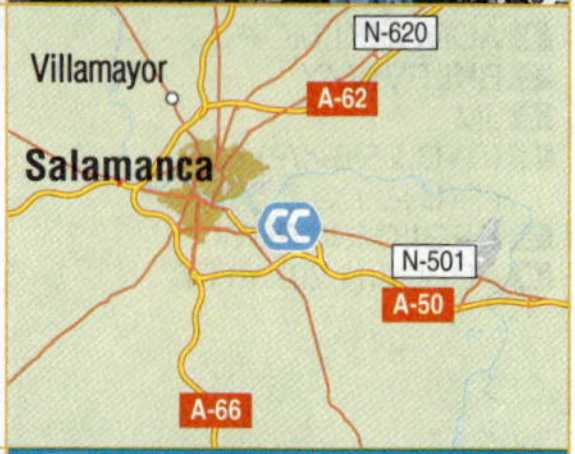

CC € 17 *1/1-15/7 1/9-31/12*

N 40°56'53'' W 5°36'53''

Villares de la Reina/Salamanca, E-37184 / Castilla y León

iD **2772**

Ruta de la Plata Cat.2
Cam. Alto de Villamayor
+34 923-289574
1/1 - 31/12
recepcion@campingrutadelaplata.com

1,2ha 60**T**(60-80m²) 5A

1 ABCFIJKLMO**PQ**
2 FGIRTVXY
3 **F**
4 (B 1/6-15/9) (Q+R+T+Z)
5 **A**DGIJKLMNOPUW
6 AEJ(N 2km)OT

The campsite is excellently located on the route to Southern Spain, Portugal and the city of Salamanca. The bus to Salamanca stops at the entrance.

On the N620 exit to Salamanca/Zamora at 238 km marker. Direction Salamanca then right immediately before 1st hotel restaurant under viaduct. Campsite on right. From Portugal exit 240 dir. Villamayor.

CC € 17 *1/1-7/7 24/8-31/12 7=6*

N 40°59'58'' W 5°40'44''

Aranjuez (Madrid), E-28300 / Madrid

iD **2773**

Camping Internacional Aranjuez Cat.1
Soto del Rebollo s/n
+34 91-8911395
FAX +34 91-8920406
1/1 - 31/12
info@campingaranjuez.com

3ha 178**T**(70-110m²) 16A CEE

1 ABCDGIJKLMOPST
2 CFRSVWXY
3 B**F**GN**O**R**W**
4 (A 15/6-11/9) (B+G 1/5-15/10) (Q+S+T+U+V+X+Y+Z)
5 **AB**DFGIJKLMNOPUWXYZ
6 ACEG**IK**(N 2km)ORSTV

Friendly, helpful staff. Site is located on the River Tajo. Plenty of vegetation. 42 km from Madrid, 40 km from Toledo. A lovely palace at Aranjuez. Gardens, avenues, fountains, flowers and plenty of walks. Trains to the heart of Madrid.

From Madrid A4 exit 37 Aranjuez Norte. Turn left after 8 km before Aranjuez and follow camping signs. From the south exit 52, then straight through the town. On the left next to 'La Rana Verde'. Follow camping signs.

CC € 19 *1/1-22/3 28/3-28/4 3/5-7/7 29/8-31/12 7=6, 14=11, 21=17*

N 40°2'32'' W 3°35'58''

El Escorial/Madrid, E-28280 / Madrid

2774

Caravaning El Escorial Cat.1
M-600 km 3,5
+34 902-014900
FAX +34 918-961062
1/1 - 31/12
@ info@campingelescorial.com

30ha 693**T**(90-120m²) 5A

1 ABCDFIJKLMO**P**ST
2 FLSTUVWXY
3 B**F**GHJKLMNRSU
4 (C+H 1/5-15/9) (Q+S) (T+U+V+X+Y+Z 1/5-30/9)
5 **AB**DFGIJKLMNOPUWXZ
6 CGJM(N 4km)ORTV

A large, spaciously laid out and well patrolled campsite. Large pitches with shade provided by many old trees and artificial sails. Also many sunny pitches. Plenty of opportunities for trips out close by (El Escorial, San Lorenzo) and further afield (Guadarama, Segovia). Madrid is easily reached by bus or train.

Located on the M600, km-marker 3.5 close by El Valle de Los Caidos. When approaching from Madrid take A6, exit 47 El Escorial/Guadarrama.

CC € 19 *1/1-17/3 29/3-28/4 3/5-19/6 1/9-31/12 7=6*

N 40°37'37'' W 4°6'0''

Gargantilla del Lozoya/Madrid, E-28739 / Madrid

2775

Monte Holiday Cat.1
C604-km 9
FAX +34 918-695278
1/1 - 31/12
@ monteholiday@monteholiday.com

30ha 125**T**(60-200m²) 7A CEE

1 ABCDGIJKLMO**P**ST
2 BFIJKLSTUVWXY
3 BGHJ**M**NRU
4 (**A**) (C+H 27/5-18/9) (Q+R)(T+U+V+X+Y+Z 18/3-27/3,19/6-18/9)
5 **AB**DFGIJKLMNOPUWZ
6 ACEGHIK(N 2km)ORTUV

Lovely, eco-conscious campsite with a view of the mountain (Sierra de Guadarama). Quiet, clean, good restaurant and pool and pitches with real green grass all year (for an extra fee). Nature reserve with hides for bird-spotting: eagles and griffon vultures.

From the A1 at the 69 km-marker exit towards Rascafria/Lozoya (M604). Turn off at the 8.8 km-marker (just after the tunnel) to the campsite (800 metres).

CC € 19 *1/1-23/3 27/3-29/4 2/5-2/6 5/6-9/6 12/6-16/6 29/8-31/12*

N 40°57'0'' W 3°43'46''

La Cabrera (Madrid), E-28751 / Madrid

2776

Pico de la Miel Cat.1
Autovia A1, salida 57
+34 918-688082
FAX +34 918-688541
1/1 - 31/12
@ info@picodelamiel.com

30ha 52**T**(50-90m²) 8A CEE

1 ABCDGIJLOP
2 FGLSTUVWXY
3 B**F**GH**M**N**S**U
4 (B+G 10/6-11/9) (Q+S 15/5-21/9) (T+U+X+Y+Z 1/6-21/9)
5 **AB**DGIJKLMNOPUWXYZ
6 AEG**K**(N 0,2km)ORTV

A campsite with a wide variety of trees, set at the foot of a beautiful mountain range, with a separate area for campers and swimming pools. A trip out to the mountain villages and a tour along the valley are well worth the visit. Beautiful panoramic views in rural nature. Ideal also as an overnight stop on your way to Portugal and the south of Spain.

Campsite located about 1 km from the A1. From Burgos and Madrid exit 57. Follow campsite signs.

CC € 19 *1/1-30/6 29/8-31/12 7=6*

N 40°51'30'' W 3°36'59''

Villaviciosa de Odón/Madrid, E-28670 / Madrid

2777

Arco Iris
M501 km 7,100
+34 916-160387
FAX +34 916-160059
1/1 - 30/11
madrid@bungalowsarcoiris.com

5ha 73**T**(60-106m²) 5A

1 ABCD**F**IJKLO**P**ST
2 FGIJLSTUVWXY
3 B**F**G**M**RU
4 (B+G 15/6-15/9) **KN**(Q)
(S 15/6-12/9)
(T+U+V+X+Y+Z)
5 **AB**DFGIJKLMNOP**S**UWXY
Z
6 ACEG**IK**(N 2km)ORTV

A deceptively small campsite. Easy to find using the Madrid ring road. Ideal for a visit to Madrid (go to Boadilla by car, free parking, then by metro to the centre). Or go by car to Villaviciosa then take the bus. Very good restaurant.

Take exit 36 on the M40 ring road around Madrid. Take M501 direction Boadilla. Then direction Villaviciosa, take exit 7. The campsite is located on the right. Coming on the M50, exit 69, M501 direction Villaviciosa. Exit 7.

CC € 19 *1/1-30/6 1/9-30/11 6=5*

N 40°22'52'' W 3°54'26''

Horcajo de los Montes, E-13110 / Castilla-La Mancha

2778

Mirador de Cabañeros
Cañada Real Segoviana s/n
+34 926-775439
FAX +34 926-775003
1/3 - 8/12
info@campingcabaneros.com

2ha 44**T**(50-70m²) 6A

1 ABCD**G**IJKLMO**P**
2 GIJKLTUVWXY
3 BGHJ**M**NRU
4 (A+E)
(Q+U+X+Z 15/6-15/9)
5 **A**DFGIJKLMNOPUWXZ
6 ACEGJ(N 0,4km)OV

A small, attractive, well run terraced site, easy access. Nature area with many opportunities for those who love flora and fauna. Beautiful views from the site. Restaurant also open at weekends.

A4 to Manzanares. Then N430 to Ciudad Real. Then CM412 to Porzuna. Turn left 2 km past Porzuna towards El Robledo and Horcajo. Campsite just before the village on the right.

CC € 19 *1/3-22/3 29/3-28/4 3/5-24/5 30/5-7/7 24/8-27/10 2/11-1/12 7=6, 14=11*

N 39°19'23'' W 4°39'0''

Mesones (Albacete), E-02449 / Castilla-La Mancha

2779

Rio Mundo
Ctra Com. 412, km 205
+34 967-433230
FAX +34 967-433287
15/3 - 11/10
riomundo@
campingriomundo.com

2,5ha 100**T**(40-100m²) 10A

1 ACD**G**IJLOPST
2 BCLSUVXY
3 AGJ**WX**
4 (B 18/6-4/9)
(Q+S+T+U+V+X+Z)
5 **A**GIJKMNOPUWZ
6 AEGK(N 7km)ORTV

Located in a mountainous nature reserve. Friendly manager. Suitable as a base for trips out. Chess, draughts and other games on loan (for use on the terrace). Excellent toilet facilities. Free WiFi.

On N322 Albacete-Bailén, turn off at Reolid direction Riópar. Campsite 7 km past Riópar on side road to your left (km-marker 205) (Mesones). Opposite direction: N301 exit to Hellin (sur), direction Elche de la Sierra/Riópar. Campsite 7 km before Riópar.

CC € 19 *15/3-20/3 28/3-15/7 1/9-11/10 7=6, 14=11*

N 38°29'18'' W 2°20'39''

Ossa de Montiel (Albacete), E-02611 / Castilla-La Mancha

2780

Los Batanes Cat.1
Ctra Lagunas de Ruidera km 8
+34 926-699020
26/2 - 31/10
camping@losbatanes.com

8,5ha 255**T**(50-100m²) 6A

1 ABCD**G**IJKLMOPT
2 BCDLSUVXY
3 BGJWZ
4 (B+G 15/6-11/9) (Q) (R+T+U+X 15/6-11/9) (Z)
5 **AB**DGIJKLMNOPRUWZ
6 CEGJ(N 8km)OTV

Very well run campsite with excellent toilet facilities. A lovely large swimming pool surrounded by lawns with trees overall for shade. A good base for trips along various lakes and towns in a beautiful area with colourful rocks.

Take the N IV. At Manzanares to the N430 direction Albacete as far as Ruidera. Then right towards Lagunas de Ruidera. From Albacete to the N430 also as far as Ruidera. The turn left towards Lagunas de Ruidera. Campsite 8 km on the right.

CC € 19 *26/2-22/3 28/3-28/4 2/5-15/6 12/9-31/10 7=6*

N 38°56'13'' W 2°50'51''

Cáceres, E-10005 / Extremadura

2781

Cáceres Camping Cat.1
Ctra N630, km 549,5
+34 927-233100
1/1 - 31/12
reservas@campingcaceres.com

5,5ha 129**T**(90-110m²) 10A

1 BCGIJKLMO**P**ST
2 FGIJLRSTVWXY
3 ABCFHRV
4 (B+G 15/6-15/9) KN (Q+R+T+U+V+X+Y+Z)
5 **AB**FGIJKLMNOPSTUWXYZ
6 ACEGK(N 3km)ORTV

A beautifully located terraced campsite with each pitch having a private cabin with excellent toilet facilities. The campsite has a large swimming pool with lawns under palm trees, a recreation building with a bar, and a restaurant with a large covered terrace. Sports centre nearby. Bus service to the historic town of Caceres.

Campsite located 4 km north of the town on the N630 next to the football stadium with tall floodlights.

CC € 17 *1/1-23/3 28/3-14/7 31/8-31/12 4=3, 8=6, 12=9, 16=12*

N 39°29'19'' W 6°24'46''

Malpartida de Plasencia, E-10680 / Extremadura

2782

Camping Parque Nacional de Monfragüe
C. Plasencia-Trujillo K10
FAX +34 927-459233
1/1 - 31/12
campingmonfrague@hotmail.com

4,8ha 128**T**(45-100m²) 10A

1 ABFIJKLMO**P**
2 FIKLRSTVWXY
3 ABGHJ**M**NRU
4 (**A**) (B+G 15/6-15/9) (Q+R+T+U+X+Y+Z)
5 **AB**FGIJKLMNOPUWZ
6 EGHK(N 6km)OQRTV

Quiet site under holm trees close to Parque Nacional de Monfragüe. 10 km from the town of Plasencia. Facilities: swimming pool with lawn, good restaurant, horse riding, guided tours, bike hire.

6 km south of Plasencia, exit EX108 Navalmoral. After 5 km exit EX208 towards Trujillo. After 4 km drive under the small viaduct. Site is located on the left directly after the viaduct. From Madrid EX-A1 exit 46, roundabout 3/4 round, follow signs of Nat. Park of Monfragüe.

CC € 15 *1/1-17/3 27/3-15/7 1/9-31/12*

N 39°56'38'' W 6°5'5''

Plasencia/Cáceres, E-10600 / Extremadura

2783

La Chopera Cat.2
Ctra Nat.110 km 3,3
+34 927-416660
1/1 - 31/12
lachopera@campinglachopera.com

6ha 150T(65-80m²) 5-10A CEE

1 ABCGIJLM
2 CLRTXY
3 ABGRU**WX**
4 (B+G 1/6-15/9) (Q) (R 1/7-31/8) (T+U+X+Y) Z
5 **A**FGIJKLMNOPUW
6 EGK(N 2km)ORTV

Campsite on level ground with spacious pitches and abundant plants on the banks of a river. In the Jerte Valley, close to the Monfragüe National Park. Just 3 km from the historical town of Plasencia, the geographical centre of northern Extremadura. Access via a foot and cycle path beside the river.

From the N630 drive into the town of Plasencia. Then via the N110 in direction Avila. The campsite is about 3 km to the left of the road in the valley. Clearly signposted.

CC € 17 1/1-15/7 1/9-31/12

N 40°2'43'' W 6°3'31''

Alcalá de los Gazules, E-11180 / Andalucia

2784

Los Gazules Cat.2
Ctra de Patrite, km 4
+34 956-420486
FAX +34 956-420388
1/1 - 31/12
info@campinglosgazules.com

40ha 140T(60-80m²) 10A

1 ABCD**G**IJKLMPST
2 CFLRSVWX
3 AGHN**O**
4 (B 15/5-15/9) (G 1/5-30/9) (Q+R+T+U+X) Z
5 **AB**GIJKMNOPUW
6 AEG**J**(N 5km)OV

Set in beautiful countryside in the heart of the Los Alcornocales nature park. Perfectly suited to all types of outdoor activities and walks. No traffic disturbance. Well equipped campsite with as much shade as you want. Advantageous menus.

Between Jerez de la Frontera and Los Barrios via Ctra 381 to Alcalá de Los Gazules. Exit 45 on the A381. Enter village. Follow road (not SatNav) into centre. Campsite signposted at end of road outside the town. Another 4 km.

CC € 17 1/1-15/7 1/9-31/12 7=6, 14=11

N 36°27'49'' W 5°39'53''

Almayate (Málaga), E-29749 / Andalucia

2785

Almayate Costa Cat.1
Ctra N340a km 267
+34 952-556289
FAX +34 952-556310
12/2 - 3/10
info@campingalmayatecosta.com

3ha 234T(40-90m²) 10A

1 BCDEIJKLMO**P**ST
2 AEFGLTVY
3 B**F**MNRWY
4 (B 1/5-30/9) (Q+S+T+U+X+Y+Z)
5 **AB**FGIJKLMNOPUWZ
6 EGIK(N 1km)ORSTV

Well maintained beachside campsite with excellent sanitation. Plenty of shade from trees. The campsite has a beautiful swimming pool.

Located on the (old) coastal road N340a at km-marker 267. On Autovia A7 Málaga-Almería from Almería exit 272 to Torre del Mar. Continue direction Málaga. From Málaga exit Benejarafe/Chilches; continue towards Almería.

CC € 17 12/2-23/3 27/3-30/6 28/8-3/10

N 36°43'28'' W 4°8'5''

Almayate (Málaga), E-29749 / Andalucia

2786

Camping Naturista Almanat
Ctra N340, km 269
+34 952-556462
FAX +34 952-556271
1/1 - 31/12
info@almanat.es

2ha 202T(50-115m²) 20A

1 B**G**IJKLMO**P**Q
2 AEFGLNTVWXY
3 B**F**GKN**OQ**RUWY
4 (**A**+B) (F 1/1-15/6,15/9-31/12) **KN** (Q+R+T+X+Y+Z)
5 **AB**GIJKMOPUWXZ
6 ACEG**K**(N 2km)ORTV

Attractive naturist campsite located right by the sea with indoor and outdoor swimming pool. Restaurant by the beach.

A7 Málaga-Motril and vice versa, exit 272 Torre del Mar. In Torre del Mar keep in direction Málaga. Located on the N340a, at km-marker 269, just outside Torre del Mar, on the seaward side of the road. Signposted.

CC € 17 *1/1-30/6 1/9-31/12*

N 36°43'58'' W 4°6'52''

Almería, E-04002 / Andalucia

2787

La Garrofa
Ctra N340a, km 435,4
+34 950-235770
1/1 - 31/12
info@lagarrofa.com

2ha 100T(10-65m²) 10A

1 BC**G**IJKLMO**P**ST
2 EFGJKNTVXY
3 AFHNWY
4 (Q+R+U+X) Z
5 **A**GIJKLMNOPUWZ
6 EG**K**(N 4km)OTV

Small and friendly campsite; lovely location, right by the sea. Well shaded in parts. The bus to Almería stops outside the campsite.

N340 Almería-Málaga v.v. At Almería towards 'Puerto'. Turn around at roundabout. Keep to the left (left hand tunnel towards Aguadulce). Turn left after about 3 km. Campsite signposted.

CC € 17 *1/1-30/6 15/9-31/12*

N 36°49'35'' W 2°30'59''

Balerma/Almería, E-04712 / Andalucia

2788

Mar Azul Balerma Cat.2
Ctra de Guardias Viejas, s/n
+34 950-937637
FAX +34 950-912126
1/1 - 31/12
info@campingbalerma.com

5ha 220T(70-100m²) 16A

1 BCDGIJKLMOPQ
2 AEFNUVWY
3 A**F**GHJNRUWY
4 (**A**) (B+G 1/4-31/10) (Q+R+T+U) Z
5 **AB**DFGIJKLMNOPUWXY
6 ABCEG**K**(N 0,5km)OTUV

NEW

Modern, new campsite. Shade still limited. Pitches with water and drainage. Excellent toilet facilities.

A7 Almeria/Motril, from both directions, take exit 400 or 403, dir. Balerma. Follow signs.

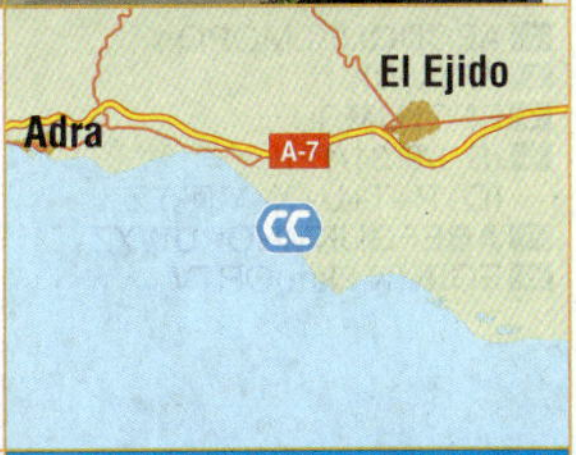

CC € 15 *1/1-30/6 1/9-31/12*

N 36°43'20'' W 2°52'40''

Beas de Granada, E-18184 / Andalucia

2789

- Alto de Viñuelas Cat. 2
- Ctra Beas de Granada s/n
- +34 958-546023
- FAX +34 958-545357
- 1/1 - 31/12
- @ info@campingaltodevinuelas.com

1ha 48T(30-60m²) 10A

1 BCDGIJKLMOPQ
2 FGJKLRTVWXY
3 GHJR
4 (B+G 1/5-30/9) (Q+T+U+X+Y+Z)
5 **AB**FGIJKLMNOPUWZ
6 ACEG**K**(N 1km)RTV

An unpretentious and peaceful campsite. Attractively laid out terraces. Lovely views of the Sierra Nevada. Good local cuisine. The bus to Granada stops outside the campsite. 2 euros are charged for a trailer. From a second pet 1 euro extra is charged.

A92 Granada-Almería/Murcia and vice versa, exit 256 direction Beas de Granada. Follow the signs.

CC € 15 *1/1-21/3 28/3-30/6 1/9-31/12*

N 37°13'29'' W 3°29'19''

Benajarafe/Málaga, E-29792 / Andalucia

2790

- Camping Valle Niza Playa Cat. 2
- Ctra N340, km 264,1
- +34 952-513181
- FAX +34 952-513476
- 1/1 - 31/12
- @ info@campingvalleniza.es

2,5ha 150T(40-120m²) 6-10A

1 BCD**G**IJKLMOPQ
2 AEFGLNRTVWXY
3 BFGHJKRVWY
4 (B+Q+R+T+U+X+Y+Z)
5 **A**FGHIJKLMNOPUWZ
6 ACDEG**K**(N 3km)OTV

The campsite is positioned by the sea, separated from it only by the old coast road 340. The toilet facilities were recently renovated. The lovely swimming pool is open year round and is surrounded by a beautiful lawn.

A7 Málaga-Motril, exit 265 Cajiz Costa. Campsite located between Benajarafe and Motril on the N340. Follow signs.

CC € 17 *1/1-7/7 24/8-31/12*

N 36°43'10'' W 4°9'53''

Cabo de Gata (Almería), E-04150 / Andalucia

2791

- Cabo de Gata Cat. 2
- Ctra Cabo de Gata s/n
- +34 950-160443
- FAX +34 950-916821
- 1/1 - 31/12
- @ info@campingcabodegata.com

3,6ha 236T(30-130m²) 16A

1 ABCD**G**IJKLMOPQ
2 AFTVWX
3 B**F**GHJ**M**RU
4 (B 1/3-31/12) (Q+R+T+U+X+Y) Z
5 **AB**EFGIJKMNOPUWXZ
6 EGI**K**(N 2km)ORTV

A very well maintained and equipped campsite. A lovely spot on the edge of a desert-like nature park, about 1 km from a long sandy beach.

A7 (N340) Almería-Murcia, exit 460; Murcia-Almería, exit 467. Follow San José signs, then Cabo de Gata, 1 km on the right.

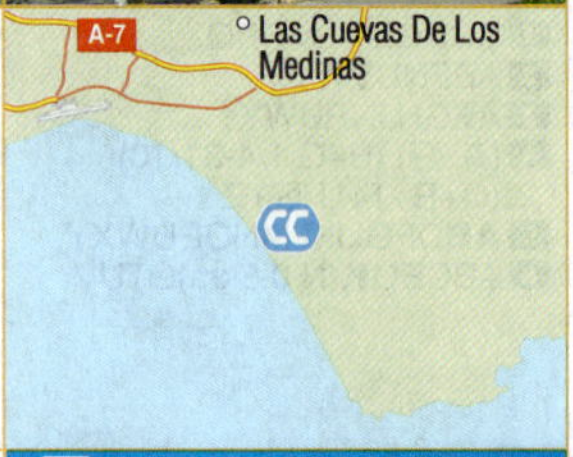

CC € 19 *1/1-15/7 10/9-31/12*

N 36°48'29'' W 2°13'55''

Caños de Meca/Barbate, E-11159 / Andalucia

2792

Pinar San José
Zahora 17
+34 956-437030
FAX +34 956-437174
1/1 - 31/12
@ info@campingpinarsanjose.com

3,7ha 150**T**(25-150m²) 15A

1 ABCD**G**IJKLMP
2 BFGJLRSVWXY
3 BK**MN**S
4 (B+G 15/5-15/10)
(Q+S+T+U+X+Y) Z
5 **AB**GIJKMNOPUWXYZ
6 ACEGIKSTV

Located in a large pine forest next to Breña nature park, with predominantly comfort pitches on fresh grass, this campsite offers plenty of natural recreation and is close to spacious beaches. The many new amenities are excellent.

On N340/E5 Cadiz-Algeciras take the Vejer/Caños de Meca exit. Left at the roundabout and the campsite is 10 km further left on, just past the bend. 1 km from the sea. Via A48, exit 36 to Los Caños de Meca and continue as above.

CC € 17 *1/1-24/3 28/3-9/6 5/9-31/12*

N 36°12'3" W 6°2'5"

Carchuna/Motril (Granada), E-18730 / Andalucia

2793

Don Cactus Cat.1
CN340, km 343
+34 958-623109
FAX +34 958-624294
1/1 - 31/12
@ info@doncactus.com

4ha 260**T**(60-70m²) 5-12A CEE

1 BCD**G**IJKLMOPST
2 AEGLNTVXY
3 BGK**M**NRUV**W**Y
4 (**A** 1/7-31/8,1/11-30/3)
(**B**+G) IJ
(Q+S+T+U+X+Y+Z)
5 **AB**EFGIJKLMNOPUWXYZ
6 CEG**IK**M(N 0,5km)OSTV

A well maintained and organised campsite. Plenty of trees. The campsite is located by the beach. The large swimming pool with water slide and bubble bath is open all year round. All pitches with water and drainage.

N340 Motril-Almería, signposted between Calahonda and Torrenueva. SatNav may cause problems due to changes in road layout.

CC € 19 *1/1-30/6 1/9-31/12* *7=6, 14=11*

N 36°41'45" W 3°26'36"

Conil de la Frontera, E-11149 / Andalucia

2794

Camping Los Eucaliptos Cat.2
Crta del Pradillo km 0200 c.p.
FAX +34 956-441272
18/3 - 25/9
@ eucaliptos@hotmail.es

2ha 133**T**(50-100m²) 10A

1 AB**G**IJL**P**
2 ABFSVXY
3 U
4 (B 1/6-30/9)
(Q+R+T+U+X) Z
5 **AB**GIKMO**P**UVW
6 EGIJQRTV

A very shaded campsite under eucalyptus trees, close to the centre. A friendly bar and restaurant with views of the swimming pool.

Take the N340/E5 between Cadiz and Tarifa to Conil. Campsite and playas well signposted in town, follow signs on ring road just before the town.

CC € 17 *18/3-15/7 1/9-24/9*

N 36°17'14" W 6°5'26"

Conil de la Frontera, E-11140 / Andalucia

2795

Camping Roche Cat.2
Carril de Pilahito s/n
+34 956-442216
FAX +34 956-442624
1/1 - 31/12
info@campingroche.com

6ha 300T(60-90m²) 10A CEE

1 ABCD**G**IJKLMO**P**ST
2 ABFGLRSVWX
3 A**F**HJ**M**R**S**VW
4 (B+G 10/5-30/10) (Q+S+T+U+X+Y) Z
5 **AB**GIJKLMNOPUWX
6 AEGK(N 3km)ORTV

Site with spacious pitches. Ideal for winter. Older section newly laid out with comfort pitches. On grass, with a lovely swimming pool in the middle and plenty of deckchairs. Barbecues permitted in winter.

N340/E5 between Cadiz and Tarifa to Conil (2 km). Follow the 'playas' and/or 'camping' signs on the ring road, then campsite's own sign. Also accessible along the N340, 2 km before the Conil exit to Cadiz. From A48/E5 exit 15 dir. N340, right at km-marker 19.

CC € 15 *1/1-30/6 1/9-31/12*

N 36°18'38'' W 6°6'46''

Conil de la Frontera, E-11140 / Andalucia

2796

La Rosaleda Cat. 1
Ctra del Pradillo km 1,3
+34 956-443327
FAX +34 956-443385
1/1 - 31/12
info@campinglarosaleda.com

6ha 335T(72-150m²) 10A

1 ABGIJKLO**P**ST
2 AGJLRTVWXY
3 B**F**GKLN**V**
4 (B 1/6-15/9) **N**(Q+S) (T+U+X+Y 1/1-30/9, 1/11-31/12)Z
5 **AB**GIJKMNOPUWX
6 EGIK(N 0,5km)RTVW

Terraced campsite with spacious pitches screened by various types of tree. Beautifully landscaped with wide avenues and borders. Variety of winter entertainment. Barbecues permitted in low season. Sauna and fitness room. Extra low rates from 16 days from 19/9 to 31/5 (except Easter).

Take the N340/E5 between Cadiz and Tarifa to Conil (2 km). On the right the 'playas' and/or 'campsite' signs are clearly indicated. Follow signs. Campsite about 1 km on the right.

CC € 17 *1/1-19/6 4/9-31/12*

N 36°17'36'' W 6°5'44''

El Puerto de Santa Maria, E-11500 / Andalucia

2797

Playa Las Dunas Cat.1
P.M. Playa La Puntilla s/n
+34 956-872210
FAX +34 956-860117
1/1 - 31/12
info@lasdunascamping.com

13ha 300T(50-80m²) 10A

1 ABCDGIJKLM**P**
2 AEGJLSVWXY
3 BFG**M**NW**Y**
4 (**B**+**G** 15/6-30/8) (Q+T+U+Y) Z
5 **AB**FGIJKLMNOPUV
6 EG**IK**(N 1,5km)OTV

Situated in pine woods with three excellent toilet blocks, this campsite offers excellent possibilities for families with children; large children's pool, huge sandy beach. Larger caravans can pitch in the newer section but there is not much shade there. Barbecues not permitted from 15/5 to 15/10. Swimming pool free during weekdays.

Follow signs from El Puerto de Santa Maria. Well signposted throughout the town. (Do not drive to the centre.)

CC € 17 *1/1-13/6 12/9-31/12*

N 36°35'15'' W 6°14'26''

El Rocío, E-21750 / Andalucia

2798

La Aldea Cat.1
Ctra del Rocío, km 25
+34 959-442677
FAX +34 959-442582
1/1 - 31/12
@ info@campinglaaldea.com

6ha 200T(27-90m²) 10A

1 ABCD**G**IJKLPQ
2 GLRVWXY
3 BGJN**O**U
4 (B 23/3-2/10) (Q+S+T+U+Y) Z
5 **AB**GIJKLMNOPUWXZ
6 EG**J**(N 1km)ORTV

An extremely well run campsite with large grassy pitches surrounded by hedges with possibility of shade. Swimming pool, well run restaurant and air conditioned recreational bar. Very unusual little town with sand tracks and close to the famous Doñana natural area.

E1/A49 Sevilla-Portugal. Exit 60 Almonte A483, this road becomes the A484 (new road). Follow El Rocio signs.

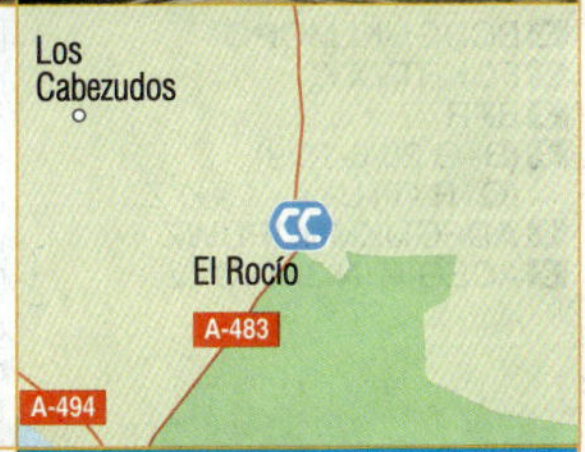

CC € 17 *1/1-10/5 18/5-14/7 1/9-31/12 7=6, 9=7*

N 37°8'29" W 6°29'27"

Estepona (Malaga), E-29680 / Andalucia

2799

Parque Tropical Cat.2
Ctra N340, km 162
+34 95-2793618
1/1 - 31/12
@ parquetropicalcamping@hotmail.com

1,2ha 82T(60-80m²) 10A CEE

1 ABCD**G**IJKLMNO**P**Q
2 EGJSTVWXY
3 BFVY
4 (D+G+Q+R+T+U+X+Y) Z
5 **AB**GIJKLMOPU
6 ABEGK(N 3km)ORT

A small campsite with plenty of tropical plants. The small indoor pool is also noticeable for its lush plants. Interesting low season rates. Some pitches are difficult for caravans. Barbecue outside the summer months.

Via A7 (not the motorway) between Marbella and Estepona (6 km) between 163 and 162 km markers. Well signposted.

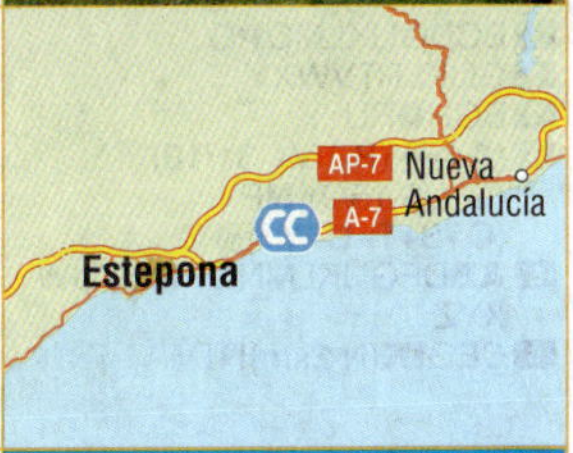

CC € 15 *1/1-15/7 1/9-31/12*

N 36°27'15" W 5°4'51"

Granada/La Zubia, E-18140 / Andalucia

2800

Reina Isabel Cat.2
Laurel de la Reina 15
+34 958-590041
FAX +34 958-591191
1/1 - 31/12
@ info@campingreinaisabel.com

0,6ha 57T(30-70m²) 6A

1 BCDGIJKLMO**P**Q
2 FGTVXY
3 **F**HJ
4 (**A**) (B 5/5-30/9) (Q+R+T+U+V+Y+Z)
5 **AB**DFGIJKMNOPUWZ
6 ABCEG**K**L(N 0,5km)RT

A well equipped campsite with stylish buildings. The site is mainly used for visiting Granada and its sights. The pitches are well marked out and offer sufficient shade. The site is well located for visiting Granada and the bus to Granada stops in front of the campsite.

Located on the edge of the village of La Zubia, south of Granada. When approaching from any direction: via Circunvalación/Autovia Granada. Exit Ronda Sur, then exit 2 La Zubia. Follow the signs.

CC € 19 *1/1-19/3 28/3-30/4 29/5-6/7 28/7-5/8 1/9-31/12*

N 37°7'28" W 3°35'12"

Granada/Otura, E-18630 / Andalucia
2801

Suspiro del Moro Cat.2
Autovia A44, exit 139
+34 958-555411
1/1 - 31/12
campingsuspirodelmoro@
yahoo.es

1ha 59**T**(60m²) 5A

1 BCDGIJKLMO**P**Q
2 FGKRTVXY
3 B**F**R
4 (B+G 20/6-15/9)
(Q+R+T+U+X+Y) Z
5 **A**DFGIJKMNOPUWZ
6 ACEGI**K**(N 3km)OTV

A peaceful, unpretentious campsite with plenty of trees and shaded pitches. Suitable as a stopover campsite and as a base for visiting Granada and surroundings. Next to a restaurant. Campsite will book for Alhambra palace. Bus service to Granada from the campsite.

A44, Granada-Motril and vice-versa, exit 139 Otura. Follow signs to Padul, Suspiro del Moro and camping signs. Take note: after leaving roundabout on the west of the A44, turn left after ± 20m to Padul.

CC € 17 *1/1-20/3 28/3-30/6 1/9-8/10 13/10-3/12 11/12-31/12*

N 37°4'6'' W 3°39'9''

Güejar Sierra (Granada), E-18160 / Andalucia
2802

Camp. & Carav. Las Lomas Cat.1
Ctra Güejar Sierra km 6
+34 958-484742
+34 958-484000
1/1 - 31/12
info@campinglaslomas.com

1,6ha 100**T**(40-110m²) 10A

1 BCDGIJKLMO**P**Q
2 GIJKLRTVWXY
3 BGH**Q**RU
4 (**A**) (B 15/4-31/10)
(G 1/6-15/9) **N**P
(Q+S+T+U+Y) Z
5 **AB**DFGIJKLMNOP**RST**UW
XYZ
6 CEGI**K**(N 2km)RTV

Comfortable campsite with lots of facilities and spacious, marked out pitches in the shade. Altitude: 1100 metres, about 200 metres above storage reservoir. Beautiful view of the mountains of the Sierra Nevada. Only 30 km away from a skiing area.

Circunvalación (Motril-Jaén v.v.) then exit 132 to Ronda Sur. Follow Sierra Nevada. Take right hand lane 3 km past the tunnel then turn left. Follow signs 'Güejar Sierra' and 'Las Lomas'. Ignore small camping signs.

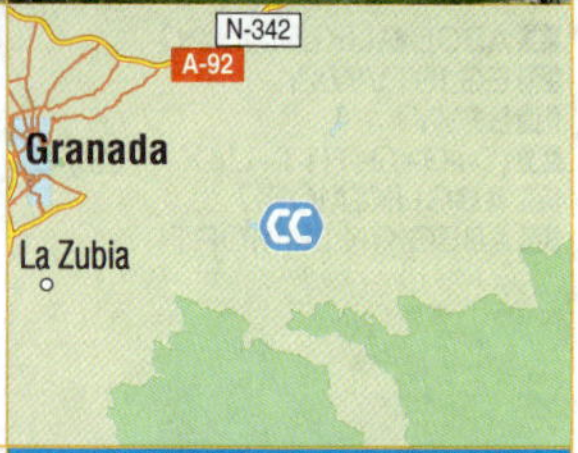

CC € 19 *4/1-23/3 28/3-30/6 1/9-5/12 11/12-23/12 21=20, 30=27*

N 37°9'36'' W 3°27'14''

Hinojos, E-21740 / Andalucia
2803

Camping Village
Doñarrayan Park
Ctra Hinojos a El Rocío 7 km
+34 959-027502
1/1 - 2/11, 1/12 - 31/12
info@donarrayan-park.com

60**T**(90-113m²) 16A

1 ABCDGIJKLMOPQ
2 BKLSVWXY
3 AGHJKN
4 (**A**) (B 1/4-15/9)
(Q+R+T+U+V+Y+Z)
5 **AB**GIJKLMNPUWXYZ
6 BCDEGK(N 5km)OQRTUV

Beautiful campsite located in the woods in the heart of the Doñana National Park. Ideal for people seeking some peace and quiet, nature lovers, walkers and families with young children. Excellent amenities, swimming pool with lawn, restaurant and a small shop.

Follow E1/A49 Sevilla-Huelva. Take exit 34 Chucona-Hinojos. Via A481 to Hinojos. Take ring road A474 dir. Alnonte. After ± 500m left to Almoradux and ± 5 km to campsite.

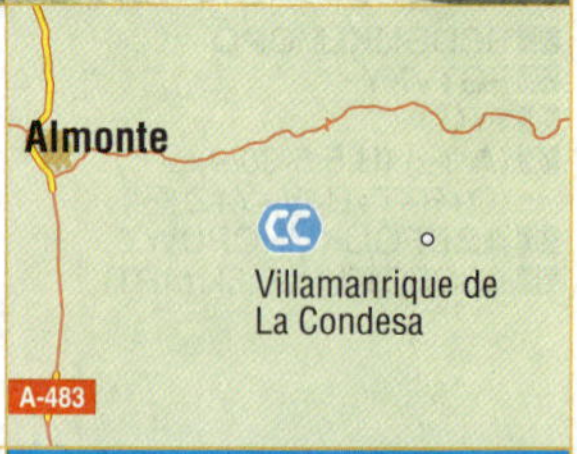

CC € 17 *1/1-18/3 29/3-10/5 17/5-30/6 1/9-2/11 1/12-31/12*

N 37°14'30'' W 6°22'58''

Humilladero, E-29531 / Andalucia

2804

La Sierrecilla
Avda de Blas Infante
+34 951-199090
1/1 - 31/12
info@lasierrecilla.com

4ha 120T(60-90m²) 10A

1 BCD**G**IJKLMOPST
2 FIJKLSTUVWXY
3 AGHJN**OP**U
4 (B+G 1/6-30/9) **N**
(Q+T+U+X+Y+Z)
5 **A**DFGIJKLMNOPUWZ
6 CEGJ(N 2km)V

A relatively new campsite in which the planting has not yet matured. High quality toilet facilities, luxuriously designed, attractive hinterland.

Autovia A92 (Antequera-Sevilla), exit 138, direction Humilladero. Left at roundabout after ±2km. Follow signs. SatNav not reliable here.

CC € 17 *1/1-15/7 1/9-31/12*

N 37°6'28'' W 4°41'47''

Isla Cristina, E-21410 / Andalucia

2805

Giralda Cat.1
Ctra la Antilla, km 1,5
+34 959-343318
FAX +34 959-343284
1/1 - 31/12
recepcion@campinggiralda.com

15ha 450T(40-80m²) 10A

1 ABCD**G**IJKLMPST
2 ABCEJSWXY
3 A**F**GJNRU**W**Y
4 (B+G+Q+S+T)
(U 31/3-8/4,1/7-31/8)
(W 31/3-7/4,1/7-31/8) Z
5 **AB**FGIJKLMNOPUW
6 EGI**K**(N 1,5km)ORTV

Small squares under the pine trees, separated by roads and slopes divide up this extensive campsite. Located close to a sandy beach and next to the Rio Carreras swamp area which can be visited by pedal boat. All types of meals, including pizza and paella are available in the snack bar. Campsite with ISO Certificate.

From the direction of Huelva towards Portugal, take exit to Isla Cristina. Then in direction La Antilla. Campsite about 1.5 km on the left.

CC € 17 *1/1-30/6 1/9-31/12 12=10, 30=20*

N 37°12'0'' W 7°18'3''

La Mamola, E-18750 / Andalucia

2806

Castillo de Baños Cat.2
CN340, km 360
+34 958-829528
FAX +34 958-829768
1/1 - 31/12
info@campingcastillo.com

3ha 240T(30-70m²) 12A

1 BCD**G**IJKLMOPST
2 EFGNORTVWXY
3 AG**WY**
4 (B+Q+S+T+U+Y+Z)
5 **AB**GIJKLMNOPUWXYZ
6 EG**K**(N 0,2km)ORTV

The campsite has marked out pitches with plenty of trees for good, natural shade. The campsite is located right by a narrow beach.

N340 exit 360 between Motril and Almeria. Look out for camping signs. Do not use SatNav.

CC € 19 *1/1-30/6 1/9-31/12 7=6, 14=11*

N 36°44'27'' W 3°18'4''

Los Escullos/Nijar (Almería), E-04118 / Andalucia

2807

Los Escullos Cat.1
Parque Natural Cabo de Gata
+34 950-389811
+34 950-106400
1/1 - 31/12
info@losescullossanjose.com

4,5ha 216T(40-80m²) 6-16A

1 ABCD**G**IJKLMOPST
2 AJNOQTVWXY
3 BGHIJK**M**NU**V**W
4 (**A**+B) **KN**(Q+S) (T 1/6-15/9) (U+V+X+Y) Z
5 **AB**FGIJKLMNOPUWZ
6 ABCEGI**K**(N 5km)TV

A campsite with pitches shaded by trees or (in summer) by sun screens. About 1 km from the sea with beautiful bays. Situated in the very dry, desert-like park Cabo de Gata. The campsite has extras such as a sauna, fitness, etc.

Located in the Parque Natural Cabo de Gata. On the Autovia A7, exit 479 direction San José (AL 3108). Follow camping signs.

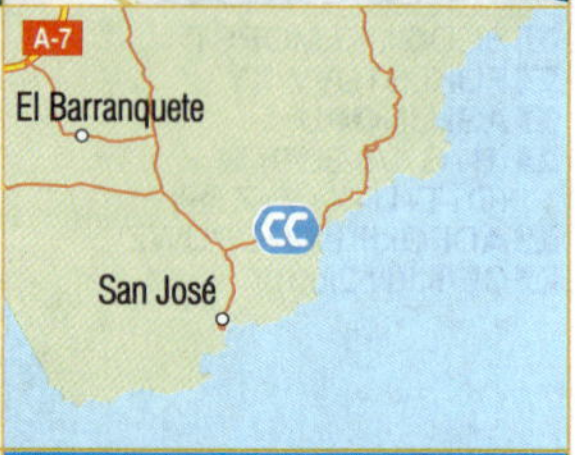

CC € 17 *1/1-30/6 1/9-31/12 7=6, 14=12*

N 36°48'24" W 2°4'53"

Marbella, E-29604 / Andalucia

2808

Cabopino
Ctra N340, km 194,7
+34 952-850106
+34 951120263
1/1 - 31/12
info@campingcabopino.com

5ha 280T(50-80m²) 10A

1 BCD**G**IJKLMO**P**ST
2 AEFGIJLSTVXY
3 B**F**GKLNRUVWY
4 (A) (B 11/4-30/9) (E) **N**(Q+R+T+U+V+X+Y+Z)
5 **AB**EFGIJKMNOP**S**UWZ
6 AFGJ**K**M(N 1km)RTUVWX

A large, well-equipped campsite with spacious pitches. Some with minimal shade, others with plenty. The campsite is just a few hundred metres from the beach. Bus connections to Marbella.

The campsite is located close to the N340. From Fuengirola, at km 194.7, exit Cabopino. Site located on the right. From Marbella, at km 194.7, exit Cabopino. At the roundabout take the motorway. Campsite in front of you.

CC € 17 *1/1-21/3 27/3-30/6 1/9-31/12*

N 36°29'21" W 4°44'35"

Marbella/Málaga, E-29600 / Andalucia

2809

La Buganvilla Cat.2
Ctra N340, km 188.8
+34 95-2831973
+34 95-2835621
1/1 - 31/12
info@campingbuganvilla.com

4,3ha 304**T**(60-80m²) 16A

1 BCD**G**IJKLMO**P**Q
2 AFGIJKLTVWXY
3 B**F**GH**M**RUW
4 (B) (G 15/6-15/9) (Q+R+T+U+V+X+Y+Z)
5 **AB**GIJKLMNOPUWXYZ
6 CEG**K**(N 0,3km)ORTV

A large, spacious camping, some pitches have limited shade, others have plenty of shade. Camping pitches for tents are completely shaded by old pine trees. The campsite is close to the N340.

Campsite on the N340 between Fuengirola (25 km) and Marbella (6 km), on the landward side of the road near 189 km marker. Short exit and sharp right.

CC € 15 *1/1-15/7 1/9-31/12*

N 36°30'11" W 4°48'12"

Motril/Granada, E-18600 / Andalucia

2810

Playa de Poniente S.L. Cat.2
Playa de Poniente s/n
+34 958-820303
FAX +34 958-604191
1/1 - 31/12
@ info@campingplayadeponiente.com

3ha 202T(60-100m²) 6-10A

1 BDGIJKLMOPST
2 AEFGLNRSTVWXY
3 BFGHJK**M**N**O**RVWY
4 (**A**) (B 1/5-30/9) (Q+R+T+U+X+Y+Z)
5 **AB**DEFGIJKLMNOPUWZ
6 ACEGIKM(N 0,5km)ORTV

A good campsite for stopovers or as a base for visiting Granada, the Sierra Nevada and its southern edge (Alpujarras). Good toilet facilities. The campsite has a quiet location and is close to the beach. Plenty of shade.

On the N340 between Motril and Salobreña take exit Granada. At the bottom, exit in the direction of Puerto (de Motril). Follow the signs. After sign to the right; then at T-junction turn right again. Campsite after about 500 metres.

CC € 17 *1/1-30/6 1/9-31/12 7=6, 21=18*

N 36°43'6'' W 3°32'46''

Olvera, E-11690 / Andalucia

2811

Pueblo Blanco Cat. 1
Ctra N384, km 69
+34 956130033
FAX +34 952-834373
1/1 - 31/12
@ info@campingpuebloblanco.com

14ha 220T(100m²) 16A

1 ABCD**G**IJKLMOPST
2 JKLSTVWX
3 ABHNU
4 (B 14/5-31/10) (Q+R+T+U+X+Y) Z
5 **A**CGHIJKLMNOPUWXYZ
6 ACEG**K**(N 3km)ORTV

A campsite established in 2011. On the top of a hill in the immense Los Gredales grounds with views out over the Olvera and the nearby Sierras. Here you will find spacious pitches, all modern amenities and several toilet blocks.

Between Antequera and Jerez de la Frontera, on the A384, at 69 km marker. About 3 km before Olvera on the right. Wide driveway 600 metres to the top.

CC € 17 *1/1-15/7 1/9-31/12 7=6, 14=11, 30=22*

N 36°56'14'' W 5°13'18''

Palomares, E-04617 / Andalucia

2812

Cuevas Mar Cat.2
Ctra Villaricos-Garrucha s/n
FAX +34 950-467382
1/1 - 31/12
@ cuevasmar@arrakis.es

3ha 180T(40-100m²) 6-10A

1 ABC**G**IJKLMO**P**Q
2 AEFLNTVWXY
3 **FGUW**
4 (B 1/5-15/10) K(Q) Z
5 **AB**EFGIJKLMNOPUW
6 EGI**K**(N 0,5km)OQTV

Well-maintained campsite with a quiet location with little natural shade at 400 metres from the beach.

On the Costa de Almería. On Autovia A7 (E15) Alicante-Almería exit 537 Cuevas de Almanzora. After a few kilometres, a short drive to Vera at the T-junction, then direction Palomares; located on the Villaricos road.

CC € 17 *1/1-30/6 1/9-31/12*

N 37°14'16'' W 1°47'57''

Roquetas de Mar (Almería), E-04740 / Andalucia

2813

- Roquetas Cat.2
- Ctra Los Parrales 90
- +34 950-343809
- FAX +34 950-342525
- 1/1 - 31/12
- @ info@campingroquetas.com

8ha 600**T**(60-80m²) 10-16A

1. ABCD**G**IJKLMO**P**Q
2. AEFJLNOTVWX
3. B**F**GKMNUV**W**Y
4. (B+G 1/4-1/10) (Q+S+T+U+X+Y ⊶) Z
5. **AB**EFGIKLMNOPUWXY
6. CEGH**K**(N 0,7km)ORTUV

A well equipped campsite, partially shaded, partially sun-drenched for the many winter visitors. The beach is accessible from the campsite via a footpath. Roquetas is about 5 km away.

Located on the Costa Almería. On motorway A7, take exit 429. In the village of El Parador turn left at the roundabout, follow signs to the campsite.

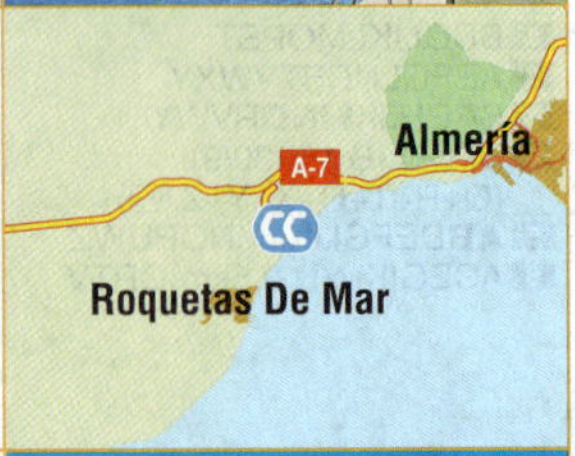

CC € 17 *1/1-7/7 25/8-31/12*

N 36°47'51" W 2°35'28"

Santa Elena (Jaén), E-23213 / Andalucia

2814

- Despeñaperros Cat.1
- Infanta Elena s/n
- FAX +34 953-664192
- 1/1 - 31/12
- @ info@campingdespenaperros.com

4ha 112**T**(70-100m²) 10A

1. BCDGIJKLMOPST
2. BFGLTVXY
3. AHJN**O**U
4. (**A** ⊶) (B+G 20/6-15/9) (Q+R ⊶) (T 15/6-15/10) (U+X+Y 20/6-15/10) Z
5. **A**FGIJKMNOPUWXYZ
6. CEG**I**KORSTV

Quiet wooded site conveniently located a short distance from the N IV/E5. Suitable for staying for some time to relax. Level grounds with sufficiently shaded pitches. The 'Batalla de Las Navas de Tolosa' museum in Sta Elena is most interesting. It shows a scene from a historical battle between the Christians and the Moors in 1212.

A4 Sevilla-Madrid, exit 259; Madrid-Sevilla, exit 257 or 258. Follow signs.

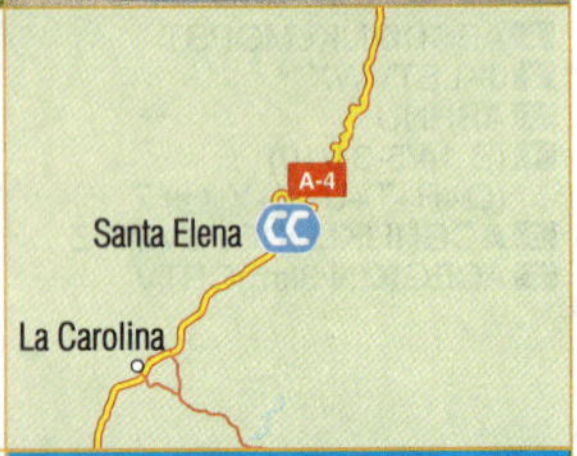

CC € 17 *1/1-19/3 27/3-16/6 15/9-23/12 25/12-30/12*

N 38°20'36" W 3°32'8"

Tarifa, E-11380 / Andalucia

2815

- Paloma Cat.2
- Ctra N340 Cadiz-Malaga, km 74
- +34 956-684203
- FAX +34 956-684233
- 1/3 - 1/12
- @ campingpaloma@yahoo.es

4,9ha 297**T**(40-120m²) 10A

1. ABCDGIJKLMPQ
2. AELRSVWXY
3. BHN**O**RWY
4. (B 15/6-15/9) (Q+S+T+X+Y ⊶) Z
5. **AB**FGIKMNOPU
6. EGJ(N 10km)ORTV

NEW

Located near to the famous Valdevaqueros sandy beach and close to the Necropolis de los Algarbes from the bronze age, this campsite offers many possibilities. The campsite is divided by hedges, and is mostly shaded. Barbecues in low season.

Located next to N340 Tarifa-Cadiz. At 10 km from Tarifa campsite indicated by signs along the road (sea at 500m with big beach).

CC € 13 *1/3-24/3 3/4-15/6 10/9-1/12*

N 36°4'35" W 5°41'37"

Tarifa/Cádiz, E-11380 / Andalucia

2816

Valdevaqueros Cat.2
Ctra N340, km 75,5
+34 956-684174
FAX +34 956-681898
1/1 - 31/12
info@campingvaldevaqueros.com

5ha 324T(50-100m²) 6A CEE

1 ABCD**G**IJKLM**P**ST
2 AELRVWXY
3 BHJK**M**S**W**Y
4 (**A**) (B+G 1/4-30/9) (Q+S+T) U(V+X+Y) Z
5 **AB**GIJKMNOPSTUWXYZ
6 CDEGIJ(N 9km)ORTV

A campsite with individual connections and spacious, marked out pitches. Shade for caravans and tents. Barbecues permitted outside the summer months.

Located by the N340 Tarifa-Cadiz. Campsite is signposted 9 km from Tarifa towards Cadiz on the right.

CC € 17 *1/1-30/6 1/9-31/12 7=6, 14=12, 21=18, 30=26*

N 36°4'9'' W 5°40'49''

Torre del Mar (Málaga), E-29740 / Andalucia

2817

Camping Caravaning Laguna-Playa Cat.1
Prol. Paseo Marítimo s/n
+34 95-2540631
FAX +34 95-2540484
1/1 - 31/12
info@lagunaplaya.com

2ha 144T(70-75m²) 10A

1 BGIJKLMOPQ
2 AEFGLNTVWXY
3 B**FO**RUWY
4 (A 1/7-31/8) (B 1/5-31/10) (G 15/6-15/9) (Q+S+T+U+X+Y+Z)
5 **AB**DEFGIJKLMNOPUWZ
6 AFGK(N 0,4km)ORTV

A quiet campsite with plenty of trees and under good management. The toilet facilities are very well maintained and the pitches are spacious. The site is almost on the beach and within walking distance of Torre del Mar.

A7 (E15, N340), exit 272 Torre del Mar. To old coast road 340a. Then Torre del Mar-West (ouest), past bus station. Follow signs.

CC € 19 *1/1-16/6 12/9-31/12*

N 36°43'46'' W 4°6'9''

Torrox-Costa (Málaga), E-29793 / Andalucia

2818

El Pino
Urb. Torrox-Park s/n
+34 952-530006
FAX +34 952-532578
1/1 - 31/12
info@campingelpino.com

5ha 290T(20-100m²) 10A

1 B**G**IJKLMO**P**ST
2 AFGJLNSTVWXY
3 B**F**GRVW
4 (B+G 1/6-15/9) (Q+R+T+U+V+X+Y+Z)
5 **AB**GIJKMOP**RST**UWZ
6 EGKM(N 2km)ORTV

A large but quietly located campsite with many (avocado) trees. The campsite is about 1 km from the beach.

A7 Motril-Malaga, exit 285 direction Torrox-Costa, follow the signs.

CC € 15 *1/1-30/6 1/9-31/12*

N 36°44'22'' W 3°56'59''

Vélez-Blanco, E-04830 / Andalucia

2819

Pinar del Rey
Paraje Pinar del Rey s/n
+34 649-901680
1/1 - 31/12
info@campingpinardelrey.com

50T(40-60m²) 6A CEE

1 ABCDGIJKLOP
2 BIKLSUVXY
3 BHJMQU
4 (B+G 1/7-31/8) (R) (Z 1/7-31/8)
5 ABDGIJKLMNOPUWXYZ
6 ABEGJ(N 1,7km)TV

Beautiful landscapes - extensive nature reserve - picturesque white villages in the area. A campsite to undertake something and then relax.

A91 dir. Granada becomes the A92N. Take exit 112. Then A317. Campsite located before Vélez Blanco on the right, opposite the petrol station.

CC € 17 1/1-15/7 1/9-31/12 7=6, 14=11, 21=17

N 37°40'51" W 2°5'43"

Villafranca de Córdoba, E-14420 / Andalucia

2820

La Albolafia Cat.2
Camino de la Vega s/n
+34 957-190835
24/2 - 9/12
informacion@campingalbolafia.com

3ha 88T(60-85m²) 10A CEE

1 BCDGIJKLMOPQ
2 FGLTVXY
3 BGHJ
4 (A) (B 15/5-15/9) (Q+R)
5 AGIKMNOPUWZ
6 CEGJ(N 0,5km)ORT

A lovely open plan campsite with spacious pitches and plenty of trees. Close to the Madrid-Cordóba-Seville motorway. Ideally located for visiting Cordóba, also for a few days of relaxation and for visiting the authentic hinterland. Restaurant only open at weekends in early and late seasons.

The village is located on route N IV/E5 Madrid-Córdoba. Exit 377. Follow the signs.

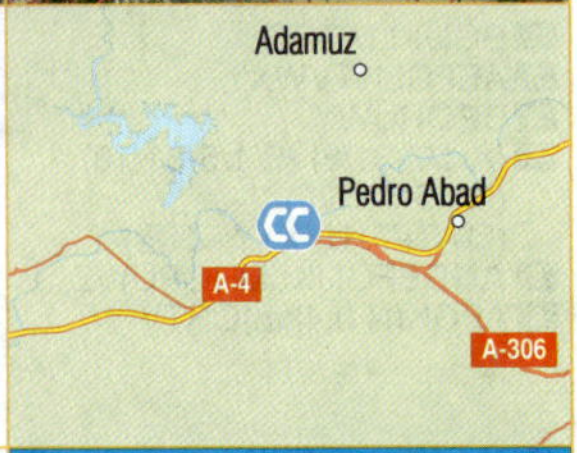

CC € 19 24/2-30/6 1/9-9/12

N 37°57'13" W 4°33'15"

Viñuela, E-29712 / Andalucia

2821

Presa La Viñuela Cat. 2
Ctra A356, km 30
+34 952-554562
FAX +34 952-554570
1/1 - 31/12
campingpresalavinuela@hotmail.com

1ha 39T(60-70m²) 10A

1 ABCDGIJKLMOPST
2 JKLTVXY
3 RW
4 (B 15/6-15/9) (Q+R+X+Y)
5 AGIJKLMNOPUWXY
6 ACEGIK(N 7km)ST

Small, peaceful campsite with good amenities and an excellent restaurant. Beautiful view of the lake and mountains.

N340, A7, exit 272 (e.g. Vélez-Malaga-La Viñuela). Follow A356 past La Viñuela. Campsite just past km 30. Indicated.

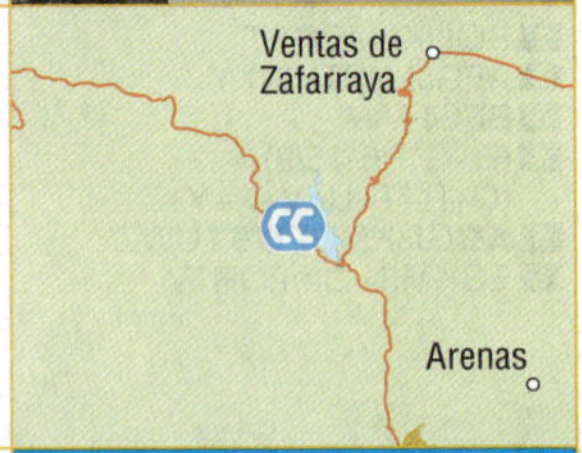

CC € 15 1/1-30/6 1/9-31/12 7=6

N 36°52'26" W 4°11'10"

Águilas, E-30880 / Murcia
2822

Bellavista*
Ctra de Vera, km 3
+34 968-449151
1/1 - 31/12
info@campingbellavista.com

1ha 65T(50-80m²) 10A CEE

1 BCDGIJKLMOP
2 AEFGTVWXY
3 AGRUY
4 (B 1/4-1/11) K(Q+R) (T+V 1/4-1/11) (Z)
5 **AB**FGIJKLMNOPUWXYZ
6 ABDEGIK(N 1km)OQTUV

Small campsite with an eye for detail. Situated quite high up, giving some of the pitches wonderful sea views (250 metres). Many small bays in the area. Good restaurant next to the campsite. No credit cards or debit cards in low season.

Located on route N332 from Águilas to Vera, km post 3.

CC € 17 *1/1-15/7 1/9-31/12*

N 37°23'31" W 1°36'34"

Águilas (Murcia), E-30889 / Murcia
2823

La Quinta Bella
Finca El Charcon 31
+34 968-438535
1/1 - 31/12
jonathan@quintabella.com

14ha 33T(125-225m²) 16A CEE

1 ABCDGIJKLMOQ
2 FUVW
3 U
4 (B+T+V+X+Z)
5 **AB**GJKLMNOPUWXYZ
6 ABCEG**K**(N 2,5km)O

New campsite (2015), small-scale, large pitches. Rural location. Lots of sun. Very friendly, helpful management.

AP7, exit 878. On 1st roundabout dir. Los Arejos RM-D24. Right at campsite sign after 2.9 km. Campsite is on right after 1.9 km.

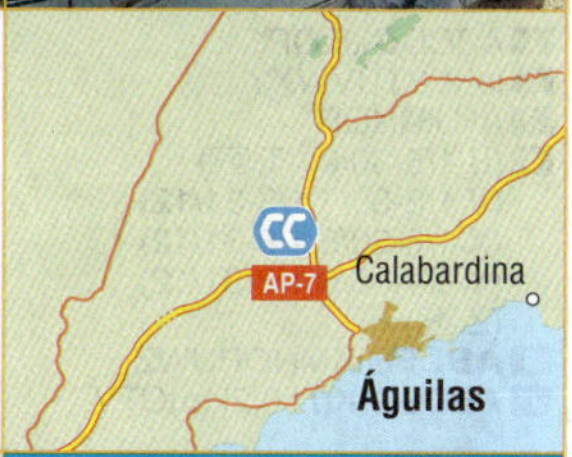

CC € 17 *1/1-7/7 24/8-31/12*

N 37°27'14" W 1°38'43"

Baños de Fortuna (Murcia), E-30626 / Murcia
2824

La Fuente
Camino de la Bocamina s/n
+34 968-685017
FAX +34 968-685125
1/1 - 31/12
info@campingfuente.com

2ha 105T(60-70m²) 10A CEE

1 ABCD**G**IJKLMO
2 GKRTUVWXY
3 HJU
4 **(C+E) KO** (Q+R+U+X+Y+Z)
5 **AB**DGIJKLMNOP**RS**UWXYZ
6 ABCEG**IK**(N 3km)OTV

A jewel in the hinterland of Alicante (province of Murcia). A small, good and charming site. Reservations between 15 December and 15 February are absolutely necessary. There is a spa heated to 36°C. Open all year.

A7, exit 559AB. Then 559A dir Fortuna. Towards Yecla RM423 at 1st roundabout, then A21 direction Baños de Fortuna. Campsite just before village on the left.

CC € 15 *1/1-15/7 1/9-31/12*

N 38°12'24" W 1°6'26"

Bolnuevo/Mazarrón, E-30877 / Murcia

2825

Playa de Mazarrón
Avda Pedro Lopéz Meca s/n
+34 968-150660
FAX +34 968-150837
1/1 - 31/12
@ camping@playamazarron.com

8ha 475T(60-80m²) 11A

1 ABCDGIJKLOPQ
2 AEFGSTVXY
3 BG**M**N**S**UWY
4 (B+G 1/5-15/10) **N**
(Q+S 15/6-15/9)
(U+X+Y+Z 1/7-15/9)
5 **AB**FGIJKLMNOPUWXY
6 ABCEG**IK**MORTV

A flower filled campsite right by the sea. Plenty of winter sun. Plenty of shade from May onwards. On one side you can walk into a lively village, on the other side you can go straight to the beach.

A7, exit 627B, via MU603 direction Mazarrón. At the end of the motorway left towards Cartagena. Right at first roundabout towards Bolnuevo (D6). Right at next roundabout. Campsite about 300 metres on the left.

CC € 17 *1/1-23/3 28/3-30/6 12/9-31/12*

N 37°33'47" W 1°18'14"

El Berro/Alhama de Murcia, E-30848 / Murcia

2826

Sierra Espuña
C/Juan Bautista s/n
+34 968-668038
FAX +34 968-668079
1/1 - 31/12
@ camping@
campingsierraespuna.com

2ha 47T(45-80m²) 6A

1 ABCD**G**IJLOP
2 IJKLSTUVWXY
3 AHJ**M**NQR
4 (B 1/5-30/9) (T 🔑)
(V 1/3-30/6,1/8-31/12)
(X 1/6-30/6,1/8-31/12)
(Y 1/1-30/6,1/8-31/12)
(Z 🔑)
5 **AB**DFGIKMNOPUWZ
6 ABCEG**I**K(N 0,2km)OTV

A small, good campsite. Village and campsite are located in an area of natural beauty. A swimming pool with a lawn, the terrace for a drink, a small restaurant. You won't want to leave!

A7 Murcia-Granada, exit 627 Alhama de Murcia. Dir. Mula on C3315. 2nd exit El Berro C25 (1st exit unsuitable). Follow signs at beginning of village. Don't go through village. Assistance available if required. Call in advance!

CC € 17 *1/1-22/3 28/3-15/7 1/9-31/12 7=6*

N 37°53'17" W 1°29'35"

El Portús/Cartagena, E-30393 / Murcia

2827

Naturista 'El Portús'*
Ctra Canteras-El Portús s/n
+34 968-553052
FAX +34 968-553053
1/1 - 31/12
@ elportus@elportus.com

10ha 350T(60-120m²) 6A

1 ABCD**G**IJKLMO**P**Q
2 AEFGIJKLNQSTUVWX
3 AGH**M**R**V**WY
4 (B 15/6-15/9) (F 🔑) **KNP**
(Q+S+T+V+X+Y+Z 🔑)
5 **AB**DFGIJKLMNOPUWXY
6 ABCEGH**IK**(N 1km)OTV

Naturist campsite. Located on a bay with its own beach, surrounded by beautiful countryside. The restaurant, bar and supermarket are located higher up, from where there are stunning views. Indoor and outdoor swimming pool, spa and wellness.

Located on the bay of El Portús, south-west of Cartagena. In Cartagena follow the signs Mazarrón N332 as far as Canteras/El Portús exit. After Canteras turn left towards El Portús. Follow the camping signs.

CC € 17 *1/1-23/3 28/3-26/6 12/9-31/12*

N 37°35'11" W 1°4'4"

Isla Plana/Cartagena, E-30868 / Murcia

2828

Los Madriles
Ctra a la Azohia km 4,5
+34 968-152151
FAX +34 968-152092
1/1 - 31/12
@ camplosmadriles@forodigital.es

6,5ha 311T(80-100m²) 10A CEE

1 ABEIJKLOPQ
2 GJKLSTUVWXY
3 BGH**M**NRU
4 (C+E) (H 15/6-15/9)
(Q+S+T+V+Z)
5 **A**DFGIJKLMNOP**RST**UXYZ
6 ABCEGH**IJK**(N 1,5km)ORT
V

Lovely terraced campsite with beautiful sea views. Attractive pitches screened by trees and bushes. You can swim all year round in warm water taken straight from the sea. The pools are emptied, cleaned and refilled every night. Dogs not permitted.

A7, exit 845, via MU603 direction Mazzarón. Left at the end of the MU603 onto the N332 and after this keep on direction Cartagena until Isla Plana is signposted (E22). Then follow camping signs.

CC € 19 *1/1-30/6 24/8-31/12*

N 37°34'47" W 1°11'42"

La Manga del Mar Menor, E-30385 / Murcia

2829

Caravaning La Manga
Autovía de La Manga, salida 11
+34 968-563019
FAX +34 968-563426
1/1 - 31/12
@ lamanga@caravaning.es

32ha 950T(84-110m²) 10A CEE

1 ABCD**G**IJKLMOPQ
2 AEFGISUVWX
3 B**F**GMNQRSU**V**WY
4 (B 1/4-30/9)
(**F** 1/1-31/3,1/10-31/12)
(G 1/4-30/9) **N**
(Q+S+T+U) (V 1/7-31/8)
(X+Y+Z)
5 **AB**DFGIJKLMNOPUWXY
6 ABCG**IK**M(N 3km)OQRTV

A good, extended campsite with pitches separated by hedges. Restaurant, bar and terrace by the sea with a beach and palms.

AP7, exit 800 to La Manga MU-312, exit 11. Across the viaduct and drive 500 metres back via the parallel road. Clearly signposted.

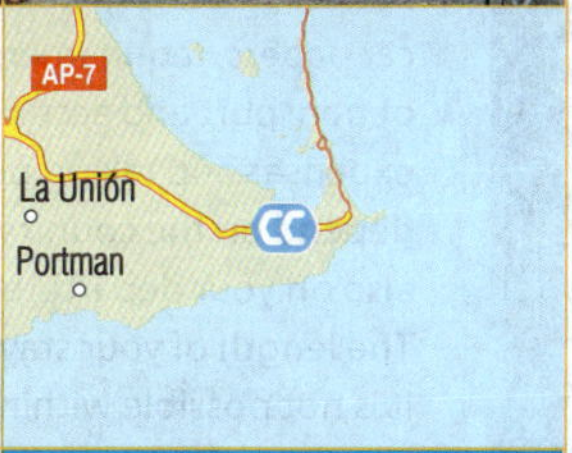

CC € 17 *1/1-30/6 1/9-31/12*

N 37°37'30" W 0°44'37"

Puerto de Mazarrón (Murcia), E-30860 / Murcia

2830

Las Torres
Ctra N332 km 26
FAX +34 968-595225
1/1 - 31/12
@ info@campinglastorres.com

5ha 210T(70m²) 16A

1 ABCD**G**IJLOQ
2 GLSTUVWXY
3 AMRU
4 (B 1/5-30/9)
(E 1/1-31/3,1/10-31/12)
(Q+R+T+U+X+Z)
5 **A**GIJKLMNOPUWZ
6 ABEGJ**K**(N 2km)OTV

A campsite among the the orange groves. The region has a favourable climate, especially in winter. Very helpful managers. Attractive bar and restaurant run by 2 charming Spanish ladies. Spanish cuisine. Entertainment programme is adapted in winter and indoor swimming in a heated pool.

A7 exit 845 via MU603 direction Mazarrón. Left at end of MU603 onto N332 and continue driving until 26 km marker.

CC € 17 *1/1-15/7 1/9-31/12*

N 37°35'23" W 1°13'45"

Portugal

General
Portugal is a member of the EU.

Time
The time in Portugal is one hour behind Amsterdam, Paris and Rome and the same as London.

Language
Portuguese, but you will usually get by in English or French.

Border formalities
Many formalities and agreements about matters such as necessary travel documents, car papers, requirements relating to your means of transport and accommodation, medical expenses and taking pets with you do not only depend on the country you are travelling to but also on your departure point and nationality. The length of your stay can also play a role here. It is not possible within the confines of this guide to guarantee the correct and most up to date information with regard to these matters.

We advise you to consult the relevant authorities before your departure about:
- which travel documents you will need for yourself and your fellow passengers
- which documents you need for your car
- which regulations your caravan must meet
- which goods you may import and export
- how medical treatment will be arranged and paid for in your holiday destination in cases of accident or illness
- whether you can take pets. Contact your vets well in advance. They can give you information about the necessary vaccinations, proof thereof and obligations on return. It would also make sense to enquire whether any special regulations apply to your pet in public places at your holiday destination. In some countries for example dogs must always be muzzled or transported in a cage.

You will find plenty of general information on ▸ ***www.europa.eu*** ◂ but make certain you select information that is relevant to your specific situation.

For the most recent customs regulations you should get in contact with the authorities of your holiday destination in your country of residence.

Currency
The currency in Portugal is the euro. Approximate exchange rates September 2015: £1 = € 1.37. You can recognise cash machines by the sign 'MB'.

Credit cards
You can pay by credit card in many places.

Opening times/Public holidays
Banks
Banks are open Monday to Friday until 15:00.

Shops
Generally open until 19:00 on weekdays. Saturdays open until 13:00.

Chemists, doctors
You can get medical assistance at the local

health centre (centro de saudé). Chemists are open on weekdays until 19:00, often with an afternoon break from 13:00 to 15:00. Chemists are open on Saturdays until 13:00.

Public holidays
New Year's Day, 9 February (Mardi Gras), Good Friday, Easter Sunday, 25 April (Revolution Remembrance Day), 1 May (Labour Day), 26 May (Corpus Christi), 10 June (Portugal Day), 15 August (The Assumption), 5 October (Republic Day), All Saints, 1 December (Independence Day), 8 December (Immaculate Conception) and Christmas Day.

Communication

(Mobile) phones
The mobile network works well throughout Portugal except in remote areas. There is a 3G network for mobile internet. You can pay for calls at payphones using a phonecard which is available from post offices and tobacconists or from Telecom Portugal shops.

WiFi, internet
You will find internet cafes in a few towns. You can use internet at post offices where 'Netpost' is displayed. WiFi is available in shopping centres, hotels and restaurants where 'wireless zone' is indicated.

Post
Post offices (correios) are normally open weekdays until 18:00.

Roads and traffic

Road network
You are advised not to drive outside the towns

during darkness. The ACP operates a breakdown service on all roads. To receive help you must have breakdown insurance. Emergency phones are located every 4 km on main roads. On other roads you should call 707509510.

Traffic regulations
Remember, all traffic in Portugal drives on the right and overtakes on the left! Headlight deflectors are advisable to prevent annoying oncoming drivers. Traffic coming from the right has priority. On roundabouts you have priority over approaching traffic. On narrow roads, the car that can move over most easily has to give way.

Maximum speed

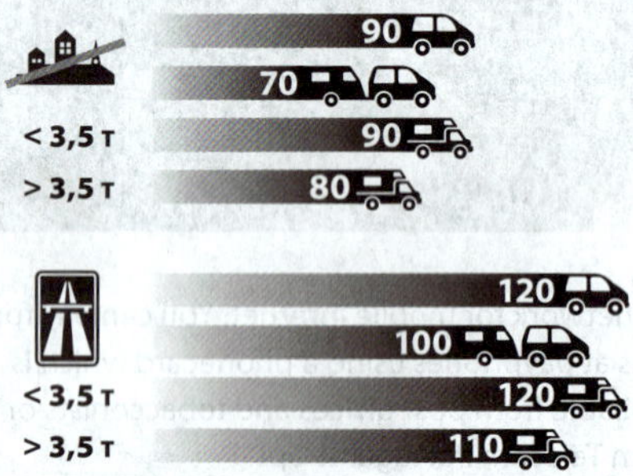

Maximum permitted alcohol level is 0.5‰. You must use a phone hands-free. In built up areas stopping and parking is only permitted where indicated or partly on the pavement in the direction of the traffic. You may not stop on bridges and in tunnels. Winter tyres are not compulsory in winter conditions but are certainly recommended.

Take note: carrying bikes on a bike rack behind the car is prohibited. You are permitted to carry them on a roof rack on the car, or on a bike rack on the back of your caravan or motorhome. The bike must not protrude on the sides and must not protrude for more than 45 cm at the back.

Navigation
Notification of fixed speed cameras by navigation systems or mobile phones is permitted.

Permitted dimensions
Height 4 metres, width 2.55 metres and length of car plus caravan 18.75 metres.

Fuel
Lead-free petrol and diesel are available everywhere.
LPG has limited availability. You can often pay by credit card.

Filling stations
Filling stations are usually open between 07:00 and 22:00.

Toll
You must pay a toll on various roads in Portugal. You can pay cash but on a number of routes you can only pay electronically. There are no barriers on these roads but your car will be registered as you enter. You can recognise these roads by the signs 'Electronic toll only'. You can buy a Toll Service card from an Easy Toll Welcome Point. This card is valid for 3 or 5 days. Another possibility is Easytoll. This is an automatic payment via credit card (MasterCard or Visa) which is registered together with your car number plate. You will need to register (free) at the border. You will receive a ticket that is valid for 30 days. You can also buy a pre-paid card (Toll card). You can purchase this at post offices, tourist offices and Easy Toll sales points. You will find more information on ▸ ***www.visitportugal.com*** ◂ and search for 'electronic tolls.

Emergency number
112: the national emergency number for fire, police and ambulance.

Camping

Portugal has its own classification system for campsites. Campsites are categorised by 1 to 4 stars in proportion to their infrastructure and services, or simply as 'rural'. In this last category the campsite is part of a farm. You are recommended to reserve in high season.

Practical

- Make sure you have a world adaptor for electrical equipment.
- Tap water is of good quality. If in doubt you can drink bottled (mineral) water.

Aboboreiras/Tomar, P-2300-093 / Santarém

iD **2831**

Pelinos -Tomar
Pelinos 77
+351 249301814
1/3 - 1/10
@ info@campingpelinos.com

1ha 30T(75-120m²) 6A

1 ABGIJKLPS
2 BFGIJRSTWXY
3 HR
4 (B+Q+T+X+Z)
5 ABCFGHIJKMOPQUWZ
6 AEJ(N 4km)V

Cosy terraced campsite with lively bar and pavement cafe. Easy-going, small and hospitable. Idyllic surroundings. Portuguese restaurant at walking distance. Information folder to discover a larger part of Portugal. Enthusiastic Dutch management.

IC9/IC3/A13, exit Tomar Norte. Left after 200m direction Aboboreiras. This is just before the (Sopor) petrol station. Follow camping signs from here.

CC € 17 *1/3-2/6 1/9-1/10*

N 39°38'18'' W 8°20'12''

Alverangel/São Pedro de Tomar, P-2300-152 / Santarém

iD **2832**

Camping Lake Portugal
Rua Principal - Castelo de Bode
+351 249371750
1/2 - 30/12
@ alverangelcampismo@gmail.com

1,4ha 55T(60-90m²) 6A

1 ABCDGIJKLMNOPS
2 ACDFGIJKNRSWXY
3 WXZ
4 (Q+R+T+U+Y+Z)
5 ACGHIJKLMNOPUWZ
6 CEGJ(N 6km)V

Located in the center of Portugal with access for all. Surrounded by nature with private and direct access to lake Castelo de Bode. Enjoy the family atmosphere, good weather, limpid waters for nautical activities, restaurant, fresh food, wines, lounge bar and beautiful gardens. Historic region, near the UNESCO town of Tomar and other interesting sights.

On A13 exit 17 dir. Tomar/Barrage Castelo de Bode. After 5 km left dir. Alverangel. Follow signs for another 3 km to site.

CC € 17 *1/2-15/7 1/9-30/12*

N 39°32'55'' W 8°18'32''

Alvor Portimão, P-8500-053 / Faro

iD **2833**

Alvor***
Estrada dos Montes
+351 282459178
1/1 - 31/12
@ info@campingalvor.com

4,5ha 400T 16A

1 AGIJKLMOPRS
2 AFGIJLQSTWXY
3 AFGJKRU
4 (B+G 1/3-30/10)
(Q+R+T+U+X) Z
5 AGIJKMNOPUVZ
6 CEGKRTV

By being divided into small terraces with plenty of shade, this large campsite always has a relaxed ambiance. Varied landscaping. Swimming pool with deckchairs at the bar.

Over two roundabouts by the white church on the N125 to Alvor (between Portimão-Lagos) then 1st exit. Campsite on the left, quite a way past the airport.

CC € 13 *1/1-30/6 1/9-31/12*

N 37°8'6'' W 8°35'26''

Arco de Baúlhe, P-4860-067 / Braga

iD 2834

Campismo Arco Unipessoal, LDA
Lugar das Cruzes
+351 968176246
5/4 - 7/10
campismoarco@hotmail.com

2ha 30T 6A

1 AGIJKLMPRS
2 CFGHJKLRSWXY
3 JWX
4 (B+G 28/5-30/9) (Q) (T+U+X+Z 5/4-2/10)
5 AGIJKLMOPUZ
6 EI(N 0,15km)V

Geert & Martine, a couple with 20 years experience in the region welcome you to this new, small, quiet site with swimming pool 100m from the centre. Centrally located near historic towns and nature parks. Plenty of documentation. Restaurant with cataplana (fish stew) and casserole. 300m from a cycle route.

A7 exit 12 Mondim/Cabeceiras. 2nd right at roundabout direction Arco de Baúlhe. Call 00351968176246 and you will be picked up.

CC € 17 *5/4-30/6 1/9-7/10 7=6, 14=12, 21=18, 28=24*

N 41°29'11" W 7°57'31"

Casfreires/Sátão, P-3560-043 / Viseu

iD 2835

Quinta Chave Grande
Rua do Barreiro 462
FAX +351 232665552
15/3 - 31/10
info@chavegrande.com

9,5ha 180T(100-150m²) 6A CEE

1 ACDGIJKLPRS
2 CGIJRSTWXY
3 AGHJMRUW
4 (A) (B+G 15/5-15/9) (Q+U) Z
5 ABGHIJKMNOPU
6 EJ(N 4km)OUV

Located in the evergreen and sunny inlands sun of Central Portugal, this beautiful campsite is set in a green valley with magnificent views. The camping pitches are very spacious and there is a lovely big swimming pool which uses salt instead of chlorine. 40 km from golf course.

A25 dir. Viseu, exit 19 dir. Sátão. Then IP5 exit 17 dir. Sátão stay on N229. Don't enter Sátão. Follow signs 'Campismo 12 km'. (With SatNav = narrow streets).

CC € 17 *15/3-14/7 1/9-31/10 10=9*

N 40°49'22" W 7°41'46"

Costa de Caparica, P-2825-450 / Setúbal

iD 2836

Orbitur Costa de Caparica
Av. Afonso de Albuquerque
+351 212901366
FAX +351 212900661
1/1 - 31/12
infocaparica@orbitur.pt

5,7ha 250T(42-80m²) 6A CEE

1 ACDGIJKLOPQ
2 AEFGSTVWXY
3 AFMNRUWY
4 (Q+R) (S 1/4-30/10) (T 1/4-30/9) (U 1/4-30/10) (X 1/6-30/9) Z
5 ABGIJKMNOPUVZ
6 CDFGJ(N 1km)ORTV

A campsite where improvements are much in evidence. Many touring pitches are very sandy. The new part has virtually no shade. The older part under the pine trees is almost completely divided into plots by hedges.

Take Caparica exit on the A2/E4. Turn right after about 6 km just before Costa da Caparica direction Trafaria. Campsite located on this bay N377-1 after 2nd roundabout.

CC € 19 *1/1-30/6 25/9-31/12*

N 38°39'13" W 9°14'19"

Entre Ambos-os-Rios/P.da Barca, P-4980-312 / Viana do Castelo

2837

- Lima Escape
- Lugar de Igreja
- +351 258588361
- 1/1 - 13/11, 28/11 - 31/12
- info@lima-escape.pt

5ha 80T 12A

1 ACD**G**IJKLNO**P**
2 BCDFGISUXY
3 AGHJ**W**XZ
4 (Q+R+T+U+X+Z)
5 **A**GIKMOPUZ
6 CDEGJ(N 1km)OTV

This campsite is a fine base for the expansive national park Peneda Geres. Lots of information at reception. Campsite is located in natural surroundings on the Rio Lima. Restaurant open all year. Basic and clean toilet facilities. Free WiFi.

A3 exit 12 IC28 to Ponte da Barca. After bridge over the Lima 2nd exit dir. Lindoso. After 10 km left site at Ambos-os-Rios. From Spain A52 Xinzo or Ourense dir. Portugal. After Lindosos right after 15 km.

CC € 13 *1/1-15/6 1/9-13/11 28/11-31/12* *7=6, 14=12, 21=18, 28=24*

N 41°49'26'' W 8°19'3''

Estela/Rio Alto, P-4570-275 / Porto

2838

- Orbitur Rio Alto****
- Estela P. de Varzim
- +351 252615699
- FAX +351 252615599
- 1/1 - 31/12
- inforioalto@orbitur.pt

9ha 620T 6A

1 BCD**G**IJKLMN**P**RS
2 ACEFLRSUVWX
3 A**F**MNRUWY
4 (B 1/6-30/9) (Q)
(R 1/1-31/5,16/9-31/12)
(S 1/6-15/9) (T)
(U+W 1/6-15/9) (X)
(Y 1/6-15/9) Z
5 **AB**FGIJKMNPUWZ
6 CEGJ(N 2km)OTV

A large campsite located in the dunes, 100 metres from the sea. The site offers little shade and has a nice restaurant and camp shop. There is a lovely swimming pool next to the campsite.

A28 take exit 17 Estela/Laundos. Follow Campismo/Orbitur signs to Rio Alto. Via N13 between Esposende/Povoa de Varzim. In Estela follow 'Campismo'.

CC € 19 *1/1-30/6 25/9-31/12*

N 41°27'46'' W 8°46'22''

Évora, P-7005-206 / Évora

2839

- Orbitur Évora***
- Estr.de Alcáçovas/
Herd. Esparragosa
- +351 266705190
- FAX +351 266709830
- 1/1 - 31/12
- evora@orbitur.pt

3,3ha 220T(60-100m²) 6A

1 BCD**G**IJKLMO**P**Q
2 FGLSTVWXY
3 B**M**
4 (B+G 17/4-30/9) (Q)
(R 15/7-31/8) (T 1/6-30/9) Z
5 **AB**GIJKMNOPUV
6 CEGIJ(N 2km)TV

A campsite with an old and shady part under the eucalyptus trees and a new section, split up into hedged areas with young trees. Large free swimming pool and lawns with deckchairs.

Take the N380 Évora to Alcáçovas, 2 km outside of Évora. When approaching the town there are signs to the campsite.

CC € 19 *1/1-30/6 25/9-31/12*

N 38°33'26'' W 7°55'34''

Gafanha da Boa Hora/Vagos, P-3840-254 / Aveiro

2840

Orbitur Vagueira***
Rua do Parque Campismo
+351 234797526
FAX +351 234797093
1/1 - 31/12
@ infovagueira@orbitur.pt

12ha 250T(80-125m²) 6A CEE

1 BCD**G**IJKLM**P**Q
2 ABFGRSVWXY
3 AC**M**NRTUV
4 (Q+R) (T+U 1/6-15/9) (X 1/6-30/9) (Y 1/6-15/9) Z
5 **AB**EFGIJKMNOPU
6 CDEGJK(N 0,5km)OTV

A family campsite located in pine woods with good amenities including internet services. The campsite is located 1500m from the sea and 1 kilometre from Vagueira. You can observe wild grey herons on the beaches of Vagueira and Areão.

Take N109 from Aveiro to Figuero da Foz. In Vagos to Vagueira. Campsite located in front of the village.

CC € 19 *1/1-30/6 25/9-31/12*

N 40°33'28'' W 8°44'41''

Gala/Figueira da Foz, P-3080-358 / Coimbra

2841

Orbitur Gala (Fig. da Foz)***
Estrada Nacional 109, km 4
+351 233431492
FAX +351 233431231
1/1 - 31/12
@ infogala@orbitur.pt

6,4ha 304T(40-80m²) 6-10A

1 ACD**G**IJKLMO**P**Q
2 ABEISWXY
3 AMNU**W**Y
4 (B+G 1/6-30/9) (Q+R+T+U+X) (Y 1/6-30/9) (Z)
5 **AB**EFGIJKMNOPUWZ
6 EGJ(N 1km)OTV

An Orbitur campsite located in the dunes by the sea with good toilet facilities. Pitches with water and waste water facilities available if desired for a supplement.

Take the N109 from Figueira da Foz to Leiria. 4 km after Figueira da Foz the campsite is clearly signposted at the bridge in Gala.

CC € 19 *1/1-30/6 25/9-31/12*

N 40°7'6'' W 8°51'24''

Gondesende/Bragança, P-5300-561 / Bragança

2842

Cepo Verde***
Lugar da Vinha do Santo
FAX +351 273-999371
1/3 - 31/10
@ cepoverde@montesinho.com

3ha 50T(15-60m²) 6A

1 ABCD**G**IJKLMO**P**RS
2 BFGIJKLRSVY
3 AHR
4 (**A** 1/3-30/6,1/9-31/10) (**B** 15/6-15/9) (Q+T+U) (X 1/3-31/5,1/10-31/10) (Y 1/6-30/9)
5 GIKMOPUZ
6 DEG**J**(N 9km)OTUV

In this wooded terraced campsite in the Montesinho nature park you can enjoy a relaxed atmosphere. Birdsong will help you to enjoy the beautiful panorama. Nearby you will discover typical villages such as Gimonde, Babe, Guadramil. Minor roads traverse the Montesinho Nature Park.

A4 exit Vinhais/Braganca (N103). 2nd exit at roundabout to Braganca/Vinhais via IP4. After 7 km exit right to N103 Braganca Oeste/Vinhais and Campismo. Follow signs.

CC € 11 *1/3-30/6 1/9-31/10* *7=6, 14=12, 21=18, 28=24*

N 41°50'56'' W 6°51'41''

Lagos, P-8600-148 / Faro

2843

Orbitur Valverde***
Estr. da Praia da Luz
+351 282789211-2
FAX +351 282789213
1/1 - 31/12
infovalverde@orbitur.pt

10ha 1000**T**(50-100m²) 10A

1 AC**G**IJKLMO**P**Q
2 FGJLSTVWXY
3 B**FM**NU
4 (B+G 1/4-30/9) (Q) (R+T+U+X 1/6-30/9) Z
5 **AB**EFGIJKMNOPU
6 ACEGIJ(N 7km)ORTV

Large campsite with several well maintained toilet blocks. Peaceful, spacious terraces with lovely views. Free swimming pool. The plots are screened by hedges. Various trees offer shade. Little shade in the new section. New toilet blocks for hibernators.

From Lagos N125 direction Sagres or Vila do Bispo, then left direction Luz and follow the signs.

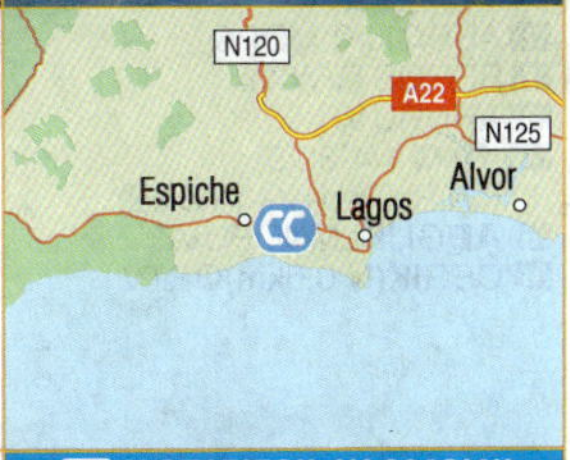

CC € 19 *1/1-30/6 25/9-31/12 7=6*

N 37°5'59'' W 8°43'4''

Luz/Lagos, P-8600 / Faro

2844

Turiscampo****
E-N 125 - Espiche
+351 282789265
FAX +351 282788578
1/1 - 31/12
info@turiscampo.com

7ha 274**T**(100-120m²) 10A

1 ACD**G**IJKLMO**P**Q
2 FGIJLTVWXY
3 A**F**GKNR
4 (B+G) K (Q+R+T+U+V+Y) Z
5 **AB**DEFGIJKLMNOPUWZ
6 CEGHI**K**L(N 4km)ORTVW

Turiscampo campsite with a Californian swimming pool. Luxurious sanitary facilities. Also individual sanitary facilities available. Thanks to the mild climate of the Algarve you are welcome here all year round on a campsite with plenty of luxurious amenities.

Drive via the IP1/E1 or the N125 to Lagos and continue in the direction of Sagres. After exit Luz, continue on the N125. The campsite is located along this road, on the right, just after the traffic lights.

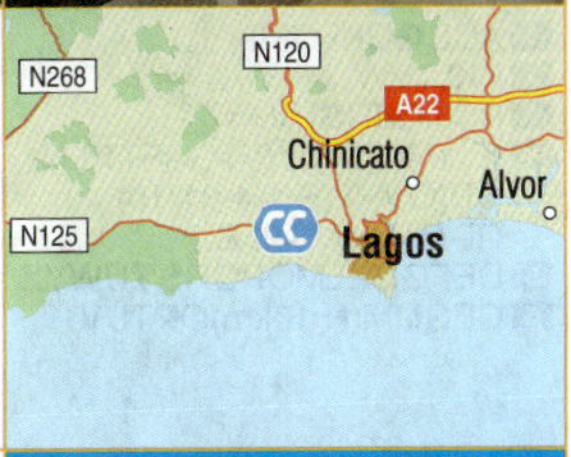

CC € 15 *1/1-12/6 11/9-31/12*

N 37°6'5'' W 8°43'56''

Meruge/Oliveira do Hospital, P-3405-351 / Coimbra

2845

Toca da Raposa
Quinta do Ameal
+351 238601547
15/4 - 10/10
campingtocadaraposa@gmail.com

1ha 30**T**(75-150m²) 6A

1 AB**G**IJKL**P**S
2 BIJKRSTWXY
3 AHIJRU
4 (B+Q+T+X) Z
5 **A**GIJKMOPUWZ
6 CEGJK(N 2,5km)

Joost and Conny will welcome you to this friendly campsite at the foot of Serra da Estrela in central Portugal. Exotic terrace and swimming pool, good sanitary facilities, bar, WiFi, restaurant. An ideal base for exploring the beautiful region. Footpaths from the campsite. You can also go cycling, horse riding and canoeing.

Oliveira do Hospital dir. Lagares da Beira/Viseu via N230. Right 6 km at roundabout Meruge via EM504. Left to campsite after about 2 km.

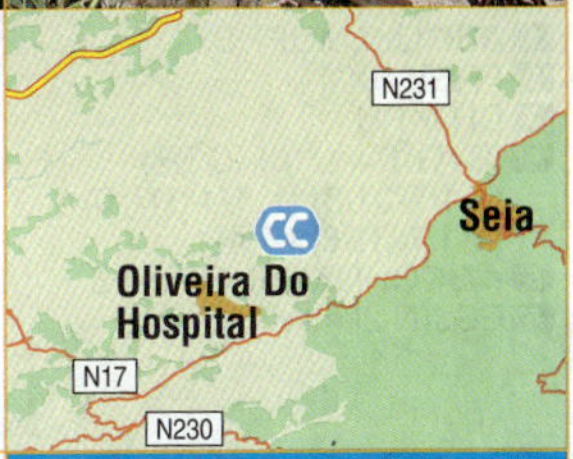

CC € 15 *15/4-30/6 1/9-10/10 8=7*

N 40°23'57'' W 7°49'34''

Nazaré, P-2450-138 / Leiria

2846

Vale Paraíso Natur Park***
Estrada Nac. 242
+351 262561800
FAX +351 262561900
1/1 - 18/12, 27/12 - 31/12
@ info@valeparaiso-naturpark.com

8ha 500T(50-120m²) 6-16A CEE

1 ABD**G**IJKLMOPQ
2 BFGIJSTVWXY
3 AHNRU**V**
4 (B+**G** 1/4-30/9) (Q+R+T+U+X+Y+Z)
5 **AB**GIJKLMNOPUVZ
6 CEGIK(N 0,5km)ORTV

Campsite Vale Paraíso is a fine campsite with an excellent restaurant and swimming pool. There is always a pleasant climate here. A short distance from the attractive fishing villages of Nazaré and Praia do Norte, ideal for surfing and bodyboarding. The lovely beaches there are among the most beautiful in Portugal.

Located on the N242 from Leiria to Nazaré, 2 km before Nazaré, on the west side of the road. Can also be reached via the new motorway A8.

CC €17 1/1-15/7 1/9-18/12 27/12-31/12 7=6

N 39°37'14" W 9°3'23"

Odemira, P-7630 / Beja

2847

Zmar Eco Campo****
Herdade-A-de-Mateus, S. Salvador
+351 707200626
1/1 - 16/1, 22/1 - 31/12
@ reservas@zmar.eu

81ha 288T(90-150m²) 16A

1 ACD**G**IJKLOPQ
2 BKLTVW
3 BCJK**M**N**S**UV
4 (B 1/4-31/10) (F+G) KLN OP(Q) (S 1/4-31/10) (T+U+V+W) Z
5 DEFGIJKLMOPQR**ST**UWYZ
6 CEGIJM(N 10km)O**P**TUV

Family campsite located on a large recreation resort for all ages. You can make use of all the amenities, such as a large indoor and outdoor pool, fitness, sauna, childcare, restaurant. All of this in an area where a clean and economical environment is important.

On the N120 in São Teotónio dir. Zambujeira do Mar. Then dir. Fataca. Stay on 393/1. Follow the arrows. From north, N390 from Milfontes to Odemira, exit São Teotónio.

CC €19 1/1-16/1 22/1-7/7 24/8-31/12

N 37°36'21" W 8°44'15"

Outeiro do Louriçal, P-3105-158 / Leiria

2848

O Tamanco (Lda.)***
Casas Brancas 11
FAX +351 236952551
1/3 - 31/10
@ tamanco@me.com

1,5ha 40T(80-120m²) 6-16A CEE

1 AB**G**IJKLMOPRS
2 FRSVWXY
3 DHJKRU
4 (B+G 1/4-1/10) (Q) (T 1/7-31/8) (X 1/4-31/10) (Y 1/7-31/8) (Z)
5 **AB**CGHIJKLMNOPUWZ
6 EGJ(N 2km)V

A forged gate swings open, and you arrive in a green oasis where you will spend a lovely time in the old orchard or among the bamboo. With clucking chickens and honking geese in the background you can dream of the rural life. Enjoy the honest and delicious food in the welcoming cantina. End the day by the campfire under the stars.

Pombal IC8 exit Outeiro do Louriçal. Take the N109 exit roundabout IC8-A1. Follow signs.

CC €17 1/3-30/6 1/9-31/10

N 39°59'29" W 8°47'20"

Italy

AT
CH
FR
SLO
HR
Trentino-Alto Adige 613
Friuli-Venezia Giulia 637
Valle d'Aosta 597
Lago di Garda 621
Veneto 629
Lombardia 609
Piemonte 598
Emilia Romagna 639
Liguria 603
Toscana 643
Marche 665
Umbria 661
Abruzzo 671
Lazio 667
Molise
Campania 673
Puglia 676
Basilicata
Calabria 679
Sardegna 683
Sicilia 688
LJUBLJANA
ZAGREB
SARAJEVO
Trento
Trieste
Bergamo
Milano
Novara
Verona
Venezia
Torino
Ferrara
Bologna
Ravenna
Rimini
Forlì
Genova
Prato
Pisa
Firenze
Livorno
Ancona
Perugia
Pescara
ROMA
Foggia
Bari
Lecce
Napoli
Salerno
Taranto
Sassari
Cagliari
Catanzaro
Messina
Reggio di Calabria
Palermo
Catania
Siracusa
Tunis

General

Italy is a member of the EU.

Time

The time in Italy is the same as Amsterdam, Paris and Rome and one hour ahead of London.

Languages

Italian is the main language in Italy but you can also get by with English, French or German.

Border formalities

Many formalities and agreements about matters such as necessary travel documents, car papers, requirements relating to your means of transport and accommodation, medical expenses and taking pets with you do not only depend on the country you are travelling to but also on your departure point and nationality. The length of your stay can also play a role here. It is not possible within the confines of this guide to guarantee the correct and most up to date information with regard to these matters.

We advise you to consult the relevant authorities before your departure about:

- which travel documents you will need for yourself and your fellow passengers
- which documents you need for your car
- which regulations your caravan must meet
- which goods you may import and export
- how medical treatment will be arranged and paid for in your holiday destination in cases of accident or illness
- whether you can take pets. Contact your vets well in advance. They can give you information about the necessary vaccinations, proof thereof and obligations on return. It would also make sense to enquire whether any special regulations apply to your pet in public places at your holiday destination. In some countries for example dogs must always be muzzled or transported in a cage.

You will find plenty of general information on ▸ ***www.europa.eu*** ◂ but make certain you select information that is relevant to your specific situation.

For the most recent customs regulations you should get in contact with the authorities of your holiday destination in your country of residence.

Currency

The currency in Italy is the euro. Approximate exchange rates September 2015: £1 = € 1.37.
If travelling to Sicily and arriving at the weekend it is advisable to take sufficient cash with you as the cash machines are often empty.

Credit cards

You can pay by credit card in many places.

Opening times/Public holidays

Banks

Banks are in general open from Monday to Friday from 08:30 to 13:30 and from 15:00 to 16:00. In tourist areas banks are open without a break until 16:00.

Shops

Shops are open from 09:00 to 13:00 and from 16:00 to 20:00. Many shops in tourist areas are open all day and on Sundays.
In Northern Italy (Milan, Venice) shops open earlier in the afternoon and they also close earlier than in the south.

Chemists

Chemists ('farmacia') are generally open from Monday to Friday between 08:30 and 12:30 and between 15:00 and 19:30. In larger towns many chemists are open without a break from 08:30 to 19:30.

Public holidays

New Year's Day, 6 January (Epiphany), Easter,

25 April (Liberation Day), 1 May (Labour Day), 2 June (National holiday), 15 August (The Assumption), All Saints Day, 8 December (Immaculate Conception), Christmas.

Communication

(Mobile) phones

The mobile network works well throughout Italy. There is a 3G network for mobile internet. You can call from payphones using a phonecard which is available from kiosks, post offices and tobacconists.

WiFi, internet

There are plenty of internet cafes in Italy, especially in towns. Most bars and restaurants offer WiFi.

Post

Most post offices are open from Monday to Friday until 14:00 and on Saturdays until 12:00.

Roads and traffic

Road network

In general, the further south you drive, the poorer the quality of the roads. You need to watch out for traffic overtaking you on the right in Italy. You should also look out for scooters and mopeds. You are not advised to drive on country roads after dark. The Italian automobile association (ACI) offers breakdown assistance on many roads. Foreigners can request free help (if they have breakdown insurance) from this service by using the emergency phones located every 2 km along the motorway: tel. 803116.

Traffic regulations

Remember, all traffic in Italy drives on the right and overtakes on the left! Headlight deflectors are advisable to prevent annoying oncoming drivers. Italy uses the metric system, so distances are measured in kilometres (km) and speeds in kilometres per hour (km/h).

Traffic from the right has priority. Trams always have priority. Vehicles entering a roundabout have priority over vehicles already on it, but take care as not everyone adheres to this rule! On narrow roads a heavier vehicle has priority over a lighter vehicle. Uphill traffic on mountain roads has priority over downhill traffic. The use of winter tyres and/or snow chains is mandatory between 1 November and 15 April anywhere in Italy where this is indicated.

Maximum speed

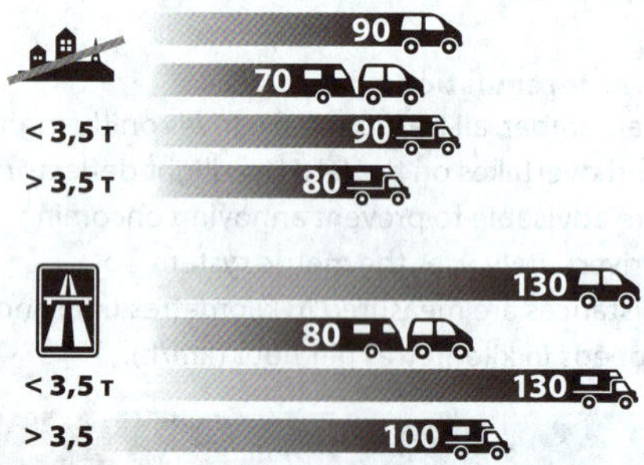

Maximum permitted alcohol level is 0.5‰. Dipped headlights must always be used during the day outside built-up areas and also in all tunnels. Phones may only be used hands-free. Nothing may protrude from a car or trailer. This means that bikes on a bike rack may not stick out at the side!

Navigation
Notification of fixed speed cameras by navigation systems or mobile phones is permitted.

Caravans, motorhomes
The SS163 south of Naples is currently closed to caravans and motorhomes between Vietri sul Mare and Positano (a distance of 40 km) due to increasing traffic congestion.

Permitted dimensions
Height 4 metres, width 2.55 metres and combined length 18.75 metres.

Zona traffico limitato (ZTL)
In a number of cities, such as Rome and Florence, a 'zona traffico limitato' (ZTL) has been introduced. This zone prohibits entry to the city centre to protect it from air pollution. Signs which denote a ZTL vary from city to city and are not always easily recognisable. Take care, as the police enforce this strictly and cameras register cars that drive into the ZTL.

Fuel
Lead free petrol and diesel are widely available. LPG is easily available in northern and central Italy, less so in southern Italy.

Filling stations
Filling stations are open between 07:00 and 19:30 with a break from 12:30 to 15:30. You can usually pay by credit card. Outside opening times you can pay at unmanned filling stations at card terminals. Filling stations alongside motorways are open day and night.

Mountain passes
The following mountain passes are prohibited for caravans:
The mountain pass between Domodossola and Locarno, Col de St. Bernard between Martigny and Aosta, Timmelsjoch (Passo del Rombo) between Sölden and Moso, Staller Sattel between Anterselve and Erlsbach, Passo di Selva between Selva and Canazei, Passo di Garden between Selva and Corvera, Passo di Costalonga between Merano and Vipiteno, Passo di Penzes between Vipiteno and Bolzano.

Tolls
Nearly all motorways are toll roads. You must also pay a toll in the following tunnels: Mont

Blanc Tunnel, Fréjus Tunnel and the Great St Bernard Tunnel. You can pay in cash or by credit card or with a prepaid card (Viacard) which contains a credit amount for toll roads. More information ▸ ***www.autostrade.it*** ◂ (in English).

Emergency number
112: the national emergency number for fire, police and ambulance.

Camping
Northern Italy (South Tyrol, Trentino, Lake Garda and Tuscany) has campsites which are among the best in Europe. Reserve in plenty of time. Campsites in Southern Italy, with a few exceptions, offer a lower level of quality than in the north of Italy. The islands of Sicily and Sardinia are becoming increasingly popular and campsites here are full in high season. The north of Sardinia is popular with divers and surfers. You must be able to identify yourself with an identity document at all Italian campsites. Your identity document will be kept at the campsite reception for the period of your stay.
Free camping is allowed with permission from the landowner.

Practical
- Tourist tax is levied in Italy. Take into account surcharges for amenities and entertainment.
- Many swimming pools only open at the end of May and a swimming cap is often compulsory. Swimming shorts are often prohibited and you will need to wear traditional swimming costumes.
- You should always take a world adaptor with you.
- You can usually drink tap water. If in doubt, buy bottled water.

Crossing to Sardinia
You can reach Sardinia by various routes. Several ferry services make the crossing to Sardinia directly or via Corsica, from France or Italy.

Etroubles, I-11014 / Valle d'Aosta

2854

Tunnel**
Str. Chevrieres 4
+39 0165-78292
1/1-9/1,29/1-30/4,27/5-15/10
info@campingtunnel.it

1,6ha 45T(60-80m²) 6A CEE

1 ACD**G**IJKLMO**P**Q
2 GJKLRVWX
3 A**F**HIRU
4 (T+U+X 1/6-10/9,26/12-6/1) (Z)
5 **AB**DGIJKLMNPUVXY
6 ACDEG**K**(N 0,4km)V

Not far from the St Bernard Tunnel, a well maintained terraced campsite with lovely panoramic views. Lovely walks in the high mountains possible from the campsite. Also a good stopover campsite. Grocery shopping within walking distance.

Turn right from the St. Bernhard past the bridge in Etroubles. Form here the campsite is signposted.

CC € 17 *29/1-30/4 27/5-15/7 1/9-15/10 2/12-16/12*

N 45°49'8'' E 7°13'45''

Morgex, I-11017 / Valle d'Aosta

2855

Arc en Ciel*
Strada Feysoulles 9
+39 0165-809257
1/1 - 3/11, 5/12 - 31/12
info@campingarcenciel.it

1,3ha 85T(70m²) 2-6A

1 ACD**G**IJKLMNOPQ
2 FJKLRWXY
3 ARU
4 (B 1/7-31/8) (Q+V) (X 1/7-31/8) Z
5 **A**GIJKLMNOPUVWZ
6 CDEGJ(N 2km)OV

This peaceful, natural terraced camp site with toilet facilities partially renovated in 2014 is located between Courmayeur and Morgex. Supermarket and thermal baths 2 km. Excellent base for exploring the beautiful surroundings; Val Veny, Val Ferret (Mont Blanc) and the valleys of the Gran Paradiso. Pizzeria at weekends.

The campsite is marked by brown signs in and just beyond Morgex on the SS26 Courmayeur-Aosta.

CC € 17 *1/1-15/7 1/9-31/10*

N 45°45'47'' E 7°0'37''

Sarre, I-11010 / Valle d'Aosta

2856

Monte Bianco**
Fraz. St. Maurice 15
+39 0165-258514
15/5 - 30/9
info@campingmontebianco.it

0,7ha 60T(80-100m²) 6A CEE

1 AGIJKLMPQ
2 CFJRVWXY
3 AR**W**
5 **A**GIJKMNO**P**UV
6 ACEGK(N 0,5km)O

Well maintained, small and green campsite under deciduous trees. Situated in the beautiful, busy Aosta Valley on the Italian side of Europe's highest mountain. Close to the high valleys of the Gran Paradiso, Val Ferret and Valpelline.

Follow the road Aosta-Courmayeur SS26. Entering Sarre it is the second openend campsite on the left.

CC € 17 *15/5-30/6 20/8-30/9*

N 45°43'0'' E 7°15'42''

Agliano Terme, I-14041 / Piemonte

2857

Camping International Le Fonti***
Via alle Fontane 54
+39 0141-954820
26/3 - 31/10
info@campinglefonti.eu

54T 6A

1 BCDGIJKLMO**PQ**
2 JKLRSUWXY
3 BHJ**MOR**
4 (**A**) (B+G 15/5-15/9) K
(Q) (T+U+X 1/6-31/8)
(Z)
5 **A**FGIJKLMNOPUVWXZ
6 ACEGJ(N 3km)**P**QTV

The campsite is located in a beautiful nature reserve. Terraces with spacious pitches. Also suitable for the whole family. Guided excursions in this wine-producing area. Friendly and helpful staff. Suitable for cycling and walking trips. Lovely swimming pool.

From A21 Torino-Alessandria, exit Asti-Est, direction Alba. Then exit Turchino, route 456, then right dir. Agliano Terme. Campsite is clearly signposted.

CC €17 *26/3-19/6 5/9-31/10*

N 44°47'49'' E 8°14'31''

Baveno, I-28831 / Piemonte

2858

Camping Village Parisi**
Via Piave 50
FAX +39 0323-924160
18/3 - 30/9
info@campingparisi.it

0,6ha 51**T**(60-80m²) 6A CEE

1 AGIJLPR
2 DFGKLNRTXY
3 A**F**WZ
4 (Q 15/7-15/8) (R)
5 **AB**GIJKMNOPUV
6 E**I**J(N 0,2km)T

A small, friendly campsite in the centre of Baveno. Located directly on Lago Maggiore.

Baveno is located between Verbania and Stresa. Follow camping signs in the centre of Baveno.

CC €17 *1/4-4/5 8/5-12/5 15/5-25/5 29/5-1/6 5/6-14/6 1/9-30/9*

N 45°54'39'' E 8°30'21''

Baveno/Oltrefiume, I-28831 / Piemonte

2859

Tranquilla
Via Cave Oltrefiume, 2
FAX +39 0323-923452
19/3 - 16/10
info@campingtranquilla.it

1,8ha 60**T**(70-80m²) 6A CEE

1 A**G**IJKLOPQ
2 FJKRVXY
3 A**F**GR
4 (B+G 1/6-15/9) (Q+R)
5 **AB**FGIJKLMNOPUV
6 EGJ(N 1,5km)OQTV

A very well maintained campsite with basic amenities, quietly located 1 km from Lago Maggiore.

In the centre of Baveno drive in the direction of Verbania. After about 1 km turn to the left in the direction of Oltrefiume. Signposted along the road.

CC €17 *19/3-15/6 1/9-16/10 7=6, 14=11*

N 45°54'44'' E 8°29'21''

Cannobio, I-28822 / Piemonte

2860

Del Sole**
Via Sotto i Chiosi 81/a
+39 0323-70732
FAX +39 0323-72387
26/2 - 6/11
info@campingsole.it

1ha 100T(32-64m²) 6A CEE

1 ABCDGIJKLMPQ
2 CLORTVY
3 BHJKMNQRWX
4 (A 1/6-30/8) (B 20/5-20/9) (Q+R+T+U+V+Y) Z
5 ABGIJKLMPUWXYZ
6 CEGKTVWX

A friendly campsite by a river close to Cannobio. The pitches are shaded. There is a swimming pool and an excellent restaurant.

E35, exit Locarno direction Brissago. In Cannobio the campsite is signposted to the left. Turn left after the first bridge, then directly right.

CC € 17 26/2-24/3 28/3-5/5 29/5-7/7 4/9-6/11

N 46°4'0'' E 8°41'42''

Castelletto Ticino/Novara, I-28053 / Piemonte

2861

Italia Lido**
Via Cicognola 104
FAX +39 0331-923032
12/3 - 23/10
info@campingitalialido.it

2ha 50T(50-70m²) 3A CEE

1 BGIJLNOPQ
2 ADFJKLRTVWX
3 AGKNRWZ
4 (Q+R+T+V+W+X+Z)
5 ABGIJKLMNOPUV
6 CEGJ(N 2km)OQTV

Quiet campsite with beautiful sandy beach on Lake Maggiore.

The campsite is located directly on Lago Maggiore on the left of the road from Dormelletto to Sesto Calende.

CC € 17 12/3-30/6 29/8-23/10

N 45°43'29'' E 8°36'36''

Dormelletto, I-28040 / Piemonte

2862

Eden
Corso Cavour 59
FAX +39 0322-497524
15/3 - 31/10
info@campingeden.it

3ha 50T 3A CEE

1 BCDFHIJKLMNOP
2 ADFGKLMRXY
3 BGKNRWZ
4 (B 20/5-20/9) (Q+R 1/4-20/9) (T+U+V+Y+Z 15/3-20/9)
5 ABGIJKMNPQUVXZ
6 EIJ(N 1km)OTV

A small and peaceful campsite with good swimming opportunities on Lake Maggiore.

From Arona direction Sesto Calende. Campsite is on the left and is clearly signposted.

CC € 15 15/3-30/6 1/9-31/10

N 45°43'53'' E 8°34'35''

Dormelletto, I-28040 / Piemonte

2863

Lago Maggiore***
Via Salvador Dalí
+39 0322-497193
FAX +39 0322-498600
24/3 - 30/9
@ info@lagomag.com

5ha 110T(60-90m²) 6A CEE

1 BC**G**IJKLMOPQ
2 ADFRVY
3 BGH**M**NRUWZ
4 (B+G 15/5-15/9)
(Q+R+T+U+V+W+X+Y+Z)
5 **A**EFGIJKLMNOPUV
6 ACEG**J**(N 1km)ORTV

Campsite with predominantly annual pitches. Inviting swimming pool located directly on Lago Maggiore.

From Arona direction Sesto Calende. Campsite is clearly marked on the left of the road.

CC € 19 *24/3-24/6 5/9-30/9*

N 45°44'7'' E 8°34'31''

Entracque, I-12010 / Piemonte

2864

Campeggio Valle Gesso**
Strada Provinciale per Valdieri 3
+39 0171-978247
FAX +39 0171-978858
26/12 - 10/1, 30/1 - 21/2,
25/3 - 16/10
@ info@campingvallegesso.com

4,9ha 145T(60-115m²) 6A CEE

1 BCD**G**HIJKLNOS
2 BCGKLRXY
3 ABGJKNRU**W**
4 (**A** 14/4-1/11) (B 1/7-31/8)
MP(Q 20/6-15/9)
(R 1/1-7/3,14/4-31/12)
(U 1/7-31/8)
(V 1/1-7/3,14/4-31/12) Z
5 **AB**DEFGIJKLMNO**P**RUVW
XYZ
6 BCDEGK(N 1km)OTV

Peacefully located campsite on a river. Wonderful nature park close by. Lovely swimming pool, open in fine weather. Well maintained toilet facilities. Climbing wall for beginners close by (Via Ferrata).

Campsite already signposted on route 20 at the T junction to the south of Bargo San Dalmazzo. Via Valdieri-Entracque. The campsite is situated 1 km before Entracque, and is clearly signposted.

CC € 19 *30/4-24/6 1/9-30/9*

N 44°15'3'' E 7°23'25''

Feriolo di Baveno, I-28835 / Piemonte

2865

Conca d'Oro***
Via 42 Martiri 26
+39 0323-28116
FAX +39 0323-28538
18/3 - 25/9
@ info@concadoro.it

5,2ha 200T(70-100m²) 6A CEE

1 B**F**IJKLMPQ
2 ADFKLRVXY
3 A**F**HJKN**O**RUWZ
4 (Q+S+T+U+V+W+X+Y+Z)
5 **A**EFGIJKMNOPUVW
6 CEG**K**(N 1km)OSTVWX

A campsite with plenty of excellent facilities. Peacefully located. Private sandy beach by the picturesque Lago Maggiore.

The campsite is located in between of the roundabout in the village of Fondotoce di Verbania and the village of Feriolo, on the shores of Lago Maggiore.

CC € 19 *18/3-3/7 29/8-25/9*

N 45°56'11'' E 8°29'11''

Feriolo di Baveno, I-28831 / Piemonte

2866

Orchidea***
Via 42 Martiri, 20
+39 0323-28257
FAX +39 0323-28573
19/3 - 9/10
@ info@campingorchidea.it

3ha 219T(60-73m²) 6A CEE

1 A**G**IJKLMPQ
2 ADFGJKLRVXY
3 B**F**GHJNWZ
4 (Q+S+T+U+V+X+Z)
5 **A**FGIJKMNOPUV
6 CFG**IJK**(N 1km)ORTV

Very well maintained campsite with a beautiful beach on the shores of Lago Maggiore, and within walking distance of the village of Feriolo. Great sports grounds for teens and special play equipment for kids.

Campsite located on road between Verbania-Fondotoce and Feriolo, just before the centre of Feriolo by the side of the lake. Signposted on the left of the road.

CC € 17 *19/3-26/6 1/9-9/10*

N 45°56'1'' E 8°28'52''

Fondotoce/Verbania, I-28924 / Piemonte

2867

La Quiete**
Via Turati 72
+39 0323-496013
FAX +39 0323-496139
19/3 - 19/9
@ info@campinglaquiete.it

2,8ha 180T(60-70m²) 6A CEE

1 B**G**IJKLPQ
2 ACDFKLRVXY
3 B**F**GHJNWZ
4 (Q+R+T+V+X+Y+Z)
5 AGIJKMOPUV
6 EGJ**K**(N 1,5km)TV

Campsite with basic amenities located directly on the clean, peaceful lake of Mergozzo. Beautiful view of the lake, you can even see the Alps.

Campsite is located between Mergozzo and Fondotoce, on the lakeside (SS34). It is about 2 km from Mergozzo centre.

CC € 17 *19/3-30/6 1/9-19/9 14=11*

N 45°57'13'' E 8°28'37''

Garbagna, I-15050 / Piemonte

2868

Piccolo Camping E Maieu**
Strada per Ramero 10
+39 339-1466287
19/3 - 30/9
@ emaieu@camping.it

6ha 45T(30-70m²) 3-10A CEE

1 B**G**IJKL**P**RS
2 GJKRTUVXY
3 **F**HJNRU
4 (**B** 16/6-1/9)
5 **A**GIJKLMNOPQUV
6 AEG**J**(N 0,5km)

A very peaceful, small campsite in a hilly area. Clean toilet facilities. Terraces. Suitable as a stopover campsite. Walking routes available. One hour's drive from the Mediterranean.

A7 Milano-Genova, exit Vignole B. Right after toll booth direction Garbagna. Follow road to the left after 7 km (direction Garbagna). 3 km beyond tunnel. In the village follow 'E Maieu' and 'camping' signs.

CC € 17 *19/3-30/6 1/9-30/9*

N 44°46'56'' E 8°59'19''

Ghiffa, I-28823 / Piemonte

2869

La Sierra**
Belvedere 337
+39 333-7815534
1/3 - 31/10
info@campinglasierra.it

8ha 42T(55-70m²) 6A CEE

1 ABCD**G**IJKLO**P**Q
2 DJKNOUVX
3 AHKRWZ
4 (Q+R+T+U+V+X+Z)
5 **A**GIKMOPUWXZ
6 AEGK(N 5km)OT

Small friendly terraced campsite situated right on Lago Maggiore. The views over the lake are breathtaking. The lively town of Verbania is close by.

Campsite located on the Verbania and Cannobio road beside Lago Maggiore. Site clearly indicated in Ghiffa.

CC € 13 *1/3-5/7 24/8-31/10*

N 45°58'36" E 8°38'2"

Orta San Giulio, I-28016 / Piemonte

2870

Orta**
Via Domodossola 28
FAX +39 0322-90267
1/3 - 31/12
info@campingorta.it

3,6ha 80T(70-80m²) 6A CEE

1 B**G**IJKLOPQ
2 DFJKLMORTVXY
3 AHKRUWZ
4 (Q+R+T+X+Z)
5 **AB**FGIJKLMNO**P**UV
6 AFG**IJ**(N 2km)OTW

Small well maintained campsite in natural surroundings on the shores of Lake Orta.

You'll find the campsite between Gozzano and Omegna 229. About 2 km past the crossing which leads to Orta San Giulio. Situated on the shores of the lake.

CC € 17 *1/3-30/6 1/9-31/12 7=6, 14=12*

N 45°48'4" E 8°25'16"

Pettenasco, I-28028 / Piemonte

2871

Camping Royal
Via Pratolungo 32
+39 0323-888945
FAX +39 0323-888100
1/3 - 30/11
info@campingroyal.com

1,8ha 30T 5A CEE

1 ACD**F**HIJKLO**P**Q
2 JKRTVXY
3 ABGHKNR
4 (**B** 1/6-15/9) (Q+S+Z)
5 **A**DGJKMNPUVW
6 CDEG**IJ**(N 3km)ORTVX

A very peacefully located and well kept campsite with beautiful views of Lake Orta below.

Pettenasco is half way between 'Gravellona Toce' and Borgomanero. Follow camping signs in centre of Pettenasco.

CC € 15 *1/3-9/7 26/8-30/11*

N 45°49'25" E 8°24'51"

Peveragno, I-12016 / Piemonte

2872

Il Melo**
Via don G. Peirone 57
+39 0171-383599
1/1-6/1,28/1-21/2,21/3-6/11
info@campingilmelo.it

1,3ha 40**T**(60-70m²) 6A CEE

1 ABGHIJKLOQ
2 CIJKLRWXY
3 A**F**GHJ**M**NR
4 (**A** 1/5-30/9) (B 1/6-1/9)
(Q 1/5-31/10)
(T+U+V+X) Z
5 **AB**DEGIJKLMNO**P**UVZ
6 ACEGIJ(N 1km)T

The campsite is located 800 metres from the village in the middle of typical mountainous countryside. Situated at a sunny, panoramic elevation at the foot of a 2400 metre high mountain. An oasis of calm for those who love nature, walking and a lovely swimming pool.

From Cuneo and from Mondovi in Peveragno village opposite gas station go uphill towards San Giovenale, then follow campsite signs. If SatNav will not find new address, use old address: Via dello Sport 1.

CC € 17 *26/3-30/6 1/9-31/10*

N 44°19'39'' E 7°36'19''

Solcio di Lesa, I-28040 / Piemonte

2873

Solcio**
Via al Campeggio
+39 0322-7497
+39 0322-7566
11/3 - 6/11
info@campingsolcio.com

1,5ha 100**T**(60-80m²) 6A CEE

1 AB**G**IJKLMOPQ
2 ADFGKMRVXY
3 AKRUWZ
4 (Q) (R 7/3-20/10) (T)
(V 7/3-20/10) (X+Y+Z)
5 **A**BFGIKLMNOPUVW
6 AEG**K**(N 0,5km)OTV

Peaceful campsite with good amenities within walking distance of the small church at Solcio, situated right on Lake Maggiore. The restaurant is of very good quality.

Solcio di Lesa is located between Stresa and Arona. Turn into the street directly opposite the church, direction 'Lago'. Entrance to the campsite is 50 metres further on.

CC € 19 *11/3-8/7 27/8-6/11*

N 45°48'57'' E 8°33'0''

Albenga, I-17031 / Liguria

2874

Delfino
Strada Comunale Villaggio Iris 23
+39 0182-591066
+39 0182-51998
24/3 - 25/9
info@campingdelfino.it

1,7ha 147**T**(52m²) 6A CEE

1 ACFHIJKLMOPST
2 AEFGNRVWXY
3 AB**F**GHRUWY
4 (**B**+G 1/5-28/9) **KP**
(Q+R+T+U+V+Y+Z)
5 **A**GHIKMO**P**UVZ
6 ACDFG**J**(N 0,5km)OTV

Campsite located by the sea. Plenty of shade from natural vegetation and overhead cover. Plenty of pitches for short stops. Good toilet facilities. The campsite has a shop and a bar/restaurant, pizzeria, swimming pool and a fitness room.

A10, exit Albenga direction Alassio/Imperia (Strada Panoramica). Left 150m after tunnel. Campsite clearly signposted.

CC € 17 *24/3-8/7 29/8-25/9*

N 44°2'9'' E 8°12'28''

Ameglia, I-19031 / Liguria

2875

River***
Località Armezzone
+39 0187-65920
FAX +39 0187-65183
12/4 - 4/10
info@campingriver.it

4ha 190**T**(60-80m²) 3-6-10A CEE

1 ABCD**G**HIJKLMNO**P**RS
2 CFGLRTVY
3 B**F**K**M**NOPRUW
4 (A 1/8-31/8) (B+G 1/5-30/9) (Q+S+T+U+V+W+X 12/4-30/9)Z
5 **AB**FGIJKLMNOPUVZ
6 CDEGJ(N 0,7km)QRTV

Peaceful campsite located on a river and close to the sea. Lovely level pitches with ample shade. The campsite has its own large swimming pool. A good base for visiting Pisa, Lucca and other places of interest. A helicopter base is located nearby the campsite.

A12 Genua-Livorno, exit Sarzana, direction Lerici. 3 km further on follow signs to Bocca di Magra (S432). Campsite clearly marked after Ameglia sign. Small entry to the campsite.

CC € 17 *12/4-5/7* *1/9-4/10*

N 44°4'33" E 9°58'12"

Arenzano/Genova, I-16158 / Liguria

2876

Caravan Park La Vesima
Via Rubens 50R
+39 010-6199672
FAX +39 010-6199686
1/1 - 6/11, 7/12 - 31/12
info@caravanparklavesima.it

2ha 70**T**(37-60m²) 3A CEE

1 ACDEIJKLMNOPR
2 EFGNOQTUVWXY
3 AB**EF**HJKRWY
4 (Q+R+T+U+V+X+Z 1/5-30/9)
5 **AB**DGIKMO**P**UVZ
6 G**K**(N 1km)RT

Campsite located right by the sea, 800m from Arenzano fishing village and 17 km from Genoa. Ideal for visiting Genoa aquarium. The site has 2 restaurants, 2 bars, a pizzeria and motorhome service. Most suitable for an overnight stop before taking the ferry to Corsica/Sardinia.

From the A10 exit Arenzano direction Genova. Campsite about 500m beyond the tunnel on the right of the road.

CC € 17 *1/3-24/3* *29/3-30/6* *12/9-16/10*

N 44°24'51" E 8°42'17"

Campochiesa/Albenga, I-17031 / Liguria

2877

Bella Vista***
Via Campore 23
+39 329-5923683
FAX +39 0182-554925
21/3 - 14/11, 15/12 - 15/1
campingbellavista@hotmail.com

1,2ha 63**T**(50-80m²) 6A CEE

1 BCD**G**IJKLMPRS
2 FJRTVWXY
3 B**F**JR
4 (A+B+G+Q+R+U+X+Z 1/5-30/9)
5 **AB**DFGIJKLMNOPUVWXYZ
6 ACGK(N 1,5km)T

Colourful, natural Dutch run campsite with local hospitality. 1,5 km from the sea. Large swimming pool. Clean toilet facilities. Activities: barbecue and eating out. Please call in advance.

A10 exit Borghetto SS dir. Ceriale. Dir. Ceriale/ Loano after 150m. Immediately dir. Ceriale after viaduct. Right at T junction. Right in Ceriale at oval roundabout and fountain. Right at traffic lights. Follow camping signs. Don't follow SatNav!

CC € 17 *1/1-15/1* *21/3-9/7* *28/8-14/11* *15/12-31/12*

N 44°5'3" E 8°12'35"

Ceriale/Savona, I-17023 / Liguria

iD 2878

Bungalow Camping Baciccia***
Via Torino 19
+39 0182-990743
FAX +39 0182-1966234
18/3 - 20/10
@ info@campingbaciccia.it

1,5ha 110**T**(45-70m²) 6A CEE

1 ACD**G**IJKLMNOPQ
2 AEFGLNORTWXY
3 AB**F**GHJKMNRUWY
4 (B+G+Q+R+T+U+V+X+Z)
5 **AB**DGIJKLMNOPUVWXYZ
6 ACEG**K**(N 0,2km)ORTV

Family campsite with shaded pitches 500m from the sea. Modern toilet facilities. Swimming pool open April to October. Larger pitches in early and late season and (where possible) cars allowed on the pitches. An ideal base for trips to Castelvecchio, Zuccarello, the caves at Toirano, Cinque Terre and Monaco.

A10, exit Borghetto Santo/Spirito, then SS1 'Via Aurelia' direction Ceriale. At Ceriale follow signs. Right at roundabout with Lidl. 200m to campsite.

CC € 19 *18/3-24/3 29/3-21/4 26/4-16/6 7/9-19/10 10=9, 14=12*

N 44°4'54'' E 8°13'4''

Déiva Marina, I-19013 / Liguria

iD 2879

La Sfinge
Località Gea
FAX +39 0187-825464
15/3 - 2/11
@ lasfinge@camping.it

1,8ha 100**T**(20-90m²) 3A CEE

1 ACD**G**IJKLMOPRS
2 FGJRTVXY
3 BH
4 (Q+S 1/4-31/10)
5 **AB**GIJKLMNPUVW
6 ACEGIJ(N 2,5km)OT

Friendly attractive campsite with plenty of shaded pitches for tents on terraces under the trees. Excellent sanitary facilities. Ideal location for trips out, for example to Cirque Terre. Déiva has a railway station with plenty of opportunity for visiting local attractions by public transport.

A12 Genova-La Spezia, exit Déiva Marina. About 4 km in the direction of Déiva Marina. Follow the signs. Cp on the right.

CC € 17 *15/3-30/6 1/9-2/11*

N 44°13'35'' E 9°33'0''

Déiva Marina, I-19013 / Liguria

iD 2880

Valdeiva**
Località Ronco
+39 0187-824174
FAX +39 0187-825352
10/2 - 6/11, 2/12 - 10/1
@ camping@valdeiva.it

4ha 65**T**(15-56m²) 3A CEE

1 ACDGIJKLMNOPRS
2 FGJRTVWXY
3 AHR
4 (B 15/6-15/9) (Q)
(R+T+U+V+X 20/5-20/9) Z
5 **AB**GIJKLMNOPUV
6 CEGIJ(N 3km)OQRT

A family campsite with plenty of shade-giving vegetation. It has a camp shop and restaurant. There is also a swimming pool. Free transport to the coast/station. Ideal for a visit to Cinque Terre.

A12 Genova-La Spezia, exit Déiva Marina. About 4 km direction Déiva Marina. Signposted to the left of the road, across new bridge.

CC € 17 *1/1-10/1 10/2-15/6 11/9-6/11 2/12-31/12*

N 44°13'31'' E 9°33'2''

Déiva Marina, I-19013 / Liguria

2881

Villaggio Turistico Arenella
Loc. Arenella
+39 0187-825259
FAX +39 0187-826884
1/3 - 31/10
info@campingarenella.it

1,8ha 75**T**(20-60m²) 3A CEE

1 ACDGIJKLMNOPRS
2 FJRTVWXY
3 AB
4 (Q+R 1/6-15/9) U
(V+X 1/6-15/9) Z
5 **AB**GIJKLMNOPUVZ
6 CEG**J**(N 1,5km)RTV

A terraced camp in a rustic location which is perfect for tourist trips to Genoa and Cinque Terre. Deiva has a (railway) station, so you can make excellent use of public transport.

A12 Genova-Livorno, exit Déiva Marina, about 5 km. Signposted to the right of the road beyond petrol station.

CC € 17 *1/3-30/6 1/9-31/10*

N 44°13'44" E 9°32'6"

Finale Ligure, I-17024 / Liguria

2882

Il Villaggio di Giuele***
Via Calvisio 37
FAX +39 019-601240
20/3 - 30/10
info@ilvillaggiodigiuele.it

2ha 120**T**(40-75m²) 6A CEE

1 ACD**G**IJKLMPQ
2 AFGRTVWXY
3 BJKLN**OP**R
4 (B+G) KP
(Q+S+T+U+V+Y) Z
5 **AB**EGIJKMOPUVW
6 EG**K**(N 1,5km)RTV

Friendly campsite located by the sea (1.5 km). Shuttle-bus to the beach. Finale Ligure: friendly village with a beautiful boulevard. Excellent base for walkers and bikers. Special facilities for mountainbikers and down-hillers. Shops, restaurant, WiFi.

From A10 exit Finale Ligure. On the SS1 turn left through the town. Left just before tunnel, direction Calvisio. Follow signs to campsite (±1.5 km). Take note: do not use SatNav, follow the signs.

CC € 19 *10/4-29/4 8/5-13/5 29/5-1/6 5/6-30/6 4/9-30/10*

N 44°11'3" E 8°21'12"

Imperia, I-18100 / Liguria

2883

De Wijnstok
Via Poggi 2
+39 0183-64986
FAX +39 0183-660323
1/1 - 31/12
info@campingdewijnstok.com

0,8ha 40**T**(30-40m²) 6A CEE

1 ABCDGIJKLPQ
2 EFGNOQSTVXY
4 (T+U+V+X+Z 1/6-15/9)
5 **A**GIJKLMNO**P**UV
6 ACFG**K**(N 0,3km)ORT

Typical Italian campsite in the centre of the Italian Riviera. Just 100m from the sea. Campsite under Italian management.

Signposted about 1.5 km west of Imperia (San Remo side) on the SS1 'Via Aurelia'. The campsite is located on the northern side of the road. Or when approaching on the A10: exit Imperia Ovest.

CC € 19 *1/1-25/3 28/3-1/6 5/6-15/7 1/9-31/12*

N 43°52'10" E 7°59'52"

Isolabona, I-18035 / Liguria

2884

Delle Rose
Regione Prati Gonter 4
+39 0184-208130
21/3 - 6/11
info@campingdellerose.eu

1ha 90**T**(30-80m^2) 3A CEE

1 BCD**G**IJKLMNO**P**RS
2 BCGJKRTVWXY
3 ABJKNRW
4 (**A** 1/7-31/8)
(B+G 1/6-30/9) (Q+R)
(T+U+V+X+Z 1/6-30/9)
5 **A**EFGIJKLMNOPUV
6 ADEGJ(N 2km)R

A friendly family campsite set in countryside. Excellent toilet facilities. Swimming pool and children's pool. The campsite is located close to the sea and is a good base for trips out to mountain villages and coastal resorts.

A10, exit Ventimiglia towards main street in Aurelia. Drive through Ventimiglia, left at Nervia roundabout and follow Strada Provinciale 64 in Val Nervia. Campsite on the right 2 km past Isolabona village. Follow the signs and not SatNav!

CC € 15 *21/3-10/7 27/8-6/11*

N 43°53'40'' E 7°38'51''

Pietra Ligure, I-17027 / Liguria

2885

Dei Fiori**
Viale Riviera 17
+39 019-625636
FAX +39 019-2211357
1/1 - 23/10, 27/12 - 31/12
info@campingdeifiori.it

2,5ha 130**T**(35-70m^2) 6A CEE

1 ACD**G**HIJKLMNPRS
2 EFJKRTUVWXY
3 BGHRUY
4 (B+G 20/5-20/9)
(Q+R+T+U+V+X 15/6-15/9)
(Z 1/5-15/9)
5 **A**GIJKMNOPUV
6 CEGK(N 0,6km)OQRT

The campsite is located in a quiet and tranquil country estate with century-old olive trees. It is 500m from the village and the sea. The campsite has a lovely swimming pool and a good restaurant. Walking, trekking and mountain bike excursions are organised.

On A10, exit Pietra Ligure. Right immediately after toll booth. Campsite about 1500m on the right.

CC € 17 *2/4-21/4 26/4-30/6 5/9-19/10*

N 44°8'52'' E 8°16'4''

Pietra Ligure, I-17027 / Liguria

2886

Pian dei Boschi***
Via Ponti 1
FAX +39 019-625425
24/3 - 31/10
info@piandeiboschi.it

4ha 215**T**(30-80m^2) 5-6A CEE

1 BCD**G**HIJKLMNPQ
2 AFJLTVY
3 B**M**R
4 (B+G 14/5-2/10)
(Q+S+T+U+V+X+Y+Z)
5 **A**IJKLMNO**P**UV
6 ABCEG**K**(N 1km)ORTV

Campsite 700m from the sea. Most shaded pitches by 'Pietra Ligure' (A10) exit. Pool, shop, restaurant, WiFi. Starting point for walks, biking, mountain biking. Pietra Ligure: lively resort, nice boulevard. English spoken. Ideal for mountain villages inland.

A10, exit Pietra Ligure. Turn right after toll booth. Campsite about 1500m on the left.

CC € 19 *30/3-21/4 27/4-31/5 6/6-26/6 29/8-31/10*

N 44°8'57'' E 8°16'7''

San Remo, I-18038 / Liguria

2887

Villaggio dei Fiori***
Via Tiro a Volo 3
+39 0184-660635
+39 0184-662377
1/1 - 31/12
info@villaggiodeifiori.it

3,3ha 131**T**(50-110m²) 6A CEE

1 BCDEIJKLMOPRS
2 EFGKNOTVWXY
3 B**F**GHIJK**M**NRWY
4 (**A**) (**B**+**G** 1/5-30/9) KP (Q+R+T+U+V+Y 1/1-10/11, 10/12-31/12) (Z 1/1-11/11,12/12-31/12)
5 **AB**DFGIJKLMNOPQ**S**UVWXYZ
6 ABCEGIK(N 0,3km)ORTV

A paved family site by the sea. Pleasant climate all year. Wide variety of excursions. Cycle path beside the sea (24 km). Reservation with CampingCard ACSI is compulsory, only by mail or fax (minimum one week in advance). Pitches are max. 6.50m (50 m²). Luxury pitches 10/15 Euros extra.

A10 exit San Remo, follw San Remo signs. Turn right onto SS1 ('Via Aurelia') at the traffic lights down in the town. Campsite 1.5 km on the left.

CC € 19 *1/5-31/5 6/6-25/6 19/9-30/9*

N 43°48'9'' E 7°44'43''

Sarzana (SP), I-19038 / Liguria

2888

Iron Gate Marina 3B
Viale XXV Aprile 54
+39 0187-676370
+39 0187-670094
15/3 - 30/9
info@marina3b.it

12ha 540**T**(40m²) 3-6A CEE

1 ACDGHIJKLMNOPRS
2 CFLMRUVY
3 BRW
4 (B+G 1/5-15/9) (Q+R 1/5-30/9) (T 1/6-30/9) (V+Y) Z
5 **AB**EFGIJKLMNOPUVXZ
6 ACDEGJLM(N 2km)OT

A large, very modern campsite by the River Magra with a restaurant, swimming pool and lawns by the river. A lovely starting point for boating enthusiasts.

A12 Genova-Livorno, exit Sarzana direction Sarzana. Right at 4th roundabout towards Carrare/ Marinella. Campsite about 3 km before motorway bridge through a small tunnel.

CC € 17 *15/3-3/7 20/8-30/9*

N 44°4'36'' E 9°58'52''

Sestri Levante, I-16039 / Liguria

2889

Fossa Lupara**
Via Villa Costa 31
+39 0185-1873287
+39 0185-1871719
1/2 - 31/10
info@campingfossalupara.it

1,5ha 30**T**(30-50m²) 6A CEE

1 AGIJKLMOPQ
2 FGRSVWXY
3 BG**M**R
4 (Q+R+T+U+V+X 1/4-30/9) Z
5 **A**GIJKLMNPUVWXZ
6 CDEGJ(N 0,3km)ORST

This basic, level campsite is located right by the A12 in Sestri Levante. Not far from the lively town centre and beach resort. There are good train connections to Genoa and the Cinque Terre, all of which are worth a visit. Free transport to train station.

A12 Genova-Livorno, take Sestri Levante exit. The campsite is well signposted from there (about 500m) close to the motorway. Warning: do not use SatNav but follow signs because of low tunnel (avoids damage).

CC € 17 *1/2-15/7 1/9-31/10*

N 44°16'26'' E 9°25'22''

Sestri Levante, I-16039 / Liguria

2890

- Mare Monti
- Via Aurelia km 469
- +39 0185-44348
- FAX +39 0185-482327
- 20/3 - 16/10
- @ info@campingmaremonti.com

2ha 50T(20-70m²) 6A CEE

1 ACDGHIJKLMOPRS
2 FJKRTVX
3 BHR
4 (B+G 1/6-30/9)
(Q+R 15/4-15/10) Z
5 **AB**EGIJKLMNOPUVXZ
6 CFGJK(N 2km)RT

An attractive and friendly family campsite with stunning panoramic views over the surroundings. The campsite is equipped with a swimming pool for both caravan and tent campers. Starting point for trips out to Cinque Terre, Portofino and Genua.

SS1 Aurelia, exit Sestri Levante A12, dir. La Spezia. 3rd campsite on the left past Trigoso. Steep access road. SatNav cannot always be trusted, choose SS1 dir. Trigoso.

CC € 17 *20/3-30/6 1/9-16/10*

N 44°15'49'' E 9°26'31''

Idro, I-25074 / Lombardia

2891

- AZUR Sportcamping Rio Vantone****
- Via Vantone 45
- +39 0365-83125
- FAX +39 0365-823663
- 22/4 - 3/10
- @ idro@azur-camping.de

4,5ha 203T(60-100m²) 6A CEE

1 AB**G**HIJKLMPRS
2 DIKLNRVX
3 BHLRU**WZ**
4 (A 1/7-31/8)
(C+H+Q 1/5-30/9) (S)
(T 1/7-10/9)
(U+Y 15/5-30/9) Z
5 **AB**DEFGIJKLMNOPUWXYZ
6 CDEG**IJ**(N 3km)OPRTV

Lovely campsite with marked out pitches. Sloping beach. Entertainment in English, German and Dutch. Modern toilet buildings. Lovely swimming pool.

From the A22 drive towards Riva. In Sarche take the SS237 towards Tione Brescia. At the end of the lake drive towards Crone-Vantone. The campsite is located by the lake.

CC € 19 *22/4-13/5 29/5-24/6 28/8-2/10*

N 45°45'16'' E 10°29'52''

Idro, I-25074 / Lombardia

2892

- Venus**
- Via Trento 94
- FAX +39 0365-83190
- 22/4 - 22/9
- @ info@campingvenus.it

1,8ha 96T(30-100m²) 3-6A CEE

1 ABC**G**IJKLMPQ
2 DKLNRTVXY
3 BHNR**WZ**
4 (B 1/5-15/9)
(Q+S+U+Y+Z)
5 **AB**FGIJKLMNOPUV
6 CEGK(N 1km)V

Located on the shores of Lake Idro with unspoiled natural surroundings. Plenty of relaxing walks in the woods near the campsite possible. The ambiance at the camp is fun and casual. There is a small swimming pool with sunbathing area. The beach slopes down gently

A22, exit Trento. In Trento exit Riva. In Sarche direction Tione Brescia. Located past the Anfo campsite on the left of the road at the lake.

CC € 17 *22/4-7/7 24/8-22/9*

N 45°44'24'' E 10°28'2''

Iseo, I-25049 / Lombardia

2893

- Covelo***
- Via Covelo 18
- +39 030-9821305
- 25/3 - 1/11
- info@campingcovelo.it

1ha 85**T**(50m²) 6A CEE

- **1** ABCD**G**IJKLMNOPQ
- **2** DGKLRTVWXY
- **3** AGKR**WZ**
- **4** (Q+R+T+V+X) Z
- **5** **AB**GIJKLMNOPUVWZ
- **6** ACEGK(N 1km)RTV

A small and friendly campsite on Lake Iseo. Pitches right by the lake with panoramic views. Restaurant with local dishes.

From the A4 exit Rovato, follow signs to Lago d'Iseo. In Iseo continue for 1 km past the supermarket, direction Pisogne at the roundabout. Campsite just after the turning on the left of the road.

CC €19 *25/3-30/6 1/9-1/11*

N 45°40'1'' E 10°4'4''

Iseo, I-25049 / Lombardia

2894

- Quai***
- Via Ipp. Antonioli 73
- +39 030-9821610
- 25/3 - 30/3, 20/4 - 25/9
- info@campingquai.it

1,3ha 83**T**(40-80m²) 6A CEE

- **1** ABCD**G**IJKLMOPRS
- **2** DFKLRVWXY
- **3** AGKR**WZ**
- **4** (Q+T+U+X+Z)
- **5** **A**GIJKLMNOPUVZ
- **6** CEGK(N 0,7km)RTV

A shaded family campsite located right by Lake Iseo with beautiful views. Boat ramp. Good toilet facilities. Restaurant with terrace and view of the lake.

A4 Milan-Brescia, exit Rovato direction Iseo. Follow the signs in Iseo.

CC €19 *20/4-18/6 1/9-25/9*

N 45°39'58'' E 10°3'47''

Ispra, I-21027 / Lombardia

2895

- International Camping Ispra****
- Via Carducci, 943
- +39 0332-780458
- FAX +39 0332-784882
- 18/3 - 2/11
- info@internationalcampingispra.it

2,5ha 106**T** 6A CEE

- **1** ABC**G**IJKLMO**PQ**
- **2** DKLMRTVY
- **3** BGHKMRU**W**
- **4** (B 15/6-15/9) (Q+R+T+U+V+X+Z)
- **5** **A**GIKMN**P**VZ
- **6** EG**K**(N 1km)TV

A campsite with a lovely swimming pool, located on the shores of Lago Maggiore in a peaceful and natural setting. Flyboarding possible.

From Sesto Calende continue towards Laveno. Campsite clearly indicated on the left of the road in Ispra.

CC €19 *18/3-3/7 20/8-2/11* *7=6, 14=11*

N 45°49'38'' E 8°37'38''

Lavena Ponte Tresa, I-21037 / Lombardia

2896

International Camping
Via Marconi 18
+39 0332-550117
FAX +39 0332-551600
1/1 - 31/12
info@internationalcamping.com

2ha 80T(60-90m²) 2-6A CEE

1 CDEIJKLOPQ
2 ADLPRVY
3 AHRUWZ
4 (Q+S+U+V+X+Z)
5 **A**FGIJKLMNOPUV
6 ACEGJ(N 1km)R

A beautifully located, tranquil campsite next to Lake Lugano. Within walking distance of the village of Ponte Tresa. Electricity supply 2-6 amps. Dogs not allowed.

A2/E35, at Lugano exit Ponte Tresa/Varese. Direction Ponte Tresa/Varese as far as Customs. Immediately after border continue towards Porto Ceresio. Campsite 800 metres on the left.

CC € 19 *1/1-9/7 28/8-31/12*

N 45°57'35'' E 8°51'48''

Marone (Lago di Iseo), I-25054 / Lombardia

2897

Riva di San Pietro***
Via Cristini 5
FAX +39 030-9827129
1/5 - 30/9
info@rivasanpietro.it

2ha 106T(45-64m²) 3-6A CEE

1 ABCD**G**IJKLNOPRS
2 DGKLRVWXY
3 A**F**HJKLRV**W**Z
4 (A 15/7-15/8)
(B+G 15/5-15/9)
(Q+R+T+U+V+X+Z)
5 **AB**EFGIJKLMNOPUWZ
6 ACEGK(N 0,3km)OTUV

Situated at the foot of the San Pietro mountain with extensive shores directly on Lake Iseo. The site has lovely landscaping and lawns and excellent views of the lake. New sanitary facilities.

A4, exit Rovato direction Iseo, follow lakeside road towards Pisogne. Campsite just before Marone on the lake.

CC € 19 *1/5-30/6 1/9-30/9*

N 45°43'56'' E 10°5'35''

Monvalle, I-21020 / Lombardia

2898

Lido di Monvalle***
Via Montenero 63
FAX +39 0332-799359
19/3 - 2/10
campinglidomonvalle@libero.it

1,5ha 80T(60-80m²) 5A CEE

1 B**G**IJKLO**P**Q
2 ADKLMRVXY
3 ARUWZ
4 (Q+R+T+U+V+Y+Z)
5 **A**GIJKMNO**P**UV
6 CEG**J**(N 4km)ORTV

Basic, peaceful campsite with ideal swimming in Lago Maggiore. The restaurant on the lake shore is very attractive and has a beautiful view over the lake.

From Laveno drive in direction Ispra. The campsite is located to the right of the road, about 10 km.

CC € 19 *1/4-3/7 29/8-2/10 7=6*

N 45°50'51'' E 8°37'13''

Piano di Porlezza, I-22010 / Lombardia

2899

Ranocchio**
Via Al Lago 7
+39 0344-70385
1/4 - 30/9
@ campingranocchio@ngi.it

3,5ha 200T(50-90m²) 3A CEE

1 ACGIJKLPRS
2 DGJKLNRTVXY
3 ARWZ
4 (B+G 15/6-15/9)
(T+U+V+X) Z
5 ABFGIJKMNOPU
6 CFGJ(N 0,15km)RTV

A family campsite with a swimming pool, good modern toilet facilities and a restaurant/pizzeria. The campsite is on Lake Piano, and surrounded by countryside with lovely walking and cycling.

N2, exit Lugano Nord dir. St. Moritz/Gandria. From Porlezza dir. Mennachio. In Piano Porlezza turn right. Alternative route via Como. New tunnel open between Gandria and Porlezza since 2013. Recommended to use coordinates.

CC € 17 1/4-13/5 17/5-9/7 27/8-30/9

N 46°2'26'' E 9°10'6''

Porlezza, I-22018 / Lombardia

2900

Darna***
Via Osteno 50
+39 0344-61597
21/3 - 31/10
@ campingdarna@hotmail.it

6ha 300T(50-80m²) 3A CEE

1 ABCDGIJKLMPRS
2 DKNRVY
3 ABGHJKMNRUWZ
4 (A 1/7-31/8)
(B+G 1/5-31/8)
(Q 1/4-30/9)
(S+T+U+V+Y) Z
5 ABCDFGIJKLMNOPUV
6 CEGHK(N 2km)OT

Located on the southern shore of Lake Lugano. The campsite has shaded pitches, 3 Amp electricity, mini-market, restaurant, swimming pool, beach, playground, tennis courts and volleyball pitch. An ideal starting point for cycling and walking tours.

N2, exit Lugano Nord direction St. Moritz. New tunnel between Gandria and Porlezza now operational. In Porlezza direction Osteno. The campsite is signposted on the right (last campsite).

CC € 17 21/3-25/6 3/9-31/10

N 46°1'31'' E 9°7'33''

Ranzanico al Lago di Endine, I-24060 / Lombardia

2901

La Tartufaia***
Via Nazionale 2519
+39 035-819259
1/5 - 25/9
@ info@latartufaia.com

1,7ha 75T(40-90m²) 4A CEE

1 ABCDGHIJKLMOPS
2 DGJKLMNRTVWXY
3 AHJKLMNRUWZ
4 (B+H 1/6-1/9) P
(Q+S+T+U+V+X) Z
5 ABGIJKLMNOPUVZ
6 ACDFGKOTV

A beautifully laid-out terraced campsite with views of Lake Endine 50 metre further on. Restaurant with produce from the campsite's own farm. Very helpful owners. Boats without motors permitted.

A4 Milan-Venice, exit Seriate. SS42 direction Lovere, campsite on the left past Ranzanico exit.

CC € 17 1/5-30/6 22/8-25/9

N 45°47'19'' E 9°56'49''

Sesto Calende, I-21018 / Lombardia

2902

Lido Okay****
Via per Angera 115
+39 0331-974235
26/3 - 9/10
campingokay@camping-okay.com

1,5ha 80T(60-100m²) 6A CEE

1 B**G**IJLOPQ
2 DFGJLMORTVWX
3 ABGKLRUZ
4 (B+G 1/6-31/8) (Q+T+V+Z)
5 FGIKMNO**P**UZ
6 AEG**K**(N 2km)OQRTV

A campsite with modern toilet facilities and a lovely swimming pool. Situated right on Lake Maggiore.

Take direction Angera from Sesto Calende. Campsite on the left of the road in Lisanza.

CC € 17 *26/3-5/7 1/9-9/10 7=6*

N 45°44'56" E 8°35'48"

Bellamonte/Predazzo, I-38037 / Trentino-Alto Adige

2903

Fiemme Village***
Via Cece 16
+39 0462-576119
FAX +39 0462-502118
14/5 - 18/9, 1/12 - 31/12
info@campingclub.it

6ha 275T(50-170m²) 3-6A CEE

1 ABCD**G**IJKLMO**P**Q
2 GIJKLRVXY
3 ABDHJLMNR
4 (A+C) **KLNP** (Q+T+U+V+X+Z)
5 **AB**DFGIJKLMNOP**QR**UVW XYZ
6 CDEGJ(N 0,4km)OTV

Bellamonte Campsite stands for nature and relaxation: a heated pool, a traditional restaurant, entertainment in the evenings, a playground and a spa. Perfect for a camping holiday in the mountains.

From Predazzo dir. Bellamonte (Passe Rolle). Follow signs in village.

CC € 17 *14/5-5/7 22/8-18/9*

N 46°18'36" E 11°39'39"

Calceranica al Lago, I-38050 / Trentino-Alto Adige

2904

Al Pescatore**
Via dei Pescatori 1
+39 0461-723062
FAX +39 0461-724212
7/5 - 11/9
trentino@campingpescatore.it

3ha 248T(70-100m²) 6A CEE

1 ABCD**G**IJKLMOPQ
2 DLNRTVY
3 BHJNR**WZ**
4 (B+G 16/5-11/9) P (R+T+U+V+X+Y+Z)
5 **AB**EFGIJKMNPUVXZ
6 EGIK(N 1km)OT

Hospitable, attractive campsite. Natural shaded pitches. New modern swimming pool with hydro massage. Located on Lake Caldonazzo. With CampingCard ACSI WiFi is free and you can occupy a larger pitch with 6A in early and late season.

A22, exit Trento. Via SS47 direction Padova. After Pergine direction Caldonazzo. After S. Cristoforo continue direction Calceranica. Campsite well signposted.

CC € 17 *7/5-8/7 25/8-11/9*

N 46°0'6" E 11°15'19"

Calceranica al Lago, I-38050 / Trentino-Alto Adige

2905

Belvedere**
Viale Venezia 6
+39 0461-723239
22/4 - 25/9
info@campingbelvedere.it

1ha 89**T**(65-100m²) 6A CEE

1 ABCD**F**HIJKLMOPQ
2 DMNRWX
3 ABJRU**W**Z
4 (Q+R+T+Z)
5 **AB**DEFGIJKLMNOP**ST**UV
6 BCEG**IJK**(N 1,5km)TV

A very friendly small campsite near the lake (on the other side of the road) close to pavement cafes and places to eat.

A22, exit Trento. Via the SS47 direction Padova. After passing Pergine drive in the direction of Caldonazzo. After passing S. Cristoforo drive in the direction of Calceranica, where the campsite is signposted.

CC €15 *22/4-6/7 23/8-25/9*

N 46°0'12'' E 11°15'29''

Calceranica al Lago, I-38050 / Trentino-Alto Adige

2906

Fleiola**
Via Trento 42
+39 0461-723153
+39 0461-724386
23/4 - 30/9
info@campingfleiola.it

1,2ha 117**T**(60-80m²) 3A CEE

1 ABCD**G**IJKLMOPQ
2 DGLNORTVX
3 ABJKRU**W**Z
4 (R+T+Z 15/5-20/9)
5 **AB**DEFGIJKLMNOP**S**UWXYZ
6 ACEG**K**ORTV

Pleasant campsite on the shore of Lake Caldonazzo. Several pitches right by the lake. Lovely views of the Trentino mountains. Your CampingCard ACSI is valid only for standard pitches.

A22, exit Trento. Take the SS47 to Padova. Past Pergine take the direction of Caldonazzo. Beyond S. Cristoforo you can just follow the signs leading to the campsite, on the left side of the road.

CC €17 *23/4-2/7 1/9-30/9*

N 46°0'23'' E 11°14'44''

Calceranica al Lago, I-38050 / Trentino-Alto Adige

2907

Penisola Verde**
V. Penisola Verde 5
+39 0461-723272
+39 0461-1820746
30/4 - 18/9
info@penisolaverde.it

3ha 129**T**(60-80m²) 4-6A CEE

1 ABCD**G**IJKLMO**P**Q
2 CDLNRVXY
3 BHJRU**W**Z
4 (A 5/7-24/8) (R+T+Z)
5 **A**BDEFGIJKLMNOPUW
6 ABCEG**J**(N 0,4km)ST

A shaded, quiet campsite with a private beach directly on the lake, flanked by small creek. Renovated toilet facilities. WiFi. Bar/terrace overlooking the lake. Bread and milk on sale. Marked out shallow water, playground and entertainment. Possibilities for excursions, hiking and cycle trips. Restaurants and village within walking distance.

A22, exit Trento. Via the SS47 direction Padova. After Pergine direction Caldonazzo. Left after the bridge in Calceranica al Lago.

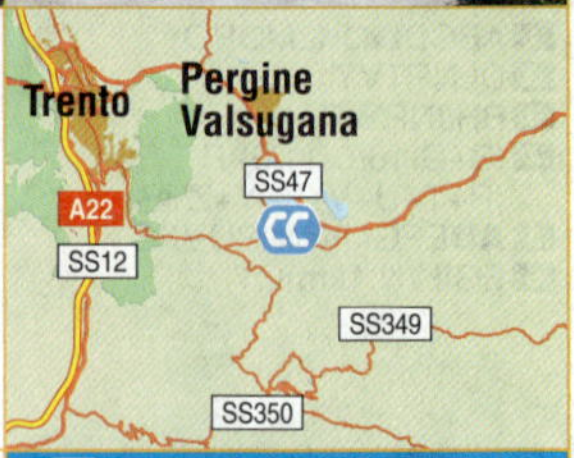

CC €17 *30/4-3/7 24/8-18/9*

N 46°0'20'' E 11°14'50''

Calceranica al Lago, I-38050 / Trentino-Alto Adige

2908

Riviera**
Viale Venezia 10
+39 0461-724464
FAX +39 0461-718689
15/4 - 13/9
@ info@camping-riviera.net

2ha 137T(75-100m²) 4-6A CEE

1 ABCD**F**IJKLMOPQ
2 DMNRVY
3 BKR**WZ**
4 (Q 🔑)
(T+U+V+X+Y 23/4-11/9)
(Z 🔑)
5 **AB**GIJKLMNOPU
6 ABEGK(N 1,5km)RTUV

Located on the southern shore of Lake Caldonazzo, 10 metres from the lake and the beach. Camping Riviera awaits you for a wonderful holiday, surrounded by countryside and in a quiet location. Many opportunities for walks and excursions in the surrounding mountains.

A22, exit Trento. Via SS47 direction Padova. After Pergine direction Caldonazzo. After S. Cristoforo direction Calceranica. Campsite well signposted.

CC € 15 *15/4-7/7 24/8-12/9 7=6*

N 46°0'13'' E 11°15'31''

Calceranica al Lago, I-38050 / Trentino-Alto Adige

2909

Spiaggia
Viale Venezia 14
FAX +39 0461-723037
15/4 - 2/10
@ info@campingspiaggia.net

1,3ha 104T(80-120m²) 6A CEE

1 ACDGIJKLMOPQ
2 DLNRTVWXY
3 AKLR**WZ**
4 (A 1/6-15/9) (Q+R 🔑)
(Z 15/4-18/9)
5 **AB**DFGIJKLMNOP**S**TUWX
Z
6 EG**K**(N 1,5km)TV

A hospitable campsite with its own beach on Lake Caldonazzo. Ideal base for mountain walks, excursions and bike trips. Spacious pitches (80-100 m²), 6 Amp. CCA users have a choice of all pitches except those with private toilet facilities. Modern toilet facilities. WiFi 100%.

A22, exit Trento-Nord, direction Padova via the SS47. Beyond Pergine take exit towards Calceranica and Caldonazzo (lake). Follow Spiaggia campsite signs beyond Caldonazzo.

CC € 17 *15/4-3/7 21/8-2/10*

N 46°0'15'' E 11°15'34''

Caldonazzo, I-38052 / Trentino-Alto Adige

2910

Camping Mario Village****
Via Lungolago 4
+39 0461-723341
FAX +39 0461-723106
28/4 - 25/9
@ info@campingmario.com

3,5ha 160T(80-150m²) 10A CEE

1 ABCDFIJKLMOPQ
2 DKLMNRTVWXY
3 ABKLNRU**WZ**
4 (A 1/7-31/8)
(C+Q+R+T+U+V+X+Z 🔑)
5 **AB**DEFGIJKLMNOP**ST**UV
WXYZ
6 BCEGIK(N 1,5km)TVW

Use CampingCard ACSI in a four stars peaceful campsite! A few metres from Caldonazzo Lake, spacious shaded pitches, 6-10A electricity, modern toilet facilities, heated swimming pool (± 28°C) and free WiFi throughout the campsite.

A22, exit Trento. Via the SS47 towards Padova. Past Pergine take direction Caldonazzo. After S. Cristoforo direction Calceranica. Then follow 'Mario' camping signs.

CC € 17 *28/4-9/7 27/8-25/9*

N 46°0'16'' E 11°15'37''

Fucine di Ossana, I-38026 / Trentino-Alto Adige

2911

Cevedale***
Via di Sotto Pila 4
+39 0463-751630
1/1 - 31/12
info@campingcevedale.it

3ha 211T(60-70m²) 3A CEE

1 ACDEHIJKLOPRS
2 CGRVY
3 AHRU
4 (Q 1/1-1/12) (R 1/7-30/9) Z
5 **AB**DGIJKLMNOPUV
6 CEGIK(N 1km)ORTV

A lovely campsite with a fresh appearance on both sides of a fast-running stream. The village can be reached by foot and the mountains are also close by. Good toilet facilities. Situated among pine trees.

SS42 Dimaro-Passo Tonale. In Fucine exit left to Ossana. The campsite is located after about 600 metres.

CC € 17 *8/1-15/7 1/9-22/12*

N 46°18'32'' E 10°44'9''

Ledro/Pieve, I-38067 / Trentino-Alto Adige

2912

Al Lago
Via Alzer 7
+39 0464-591250
+39 0464-905467
22/4 - 2/10
info@camping-al-lago.it

1ha 90T(56-80m²) 3-4A CEE

1 ABCD**G**IJKLMOPRS
2 DGKNRTVWXY
3 BGHJK**M**R**WZ**
4 (**A** 1/7-31/8)
(T+U+V+X+Y+Z)
5 **AB**GIJKLMNOPUV
6 ACEGJK(N 0,5km)RTV

Beautiful, peaceful campsite on the lovely Lake Ledro. Swimming, surfing, mountain biking, and afterwards a fine meal in the restaurant. Staff speaks English, Dutch and German. Free WiFi.

In Riva del Garda towards Val di Ledro. Through a newly built tunnel N240 you will reach the pass. Beyond Molina drive along the lake on the SS240 and turn left in the town of Pieve di Ledro.

CC € 17 *22/4-1/7 1/9-2/10*

N 45°53'1'' E 10°43'54''

Ledro/Pieve, I-38067 / Trentino-Alto Adige

2913

Azzurro***
Via Alzer 5
+39 0464-591276
+39 0464-592333
22/4 - 30/9
campingazzurro@virgilio.it

2ha 120T(60-125m²) 6-10A CEE

1 AB**G**HIJKLMO**P**RS
2 DGKLMNRVXY
3 AHJK**QR**W**Z**
4 (A 1/7-31/8) (B 15/5-30/9) P
(Q+V+X+Z)
5 **A**BCDGIJKLMNOPUVWXY
Z
6 ACEG**IJ**QTV

The campsite is situated right by Lago di Ledro with a spacious beach and beautiful surroundings. Many mountain sport opportunities (including mountain walks and mountain biking). Very good toilet facilities. Special pitches for CampingCard guests. Pitches by the lake (6A) for a supplement.

In Riva del Garda direction Val di Ledro. You reach the top via a tunnel (N240). After Molina turn left by the lake in Pieve di Ledro.

CC € 17 *1/5-18/6 10/9-30/9*

N 45°53'6'' E 10°43'53''

Levico Terme, I-38056 / Trentino-Alto Adige

2914

2 Laghi****
Località Costa 3
+39 0461-706290
FAX +39 0461-707381
14/5 - 18/9
info@campingclub.it

11ha 426T(80-120m²) 6-10A CEE

1 ABCD**G**IJKLMOPQ
2 LMRVXY
3 BGJKLMNRU**W**
4 (A+C+G+R+T+U+V+W+Y)
5 **AB**FGIJKLMNOP**S**TUVXYZ
6 CDEGJ(N 1km)ORTUV

A campsite located between the Levico and Caldonazzo lakes. The site has tennis courts, a swimming pool and very good toilet facilities. Pitches with plenty of shade and a very quiet campsite in early and late seasons.

A22, exit Trento. Drive via the SS47 towards Padova. Take the first exit towards Levico. Turn left after 300m opposite petrol station. Campsite on the left at slip road.

CC € 15 *14/5-5/7 22/8-18/9*

N 46°0'16'' E 11°17'21''

Levico Terme, I-38056 / Trentino-Alto Adige

2915

Lago di Levico****
Loc. Pleina 1
+39 0461-706491
FAX +39 0461-707735
8/4 - 16/10
info@campinglevico.com

4,5ha 430T(70-120m²) 6-10A CEE

1 ABCD**G**IJKLMOPQ
2 CDKLMNRSVWXY
3 ABCD**F**HJKLMN**Q**R**T**U**WZ**
4 (A 1/7-31/8)
(C+G 15/5-15/9) J**O**
(Q+R+T)
(U+V+X+Y+Z 20/4-16/10)
5 **AB**CDEFGIJKLMNOP**QRS**
TUVWXYZ
6 ABCDEGIKL(N 1,5km)OQR
TUV

A peaceful family campsite located on Lake Levico. A beautiful private beach that is suitable for children. It has three small swimming pools. WiFi is available. A ferry takes you from the campsite to the beach opposite. There are designated areas where your dog can swim.

A22, exit Trento. Take the SS47 to Padova. First exit Levico. Turn left to the campsite, following the signs.

CC € 17 *8/4-7/7 26/8-16/10*

N 46°0'29'' E 11°17'5''

Meran, I-39012 / Trentino-Alto Adige

2916

Camping Hermitage****
Via Val di Nova 29
+39 0473-232191
FAX +39 0473-256407
28/3 - 1/11
info@einsiedler.com

1ha 71T(60-90m²) 10-15A

1 BCDGQ
2 GRST
3 AB
4 (B 15/5-15/9) (**F**) M**N**
(Q+U+X+Y+Z)
5 **A**IJLMNOP**ST**U
6 K(N 1km)

Quiet, modern campsite with a view of the town of Meran and the surrounding mountains. There is a bus connection to Meran, 3 km. There is an outdoor swimming pool and covered pool. Free WiFi.

From the Brenner Pass, direction Bolzano south. Motorway Bolzano/Merano south, 4 km towards Meran 2000.

CC € 19 *2/4-4/5 8/5-12/5 16/5-25/5 29/5-9/7 18/9-28/9 3/10-30/10*

N 46°40'18'' E 11°12'11''

Pergine, I-38057 / Trentino-Alto Adige

2917

- Punta Indiani
- Valcanover
- +39 0461-548062
- FAX +39 0461-548607
- 29/4 - 30/9
- info@campingpuntaindiani.it

1,5ha 115**T**(60-100m²) 4A CEE

- **1** ABCD**G**IJKLMOPQ
- **2** ADGJLMNRVWXY
- **3** ABJR**WZ**
- **4** (S+T+U+V+Y)
- **5** **AB**GIJKLMNPUVWZ
- **6** EG**J**ORT

A family campsite right by Lake Caldonazzo with a private beach. Spacious, grassy and leafy pitches. Supermarket, bank, restaurant and bus all within 100m. Cycle track close to the campsite, an ideal starting point for excursions and walks. CampingCard ACSI is valid on pitches in Zone C.

From Trento drive in the direction of Padova. After Pergine exit Caldonazzo. The campsite is located on the lake, after the small town of S. Cristoforo.

CC € 17 *29/4-7/7 26/8-30/9*

N 46°1'39'' E 11°13'54''

Pergine Valsugana, I-38057 / Trentino-Alto Adige

2918

- S. Cristoforo**
- Loc. Cristoforo
- FAX +39 0461-512707
- 14/5 - 18/9
- info@campingclub.it

2,5ha 157**T**(80-120m²) 6A CEE

- **1** ABCD**G**HIJKLMO**P**RS
- **2** DLMRVWX
- **3** B**F**JKL**M**QRU**W**
- **4** (A+B+G+T+U+V+Y+Z)
- **5** **AB**GHIJKLMNOPUWXZ
- **6** EG**J**(N 0,8km)RTV

San Cristoforo campsite has the perfect location for a family holiday in Valsugana, Trentino... Magical surroundings to discover all that the area has to offer.

A22, exit Trento. Via the SS47 direction Padova. Take exit S. Cristoforo (Lago di Caldonazzo). Follow camp signs in the village.

CC € 15 *14/5-5/7 22/8-18/9*

N 46°2'19'' E 11°14'12''

Predazzo, I-38037 / Trentino-Alto Adige

2919

- Valle Verde**
- Loc. Ischia 2, Sotto Sassa
- FAX +39 0462-502394
- 1/5 - 1/10
- camping.valleverde@tin.it

1,4ha 117**T**(60-110m²) 6A CEE

- **1** ABCD**G**HIJKLMOPQ
- **2** CRVWXY
- **3** ABHKLNR**WX**
- **4** (Q) (R 15/6-15/9) (T+U+V+X+Y 1/5-30/9) (Z 1/6-30/9)
- **5** **AB**DEFGJLNP**S**UVWXZ
- **6** ACEGIK(N 2km)ORSV

An ideal campsite for those who like walks in the middle of mountains, lakes, streams, flora and fauna. 2 km from Predazzo. The Guest Card is included in the extra tax.

A22, exit Ora, N48 direction Cavalese/Predazzo. In Predazzo exit S. Martino di Castrozza. Follow campsite signs.

CC € 19 *1/5-8/7 25/8-1/10*

N 46°18'38'' E 11°37'54''

Racines/Casateia, I-39040 / Trentino-Alto Adige

2920

Gilfenklamm*
Jaufenstraße 2
+39 0472-779132
1/2-14/2,19/3-1/4,30/4-23/10
info@camping-gilfenklamm.com

4ha 135**T**(50-90m²) 8A

1 ABC**G**IJKLMNO**P**Q
2 BFGRTUWXY
3 A**C**GRU**W**
4 (Q+R 1/7-31/8)
(T+U+V+X+Y+Z)
5 **AB**DFGIJKLMNO**P**UVW
6 BCGJ(N 0,3km)S

The first campsite after the Brenner Pass. The site is located just 3 km from the motorway. The unmarked pitches are located in several small lawns surrounded by lawns with seasonal pitches. Starting point for mountain walks or ski trips.

Take the Vipiteno-Sterzing exit from the Brenner pass. Another 2 km towards Racines/Casateia.

€17 *30/4-30/6 1/9-23/10*

N 46°52'58'' E 11°24'29''

Rasen/Rasun, I-39030 / Trentino-Alto Adige

2921

Corones****
Rasun di Sotto 124
+39 0474-496490
FAX +39 0474-498250
5/5 - 23/10, 6/12 - 3/4
info@corones.com

2,5ha 135**T**(70-110m²) 10A CEE

1 ACD**F**IJKLMPST
2 CLRTUVWX
3 BFHJN**OPQ**RU**VW**
4 (A 1/7-31/8)
(B+G 24/5-25/10) **N**
(Q+R+T+U+X+Y+Z)
5 **AB**DEFGIJKLMNOPR**ST**U
WZ
6 CDEG**IK**(N 1km)O**P**RSTV

A comfortable and luxuriously equipped campsite on the edge of a large nature and ski area in the Dolomites ('Der Kronplatz'). The perfect base for all summer and winter sports including mountain climbing, cycling, walking, and both downhill and cross country skiing. Back at the campsite there is a swimming pool, a restaurant and a sauna.

From Bruneck (Brunico) continue towards Toblach. Past Olang 600m, left to Rasen. Follow camping signs from here.

€19 *13/5-30/6 17/9-23/10*

N 46°46'33'' E 12°2'13''

Sankt Sigmund/Kiens, I-39030 / Trentino-Alto Adige

2922

Gisser***
Pustertalerstraße 26
+39 0474-569605
FAX +39 0474-569657
1/5 - 31/10
reception@hotelgisser.it

2ha 130**T**(40-70m²) 7A

1 ACD**F**IJKLMN**PQ**
2 BCGLRWXY
3 ANR
4 (B 15/6-15/9)
(D 31/3-15/10) (Q)
5 **A**GIJKLMNOPUW
6 BEG(N 1,5km)V

Peaceful basic campsite in the Pustertal valley. Pitches with or without shade on grassland. Other unmarked pitches have plenty of shade in the pine woods. You can stay in the hotel in bad weather.

From motorway junction Brixen (Bressanone) take the direction of Bruneck (Brunico) and Pustertal till you reach St. Sigmund. Then follow the signs.

€19 *1/5-30/6 15/9-31/10*

N 46°48'29'' E 11°48'42''

Sarnonico/Fondo, I-38010 / Trentino-Alto Adige

2923

Camping Park Baita Dolomiti***
Via Cesare Battisti 18
+39 0463-830109
FAX +39 0463-870000
25/5 - 30/9
info@baita-dolomiti.it

4ha 150T(70-100m²) 3-6A CEE

1 ABCD**G**HIJKLMNOPQ
2 GKLRTVXY
3 AB**F**HJNRU
4 (C+H+Q+T+U+X+Z)
5 **AB**FGIJKLMNOPUVWZ
6 BCEGJ(N 1km)QRTV

Beautiful, quiet campsite on the edge of the village of Sarnonico at 1000 metres altitude in a mountainous area (Dolomites). Campsite has a heated outdoor pool and paddling pool and is an ideal base for walks and cycling tours. 3 km away from an 18-hole golf court.

A22 exit S. Michelle Mezzocorona. Follow dir. Val di Non-Fondo-Sarnonico. On fork in Dermulo keep right, dir. Fondo-Sarnonico. NOT recommended: trying to reach Fondo from Bolzano via Mendolapas.

CC € 19 25/5-15/7 1/9-30/9 7=6

N 46°25'17'' E 11°8'23''

Terlago, I-38070 / Trentino-Alto Adige

2924

Laghi di Lamar***
Via alla Selva Faeda 15
+39 0461-860423
FAX +39 02-700538636
1/4 - 30/10
campeggio@laghidilamar.com

2ha 113T(80-100m²) 3-10A CEE

1 ABCD**G**IJKLMNOPQ
2 BGHJKLMRVX
3 ABCHIJ**Q**RU
4 (**A** 1/7-31/8) (C 1/6-15/9) (Q+R+V+Y+Z)
5 **AB**DEFGIJKLMNOP**S**UXYZ
6 ACEGIK(N 4km)ORTV

Campsite located in the wonderful setting of the Dolomites, in the Valle de Laghi. An oasis combining nature and hospitality. The grounds offer total peace and quiet and make an excellent starting point for walks, mountain bike trips and visits to Trento. New facilities.

Exit Trento Nord or Trento Sud. Follow SS45B and take exit 6 dir. Riva del Garda. Continue dir. Valle dei Laghi and follow signs. Route is through Terlago. Less suitable for caravans. Alternative via Vezzano.

CC € 19 1/4-30/6 1/9-30/10

N 46°6'38'' E 11°2'52''

Toblach/Dobbiaco, I-39034 / Trentino-Alto Adige

2925

Toblacher See***
Toblacher See 3
+39 0474-973138
FAX +39 0474-976647
1/1 - 31/10, 20/12 - 31/12
camping@toblachersee.com

2,5ha 132T(80-130m²) 6A CEE

1 ABCD**G**IJKLM**P**Q
2 BDGIJLMRTVWX
3 AHJKNR**W**
4 (Q+T+U+V+Y+Z)
5 **AB**DEFGIJKLMNOPR**S**TU WXYZ
6 CEG**IJ**(N 2km)OSTU

A lovely comfortable summer and winter campsite located on the Toblacher lake. The site is an excellent base for summer and winter sports. Back at the campsite you can take advantage of the restaurant. Very easily accessible, located beside the N51 Toblach to Cortina d'Ampezzo road.

From the Pustertal take the exit towards Cortina via the SS51. Campsite on the right 2 km further on.

CC € 19 7/1-8/7 29/8-31/10

N 46°42'23'' E 12°13'5''

Bardolino, I-37011 / Lago di Garda

2926

La Rocca Camp***
Via Gardesana dell' Acqua 37
+39 045-7211111
FAX +39 045-7211300
18/3 - 4/10
info@campinglarocca.com

8ha 272T(20-120m²) 6-16A CEE

1 ABCD**G**IJKLMOPRT
2 DFGJLMNRVWXY
3 BCKNRUV**WZ**
4 (A 15/5-15/9)
(C+H 27/3-4/10) J**KM**
(Q+S+T+U+V+Y) Z
5 **AB**EFGIJKLMNOPRUVWZ
6 CEGH**IK**(N 1km)QRSTUV

A lovely well-equipped campsite with swimming pool and sports facilities, located directly on Lake Garda. Within walking distance of Garda and Bardolino. CampingCard ACSI pitches in the higher section and in the lower section only in the first three rows from the office.

A22, exit Lago di Garda Sud, then direction Bardolino/Lago di Garda. In Bardolino turn right in the direction of Garda, via the N249. Clearly signposted. Located at the lake.

CC € 17 18/3-23/3 3/4-4/5 9/5-13/5 29/5-3/7 9/9-29/9

N 45°33'52'' E 10°42'46''

Bardolino, I-37011 / Lago di Garda

2927

Serenella***
Località Mezzariva 19
+39 045-7211333
FAX +39 045-7211552
12/3 - 23/10
serenella@camping-serenella.it

5ha 276T(65-100m²) 6A CEE

1 ABCDEIJKLOPRS
2 DFGILMNRVWXY
3 BKRV**WZ**
4 (B 1/5-20/9) (H 1/4-30/9)
(Q+S+T+U+V+Y+Z)
5 **AB**EGIJKLMNOPR**S**TUVZ
6 ACEG**K**(N 2km)ORTV

A well maintained campsite on the shores of Lake Garda, just 1 km from both Garda and Bardolino. Modern facilities and water sports opportunities. The first three rows of pitches on the campsite (as seen from the lake) are not available to CampingCard ACSI holders.

A22, exit Lago di Garda-Sud, then direction Bardolino/Lago di Garda. Turn right in Bardolino direction Garda via de N249. Campsite located by the lake beyond Bardolino.

CC € 17 12/3-2/7 27/8-22/10

N 45°33'33'' E 10°42'59''

Cisano di Bardolino, I-37010 / Lago di Garda

2928

Cisano/San Vito****
Via Peschiera 48
+39 045-6229098
FAX +39 045-6229059
19/3 - 9/10
cisano@camping-cisano.it

15ha 460T(50-110m²) 6-16A CEE

1 ABCDEIJKLMOPQ
2 ADGIJLRTVXY
3 BKMNQRUV**WZ**
4 (B+G 1/5-19/9) JP
(Q+S+T+U+V+Y+Z)
5 **AB**EFGIJKLMNOP**QRST**U
VWZ
6 CEG**J**M(N 0,3km)QRTV

Cisano campsite with its narrow sandy beach on Lake Garda has an area on the other side of the road where you will find the swimming pool and the restaurant. The two parts are connected by an underpass.

A22, exit Lago di Garda Sud, then direction Bardolino/Lago di Garda. At Bardolino turn left in the direction of Lazise via the N249. The campsite is located just after Cisano, by the lake.

CC € 17 19/3-2/7 20/9-8/10

N 45°31'32'' E 10°43'43''

Desenzano del Garda, I-25015 / Lago di Garda

2929

Camping Village San Francesco*****
Str.Vic.S.Francesco
+39 030-9110245
22/4 - 10/10
booking@campingsanfrancesco.com

10,4ha 348T(60-96m²) 6A CEE

- **1** ABCDGIJKLMOPQ
- **2** DFGLMNORTVWXY
- **3** AFK**M**NRUWZ
- **4** (B+G 25/4-13/9) (Q+S 🔑) (T 6/6-5/9) (U+V+Y+Z 🔑)
- **5** **AB**EFGIJKLMNOPUWXY
- **6** CDEGH**IK**(N 2km)OTUVW

This campsite has its own 300-metre beach on the south side of Lake Garda and is located close to the village of Sirmione. The site boasts luxurious modern facilities. Excellent (water)sports activities. The modern swimming complex is surrounded by terraces and landscaping. The CampingCard ACSI rate is valid for the standard pitches and the equipped pitches.

A4 Milano-Venezia, exit Sirmione. Campsite signposted.

CC € 19 22/4-10/7 27/8-9/10 14=12, 21=18, 28=24

N 45°27'56'' E 10°35'41''

Lazise, I-37017 / Lago di Garda

2930

Park Delle Rose***
Strada San Gaetano 20
+39 045-6471181
FAX +39 045-7581356
16/4 - 2/10
info@campingparkdellerose.it

9,2ha 423T(70-95m²) 6A CEE

- **1** ABCDEIJKLMOPRS
- **2** ADFGIKLRVWXY
- **3** BFG**M**QRV**W**Z
- **4** (B+G 23/4-25/9) JP (Q+S+T+U+V+Y+Z 🔑)
- **5** **A**EFGIJKLMNOP**ST**UVZ
- **6** CEG**J**M(N 2km)ORTV

A spaciously appointed campsite, right on Lake Garda, with its own sandy beach, swimming pool, sports facilities and a restaurant with an extensive menu. Pitches from the beach to Via Moniga (1-80) are not available to CampingCard ACSI.

A22, exit Lago di Garda Sud, via N249 direction Lazise. Follow signs at Lazise.

CC € 17 16/4-13/5 30/5-1/7 1/9-1/10

N 45°29'21'' E 10°43'54''

Lazise sul Garda, I-37017 / Lago di Garda

2931

Belvedere***
Strada del Roccolo 11
+39 045-7590228
FAX +39 045-6499084
18/3 - 3/10
info@campingbelvedere.com

6ha 266T(70-90m²) 4-6A CEE

- **1** ABCD**G**IJKLOPQ
- **2** ADFGIJKLNRVWXY
- **3** BC**F**KMNR**WZ**
- **4** (B+G 1/5-22/9) JK (Q+S+T+U+V+Y 🔑) Z
- **5** **AB**FGIJKLMNOPUVZ
- **6** ACEG**J**M(N 2km)QTV

A campsite with a swimming pool and stony beach by a lake, behind the Acquasplash Caneva sports centre. A good restaurant with lovely views over the lake. The first two rows by the lakeside (pitches 1 to 32) are not for CampingCard ACSI. 10% discount in the restaurant in low season with CampingCard ACSI.

A22, exit Lago di Garda Sud, then direction Lazise/Lago di Garda via N249. Follow signs beyond Lazise. The campsite is located before Caneva Sport, by the lake.

CC € 17 18/3-29/6 1/9-2/10

N 45°28'47'' E 10°43'22''

Lazise sul Garda, I-37017 / Lago di Garda

2932

Fossalta***
Loc. Fossalta str. del Roccolino 22
+39 045-7590231
FAX +39 045-7590999
18/3 - 30/9
@ info@fossalta.com

6ha 272T(60-135m²) 4-6A CEE

1 BCD**G**IJKLMOPRS
2 ADFGIJKLNRVWXY
3 B**F**KMNR**W**Z
4 (B+G 1/5-30/9) (Q+S+T) Z
5 **A**DEFGIJKLMNOPUVZ
6 CEGHKM(N 2km)ORTV

A quiet, well-maintained campsite right next to Lake Garda. Spacious shaded pitches with plenty of greenery and flowers. The first two rows from the lake (0-29) are not available with CampingCard ACSI. 10% discount at the bar during CampingCard ACSI acceptance period.

A22, exit Lago di Garda Sud, then direction Bardolino/Lago di Garda. At Bardolino turn left in the direction of Peschiera. Clearly signposted after Lazise.

CC € 17 *18/3-26/6 22/8-30/9*

N 45°28'49'' E 10°43'21''

Limone, I-25010 / Lago di Garda

2933

Campingpark Garda***
Via IV Novembre 10
FAX +39 0365-954550
1/4 - 16/10
@ info@hg-hotels.com

2,3ha 200T(40-60m²) 3A CEE

1 B**G**IJKLMO**P**RS
2 DJLNRTVXY
3 **MWZ**
4 (B+G+Q) (S 15/6-30/9) (U+V+Y+Z)
5 **A**GIJKLMOPUVZ
6 CFG(N 1km)OQRTV

Natural surroundings, close to the old town, view of the lake with private beach. You can sunbathe by the two new pools. Restaurant, bar, pizzeria, supermarket and barbecue on the beach. Sailing and surfing lessons. Mooring for motor and sailing boats. Peace and beauty for lovers of nature and sports.

From Riva del Garda take SS45bis dir. Salò. After many tunnels you reach Limone. After Limone, at Tamoil service station, campsite is located left of the road.

CC € 19 *1/4-13/5 31/5-1/7 4/9-16/10*

N 45°48'20'' E 10°47'16''

Manerba del Garda, I-25080 / Lago di Garda

2934

Baia Verde****
Via dell'Edera, 19
+39 0365-651753
FAX +39 0365-651809
19/3 - 8/10
@ info@campingbaiaverde.com

3ha 89T(80-90m²) 16A CEE

1 ABC**G**IJKLMOPQ
2 CGLRVX
3 BNRW
4 (A 1/6-26/9) (B+G 7/4-3/10) KP(Q+S+T+U+V+X+Z)
5 **ABC**DEFGIJKLMNOPR**ST** UVWXYZ
6 DEG**K**(N 1km)QRTV

This luxury campsite with 2 swimming pools, whirlpools, hydromassage, roof solarium, modern toilet facilities, and much more is located 300m from Lake Garda. All this is situated in an oasis of greenery and peace in the breathtaking surroundings of Lago di Garda. Lovely spacious pitches.

A4 exit Desenzano, then direction Salò via the SS572. Follow camping signs at Manerba del Garda.

CC € 19 *19/3-30/6 28/8-7/10*

N 45°33'41'' E 10°33'13''

Manerba del Garda, I-25080 / Lago di Garda

2935

Zocco***
Via del Zocco 43
+39 0365-551605
+39 0365-552053
22/4 - 3/10
info@campingzocco.it

5ha 206**T**(60-80m²) 6A CEE

1 ABC**F**HIJKLMOPQ
2 DGJKNRTVWXY
3 B**F**GKL**M**NRU**W**Z
4 (B+G) P
(Q+S+U+V+X+Z)
5 **AB**EFGIJKLMNOPUV
6 CEGK(N 2km)QRTV

This lovely, well kept campsite is close to Lake Garda. Lovely views. Partly terraced under olive trees. The staff, the central bar, the pizzeria and the small shop ensure a relaxing atmosphere. The lovely swimming pool will tempt you.

A4, exit Desenzano, then towards Salò via the SS572. Leave this road at Manerba del Garda. Follow the brown camping signs. The campsite is located by the lake.

CC € 17 *22/4-13/5 29/5-1/7 9/9-2/10*

N 45°32'24" E 10°33'22"

Moniga del Garda, I-25080 / Lago di Garda

2936

Fontanelle s.r.l.****
Via del Magone 13
+39 0365-502079
+39 0365-503324
15/4 - 2/10
info@campingfontanelle.it

4,5ha 166**T**(65m²) 6A CEE

1 ABC**F**IJKLM**P**Q
2 DFGJKNRTVWXY
3 B**FM**NRU**W**Z
4 (B+G 15/5-15/9)
(Q+S+T+U+V+Y+Z)
5 **AB**GIJKLMNOPUWXY
6 CEG**I**K(N 1km)ORTV

A friendly family campsite under olive trees on a 450m long beach. Located within walking distance of the pavement cafes in the small village of Moniga. Lovely day trips to Salò and Sirmione, among other places. Verona is also within easy reach. CampingCard ACSI is only valid for standard pitches.

A4, exit Desenzano, then direction Salò via the SS572. Leave road at Moniga del Garda. Follow the brown campsite signs. Campsite located by the lake.

CC € 17 *15/4-13/5 4/6-1/7 3/9-1/10*

N 45°31'32" E 10°32'35"

Moniga del Garda, I-25080 / Lago di Garda

2937

Piantelle****
Via San Cassiano 1a
+39 0365-502013
+39 0365-502637
19/3 - 2/10
info@piantelle.com

8,5ha 150**T**(60-100m²) 6A CEE

1 ABC**G**IJKLMOPQ
2 DFJKLNRWXY
3 BGKNRWZ
4 (B+G 10/5-2/10) **N**
(Q+R+U+V+Y+Z)
5 **AB**GJLNPUVWXYZ
6 CDEGJ(N 0,5km)RT

A lovely campsite on Lake Garda with its own 250m beach and private landing stage. Modern swimming pool. Well-maintained marked-out pitches. Four free WiFi points. Pitches on the lake are not available for CampingCard ACSI.

A4, exit Dezenzano. Then towards Salò via the SS572. Leave the road at Moniga del Garda. Follow brown camping signs.

CC € 19 *19/3-30/6 1/9-2/10*

N 45°31'12" E 10°31'48"

Moniga del Garda, I-25080 / Lago di Garda

2938

Sereno Camping Holiday***
Via San Sivino 72
+39 0365-502080
FAX +39 0365-503893
19/3 - 26/9
@ info@sereno.info

4ha 32**T**(50-90m²) 6A CEE

1 ABCGHIJKL**P**Q
2 DKLNRTVWXY
3 B**EF**GM**NQ**RU**W**Z
4 (B+G 1/5-26/9) (Q+S+U+V+Y+Z)
5 **A**GIJKLMNOPUVX
6 CEGK(N 2km)TV

A campsite with a large swimming pool and an extensive entertainment team. Good toilet facilities. Peacefully located touring pitches. Good restaurant.

A4, exit Desenzano, then direction Salò via the SS572. Follow the brown camping signs at Moniga del Garda. Campsite located by the lake.

CC € 15 *19/3-27/6 29/8-26/9*

N 45°31'48'' E 10°33'12''

Pacengo di Lazise, I-37017 / Lago di Garda

2939

Camping Le Palme***
Via del Tronchetto 2
+39 045-7590019
FAX +39 045-7590554
18/3 - 24/10
@ info@lepalmecamping.it

2,5ha 112**T**(50-100m²) 6A CEE

1 ABCD**F**IJKLMOPQ
2 ADFGJLNRVXY
3 AB**F**GKNRV**WZ**
4 (C+H) JKP (Q+R+T+U+V+X) Z
5 **AB**DFGIJKLMNOP**ST**UWXYZ
6 CEG**K**M(N 0,5km)RSTV

Campsite with excellent toilet facilities and where all pitches have electricity, water and drainage connections. The site has two swimming pools with hydro massage and a slide. One third of the pitches are available for CampingCard ACSI holders.

A22, exit Lago di Garda Sud. Follow SR450 direction Lago di Garda Sud/Peschiera. After 7 km head towards Lazise. S249 direction Pacengo. Campsite signposted in Pacengo.

CC € 17 *18/3-24/3 29/3-13/5 29/5-20/6 4/9-24/10*

N 45°27'54'' E 10°42'52''

Pacengo di Lazise, I-37017 / Lago di Garda

2940

Lido***
Via Peschiera 2
+39 045-7590030
FAX +39 045-7590611
18/3 - 9/10
@ info@campinglido.it

12ha 561**T**(60-100m²) 6-10A CEE

1 ABCD**G**IJKLMOPRS
2 DFGIJLNRVWXY
3 B**F**GKL**M**NR**VWZ**
4 (C 24/4-9/10) (G 15/5-30/9) J**P**(Q+S+U+V+Y+Z)
5 **AB**DEFGIJKLMNOP**ST**UVXYZ
6 CEG**J**RTV

Spacious, shaded campsite with marked out pitches, mostly surrounded by hedges, new toilet facilities. Lovely new swimming pools with waterslide, children's pool and modern fitness centre. Site is located on Lake Garda. Dogs are very welcome. 10% discount in the restaurant in low season with CampingCard ACSI.

A22, exit Lago di Garda Sud, then take SR450 dir. Peschiera. After 7 km exit Lazise. In Lazise dir. Pacengo. Campsite is south of Movieland.

CC € 17 *18/3-29/6 1/9-9/10*

N 45°28'12'' E 10°43'15''

Padenghe sul Garda, I-25080 / Lago di Garda

2941

La Ca'****
Via della Colombaia 6
+39 030-9907006
FAX +39 030-9907693
13/2 - 31/10
info@campinglaca.it

2ha 135T(60m²) 5-6A CEE

1 ABGIJKLOP
2 DFGHJKNRTVX
3 BFNRWZ
4 (B 1/3-31/10) (G) P
(Q+U+V+W+Y+Z)
5 AGIJKLMNOPRSTUW
6 EGK(N 0,2km)QT

A beautifully maintained terraced campsite. Beatiful view of Lake Garda, also from the swimming pool and the welcoming restaurant. 13 Euros in February, March, April and October.

A4, exit Desenzano, then towards Salò via the SS572. Follow the brown camping signs at Padenghe sul Garda. Enter 'Via San Cassiano' at roundabout. Campsite located by the lake.

CC € 15 *13/2-10/7 27/8-31/10*

N 45°30'45'' E 10°31'27''

Peschiera del Garda, I-37019 / Lago di Garda

2942

Bella Italia*****
Via Bella Italia 2
+39 045-6400688
FAX +39 045-6401410
12/3 - 23/10
info@camping-bellaitalia.it

32ha 400T(90m²) 16A CEE

1 BCDEIJKLQ
2 DFGKLNRTVY
3 BFGKMNRUWZ
4 (C+H 26/3-20/9) IJKMP
(Q+S+T+U+V+X+Y+Z)
5 ABEFGIJKLMNOPUWXYZ
6 CEGHIJM(N 1km)RTV

A large family campsite with an extended pebble beach located on Lake Garda, with an enormous leisure pool for all ages, many facilities. You can reach the centre of Peschiera in 10 minutes along a promenade passing the beach.

A22, exit Lago di Gardo Sud, SR450 to Peschiera. SR11 to Peschiera/Brescia at roundabout, stay on the SR11 in the direction of Brescia. Follow camping signs.

CC € 19 *12/3-29/6 1/9-22/10*

N 45°26'31'' E 10°40'39''

Peschiera del Garda, I-37019 / Lago di Garda

2943

Butterfly****
Lungo Lago Garibaldi 11
+39 045-6401466
FAX +39 045-7552184
12/3 - 6/11
info@campingbutterfly.it

3,8ha 50T(70-100m²) 6A CEE

1 ABGIJKLMOPRS
2 ADFGNRTVXY
3 BFKNRWZ
4 (B+G 25/4-15/9)
(Q+S+T+U+V+Y+Z)
5 ABFGIJKLMNOPUVWXYZ
6 CDEGJ(N 0,8km)RTV

Quiet, comfortable family campsite located on Lake Garda, close to the yacht harbour, train station and historic centre of Peschiera. The site has a swimming pool, children's pool, restaurant/pizzeria and supermarket. Dogs very welcome.

A22 exit Lago di Garda-Sud. On SR450 dir. Lago di Garda-Sud/Peschiera (SR11). Follow Centro in Peschiera. Then follow signs.

CC € 17 *12/3-2/7 20/8-5/11*

N 45°26'42'' E 10°41'40''

Peschiera del Garda, I-37019 / Lago di Garda

2944

Wien
Loc. Fornaci
+39 045-7550379
+39 045-7553366
1/4 - 30/9
info@campingwien.it

4ha 97T(75m²) 3A CEE

1 AB**F**IJKLPQ
2 DFGNRTY
3 A**W**Z
4 (B+G 25/4-23/9) (Q+S+T+V+X+Z)
5 **AB**GIJKLMNOPUV
6 CEG**J**(N 0,2km)RTV

A peaceful, shaded campsite with views of the lake. The swimming pool has a beautiful location by the lake.

A22, exit Lago di Garda Sud, SR450 to Peschiera. At the roundabout SR11 towards Peschiera/Brescia. Stay on the SR11 towards Brescia. Follow camping signs.

CC € 19 1/4-7/5 1/6-30/6 5/9-30/9

N 45°27'4'' E 10°39'56''

San Benedetto/Peschiera, I-37019 / Lago di Garda

2945

Villaggio Turistico Camping S. Benedetto***
Strada Bergamini 14
+39 045-7550544
+39 045-7551512
19/3 - 9/10
info@villaggiosanbenedetto.it

6,6ha 60T(40-100m²) 6-10A CEE

1 ABCDGHIJKLM**P**RS
2 DFGILMNRTVY
3 B**F**GJKNR**WZ**
4 (B+G 1/5-30/9) (Q+T+U+V+Y+Z 1/4-4/10)
5 **AB**CEFGHIJKLMNOPQRUV WXYZ
6 CEG**IK**(N 2km)RTUV

Located directly on Lake Garda next to a small marina. Atmospheric family campsite with many amenities, including a pool, entertainment and restaurant with specialities.

A22, exit Lago di Garda Sud. Take the SR450 to Peschiera, at the roundabout SR11 direction Peschiera/Brescia. Continue on the SR11 towards Brescia. Turn right in San Benedetto towards the lake. Campsite signposted.

CC € 17 29/3-14/5 29/5-18/6 3/9-9/10

N 45°26'53'' E 10°40'11''

San Felice del Benaco, I-25010 / Lago di Garda

2946

Fornella****
Via Fornella 1
+39 0365-62294
+39 0365-559418
23/4 - 24/9
fornella@fornella.it

9,2ha 263T(60-140m²) 10-16A CEE

1 BCGIJKLMO**P**Q
2 DIJKLNRTVXY
3 BC**F**JKL**M**NR**WZ**
4 (B+G 15/5-15/9) (Q+S+U+V+X+Y) Z
5 **AB**EFGIJKLMNOPUVWXY
6 CDEG**IK**(N 2km)ORTV

A well kept, very large campsite with two swimming pools. The layout of the site is well thought out and pleasant. Suitable for families with older or younger children. New toilet facilities, a new supermarket and beautifully laid out new pitches (2013).

A4, exit Desenzano, on the SS572 to Salò, or A22, exit Trento, SS45bis direction Riva. Drive along the lake in the direction of Salò. Campsite is signposted in Salò.

CC € 19 23/4-15/5 29/5-3/7 5/9-24/9

N 45°35'6'' E 10°33'57''

Sirmione, I-25019 / Lago di Garda

2947

Tiglio
Loc. Punta Grò
+39 030-9904009
24/3 - 30/9
info@campingtiglio.it

3ha 168T(60-80m²) 4A CEE

1 ABCFIJKLPQ
2 DFGMNRTVWXY
3 BFJRWZ
4 (B+G 1/5-30/9)
(Q+S+U+V+Y 1/4-27/9)
(Z)
5 AGIJKLMNOPUZ
6 EGK(N 3km)RSTV

The campsite, a family business is located on the shores of Lake Garda in a quiet setting between the picturesque villages of Sirmione and Peschiera. An ideal campsite for city trips to Verona, Milan and Venice.

A4 Milano-Venezia, exit Sirmione. On the SPBS11 roundabout direction Peschiera-Verona. Campsite signposted 4 km after roundabout.

CC € 19 24/3-15/7 1/9-30/9

N 45°27'27'' E 10°38'25''

Toscolano Maderno, I-25080 / Lago di Garda

2948

Riviera***
Via Promontorio 59
+39 0365-643039
25/3 - 3/10
info@camping-riviera.com

3,8ha 170T(64-100m²) 3A CEE

1 ABGIJKLMOPQ
2 DGKNRTVWXY
3 BFRWZ
4 (B 1/4-30/9)
(Q+R+U+V 27/3-30/9) Z
5 AEGIJKLMNOPUVX
6 CEGJ(N 0,2km)OT

Located right by a lake in a peaceful area with plenty of greenery. The centre can be reached within minutes via a promenade beside the lake. The water is very clear and clean and suitable for divers, anglers and windsurfers. The pebble beach slopes gently into the water, making it suitable for small children.

From Riva del Garda towards Salò via the SS45Bis. After Gargnano drive towards Toscolano. Campsite well indicated. Site by a lake.

CC € 17 25/3-30/6 29/8-3/10

N 45°38'4'' E 10°36'47''

Toscolano Maderno, I-25088 / Lago di Garda

2949

Toscolano***
Via Religione 88
+39 0365-641584
+39 0365-642519
23/3 - 1/11
campeggiotoscolano@virgilio.it

5ha 350T(80m²) 3A CEE

1 ABGIJKLMPQ
2 ADGNRTVWXY
3 BFMNWZ
4 (B+G 1/4-30/9) K
(Q 30/5-25/9) (S 1/5-20/9)
(U+V+X+Y 1/4-30/9) Z
5 ABGIJKLMNOPUVZ
6 CFGJ(N 0,3km)TV

NEW

Located within the walls of a 14th century monastery. Surrounded by a flower garden. Private beach, spacious pitches, modern toilet facilities, shop, fish restaurant, bar and pizzeria. Pools, tennis courts and football field. Entertainment all week in summer for children and adults, e.g. sports tournaments. Horseback excursions bookable.

From Riva del Garda dir. Salò via SS45bis. After Gargnano dir. Toscolano. Site is well signposted from here. Site is on a lake.

CC € 19 1/4-13/5 31/5-1/7 4/9-7/10 24/10-31/10

N 45°38'15'' E 10°36'46''

Arsiè, I-32030 / Veneto

2950

Al Lago***
Via Campagna 14
+39 0439-58540
+39 0439-58471
20/4 - 18/9
info@campinglago.info

2ha 168T(60-100m²) 4A CEE

1 ABCD**G**IJKLMO**P**RS
2 BCDGKLMRTUVWXY
3 ABHJKLNRU**W**XZ
4 (Q+R+T+U+V+Y+Z)
5 **AB**EGIJKLMNOPUWXYZ
6 ABCDEGKL(N 3km)OTV

A peaceful small campsite located on Lake Corlo. Come to visit a very natural place, surrounded by the breathtaking Belluno Dolomites. This 'off the beaten track spot' is perfect for those who love to relax and doing activities such as walking and fishing. Dog are welcome.

From Trento follow the SS47 direction Padova as far as the Feltre exit onto the SS50bis. Take Rocca exit after the tunnel. Campsite is then signposted.

CC €17 *20/4-7/7 24/8-18/9*

N 45°57'52" E 11°45'33"

Arsiè, I-32030 / Veneto

2951

Gajole
Loc. Gajole
+39 0439-58505
1/4 - 30/9
info@campinggajole.it

1,7ha 70T(> 50m²) 6A CEE

1 ABGHIJKLMNO**P**RS
2 DIJKLMRTUVX
3 AHJKLMR**W**Z
4 (A 1/4-31/5,1/9-30/9) (R+T 1/6-15/9) (U 1/6-1/9) (X 1/6-15/9) (Z)
5 **AB**FGIJKLMNOP**T**UVXYZ
6 CDEG**K**(N 3km)TVW

Gajole campsite is probably the most peaceful campsite in the world. Gajole campsite was started in 1975 by the Turra family which is still in charge of it. The site is located on the shores of Lake Corlo, a strategic starting point for trips out to various coastal towns and the Dolomites.

From Trento take the SS47 dir. Padova, exit Feltre. Take the SS50B. After tunnel exit Rocca. Campsite then signposted with big, clear signs.

CC €17 *1/4-30/6 1/9-30/9*

N 45°58'4" E 11°45'58"

Campalto/Venezia, I-30173 / Veneto

2952

Rialto
Via Orlanda 16
+39 041-5420295
24/3 - 20/11
rialto@camping.it

2ha 150T(20-80m²) 6A CEE

1 ABCGIJKLMPQ
2 FGRWXY
4 (Q) (R+V+Z 1/5-30/9)
5 **A**GIJKLMOPUV
6 CEGJ(N 0,3km)T

A small, attractive and modest campsite with grass and deciduous trees. Near the approach road to Venice. New toilet facilities since February 2013. By bus (7 minutes away) just a 15 minute ride to the centre of Venice (Piazzale Roma).

A4 continue towards Venice. Immediate right after bus stop and car park on SS14 towards Trieste. Over viaduct, follow Trieste-Aeroporto road. Campsite another 1km on the right.

CC €19 *5/4-4/5 23/5-30/6 11/9-20/10 6=5*

N 45°29'4" E 12°17'0"

Caorle, I-30021 / Veneto — 2953

Laguna Village***
Via dei Cacciatori 5
+39 0421-210165
FAX +39 0421-217085
22/4 - 18/9
@ info@campinglagunavillage.com

10ha 500**T**(60-90m²) 6A CEE

1 ABCDGHIJKLMPQ
2 AEGRVY
3 AB**F**JKNRY
4 (B 7/5-18/9) JK
(Q+S+U+V+Y 7/5-18/9) Z
5 **AB**FGIJKLMNOPUVWXYZ
6 EG**K**MQRT

A lovely quiet campsite with a pleasant ambiance, partly in pine woods. Excellent toilet facilities. The campsite is located by the sea with a wide beach. CampingCard ACSI is only valid on the 'Laguna' pitches.

When entering Caorle follow signs left 'Spiaggia di Levante' (corso Chiggiato-Viale Falconera). Then follow camping signs.

CC € 15 *22/4-30/6 29/8-18/9*

N 45°36'59'' E 12°54'25''

Caorle, I-30020 / Veneto — 2954

San Francesco****
Via Selva Rosata
+39 0421-2982
FAX +39 0421-299284
21/4 - 3/10
@ agency@villaggiosfrancesco.com

32ha 898**T**(70-100m²) 10A CEE

1 ABCD**F**HIJKLMOPQ
2 AEGLRSVXY
3 B**F**GJK**MNQ**RUVY
4 (B+H) **JK**M
(Q+S+T+U+V+W+X+Y) Z
5 **AB**EFGIJKLMNOPR**ST**UW
XYZ
6 CEG**IJK**MORTV

A lively holiday village in a pine forest, close to the sea. The campsite has a private beach more than 500m in length. The campsite is an ideal base for exploring the area, including the small town of Caorle, a traditional fishing village.

In Caorle drive first in the direction of Porto S. Margherita, then Duna Verde. The campsite is signposted and is located on the left side of the road.

CC € 15 *21/4-11/6 27/8-3/10*

N 45°33'59'' E 12°47'40''

Cavallino, I-30013 / Veneto — 2955

Europa Camping Village****
Via Fausta 332
+39 041-968261
FAX +39 041-5370150
22/4 - 2/10
@ info@campingeuropa.com

10,7ha 564**T**(60-90m²) 8A CEE

1 ABCD**G**HIJKLMO**P**Q
2 AEGRSVXY
3 BGK**M**NR**V**Y
4 **(C+G) JKLNP**
(Q+S+T) (U 15/5-10/9)
(V+Y+Z)
5 **AB**EFGIJKLMNOPUVWXYZ
6 CEGH**IK**M(N 1km)ORSTV

A peaceful campsite by the sea where you can take your dog. Very centrally located. Deciduous trees provide shade. Newly designated beach for dogs (2013).

The campsite is located on the road between Jesolo and Punta Sabbioni. Clearly signposted.

CC € 17 *22/4-13/5 28/5-16/6 1/9-2/10*

N 45°28'26'' E 12°32'55''

Cavallino, I-30013 / Veneto

2956

Italy****
Via Fausta 272
+39 041-968090
FAX +39 041-5370076
28/4 - 25/9
@ info@campingitaly.it

3,9ha 260T(50-80m²) 6A CEE

1 BCDEHIJLMPST
2 AEGRSVY
3 AB**F**JK**MOPQ**RUY
4 (C+H 1/5-20/9)
(Q+S+T+U+V+Y+Z)
5 **A**BEFGIJKLMNOPUWYZ
6 CEG**I**K(N 2km)ORTV

A small campsite with deciduous trees and plenty of attention to the environment, close to the sea. The guests can make use of the many sports facilities at the Union Lido campsite. All pets are prohibited (not just dogs!). Luxurious toilet facilities with a separate, nicely decorated space for children.

Campsite located in Cavallino, on the main road (Via Fausta). Campsite signposted.

CC € 15 *28/4-14/5 28/5-29/6 10/9-25/9*

N 45°28'6'' E 12°31'59''

Cavallino, I-30013 / Veneto

2957

Villa Al Mare***
Via del Faro 12
+39 041-968066
FAX +39 041-5370576
20/4 - 22/10
@ info@villaalmare.com

2ha 100T(60-100m²) 6A CEE

1 ABCEHIJKLMOPQ
2 AEGLRSVY
3 B**F**GJKRV**W**Y
4 (H 4/5-14/9) **KP**
(Q+S+T+U+V+Y+Z)
5 **A**FGIJKLMNOPUVWXYZ
6 CDEGK(N 2,5km)OQRSTV

A peaceful campsite located on the beach next to the marina and fishing harbour. Shaded pitches, all with electricity, water supply and drainage and satellite TV socket. Direct connection to St. Mark's Square in Venice. Excellent cuisine with fresh vegetables and fish at a very reasonable prices and local Italian dishes. WiFi available.

From the Jesolo roundabout choose direction Cavallino. Campsite close to the lighthouse (Faro) and is signposted

CC € 17 *20/4-14/5 30/5-28/6 12/9-21/10*

N 45°28'45'' E 12°34'52''

Cavallino, I-30013 / Veneto

2958

Village Cavallino****
Via delle Batterie 164
+39 041-966133
FAX +39 041-5300827
17/3 - 13/11
@ info@campingcavallino.com

11ha 560T(64-120m²) 6A CEE

1 ABC**F**HIJKLMO**P**Q
2 ABEGRSVWXY
3 ABK**Q**RY
4 (B+G 1/5-15/9) K
(Q+S+T+U+V+Y+Z)
5 **AB**DFGIJKLMNOP**QRS**UX
Y
6 CEGH**IK**M(N 2km)RTV

A family campsite with lovely, modern toilet facilities set close to the sea in a pine forest. The abundant flowers add a splash of colour to the site. You cannot pitch by the sea if using CampingCard ACSI. New toilet facilities (2014).

From Cavallino direction Punta Sabbioni on the Via Fausta, turn left just after Ca'Ballerin. Follow the campsite signs.

CC € 19 *17/3-11/5 30/5-29/6 4/9-12/11*

N 45°27'24'' E 12°30'3''

Cavallino/Treporti, I-30013 / Veneto

2959

Scarpiland***
Via Poerio 14
+39 041-966488
21/4 - 24/9
info@scarpiland.com

3ha 204T(70-90m²) 6A CEE

1 ABCD**F**HIJKLMPRS
2 AEGRSVY
3 AKRY
4 (Q+R+S+T+U+V+Y+Z)
5 **A**BFGIJKLMNOPUVWXYZ
6 ACEG**K**M(N 2km)OQRSTV

A small but very neat campsite by the sea with separated pitches as well as open ones. It is cosy and peaceful to camp here between the pine trees.

From Cavallino via Fausta to Punta Sabbioni. Past Ca'Ballarin turn left at first traffic lights, then right at first intersection and follow the camping signs.

CC € 17 21/4-2/7 20/8-24/9 10=9

N 45°27'19'' E 12°29'20''

Fusina/Venezia, I-30030 / Veneto

2960

Fusina***
Via Moranzani 93
+39 041-5470055
+39 041-5470050
1/1 - 31/12
info@campingfusina.com

5,5ha 275T 6A CEE

1 ABCDGIJKLMNOPST
2 CFGKLRXY
3 ABJK**VW**
4 (Q+R+T+U+V+X+Z 1/4-30/10)
5 **AB**DEFGIJKLMNOPUW
6 CG**IJ**M(N 5km)ORTV

A peacefully located campsite on the lagoon with a landing stage close by. Plenty of deciduous trees on the site. Views of Venice. Perfect for visiting the town.

Signposted on the SS309 Ravenna-Venice, direction Malcontenta/Fusina. The campsite is at the end of the road next to the Fusina-Venice landing stage.

CC € 19 1/5-8/5 16/5-31/5 13/6-21/6 1/9-30/9

N 45°25'10'' E 12°15'22''

Lido di Jesolo, I-30016 / Veneto

2961

Camping Park dei Dogi
Viale Oriente 13
+39 0421-1885626
+39 0421-1885619
1/3 - 31/10, 23/12 - 6/1
info@campingparkdeidogi.com

2,8ha 250T 6A CEE

1 ABCDGHIJKLMOPQ
2 AEGRTVX
3 BJY
5 **AB**EFGJKN**PRT**UWXZ
6 DE**K**(N 0,3km)TU

A basic campsite with an excellent toilet block. Washing machines available. The pathways are separated by trees and conifers, giving both shade and sun. Very suitable for motorhomes and caravans. At walking distance from the sea.

Campsite on the Viale Oriente. Well signposted, use of coordinates recommended.

CC € 13 1/1-6/1 1/3-30/6 1/9-31/10 23/12-31/12

N 45°31'18'' E 12°41'17''

Lido di Jesolo, I-30016 / Veneto

2962

Malibu Beach****
Viale Oriente 78
+39 0421-362212
+39 0421-961338
7/5 - 18/9
info@campingmalibubeach.com

9,5ha 120T(20-90m²) 6A CEE

1 ABEHIJKLMOPQ
2 AEGRSVXY
3 BFKRVY
4 (B+G) KP(Q 11/5-14/9) (S+T+U+V+Y)
5 **AB**GIJKLMNOPUVWXYZ
6 CEGH**K**M(N 1,2km)OQRTV

A lovely, well run campsite offering both sun and shade close to the sea. There is excellent cycling and shopping in Jesolo. After a day on the beach you can eat well in the large restaurant. In 2015 the swimming pool and the restaurant were renovated. A combined bus and boat ticket to Venice can be purchased at reception.

Campsite well indicated with brown signs in Jesolo on the Viale Oriente.

€17 *7/5-31/5 6/6-30/6 5/9-18/9*

N 45°31'27" E 12°42'2"

Lido di Jesolo, I-30016 / Veneto

2963

Parco Capraro***
Via Corer 2° ramo, 4
+39 0421-961073
+39 0421-362994
1/4 - 25/9
info@parcocapraro.it

5,7ha 400**T**(60-90m²) 16A CEE

1 ABCDGHIJKLMO**P**Q
2 AEGRUVXY
3 B**F**GNRVWY
4 (B+G 22/4-25/9) (Q) (S+U+V+Y 22/4-25/9) Z
5 **AB**GI**J**K**L**MNO**P**RUVWXY Z
6 ACDEG**K**(N 1km)ORTV

Staying on this shaded campsite with its large swimming pool is the guarantee of a good holiday. During the day you can walk along a wide woodland path and be on the beach in 5 minutes, while in the evenings you can have a delicious Italian meal in the large restaurant. Special site for plenty of motorhomes. A combined bus and boat ticket to Venice can be purchased at reception.

In Jesolo turn off the Viale Oriente. Follow brown camping signs. Campsite clearly indicated.

€15 *1/4-24/6 22/8-25/9*

N 45°31'37" E 12°41'49"

Lido di Jesolo, I-30016 / Veneto

2964

Waikiki***
Viale Oriente 144
+39 0421-980186
+39 0421-378040
7/5 - 18/9
info@campingwaikiki.com

5,2ha 100T(20-90m²) 6A CEE

1 ABGHIJKLOPQ
2 AEGRSVXY
3 B**F**KRV**W**Y
4 (B+G) KP (S+T+U+V+Y) Z
5 **AB**GIJKLMNOPUVWXYZ
6 CEGH**K**M(N 3,2km)OQRTV

A lovely, well-run campsite offering both sun and shade. Close to the sea. Friendly staff and a welcoming restaurant. Cycle trips possible in the locality. Swimming pool was renovated in 2015. Combined tickets for bus and boat can be bought for a day trip to Venice at reception.

The campsite is well indicated in Jesolo on the Viale Oriente with brown signposts.

€15 *7/5-31/5 6/6-30/6 5/9-18/9*

N 45°31'52" E 12°43'19"

Malcontenta/Venezia, I-30176 / Veneto

2965

Serenissima***
Via Padana 334a
+39 041-921850
+39 041-920286
21/3 - 5/11
info@campingserenissima.it

2ha 120T 10A CEE

1 ABCGIJKLMOPQ
2 CFRY
3 AKR**W**
4 (Q+S)
(U+V+X 10/6-30/9) (Z)
5 **AB**FGIJKLMNOPUVW
6 CEG**I**(N 2km)ORV

A shaded and very peaceful family campsite with well maintained toilet facilities. Bus (3 Euros) to Venice centre 100m from the entrance. Lovely level cycle path along the Brenta River. The centre of Malcontenta with its Renaissance villas is very pleasant. A peaceful retreat after a busy day in Venice.

A4 exit Oriago/Mira. Follow signs at the first roundabout to Ravenna and Venezia and at the second roundabout to Padova / Riviera del Brenta (SR11).

€ 19 *21/3-30/6 24/8-5/11*

N 45°27'14" E 12°11'0"

Mestre/Venezia, I-30170 / Veneto

2966

Venezia**
Via Orlanda 8/C
+39 041-5312828
+39 041-5327618
4/2 - 2/11, 27/12 - 31/12
info@veneziavillage.it

2ha 140**T**(50-80m²) 6A CEE

1 ABCDGHIJKLMOPQ
2 FGLRSVXY
3 AB
4 (**F**) **KNP**
(Q+R+U+V+X+Y+Z)
5 **AB**DEFGIJKLMNOPUWXZ
6 CDEG**K**(N 3km)O

A quiet family campsite with a heated indoor pool, sauna and jacuzzi, charges apply. New modern toilet facilities. Good cuisine with local specialities. 8 minutes by city bus to Piazzale Roma. Then 20 minutes by boat on the Grand Canal to San Marco.

Stay on the A4 at first towards Venezia. Keep right after bus stop and car park towards Trieste (SS14). Drive over the viaduct, follow Trieste-Aeroporto road. The campsite is on the right after a few hundred metres.

€ 19 *4/2-23/3 30/3-8/7 29/8-2/11*

N 45°28'51" E 12°16'31"

Rosolina Mare, I-45010 / Veneto

2967

Vittoria***
Strada Sud 340
+39 0426-68128
+39 0426-68148
5/5 - 11/9
info@campingvittoria.it

17ha 350**T**(60-120m²) 6A CEE

1 ABCD**F**HIJKLMO**P**ST
2 ABEGIKSY
3 AB**C**GJWY
4 (B+G 1/6-13/9) J
(Q+S+U+V+X)
(Y 9/5-13/9) Z
5 **AB**GIJKLMNPUVZ
6 EGJ(N 1km)OT

A friendly, informal campsite with large pitches in the wood or on the beach. Large, sloping child-friendly beach in the Parco Delta del Po. There is a good restaurant with fish specialities and many traditional dishes.

On the SS309 exit to SP65. Via Rosolina Mare. Keep right past the lake. Bear left just before the next lake, Strada Sud.

€ 17 *5/5-25/6 28/8-11/9*

N 45°7'0" E 12°19'31"

Rosolina Mare/Rovigo, I-45010 / Veneto
2968

Villaggio Turistico Camping Rosapineta***
Strada Nord 24
+39 0426-68033
FAX +39 0426-68105
11/5 - 13/9
info@rosapineta.it

46ha 1151**T**(60-70m²) 10A CEE

1 ABCD**F**IJKLMP
2 ABEGIKRSTWXY
3 ABHJKMQRT**V**
4 (B+G) J**KP** (Q+S+T+U+V+Y+Z)
5 AGIJKLMNOPUVXYZ
6 EG**IJ**(N 1km)RT

46 hectares to enjoy the flora in peaceful surroundings near the beach. Good cuisine and a romantic pavement cafe. An ideal base for Venice with own transport. Campsite with entertainment and shopping facilities near the village centre. Several swimming pools, one with a whirlpool.

A4 Milano-Venezia, exit Padova Interporto. SS Romea direction Chioggia/Ravenna. Turn right 14 km beyond Chioggia and 200m past bridge over the Adige and follow signs to Rosolina Mare.

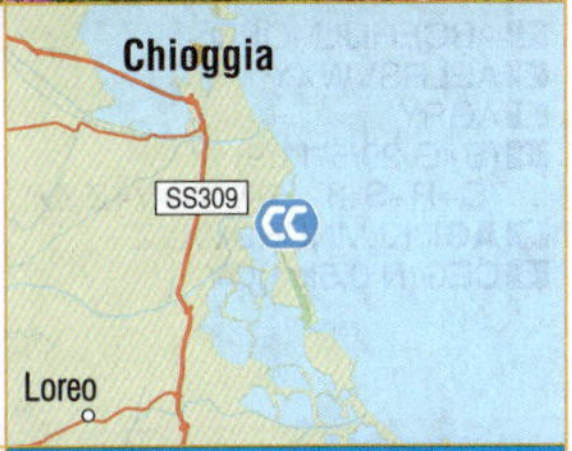

CC € 17 *12/5-30/6 1/9-13/9*

N 45°8'20'' E 12°19'25''

Sappada, I-32047 / Veneto
2969

Alpin Park Sappada
Borgata Cima, Località Eirl
+39 340-6353354
27/5 - 9/10, 1/12 - 28/3
info@alpinpark.it

2ha 44**T**(> 80m²) 4A

1 ACDGIJKLMPQ
2 BCGJKLRTVX
3 AB**EF**HJ**M**NOP**Q**
4 (A) (Q 1/1-6/4,29/5-31/12) (Z)
5 FXYZ
6 CHJ(N 0,7km)Q

Peacefully located in the beautiful Dolomites. An adventure park for adults and children where you can climb in the treetops. There is a beer garden and a good restaurant. Free WiFi at reception.

From Brenner direction Brixen-Bruneck-Dobbiaco (Toblach)-Sexten-San Stefano di Cadore-Sappada.

CC € 17 *9/1-28/3 27/5-14/7 1/9-9/10 1/12-22/12*

N 46°34'16'' E 12°43'6''

Sottomarina, I-30015 / Veneto
2970

Adriatico***
Lungomare Adriatico 82
+39 041-492907
FAX +39 041-5548567
25/3 - 2/10
info@campingadriatico.com

1,7ha 121**T**(45-80m²) 5A CEE

1 ABCDFHIJKLOPRS
2 AEGLRSVY
3 BGKRVY
4 (B+G 14/5-30/9) (Q+R+S+T+U+X+Z)
5 **A**FGIJKLMNOPUVXYZ
6 CEG**K**ORV

A small, friendly campsite by the boulevard near the beach. Close to the town centre. Ferry to the heart of Venice within walking distance. A family run business for 50 years.

Clearly signposted on the SS309. In Sottomarina follow the boulevard. Campsite is located on the landside, near the middle of the boulevard.

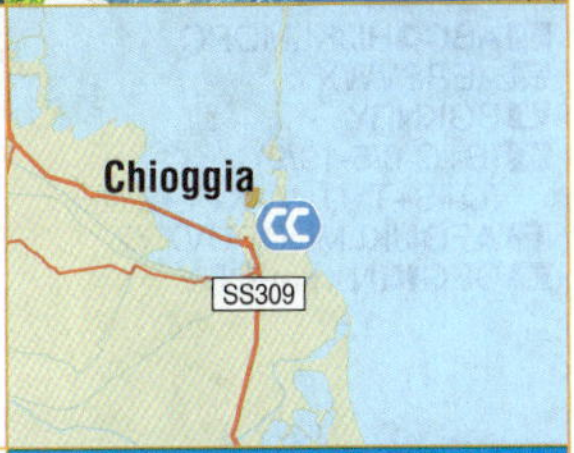

CC € 17 *25/3-21/4 26/4-31/5 6/6-19/6 22/8-30/9 14=12*

N 45°12'17'' E 12°17'55''

Sottomarina, I-30015 / Veneto

2971

Atlanta***
Via Barbarigo 73
+39 041-491311
FAX +39 041-4967198
22/4 - 15/9
@ info@campeggioatlanta.com

4ha 220**T**(50-70m²) 6A CEE

1 ABCEHIJLMOPQ
2 AELRSVWXY
3 AGRY
4 (B+G 29/5-11/9) (Q+R+S+T+U+V+X+Y+Z)
5 **A**GIJKLMNOPUVXYZ
6 CEG(N 0,5km)OV

A friendly family campsite with lovely, modern toilet facilities, right by the sea. Mostly Italian guests.

Clearly signposted on the SS309 Ravenna-Venice. In Sottomarina turn right before the beach, follow country road. Campsite is signposted.

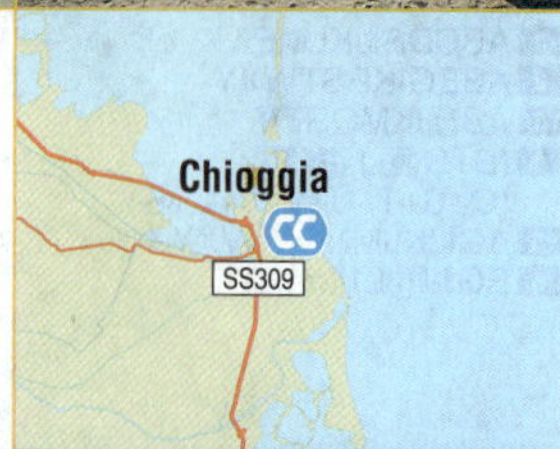

CC € 17 *22/4-30/6 1/9-15/9 7=6*

N 45°11'34'' E 12°18'7''

Sottomarina, I-30015 / Veneto

2972

Internazionale***
Via A. Barbarigo 117
+39 041-491444
FAX +39 041-5543373
15/4 - 20/9
@ info@campinginternazionale.net

7ha 300**T**(60-90m²) 6A CEE

1 ABCEHIJKLMNOS
2 AERSVWX
3 AGKY
4 (B+G 1/6-31/8) (Q+S+T+U+V+X+Y+Z)
5 **A**GIJKLMNOPUVXYZ
6 EGIJ**K**(N 1km)OV

This campsite is located right by the beach and has modern toilet blocks. There is a supermarket, bar, pizzeria and bazaar. WiFi right down to the beach. In the middle of the site there is a lovely swimming pool next to an enchanting castle that certainly adds to the atmosphere.

Clearly signposted from the SS309 Ravenna-Venice. In Sottomarina-Lido turn right before the beach on the the country road. The campsite is located left on the seaward side.

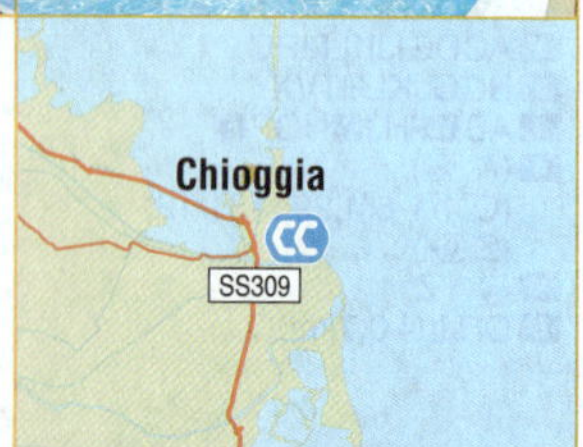

CC € 17 *15/4-30/6 22/8-20/9*

N 45°11'19'' E 12°18'16''

Sottomarina, I-30015 / Veneto

2973

Miramare***
Via A. Barbarigo 103
FAX +39 041-490610
21/4 - 19/9
@ info@miramarecamping.com

5,5ha 350**T**(60-100m²) 6A CEE

1 ABC**G**HIJKLMOPQ
2 AERSVWXY
3 BGKNRY
4 (B+G 8/5-19/9) (Q+S+T+U+V+X+Y+Z)
5 **A**FGIJKLMNOPUVXYZ
6 CEG**K**(N 1km)ORV

This campsite run by the Boscolo family is located right by the sea and offers modern toilet buildings, a bar, restaurant, minimarket and swimming pool. There is a wide beach with many facilities. The modern comforts will bring even more pleasure to your holiday.

Clearly signposted on the SS309 Ravenna-Venice. In Sottomarina turn right before the beach, follow country road.

CC € 17 *21/4-30/6 22/8-19/9 7=6, 14=12, 21=18*

N 45°11'25'' E 12°18'12''

Sottomarina, I-30015 / Veneto

2974

Oasi***
Via A. Barbarigo 147
+39 041-5541145
FAX +39 041-490801
25/3 - 2/10
info@campingoasi.com

NEW

2,5ha 150T(56-100m²) 6A CEE

1 AC**G**HIJKLMNO**P**ST
2 ACELRSVXY
3 AGK**M**N**O**P**R**U**W**Y
4 (B+G 15/5-15/9) **KP**
(Q+R+S+T+U+V+W+X) Z
5 **AB**FGIJKLMNOP**T**UVXYZ
6 CEG**K**(N 2km)QRV

Small, neat and very quiet family campsite on the sea with well-maintained toilet facilities and an own marina on the mouth of the Brenta. Very neat fish restaurant.

Clearly signposted on the SS309 Ravenna-Venice. In Sottomarina follow the signs. Turn right before the beach, then follow the country road as far as the end.

CC €17 *25/3-8/7 27/8-2/10*

N 45°10'54" E 12°18'28"

Tarzo, I-31020 / Veneto

2975

Camping al Lago di Lago
Località Fratta 89
+39 0438-586891
19/3 - 16/10
info@campingallagodilago.it

NEW

2,2ha 83T(60-120m²) 8A CEE

1 ABGIJKLMO**P**RS
2 DFKLMRY
3 ABJRWZ
4 (B+G 1/6-30/9)
(Q+V+X+Z)
5 **AB**GJLNPQRUWXYZ
6 AEGJ(N 1,4km)OQT

In the foothills of the Alps you will find this campsite in a national park on a beautiful small lake. The surroundings are perfect for active and cultural outings, such as a visit to Venice, Vicenza or other historic locations.

From A27 9 km Bellum-Treviso exit Vittorio Venero Nord. From SSS1 to SP35 dir. Tarzo, via SP153 or SP635 follow road. Follow campsite signs.

CC €17 *19/3-3/7 22/8-16/10*

N 45°58'57" E 12°13'40"

Alesso/Trasaghis, I-33010 / Friuli-Venezia Giulia

2976

Lago 3 Comuni**
Via Tolmezzo 52
FAX +39 0432-979464
1/4 - 2/10
camping@lago3comuni.com

1,2ha 66T(64-80m²) 6A CEE

1 ACD**G**IJKLMOPQ
2 CDKLMNRVWXY
3 AHJKWZ
4 (Q+T) Z
5 **A**DGHIKMNOPUZ
6 AEGHJ(N 1,5km)OT

Renovated in 2011 and set in lovely countryside by a lake, is located about 15 km from the autostrada. Also suitable as stopover campsite. Groceries on sale 1500m from the site. Of the two adjacent campsites this site, coming from the north is the second site on the left. Entrance is round the bend in the road.

From Villach on the A23 direction Udine. Exit at Gemona-Osoppo. Take the SS13 towards Trasaghis and continue on the SR512 until Alesso. Campsite signposted.

CC €17 *1/4-30/6 1/9-2/10*

N 46°19'31" E 13°3'53"

Aquileia, I-33051 / Friuli-Venezia Giulia

2977

Aquileia**
Via Gemina 10
+39 0431-91042
FAX +39 0431-30804
1/4 - 30/9
@ info@campingaquileia.it

3,2ha 115T(70-140m²) 6A CEE

1 ACDGIJKLMOPQ
2 CGLRVWXY
3 AJKR
4 (C+G+Q+S+U+Y) Z
5 AGIJKLMNOPUV
6 ACDEGIK(N 0,2km)OQTV

A peaceful campsite with a swimming pool, located 10 km from Grado and about 7 km from the sea. Plenty of grass and lovely shaded pitches. There is a supermarket opposite the campsite. There is a large culture park right next to the site with Roman excavations.

Coming from the north in Aquilea turn left at the first traffic lights. After about 450 metres you will see the campsite entrance.

CC € 19 *1/4-30/6 21/8-30/9*

N 45°46'34'' E 13°22'15''

Grado, I-34073 / Friuli-Venezia Giulia

2978

Tenuta Primero****
Via Monfalcone 14
+39 0431-896900
FAX +39 0431-896901
22/4 - 25/9
@ info@tenuta-primero.com

22ha 760T(60-110m²) 6A CEE

1 ABCDEIJKLMOPQ
2 AEGLRSTVXY
3 ABEGJKMNRUWY
4 (A 1/5-10/9)
(B+G 1/5-16/9) K(Q+S)
(T+U+V 15/5-16/9) (X)
(Y 15/5-16/9) Z
5 ABFGIJKLMNOPRUVWXYZ
6 CDEGIJ(N 5km)OQRTV

This well maintained campsite is located 8 km from Grado village. Pine trees provide shade and you can enjoy the sun on the beach. A very good swimming pool and all the facilities available ensure carefree holiday pleasure. There is a golf course next to the campsite which can be used (for a payment) by campers.

Exit the A23 towards Palmanove, and then drive in the direction of Monfalcone. Follow the camping signs in Grado. The campsite is the fourth on the right.

CC € 17 *22/4-13/5 1/6-30/6 5/9-24/9 7=6*

N 45°42'19'' E 13°27'51''

Sistiana, I-34019 / Friuli-Venezia Giulia

2979

Mare Pineta Baia Sistiana****
Via Sistiana 60/D
+39 040-299264
FAX +39 040-299265
24/3 - 3/10
@ info@marepineta.com

107ha 500T(80-100m²) 6A CEE

1 ABCDFIJKLMNPQ
2 BEFGJKLMNQRTVWXY
3 ABHJMNRUVW
4 (B+G 1/6-10/9)
(Q+S+T+U+V)
(X+Y 15/4-15/9) Z
5 ABEFGIJKLMNOPSUVXZ
6 CEGK(N 1km)ORTV

Lovely well kept site located right by the A4 motorway. Views of the sea and 1500m from the beach. Marked out pitches. The site is also suitable as a stopover site, for example on the way to Croatia. In June, July and August a small train rides between the campsite and the beach lower down from 10:00 to 18:00 (free for campsite guests).

Take A4 direction Trieste, exit Duino. Direction Trieste via the coast road. Campsite located on the right beyond Duino.

CC € 17 *24/3-11/5 30/5-29/6 1/9-2/10*

N 45°46'19'' E 13°37'27''

Casal Borsetti, I-48010 / Emilia Romagna

2980

Adria***
Spallazzi 30
+39 0544-445217
FAX +39 0544-442014
23/4 - 15/9
@ info@villaggiocampingadria.it

3,4ha 528T(60-120m²) 10A CEE

1 ABC**F**HIJKLMPQ
2 AEGLRSVWXY
3 BGHJK**M**NRUWY
4 (B+G 15/5-14/9) (Q+R+T+U+V+X+Y) Z
5 **AB**EFGIJKLMNOPRUVWXY Z
6 CDG**IJK**(N 0,2km)ORSTV

A good campsite close to the sea. A regular and a new swimming pool up to 1m in depth and a large bubble bath. Lovely trips out from here to Venice, Rimini, etc.

Take A14 to Ravenna. Then via the SS309 direction Venice. You will shortly see signs to 'Casal Borsetti' and campsite 'Adria'.

CC € 15 *23/4-27/6 24/8-15/9 7=6, 14=12*

N 44°33'32'' E 12°16'47''

Cervarezza Terme, I-42032 / Emilia Romagna

2981

Le Fonti****
Via Santa Lucia 1
+39 0522-890126
FAX +39 0522-890390
1/1 - 31/12
@ info@campinglefonti.com

10ha 70T(25-80m²) 4A CEE

1 ABCD**F**HIJKLOPQ
2 BGIJKLRTUVWXY
3 BGHJNRU**V**
4 (A 1/7-30/8) (F) **KLP** (Q+S) (T+U+V+X 15/6-15/9) Z
5 **AB**DFGIJKLMNOPUVW
6 ACEG**J**(N 2km)OT

A site which still offers genuine camping and stunning panoramas. The perfectly run site with heated toilet blocks has an indoor pool (open all year). The friendly, helpful owners organise activities all year round and will happily assist you in plannning trips out and excursions.

A1, exit Reggio Nell 'Emilia. S63, Cervarezza Terme. Campsite signposted beyond Castelnovo ne Monfi.

CC € 19 *23/3-15/7 1/9-30/10 7=6*

N 44°23'42'' E 10°19'33''

Gatteo Mare, I-47043 / Emilia Romagna

2982

Delle Rose***
Via Adriatica 29
+39 0547-86213
FAX +39 0547-87583
1/5 - 18/9
@ baiocchi@villaggiorose.com

4ha 400T(50-70m²) 6A CEE

1 ABC**F**HIJKLMPQ
2 AEGLRTVY
3 BGKNRUW
4 (B+G 30/5-18/9) (Q+S+T+U+V+Y) Z
5 **AB**EFGIJKLMNOPUVW
6 CEG**J**M(N 0,5km)OQRTUV

A shady campsite 500m from the sea. Swimming pool. A perfect place for people who want to relax, although there is a railway line close by. Many lovely sights in the immediate vicinity.

On the A14 take exit Rimini-Nord. Then direction Ravenna and take exit Gatteo Mare.

CC € 17 *1/5-26/6 26/8-18/9 7=6*

N 44°9'58'' E 12°25'56''

Lido di Dante, I-48100 / Emilia Romagna

2983

Classe***
Via Catone 1
+39 0544-492005
+39 0544-492058
26/3 - 9/10
info@campingclasse.it

70ha 400**T**(60-80m²) 4A CEE

1 ABC**F**HIJKLMPQ
2 AEGLRSVXY
3 BGHKNRUVWY
4 (B+G 22/5-30/9) (Q+S+T+U+V+X+Y 🔑) Z
5 **A**EFGIJKLMNOPSUVXYZ
6 CEG**J**(N 0,5km)ORTV

Partly naturist campsite. A peaceful site by the sea with its own swimming pool and reasonably sized pitches. Perfect for sea and sun worshippers.

Follow signs to Lido Sud from the Ravenna area, then to Lido di Dante. Then follow Porto Fuori. Follow signs if in the village, it's closer.

CC € 19 *26/3-10/7 1/9-9/10*

N 44°23'5'' E 12°18'57''

Lido di Dante, I-48122 / Emilia Romagna

2984

Ramazzotti***
Via Paolo e Francesca
+39 0544-492250
+39 0544-492009
1/5 - 25/9
info@campingramazzotti.it

2,8ha 300**T**(60-80m²) 3-10A CEE

1 ABC**G**HIJKLMPQ
2 AEGRSV
3 BGJ**M**NRWY
4 (Q+T+U+V+W+X+Y 🔑) Z
5 **AB**EFGIJK**L**MNOPUV
6 CEGIJ(N 0,5km)OQRTV

Located by the sea in a small village. A basic campsite with adequate amenities. An excellent base for visiting Ravenna and the famous church at Lido di Dante.

From surroundings of Ravenna follow the Lido Sud signs, then follow signs to Lido di Dante.

CC € 17 *1/5-15/7 1/9-25/9 7=6*

N 44°23'6'' E 12°19'8''

Novafeltria, I-47863 / Emilia Romagna

2985

Perticara***
Via Serra Masini 10/d
+39 335-7062260
13/5 - 20/9
info@campingperticara.com

8ha 77**T**(100-120m²) 10A CEE

1 AGIJKLPQ
2 GJKLRVWX
3 BHIJNRU
4 (C+Q+R+T 🔑) (U 1/7-31/8) (Z 🔑)
5 **A**FGIJKLMNOPRUWXYZ
6 ADEGH**K**(N 1km)TV

A very well equipped campsite. You will be warmly welcomed by the owners. Excellent service. The panoramic views of the picture postcard hills are a bonus (also from the lovely swimming pool). Very well maintained toilet facilities. No mosquitoes. An excellent base for excursions.

Exit Rimini Nord, direction San Leo-Montefeltro. Right onto SP258 towards Novafeltria, turn off SatNav. Right at Pascucci Bar to Perticara. Follow camping signs.

CC € 19 *13/5-30/6 1/9-20/9*

N 43°53'43'' E 12°14'32''

Pinarella di Cervia, I-48015 / Emilia Romagna

2986

Adriatico***
Via Pinarella 90
+39 0544-71537
FAX +39 0544-974411
14/4 - 19/9
@ info@campingadriatico.net

3,4ha 280**T**(60m²) 6A CEE

1 ABC**G**HIJKLMPQ
2 AEGRTVY
3 B**F**HIJKRU**W**
4 (**B+G** 15/5-10/9)
(Q+R+T+U+V+X) Z
5 **AB**FGIJKLMNOPUVWZ
6 CDEG**J**(N 0,8km)ORTUV

A friendly, well-kept family campsite with attractive amenities. This campsite is well worth a visit in the early season.

Follow the SS16 between Rimini and Ravenna. Exit at Cervia and follow signs.

CC € 17 *1/5-29/6 22/8-19/9 14=12*

N 44°14'51'' E 12°21'32''

Ponte Messa di Pennabilli (RN), I-47864 / Emilia Romagna

2987

Marecchia 'Da Quinto'****
Via Mulino Schieti 22
+39 338-7226690
FAX +39 0541-928936
1/5 - 10/9
@ info@campingmarecchia.it

0,8ha 30**T**(20-80m²) 6A CEE

1 ABCDFIJKLNOP
2 CGLRVWXY
3 AHN
4 (B+G 1/6-10/9) **K**
(T+U+X+Z 1/6-10/9)
5 **A**CGIJKMNO**P**UWZ
6 EGK(N 0,8km)V

A unique campsite decorated with art and culture in Emilia Romagna on the River Marecchia and close to the town of Pennabili. A large natural site paying attention to the environment. Lovely swimming pool and excellent restaurant. Nature walks and cultural centres close by.

A14, exit Rimini Nord, direction Sanleo-Montefeltro (SP258). Novafeltria-Pennabilli at roundabout direction Ponte Messa (follow camping signs). The campsite is on the right before the village.

CC € 19 *1/5-30/6 1/9-10/9*

N 43°49'32'' E 12°15'1''

Repubblica San Marino, I-47893 / San Marino

2988

Centro Vacanze San Marino****
Strada S. Michele 50
+378 0549-903964
FAX +378 0549-907120
1/1 - 31/12
@ info@
centrovacanzesanmarino.com

10ha 200**T**(50-80m²) 5A CEE

1 ABCD**F**IJKLMOPRS
2 GJLRUVXY
3 ABDGMNRU
4 (B 1/6-31/8) K
(Q+R 1/4-30/9)
(T+U+V+Y+Z
1/1-15/1,1/3-31/12)
5 **AB**DEFGHIJKLMNOPW
6 CEGIK(N 3km)OTV

Large, well equipped terraced campsite at an altitude of 250m in San Marino. Swimming pool and good sports fields. Spacious marked out pitches. Bus service to Rimini beach. Well placed for cultural trips out. CampingCard ACSI not valid for groups.

Exit Rimini Sud, direction San Marino, follow the SS72. On entering the Republic follow the main road and you will see the camping sign high up on the right 3 km further on. Turn right at the Brico ID Shop. Look out for signs.

CC € 17 *4/1-8/7 25/8-4/10 16/10-27/12*

N 43°57'33'' E 12°27'41''

Riccione, I-47838 / Emilia Romagna

2989

Adria***
Via Torino 40
+39 0541-601003
+39 0541-602256
24/3 - 2/10
info@campingadria.com

6,2ha 516T(60-70m²) 6A CEE

1 ABCD**G**IJKLMOPQ
2 AEFGRVY
3 ABD**F**UWY
4 (Q 15/4-2/10)
(S+T+U+V+X+Y) Z
5 **AB**EFGIJKLMNOPUVYZ
6 CDEGHI**JK**M(N 1km)ORTU
V

A family campsite right next to the sea. Within walking distance of the resort of Riccione. Lovely excursions possible in the area. WiFi is free for CampingCard ACSI holders.

Take A14 as far as Riccione. Then the SS16 for about 500 metres then follow the large signs.

CC € 19 *24/3-30/6 1/9-1/10*

N 43°59'28'' E 12°40'43''

Riccione, I-47036 / Emilia Romagna

2990

Alberello***
Viale Torino 80
+39 0541-615402
+39 0541-615248
14/4 - 19/9
direzione@alberello.it

4ha 170T(60-70m²) 4-6A CEE

1 ABCEHIJKLOPRS
2 AEFGRTVWXY
3 AB**F**JNRSUWY
4 (Q+R+T+U+V+X+Y+Z)
5 **AB**EFGIJKLMNOPQUVZ
6 CEG**IK**M(N 0,3km)ORTV

A very peaceful campsite with simple, but clean sanitary facilities.

Motorway A14 exit Riccione. Take the SS16 Rimini to Ancona and follow the signs.

CC € 17 *22/4-24/6 1/9-19/9*

N 43°59'10'' E 12°41'15''

Riccione, I-47838 / Emilia Romagna

2991

Riccione****
Via Marsala 10
+39 0541-690160
+39 0541-690044
22/4 - 25/9
info@campingriccione.it

6,5ha 450T(65-100m²) 5A CEE

1 ABCFIJKLMPQ
2 AEFGLRSTVY
3 B**F**GK**M**N**Q**RUY
4 (B+G 23/4-21/9) J
(Q+S+T+U+V+W+X+Y+Z)
5 **AB**EFGIJKLMNOPUVWX
6 CFG**IJ**M(N 1km)ORTV

A friendly campsite with lovely swimming pools. The toilet facilities are very well maintained. Shuttle train to the centre. The surroundings invite you to go out for enjoyable trips. CampingCard ACSI users must pay their bill in cash.

On the motorway take exit Riccione. Follow the signs.

CC € 19 *22/4-12/6 4/9-24/9 7=6*

N 43°59'7'' E 12°40'45''

Rioveggio, I-40040 / Emilia Romagna

2992

Riva del Setta****
Ginepri 65
+39 051-6777749
1/4 - 30/9
info@rivadelsetta.com

3,5ha 86T(70-80m²) 3A CEE

1 ACGHIJKLMOPRS
2 CFRVXY
3 AMRW
4 (B 15/6-31/8)
(Q+R+T+V+Y) Z
5 AGIJKLMNOPUV
6 CFGJ(N 0,5km)

The campsite is situated in the Setta valley between Bologna and Florence. Close to the autostrada. It has a pizzeria and swimming pool. Good base for cultural visits to Bologna and Florence. Reception closed for lunch 13:00 - 15:00.

A1, exit Rioveggio, turn right and follow the signs.

CC € 17 *1/4-15/7 1/9-30/9*

N 44°17'29'' E 11°13'5''

San Mauro Mare, I-47030 / Emilia Romagna

2993

Camping Green**
Via Amerigo Vespucci 6
+39 0541-1743047
9/4 - 25/9
info@campinggreen.it

100T(36-80m²) 6A CEE

1 ABCGHIJKLMPQ
2 AEGRY
3 BFGKRWY
4 (T+U 11/6-11/9) Z
5 AFGIJKMNOPUV
6 EK(N 0,3km)O

Not by the sea, but in a village. Everything easily accessible, including the beach. The surroundings are very attractive. Lovely villages and good cycling opportunities. A modest site with plenty of relaxation.

A14, exit Rimini Nord. Follow SS16 towards Ravenna as far as San Mauro Mare. Enter village and turn left at the 'Green' sign.

CC € 15 *9/4-30/6 1/9-25/9*

N 44°9'45'' E 12°26'32''

Arezzo, I-52100 / Toscana

2994

Villaggio Le Ginestre***
Loc. Ruscello 100
+39 0575-363566
+39 0575-366949
1/3 - 5/11
info@campingleginestre.it

2,2ha 40T(81m²) 6A CEE

1 ABCGIJKLOPQ
2 FGJLRVWXY
3 BJMNRU
4 (B 15/5-15/9)
(T+U+V+Y) Z
5 ABDEGJLMNPUVZ
6 ACDEGIK(N 0,3km)RTV

A peaceful rural campsite. Very convenient for visiting Arezzo and surroundings. Also suitable as a stopover campsite. Restaurant with Tuscan cooking.

A1 Firenze-Roma, exit Arezzo. Direction Battifolle. Then direction Ruscello. Follow the camping signs, 2 km from the motorway.

CC € 19 *1/3-30/6 1/9-5/11*

N 43°26'59'' E 11°47'25''

Barberino di Mugello, I-50030 / Toscana

2995

Il Sergente***
SS 65 Monte di Fo
+39 055-8423018
+39 055-8423907
1/1 - 31/12
info@campingilsergente.it

3ha 25T(40-80m²) 10A CEE

1 ACDGIJLMO**P**Q
2 GIJRTVXY
3 BGMNR
4 (C 15/5-30/9) (Q+R) (T+U+V+Y 1/1-30/12) Z
5 **AB**DEFGIJKLMNOPUVWZ
6 CEGIJK(N 7km)OQRTV

A modern family campsite with a swimming pool and restaurant located in the Mugello area of Tuscany. The campsite is close to the Futa pass. It is a good base for visiting Florence or Siena and other historic Tuscan towns.

A1 Bologna-Firenze, exit Roncobilaccio or Barberino Mugello. Take the SS65 to Passo della Futa. Located about 12 km from the motorway.

CC €17 *1/1-15/7 1/9-31/12*

N 44°4'39'' E 11°16'53''

Bibbona, I-57020 / Toscana

2996

Le Capanne***
Via Aurelia km 273
+39 0586-600064
+39 0586-600198
22/4 - 18/9
info@campinglecapanne.it

9ha 324T(60-130m²) 10A CEE

1 ABCD**G**IJKLMOPST
2 BGLRVXY
3 B**F**JKL**M**N**Q**RU
4 (B+G) IJKP (Q+S+T+U+V+W+Y+Z)
5 **AB**EFGIJKLMNOPTUWXYZ
6 CDEGHKM(N 2km)OPRSTU V

The campsite is situated in a park with olive, pine and eucalyptus trees. Excellent toilet facilities. Lovely swimming pool with large sunbathing area, children's pool, water slide and hydro massage.

A12, exit towards Rosignano Marittimo, and take the SS1 Livorno-Grosseto in the direction of Grosseto. Then exit towards La California and take the SP39 and drive south. Campsite entrance after ± 3 km.

CC €17 *22/4-30/6 1/9-18/9*

N 43°15'13'' E 10°33'10''

Capannole-Bucine, I-52020 / Toscana

2997

La Chiocciola***
Via Giulio Cesare
+39 333-6494983
+39 055-995776
24/3 - 30/9
campinglachiocciola@hotmail.it

3ha 125T(90m²) 6A CEE

1 BC**G**IJKLMO**P**Q
2 CGLRVWXY
3 AHKMNR
4 (B+G 1/5-1/9) (Q+S+T+U+V+X+Y) Z
5 **AB**GIJKLMNOPUWXZ
6 ACEGK(N 0,2km)OTVW

A campsite in the Chianti region. Spacious marked out pitches with your own sink, three large swimming pools. Ideal for visiting Florence, Siena, Arezzo, Chianti and the Crete area. English, Dutch and German spoken at the reception.

A1 Firenze-Roma, exit Val d'Arno direction Montevarchi. Then direction Lévane. In Lévane direction Siena. Follow the camping signs.

CC €19 *24/3-2/7 27/8-30/9*

N 43°26'42'' E 11°37'6''

Capoliveri, I-57031 / Toscana

2998

Lacona Pineta
Viale dei Golfi 249
+39 0565-964322
FAX +39 0565-964087
22/4 - 15/10
@ info@campinglaconapineta.com

4ha 179T(50-80m²) 3-5A CEE

1 ACD**G**HIJKLMNOPQ
2 AEGJLNOQUVY
3 ABCWY
4 (A) (B 30/5-20/10) KP (Q+R+S+T+U+V+X+Y+Z)
5 ABFGIJKLMNOPUVWZ
6 ABEGHI**IK**LM(N 2km)OQRS TU

Terraced campsite located in a pine forest at 50 metres from the beach.

In Portoferraio, dir. Porto Azzurro. Then dir. Lacona. Campsite is located on right after the bend.

CC € 17 *22/4-18/6 5/9-15/10*

N 42°45'33'' E 10°18'49''

Casale Marittimo, I-56040 / Toscana

2999

Valle Gaia****
S.P. Cecina Casale
+39 0586-681236
FAX +39 0586-683551
19/3 - 1/10
@ info@vallegaia.it

4,3ha 240T(80-120m²) 6A CEE

1 AB**G**HIJKLMOPST
2 FJRTVXY
3 BGHJK**M**NRU
4 (B+G+Q+S+T+U+V+Y+Z)
5 **A**DEFGIJKLMNOPUV
6 CEG**IK**M(N 3,5km)RTV

Valle Gaia campsite, with its good toilet facilities, various swimming pools, restaurant and pizzeria is located on the edge of the Tuscan hills 9 km from the sea. Ideally positioned for trips out to the Tuscan art cities.

A12, exit Rosignano Marittimo, SS1 direction Roma, exit Cecina-Centro (NOT Cecina-Nord). At the roundabout direction Casale Marittimo; turn left at the intersection in the direction of Casale Marittimo. Campsite located 3 km down the road.

CC € 15 *19/3-9/7 1/9-1/10*

N 43°18'2'' E 10°34'54''

Casciano di Murlo/Siena, I-53016 / Toscana

3000

Le Soline***
Via delle Soline 51
+39 0577-817410
FAX +39 0577-817415
1/1 - 31/12
@ camping@lesoline.it

6,5ha 170T(24-90m²) 6A CEE

1 ABC**G**IJKLOPQ
2 JKRTWXY
3 A**F**JN**OP**R
4 (A 25/6-31/8) (B+G 15/4-10/10) KP (Q+R 15/3-30/9) (U+V+Y 15/3-20/10) (Z 15/3-30/9)
5 **AB**DFGIJKMNO**PS**UVWZ
6 CEGK(N 1km)ORTV

The campsite is made up of terraces set into the hillside. Both the pitches and the large swimming pool have lovely views of the surrounding countryside. Very good restaurant.

SS223 Siena-Grosseto. Exit Fontazzi/Cassiano. Follow campsite signs.

CC € 19 *1/1-30/6 1/9-31/12*

N 43°9'18'' E 11°19'55''

Castagneto Carducci, I-57022 / Toscana

iD **3001**

Le Pianacce***
Località Le Pianacce
+39 0565-763667
FAX +39 0565-766085
22/4 - 18/9
@ info@campinglepianacce.it

9ha 156T(60-80m²) 6-10A CEE

1 ABCD**G**IJKLMPST
2 BJKRUVXY
3 BHJKL**M**NQR
4 (B+G) M
(Q+S+T+U+V+W+Y) Z
5 **AB**EFGIJKLMNOPUWXYZ
6 ACEGHKM(N 2km)ORTU

A peaceful campsite 6 km from the sea and beach. Laid out in terraces with accessible pitches of different sizes. Unusual swimming pool and lovely playground. Ideal for small children.

SS1 Aurelia exit Donoratico, direction Castagneto Carducci. Before Castagneto Carducci turn left in the direction of Bolgheri. The campsite is located on the right.

CC € 13 *22/4-30/6 1/9-18/9*

N 43°9'57'' E 10°36'49''

Castiglione della Pescaia, I-58043 / Toscana

iD **3002**

Camping Village Rocchette***
SP. 62 delle Rocchette
+39 0564-941123
FAX +39 0564-941213
24/3 - 22/10
@ booking@rocchette.com

12ha 195T(30-70m²) 6A CEE

1 ACD**F**HIJKLNO**P**S
2 AERVWXY
3 BJK**M**NR
4 (B 16/4-22/10)
(G 20/4-17/10) **KLP**
(Q+R+T+U) (V 15/5-15/9)
(W+Y 8/4-17/10) Z
5 **AB**EGIKMNOP**QRST**
6 EJM(N 7km)O

Village Rocchette Campsite has two superpools of 2000m² with 3 jacuzzis. The campsite is close to a beautiful beach. The loveliest locations in Tuscany are close enough for great daytrips.

From Follonica take SS322. A few kms before Castiglione della Pescaia turn right to Le Rocchette. Site is on right after 2.5 km.

CC € 15 *24/3-1/7 3/9-21/10 7=6*

N 42°46'46'' E 10°48'5''

Castiglione della Pescaia, I-58043 / Toscana

iD **3003**

Maremma Sans Souci***
+39 0564-933765
FAX +39 0564-935759
26/3 - 2/11
@ info@maremmasanssouci.it

30ha 372T(30-100m²) 3A CEE

1 ABCD**F**HIJKLNOPST
2 ABEGSVY
3 B**F**JKLUWY
4 (Q+R+S+T+U+V+W)
(Y 28/3-15/10) Z
5 **AB**FGIJKMNOPQUVZ
6 CEGH**I**J**K**M(N 2,5km)RST
V

Atmospheric campsite with private marked-out pitches of various sizes, in a pine forest, located directly on a beach on the sea. Good restaurant and welcoming bar.

In Grosseto or in Follonica, take route SS322 direction Castiglione della Pescaia. The campsite is 2 km north of Castiglione della Pescaia, sea side.

CC € 15 *26/3-30/6 1/9-1/11*

N 42°46'25'' E 10°50'39''

Castiglione della Pescaia, I-58043 / Toscana

3004

Santapomata
Strada delle Rocchette
+39 0564-941037
FAX +39 0564-941221
24/3 - 22/10
info@campingsantapomata.it

6ha 342T(50-80m²) 3A CEE

1 BCGHIJKLNRS
2 ABEGRSVXY
3 WY
4 (Q+S+T+U+V+Y) Z
5 AGIJKMNOPUV
6 CEGIK(N 5km)ORTV

This campsite with plenty of shade and good toilet facilities is located directly on a gently sloping beach.

From Follonica take the SS322. A few kilometres before Castiglione della Pescaia turn right towards Le Rocchette. Signposted.

CC € 15 *24/3-1/7 3/9-21/10 7=6*

N 42°46'36" E 10°48'34"

Castiglione della Pescaia, I-58043 / Toscana

3005

Stella del Mare****
Strada Provinciale delle Rocchette
FAX +39 0564-947100
16/4 - 16/10
info@stelladelmarecamping.it

7ha 150T(30-90m²) 3A CEE

1 ABCGHIJKLMNOPST
2 AEJQRTVXY
3 BGMNRWY
4 (B+G+Q+S+T+U+V+Y) Z
5 ABEFGIJKLMNOPUW
6 ACEGJ(N 7km)ORTV

Stella del Mare campsite with its lovely swimming pools and children's pool, lawns and deckchairs is positioned on the Mediterranean coast of Maremma opposite the island of Elba. It is partly level and partly laid out in terraces. Sandy beach and a rocky coastline close to the site. Castiglione delle Pescaia is within cycling distance.

From Fallonica the SS322 southwards direction Castiglione della Prescaia. Take exit Le Rocchette. Campsite at the end of the road.

CC € 17 *16/4-30/6 1/9-16/10*

N 42°46'38" E 10°47'34"

Cavriglia, I-52022 / Toscana

3006

Camping Orlando in Chianti
Località Cafaggiolo
FAX +39 055-967422
28/4 - 9/10
info@campingorlandoinchianti.it

6ha 70T(70-120m²) 6-10A CEE

1 ABCDGIJKLNOPST
2 BIJKSTVXY
3 ABHR
4 (A+C+H) JK
(Q+S+T+U+V+Y) Z
5 ABGIJKLMNPUV
6 ACEGHJ(N 7km)OTVX

Situated in a nature reserve in the Chianti region, in the middle of a forest. The campsite provides a good restaurant, pizzeria with wood oven, minimarket, three swimming pools (heated) and a jacuzzi. Perfect location for hiking, mountain biking, visits to wine castle and for trips to Florence, Siena, Arezzo.

Leave the A1 at Incisa, direction Figline Valdarno, then direction Greve in Chianti. Follow camping signs towards Lucolena and Park Cavriglia. Don't follow SatNav.

CC € 15 *28/4-1/7 3/9-9/10 7=6, 14=11*

N 43°32'18" E 11°24'50"

Cecina Mare/Livorno, I-57023 / Toscana

3007

New Camping Le Tamerici SRL***
Via della Cecinella 5
+39 0586-620629
FAX +39 0586-687811
11/5 - 3/10
@ info@letamerici.it

8ha 130T(50-80m²) 6A CEE

1 ABCD**F**HIJKLMNO**P**
2 AEFGNRSTUVXY
3 BGK**M**NRUWY
4 (B+G+Q+S+T+U+V+Y) Z
5 **AB**GJKMNOPUV
6 DFGJM(N 1km)ORT

This campsite is separated from the sea and the beach by a lovely walking area (pine forest) 600m from the sea and a short distance from Cecina and Cecina Mare. Swimming and children's pools, sports fields, shops and a good restaurant. Special camping pitches.

A12, exit Rosignano Marittimo, then the SS1 (Aurelia) direction Roma, exit Cecina Nord direction Cecina Mare. Straight on at traffic lights, campsite signposted.

CC € 17 *11/5-15/6 1/9-2/10*

N 43°17'31'' E 10°30'38''

Certaldo/Marcialla, I-50020 / Toscana

3008

Camping Panorama Del Chianti**
Via Marcialla 349
FAX +39 0571-669334
24/3 - 31/10
@ info@campingchianti.it

2,1ha 65T(60-80m²) 10A CEE

1 ABCD**G**IJKLOPQ
2 JKLRTVWXY
3 HIJ
4 (B 25/5-30/9) (Q+R+T+U) Z
5 **AB**GIKMNOPUVWZ
6 ACEGJ(N 1,6km)T

A rural terraced campsite. From the campsite you can see the Tuscan countryside in the distance. Peacefully located on the green hills of Tuscany and close to cultural cities such as Florence, Siena, San Gimignano, Certaldo and Volterra.

From motorway Florence-Siena, take exit Tavarnelle. In Tavarnelle direction Marcialla/ Certaldo. In Marcialla direction Fiano and follow campsite signs.

CC € 15 *24/3-5/7 22/8-31/10*

N 43°34'55'' E 11°8'19''

Coltano, I-56121 / Toscana

3009

Camping Lago Le Tamerici
Via della Sofina 6
+39 050-989007
FAX +39 050-989935
21/3 - 16/10
@ info@lagoletamerici.it

18ha 44T(100-120m²) 6A CEE

1 ABCDGIJKLMPRS
2 DFLRTUVWXY
3 AGN**OPW**
4 (B 1/6-15/9) (Q+R+U+X) Z
5 **AB**GIJKLMNOPUWXZ
6 ACFGJ(N 2km)

Campsite located in a nature reserve between Livorno and Pisa. Spacious pitches on grass, with or without shade, by a lake. View of the Pisan mountains. Savour the organic meats, wine and other regional dishes in the restaurant. Bikes and kayaks available for use for free. Also motorhome pitches.

Firenze-Pisa-Livorno exit Darsena Pisna, to SS1 direction Coltano, right after ± 3 km dir. Caltano, then follow camping signs, or use coordinates with SatNav (do not use address).

CC € 17 *21/3-15/7 1/9-16/10 7=6*

N 43°38'14'' E 10°22'3''

Elba/Lacona/Capolíveri, I-57037 / Toscana

3010

Lacona***
C.P. 65
+39 0565-964161
FAX +39 0565-964330
22/4 - 19/10
@ info@camping-lacona.it

2,6ha 158T(40-80m²) 6A CEE

1 ABCD**G**HIJKLMNOPS
2 ABEGJLNQTVXY
3 B**F**HJKRUVWY
4 (B+Q+R+T+U+V+X) Z
5 **AB**FGIJKLMNOPUVW
6 ACEGIJK(N 8km)OQRTVX

This shady campsite, set among eucalyptus trees, is laid out in easily accessible terraces on a narrow headland with a pebble beach, marker buoys and a boat winch close by on one side, and a long sandy beach on the other. Scooter rental. Bikes, safe and kayaks free.

Follow 'tutti direzioni' in Portoferraio. Direction Porto Azzurro at 3rd roundabout. Straight on at traffic lights. Take next exit to Lacona. Campsite after the bend on the left.

CC € 17 *22/4-20/6 1/9-19/10*

N 42°45'37" E 10°18'56"

Elba/Marina di Campo, I-57034 / Toscana

3011

Ville degli Ulivi***
Via della Foce 89
+39 0565-976098
FAX +39 0565-976048
16/4 - 15/10
@ info@villedegliulivi.it

NEW

7ha 285T(40-95m²) 6A CEE

1 ACD**F**HIJKLMNO**P**ST
2 ABEQSTVXY
3 BHJK**M**NQR**V**WY
4 (**B** 1/5-30/9) (G 10/5-30/9) **IKLNP**(Q+S+T+U+V+Y) Z
5 **AB**EFGIJKLMNOP**ST**UVW XY
6 CDEG**K**M(N 1km)ORTUVW X

Luxury family campsite with beautiful swimming pools and playground, long sandy beach at 200 metres. This well-maintained campsite is located on the edge of a lively seaside resort.

From Portoferraio follow 'tutti direzioni'. At the third roundabout direction Procchio. In Procchio direction Marino di Campo. Before the town direction Lacona. Over the bridge on the sea side.

CC € 19 *16/4-11/6 10/9-15/10*

N 42°45'7" E 10°14'42"

Marina di Bibbona, I-57020 / Toscana

3012

Camping I Melograni
Via dei Cipressi 11
+39 0586600222
FAX +39 0586602717
1/4 - 30/9
@ info@campeggioimelograni.it

NEW

4,5ha 100T(55-90m²) 4A CEE

1 ACD**G**HIJKLNOP
2 AFGUVXY
3 BGJK**Q**R
4 **A**(Q+S+U+V+Y+Z)
5 **A**EFGJKNPUVXY
6 CDEG(N 0,2km)OT

The campsite is located in the little bathing resort Marina di Bibbona at walking distance from the beach.

SS1, exit Cecina Sud dir. Marina di Bibiona, straight on on roundabout. Right on mini-roundabout. Site is located on left of road.

CC € 15 *1/4-30/6 1/9-30/9* 7=6, 14=11

N 43°14'58" E 10°31'59"

Marina di Bibbona, I-57020 / Toscana

3013

Free Beach***
Via Cavalleggeri Nord 88
+39 0586-699066
FAX +39 0586-696041
19/3 - 16/10
@ info@campingfreebeach.it

9ha 150T(75-80m²) 3A CEE

1 BCD**G**HIJKLMNOPS
2 AEGRSVXY
3 BGKNRU**W**Y
4 (B+Q+S+T+U+V+X) Z
5 **AB**GIJKMNOPUW
6 AEG**J**(N 0,3km)PTV

A campsite located a few steps from the beach, pine woods and the small town of Marina di Bibbona, with new toilet facilities, restaurant, shops, bike rental and two swimming pools.

A12, exit Rosignano Marittimo, then SS1 'Aurelia' towards Roma. Exit La California/Cecina Sud towards Marina di Bibbona. Straight ahead at roundabout; straight ahead at mini-roundabout. Right after small bend. Follow the signs. Campsite at the end of the road around the corner on the right.

CC € 17 *19/3-30/6 1/9-16/10*

N 43°15'6'' E 10°31'41''

Marina di Bibbona, I-57020 / Toscana

3014

Free Time***
Via dei Cipressi
+39 0586-600934
FAX +39 0586-602682
21/4 - 16/10
@ info@freetimecamping.it

4ha 100T(80-105m²) 6A CEE

1 ACDGHIJKLMN**P**RS
2 AEGRVWXY
3 BKNRV**W**
4 (B+G 25/4-18/10) JN
(Q+S+U+V+Y) Z
5 **AB**EFGIJKLMNOP**S**TUWX
YZ
6 ACDEG**IJ**(N 0,5km)RTV

Close to town of Marina di Bibbona with many modern amenities: fitness centre, massage and internet point. Large pool. Plenty of sunny or lightly shaded pitches. 500 metres from sea and a sandy beach, accessible through a pine forest. Fishing lake. Pitches with private toilet facilities for 5 Euros extra.

A12, exit Rosignano Marittimo, then SS1 Aurelia to Roma, exit La California/Cecina Sud. Dir. Marina di Bibbona. Right 'Via dei Cipressi', site just before the bend.

CC € 17 *21/4-30/6 1/9-16/10*

N 43°15'9'' E 10°31'51''

Marina di Castagneto, I-57022 / Toscana

3015

Belmare Camping S.R.L.**
Via del Forte 1
FAX +39 0565-744264
1/4 - 30/9
@ info@campingbelmare.it

7ha 225T(50-90m²) 4A CEE

1 ABCFHIJKLMNOST
2 ABEGSVXY
3 UWY
4 (Q+S+T+U+V+W+Y) Z
5 **A**GIKMO**P**UVWZ
6 CEGJOTV

A genuine Italian campsite. Positioned by the sea in the middle of pine trees. Here you will find both free and paying sandy beaches. You can walk into the village from the campsite. The site has a good and affordable self-service restaurant. Dogs only allowed in April, May and September.

A12, exit Rosignano Marittimo, then SS1 'Aurelia' direction Rome. Exit Donoratico direction Marina di Castagneto. Continue straight ahead and follow signs.

CC € 17 *1/4-30/6 1/9-30/9*

N 43°10'38'' E 10°32'34''

Marina di Castagneto, I-57022 / Toscana

3016

Continental
Via 1° Maggio C.P. 5
☎ +39 0565-744014
FAX +39 0565-744168
1/4 - 18/9
@ info@campingcontinental.it

13ha 265T(40-85m²) 3A CEE

1 ABCDGHIJKLMNOPST
2 ABEGISVXY
3 BGJKNY
4 (Q+S+U+V+W) Z
5 **A**GIKMO**P**UVWZ
6 ACEGJ(N 0,5km)ORT

A spaciously laid out campsite in a pine wood right by a lovely beach. In addition to many permanent pitches there are plenty of touring pitches of varying sizes. The seaside resort is within walking distance.

A12, exit Rosignano-Marittimo, then SS1 'Aurelia' direction Rome, exit Donoratico; direction Marina di Castagneto, continue straight and follow signs.

CC € 15 1/4-18/6 22/8-18/9 7=6, 14=11

N 43°10'24'' E 10°32'38''

Marina di Castagneto, I-57022 / Toscana

3017

Int. Camping Etruria**
Via della Pineta
☎ +39 0565-744254
FAX +39 0565-744494
23/4 - 9/10
@ info@campingetruria.it

24ha 600T(60-100m²) 2A CEE

1 ABCD**G**IJKLMOPS
2 ABEGSVXY
3 BRWY
4 (Q+S+T+U+V+W) Z
5 **AB**GIKMO**P**UV
6 CEGK(N 1km)ORT

A campsite right by the sea with a large sandy beach, located in a wood with winding roads and many hidden places.

A12 Genova-Rosignano. Then SS1 'Aurelia', direction Roma, exit Donoratico, direction Marina di Castagneto. Follow the camping signs.

CC € 17 23/4-30/6 4/9-9/10

N 43°11'16'' E 10°32'30''

Marina di Grosseto, I-58100 / Toscana

3018

Cieloverde****
Via della Trappola 181
☎ +39 0564-321611
FAX +39 0564-30178
14/5 - 18/9
@ info@cieloverde.it

60ha 1260T(80-100m²) 3A CEE

1 ABCDGHIJKLNOPS
2 ABEGRSVXY
3 BGHJKNRUWY
4 (A+B+G+Q+S+T+U+V+W+Y)Z
5 **AB**FGHIJKLMNOP**S**UV
6 EGHJM(N 2km)ORTUV

Very nicely appointed campsite in a park with e.g. many play options for children. The site seems far from the sea by its size, but a train will get you to the end of the campsite, from where there is a walking/cycle path to the sea.

In Grosseto drive in the direction of Marina di Grosseto (mare). In Marina di Grosseto drive in the direction of Principina a Mare. The campsite is located on the right side of the road, before the exit towards Principina a Mare.

CC € 17 14/5-1/7 1/9-17/9 7=6

N 42°42'47'' E 11°0'27''

Marina di Grosseto, I-58046 / Toscana

3019

Le Marze**
S.P. 158 km 30.200
+39 0564-35501
FAX +39 0564-744503
24/3 - 5/10
@ info@lemarze.it

20ha 452T(50-110m²) 10A CEE

1 ABCD**G**HIJKLMN**P**RT
2 ABEGRSUVWXY
3 B**F**JKR**W**Y
4 (B 15/6-15/9) (Q+S+T+U+V+W+Y) Z
5 **AB**EFGIJKLMNOP**ST**UV
6 CDEGJM(N 5km)OTX

Located in a beautiful pine forest with pitches of varying dimensions. Several toilet blocks including private and children's toilets. Large built-up swimming pool 6 x 24 metres with supervision. A lovely walking and cycle path takes you to the sandy beach.

From Follonica take the SS322 south direction Castiglione della Pescaia. In the town cross the bridge towards Marina di Grosseto. The campsite is on the left after about 5 km.

CC € 15 *24/3-27/6 27/8-5/10*

N 42°44'42" E 10°56'44"

Marina di Massa, I-54100 / Toscana

3020

Camping Giardino
Via delle Pinete 382
+39 0585-869291
FAX +39 0585-240781
16/4 - 25/9
@ info@campinggiardino.com

3,8ha 140T(40-60m²) 3A CEE

1 BCDGHIJKLMOPQ
2 AEFGLORVXY
3 B**F**KRWY
4 (B 21/5-25/9) (Q+S+U+V+X 1/6-27/9)
5 **AB**GIKMO**P**UVZ
6 ACEGHKORTV

A spacious, well run campsite with good amenities, close to the sea, a good restaurant and an attractive terrace. Excursion possibilities to the marble quarries, caves and the famous cultural towns.

A12 exit Massa, 1st roundabout right to Massa, 2nd roundabout right, 3rd roundabout right ± 2 km straight ahead. Campsite on the right.

CC € 17 *16/4-1/7 1/9-25/9*

N 44°1'30" E 10°4'27"

Marina di Massa, I-54037 / Toscana

3021

Luna***
Via delle Pinete 392
+39 0585-780460
FAX +39 0585-784058
21/4 - 1/10
@ info@campingluna.it

6,5ha 36T(50-60m²) 6A CEE

1 ABCDFHIJKLMPS
2 AEFGRSTVWXY
3 **F**RWY
4 Z
5 **A**GIJKMOPUVX
6 AEG**IK**TV

A friendly, peaceful and presentable campsite close to the beach. Ideal for those seeking relaxation. A good base for trips to the Cinque Terre, the marble quarries and the Tuscan art towns.

A12 exit Massa. Immediate right on roundabout over viaduct A12. To next roundabout, campsite about 2 km on the right. (Route differs from most navigation systems).

CC € 19 *21/4-19/6 1/9-30/9*

N 44°1'38" E 10°4'14"

Marina di Massa, I-54037 / Toscana

3022

Partaccia 1***
Via delle Pinete 394
+39 0585-780133
FAX +39 0585-784728
23/4 - 2/10
@ info@partaccia.it

4,3ha 80T(20-50m²) 5A CEE

1 BCEIJLPS
2 ABEFGSVWXY
3 AY
4 (Q) (S+U 1/5-15/9) (V+Y) Z
5 **A**IKMO**P**UV
6 CEGK(N 0,5km)ORTV

A park-like established campsite, a natural oasis with shady trees and colourful flowers, well maintained, 65m from a free beach. The campsite is situated on lively vibrant coastal road. Many opportunities for excursions.

A12 La Spezia-Livorno, exit Massa, left after toll booth. Follow road to intersection bar/café 'La Dolce Vita'. Turn left and follow camping signs.

CC € 17 *23/4-9/7 26/8-2/10 7=6, 14=11*

N 44°1'37'' E 10°4'11''

Marina di Massa, I-54100 / Toscana

3023

Taimì****
Via del Cacciatore, 30
+39 0585-789262
FAX +39 0585-632504
21/4 - 18/9
@ info@campingtaimi.it

2ha 60T(< 90m²) 6A CEE

1 ABCDFIJKLMOPS
2 AEFGLSVXY
3 ARY
4 (B 1/5-18/9) (U+X+Z)
5 **AB**FGIJKLMNOPUWXY
6 ABCGJOTV

Spaciously appointed, luxury campsite with royal pitches (lots of shade). Relaxation is valued at this campsite. The beach is a short cycle away, shops within walking distance.

A12 exit Massa. Left dir. Carara. Left at 1st traffic light. 5th exit turn right. Campsite on right after 500 metres.

CC € 19 *21/4-19/6 1/9-18/9*

N 44°1'49'' E 10°4'24''

Marina di Massa/Partaccia, I-54037 / Toscana

3024

Dal Pino Srl
Via Flavio Baracchini 119
+39 0585-630164
FAX +39 0585-648693
21/4 - 18/9
@ info@campingdalpino.com

3ha 60T(35-55m²) 6A CEE

1 ABC**F**HIJKLMNOPRS
2 ABEFGSXY
3 BGNRY
4 (Q+R+U+Y) Z
5 ABGIJKMOPUV
6 ACEGHKTV

Spaciously laid out, shady beach campsite. Within walking distance of the sea. Every day there is fresh bread from the wood-fired pizza oven.

Genova-Livorno exit Massa. Turn left at roundabout ± 1 km. Left at Bar La Dolce Vita. Campsite on the left.

CC € 17 *21/4-10/7 30/8-18/9*

N 44°1'48'' E 10°4'15''

Montecatini Terme, I-51016 / Toscana

3025

Belsito***
Via delle Vigne 1/a
+39 0572-67373
FAX +39 0572-549100
24/3 - 30/9
@ info@campingbelsito.it

3,7ha 250**T**(50-100m²) 15A CEE

1 ABCD**G**HIJKLMOPST
2 FGIJKLRTVWXY
3 AHNRU
4 (B+G 1/5-30/9) KP
(Q+S+T+U+V+X) Z
5 **AB**EFGIJKLMNOPQR**S**UV
XYZ
6 ACDEG**K**(N 3km)OTV

A peaceful shaded campsite, many of the camping pitches have lovely views of the Tuscan countryside. There are two lovely swimming pools where you can cool off after a trip of discovery through Tuscany.

A11 Firenze-Pisa, exit Montecatini Terme. Straight ahead after toll booths direction Montecatini Terme. Follow camping signs and Montecatini Alto signs. Do not use SatNav.

CC € 19 *24/3-30/6 1/9-30/9*

N 43°54'19" E 10°47'17"

Montescudaio, I-56040 / Toscana

3026

Camping & Village
Montescudaio****
Via del Poggetto km 2
+39 0586-683477
FAX +39 0586-090373
11/5 - 18/9
@ info@camping-montescudaio.it

25ha 370**T**(60-200m²) 5A CEE

NEW

1 ACDGIJKLPQ
2 BFIRTVXY
3 BGK**M**NRU
4 (B 15/5-15/9) (G) P
(Q+S+T+U+V+Y) Z
5 **AB**EGIJKLMNOPUW
6 CEGJ(N 0,5km)OTV

Large campsite with different altitudes located in a forest. Campsite is about 5 km from the sea. Green surroundings.

A12, exit Rosignano Marittimo. SS1 dir. Roma, exit Cecina Centro (NOT Cecina-nord!). On roundabout dir. Guardistallo (not Montescudaio). Campsite left after 2 km.

CC € 17 *11/5-1/7 20/8-18/9*

N 43°18'57" E 10°33'15"

Montopoli, I-56020 / Toscana

3027

Toscana Village***
Via Fornoli 9
+39 0571-449032
FAX +39 0571-449449
1/1 - 31/12
@ info@toscanavillage.com

3,8ha 139**T**(60-100m²) 6A CEE

NEW

1 ABCDGHIJKLMOPRS
2 FIJKLTVWXY
3 A**F**GNRU
4 (B 1/6-30/9)
(Q+R+U+V+W 1/5-30/9) Z
5 **AB**EGIJKLMNOPUVXZ
6 CG**IK**(N 0,5km)OTV

Campsite is centrally located between Pisa, Florence, Lucca, Pistoia and other Tuscan art towns. The campsite is at a walking distance from the authentic village of Montopoli. Beautiful pool on the site. The campsite offers all amenities for a pleasant stay.

Superstrada Fi-Pi-Li, Livorno-Firenze. Exit Montopoli val d'Arno; follow SS67 to Montopoli; follow campsite signs from Capanne village. When using SatNav: pay attention to traffic signs and illegal routes.

CC € 15 *1/1-30/6 1/9-31/12*

N 43°40'32" E 10°45'11"

Passo de la Futa/Firenzuola, I-50033 / Toscana

3028

La Futa**
Via Bruscoli, 889/H
+39 055-815297
15/4 - 30/9
info@campinglafuta.it

10ha 80T(60-80m²) 10A CEE

1 ABCDGHIJKLMOPQ
2 BFJKRTWXY
3 AHJR
4 (B 15/5-16/9) (Q+R+V) Z
5 ABFGIJKLMNOPUWZ
6 CEGJ(N 3km)OTV

This lovely campsite with stunning panoramic views is located in the Futa Pass (about 900 metres). The campsite is equipped with a swimming pool. Starting point for walks in the mountain areas. Florence, Siena and other historic towns are within easy reach of this Tuscan campsite.

A1 Bologna-Firenze, exit Roncobilaccio (or Barberino-Mugello). SS65 to Passo della Futa. Campsite close to the Futa Pass (war cemetery).

CC € 17 15/4-30/6 25/8-30/9

N 44°5'52'' E 11°16'7''

Punta Ala, I-58040 / Toscana

3029

Baia Verde***
Loc. Casetta Civinini
+39 0564-922298
FAX +39 0564-923044
22/4 - 15/10
info@baiaverde.com

20ha 1138T(60-100m²) 3A CEE

1 ABCGHIJKLMNOPRS
2 ABEGRSVY
3 BFGJKNOPRTUWY
4 (Q+S+T+U+V+W+X+Y) Z
5 ABFGIKMOPUV
6 CEGHIJM(N 6km)ORTV

The campsite is located right on an extensive sandy beach inviting you to take long beach walks. The site has spacious pitches and many amenities including several shops.

From Follonica take the SS322 in the direction of Castiglione della Pescaia. At Pian d'Alma drive in the direction of Punta Ala. The campsite is located on the right.

CC € 17 22/4-15/6 14/9-15/10

N 42°50'2'' E 10°46'46''

Riotorto, I-57020 / Toscana

3030

Campo Al Fico
Loc. Campo al Fico 15
+39 0565-21008
FAX +39 0565-21118
25/4 - 18/9
info@campingcampoalfico.com

4,5ha 80T(42-60m²) 3A CEE

1 BCFHIJKLMNR
2 GLRVY
3 BKMR
4 (B+G 1/6-29/9)
(Q+R+T+U+V+Y) Z
5 AGIKMOPUVZ
6 CEGJK(N 7km)OTV

Located 1 km from the sandy beach with floodlit tennis courts and a swimming pool with two sections. Ideally located for a trip to Elba.

SS1 Aurelia, exit Vignale/Riotorto. On the roundabout Piombino. The campsite is located on the left hand side of the road.

CC € 15 25/4-15/7 1/9-18/9

N 42°58'0'' E 10°39'0''

Riotorto, I-57025 / Toscana

3031

Pappasole****
Loc. Carbonifera 14
+39 0565-20414
FAX +39 0565-20346
23/4 - 22/10
info@pappasole.it

18ha 476T(90-100m^2) 10A CEE

1 ABCD**G**HIJKLMNOPQ
2 AEFGLRTUVXY
3 BGK**M**N**Q**RUWY
4 (B+G 23/4-14/10) IKP (Q+S+T+U+V+Y+Z)
5 **AB**EFGIJKLMNOP**ST**UWX YZ
6 ACEG**IK**M(N 7km)OQRTUV

Luxurious campsite, a 4 minute walk from a long sandy beach has a separate new area with a modern toilet block for CampingCard ACSI holders. The 90-100 m^2 marked out pitches are covered with a light gauze sail which provides shade. Beach accessible by wheelchair and the minigolf is also suitable for the disabled.

SS1 Aurelia exit Riotorto direction Folllonica/ Grosseto. Take the flyover over the motorway about 5 km before Follonica, then turn right and follow the signs.

CC € 19 *23/4-31/5 6/6-10/6 4/9-21/10*

N 42°57'3'' E 10°41'14''

San Baronto/Lamporecchio, I-51035 / Toscana

3032

Barco Reale****
Via Nardini 11
+39 0573-88332
FAX +39 0573-856003
26/3 - 30/9
info@barcoreale.com

10ha 253T(60-110m^2) 10A CEE

1 ABCDFIJKLMPQ
2 BHIJKLRTVWXY
3 A**F**GHJKNRU
4 (A+C+G+Q+S+T+U+V+Y Z)
5 **AB**EFGIJKLMNOPUWXYZ
6 ACEG**IJ**K(N 1km)OTV

Peacefully located campsite in a wood with beautiful views of the surrounding Tuscan landscape.

Motorway A11 Firenze-Pisa, exit Pistoia. Take the direction of San Baronto/Lamporecchio/Vinci. Follow the signs.

CC € 19 *26/3-17/6 3/9-30/9*

N 43°50'30'' E 10°54'38''

San Piero a Sieve, I-50037 / Toscana

3033

Camping Village Mugello Verde***
Via Massorondinaio 39
+39 055-848511
11/3 - 1/11
mugelloverde@ florencevillage.com

12ha 250T 6A CEE

1 BCGIJKLMO**P**Q
2 BIJRSTWXY
3 A**F**HJMR
4 (B 1/6-15/9) (Q+R+T+U+V+X+Z)
5 **AB**GIJKLMNOPUVW
6 CEGHJ(N 1km)ORTV

A quietly located, basic campsite in natural, wooded surroundings with pitches next to a hillside. 3 children up to 11 years are included.

A1 Bologna-Firenze, exit Barberino. Direction Borgo San Lorenzo. Follow the signs and turn to the right at the service station.

CC € 17 *11/3-15/5 25/5-5/7 22/8-1/11*

N 43°57'40'' E 11°18'37''

San Vincenzo, I-57027 / Toscana

3034

Park Albatros****
Pineta di Torre Nuova 2
+39 0565-701018
FAX +39 0565-701400
22/4 - 11/9
@ parkalbatros@ecvacanze.it

23ha 500T(80-100m²) 10A CEE

1 BCD**G**IJKLMOPST
2 ABRSVWXY
3 BKN**Q**R
4 (E+F+H) IJP (Q+S+T+U+V+W+Y) Z
5 **AB**EFGIJKLMNOPUWXYZ
6 FG**IJ**M(N 6km)ORTV

The moment you enter Park Albatros you won't help noticing the swimming pools with 3000 m² of lagoons encircled by deckchairs. Keep going and you will find the very modern toilet facilities, a large supermarket, an excellent restaurant and large touring pitches in sunny surroundings with gentle shade.

SS1 'Aurelia', exit San Vincenzo Nord, follow the SP23 direction Piombino through the town. Entrance to campsite on the left near 7.0 km-marker.

CC € 19 *22/4-24/6 1/9-10/9*

N 43°1'40" E 10°32'1"

Scarlino, I-58020 / Toscana

3035

Vallicella
Loc. Vallicella
+39 0566-37229
FAX +39 0566-37232
23/4 - 1/10
@ info@vallicellavillage.com

10ha 242T(60-100m²) 4A CEE

1 ABC**G**HIJKLMN**P**ST
2 FGIJKRTVWXY
3 BFGH**M**NPRU
4 (B+G 1/5-30/9) **P** (Q+R+T+U+V+Y) Z
5 **AB**IJKLMNOP**T**UV
6 ACEGIJ(N 4km)ORTV

An attractive new terraced campsite in a mediterranean setting. A romantic atmosphere is created by the illuminated terraces and the soaring castle and by the village of Scarlino. A well maintained campsite on a hillside.

SS1 Aurelia exit Scarlino/Scalo, direction Scarlino/Punta Ala (Sp.84). Continue straight ahead at the crossroads and straight ahead at the next crossroads. The campsite is in the bend of the road.

CC € 13 *23/4-9/7 27/8-1/10 7=6, 14=11*

N 42°54'46" E 10°51'10"

Sovicille, I-53018 / Toscana

3036

La Montagnola
S.P. 52 della Montagnola
FAX +39 0577-314473
24/3 - 30/9
@ montagnolacamping@libero.it

2,5ha 66T(80m²) 5A CEE

1 ABCGIJKLMOPQ
2 BGJRSTUVY
3 AKR
4 (Q+R) Z
5 **AB**GJKMNOPUVW
6 CEG**K**(N 1km)ORTV

A quiet campsite in wooded rural surroundings, with level marked-out pitches. Good opportunities for walking. The bus to Siena stops at the campsite.

Left at the Ovest exit on the Florence-Siena motorway towards Sovicille and follow camping signs.

CC € 19 *24/3-10/7 27/8-30/9*

N 43°16'51" E 11°13'8"

Torre del Lago Puccini, I-55049 / Toscana

3037

Europa*
Viale dei Tigli, 51
+39 0584-350707
FAX +39 0584-342592
9/4 - 9/10
@ info@europacamp.it

5,3ha 200T(54-70m²) 6A CEE

1 ABCD**G**IJKLMOPRS
2 AFGRSVXY
3 BGHJKMNRU
4 (A) (B 14/5-25/9) (Q+S+T+U+V+Y+Z)
5 **AB**GIJKMO**P**UVWZ
6 ACFGI**JK**(N 1km)ORTV

Well-maintained campsite close to the free beach. Trips to Tuscan cultural cities. Cash payment required for CampingCard ACSI. Free bottle of Chianti when staying at least a week. Attention: dogs allowed entire season.

A12 La Spezia-Livorno, exit Viareggio, along the dual-carriageway Aurelia road to Torre del Lago, exit Marina di Lago, follow the 'Mare' signs. Follow camping signs.

CC € 17 *9/4-1/7 22/8-9/10 7=6, 14=12, 21=18*

N 43°49'52'' E 10°16'14''

Torre del Lago Puccini, I-55048 / Toscana

3038

Italia
Viale dei Tigli 52
+39 0584-359828
FAX +39 0584-341504
20/4 - 30/9
@ info@campingitalia.net

10ha 150T(50-80m²) 6A CEE

1 ABCDGIJKLMOPQ
2 ABFGRSWXY
3 BGHJK**M**NRU
4 (**B** 1/6-30/8,1/9-7/9) (Q+S+T+U+V) (Y 16/4-25/9) Z
5 **AB**EFGIJKMNO**P**UVWZ
6 CEG**K**(N 0,8km)ORTV

If you appreciate art, nature and endless beaches you should visit Versilia in the heart of Tuscany with the Alpi Apugne in the background. Here you will find the Italia campsite in Torre del Lago Puccini, a shady campsite with good facilities. Dogs permitted 20/4-31/5 and from 1/9-30/9. CampingCard ACSI holders can swim free.

A12 La Spezia-Livorno exit Viareggio, then SS1 direction Pisa. Take Marina di Torre del Lago exit, then follow camping signs.

CC € 17 *20/4-30/6 22/8-30/9 7=6*

N 43°49'45'' E 10°16'14''

Troghi/Firenze, I-50067 / Toscana

3039

Il Poggetto
Strada Provinciale 1 Aretina km 14
FAX +39 055-8307323
19/3 - 15/10
@ info@campingilpoggetto.com

4,5ha 110T(60-85m²) 7A CEE

1 ABCD**G**IJKLMNO**P**Q
2 FGJKLRTVWXY
3 B**F**GHJKN**OP**RUV
4 (A 15/6-15/9) (B+G 1/5-30/9) (Q+S+T+U+V+Y+Z)
5 **AB**EFGIJKLMNOP**S**UVW
6 CEGH**K**(N 0,5km)ORTV

Campsite is situated on wide terraces against a mountainside. The bus to Florence stops by the entrance. Beautiful swimming pool and well-maintained toilet facilities.

A1 Firenze-Roma, exit Incisa. Turn right, after about 4 km turn left. After the bridge crossing the Arno river left. Then follow the camping signs.

CC € 19 *19/3-30/6 1/9-15/10*

N 43°42'6'' E 11°24'19''

Vada/Livorno, I-57016 / Toscana

3040

Baia del Marinaio***
Via dei Cavalleggeri 177
+39 0586-770164
23/4 - 9/10
info@baiadelmarinaio.it

6ha 286T(40-85m²) 6A CEE

1 ABCD**G**IJKLNOQ
2 AEFGRTUVWXY
3 BDJK**M**NR**W**Y
4 (B 25/4-27/9) (G) IJP
(Q+S+T+U+V+X+Y) Z
5 **A**BGIJKLMNOPUVW
6 EGJ(N 1km)ORTV

Campsite with a new sanitary building. A swimming pool with a slide. Located 300 metres from the sea, merely separated from it by a road and a pine-tree forest. Sand- and pebble beach.

A12, exit Rosignano Marittimo. Then take the SS1 Aurelia to Roma, exit Vada. In Vada take the direction of Mazzanta. Campsite is on the landward side of the road.

CC € 17 *23/4-1/7 5/9-9/10*

N 43°20'5'' E 10°27'41''

Vada/Livorno, I-57018 / Toscana

3041

Campo dei Fiori**
Via Cavalleggeri
+39 0586-770096
FAX +39 0586-770323
23/4 - 25/9
info@campingcampodeifiori.it

15ha 500T(60-105m²) 3A CEE

1 ACD**G**IJKLMO**P**RS
2 BFGRTVWXY
3 ABDGK**M**NRU
4 (B 15/5-11/9) KP
(Q+S+T+U+V+W+Y) Z
5 **A**GIJKLMNOPUVXYZ
6 AEJK(N 1km)ORTV

A large, mostly shaded campsite with basic toilet facilities and ± 800m from a sandy beach. Central restaurant, pizzeria, bar, shops, swimming pool with children's pool, plenty of room for sports.

A12, exit Rosignano, then take the SS1 Aurelia in the direction of Roma, exit Vada. In Vada drive in the direction of Mazzanta (Vada-Celina-Mare). After about 1 km turn left and follow the signs.

CC € 15 *23/4-25/6 28/8-25/9 14=12*

N 43°20'8'' E 10°27'56''

Vada/Livorno, I-57018 / Toscana

3042

Molino a Fuoco***
Via Cavalleggeri 32
+39 0586-770150
FAX +39 0586-770031
14/4 - 15/10
info@campingmolinoafuoco.com

5ha 120T(40-75m²) 4A CEE

1 ABCD**G**HIJKLMNPS
2 AEFNRVXY
3 BHJK**M**NR**T**UVWY
4 (**B**+G+Q+S+T+U+V+Y) Z
5 **AB**EFGIJKLMNOPUZ
6 ACDEG**IJK**M(N 2km)ORTU
V

Lovely surroundings with various places to visit; Vada, Volterra and Cecina. A day trip to the island of Elba is worth the visit. Cyclist will love it here (bikes for hire). In the evening enjoy an excellent meal in the restaurant. Larger pitches for a surcharge. Now with new swimming pool.

A12, exit Rosignana-Marittimo then the SS1 Aurelia direction Rome, exit Vada. In Vada direction Mazzanta, the campsite is on the seaward side 2 km further on.

CC € 17 *22/4-25/6 10/9-15/10*

N 43°19'55'' E 10°27'37''

Vada/Livorno, I-57016 / Toscana

3043

Rifugio del Mare
Loc. I. Mozzi
+39 0586-770091
FAX +39 0586-770268
25/4 - 25/9
@ info@rifugiodelmare.it

6ha 120T(40-80m²) 6A CEE

1 ABCD**G**HIJKLMNOPQ
2 AFGLRVXY
3 BGKNRU
4 (B 30/5-15/9) (G 30/5-11/9) (Q+S+T+U+V+X) Z
5 **AB**GIJKMNOPUVZ
6 CEGJ(N 0,6km)OTV

'Rifugio del Mare' located 600 metres from the beach extends over a natural area of 60,000 m². It offers a new swimming pool for children, playground, bar, supermarket, bazaar and restaurant. Marked out pitches. A good base for making excursions to the art towns in Tuscany.

A12, exit Rosignano Marittimo. Then SS1 Aurelia to Roma, exit Vada. In Vada take the direction of Mazzanta. You'll reach the campsite after about 2 km. It is on the landward side.

CC € 11 *25/4-1/7 21/8-25/9*

N 43°19'50'' E 10°27'50''

Viareggio, I-55049 / Toscana

3044

La Pineta**
Via dei Lecci 105
FAX +39 0584-383397
24/3 - 22/9
@ campinglapineta@interfree.it

3,2ha 85T(35-70m²) 5A CEE

1 ABCD**G**HIJKLMOPQ
2 AFGRSVXY
3 AK**OP**RU
4 (B+G 15/5-25/9) **N** (Q+R+T+U+X) Z
5 **A**GIKMOPUVWZ
6 EG**K**(N 0,3km)OTV

A very peaceful campsite with shaded pitches; 1300 metres from the sea with a large, free beach. 2 km from the centre of Viareggio, 3 km from Torre del Lago Puccini; 20 km from Lucca and Pisa; Florence 90 km. 1 hour free WiFi with CampingCard ACSI. Free swimming pool.

A12, exit Viareggio and follow 'campings' signs towards Torre del Lago Puccini.

CC € 17 *24/3-30/6 25/8-22/9 7=6, 14=12*

N 43°51'2'' E 10°15'56''

Viareggio, I-55049 / Toscana

3045

Viareggio
Via Comparini 1
FAX +39 0584-391012
1/4 - 2/10
@ info@campingviareggio.it

3ha 250T(36-80m²) 4A CEE

1 ABCD**G**IJKLMOPQ
2 BFGRSVY
3 BHJKNRU
4 (**B** 1/6-30/8) (Q+S+T+U+V+Y) Z
5 **AB**EFGI**J**KMO**P**UWZ
6 EG**IK**(N 0,2km)ORTV

The campsite is located about 1.5 km from the town. The beach is accessible from the campsite through a wood (800m distance). Hospitable and friendly atmosphere. Outstanding toilet facilities. The campsite offers many facilities such as a restaurant and a supermarket. Countless opportunities for trips out.

Take direction Torre del Lago from the centre of Viareggio and then follow the signs to the campsite.

CC € 17 *1/4-30/6 25/8-2/10 7=6*

N 43°51'5'' E 10°15'35''

Assisi/Perugia, I-06081 / Umbria

3046

Camping Village Assisi***
Via S.G. in Campiglione 110
+39 075-816816
FAX +39 075-812335
19/3 - 2/11
@ info@campingassisi.it

3ha 95T(50-120m²) 6A CEE

1 ABCDGIJKLMNO**P**Q
2 BLRVY
3 ABGHJKMNRUV
4 (**B**+**G** 1/6-1/9) (Q+R+T+U+V+Y) Z
5 **AB**GIJKLMNOPUVWZ
6 CDEG**IK**(N 2km)OQTUV

A fairly large campsite with spacious, shaded pitches. Suitable for campers who want to spend some time in Assisi. The campsite is right on the road to Assisi and has its own shuttle bus. Good restaurant. Assisi campsite is a good base for visiting other towns: Spello, Perugia, Gubbio and Lake Trasimeno.

A1/E6, take exit Perugia (SS75). After Perugia take the Ospedallicchio-Sud exit, under the motorway and right at the roundabout. Follow signs to Assisi (SS147).

CC € 19 *28/3-21/4 26/4-15/7 1/9-2/11*

N 43°4'33'' E 12°34'24''

Bevagna, I-06031 / Umbria

3047

Pian di Boccio***
Via Pian di Boccio 10
+39 0742-360164
FAX +39 0742-360391
1/4 - 30/9
@ info@piandiboccio.com

8ha 70T 6A CEE

1 ABCDGHIJKLMO**P**Q
2 BFJRTWXY
3 BGHJ**M**NQRU
4 (B 15/5-30/9) (G 1/7-30/9) P (Q+R) (U+V 1/7-31/8) (Y) Z
5 **A**EGIJKLMNO**P**UV
6 CEG**IK**(N 3,5km)ORV

This campsite is situated on hilly grounds in a mixed forest. There are no marked out pitches, which means campers are free to chose their own space. An ideal base for visiting Umbria.

In Foligno exit Foligno Nord dir. Bevagna. Without caravan: just past Bevagna first road on the right past the bridge. With caravan straight on S316 and after 3 km turn right. Follow the signs.

CC € 17 *1/4-30/6 1/9-30/9*

N 42°54'44'' E 12°35'10''

Cascia, I-06043 / Umbria

3048

Campeggio il Drago
Loc. San Giorgio di Cascia 1
+39 0743-751070
FAX +39 0743-755944
20/3 - 31/10
@ info@campeggioildrago.it

1ha 35T(25-40m²) 6A CEE

1 BCDGILM**P**Q
2 GJKLRTUVWXY
3 ABGHJ**MNO**
4 (A 15/5-30/9) (C 1/6-7/9) (Q+R+T+U+V+Y+Z)
5 **A**GIJKLMNOPUWXZ
6 CDEGK(N 5,5km)OTV

Il Drago campsite combines unspoiled countryside with comfort (e.g. large pool). Ideal for exploring Umbria and the Italian interior.

From Cascia take the SP474 direction Agriano. Turn left after 7 km to San Giorgio. Follow camping signs. If coming past San Anatolia, don't use SatNav but continue to Cascia.

CC € 15 *20/3-15/7 1/9-31/10*

N 42°45'7'' E 13°0'56''

Castiglione del Lago, I-06061 / Umbria

3049

Badiaccia Camping Village****
Via Pratovecchio 1
+39 075-9659097
FAX +39 075-9659019
1/4 - 30/9
info@badiaccia.com

5,5ha 260T(55-110m²) 10A CEE

1 BCD**G**HIJKLMNOPQ
2 ADKLRSTVXY
3 ABGHJKMNQRU**V**WZ
4 (A 1/7-31/8) (B 15/5-30/9) (G 1/5-30/9) KP (Q+R+S+T+U+V+X+Y) Z
5 **AB**EFGJKLMNOPSTUVWX YZ
6 ACDEGIJ(N 0,8km)OQRTV

A large campsite with many shaded pitches, its own harbour, swimming pool and hydro massage baths. The campsite is located on the lake between Tuscany and Umbria. Close to the towns of Florence, Siena and Perugia.

A1/E6, via Val di Chiana SS75 exit to Castiglione del Lago exit. Then via route 71 southwards, turn off towards Borghetto.

CC € 19 *1/4-5/7 22/8-30/9*

N 43°10'52'' E 12°0'59''

Castiglione del Lago, I-06061 / Umbria

3050

Listro**
Via Lungolago
FAX +39 075-951193
1/4 - 30/9
listro@listro.it

1ha 100T(40-85m²) 3A CEE

1 BCD**G**HIJKLMOPQ
2 ADKLRTXY
3 A**F**HJK**M**RWZ
4 (**F**+Q+R) Z
5 **A**GIKNOPUV
6 CEGI**J**(N 0,8km)OTV

Small, shaded and hospitable campsite right by the lake and close to the town centre. This site is part of the Trasimeno National Park.

A1/E6, exit Val di Chiana, take the Perugia SS75. Then take exit Castiglione del Lago (SS71) to the south. In Castiglione second street left. Follow the signs.

CC € 15 *1/4-30/6 1/9-30/9*

N 43°8'4'' E 12°2'39''

Monte Santa Maria Tiberina, I-06010 / Umbria

3051

Luna del Monte
Loc. S. Pietro 8
+39 366-8906331
15/4 - 15/9
info@campinglunadelmonte.nl

1ha 46T(40-65m²) 6A CEE

1 ABGIJKLMO**PQ**
2 GKUVWXY
3 BHJR
4 (Q+R+V+X+Z)
5 **A**GIKMNOPUVWZ
6 CDEGJK(N 2km)OQTV

Small, rustic campsite located at the top of a mountain. Directly adjacent to a beautiful castle village with an amazing view. The pitches are surrounded by high hedges, which gives the idea of privacy. Very suitable for people who love peace and quiet, culture and nature.

E45, exit Citta di Castello Nord. Dir. Arezzo. Turn left after 2 km to Monte Santa Maria Tiberina. Follow signs to campsite and restaurant 'Il Poggio'.

CC € 19 *15/4-3/7 29/8-15/9*

N 43°26'17'' E 12°9'33''

Narni/Borgheria, I-05035 / Umbria

3052

Monti del Sole**
Strada di Borgaria 22
+39 0744-796336
23/3 - 4/9
info@campingmontidelsole.it

8ha 80**T**(45-80m²) 6A CEE

1 CFHIJKLMOPRS
2 BGJLRTVWXY
3 ABGHMNR
4 (B+G 15/6-31/8) (Q)
(U+V+X 1/7-31/8) Z
5 **A**GIJKLMNOPUVZ
6 ACEGJ(N 3km)R

A peaceful, friendly family campsite with spacious shaded touring pitches and very well maintained sanitary facilities. Swimming pools, tennis, bar, restaurant, little stone cottages. An ideal base for excursions to Umbria and Lazio. Rome can be reached by train in 40 minutes.

A1 between Siena and Rome. Take Magliano Sabina exit towards Narni. SS3 km 80.800. From the SS3/E45 Perugia-Cesena, take Narni/Scalo exit. Direction Narni, then follow camping signs.

CC € 17 *23/3-9/7 27/8-4/9*

N 42°29'5'' E 12°30'55''

Passignano sul Trasimeno, I-06065 / Umbria

3053

Kursaal***
Viale Europa 24
+39 075-828085
FAX +39 075-827182
16/4 - 31/10
info@campingkursaal.it

2,5ha 70**T**(40-70m²) 6A CEE

1 ABCD**G**IJKLMNOPRS
2 ADGKLMNRSVY
3 AGHJKNRWZ
4 (B+G 1/5-15/10) J**K**(Q)
(R 10/5-30/9) (U+Y) Z
5 **AB**FGIJKLMNOPUW
6 ACEG**IJ**(N 0,8km)RTV

A small campsite by the lake set in the exotic gardens of a stylish villa hotel with an excellent restaurant. The fact that camping guests may use the same outdoor facilities as the hotel guests is a sign of the kind-heartedness of the owners.

A1/E6, exit Val di Chiana, SS75 direction Perugia. Then exit Passignano Est. Drive in the direction of Passignano. The campsite is located on the left after the tracks.

CC € 19 *16/4-30/6 25/8-31/10*

N 43°11'2'' E 12°9'2''

Passignano sul Trasimeno, I-06065 / Umbria

3054

La Spiaggia**
Via Europa 22
+39 075-827246
FAX +39 075-827276
24/3 - 1/11
info@campinglaspiaggia.it

1,8ha 50**T**(50-100m²) 6-10A CEE

1 ABCD**G**HIJKLMNO**P**RS
2 ADGKLMRWXY
3 ABGHJKRWZ
4 (A 1/4-15/9) (B 28/5-18/9)
(Q+R 27/3-13/10)
(T+U+V+X) Z
5 **AB**EFGIJKLMNOPUV
6 ADEGK(N 0,7km)OTV

A quiet lakeside campsite with its own private beach, large shaded pitches and friendly management. Minimarket and bar where you can order pizza and other snacks. Bikes and canoes for rent. Well maintained toilet facilities, numerous camping pitches on soft grassy ground. Lawns by the lake.

A1/E6, take Val di Chiana exit, direction Perugia SS75. Take exit Passignano Est. Keep right direction Passignano. Second campsite over the railway line.

CC € 19 *24/3-5/7 22/8-31/10*

N 43°11'2'' E 12°9'3''

Piediluco, I-05100 / Umbria

3055

Lago Di Piediluco**
Via dell'Ara Marina 2
+39 328-1099396
25/3 - 30/10
campinglagodipiediluco@gmail.com

3,3ha 150T(60-80m²) 6A CEE

1 ABC**G**IJKLMNOPQ
2 DGKLMRVXY
3 BGH**M**NRWZ
4 (**C** 11/6-31/8) (Q 25/3-30/9) (R+V 1/6-6/9) Z
5 GIJKLMOPUVZ
6 CEGJ(N 0,6km)OTV

This campsite has everything you need for a successful holiday. Located on the shores of Lake Piediluco. Quiet pitches among greenery. Extensive sports facilities including an Olympic size swimming pool. An ideal location for visiting Rome and Assisi.

A1 exit Orte direction Terni. Exit Terni Est, follow dir. Rieti. After 2 tunnels exit Marmore. In Marmore dir. Piediluco. In Piediluco follow ('piscina') signs.

CC € 15 25/3-5/7 25/8-30/10

N 42°32'6'' E 12°46'20''

Preci, I-06047 / Umbria

3056

Il Collaccio****
Fraz. Castelvecchio
+39 0743-939084
FAX +39 0743-939094
1/4 - 30/9
info@ilcollaccio.com

10ha 120T(25-80m²) 6A CEE

1 ACDFIJKL**P**Q
2 JKLRTVXY
3 BGK**M**NRU
4 (**A** 1/6-15/9) (B+G 20/5-20/9) (Q+S+U+V+Y) Z
5 **A**GIJKMNOPUV
6 ACEG**IK**(N 2km)OTV

A beautifully situated terraced campsite with fine panoramic views of the Umbrian hills. The site makes a really good impression.

SS3 from Foligno to Spoleto. Turn left towards Norcia. Then S209 direction Visso. Before Preci exit left towards Castelvecchio. Then follow camping signs. (Do not use SatNav!)

CC € 17 1/4-9/7 27/8-30/9

N 42°53'18'' E 13°0'53''

Tuoro sul Trasimeno, I-06069 / Umbria

3057

Camping Village Punta Navaccia***
Via Navaccia 4
+39 075-826357
FAX +39 075-8258147
24/3 - 15/10
navaccia@camping.it

6,5ha 190T(75-100m²) 6A CEE

1 ABCDGIJKLMO**P**Q
2 ADFKRUVY
3 B**F**HJKMNRUVWZ
4 (A 1/7-30/8) (B+G 1/5-30/9) KP(Q+R+T+U+V+Y) Z
5 **AB**EFGIJKLMNOPUWXZ
6 ACDEGK(N 1km)ORTVX

A large, friendly campsite by the lake. Also suitable for young children and teenagers. Shaded pitches by Lake Trasimeno with panoramic views. Touring pitches by a private harbour with free boat trips. Sandy beach, bars and adult disco close by.

A1/E6, exit Val di Chiana. Take the SS75 to Perugia. Exit Tuoro, then left under the bridge. At the end of the road on the shore of the lake you will find the campsite.

CC € 17 24/3-30/6 1/9-15/10

N 43°11'30'' E 12°4'35''

Cupra Marittima, I-63012 / Marche

3058

Calypso***
Via Boccabianca 7
+39 0735-778686
+39 0735-778106
1/4 - 30/9
info@campingcalypso.it

2,6ha 220T(50-80m²) 6A CEE

1 ACDFIJKLQ
2 AEFGRVXY
3 ABKMNRUVWY
4 (B 15/5-30/9) J(Q)
(S+T+U+V+W+Y 5/5-15/9) Z
5 **AB**GIJKLMNOPUV
6 GIK(N 1km)ORSTV

Well-maintained, large campsite. Private beach, swimming pool and sports facilities. The railway line is just next to the beach and the campsite.

From the north, the campsite is accessible via the A14, exit Pedaso. A further 6 km southwards. Follow camping signs. From the south via the A14 exit Grottamare; direction Ancona; 5 km northwards then follow signs.

CC €17 20/4-4/6 28/8-30/9

N 43°2'39'' E 13°51'12''

Fiorenzuola di Focara/Pesaro, I-61121 / Marche

3059

Panorama***
Strada Panoramica
+39 0721-208145
+39 0721-209799
15/4 - 30/9
info@campingpanorama.it

2,5ha 140T(45-100m²) 6A CEE

1 ABCD**F**HIJKLMNOPRS
2 EFJLORUVXY
3 AB**F**HJNRUWY
4 (B+G 15/5-15/9)
(Q+S+T+U+V+X+Z)
5 **A**GIJKMNOPUVZ
6 CDEGK(N 3km)OQRTV

Camping Panorama is located in the region of La Marche in the green heart of the San Bartolo Nature Park, 100m above sea level on the scenic Strada Panoramica route. An ideal place for rest and recreation. The campsite includes a swimming pool, bar, pizzeria and free WiFi. Activities in the area include golf, fishing and diving. Nearest beach 10 to 15 minutes by car.

A14 exit Pesaro. SS16 direction Gabicce Mare. In Cattabrighe follow camping signs.

CC €19 15/4-30/6 1/9-30/9

N 43°56'30'' E 12°50'45''

Monteciccardo, I-61020 / Marche

3060

Podere Sei Poorte
Via Petricci 14
+39 333-1406043
+39 0721-910286
29/4 - 1/10
info@podereseipoorte.it

6ha 110T(100-200m²) 6A CEE

1 ACD**G**IJKLMNOPQ
2 CIJKLRSTVWX
3 AGHJNRU
4 (B 29/4-24/9)
(Q+R+Y+Z)
5 **AB**CGHIJKLMNOPRUVWX
Z
6 ACEGHJ(N 7km)O**P**V

Picturesque area. Swimming pool with panoramic views, hospitable atmosphere, good toilets, spacious pitches. Authentic farm, Italian cuisine, communal brunch on Sundays. Free olive/wine tasting on Thursdays including food. Dutch couple.

A14, exit Pesaro/Urbino towards Urbino. Then S. Angelo in Lizzola; follow brown 'Camping P6P' signs (not GPS). Then Mombaroccio (SP26). In Villa Ugolini in the same direction enter Via Petricci (narrow road), 1400m on the right.

CC €19 29/4-8/7 25/8-1/10

N 43°48'4'' E 12°49'18''

Numana, I-60026 / Marche

3061

Camping Village Numana Blu****
Via Costaverde 37
+39 071-7390993
FAX +39 071-7391793
22/4 - 25/9
@ info@numanablu.it

8,6ha 330T(60-80m²) 5A CEE

1 BCD**G**HIJKLOPQ
2 AEFGLRTVXY
3 BFJK**M**N**OP**RUWY
4 (A 1/6-14/9)
(B+G 14/5-20/9) KP
(Q+S+T+U+V+W+Y+Z)
5 **AB**CEFGHIJKLMNOPRUV
W
6 ACDEG**IK**(N 2km)OQRTUV

Large palm trees and beautiful flowers welcome you to this well maintained family campsite. 4 stars. A professional team organises daily entertainment from 1 June to mid September. ± 300m from a private beach. Excellent sports fields, swimming pool and modern toilet facilities.

A14, in the direction of Loreto, and then drive in the direction of Porto Recanati. When the coastal road is in sight drive in the direction of Sirolo/Numana. Turn left at the sign 'Numana Blu'.

CC € 17 *22/4-19/6 1/9-25/9*

N 43°28'35" E 13°38'4"

Porto Recanati, I-62017 / Marche

3062

Bellamare***
Lungomare Scarfiotti 13
+39 071-976628
FAX +39 071-977586
2/4 - 30/9
@ info@bellamare.it

5ha 360T(30-60m²) 6A CEE

1 ACDEHIJKLMOPQ
2 AEFGNRVWX
3 AB**F**KL**M**N**O**RUWY
4 (B+G 1/5-20/9)
(Q+R+T+U 19/4-30/9)
(V 1/5-30/9) (Y 19/4-30/9) Z
5 **AB**FGIJKMO**P**UV
6 ACDEG**IK**(N 3km)OTVX

A large friendly campsite positioned directly next to its own beach. There are plenty of shaded pitches and the whole place gives a well maintained impression. There are plenty of comfortable amenities on the site. The 'Rivièra de Conero' with beautiful views is close by.

A14. take exit Porto Recanati. After the toll booth turn directly right at the sign 'P.Rec'. Turn left (centre). Follow Numana. Follow the road over the hill along the beach (about 6 km in total).

CC € 17 *2/4-8/7 27/8-30/9*

N 43°28'17" E 13°38'29"

Sarnano, I-62028 / Marche

3063

Quattro Stagioni***
Contrada Brilli
+39 0733-651147
FAX +39 0733-651104
1/1 - 31/12
@ quattrostagioni@camping.it

4,5ha 50T(80-100m²) 6A CEE

1 ACDFHIJKLNOPQ
2 CGIJKLRVY
3 BGJ**M**N**O**RU
4 (B+G 1/6-10/9)
(Q+R 1/7-31/8)
(T+U+V+Y 1/6-30/9) Z
5 **A**EGIJKLMNOPUV
6 ACEGI**J**(N 3km)OTV

A terraced campsite near the Sibilini National Park. Lovely views of the mountains. Spacious pitches with plenty of shade. A perfect spot for lovers of peace and the countryside. This campsite is ideal for people of a sportive nature.

A14, exit Civitanova Marche. Motorway to Macerata as far as Sarnano exit. In Sarnano turn right at square (follow main road). Campsite a few km outside Sarnano.

CC € 17 *1/5-10/7 1/9-30/9*

N 43°1'4" E 13°16'55"

Stacciola/San Costanzo, I-61039 / Marche — 3064

Camping Village Mar y Sierra***
Strada San Gervasio, 3
+39 0721-930044
15/4 - 2/10
info@marysierra.it

4ha 130T(45-60m²) 6A CEE

1 BCDFIJKLPRS
2 FJKLRTUWXY
3 ABKMNRU
4 (B 15/5-1/9) (G 15/6-1/9) P (Q) (T+U+V+Y+Z 1/6-30/9)
5 **A**GIJKLMNOPUVXYZ
6 EG**I**J(N 3km)RTV

Friendly and hospitable terraced campsite with swimming pool and excellent restaurant. Beautifully situated with panoramic views. Suitable as a stopover campsite. Renewed sanitary facilities (2014)

Leave A14 from Rimini-Ancona at Marotta Mondolfo. At the exit turn right. Follow this route (SS424) for about 4 km. In Ponte Rio turn right towards Stacciola (SP154). The campsite is at the top of the hill. Follow Mar y Sierra signs.

CC € 19 *15/4-24/6 27/8-1/10*

N 43°44'44" E 13°4'56"

Bolsena, I-01023 / Lazio — 3065

BLU International Camping***
Via Cassia km 111,650
+39 0761-798855
21/4 - 8/10
info@blucamping.it

3ha 230T(50-70m²) 8A CEE

1 BCD**G**HIJKLMNOPQ
2 ADKLRTVXY
3 ARWZ
4 (B 14/5-17/9) (Q 21/4-29/9) (S 28/5-17/9) (U+V+Y+Z 21/4-29/9)
5 **AB**GIJKMOPUZ
6 CEG**K**(N 1,5km)OTV

All pitches are clearly marked-out and shaded. The campsite is located directly on the lake and has a neat and excellent restaurant.

From A1/E6 via SS71 to Bolsena. In the centre at the traffic lights direction Montefiascone/Viterbo. The campsite is located 1.4 km past Bolsena alongside the lake.

CC € 17 *21/4-30/6 1/9-8/10*

N 42°37'53" E 11°59'41"

Bolsena, I-01023 / Lazio — 3066

Lido Camping Village****
Via Cassia km 111
+39 0761-799258
FAX +39 0761-796105
24/4 - 30/9
info@lidocampingvillage.it

10ha 600T(49-70m²) 3A CEE

1 CD**F**HIJKLMNOPQ
2 ADGKLRSVXY
3 AGHJK**M**NRWZ
4 (**B**+**G** 15/6-31/8) (Q+S+T+U+V+W) Z
5 **AB**EFGI**J**KMNO**PS**U
6 CFG**K**(N 2km)ORTV

An extensive campsite with shaded pitches right by Lake Bolsena. Every amenity and excellent toilet facilities.

From the A1/E6 via route SS71 (past Orvieto) to Bolsena. In the centre, at the traffic lights, turn in the direction of Montefiasone/Viterbo. The campsite is located at the lake, 1.5 km past Bolsena.

CC € 19 *24/4-30/6 5/9-30/9*

N 42°37'39" E 11°59'39"

Bracciano, I-00062 / Lazio

3067

Porticciolo
Via Porticciolo
☎ +39 06-99803060
FAX +39 06-99803030
1/4 - 30/9
@ info@porticciolo.it

3,3ha 170T(40-80m²) 3-6A CEE

1 ABCD**F**IJKLMNOPRS
2 ABDGKLMORVY
3 AKNRWZ
4 (Q+R+T+U+V+X) Z
5 **A**EFGI**JK**L**M**NO**P**UVZ
6 ACEGI**K**(N 2km)ORTVW

The lake and Rome, good food and a relaxed atmosphere on the terrace, sailing and excursions, also by bike and boat. Take our private bus to the train station; maps, timetables and tickets available at the reception. Free WiFi on all pitches.

SS2 Viterbo-Roma, at Sutri right towards Bracciano. Keep right in Bracciano and follow road round the lake. There are signs. Or: follow Maglino-Nepi SS2 dir. Sutri. Before Sutri head to lake keep right. Avoid Bracciano.

CC € 17 *1/4-30/6 1/9-30/9*

N 42°6'21'' E 12°11'11''

Bracciano, I-00062 / Lazio

3068

Roma Flash***
Via Settevene Palo km 19,800
☎ FAX +39 06-99805458
1/4 - 30/9
@ info@romaflash.it

7ha 250T(50-120m²) 6A CEE

1 ABCD**G**HIJKLMNO**P**Q
2 ABDGKLMRVWXY
3 BGK**M**NRWZ
4 (B+G 1/6-31/8) (Q+R)
(T 15/4-20/9) (U+V+X) Z
5 **AB**EFGIJKLNPUVX
6 ACEGH**K**(N 4km)RTVW

The campsite is located 35 km from Rome and has a good restaurant/pizzeria. The bus to Bracciano station stops at the campsite 12 times a day. Excursion to Pompeii once a week on Sunday. WiFi is available for a payment and covers the entire site.

SS2 Viterbo-Roma, head right towards Trevignano at Sutri. On reaching the shore of the lake take direction Bracciano, campsite clearly signposted on the left.

CC € 15 *1/4-7/7 24/8-30/9*

N 42°7'48'' E 12°10'25''

Fiano Romano/Roma, I-00065 / Lazio

3069

I Pini Family Park****
Viale delle Sassete 28
☎ +39 0765-453349
FAX +39 0765-1890941
22/4 - 20/9
@ ipini@ecvacanze.it

5ha 100T(60-90m²) 6A CEE

1 ABCD**F**IJKLMOPQ
2 BFILRVWXY
3 BGJK**M**NRU
4 (B+G) M
(Q+S+U+V+Y) Z
5 **AB**EFGIJKLMNOPUWXZ
6 CEG**I**JM(N 2,5km)ORTVW
X

A rural campsite north of Rome. From time to time from May to September they arrange buffets with delicious local hot and cold dishes. The site is very homely and suitable for families with young children.

A1 Roma Nord. After the toll booth exit Roma Nord-Fiano Romano. After the Holiday Inn at roundabout right. Drive 2 kilometres, 2nd roundabout straight on to crossing, then turn left. The campsite is signposted after 2 km.

CC € 17 *22/4-30/6 29/8-20/9*

N 42°9'20'' E 12°34'23''

Marina di Montalto di Castro, I-01014 / Lazio

3070

Pionier Etrusco***
Via Vulsinia 2
+39 0766-802807
FAX +39 0766-801214
21/3 - 30/9
@ info@campingpe.it

6,5ha 250T(50-100m²) 3A CEE

1 BCDEHIJKLMNO**P**
2 ABEGSTY
3 BG**M**RWY
4 (A 1/7-30/8) (B 1/6-30/9) (Q+R+T+U+V+W+X) Z
5 **A**GIJKMNOPRUV
6 EGJ**K**TV

This shaded campsite located by the Tyrrhenean Sea is an ideal base for visiting the countless historical and cultural sites in the area.

A1, exit Firenze, then SS1 direction Grosseto/Rome. Turn right at the 108 km-marker and follow the campsite signs.

CC €17 *21/3-26/6 29/8-30/9*

N 42°19'38'' E 11°34'54''

Roma, I-00125 / Lazio

3071

Camping Village Fabulous
Via di Malafede 205
+39 06-5259354
FAX +39 06-83517789
25/3 - 31/10
@ fabulous@ecvacanze.it

30ha 70T(< 100m²) 6A CEE

1 ABCD**G**IJKLMO**P**Q
2 BFGKLSTUVY
3 BG**MN**QRU**V**
4 (B+G 1/5-30/9) KM (Q 25/4-30/9) (S 1/5-31/8) (U 1/4-31/10) (V 1/5-30/8) (Y 1/4-31/10) Z
5 **AB**EFGIJKLMNOPU
6 CEGH**I**JM(N 3km)OTV

Camping Fabulous is located in a 30 hectare pine forest between Rome and Lido di Ostia. It has every comfort and large swimming pools. There is an aqua park. It has a disco for teenagers and an inline skate track. A good, friendly restaurant. Excursions are organised regularly.

Follow direction Aeroporto Fiumicino on the G.R.A. ring road. Take exit 27 via Colombo towards Ostia. Turn right at the traffic lights by 18 km marker. Campsite on the right.

CC €17 *25/3-28/6 29/8-31/10*

N 41°46'38'' E 12°23'46''

Roma, I-00189 / Lazio

3072

Flaminio Village Camping & Bungalow Park****
Via Flaminia Nuova, 821
+39 06-3332604
FAX +39 06-3330653
1/1 - 31/12
@ info@villageflaminio.com
8,6ha 260T 6A CEE

1 ABCD**G**IJKLMO**P**Q
2 FGIJLRTY
3 A**F**HJK
4 (B 15/5-30/8) (Q+R+T) (V 1/1-6/1,1/2-31/12) (Y) Z
5 **AB**DEFGIJK**L**MNOPUW
6 CEGIJ(N 0,3km)ORTVW

Well shaded, numbered or free choice pitches, this site is perfect for visiting the city of Rome. Bus stop outside the entrance and metro station just across the road. Good restaurant. An unusual feature is the classical music in the toilet blocks. WiFi is free.

On the G.R.A. (Rome ring road) exit 6 Via Flaminia, and continue towards Flaminio/Centro. At fork in road turn left towards Flaminio. Take note: campsite entrance is immediately on the right.

CC €19 *7/1-17/3 1/4-15/4 2/5-27/5 6/6-30/6 17/8-31/8 16/9-30/9*

N 41°57'23'' E 12°28'56''

Roma, I-00123 / Lazio

3073

Happy Village & Camping***
Via del Prato della Corte 1915
+39 06-33626401
FAX +39 06-33613800
1/3 - 18/12, 27/12 - 31/12
@ info@happycamping.net

4ha 220T(30-75m²) 6A CEE

1 ABCD**G**IJKLMO**P**Q
2 FGIJKLRTVY
3 A
4 (B+G 15/5-30/9) (Q+R+T+U+V) (Y 1/3-2/11) Z
5 **AB**DEFGIJKLMNOPU
6 CEG**J**(N 3km)RTV

Ideal campsite for a visit to Rome. Free bus to Prima Porta metro station from where you can be in the centre of Rome in 20 minutes. Well laid-out campsite with good toilet facilities (plenty of hot water). 2 fantastic swimming pools, new restaurant and an excellent, inexpensive pizzeria. WiFi free for first half hour.

GRA (Rome Ring Road), exit Cassia Veientana/ Viterbo. Then 1st exit, 10 m. on the right, then left uphill. Look out for signs; it is well indicated.

CC €17 *1/3-30/6 17/8-18/12 7=6*

N 42°0'2" E 12°27'12"

Roma, I-00188 / Lazio

3074

Tiber***
Via Tiberina km 1,4
+39 06-33610733
FAX +39 06-33612314
20/4 - 25/10
@ info@campingtiber.com

6ha 300T 6A CEE

1 ABCD**G**IJKLMOQ
2 CFRTXY
3 AW
4 (B 1/5-30/9) (Q+R+T+U) (V+Y 1/4-30/4) Z
5 **AB**EFGIJKLMNOPUWZ
6 ABCDEG**IK**M(N 1,5km)ORTUV

Tiber campsite is situated at the River Tiber and offers shade and rest. The shuttle bus will take you to Prima Porta station for one euro every half hour. Tiber campsite offers a swimming pool, WiFi, bar, excellent restaurant and shop. The site also has new toilet facilities. New: Tiber dog park.

On the G.R.A. (Rome ring road) exit 6, direction Flaminia-Prima Porta, after 2 km turn right on the Via Tiberina. Campsite clearly signposted.

CC €17 *20/4-30/6 29/8-25/10*

N 42°0'36" E 12°30'13"

Tarquinia, I-01016 / Lazio

3075

Europing 2000 srl****
Via Aurelia km 102
+39 0766-814010
FAX +39 0766-814075
30/4 - 18/9
@ europing@europing.it

25ha 700T(60-90m²) 3A CEE

1 BCDEHIJKLMNOPQ
2 AELRSVXY
3 BK**M**N**O**RU**V**WY
4 (**B** 15/6-15/9) (**G** 15/5-15/9) (Q+S+T+U+V+W+X+Y) Z
5 **A**GIKMOPUVWXY
6 CEGK(N 5km)OPRTV

An extended campsite located in pine woods. The private beach is 200 metres from the site. Various Etruscan archaeological sites in the immediate vicinity.

SS1 'Via Aurelia' Grosseto-Roma. At the 102 km-marker turn right exit Riva dei Tarquini. Immediately after the railway bridge turn right. Follow the camping signs.

CC €17 *30/4-10/7 27/8-18/9*

N 42°17'53" E 11°38'12"

Trevignano Romano, I-00069 / Lazio

3076

Camping Internazionale Lago di Bracciano***
Via Settevene Palo km 7.400
+39 06-9985032
FAX +39 06-99826770
1/4 - 30/9
@ camping.village@gmail.com
2ha 100T(60-80m²) 4A CEE

1 ABCD**G**HIJKLMO**P**RS
2 ADGKLRVXY
3 ABHJKNRUWZ
4 (G 15/5-30/9) (Q) (R+V+X 25/5-15/9) (Z 15/4-30/9)
5 **A**BCEGIJKLMNOPUV
6 CEG**I**J(N 3,5km)TVW

A quiet, friendly and well maintained campsite with a swimming pool, bar and restaurant. Close to Rome. Private beach on Lake Bracciano. New children's toilet facilities and a disabled toilet with shower. Private bus service to Anquillaro station.

SS2 'Via Cassia' exit Lago Bracciano. At the lakeside take the direction of Trevignano, then Anquillara. A sudden turn to the right to a small country road that leads to the camping.

CC € 15 1/4-6/7 27/8-30/9

N 42°8'48'' E 12°16'9''

Alba Adriatica, I-64011 / Abruzzo

3077

Eucaliptus***
Via Abruzzo 69
+39 0861-713356
FAX +39 0861-752382
18/5 - 19/9
@ info@campingeucaliptus.it
2ha 160T(> 60m²) 7A CEE

1 BCGHIJLPQ
2 AEFLRVY
3 BGKRY
4 (B+G) PZ
5 **A**EIJKLMNO**P**UVZ
6 EG**IJ**(N 0,2km)RTV

A small, modest campsite with a swimming pool. Friendly welcome.

From north on SS16 turn left at km marker IX 399. 1st right after rail tunnel. Follow road until it leaves train track. Then 2nd left. Campsite entrance is on left.

CC € 15 18/5-30/6 1/9-19/9

N 42°49'21'' E 13°55'48''

Giulianova Lido, I-64022 / Abruzzo

3078

Camping & Residence Don Antonio
Via Padova
+39 085-8008928
FAX +39 085-8006172
14/5 - 16/9
@ info@campingdonantonio.it
5ha 280T(50-100m²) 6A CEE

1 ABCFHIJKLMNOPQ
2 AEFGLRSTVWXY
3 ABGHJK**MW**Y
4 (B+G) IJKP (Q+R+U+V+W+Z)
5 **AB**FGIJKLMNOPS**T**UVXYZ
6 ACDEGHI**K**M(N 1km)ORTV

A campsite located by the sea with large and small pitches, sandy beaches, swimming pool, cycle route (42 km). 2 km from the centre. Bus from the site to the centre, 2 bars, WiFi.

E2/A14, exit Val Vibrata. Via the SS259 dir. Alba Adriatica located on the intersection of the SS259 and the SS16 to Giulianova. Follow indications. From the south, take Teramo exit on the E2/A14, follow the SS80 to the intersection with the SS16, then follow the signs Via Padova.

CC € 17 14/5-30/6 1/9-15/9

N 42°46'39'' E 13°57'10''

Opi, I-67030 / Abruzzo

3079

Il Vecchio Mulino
SS83 Marsicana km 52
+39 0863-912232
1/1 - 31/12
ilvecchiomulino@tiscali.it

6ha 300**T**(100-120m²) 6A CEE

1 ACD**F**IJKLMOPRS
2 BCGLRTVWXY
3 ADHIJR
4 (Q+R+U+Y+Z)
5 **AB**DGIJKLMNOPUVZ
6 CEJ(N 2km)OV

After a cultural visit to hectic cities such as Rome and Naples, this campsite is in a fantastic setting in the Abruzzen national park. You can enjoy the beautiful countryside, footpaths and even spot bears and wolves here.

The campsite is located on the SS83 from Opi direction Barrea/Alfedena. Clearly signposted.

CC €19 *1/1-15/7 1/9-31/12*

N 41°46'45" E 13°51'46"

Pineto, I-64025 / Abruzzo

3080

Pineto Beach***
SS16 Adriat. km 425
+39 085-9492724
+39 085-9492796
20/4 - 24/9
info@pinetobeach.it

2,5ha 300**T**(21-105m²) 6A CEE

1 ACGHIJKLMNQ
2 AEFNRUVY
3 ABGJKNRUVWY
4 (B+G 15/5-24/9) P (Q+R+S+T+U+V+W+X+Y+Z)
5 **AB**GHIJLMNOP**ST**UVXYZ
6 ACDEGIJ(N 0,8km)ORTUV

A beautiful campsite by the sea with plenty of amenities. New restaurant, pizzeria and bar suitable for all types of weather. WiFi and a solarium. Ask for the discounts with CampingCard ACSI in the last part of June.

Motorway E2/A14 to Bari, exit Pineto (SatNav off). Follow 'Pineto Beach' signs on the SS16. Tunnel (4m20 headroom).

CC €17 *20/4-23/6 29/8-24/9*

N 42°37'26" E 14°3'21"

Roseto degli Abruzzi, I-64026 / Abruzzo

3081

Eurcamping***
Lungomare Trieste 90
+39 085-8993179
+39 085-8930552
1/5 - 22/10
info@eurcamping.it

5ha 265**T**(50-100m²) 6A CEE

1 A**G**HIJKLMNPQ
2 AEFQRVWXY
3 ABGK**M**NRU**W**Y
4 (B+G 20/5-15/9) (Q+R+T+U+V+X 15/5-30/9) Z
5 **AB**FGIJKLNPUVZ
6 EG**IK**(N 2km)OTV

A lovely campsite positioned right by the sea. It has its own private beach and service. Large playground and jogging track. Many things are organised on the campsite. Spacious grounds! The site has a wonderful swimming pool.

E2/A14, exit Roseto. Roseto degli Abruzzi. In Roseto direction Pineto SS16. For gas station left and follow signs. Tunnel height 5 m.

CC €17 *1/5-9/7 26/8-22/10 7=6*

N 42°39'28" E 14°2'7"

Capaccio/Paestum, I-84047 / Campania

3082

La Foce dei Tramonti***
Via Foce Sele 2
+39 0828-861220
1/4 - 31/10
info@lafocedeitramonti.com

1,2ha 30T(75m²) 3A CEE

1 ACDGHIJKLMNOPQ
2 ACEGKLRTUVWY
3 BGKNRWY
4 (Q+S 15/6-15/9) (T+U+V+X 2/6-15/9) (Z 15/5-15/9)
5 **A**GIKMOPUVXYZ
6 CDEGJ(N 5km)OT

A beautifully located campsite at the mouth of a river. The ideal place to relax next to the sea, with views of the sunset every evening.

Along the coast road about 7 km north of Paestum direction Salerno, at the mouth of the Sele.

CC €17 1/4-10/7 27/8-31/10 14=12

N 40°28'51'' E 14°56'41''

Massalubrense/Marina d.Cantone, I-80061 / Campania

3083

Nettuno
Via A. Vespucci 39
+39 081-8081051
+39 081-8081706
15/3 - 1/11
info@villaggionettuno.it

0,5ha 60T(10-40m²) 4A CEE

1 ABDFIJLN**P**RS
2 EGHIJKNQSTWXY
3 H**M**RUWY
4 (**A**+R+T+U+V+Y+Z)
5 GIJKLMNOPU
6 EG**J**(N 2km)OPRV

Between Positano, Sorrento and Capri, on Marina del Cantone Bay on the gorgeous Amalfi coast. Direct access to crystal clear sea with private beach access. Ideal spot for relaxing, peaceful holiday. Diving centre. Small pitches (40 m²).

Coastal road to Sorrento. In Meta di Sor. dir. Positano. Then dir. San Agata and Marina del Cantone. (At site keep going, turn around). Difficult road for cars with caravans and motorhomes longer than 6m.

CC €19 15/3-24/3 2/4-13/5 28/5-1/7 12/9-1/11

N 40°35'0'' E 14°21'15''

Paestum, I-84063 / Campania

3084

Athena***
Via Ponte di Ferro
+39 0828-851105
1/4 - 31/10
info@campingathena.com

2,5ha 130T(80-100m²) 5A CEE

1 ACDFHIJKLMNOPQ
2 AEGKRSWXY
3 BGUWY
4 (Q+S 15/5-20/9) (T+V+X+Z 1/6-31/8)
5 **A**GIKMOPUV
6 CDEGJ(N 2km)RTV

A lovely campsite by the sea (sandy beach). Well situated for a visit to ancient Paestum.

Follow the campsite signs in the centre of Paestum. The site is located right by the sea.

CC €17 1/4-10/7 27/8-31/10 7=6

N 40°25'44'' E 14°58'56''

Paestum, I-84063 / Campania

3085

Villaggio dei Pini***
Via Torre di Mare
+39 0828-811030
FAX +39 0828-811025
1/1 - 31/12
info@campingvillaggiodeipini.com

3ha 158**T**(40-100m²) 6A CEE

1 ACD**G**HIJLMOPQ
2 ABEGLRTUVXY
3 ABGJKMN**Q**RWY
4 (**A**) M(Q+R) (U+V+Y 1/3-31/10) (Z)
5 **AB**EGHIJKLMNOPUV
6 BCDFGIJ(N 0,3km)ORTUV

Beach campsite with plenty of greenery and excellent location. Enclosed touring pitches. Beautiful private beach. Delicious cuisine with fresh local dishes.

In Paestum centre follow signs to campsite. Campsite is located directly on sea.

CC € 17 *1/1-30/6 20/9-31/12*

N 40°24'39'' E 14°59'43''

Pompei, I-80045 / Campania

3086

Fortuna Village Pompei
Via Plinio 115
FAX +39 081-8508439
1/1 - 31/12
info@fortunavillagepompei.it

0,5ha 50**T**(30-60m²) 6A CEE

1 ACDGIJKLMO**P**ST
2 FGKRVWX
4 (Q+T+U+V+Y+Z 19/3-10/11)
5 **A**GIJKLMNOPUW
6 CEGJ(N 1km)R

Campsite is located at 100 metres from the entrance to the Pompei ruins and is also an excellent base for visits to Napels, Sorrento and the Vesuvius crater.

From A3 Napels-Salerno, exit Pompei Quest left. Site is on right after 300 metres.

CC € 15 *8/1-18/3 4/4-22/4 9/5-28/5 6/6-15/7 1/9-4/12 12/12-23/12*

N 40°44'48'' E 14°29'3''

Pompei, I-80045 / Campania

3087

Spartacus***
Via Plinio 127
FAX +39 081-8624078
1/1 - 31/12
staff@campingspartacus.it

1ha 80**T**(25-32m²) 8A CEE

1 BCDFIJLPRS
2 FGRVWXY
3 U
4 (B 1/6-15/9) (Q 1/3-15/9) (V 1/7-31/8) (Z 1/3-15/9)
5 **AB**GIJKMNOPUVX
6 CG**J**(N 0,5km)R

A shaded, small-scale campsite close to the Pompeii excavations.

A3 Napoli-Salerno, exit Pompei Ovest, then left. Campsite about 250 metres on the right.

CC € 17 *7/1-20/3 4/4-30/6 1/9-20/12*

N 40°44'44'' E 14°29'2''

Pompei, I-80045 / Campania

3088

Zeus
Villa dei Misteri
+39 081-8615320
FAX +39 081-8617536
1/1 - 31/12
info@campingzeus.it

2ha 80T(40-100m²) 10A CEE

1 BCDFHIJL**P**Q
2 FGRSTVWXY
4 (R 1/4-31/10)
(T+U+V+X+Y 1/4-30/10)
(Z 1/4-15/11)
5 **AB**GIKMOPU
6 CEG**IK**(N 1km)ORT

Zeus campsite is located near the famous archaeological excavations at Pompeii; evening visits are possible until 19:30. In a lovely park with tropical plants at the foot of Vesuvius. Many facilities: bar/restaurant, souvenir shop and internet point. Good location for excursions by public transport to Naples, Sorrento, Amalfi, Positano and Capri.

A3 from Naples or Salerno: exit Pompei Ovest, left. After 200 metres left again, then left uphill.

CC € 19 *7/1-25/3 29/3-29/4 2/5-1/6 6/6-15/7 1/9-23/12*

N 40°44'57'' E 14°28'51''

Pozzuoli, I-80078 / Campania

3089

Int. Vulcano Solfatara***
Via Solfatara 161
+39 081-5267413
FAX +39 081-5263482
1/1 - 31/12
camping@solfatara.it

3ha 160T(40-70m²) 4A CEE

1 BCDFIJKLMOPRS
2 BFGRSWXY
3 AGR
4 (B+G 1/6-30/9) N
(Q+S+T+U 1/4-31/10)
(Z)
5 **AB**GIKMNOPUVW
6 CEGK(N 1km)ORT

The campsite is located in the Solfatara volcanic crater. Basic toilet facilities. An ideal place for visiting Naples, Pompeii etc.

Located just outside Pozzuoli direction Napoli. ('Tangenziale' exit 11 Agnano). The campsite is clearly signposted. Gate at entrance 2m 70 wide and 3m 40 high.

CC € 19 *8/1-24/3 1/4-28/4 2/5-30/6 1/9-24/12*

N 40°49'43'' E 14°8'12''

Vico Equense, I-80069 / Campania

3090

Sant'Antonio****
Via Marina d' Equa 21
FAX +39 081-8028570
15/3 - 31/10
info@campingsantantonio.it

1ha 60T 5A CEE

1 ACDFHIJKLPRS
2 AEGHNRWXY
3 **WY**
4 (Q+S+Y+Z)
5 **A**GIKMO**P**U
6 EG**J**(N 1km)OR

A peaceful campsite under lemon, olive and walnut trees by a picturesque harbour. The restaurant serves typical Italian home cooking. Basic toilet facilities. Boat trips to Capri. The campsite has WiFi.

A3, exit Castellamare direction Sorrento. Take tunnel left dir. Sorrento. After tunnel and bridge turn right and drive slowly.

CC € 19 *15/3-30/6 1/9-31/10*

N 40°39'34'' E 14°25'8''

Foce Varano (Isola Varano), I-71010 / Puglia

3091

Camping 5 Stelle***
SP41 Località Isola Varano
+39 0884-917583
FAX +39 0884-917561
16/4 - 17/9
@ info@camping5stelle.it

4ha 150T(80-100m²) 4A CEE

1 ABCGIJKLMPRS
2 ABDEGSY
3 ABKMNRY
4 (A+**B** 1/5-21/9) (**G** 26/5-10/9) (Q 1/5-21/9) (S 29/5-15/9) (T 15/5-15/9) (U+V 1/6-15/9) (X 15/5-15/9) (Z)
5 **A**FGIKMOPR**ST**UVXY
6 CDEG**IJ**(N 5km)OTV

Located between the sea and the lake. Large pitches encircled by the Parco Nazionale del Gargano. A beach several kilometres long slopes down gently to the clear blue sea. Swimming pool, supermarket, restaurant/pizzeria. Trips out include Pater Pio and Foresta Umbra.

A14, exit Poggio Imperiale towards Vieste Strada as far as Sannicandro Garganico (SS693). 20 km Litoranea SP41 Isola Varano dir. Torre Mileto (provincial road 14). Campsite on the right.

CC €15 *16/4-30/6 27/8-17/9*

N 41°54'45'' E 15°43'56''

Gagliano del Capo (LE), I-73034 / Puglia

3092

S. Maria di Leuca***
SS 275, km 35.700
+39 0833-548157
FAX +39 0833-548485
1/1 - 31/12
@ info@campingsmleuca.com

3ha 200T 3A CEE

1 ABC**G**HIJKLMNO**P**RS
2 BGTUXY
3 ABHKMNRW
4 (**A** 1/6-30/9) (B 1/5-1/11) P (Q) (R+T+U 1/6-31/8) (V 1/7-31/8) (W 1/6-31/8) Z
5 **A**GIJKLMNO**PT**U
6 EG**I**KM(N 2km)OQRTV

Surrounded by green trees on 3 hectares. 3 km from the crystal clear sea of Santa Maria di Leuca. The campsite has its own shuttle bus. The pitches are comfortable with plenty of shade and electricity. 3 bath houses with hot showers and motorhome service. The 2 swimming pools and sports field are central. Bar, restaurant, shop open from end of May to mid September.

From S. Maria di Leuca follow the Litoranea till past Gagliano del Capo. Well marked by signs.

CC €17 *1/1-15/7 1/9-31/12*

N 39°49'28'' E 18°22'7''

Gallipoli, I-73014 / Puglia

3093

Baia di Gallipoli Camping Resort****
S.P. 215 km 0,100
+39 0833-273210
FAX +39 0833-275405
1/4 - 15/9
@ info@baiadigallipoli.com

11ha 600T(40-120m²) 6A CEE

1 ABCD**G**HIJKLMN**P**S
2 AGKORSY
3 ABGHJK**M**N**O**RUW
4 (A+B 1/5-30/9) (Q) (R 1/4-1/6) (S 1/6-31/8) (T+U+V+W+Y) Z
5 **AB**FGIJKLMNOPUV
6 EG**K**(N 4km)QTV

A quiet, rural campsite with large shaded pitches set on a hill. When staying for 7 or more nights you will receive a regional product as a gift.

From the south take the SS101 Lecce-Gallipoli. Keep left before Gallipoli on the SS274 to S. Maria di Leuca. Lido Pizzo exit about 2 km further on. After about 5 km turn left at end of road. Campsite on the left.

CC €17 *1/4-24/6 29/8-15/9*

N 39°59'54'' E 18°1'34''

Manfredonia, I-71043 / Puglia

3094

Lido Salpi
SS159, km 6,2
+39 0884-571160
1/1 - 31/12
@ lidosalpi@alice.it

1ha 52T(50-70m²) 6A CEE

1 ABCGHIJKLMPRS
2 AEGKTVY
3 ABGRUWY
4 (Q+R+T+V+X+Z)
5 **A**GHIJKMNO**P**UVYZ
6 CDEGIK(N 7km)ORTV

Campsite is open all year and is located on a sandy beach. Ideal for long beach walks and right by the sea. There are new toilet facilities and limited provisions are always available. A good bar with delicious food. Excursions to Gargano, S. Giovanni Rotondo, Foresto Umbra, Monte S. Angelo, Vieste. An ideal stopover site from the A14.

A14, exit Foggia, direction Monfredonia. SS89 exit Monfredonia Sud. Southwards on the SS159 to the campsite sign on the left.

CC € 13 1/1-15/7 1/9-31/12 7=6

N 41°33'18'' E 15°53'45''

Peschici (FG), I-71010 / Puglia

3095

Cp. Internazionale Manacore****
Lit. Pes.-Vieste
+39 0884-911020
FAX +39 0884-911049
7/5 - 23/9
@ manacore@grupposaccia.it

22ha 700T(40-60m²) 3A CEE

1 ABC**G**HIJKLMN**P**RS
2 AEGJKRSVY
3 BGK**M**NRWY
4 (B 16/5-26/9)
(Q+S+T+U+V+W+X+Y+Z)
5 **A**GIJKLMNOPUVZ
6 CFG**I**M(N 10km)OQT

This site is a village by itself. Right by the sea and with a lovely swimming pool. This is a good area for surfing and snorkelling. A beautiful coastline near Gargano and just 10 minutes from Peschici. Excursions possible to Monte S. Angelo, Padre Pio and Foresta Umbra. XL pitch by the sea for a supplement

A14, exit Poggio Imperiale, SS89 direction Vieste as far as Peschici. Then take coast road towards Vieste (Litoranea) as far as service station. Then onto campsite road.

CC € 19 7/5-25/6 20/8-23/9

N 41°56'14'' E 16°4'12''

Peschici (FG), I-71010 / Puglia

3096

Parco Degli Ulivi***
Baia di Peschici-Gargano
+39 0884-962299
13/5 - 30/9
@ contatti@parcodegliulivi.it

16ha 300T(50-90m²) 5A

1 ABFHIJKLMN**P**RS
2 AEGKQRY
3 AGK**M**NRWY
4 (A 1/6-13/9)
(B+G 21/5-13/9) J(Q+S)
(T+U+V+Y 1/6-8/9) (Z)
5 **A**GIKMOPUVZ
6 CEG**J**(N 1,5km)OQRT

The 'Park of Olives' is near the bay in the picturesque village of Peschici, 150m from the sea, surrounded by olive groves and forests. Not far from the marina, private beach, 140,000 m² and well equipped for a good holiday. The sports and leisure facilities: swimming pool, tennis, volleyball, children's playground, bowling, disco and entertainment with shows and games.

A14, exit Poggio Imperiale, SS89 direction Vieste as far as Peschici. Then follow camping signs.

CC € 13 13/5-30/6 27/8-30/9 7=6

N 41°56'35'' E 16°0'23''

Specchiolla di Carovigno, I-72012 / Puglia

3097

Pineta al Mare***
Via di Tamerici
+39 0831-987803
FAX +39 0831-994057
6/5 - 25/9
info@campingpinetamare.com

5,5ha 135T(49-80m²) 3A CEE

1 ABCDFIJKLMNPRS
2 ABEGLORVY
3 ABJKNRUWY
4 (B 1/5-20/9) (G) JKP (Q+S+T+U) (V 1/5-15/9) (Y) Z
5 AEGIKMOPUV
6 CEGIJORTV

Family campsite located by the sea and within walking distance of Specchiolla. Shaded, marked out pitches. Separate section specially equipped for motorhomes. Free WiFi, also for CampingCard ACSI holders.

On the SS379 coast road take at km-marker 32.5 the exit to Specchiolla. Follow the camping signs.

CC € 19 6/5-15/7 1/9-25/9

N 40°44'27'' E 17°44'10''

Torre dell'Orso, I-73026 / Puglia

3098

Sentinella***
Via degli Eucaliptus
+39 0832-842030
FAX +39 0832-842235
1/4 - 15/10
info@campeggiosentinella.it

5ha 160T(60-80m²) 6A

1 ABCDFJKLMNOPR
2 ABGTY
3 AJKMNRW
4 (B 1/6-15/9) (Q+R 15/6-15/9) (U+V+Y 1/6-15/9) Z
5 ABGIKMNOPSUVY
6 AEGIJ(N 0,5km)OTWX

Almost in the centre of the village so it is enjoyable to go out in the evening.

From the north: SS16 direction Otranto/Maglie. Tangenziale Est di Lecce, exit 7b. On the SP364 turn right after 7.2 km onto SP366. Follow signs.

CC € 17 1/4-7/7 1/9-15/10

N 40°16'22'' E 18°25'6''

Vieste del Gargano, I-71019 / Puglia

3099

Baia e Cala Campi***
Litoranea Vieste-Mattinata, km 11
+39 0884-700000
FAX +39 0884-700003
1/4 - 30/9
info@baiadicampi.it

11ha 416T(80-100m²) 16A CEE

1 ABCFHIJKLMPQ
2 EGKNTY
3 BMRW
4 (Q+S 10/5-20/9) (V+Y 24/5-30/9) (Z)
5 ABGIKMPUVZ
6 EGJ(N 11km)RTV

Village Baia di Campi is a perfect destination for campers who want to spend their holiday in contact with nature. The pitches are positioned among the dense vegetation of Aleppo pine trees and olive trees, guaranteeing coolness and shade. Free WiFi in early season.

Exit Poggio Imperiale A14, then main road to Vico del Gargano. Then towards Rodi Garganico, Peschici, Vieste. From Vieste follow coast road south for about 10 km.

CC € 17 1/4-30/6 21/8-30/9

N 41°48'53'' E 16°11'24''

Vieste del Gargano, I-71019 / Puglia

iD **3100**

Vill. Baia degli Aranci***
Lungomare Europa 48
+39 0884-706591
FAX +39 0884-705064
22/4 - 16/10
info@baiadegliaranci.it

11ha 400T(30-40m²) 6A CEE

1 ABEHIJKLMNPRS
2 AEGJKRTVXY
3 BGNRU**V**WY
4 (B+G 1/5-22/10) P
(Q+S 15/5-10/10)
(T+U 20/5-14/10)
(V 1/6-15/9) (Y+Z)
5 **A**GIJKMOPUVZ
6 CFGIJ(N 0,7km)ORTV

A camping village with hotels, within walking distance of the town of Vieste. Situated by the beach, accessible through an underpass, views of Vieste, the rocky coast, the beach and the yacht harbour from the higher pitches on the site.

A14, exit Poggio Imperiale, SS89 direction Vieste inner road. Go as far as Vieste, there turn left and drive to the coast road. Campsite located on the road before the village.

CC € 17 *22/4-9/7 1/9-16/10*

N 41°53'13" E 16°9'59"

Vieste del Gargano (Fg), I-71019 / Puglia

iD **3101**

Camping Village
Molinella Vacanze***
Località Molinella nr. 72
+39 0884-707530
FAX +39 0884-704399
1/4 - 30/10
info@molinellavacanze.com

2ha 100T(30-60m²) 6A CEE

1 ABCGIJKLMNPQ
2 AEJKQSVX
3 AGKRUVWY
4 (Q+R+S+T+V+X+Z)
5 **A**GIJKLMNOPUVZ
6 ACDEG**IJK**(N 3km)OQRST
VW

Ideal for a relaxing holiday, perfect for excursions. Right by the sea, 3 km from Vieste. Bar, restaurant and pizzeria on the beach. Shuttle bus (free) to Vieste from 15/5-15/9. 1 parasol + 2 deckchairs free from 14/5-18/6 and 28/8-25/9. Free WiFi and bicycles at bar.

A14 exit Poggio Imperiale, SS89 dir. Vieste. Side road after Peschici (not Littoranea) past Foresta Umbra exit, 1st road left, right at T-junction as far as traffic lights, then left, see signs.

CC € 17 *1/4-25/6 28/8-30/10*

N 41°54'28" E 16°9'2"

Cirò Marina, I-88811 / Calabria

iD **3102**

Punta Alice***
Via Punta Alice
+39 0962-31160
FAX +39 0962-373823
1/1 - 31/12
info@puntalice.it

5,5ha 280T 6A CEE

1 ABC**F**HIJKLM**P**RS
2 AENSTVY
3 BK**M**NRUWY
4 (B 30/5-15/9)
(**G** 20/5-30/9) P(Q)
(R 20/6-15/9) (T 1/4-30/9)
(U+V+W+Y 1/6-30/9) Z
5 **AB**GIJKLMNO**P**UVXYZ
6 CDEG**IK**ORTV

There is plenty of opportunity to enjoy the beautiful surroundings among the vineyards of the famous 'Ciro' wines. The campsite is right by the sea. The beach has Blue Flag status. You will find a real mediterranean ambiance on the site.

From the SS106, at the Ciro Marma exit km-marker 279 enter the town below on the left. From the north at km-marker 280 right. Then follow signs.

CC € 13 *1/1-30/6 13/9-31/12*

N 39°23'6" E 17°8'34"

Corigliano/Calabro, I-87060 / Calabria

3103

Thurium****
Contrada Ricota Grande
+39 0983-851101
1/1 - 31/12
info@campingthurium.com

10ha 500T(60-80m²) 6A CEE

1 ABC**F**HIJKLM**P**
2 AERSY
3 AB**F**GJKMNRUWY
4 (A 1/6-15/9)
(**B**+G 1/6-30/9)
(S+T+U+V+W+Y 1/5-10/10)
Z
5 **AB**DEFGIJKLMNO**P**UV
6 CEG**IJ**(N 7km)ORTV

A beautiful, well-kept campsite located in the middle of countryside. Peace and privacy on spacious pitches. The Calabria region offers many opportunities for trips out. Visit the mountains of Sila and Pollino or historical cities such as Corigliano, Rossano or Altomonte. Extensive sports facilities and an attractive swimming pool on the campsite.

Turn off the SS106-Bis coast road towards the sea at 21 km post. Campsite then signposted.

CC € 15 *1/3-15/7 1/9-30/11 7=6*

N 39°41'29'' E 16°31'20''

Cropani Marina, I-88050 / Calabria

3104

Camping Case Vacanza
Lungomare***
Viale Venezia 40
+39 0961-961167
+39 0961-961600
20/3 - 31/10
info@campinglungomare.com

2,1ha 100T(20-42m²) 6A CEE

1 ABC**F**HIJKLMN**P**RS
2 AEUVXY
3 BNY
4 (T+U+V+W+Y 1/7-15/9) Z
5 **A**IKMOPUV
6 EGK(N 0,5km)TV

A family campsite with modest but attractive facilities right in the village.

From Catanzaro coast road SS106 to the north direction Crotone. Follow signs in Cropani Marina village.

CC € 15 *20/3-15/7 1/9-31/10*

N 38°54'32'' E 16°48'34''

Marina di Nicotera, I-89844 / Calabria

3105

Maris Villaggio Camping***
Località Mortelletto
+39 0963-887834
20/4 - 30/9
info@mariscalabria.it

45T(60-120m²) 10A CEE

1 ABCDGIJKLMNOPRS
2 AEFKTUXY
3 ABGKM**OP**RWY
4 (B 1/6-30/9) (G) P
(Q+R+T+X) Z
5 **A**GIKMO**PST**UV
6 EGJ(N 2,5km)OTV

Quiet campsite, located by a beautiful sandy beach, with spacious pitches. Very many amenities and a beautiful pool.

A3 Salerno-Reggio Calabria. Exit Rosarno dir. San Ferdinando Porto. On SP50 follow campsite signs for ± another 7 km.

CC € 17 *20/4-15/7 1/9-30/9*

N 38°30'37'' E 15°55'22''

Marina di Nicotera, I-89844 / Calabria

3106

Villaggio Camping Mimosa***
Loc. Mortelletto
+39 0963-81397
FAX +39 0963-81933
1/1 - 31/12
@ info@villaggiomimosa.com

3ha 50T 12A CEE

1 ABCGHIJKLMNO**P**RS
2 AEFLRTUXY
3 B**F**GJKN**O**RWY
4 (B+G 15/4-20/10) (Q)
(R+U 15/4-20/10)
(V 15/4-15/9)
(Y 15/4-20/10) Z
5 **A**GHIKMOPR**ST**VXZ
6 CEG**I**K(N 2km)ORTWX

Right by the sea with a long beach of white sand. An oasis of peace surrounded by a lovely pine forest. Market, pizzeria, bar-restaurant, swimming pool, tennis, horse riding. Excursions directly from Tropea (15/3-15/10) and Nicotera (1/7-30/8) to the Aeolian Islands.

A3 Salerno-Reggio Calabria, exit Rosarno direction San Ferdinando Porto. Follow camping signs on the SP50. Another ±7 km.

CC €17 *1/1-15/7 1/9-31/12*

N 38°30'27'' E 15°55'36''

Marina di Zambrone, I-89868 / Calabria

3107

Villaggio Camping Sambalon****
SS 522 per Tropea
+39 0963-392828
FAX +39 0963-392836
20/5 - 23/9
@ info@sambalon.com

1,5ha 110T(35-80m²) 6A

1 ACD**F**HIJKLM**P**RS
2 AEGKTUVY
3 ABGR**WY**
4 (Q+R 1/7-30/8)
(T+U+V+W+X+Y 20/6-30/8)
5 AGIJKLMNOPQRSTUVXYZ
6 DEGIJ(N 4km)ORT

A large, hospitable campsite in fantastic surroundings located on the so-called 'coast of the gods', the Tyrrhenian Sea. The sea really is blue here. Culinary delights at affordable prices. Lovely trips out to the nearby Tropea and Capo Vaticano.

Coming from the north A3 Salerno-Reggio Calabria exit Pizzo Calabro, then to the SS522 direction Tropea. Exit Zambrone Marina (± 20 km). Follow camping signs.

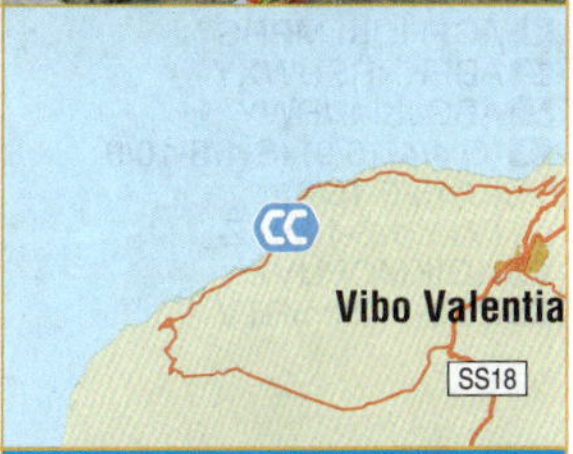

CC €17 *20/5-15/7 1/9-23/9*

N 38°42'23'' E 15°58'12''

Praia a Mare, I-87028 / Calabria

3108

International Camping Village***
Lungomare F. Sirimarco
FAX +39 0985-72211
1/5 - 26/9
@ reception@campinginternational.it

5,7ha 360T(30-45m²) 4A CEE

1 ACGHIJKLMNQ
2 EKNQRTVY
3 ABGMNRWY
4 (G 1/7-20/9)
(Q+S+U+V+Y 1/5-21/9)
(Z)
5 **A**GIKMOPUVZ
6 CDEGJ(N 0,5km)OT

A campsite for the camper in search of a Mediterranean atmosphere and 100% chance of sun, sea and beach. For the culinary traveler ristorante 'L'Isola' on this campsite is a must!

In Praia a Mare follow signs to 'Lungomare'. Campsite located on the Isola di Dino.

CC €11 *1/5-3/7 29/8-26/9 7=6, 14=11*

N 39°52'55'' E 15°47'8''

Praia a Mare, I-87028 / Calabria

3109

La Mantinera****
C. da Mantinera
+39 0985-779023
FAX +39 0985-779009
22/4 - 30/9
@ lamantinera@tiscali.it

12ha 350**T**(30-50m²) 3A CEE

1 ACFHIJKLMPQ
2 EGLNRTVY
3 ABGK**M**NU**W**Y
4 (**A**+**B**+**G**+Q) (S 1/6-15/9) (T+U+V 15/6-15/9) (W+Y+Z)
5 **AB**GIKMNOPUVXZ
6 CEGJ(N 2km)ORTV

Beautifully landscaped campsite with a luxurious reception and plenty of facilities. Swimming pool on the site, free until 27 June and from 29 August. The beach is 300 metres away by an azure blue sea and will make your stay complete.

Take the Praia a Mare exit on the SS18 and then follow the camping signs. The campsite is located just south of Praia a Mare.

CC € 15 22/4-30/6 1/9-30/9 7=6

N 39°52'36'' E 15°47'19''

Sibari/Cosenza, I-87011 / Calabria

3110

Camping-Village Pineta di Sibari***
Contrada Fuscolara
FAX +39 0981-74135
25/3 - 25/9
@ info@pinetadisibari.it

17ha 500**T**(100-120m²) 5A CEE

1 AC**F**HIJKLMPRS
2 ABEKNRSUWXY
3 ABGJKMNRWY
4 (Q 4/4-15/9) (S 1/6-10/9) (U 15/5-15/9) (V+Y 1/6-10/9) Z
5 **A**GIKMOPUVZ
6 EG**J**(N 2km)RTV

A large and very peaceful campsite by the sea. Tall pine trees provide shaded pitches.

Coast road SS106 dir.Reggio di C. Villapiana Scalo exit. Right in village dir. Sibari. Past village cross over the railway. Left at sign. Dirt road. Keep right. Follow camping signs. Beware 2.7m high tunnel. Use other entrance over railway track ±300m towards village.

CC € 17 25/3-15/7 1/9-25/9 7=6

N 39°46'47'' E 16°28'46''

Tropea, I-89861 / Calabria

3111

Marina del Convento**
Via Marina del Convento
FAX +39 0963-62501
10/5 - 15/10
@ info@marinadelconvento.it

1,3ha 130**T**(36m²) 6A CEE

1 AFIJKLMN**P**Q
2 EGKNQRVXY
3 AH**W**
4 (Q+R 15/6-30/9) (T 1/8-31/8) (U 1/6-1/9) Z
5 **A**GIKMO**P**UVZ
6 EGKTV

A campsite located at the foot of a rocky cliff with the old town of Tropea at the top. The tourist village looks out over a lovely white sandy beach and a calm, clear sea.

A3 exit Pizzo Calabro. SS522 direction Tropea. Follow Beach/Porto (harbour) signs. Avoid centre coming from south. After Tropea follow Porto signs. Then follow camping signs.

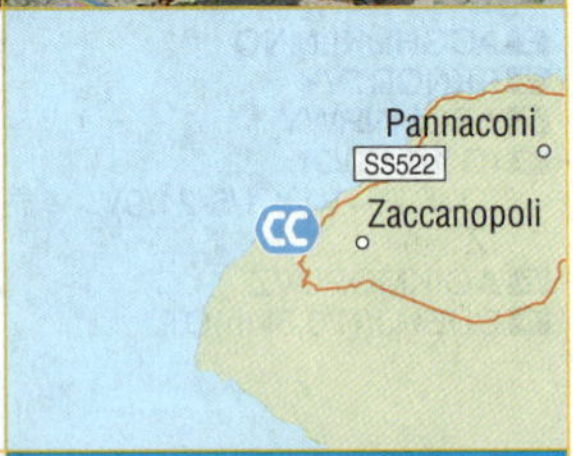

CC € 17 10/5-30/6 1/9-10/10

N 38°40'30'' E 15°53'23''

Aglientu, I-07020 / Sardegna

3112

Camping Village Baia Blu La Tortuga****
Pineta di Vignola Mare
+39 079-602060
FAX +39 079-602040
21/4 - 3/10
@ info@campinglatortuga.com

17ha 700T(40-120m²) 3A CEE

1 ACD**F**HIJKLMOPST
2 ABEGJRSTVWXY
3 BGK**M**NRUVWY
4 (Q+S+T+U+V+W+Y+Z)
5 **AB**EFGIJKLMNOP**ST**UVXZ
6 CDEG**IJ**M(N 9km)ORTVWX

Extensive campsite mostly located in pine forests with plenty of shade. Close to the sea and with a private beach. The spacious pitches are marked out by small trees. First class comfort. Numerous water sports opportunities.

SP90 at exit to Aglientu and Vignola Mare. Entrance to the campsite direction Vignola Mare.

CC € 19 21/4-29/6 1/9-2/10

N 41°7'28'' E 9°4'3''

Alghero, I-07041 / Sardegna

3113

Camping Village Laguna Blu (Calik)****
SS 127 bis km 41 Fertilia
+39 079-930111
FAX +39 079-930595
24/3 - 6/11
@ info@campinglagunablu.com

11ha 450T 10A CEE

1 ABCDGIJKLMO**P**Q
2 ABDEGKRSUVWXY
3 B**E**JKNRUWY
4 (Q+U+V+W+Y+Z)
5 **AB**CEFGIJKLMNOPUXYZ
6 ACEG**K**(N 0,5km)ORSTUV WX

A large open campsite offering all amenities. One section is in pine woods and one section is open. Modern toilet facilities. 20 metres from the sea.

From Alghero direction Fertilia on the SS127bis at km 41 marker.

CC € 17 24/3-29/6 1/9-5/11

N 40°35'41'' E 8°17'29''

Alghero, I-07041 / Sardegna

3114

La Mariposa***
Via Lido 22
+39 079-950480
FAX +39 079-984489
1/5 - 30/9
@ info@lamariposa.it

4ha 256T(80-90m²) 6A CEE

1 ABCDFIJKLMNOP
2 AEGIRSTVXY
3 KUWY
4 (A 15/7-31/8) (Q+S) (T 15/7-31/8) (V 1/6-30/9) (W 1/8-31/8) Z
5 AGIKMO**P**UW
6 CEG**IJ**(N 1,5km)OQRTV

A campsite located in a slightly hilly area with fields for tents. There are flat, open pitches for caravans and campers. Some of them are located in the shadow of the trees, others lie in the sun on the beach. You will find the toilets in a pleasant square. There are a lot of possibilities to practice water sports. Old excavations and Alghero are worth visiting.

The campsite is located on the seaward side of the road Alghero Centro-Fertilia. Follow the signs.

CC € 19 1/5-30/6 1/9-30/9

N 40°34'46'' E 8°18'45''

Cannigione di Arzachena, I-07021 / Sardegna

3115

Centro Vacanze Isuledda****
Loc. Isuledda
+39 0789-86003
FAX +39 0789-86089
17/3 - 6/11
info@isuledda.it

15ha 650T(25-90m²) 4A CEE

1 BCDEHIJKLMNO**P**Q
2 AEGIJKLMNOQSTUVXY
3 ABKNRU**V**WY
4 (Q 26/3-30/11)
(S+T+U+V+W+Y+Z)
5 **AB**GIJKLMNOPUV
6 EG**IJ**M(N 2km)OQRTV

A beautiful campsite (15 hectares) on a bay with a private beach. Shaded pitches on gently sloping grounds. Restaurant, bar, shop, diving and sailing school and many watersports opportunities. Boat trips to La Maddalena Archipelago. Archaeological sights in the neighbourhood. A visit to Porto Cervo is most fascinating.

Route 125 from Olbia to Paula-Arzachena for 20 km, continue towards Cannigione. The campsite is located about 3 km past Cannigione.

CC € 19 *17/3-11/5 30/5-23/6 4/9-5/11*

N 41°7'54'' E 9°26'26''

Cuglieri, I-09073 / Sardegna

3116

Camping Village Bella Sardinia***
Torre del Pozzo
+39 0785-38058
FAX +39 0785-389218
22/4 - 3/10
info@camping-bellasardinia.it

33ha 275T(40-100m²) 6A CEE

1 ABCDFIJKLMO**P**
2 ABEGRSY
3 AB**F**GMNQRUWY
4 (A 1/5-30/9) (B 23/4-5/10)
(G+Q+S+V+W+Y+Z)
5 **AB**EFGIJKLMNOPUZ
6 ACEG**I**J(N 7km)OTV

A very large campsite on sloping grounds, sufficiently shaded. Several sunny pitches. Free choice on unmarked pitches. Wide sandy beach and watersports opportunities. There is a bar/restaurant with a large terrace and a swimming pool. A visit to the excavations is highly recommended.

Route 292 between Cuglieri and Riola Sardo. Campsite signposted at exit post 109. Follow Bella Sardinia.

CC € 17 *22/4-3/7 20/8-2/10 7=6*

N 40°4'15'' E 8°29'40''

Palau, I-07020 / Sardegna

3117

Capo d'Orso***
Loc. Le Saline
+39 0789-702007
FAX +39 0789-702006
21/4 - 26/9
info@capodorso.it

13ha 450T(40-80m²) 3A CEE

1 ABCDFHIJKLMNOPQ
2 AEGJKOSTVXY
3 ABMNUWY
4 (A 1/7-31/8) (Q)
(S 15/5-15/9) (T)
(U 15/7-20/8) (V 30/5-15/9)
(W 15/7-20/8) (X 20/5-25/9)
(Y+Z)
5 **A**GIKMOPUV
6 CEGHJ(N 5km)ORT

A big campsite with a series of partially shaded terraces by the sea with a private beach. Ideal for practicing or taking various water sports lessons (surfing, diving). The facilities on the site are luxurious. Palau and the Maddalena Archipelago are well worth visiting. Only small dogs allowed.

From Sta Teresa follow the panoramic road around Palau (is indicated!). From Cannigione follow Palau, site is signposted on the roundabout.

CC € 17 *21/4-29/6 1/9-25/9*

N 41°9'41'' E 9°24'10''

Piscina Rei/Costa Rei, I-09043 / Sardegna

iD 3118

Le Dune***
☎ +39 070-9919057
FAX +39 070-991110
22/4 - 3/10
@ info@campingledune.it

6ha 180T(80m²) 3A CEE

1 ABCD**F**HIJKLMNO**PQ**
2 AEGRSUVWXY
3 BHK**M**N**O**UW**Y**
4 (**A** 15/6-30/9)
(**B** 24/4-30/9) (**G** ⊶)
(Q 18/4-30/9)
(S+T+U+V+W+Y ⊶) Z
5 **A**GIKMNOPUZ
6 CDEGHJ(N 2km)RTVW

A level campsite with pitches marked out by poplar and plane trees. A footpath leading through a lagoon with water birds takes you to the beach.

New road SS125var direction Muravera/ Villasimius/Costa Rei, dir. Costa Rei (see brown sign). Follow signs to Le Dune.

CC € 17 *22/4-30/6 1/9-3/10*

N 39°16'36'' E 9°34'56''

Porto San Paolo, I-07020 / Sardegna

iD 3119

Tavolara***
Soc. Ariel S.r.l. SS125 km 300
☎ +39 0789-40166
FAX +39 0789-480778
1/5 - 15/10
@ info@camping-tavolara.it

5ha 260T(9-60m²) 10A CEE

1 ABCD**G**HIJKLMNOPS
2 AEIKLORSTUVWXY
3 AB**M**NRW
4 (**A**+Q ⊶) (S 15/5-15/9)
(T+U 1/5-15/9)
(V 15/5-15/9) (Y 1/5-15/9)
(Z ⊶)
5 **A**GIJKMOPUVW
6 ACDEGJ(N 2km)ORTVWX

A natural campsite, particularly in spring with many flowers and birds. Enclosed pitches with excellent views provided by many bushes and flowers. The beach with its views of the Tavolara rock is highly recommended. A 500 metre walk.

Located on the SS125 close to 300 km-marker.

CC € 19 *1/5-13/7 30/8-15/10*

N 40°51'33'' E 9°38'34''

Pula, I-09010 / Sardegna

iD 3120

Flumendosa
Flumendosa 12
☎ +39 070-4615332
FAX +39 0707731551
1/1 - 31/12
@ info@campingflumendosa.com

NEW

6ha 136T(40-60m²) 8A CEE

1 ABCDFHIJKLMO**P**R
2 ABEGLSTWXY
3 BGHJKVWY
4 (**A**+B+G+Q+R+T+U+V+
X+Z ⊶)
5 **A**GIJKLMNOPUZ
6 ABCEGJ**K**(N 3km)OT

On the beach of Santa Margherita di Pula, a short distance from Chia, 5 minutes from the Phoenician town of Nora and only 30 km from Cagliari. Campsite Flumendosa is surrounded by unspoilt nature and the typical smells and colours of the Mediterranean Sea. An oasis of peace and relaxation. Enjoy the crystal clear sea a few metres from the campsite. All necessary amenities.

Campsite clearly signposted on the SS195, km-marker 33,8.

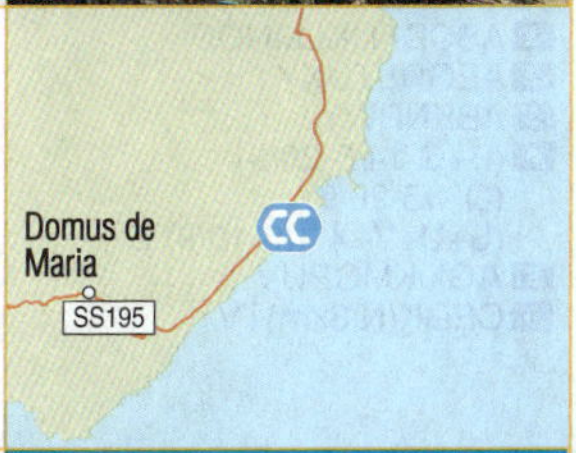

CC € 17 *1/1-30/6 1/9-31/12*

N 38°58'4'' E 8°58'41''

Santa Lucia/Siniscola, I-08020 / Sardegna

3121

Selema Camping***
Thiria Soliana
+39 0784-819068
1/4 - 15/10
@ info@selemacamping.com

7,5ha 350T(30-120m²) 6A CEE

1 ABCDGHIJKLMNO**PQ**
2 ABCEGJKOSUY
3 ABK**M**NRWY
4 (B+G 15/6-15/10) **KP**
(Q+R+T+U+V 15/5-15/10)
(X 15/5-10/10) (Z)
5 **A**FGIJKMNOPUVWZ
6 ADEGIJ(N 0,3km)OTVWX

A large campsite, partly level, partly sloping, partly terraced, in a pine forest by the sea. There are even trees halfway down the beach! The pitches are numbered. The campsite offers every comfort. There is a small village within walking distance. The sandy beach is ideal for families with (small) children.

From the SS125 take the S. Lucia exit at the 252 VIII km marker. Campsite signposted.

CC € 19 *1/4-30/6 1/9-15/10*

N 40°34'43'' E 9°46'23''

Torre Grande, I-09170 / Sardegna

3122

Spinnaker****
Strada per il Pontile
+39 0783-22074
FAX +39 0783-22071
14/5 - 2/10
@ info@spinnakervacanze.com

3,5ha 120T(40-90m²) 6A CEE

1 ABCD**G**HIJLMNO**P**
2 ABEGISTVY
3 ABGNQRWY
4 (B+G+Q+S+U+V+Y+Z)
5 **A**EGIKMNOPUZ
6 ABCDEG**IJ**(N 1,5km)OTV

A campsite beneath the pine trees with pitches partly marked out by tree trunks. Slightly sloping grounds near the sea with a sandy beach (± 150 metres away). Centrally located swimming pool with adjacent restaurant, bar and market. A visit to the excavations and to the bird sanctuary are highly recommended.

SS131, exit Oristano N. Follow Tharros (brown sign on the big blue one). Then follow signs to Torre Grande. The campsite is signposted before Torre Grande.

CC € 19 *15/5-30/6 1/9-30/9*

N 39°54'14'' E 8°31'51''

Tortolì/Arbatax, I-08048 / Sardegna

3123

Camping Village Orrì***
Loc. Orrì
+39 0782-624695
FAX +39 0782-624685
1/5 - 30/9
@ orricamping@tiscali.it

3ha 100T(80m²) 4A CEE

1 ABCDFIJKLMNOP
2 AEGRSTUXY
3 ABKNRWY
4 (B+G 14/5-20/9)
(Q 1/5-20/9)
(S+U+V+X 1/6-10/9) Z
5 **A**GIJKMOPUV
6 CEGK(N 3km)TV

The campsite is located 4 km from Arbatax harbour on the east coast of Sardinia on a large sandy beach, right next to the crystal clear sea. The campsite has a bar, mini-market, restaurant, pizzeria and swimming pool.

SS125 exit Tortolì/Lido di Orri; take Lido di Orri (turn right after 500 metres); follow the camping signs.

CC € 17 *1/5-30/6 1/9-30/9*

N 39°54'24'' E 9°40'52''

Tortolì/Arbatax, I-08048 / Sardegna

3124

Cigno Bianco***
Loc. Orri
+39 0782-624927
FAX +39 0782-624565
16/4 - 16/10
info@cignobianco.it

4ha 100**T**(60-80m²) 6A CEE

1 ABCDFIJKLMOP
2 AEGSTUVWXY
3 ABK**M**RUWY
4 (Q+S+T+U 1/5-30/9) (V+Y 1/6-30/9) Z
5 **A**GIKMOPUVZ
6 CEGJ(N 3km)OQRTV

A rectangular level campsite 300 metres long and 80 metres wide, shaded by tall trees with numbered but unmarked pitches. Washing facilities are centrally located. The site is right by the sea with a lovely sandy beach.

SS125 exit Tortolì/Lido di Orri; Follow Lido di Orri (right after 500 metres); follow camping signs.

CC € 15 *16/4-30/6 1/9-16/10* N 39°54'28'' E 9°40'45''

Tortolì/Arbatax, I-08048 / Sardegna

3125

Villaggio Camping Sos Flores s.r.l.***
San Gemiliano
+39 0782-667485
FAX +39 0782-624627
15/4 - 30/10
sosflores@tiscali.it

5ha 170**T**(40-100m²) 5A CEE

1 ABCD**F**IJKLMNO**P**R
2 AEGRSTVXY
3 ABHJK**MNO**RUVWY
4 (Q 1/5-30/9) (R+T+U+V+X+Y 1/6-15/9) Z
5 **A**GIKMOPUV
6 CDEGHI**J**(N 2km)QTV

Idyllic natural campsite by the sea. Offers every comfort. Free choice of pitches. Located in the vicinity of Tortolì. A visit to the rocks at Arbatax is a must.

Follow the airport at Tortolì. Campsite indicated on this road.

CC € 17 *15/4-30/6 1/9-30/10* N 39°55'15'' E 9°41'33''

Valledoria/Sassari, I-07039 / Sardegna

3126

La Foce****
Via Ampurias 110
+39 079-582109
FAX +39 079-582191
25/4 - 30/9
info@foce.it

20ha 400**T**(100m²) 4A CEE

1 ABCDGIJKLMNO**P**S
2 ABCEGIKRSVY
3 BJK**MNOP**RWXY
4 (B+G+Q+S+T+U+V+Y+Z ⊶)
5 **AB**GIJKLMNOPUV
6 CEG**I**J(N 0,8km)RT

The campsite has spacious, free pitches. There are swimming pools, tennis and football pitches. Showers with hot water. There is a restaurant on site with a wide selection, a bar and a well-stocked supermarket. Also opportunities for kite surfing, windsurfing, kayaking, sailing and bird watching. Free ferry to the beach.

Campsite located on the coast road from Castelsardo to S. Teresa. Signposted in Valledoria.

CC € 17 *25/4-13/7 30/8-30/9* N 40°56'1'' E 8°49'1''

Acireale, I-95024 / Sicilia

3127 · iD

- ▲ La Timpa International Camping Acireale***
- Via Santa Maria La Scala 25
- ☎ +39 095-7648155
- FAX +39 095-7640049
- 1/1 - 31/12
- @ info@campinglatimpa.com

1,8ha 150T(41-80m²) 3A CEE

- **1** ABC**G**IJLRS
- **2** EFJKOQRTWXY
- **3** ARWY
- **4** (Q+V+Y) (Z 1/7-31/8)
- **5** **A**GIKMNOPUXYZ
- **6** CG**J**(N 1,1km)T

A lovely shaded campsite in terrace form, with citrus trees. Panoramic views of the Tyrrhenian Sea. Renovated catering. A lift takes you down to the bay. Trips out to Catania and Acireale are possible by public transport. Free WiFi if staying minimum 3 days. Payment by credit card is possible from 50 Euros. Basic toilet facilities.

A18, exit Acireale. SS114 km 80.3 in Santa Maria la Scala village. Campsite clearly signposted.

CC € 17 *1/1-10/7 18/9-31/12 7=6, 14=11, 30=22*

N 37°37'12'' E 15°10'23''

Avola, I-96012 / Sicilia

3128 · iD

- ▲ Paradiso del Mare
- c/da Gallina Fondolupo
- ☎ +39 347-8763305
- FAX +39 0931-561147
- 16/4 - 31/10
- @ camping@paradisodelmare.it

0,4ha 40T(60-100m²) 10A CEE

- **1** ABCDGHIJLQ
- **2** AEFNSXY
- **3** R**W**Y
- **4** (Q+T+U+V+Z)
- **5** **A**IKMO**P**UW
- **6** ABEGJ(N 3km)T

Quiet campsite close to a free-to-use, sandy beach. Managers Loes and Paolo have created a homely atmosphere. Beautiful nature (Avola gorge) and culture, you can admire e.g. Noto and Siracusa.

From E45 take exit Cassibile or Avola. Campsite is along the SS115 (side with sea) between both exits. Narrow entryway (350 metres) leads to campsite.

CC € 15 *16/4-26/6 12/9-31/10*

N 36°56'18'' E 15°10'39''

Avola, I-96012 / Sicilia

3129 · iD

- ▲ Sabbiadoro
- Via Chiusa di Carlo 45
- ☎ FAX +39 0931-822415
- 1/1 - 31/12
- @ info@campeggiosabbiadoro.it

2,2ha 150T 10A CEE

- **1** ABCGHIJKLNRS
- **2** AEFIJUY
- **3** WY
- **4** (Q+R) (T 1/5-30/9) (V 15/5-30/9) (X 1/5-30/9) (Z)
- **5** **A**GIKMNO**P**UVZ
- **6** CFG**IJ**(N 4km)T

A gem of a campsite, situated in a tropical botanical garden on a beautiful sandy bay. Ideal for a visit to Siracusa, Noto, Cava Grande. Modern toilet facilities. Access can be difficult for caravans and motorhomes because of the narrow road.

New E45/A18 autostrada Catania-Gela exit Avola. About 700m left on the SS115. 500m narrow access road.

CC € 17 *1/1-10/7 12/9-31/12*

N 36°56'11'' E 15°10'29''

Catania/Ognina, I-95126 / Sicilia

3130

Jonio***
Via Villini a Mare 2
+39 095-491139
FAX +39 095-492277
1/1 - 31/12
info@campingjonio.com

1,2ha 80T 6A CEE

1 ABCGIJKLNRS
2 EFGJKLOTWXY
3 BRU**WY**
4 (Q+R+T) (U 1/6-30/9) (V+X+Z)
5 **AB**GI**J**KMNOPU
6 ACEG**IK**(N 3km)ORTV

Beautifully located above the Ionian Sea. Wonderful swimming among the lava islands. Trips out to Catania, Etna, Syracuse and Taormina.

SS114 north of Catania, exit Ognina. From the Catania ring road, take exit Catania centro (San Gregorio) and then Catania Est. Campsite clearly signposted. On SatNav enter via Salvatare Quasimodo.

CC € 15 *1/1-15/7 1/9-31/12*

N 37°31'58" E 15°7'12"

Falconara/Sicula, I-92027 / Sicilia

3131

Eurocamping Due Rocche***
SS115 km 241,800
+39 0934-349006
FAX +39 0934-349007
1/1 - 31/12
duerocche@duerocche.it

2,8ha 50T(40-75m²) 3A CEE

1 ABCGHIJKLMNRS
2 AEOWXY
3 ABGNRUWY
4 (Q+R) (T+U 1/7-31/8) (V+Y 1/6-31/8) (Z)
5 **A**GIJKMNOPUV
6 AEG**K**(N 8km)ORTV

A campsite by the sea with its own sandy beach. It has many loyal Italian guests who create a lively Sicilian atmosphere. The toilet facilities are outdated but well maintained. Trips out to Agrigento (60 km) and Piazza Armerina (50 km) possible.

SS115 Gela direction Agrigento. The campsite is signposted with a large yellow sign on the SS115 at the km-marker 241.8.

CC € 17 *1/1-15/7 1/9-31/12*

N 37°6'35" E 14°2'19"

Finale di Pollina, I-90010 / Sicilia

3132

Camping & Village Rais Gerbi***
SS113 km 172,9
+39 0921-426570
FAX +39 0921-426577
1/1 - 31/12
camping@raisgerbi.it

4,2ha 216T(60-80m²) 6A CEE

1 ABCGHIJKLMO**P**Q
2 EFGJKLNOQTUVY
3 AB**MNO**RUWY
4 (B 1/4-30/10) (Q+S 15/5-30/9) (U+V+Y) Z
5 **A**GIKMNOPUZ
6 ACDFG**I**K(N 0,7km)OQRTV

Ideally equipped for receiving groups. Lovely free swimming pool with unique sea views. Various day trips possible. Very comfortable toilet facilities. Free WiFi throughout the campsite.

A20 direction Messina, exit Tusa, SS113. Turn left towards Palermo. Coming from Palermo exit Castelbuono/Pollina direction SS113 (on the sea) then turn right. Campsite on the SS113 at 172,9 km-marker.

CC € 19 *1/1-23/3 29/3-20/4 2/5-1/6 6/6-14/7 1/9-31/12*

N 38°1'22" E 14°9'14"

Fondachello/Mascali, I-95016 / Sicilia

3133

Mokambo**
Via Spiaggia 211
+39 095-938731
FAX +39 095-7799243
1/4 - 30/9
@ mokambo@camping.it

2,8ha 180T(40-75m²) 3A CEE

1 ABCGHIJKLMNORS
2 EFGKNRSVWXY
3 BNRUWY
4 (Q+R) (T+U 1/7-31/8) (V+Y+Z)
5 **A**GIKMO**P**UV
6 ACEG**K**(N 1km)ORTV

An attractive unpretentious campsite right by the sea with WiFi zone. Lovely pebble beach. Unique views of Etna. Good bar, restaurant and pizzeria. The campsite is located on the coast road.

A18. Campsite by the sea between Giarre and Fiumefreddo exits. Via SS114 as far as Mascali then continue towards the sea.

CC € 17 *1/4-30/6 1/9-30/9 7=6*

N 37°44'58" E 15°12'27"

Isola delle Femmine, I-90040 / Sicilia

3134

La Playa**
Viale Marino 55
FAX +39 091-8677001
21/3 - 15/10
@ campinglaplaya@virgilio.it

2,2ha 80T(40-70m²) 6A CEE

1 ABGHIJKLMO**P**Q
2 AEFGKOSTVWXY
3 BWY
4 (Q 1/4-30/9) (R 1/4-15/9) (Z 1/4-30/9)
5 **AB**GIJKLMNO**P**UVZ
6 ACG**K**QRT

A shaded, medium sized campsite. Situated by the sea with well maintained toilet facilities. Some noise disturbance in the summer from the nearby disco. Extensive information available at the reception concerning visits to Palermo. Payment by credit card is not possible under 100 Euros. Better not to use SatNav if arriving by car.

A29, exit Isola delle Femmine. Better not use SatNav (too many one-way streets). Follow signs to campsite.

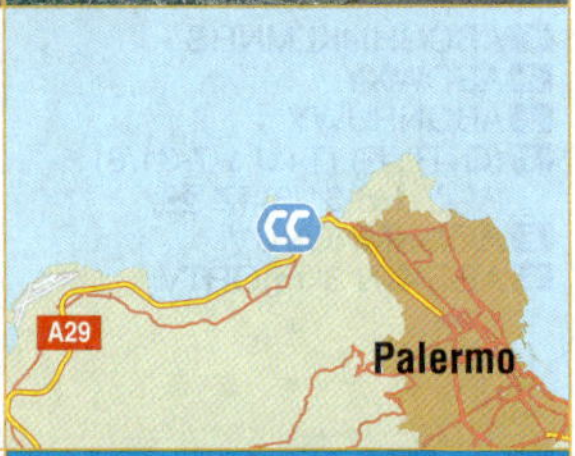

CC € 17 *21/3-30/6 1/9-15/10*

N 38°11'49" E 13°14'39"

Mazara del Vallo, I-91026 / Sicilia

3135

Sporting Club Village & Camping***
C. da Bocca Arena
+39 0923-947230
FAX +39 0923-909569
1/4 - 9/10
@ info@sportingclubvillage.com

60ha 300T(80-110m²) 6A CEE

1 ABC**G**HIJKLMORS
2 AEFGRWX
3 BKMNQRUWY
4 (B 1/4-30/9) (Q 1/7-1/9) (R 1/5-30/9) (T 1/6-15/9) (V+Y 1/4-30/9) (Z)
5 **A**GIKMNOPUVXZ
6 ACEGK(N 2km)ORTV

A large campsite with plenty of opportunities for sport. The site is located between a small river and a railway line. The two lovely swimming pools are located next to the excellent restaurant.

From Palermo: End of motorway A29, exit Mazara del Vallo. From Marsala: the SS115 becomes the A29 motorway. Take the Mazara exit where the roads change number. Campsite signposted after about 1 km.

CC € 17 *1/4-15/6 1/9-9/10 7=6, 14=11*

N 37°38'11" E 12°37'2"

Oliveri/Marinello, I-98060 / Sicilia

3136

Villaggio Marinello****
Località Marinello
+39 0941-313000
FAX +39 0941-313702
1/1 - 31/12
@ villaggiomarinello@gmail.com

3,2ha 250T(40-75m²) 6A CEE

1 ABCGHIJKLMNORS
2 AEFKSVY
3 ABGK**M**RWY
4 (Q+S 1/3-31/10) (T+U+V+Y+Z 20/3-15/9)
5 **A**GIKMNOPUW
6 ACEGIK(N 1km)OQRTV

Well run 4 star campsite with a pebble beach. Attractive marked out pitches among the trees. Sophisticated Sicilian gastronomy. Internet point and wireless internet available. Tyndaris and the Aeolian islands are close by.

A20, exit Falcone, then SS113 direction Palermo. Then follow the campsite signs and/or 'Laghetti Martinello'.

CC € 19 *1/1-10/7 1/9-31/12 7=6*

N 38°7'56'' E 15°3'16''

Punta Braccetto/S. Croce Cam., I-97017 / Sicilia

3137

Camping Luminoso***
Viale dei Canalotti
+39 0932-918401
FAX +39 0932-918455
1/1 - 31/12
@ info@campingluminoso.com

1,5ha 50T(< 65m²) 6A CEE

1 ABCDGIJKLMNOR
2 AEUVY
3 ABHKRUVWY
4 (Q+S+Z)
5 **AB**GIJKLMNOPUXZ
6 AEG**K**(N 5km)TUV

A campsite with private beach, fully renovated and reopened in 2009. Spacious and offering every comfort. Ideal for families and those seeking relaxation. Many sights in the area. Very attentive management. Free use of deckchairs and parasol on the beach.

Take the SS194 from Catania to Ragusa. Then take the SS514 to Ragusa. From Ragusa take exit towards S.Croce Camerina SP60. From S. Croce Camerina continue via the SP85 then SR25 to Punta Bracetto.

CC € 17 *1/1-15/7 1/9-31/12 7=6, 14=11*

N 36°49'2'' E 14°27'57''

Punta Braccetto/S. Croce Cam., I-97017 / Sicilia

3138

Scarabeo Camping**
Via dei Canalotti
+39 0932-918096
1/1 - 31/12
@ info@scarabeocamping.it

12ha 50T(50-70m²) 6A CEE

1 AB**G**HIJKLMNORS
2 AESUVY
3 ARUWY
4 (Q+R)
5 **AB**GIJKLMNO**P**STXYZ
6 ACEG**K**(N 3km)**P**QTUV

Small, well-kept quiet campsite with lots of flowers and greenery. Spacious, marked out pitches. Lovely sandy beach on the site. Private toilet facilities for every pitch. Atmospheric lighting. From 1 October to 31 March extra discounts with longer stays.

Coming from Comiso to Santa Croce. From there follow the signs 'Punta Braccetto' (4 km).

CC € 17 *1/1-8/7 1/9-31/12*

N 36°49'2'' E 14°28'2''

Punta Secca/Santa Croce Camer., I-97010 / Sicilia

iD **3139**

Capo Scalambri
Via Torre di Mezzo
+39 0932-915600
FAX +39 0932-616359
1/1 - 31/12
@ info@caposcalambri.com

5ha 150T(50-100m²) 6A CEE

1 ABGIJKLMOPRS
2 AESTUVY
3 BGKWY
4 (Q 1/6-31/8)
5 AGIKMOPUZ
6 CDEG(N 0,8km)T

This very modest campsite is set in natural surroundings. Free beach, shaded by trees. The site has limited and outdated toilet facilities. There is plenty of space and no noise.

From Comiso to Santa Croce Camerina, then continue to Punta Secca. Campsite is well signposted.

CC € 13 1/1-15/7 1/9-31/12 7=6

N 36°47'37'' E 14°29'24''

Ribera/Seccagrande, I-92016 / Sicilia

iD **3140**

Kamemi Camping Village**
Contrada Cam. Sup.
FAX +39 0925-69212
1/1 - 31/12
@ info@kamemivillage.com

4,8ha 50T(40-75m²) 6A CEE

1 ABCGHIJKLMNORS
2 RTVXY
3 ABGMNU
4 (B 15/5-7/9) (G 3/5-7/9) (Q) (R 1/3-31/10) (T+U+V+W+Y 21/6-10/9) (Z)
5 AGIKMOPSTU
6 CEGJ(N 5km)QTV

A well-organised campsite with two lovely swimming pools. Enthusiastic campsite managers. Located close to the sea. Agrigento, Scala dei Turchi, Eraclea Minoa and Selinunte are all within easy reach. Substantial discounts if you stay longer.

From the SS115 (south coast) turn off at 142 km marker (follow signs).

CC € 17 1/1-15/7 1/9-31/12 7=6, 14=11, 30=17

N 37°26'21'' E 13°14'29''

San Vito Lo Capo, I-91010 / Sicilia

iD **3141**

El-Bahira****
Contrada Salinella
+39 0923-972577
FAX +39 0923-972552
1/1 - 31/12
@ info@elbahira.it

8ha 400T(25-65m²) 6A CEE

1 ABCGHIJKLMNOPQ
2 EGLNOQSTUVXY
3 ABGHKMNUY
4 (B+G+Q+S+T+U 1/4-10/10) (V 1/7-30/8) (W 1/4-30/9) (Y 1/4-10/10) Z
5 AGIKLMNOPUVXYZ
6 AEGIJ(N 4km)OQRTV

Lovely, large campsite with many amenities such as wonderful seawater pool. Beautiful location on north-west cape of Sicily, close to nature area of 'Lo Zingaro' and the resort of San Vito Lo Capo. Much attention has been given to landscaping and cosy little areas. Cyclists are very welcome (repairs done).

From Palermo A29 dir. Trapani. Exit Castellammare del Golfo. Follow SS187. Follow San Vito Lo Capo between km-markers 18 and 17. Follow sign after km-marker 18.

CC € 17 1/1-15/7 1/9-31/12 7=6, 15=12

N 38°9'1'' E 12°43'54''

Sant'Alessio Siculo/Taormina, I-98030 / Sicilia

3142 iD

La Focetta Sicula**
Contrada Siena 40
+39 0942-751657
FAX +39 0942-756708
1/1 - 31/12
@ info@lafocetta.it

1,2ha 120T 6A CEE

1 ABCGHIJLMNORS
2 AEFGKNRSXY
3 ANUWY
4 (A 9/8-23/8) (T 1/7-31/8) (Z)
5 **AB**GIJKMO**P**UV
6 CEG**IK**ORT

A small, peaceful campsite, beautifully located on the Ionian Sea with a fine, black shingle beach. Basic accommodation located close to Taormina.

SS114, km 34 exit Sant'Alessio Siculo. The first campsite south of Messina. A18, exit Roccalumera.

CC € 17 *1/1-15/7 1/9-31/12 7=6, 14=11, 30=20*

N 37°55'54'' E 15°21'20''

Place name index

A

B

C

D

E

M

N

O

P

Q

R

S

T

W

X

Y

Z

Naturist camp sites

In this CampingCard guide you will find the following naturist camp sites or camp sites with a naturist section. Be aware that on most of these sites you will need to be a member of a naturist association.

Naturist camp sites

France